*Directory Listings of the 1996 New York & New England Edition*

How to Use This Directory ....................I
Woodall's Rating System ....................IV

**Connecticut**
**Maine**
**Massachusetts**
**New Hampshire**
**New York**
**Rhode Island**
**Vermont**
**Ontario, Canada**

Alphabetical Quick Reference
GUIDE TO SEASONAL SITES IN RV PARKS/CAMPGROUNDS
Yellow pages
Reader Input Survey

Cover Credit
Nubble Lighthouse, York, Maine
by Dick Dietrich

Book Trade Distribution by
The Globe-Pequot Press
6 Business Park Drive
P.O. Box 833
Old Saybrook, CT 06475
ISBN# 0-671-53506-4

# WOODALL'S

*invites you to...*

# DISCOVER THE FESTIVAL THAT IS NORTH AMERICA

**Festivals of New York and New England:** CT, ME, MA, NH, NY, RI, VT. Come to Maine's 146-year-Old Fryeburg Fair for farm exhibits and much more; Enjoy cranberry muffins at the Massachusetts Cranberry Harvest Festival; c'mon over for pancakes at the Vermont Maple Festival; learn to sail at Discover Sailing Day in Burlington, Vermont.................Page 3

**Mid-Atlantic Festivals:** DE, DC, MD, NJ, PA, VA, WV. Bring the children to historic Cold Spring Village in New Jersey for Children's Jubilee; DC's Cherry Blossom Festival is a not-to-be missed floral extravanganza; enjoy a spooky Halloween at Huntingdon PA's Ghosts & Goblins Weekends.................Page 34

**Festivals of the South:** AL, FL, GA, KY, LA, MS, NC, SC, TN. Come party hearty at Mardi Gras festivals in New Orleans, and throughout the South; enjoy West Palm Beach's SunFest, billed as Florida's largest jazz, art and water festival; celebrate the "Run for the Roses" at the Kentucky Derby Festival; learn banjo pickin' at Hattiesburg, Mississippi's Elks Dixie Bluegrass Festival.................Page 52

**Festivals of the Great Lakes Region:** IL, IN, IA, MI, MN, OH, WI. Taste some fresh sweet corn dripping with butter at Mendota, Illinois' National Sweet Corn Festival where more than 160,000 ears are served!; visit Holland, Michigan in May for Tulip Time; tap your feet to the music at Milwaukee's 11-day Summerfest, with more than 2,500 performers to entertain you; view the world's largest single-day sporting event, the Indianapolis 500.................Page 82

**Frontier West Festivals:** AR, KS, MO, NM, OK, TX. Attend Gallup, New Mexico's Inter-Tribal Celebration with a rodeo, arts & crafts, ceremonial dances and more; head down to the Rio Grande Valley for Weslaco's OnionFest; visit Branson, Missouri for their National Festival of Craftsmen, a 7-week-long, 1890s-themed event.................Page 90

**Festivals of the Great Plains & Mountain States:** CO, MT, NE, ND, SD, UT, WY: Come to the Lewis and Clark Festival in Great Falls, Montana for history and fun; step back in time 400 years at Larkspur, Colorado's Renaissance Festival; head to Cody, Wyoming for the Cody Stampede with rodeos, parades, and art shows.................Page 100

**Far West Festivals:** AK, AZ, CA, ID, NV, OR, WA. Go way up north to Nome, Alaska for their Midnight Sun Festival, when the sun shines around the clock; rockhounds love the Quartzsite (Arizona) Pow Wow Gem & Mineral Show; Carnaval San Francisco offers up a big city-style mega celebration; Vegas is a festival that is celebrated 24 hours a day, 365 days a year .................Page 106

**Festivals of Canada:** Alberta's Calgary Stampede offers true western hospitality, Canada style; spend a day at the beach at the Annual International Sandcastle Competition on BC's Vancouver Island; come to the world's largest outdoor free picnic at Toronto's Chin International Picnic; thrill to a spectacular fireworks show at the Benson & Hedges International Fireworks Competition in Montreal; head to Summerside, Prince Edward Island for their Lobster Carnival.................Page 12

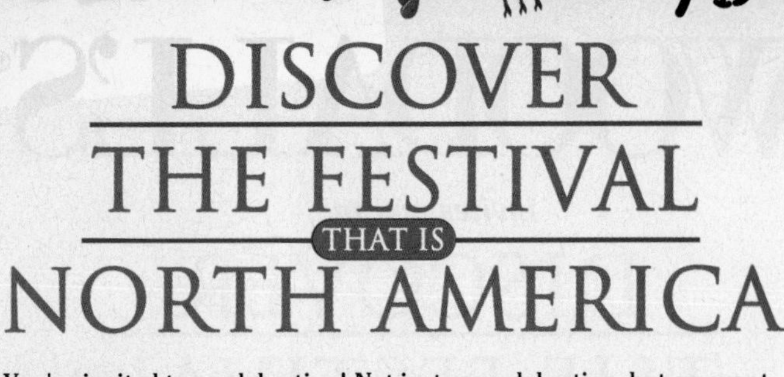

# DISCOVER THE FESTIVAL THAT IS NORTH AMERICA

You're invited to a celebration! Not just any celebration, but an event that is happening somewhere near you . . . or near where you want to go. From small town, one-day civic celebrations to a summer-long, nightly outdoor drama, attending fairs and festivals is an increasingly popular vacation activity. Think for a moment how enjoyable a good party can be. It can tempt your palate by serving up delicious food; lift your spirits by amusing and entertaining you; and, it can rekindle your relationships, whether with your own next door neighbors or with friends you haven't met yet. More importantly, you and your family will learn about folks from all over North America if you attend one of their special celebrations. You'll relearn that we *all* have a common thread: hobbies, interests, ethnicity, history, and most often, the need to just kick back and have a good time!

Do you enjoy fresh seafood? Combine a postcard-perfect New England town with fresh-caught lobster, clams and scallops and you've got the Yarmouth, Maine Clam Festival. If you're a history buff, attend the Gettysburg Civil War Heritage Days, reliving the era through a Living History Camp. Did Mom ever tell you that woolly worms can predict the severity of the coming winter? Come honor these little critters at the Beattyville, Kentucky Woolly Worm Festival. Do you like music? Plan to attend the world-famous Monterey, California Jazz Festival for fun, food, and some of the finest jazz anywhere.

State fairs are a wonderful way to explore an entire state in one visit, and one of the best is the Texas State Fair in Dallas. As you'd expect from a state like Texas, this is one of the biggest anywhere, covering over 277 acres with livestock and farm exhibits, food concessions, and much more. Ever wanted to be a train engineer? Attend Railfan Weekend in Union, Illinois, and you can operate a train under the guidance of an engineer. The Stratford Festival in Stratford, Ontario has grown to become North America's largest repertory theater, and includes a film festival, a music festival, and art exhibits.

This is a special year for us all here at WOODALL, as we are celebrating our own happy event — our 60th anniversary (1935-1995). Back in 1937, WOODALL'S first *Directory of Trailer Parks and Camps* sold for 25 cents, weighed a few ounces, and listed about 2,000 parks. Now, *WOODALL'S North American Campground Directory* weighs about 5 pounds and lists more than 15,000 locations. At 60 years young, we're going stronger than ever! So, gas up the car or RV, put on your most comfortable shoes and your brightest smile. Join us in our anniversary celebration by making plans today to attend festivals, rodeos, fairs, sporting events, races, cultural events, and theater productions throughout North America, as we *Discover The Festival That Is North America.*

*Barbara Tinucci*

Barbara Tinucci
Editor

WOODALL'S IS THE OFFICIAL CAMPGROUND DIRECTORY RECOGNIZED by the FAMILY MOTOR COACH ASSOCIATION and FAMILY CAMPERS and RVers

This directory is printed on recycled paper. PRINTED IN THE U.S.A.

**Published by Woodall Publications Corp.**
**13975 West Polo Trail Drive**
**Lake Forest, Illinois 60045-5000**
**708-362-6700**

**Also Publishers of**
Woodall's Plan It • Pack-It • Go...
*Great Places to Tent • Fun Things to Do*
Go & Rent, Rent & Go
Woodall's Campground Management
Woodall's RV Buyer's Guide
Woodall's Camperways
Woodall's RV Traveler
Woodall's Camp-orama
Woodall's Southern RV
Woodall's California RV Traveler
Woodall's Texas RV

# DISCOVER THE FESTIVALS of New York and New England

## *CONNECTICUT FESTIVALS*

**Spring:**

It has been called the "gentlest of festivals" by *The New York Times*, and May's annual **Dogwood Festival** in Fairfield lives up to that nickname. The festival has been held for over 59 years, and is situated on a picturesque hilltop setting dominated by the white steepled Colonial style church and the blossoming pink and white dogwoods. The daily musical programs often include the Westport Madrigal Singers, the Park Street Singers, piano duets, and the Greenfield Hill Church Choir. There is also a juried art show, crafts from area artisans, guided walking tours, baked goods and snacks, handmade clothing and handicrafts, weekend children's activities and a sit-down luncheon each day (reservations required for the luncheon).

**Summer:**

Visit Sunrise Resort in Moodus, Connecticut for their **Great 1996 Connecticut Traditional Jazz Festival** which will be held August 2nd, 3rd and 4th. Now in its 10th year, the festival hosts as many as 18 different traditional jazz bands from around the world who play in various locations throughout the resort. A recent festival provided five large canvas tents so the event may be held rain or shine.

Mark your calendar for the last Sunday in June and visit **Trumbull Day** in Trumbull, Connecticut. The event was started in 1965 as a picnic for town residents, and over the years has grown to the second largest one-day event in the state, with recent attendance figures hovering around 60,000. A truly family-oriented event, it is famous for its fireworks display, over 25 food vendor booths in an international food court, a 100-booth flea market with emphasis on arts and crafts, over 30 full-sized carnival rides, and special entertainment each year.

**Fall:**

The 1996 **Oyster Festival of East Norwalk** will be held September 6th through 8th. The festival was begun in 1978 by the Norwalk Seaport Association to build awareness of marine resources, environment and maritime heritage. Today, the festival includes entertainment on four stages; a tall ships and vintage oyster boats parade; the Oyster Pavilion with oyster shucking and slurping contests; Kid's Cove with games, rides, music and storytelling; model train exhibits; and special nightly shows including a laser light show. More than 200 juried fine artists and crafters come from all over North America and are said to represent one of the largest and highest quality arts and crafts shows on the East Coast.

Come to Canterbury on one of the last three weekends in October for **The Spooky Hayrides** that are held at Wright's Mill Farm each year. The Spooky Hayrides are held Thursday, Friday and Saturday evenings and are either horse-drawn or tractor-drawn. Strategically placed actors offer scary surprises that just might send shivers up your spine — this ride is not for the faint of heart! For a gentler ride, try a Pumpkin Hunt Hayride which includes a leisurely tractor-drawn hayride through the 250-acre Christmas tree farm, passing antique mill sites and the miller's homestead.

## *MAINE FESTIVALS*

**Spring:**

The town of Greenville kicks off the local tourism season each year in May with **Moosemainea**, an event that has become a

*Maine Festivals continued on page 8*

# Beneath Ever
# There's A Sol

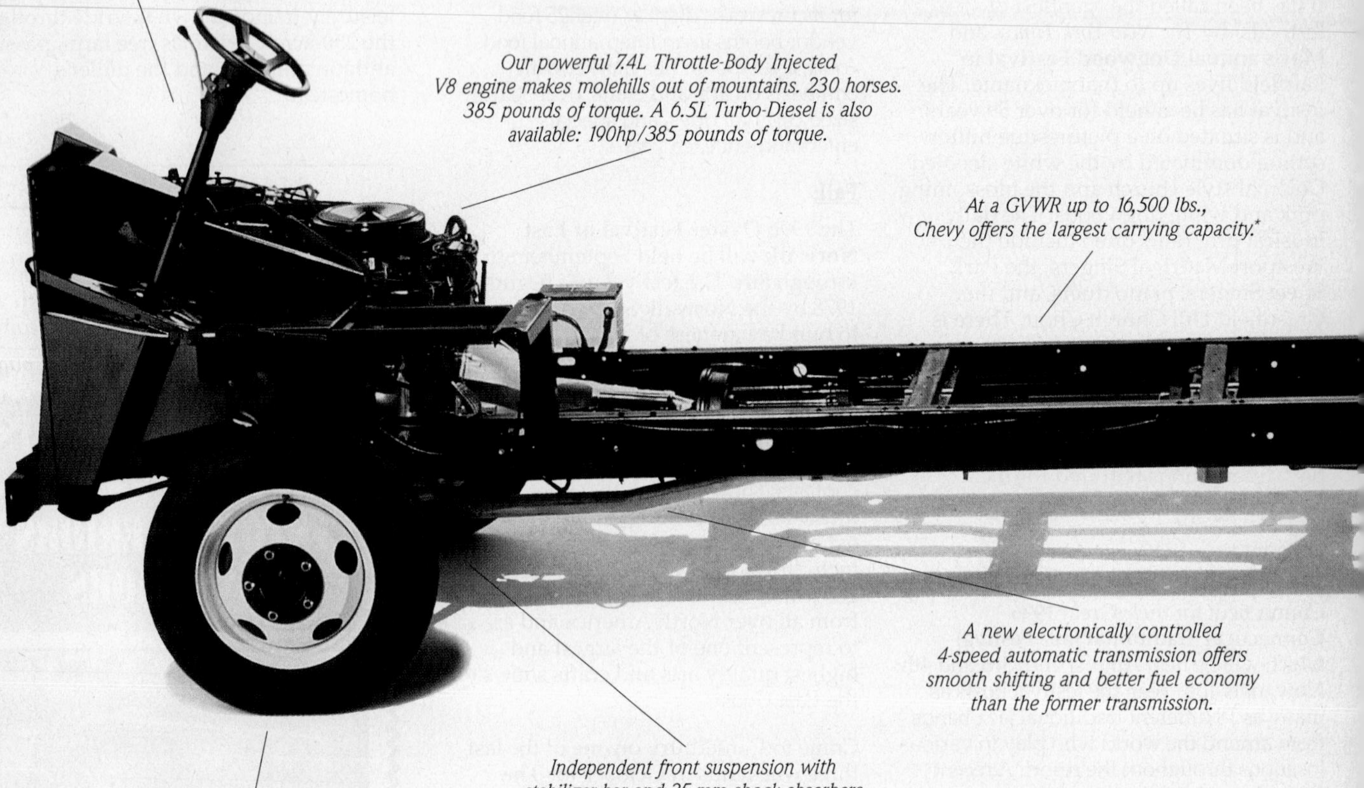

Variable-ratio power steering.

*Our powerful 7.4L Throttle-Body Injected V8 engine makes molehills out of mountains. 230 horses. 385 pounds of torque. A 6.5L Turbo-Diesel is also available: 190hp/385 pounds of torque.*

*At a GVWR up to 16,500 lbs., Chevy offers the largest carrying capacity.**

*A new electronically controlled 4-speed automatic transmission offers smooth shifting and better fuel economy than the former transmission.*

*Independent front suspension with stabilizer bar and 35 mm shock absorbers soak up bumps like a sponge.*

*Large rotor front disc brakes provide excellent stopping power.*

The Chevy P-30 Motor Home Chassis is the solid support you need to build your dream home. We've made major improvements in virtually every category. And

*Front gas engine chassis only. †14,800 lbs. and above GVWs. **Rear drum brakes on GVWRs 11,800-12,300 lbs. The Chevrolet Emblem is a registered trademark a

# y Great Home,
# d Foundation.

Sturdy frame side rails and riveted cross members.

Tapered-leaf rear suspension. Stabilizer bar.† 35 mm shock absorbers.

Rear disc brakes on GVWRs 14,800-16,500 lbs.**

Six wheelbase choices. (137.0" to 228"). 4 GVWR choices (11,800 lbs. to 16,500 lbs.).

Available as an option, the widest rear axle in the market allows up to a 102" wide body. That's a lot of elbow room. Slide-outs mean even more room.

then some. The open road is calling. And we're answering at the CSV Express line at 1-800-759-5550 or 1-800-FOR-CHEV.

**Chevy Trucks**
**LIKE A ROCK**

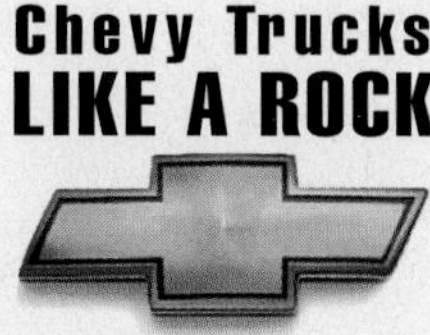

THE STAY AND PLAY UNIQUE GETAWAY

# The Perfect 3-Season Vacation or Second Home Alternative

**The Challenge**
*Our exquisite, new, championship 18-hole golf course adjacent to our private, sandy beaches is already hailed as one of the best in Maine. The perfect course for every level of golfer.*

**The Charm**
*Nature at its very best with over 800 acres of pristine Maine woodlands. Featuring comfortable accommodations in RV park models, travel trailers or sites nestled in the trees or near Sebago Lake.*

**The Choices**
*A large variety of seasonal outdoor activities for all ages including golf clinics, tennis, boating, fishing, waterskiing, shuffleboard, arts and crafts, games, tournaments and daily entertainment.*

**The Cuisine**
*Our Lakeview Restaurant features gourmet specialties including lobster, prime rib and special buffets in addition to our extensive regular nightly menu. For casual and quick meal options, enjoy our convenient outdoor cafe and beach barbeque.*

**The Crew**
*Our team of friendly, trained staff will assist your family day and night. We offer PGA teaching pros, a tennis pro and other experts to provide the best instruction in outdoor recreation.*

**The Call**
***1-800-872-7646*** *to make reservations or to receive our free video brochure. Write to:*
*Point Sebago*
*RR #1, Box 712W*
*Casco, ME 04015*
*Internet Access:*
*http//www.pointsebago.com/*

POINT SEBAGO
GOLF AND BEACH RV RESORT

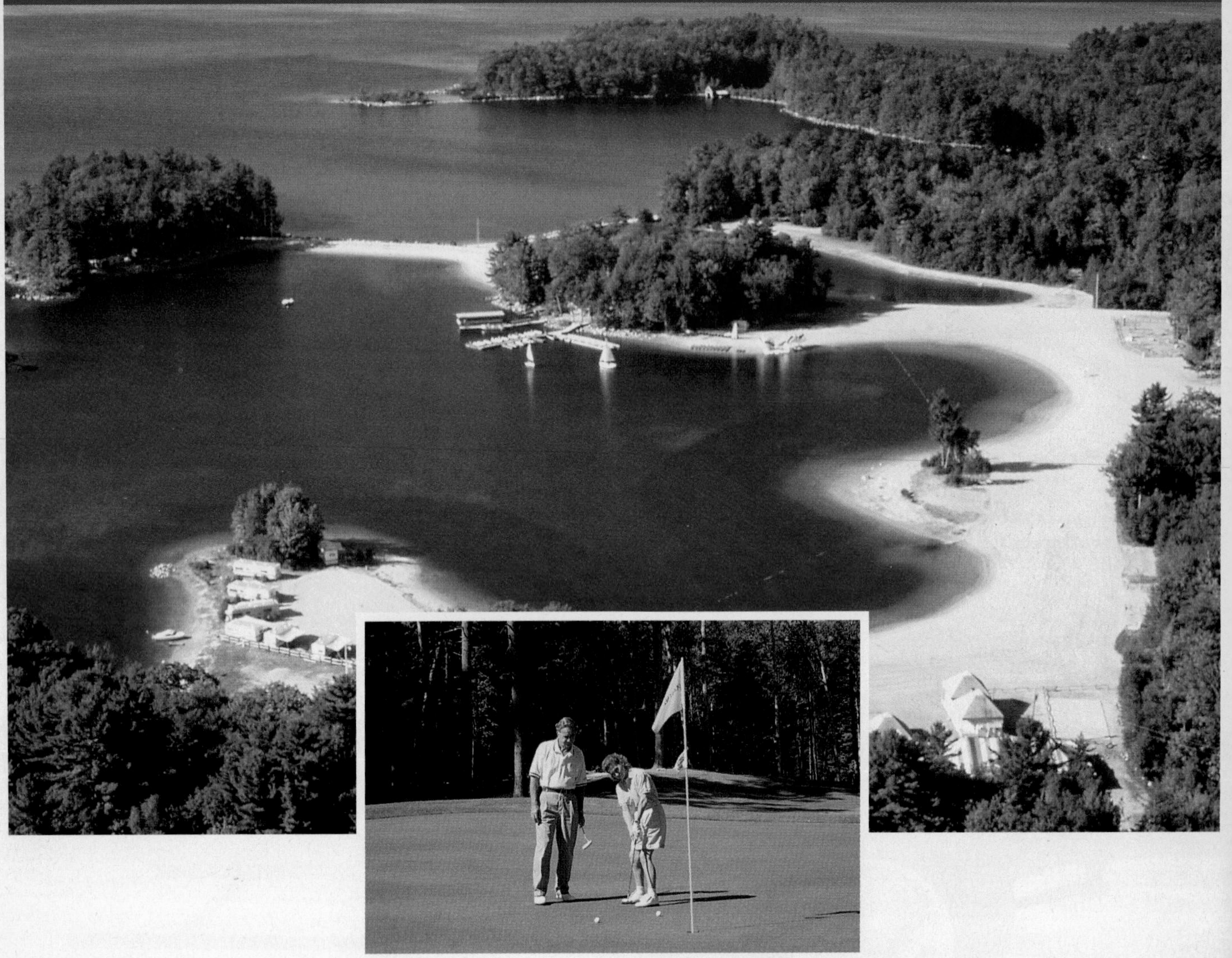

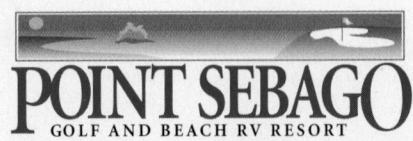

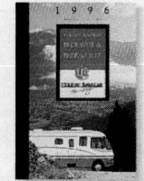

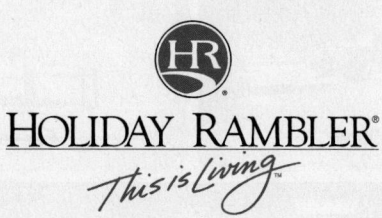

*Maine Festivals continued from pg. 3*

month-long celebration. Activities include a craft fair, a fun run for children and the Tour de Moose Mountain Bike Marathon which is a 10-mile ride through moose-favorable terrain. The Moose Ball and Auction is billed as the "Annual Black Fly Affair," so you can be sure that residents and guests have their senses of humor intact. This "dressy" event showcases the latest fashion crazes in backwoods wear and often includes hard hats, so leave the white gloves and tuxedos at home.

The **Fishermen's Festival** will be held in Boothbay Harbor on April 19th, 20th and 21st. The festival originated in 1973, and consistently draws between 2,500 and 3,000 visitors. There's a codfish race, lobster trap hauling, crate races and fish and shellfish picking and shelling contests.

Wells Beach is a bustling resort community that is like a beachfront festival all summer long. It's blessed with more than 7 miles of beautiful, wide, white sandy beaches for unlimited outdoor fun. Anyone who enjoys the ocean will love it here. There's swimming, walking, running to keep busy, and just plain relaxing. In town there are rare bookshops, flea markets and antique shops to keep vacationers intrigued after a morning on the beach.

**Summer:**

Visit Boothbay Harbor the last week in June for **Windjammer Days**, which will be celebrated for the 34th year in 1996. Join the residents as the entire community celebrates the by-gone days of the majestic sailing vessels, as well as food, fireworks, music, a big parade, and, of course, the beautiful antique boats.

The 3rd weekend in July, 1996 brings one of southern Maine's biggest and most family-oriented festivals to Yarmouth — the 31st annual **Yarmouth Clam Festival.** Combine a postcard-perfect New England town with three days of Down-East food, free music and entertainment from morning 'til night, a craft show and special competitions, and you've got the Yarmouth Clam Festival. Starting out as a local clam bake in 1966, the festival has grown into one of Maine's biggest and most popular events with recent attendance hovering around 50,000 visitors per day. The festival is a celebration of clams, in all their delicious forms from chowders, rolls, and fried clam dishes. There are lots of other culinary delights, too, including fresh peach shortcake and lobster and scallop

*Maine Festivals continued on page 10*

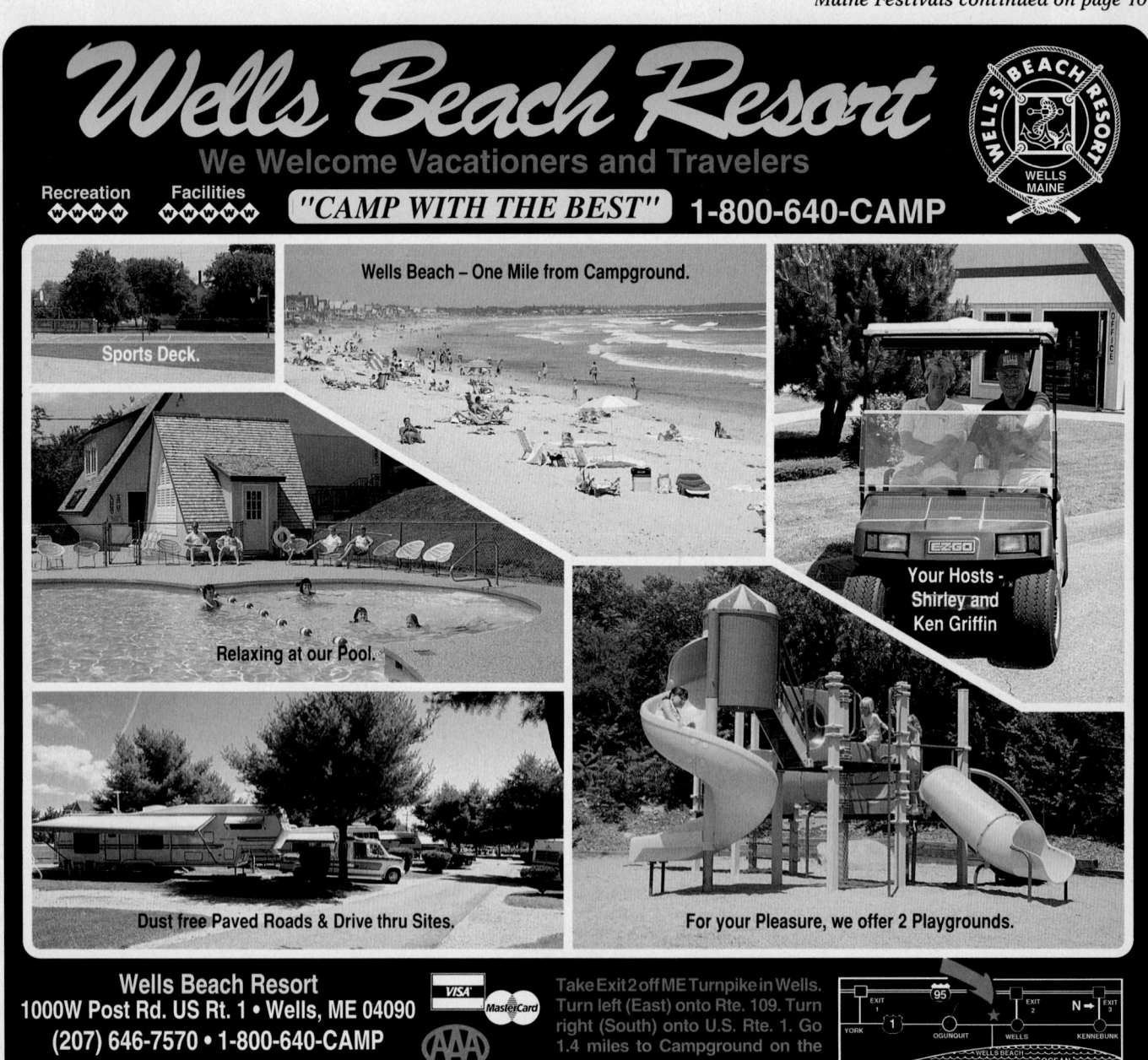

*Maine Festivals continued from pg. 8*

rolls. Entertainment is provided by theatrical groups, musicians, a barbershop chorus, and a juggling comedian. A craft show is provided by over 115 artisans who have brought their best works from fine quilts to baskets to jewelry.

Rockport plays host to the **Maine Lobster Festival** which will be held for the 49th time on August 1st through the 4th, 1996. Tie on a plastic bib and get your taste buds ready for succulent Maine lobster which is cooked in the world's largest lobster cooker — 300 to 400 pounds at a time. Or how about a Maine shrimp cockail, or some steamed or smoked mussels, or fried shrimp, lobster rolls, or a steaming bowl of seafood chowder? It's all here in Rockland, along the coast between Portland and Bar Harbor. It's an ideal destination for your vacation to Maine, or as a stop on the way to Acadia National Park, Bar Harbor, Boothbay Harbor, or Camden. Continuous entertainment provides the backdrop for all this great food, as you enjoy jazz, blues, country, and big band music all day.



**Fall:**

Tenters and RVers will want to make plans to visit Maine's midcoast region the last weekend in September in 1996 for their second annual **Fall Harvest Camping Festival**. If you don't own a tent or RV, rent or borrow one and come enjoy the spectacular fall scenery and fun activities. The midcoast region is delightful to explore, as it's one of the least crowded areas of Maine, and is especially peaceful after Labor Day. Included in the region are the harbor towns of Rockport, Rockland, Camden, Thomaston, and Belfast along Penobscot Bay. The weekend includes lots of activities and events for campers/RVers only — including harbor cruises, train rides, hiking excursions, apple picking and farm tours, and special discounts are offered at local shops, attractions and restaurants. The event is coordinated by 13 member campgrounds and campers registering at the parks are given a list of the weekend's activities and events.

The first week in October is **Fryeburg Fair** time, and this year the fair will celebrate its 146th anniversary! The Fryeburg Fairgrounds come alive for the 8-day event that features agricultural exhibits, farm displays, farm and home products, a giant midway, evening entertainment and shows on four stages, and much more. One of the fair's most popular events is the ox pulling contest, and fair officials boast that they have the largest steer show in the world. All in all, there are more than 1,000 animals on the grounds during the fair, and some of the most popular are the huge draft horses. The grounds have limited camping available, but there are plenty of nearby privately-operated campgrounds and RV parks, including Woodland Acres Camp N Canoe.

## *MASSACHUSETTS FESTIVALS*

**Spring:**

The Cranberry World Visitors' Center in Plymouth is the site of the annual **Cranberry World Wildlife Festival** that is held in March. Festival-goers will find themselves surrounded by fuzzy, furry and slimy animals, hailing from as far away as the tropical rain forest, and as close as a New England backyard. You might see a golden eagle, a great horned owl, or a baby brown bat. Slithering attendees may include a timber rattlesnake, northern copperhead snake or a Madagascar jumping cockroach.

*Massachusetts Festivals con't. on page 12*

**FREE INFO?** Home & Park, enter #734 on Reader Service Card following page 16.

*Mass. Festivals cont. from page 10*

Experts will discuss the animals' lifestyles, habitats and what humans can do to protect those environments. Information will also be available on national marine sanctuaries and local wildlife organizations.

Lace up your best running shoes and join the more than 1-1/2 million spectators to view (or maybe run in?) the 100th running of the world famous **Boston Marathon** held on April 15th. In April of 1897, fifteen men started the first Boston marathon, the second marathon ever held in the United States. Not just a sporting event, but an historic and patriotic event, the marathon is held on Patriots' Day, a holiday celebrated in Massachusetts in honor of Paul Revere's famous ride signaling the start of the American Revolution. The race generates enthusiasm and teaches sportsmanship and each year produces American and international heroes and outstanding role models for young athletes around the world.

May in Brimfield brings the **Brimfield Antique and Collectible Shows** that have been held there for about 30 years. Three shows are held each year — one in May, one in July, and the last in September. The show is billed as the largest outdoor antique and collectibles show in the world, and it's easy to see why — there are more than 3,000 dealers at each show. Around 1958, the late Gordon Reid Sr. brainstormed the idea of gathering antique dealers together for a large sale. Mr. Reid and his wife traveled throughout New England, persuading their many friends in the antique business to come to Brimfield for the beginnings of the sale and flea market. The next year, the first Brimfield Antique Flea Market was held at Gorden Reid's Antique Acres on Route 20. Today, the flea market has grown to include displays from thousands of antique dealers as over 20,000 antique lovers converge upon the town each year to restock their stores or to add to their own personal collections.

Celebrate Memorial Day weekend at the **Salem Seaport Festival** in Salem. Throughout the weekend, over 100 professional artists and craftspeople from throughout the country display and sell their wares under the bigtop. There's a delicious assortment of food, too, with barbecue ribs, fried dough, homemade fudge, and fresh-squeezed lemonade just waiting for hungry and thirsty festival goers. Entertainment is family-oriented, with a wandering minstrel who brings her program of multicultural stories, folksongs and puppets to the delight of young and old alike. Musical entertainment includes traditional jazz, country, rock, Renaissance music and Dixieland. There's even a vaudeville act.

**Summer:**

Up to 50 kayaks will hit the waters off the Provincetown beach during mid-June to follow the route of the Mayflower across Cape Cod Bay to Plymouth in this celebration of the Pilgrims' arrival in a race sponsored by Finlandia Vodka. The local paddlers are part of Finlandia's efforts to reach more people with its clean water message, and the **Provincetown to Plymouth Race** is an extension of the third annual 1,000-mile Finlandia Vodka Clean Water Challenge kayak endurance race that kicked off in Chicago and finished in New York.

Plymouth is host to a **Waterfront Festival** held in mid-July each year. More than 100 crafters from throughout the Northeast display their finest works in a juried show along the waterfront; there are 17th-century children's games, amusement rides, a food tent and day-long musical performances. Sunday evening tops off the festival with a free recital on a 4,000-pipe organ at the Church of the Pilgrimage in the Town Square.

Late August brings the **Lobster Festival** to Plymouth. See live lobster "races," browse through the craft fair, and tap your feet to a folk music concert punctuated with English folk tales aboard the *Mayflower II*, a full-scale reproduction of the original ship docked next to Plymouth Rock. Costumed crewmen and passengers recount experiences of the Pilgrims' 1620 voyage, giving visitors a true sense of that historic journey.

**Fall:**

Massachusetts cranberry growers invite everyone to feast their eyes on a sea of cranberries at the Third Annual **Massachusetts Cranberry Harvest Festival**. The event, a celebration of the "fruits" of the growers' year-round labor, takes place at the Edaville Cranberry Bogs in South Carver, and at Cranberry World Visitors' Center in Plymouth, during early October. Activities for all ages are scheduled throughout the Columbus Day weekend festival. At the Edaville Bogs, cranberry growers and guides offer facts and stories about the cranberry and its wetland habitat; there are cranberry arts and crafts, a cooking contest, a farmers' market, hay rides, helicopter rides and country western music. At Cranberry World, visitors may watch re-creations and demonstrations of the traditional cranberry harvesting method, using hand-held wooden scoops common in the 1800s and early 1900s, and present day dry harvest machines. Visitors may sample free Ocean Spray juice drinks and harvest muffins.

Visit Newburyport over Labor Day weekend and attend the **Newburyport Waterfront Festival** that has been held here for over 18 years. Located at Plum Island Fairgrounds midway between the restored downtown area and the dunes of Parker River Wildlife Refuge, the festival usually attracts over 10,000 visitors. Activities include musical entertainment, arts and crafts exhibits and the "Great American Picnic" with a multicultural variety of foods.

*Massachusetts Festivals con't. on page 14*

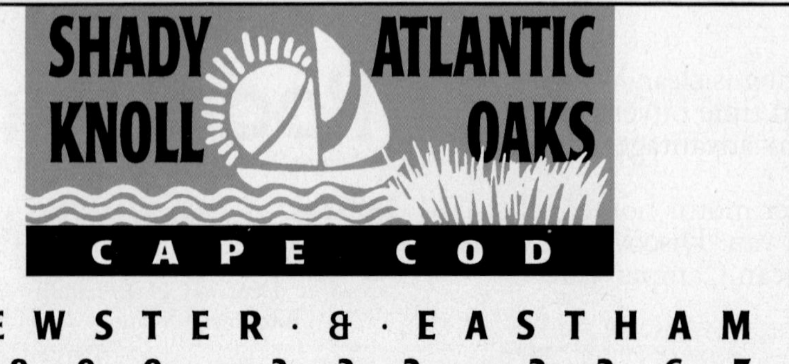

Yogi Bear™ ©1996 Hanna-Barbera Productions, Inc.

**FREE INFO?** Yogi Bear's Jellystone Park Camp-Resorts/Leisure Systems, Inc., enter #733 on Reader Service Card following page 16.

*Mass. Festivals con't. from page 12*

Ranked as the nation's 11th largest fair and the largest fair in the Northeast, the **Eastern States Exposition** (The Big E) will be held September 13th through the 29th, celebrating their 75th anniversary. Each year the fair hosts more than one million visitors who partake in free entertainment, midway rides, agricultural competitions and programs, and favorite fairtime foods. Within the fair, visitors will enjoy historic Storrowton Village, an authentic 19th-century American township of buildings gathered from throughout New England and reconstructed around a traditional village green. Activities include entertainment, antique craft making and demonstrations, children's games and guides tours of the buildings. There's also a huge livestock show with cattle, sheep, goats and hogs; a petting zoo, horse show, band concerts, an auto thrill show, hundreds of crafts exhibits and The Grand Parade which is held daily at 4:30 p.m.

See how families celebrated the first great American holiday more than 160 years ago by attending the November 24th **Thanksgiving Day Celebration at Old Sturbridge Village** in Sturbridge, a re-created village where historically costumed staff demonstrate the daily life, work, and community celebrations of a rural New England town of the 1830s. The village covers over 200 acres with more than 40 exhibits including restored houses, gardens, meetinghouses, mills, a district school, working farm and craft shops.



As a living history museum faithfully reflecting early American life, Old Sturbridge re-creates this 1830s New England celebration. Thanksgiving in the 1830s was a time when families gathered together to share the harvest from their own farms and gardens. Attend a re-created Meetinghouse service and watch the village men compete in a shooting match. Enjoy early American songs and stories. Advance reservations required for the Thanksgiving Celebration. The Village is open 10 a.m. to 4 p.m. daily, and is located on Route 20, near exit 9 of the Massachusetts Turnpike and exit 2 off I-84.

## *NEW HAMPSHIRE FESTIVALS*

**Spring:**

Amherst is a town near and dear to the hearts of classic car enthusiasts who flock here on the last Sunday of each month from April through October each year to celebrate **Cruising to Amherst.** On those days, Amherst plays host to an event that is part flea market, part car show and part living museum. 1996 will be the 36th year of the event that is represented by over 3,000 regulars who arrive to buy, swap, sell or simply engage in lively conversations about the "love of their life," antique cars and all things relating to them. Serious buyers show up as early as 6:00 a.m., and operating hours are from that time until around 3:00 p.m. So if you are looking for a fender for your 1957 Dodge or a hood for a 1940 Ford truck, come to Amherst. Happy hunting!

**Summer:**

Since 1985 the **Attitash Equine Festival** has brought world-class show jumping excitement to New Hampshire's scenic White Mountains resort area. Nestled in the rugged Mt. Washington Valley and remote from large population centers, the event has become one of the high points of the summer season here. From its first year, the festival has attracted the best show jumpers from the U.S. and Europe. The grand finale, the Grand prix of New Hampshire draws former and future Olympic stars, both human and equine. The festival runs for 10 days — filled with top-notch equestrian competition and family-oriented activities.

The **Somersworth International Children's Festival** is held each year on the 3rd Saturday in June on Main Street and at Noble Pines Park. Visitors enjoy the international entertainment, exhibits and foods combined with children's entertainment and activities. The downtown site contains four stages providing continuous entertainment by ethnic and traditional American folk performers. Arts and crafts exhibits and sales, a children's art gallery, and an Expo tent providing hands-on demonstrations are also featured.

Gunstock Resort in the heart of the Lake Winnipesaukee Region is the site of an **Annual Crafts Festival.** Held July 5th through the 7th, this will be their 25th year. About 150 artists and craftspersons display everything from hand-made baby clothes to beautiful Shaker furniture. Along with the crafts, there is live music throughout the festival and lots of hearty food such as hamburgers and hot dogs, barbecued chicken and ribs.

Come to Branch Brook Campground in Campton for their annual **Pemi Valley Bluegrass Festival.** The 1996 dates are August 2nd, 3rd and 4th (held the first weekend in August each year). Come learn what the area has to offer and enjoy the quality family entertainment, promoting the enjoyment of bluegrass music, all the while benefiting the local businesses. For those of you who are unfamiliar with bluegrass, it was named for its native Kentucky, and its origins are credited to Bill Monroe, still pickin' today at well over age 80. Bluegrass has been described as "country jazz" for the way it brings together traditional mountain and folk music with a faster tempo. Along with the lively music, you'll find T-shirts, musical instruments, tapes and CDs, and all types of food from breakfasts provided by the local church of Thornton to pizza, salads, fresh fruit drinks, and much more. The musicians in your group or family will enjoy the workshops, and the dancers can join in on the country dancing on Saturday evening.

The 63rd annual **Craftsmen's Fair** will be held at Mt. Sunapee State Park in Newbury August 3rd through August 11th. Situated in the heart of the Dartmouth/Lake Sunapee region, the fair is held in large tents in view of the mountains. Special exhibits are held in the park's ski lodge and out-buildings, and craftspersons offer demonstrations and workshops for all ages. Visitors may watch the blacksmiths working or participate in weaving and sculpture projects. Work up an appetite and enjoy the variety of food concessions or stroll among the booths to choose lovely crafts to purchase. You'll find over 170 booths featuring pottery, jewelry, hand-woven clothing, quilts, leather goods and more.

**Fall:**

Put on some comfortable walking shoes and bring your appetite to the 7th annual **Hampton Beach Seafood Festival** in September. Seafood is the main attraction, as more than 50 area restaurants and service groups cook up

*New Hampshire Festivals cont. on pg. 26*

# Vacation where the American Spirit took Flight

## The Heart of New England – Historic and Scenic
## Brookfield-Sturbridge, Massachusetts

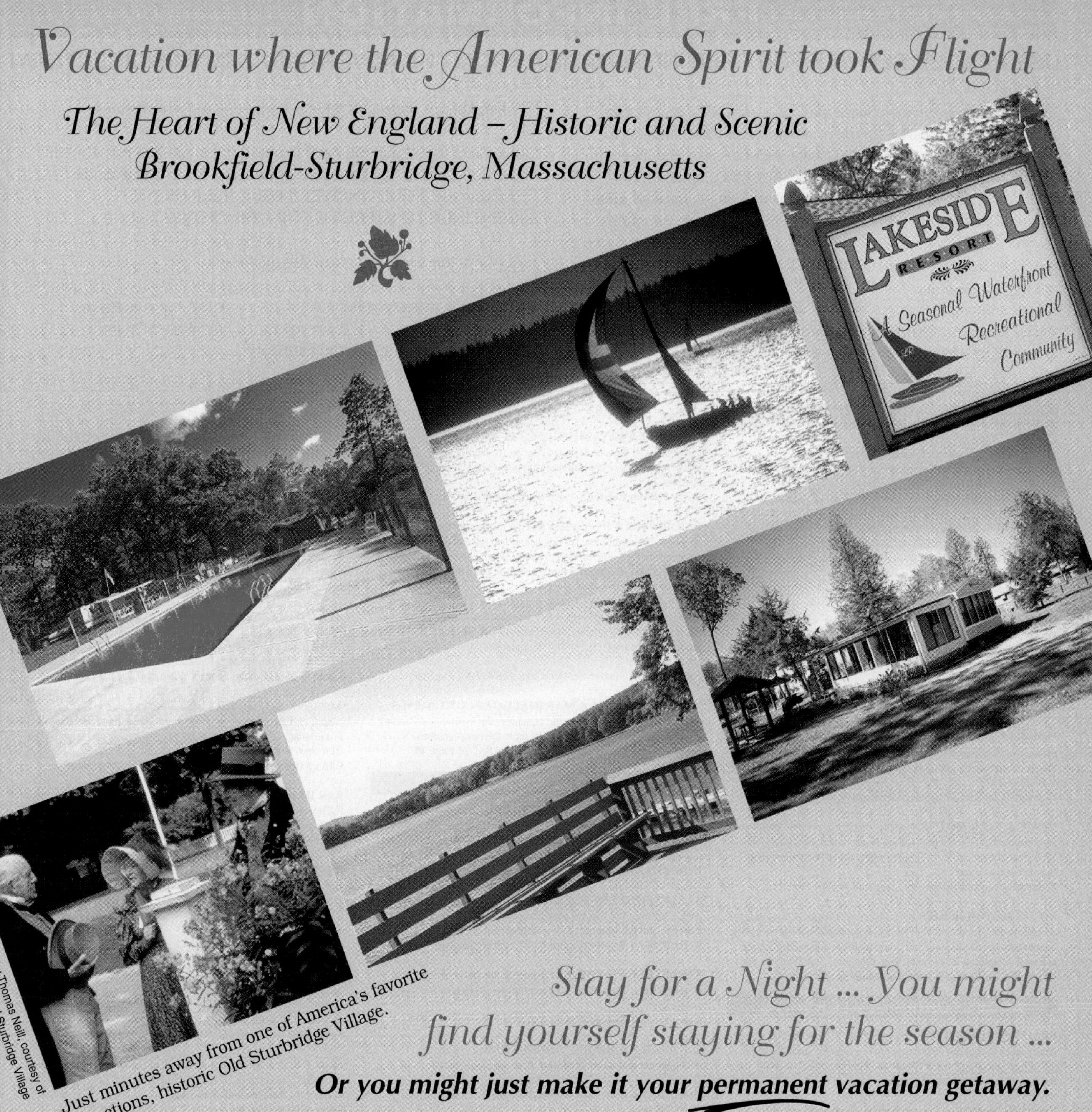


Just minutes away from one of America's favorite attractions, historic Old Sturbridge Village.

by Thomas Neill, courtesy of Old Sturbridge Village

*Stay for a Night ... You might find yourself staying for the season ...*

***Or you might just make it your permanent vacation getaway.***

Lakeside Resort is an innovative new camping community specializing in relaxed, vacation home living. Sites will accommodate all types of recreational vehicles ... whether you prefer a travel trailer, fifth-wheel, motor home, park model or cabin. Full hook-ups are available, as are pull-throughs. Come by and see for yourself why our resort park can offer you the finest vacation destination – whether you buy your campsite, stay for the season, or simply enjoy ... a Lakeside weekend.

# LAKESIDE RESORT

12 Hobbs Avenue, Brookfield, MA 01506
(508) 867-2737 1-800-320-CAMP

**FREE INFO?** Lakeside Resort, enter #797 on Reader Service Card following page 16.

# FREE INFORMATION

## USE READER SERVICE FOR FREE INFORMATION FROM THE ADVERTISERS IN THIS DIRECTORY!

Use this no-hassle way to learn more about the RVs, accessories, campgrounds/RV parks, travelers services, and travel and tourist areas. WOODALL'S advertisers want your business, and they are eager to send you pricing information, brochures, and more, to help you make your travel and buying decisions . . . the easy, time-saving way, right from your home! Follow these three easy steps:

1.) Read the advertisements and the following descriptions which are organized alphabetically within 5 catetories: RV manufacturers, RV accessories and dealerships, campgrounds/RV parks, tourism information and tourist attractions, and general. Reader Service Numbers will appear at the bottom of the pages where the ads appear, as well as in these descriptive listings.

2.) Enter the Reader Service Numbers on the postage-paid Reader Service Card. Also, please take a few moments to complete the brief survey. YOUR ANSWERS WILL HELP US TO CONTINUE TO IMPROVE OUR DIRECTORY.

3.) Drop the card in the mail. It's that easy!

PS - When using telephone numbers to contact our advertisers, please make sure to tell them you found out about them in WOODALL'S Campground Directory!

---

### RV MANUFACTURERS

**CARRIAGE** is a full-line manufacturer of such well-known vehicle names as Carriage, Carriage Commander, Royals International, Carri-Lite, Carri-Lite Cashay, Callista Cove Class C motorhomes and Carriage Van Conversions.
**Enter #738 on Reader Service Card and See Ad Page 27.**

**COACHMEN RECREATIONAL VEHICLE COMPANY** offers beautiful livability, reliable performance, safety, ease of maintenance, high resale value, and a company and warranty you can count on. It's value for the long haul.
**See Ad Page 45.**

**GULF STREAM COACH,** Inc., Nappanee, Ind., is one of the few RV manufacturers to rank near the top in both motorized and towable production. Located in the heart of Amish country. Innsbruck travel trailers to Tour Master Buses — tours daily! Phone 219/773-7761.
**Enter #735 on Reader Service Card and See Ad Inside Back Cover.**

**HOLIDAY RAMBLER** represents the ultimate quality of RV life because of its superior reliability, dependability, safety and comfort. For information on motorhomes, travel trailers and fifth wheels, call 1-800/245-4778.
**Enter #853 on Reader Service Card and See Ad Page 7.**

**HOME & PARK MOTORHOMES** manufactures the "Roadtrek Motorhome Van" — the best selling North American camper van! Visit your nearest dealer to find out more about "the motorhome that drives like a van".
**Enter #734 on Reader Service Card and See Ad Page 11.**

**TIFFIN MOTOR HOMES** are builders of Allegro, Allegrobay and Allegrobus motorhomes. Quality, dependable motorhomes with an outstanding 10-year unitized construction warranty and 5-year sidewall delamination warranty. Free brochure. Call: 205/356-8661.
**Enter #731 on Reader Service Card and See Ad Page 43.**

### ACCESSORIES/DEALERSHIPS

**BEAUDRY RV CENTER** is the world's #1 Fleetwood Motorhome dealer and has been for four consecutive years. Inventory features the largest selection of new Fleetwood products in one location in the U.S.A. Facilities include the largest indoor RV showroom in the Southwest.
**Enter #114 and #91 on Reader Service Card and See Ad Page 107 and Convenient East/West Divider.**

**CAMPER & RECREATION** has provided quality service for over 37 years, with new canvas replacement for all tent camper types. Guaranteed fit and quality. Call or write for information.
**Enter #358 on Reader Service Card and See Ad Page 88.**

**DUCANE FIRELIGHT II,** the dual purpose barbecue grill/campstove, is perfect for tailgating, RVs, boating, camping or any other outdoor activity. It folds up like an attache and tucks neatly into its accessory carrying case. Call 800/489-6543.
**Enter #854 on Reader Service Card and See Ad Page 63.**

**CAMPER'S CHOICE** — a complete line of RV accessories from TV antennas to kitchen appointments at fantastic savings. Free color catalog. Call: 800/833-6713.
**Enter #739 on Reader Service Card and See Ad Page 71.**

**CAMPING WORLD** is the world's largest retailer of RV accessories, supplies and service. Plus, they now offer custom decorating services. For a FREE catalog, call 1-800/626-5944.
**Enter #741 on Reader Service Card and See Ad Inside Front Cover.**

**CUSTOM LAND YACHTS** is a bus conversion company specializing in custom designed coaches of the highest quality and workmanship. Also specializing in renovations and updating of coaches.
**Enter #362 on Reader Service Card and See Ad Page 3.**

**EARNHARDT'S RV** has been serving the greater Phoenix area for 45 years. Their complete service center and fine indoor showroom complement their line of vans, trailers, 5th wheels and motorhomes.
**Enter #112 on Reader Service Card and See Ad Page 109.**

**JWH DISTRIBUTING** Eco-Save products are the natural, non-toxic, non-chemical, ecologically safe answer for cleaning and for RV/marine holding tanks. Liquid bacteria start digestion of waste products in the tanks, providing odor control. Won't stain or harm anything.
**Enter #742 on Reader Service Card and See Ad Page 60.**

**MARSHALL BRASS & MARSHALL GAS CONTROLS,** div. of the S.H. Leggitt Co., give the consumer the assurance of finding products made in America that will meet their expectations.
**Enter #732 on Reader Service Card and See Ad Page 40.**

### CAMPGROUNDS/RV PARKS

**A DEMING ROADRUNNER RV PARK** is your base camp for southern New Mexico — Gila Cliff Dwellings, museums, City of Rocks State Park. Hot tub & heated pool, near 18-hole golf course, rockhounding — great for snowbirds!
**Enter #363 on Reader Service Card and See Ad Page 92.**

**ALAMO FIESTA RV PARK** is the San Antonio area's newest RV park. Conveniently located near San Antonio, Fiesta Texas, Cascade Caverns, and the beautiful Texas hill country.
**Enter #105 on Reader Service Card and See Ad Page 98.**

**ALAMO REC VEH PARK** is located in the heart of the Rio Grande Valley. They offer full amenities and activities for your enjoyment!
**Enter #104 on Reader Service Card and See Ad Page 99.**

Stay at **ALBUQUERQUE NORTH-KOA** and visit both Albuquerque and Santa Fe! Enjoy Albuquerque's historic "Old Town," Indian Pueblo Cultural Center, Rio Grande Zoo/Nature Center, Sandia Tram, International Balloon Fiesta, and famous Santa Fe Plaza.
**Enter #315 on Reader Service Card and See Ad Page 92.**

**ALPINE LAKE CAMPING RESORT** is located in a beautiful, natural setting with two private spring-fed lakes, full facilities and many activities. Near Lake George and Saratoga Springs.
**Enter #130 on Reader Service Card and See Ad Page 26.**

The **AMANA COLONIES,** located in east central Iowa, is a National Historic Landmark, comprised of seven "old world" villages. RV park available. Call Amana Colonies Convention & Visitors Bureau at 1-800/245-5465.
**Enter #724 on Reader Service Card and See Ad Page 84.**

**AMERICAN RV PARK** is New Mexico's finest. Close to Albuquerque attractions—historic Old Town, Indian Pueblo Cultural Center, Rio Grande Zoo & Nature Center, International Balloon Fiesta, and more. 184 paved, landscaped sites.
**Enter #333 on Reader Service Card and See Ad Page 92.**

**AQUIA PINES CAMP RESORT** features both tours and shuttle to Washington, D.C. directly from the campground. All campsites are shaded and some include instant telephone hook-ups. Varied recreation and sparkling restrooms.
**Enter #334 on Reader Service Card and See Ad Page 48.**

**ASPEN-BASALT CAMPGROUND** is the closest full-service campground to Aspen where you can experience the music festival, balloon races, Bell Peaks and ghost town. Also close to world's largest hot springs pool. Ski Aspen, Snowmass, Buttermilk & Highlands. Open all year.
**Enter #338 on Reader Service Card and See Ad Page 102.**

**ATLANTIC CITY BLUEBERRY HILL** at Port Republic, New Jersey offers special weekend activites, wooded and open sites, and transportation (fee) to Atlantic City.
**Enter #339 on Reader Service Card and See Ad Page 37.**

**ATLANTIC CITY NORTH KOA** is centrally located between Atlantic City and Long Beach Island. Free shuttle to Atlantic City with 2-night stay. Free beach passes and shuttle to Long Beach Island during July & Aug. Planned activities with social director.
**Enter #374 on Reader Service Card and See Ad Page 37.**

**AUSTIN CAPITOL-KOA** has it all. It's located in Austin, the capital of Texas. Enjoy the area's music, museums, lakes, restaurants and golf. This 5◆ RV park is sure to please you. Visit their new, large gift shop, too!
**Enter #103 on Reader Service Card and See Ad Page 98.**

**BAR HARBOR RV PARK** at Abingdon, Marlyland is the closest full-service campground to Baltimore attractions. Come visit this quiet, secluded neighborhood on the bay.
**Enter #340 on Reader Service Card and See Ad Page 37.**

**BATTLE OF CEDAR CREEK CAMPGROUND** is located only 1 mile off I-81, with easy on/off access. In the heart of the Shenandoah Valley and close to Belle Grove Plantation and the historic attractions of Old Winchester and near Front Royal and Skyline Drive.
**Enter #341 on Reader Service Card and See Ad Page 48.**

At **BATTLEMENT MESA,** a 4-season mountain resort community, enjoy a vacation at the 3,200-acre master-planned community and you'll discover why so many others who came to visit decided to stay.
**Enter #342 on Reader Service Card and See Ad Page 103.**

**BEACON CAMPING** lies atop a scenic hill in the heart of Amish farmlands, just outside of Lancaster, Pa. A short drive will take you to Hershey, Reading and Gettysburg.
**Enter #350 on Reader Service Card and See Ad Page 46.**

**BENBOW VALLEY RV RESORT & GOLF COURSE** is a premier destination park in the heart of Northern California's Redwood Empire. With its full range of recreation–including golf–this is the resort you've been looking fore!
**Enter #352 on Reader Service Card and See Ad Page 112.**

**BEST HOLIDAY/HOLLY ACRES** in Egg Harbor City, NJ is a family-oriented RV park with weekend activities for all ages. Short drive to Atlantic City beaches and casinos; member of the Best Holiday Trav-L-Park system.
**Enter #343 on Reader Service Card and See Ad Page 39.**

**BETHPAGE CAMP-RESORT**'s location on the Rappahannock River just off Chesapeake Bay provides a perfect setting for family or group camping. Scheduled entertainment, crabbing, fishing, boating & swimming will make your stay memorable.
**Enter #351 on Reader Service Card and See Ad Page 47.**

**BIRCHVIEW FARM CAMPGROUND** features spacious wooded or meadow sites, and is set in picturesque Amish Country, yet near to Philadelphia, Valley Forge, Reading and Longwood Gardens.
**Enter #353 on Reader Service Card and See Ad Page 44.**

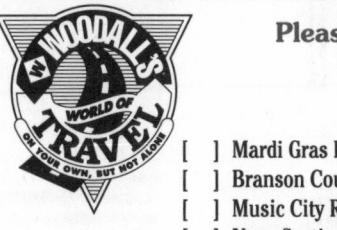

NO POSTAGE
NECESSARY
IF MAILED
IN THE
UNITED STATES

**BUSINESS REPLY MAIL**

FIRST CLASS MAIL PERMIT NO. 407 LAKE FOREST, IL

POSTAGE WILL BE PAID BY ADDRESSEE

**WOODALL'S®**
**CAMPGROUND DIRECTORY**

CREATIVE DATA CENTER
650 S CLARK
CHICAGO, IL 60605-9913

NO POSTAGE
NECESSARY
IF MAILED
IN THE
UNITED STATES

**BUSINESS REPLY MAIL**

FIRST CLASS MAIL PERMIT NO. 407 LAKE FOREST, IL

POSTAGE WILL BE PAID BY ADDRESSEE

**WOODALL'S®**
**CAMPGROUND DIRECTORY**

CREATIVE DATA CENTER
650 S CLARK
CHICAGO, IL 60605-9913

NO POSTAGE
NECESSARY
IF MAILED
IN THE
UNITED STATES

**BUSINESS REPLY MAIL**

FIRST CLASS MAIL PERMIT NO. 407 LAKE FOREST, IL

POSTAGE WILL BE PAID BY ADDRESSEE

**Woodall's World of Travel**
**306 Maplewood Dr.**
**PO Box 247**
**Greenville, MI 48838-9901**

**(questions continued)**

**F. What is your family income?**
31 Under $10,000
32 $10,000 to $19,000
33 $20,000 to $29,999
34 $30,000 to $39,999
35 $40,000 to $49,999
36 $50,000 to $59,999
37 $60,000 to $69,999
38 $70,000 to $79,999
39 $80,000 to $89,999
40 $90,000 to $99,999
41 $100,000 and over

**G. What is your age?**
42 Under 25
43 25 - 34
44 35 - 49
45 50 - 64
46 65 - 74
47 75 and over

**H. Where did you buy this book?**
48 Bookstore
49 Newsstand
50 RV Dealer
51 Other

**I. What portion of your camping stops do you preplan before leavin home?**
52 None
53 25%
54 50%
55 75%
56 All

**J. How many times (approximately) hav you used a WOODALL Campground Directory in the past 12 months?**
57 Zero
58 1 to 5
59 6 to 10
60 11 to 15
61 16 to 20
62 21 to 25
63 More than 25

**K. How many times have you lent ou your WOODALL Campground Directory in the past 12 months?**
64 Zero
65 1
66 2
67 3
68 4
69 5 or more times

**L. Are you more inclined to select locations that advertise their unique features over those who don't?**
70 Yes
71 No

# Points of interest

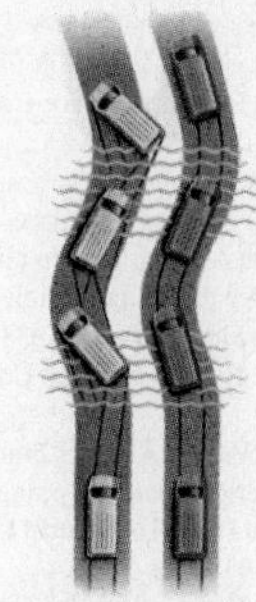


**Standard anti-lock brakes.** *For safe stops, Ram Vans feature standard rear or available four-wheel anti-lock brakes.*

**Custom tours.** *Ram Van comes in three different body lengths. And whichever length you choose, you can convert your Ram Van to suit your own needs.*

**Magnum® power.** *Dodge has, overall, the most powerful line of truck engines on the planet. So it's no surprise that Ram Van's 3.9L Magnum V-6 engine gives you more standard horsepower than any other van. What's more two Magnum V-8s are available – a 5.2L and a 5.9L.*

**Standard driver's airbag.** *Dodge is the only full line truck manufacturer to put a standard driver's airbag in every single truck it builds. So of course, Dodge Ram Van has one.*

**Travel insurance.** *Ram Van is backed by our Customer One Care™ 3-year or 36,000-mile bumper-to-bumper warranty and 3/36 Roadside Assistance. There's a 7-year/100,000-mile outer body rust-through warranty, too.**

**Accommodating rates.** *We're offering an affordable Ram Van Ready Conversion Package that features many of the amenities you're looking for. Including air conditioning and speed control. So pay us a visit. For the name of your nearest Dodge dealer, or for more information, call 1-800-2-RAM VAN.*

# for people who like to travel.

Always wear your seat belt for a fully effective airbag.

*See limited warranties and restrictions at your dealer. Excludes conversion alterations and normal maintenance & wear items.

America's Truck Stop  The New Dodge

A DIVISION OF THE CHRYSLER CORPORATION

# FREE INFORMATION

As "The Best in the West", **BOOMTOWN'S** new beautifully landscaped RV complex, off I-15 just south of the Las Vegas strip, provides phone service and cable TV to every site. Be sure to visit their adjacent casino. Call 1-800-588-7711.
**Enter #108 on Reader Service Card and See Ad Page 117.**

**BOOMTOWN** offers western hospitality at "America's favorite" casino plus 200 full-hookup spaces, out under the stars, away from Reno's city lights . . . but next to all the action. Enjoy the new family fun center featuring 18-hole mini-golf course, motion theater, and arcade games. Call 1-800-648-3790.
**Enter #795 on Reader Service Card and See Ad Page 120.**

**CAL EXPO RV PARK** offers brand-new facilities, walking distance to entertainment, shopping & bike trail. Home of the California State Fair, Waterworld USA, & Paradise Island Family Fun Park. Call 916/263-3187.
**Enter #728 on Reader Service Card and See Ad Page 112.**

The **CALIFORNIA** provides a convenient downtown RV park for enjoying the fabulous new Fremont Experience! At **SAM'S TOWN**, don't miss the new Atrium, a wonderland of waterfalls, walkways & light shows. Their two RV parks offer all the comforts of home. Call 1-800-634-6255 or 1-800-634-6371.
**Enter #122 on Reader Service Card and See Ad Page 123.**

**CAMP AT FERENBAUGH** provides family camping and is the closest campground to Corning. Offering cable TV, pull-thrus, 50 amps and a pool. The best location for all area attractions. Call 607/962-6193.
**Enter #356 on Reader Service Card and See Ad Page 26.**

**CAMP HATTERAS** is a complete resort facility located between the ocean and the sound on the beautiful Outer Banks of North Carolina. Convenient to activities and restaurants.
**Enter #357 on Reader Service Card and See Ad Page 74.**

**CAMPARK RESORTS,** Niagara Falls, Ontario, is only minutes from the Falls and other attractions.
**Enter #819 on Reader Service Card and See Ad Page 135.**

**CAPE ISLAND CAMPGROUND** in beautiful, historic Cape May, New Jersey. Come enjoy the pool or nearby ocean beaches and attractions.
**Enter #355 on Reader Service Card and See Ad Page 39.**

**CHERRY HILL PARK** is the closest full service RV resort to Washington, D.C.
Offers a variety of tours to the Capitol. Complete RV service facility on premises. Member of the Best Holiday Trav-L-Park system.
**Enter #116 on Reader Service Card and See Ad Page 35.**

**CHERRYSTONE CAMPING RESORT** on Virginia's Eastern Shore. Enjoy 300 acres of waterfront on the Chesapeake Bay with 700 campsites; 3 swimming pools; mini-golf; planned activities in season.
**Enter #359 on Reader Service Card and See Ad Page 47.**

Enjoy the unique Western atmosphere at **CIRCLE CG FARM.** Natural beauty, thoughtfully planned sites, and Western entertainment welcome you. Call to inquire about the Chuckwagon Dinner Shows and special events. 508/966-1136.
**Enter #273 on Reader Service Card and See Ad Page 10.**

**CIRCLE RV RANCH,** El Cajon, California — a beautifully landscaped RV park close to Mexico and all San Diego area attractions.
**Enter #90 on Reader Service Card and See Ad Page 114.**

**CIRCUSLAND,** located right on the famed Las Vegas Strip, offers non-stop fun for all. The full-service RV park is linked by monorail with the exciting Circus Circus Midway, and the new Grand Slam Canyon, a themed amusement park. Call 1-800/444-CIRCUS.
**Enter #750 on Reader Service Card and See Ad Page 120.**

**COCOPAH RV & GOLF RESORT** is the friendly park where golf is free any day the sun doesn't shine. Residents golf free on an 18-hole, par-70 course during Sept. & Oct. 806 full hookups with phones at each site.
**Enter #113 on Reader Service Card and See Ad Page 106.**

**COEUR D'ALENE RV RESORT** offers campers year-round luxury with indoor pool, spas, fitness center, and even a massage. Located in a scenic area, convenient to outdoor sports and other attractions.
**Enter #749 on Reader Service Card and See Ad Page 116.**

Enjoy quiet, country-style family camping at **CRYSTAL LAKE BEST HOLIDAY TRAV-L-PARK,** then join the activity in the port town of Ludington, home of the car ferry and great sportfishing on Lake Michigan.
**Enter #757 on Reader Service Card and See Ad Page 87.**

Welcome to the world of **DEER CREEK RV/GOLF RESORT** in the center of Florida attractions. Enjoy the sporting life — golf, tennis, swimming, plus great activities calendar.
**Enter #123 on Reader Service Card and See Ad Page 57.**

Enjoy all the comforts of home and all the magic of Disney at **DISNEY'S VACATIONLAND CAMPGROUND** in Anaheim, California, across the street from Disneyland Park.
**Enter #751 on Reader Service Card and See Ad Page 113.**

**DRUMMER BOY CAMPING RESORT,** only 5 minutes from the battlefield. Step back into history as you take a bus tour from camp or rent an auto tape of historic Gettysburg.
**Enter #752 on Reader Service Card and See Ad Page 44.**

**DUNCAN'S FAMILY CAMPGROUND** — quiet, secluded campground only 30 minutes to Washington, D.C. and Annapolis. Wooded sites, rental cabins. 410/627-3909.
**Enter #117 on Reader Service Card and See Ad Page 35.**

**EAGLES PEAK CAMPGROUND,** in the heart of Pennsylvania Dutch Country, boasts a warm, friendly atmosphere, lots of activities, and fresh mountain air. Visit Lancaster and Reading while camping here.
**Enter #766 on Reader Service Card and See Ad Page 46.**

**EAST SHORE RV PARK** has spacious sites with panoramic lake views; close to all Los Angeles and Anaheim attractions. In a huge county park with lots of recreation, including golf, tennis and excellent fishing.
**Enter #110 on Reader Service Card and See Ad Page 114.**

**ENCHANTED VALLEY RV RESORT** is RV camping at its finest on the banks of the Hiawassee River. Nestled between Helen & Hiawassee, offering lot sales & rentals; excellent golfing nearby and fishing in river & lake.
**Enter #494 on Reader Service Card and See Ad Page 60.**

**FAR HORIZONS 49ER TRAILER VILLAGE** is a complete full-service RV resort in the heart of Gold Country. Follow the original 49er's trail. Discover RV gold in the California Mother Lode! Call 209-245-6981 or 1-800-339-6981 (California only).
**Enter #830 on Reader Service Card and See Ad Page 113.**

**FERRYBOAT CAMPSITES,** an active campground a short distance from Harrisburg, lies along the Susquehanna River. Campers are frequently entertained by the historic Millersburg Ferry, which docks at the campground.
**Enter #386 on Reader Service Card and See Ad Page 40.**

Bald eagles soar over beautiful, new **FIDALGO BAY RESORT.** Enjoy over 1,000 feet of beachfront. Located between historic Mt. Vernon, the quaint shops of La Connor and scenic Anacortes.
**Enter #364 on Reader Service Card and See Ad Page 126.**

Let **FLORIDA CAMP INN** at Baseball City become your winter home. Enjoy swimming, shuffleboard and great activities. Its location is convenient for touring all central Florida's major attractions.
**Enter #124 on Reader Service Card and See Ad Page 54.**

While at **FORT CASPAR CAMPGROUND,** visit Fort Caspar Museum, site of old Fort Caspar, restored frontier trading post and military outpost that guarded the Oregon Trail in Wyoming. Circle drive & hiking trails on Casper Mtn.
**Enter #857 on Reader Service Card and See Ad Page 105.**

Come join us at **FRIENDSHIP VILLAGE CAMPGROUND** and RV PARK in Bedford County, PA, crossroads of heritage and hospitality, near golf courses, ski resort and historic Old Bedford Village.
**Enter #758 on Reader Service Card and See Ad Page 46.**

**FRONTIER TOWN,** an oceanside park within a short driving distance to the Ocean City beach resort, has many amenities including a Western theme park. Free waterslide and beach shuttle from Memorial Day to Labor Day.
**Enter #365 on Reader Service Card and See Ad Page 37.**

**GARDEN OF THE GODS CAMPGROUND** offers full amenities and activities. A great base camp for visiting major scenic and cultural attractions in the Colorado Springs area.
**Enter #514 on Reader Service Card and See Ad Page 101.**

Make **GAYLORD ALPINE RV PARK & CAMPGROUND** your base camp while experiencing the "Golf Mecca of the Midwest." A wooded setting, yet within walking distance to shops, restaurants, and the Alpenfest.
**Enter #824 on Reader Service Card and See Ad Page 87.**

**GETTYSBURG CAMPGROUND,** with modern facilities, is minutes away from the Gettysburg Battlefield where history comes alive. Stroll through America's premier battlefield and view over 1000 monuments and cannons.
**Enter #767 on Reader Service Card and See Ad Page 40.**

**GOLDEN'S SCENIC ROCK RV PARK,** Denver's top-rated park, offers lots of amenities: landscaped, shaded sites, paved roads, sparkling restrooms & laundry, full-service store, lounge, and rec room. Climb the rock for a breathtaking view of Denver's city lights.
**Enter #366 on Reader Service Card and See Ad Page 101.**

**GRAND JUNCTION KOA** in western Colorado is the perfect base camp for exploring the Grand Mesa and Colorado National Monument while enjoying the breakfast & dinner pavilion and large, shaded sites.
**Enter #379 on Reader Service and See Ad Page 101.**

**GUADALUPE RIVER RV RESORT** is Texas Hill Country's top rated RV resort providing phone hookups and cable TV to your site. Luxury cottages & many extra amenities. Phone: 800/582-1916 for reservations.
**Enter #102 on Reader Service Card and See Ad Page 94.**

**HAPPY TRAILS FAMILY CAMPGROUND** is a full-service campground in beautiful western Maryland, convenient to I-70 & I-68. Activity program is oriented toward families. Lots of opportunities to hike & bike.
**Enter #118 on Reader Service Card and See Ad Page 36.**

**HATCH RV PARK** is the most centrally located RV park in Corpus Christi. Close to beaches, restaurants & shopping, and many area attractions. Call 800/332-4509 for reservations now!
**Enter #101 on Reader Service Card and See Ad Page 98.**

**HAVRE RV PARK & TRAVEL PLAZA** is a new, beautifully landscaped RV complex in historic Havre, Montana. The state's finest dining & two casinos within walking distance. Superior facilities & valet parking.
**Enter #369 on Reader Service Card and See Ad Page 103.**

**HICKORY RUN FAMILY CAMPING RESORT** is located in Denver, in the heart of Pennsylvania Dutch Country, within easy driving distance of Hershey, Lancaster, Reading, Philadelphia, Valley Forge and Gettysburg.
**Enter #525 on Reader Service Card and See Ad Page 46.**

Enjoy your winter home at **HIDE-A-WAY** or **ALAFIA RIVER RESORT.** Each offers great fishing, swimming and varied activities. Their location is convenient for visiting central Florida attractions & gulf beaches.
**Enter #125 on Reader Service Card and See Ad Page 53.**

**THE HIDEOUT CABINS & CAMPGROUND** in picturesque Glenwood Springs offers quiet, wooded RV and tent sites close to famous hot springs pool, white water rafting, fishing, and other area attractions.
**Enter #747 on Reader Service Card and See Ad Page 103.**

Camp on an island, fish for that big one in the waters off the dam, square dance in the barn, enjoy the restaurant and adult lounge at **HOLIDAY ACRES JELLYSTONE PARK**-Belvidere, Illinois. Call 815-547-7846.
**Enter #748 on Reader Service Card and See Ad Page 83.**

Enjoy "resort camping" on Florida's Suncoast. **HOLIDAY CAMPGROUND** in Seminole for all the recreation and super activities, plus INDIAN ROCKS BEACH RV RESORT located just across the street from a beautiful beach.
**Enter #825 on Reader Service Card and See Ad Page 59.**

Enjoy the beautiful sun and sea of North Carolina's Crystal Coast on Emerald Isle. Swim in the ocean and the pool and enjoy all the activities at **HOLIDAY TRAV-L-PARK**.
**Enter #138 on Reader Service Card and See Ad Page 74.**

Come to Virginia Beach, Virginia and get into the swing of things at **HOLIDAY TRAV-L-PARK,** where you'll have a full range of recreation activities at the campground, plus free beach parking.
**Enter #422 on Reader Service Card and See Ad Page 47.**

Enjoy the beaches of Cape Cod National Seashore; visit historic lighthouses & quaint villages from **HORTON'S CAMPING RESORT.** View Provincetown Monument from our secluded "honeymoon" site! Call 800/252-7705 for brochure.
**Enter #272 on Reader Service Card and See Ad Page 12.**

**JAMES ISLAND COUNTY PARK CAMPGROUND** is located in a beautiful 640-acre park on a saltwater lagoon, and it's only 10 minutes from historic Charleston, South Carolina. Phone 1-800-743-PARK.
**Enter #140 on Reader Service Card and See Ad Page 75.**

**JANTZEN BEACH RV PARK** on Hayden Island in the Columbia River has the feel of the country, the convenience of the city, with entertainment and recreation for the entire family. Portland Metro transportation available.
**Enter #858 on Reader Service Card and See Ad Page 124.**

**JELLYSTONE PARK** at Amherstburg is located in the hub of Essex County. Convenient to many local attractions. 20 minutes from Detroit-Windsor Bridge. Come visit with Yogi and his friends — hope to see you soon!
**Enter #373 on Reader Service Card and See Ad Page 142.**

**KOA (Kampgrounds of America, Inc.)** is North America's largest system of full-service family campgrounds. Open to the public with nearly 600 locations, they're on the way to wherever you're going.
**See Ad Pages 68 and 69 and Back Cover.**

**KOA KAMPING KABINS**. Check-in to one of KOA's cozy kamping kabins, where you and your family can enjoy all the adventure of camping even if you don't have much equipment.
**See Ad Page 9.**

Stay and play at **KOA-HOUSTON CENTRAL,** only 13 miles from the heart of the great city of Houston. Enjoy an oasis of trees, grass and country living. Call now! 713/442-3700.
**Enter #526 on Reader Service Card and See Ad Page 99.**

**KOA-KERRVILLE** is your home base for visiting Texas Hill Country. An hour or less from Fiesta Texas, San Antonio, Fredericksburg, LBJ Country & Bandera. Call: 800/874-1665.
**Enter #100 on Reader Service Card and See Ad Page 94.**

**KOA-LAKE PLACID-WHITEFACE MOUNTAIN** is a beautiful campground along a 1/2-mile of the trout-famous Ausable River with magnificent gorge and waterfalls.
**Enter #772 on Reader Service Card and See Ad Page 30.**

**KOA MACKINAW CITY** is located at the southern end of the Mackinac Straits. A perfect camping spot while touring world-famous Mackinac Island and Mackinaw Bridge — the world's longest suspension bridge.
**Enter #826 on Reader Service Card and See Ad Page 86.**

**KOA NEWBURGH-NEW PALTZ/NEW YORK CITY TOURS.** Tours of "The Big Apple" depart from this wooded, full-service campground in the historic Hudson Valley. Free brochure available.
**Enter #746 on Reader Service Card and See Ad Page 30.**

While visiting New Orleans, stay at **KOA NEW ORLEANS** and enjoy 5◆ facilities. New Orleans tours pick up at the campground, or use the KOA shuttle van. Casinos nearby.
**Enter #131 on Reader Service Card and See Ad Page 64.**

**KOA NIAGARA FALLS NORTH** — a quite, wooded campground within 15 minutes of Niagara Falls, Fantasy Island, Fort Niagara, Canada, golfing, Fatima Shrine, outlett mall. Call: 716/754-8013.
**Enter #375 on Reader Service Card and See Ad Page 26.**

Make **KOA-PHILADELPHIA/WEST CHESTER** your base camp for visiting historic Philadelphia and Valley Forge, and the Amish Country. Located on Chester County's famous and historic Brandywine River.
**Enter #376 on Reader Service Card and See Ad Page 39.**

**KOA PORT HURON**, located in the eastern port city, is the gateway to Ontario, Canada. The little Western town, Sawmill City, features a variety of adventures for the whole family.
**Enter #822 on Reader Service Card and See Ad Page 86.**

**KOA WYTHEVILLE** is where you will discover the beautiful Southwest Virginia Mountains. The campground takes pride in being locally owned and operated for over 15 years, and provides the best in service & facilities. Need help setting up? Just ask!
**Enter #377 on Reader Service Card and See Ad Page 50.**

**LAKE GEORGE CAMPSITE** is in the heart of beautiful Lake George region. Offering lake activities, and near the Great Escape Fun Park, restaurants, mall, factory outlet centers. Give them a call!
**Enter #820 on Reader Service Card and See Ad Page 28.**

At **LAKE GEORGE RV PARK** one value-packed nightly rate includes: transportation to Lake George Village, live entertainment, paved bike trails, indoor heated pool, and 2 outdoor pools.
**Enter #775 on Reader Service Card and See Ad Page 26.**

**LAKESIDE RESORT** is an innovative new camping community in Massachusetts specializing in relaxed vacation home living. See for yourself why they offer you the finest vacation destination — whether you buy your campsite, stay for the season, or enjoy a lakeside weekend. Call 800/320-CAMP.
**Enter #797 on Reader Service Card and See Ad Page 15.**

**LAKESIDE RV PARK** and **SILVER LAKE RV PARK** in Everett, **GIG HARBOR RV RESORT** in Gig Harbor, and **TWIN CEDARS RV PARK** in Lynnwood offer quality camping within minutes of downtown Seattle, and are conveniently located for exploring western Washington.
**Enter #415 on Reader Service Card and See Ad Page 125.**

Beachfront beauty and an ocean of activity await you at **LAKEWOOD CAMPING RESORT.** THE place for your total vacation pleasure in Myrtle Beach. Call for free color brochure 1-800-258-8309.
**Enter #821 on Reader Service Card and See Ad Pages 76 and 77.**

**MAGIC VALLEY RV PARK** is located in the middle of the Rio Grande Valley—make it your winter home!
**Enter #99 on Reader Service Card and See Ad Page 94.**

**MAMMOTH CAVE JELLYSTONE** — an **AWARD WINNING** park — family campground emphasizing cleanliness & always a free cup of coffee. The friendly staff and convenient location offer all you need for a fun vacation. Mammoth Cave, KY.
**Enter #381 on Reader Service Card and See Ad Page 62.**

"Sea" for yourself . . . Camping is great on Martha's Vineyard! Enjoy miles of beaches and bike trails while camping at **MARTHA'S VINEYARD FAMILY CAMPGROUND**. Inquire about our new cabins. Call 508/693-3772.
**Enter #380 on Reader Service Card and See Ad Page 10.**

**MARY'S LAKE CAMPGROUND** is Estes Park's finest family-oriented campground. Adjacent to Mary's Lake, there are 40 acres of camping on meadow or tree-shaded sites, or near the pond. Special spring & fall rates.
**Enter #316 on Reader Service Card and See Ad Page 101.**

Enjoy scenic, lakefront or wooded sites 96 miles from Chicago at **MENDOTA HILLS CAMPGROUND**. FREE weekend activities. Golf course — 1/2 mile. Reserve your site now! 815/849-5930.
**Enter #814 on Reader Service Card and See Ad Page 82.**

**MILL BRIDGE CAMPRESORT** is a modern campground adjoining a reconstructed Early American Village in Lancaster. Free admission to Village while camping, including Amish buggy rides in Pennsylvania Dutch Country.
**Enter #387 on Reader Service Card and See Ad Page 40.**

**MILTON HEIGHTS CAMPGROUND** is just minutes from the 401. Sixty-two acres beneath the beautiful Niagara Escarpment, surrounded by conservation areas, and just 35 minutes from downtown Toronto. Phone: 905/878-6781; Fax: 905/878-1986.
**Enter #383 on Reader Service Card and See Ad Page 138.**

**MISSION RV PARK**—the finest luxury park in El Paso. Enclosed heated swimming and therapy pools. Daily tours to Mexico.
**Enter #97 on Reader Service Card and See Ad Page 96.**

**MODEL T CASINO/MOTEL/RV PARK,** "your fun place," is conveniently located right in downtown Winnemucca. A 24-hour "must stop" midway between Salt Lake City & San Francisco. Call: 702/623-2588.
**Enter #760 on Reader Service Card and See Ad Page 118.**

**MONARCH VALLEY RANCH** — your Colorado vacation destination is surrounded by snow-capped peaks and Gunnison National Forest. Featuring horse rentals, stocked trout fishing, Tin Cup Restaurant, RV park, lodge & cabins.
**Enter #389 on Reader Service Card and See Ad Page 102.**

**MORRIS MEADOWS RECREATION FARM** is a beautiful full-service resort close to Baltimore, Maryland and Hershey, Lancaster & Gettysburg, Penn. Extensive recreation facilities.
**Enter #119 on Reader Service Card and See Ad Page 36.**

**MYRTLE BEACH, S.C. CAMPGROUND OWNER'S ASSOCIATION** — call toll free and receive a 12-page, 4-color guide on all seven beautiful family campgrounds in Myrtle Beach, offering oceanfront, wooded and lakeside sites and great family amenities. 800/356-3016.
**Enter #788 on Reader Service Card and See Ad Page 79.**

Southern California's premier RV destination, **NEWPORT DUNES RESORT**, offers first class amenities on the waterfront.
**Enter #827 on Reader Service Card and See Ad Page 115.**

**NIAGARA GLEN-VIEW TENT & TRAILER PARK** is the closest camp to the Falls. Nestled high above the banks of the mighty Niagara River, they offer complete tour packages for groups or individuals along with daily shuttle service to the Falls.
**Enter #391 on Reader Service Card and See Ad Page 139.**

Explore historic Boston & Cape Cod's villages from **NORMANDY FARM,** the resort that offers something for everyone. Enjoy nonstop activities year-round at the Northeast's most popular campground. "We treat you like we'd want to be treated." Send for 16-page color brochure.
**Enter #392 on Reader Service Card and See Ad Page 10.**

**OAK SHORES RESORT**, located just southwest of Kalamazoo, Mich., mixes country flavor with boundless activities. Great fishing, canoeing, row boating and swimming take place on a private 115-acre lake.
**Enter #393 on Reader Service Card and See Ad Page 87.**

**OAKWOOD LAKE RESORT** is California's largest water theme park and campground. 357 sites in a woodsy setting with lake & river fishing. Campground is open year-round.
**Enter #109 on Reader Service Card and See Ad Page 114.**

**OASIS-LAS VEGAS,** Las Vegas' newest RV resort offers 700 deluxe sites, lush landscaping, meandering streams, and a champagne assortment of amenities, including an 18-hole putting course; 24,000-sq. ft. clubhouse and shuttle service to Las Vegas attractions. Call 800/566-4707.
**See Ad Page 119.**

**OCEAN VIEW RESORTS CAMPGROUND,** located in Cape May, New Jersey, is halfway between Atlantic City and Wildwood. Enjoy nearby ocean beaches or lake and pool swimming at this wooded resort.
**Enter #317 on Reader Service Card and See Ad Page 37.**

We pamper the camper at **O'CONNELL'S YOGI BEAR'S JELLYSTONE PARK CAMP-RESORT** — the finest in family camping — the camping center of Illinois. 5,000-sq. ft. convention center with climate control. Reservations only 1-800-FOR-YOGI or 815-857-3860.
**Enter #737 on Reader Service Card and See Ad Page 82.**

**OREGON DUNES KOA** is located north of Coos Bay at the southern part of Oregon Dunes National Rec. Area. Close to ATV rentals, Dunes Towers, hiking trails, casino, world-class fishing & kite flying.
**Enter #744 on Reader Service Card and See Ad Page 124.**

**OTTER LAKE CAMP RESORT** is open year-round for your camping pleasure. Situated in Pennsylvania's Pocono Mountains, it features an indoor pool complex, 60-acre lake, and winter seasonal facilities.
**Enter #762 on Reader Service Card and See Ad Page 46.**

Amarillo's most convenient RV park, **OVERNITE RV PARK** offers pull-thrus for all sizes, 50 amps & heated pool. Walk to restaurants, visit Palo Duro Canyon & see the musical, Texas.
**Enter #96 on Reader Service Card and See Ad Page 96.**

**PARK PLACE CAMPING RESORT** in beautiful Estes Park has scenic mountain views in a secluded mountain setting, only minutes to Estes Park attractions and Rocky Mountain Nat'l. Park. Off season rates available.
**Enter #394 on Reader Service Card and See Ad Page 102.**

**PAUL'S RV PARK** and **RIO RV PARK** offer year-round camping and recreation. Visit exciting Mexico and South Padre Island beaches from their convenient location!
**Enter #95 on Reader Service Card and See Ad Page 95.**

Located on the shores of Little Traverse Bay, the newest built KOA Kampground in Michigan, **PETOSKEY KOA,** is the perfect home base while visiting the Petoskey/Charlevoix area. Visit **KILWINS CANDY KITCHEN** for some delicious treats.
**Enter #770 on Reader Service Card and See Ad Page 87.**

Whatever your pleasure, you will find more than enough vacation enjoyment when you plan your next New Hampshire getaway at **PINE ACRES FAMILY CAMPGROUND**. Send for free brochure.
**Enter #396 on Reader Service Card and See Ad Page 14.**

**PINE CREST RV PARK** in Slidell, Louisiana, offers southern hospitality in their beautiful pine forest campground. Strategically located for easy access to New Orleans and southern Mississippi attractions.
**Enter #134 on Reader Service Card and See Ad Page 62.**

**PINE VALLEY RV RESORT** is a wooded campground near Quechee Gorge and other Vermont attractions, and convenient to I-89 and I-91. Large rigs welcome.
**Enter #777 on Reader Service Card and See Ad Page 31.**

Plymouth camping at **PINEWOOD LODGE,** your family's vacation retreat, nestled in the pines by the lake. Centrally located near Boston, Cape Cod and all Plymouth attractions. Send for brochure and area information.
**Enter #395 on Reader Service Card and See Ad Page 10.**

Experience the fun and excitement of Pennsylvania's Pocono Mountains at **POCONO VACATION PARK.** They offer a complete vacation in a most accessible park, less than five minutes from I-80.
**Enter #778 on Reader Service Card and See Ad Page 42.**

**POINT SEBAGO RV & GOLF RESORT** offers an extensive activity program for all ages. Resort property available for sale surrounding the golf course.
**Enter #813 on Reader Service Card and See Ad Page**

# FREE INFORMATION

**PRIMADONNA RESORTS** offers nonstop entertainment on the California/Nevada border at Stateline. Ride trains and a monorail between Buffalo Bill's, Whiskey Pete's, and the Primadonna. Experience the Desperado, the world's tallest, fastest rollercoaster. Call 1-800-367-7383.
**Enter #779 on Reader Service Card and See Ad Page 121.**

Camp at **RANCHEROS DE SANTA FE CAMPGROUND** in the quiet countryside just outside historic Santa Fe, New Mexico. Visit the famous downtown plaza, museums, Santa Fe Opera, Fiestas, Markets, rodeo, Indian Pueblos (dances).
**Enter #397 on Reader Service Card and See Ad Page 93.**

**ROAMER'S RETREAT CAMPGROUND** features great camping in the heart of beautiful Pennsylvania Dutch Country. Located next to a working Amish farm, you can watch the horse-drawn buggies pass by.
**Enter #780 on Reader Service Card and See Ad Page 44.**

**ROSEMOUNT CAMPING RESORT** is an exclusive family resort in the Appalachian Mountains of Pennsylvania. Offering beautiful wooded sites and activities galore. Rosemount's motto is "We keep your kids happy".
**Enter #402 on Reader Service Card and See Ad Page 41.**

At **RV RIVER CHARTERS,** drive your RV onto the barge decks and leave the cruising to us. Enjoy off-board activities at different ports of call. Phone: 1-800-256-6100 for available dates.
**Enter #135 on the Reader Service Card and See Ad Page 66.**

**SAFARI CAMPGROUND** in Williamsport, MD is a family-oriented and family-operated campground located in the historic Civil War area. Wooded and open sites in a park convenient to I-81 & I-70.
**Enter #120 on Reader Service Card and See Ad Page 36.**

An interesting place to stay while visiting the Mackinac Straits, **ST. IGNACE/MACKINAC ISLAND KOA** offers an on-site petting zoo and authentic Indian trading post.
**Enter #761 on Reader Service Card and See Ad Page 86.**

Dallas' **SANDY LAKE RV PARK** is the closest large RV park to downtown Dallas. Also convenient to Cowboy Stadium, DFW Airport, Six Flags, and great restaurants and shopping.
**Enter #94 on Reader Service Card and See Ad Page 96.**

Beautiful resort camping only minutes from the Chicago attractions at **SCHAUL'S COUNTRY LAKES CAMPGROUND.** Ask about weekend vacation packages. Fun for everyone in the family! Call 708/546-1515.
**Enter #781 on Reader Service Card and See Ad Page 83.**

**SCOTTYLAND CAMPING RESORT** is located in the scenic Laurel Highlands of western Pa. Featuring down-home hospitality on 300 acres, they specialize in family fun-filled camping activities.
**Enter #782 on Reader Service Card and See Ad Page 41.**

**SEASHORE CAMPGROUND** is a Christian-oriented campground located in historic Cape May, New Jersey. Close to beaches & various attractions.
**Enter #823 on Reader Service Card and See Ad Page 38.**

Choose from two fine campgrounds located in the heart of Cape Cod. From **SHADY KNOLL** or **ATLANTIC OAKS** you may explore historic villages, windmills, museums; ride on miles of bike trails, and enjoy the beautiful beaches. Call 1-800-332-CAMP.
**Enter #405 on Reader Service Card and See Ad Page 12.**

**SHERKSTON SHORES** may well be the ideal family camping and recreational facility in Ontario with its 500 acres and 2-1/2 miles of lakefront. Phone: 800-263-8121.
**Enter #404 on Reader Service Card and See Ad Page 142.**

**SPRING GULCH RESORT CAMPGROUND** is convenient to all Lancaster County attractions. Enjoy resort camping at its finest. We take your leisure seriously with our complete recreation program for all ages.
**Enter #406 on Reader Service Card and See Ad Page 41.**

**SUN N FUN,** one of Florida's largest parks, offers activities galore, an olympic size pool, lawn bowling, 24-hour security, a restaurant and more. Centrally located near theme parks & close to Gulf beaches.
**Enter #128 on Reader Service Card and See Ad Page 56.**

Only 34 miles northwest of Corpus Christi, **SUNRISE BEACH** is on Lake Corpus Christi, and features the longest freshwater pier in Texas. Enjoy this spacious campground soon!
**Enter #93 on Reader Service Card and See Ad Page 96.**

**SUNRISE TOURIST TRAILER PARK** is a friendly, clean campground where campers are pampered. On the northwest shore of Rice Lake, famous for bluegill, crappie, walleye, large & smallmouth bass & the mighty muskie.
**Enter #409 on Reader Service Card and See Ad Page 140.**

**SURFSIDE RV RESORT** in Parksville, British Columbia offers oceanfront sites with spectacular sea, mountain & estuary views.
**Enter #408 on Reader Service Card and See Ad Page 130.**

At **TALL PINES CAMPGROUND,** "We care about your good times". Fun family camping on large, shaded sites in the heart of historic, rural southwestern New Jersey. Call for more information 1-800-252-2890 or . . .
**Enter #318 on Reader Service Card and See Ad Page 38.**

**TAOS VALLEY RV PARK & CAMPGROUND** is located in the southern Rockies of northern New Mexico. Nearby are the famous Taos Indian Pueblo, Kit Carson Museum, historic sites and many art galleries.
**Enter #319 on Reader Service Card and See Ad Page 93.**

Stay at **TERRY BISON RANCH** and pretend you're back in the Old West. Weekly summer rodeos, chuckwagon dinners, bison herd, horseback riding, dude ranch packages, 100-space RV park, cabins, bunkhouse. Cheyenne Frontier Days in late July.
**Enter #410 on Reader Service Card and See Ad Page 105.**

**THREE SEASONS CAMPING RESORT.** Closest RV resort to Delaware beaches; near outlet stores, amusements, and restaurants. Phone: 800/635-4996.
**Enter #278 on Reader Service Card and See Ad Page 34.**

**TIGER RUN RESORT,** Colorado's finest RV resort with the finest amenities: large, landscaped sites, beautiful clubhouse, free cable TV, and a mountain setting close to Breckenridge's year-round activities. Open year around.
**Enter #412 on Reader Service Card and See Ad Page 101.**

**TIMBERLINE LAKE CAMPING RESORT**. Swim in our lake, pool, or take a short ride to ocean beaches. Bring your canoe or rent one nearby. Short drive to Atlantic City casinos.
**Enter #816 on Reader Service Card and See Ad Page 38.**

**TREETOPS VILLAGE RV PARK** in Arlington, TX — in the heart of the Dallas/Ft. Worth metroplex. Beautiful 5✪ park with large, shaded sites, A/C restrooms & laundry. Easy access, near great restaurants & shopping.
**Enter #92 on Reader Service Card and See Ad Page 96.**

**UNITED CAMPGROUND of DURANGO** is located at the north edge of town featuring modern full facilities. Campers are entertained by the Silverton Narrow Gauge Railroad passing through the campground. A great base for visiting historic Durango, Colorado.
**Enter #784 on Reader Service Card and See Ad Page 102.**

In the shadow of the fabled Sleeping Ute Mountains lies the Four Corners' only casino gaming at **UTE MOUNTAIN CASINO.** Have a memorable vacation at the casino and new **SLEEPING UTE RV PARK & CAMPGROUND** while visiting other Anasazi Indian sites.
**Enter #817 on Reader Service Card and See Ad Page 100.**

Enjoy the old-fashioned charm of the new **VICTORIAN RV PARK** in Sparks, Nevada. Just minutes away from Reno/Sparks attractions & glitter. Shuttle service to casinos. Call 1-800-955-6405.
**Enter #107 on Reader Service Card and See Ad Page 117.**

Camp in the heart of historyland. Make **WARWICK WOODS FAMILY CAMPING RESORT** your headquarters for visiting Philadelphia, Hershey, Lancaster and Valley Forge, or enjoy peaceful beauty away from it all.
**Enter #785 on Reader Service Card and See Ad Page 41.**

**WELLS BEACH RESORT** offers a quality camping experience in the heart of southern Maine's resort area.
**Enter #798 on Reader Service Card and See Ad Page 8.**

**WEST WORLD** in Scottsdale, Ariz., offers an RV park with an equestrian emphasis and numerous outdoor interests and special events throughout the year.
**Enter #818 on Reader Service Card and See Ad Page 108.**

At **WHIPPOORWILL CAMPGROUND** you can choose the beach nearby or the pool in the park. Beautiful wooded sites in the heart of the New Jersey shore.
**Enter #745 on Reader Service Card and See Ad Page 38.**

**WHISPERING PINES CAMPGROUND & RESORT** is in Tyler, the home of the Rose Festival & Azalea Trail. Convenient to East Texas, Dallas, Canton First Monday & Louisiana casinos.
**Enter #141 on Reader Service Card and See Ad Page 99.**

Escape to **WOGENSTAHL'S RESORT AND TRAILER PARK** with ultra-modern housekeeping cabins and full-hookup sites in a beautiful, secluded setting on Cedar Lake in Ontario. A fishing & hunting paradise for mom and dad; kids love the sand and playground.
**Enter #786 on Reader Service Card and See Ad Page 142.**

**WOLF'S CAMPING RESORT,** located in northwestern Pennsylvania, offers complete recreational facilities, including daily activities and a water complex with whirlpool and waterslide; also a golf course and Wolf's Den Restaurant.
**Enter #763 on Reader Service Card and See Ad Page 44.**

**WOODLAND ACRES CAMP N CANOE** offers riverside sites on the beautiful Saco River with canoe rentals and transports available.
**Enter #812 on Reader Service Card and See Ad Page 3.**

**WOODLAND PARK,** a family campground emphasizing cleanliness & quiet, is within walking distance of a beautiful sandy beach on Lake Huron. Indoor heated pool, full services, cement patios, store, laundry, satellite TV and game room.
**Enter #330 on Reader Service Card and See Ad Page 140.**

**WOODY MOUNTAIN CAMPGROUND** offers tree-shaded sites in a forest setting. Owners escort each vehicle to their site for the extra attention visitors love. A great base camp to visit Grand Canyon and the Williams Steam Train.
**Enter #111 on Reader Service Card and See Ad Page 111.**

**YELLOWSTONE GRIZZLY RV PARK** is a new RV park scheduled to open in spring of 1996. Located in a prime Montana tourist area at the west entrance to Yellowstone National Park and close to many attractions & shopping.
**Enter #764 on Reader Service Card and See Ad Page 103.**

Stay inside **YELLOWSTONE NATIONAL PARK** at one of their campgrounds and wake up with geysers, elk and bison. Reserve your site by phoning **TW Recreational Services** at 307/344-7311.
**Enter #729 on Reader Service Card and See Ad Page 105.**

**YOGI BEAR'S JELLYSTONE PARK CAMP-RESORT** is an activity-oriented campground in central New Jersey. Closest campground to Great Adventure Safari & Amusement Park.
**Enter #787 on Reader Service Card and See Ad Page 39.**

**YOGI BEAR'S JELLYSTONE PARK CAMP-RESORT** is located in the heart of Ontario's beautiful Niagara Peninsula, 3-1/2 miles from the breathtaking Horseshoe Falls. Come join the famous bears for a fun-filled family vacation at Jellystone Park — where you camp with friends.
**Enter #419 on Reader Service Card and See Ad Page 135.**

At **YOGI BEAR'S JELLYSTONE PARK CAMP-RESORT** in Luray, Virginia, you are only minutes from Luray Caverns and the Skyline Drive. Enjoy the full range of recreation as you relax at this full service campground.
**Enter #421 on Reader Service Card and See Ad Page 48.**

**YOGI BEAR'S JELLYSTONE PARK CAMP-RESORT AT BIRCHWOOD ACRES** is a luxury camping resort with outstanding recreation & camping facilities. Located in the heart of the Catskills.
**Enter #829 on Reader Service Card and See Ad Page 26.**

**YOGI-BEAR'S JELLYSTONE PARK CAMP-RESORTS** are "Where You Camp With Friends!" Enjoy any one of their over 70 entertaining full-facility Camp-Resorts. For reservations, please call 1-800-558-2954.
**Enter #733 on Reader Service Card and See Ad Page 13.**

The RV Park & Campground is just a part of **ZEPHYR COVE RESORT**— there's the beach, marina, the new *M.S. Dixie II*, stables, restaurant, cabins, snowmobile center & more... all on the shores of Lake Tahoe!
**Enter #106 on Reader Service Card and See Ad Page 120.**

## TOURISM/ATTRACTION INFORMATION

**ALASKA MARINE HIGHWAY** — Drive the other Alaska Highway. Explore the byways of the Inside Passage which connects you with exciting places off the beaten path. Accommodates vehicles or walk-on passengers.
**Enter #722 on Reader Service Card and See Ad Page 106.**

Visit **ALBERTA'S CULTURAL & HISTORIC SITES** throughout the province, where history can be experienced at museums, historic sites and interpretive centres. Phone: 800/661-8888.
**Enter #723 on Reader Service Card and See Ad Page 131.**

**BATON ROUGE CONVENTION & VISITORS BUREAU** is the information center for Louisiana's capital city. The perfect place to begin your adventure of plantation homes, Southern hospitality, colorful festivals and Creole cuisine at its best!
**Enter #129 on Reader Service Card and See Ad Page 67.**

The **BATTLESHIP NORTH CAROLINA,** a faithfully restored WWII warship, offers daily tours. During the summer its history is recreated in an outdoor sound and light spectacular.
**Enter #137 on Reader Service Card and See Ad Page 72.**

Call the **BRANSON LAKES AREA CHAMBER OF COMMERCE** for information on the country music entertainment capital of the world! Information packages available for campgrounds, shows, restaurants and attractions. 417-334-4136.
**Enter #726 on Reader Service Card and See Ad Page 91.**

Experience Christmas all year around at the world famous **BRONNER'S CHRISTMAS WONDERLAND,** set in the heart of Frankenmuth, Michigan's quaint Little Bavarian Town.
**Enter # 727on Reader Service Card and See Ad Page 86.**

**CAPE BRETON ISLAND** is a part of Nova Scotia, yet apart. From the historic coastline to the scenic Cabot Trail, there's a campground waiting for you. Phone: 1-800-565-9464.
**Enter #951 on Reader Service Card and See Ad Page 134.**

Preserving its 1900s appearance, historic **CRATER LAKE LODGE** at Rim Village has been newly re-opened on the rim of beautiful Crater lake in the National Park. Rim Village also includes a visitor center, large cafeteria and gift shop.
**Enter #828 on Reader Service Card and See Ad Page 124.**

Make Durango your base camp for western attractions, rafting, mountain biking, fishing, and many "off-road" experiences. The **DURANGO AREA CHAMBER RESORT ASSOCIATION** will help with your vacation plans. Phone: 800/463-8726.
**Enter #753 on Reader Service Card and See Ad Page 100.**

**DUTCH VILLAGE** — Along the shores of Lake Macatawa, an inlet of Lake Michigan, is Holland, Michigan, which is home to an authentic reproduction "Dutch Village" complete with shops, performances and a restaurant.
**Enter #725 on Reader Service Card and See Ad Page 84.**

**ENSENADA,** "Baja's Best Kept Secret," is only 70 miles south of the border, but a world away. Experience the history and culture of Baja and the many activities, tours, shopping and dining. Phone: 800/310-9687 or Fax: 011-52-8-8588.
**Enter #121 on Reader Service Card and See Ad Page 127.**

**GRAND CASINO AVOYELLES** is Louisiana's newest and largest land-based casino featuring: 3 great restaurants, supervised child care, and gaming at its best. Open 7 days a week, 24 hours a day.
**Enter #768 and #367 on Reader Service Card and See Ads Pages 67 and 70.**

**THE GREAT PASSION PLAY**, in Eureka Springs, Arkansas, presents America's #1 outdoor drama — a re-enactment of Christ's life, death, resurrection and ascension.
**Enter #498 on Reader Service Card and See Ad Page 90.**

No trip to Arkansas is complete without a visit to **HOT SPRINGS!** Top family attractions are everywhere, as well as great campgrounds and RV parks.
**Enter #692 on Reader Service Card and See Ad Page 90.**

Riverboat gambling in one of the South's most historic cities with full service upscale RV park and free shuttle to the casino; friendly staff and gorgeous location. **ISLE OF CAPRI** — Vicksburg, Miss. Come for a visit — you'll return often!
**Enter #372 on Reader Service Card and See Ad Page 73.**

**THE JOHN CABOT 500TH ANNIVERSARY** (1997), is a full year of celebrations honoring Cabot and the spirit of his voyage to Newfoundland and Labrador in 1497. Art, song, research and a sailing replica of his ship are just some of the events. Phone: 1-800-563-NFLD.
**See Ad Page 133.**

Bluegrass music, burgoo and barbecue. Fiddlers & fairs. Arts & crafts. Whatever you love, you'll find it **KENTUCKY!** Come fiddle around and have some fun. Discover the uncommon wealth of Kentucky — Phone KY Dept. of Travel: 1-800/225-TRIP for free information.
**Enter #720 on Reader Service Card and See Ad Page 63.**

**KITTATINNY CANOES COUNTRY** — where great times are natural! Camp, raft and canoe on the Delaware River in Pennsylvania or New York. Adventure in either calm or whitewater; also tubing and kayaking.
**Enter #771 on Reader Service Card and See Ad Page 40.**

For a memorable holiday or meeting, c'mon, get caught in the spell of that Smoky Mountain magic in **KNOXVILLE,** the World's Fair City in East Tennessee.
**Enter #773 on Reader Service Card and See Ad Page 80.**

Feel the pulse of Cajun Country in **LAFAYETTE, LOUISIANA,** the heart of Acadiana. This unique city blends eclectic cultural traditions with contemporary sophistication. Stop by for ideas and information.
**Enter #132 on Reader Service Card and See Ad Page 66.**

Let **LaGRANGE AREA CHAMBER OF COMMERCE** tell you about one of Texas' best little hidden treasures.
**Enter #743 on Reader Service Card and See Ad Page 98.**

A resort community specializing in year-round water activities on the Colorado River including fishing, houseboating and water skiing. **LAKE HAVASU CITY** is home to the famous London Bridge.
**Enter #774 on Reader Service Card and See Ad Page 110.**

**LIVE OAK GARDENS** in New Iberia, Lousiana, offers a unique semi-tropical garden with a magnificent Victorian house, an art gallery with changing exhibits, a restaurant, museum and store.
**Enter #133 on Reader Service Card and See Ad Page 71.**

In **LOUISIANA,** our food, music and words are different. Very different. So, come on down, and say things you've never seen before. For your FREE tour guide and planning kit, call 1-800/753-6799.
**Enter #695 on Reader Service Card and See Ad Page 64.**

Experience **MARK TWAIN CAVE** where Tom Sawyer and Huck Finn had all their adventures. Tours daily for all ages. Camp in their quiet, secluded valley and dine at new Olivia's Restaurant.
**Enter #382 on Reader Service Card and See Ad Page 91.**

**McALLEN CHAMBER OF COMMERCE** provides information on things to do and places to go in the "Texas Tropics". Phone 512-682-2871.
**Enter #98 on Reader Service Card and See Ad Page 99.**

**McKENZIE COUNTY,** North Dakota is the gateway to the North Unit of Theodore Roosevelt National Park. The Old West is kept alive in area museums, rodeos, trail rides, working ranches and wide open spaces.
**Enter #776 on Reader Service Card and See Ad Page 104.**

**MESA CONVENTION & VISITORS BUREAU.** Mesa, Arizona has it all! Shopping, restaurants, museums, the Symphony, and great RV parks and resorts. It's the perfect destination for the active 55 and older senior lifestyle.
**Enter #759 on Reader Service Card and See Ad Page 108.**

A **MICHIGAN** vacation allows you to enjoy the outdoors without leaving the city too far behind. Phone 1-800-5432-YES for a free Michigan Travel Planner.
**Enter #696 on Reader Service Card and See Ad Page 85.**

The **MOBILE CONVENTION and VISITORS' BUREAU** offers information on the city of Mobile, Alabama. Free maps & guides available.
**Enter #388 on Reader Service Card and See Ad Page 52.**

Let **MONROE COUNTY TOURIST COUNCIL** be your guide while in the Florida Keys. Choose from two oceans with many waterfront camping & RV sites. Enjoy water sports or just relax. Phone 1-800-FLA-KEYS.
**Enter #527 on Reader Service Card and See Ad Page 53.**

**NATURAL BRIDGE CAVERNS,** between San Antonio and New Braunfels, are Texas' largest caverns. Guided tours 9 a.m.-4 p.m. (9 a.m.-6 p.m. June thru Labor Day). Open all year. Call: 210/651-6101.
**Enter #390 on Reader Service Card and See Ad Page 94.**

**NEVADA COMMISSION ON TOURISM.** Discover both sides of Nevada. Call 1-800-NEVADA-8 for a free color brochure and state map.
**Enter #698 on Reader Service Card and See Ad Page 122.**

**THE NIAGARA PARKS COMMISSION,** Niagara Falls, Ontario, operates a great Niagara Falls attractions package, all-day transportation on the modern People Movers, fully-serviced campsites and fine restaurants.
**Enter #863 on Reader Service Card and See Ad Pages 136 and 137.**

**QUEBEC** offers pristine wilderness, wildlife reserves, national and provincial parks and fully-equipped camping facilities. A unique experience for the true wildlife enthusiast. For a FREE Quebec Campgrounds Guide phone: 1-800/363-7777, operator 001.
**Enter #697 on Reader Service Card and See Ad Page 144.**

**REMINGTON-ALBERTA CARRIAGE CENTRE** — one of the finest displays of horsedrawn transportation with more than 200 vehicles. Features a working stable, a fire hall, carriage factory and numerous videos.
**Enter #398 on Reader Service Card and See Ad Page 129.**

Visit **ST. TAMMANY PARISH** and enjoy historic towns and villages, affordable hotels & restaurants, distinctive shops, family attractions and festivals. All a short drive from casinos and the French Quarter.
**Enter #407 on Reader Service Card and See Ad Page 64.**

**SARASOTA** — "The Vacation Location," centrally located on the west coast of Florida. Come tour and enjoy the beautiful beaches & islands, plus visit the many attractions.
**Enter #127 on Reader Service Card and See Ad Page 55.**

**SASKATCHEWAN TOURISM** has the information you need for your camping adventures, as well as other vacation experiences–from visiting historic sites to participating in outdoor sports. Phone: 1-800-667-7191.
**Enter #721 on Reader Service Card and See Ad Page 145.**

**SOUTHERN WEST VIRGINIA CONVENTION & VISITORS BUREAU**
Escape to the Heart of the Appalachians. Exciting outdoor adventures — whitewater rafting, comfortable campgrounds, tours of mines, caves and historic towns, plus outdoor musical entertainment. Free vacation planning kit.
**Enter #815 on Reader Service Card and See Ad Page 50.**

**STRATFORD,** Ontario is home to one of the world's finest classical theatres, the Stratford Festival. This Victorian city features excellent shopping, dining, galleries and a beautiful parks system. Additional special events compliment theatre activities. Phone: 1-800/561-SWAN.
**Enter #783 on Reader Service Card and See Ad Page 140.**

**TURNING STONE CASINO** offers all you need for a fun vacation. Full service, upscale RV park with on-site recreation and free shuttle to the casino; friendly staff and convenient location.
**Enter #794 on Reader Service Card and See Ad Page 28.**

Stay awhile in beautiful **WACO, TEXAS,** with over 100 riverside RV spaces at Fort Fisher Campground and over 1000 rally sites at Heart O'Texas Fair Complex. Phone 1-800-WACO-FUN.
**Enter #416 on Reader Service Card and See Ad Page 95.**

Contact **WESTERN KENTUCKY'S AUDUBON REGION** for great hunting, fishing, bluegrass and blues festivals, camping and scenic beauty. Write Travel Dev. GR 17, PO Box 2011, Frankfort, KY 40602-2011.
**Enter #796 on Reader Service Card and See Ad Page 62.**

## GENERAL

The **AMERICAN ASSOCIATION FOR NUDE RECREATION** is the oldest and largest nudist organization in North America. Represents over 200 private clubs & parks located throughout the U.S.A. & Canada. Call 1-800/879-6833.
**Enter #332 on Reader Service Card and See Ad Page 54.**

**CAMPER CLUBS OF AMERICA** offers $5 RV hookups at over 230 quality RV parks nationwide, 365 days a year. For information call: 1-800/369-CAMP (2267).
**Enter #765 on Reader Service Card and See Ad Page 33.**

**CAMPER FORCE** Directory offers more than 1,500 listings of campgrounds and resorts that will pay you while camping. For information, call: 414/793-4088.
**Enter #740 on Reader Service Card and See Ad Page 84.**

**CHEVROLET,** the manufacturer of the most dependable, longest-lasting trucks on the road, introduces the all-new Chevy Blazer, the only sport utility vehicle with the Exclusive Driver Control System for better handling and more control. For more information call 1-800/950-0540.
**See Ad Pages 4 and 5.**

**THE NEXT EXIT** saves time, money and frustration. It is an invaluable aid in locating desired services along interstate highways in an unprecedented way.
**Enter #139 on Reader Service Card and See Ad Page 72.**

**RRR RV EMERGENCY ROAD SERVICE** is the original RV program. Deal directly with the service provider. Dependable assistance from RV experts anywhere in the U.S. and Canada. Unlimited coverage with one call. Only $69.95. To enroll, call 1-800/999-7505.
**Enter #864 on Reader Service Card and See Ad Page 49.**

**WOODALL'S ERS** is the premier 24-hour emergency road service plan for travelling throughout North America. RVers came up with the plan, so you know it's comprehensive. Woodall's benefits package is not found in any other road service plan. Call 1-800-626-ROAD.
**Enter #855 on Reader Service Card and See Ad Page 32.**

**WORLDWIDE MOTORHOME RENTALS, INC.** is an independent broker dealing exclusively in motorhome rentals, distributing rates and information of over 900 rental companies and private owners in the United States, Canada and Europe.
**Enter #730 on Reader Service Card and See Ad Page 118.**

# FREE CAMPING INFORMATION

# Travel Sections

**SAVE HOURS OF RESEARCH!**

The campgrounds/RV parks, RV service centers and attractions listed below want your business! To help plan your next trip, here is a quick and easy way to receive **free travel and camping information**. Simply enter the **Reader Service Number** (listed below) on the **Reader Service Card**, which is located opposite page 16. Your request will be forwarded to the businesses you've indicated. Then, **you'll receive brochures and/or pricing information**, sent directly to your home. It's the no-hassle way to plan your next trip!

**Enter Number**

**ALABAMA**

607 Alabama Bureau of Tourism
324 Alabama State Parks
534 Army Aviation Museum
177 Ave Maria Grotto
323 De Soto Caverns
531 Mobile Convention & Visitors Bureau
597 Natchez Valley Campground
178 Noccalula Falls
523 Ozark Area Chamber of Commerce
176 Sequoyah Caverns
533 Talladega Super Speedway

**ALASKA**

605 Alaska Marine Highway System
287 Alaska Recreational Rentals
470 Anchorage Convention & Visitors Bureau
288 Beluga Lookout RV Park
205 Fireweed RV Rentals
456 Golden Nugget Camper Park
289 McKinley KOA Kampground
606 Phillips Cruises & Tours
206 Santa Claus House
348 Smith's Green Acres RV Park
207 Tickets, Tours, Trips & Things

**ARIZONA**

336 Apache Skies Mobile Home Park
535 Grand Travel
208 Hon-Dah Casino
335 Papillon Grand Canyon Helicopters
611 The Peanut Patch
516 Roger's RV Resort Golf & Country Club
536 Sanborn's Mexico Insurance
337 Venture In RV Resort

**ARKANSAS**

608 Hot Springs Convention & Visitors Bureau
290 Parkway Travel Park
609 Pine Mountain Jamboree
610 Springdale Chamber of Commerce
192 White River Campground
596 Wiederkehr Village

**CALIFORNIA**

226 Anaheim Harbor RV Park
613 California Campground Consultants
582 California Travel Parks Assn.
612 Camper Clubs of America
346 Campland on the Bay
345 Circle RV Ranch

**Enter Number**

578 Fairplex RV Park
577 International Recreation Enterprises
209 Mike Daugherty Chevrolet RV Center
615 Napa Town & Country Fairgrounds
614 Newport Dunes Resort
347 Oak Creek RV Park
210 Orangeland RV Park
211 Paradise by the Sea
349 Rancho Casa Blanca
344 Rancho Los Coches RV Park
712 San Bernardino County Regional Parks Dept.
704 Sun N Fun
484 Trailer Villa
579 Two Harbors Campground

**COLORADO**

537 A & A Mesa Verde RV Park & Resort
291 Battlement Mesa
590 Blue Mountain Village
491 Cripple Creek Chamber of Commerce
489 Cross D Bar Trout Ranch
213 Denver North Campground
622 Durango Area Chamber of Commerce
292 East Tin Cup Village
540 Great Sand Dunes Oasis Campground
621 Gunnison Country Chamber of Commerce
490 Koshare Indian Museum & Kiva
197 Mollie Kathleen Gold Mine
492 Pagosa Springs Area Chamber of Commerce
488 River's Edge RV Resort
620 Wilderness Aware Rafting
293 Winding River Resort Village
493 Wogenstahl's Canadian Resort & Trailer Park

**CONNECTICUT**

445 CT Campground Owners

**DISTRICT OF COLUMBIA**

294 Aquia Pines Camp Resort
385 Capitol KOA
215 Cherry Hill Park
384 Duncan's Family Campground
216 Jamestown Beach Campsites
295 KOA-Fredericksburg/D.C.
217 KOA-Virginia Beach
623 KOA-Williamsburg
593 Mountain View Campground
296 Prince William Travel Trailer

**Enter Number**

193 Williamsburg Pottery Fair-oaks Campground
297 Yogi Bear's Jellystone Park

**FLORIDA**

179 Arrowhead Campsites
624 Brookville Campground
625 Camp Mack's River Resort
628 Camper Clubs of America
218 Dunedin Beach Campground
444 Florida Assn. of RV Parks and Campgrounds
219 Florida Camp Inn
629 Florida State Parks
214 Giant Recreation World
626 Ginnie Springs Resort
401 Holiday Travel Park
627 KOA-Williamsburg
221 Orlando Southeast KOA
630 Panama City Beach Convention & Visitors Bureau
400 Pleasant Lake
706 South Walton Tourist Dev. Council

**GEORGIA**

631 Camper Clubs of America
496 Chehaw Park
495 Flat Creek Ranch
417 Georgia Mountain Fair
499 Georgia State Parks & Historic Sites
222 Georgia Stone Mountain Park

**IDAHO**

399 Idaho RV Campground Assn.

**ILLINOIS**

632 Gages Lake Camping
541 Holiday Acres Jellystone Park
542 O'Connell's Yogi Bear Jellystone Park

**INDIANA**

446 Camp-Land
475 Pla-Mor Park
543 RV America
544 Williams Broken Arrow CG & Trailer Sales

**IOWA**

425 Grotto of the Redemption RV Park
223 Keokuk River Museum
298 Sleepy Hollow RV Park & Campground
426 Walnut Acres Campground

**KANSAS**

424 Boot Hill Museum
545 Dalton Gang Hideout
497 Kansas Campground Owners Assn.

**Enter Number**

**KENTUCKY**

468 Land Between the Lakes
225 Mobile Parts

**LOUISIANA**

587 Louisiana Travel Promotion Association
546 Sabine River Authority

**MAINE**

636 Acres of Wildlife
547 Bayley's Pine Point Resort
548 Brake Service & RV Parts
635 Desert of Maine
637 Kezar Lake Camping Area
549 ME Campground Owners
634 Moosehead Marine Museum/Katahdin Cruises
473 Timberland Acres RV Park

**MARYLAND**

228 Cherry Hill Park
144 Eagle's Nest Park

**MASSACHUSETTS**

583 MA Assn. of CG Owners
633 Plymouth Co. Attractions
299 Springbrook Family Camping

**MICHIGAN**

443 Acres & Trails KOA of Oscoda
638 Bronner's Christmas Wonderland
640 Cook Energy Information Center
457 Holiday Park Campground
550 Houghton Lake Travel Park
300 Jellystone Park
552 Pine Crest Campground
455 Poncho's Pond
301 Sutter's Recreation Area
Happy Mohawk Canoe Livery
551 Vegas Kewadin Casino
554 White River Campground

**MINNESOTA**

556 Beaver Trails Campground
641 Lake Byllesby Campground
584 Minnesota Assn. of Campground Operators
302 Shooting Star Casino
555 Thompson Motorhome Sales

**MISSISSIPPI**

230 Columbus Convention & Visitors Bureau
509 Grand Gulf Military Park
644 Mississippi Division of Parks & Recreation
231 Oxbow RV Park
232 Pat Harrison Waterway District

**Enter Number**

233 Reliable RV Sales
643 Washington County Conven. & Visitors Bureau

**MISSOURI**

188 Jason Place Campground
642 Missouri Assn. of Parks & Campgrounds
229 Old Dawt Mill
184 Willow Springs Campground

**MONTANA**

180 Montana CG Owners Assn.

**NEBRASKA**

586 Nebraska Dept. of Economic Dev. & Tourism

**NEVADA**

538 Safari Stores

**NEW HAMPSHIRE**

467 Arcadia Campground
507 Hart's Turkey Farm Restaurant
647 NH Div. of Parks & Rec.
558 Terrace Pines
528 White Mtn. Attractions

**NEW JERSEY**

303 Cold Spring Village
182 Frontier Campground
648 KOA-Williamsburg
234 NJ CG Owners Assn.
242 Whippoorwill Campground

**NEW MEXICO**

214 Red Rock State Park & City of Gallup

**NEW YORK**

652 Buckridge Nudist Park
649 Campark Resorts
553 Campground Owners of NY
714 Chautauqua-Allegheny Region
651 Fulton Co. Tourism Office
653 Kittatinny CG & Canoes
181 KOA-Niagara Falls
656 KOA-Williamsburg
655 Leatherstocking Country
650 New York State Department of Environmental Conserv.
705 Oswego County Dept.
142 Shalamar Lake Niagara
654 Sullivan County Office of Public Information
508 Yogi Bear's Jellystone Park Camp-Resort–Flatrock
244 Yogi Bear's Jellystone Park Camp-Resort–Niagara Falls, ON

**NORTH CAROLINA**

646 Camper Clubs of America
240 Hot Springs RV Park & Campground
304 Midway Campground & RV Resort
581 Paramount's Carowinds
241 Sassafras Gap Campground
645 Singing Waters Camping Resort

**NORTH DAKOTA**

460 Bonanzaville USA–A Pioneer Village

**OHIO**

657 Amish Farm & Home
661 Camper Clubs of America
660 Convention & Tourist Bureau of Greater Logan County

**Enter Number**

245 Hickory Grove Lake Campground
662 KOA–Williamsburg
664 Marietta Area Tourist & Convention Bureau
246 MohicanWilderness
663 Ohio Dept. of Natural Resources
247 Sauder Farm & Craft Village
658 Whispering Hills Family Campground
560 Yogi Bear's Jellystone Park

**OKLAHOMA**

305 Indian Nation RV Resort
248 KOA-Checotah/Henryetta

**OREGON**

668 Astoria/Warrenton Chamber of Commerce
483 Baker Co. Visitor & Convention Bureau
715 Flying M Ranch
669 La Grande/Union County Chamber of Commerce
306 Northcoast Myrtle Wood Outlet
667 Pear Tree Motel & RV Park
465 Pendleton Roundup Assn.
562 Philomath Frolic & Rodeo Grounds
563 Reedsport/Winchester Bay Chamber of Commerce
564 Sumpter Valley Railroad

**PENNSYLVANIA**

707 Bucks County Tourist Commission
671 Gettysburg Travel Council
510 Kittatinny Canoes
670 KOA-Williamsburg
511 PA CG Owners Assn.

**SOUTH CAROLINA**

255 Discover Upcountry Carolina Assn.
256 Pendleton Dist. Commission

**SOUTH DAKOTA**

183 Camp McKen–Z
308 4 B's Campground
672 Pierre Area Chamber
307 Sitting Bull Crystal Caverns
257 Tee Pee Campground
569 Wylie Park Campground

**TENNESSEE**

190 Countryside Resort
189 Holiday Nashville Travel Pk.
258 Lazy Daze Campground
187 Two Rivers Campground

**TEXAS**

617 Alamo–KOA
148 Alamo Rec-Veh Park
259 Ancira Motorhomes
619 Baehre Real Estate
675 Cameron County CG Owners
676 Camper Clubs of America
260 The Country Place
261 East Lucas RV Park
616 Fort Clark Springs
673 Fun N Sun
263 Lakeside RV Resort & Marina
708 Mountain View RV Park
570 Natural Bridge Caverns
674 Oak Forest RV Park
264 Rio Vista Resort
262 Sanborn's Mexico Insurance
618 Weslaco Area Chamber of Commerce

**Enter Number**

**UTAH**

717 Dinosaurland Travel Board
592 Sevier County Travel Council
677 UT Campground Owners
678 Washington County Travel & Convention Bureau

**VERMONT**

487 Rest N' Nest

**VIRGINIA**

309 Bethpage Camp–Resort
679 Bull Run Regional Park
265 Cherrystone Camping Resort
266 Colonial Campground
267 Holiday Trav-L-Park
268 Jamestown Beach Campsites
594 KOA-Chesapeake Bay/Smith Island
680 KOA–Williamsburg
269 KOA-Virginia Beach
191 KOA–Wytheville
270 Williamsburg Pottery Fairoaks Campground

**WASHINGTON**

572 Centralia Factory Outlets
573 Conestoga Quarters RV Park
682 Copalis Beach Surf & Sand RV Park
683 Driftwood RV Park & Cabins
574 Elma RV Park
427 Eric's RV Performance Center
436 Harmony Lakeside RV Park
684 Lake Bronson Club Family Nudist Park
186 Lakeside RV Park
575 Ocean Park Resort–La Push
600 Ocean Park Resort–Ocean Park
454 Peabody Creek RV Park
175 Ponderosa Hill–A Park Washington Facility
474 Willapa Harbor Golf Course & RV Park

**WEST VIRGINIA**

576 Southern West Virginia Convention & Visitors Bur.

**WISCONSIN**

271 Sanders Park

**WYOMING**

685 Cody Country Chamber of Commerce
686 Lionshead RV Park Resort
476 Thermopolis Chamber of Commerce

**ALBERTA**

204 Mirage Adventure Tours
450 Shoreline Camping & Fishing Resort

**BRITISH COLUMBIA**

703 BC Motels, Campgrounds & Resorts Assn.

**MANITOBA**

227 Magic Valley Park
479 Shady Oaks RV Resort & CG

**NEW BRUNSWICK**

701 Natural Resources & Energy

**NEWFOUNDLAND**

517 O'Briens Bird Island Charters

**NOVA SCOTIA**

224 Anne Murray Centre
559 Dunromin Campsites
310 Fundy Trail Campground
452 Ovens Natural Park

**Enter Number**

**ONTARIO**

440 Birchwood Cottages Tent & Trailer Park
689 Campark Resorts
500 Cedar Valley Resort
311 The Dunes Oakridge Park
501 Glenrock Cottages & Trailer Park
249 Grand River Conservation Authority
469 Huronia Historical Park
250 Knight's Hide-Away Park
502 Lafontaine Campground & RV Park
312 Little Austria Campground
503 Narrows Lock Campground
504 Nighthawk Retreat
561 Nottawasaga Valley Conser. Authority
471 Ontario Gem Mining Co.
852 Ontario Private Campground Owners Association
438 Roth Park
690 St. Lawrence Parks Comm.
251 Sand Hill Park
313 Saugeen Valley Conservation Authority
314 Stratford Tourism Department
505 West Lake Willows

**QUEBEC**

529 Camping Annie
580 Camping Domaine de la Chute
253 Camping Panoramique de Portneuf
530 Domaine Parc Estrie
566 Pourvoirie Domaine Lac Malcom
585 Quebec Camping Guide
568 Societe Des Casinos du Quebec
567 Winter Location

**SASKATCHEWAN**

691 Heart of Canada's Old Northwest

**YUKON**

143 MacKenzie's RV Park

**BAJA MEXICO**

235 Experience Baja
754 Discover Baja Travel Club
236 Ensenada Tourism & Conven. Bureau
237 Happy Camper Mobile RV Service
238 Instant Mexico Auto Insurance Specialist
694 MacAfee & Edwards Mexican Insurance
239 Mulege Chamber of Commerce
755 Solmar Fishing Fleet
603 Special Interest Videos
604 Vagabundos Del Mar Travel Club

**MAINLAND MEXICO**

557 Sanborn's Mexico Insurance

# FREE CAMPING INFORMATION
# Seasonal Guide

## SAVE HOURS OF RESEARCH!

The campgrounds/RV parks, RV service centers and attractions listed below want your business! Here is a quick and easy way to receive **free information** about seasonal camping, fun things to do, and where to service your RV or buy a new one. Simply enter their **Reader Service Number** (listed below) on the **Reader Service Card,** which is located opposite page 16. Your request will be forwarded to the names you've indicated. Then, **you'll receive brochures and/or pricing information,** sent directly to your home. It's the no-hassle way to shop for the campground, attraction or RV dealership you are interested in!

**Enter Number**

**ALABAMA**
149 Lake Eufaula Campground

**ARIZONA**
789 Fiesta Grande, An RV Resort
151 Gringo Pass RV Park
790 Quail Run RV Park
515 Roger's RV Resort Golf & Country Club
791 Silveridge RV Resort
793 Venture In RV Resort
792 Villa Alameda RV Resort

**ARKANSAS**
321 Riverside Mobile & RV Park

**CALIFORNIA**
718 Big River RV Park
196 The California RV Resort
803 Campland on the Bay
875 Carbonero Creek Travel Trailer Village
802 Circle RV Ranch
174 Clio's River's Edge Trailer Resort
804 De Anza Harbor Resort
700 Desert Trails RV Park & Country Club
810 East Shore RV Park
173 Emerald Desert Country Club
805 Escondido RV Resort
874 Fairplex RV Park
873 Far Horizons 49er Trailer Village
811 Golden Village RV Resort
435 Mammoth Mountain RV Park
871 Mountain Valley RV Park
150 Mountain View RV Park
870 Newport Dunes Resort
800 Oak Creek RV Park
806 Palm Canyon Resort RV Park
801 Paradise by the Sea RV Park
809 Rancho Casa Blanca
799 Rancho Los Coches RV Park
172 Salton City Spa & RV Park
807 Santee Lakes Regional Park & Campground
876 Sun & Fun RV Park
482 Tahoe Valley Campground
808 29 Palms RV Resort
872 Valencia Travel Village
950 Yosemite Pines RV Park

**Enter Number**

**COLORADO**
880 Alpen–Rose RV Park
878 Coachlight RV Park & Motel
877 Conejos River Campground
879 Diamond Campground & RV Park
513 Garden of the Gods Campground
881 Monarch Valley Ranch
522 Navajo Trail Campgorund
521 Riversedge RV Resort
882 Stagecoach Campground & Lodging
883 Ute Bluff Lodge RV Park

**CONNECTICUT**
884 Strawberry Park Resort Campground

**FLORIDA**
849 Bryn Mawr Ocean Resort
890 Camp Mack's River Resort
169 Central Park
893 Crystal Lake Village
894 Emerald Pointe RV Resort
842 Holiday Campground
850 KOA-Punta Gorda/Charlotte Harbor Kampground
888 Many Mansions RV Park
891 Meadowlark Campground
168 Naples RV Resort
414 Orange Harbor Mobile Home & RV Park
851 Panacea RV Park
845 Quail Roost RV Campground
170 Road Runner Travel Resort
892 Rock Creek Campgrounds
846 Sarasota Bay Travel Trailer Park
283 Southern Comfort RV Resort
843 Sumter Oaks RV Park
719 Tampa East Green Acres RV Travel Park
887 Travel Towne Travel Trailer Resort
279 Travel World
171 Upriver Campground
847 Village Park Luxury RV Park
889 Woodsmoke Camping Resort
844 Yogi Bear's Jellystone Park Camp-Resort

**Enter Number**

**GEORGIA**
868 Cherokee Campground
167 Deen's RV Park
524 Lake Nottely RV Park
710 Pine Mountain Campground
866 South Prong Creek Campground & RV Park
867 Sugar Mill Plantation RV Park

**ILLINOIS**
896 Hide-A-Way Lakes
895 Mendota Hills Campground
486 Shady Lakes Campground

**INDIANA**
897 Elkhart Campground
899 Hidden Paradise Campground
451 KOA-Brown County/Nashville
203 Last Resort Campground
326 Manapogo Park
898 Mini Mountain Campground
478 Mohawk Campground & RV Park
466 Yogi Bear's Jellystone Park Camp-Resort

**KENTUCKY**
434 Lakewood Resort

**LOUISIANA**
886 Great Discovery Campgrounds
166 KOA-Baton Rouge East
165 KOA-New Orleans/Hammond
885 KOA-Vinton/Lake Charles
900 Yogi Bear's Jellystone New Orleans-Hammond

**MAINE**
903 Beach Acres Campground
904 Libby's Oceanside Camp
902 Orr's Island Campground

**MARYLAND**
145 Eagles Nest Park

**MASSACHUSETTS**
329 Pout & Trout Campground
901 Springbrook Family Camping Area
194 Sweetwater Forest RV
199 Windy Acres Camping

**MICHIGAN**
195 Andry's Acres on the Lake

Enter Number

448 Birchwood Resort & Campground
146 Camelot Campground
906 Cedarville RV Park Campground
711 Creek Valley Campground
907 Greenwood Acres Family Campground
905 Juniper Hills
462 Sandy Oak RV Park & RV Sales
908 Sharp Park
459 White River Campground

**MINNESOTA**

331 Pelican Hills Park

**MONTANA**

910 The Elkhorn Guest Ranch
909 Yellowstone's Edge RV Park

**NEVADA**

164 Holiday Travel Park

**NEW HAMPSHIRE**

428 Angle Pond Grove
520 Beachwood Shores Campground
914 Chocorua Camping Village
588 Crazy Horse Campground
485 Friendly Beaver Campground
115 Goose Hollow Campground
477 Mile Away Campground
320 Oxbow Campground
589 Terrace Pines
429 Woodmore Campground

**NEW JERSEY**

915 Brookville Campground
831 Cape Island Campground
916 Echo Farm Campground
185 Indian Branch Park
274 Ocean View Resorts Campground
447 Pleasant Acres Farm Campground
201 Pleasantville Campground

**NEW MEXICO**

917 Little Creek RV Park

**NEW YORK**

595 Allen's Boat Livery Marina and Campground
518 Brennan Beach RV Park
709 Deer Run Campgrounds
920 Delaware Valley Campsite

**NORTH CAROLINA**

437 Camp Hatteras
280 Rivercamp USA

**OKLAHOMA**

962 Holliday Outt Mobile Home & RV Park

**OREGON**

481 Driftwood Village RV Park
449 Sweet Home/Foster Lake KOA

**PENNSYLVANIA**

935 Family Affair Campgrounds
937 The Locust Campground
938 Mountain Springs Camping Resort
939 Pocono Vacation Park
936 Round Top Campground
934 Shady Acres Camp Grounds

Enter Number

**SOUTH DAKOTA**

325 Lake Park Campground

**TEXAS**

983 Alamo-KOA
156 Ancient Oaks Campground
163 Austin Capitol-KOA
162 Autumn Acres RV & Mobile Home Park
942 Bahia Vista Waterfront RV Park
985 Bayside RV Park
158 Breeze Lake Campground
441 Cowtown RV Park
699 Fun N Sun
154 Guadalupe River RV Resort
159 Honeydale Mobile Home & RV Park
984 Lakeview Mobile Home & Travel Trailer Park
155 McAllen Mobile Park
986 Meadowlark Park
941 Palmdale RV Resort
160 Paul's RV Park
284 Port Isabel Park Center
161 Twin Palms RV Park

**UTAH**

153 Camp VIP
152 The Canyons RV Resort
157 Harrisburg Lakeside RV Resort

**VERMONT**

945 Apple Tree Bay Resort
519 Lone Pine Campsites

**VIRGINIA**

202 Blue Ridge Campground
944 Gloucester Point Campground
277 Inlet View Waterfront Family Campground
943 Tom's Cove Camping
198 Yogi Bear's Jellystone Park Camp-Resort

**WASHINGTON**

946 Elma RV Park
591 Ferndale Campground & RV Park
463 Fidalgo Bay Resort
136 Ponderosa Hill RV Park–A Park Washington Facility

**WISCONSIN**

947 Wilderness Campground

**WYOMING**

254 Big Horn Mountains RV Resort
949 Fountain of Youth RV Park
948 Greenway Trailer Park

**NEW BRUNSWICK**

423 Camper's City

**NOVA SCOTIA**

919 E & F Webber Lakeside
286 Green Valley Campgrounds
918 Holiday Haven
430 Klahanie Trailer Sales

**ONTARIO**

921 Ahmic Lake Resort

Enter Number

328 Alpine RV Resort-Campsite
439 Bensfort Bridge Resort
927 Campark Resorts
930 Cedar Beach Park
285 Double M RV Park & Campground
282 Dressel's Still Acres
925 The Dunes Oakridge Park
924 Duttona Trailer Park
431 Elm Grove Trailer Park
281 Grand River RV Resort
923 The Homestead Trailer Park
275 Indian Lake Campgrounds
929 Kenorus Quiet RV Resort
932 KOA-Sherwood Forest
928 LaFontaine Campground & RV Park
926 Marydale Estates
922 Nottawasaga Valley Conservation Authority
931 Ol Jo Mobile Village RV Park & Campground
933 Osprey Point RV Resort
200 Riverside Park Motel & Campground
322 Willow Lake Park
327 Woodland Lake Camp & RV Resort

**PRINCE EDWARD ISLAND**

940 Marco Polo Land

**QUEBEC**

461 Camping "Domaine Du Repos"
480 Camping Jardin du Campeur
453 Camping Tropicana
433 Camping Wigwam
442 Domaine Du Lac Louise

**BAJA MEXICO**

912 Baja Seasons Resort
913 Estero Beach Resort
602 Juanito's Garden RV Park
911 Vagabundos Del Mar RV Park
601 Villas De Loreto Resort

*New Hampshire Festivals con't. from pg. 14*

fresh shrimp, calamari, clams and, of course, lobster. Many visitors enjoy "grazing" while strolling between two stages featuring continuous entertainment from local and regional bands.Plan to make Pine Acres at Raymond your home base while attending the festival. You'll find a friendly welcome, and plenty of on-site recreation.

## NEW YORK FESTIVALS

**Spring:**

If your "festival budget" is on a shoe string, Rochester's annual **Lilac Festival,** held May 10th through the 19th in 20 acres of rolling hills of the city's Highland Park, offers family-oriented entertainment with no admission charge, and no charge for any of the entertainment. All activities, with the exception of a few for children, are completely free. Although there are no carnival-type rides or attractions, there is plenty of fun for the more than half-million visitors who attend each year. Over 500 varieties of lilacs cover 22 of Highland Park's 155 acres, and the festival is a lavish array of flowers, attractions and special events that signal the arrival of spring. The focus is on the flowers, foods, and music, and a seemingly unlimited selection of international foods is available for purchase. There are opening day ceremonies, the Lilac Parade, a craft and gift show, a golf tournament, and a lilac art show. Highland Bowl, a natural open-air amphitheater that can hold over 5,000 people, hosts free music festivals with well-known entertainers.

May 10th through the 12th are the dates to mark on your calendar for the 5th annual **Great Hudson Valley Balloon Race** held at the Dutchess County Airport in Wappingers Falls, just 1-1/2 hours from New York City. Festivities begin Friday evening with opening ceremonies, a band concert and the first of 5 flights by more than 40 balloons. Other events include hot air balloon rides and races, stunt pilots and parachutists performing aerobatic maneuvers, bicycle and running races, arts and crafts, a fireman's muster, simulated rock climbing demonstrations, and lots of activities for children including special appearances by Smokey the Bear. Admission to the event, including air shows and all activities, is free.

**Summer:**

The **German Alps Festival** is held each year at Hunter Mountain, a stately mountain setting in the northern Catskill Mountains that is famous for its great winter skiing. Covering two weekends in

July, the mountain festival features a huge gathering of authentic German and Austrian entertainers. The International Beer Expo features more than 100 brews from around the world. There are several daily expositions, craft shows and special entertainment for children.

August at Hunter Mountain brings **RockStalgia,** a musical festival taking you back to the '50s, '60s and '70s. RockStalgia 1995 brought the Association who have sold over 30 million records since their heyday in the '60s. The Buckinghams provided lots of memories as they performed some of their hits including Kind Of A Drag and Susan.

For an event that lasts all summer, plan a visit to Caramoor Center for Music and the Arts, off Route 22 in Katonah, just 45 miles north of midtown Manhattan. Caramoor is home to metropolitan New York's largest annual **Summer Music Festival,** and is also known for year-round concerts, lectures and educational programs. The center is an oasis of music, art, gardens and woodlands, and is an ideal starting place for a relaxing day or weekend in the country. Modeled after the great palazzos of southern Europe, Caramoor's House Museum contains treasures from Renaissance Europe and the Far East, and surrounds the Spanish Courtyard that is used for chamber mucis concerts. Andre Previn is Caramoor's Artistic Advisor, and is among the many varied artists who perform here, including Dave Brubeck, Marilyn Horne, and Emerson String Quartet.

**Taste of Buffalo,** held in early July for the past 12 years, has evolved into the 2nd largest "taste of" festival in the country. The weekend festival of food and music showcasing Western New York's top restaurants, musicians and entertainers attracts more than 400,000 people each year. More than 55 restaurants and wineries represent over 13 different ethnic groups and culinary specialities. They serve 150 different taste-size items with no duplication and all food items are priced between 50 cents and $2.50. Festival goers will find 4 stages of continuous entertainment including a children's activities stage, a country western state, sing-a-long, top ten, jazz, blues and contemporary music.

**Harborfest** held in Oswego in July boasts more than 200 admission-free performances on seven stages, as well as other special events. The popular New York Power Authority Fireworks display is the festival centerpiece with its annual symphony of sight and sound choreographed to music that turns the shores of Lake Ontario into a large, outdoor theater. Children take center stage during the Children's Parade as youngsters can either march in or enjoy watching Central New York's largest children's procession.

Early July in Tupper Lake is your opportunity to learn exactly what lumberjacks do. Plan on attending the **Tupper Lake Woodsmen's Days** and watch amateurs compete for the title of "Lumberjack of the Year." There's a chain saw carving demonstration and auction, and the Adirondacks' Largest Horse Pull.

Held the 2nd full weekend each August for the past 51 years, the **Gerry Rodeo** in Gerry, New York proves that true Western entertainment can be found in New York state. The "oldest consecutive rodeo east of the Mississippi" is held in the small rural community, providing bareback bronc riding, calf roping, saddle bronc riding, bull riding, and clowns. The midway provides freshly-prepared barbecue with their famous locally made sauce. Gerry is located just 6 miles north of Jamestown on Route 60.

**Sky-Fest '96** is held in Cooperstown in August at the Cooperstown Fun Park, 3 miles south of town. The exciting 3-day event includes giant hot air balloon launches, bands, entertainment, sky diving, a variety of food and beverages, a car show, a craft show, carnival rides — in short, something for everyone. The family-oriented event has been celebrated during the last weekend in August for over five years, and attracts thousands of visitors each year.



**Fall:**

Hunter Mountain in the northern Catskills is the site of the **Mountain Eagle Indian Festival** held in September. Visitors enjoy three exciting days of authentic American crafts, tribal dancing competitions and a rich cultural and educational atmosphere. The Great Tent provides storytelling, dancing competitions from tiny tots to adults, men's grass dancing, and more. Crafts include fine handmade dolls, drums and outstanding display of Native pottery. Other fall weekends at Hunter Mountain include the **AutumnMobile Show**, **Oktoberfest**, and **Craft Expo**.

When the leaves begin to turn, let your thoughts turn to the 21st annual **Letchworth Arts & Crafts Show and Sale.** It'll be held in 1996 on October 12th, 13th and 14th in Letchworth State Park. Visitors will find beautiful displays of pottery, watercolors, quilts and fiber arts, handmade jewelry, photography, decorative painting and dried flowers. You'll be entertained by stilt walkers, dancers, actors and musicians, all roving about to add a delightful dimension to the show. Convenience is a consideration at this highly organized show. Shuttle service is provided from Perry to the park where there are ATM machines, and a post office to ship your purchases anywhere in the world. The show, which originated in 1975, began with about 20 local crafters and because of the great response has grown to represent over 300 artists/crafters. Careful selection of works ensure only the finest representations of regional artists and crafts people.

Queensbury, New York's Warren County Airport is the site of the **Adirondack Balloon Festival** which will be held again in 1996 on September 19th through the 22nd. The festival was started in 1973 with 18 balloons and has grown to over 100 balloons that come from all parts of the United States, Canada, England, Germany, Italy and Japan. These spectacular balloons defy description — many are over 100 feet tall. A special "Smokey Bear" balloon made an appearance at the 1995 festival — this one is 9 stories tall and 55 feet in diameter. Balloon launches and landings can only occur early in the morning, or at dusk, so what to do all day? There is kite flying, musical entertainment, radio-controlled model aircraft demonstrations, military aircraft demonstrations, and a photography contest to keep you entertained until the next launch.

The fourth full weekend in September each year since 1980 has been the time to

*New York Festivals continued on page 30*

# CRUISE AMERICA'S RV VACATIONS

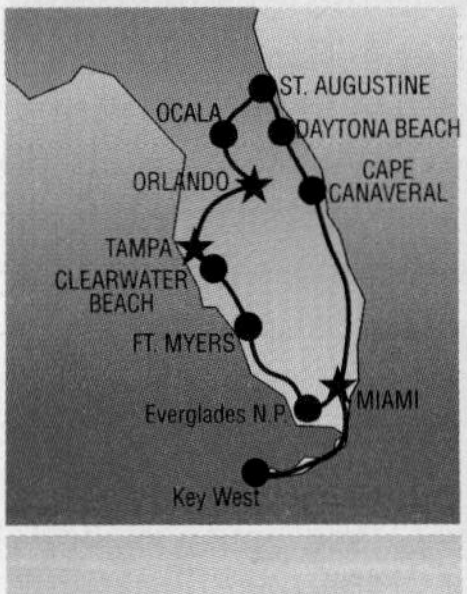

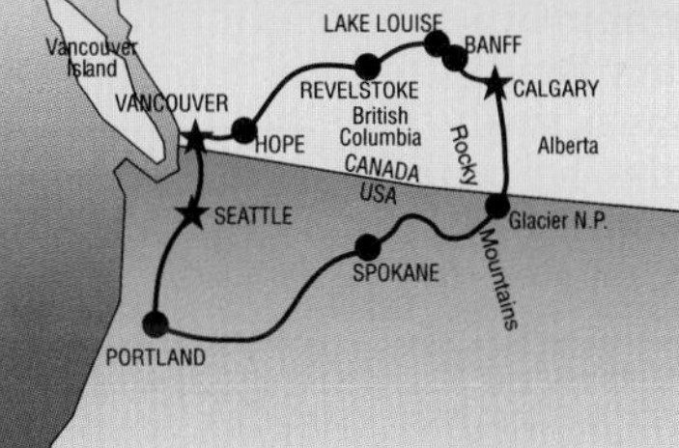

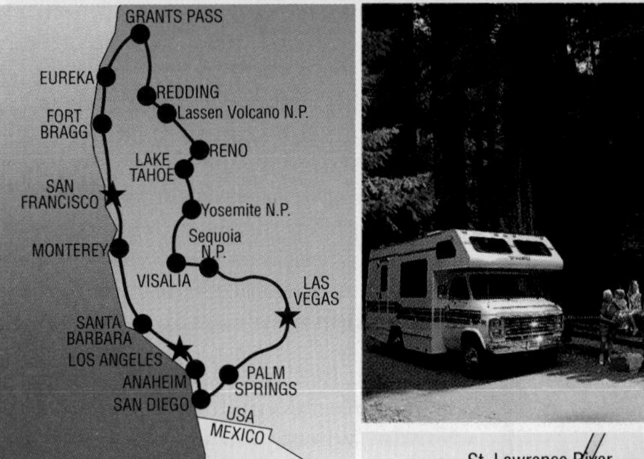

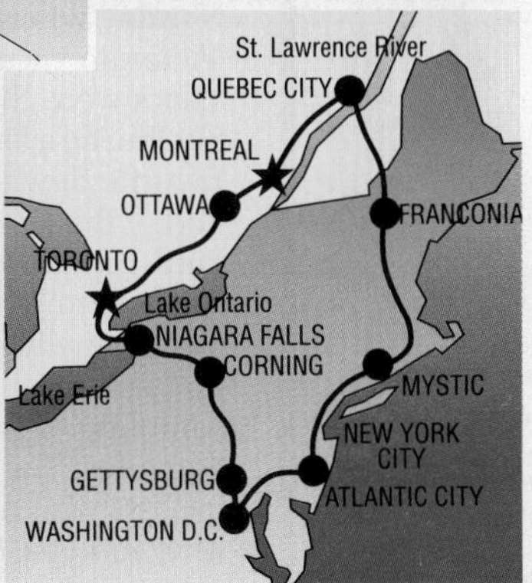


## RENT A ROLLING HOLIDAY AND DISCOVER NORTH AMERICA YOUR WAY

Smart vacationers are discovering the fun and adventure of touring by RV. With an RV you are free to select the itinerary and scenery that you desire. Tour wherever you want for as long as you want.

You can take your RV adventure tour locally or drive one way clear across the continent. Or, fly to your destination and start your RV adventure tour there.

We'll make it easy. There are over 100 rental locations in North America with the largest motorhome fleet in the world. With just one toll free call to our reservation center, we'll have the right size, fully equipped RV you need ready-to-go on your RV adventure vacation.

Call today and let's get rolling.

**1-800-327-7799**

CRUISE AMERICA FEATURES RELIABLE CHEVROLET MOTORHOME CHASSIS.

*New York Festivals continued from pg. 28*

visit Main Street, Remsen, New York for their **Remsen Barn Festival of the Arts**. Just 12 miles north of Utica on Route 12, the festival provides arts & crafts, a farmers' market, food concessions and other exhibitors. Over 300 arts and crafts booths display a variety of works including painted china, sheepskins, silk-screens, furniture, floral arrangements, etching, candles, beadwork, and lots of other crafts. Entertainment includes workshops on juggling, line dancing in the firehouse, pancake breakfasts, a strolling barbershop quartet and a Welsh hymn sing.

## *RHODE ISLAND FESTIVALS*

**Summer:**

One of the most popular fishing competitions in the region is held at Snug Harbor Marina in Wakefield. The **Snug Harbor Shark Tournament** will be held the 1st weekend after July 4th. Visitors may expect to see several species of sharks such as mako, blue, thresher, and maybe even a great white during the competition. Weigh-ins occur between 2 p.m. and 4:30 p.m. While people wait for anglers to enter their fish, they can participate in the "Dockside Feeding Frenzy." Snug Harbor is also the site of the **Snug Harbor Ladies' All Release Tournament** that is held the last weekend in July. Created exclusively for female competitors, the event is the only all release tournament in the area. In addition, it's the first tournament in New England to provide cameras to all registered anglers so they may record the various species they catch and release.

The **Newport Music Festival** will celebrate its 28th season July 6th through 21st, continuing its tradition of presenting unique chamber music programs, American debuts, world-class artists and special events in the grand "summer cottages" of Newport, Rhode Island. Selected works from 19th-century chamber music, vocal performances, and the Romantic era piano compositions create one of the most extraordinary festivals in the world. The Festival will present 55 concerts (3, 4 and 5 per day) in Newport's famed mansions. Over 60 artists from around the world will participate in the famous event.

Plan on attending the **Charlestown Seafood Festival** which is always held the first Sunday in August in Ninigret Park and for 1996 will be expanded to both Saturday and Sunday. You'll find a huge midway with over 150 vendors, with about 60% crafts and 40% food. The food consists of all types of seafood: lobsters, crab, clams, mussels, fish and chips, scallops, calamari, sushi as well as various ethnic foods. There's continuous live entertainment each day from live bands including the U.S. Navy Band (when available), strolling musicians, singers, kiddie rides, hay rides, helicopter rides and other midway performers. Try your luck at the raffle where the first prize is usually a boat, motor and trailer. Amateur cooks will want to show off their culinary skills in the Amateur Seafood Cook-off with monetary prizes awarded to the top three winners.

Pawtucket is the site of the **International Steamboat Muster** in August. This event is one of the premier summer time events in the state and is a celebration of over 200 years of steamboating on the headwaters of Narragansett Bay, Rhode Island's largest water resource. View historic and operating steam launches; canoes and kayaks on the river; the Pawtucket Red Sox Family Muster baseball game; enjoy an international music concert or take a Steamboat Muster sunset cruise aboard the *Vista Jubilee*, and top off each day's entertainment with a Rhode Island Shore dinner.

**Fall:**

The **Providence Waterfront Festival** is a 2-day celebration along the Providence waterfront, hosting exhibits by major non-profit groups in the area including Save The Bay and the Rhode Island Audubon Society. The festival features Tall Ships, tours of the upper bay by the Block Island Ferry, river tours, boat building demonstrations, sail boat rides, a match racing regatta and rowing workshops. There is an international food court, and vendors selling craft items and folk art pieces. The children will enjoy the jugglers, magicians, face painters, balloon art and stilt walking lessons.

## *VERMONT FESTIVALS*

**Spring:**

Since 1967, the **Vermont Maple Festival** has celebrated the first maple harvest of the year in St. Albans, and this year's dates are April 19th through 21st. Franklin County produces more maple syrup than any other county in the United States. Friday kicks off the festival with an arts & crafts show, and exhibits in the Maple Hall on Kingman Street include displays of maple syrup and other maple products. There's an antique show and sale, clogging performances, children's story time, a carnival at the city parking lot, a youth talent show, and a variety talent show. The educational displays include candy making demonstrations, taste testing, the world's largest maple syrup contest and championship maple cooking contests. Pancake breakfasts are alway a hit of the festival, and, of course, feature pancakes drenched in maple syrup.

Visit the Shelburne Museum on May 19th, 1996 and you'll be treated to **Lilac Sunday** where you can experience a Victorian vacation (at least for a day!). Lilacs were chosen as integral to Shelburne's landscaping as they were a favorite flower of the museum's founder. Today the 45 acres of grounds are landscaped with over 400 lilac bushes representing over 90 varieties of the sweet-smelling flowers. The Victorian-era ambiance is evidenced by a brief sampling of recent Lilac Sunday activities: The Wheelmen are costumed cyclists who demonstrate the Sunday afternoon pastime of bicycle riding —

19th century style; shuttlecock and other 19th-century games for children; demonstrations of the fine art of pastel painting using lilacs as subject matter, of course!; the lawn game of croquet; the Vermont Youth Orchestra's string quartet performing selections that were popular during the Victorian era and traditional New England music and dancing.

**Summer:**

If you've ever dreamed of learning to sail, but felt the expense was out of reach, think again. Now you can combine your vacation with an introduction to sailing. The International Sailing School in Burlington will hold its annual **Discover Sailing Day** Sunday, August 3rd from Noon to 5:p.m, as the school celebrates its 16th season. This is an excellent opportunity for the public to try sailing on a first-come, first-served basis. The event is open to all and is free of charge. A wide array of sailing craft will be available ranging in size from 21 feet to 30 feet in length. Veteran instructors and club members will be on board to answer questions and explain the basic concepts of sailing. ISS has provided hands-on sailing instruction for the beginning to advanced sailor since 1981. Two and six-day programs are offered with a free week of sailing club privileges/membership with every course.

Stowe, Vermont hosts the **Stowe Flower Festival** during the last weekend in June each year. (This year's dates are June 28th through 30th). The local festival was begun by local businesses and garden enthusiasts because there were so many gardens in the community that it seemed natural to create a weekend of celebration, tours and education. Exhibits include over 75 booths displaying flower and garden related themes, and more than 40 restaurants provide food booths. A brief sampling of past workshops and events: Learn to capture the beauty of your own gardens and flowers in the wild with a photography workshop; tips and techniques for keeping your container garden healthy; creation of arrangements using wildflowers; a ride on the Stowe Trolley as you tour three of Stowe's private gardens.

**Winter:**

Voted one of the top ten winter events in Vermont by the state chamber of commerce is the **Brattleboro Winter Carnival** which will be held February 17th through the 25th. It's the oldest witner carnival in New England and will celebrate its 40th anniversary this year. The entire family will find plenty to do as the carnival kicks off with sleigh rides, a torchlighting ceremony, special luncheons, junior olympics, skydiving demonstrations, snow sculpture contests, skiing, ice skating and much more.

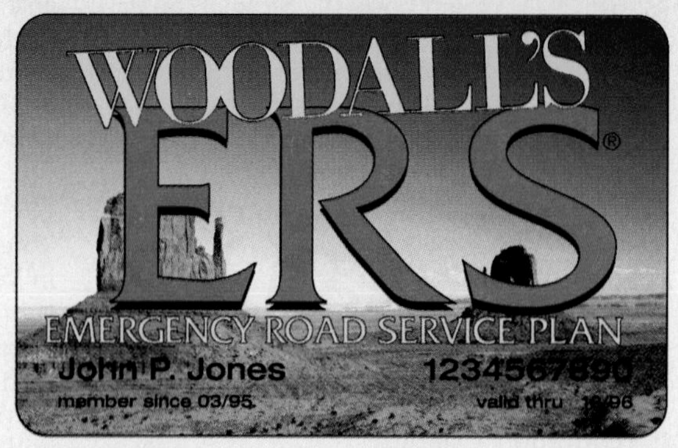


# Think of Woodall's ERS as a safety net, a helping hand, and a personal pit crew ...... that fits in your wallet.

***Introducing Woodall's Emergency Road Service*** — the premier RV road service plan from the leaders in RV travel — Woodall's.

Let's face it, unexpected things can and do happen when you're on the road. Sometimes we laugh and share the stories with friends ... sometimes the trip is ruined. Unless of course you're carrying the card that protects you, your family, your vehicle and your vacation from those unforeseen events. The ***Woodall's Emergency Road Service*** plan card.

This is a brand new complete protection plan from the company you can trust — Woodall's. Just as you've been able to depend on our camping and RV park information for over 60 years, now you can trust us to help you when you need it most ... when something happens and you're away from home.

*Think of us as your 'round-the-clock RV Safety Net.*

You might already have some form of road service. Maybe you got it when you joined a club, or got it through your auto insurance. Or maybe you choose to travel without it.

Consider this before you go too far: RV'ers came up with this plan. People just like you told us what they needed. They told us what was missing from their current plans, and what we should provide. They even told us how much to charge. And we delivered.

*"Top-notch benefits and no unnecessary add-ons."*

## Look at these benefits:

- **24 Hour emergency roadside service.**
- **Covers all your enrolled vehicles ... motorhomes, travel trailers, cars, motorcycles ... even boat trailers.**
- **Covers you in the U.S.A, Canada, and Mexico.***
- **No Mileage / Dollar Limits.**
- **No Out-of-pocket Towing Expense — ever!**
- **$1,200 Travel Delay Assistance for unexpected covered expenses as a result of a collision.**
- **$600 Travel Delay Assistance for unexpected covered expenses as a result of a major mechanical breakdown.**
- **24-hour Travel Delay Assistance "Help Desk".**
- **Use of the exclusive Woodall's Trip Routing System.**
- **Discounts on Car Rentals.**
- **Discounts on Hotels, Motels, & Restaurants.**
- **One Toll-Free Number to Call.**

For a complete listing of specific benefits, coverages and limitations, please refer to the Member Handbook.

*Now this is the comprehensive road service plan that RV'ers asked for!*

Think of it!! 24-hour response to your toll-free call — no matter where you are. Traveling with the Woodall's Emergency Road Service plan means traveling worry-free. That could help make your next vacation your best vacation ever!

Woodall's benefits package is not found in any other road service plan.

For instance ...

*Will the road service plan that came with your auto coverage tow your pick-up truck and fifth-wheel when it's only the tow vehicle that has a problem?* Woodall's will.

*Will your road service plan tow the car you pull behind your motorhome when your motorhome breaks down?* Woodall's will.

*Where would you be if you had to leave your trailer or towed auto behind when your primary vehicle is in need of service?* With Woodall's you won't have to answer that question .

Other Road Service Plans may charge you as much as $150.00 per year for a plan this comprehensive.

## Woodall's Emergency Road Service Plan is only $89.95 !

Consider the value of this plan and the cost of towing your RV. You'll realize that one single use can pay for your membership dues for two or three years. Call now to join Woodall's Emergency Road Service plan and travel worry-free "on your own, but not alone."

To activate your coverage immediately with payment by credit card, call us between 6:30 am and 6:30 pm (mountain time) weekdays, or Saturday 7 am to 1 pm (mountain time).

Join us today!

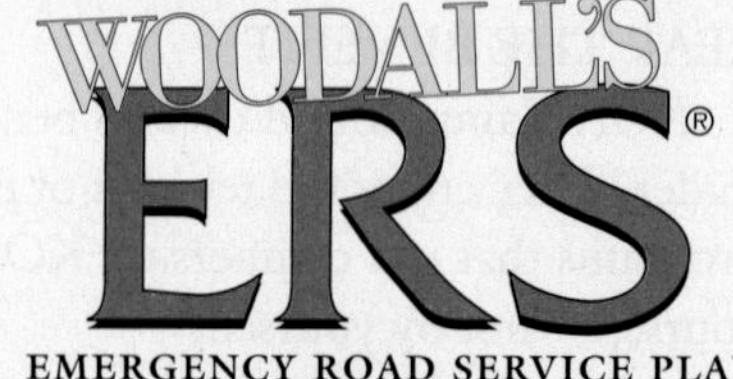


**EMERGENCY ROAD SERVICE PLAN**

**call toll-free**

**1-800-626-ROAD (7623) ext. 210**

*** Woodall's ERS will only provide claims reimbursement for covered breakdown services in Mexico. Roadside Service will be provided to enable your vehicle to either proceed under its own power, or be towed to our nearest network service center for repair.** 

5R-WDLS-139



**FREE INFO?** Woodall's ERS, enter #855 on Reader Service Card following page 16.

# EXPRESS ENROLLMENT CARD

TEAR ALONG DOTTED LINE, FOLD, TAPE AND MAIL

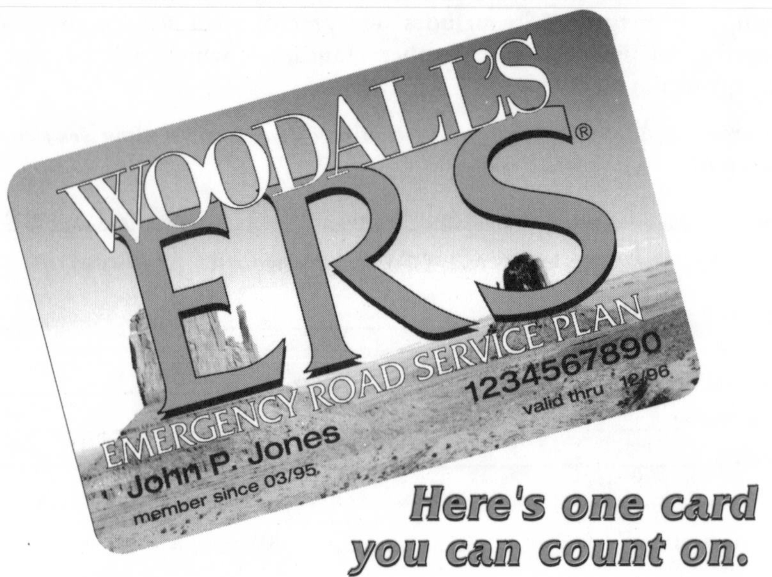


**Here's one card you can count on.**

TEAR ALONG DOTTED LINE, FOLD, TAPE AND MAIL

NO POSTAGE NECESSARY IF MAILED IN THE UNITED STATES

5R-WDLS-139

**BUSINESS REPLY MAIL**
**First Class Permit No. 312 Englewood, CO**

**POSTAGE WILL BE PAID BY ADDRESSEE**

WOODALL'S EMERGENCY ROAD SERVICE PLAN
PO BOX 6851
ENGLEWOOD CO 80112-9606

## Questions for Comparison

Will the road service plan that came with your auto coverage tow your pick-up truck and fifth-wheel when only the tow vehicle has a problem? **Woodall's will.**

Will your road service plan tow the car you pull behind your motorhome when your motorhome breaks down? **Woodall's will.**

Where would you be if you had to leave your trailer or towed auto behind when your primary vehicle is in need of service? **With Woodall's you won't have to answer that question.**

## DELAWARE FESTIVALS

**Spring:**

Good Friday is the big day for kite enthusiasts because that's the day of the Annual **Great Delaware Kite Festival**. The festivities begin at 10:00 a.m. at Cape Henlopen State Park in Lewes. In addition to contests for novices and experts alike, special recognition is given for extremes of contestant age, distance traveled and size of kite. In all, 28 trophies are awarded. Great food, beverages and souvenirs are also available.

Plan on a visit to Milton in May to attend the 7th annual **Delmarva Hot Air Balloon Festival.** The free event is sponsored by the American Diabetes Association.

**Summer:**

Spend an **Olde Fashioned Sussex County July 4th** and enjoy swimming, a horseshoe tournament, pork or chicken barbecue and the Biggest, Best, Most Spectacular fireworks display in Sussex County!

August in Rehoboth beach brings a daily **Whale Sandcastle Contest** at Fisherman's Beach. Or, for some beautiful arts and crafts, attend the annual **Art & Craft Members' Outdoor Show** sponsored by the Rehoboth Art League. The free show is held Saturday and Sunday over two weekends in mid-to-late August. Later in the month, the 47th **Annual Kiwanis Charitable Auction** is held at the Rehoboth Beach Convention Center.

The **Annual Old Fashioned Victorian Ice Cream Festival** held each year on the grounds of the Rockwood Museum in Wilmington in early July began in the early 1980's as a family picnic. An event for everyone in the family, children to grandparents, the 2-day festival offers music, demonstrations and exhibits of crafts and skills of the turn of the century. Of course, everyone must sample each of the 25 flavors of ice cream available.

**The Delaware State Fair** will celebrate its 77th birthday when it opens on the third Thursday in July in for its 10-day run in Harrington. Competitive judging occurs in livestock, flower, garden vegetable, arts and crafts, and culinary and needlework categories. Visitors can enjoy lots of free attractions and entertainment included with the admission price. Recent performers included Lilli Ana's Leopards, local country and rock bands and the Bikes, Blades & Boards show. Additional performances are provided by top-name groups such as BoyzII Men, Amy Grant, Clint Black and others. In addition to the variety of fair offerings of livestock, midway, 4-H and arts and crafts, the food vendors serve regional fare such as oyster sandwiches and crab cakes.

**Fall:**

**The Sea Witch Halloween Festival & Fiddler's Convention** in Rehoboth Beach includes haunted houses, pet costume contest, pony rides, horse show on the beach, hay rides, broom tossing contest, Mummers String Band performances and trick or treat with the merchants. 300 runners participated in the costumed 5K race in 1994. The Fiddler's Convention is a contest offering cash prizes for the best fiddler player, banjo player and best blue grass band. The namesake event is a day-long treasure hunt for the invisible Sea Witch.

## DISTRICT OF COLUMBIA FESTIVALS

*For additonal festivals in the D.C. area, please refer to the Maryland and Virginia festivals pages.*

The **Smithsonian Institution** is a museum, education and research complex of 16 galleries and museums, and the National Zoo, and all but two are located in Washington, D.C. The total number of objects, works of art and specimens is estimated at approximately 141 million, most of which is in the National Museum of Natural History. The "nation's museum" will celebrate its **150th anniversary** this year with a host of special programs including an exhibition that will tour the country, a public celebration on the National Mall on August 10th and 11th, and special programs and events throughout the year including: March — 30th annual Kite Festival, April 24th through the 28th — 14th annual Craft Show, August 10th — public birthday party on the National Mall.

**Spring:**

The **National Cherry Blossom Festival** had its beginnings in 1909, when first lady, Helen Herron Taft, arranged for the importation of 90 Japanese cherry trees. Unfortunately, after they arrived they were found to be diseased, and had to be destroyed. Having learned of Mrs. Taft's thwarted beautification efforts, the Mayor of Tokyo sent a donation of 3,000 cherry trees to Washington, to be a "memorial of national friendship between the U.S. and Japan." Soon after, Mrs. Taft and the wife of the Japanese Ambassador, planted the first of the trees on the north bank of the Tidal Basin in a simple ceremony, which today, has evolved into the Cherry Blossom Festival. Events are subject to change without notice depending upon the weather, however, the festival is planned around the average date of blooming which is April 7th. Among the festivities are art and craft shows, concerts, ceremonial tree plantings, a golf tournament, a rugby tournament, parades and a Monte Carlo Cruise aboard the *Spirit of Washington.*

The fourth annual **Worldfest** takes place over Memorial Day weekend and includes 3 outdoor music stages featuring Zydeco, Latin Jazz, African Pop and more. Visit the Global Village for a stunning array of music, dance, crafts and customs presented by embassies. Enjoy a block-long area of magicians, international games, dancers and exciting folklore exhibits.

**Summer:**

Across the nation this summer, dogs and their owners will be practicing for the best "doggone" event in the country, the **Friskies Canine Frisbee Disc Championships**. The World Finals are traditionally held in mid-September on the grounds of the Washington Monument. Competition is held in two events: freestyle and mini-distance. There is no entrance fee for contestants and no charge to spectators. It's truly a grass-roots event with men and women, boys and girls, young and old attending.

**Fall:**

Set aside Columbus Day weekend for the **Sixth Annual Taste of DC** and enjoy the Little Monster Parade, 2 outdoor music stages featuring the hottest performers in reggae, salsa, jazz, pop, country, blues, rock and more, the Science Fiction Factory and the Eat & Run 5K. So much food, so little time...a trip around the world with food — from Jamaica to China, from Italy to Mexico, from Ethiopia to Greece, from Spain to Thailand.

## *MARYLAND FESTIVALS*

*For additional festivals in the Maryland area, please refer to the District of Columbia and Virigina festivals pages.*

**Spring:**

The 18th annual **Southern Maryland Celtic Festival** will be the last Saturday in April at the Jefferson Patterson Park & Museum in St. Leonard. Competitions include Highland dance, fiddling and piping and band. There will be demonstrations of spinning and weaving as well as sheep shearing and fencing. Stroll the Celtic Marketplace, relax with the storytellers and cheer on your favorite at the Kilted Mile Race.

Sugarloaf's 21st annual **Spring Crafts Festival** is held in early April. The show features more than 500 artists and craftspersons who display and sell their beautiful, original creations. There's also live music, ongoing demonstrations, a children's theater, a large selection of delicious food, and hourly gift certificate drawings. Held at the Montgomery County Fairgrounds in Gaithersburg, festival-goers will find plenty of free parking.

Dateline: Chestertown, May 23, 1774 — local citizens boarded the Geddes and dumped the English shipment of tea overboard. Spend Memorial Day weekend at the **Chestertown Tea Party Festival** for early American food, fun, crafts and demonstrations. The highlight event is, of course, a re-enactment of the original "Tea Party."

**Summer:**

The 8th annual **Columbia Festival of the Arts**, running from June 14th through the 23rd, presents the best in music, theatre, dance and visual arts in 11 different venues in and around Columbia. Recent performers include renowned jazz vocalist, Cassandra Wilson, the Uptown String Quartet, flutist and television personality Eugenia Zukerman, Grammy Award-winning jazz vocalist, Diane Schuur, and legendary actress Claire Bloom who performed an unusual and charming chamber concert entitled, *Words and Music.*

Every weekend is a festival at **Deep Creek Lake** where **sailboat races** are held all summer long from Memorial Day through Labor Day. Even if you don't know a spinnaker from a keel, you'll enjoy watching the beautiful boats, and now just might be the time to think about sailing lessons. Head over to the southern portion of Deep Creek Lake in western Maryland to watch the beautiful sailboats and special regattas for Flying Scot and Laser sailboat classes.

Crisfield plays host to the 6th annual **Tangier Sound Country Music Festival** the last weekend in June. Fun for the whole family, the festival offers dance activities, children's activities and music workshops. Water activities will provide kids of all ages a refreshing break. Fresh seafood from the Eastern Shore and a wide variety of other foods and beverages will be available to quench the thirst and appetite of festival-goers. For the 2nd year the festival will also hold a juried craft show, exhibiting creative and collectible crafts from all around the mid-Atlantic.

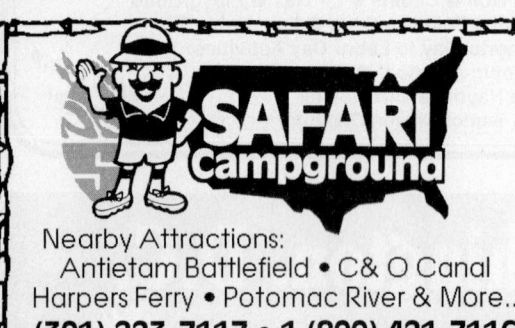

The **Western Maryland Loggers/Forestry Field Day & Equipment Show** takes place in early June. Held at the Garrett County Fairgrounds in McHenry, the festivities include logging and sawmill equipment exhibits and demonstrations, lumberjack demonstrations, logging competitions, wildlife and fisheries exhibits, and birds of prey demonstrations and exhibits.

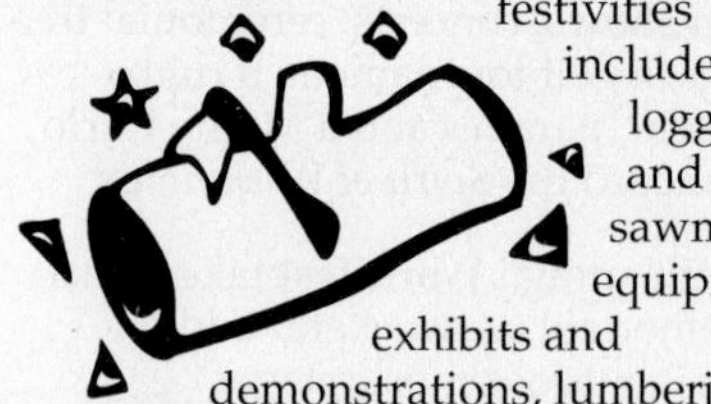

Fun and fellowship on the banks of the Choptank River — this year's **Seafood Feast-I-Val** will be held on the 2nd Saturday in August at Sailwinds Park in Cambridge. The Feast, from 2:00 to 6:00 pm will include Maryland blue crabs, fried fish, fried clams, crab soup, Eastern Shore crab cakes, ranch fries, watermelon, corn on the cob, hot dogs; soft drinks and beer will be sold by the cup. Musical entertainment, arts and crafts displays and free parking round out the featured events.

**Fall:**

The historic Carroll County Farm Museum in Westminster is the home of **The Maryland Wine Festival** every 3rd weekend in September. The festival is not only a showcase for the wines and foods of Maryland, but also an opportunity to learn about wine, how it is made, and the significance of the grape, climate and soil. Wine experts will be on hand to explain the art of wine tasting. A family affair, the festival includes wine, food, music, crafts and visual arts.



**The strength of a nation derives from the integrity of the home.**
***Confucius***

Antiques, crafts, plenty of food, entertainment, fine arts exhibits, farmer's market…all can be found at the 29th annual **Autumn Glory Festival in Oakland**, October 10th through the 13th. In addition to parades and concerts, and more than 20 food booths, the festival specialty is a complete turkey dinner with all the trimmings. Special selected events include a Tall Tale Liar's Festival where local and out-of-town storytellers tell tall tales and "true" personal stories; a bagpipe band concert; a baseball & sports card show; the Western Maryland Gun Show; an Oktoberfest meal; fireman's parade, and many others. If you are a craft lover, you'll enjoy the two craft shows, totalling nearly 100 booths, as well as a fine arts exhibit at the local library.

Kent County on Maryland's Eastern Shore is the site of the annual **Cruisin' Kent festival** held over the Columbus Day weekend. With the *Pride of Baltimore II* as their flagship, boaters cruise with her around the western edge of Kent County, exploring natural vistas and waterfowl, as well as attending festivities at each port. The festival is launched in Georgetown, a yachting center on the Sassafras River. There will be activities at each port for boaters and landlubbers alike, as festivities are held in Worton, Fairlee Creek, Tolchester, and on into the mouth of Rock Hall Harbor. A seafood festival is held in Rock on Saturday, and Chestertown hosts an antique boat show and market day fair with sidewalk sales, refreshments, and entertainment.

Huzzah! The sound of musket fire and the scent of hearth-cooking will fill the air at Historic St. Mary's City during the **Grand Militia Muster** on October 19th and 20th. Seventeenth-century reenactment units from all over the East Coast will participate in competitions to test their skills at pike drill, crossbow artistry, swordplay, camp-cooking and historic costuming in the Governor's Field at Maryland's first capital. This gathering of 17th-century military reenactors is the largest of its kind. As with any gathering of this kind in the colonial period there will be sutlers — merchants selling period items — on hand.

The **Waterfowl Festival**, November 8th through the 10th, is one of the world's premier wildlife art shows and sales featuring 450 of the country's finest artists displaying paintings, sculpture, carvings, duck stamps, photography, crafts and antique decoys. There is free shuttle service to 17 exhibit locations throughout the charming historic town of Easton. There will also be retriever demonstrations, world championship goose and regional duck calling contests, shooting exhibitions, seminars and a decoy auction. Proceeds are donated to wildlife conservation.

## *NEW JERSEY FESTIVALS*

**Spring:**

This year, April 27th and 28th mark the fifteenth annual **Shad Festival**

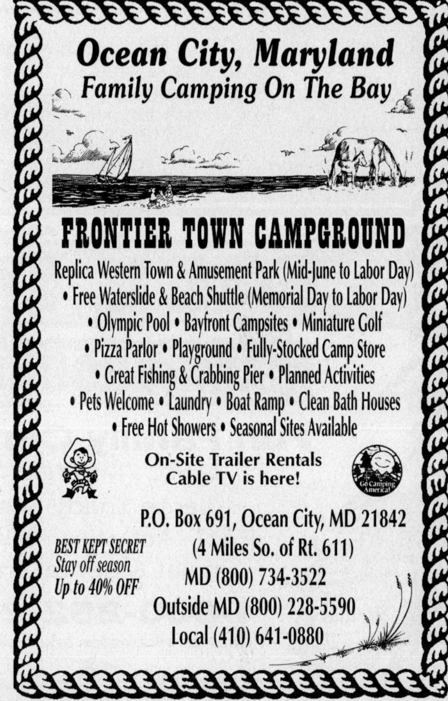


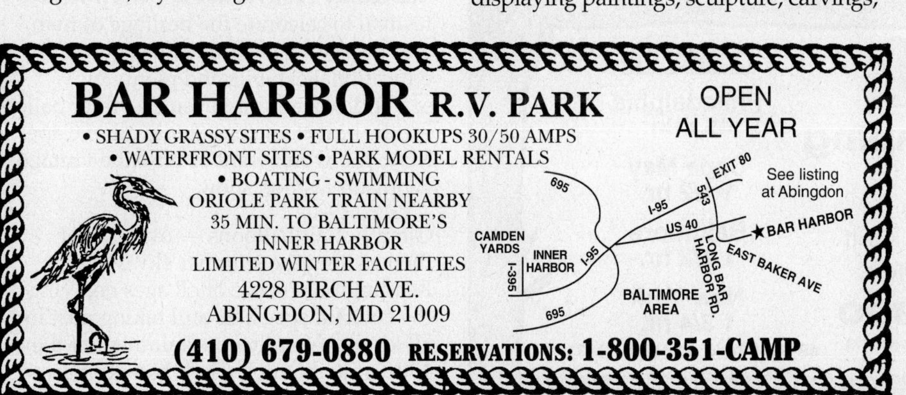

**FREE INFO?** Bar Harbor, enter #340; Frontier Town, enter #365; Ocean View, enter #317; Atlantic City Blueberry Hill, enter #339; KOA Atlantic City North, enter #374 on Reader Service Card following page 16.

highlighting the arts, crafts, the Delaware River, the City of Lambertville and their favorite fish — the shad. The Shad Festival has evolved from a local art show to a nationally recognized festival to welcome Spring to the region. Put on by an all-volunteer staff, the event acts as a fund raiser for many non-profit community based organizations.

The **Cape May Music Festival** is a 6-week fanfare heralding the arrival of high summer in the nation's oldest seaside resort. There's always something exciting happening. Spend a day basking the warm sunshine, stroll the charming Washington Street Mall, enjoy dinner at one of the many famous restaurants in town, then finish your evening in the intimate company of some of America's most distinguished performing artists.

Spring at Historic Cold Spring Village in Cape May offers **May Tag Day**, a community yard sale sponsored by the Lower Township Chamber of Commerce on the third Saturday. The weekend before Memorial Day is the **Festival of American Crafts** at which over 100 juried crafters demonstrate and sell their wares.

**Summer:**

Called the Kentucky Derby of cycling, the **Tour of Somerville** is the oldest, continuous major bike race in the country. The Tour takes place on Memorial Day and attracts top national bike racing competitors.

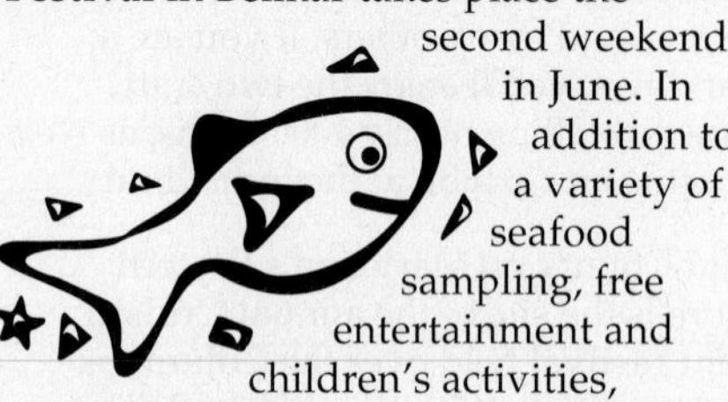

The 9th annual **New Jersey Seafood Festival** in Belmar takes place the second weekend in June. In addition to a variety of seafood sampling, free entertainment and children's activities, Garden State wineries will offer exhibits and tastings. A craft fair, contest with prizes and educational exhibits are also available.

Also on the second weekend in June is the **Sea & Sky Festival** in Cape May. This festival to celebrate the heritage of man and the sea will feature entertainment, educational exhibits and plenty of seafood. Visitors can even cast thier ballot for the best clam chowder in all of Cape May. You won't want to miss the vintage swimsuit fashion show.

Giant hot-air balloons — over 125 of them, filling the summer sky over Readington. People of all ages enjoying the colorful spectacle and taking part in all kinds of family entertainment at the 13th annual **Quick Chek New Jersey Festival of Ballooning**. Other activities include live concerts, Lamb Chop show, New Jersey Monthly Storytelling Festival and much more over the last weekend in July.

The first Saturday in August is **Hambletonian Day** at Meadowlands Racetrack in East Rutherford. America's premier championship harness race features the world's best 3-year-old trotters in competition for a more than $1 million purse. This family fun day, held in a country fair setting, also includes free pony and kiddie rides, carnival games, specialty foods, live entertainment, clowns, jugglers, music and free giveaways.

There is no more spectacular sight than watching 75-100 hot-air balloons float gently upward, lighting up the sky with a rainbow of colors. Whether on the ground watching the breathtaking mass ascension or savoring the beauty of the landscape while floating more than 500 feet above the ground, The **Magic of Alexandria Balloon Festival** is an

**FREE INFO?** Tall Pines, enter #318; Whippoorwill, enter #745; Seashore, enter #823; Timberline, enter #816 on Reader Service Card following page 16.

unforgettable experience. Concerts, sports demonstrations and dance exhibitions are featured as part of the weekend of family fun. Portions of the proceeds are donated to the Make-A-Wish Foundation. Up, up and away in Pittstown on the first weekend in August.

Historic Cold Spring Village in Cape May offers many summer events, including the **Children's Jubilee** on the last weekend in June. The Jubilee will have puppets sheep shearing, games, children's crafts, music, storytelling, cornhusk dollmaking, folk songs, and lots of fun, fun, fun! The weekend after the Fourth of July is set aside for **Music And Dance of the 1800's** — traditional music and dance of the period including folk, ragtime, march music, clogging, 17th Virginia military encampment and the Cape May Victorian Dancers. The third weekend in August brings **Farmfest '96** — join villagers in celebrating the harvest with food, games, animals, square dancing, pony rides, butter-churning and soap-making at an old fashioned country fair.

__Fall:__

On September 21st and 22nd, the Wetlands Institute of Stone Harbor, a nonprofit research and education facility, will hold the 14th annual **Wings 'n Water Festival**. Timed to coincide with the arrival of autumn, the fund-raiser will feature the work of bird and fish carvers, wildlife artists and photographers, quilters and nature related crafters. Live folk music, narrated boat cruises, retriever demonstrations, fly tying and casting, children's nature games, environmental exhibits, a four block long kite festival on the beach, plus two food courts featuring local seafood all add up to a great weekend.

**Victorian Week** is Cape May's 10-day extravaganza in celebration of the Victorian lifestyle. There's something for everyone — historic house tours, mystery dinners, antiques and crafts shows, lectures, vaudeville, workshops, and more — a virtual kaleidoscope of activities in America's first seashore resort! Starting the first Friday in October, **Victorian Week** runs for 10 days and is sponsored by the Mid-Atlantic Center for the Arts, a non-profit organization.

The fourth weekend in September at Historic Cold Spring Village in Cape May is time for **Civil War Weekend** — a military encampment hosted by the 17th Virginia and 7th New Jersey Regiments, military battle, regimental music, 19th century camp wedding, military trial, candlelight tour of both confederate and Union camps. The **5th Annual Pumpkin Festival** is a special program sponsored by the Lower Township Rotary Club. In addition to the Halloween parade, enjoy games, over 100 exhibitor craft show, scarecrow decorating, music, food and pumpkin painting all on the third weekend in October.

## *PENNSYLVANIA FESTIVALS*

__Winter:__

Celebrate the 80th annual **Pennsylvania Farm Show** January 6th through the 11th in Harrisburg. The show has grown from its modest beginnings in 1917 into the



**FREE INFO?** KOA Philadelphia, enter #376; Yogi Bear's, enter #787; Best Holiday Holly Acres, enter #343; Cape Island, enter #355 on Reader Service Card following page 16.

nation's largest indoor agricultural exposition, now occupying 622,000 square feet. An institution in itself, the **Farm Show** is a showcase of Pennsylvania's leading industry. Not only is the **Farm Show** a great place to see agriculture — it's also a great place to taste agriculture! The Food Market has been recreated for you to buy and sample food products from local companies. The Food Pantry features cooking demonstrations all week. More than $10 million has been spent over the last 8 years to up grade the complex to make it more enjoyable and educational.

Like to kick tires and slam doors? Stop by the **Pennsylvania Auto Show** in Harrisburg, January 20th through the 28th or the **Philadelphia International Auto Show**, January 27th through February 4th. Both shows will feature the newest model vehicles, along with never seen before concept cars. Produced by Liberty Productions, Inc., these shows have a unique highway theme carpet and signage displays.

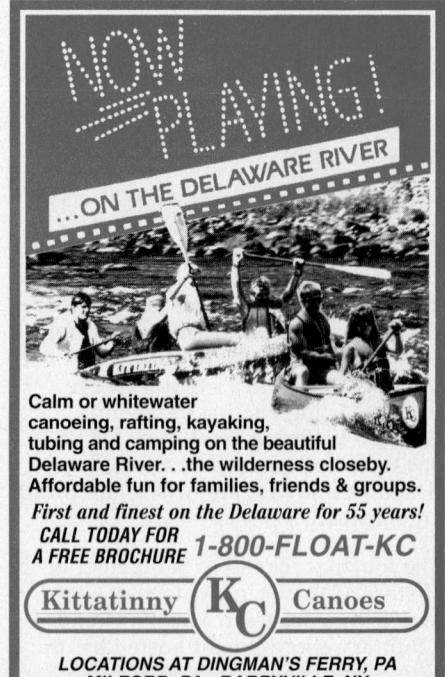

**FREE INFO?** Marshall Brass, enter #732; Gettysburg Campground, enter #767; Millersburg Ferry, enter #386; Mill Bridge Vlg., enter #387; Kittatinny Canoes, enter #771 on Reader Service Card following page 16.

**Spring:**

The City of Philadelphia invented **The Book and The Cook** in 1985 to showcase the extensive range and exceptional quality of dining experiences that are to be found in the city. This 12th annual **The Book and The Cook** has doubled in size and patrons and the reputation of Philadelphia's chefs and restaurateurs has been acclaimed throughout the country. When you reserve your place (April 21st through the 28th) at one or more of the participating restaurants, you will have the opportunity to meet and talk with the authors and the chefs who will be present as you savor the special dishes and meals, the wines and other beverage tastings they have planned and created in partnership for your delectation. Or taste you way through the 7th annual **The Book and The Cook Fair** — showcasing over 100 exhibitors, including free samplings from gourmet food purveyors, kitchen cabinetry, state-of-the-art appliances, herbs and spices, specialty coffees and much more (April 26th through the 28th).

**Gettysburg Bluegrass Camporee** at Granite Hill Family Campground is a 4-day, mostly outdoor event, featuring live performances by approximately 18 bluegrass bands, most of which are nationally or internationally known. Also featured is a selection of music related workshops put on by favored artists, plus a band contest that gives rising young bands an opportunity to perform before a large audience. Bluegrass Camporee happens twice yearly — May 2nd through the 5th and August 22nd through the 25th.

From horse show neophytes interested in seeing may different breeds of horses and types of competitions to experts concentrating on the best, the **Devon Horse Show and Country Fair** offers the tops in entertainment. Starting the Friday before Memorial Day and finishing up on the Saturday after, the **Show** is celebrating its 100th anniversary this year. The **Country Fair**, open daily, offers boutique shopping for fine sporting clothes, paintings, prints and sculptures, garden statuary, gold and silver jewelry, leather goods and souvenirs. Food ranges from hot dogs and hamburgers to dainty tea sandwiches. And don't forget the famous Devon fudge. Proceeds benefit the Bryn Mawr Hospital.

**Summer:**

On your mark…get set…GO! Everyone is getting geared up for two weeks of amateur bike rides, pro-am bike races, an art show, a Victorian-themed Stroll, fabulous foods, a spectacular block party and many other events culminating in two heart-pumping professional bike races. In short, its time for the annual **CoreStates Championship Festival.** It all begins the third Saturday in May in Philadelphia.

The first **Three Rivers Arts Festival** was in 1960, lasted three days and was organized as "a little art show;" it now boasts 1000 artists, over 126 concerts, over 12 types of food booths, over 125 performers on 8 different stages and over 540 exhibitors over 17 days. Enjoy the parks and plazas of downtown Pittsburgh from June 7th through the 23rd.

Combine 18th and 19th century Pennsylvania Dutch culture and traditions with taste-tempting foods, pageantry, outstanding demonstrations of authentic craftsmanship, quilting, folklore seminars and children's activities, and you have the **Kutztown**

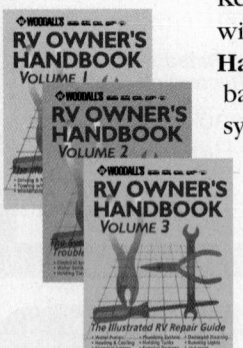

**Pennsylvania German Festival.** Visitors discover the past June 29th through July 7th.

Historic Gettysburg extends a cordial welcome to all visitors during the 14th Anniversary of **Gettysburg Civil War Heritage Days,** held in conjunction with the 133rd Anniversary of the historic battle fought in Gettysburg. Stay a few days and enjoy the Living History Camp, Heritage Days evening Lecture Series, band concerts, Firemen's Festival, Civil War battle re-enactments, train raids, Civil War book show and collector's show. It all takes place from June 19th through July 7th.

The largest Fourth of July Commemoration in Central Pennsylvania, the **Harrisburg Independence Weekend Festival** is truly an event for the whole family. This year's five-day celebration features a lively combination of food, rides, games, children's theatres, educational activities, arts & crafts, boat races, sporting events, concerts, bingo and other family activities. The festival runs July 3rd through the 7th with a Gala Fireworks extravaganza on July 4th.

The **South Side Summer Street Spectacular** features such activities as 3 stages of musical entertainment, a carnival, a parade, food courts, a children's area, an artists' market and "Pittsburgh's Perfect Pierogie Cook-off." Many community groups use this event in mid-July to raise funds for their causes.

**Musikfest** is a nine-day extravaganza that features more than 650 free performances by more than 300 national, regional and local musicians and groups. Styles range from Bach to bluegrass and folk to reggae. Musikfest also features ethnic dance troupes as well as programs teaching individuals. For children, Musikfest has a site devoted to activities such as souvenir making as well as a backyard circus, puppet shows, storytellers, magicians and more! It's August 10th through the 18th in Bethlehem.

Experience the fantasy! The **Pennsylvania Renaissance Faire** at the Mount Hope Estate & Winery north of Lancaster runs 10 weekends: Saturdays, Sundays & Mondays August 3rd through September 2nd and Saturdays and Sundays only September 7th through October 6th.

*Pennsylvania Festivals con't. on pg. 44*

*Pennsylvania Festivals con't. from pg. 42*

Starting as a small one day festival held in the yard of the York County Colonial Courthouse, the 15th annual **Riverwalk Arts Festival** has grown to 6 entertainment stages, a children's festival area, an adult juried art exhibition, festival marketplace, literary competitions and a film competition. It will be held August 24th and 25th in Center City York.

An exciting weekend of activities for the whole family, it is no wonder that **Harrisburg's Kipona Celebration** is considered one of the top ten festivals in the state. The celebration features a variety of food, rides, games, children's theatres, educational activities, arts & crafts and other family activities. One of the oldest waterfront festivals in the United States, Kipona plays host to the March of Dimes Rubber Duck Regatta, the PA State Chili Cook-Off, the Breath of Nature Karate Tournament and other tournaments. The celebration culminates with its renowned fireworks display. Held over Labor Day weekend each year, this year from August 30th through September 2nd.

Where can you find Grammy Award-winning musicians munching on halupki, pierogies and bratwursts between sets? Where can you walk, and within a few blocks, experience the artistic mastery of Irish, German, Slovenian, Polish, Serbian, Ukrainian and Croatian immigrants? Where can you look over your shoulder and see the beauty of the Allegheny Mountains shadowing it all? And where can you do it all for free? There's only one place — **Johnstown FolkFest '96,** Labor Day weekend!

Greater Hazleton's **FUNFEST** is held the weekend following Labor Day, September 7th and 8th. Activities include a craft show, muscle car and street machine show, a Hot Wings contest, a bed race, the sports card and comic book show, a parade and over 100 booths benefiting nonprofit organizations.

Fun for all in the heart of the Alleghenies — **Hoss's Keystone Country Festival** is on the calendar for September 6th through the 8th. You'll enjoy over 300 art and craft booths, an ethnic food village with 14 vendors, petting zoo and farmers' market. Entertainment consists of country, big band, jazz and folk music plus puppet shows, story telling and much more.

**The Pennsylvania National Quilt Extravaganza III,** the center of it all for quilt, fiber, wearable and textile arts, will take place September 19th through the 22nd at the Expo Center in Fort Washington. In addition to the over 400 quilts on display and the Fairfield Fashion Show, appraisals, special exhibitions and special tours are available. Over 60 workshops and lectures with instructors from across the country will be offered.

**Fall:**

**Penn's Colony Festival** celebrates Early America and its decorative arts, crafts and entertainments. The Festival is a re-creation of the 18th century "Publick Times" which assembled artists, craftsmen and entertainers to sell their goods and entertain the community. The market-place fair features over 185 colonial-dressed craftsmen selling fine furniture and handcrafted decorative accessories in the Americana and folk art traditions. The "Publick Times" atmosphere is replicated through 18th

*Pennsylvania Festivals con't. on pg. 46*

*Pennsylvania Festivals con't. from pg. 44*

century events which include rousing bagpipe and drum performances, authentic dance, Irish and classical music, battle re-enactments, colonial children's games, educational children's exhibits, living history demonstrations and traditional foods. Held the last two weekends in September, the 21st and 22nd and the 28th and 29th at North Park just 10 minutes north of Pittsburgh.

Save the last weekend in September for the **Celtic Classic Highland Games and Festival** in Bethlehem. Free admission includes the following: entertainment and craft tents, bleacher seating for Highland events, children's entertainment. Also available are the Afternoon Tea and grandstand seating.

On **Apple Harvest Day**, Hopewell Furnace National Historic Site will again appear as a thriving community as costumed crafts people and interpreters demonstrate harvest activities and the operations of a charcoal burning iron furnace. Local crafts people will demonstrate their skills and park rangers will demonstrate 19th century cooking and farming. Enjoy all of these activities on the last Saturday in September.

Your harvest of memories begins here — The **National Apple Harvest Festival** at the South Mountain Fairgrounds in Arendtsville. Spend the first two weekends in October enjoying traditional apple products such as sauce, cider, pie, jelly and candied apples. There will be continuous free entertainment, orchard tours, mini tractor pull, pony rides, contests and plenty of food.

Lincoln Caverns and Whisper Rocks, neat Huntingdon, will be transformed into a unique haunted house for **Ghosts & Goblins** weekends in October. One hour tours offer a spirited narrative explaining the wonders and highlights of two beautiful crystal caverns, while more than twenty supporting characters greet visitors along the way.

Ghouls and goblins and ghosts, oh my! For Halloween season there is no place like Frightsville. This is the time of year when creatures watch from every shadow, waiting to be summoned forth to take the living on a nightmarish journey through the darkest recesses of the imagination. Are you brave enough to venture in to the realm of the unknown? If so, the inhabitants of

Frightsville are *dying* to guide you. **Halloween Fright Night** opens on October 11 and continues Fridays, Saturdays and Sundays through October 27 with the finale on Thursday, October 31 at the Victorian gardens of Mount Hope Estate and Winery north of Lancaster.

**Winter:**

Christmas night — 1776! Washington crossing the Delaware! A night destined to become the most significant in America's history. The 44th re-enactment of **General George Washington's Crossing of the Delaware** takes place on Christmas Day in Washington Crossing, sponsored by the Washington Crossing Foundation. A major goal of the Washington Crossing Foundation is to establish and perpetually endow scholarships for study in areas preparing the recipient to enter the field of public service.

## VIRGINIA FESTIVALS

*For information about additional festivals in the Virginia area, please refer to the Maryland and District of Columbia festivals pages.*

**Spring:**

If you want up-close and personal, action-packed racing, beautiful surroundings and comfort, then **Martinsville Speedway** in the foothills of the Blue Ridge Mountains is the place for you. This year's race dates are: March 17 – Miller Genuine Draft 300, NASCAR Late Model Stock Car race; April 20 – Goody's 500, division to be determined; April 21 – Goody's 500, NASCAR Winston Cup race; September 21 – Hanes 150, division to be determined; September 22 – Hanes 500, NASCAR Winston Cup race; October 13 – Taco Bell 300, NASCAR Late Model Stock Car race.

A continuation of the Deep Run Races which originated in 1898, the **Strawberry Hill Races** on Saturday, April 13th in Richmond are a full day of steeplechase horse racing sanctioned by the National Steeplechase Association. Picnicking and tailgating are the order of the day. Pre-race opening ceremonies take place at 11:45; gates open at 9 a.m.

Spring is an especially beautiful time of year in the Shenandoah Valley. Acres of pink and white apple blossoms explode against the new green of the rolling hills promising a bountiful harvest. In 1924, the First **Shenandoah Apple Blossom Festival** introduced the springtime beauty of the Shenandoah Valley to the world. The coronation of Queen Shenandoah and the Grand Feature Parade were the main attractions. This year continues those traditions along with annual additions including presidential visits, Sports Breakfast, high school band competitions, Weekend in the Park, the 10K Race, the Clyde Beatty-Cole Bros. Circus and the latest addition, the Bluegrass Festival. As the Winchester-Frederick County community grows, the Festival continues to develop new ways to celebrate in early May.

Take the whole family out for a fun filled day to the **Annual Ramp Festival** in Whitetop on the third Sunday in May. Organized as a fund-raiser for the Mt. Rogers Volunteer Fire Department & Rescue Squad, the festival has grown to include: arts and crafts; clowns, games and face painting; buegrass, country and Gospel music; a fantastic open pit barbecue chicken dinner and the highlight of the festival...the Ramp eating contest. A ramp is a wild leek that grows in the moist woodlands of the Eastern United States, usually in high altitudes, not to be confused with ordinary wild onions.

**Festival in the Park**, long considered the harbinger of summer, opens in Roanoke this May 23rd to celebrate its 27th anniversary. Once a weekend outgrowth of the small yet significant Sidewalk Art Show, **Festival in the Park** has become a major 11-day celebration, offering art, entertainment, food, parades and sporting events for all ages and interests. The Sidewalk Art Show has grown much more sophisticated; it's now one of the largest shows on the East coast.

**Summer:**

Wytheville natives and visitors gather every June, beginning the third Saturday and continuing for nine consecutive days, to celebrate the fine arts featured at the **Annual Chautauqua Festival**. The **Chautauqua Festival** is held in Elizabeth Brown Memorial Park in Wytheville — a small, quaint, southern town located in the heart of the Blue Ridge Mountains. Nationally-known and local musicians, actors, dancers, storytellers and

**FREE INFO?** Holiday Trav-L-Park, enter #422; Bethpage, enter #351; Cherrystone, enter #359 on Reader Service Card following page 16.

magicians perform each night. Antiques and crafts, children's activities, photography and art contests, creative writing and dancing workshops combine to provide daytime entertainment. All events are free of charge. Featured events at the **Chautauqua Festival,** outside of the nightly performances, include: an antique car show, an archeology display, a balloon rally, face painting, cooking show, chili cook-off, a chess tournament, bingo, a flower show, the hospitality house, historical tours, quilt and needlework show, kick-off parade, petting zoo, pet show, wine-tasting, golf tournament, western two-step dance workshop and doll show.

Popularized by Margarite Henry's books, *Misty of Chincoteague* and *Stormy, Misty's Foal,* the annual **Chincoteague Volunteer Firemen's Carnival and Pony Round-up and Swim** celebrates its 71st anniversary this year. Starting the Fourth of July weekend and continuing through the end of July, the carnival offers rides, games, entertainment, fireworks, drawings and great food. The namesake event is the round-up of ponies on Assateague Island and their swimming the channel to Chincoteague. The first foal to come ashore is raffled away later in the day. Other foals are available at auction. Later that week the adult ponies are returned to Assateague. All proceeds benefit the Chincoteague Volunteer Fire Company.

Historic Abingdon is the site of the **Virginia Highlands Festival**, held annually the first two weeks in August. Abingdon is the oldest town west of the Blue Ridge Mountains and provides the ideal setting for this annual event. Music and performing arts events are central to the festival. Demonstrations, workshops, tours, special events for youth and a host of other offerings geared to diverse ages and interests make this a festival for the whole family.

On September 7th and 8th, the Museum of American Frontier Culture will host its annual celebration of America's heritage, the **Traditional Frontier Festival**. Visitors will be entertained with non-stop music and dance of early America and the old-country, while visiting nearly 100 selected crafters demonstrating traditional skills and sampling some of the foods our ancestors enjoyed. Besides the wide variety of traditionally made crafts and heritage arts, special performances at each of the historic farmsites are offered throughout the day. You might hear the lilting tones of someone playing a Celtic harp, see German schuplatter dancing, catch a puppet show, see Morrismen perform, hear some tall tales or listen to some old-time Appalachian favorites on a banjo. Other festival highlights include a children's activity tent and a collection of uncommon and rare animals.

## Fall:

The historic town of Occoquan will host the **Fall Arts and Crafts Show** the fourth weekend in September with over 350 juried artists and crafters in a lively street festival. There will also be a variety of tantalizing foods and live entertainment. The exhibitors come from over 35 states to display a fabulous selection of handmade wares, fine art and crafts in the streets of the charming gas-lighted downtown area, creating a shoppers' delight. Over 125 specialty shops and restaurants in town will also be open.

The confirmed festival-goer can expect to hit the Boardwalk on Virginia Beach's oceanfront anytime after 3 p.m. on Friday, September 27th for the 23rd annual **Virginia Beach Neptune Festival**. All 65 food and beverage vendors are open, along with the juried art and crafts show, consisting of 230 to 250 exhibitors. The King's Concert in the 24th Street park bandshell traditionally kicks off all the music entertainment. There's a 2-day mens and womens open volleyball tournament, the Virginia finals 8K run, an all-ages surfing competition, the traditional fireworks spectacular and the Grand Parade on Sunday afternoon. The sand sculptures which are built on the beach on Sunday attract thousands of viewers and photographers before the last tides sweep in and the weekend is officially closed at 6 p.m.

The **Urbanna Oyster Festival** has become a great tradition, enjoyed by thousands of residents and visitors alike. As a tribute to the oyster, this festival features the finest varieties of oyster presentation and preparation: steamed, fried, frittered or on the half-shell. Festivalgoers are

*Virginia Festivals con't. on pg. 50*

*Virginia Festivals con't. from pg. 48*

invited to meander through the streets, visit the waterfront and sample fantastic food fare prepared by civic, church and charitable organizations. Each booth has its own special recipe and each delicacy tastes as good as the next. Come ready to eat oyster, crabs, shrimp and seafood of every variety. They promise you won't go away hungry. Come celebrate the oyster the first weekend in November!

## *WEST VIRGINIA FESTIVALS*

**Summer:**

The **Bowden Fishing Derby** is an annual event during National Fishing Week (the first full week of June) to introduce the pleasure of fishing to kids. It is held at the Bowden National Fish Hatchery, which is ten miles east of Elkins. All the names of the participants are entered for a random drawing. Entertainment is provided by fishing pros and "Woodsy the Owl."

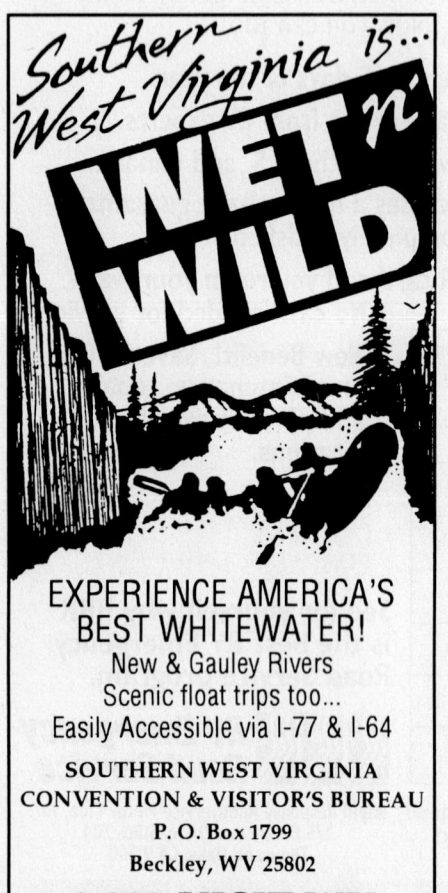

For a third of a century, the **Mountain State Art & Craft Fair** has provided a master showcase for authentic, traditional Appalachian art and craft work. A variety of heritage crafts are demonstrated daily during the Fair by skilled craftspeople. Other elements of the region's rich history are kept alive by musicians, singers, dancers and story-tellers in almost continuous performances. Take time to stop by the concession stands for a taste of unique Appalachian foods. It all takes place June 3rd through the 7th amid the beautiful setting of Cedar Lakes in Ripley.

When you arrive at the **West Augusta Historical Society Round Barn Quilt Show** you will see a beautifully located Round Barn (the only one in the state) in a beautiful valley. In addition to quilts, wallhangings, miniature quilts and quilting supplies, souvenirs from the Historical Society are available. Classes and/or demonstrations are also offered over the Father's Day weekend at this show in Mannington.

The **State Fair of West Virginia**, held annually in August, represents the traditions of the "country" fair. Everything from thrilling carnival rides to harness racing to top-name music entertainers can be found at this mountain state event in Lewisburg.

Labor Day weekend in Clarksburg is the place for the **Italian Heritage Festival.** Feast on Italian pastry, famous Italian bread, pepperoni rolls, handmade pasta and other delicacies. This 17-year old festival features concerts, strolling minstrels, authentic Italian dancers and sacred Italian religious observances.

**Fall:**

A person arriving at the **Honey Festival** will be both entertained and educated about honey and honey products. There are several exhibits and demonstrations which take place such as beekeepers working and explaining a live beehive, candle making, extracting honey from the comb and much more. Honey and honey products are available. In addition, there's a car show, baking contest, baking auction and honey and wax auction. It all takes place on the second weekend in September in Parkersburg.

The **Heritage and Harvest Festival** takes place in Moorefield in late September. The people of Hardy County share their historic homes and buildings, old-time crafts, festivities and beautiful countryside. Some of the homes are occupied by descendants of the families who built them. Heritage crafts are still a part of their daily lives. The festival includes meals prepared and served by different community groups.

The last weekend in September is time for the **Burlington Old Fashioned Apple Harvest Festival**. The Apple Harvest Dance kicks off the festivities on Friday evening, and voting for Baby Apple Dumpling takes place all weekend with the crownπing on Sunday afternoon. In addition, enjoy music, food, the vintage auto show and the chicken barbecue.

The Gauley River, ranked 7th among the world's great whitewater rivers, and one of the two most popular in the United States, presents the ultimate thrill in whitewater rafting. A technical river, demanding skill and experience, out of 100 rapids in the 38-mile trip, 50 are considered "major", drawing rafting enthusiasts from all over North America. **Gauley Season** runs Friday through Monday beginning September 6th and continues for 22 exciting days. Visitors can experience whitewater rafting or watch from the shores, as water is released from the Summerville Dam into the river. To view the grand finale of these celebratory days, visitors are encouraged to be at the New River Gorge Bridge on the 3rd Saturday in October. You'll see displays of parachuting off the bridge and other exciting activities around the New River Bridge, the largest expansion bridge in the world.

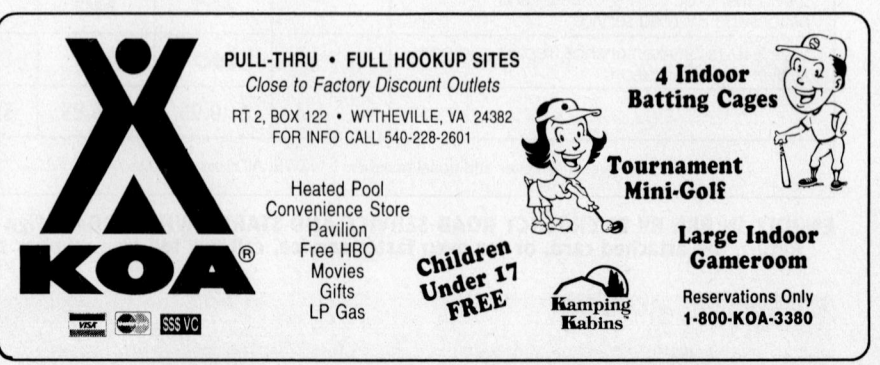

# DISCOVER THE FESTIVALS of The South

## ALABAMA FESTIVALS

**Spring:**

The beautiful **Bellingrath Gardens and Home** in Theodore is the site of a museum home filled with antique treasures surrounded by extensive gardens. It is truly a must-see floral paradise when visiting Alabama's Gulf Coast. The Gardens offers a year-round calendar of floral displays, including their **spring bulb extravaganza.** Azaleas electrify the landscape in hues of pink and crimson, and are preceded by one of the largest bulb displays this side of Holland. A visit during February will show displays of tulips, daffodils, hyacinths, Japanese magnolias, pansies and camellias. If you arrive during April, you can also take in the Camellia Classic Car Show held on the Great Lawn.

Cullman is the site of the **Bloomin' Festival** which has been held during early April for more than eleven years and annually draws more than 20,000 visitors. There are over 130 arts and crafts dealers from across the United States. You'll see (and perhaps purchase!) handmade furniture, baskets, wildlife sculptures made of bronze, leather goods, watercolor art, and much more.

The **Battle of Selma** has been reenacted annually for more than nine years. Held in April, you can experience authentic Civil War camps, music and entertainment, artillery night firings, and even cruise the Alabama River aboard the *Betsy Ann* riverboat.

The **19th Annual Alabama Jubilee** festival will be held in late May. It's Alabama's largest hot-air balloon festival and is held each year at Decatur's Point Mallard Park. Bring the camera and be prepared to be awed by more than 60 colorful balloons — each as tall as a 7-story building! There are also arts and crafts exhibits, music, dancing, antique and classic automobiles, and, best of all, the admission is free!

**Summer:**

Bargain hunters will love the **World's Longest Yard Sale** that is held the third weekend in August. If you are traveling north, the sale begins at Noccalula Falls Park in Gadsden and extends north along the Lookout Mountain Parkway to Chattanooga, Tenn. where it joins the U.S. Highway 127 Vacation Corridor and continues to Covington, Ky. and Cincinnati, Ohio. All kinds of items are lined up in vendors' booths alongside the road — you might find antiques, quilts, pots and pans, china, cutlery, and arts and crafts. It's a great reason to get off the interstate and back onto the smaller, more local highways.

**Fall:**

The **Annual National Shrimp Festival,** held the second full weekend of October, has been celebrated in Gulf Shores for over 24 years. The festival has been included in the 200 Best Shows list for traditional crafts, and features more than 200 fine arts, crafts and commercial exhibitors. Musical entertainment for all ages and tastes highlight the festival, as does the Seafood Boardwalk, where shrimp and other succulent seafood specialties are offered.

**Kentuck** is one of the South's major arts and crafts festivals. A tradition for over 24 years, the festival, which is held in Kentuck City Park in Tuscaloosa in mid-October, is host to more than 30,000 visitors who are treated to storytelling, jazz, and blacksmith demonstrations. Over 200 artists from across America display their works at this major festival. There's plenty of food, and, of course, wonderful Southern hospitality!

**Winter (through Spring):**

**Mardi Gras** in Mobile was the nation's first Mardi Gras celebration, dating back to 1703 (yes, before New Orleans'). Today, Mobile's carnival season begins with the International Ball in November. More than 50 nations are represented and the Ball is open to the public. The beginning of Lent is celebrated by masked balls, pageants and candy-throwing revelers on parade floats. While not the *biggest* Mardi Gras celebration along the Gulf, Mobile's parties and parades offer plenty of fun suitable for the whole family. There is a huge variety of fun and activities, but the parades alone are worth the visit — last year's themed floats included a Hawaiian Islands float complete with a waterfall! The food is abundant, too, with everything from turkey legs to funnel cakes.

## *FLORIDA FESTIVALS*

**Winter:**

January 8th through the 15th is an exciting time to visit the Florida Keys to enjoy the 12th annual **Florida Keys Renaissance Faire.** Ensembles of musicians and actors travel along the Upper and Lower Keys to create excitement for the upcoming 3-day Faire held in Marathon. Each day of the Renaissance Market Fair has a different theme, and there are over 30 stage shows featuring the finest Renaissance performers, full-armored horseback jousting tournaments, and human chess matches twice daily. Artisans and crafters from all over the United States demonstrate and offer their wares for sale.

Stop at Sandestin on January 20th for the 7th annual **Great Southern Gumbo Cook-Off.** Approximately 20 local restaurants participate in the competition, and awards are given for best gumbo. Best of all, a one-ticket admission includes unlimited sampling at all booths! There's music to go with the gumbo, as a Dixieland band performs Cajun and Dixieland music all day.

Plant City will host the 61st **Florida Strawberry Festival** February 29 through March 10, 1996. Plant City, the Winter Strawberry Capital of the world, is located about 24 miles east of Tampa. The 11-day event includes daily entertainment by famous country music stars, exhibits focusing on agriculture and livestock, education, industry and the arts. Competitions range from cook-offs and clogging to diaper decorating and strawberry shortcake eating contests.

February and March are busy months in Naples, Florida. Enjoy **Dancing Under the Stars** with big bands like Perry Fotos, Don Glasser and The Gulf Coasters, and bands playing the music of the 1950s and 1960s. **Celebrating Old Naples**, March 2nd through 5th, features a historic walking tour and four days of activities including a parade with a fashion competition of yesteryear, horse and buggy rides, and more. Beginning in November you can purchase fresh produce at the **Old Naples Farmers Market** on Third Street and the Avenues. The market has become a place where folks come to stroll and socialize.

February is also the month to enjoy art in Coconut Grove at the 33rd annual **Coconut Grove Arts Festival.** Located by the turquoise waters of Biscayne Bay, the festival takes over this charming Miami neighborhood. There are musicians, food vendors, and a variety of arts media including sculpture, paintings, photography, jewelry, watercolors, pottery, and more. The works of more than 2,000 artists are represented at over 325 booths. The food is world-class, too, with a variety of international delicacies featured. Huge Greek salads, Bahamian crab cakes, conch fritters, and other gourmet treats await visitors to this event.

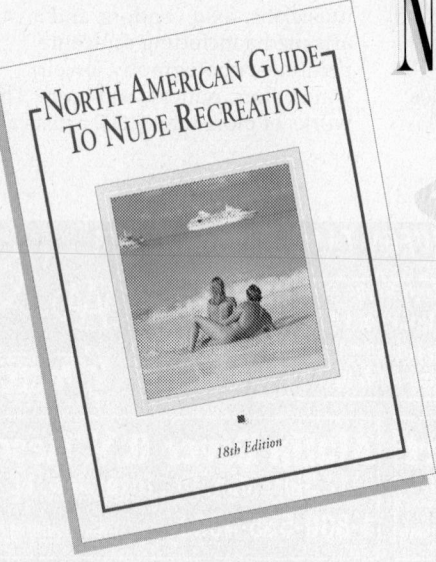

Enjoy a visit to the 92nd annual **Florida State Fair** February 2nd through the 18th at Florida Expo Park in Tampa. It's the biggest fair in the Southeast and features one of the largest midways in the country. More than 86 rides and shows are featured on the 325-acre site, located 7 miles east of Tampa off I-4. A special feature of the fair is Cracker Country, a re-enactment of life in Florida from 1870 to 1912 with hundreds of volunteers dressed in period costumes. The Craft Center showcases working craftsmen with their handmade products for sale.

February 16th, 17th and 18th are the dates for the **Olustee Battle Festival and Re-enactment,** a major Civil War re-enactment with over 1,500 participants. The event began over 17 years ago and has grown ever since. Enjoy authentic Civil War villages; arts, crafts and collectibles; a parade; a Blue-Grey square dance; food booths and a 1-mile fun run.

The Daytona International Speedway opened in 1959 with the inaugural Speedweeks and the **Daytona 500**. Today it is internationally-known as the "World Center of Racing." The Speedway, which is the site of world-renowned stock car, sports car and motorcycle racing events, is also a major year-round attraction. The 450-acre facility includes a 2.5-mile trioval course and a 3.56-mile road course, both of which use the famed 31-degree high-banked turns. Guided tours are conducted daily, starting at the World Center of Racing Visitors' Center.

**Spring:**

Sandestin makes a unique toast on the Northwest Florida coast as the resort town celebrates **Sandestin Women in Wine Festival** in April. One of the area's largest and most well-known wine tastings in Northwest Florida, the festival is attended by thousands of visitors. Live jazz music is featured throughout the event and there are watercolor art exhibits to feast the eyes after soothing the palate with wine.

New Smyrna Beach's 20th annual **Images, A Festival of the Arts** in March brings innovative and talented artists together for entertainment, fine art, and lots of hands-on activities. Continuous musical entertainment provides a lively atmosphere, and a few highlights of the food menu included Philly steak sandwiches, BBQ ribs, grouper sandwiches, funnel cakes, and a variety of ice-cream treats.

The **Florida Heritage Festival** in Bradenton from Saturday, March 23rd through Saturday, April 20th is an Indian arts and heritage festival featuring about two dozen displays by Native American Indians, including arts and crafts, food and reconstructed living quarters. The three-day RiverFest begins Friday evening, April 19th, and is held at a large park along the Manatee River with 15 to 20 food booths, 80 arts and crafts booths, live music, children's rides, a boat show, and often, an RV show. The Bottle Boat Regatta features homemade boats whose hulls consist of plastic gallon jugs. The crews of these boats race their colorful and cleverly-designed craft across Palma Sola Bay. A highlight of the event is the Grand Parade, which begins around sundown. Consisting of a long line of floats constructed by groups from across the state, this parade has become the largest nighttime parade in Florida.

Situated on the banks of the St. Johns River, downtown Jacksonville plays host to a large number of exciting outdoor festivals each year. **Feast & Fest . . . A Taste of Jacksonville**, April 20th and 21st, is an opportunity to enjoy this beautiful waterfront city. This springtime tradition offers a variety of good food, entertainment and fun. Approximately 20 local restaurants serve their specialties each year. Big name chains and local restaurants alike are represented.

Celebrate the Easter season in St. Augustine and the beaches of Anastasia Island by attending the **St. Augustine Easter Festival,** a tradition for over 40 years. You'll be treated to the Twilight Lighthouse Run, where hundreds of runners sprint along The Beaches of Anastasia Island toward the glowing beacon of an 1887 lighthouse; the St. Augustine Passion Play, a portrayal of the resurrection of Christ; a Spring Arts and Crafts Festival; the Blessing of the Fleet; and a Seafood Festival. Relive the joy of yesteryear during Easter in St. Augustine.

Visit Fort Walton Beach beginning April 19th for the three-day, 13th annual **Fort Walton Beach Seafood Festival**. In addition to the fresh seafood, you'll be treated to view more than 100 classic and antique cars on display, and an arts, crafts and commercial show exhibition.

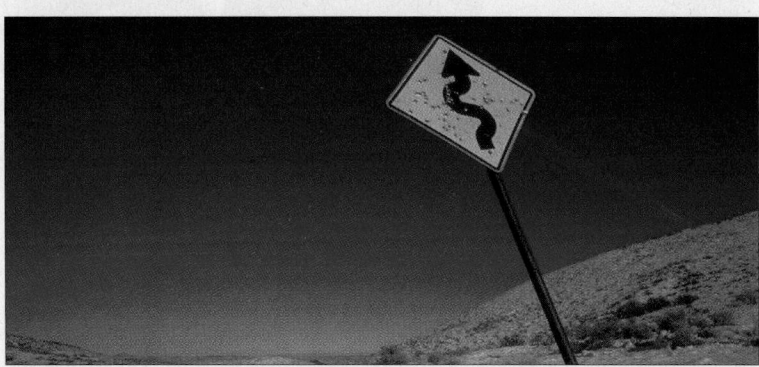

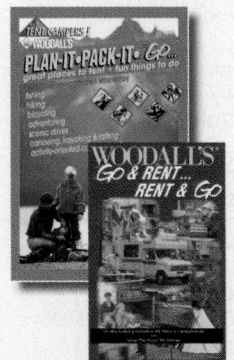

The Jazz Club of Sarasota is the sponsor of the 16th annual **Sarasota Jazz Festival,** April 10th through the 13th. The '96 musical lineup was not determined at press time, but highlights of last year's event included musical direction by Bob Rosengarden, a salute to Benny Goodman, Piano Explosion, and All In The Family, King of Mambo.

**Springtime Tallahassee,** beginning in March, is a season-long celebration of the city's historic, cultural and natural history. The events include the Springtime Grand Parade with horses, marching bands and floats. The Arts & Crafts Jubilee is an open-air market with over 250 craft and food vendors and live musical performances. Over 500 volunteer groups (krewes) organize historical eras that date from the early 1500s through modern times. Each krewe member is costumed to his or her historic period, and the parade floats are geared to a specific historic time.

For jazz and more jazz, plan to attend the **Pensacola JazzFest**, held the third weekend in April each year for over 14 years. The event presents a wide variety of jazz performances from big band to be-bop; progressive to Dixieland, and the spicy sound of New Orleans blues. The musicians perform "in the round" as the setting of JazzFest is rather intimate. The performance stage is actually an historic gazebo set against a background of centuries-old oak trees. The fest also provides local Pensacola cuisine, as area restaurants offer a variety of treats: specialty breads, yogurt, seafood, vegetarian specialties, low-fat menus, sandwiches, beer, wine and soft drinks.

Come and join in the fun in Fort Lauderdale on April 12th through the 14th for the 12th annual **Fort Lauderdale Seafood Festival,** held downtown at Bubier Park. According to Dan Hobby, Executive Director of the Fort Lauderdale Historical Museum, "Seafood hasn't always been commercially plentiful in Fort Lauderdale. In 1910, if you wanted local seafood, you had to catch it yourself or know a fisherman." Today, it's much easier, especially when you attend this festival. Chefs from over 20 of South Florida's most popular restaurants will prepare their seafood specialties for the

*Florida Festivals continued on pg. 58*

# ENJOY FLORIDA LIVING AT THE PREMIER RV RESORT/GOLF CLUB IN FLORIDA!

Rentals

Rally Groups Welcome

Park Homes & Lots

Lot Sales

Wilson

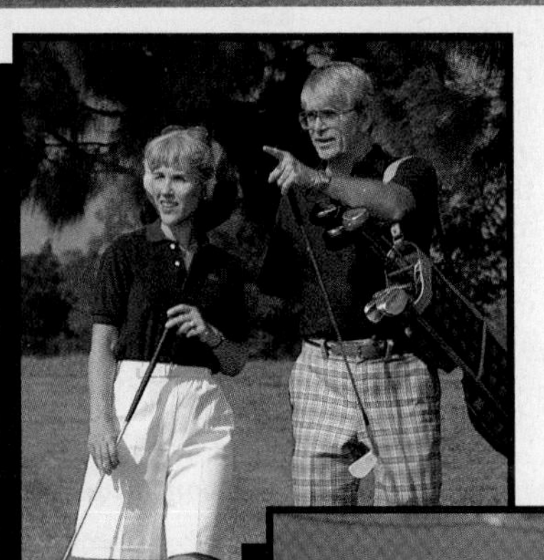

**Located in the Heart Of Florida**

75
4
ORLANDO
Disney World
528
BASEBALL CITY
Sea World
Deer Creek
Florida Turnpike
4
27
Cypress Gardens
60

Come to centrally located Deer Creek and enjoy the luxury of a community designed and developed specifically for the RV Lifestyle. Play a challenging round of golf on our beautiful 18-hole golf course, relax in our heated pools and spa or indulge in the numerous planned and unplanned activities at Deer Creek.

***Relax...Enjoy Your Time***

We offer 24-hour gated and manned security on our 200 acres of the most unique, master planned community that boasts of the finest recreational facilities found in Florida...or anywhere else in the U.S.

***Stay for a day, a week, a month or all year long...***

Bring your motor home, trailer, fifth wheel or reside in a spacious park model.

***Everything You Need...***

All Deer Creek sites are fully landscaped and sodded with concrete pads and patios, full hookups to county water and sewer, 50/100 amp electrical service, TV cable and garbage pick-up.

***and there's more...***

Restaurant and Lounge
Full-time Social Director
Arts & Crafts
Recreational Building
Heated Pools & Spa
ATM Machine
Elegant, 2 Story Clubhouse
Tennis & Vollyball Courts

***Beautiful Park Homes for Rent or Sale***

**4200 U.S. Highway 27 N.
Davenport, FL 33837**

**1-800-424-2931**

· *Central location near medical facilities and shopping* ·
· *Disney World and many other major attractions within 15 minutes* ·

*Florida Festivals continued from pg. 56*

more than 50,000 expected visitors to the three-day event. It's a music festival, too, with more than 15 of the hottest jazz, pop, reggae, blues, oldies, rhythm & blues, Zydeco and country bands performing continuously.

**SunFest** is held over a five-day period beginning the first weekend in May in downtown West Palm Beach. An estimated 300,000 people attended the event in '95, and enjoyed the large musical lineup as well as the arts, music and fireworks. Billed as Florida's largest jazz, art and water events festival, SunFest's setting is the beautiful waterfront along palm tree-lined Flagler Drive. Past headline acts have included Harry Connick, Jr., Bonnie Raitt, Crosby, Stills and Nash and B.B. King. Activities include a professional art exhibit, water sports and powerboat races, an eclectic marketplace with unusual arts and crafts, a youth park, and international cuisine. Don't worry about parking — a continuous bus shuttle between the Palm Beach Mall parking lot and the festival entrance gates will be available for a nominal fee.

Late May is the time to attend the 44th annual **Florida Folk Festival** at the Stephen Foster State Folk Culture Center in White Springs. The festival celebrates the diverse folklife of the state as performers, crafters and over 25,000 visitors join in the activities. There are many beautiful, handmade crafts to purchase, and workshops provide lessons in music, crafts and storytelling. Food is abundant, with vendors tempting visitors with Seminole fry bread, barbecue dinners, hoppin' john, and other delicious ethnic and historic foods.

**Summer:**

The **Hemingway Days Festival**, held each July for over 15 years in Key West, brings novelists, editors and Hemingway scholars together for a three-day writers' workshop and conference. The festival was founded in 1981 to honor the famous author. There's a 5-K sunset run, a First Novel Contest, and even a Hemingway look-alike contest.

**Fall:**

At the 19th anniversary of the **Boggy Bayou Mullet Festival** in October you'll be treated to a wide variety of food from more than 60 vendors serving up some tasty Greek, Italian, German, and Oriental cuisine, and, of course, fresh seafood. Mullet, shrimp, crab, gumbo, shark, alligator, amberjack and grouper are skewered, fried, baked, steamed and grilled to perfection. There's also a juried art & crafts show with over 100 artists and artisans represented. Continuous free entertainment begins late Friday afternoon, and continues all weekend.

**The Florida Horse & Agriculture Festival** held in October in Ocala is sponsored by the Ocala Marion County Chamber of Commerce. The festival showcases over 400 professional equestrians representing over 40 breeds of horses and 15 breeds of cattle and exotic animals. There is a 50-booth trade show with displays ranging from fine jewelry and clothing to the latest in horse and agricultural products. Other activities include educational seminars and hands-on activities where guests may experience calf roping, race riding, or learn country dance steps.

*Florida Festivals continued on pg. 60*

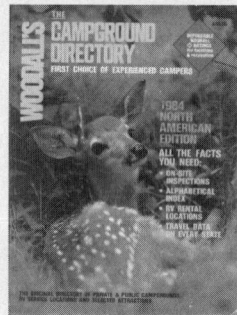

*Florida Festivals continued from pg. 58*

Historic Naples hosts the **Festival of Lights on Third Street South** each Monday before Thanksgiving, which in 1996 will be November 18th. The festival takes place from 6 to 9 p.m. with an official tree-lighting ceremony conducted by the mayor and Santa Claus. Over 20 groups of entertainers provide music, dance and choral singing, and the entire area is decorated with over a quarter-million white lights.

## *GEORGIA FESTIVALS*

**Spring:**

**The Mossy Creek Barnyard Festival** is held twice annually, during the 3rd weekend in April, as well as October. The setting is made up of heavily wooded terraces with tall pines around two old houses, an old store, barn and barnyard. Hostesses in calico and bonnets greet all guests. Wide paths are covered with golden straw. You'll find pioneer craft demonstrations, heritage music, hayrides, food (including hush puppies, fried chicken and home-baked cakes), fine art, and best of all, the festival is known for its ability to encourage friendships while experiencing things "the way they used to be." Located just 90 miles south of the Atlanta airport, 3 miles east of I-75 near Perry.

The **Atlanta Dogwood Festival** has been held since 1936. Over 150,000 visitors in April enjoy the children's activities, main stage concerts featuring continuous music, a wildlife sanctuary learning center, hot-air balloons, a garden center and dogwood markets, and much more.

The **Prater's Mill Country Fair** (May 11th & 12th, and October 12th & 13th), is one of the finest rural festivals in the country, celebrating the best of Southern folklife and the rich traditions of crafts and heritage of the region. Visitors will find craft demonstrations including blacksmithing, weaving, quilting, rug hooking and hand tufting. There are also pony rides, canoeing on the mill pond, and nature trails to enjoy. Located on Georgia Highway 2, ten miles northeast of Dalton and about 30 miles south of Chattanooga, Tennessee.

**Summer:**

Make plans to visit the 46th annual **Georgia Mountain Fair** in Hiawassee during August and you'll be treated to a mountain village of yesteryear where you can explore stores, blacksmith shops, a farm museum, one-room school, and a corncrib and barn. There are no commercial exhibits, just products and talents of the mountain folks. Fresh and canned fruits and vegetables, antiques, and lovely needlework are here to view, enjoy, and, maybe, purchase! There is also an antique auto parade along with marching bands, buggies and floats.

Let the Games begin! When those four words are announced again on July 19th, the **XXVI Olympic Games** will begin in Alanta, running through August 4th. It's the first time in Olympic history that the Southern United States will host the games. The Olympics have not been held in the United States since the 1984 Summer Games in Los Angeles, and have never been held in a U.S. city east of the Mississippi, but international attention and growth in the past decade have afforded Atlanta with exciting opportunities to host major events. Seven and a half million tickets to the events will be available to the public. Parking need not be a problem as the Olympic Transportation System has been designed to funnel people from across the metro area to concentrations of Olympic events downtown and in the suburbs. From there, walking is recommended, but there will also be an additional 2,000 leased buses, remote park-and-ride lots and shuttles, high-occupancy vehicle lanes on freeways, and staggered work schedules for employees of downtown businesses to make things less congested.

**Fall:**

Come celebrate the **Labor Day Holiday at Agrirama**, an authentic living history museum in Tifton, Georgia. You'll step back in time to a nostalgic county fair, circa 1896. Explore the farms, see bacon and ham curing in the smokehouse, all under the guidance of costumed staff who will make you aware of the life and work of the era.

Cooks from all across Georgia will arrive October 5 to compete in the **"Big Pig Jig," the Georgia barbecue cooking championship.** The event, which will be held October 5th, 11th and 12th , has attracted over 35,000 spectators and at least 120 teams of barbecue specialists. Twice named one of the top 100 events in America and a top 20 event in the Southeast, the wonderful food is augmented by arts and crafts, games, art contests, a 5K run called the Hog Jog, skydiving events and a parade. The event is held in south central Georgia in the town of Vienna (Dooly County), whose other claims to fame are the processing and sale of pecans, peanuts, and wonderful candies.

Jasper, Georgia is home to the annual **Marble Festival** where you can see the results of over 100 years of quarrying the most beautiful and durable marble in the world. Each year, the world's largest open pit marble quarry is open to the public as the Marble Valley of Pickens County becomes the site of the annual Marble Festival. The Festival is held the first weekend in October and provides crafts, plenty of food and music. Historic buildings to tour, fabulous Georgia food, and the annual Marble Sculpture Exhibits make this a worthwhile stop during your travels.



*South Festivals continued on pg. 62*

*South Festivals continued from pg. 62*

## *KENTUCKY FESTIVALS*

**Spring:**

Each year, quilters and folks who just plain appreciate fine quilts, show up in Paducah, Kentucky to attend one of the largest displays of quilts in the world, the **American Quilter's Society Quilt Show and Contest.** Held from April 25th through the 28th, the show will feature over 400 competition quilts displayed, as well as many wall hangings and other creative works. The fashion show of quilted wearables is a "must see" event, and the whole town welcomes visitors with special restaurant meals, free bus tours of the city, and more.

Kentucky is horse country, and what better way to celebrate these majestic animals than by attending the 16th annual **three-day qualifying trials for the U.S. Olympic Equestrian Team.** The event showcases the strength, courage, stamina and refined beauty of the horses, and illustrates the harmony and trust that are developed between horse and rider. The event was held in 1995 on April 27th through the 30th. Phone Kentucky Horse Park in Lexington for the 1996 dates.

For the largest and most famous event in Kentucky, come on down for the **Kentucky Derby Festival** which will be held in Louisville April 19th through May 5th. What the Run for the Roses is to horse racing, the award-winning Derby Festival is to community celebrations. The event begins with "Thunder Over Louisville," now considered to be the nation's largest annual fireworks extravaganza. The ensuing two weeks offer something for everyone, and encompass over 70 different festivals. Some highlights are: The Derby Festival Chow Wagon, the Fillies' Derby Ball, McDonald's Derby Festival Basketball Classic, Derby Festival Great Balloon Race, the Giant Steamboat Race, a marathon, and more.

**Summer:**

For a memorable weekend of free concerts in June, attend the **Great American Brass Band Festival** in Danville. In addition to the concerts, there are antique bicycles, hot-air balloons, street musicians and parades, all set against the backdrop of historic, picturesque Danville. While not the oldest festival in North America (1996 will be their 7th year), the event draws more than 40,000 guests.

When planning a June visit to western Kentucky, stop and join the fun, sample the food, and listen to the music of **The Taste of Madisonville.** The festival provides rides and games, booths displaying arts and crafts, local food specialties, and lots of music from blues to bluegrass.

**Fall:**

If Bluegrass music is your "thing," don't miss the **International Bluegrass Music Association (IBMA) FAN FEST** from September 27th through 29th in Owensboro.

We owe a special thank you to Colonel Sanders for inspiring the **World Chicken Festival** that has been held in London, Kentucky for over five years. The original Kentucky Fried Chicken restaurant is located in the county, so the local people thought it would be a nice tribute to the Colonel to have a special occasion celebrating chicken. The festival is staged on the streets and parking lots of downtown London/Laurel County. In addition to delicious chicken, there are over 25 food booths, music, a car show, hot-air balloon rides, a magic show for the children, and even a chicken wing eating contest. The festival will be held September 21st through the 24th.

The 9th annual **Woolly Worm Festival**, held each October in Beattyville (Lee County), honors these little critters that supposedly have the power to predict how severe or mild the forthcoming winter will be. Festival highlights include a Woolly Worm race (look out, Kentucky Derby!) a 5K race (for humans), a classic car show, parades, food booths, arts and crafts, and much more. No small celebration, the event annually draws more than 50,000 visitors from all over the world.

**Winter:**

For a different "down under" Christmas Celebration, visit Mammoth Cave National Park for their **Annual Christmas Sing in the Cave** celebration. Each December (usually on the 2nd Sunday of December), various singing groups perform in selected rooms of the cave, as visitors make their way from chamber to chamber, enjoying both fellowship and the delicate cave acoustics. Some special notes to help you enjoy this unique visit: Dress for winter weather, it's cold! Wear appropriate footwear, and be aware there is no seating provided in the cave. Cave lighting will be dim.

## *LOUISIANA FESTIVALS*

**Spring:**

DeSoto Parish hosts the **River City Fest** held in Logansport the first weekend in May, as well as a fun boat race later in the summer. Visit beautiful and historic DeSoto Parish during the spring and early summer and you'll be treated to their **Blueberry Festival** which is held the last weekend in June. Blueberries are a growing industry (no pun intended!) in this part of Louisiana, and the Festival showcases the delicious fruit with servings of blueberry pancakes, blueberry cobbler, cakes, and a blueberry cook-off contest. There are also arts and crafts, entertainment, and a parade on Saturday. You can even purchase your own blueberry bushes to grow at home. Come to the Courthouse Square in Mansfield and enjoy the fun and sample some Louisiana blueberries.

Get your taste buds ready for some delicious, juicy Louisiana strawberries and visit Tangipahoa Parish and especially the town of Ponchatoula in April for **Ponchatoula's Strawberry Festival**, one of the largest festivals in the state. A vast variety of strawberry desserts, a parade, music and street dancing await your visit. Besides the world-renowned strawberries, the area is famous for its great antique shops.

A visit to St. Tammany Parish during April will be a real treat for antique lovers, particularly during the **Slidell Antique District Street Fair** (also held again during October.) If you are visiting Slidell during May, you'll be treated to three days of continuous jazz performances and family entertainment at the **Slidell Jazz Festival.**

Stop by the Shreveport-Bossier area for **Mudbug Madness**, which is held in late May. This popular festival celebrates the crawfish season with Cajun foods, music, children's activities and fun.

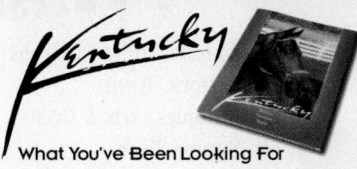

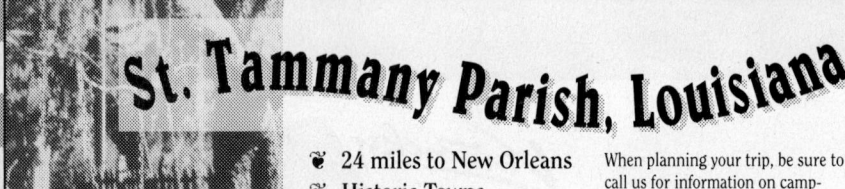

**FestForAll,** Baton Rouge's largest community "Celebration of the Arts" takes place on May 18th and 19th. It's an exciting blend of fine arts and crafts, as well as performing arts, all displayed along winding brick walkways in downtown Baton Rouge. You'll find plenty of great food (of course you will, this is Louisiana!) including fresh seafood, pasta, and desserts, all of which can be enjoyed as you stroll through the festival marketplace. Stroll along historic oak-lined boulevards and enjoy a wide variety of music, all in Baton Rouge at FestForAll.

May is a good time to visit Eunice, Sunset, Grand Coteau and Washington, all of which are in St. Landry Parish. Their annual food and music festival called the **St. Landry Parish Heritage Festival** is held the second week in May with most activities held over Mother's Day weekend. You'll be treated to cooking classes, a tasting party, Cajun and Zydeco music, a tour of Antebellum homes, and a crafts show.

Opelousas hosts the **International Cajun Joke Telling Contest** each year during the third weekend of April. Contestants gather from throughout Louisiana and other states to tell their best Cajun jokes.

**Summer:**

Visit the **Bayou Lacombe Crab Festival** the first week in July for a taste of fresh Louisiana seafood prepared in many different ways.

July 1st through the 4th brings the **Freedom Festival: Gospel & Soul on the Bayou** to Houma, Louisiana. It's a unique celebration of America's religious music heritage, and features a relaxing atmosphere, Cajun food, a parade, spectacular fireworks and music, music, music!

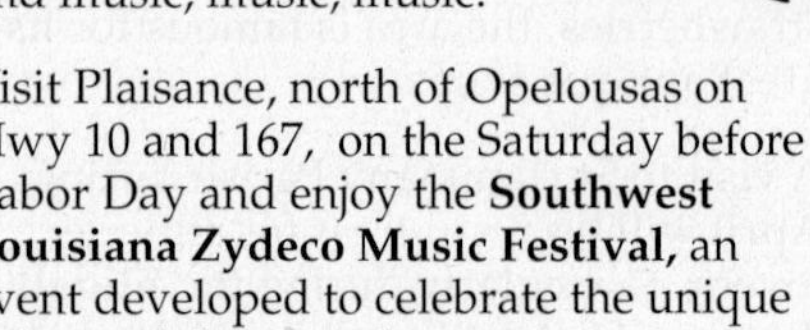

Visit Plaisance, north of Opelousas on Hwy 10 and 167, on the Saturday before Labor Day and enjoy the **Southwest Louisiana Zydeco Music Festival,** an event developed to celebrate the unique culture of this popular music.

**Fall:**

Labor Day weekend is the time to visit Morgan City for the **Louisiana Shrimp and Petroleum Festival**, the state's oldest chartered harvest festival. Dubbed one of Louisiana's top 20 festivals, the main event is the historic blessing of the fleet, followed by a water parade featuring elaborately decorated shrimp boats, pleasure boats, and oil industry vessels. On land, there's a street carnival and

*Louisiana Festivals continued on pg. 66*

**FREE INFO?** Louisiana Office of Tourism, enter #695; St. Tammany Parish CVB, enter #407; KOA New Orleans West, enter #131 on Reader Service Card following page 16.

## TO SEARCH FOR AN RV, SEND US THIS CARD

**Yes,** I would like to request an RV Search (only $5!) that will give me five matches in my geographical area. I have indicated the details regarding the RV that I am seeking directly below.

**My Name** ______________________________

**Address** ______________________________

**City**____________________ **State** ________ **Zip**__________

**Phone (** **)** ______________________________

**Good Sam/Coast to Coast Member No.**__________________

❑ **My check for $5 is enclosed** ❑ **Bill my:**

❑ **Visa** ❑ **MasterCard** ❑ **Discover**

**Account No.** ____________________ **Exp. Date**________

Type of RV (Motorhome, Fifth Wheel, etc.)____________________

Make (Manufacturer) ______________________________

Model ____________ Length ________ Year(s) ______ Price Range ________

Make check payable to **RV Search Network**; P.O. Box 6850, Englewood, CO 80155-9604
Attention RV Search Coordinator or call:

**1-800-SHOP 4 RV** Operator 9605 (1-800-746-7478) (8:30 am - 8:00 pm EST)

051996

## TO LIST YOUR RV, SEND US THIS CARD

**Yes,** I would like to list my RV with the RV Search Network (only $59.95 for a full year!) I have indicated the details regarding my RV below.

**My Name** ______________________________

**Address** ______________________________

**City**____________________ **State** ________ **Zip**__________

**Phone (** **)** ______________________________

**Good Sam/Coast to Coast Member No.**__________________

❑ **My check for $5 is enclosed** ❑ **Bill my:**

❑ **Visa** ❑ **MasterCard** ❑ **Discover**

**Account No.** ____________________ **Exp. Date**________

Year________ Make__________ Model__________ Type__________ Price__________

Fuel________ Engine Size (cu. in.)________ Mileage__________ Sleeps______ Length______

Original Owner______ Non-Smoking______ Alternate Vehicle Location____________________

**Alternate Address** ______________________________

City____________________State____________Zip____________

**Features:** Awning___ Central Control___ Fresh Water___ Stove___ Generator___ Holding Tank____

Hot Water____ Leveling Jacks____ Propane____ Refrigerator____ Air Cond.____ Slide-Out____

Microwave___ TV/VCR___ Stereo___ CB Radio___ Satellite Dish___ Disposal___ Other__________

Make check payable to **RV Search Network**; P.O. Box 6850, Englewood, CO 80155-9604
Attention RV Search Coordinator, or call:

**1-800-5 SELL RV** Operator 9605 (1-800-573-5578) (8:30 am - 8:00 pm EST)

051996

## SEARCH OUR NATIONAL NETWORK FOR LISTINGS OF PREVIOUSLY OWNED RVS

**Complete the information on the reverse and mail it today, or call**

## 1-800-SHOP 4 RV

**(8:30 A.M. TO 8:00 P.M. EST)**

## SELL YOUR RV THROUGH OUR NATIONWIDE LISTING SERVICE

**Complete the information on the reverse and mail it today, or call**

## 1-800-5 SELL RV

**(8:30 A.M. TO 8:00 P.M. EST)**

# Buying? Selling?

**RV Search Makes It Easy To Buy Or Sell Your Pre-owned RV!**

## To Buy:

It's time to move up. Time to purchase that model you've had your eye on ever since you hooked up next to one in Maine that summer. Or maybe it's time to buy your very first rig.

### Introducing RV Search!

RV Search is a new national network of RV buyers and sellers developed by the parent company of Trailer Life Enterprises, Coast to Coast Resorts and Woodall's. As part of the corporate family that publishes RV magazines and directories that reach literally millions of RV owners each month, RV Search benefits from advertisements and direct mail communications to the largest database of RV owners in the world! And because of this incredible resource, RV Search can put you in touch with the exact seller you are looking for. Fast.

### We Find the RV You Want.

All you do is make one toll-free call and give us the make, model, size, year, accessories and price range you are looking for. Our computer does the rest. We will send you the listings in your area that meet your needs for the price you want to pay! Why not call right now!

**1 800 SHOP 4 RV**

**(1 800 746-7478, 8:30 am - 8:00 pm, M-F, EST Ask for operator 9605)**

## To Sell:

Here you are. Faced with the need to sell your RV. Maybe you're ready to move up to a bigger unit. Or maybe you want something more compact now that the kids are gone. Either way, you need the cash out of your current rig. Now.

### RV Search to the Rescue!

Simply list your RV with a new, nationwide network of buyers and sellers called RV Search. Once listed, your rig and asking price are computer matched to RV Search's giant database of buyers who are looking for pre-owned RVs. And yours may be just the unit they have asked for! If so, we rush those buyers (located in your area) your name, address and phone number, so you can get down to business.

And here's another RV Search bonus! After your sale, send us the name of your buyer and we'll rebate $10 to you—making your RV Search listing a great value!

### We Find the Buyer You Need.

All you do to list your rig with RV Search is call one toll-free 800 number. Our computer will do the rest.

RV Search is part of the Trailer Life Enterprises/ Woodall's / Coast to Coast Resorts family of companies—with all of the resources those industry leaders bring with them. So you can trust you are getting all the selling clout you need! Why not call right now!

RV Search NETWORK

Part of the TL Enterprises, Woodall's and Coast to Coast family

**1 800 5 SELL RV**

**(1 800 573-5578, 8:30 am - 8:00 pm, M-F, EST Ask for operator 9605)**

**FREE INFO?** RV Search, enter #659 on Reader Service Card following page 16.

*Louisiana Festivals continued. from pg. 64*

parade, arts and crafts featuring more than 100 artists, and a children's village, a fantasy land filled with games for all ages. Listen to lively music from over a dozen bands featuring traditional Cajun, Zydeco, Zyde Cajun, and other styles of music. There's even a gospel tent. Eat a variety of some of the best shrimp dishes in the country, and visit the beautiful Atchafalaya Basin, with its rivers, lakes and streams.

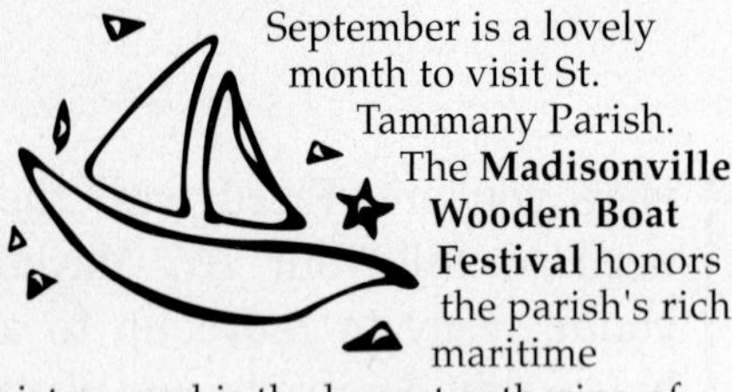

September is a lovely month to visit St. Tammany Parish. The **Madisonville Wooden Boat Festival** honors the parish's rich maritime history and is the largest gathering of antique, classic and contemporary water craft on the Gulf Coast.

Lafayette is home to **Festivals Acadiens**, held each fall on the third weekend of September. Actually, it's a combination of several festivals all rolled into one: the Louisiana native Crafts Festival, the Bayou Food Festival, Festival de Musique Acadienne, and Downtown Alive! and Kids Alive! The festivities attract over 150,000 visitors each year who come to hear, taste and experience the rhythm of Cajun life in Acadiana. The Native Crafts Festival showcases the works of over 300 craftspersons, singers, musicians, cooks, artisans and storytellers who explain and demonstrate their artistry. Festival de Musique attracts Louisiana's best Cajun and Zydeco bands, using music to entertain and teach about the fascinating culture of Louisiana.

Downtown Alive! and Kids Alive! kick off the festival with music in downtown Lafayette's Parc de Lafayette, and provide special performances and activities for children.

**The Louisiana Shrimp Festival** is held the 3rd weekend of September on the campus of Archbishop Hannan High School in Meraux, Louisiana. The event boasts many food booths serving shrimp fettuccini, shrimp kabobs, po-boys, jambalaya, char-broiled oysters, and much more. Entertainment is provided around the clock with major local bands performing nightly.

September 29th through October 1st are the dates to mark on your calendar if you love this combination: **Balloons & BBQ,** a popular Baton Rouge festival. Watch scores of the colorful hot-air balloons and enjoy some great Louisiana barbecue.

**The Super Derby Festival (Riverfront Festival)** is held in Shreveport-Bossier City in September/October. It's an eleven-day festival featuring more than 40 fun-filled events.

Witness the blues in Baton Rouge by arriving October 12th or 13th to enjoy the **Baton Rouge Blues Festival.** This is one of the largest blues festivals in the country, and attracts many legends of blues such as Elvin Bishop, Doctor John, Albert Collins, and others. Non-stop music on four stages make this a "blues extravaganza."

*Louisiana Festivals continued on pg. 70*

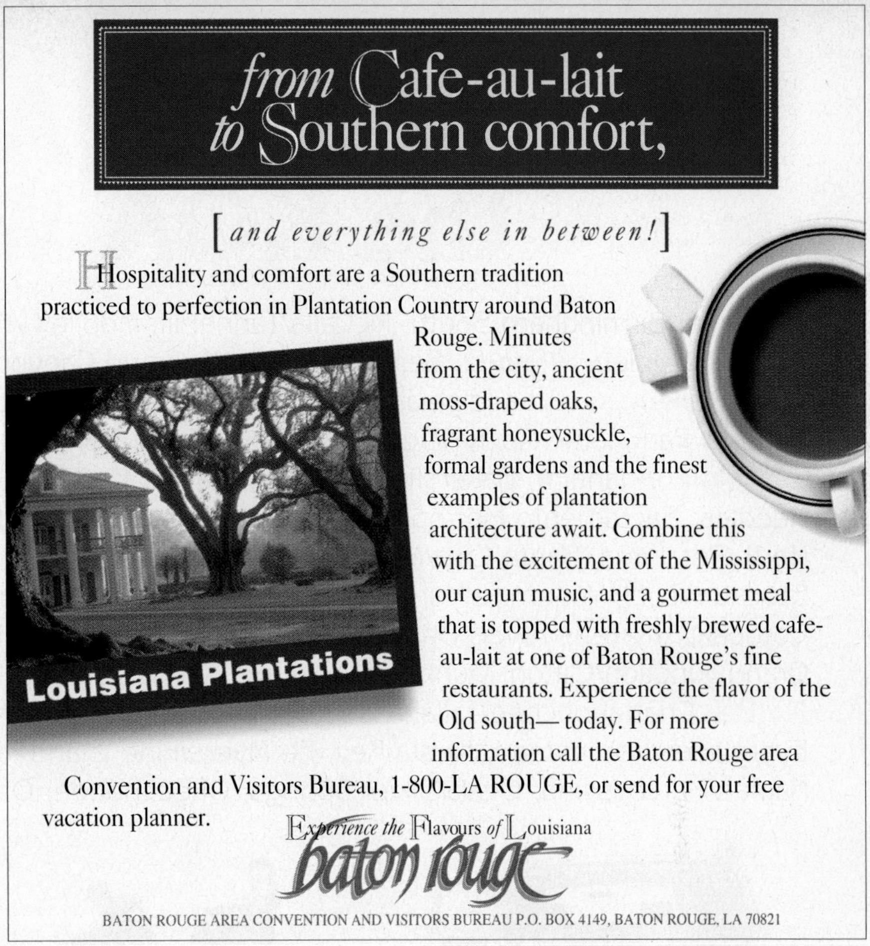

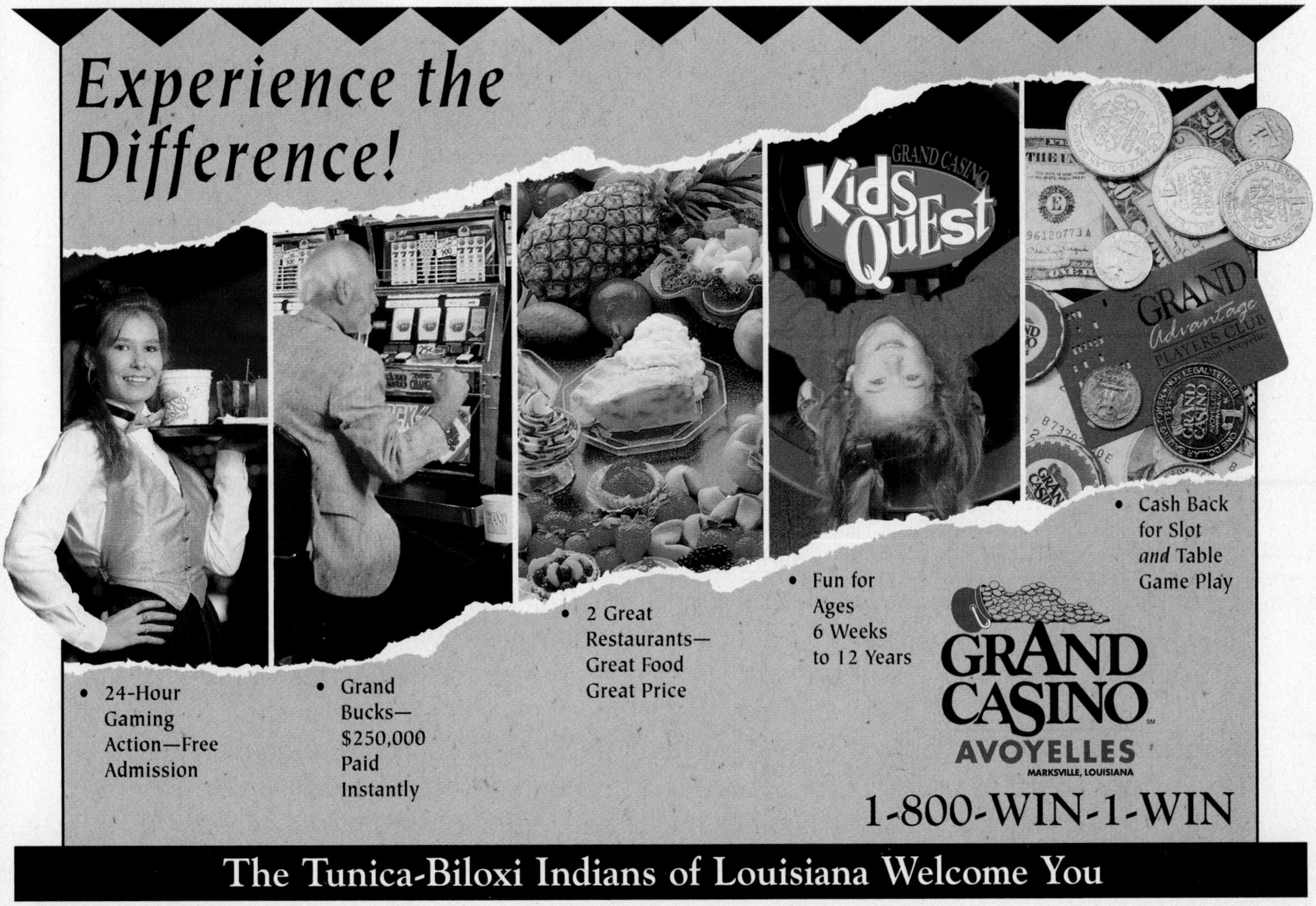

# Discover North America... the KOA Way

**Alabama:** Birmingham South, McCalla/Tannehill, Mobile N/River Delta. **Alaska:** Denali/McKinley. **Arizona:** Benson, Flagstaff, Grand Canyon/Williams, Kingman, Phoenix West. **Arkansas:** Arkadelphia/Exit 78, Eureka Springs, Fort Smith/Alma, Hot Springs National Park, Little Rock N/Jct I-40, Morrilton/Conway, Rogers/Pea Ridge, Texarkana. **California:** Anaheim, Bakersfield, Barstow/Calico, Eureka, Lake Tahoe South Shore, Needles, Sacramento Metropolitan, San Bernardino, San Diego Metro, San Francisco North/Petaluma, Santa Cruz/Monterey Bay, Santa Margarita/San Luis Obispo, Stockton/Lodi, Yosemite/Mariposa. **Colorado:** Colorado Springs South, Cotopaxi/Arkansas River, Denver East/Strasburg, Denver NE/Hudson, Durango East, Grand Junction/Clifton, Gunnison, La Junta, Lamar, Limon, Pueblo, Steamboat Springs. **Florida:** Chattahoochee/Tallahassee W., Daytona S/New Smyrna Beach, Everglades/Homestead, Fiesta Key, Ft. Myers/Pine Island, Kissimmee/Orlando, Naples/Marco Island, Ocala/Silver Springs, Okeechobee, Orlando SE/Lake Whippoorwill,

Panama City Beach, Punta Gorda/Charlotte Harbor, St Augustine Beach, St Augustine/Jacksonville S, St Petersburg/Madeira Beach, Sugarloaf Key, Wildwood. **Georgia:** Atlanta North, Commerce/Athens, Forsyth, Savannah South. **Idaho:** Boise, Idaho Falls, Montpelier, Pinehurst/Kellogg, Twin Falls/Jerome. **Illinois:** Benton, Casey, Chicago/I-90/Marengo. **Indiana:** Brown County/Nashville, Crawfordsville, Elkhart Co/Middlebury Exit, Richmond, South Bend East. **Iowa:** Des Moines West. **Kansas:** Garden City, Goodland, Topeka, Wellington. **Kentucky:** Bowling Green, Franklin, Louisville Metro. **Louisiana:** Alexandria West/Kincaid Lake, Baton Rouge, Lafayette, Lake Charles/Vinton, New Orleans East, New Orleans/Hammond, New Orleans West, Shreveport/Bossier. **Maine:** Augusta/Gardiner, Saco/Portland South, Skowhegan/Canaan. **Maryland:** Hagerstown/Snug Harbor, Washington DC, NE. **Massachusetts:** Northwest/Concord/Salem, South/Middleboro/Plymouth, Southwest/Wrentham. **Michigan:** Indian River/Cheboygan, Mackinaw City, Monroe Co/Toledo North, Oscoda, Petoskey, Port Huron, St Ignace/Mackinac Island. **Minnesota:** Minneapolis NW/Maple Grove, Mpls SW/US 169/Jordan-Shakopee, Moorhead/Fargo, Rochester/Marion, St Cloud/Clearwater/I-94, St Paul East, Winona. **Mississippi:** Meridian East/Toomsuba. **Missouri:** Branson, Jonesburg/Warrenton, Joplin, Kansas City East/Oak Grove, Lebanon, Osage Beach/Lake Ozark, Springfield, St Louis South, St Louis West, Stanton/Meramec, Sullivan/Meramec. **Montana:** Bozeman, Choteau, Dillon, Polson/Flathead Lake, St Regis, West Glacier, Whitefish/Kalispell N. **Nebraska:** Gothenburg, Kimball, West Omaha. **Nevada:** Las Vegas.

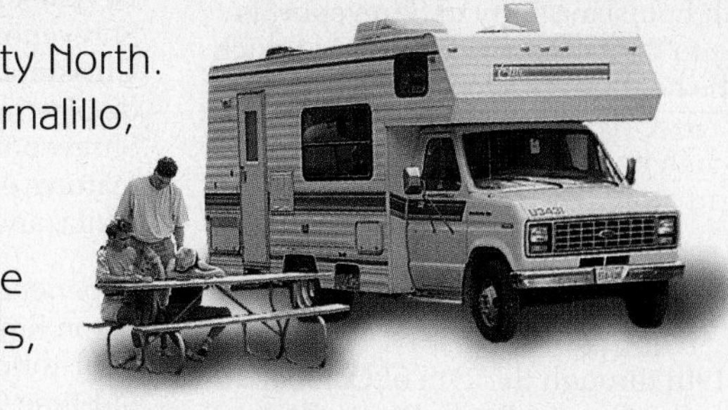

**New Hampshire:** Woodstock. **New Jersey:** Atlantic City North. **New Mexico:** Albuquerque Central, Albuquerque N/Bernalillo, Bloomfield, Clayton, Gallup, Santa Fe, Silver City, Tucumcari. **New York:** Ausable Chasm, Canandaigua/Rochester, Cooperstown, Herkimer, Lake Placid/Whiteface Mt, Newburgh/New Paltz, Niagara Falls, Niagara Falls N/Lewiston, Ogdensburg/1000 Is, Old Forge, Rome/Verona, Saugerties/Woodstock. **North Carolina:** Cherokee/Great Smokies, Fayetteville/Wade, Statesville. **North Dakota:** Bismarck, Jamestown. **Ohio:** Buckeye Lake/Columbus East, Dayton, Cincinnati South, Toledo East/Stony Ridge, Toledo/Maumee. **Oklahoma:** Checotah/Henryetta, El Reno West, Elk City/Clinton, Oklahoma City East, Tulsa NE. **Oregon:** Astoria/Seaside, Bandon/Port Orford, Cascade Locks/Portland E, Corvallis/Albany, Eugene S/Creswell, Lincoln City, Madras/Culver, Medford-Gold Hill, Sweet Home/Foster Lake. **Pennsylvania:** Allentown, Bellefonte/State College, Delaware Water Gap, Erie, Gettysburg/Battlefield, Hershey, Jonestown/I-81,78, Kinzua East, Lancaster/Reading, Madison/New Stanton, Mercer/Grove City, Philadelphia/West Chester, Tunkhannock. **South Carolina:** Anderson/Lake Hartwell, Charleston, Florence, Joanna/Columbia West, Myrtle Beach, Point South. **South Dakota:** Badlands/White River, Belvidere East, Custer/Crazy Horse, Custer/Mt Rushmore, Deadwood, Kennebec, Mt Rushmore/Hill City, Sioux City North, Rapid City, Sioux Falls, Spearfish. **Tennessee:** Bristol/Kingsport, Chattanooga North/Cleveland, Dickson/I-40, Lookout Mtn/Chattanooga West, Manchester, Memphis East, Memphis/Graceland, Nashville/North, Nashville/Opryland, Newport/I-40/Smoky Mtns, Paris Landing, Pigeon Forge/Gatlinburg, Pulaski/I-65 Exit 14, Sweetwater. **Texas:** Abilene, Amarillo, Austin, Belton/Temple/Killeen, Houston Central, Houston E/Baytown, Houston West/Brookshire, Kerrville, Midland/Odessa, San Antonio, Van Horn. **Utah:** Bear Lake/Garden City, Brigham City/Perry South, Fillmore, Nephi, Panguitch, Vernal. **Vermont:** Brattleboro North. **Virginia:** Bowling Green/Richmond N, Chesapeake Bay/Smith Island, Charlottesville, Fredericksburg/Wash DC S, Front Royal/Wash DC W, Natural Bridge/Lexington, Staunton/Verona/I-81 Exit 227, Virginia Beach, Williamsburg/Busch Gardens, Wytheville. **Washington:** Burlington, Leavenworth/Wenatchee, Seattle/Tacoma, Yakima. **Wisconsin:** Hixton/Alma Center, Rice Lake/Haugen, Wisconsin Dells. **Wyoming:** Arlington, Casper, Cody, Devils Tower, Douglas, Grand Teton Pk/Moran Jct, Greybull, Laramie, Lyman/Fort Bridger. **Alberta:** Calgary West. **British Columbia:** Burns Lake, Lac La Hache, Oliver/Gallagher Lake. **New Brunswick:** Penobsquis/Sussex. **Nova Scotia:** Baddeck/Cabot Trail. **Ontario:** Barrie, Kingston, London/401, Niagara Falls, Parry Sound, Renfrew, Toronto West, Wawa. **Prince Edward Island:** Cavendish. **Quebec:** Quebec City. **Saskatchewan:** Saskatoon.

KOA® KAMPGROUNDS

**These and other KOAs to serve you.**

*Louisiana Festivals continued from pg. 67*

North Louisiana's city of Shreveport is home to the **Louisiana State Fair,** which will be held from October 17th through the 27th. Originating in 1906, the fair has grown in popularity each year to its current attendance of more than 280,000 guests. Plan your visit when you're extra hungry because there are over 200 food booths to choose from!

The 19th through the 29th of October brings the **Greater Baton Rouge State Fair** to the Airline Highway Park/Fairgrounds in Baton Rouge. Come down and enjoy a wonderful state fair, Louisiana style!

Winter:

December is a great time to visit the Shreveport-Bossier City area and enjoy **Christmas on the Red,** a spectacular light display in the heart of downtown Shreveport. The kickoff celebration features entertainment, the arrival of Santa, and much more.

Experience **Christmas on the River** as Baton Rouge "lights up for the holidays" in historic downtown Baton Rouge. The old-time Christmas celebration runs for the entire month of December. There are Christmas parades, bonfires on the levee, a fireworks display and a Cajun Christmas Wonderland. As an added treat, many of the surrounding plantations offer candlelight tours to view their elegant 19th-century Christmas decorations.

For a visit to one of the most famous parties in the world, visit New Orleans during **Mardi Gras**, held each year since 1857, beginning anywhere from February 3rd to March 9th. (In 1996, the date for Mardi Gras is February 20th.) For the twelve days that precede Mardi Gras, there is a vast assortment of parades, parties, balls, and any sort of celebration you can think of. In a town famous for night life, great restaurants, and exciting music, the pure grand scale of Mardi Gras is the icing on the cake. While the somewhat risqué side of Mardi Gras is alive and well, thank you, there is a new trend toward attracting families. Accents on Arrangement, Inc., owned by a former teacher (and mother of two) will take your children on a behind-the-scenes tour of parade float building companies, or a carriage ride with stops at the U.S. Mint or a wax museum. If your travels take you to other areas of Louisiana, remember Mardi Gras is a statewide celebration, and may be enjoyed on a slightly smaller (but not lesser) scale throughout the state.

## *MISSISSIPPI FESTIVALS*

**Spring:**

The **Atwood Music Festival** in Monticello is a nice way to say good-bye to spring, and to welcome the summer season. Held on Memorial Day weekend each year, the festival offers arts and crafts, tasty food, a balloon race, children's races and games, a car race and an art show.

Civil War buffs will want to attend the **Vicksburg Civil War Reenactment** May 25th and 26th. The mock siege begins Saturday morning as the camps open to the public. Next comes a brief truce, with the troops bartering with one another for food, coffee and tobacco. The truce ends, and fighting resumes. Saturday evening brings a period dance that is held at the City Auditorium. If the children in your family think history lessons are dry and uninteresting, bring them along!

1996 will be the 25th anniversary of the **Gum Tree Art Festival** that is held in May in Tupelo. Artists and craftspersons from the southeastern states gather to sell their works and to compete for prizes. There are carnival rides for children, storytellers, and a play. Art and craft items may include watercolor paintings, sculpture, metalwork jewelry, pottery, and hand painted fabrics. In past years, the food menu has included pit-cooked barbecue, overstuffed sandwiches, funnel cakes, blossom onions, and much more. Most events are held on the lawn of the Lee County Courthouse.

**Summer:**

The 7th annual **Mississippi International Balloon Classic** will be held in Greenwood on June 26th through the 30th. The sky will be filled with more than 75 beautiful hot-air balloons from all over North America and Europe. In addition to the balloons, there will be live entertainment each night and Saturday and Sunday afternoons. Amusement rides are open throughout the event, and a variety of refreshments are available.

The summer season brings more music celebrations to Mississippi. Visit Hattiesburg for the **Elks Dixie Bluegrass Festival,** which will be held from July 11th through the 13th. This three-day family-style festival features professional stage shows daily; classes in instrument playing, song writing and harmony vocals; a talent search; teen activities and plenty of Southern hospitality. Enjoy top-quality regional and national performing artists.

**Fall:**

Visit Quitman, Mississippi in the Fall and you'll be treated to two lovely festivals. The **Southern Gospel Music Festival** is held annually on the third or fourth weekend in September. Created in 1991 as a celebration of Southern Gospel music by Jackie Smith, today over 12 gospel music groups perform on Friday night and Saturday, with a talent show on Saturday afternoon.

October brings **Clark County's seventh annual Forestry and Wildlife Festival,** held on the first Saturday in October at Archusa Water Park, also in Quitman. There are lake and park tours, aircraft demonstrations, an arts & crafts fair, and a wide variety of booths and displays.

Columbus, Mississippi may be called the "place where swine is divine," as it's the site of their 14th annual **Possum Town Pig Fest**, which will be held on September 26th through 28th. Highlights of the festivities include a scrumptious cooking contest, an auction that benefits the Mississippi Sheriffs' Boys and Girls Ranches, musical entertainment, and the annual Parade of Pigs. The event is held on the Fairgrounds on Hwy 69.



Stop by the Mississippi Crafts Center one mile north of Jackson for the 19th annual **Pioneer & Indian Festival** that is always held on the first Saturday in October. The heritage of the Choctaw tribe is represented by their beautiful baskets and beadwork, as well as by their delicious fry bread and hominy. The heritage of the pioneers is represented by artisans selling and demonstrating woodcarving, basketry, spinning, and pottery. Pioneer food such as homebaked bread and vegetable stew are available for sampling.

The **Natchez Fall Pilgrimage Tour** provides history buffs and those who long for the romantic traditions of the Old South a chance to step back in time. (Also held each spring early March through early April.) Visitors may stroll through old-fashioned gardens and enjoy a welcome by ladies in hoop skirts to tour 24 beautiful Antebellum homes, which still hold the relics and furnishings of this vanished era. Held annually in October as well as March, the tour has been named one of the Top 100 Events in North America by the American Bus Association and one of the Top 20 Events in the Southeast by the Southeast Tourism Society. One highlight of the Tour is Natchez' most visited house, Longwood. The famous octagonal mansion also is open as part of a regular, rotating tour along with other houses.

## *NORTH CAROLINA FESTIVALS*

### Spring:

For some fine blues music, North Carolina style, plan on attending the 7th annual **Hatteras Island Blues Festival**, held during the last week in April at Camp Hatteras in Rodanthe. "Chase the Blues" starts at noon on Friday with a fishing tournament, followed by a fish fry and 1st night food fest. Saturday, the fishing contest continues, and the fair opens with food, beverages, children's games, a craft fair and many exhibits. Sunday morning brings a jazz brunch and a beach casting contest.

North Carolina's Crystal Coast area is situated along the Southern Outer Banks, on the central coastline of the state. The area is world-famous for its beautiful beaches and magnificent sunsets, and there are several fun festivals to attend each year. In March, plan on attending the **Emerald Isle St. Patrick's Day Festival,** where even non-Irish folks will enjoy music, arts and crafts, as well as traditional meals of corned beef and cabbage. April brings the **Newport Pig Cookin' Contest** to that town. It's the largest barbecue contest in the state, and features live entertainment and children's activities. May brings the **Salter Path Clam & Scallop Festival** when you'll get to enjoy lots of these tasty treats from the sea, as well as a variety of gospel, country and jazz musical presentations. The children won't be bored, as there are children's activities and carnival rides.

April is the month for the **Beaufort By-The-Sea Music Festival** — the 8th annual event will be held in 1996. The event features almost 50 musical groups who perform at four downtown locations including two waterfront stages. All performances are free at this family-oriented festival. Guests are encouraged to bring lawn chairs or blankets for seating, and keep in mind that Beaufort ordinances prohibit alcoholic beverages on public property.

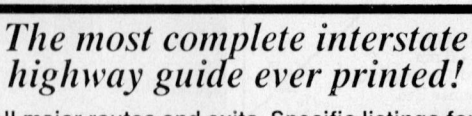

Mark your calendars for the 3rd Saturday in May and attend the 17th annual **Emerald Isle Beach Music Fest** that is held on the grounds of the Holiday Trav-L-Park in Emerald Isle. Billed as "the grandaddy of all beach music festivals," the musical event features "beach music." What is beach music? The actual definition is somewhat elusive, but a reliable source tells us that if you have enjoyed the Spinners and the Four Tops, you'll enjoy beach music. In fact, these two famous groups have appeared here in past years. There's continuous music from 9:30 a.m. until 5:30 p.m., and local community groups provide food and beverages. Parking is not a problem, as there is a nominal fee shuttle provided by the Shriners from the Emerald Plantation Shopping Center to the festival site.

In May it's time for the **Rally in the Valley,** the Maggie Valley's hot-air balloon rally. Each year visitors to the

*North Carolina Festivals con't. on pg. 74*

*North Carolina Festivals con't. from pg. 72*

event enjoy lively bluegrass music, food, crafts, and, of course, the beautiful hot-air balloons. The array of interesting crafts include wood carvings, hand-made cutlery, and "Rally in the Valley" T-shirts. Local bands provide the musical culture of the mountains. There are some fun local attractions in the area, so while you are here, plan on visiting Ghost Town in the Sky or the Soco Gardens Zoo and Great Smoky Mountain National Park as well as the Blue Ridge Parkway.

The first **Ole Time Fiddler's & Bluegrass Festival** was begun in 1924 as a fiddler's convention held at Fiddler's Grove in Union Grove, North Carolina. The traditional music fest has been held ever since, becoming the oldest event of its kind in the nation. The festival takes place on Memorial Day weekend each year and draws traditional old-time and bluegrass bands and individual musicians from all over the United States, and a few foreign countries. In addition to the enjoyable family entertainment, there are workshops in related arts as well as clogging, storytelling, shape note singing, children's folk music and more.

**Summer:**

June brings the **Beaufort Old Homes Tour,** as visitors tour the historic homes, gardens and public buildings, led by guides dressed in traditional colonial clothing. In August at the North Carolina Maritime Museum in Beaufort, you'll be treated to some local flavor as cooks gather and provide you with their favorite and strangest seafood concoctions at the **Strange Seafood Exhibition**.

Early July is the time for a "wee bit of the Scottish Highlands" in North Carolina, as Linville celebrates its 41st annual **Grandfather Mountain Highland Games and Gathering of Scottish Clans**. Cheer on your favorites in several competitions such as highland dancing, Scottish athletics, Scottish fiddling, marathon and hill climbing, piping and drumming, Scottish harp, track and field and children's activities. Arrive early and take some time to enjoy the area's many family attractions including Grandfather Mountain and the Blue Ridge Parkway.

For more than 50 years, **The Lost Colony** has been entertaining audiences with its fascinating story of the English colonists' struggles to set down their roots in the New World. Actors, dancers, singers and musicians join in portraying the story of the English colonists who journeyed to Roanoke Island over 400 years ago, only to vanish, leaving historians with an unsolved mystery. The performances are held in the scenic Waterside Theater, three miles northwest of Manteo.

A visit to the **Battleship *North Carolina* Memorial** in Wilmington is like a festival in itself. If you missed out on the 50th anniversary of the end of World War II during 1995, there is still plenty to enjoy this year at the Battleship. The ship was painted for the commemoration with the same gray and blue camouflage pattern she served with in the Pacific during W.W.II, and the new look will last from 5 to 7 years. Approximately 800 gallons of paint were used to complete the task. Memorial Day is a special holiday here, and you will enjoy the Color Guard presentation, patriotic music, and, of course, there is a spectacular July 4th fireworks display.

This year marks the 13th annual **Folkmoot U.S.A. Festival,** an 11-day event in July whose opening day parade is held in the town of Waynesville. Other participating communities are Maggie Valley, Hendersonville, Mars Hill, Fletcher, Asheville, Franklin, Cullowhee, Bryson City, Brevard, and others. Each year 10 premier folk groups representing different parts of the world are featured. They demonstrate their cultural heritage via colorful costumes, dance, and music that is played on unique hand-crafted instruments. Fookmoot has been named one of the top 20 events in the Southeast for many years.

**Fall:**

The South Brunswick Islands' **North Carolina Oyster Festival** is held during the 3rd weekend of October. If you love fresh seafood, don't miss this event. You'll get to sample fresh fish, shrimp, and, of course, the main attraction — oysters. Served steamed by the bucket, fried, or as oyster cocktails, these fresh shellfish are the stars of this festival. You can walk off your meal by visiting more than 100 arts and crafts booths displaying lovely, handmade original works. Several foot races, carnival rides, live musical entertainment, and the Oyster Shucking Championships all round out the two days of fun. The South Brunswick Islands are located just 35 miles north of Myrtle Beach and 35 miles south of Wilmington. Plan on extending your stay and visiting the towns of Calabash, Shallotte, Holden Beach, Ocean Isle Beach, Sunset Beach, Seaside and Varnumtown.

Late October is the time for the **North Carolina Festival By The Sea**, held annually since 1980 in Holden Beach. There's a traditional Halloween carnival for the children, with costume contests, game booths and lots of food. There's a parade that kicks off the festival, an arts & crafts show with over 125 participants, and food vendors to tempt visitors with an array of mouth-watering treats. A few blocks away you'll find the horseshoe pitching contest, and other activities include a golf long-driving competition, kite flying contests, and volleyball tournaments. An annual gospel sing headlines Sunday's activities.

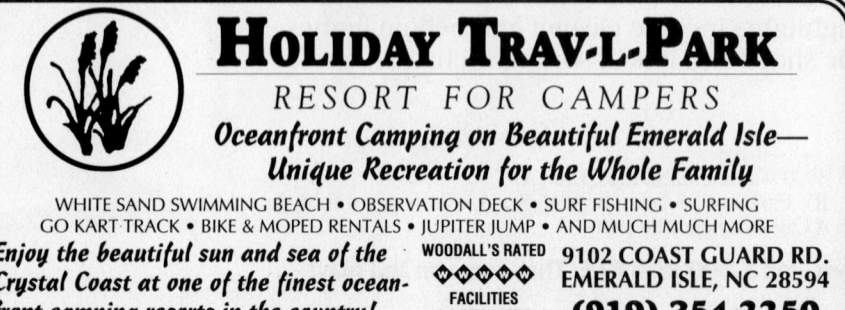

**Winter:**

A visit to the Crystal Coast in the winter brings the **Mill Creek Oyster Festival,** held in early November. It's a family event featuring arts, crafts, and lots of oysters. During late November, the **Swansboro Christmas Flotilla** offers Santa the opportunity to parade the waterway with his fleet of brilliantly decorated boats.

Celebrate the coming of the new year with **First Night Raleigh, '96.** There is a People's Procession which kicks off the evening activities, consisting of thousands of people marching through the streets of Raleigh, led by two bands, floats and street performers. Entertainment is provided by Chuck Davis and the African American Dance Ensemble, and there is truly something for everyone, including jazz, blues, magic shows, even ballroom dancing. Activities take place inside bank lobbies, church atriums, in restaurants and outside (weather permitting.)

Southport/Oak Island provides **Christmas By the Sea,** a festival that lasts from November 25th with the Merchants Open House and ends on December 18th with the announcement of the winner of the Best Decorated Home contest. The first and second weekends in December are filled with numerous events, such as the Christmas Parade in Yaupon and Long Beach. This parade with its homemade floats and old-fashioned fun is an example of a small, hometown event that is sure to instill the Christmas spirit in all who attend.

## *SOUTH CAROLINA FESTIVALS*

**Spring:**

Plan to visit Rock Hill from April 12th through the 20th, 1996, and you will be treated to the town's 35th annual **Come See Me Festival.** The festival had its beginnings in 1961 as a weekend event where friends and relatives were invited to see Rock Hill at its most beautiful. One of the many highlights of the festival continues to be the Glencairn Garden, with its more than 3,500 azaleas are surrounded by camellias, dogwood, wisteria and other flowering trees and shrubs. A sample of the featured events at the festival are: Home Garden Tours of 7 home gardens with exhibits and lectures; the Downtown Gala; a fireworks extravaganza; an antique show; horseshoe, tennis, golf, volleyball and softball tournaments; Mayor's Frog Jump; and much more.

April is the month for the **Striped Bass Festival of Clarendon County,** which was begun in 1978 as part of a program to promote tourism in the smaller communities of South Carolina. The festival, said to be "bigger than Christmas" to those who live here, celebrates the beginning of spring, and is a tribute to the beauty of the area, along with a special salute to its star, the Striped Bass, the fish that put the Santee Cooper lakes on the fishing map of the world. In fact, Clarendon County borders Lake Marion, the upper of the Santee Cooper lakes.

Visit Charleston from March 14th through April 13th, 1996 and you will have the opportunity of attend one of the **Plantation Oyster Roasts** which are part of the Spring Festival of Houses and Gardens in this lovely, historic city. Admission includes a guided tour of historic Drayton Hall, roasted oysters, barbecue sandwiches, and refreshments, plus entertainment by a local bluegrass band.

Another historic South Carolina town celebrates their **Spring Jubilee** April 1st through 2nd in 1996. The event in 1996 will mark their 19th annual celebration with a weekend highlighting quality arts and crafts, antiques, a variety of musical entertainment, and lots of food. The festival also marks the opening of many local attractions, and was begun as a means to inaugurate the tourism season of the area.

Come and join the residents of St. George for their 11th annual **World Grits Festival,** which was held in 1995 from April 22nd through the 23rd. Hot grits, friendly people and loads of entertainment add up to a weekend of Family Fun — Southern style!

Historic Pendleton holds its **Spring Jubilee** during the first weekend in April each year. The fun consists of entertainment, museum exhibits, house tours, arts and crafts, antique shows and delicious food.

Mid-April brings the **Azalea Festival** to Pickens, South Carolina, where visitors will be able to enjoy the displays of beautiful azaleas, arts and crafts, a classic car show, music and food.

*South Carolina Festivals con't. on pg. 78*

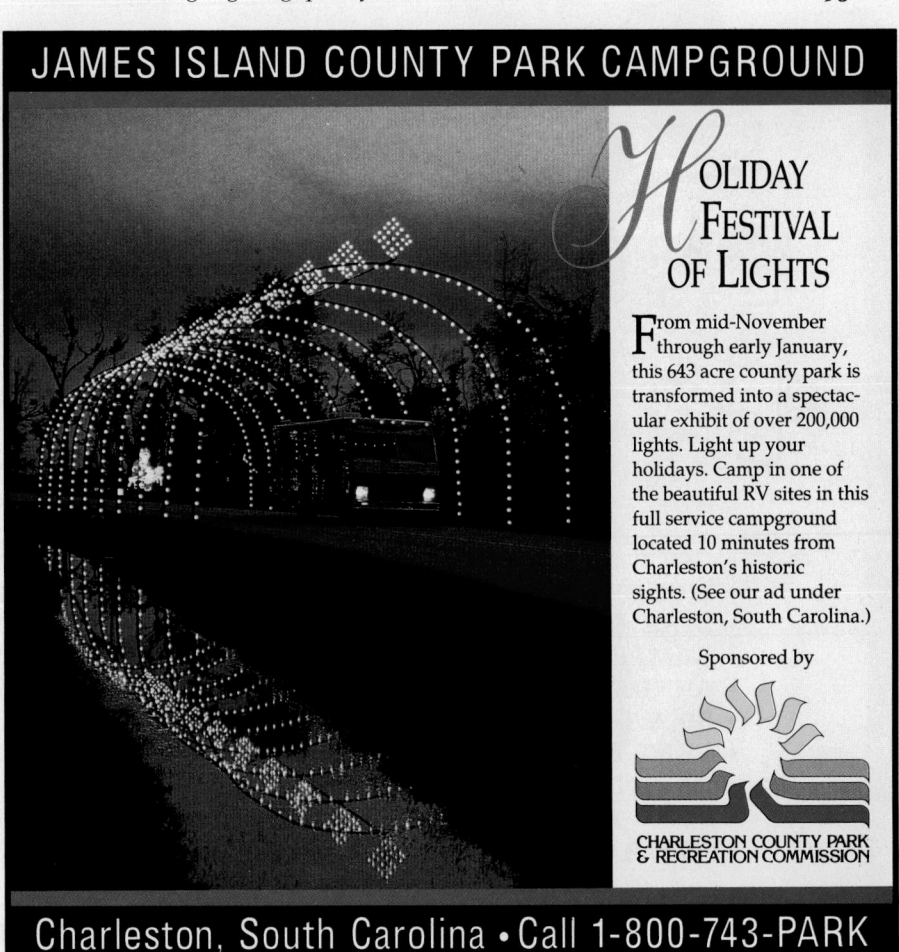

*South Carolina Festivals con't. from pg. 75*

Visit Mt. Pleasant on the last Sunday of April and join in the **Blessing of the Fleet Seafood Festival**. The main attraction and tradition of the festival consists of a local pastor blessing the shrimp fleet as it parades by in Charleston Harbor, wishing the shrimpers a healthy and prosperous year. Local restaurants provide restaurant booths with fresh, local seafood dishes. About 45 craft booths display their treasures, and there is live music on stage.

May 10th through the 11th bring the **South Carolina Poultry Festival** to Batesburg-Leesville (always the second full weekend in May). The festival originated in 1987 as a means of not only recognizing the importance of the poultry industry to the state, but also for providing a wholesome, family-oriented festival for the Batesburg-Leesville area. The towns in the area serve as the home base for the majority of South Carolina's poultry production, and local businesswoman, Sara Shealy, owner of the regionally renowned Shealy's Bar-B-Que House, is credited with "hatching" the poultry festival.

Festival goers will find 20 vendors offering an ever-increasing variety of food, including Cajun cuisine, cotton candy, kabobs, sausage dogs, funnel cakes, barbecue, Oriental dishes, and, of course, plenty of chicken! It's a delight for craft lovers, too, as there are more than 125 arts and crafts booths displaying their finest works.

Carnival rides open on Friday evening, and remain open all day Saturday. A Saturday morning parade displays more than 120 units including bands, beauties, dignitaries, performing entries and hometown floats. Also on Saturday, five outdoor stages offer continuous, live music and showcase local dancers and singers. Street dances on Friday and Saturday nights feature popular area bands. Throughout the day, visitors can experience a number of contests including the popular Chicken Calling Contest that is always a crowd pleaser. The festival ends just after darkness when the state's largest annual fireworks extravaganza illuminates the sky. For some great tasting chicken and one of South Carolina's most popular family festivals, "shake a leg" and get to the South Carolina Poultry Festival!

Head to Myrtle Beach at the end of April for **Myrtle Gras.** You'll be treated to Cajun cuisine, and jazz and blues music will bring a New Orleans flavor to Myrtle Beach. Visitors will enjoy lots of entertainment, food, and arts and crafts displays.

**Summer:**

Myrtle Beach will host its 45th **Sun Fun Festival** on June 7th through the 10th, 1996. National celebrities are a part of each festival, and in 1995 Vanna White and Roy Clark were the headliners. The event kicks off the celebration of summer in the Myrtle Beach area, as vacationers flock to the area's 60-mile stretch of sandy beaches to enjoy the week-long festival packed with exciting events.

Festival events which attract thousands of spectators, as well as national media attention, include an air show, the Sun Fun Parade, the Miss Sun Fun Pageant and Miss Bikini Wahine Contest, beach games for children of all ages and musical and sporting events.

Recent performances at the air show include a dynamic line-up of performers including the U.S. Army Golden Knights, Northern Lights, Star Aerobatic Team, Chuck Boyd Airshow and Hawaiian Eagle jet Dragster, according to Carson Benton chairman of the '95 Sun Fun Festival. The amazing precision and aerial demonstration of the Golden Knights parachute Team has become a favorite tradition at the Sun Fun Air Show. The team, which is based at Fort Bragg, N.C., traces its origins back to 1957 when seven soldiers from the Army's Special Forces received training in what was then called "delayed fall" parachuting. Today, this technique has been developed into exciting skydiving skills that earn national and world championships for the Golden Knights.

Northern Lights is comprised of three former members of the internationally known Canadian Forces Snowbirds and a Swiss woman, who is an aerobatics gold medalist. The team flies custom, German-built Extra 300 aircraft capable of airspeeds in excess of 225 mph and performs exciting, synchronized four-ship aerobatic maneuvers.

The Star Aerobatic Team consists of four pilots who fly Pitts Special S-2 biplanes designed for specialized formation flying and precision aerobatics. Chuck Boyds files a smooth, professional solo performance demonstrating the capabilities of the Pitts S-2A, using both inside and outside maneuvers.

The metallic gold-green Incredible Hawaiian Eagle Jet Dragster car entices crowds with its capability of reaching speeds of 378 mph in under seven seconds. Weighing 1,350 pounds, the 25-foot car takes approximately 50 gallons of jet fuel per quarter mile run, and is powered by a GE J-85 engine producing over 5,000 hp in after burner.

Each year, young ladies from across South Carolina anticipate the exciting moment when the winners of the Sun Fun Festival pageants, sponsored by Hawaiian Tropic Suntan Lotion, are announced. Contestants first vie for the title of Miss Sun Fun 1997, and will then compete for the Miss Bikini Wahine 1997 crown.

The festival includes a Sun Fun Kids Fair featuring a day full of fun designed for children ages 12 and under with contests, games, clowns and mimes. The Sun Fun Parade featuring military and high school bands takes place on Saturday, with many celebrities, visiting queens and dignitaries. Other exciting events include a Jazz in the Park concert, various sand sculpting contests, a beach run, fishing tournament, miniature golf tournament, watermelon eating contests, and a beach volleyball tournament.

Early July brings another festival to Myrtle Beach — their **Art In The Park** show. Visitors will find fine art and handmade crafts that have become the trademark of this juried festival that is held in pretty Chapin Park. The show is held again in August.

Late May through early June marks the arrival of the **Spoleto Festival U.S.A.** each year in historic Charleston. Originated in Italy in 1958, the Spoleto, Italy Festival dei Due Mondi (Festival of Two worlds), the Festival was conceived as a trans-Atlantic affair, and today continues that tradition with artists from around the world. A true comprehensive arts festival, it presents both traditional and contemporary works of opera, chamber music, jazz, as well as others, and drama, ballet, literature and visual arts. It's a city-wide festival, with celebrations and performances held in the city's historic theaters, in front of City Hall, and elsewhere throughout the city. Historic Charleston and its surrounding area is home to the oldest playhouse still in use in the United States, the oldest museum is the Charleston Museum which was founded in 1773, and the oldest landscaped gardens, Middleton Place which is often the site of the festival's gala finale.

*Tennessee Festivals con't. on pg. 80*

# Camp Myrtle Beach, South Carolina

## Nature's Trail By The Sea

Choose from, seven beautiful campgrounds, over 7000 sites, spacious white sandy beaches, amusement parks, water parks, restaurants , shopping, fishing, over 80 championship golf courses, country music theaters, numerous miniature golf courses, tennis, sailing and so much more ! CHECK SPECIAL RATES FOR FALL, WINTER AND SPRING! You don't have to bring your own recreational vehicle as FULLY-FURNISHED RENTAL UNITS are available.

**1. APACHE FAMILY CAMPGROUND**
9700 Kings Road
Myrtle Beach, SC 29572
(803) 449-7323 or (803) 449-3357
Toll Free 1-800-553-1749

**2. BAREFOOT RV RESORT**
4825 Hwy. 17 South
P.O. Box 2116
North Myrtle Beach, SC 29598
(803) 272-1790
Toll Free 1-800-272-1790

**3. LAKEWOOD CAMPING RESORT**
5901 S. Kings Hwy.
Myrtle Beach, SC 29575-4497
(803) 238-5161
Toll Free 1-800-258-8309

**4. MYRTLE BEACH KOA KAMPGROUND**
Bus. Hwy. 17, 5th Ave. South
Myrtle Beach, SC 29577
(803) 448-3421
Toll Free 1-800-255-7614

**5. MYRTLE BEACH TRAVEL PARK**
10108 Kings Road
Myrtle Beach, SC 29572
(803) 449-3714
USA and Canada 1-800-255-3568

**6. OCEAN LAKES FAMILY CAMPGROUND**
6001 S. Kings Hwy.
Myrtle Beach, SC 29575
(803) 238-1451
Toll Free 1-800-722-1451

**7. PIRATELAND FAMILY CAMPGROUND**
5401 S. Kings Hwy.
Myrtle Beach, SC 29575
(803) 238-5155
Toll Free 1-800-443-CAMP

**CALL TOLL FREE TODAY and receive our 12-page color booklet with information on all seven campground including location maps and more, or call direct to campgrounds listed above.**

**1-800-356-3016 Ext. 110**

**FREE INFO?** Myrtle Beach Campground Assn., enter #788 on Reader Service Card following page 16.

*Tennessee Festivals con't. from pg. 78*

**Fall:**

**Fall for Greenville — a Taste of Our Town** is held in mid-October. The fun consists of a waiter's race, ice sculpting, bicycle races, a soccer tournament, free concerts, a food fair and a spectacular fireworks display.

**The South Carolina Apple Festival** in Westminster celebrates this juicy fruit with apple orchard tours, a road race, white-water rafting, a crafts show, beauty pageant, square dancing, and a world championship rodeo.

Bargain hunters won't want to miss Myrtle Beach's **South Carolina's Largest Garage Sale.** You'll find an abundance of vendors set up in a large parking garage to sell clothing, furniture, "junque", household goods and other bargains.

Bring your sense of humor and stop by the town of Woodruff for their annual **Bubbafest,** held each year the weekend after Labor Day. This celebration of brotherhood and good humor highlights the way of life of the area: patriotism, pig roasts, good humor, and not taking oneself too seriously. Activities include the crowning of the official Bubba and Bubbette; Bubbajam featuring a night of dancing, music and food; BubbaLympics featuring team competition, and of course a Bubba-Q where whole hog cooks come from far and wide to compete in the cooking contest.

**Winter:**

The Myrtle Beach Convention Center hosts the **Myrtle Beach Wildlife Expo** in late January. Visitors will find all types of outdoor gear displayed including fishing and hunting gear in this festive expo.



Drayton Hall in Charleston will be the site of the 15th annual **Spirituals Concert** on December 20th — 21st. This is a rare opportunity to experience music which is rooted in the work songs of West Africa that developed in this area. The spirituals reflect a tradition of faith, love and yearning for salvation among the people of the Georgia and South Carolina sea islands.

**The Southeastern Wildlife Exposition** will be held February 16th through 18th in Charleston, and for over 14 years, the Exposition has grown into the largest wildlife art show in the United States, attracting more than 500 exhibitors and over 40,000 visitors annually. Its purpose was to provide the public with a comprehensive collection of wildlife art and to educate the public about wildlife conservation. Art lovers will find wildlife and nature paintings, prints, sculpture, carvings, crafts and collectibles, displayed throughout Charleston's historic district.

## *TENNESSEE FESTIVALS*

**Spring:**

The **Dogwood Arts Festival** held in April each year in Knoxville has been called the "best 17 days of Spring in America." Actually a variety of festivals in one, there are arts and crafts, music and dance, sports events and more than 60 miles of glorious dogwood trails and fabulous garden tours, all amid the natural scenic beauty of Knoxville.

This year **Memphis in May** will celebrate its 20th Anniversary, and the festival will be more grand than ever. The history, art and culture of more than 18 countries will be honored and celebrated, providing a spectacular theme for all events. In the past, the festival featured one country each year, showcasing its people, art and culture. A visit to this celebrated festival during 1996 will be a "trip around the world," as visitors sample the food and culture from Japan, Canada, Italy, Israel, Kenya, and many more countries from six continents. The Festival is held throughout the month of May in Tom Lee Park overlooking the Mississippi River.

**Summer:**

Visit Nashville in early June for the **Summer Lights Festival.** This event showcases the Music City's excellence in the arts, entertainment and hospitality. A wide variety of music is performed on both indoor and outdoor stages, and there's a marketplace with selected visual art exhibits, restaurants and shops. Country music and lots more drew an estimated 150,000 visitors last year.

Ross's Landing in Chattanooga is host to the **Riverbend Festival** in mid-June. It's an urban celebration presenting the arts, fantastic sporting events, children's events and activities, and music.

For a taste of Italy without ever leaving the United States, visit the **Italian Street Fair** that has been held each year for over 42 years in Nashville. Truly a family affair, the festival features some of the finest Italian cuisine anywhere, along with non-stop stage entertainment, top quality arts and crafts exhibits, dozens of market boutiques, carnival rides and an array of special performers and events just for kids. Held each Labor Day weekend in downtown Nashville at Riverfront Park.

Horse lovers will want to mark their calendars for August 6th through 12th and plan a visit to Murfreesboro for the **International Grand Championship Walking Horse Show.** Held each year since 1979, the show features competitions from amateur to professional, all showcasing these stately and beautiful horses, a throwback to the plantation era when their smooth gait allowed comfortable rides over thousands of plantation acres.

**Fall:**

Centennial Park in Nashville is home to the annual **Fall Crafts Fair** which will be held again in 1996 from September 27th through 29th. The 1996 Fair is extra special, as it's their 25th anniversary. The fair features over 165 craft artists selected nationally for the quality of their work. Visitors will enjoy the best of American crafts including traditional and contemporary work in clay, wood, leather, glass, metals, mixed media, photography and original prints. Shopping takes energy, so to replenish yours, stop by the food court for some fresh-squeezed lemonade, fried pies, barbecue or funnel cakes.

**The National Storytelling Festival** is held the first full weekend in October each year, with the 1996 dates set for October 4th through 6th. Throughout the world, in every culture, people have told stories that have provided the pride and sense of history and family that is so important. People from all walks of life from lawyers to teachers to songwriters converge at Jonesborough for this very special festival where legends, fables, myths and yarns unfold each year.

# RESERVE YOUR COPY NOW!

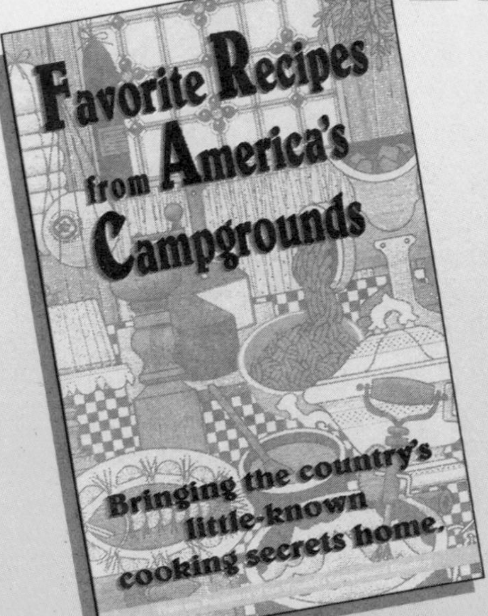


200 prompt responders will receive the famous cookbook

**"FAVORITE RECIPES FROM AMERICA'S CAMPGROUNDS."**

Absolutely free. No purchase necessary.

*Just fill in your full name and address* (PLEASE PRINT) *on this reservation card and mail it back, and you qualify for a copy of this 240-page cookbook containing favorite recipes from campgrounds and RV parks across North America. Maybe you will find a recipe from one of the parks where you've enjoyed camping.*

Winners will be selected from early respondents, allocated on a geographical basis to ensure fairness. Plus, your name will be kept on file for notification of future FREEBIES!

**HURRY, THIS IS A LIMITED OFFER. SEND TODAY!**

Name ______________________________________________

(PLEASE PRINT)

Address ______________________________________________

City ______________________ State __________ Zip __________

Do you currently own an RV? ❑ Yes ❑ No

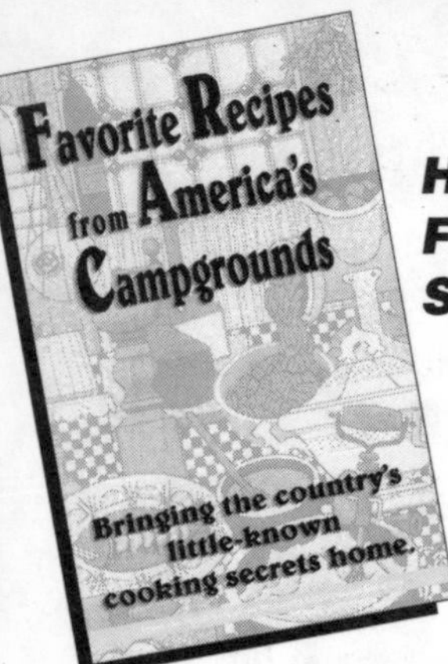
Favorite Recipes from America's Campgrounds
Bringing the country's little-known cooking secrets home.

**HURRY!**
**FREE LIMITED OFFER**
**SEE OTHER SIDE.**

PLACE STAMP HERE
32¢
FIRST CLASS POSTAGE REQUIRED

AFFINITY GROUP, INC.
PO BOX 280866
LAKEWOOD, CO 80228

The **Tennessee Fall Homecoming** is held October 10th through the 13th at the Museum of Appalachia in Norris, just 16 miles North of Knoxville on I-75, exit 22, then 1 mile east. Visitors will find the spacious Museum of Appalachia mountain farm and homestead complex, once described at "the most authentic & complete replica of pioneer Appalachian life in the world." The festival offers over 175 mountain activities, crafts demonstrations, artists, and much more. Hundreds of old-time mountain, folk, hymn, traditional and bluegrass musicians, plus buck dancers and cloggers.

With the gathering of over 400 old-time Southern Appalachian musicians and singers, and genuine mountain craftspersons and artisans, the event is reminiscent of an old-time mountain homecoming. Demonstrations include such rural and pioneer activities as rail splitting, molasses boiling, wool spinning, saw milling, lye soap making, sheep herding, and white oak basket making. Over 250 locally and nationally-known musicians perform simultaneously on 4 "stages" while regional authors autograph their books and local cooks serve traditional Southern food such as pinto beans and cornbread and fried pies. Participants and visitors return each year to celebrate and commemorate the heritage and culture of Southern Appalachia.

The musicians and entertainers represent some of the nation's best and most respected old-time performers, as well as being "just plain folks." Recent performers include Roy Acuff's Smoky Mountain Boys who perform regularly for Opryland U.S.A. Their music and humor has evolved from the rural, mountain culture of Appalachia, and through their many performances, has touched people from around the world. Octogenarian, Minnie Black and Her All Gourd Band were recent performers. All sixteen members of the band play on fiddles, guitars, banjos, harps, harmonicas and more, all made by Minnie Black from gourds she grew in her garden.

There's a writer's table with local and regionally known authors, and a genealogy table to help all "cousins" find their roots. Sheep and duck herding competitions with dogs are held throughout the festival, and daily hymn singing in the log "Church in the Wildwood".

Don't miss this festival if you like to shop for unique, mountain crafts. You'll find hand woven baskets, hand sculpted clay jewelry, handmade teddy bears, hand-dipped beeswax candles, furniture, native herbs and plants, needlecrafts, and Appalachian photography. All craftspersons provide daily demonstrations of their skills.

This is a wonderful festival if you are in need of some delicious Appalachian Mountain food. Recent menu items include corn-on-the-cob, beans and cornbread, barbecue, Indian fry bread, fresh made cider, mince meat pies, apple butter, ham/sausage & biscuits, funnel cakes, fresh made molasses, and home made bread.

**Winter:**

Celebrate the birthday of the King of Rock and Roll in Memphis at the **Elvis Presley Birthday Celebration**, January 6th through 8th. The birthday bash begins on Friday evening at the Best Western Hotel with a popular disk jockey hosting a full evening of Elvis records, trivia, prizes and dancing. The hotel's cash bar and dinner menu are available. It's recommended that you make reservations well in advance for this party. Saturday brings a "by invitation only" Elvis Fan Club President's Luncheon where fan club leaders enjoy a special program which included updates from RCA representatives regarding Elvis recording projects, and a preview of a collection of Elvis' classic love songs. There are usually special guests including friends and colleagues of Elvis.

The Elvis Presley Birthday Proclamation Ceremony & Activities are held on Sunday when guests enjoy complimentary birthday cake and coffee served all afternoon at the Heartbreak Hotel Restaurant.

**Smoky Mountain Lights** runs from November through February in Gatlinburg, the gateway to the Great Smoky Mountains National Park. If you look to the sky and follow the brightest star, you'll probably find yourself in Tennessee at Gatlinburg's annual event, part of a county-wide Winterfest Celebration. Displays, complete with animation standing 20-60 feet high, light up the night skies. The event has been awarded the #1 Special Event in the South by the Southeast Tourism Society, and a Top 100 Event in the United States by the American Bus Association. Over 20 new lighting displays of lights have been recently added. The program is already worth over $1 million dollars in value, showcasing many unique and exciting displays. Gatlinburg brings to life through animation the black bear of the Smokies. Standing 20-feet high on one corner of the city, the "Gatlinbear" is making hot cider at his still. He can also be found catching a fish down at the Little Pigeon River that runs through the city. This year's additions will enhance the sparkle of the mountain village through several Bavarian themed displays custom designed for the Smokies.

Visitors will be greeted warmly by chandeliers of light draped across the parkway and tunnels of lighted branches along the sidewalks. This is an event you must see to believe! A convenient way to view the lights is via a guided trolley tour. A professional guide will be on board to tell about the history and the meaning of each lighted display. The tours run Sunday through Thursday beginning early November. Tours are suspended over Thanksgiving and will run only on Saturdays in January. Hop on the trolley at the trolley stop in front of the Gatlinburg Chamber of Commerce Welcome Center located at traffic light #3.

**First Night Kingsport** is when the downtown area of Kingsport is transformed into a lively stage where more than 70 musicians, dancers, singers, actors, musicians, clowns, comedians, storytellers and artists all band together to ring in the New Year! The fun begins at 5:30 p.m. with the First Night Kickoff spectacular at Church Circle. Performances begin at 6:p.m. at 40 locations throughout town, and from that point on, the entertainment is non-stop. From First Union Bank at the train station to Church Circle and every area in between along Broad Street, visitors will find performers to "light up your night."

The event is a family-oriented, alcohol-free celebration of the arts that is held each New Year's Eve. They hold the only First Night in Tennessee, and are members of the International First Night Alliance and one of 136 cities in North America with similar festivals.

Downtown churches and businesses open their doors to provide indoor performing sites. In addition, 5 large tents are constructed to house country music, a teen dance, oldies music, comedians, and dining space for the food court. The four blocks of Broad Street are alive with roving entertainers, Moonjump and train rides for children, K-9 police demonstrations, ice carving, cloggers, clowns, costumed characters, and sidewalk art displays. Typically, New Year's Eve celebrations are adult oriented, and tend to exclude the very old and the very young. At First Night Kingsport, the streets are filled with teenagers, children, even babies in strollers accompanied by parents and grandparents, all together in a wholesome environment with entertainment to please all tastes.

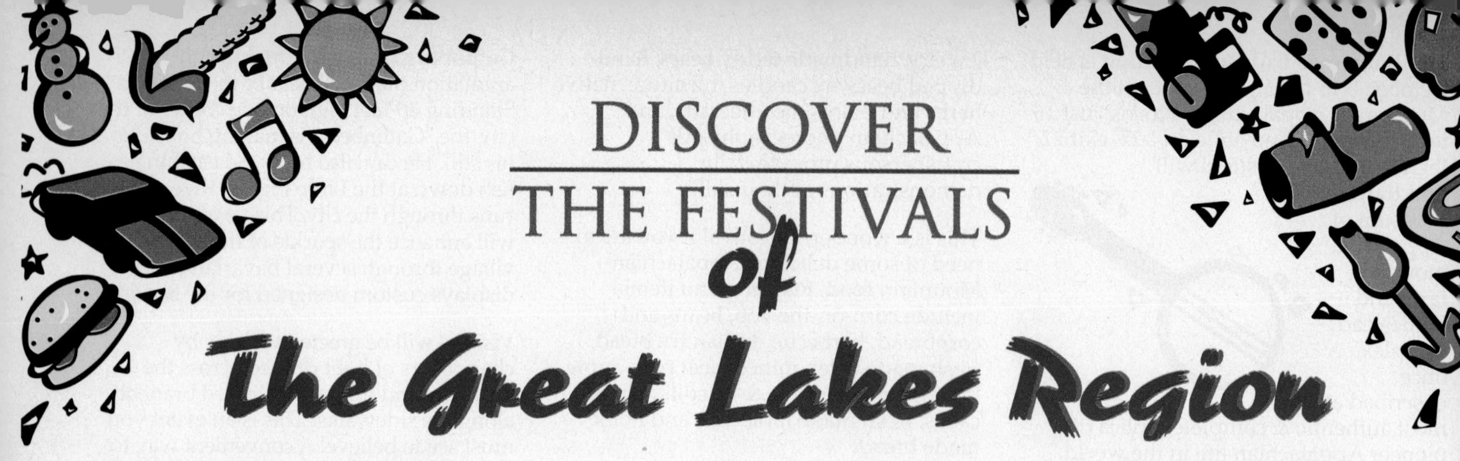

# DISCOVER THE FESTIVALS of The Great Lakes Region

## ILLINOIS FESTIVALS

**Summer:**

Chicago winters being what they are, locals and visitors alike take to the outdoors to enjoy the warm weather. Neighborhood festivals are held just about every weekend during the summer, and several major "superfests" really keep things hopping. (There is plenty of RV/camping in outlying areas.) Some of the biggest are: The **Chicago Blues Festival** held in early June in Grant Park along Lake Michigan; **Chicago Gospel Festival; Grant Park Music Festival; Taste of Chicago**, *the* major Chicago food extravaganza where scores of the city's world-famous restaurants bring out their best samples; **Venetian Night** where beautifully-decorated boats cruise the shoreline; **Chicago Air & Water Show** in August at North Avenue Beach; and the **Chicago Jazz Festival** in early September which closes the summer festivities.



Food and fun await travelers at the annual **National Sweet Corn Festival** held in Mendota August 9th through 11th. The celebration began in 1948 as a harvest festival with the serving of free, hot buttered sweet corn. Today, the event, sponsored by the Mendota Area Chamber of Commerce, attracts over 50,000 people during its three day run, and more than 62 *tons* of delicious Del Monte Sweet Corn is consumed. Del Monte donates all the sweet corn, which is cooked to golden goodness with the help of a vintage steam engine. Local clubs and organizations provide the hands to serve over 160,000 ears of the fresh ears, dripping with butter and salted to your taste on Sunday afternoon of the festival.

Mid-June brings the **Oldsmobile Balloon Classic Illinois** to Danville at the eastern border of the state. Head over to the Vermilion County Airport for the largest hot air balloon race in Illinois where you'll gaze in wonder at more than 100 of the beautiful hot air balloons billowing over the Illinois prairie. This major event attracts thousands of spectators and also includes concessions and entertainment. The Midway is a collection of food booths offering local favorites like pork chop sandwiches, fresh strawberry shortcake along with the usual hot dogs and cotton candy. If your feet get tired, stop by the beer gardens to sit, relax and have some refreshments. There's also a play area for children, so they can work off some steam.

Amboy celebrates its **Depot Days** for three days at the end of August. Visitors will be treated to the Miss Amboy Pageant at the Depot Museum; a carnival with more rides than ever before; garage sales throughout town; and an arts and crafts show. Head over to the Depot Museum south parking lot on Friday evening for country line dancing complete with free lessons. After steppin' out with your partner, stroll over to the Knights of Columbus Beer Garden for more free music and a tall, cool one. Saturday brings more food and music and a petting zoo for the children; and Sunday everyone enjoys more great Depot Museum foods at the pavilion, a co-ed volleyball tournament and a car show.

The 32nd annual **Dixon Petunia Festival** will be held the last weekend in June. Festival goers will enjoy what is billed as the "best midway in Northern Illinois," with more exciting rides than ever. The Matt Armstrong Shows offer a family-oriented carnival and midway with moneysaving specials each day. Spectators enjoy a full day of bicycle races through the streets of Dixon as both local citizens' and United States Cycling Federation races take place. At the airport, you'll thrill to a skydiving show. Other events include an ice cream social, a municipal band concert, tours of the Ronald Reagan home, pancake breakfasts, a beer garden, jazz and country musical performances, a drum corps show, a gospel show, and a 5k walk/run/rollerblade race.

**Fall:**

Rockford celebrates its **On The Waterfront Festival** over Labor Day weekend each year. What began as a neighborhood block party 11 years ago, has evolved into a major festival attracting more than 300,000 visitors. Held along the streets of downtown Rockford along both the east and west banks of the Rock River, the festivities include 7 outdoor music stages featuring contemporary jazz, blues, country, rock, reggae, and oldies music. Special events include a carnival and kiddie carnival, street performers, electronic dart and fishing tournaments, a 5k race, and great food. Get your taste buds ready for tender pork chop sandwiches, tempura, pastries, pizza, and country apple fritter to name just a few of the delicacies.

Labor Day weekend is **Railfan Weekend** at the Illinois Railway Museum in Union, Illinois, the largest operating railway museum in the country. If you are a train buff, a model railroader, or anyone with an interest in transportation history, this is one event you won't want to miss. Take your pick of learning about and enjoying steam trains, electric cars and trolleys, or diesel trains on all three days. If you have ever wanted to sit next to the motorman on a trolley or have dinner in a railroad diner, or try your hand at pumping your way down the track on a hand car, you'll especially want to be here for this event. Seeing and riding the trains is a treat in itself, but have you ever had the fantasy of being the engineer? Your wish can come true at the museum with the "Take The Throttle" program, where visitors can operate their choice of a steam engine, a diesel, or an electric car under the instruction and supervision of a qualified museum crewman. Space in this program is limited and advance reservations are essential.

For some small-town beauty and serenity, head south to Union County for their annual **Union County Fall Colorfest** the 2nd weekend in October. The small communities in Union County celebrate the fall colors of the Shawnee National Forest with guided bus tours, horse and buggy rides, bicycle tours, arts and crafts shows, washer pitching contests, games, raffles, quilt shows, a wine festival and lots of good southern Illinois food.

## *INDIANA FESTIVALS*

**Spring:**

Held annually in May, the **500 Festival** is a city-wide celebration in Indianapolis that enhances the 500-mile race with such events as the nations' largest half-marathon and only interactive parade. From 15,000 half-marathon runners racing toward the finish line downtown to 30,000 children playing games on Monument Circle to 52,000 spectators playing kazoos in unison, the 500 Festival involves thousands of Indianapolis visitors and residents. Special mini-festivals within the big festival abound. 500 Festival Kids' Day is a free event where children race Big Wheels, make arts and crafts, play games and participate in fun and educational activities. It's the city's largest outdoor festival just for children, and more than 12,000 prizes are awarded ranging from jump ropes to bicycles. The month of May culminates with the world's largest single-day sporting event, the **Indianapolis 500.** Indianapolis Motor Speedway opens for racing three weeks and one day before the race, and is brimming with practice activity throughout the month of May.

**Summer:**

The annual **Amish Acres Arts & Crafts Festival** will celebrate its 34th anniversary in mid-August. The festival is held on the grounds of Amish Acres, an 80-acre historic farm restoration, and is reflective of the heritage and folk art of the plain people who homesteaded this land. Visitors will find plenty of free parking, and over 300 artists and craftspersons who display and sell their work in a marketplace atmosphere. Entertainment includes barbershop quartets, folk singers, square dancing, and strolling musicians, and there's live musical comedy at the Plain & Fancy Theater.

**Fall:**

Don't miss the annual **Persimmon Festival** held in late September in Mitchell. For non-Hoosiers, the persimmon is a prized wild fruit found in secret locations in southern Indiana, and is as valued as any wild mushroom, wild asparagus or blackberry bush. The fruit is the largest berry produced by any tree in North America, and is sometimes described as looking like a small jack-o-lantern. Although the taste of an unripe persimmon is described as "puckery," and Hoosiers have been known to good-naturedly test unwary out-of-staters by offering them a taste of an unripe persimmon, they do become sweet upon ripening. The festival includes a candlelight tour of Spring Mill Village at Spring Mill State Park where volunteers dress in period costumes and reenact 1800s pioneer life. There's an arts & crafts show; an art exhibit; a road rally; a 5k run; and many variations of persimmon food delicacies including puddings, cookies, cakes, ice cream and candy.

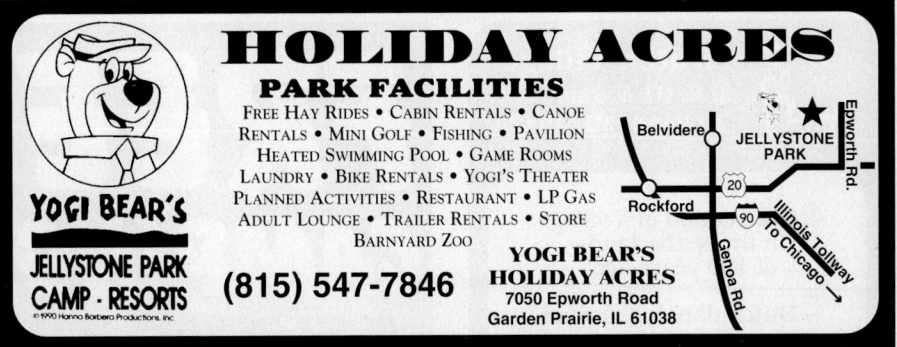

## IOWA FESTIVALS

**Spring:**

Amana Society, Inc. was founded by German immigrants who came first to New York State, then moved on to Iowa in 1855, eventually purchasing 25,000 acres in Iowa County where it established the seven villages known as the Amanas. Originally a religious-communal organization, the Society was incorporated in 1932. Today, it's a privately-held corporation with the largest single farm and forest holding in Iowa, hand-crafted furniture manufacturing, baker and meat markets, and much more. The Colonies are also a National Historic Landmark and Iowa's leading visitor attraction. Festivals are held to celebrate the various seasons, beginning in spring. **Maifest,** held the first weekend in May, features maipole dancers, German music and a "Taste of the Amana Colonies" food extravaganza.

**Summer:**

The **Iowa State Fair,** nicknamed the "Fun and Only," will be held in Des Moines August 8th through the 18th. The Fair has been held since 1854, and many of the buildings are outstanding examples of exposition-style architecture. The extravaganza is known as the classic American state fair because it has all the traditional features of a fair, from one of the largest livestock shows in the world to the whirling excitement of the midway. It is one of the most famous state fairs in the country: The original novel, *State Fair*, written by Iowan Phil Strong, and three motion pictures were based on this event.

The **Midwest Old Thresher's Reunion** is held August 3rd through September 4th in Mount Pleasant. Visitors enjoy the scores of steam traction engines, antique tractors and agricultural implements and tools on display. There are also agricultural and historical exhibits, educational programs and tours of the area.

**Fall:**

**Oktoberfest** is held the first weekend in October at the Amana Colonies in east central Iowa, and celebrates the harvest season with German entertainment, crafts, a beer tent, parade and more.

**Winter:**

Winter at the Amana Colonies in east central Iowa is celebrated with their **Prelude to Christmas** event the first weekend in December. The village of Amana provides the perfect setting with old-fashioned decorations, special entertainment at the Museum of Amana History, candlelit streets, carolers, Santa and holiday crafts.







## MICHIGAN FESTIVALS

**Spring:**

**The Blossomtime Festival** comes to Benton Harbor, St. Joseph and surrounding communities at the end of April through the first week in May. This multi-community celebration begins, as it has every year since 1908, with the Sunday blessing of the blossoms. Before it concludes with the metric century bicycle ride the following Sunday, the celebration will have encompassed three parades including the Grand Flora Parade on Saturday, the Queen's Fashion Show, arts and crafts shows, an antique show, a Las Vegas night, 5- and 10-k runs and walks, and the Grand Floral Ball.

May brings a major event, **Tulip Time**, to Holland, Michigan, which celebrates the area's Dutch heritage along with the beautiful blossoms of millions of tulips. Visitors will enjoy musical shows, parades, over 1,400 costumed Klompen Dancers, and 8 miles of Tulip Lanes. One of the most popular parades is the Volksparade, which is preceded by the town crier's announcement that the streets are too dirty for a special Dutch parade. He orders a brigade of costumed scrubbers who splash and scrub until the parade begins. There are a variety of special shows and events including a Dutch Heritage Dinner Show where you will experience authentic Dutch costumes, songs and folk dances along with a plentiful Dutch meal. *A Trip Through Time* portrays Holland's past with fascinating stories of Dutch pioneers and other Dutch stories. Special group services include "Step-On Guides," which are locals who will provide your group with a special festival tour; and groups of 20 or more can make reservations for a meal at one of the local churches which have been transformed into restaurants for groups. You'll experience smiling cooks and delicious meals in the "Dutch tradition."

**Summer:**

Battle Creek is home to the 13th annual **World Hot Air Balloon Championship**

***Michigan Festivals continued on page 86***

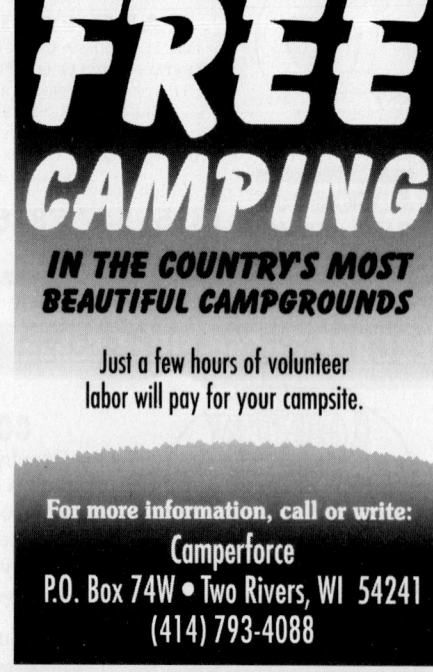

# How To Get Better Mileage Out Of Your RV.

In Michigan, you get more per mile out of your RV. Because there's more to do. And more to see.

There are state parks galore. Campgrounds by the hundreds. And lakes and beaches that never seem to end.

Plus a mind-boggling choice of things to do: Fish a quiet lake. Shop a luxurious mall. Visit a famous museum. Eat at a great restaurant.

Take in a terrific show. Go to a spectacular festival.

Or simply relax and enjoy the breathtaking splendor of Michigan's natural beauty.

From the trees to the lakes to the big open skies.

We even have a way to get you there quicker. Call **1-800-5432-YES ext. 199.** Our friendly travel advisors can help you plan a great getaway. We'll fax or mail the info right away. It's just one more way Michigan goes the extra mile for you.

# Start Here.

XWD

For free Michigan travel information, return coupon to Michigan Travel Bureau, P.O. Box 3393, Livonia, Michigan 48151-3393. Or call Michigan's travel advisors at **1-800-5432-YES ext. 199,** Monday-Friday 8am-11pm and Saturday-Sunday 8am-5pm. (For the hearing impaired, TDD 1-800-722-8191).

NAME

ADDRESS

CITY

STATE

ZIP

SAY**YES**TO**MICHIGAN**

*Michigan Festivals cont. from page 84*

held in early July. Visitors will see more than 175 beautiful hot air balloons from 32 countries, some designed in fanciful shapes such as Disney characters, Tony the Tiger, Post Cereals' Sugar Bear, Garfield the cat, a huge flying insect and more. The evening show presents "Balloon Night Illumes," when the balloons are illuminated. Other events include the precision flying team, the U.S. Air Force Thunderbirds; Team America, a three-ship operation that offers spectators the chance to fly the "Dog Fight"; a giant fireworks display; and Funland Amusement Park with over 40 rides including the ever popular "Skycoaster."

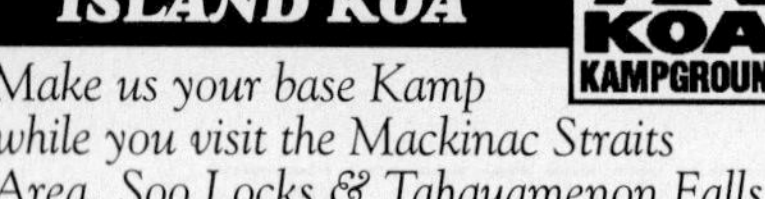



Petoskey's Pennsylvania Park is filled with wonderful art objects in celebration of their **Art in the Park** festival held on July 19th. The juried show has grown over the years to include the works of more than 138 artists from around the country. Truly the "cream of the crop," the chosen artists are picked from more than 400 applicants, ensuring a high-quality show. There's a children's tent featuring works of art that children can afford, costing between $2 and $5. There are also art projects that children can participate in such as paper sculpture and face painting. Parents are not permitted in the children's tent, and children may stay in the tent for up to 45 minutes, providing time for parents to shop and kids to have their fun, also.

Plan on a July visit to Port Huron for the **Port Huron to Mackinac Island Yacht Race**, an event that has been held for over 71 years. Sponsored by the Bayview yacht Club of Detroit, the race is one of the most popular events in the area, and the largest freshwater sailing event in the world. Thousands of visitors and locals head to downtown Port Huron to enjoy the week-long festivities that surround the race, and many local businesses and service organizations sponsor games, dinners and offer souvenirs for sale. There's a magnificent grand parade of water craft of all types that heads up the St. Clair River and out toward the Lake Huron starting line, and some of the best viewing spots for the parade are under the Bluewater Bridge in Port Huron or at Point Edward, along the Black River.

The Osceola County Fairgrounds in Evart is the site of the **Dulcimer Musical Funfest**, a non-electrical musical event that is always held the 3rd weekend in July. There are concerts featuring the melodic dulcimers, workshops, old-time square dancing, and an instrument sales area so you can take one home and learn to play. The friendly event is billed as "good old fashioned fun and friends," and visitors who arrive in Evart not knowing anyone will surely leave some new, good friends behind.

The **Ypsilanti Heritage Festival** is held August 16th through 18th (each year on the 3rd weekend in August), and this year marks its 18th anniversary. See nearly 200 arts and crafts exhibits, explore historic Depot Town, sample delicious treats from vendors throughout the site or relax for an afternoon of music. Diversity abounds with a line-up of jazz, blues, country, gospel and more at three performance stages. Visit the Living History Encampment (1700s to 1860s) and the Family Village activities in the pastoral setting of Riverside Park along the Huron River. Take an opportunity to view the unique architecture of the historic district during the Heritage Home Tour. These and many more activities add up to a weekend full of fun for everyone who attends this popular festival.

Mid-July brings the annual **Cherry Festival** to Traverse City. Visitors will be able to feast on the best cherries anywhere at this, the

"Cherry Capital of the World." The celebration includes fireworks displays, parades, an arts and crafts show, and every shape and size of cherry creation. View the sky-high thrills at the air show or enjoy the nightly entertainment at the concerts, shop for arts and crafts at the more than 70 booths, or watch the open-band and drum-and-bugle corps contests. Speaking of cherry creations, there's a Very Cherry Luncheon buffet, or you can sample some the goodies made by the winners of the Taste of Cherries contest. How about some great tasting cherry-bran chewies or the unique cherry-chicken-almond casserole?

Late August brings the **Kalamazoo Scottish Festival** to Michigan at River Oaks Park on Highway 96 east of Kalamazoo. The one-day festival celebrates the Scottish heritage of the area with pipers and pipe bands, fiddlers, dancers, weavers, Scottish wares and crafts, food vendors, clan tents, children's activities and games.

**Fall:**

Frankenmuth celebrates **Oktoberfest** each year on the 2nd full weekend in September (Thursday through Sunday). German music, food and dancing are enjoyed in the festival tent, while the European marketplace atmosphere of Frankenmuth's Main Street is dressed in fall colors. You'll be greeted by the aroma of fresh grilled bratwurst and soft German pretzels hot from the oven. Sip a frosty cold Frankenmuth beer as you listen to the "oom-pah-pah" sounds filling this German platz. Visitors to Frankenmuth will delight in the Bavarian architecture found throughout the quaint shops lining Main Street. The multitude of fall blooms and the cleanliness and hospitality (gemuelichkeit) of the community blend to create an experience as enchanting as a German fairy tale.

Labor Day morning brings the 39th annual **Labor Day Mackinac Bridge Walk** to St. Ignace and Mackinaw City, Michigan. Since its inception in 1958, the Walk has been enjoyed by persons of all ages, including a 100-year-old lady who participated in 1988. Labor Day is the only day of the year when pedestrian traffic is allowed on the world's longest suspension bridge. You won't need to get in shape for this event, as the walk is not a timed event, and the average walker completes the 4-1/2-mile trek in about an hour and twenty minutes. It's an event that can be enjoyed by the whole family and fits in well with our increased awareness that walking is a nice fitness activity, but is not too strenuous for most people. Each participant receives a numbered bridge walk certificate upon completion of his or her walk, with a drawing held for a winning number. For the extra energy needed for the event, many local restaurants are open early for "walkers' breakfasts."

Visit the Kalamazoo and Paw Paw areas in mid-September for their **Michigan Wine and Harvest Festival.** It's the state's largest wine and harvest festival and offers the "Best of Michigan" wine tasting, where more than a dozen wineries serve a sampling of more than 60 award winning wines. Kalamazoo chefs serve a wide variety of their best dishes at an ethnic food fair, cooking up everything from Chinese to American to Greek specialities. There's a fun "bed race" and a celebrity grape stomp for some laughs, and visitors can turn back the clock at the classic car show and vintage rock n' roll concert. Paw Paw offers a carnival; steamboat rides; an arts and crafts show with more than 250 exhibits; and face painting, magicians and storytelling for the children.

## MINNESOTA FESTIVALS

**Spring:**

Everything ethnic from all over the world is showcased at the **Festival of Nations**, Minnesota's largest multi-ethnic event held May 2nd through 5th at the Saint Paul Civic Center. Ninety-five ethnic groups present exciting folk dance performances, folk art demonstrations, cultural exhibits, and an international shopping bazaar, plus other attractions to delight all ages. You'll feel as if you have embarked on a trip around the world, as traditional ethnic foods are served with over 240 menu items at 40 sidewalk cafes circling the arena, surrounded by authentic building replicas of each group. The bazaar consists of a fascinating assortment of 58 shopping booths for browsing and buying gifts from around the globe.

**Summer:**

The **Minnesota State Fair** is held August 22nd through September 2nd in St. Paul, and promises to be bigger and better than ever! It's one of the largest and best-attended agricultural and educational entertainment events in the nation, in recent years attracting over 1.5 million people. Fairgoers enjoy scores of free performances, top-name grandstand presentations, agricultural exhibits including livestock and farm crops, creative and fine arts presentations, special exhibits and thrilling midway rides such as the Ejection Seat (a reverse bungee ride!), and many more. There's an auto race, performances by the Royal Canadian Mounted Police, a vintage motorcycle display, and the opportunity to perform with real circus performers at the "Be A Star Circus."

## OHIO FESTIVALS

**Summer:**

Each June (with fall shows run again in October) guests can venture back in time to the 1880s at the **Prairie Peddler Old West Festival.** The festival is held in Bunker Hill Woods on Highway 97 between Butler and Loudonville. Over 160 traditional craftspersons demonstrate and sell their handmade items while dressed in cowboy garb, complete with boots, hats, spurs and chaps. There are lovely, well-groomed paths to stroll while you shop, all the while being entertained by musicians and storytellers. When you have had enough shopping for awhile, excellent country foods cooked over open fires are available.

Loudonville is the site of the **Great Mohican Indian Pow-Wow and Rendezvous** that is held in early July and again during mid-September. The entire family will enjoy learning about the Native American culture via first-rate entertainment provided by Native Americans from all over the United States, representing tribes such as the Navajo, Cherokee, Lakota, Sioux, Seneca, Ottawa and others. Visitors will hear Native Americans tell stories of their heritage, taste traditional Indian foods, and watch the hand-crafting of traditional musical instruments. Tribal members compete in spiritual dance contests while dressed in colorful, elaborate costumes.

**Fall:**

Visit Sugarcreek the 4th Friday and Saturday after Labor Day for the 44th annual **Ohio Swiss Festival**. Sugarcreek is located in the rolling hills of western Tuscarawas County, 8 miles west of Dover and 18 miles east of Millersburg, on Route 39. Beginning at noon on Friday, festival goers can enjoy continuous free entertainment by Swiss yodelers, polka bands and spin their partners by dancing in the pavilion. Guests enjoy the best in Swiss delicacies this side of the Alps including locally-produced Swiss cheese sold in sandwiches and by the pound. Meals are served in a huge cafeteria operated by the Sugarcreek Rotary Club, and there is lots of Swiss-style entertainment such as Swiss yodeling contests, Steinstossen (stone throwing), Schwingfest (Swiss wrestling), and the ever-popular Swiss Cheese Chase (a five-mile run).

## WISCONSIN FESTIVALS

**Spring:**

Always held the first weekend after Memorial Day, the 21st annual **Great Wisconsin Dells Balloon Rally** will be celebrated June 1st and 2nd on the field across from the Wisconsin Dells Greyhound Park. Pilots compete during each of three balloon launches scheduled for the early morning and evening hours to take advantage of light winds. The "tasks" have names like the "Hare and Hound" chase, "Watership Down" target drop and the "Elbow" flight maneuver. Named one of the Top 100 Events in the nation by the American Bus Association in 1995, the 21st annual rally will continue the tradition with nearly 100 hot air balloons and is expected to attract more than 80,000 spectators.

**Summer:**

The 141st edition of the **Wisconsin State Fair**, held August 1st through 11th, will appeal to people of all ages and from all walks of life. The fair, which is the state's largest and oldest annual event, is held at Wisconsin State Fair Park in West Allis, conveniently located west of downtown Milwaukee. It has grown from a 2-day event in 1851 with attendance of 18,000 to an 11-day fair with attendance of almost one million in recent years. In addition to a vast midway, and numerous agricultural exhibits, free entertainment on 25 stages runs the gamut from regional and local musical acts to cooking demonstrations to educational programs on Wisconsin's natural resources. Not to be missed are the fair's most famous treats: cream puffs! For more than 70 years, the Wisconsin Bakers Association has used its special recipe to make and sell more than 200,000 of these Dairy State delicacies each year. There is lots of parking available, including spaces for RVs.

Milwaukee's **Summerfest** that begins the last weekend each June, is often touted as the "World's Greatest Music Festival." It's an 11-day extravaganza of musical entertainment with over 2,500 performers on 11 permanent stages on the Summerfest's grounds. Everything from big band to jazz to country and heavy metal bands are featured, and the top names in music appear here, many in free concerts. Food, fun and a host a activities are available for the entire family.

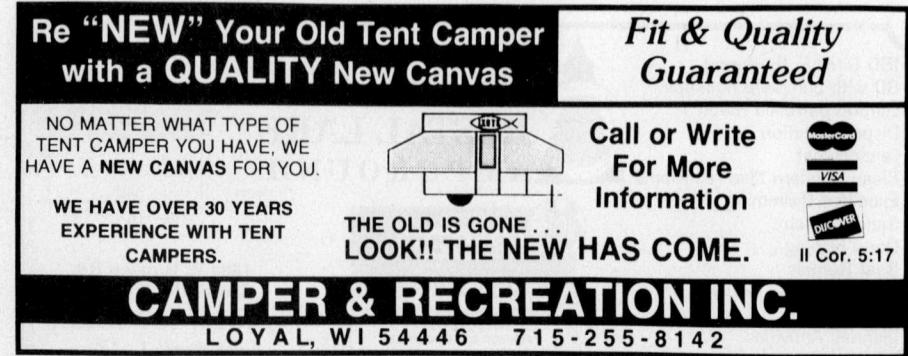

If you love airplanes and aviation, nothing compares to **EAA Oshkosh**, a huge convention put on each summer by the Experimental Aircraft Association at Wittman Regional Airport near Oshkosh. The event provides more than 600 exhibitors, 2,500 showplanes, seminars, workshops, and new exhibit hangars offering everything from complete airplanes to souvenirs. ◆

# DISCOVER THE FESTIVALS *of* The Frontier West

## ARKANSAS FESTIVALS

**Spring:**

For an event that lasts all spring and summer, plan on attending **The Great Passion Play** in Eureka Springs. The 29th season begins on the last Friday in April and runs through the last Saturday in October. The play, which is the #1 attended outdoor drama in the United States, depicts the life, death, resurrection and ascension of Jesus Christ. More than 5 million people have come to Eureka Springs since the first performance in1968. Today the two-hour play is presented by a cast of 250 actors and live animals and includes authentic Biblical costumes, a multi-level stage and the latest in sound and lighting technology. Other exhibits on the beautiful 600-acre grounds include the Christ of the Ozarks statue; a 10-foot section of the Berlin Wall adjacent to a 100-year-old church; the Smith Memorial Chapel, a quiet place for prayer and meditation; the Bible Museum with exhibits of over 6,000 old and rare bibles; and the Sacred Arts Center with over 1,000 works of Christian art.

**Summer:**

Historic Wiederhehr Village, on the National Register of Historic Places, celebrates its **Summer Grape Festival** in late July. The first celebration was held in 1984 to show appreciation to the local grape growers. The festival activities change each year, but some traditions are kept, such as grape stomping, the blessing of the harvest and the vine cutting ceremony. Both days of the 2-day festival are filled with music, grape-related games, and free wine and juice sampling. The amateur winemaking contest is a favorite among do-it-yourselfers, and arts and crafts and food vendors come from far and wide to participate in the festival. While in town, plan on a leisurely, candle-lit meal at Weinkeller Restaurant, located on the site where Johann Andreas Wiederkehr hand-dug the first wine cellar here in 1880.

**Fall:**

On the National Historic Register of Historic Places, and settled in 1880, Wiederkehr Village near Altus has first-class food and wine service, sightseeing, trail riding, canoeing the rapids on the Mulberry River, hiking the Ozark Mountains, and several fun festivals. Come help celebrate the harvest by attending **Weinfest,** considered to be the most authentic Alpine-style festival in the United States. Held the last weekend in September in historic Wiederkehr Village, Weinfest celebrates the Swiss wine-making heritage of some of the oldest and most fascinating wineries in mid-America. Free tours and wine tastings are held year around.

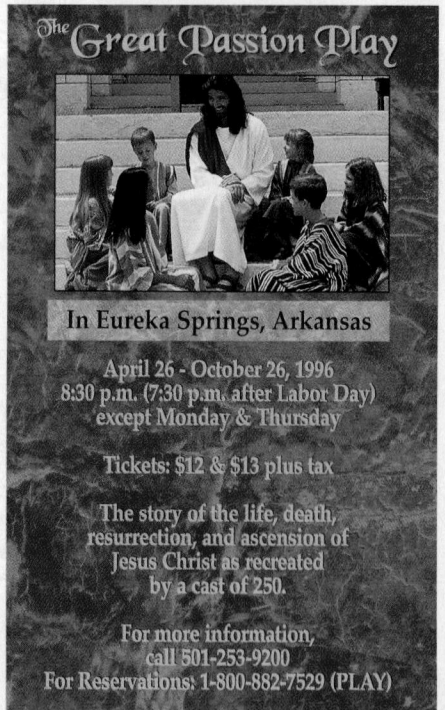

**FREE INFO?** Hot Springs CVB, enter #692; The Great Passion Play, enter #498 on Reader Service Card following page 16.

## KANSAS FESTIVALS

**Spring:**

Larned's **Santa Fe Trail Days** celebration is held each Memorial Day weekend, and 1996 is a special year for them as it commemorates the 175th anniversary of the Santa Fe Trail. The relatively small festival has grown each year since its beginnings with about 2,500 in attendance recently. There are more than 65 craft and food booths and 8 outdoor flea market booths inviting visitors to search for that "special treasure." Join the living history staffers at nearby Fort Larned as they help guests experience the sights, sounds and smells of the 1860s fort through talks and demonstrations on frontier life.

**Summer:**

Railroad buffs will want to visit Topeka on Labor Day weekend for the **Topeka Railroad Days** festival which celebrates the city's railroad heritage. The event was started in 1986 as a fund-raiser and has grown into a major festival. Visitors will find over 90 arts, crafts and commercial exhibits and 20 food vendors. Entertainment includes railroad equipment displays, railroad expo, motor car rides and model train displays. Continuous musical entertainment is provided all weekend with top local, regional and national groups. Evening shows feature popular headline country entertainers. The children will enjoy Choo Choo Junction, a play area with activities, clowns and magicians. There are also horse and pony rides. A special activity is the "Excursion Train" ride, a 60-mile round trip to three area cities.

**Fall:**

The 83rd annual "great Kansas get-together" will again turn the state fairgrounds in Hutchinson into a 280-acre stage for the 10-day variety show that is the **Kansas State Fair.** Held September 6th through the15th, it's the largest event in the state, with nearly 350,000 fairgoers attending to celebrate Kansas' agricultural heritage. There's a 10,000-seat grandstand which is the focal point for major entertainment events and most evenings are filled with concerts by some of the country's biggest country and pop music entertainers. There's also a big and colorful midway featuring carnival rides, attractions and food concessions. If your feet get tired, take the train ride around the grounds or enjoy a boat ride on Lake Talbott. There are many free, one-day events within the fair such as a chili cook-off, antique tractor pull, nostalgia car show, arm wrestling championships and more.

## MISSOURI FESTIVALS

**Spring:**

Visit historic St. Charles, the oldest town on the Missouri River, for **Lewis & Clark Heritage Days** held each May. With the shrill of fifes and color of flags, visitors can step back into a world of candlelight, buckskins, teepees and explorers as citizens celebrate the Lewis & Clark Rendezvous. The event commemorates the encampment and departure of the celebrated Lewis & Clark expedition which explored and mapped the "world's largest real estate deal," the Louisiana Purchase. Traditional pioneer artisans demonstrate the crafts of the 1804 period and succulent foods such as game meat and cobbler are served. Each day the 1804 fifteen star flag is raised at Reville accompanied by musket fire and fife and drummer corps. Re-enactment groups skirmish and demonstrate19th-century drill tactics and visitors are invited to visit the campsites in Frontier Park.

May brings the **St. Louis Storytelling Festival** to this state. This 17th annual event celebrates stories and storytelling from diverse cultures and features nationally recognized as well as local storytellers. The festival is held at the Gateway Arch and various other locations.

**Summer:**

The **National Tom Sawyer Days** are held on the Fourth of July weekend each year in downtown Hannibal, and have been celebrating this Mark Twain hero for over 40 years. Visitors may watch or join in activities such as the National Fence Painting Championships, a frog-jumping contest, the Tomboy Sawyer Competition, the Sam Clemens-Kiwanis Arts and Crafts Show, Mississippi Mud Volleyball, bingo, live entertainment, and much more. A gigantic fireworks display is held at the riverfront on the evening of July 4th. A highlight of the event is the Tom Sawyer and Becky Thatcher contest.

Located in Sedalia at the crossroads of highways 50 and 65, the **Missouri State Fairgrounds** have hosted this midwestern extravaganza each August since 1901 with the exception of 1943 and 1944 during World War II. Today more than 400,000 visitors stroll along the 396 acres of livestock and agricultural exhibits and booths. From sellout grandstand shows featuring big-name entertainers to auto racing, and a variety of commercial exhibits, there is truly something for everyone. The AgriMissouri market is filled with Missouri-grown and -processed food products. Elsewhere, hungry fairgoers can feast on soybean doughnuts, pork chops, steaks, chicken, turkey, corn-on-the-cob — all products produced in the state. Other special events include a draft horse pull, demonstrations of traditional blacksmithing, the state finals rodeo and an antique tractor pull. Recent entertainers include saxophonist Kenny G, the Beach Boys, singer Lorrie Morgan and Travis Tritt.

**Fall:**

Hannibal's historic district is the site of the **Autumn Historic Folklife Festival** held the third weekend in October. Visitors stroll the quaint streets amid the artisans demonstrating the lifestyles and crafts of the mid-1800s. There are street musicians playing traditional music of the era, and storytellers whose yarns and tales entertain young and old alike. Traditional wood fires are used to cook up tempting dishes, and if you take a moment (right now) you can almost smell the roasted corn or pumpkin pie!

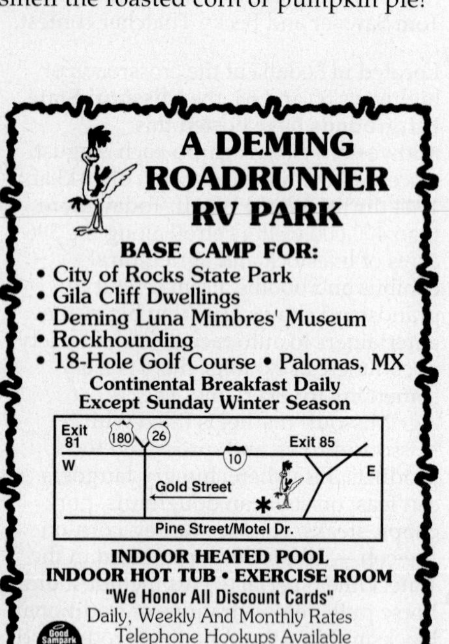


Branson, Missouri is the home of Silver Dollar City, an attraction that mixes the sights and sounds of the 1890s with the fun and excitement of the 1990s, and Silver Dollar City is host each year to the **National Festival of Craftsmen**. The event begins in mid-September and runs through the last weekend in October. Visited by over 300,000 festival-goers each year, the event was started in 1961 as a small weekend festival which has grown to a seven week event. Crafts must fit within the 1890s theme and are demonstrated by craftsmen in over 75 booths showcasing pioneer crafts, fine crafts and fine art. Guests sample specialty and home-cooked foods; a variety of music shows and musical groups representing western, Cajun and gospel music; crafts; rides; shops and more. The Quiltmaker's Collection Show and Sale features a competition and show of hundreds of the country's best quilts competing for prizes.

## *NEW MEXICO FESTIVALS*

**Spring:**

For what is billed as the "hottest show on earth," visit the **8th Annual National Fiery Foods Show** at the Albuquerque Convention Center March 1st through 3rd. Here, lovers of the chile pepper gather to taste, sell and talk peppers. Exhibitors display everything from exotic Caribbean hot sauces and pepper seeds to Texas-shaped tortilla chips and jalapeno brittle candy. You'll

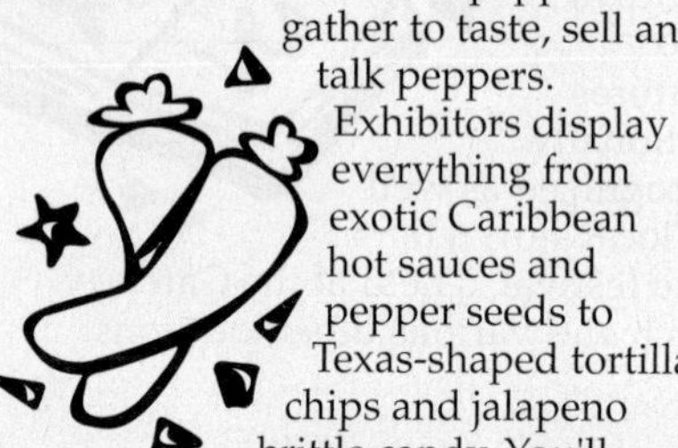

receive an instant education on the fiery foods industry by talking to food brokers, distributors, and owners of shops specializing in the palate-singeing peppers. Special events include cooking demonstrations and cookbook signings by fiery foods authors.

Native American culture comes alive at the **Gathering of Nations Powwow, Indian Trader's Market** and the crowning of Miss Indian World at this event held in Albuquerque April 25th through 27th. Visitors will be treated to over 2,000 American Indian dancers and singers, representing more than 700 tribes from Canada and the United States. The Indian Trader's Market offers a special shopping experience and exhibits of Native American artifacts and works of art. Over 800 artists, crafters and traders place their treasures on display and for sale. The selection of Miss Indian World is based on an assessment of personality, knowledge of tribal tradition and dancing ability. It's an ideal way to learn more about these cultures, amid the art and music of an enjoyable festival.

**Summer:**

Fort Union near Watrous, New Mexico, once guarded the intersection of the Mountain and Cimarron Branches of the Santa Fe Trail, and was once the largest U.S. military installation on the 19th-century frontier. Today, the ruins reveal the stone foundations of the original buildings that housed the guards, the post commander, the company quarters and the prison. Summer brings three special events to the Fort. On June 22nd, visitors glean a rare opportunity to visit the site of the **First Fort Union**, open to the public only once a year. July 20th and 21st brings **Cultural Encounters on the Santa Fe Trail,** a living history camp, talks and demonstrations offered by costumed guides dressed as soldiers, frontier women, teamsters and traders, all telling the story of life on the Santa Fe Trail. August 24th brings **An Evening at Fort Union** when visitors can experience Fort Union's past on an evening walk through the ghostly ruins. Scenes of past times at the fort will be re-created. Make reservations early for this popular tour.

Fathers' Day is extra-special in Santa Fe as it is the weekend the city holds its **Annual Santa Fe Plaza Arts & Crafts Festival.** Approximately 240 artists and craftspersons display their work on the Plaza and surrounding streets. An array of jewelry, ceramics, clothing, crafts, sculpture, paintings, and more decorate the Plaza — brought here by artists and craftspersons from all over the country. Visitors won't go hungry after a long day's shopping as there are rows of food booths featuring tasty New Mexican and Navajo dishes, fajitas, hamburgers and cappuccino. While enjoying this special

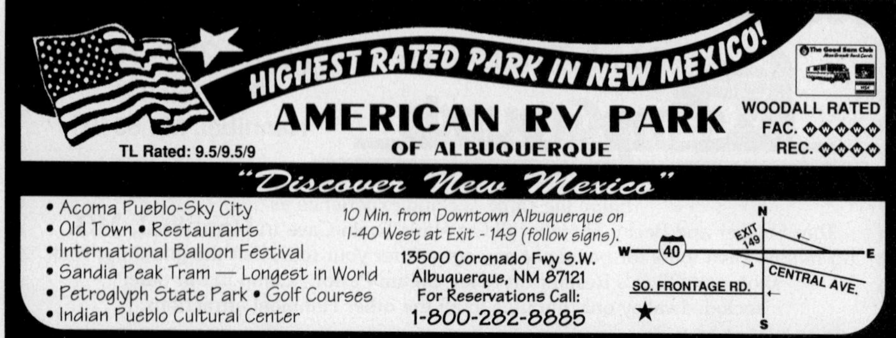


FREE INFO? A Demming Roadrunner, enter #363; Albuquerque North KOA, enter #315; American RV Park, enter #333 on Reader Service Card following page 16.

festival, visitors also help a local non-profit organization called Challenge New Mexico, which serves mentally and physically challenged children and adults. The group's programs fund performing arts programs, skiing, horseback riding and other sporting events.

The fourth of July weekend brings the **One World Music Festival** to Angel Fire Ski Area near Taos. The event is held outside high up in the beautiful Rocky Mountains surrounded by 13,000-foot peaks. Each day 6 or 7 musical acts perform on the main stage with local talent opening the day, lesser-known world beat performers in the middle of the day, and 1 or 2 headline entertainers closing the day's festivities. Recent headline acts included Los Lobos, Blues Traveler, Ivan Neville, Stephen Stills, and Steel Pulse, the Grammy Award-winning roots reggae band.

Mid-July brings **Wings Over Angel Fire** to the area. Learn about aviation from man's gazing at the mysterious heavens, to contemplating nature's wonder of birds in flight, on to capturing hot air for man's first view of the earth from aloft, to the science of space flight and exploration. Visitors can take a peek at the heavens via "Starlab" a portable planetarium courtesy of the Space Center in Alamogordo. Colorful balloons dot the skies both days, with pilots competing in targeted flight challenges. For a different sort of flight craft, there will also be helicopter demonstrations, with rides available at bargain rates.

The **Inter-Tribal Indian Ceremonial 75th Diamond Anniversary Celebration** will be held August 6th through the 11th in Gallup. Visitors will be treated to Ceremonial Dances, a Pow Wow, an All Indian Rodeo, a juried arts and crafts show, the Queen Contest, a 1/2 Marathon and other runs, performing arts, Native foods, and an indoor/outdoor marketplace. Representing more than 50 Native American tribes, this festival is a chance to experience and learn about the Native American culture at beautiful Red Rock State Park in Gallup, New Mexico.

**Fall:**

As northern New Mexico's quaking aspens turn from green to brilliant gold, the artists of Taos come out of their studios and galleries for a 17-day festival, showcasing a wide variety of art and artists that comprise this unique community. **The 21st Annual Taos Arts Festival** takes place September 15th through October 1st, featuring special art exhibits, craft fairs, and receptions in many of Taos' numerous art galleries. The Taos Open is a juried exhibition featuring recent works by new and established artists of Taos. As part of the festival, the Plaza Arts and Crafts Fair is held on Taos Plaza and features the talents of local jewelers, potters, metalworkers and other fine crafters. The Old Taos Trade Fair offers fine native foods, demonstrations in traditional northern New Mexican skills, Mountain Men, Indians, music, dancing and other performances.

Ballooning is one of the most visually spectacular sports in the world, and the **Kodak Albuquerque International Balloon Fiesta** held for 9 days in early October has become *the* ballooning event of the year. It's billed as the world's biggest, with more than 650 balloons participating — a far cry from the modest start in 1972 when 13 balloons participated. Approximately 1.6 million spectators attend, and contestants travel here from 16 countries. The vast and striking New Mexico sky is the perfect backdrop for these magnificent works of art. It is the most photographed event in the world — last year it is estimated that 25 million photographs were taken. Few events can rival the sight of hundreds of balloons lifting up into the morning sky, as five of the nine mornings begin with mass ascensions.

## *OKLAHOMA FESTIVALS*

**Spring:**

Historic Guthrie, Oklahoma is the site of the annual **Guthrie Jazz Banjo Festival** held each year Friday through Sunday on Memorial Day weekend. The event is the result of a long time dream held by the originator, Brady Hunt, to create a festival that helps preserve and perpetuate the music of the 4-string tenor and plectrum banjo in Oklahoma. The instrument was very popular during the 1800s through the 1930s, but has been on the decline since then. It is hoped that this festival will introduce (or re-introduce) people to its toe-tappin' music. The streets of historic, Victorian Guthrie add a special ambiance to the festival, as they are lined with dozens of beautifully restored 1890s and 1900s era buildings. Each year over 150 banjo players converge on the town from all over the United States. Banjo bands and soloists combine for over 90 performances in six downtown locations and two amphitheater concerts.

**Summer:**

July 11th through the 14th are the dates for the annual **American Music Festival** that had its beginnings three years ago in Duncan, Oklahoma at their new civic and sports complex, the Simmons Center. Visitors from far and near come to hear nationally-recognized musicians such as Mason Williams, and standard show tunes from Rogers and Hammerstein. Duncan, which is located in south central Oklahoma, with a population of approximately 22,000, is known for its various arts activities, and is also the site of one of the world's largest garage sales. There are lots of antique shops in the thriving downtown area, as well as four lakes nearby.

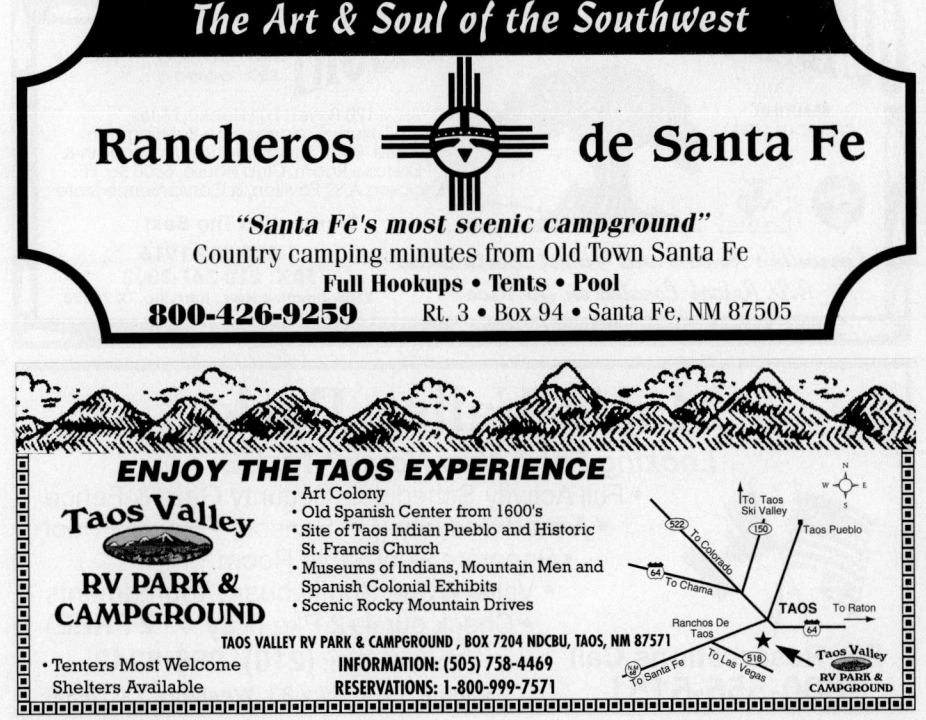

Oklahoma City welcomes visitors from far and wide to its celebration of Native

American cultures, **Red Earth Festival.** For three days in early June people representing more than 100 tribes from throughout North America gather in downtown Oklahoma City, ready to share the richness and diversity of their heritage with the world. In the nine years since its inception, Red Earth has grown into one of the world's largest and most respected visual and performing arts events of its type. Nearly 150,000 visitors view more than 1,800 of the world's finest Native American dancers and artists as they share their works and talents. Presentations held throughout the festival include storytelling, art, dance and music.

## *TEXAS FESTIVALS*

**Spring:**

Held annually the last weekend in April, the **Pleasure Island Music Festival** in Port Arthur celebrates the music and ethnic heritage of southeast Texas. Located on Pleasure Island's 10-acre music park, the naturally-landscaped surroundings feature a 36-foot stage along with two smaller stages. Continuous musical entertainment keeps visitors happy all weekend with local and regional talent performing during the day and big-names contracted for evening performances. Past festival entertainers include The Platters, Mickey Gilley, Miami Sound Machine, Roberta Flack and many more. There's plenty of parking, an arts and crafts tent, and a nice variety of ethnic and all-American foods.

The children in your family will love the **Safari Outdoor Family Festival** held at the Austin Nature Center in West Zilker Park in Austin, Texas. There are hands-on activities for children, native wildlife exhibits, entertainment, environmental education and demonstrations. Always the third weekend in May, and also in Austin, **Fiesta Laguna Gloria** offers arts, crafts, food, music, games and entertainment on the beautiful grounds of the Laguna Gloria Art Museum.

For one of the largest agricultural festivals of its kind in Texas, plan on attending the 49th annual **Strawberry Festival** in Poteet in early April. Just 25 miles south of San Antonio, in addition to tasty treats made from delicious Texas strawberries, the festival features nationally recognized country and western artists and Tejano stars at five outdoor concerts. There's also entertainment for children, an arts and crafts show, animal shows, helicopter rides and a "Taste of Texas" food show.

Late April through early May welcomes the annual **Buccaneer Days Festival** to Corpus Christi, when the town's history as a hideaway for pirates is commemorated. There's a carnival, parades, fireworks, a sailboat regatta, sporting events and lots of music.

April in Waco, Texas brings the **Cotton Palace Pageant** that re-creates Waco's history and heritage from its beginnings in 1849 when cotton was first cultivated here. There's a coronation of King and Queen Cotton and their royal court. Later in the month, plan on attending the **Brazos River Festival.** The fun includes an historic homes tour, music, food, live entertainment and more, all held at Fort Fisher Park.

**Spring Break on South Padre Island** offers headliner bands, Mexican markets, sandy white beaches, crystal blue water, and more than 100,000 sunbathers! Great music, clean beaches, watersports galore and a legendary nightlife are just a few of the reasons why so many college students are drawn to this hot spot each year — not to mention the array of beachside activities and games that the Collegiate Health and Fitness Tour has to offer. Located on the tropical tip of Texas, South Padre Island is easily accessible and a great "two nation vacation" with Mexico just 25 minutes away.

Weslaco in the Rio Grande Valley is host to **OnionFest** each April. Located 13 miles east of McAllen, Weslaco's annual festival is an enjoyable day of family fun. There are rides, games, face-painting, and

storytelling for the children. The "Onion Fest Beauty Pageant" and the "Onion Ring Frying Competition" are among the favorite events of the festival, and there is musical entertainment as well.

April 19th through the 28th, San Antonio comes alive with its **Fiesta,** a 10-day event that celebrates the rich and diverse history and culture of one of America's favorite cities. More than a festival, Fiesta is a series of glittering parades, exciting carnivals, challenging sports, fireworks, music, ethnic feasts, art exhibits, dances, floats gliding down the river and streets spilling over with fun lovers of all ages. In all, there are more than 150 exciting events to satisfy all interests and draw over 3 million spectators and participants. A true city-wide event, Fiesta takes place in the heart of historic downtown San Antonio, where the major events are held, to special events in every part of the city, involving universities, churches, military installations, civic groups and people from all walks of life.

Come to Kerrville late May through early June for the 25th annual **Kerrville Folk Festival,** an 18-day event which includes eleven 6-hour evening concerts, 3 New Folk concerts for emerging songwriters, three Chapel Hill services on Sunday mornings, and six 2-hour children's concerts. The festival began in 1972 as a gathering of thirteen folk music performers playing at three concerts at the Municipal Auditorium. Today the festival is held at Outdoor Theater, Quiet Valley Ranch, 9 miles south of Kerrville on Highway 16. No coolers or pets are allowed in the theater, but cold beer, soft drinks, delicious smoked barbecue, smoked sausage, health foods and other food is available throughout the hours that the theater is open every day of the festival.

**Summer:**

Where can you find explosive entertainment, song, dance and a romantic tale of the Old West? It's all in ***Texas,* the musical drama** played nightly except Sunday each summer under the stars in the Palo Duro Canyon State Park near Amarillo and Canyon, Texas. The 2-1/2-hour play (which has been running since 1966) unfolds as cowboys ride the range, Indians leap from rocks, and magnificent songs and dancing fill the stage. State of the art technical effects make it all possible, as does the magnificent outdoor setting with a natural rock cliff as its backdrop. Spectators are riveted when a prairie fire leaps onto the stage, and a simulated thunderstorm sends them searching for an umbrella. Showtime is 8:30 p.m. and advance reservations are recommended.

Early June brings the **Texas Scottish Festival & Highland Games** to Arlington. It's a celebration of Scot and Celtin culture held at the University of Texas at Arlington's Maverick Stadium. Lads and lasses will enjoy the Highland dancing, bagpipe entertainment, drumming, Scottish clan tents, caber toss, and authentic Scottish food and ale.

Mid-June through early September is time for ***Viva! El Paso,*** a celebration of the rich history of El Paso del Norte, unfolded against the dramatic backdrop of the Franklin Mountains. This

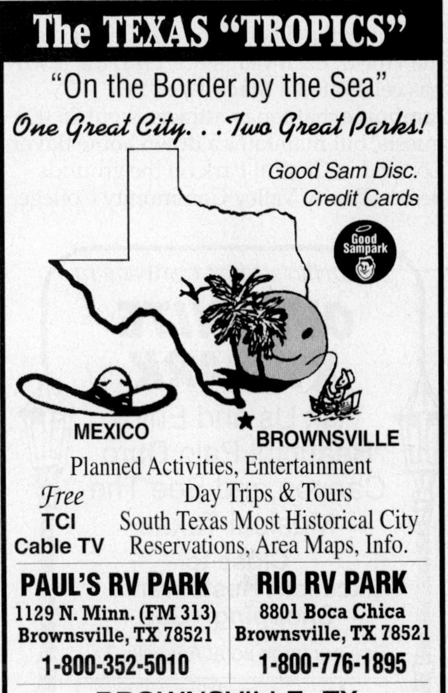

**FREE INFO?** Paul's RV Park, enter #95; Waco Convention & Visitors Center, enter #416 on Reader Service Card following page 16.

entertaining outdoor musical drama tells the exciting story of Indians, conquistadors, cowboys and cavalry. Evening performances are held Thursday through Saturday at McKelligon Canyon Amphitheater.

For many years, the growing, processing, canning and eating of black-eyed peas was a major part of life in Athens, Texas, and so much so, that Athens became known as the Black-Eyed Pea Capital of the World. Each year since 1971, the town has celebrated a **Black-Eyed Pea Jamboree** that today attracts about 25,000 guests, but maintains a down home flavor. Located in Central Park on the grounds beside Trinity Valley Community College, visitors are welcomed to join in on the fun the 3rd weekend in July. The main event is a black-eyed pea cookoff, with about a hundred entrants each year trying to win part of the prize money, as well as the fame that goes with being a champion cook. There's an arts and crafts show and the ever popular "pea poppin'" and "pea eatin'" contests.

The Alamo City of San Antonio is about as popular a tourist destination as you'll find anywhere, and the city is careful to ensure that visitors have a memorable time during their stay. The Institute of Texan Cultures takes its role as a tourist attraction seriously, as well, by producing an event that assembles over 70,000 visitors and 10,000 participants each year — the **Texas Folklife Festival** that has been held here each year in early August for 25 years. Visitors are treated to musical entertainment, tasty ethnic and cultural foods, traditional crafts and customs, and a variety of cultural dancing. You can learn how to make a pinata, care for goats, learn blacksmithing, create bobbin lace, spin horsehair into rope, or learn clog dancing. No matter how modern the world has become, it's always fun to learn about the skills and crafts of those who have come before us.

Come on out to the **Texas International Apple Festival** always the last Saturday in July in Medina, the Apple Capital of Texas. Visitors enjoy ice cold apple cider and more apple goodies than anyone can eat in a day, including everything from apple pie to apple pizza! There are three stages of continuous live music and entertainment and more than 100 arts and crafts booths to shop. A spectacular fireworks display is scheduled right after dark, so plan to spend the entire day at the festival.

<u>Fall:</u>

A sure sign of autumn in Texas is the excitement that precedes the opening of the **State Fair**, held in Fair Park in Dallas during October. The State Fair notwithstanding, Fair Park is an attraction unto itself, with fountains, reflecting pools, flowers, walkways and grassy lawns. There are museums of science, history and transportation, a garden center and aquarium on the grounds, too. As you'd expect from a state that does few things on a small scale, the Fair is nicknamed "The Big

*Texas Festivals continued on pg. 98*

# Safety Alert!

**At Last! All You Need To Know To Protect Your Loved Ones... Yourself ... Your Gear... And Your Rig From Danger.**

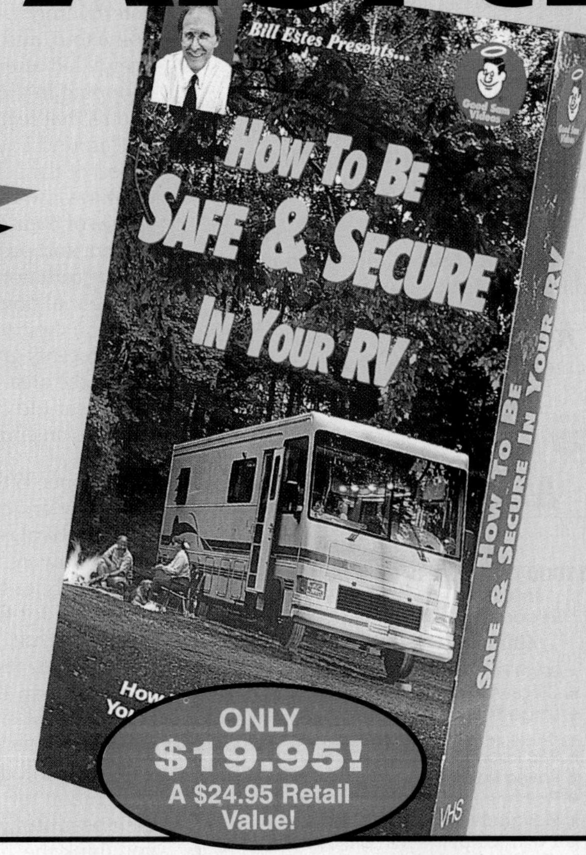


Don't miss this important video event! Bill Estes, publisher of *Trailer Life* and *MotorHome* magazines, and Good Sam Videos, are proud to present one of the most important VHS tapes you or any RVer will ever own! *How To Be Safe & Secure In Your RV* is a comprehensive how-to video that candidly explores all the dangers of the open road and gives you smart, *proven* ways to avoid them.

- **AWARENESS**—surroundings… suspicious characters and vehicles… trusting—*and training*—your instincts
- **PREPARATION**—destination security… law enforcement communication… local crime check
- **VEHICLE MAINTENANCE**—engine… fluids… systems… tires… tools… and more
- **FIRST AID**—supplies… personal medications… CPR
- **FIRE PREVENTION**—smoke detectors… fire extinguishers… fire suppression systems… poison gas detection
- **LOCKS**—dead bolts… exterior padlocks… fuel supply locks… wheel locks… floor safes
- **LIGHTS**—exterior… interior… infrared motion sensors… street lighting
- **ALARM SYSTEMS**—wireless alarm systems… dogs… ignition kill switches… theft tracking systems (and tips)… system ID stickers
- **WEAPONS**—fire arms safety… ordinances… mace and pepper sprays
- **TRAVEL TIPS**—convoys… if you break down… roadside criminals… being followed… personal and vehicle documents… cellular phones… CBs… holdups… abductions

**This full-color, 30-minute tape includes a COMPLETE, LIFESAVING CPR DEMONSTRATION!**
**Now you can learn this vital technique at home!**

## SAVE $10 ON SET OF TWO VIDEOS ... BOTH "MUSTS" FOR THE RVer!

Two-tape set includes ***How To Be Safe & Secure In Your RV*** and ***The Best of 10-Minute Tech***— 25 valuable tips to save you time, money and frustration.

- Make your own inexpensive tire covers!
- Measure your trailer's tongue weight with a bathroom scale!
- Stay dry under your awning when rain blows!
- Burglar-proof your locks!
- Spot tiny leaks in your LP gas system!
- And much, much more!
- Save $10—Only $29.95 For Both!

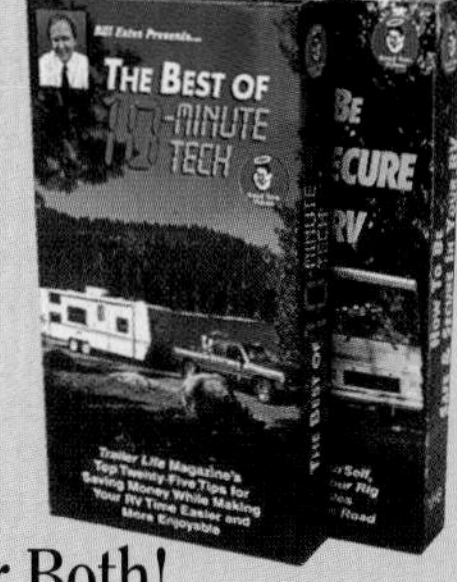


**CALL NOW! 1-800-847-8773**

**Or mail payment to: P.O. Box 8555, Ventura, CA 93001**

**Include $3.95 shipping & handling for one tape, $5.95 for two tapes. CA residents add 8.25% sales tax.**

**FREE INFO?** Safety Alert!, enter #666 on Reader Service Card following page 16.

*Texas Festivals continued from pg. 96*

One," and it lives up to its name. The exposition sprawls over 277 acres, just minutes from downtown Dallas. During its annual 24-day run, more than 3 million fun seekers stroll its midway and exhibit halls. First greeted by Big Tex, the smiling 52-foot cowboy who greets one and all with a hearty "Howdy, folks!", guests will next find the tallest Ferris wheel in the western hemisphere, a gigantic car show, a laser light show, livestock and horse shows, parades, a rodeo, fireworks displays, over 175 food booths, around 100 arts and crafts booths, and much more.

The 3-day **Jail House Cell-Abration** is held the last weekend of September each year on thr grounds of the 100+ year-old Fayette County Jail in LaGrange. The fun features a Jail Break 5k Fun Run and a 1-mile walk, the Golden Badge Gala, an antique and vintage car show, a country-wide road rallye, a pet parade and blessing, children's activities, live entertainment, bingo, a street dance, a home tour, and if you've still got a little energy left after all these fun events, shopping in the many arts and crafts booths that feature products produced in and around Fayette County. A special aspect of the celebration is the gathering of old-time law enforcement officers to recall stories of their days associated with the jail. Present and past peace officers are honored during ceremonies on Saturday morning. The special home tour allows visitors to drive on their own or be driven in wagons with docents giving histories of each home and of the area. Inside tours of a home and a 140-year-old church bring the three days of fun to an end.



On October 17th through the 20th plan a visit to Tyler, Texas, home of the annual **Rose Festival,** which celebrates these field grown flowers. The growing of roses began in Tyler because it was an area conducive for the growing of nursery stock and fruit, specifically peaches. The festival itself began in 1933 because local garden club women wanted recognition for their beautiful roses. If you think the Texas landscape provides only views of cactus and oil wells, you are in for a real treat when you visit east Texas, and specifically Smith County, the site of one fifth of all commercial rose bushes produced in the United States. The festival includes a variety of events such as the Rose Queen's Coronation, square and round dances, rose field tours, an arts and crafts fair, and a grand march. Any time of the year, from early May until frost, travelers may visit the Tyler Municipal Rose Garden which blooms with 30,000 bushes exhibiting over 400 varieties of roses.

Waco is the site of a Texas tradition: the **Heart O'Texas Fair & Rodeo** held at the Heart O'Texas Fair Complex. Each year cowboys and cowgirls perform for thousands at the PRCA rodeo, which also offers live country music, a carnival midway, horse and livestock shows, exhibits and more.

One of the top five airshows in the United States, the **Wings Over Houston** airshow annually honors one of the nation's leading aviators each year at Ellington Field the third week in October. Visitors enjoy the Reactor Motion Simulation Theatre, a thrilling flight simulator that allows participants to ride in the cockpit of a U.S. Navy F-18 Hornet in the Blue Angels Aerial Demonstration Squadron. It's a complete festival of aviation and entertainment with thrilling air demonstrations, rows of vintage World War II and modern-day military aircraft, a recreated World War II military camp, as well as entertainment by local music groups.

**Winter:**

For an old-fashioned Christmas, Texas style, visit Wichita Falls during the month of December. Your eyes will be treated to the dazzling display, **Fantasy of Lights**, thousands of colored lights, life-sized storybook characters and animated scenes, all on the campus of Midwestern State University.

The annual **Mobil Cotton Bowl Classic** game is played each year in the Cotton Bowl in Dallas on January 1st. The game was started in 1936 through the efforts of Texas oilman J. Curtis Stanford whose efforts were so dedicated that he paid for the first four games out of his own pocket. Joe Montana played here in 1973 for Notre Dame, and the temperature was so cold that year that Montana sat out most of the third quarter trying to warm up.

Sunday, January 21st will mark the 24th running of the **Houston-Tenneco Marathon** which begins and ends in front of the George R. Brown Convention Center in Houston. The first Houston Marathon took place in 1972 with 113 runners. The 1995 race had over 6,300 participants representing almost every state in the U.S. and over 22 foreign countries. The Marathon combines a competitive athletic event with a city-wide festival of fun. Runners and spectators enjoy miles of non-stop entertainment provided by the unique "Hoopla Brigade," a group of professional and non-professional performers ranging from jump rope squads to jazz bands, whose main purpose is to entice the runners to keep running. Shorter distance runners should attend, also, as there's a 5-kilometer race that takes runners on a course through downtown Houston, and joins the marathon course for a mile along Main Street.

**Charro Days Fiesta** is held in Brownsville each year on the last Thursday in February. The fiesta originated in 1938 when about 1,000 people attended, and today it is world renowned as an example of international harmony and cooperation with more than 175,000 attendees. The link of friendship between Mexico and the United States is strengthened by mutual respect, appreciation and frivolity during this unique international fiesta. The name comes from the dashing horseman, hero of Mexican history, song and folklore, who were the forerunners of the American cowboys. Visitors will find the festival opening with a "Grito," the Mexican cousin to the Rebel yell, then Mariachi music begins. This is the signal for days of fun and myriad activities for visitors and townspeople alike. People from both nations stage three parades featuring bands, orchestras and theme floats depicting the legends, flowers, states and songs of Mexico. There are costume balls and public dances sponsored by local clubs and churches.



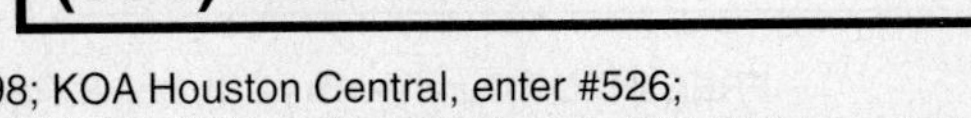

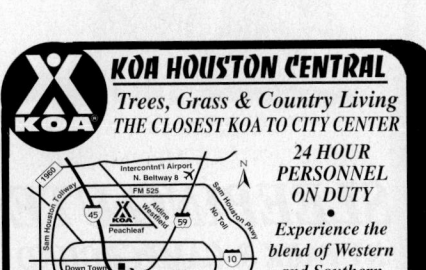

## COLORADO FESTIVALS

**Summer:**

For a unique Father's Day weekend, enjoy Salida's **FIBArk** (First in Boating on the Arkansas) **Boat Races**. There are no entry fees to the park and you'll enjoy the boat races, US Canoe and Kayak Team, sanctioned slalom races and a white water rodeo event; food booths serving frybread, funnel cakes, baklava, hot dogs, and more; and arts and crafts booths located in Alpine Park. This 47 year old event also offers nightly entertainment. Starts Thursday and runs through Father's Day.

The **6th Annual Wool Market** in Estes Park takes place the second weekend in June. It includes exhibits, demonstrations and vendors of products derived from animal fibers; with competitions, children's exhibits and more.

Colorado's oldest civic celebration is **Strawberry Days** in Glenwood Springs. A full week of fun and activities including a rodeo, talent show, music, dancing, arts and crafts fair, parade, food booths, carnival and strawberries and ice cream following the parade. Also, the Strawberry Short Cut foot race and softball tournament. It all happens the third weekend in June.

Learn about brewing and escape the heat by attending the **Colorado Brewers' Festival** in downtown Fort Collins. The last weekend in June is the time to tap the kegs of over 40 brewers. Tickets include t-shirt, mug and entry.

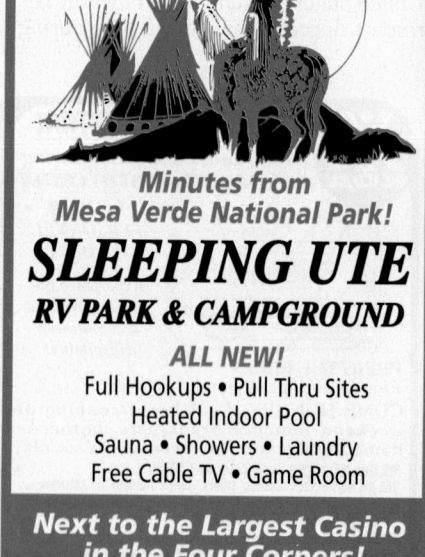

Want to see a city in celebration? Get to Colorado Springs for **Springspree** on the last weekend in June and enjoy the parade of beds and bed race, symphony concert in the park, exciting performances, many demonstrations, beautiful fine arts & crafts festival, fantastic food court, numerous children's activities and extensive entertainment; all in Monument Valley Park. Cruise the sidewalk sales at the downtown merchants for great values and relax in the Beer Garden. The complete event is managed by volunteers and there is no admission fee.

Rendezvous with country stars under the western sky this summer at **Colorado Country Jam USA** in Grand Junction. There will be four days of great music, food, vendors and good times. Billed as the premier outdoor country music, camping and food festival, **Jam USA** takes place the last weekend in June. Camping area opens Wednesday, **Jam USA** starts Thursday.

Step back in time 400 years for the 20th annual **Renaissance Festival** in Larkspur. There's music, mirth and merriment! Open eight weekends from mid June until the end of July, you'll experience combat jousting, an artisan's marketplace, strolling minstrels, and continuous entertainment, food and drink.

**Bach, Beethoven and Breckenridge**, the National Repertory Orchestra series includes classical concerts, workshops and a camp program the month of July.

The acclaimed **Colorado Dance Festival** presents the third year of a three-year exploration of "Dances of the Spirit," an investigation of dance and the arts, spirituality and environment from five world views. In addition to performances there are classes, talks, lectures, demonstrations, workshops and other presentations. **Colorado Dance Festival** is co-sponsored by the University of Colorado/Boulder, Department of Theatre and Dance and runs the month of July.

Rest up over the Fourth of July weekend so you can spend the next weekend in Breckenridge at **Genuine Jazz in July.** Friday and Saturday are cool jammin' nights and Saturday and Sunday are hot jazzin' days. There'll be free jazz on Maggie Pond in the Village at Breckenridge.

The **Crested Butte Wildflower Festival** celebrates designation as the Wildflower Capital of Colorado in 1989 and, of course, the annual bloom of incredible natural wildflowers. The week-long festival events include: daily hiking, walking and mountain biking tours for flower identification as well as local garden and wetlands tours. Workshops, botanical art show and antique botanical print exhibit and sale are part of the fun. Set aside the second week in July for this festival high in the central Rockies.

Re-live the excitement of the Old West for five days — head to Gunnison for the 96th annual **Cattleman's Days** starting mid-July. In addition to the PRCA Rodeo (the oldest running rodeo in Colorado), the folks of Gunnison will be putting on a race meet, 4-H stock show, carnival, parade, dance and bar-b-que. At first the rodeo was held at the intersection of Main Street and Tomichi Avenue, then moved to the property of the Colorado State Normal School; in time the County rodeo grounds came into being and this is the present location.

Concerts, dances, and world class performers highlight the **Fifth Annual Rocky Mountain Ragtime Festival** coming to Boulder in late July. The festival will feature at least fifteen musical events plus ragtime dancing every day including the popular Sunday afternoon tea dance. To encourage young people to learn about ragtime, a special ragtime competition is open to students ages 12-18.

Celebrate a world-renowned product of Colorado's western slope — the perfect peach at the Palisade Peach Festival in Grand Junction. Festivities include a parade, food and crafts.



The first **Colorado State Fair and Exposition** was held in 1872 in Pueblo, making it one of the oldest of the western fairs in the nation. Set aside the last week of August and the first week of September to attend. Enjoy food, livestock, 4-H exhibits, the midway, 9 PRCA rodeos, commercial exhibits, horse shows, live entertainment, children's zoo, fine arts, Kid's Korner, the Coor's Grandstand, racing pigs, cow milking, monster trucks and other educational and fun activities. The **Colorado State Fair and Exposition** is the 11th largest fair/festival in the United States. Be a part of it!

**Fall:**

Early September in Estes Park is set aside for the annual **Scottish-Irish Festival.** Four days of Celtic competitions, concerts, demonstrations and a parade, all celebrating the Celtic tradition.

Chaffee County, in the "Heart of the Rockies," offers two weeks of home-grown fun in mid-September — the **Snowbird Festival**. Local citizens and special groups in the 3 towns of Salida, Buena Vista and Poncha Springs have joined the Chaffee County Visitors Bureau to schedule daily activities to entertain and engage visitors including an art and antique auction, US Air Force Academy Country Western Band concert, hang gliding demonstration, fish hatchery tours, square dancing, farm machinery demonstrations, historical tours, senior olympics swim meet, merchant sidewalk sales and much, much more.

Some like it hot! If you're one, get to Pueblo the third weekend in September for the **Chile & Frijole Festival**. It takes place in the heart of downtown Pueblo at the actual site of the original trading post, El Pueblo. In addition to a farmer's market and chile roasting, watch barrel making, adobe block making, techniques of adobe construction; experience salsa music, and be treated to displays of Pueblo and regional artists.

The **Annual Fall Arts Festival** takes place in Glenwood Springs in late September. The festival features the works of renowned artists in amateur and professional categories, sponsored by the Glenwood Springs Arts Guild.

Late September is the time to head out to Delta for the **Council Tree Pow-Wow.** There'll be 3 days of dance competition, a drum contest, a Native American art show, outdoor Indian market booths and outdoor traditional tepee encampment and demonstrations. People representing Native American tribes throughout the continent will gather to share the richness and diversity of their heritage and their world. Also located in Delta is the Fort Uncompahgre Living History Museum.

**Coloradofest** at the Royal Gorge Bridge outside of Canon City is steeped in the traditional Bavarian Oktoberfest atmosphere of festivity, singing and dancing. Revelers indulge in authentic German food, beer, Bavarian music and one of the most spectacular views in the world! Taking place the last weekend of September and the first weekend of October, the Royal Gorge Bridge Coloradofest offers genuine German food, several of Colorado's premier German bands and demonstrations of German folk dances. Royal Gorge admission prices are cut in half during the two weekends of Coloradofest. Plan on attending this popular event and viewing one of America's most spectacular attractions while feasting on German delicacies.

What do great food, Boulder brew, Colorado wine, arts & crafts, dancing, farm-fresh produce, carnival rides for the kids and Oom-Pah-Pah bands have in common? They're all part of the sights and sounds of the **Boulder Fall Festival,** a 3-day family event located in the heart of Boulder. The Festival takes place during the first weekend in October, and is Boulder County's premiere autumnal celebration. Fashioned after the traditional German Oktoberfest, the event has grown to include an Oktoberfest beer tent, a full entertainment schedule, 4 blocks of arts & crafts booths, carnival rides, a petting zoo and a dozen food booths.

## *MONTANA FESTIVALS*

**Spring:**

The **Helena Railroad Fair** is in its 16th year, and is now the largest railroad hobby event in Montana and the northern Rockies. It is unique in that you'll see not only scale model and toy train interests represented, but also a substantial railroad antique and collectibles focus. Exhibitors are primarily from the western part of the country, with several Canadian provinces represented. The event is limited to one day, and uses nearly 21,000 square feet of the Civic Center. This year's Fair will be Sunday, April 21 from 9:30 am until 4:00 pm.

**Summer:**

The **Lewis and Clark Festival** will be held Thursday, June 27th through Sunday, June 30th, in Great Falls. Choose between auto tours or float trips; experience buffalo burgers or bar-b-que. Activities for children include building a model canoe



**FREE INFO?** Battlement Mesa, enter #342; The Hideout, enter #747; Havre RV Park, enter #369; Yellowstone Grizzly, enter #764 on Reader Service Card following page 16.

and then racing it on the river, water bucket relay and camp games. Don't miss the special display of hides and furs of the Montana plains animals. College credits are available.

**Little Big Horn Days; A Celebration of Cultural Heritage** in Hardin, features re-enactments of Custer's Last Stand, Pony Express riders, and an 1876 Military Ball. The exciting, fun-filled 4-day celebration of plays, pageants, street fairs, games, and professional rodeo are all in observance of the anniversary of the Battle of the Little Big Horn. Held the last weekend in June.

It began back in the 1970's as a simple birthday party to commemorate the opening of the site to the public, and now spans two days — **Western Heritage Days Celebration** at the Grant-Kohrs Ranch National Historic Site. No entrance fee is charged. Scheduled annually on the second full weekend in July, events include rope-making and wheelwright demonstrations, branding cattle, tours of part of the elegant ranch house and chuckwagon cooking.

**North American Indian Days** is held annually during the month of July in Browning. Located at the Blackfeet Tribal Fairgrounds, adjacent to the Museum of the Plains Indian, it comprises one of the largest gatherings of United States and Canadian tribes in the northwest. The 4-day program includes Indian dancing, games and sports events, an encampment and parades.

In its 10th season, the **Flathead Music Festival** has continually grown to provide the Flathead Valley with the caliber of musicians found in symphonies from around the world. Held the last two weeks of July, the festival offers a scholarship program, master classes and music camp as well as varied concerts. Some recent offerings included jazz, country, Ccassical and Native American.

Mid-August in West Yellowstone is the place for **The Burnt Hole Rendezvous**, an event designed to help educate the public to the life and times of the early explorers of the region. Besides demonstrations of fire starting with flint and steel or bow and drill, Native American beadwork and beaver trapping, there's a 2-day Blackpowder Shoot Aggregate Competition. Sample food from the era as well as joining in the ladies frying pan throw or tall tale competition. Be sure to visit Trader's Row.

From eloquent to raucous, cowboy poets capture a part of America we all love. And they offer something for everyone. The 11th annual **Montana Cowboy Poetry Gathering** will be held in Lewiston in mid-August. In addition to poetry, past years have offered country music, a Western arts & crafts show and a raffle for unique cowboy gear.

Held the 1st Thursday after Labor Day, **The Taste of Whitefish** features gourmet cuisine from thirteen of Whitefish's finest restaurants. This open air event is held in a local park next to the historic chalet Great Northern Depot and includes live entertainment. No particular food theme is followed, so the variety is magnificent, ranging from barbecued ribs to decadent deserts! Enjoy the alpine setting, the cascading fountain and an auction of local artisans' work.



## *NEBRASKA FESTIVALS*

**Summer:**

The **Cottonwood Prairie Festival** is an annual fine arts event. 1996 will mark the 7th year of the festival which is held the first full extended weekend in June. The Festival hosts a wide variety of activities including the show and sale of fine arts and sculpture, quality antiques, crafts, continuous live entertainment, fur traders and children's activities. A highlight of the Festival is Saturday night's amphitheater concert featuring nationally recognized entertainment. Fun and excitement are waiting for you and your family at Brickyard Park in Hastings.

Head out to North Platte for **NEBRASKAland Days** June 17 through the 24th, for old-fashioned family fun. In addition to four nights of great PRCA rodeo, check out parades, good western food, craft fairs and Country Western stars. Adjacent attractions include Buffalo Bill's Scouts Rest Ranch and the Lincoln County Historical Museum. The Buffalo Bill Award is to honor someone who portrays good family/Western entertainment; previous recipients have included Louis L'Amour, Sam Elliot, Charleton Heston and Henry Fonda — aren't you curious about this year's winner?

## *NORTH DAKOTA FESTIVALS*

**Summer:**

An annual festival entitled **Dinosaur Days** has been created in conjunction with the new Dakota Dinosaur Museum in Dickinson. The feature attraction is the only known Dinosaur Hollering Contest in the world. Other activities include a hot air balloon rally, a Triceratops Tromp, outdoor musical entertainment, a dinosaur egg hunt and a dinosaur bone treasure hunt. The festival takes place over Father's Day weekend.

Bonanzaville and its village of museums comes alive by hosting the annual **Pioneer Days**, begun in 1969 in the rural community of Davenport. 1996 will host the 27th annual **Pioneer Days**, August 17 & 18. There are over 100 demonstrations including butter making, feather stripping, wool spinning, hand made ice creams and candle making.

## *SOUTH DAKOTA FESTIVALS*

**Summer:**

The **Fort Sisseton Historical Festival**, first held in 1977, continues to provide quality programming which seeks to involve visitors in tangible firsthand experiences regarding lifestyles, cultures, crafts and hardships which may have occurred during the Fort's military occupation between 1864-1889. Always held the first full weekend in June, the Festival offers family-oriented activities that are one-hour in length and are offered two to four times daily. All of the programs presented relate to the arts and humanities.

Do not miss the **Days of '76** in Deadwood! Experience a three mile long parade which depicts the history of Deadwood, 3 PRCA rodeos, and the Old West Fest. Watch the West come alive as you enjoy this 73 year old event.

The **Corn Palace Festival** is held each September in Mitchell, in honor of the agricultural harvest. The Corn Palace is decorated annually with over 3000 bushels of corn and colored grain. The festival begins the Friday following Labor Day and runs for 10 days. Entertainment includes rock, country, gospel, big band, and polka music.

**Fall:**

The **Annual Buffalo Roundup** will take place in early October at Custer State Park in Custer. Monday, September 30 is the actual roundup; branding, sorting and vaccinating continue October 1 and 2. The roundup began as a way to regulate the number of buffalo on the range, but the herd has grown to exceed the carrying capacity so the sale was begun as a way to reduce the herd size and generate income to help maintain and operate the park. The auction is held the third Saturday in November. In 1994 an Arts Festival was established to coincide with the roundup.

## *UTAH FESTIVALS*

During 1996, thousands of activities are planned throughout the state. From metropolitan galas to small-town festivals, every county in Utah has planned their own celebrations. To guide Utah visitors through the state, a Centennial passport will be available for free. Visitors and residents can have the passport stamped at designated locations in each county.

**Special Centennial events** include: January 2 — Grand Centennial Ball, January 4 — Re-enactment of Utah's statehood inaugural ceremony, Salt Lake Main Street historic re-enactment; June — Month-long wagon train trek from north to south; December — Utah provides nation's capitol with the official holiday tree.

**Summer:**

Before the stars come out and the curtain rises, visitors coming to see **UTAH!** will be treated to taste of the old west, including western style Dutch Oven cooking and pre-show Indian and pioneer dance and song. This spectacular outdoor musical runs June through September in St. George.

## *WYOMING FESTIVALS*

**Spring:**

Jackson Hole's **Old West Days** includes parades, special rodeo, mule show, street dancers, amateur western swing contest, beard-growing contests, stagecoach rides, Indian dancers and a cowboy poetry gathering, plus an authentic Mountainman Rendezvous. Takes place in late May.

**Summer:**

The Chugwater **Chili Cook-Off,** the largest single-day event in Wyoming, will be held at the Diamond Guest Ranch in mid-June. This family affair is the annual Wyoming State Championship Chili Cookoff. In addition to day-long entertainment, samples of chili are available to all. End the day with an evening dance.

For the 15th year, the Buffalo Bill Historical Center in Cody presents its **Plains Indian Powwow** in late June. For Indian people, the powwow provides an opportunity to come together in a celebration of their cultures, histories and unique traditions. Visitors are invited to share in these traditions as they learn more about Plains Indian people and their lives and heritages. After 2 days of dancing, winners are announced on Sunday evening.

Cody's major event each year is a real old-fashioned Fourth of July — the **Cody Stampede**. Featuring 4 action-packed rodeos, 3 colorful parades down main street, western entertainment, street dance and art shows culminating in a grand fireworks display. Cody is also the home of the Buffalo Bill Historical Center.

America's premier Western family celebration takes place in Cheyenne each year during the last full week of July. **Cheyenne Frontier Days** is a 10-day wingding of street dances, parades, carnival rides, top-name entertainers, free pancake breakfasts, cowboys, Indians and horses. It's topped off by the rodeo known among the cowboys as the "Daddy of 'em All." It's one-of-a-kind…the real thing, packed with action and entertainment and all the other trappings that made the West a legend!

**Fall:**

Mid October in Riverton features a **Cowboy Poets Round-Up** for 2 days at Central Wyoming College. Events are free and open to anyone to share western music and poetry. Western art, tack and accessories are available.

The last stop for the pros who want to increase earnings and get a chance to make the National Finals is the **PRCA Season Finale Rodeo** in Casper. A fine, indoor arena provides comfortable seating for fans; necessary in Wyoming in late October.

# DISCOVER THE FESTIVALS of

# The Far West

## ALASKA FESTIVALS

**Spring:**

Early March is the time for the 23rd annual **Alaska Folk Festival** held in Juneau. It's Alaska's largest gathering of musicians, and music lovers from all over North America are invited to attend this free event, or if you have musical talents, consider signing up as a performer. The performances are held all over town including at Centennial Hall.

**Summer:**

**The Midnight Sun Festival** in Nome is a celebration of the summer solstice, which is when the city experiences the midnight sun. A variety of activities are scheduled around June 21st, the longest day of the year, with more than 22 hours of direct sunlight. The Nome Chamber of Commerce coordinates most of the events, although many organizations and individuals are involved in the festivities. In past years, some of the activities have included a street dance, blanket toss, a barbecued chicken dinner, Eskimo dances, Monte Carlo Night, a teen party, and a parade along Front Street. The Bank Hold-Up and Jail are annual events held during the festival. A portable jail is brought to Front Street to house any person caught without a "Midnight Sun Festival" button. To be released from jail the person must pay for a button or be bailed out by a sympathetic by-stander.



Late July through early August is the time for the **Fairbanks Summer Arts Festival.** Begun in 1980 as a one-week jazz festival, the event has grown into various performances of jazz, ice-skating theater, dance theater, classical music and visual arts. Today, the celebration lasts two full weeks and also includes a unique opportunity for summer studies in the arts.

Come to Juneau in late June and you'll be treated to **Gold Rush Days,** a celebration of Juneau's golden past via a fun, family-oriented weekend. There are mining and logging events and lots of other activities at the festival site in Riverside Park.

## ARIZONA FESTIVALS

**Spring:**

The **Midnight at the Oasis Festival** will hold its fourth annual event in Yuma March 8th through 10th. Stroll down memory lane to an incredible nostalgic festival that features the cars and music of the 1950s and 1960s. Guests enjoy the car show, "Show & Shine", a rock n' roll concert and dance, arts & crafts and other activities.

**Spring training** is a spectator sport in Mesa that begins each March. Visitors can watch major league baseball teams warm up for their summer season. Catch the Chicago Cubs at Ho Ho Kam Stadium. Other teams include the California Angels, the Milwaukee Brewers, Oakland Athletics, San Diego Padres, San Francisco Giants and the Seattle Mariners.

April 2nd through the 6th brings the **Arizona Temple Easter Pageant** to Mesa. The nightly pageant begins one week before Easter, and is considered the largest annual Easter pageant in the world, with a cast of 300, and seats for 10,000 spectators.

*Arizona Festivals continued on page 108*

*Arizona Festivals continued from pg. 106*

The 25th annual **Arizona State Championship Chili Cookoff** will be held in Bullhead City's Riverview Park on April 27th. Here, semi-finalists compete after winning district and regional contests, and the top winner goes on to the world championship competition in Reno, Nevada. In addition to free samples of the great-tasting chili, there's Little Miss Chili Pepper and Little Mr. Hot Sauce costume contests, live country music entertainment, beverages and booths selling burgers, beef on a stick, arts and crafts, and more.

The last weekend in April brings the annual **Route 66 Fun Run**, in which participants from across the world race along the longest remaining continuous stretch of historic Route 66 from Seligman to Topock. Spectators and runners alike enjoy the classic and vintage automobiles, and visiting with celebrities who became famous during the heydey of Route 66 including Charlie Ryan (Mr. Hot Rod Lincoln), Bobby Troup and others.

**Summer:**

In Whiteriver, the White Mountain Apache Tribe is holding its 70th annual **White Mountain Apache Fair & Rodeo** from late August through early September. Saturday's events include a sunrise dance ceremony, the All-Indian Rodeo, a softball tournament, horseshoe and frybread contests, a carnival, various entertainment acts, a fireworks display and a country-western dance. On Sunday, there will be the softball tournament championship, the carnival, the All-Indian Rodeo, a gospel jam session, a tiny-tot fashion show and a country-western dance. On Monday, there's a 16-mile team relay race, the finals of the rodeo and the last day of the carnival.

Flaggstaff's 14th annual **Festival in the Pines** will be held August 2nd through the 4th at Ft. Tuthill, Coconino County Fairgrounds. Recognized as one of Arizona's top events, this huge outdoor arts and craft show and sale attracts artisans from throughout the United States. There are more than 250 displays from some of the finest artists and crafts people in the west. The juried arts and craft show features everything from massive bronze sculptures to delicate dried floral arrangements. Festival goers will find dozens of tantalizing food selections, children's activities and three stages providing non-stop entertainment all presented in the cool climate of the Northern Arizona pines.

**Fall:**

The **IJSBA World Final Boat Races** are held in front of the Nautical Inn in Lake

*Arizona Festivals continued on pg. 110*

**FREE INFO?** Earnhardt RV, enter #112 on Reader Service Card following page 16.

*Arizona Festivals continued from pg. 108*

Havasu City. Top-ranked competitors vie for titles and prize money in world-class high speed races in several areas of competition. Sanctioned by the International Jet Sport Boating Association, this is one of the richest boating events in the world with the highest purse offered in the sport. Riders compete in slalom, closed course and freestyle events. Competitors in distance jumping will vie for their own World Champion titles. The event draws thousands of spectators and competitors for five exciting days of racing, and has grown into a very popular event. It is recommended that accommodations be reserved 3 to 6 months prior to the event.

The 18th annual **Apache "Jii"** (Apache word for day) celebration will be held October 26th and 27th, honoring Globe-Miami's San Carlos' Apache neighbors. This colorful Native American event transforms Globe's historic downtown into a street fair lined with booths offering authentic Indian jewelry, baskets, clothing, dolls, pottery and works of art from various southwestern tribes. Foods offered include traditional fry bread, Indian tacos and Apache acorn syrup. The streets come alive during the festival with colorfully-costumed dancers, singers, and storytellers, plus a Native American fashion show. The famous Apache Crown Dancers will be performing throughout the day. Don't be surprised if you become especially happy after watching their performance — a legend says that the Crown Dancers were originally spirit dancers who came down from the mountain into the Apache Villages to drive away evil spirits.

Fall brings two exciting events to Mesa. The 14th annual **Native American Pow Wow** is held in mid-October. Visitors will enjoy more than 300 Native American dancers from throughout the nation as they compete in the colorful event. There are also arts, crafts and plenty of delicious food. Early November brings the 12th annual **Fine Folk Festival.** Its a large arts and crafts fair with a carnival, 3 stages providing local entertainment and childrens events. Admission and parking are both free.

The last weekend in September brings the **Kingman Army Airfield Reunion,** which reunites many of the more than 30,000 pilots and gunners who trained at the Kingman Army Airfield in 1942. The annual reunion celebrates this chapter in our nation's past with vintage Warbirds on display, airshows, military displays, classic and antique car cruise, walking tours, dinners, dancing, and more.

Over 150 balloons take part in one of the most colorful, photographed events in the Valley of the Sun — the **Thunderbird Balloon Classic & Airshow** in Glendale. Always held the 1st weekend in November, each day of the event brings an air show, a balloon glow and street dance. You won't go hungry amid the more than 30 food booths providing plain ol' American hot dogs and hamburgers as well as more exotic ethnic foods such as Japanese, Thai, Chinese, Italian and Mexican. Over 85 arts and crafts booths provide plenty of shopping.

Fans of the late character actor, Andy Devine, flock to the Kingman area for the annual **Andy Devine Days**, during which Kingman honors its famous native son. There are Andy Awards for outstanding volunteer community service, softball and golf tournaments, a PRCA rodeo, parade, barbecue, and a gem and mineral show.

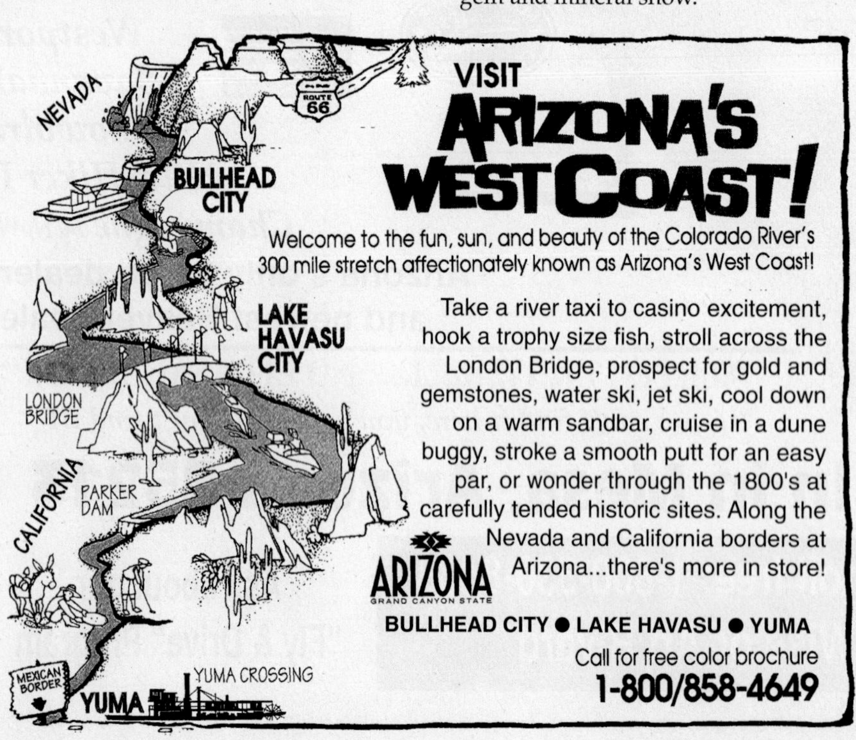


**Winter:**

The streets of downtown Tempe will be filled with over 550 artists and crafts people December 6th, 7th and 8th for the 28th annual **Old Town Tempe Fall Festival of the Arts**. As one of the largest shows of its kind in the southwest, it's a highly competitive, juried show with award winning artists from throughout the nation. Artists exhibit an incredible variety of items including watercolor paintings, metal sculptures, pottery, fine jewelry, dried floral arrangements and wood carvings. All items are hand crafted with the artist presenting his or her works. The festival also includes a great selection of activities and booths for the non-shoppers in your group. There are four stages with non-stop entertainment, more than 60 food booths, carnival rides, and hands-on activities for children.

1988 marked the first year of Lake Havasu City's annual **Dixieland Jazz Festival** held on January 12th through the 14th. The event kicks off the first festival of the year, and features 9 bands with the sweet sounds of Dixieland jazz. Over 30 hours of jazz in 4 locations with 3 large dance floors for festival goers who just can't sit! Highlights of the weekend include a parade, music aboard the *DixieBelle* riverboat, and a Sunday morning gospel concert.

The 30th annual **Quartzsite Pow Wow Gem & Mineral Show** will begin Wednesday, February 7th (always the first Wednesday in February) and run through Sunday, February 11th. The show features over 300 vendors in more than 500 selling spaces with rough as well as polished rocks and gems, jewelry, lapidary equipment and related items from all over the world. The Roadrunner Gem & Mineral Club offers daily guided field trips to nearby digging areas. Begun in 1967 as a "tailgate" show by 20 "rockhounds" and attended by about 1,000 visitors, today the show draws between a quarter million to 1 million visitors who peruse the show's fine gems and jewelry as well as colorful rocks, minerals, fossils and stones.

February brings the Annual **Snowbird Jamboree** to Lake Havasu City's Community Center, and this year the event celebrates its 11th anniversary, beginning on President's Day. There's a nice lineup of events including entertainment and a big band concert. Sunday, the Chili Society holds their annual Chili Cookoff at Windsor Beach State Park, and Sunday evening there is a free, one-hour display of fireworks. Both this event and the Jazz Festival offer ample bus parking.

January 9th through the 11th in Tucson marks the evenings of the **Triple C Chuckwagon Suppers annual Chuckwagon Jamboree.** Guests will let their "diets" go for awhile, and indulge in some old fashioned western food: barbecue beef or chicken, biscuits with honey and butter, cowboy beans, and much more. Entertainment is provided by eight western entertainment groups who put on a "three-night show" for the guests.

Bullhead City, Arizona plays host to its annual **Turquoise Circuit Finals Rodeo** January 12th through the 14th. Located at the corner of Hwy 95 and Marina Blvd., the rodeo is a Professional Cowboys Association sanctioned event and features calf roping, bareback bronc riding, bull riding, team riding and other competitions. Visitors also enjoy the variety of food and arts & crafts displays as well as a rodeo dance.

**Super Bowl XXX** will be held at Arizona State University's Sun Devil Stadium in Tempe on January 28th. If you don't already have your tickets, you probably won't get to attend. The NFL sells tickets only by a random drawing in which names are selected on June 1st of the preceding year. Not to worry! If you're not one of the lucky ones to attend the game, the NFL has an exciting alternative: the NFL Experience, a 20-acre pro-football theme park with 50 interactive displays. For the price of admission, fans *can* experience the Super Bowl. You can test your skills against Joe Montana, run a 60-yard dash against Emmitt Smith, or take the mike from Al Michaels to do your own play-by-play. The NFL experience is scheduled for January 20th & 21st and January 24th to 28th, and will be located north of Sun Devil Stadium along the new Rio Salado development.

The **Phoenix Open golf tournament** held in Scottsdale during late January, is billed as Arizona's largest spectator event. This tournament attracts the PGA Tour's finest golfers to one of the oldest (over 50 year) and most revered golf tournaments. Sponsored by the Thunderbirds, the Special Events Committee of the Phoenix Metropolitan Chamber of Commerce, the tournament is played at thr Tournament Players Club of Scottsdale, one of the country's most picturesque golf courses. There is ample bus parking and a shuttle service is available.

Other winter activities in Scottsdale include the **Scottsdale All-Arabian Horse Show** held in February. The show brings the beauties of the equine world to the sunshine of Arizona in February. Quarter horses take the center stage in the **Sun Country Quarter Horse Show** held toward the end of January. These beautiful western horses prove once again they have the abilities of the finest working horses in the country. While in the Scottsdale area, visit **WestWorld of Scottsdale**, a 360-acre park with more than 400 RV spaces on site. The emphasis is on outdoor activities, major special events and equestrian shows. From junction of I-17 & Bell Road E (exit 212), go 11 miles east on Bell Road, then 3/4 mile N on Pima Road.

Flaggstaff's **Winterfest** is the city of Flaggstaff's largest winter event, scheduled annually in February to celebrate the town's bright winter season of sunshine and snow. The 10th annual event will be held January 26th through February 4th to coincide with Super Bowl celebrations. There are more than 100 individual events and recreational opportunities, entertainment and education, including championship sled-dog races, Alpine and Nordic ski events, a children's performing arts festival, wine tastings and auction, snowshoe events, a national headline band, a film festival, and much more.

Wickenburg celebrates its annual **Gold Rush Days** the 2nd full weekend each February, an annual event for over 48 years. February 9th through 11th, for three action-filled days, thousands of visitors and participants enjoy the multitude of activities that celebrate the rich western heritage of the town. Festivities begin with a shootout on Frontier Street. Then, one of Arizona's largest parades begins, and later cowboys from all over the country gather to compete in the Senior Pro Rodeo. In the area around the Wickenburg Community Center the entire family will enjoy the carnival, food booths, a gem and mineral show and over 250 arts and crafts booths. Contests include a gold panning contest and a mucking and drilling contest - just like the miners used to do. Music, dancing, an old-fashioned melodrama, horses, floats and food — all are part of Wickenburg's action packed weekend.

**Yuma Crossing Day** is held the last Saturday of February each year, and is a wonderful way to learn about the history and culture of the area. Located in the heart of the downtown historic district of Yuma, visitors will find a variety of activities highlighting life from the 1500s until the 1950s. There are historic re-enactments, gunfights, train rides, historic site tours, dancing entertainment, craft demonstrations, and southwestern music.

The western Arizona desert becomes the center of the RV universe February 3rd through 11th when the 13th **Annual Quartzsite Sports, Vacation and RV Show** opens in Quartzsite on its new, larger 23-acre site across the interstate and located next to the Tyson Wells Sell-A-Rama on Hwy 95. The additional space will provide show goers more high-caliber exhibits, and the addition of service bays for the installation of many of the products sold at the show, adding a dimension to the show making it unique and clearly service-oriented. Everything from awnings, to jacks, tow bars and more can be installed right on site. Visitors also enjoy daily entertainment and informative seminars on everything from travel destinations to how everything works in an RV.

It's time to polish the King's crown and tune up the jester's bells for the annual **Arizona Renaissance Festival** held on weekends in Apache Junction February 3rd and 4th *through* March 23rd and 24th. Set against the magnificent backdrop of the Superstition Mountains, the faire is an authentic re-creation of a 16th Century European market faire comprised of a mixture of food, arts, theater, concerts, strolling musicians, comedy, storytelling, dance, crafts, equestrian events, and a three-times daily jousting event. An elaborate Artisan Market is the core of the 25-acre theatrical village site, and the crafters are joined by purveyors of food and drink, living history exhibits and seven stages offering continuous entertainment. Open weekends from 10:00 a.m. to 5:30 p.m. rain or shine.

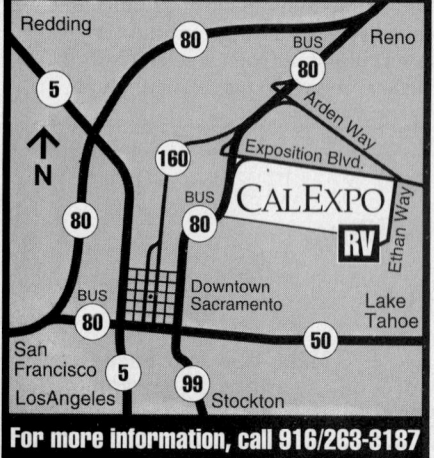

## *CALIFORNIA FESTIVALS*

**Spring:**

For over 72 years, the **Ramona Pageant** has been presented in the beautiful Ramona Bowl by the people of Hemet and San Jacinto, California. With an entire mountain as a stage, a cast of over 350 present a romantic story of early California in this unique, outdoor setting.

**Carnaval San Francisco** is a massive 2-day festival and parade that takes place Memorial Day weekend, May 25th through 26th, in San Francisco's Mission District. Attendance in its first year, 1979, was 2,000, and has grown steadily each year to its 1995 level of 600,000 plus. The event includes a spectacular parade which snakes its way through the Mission District led by the sumptuous floats of the Carnaval King and Queen. Dozens of contingents of dancers and musicians bedecked with feathered and sparkling costumes follow, along with extravagant floats and comparsas (Central and Latin American groups), pulsating Caribbean steel bands, Native American warrior dancers, lively Mariachi and Dixieland bands.

The seventh oldest community in California, San Juan Capistrano, is a city known for its history and tradition, but it's probably best known for an annual event which has occurred since the beginning of time — the return of the swallows, first recorded by missionaries in the late 1700s. The swallows do return to Southern California faithfully each spring from their winter home in South America, but the date of their return may vary according to the weather. Nevertheless, **Swallow's Day Activities** are celebrated on the Feast of St. Joseph each year at Mission San Juan Capistrano. Visitors will find food and refreshments, outdoor exhibits giving information about the swallows, and performances by singers, dancers and local choral groups.



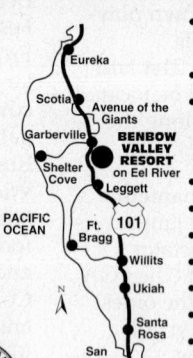

 **FREE INFO?** Cal Expo RV Park, enter #728; Benbow Valley RV Resort &Golf, enter #352 on Reader Service Card following page 16.

**Summer:**

Travel to Gilroy, California in late July and you'll know it's garlic harvest time by the aroma! Gilroy, known as the "garlic capital of the world," celebrates this pungent, onion-like plant with its annual **Gilroy Garlic Festival.** Since the 1920s, Garlic has been big business in Gilroy, and since 1972, the town has been celebrating its bounty with a festival. Visitors will find ample parking at the festival site along Uvas Creek, and there is shuttle service if you park "way out" in the lot. Stroll through Gourmet Alley, the festival's food showcase, and you'll be treated to delicious garlic-flavored dishes such as the show favorite, a pepper steak sandwich. Or try the large, grilled mushrooms served stuffed with breadcrumbs, cheese, sausage and garlic. There's a garlic recipe cook-off complete with "secret recipes" and notable judges, an arts and crafts show, musical entertainment, and much more. . . including, for the really daring . . . garlic ice cream!

The San Diego Museum of Man hosts its 13th annual **Indian Fair** June 15th and 16th. American Indians from Hopi, Sioux, Zuni, Navajo, Luiseno and many other tribes journey each year to this authentic, educational event for the whole family. Renowned American Indian artists are invited to sell their top quality works of art and jewelry at the "Indian Market," and traditional dancing is presented by various tribes in full costume. American Indian foods such as fry bread and parched corn are prepared and sold. Children can create their own art at the Crafts Corner.

The **Redwood Acres Fair and Rodeo** is held June 26th through 30th at Redwood Acres Fairgrounds in Eureka. The 15th annual event will include concerts, stock car races, live musical entertainment, tractor pulls and a rodeo. Visitors enjoy the commercial exhibits, art and photography displays, livestock exhibits, and 20 craft booths displaying dolls, antiques, needlecraft and more.

Shine those boots, polish that belt buckle and mosey over to the **Orange County Fair**, where bucking broncos, bull riding, wild cow milking and other western-style events are back and better than ever during four days of rodeo performances. The fair itself is held over a 17-day period early July through late July and includes free entertainment, exhibits and attractions daily throughout the run. Fairgoers at recent fairs have enjoyed the motorcycle speedway racing, the Southern California Firefighter Combat Challenge, and traditional competitions and attractions including a gem and mineral show, a flower and garden show, photography, fine arts, hobbies and crafts, aquariums, a wine pavilion, and more.

Concerts at the fair have been performed by Stephen Stills, Paul Revere & the Raiders, Kool & The Gang, and The Association. Livestock exhibits include pot bellied pigs, dairy goats, cattle, sheep, pygmy goats, a maternity barn, and a junior livestock auction.

Ferndale's Humboldt County Fairgrounds is the site of the 46th annual **Mid-Summer Scandinavian Festival** the third weekend in June. Their theme, "Take a Liking to a Viking!" is meant to offer a light-hearted look at this interesting culture. Celebrate the summer solstice with traditional Scandinavian music, authentic foods, dances, a flag ceremony and a Grand March of costumes. Festivities take place on Main Street on Saturday, and in Belotti Hall at the fairgrounds on Sunday.

This year marks the 14th season of **Shakespeare on the Lake** at Benbow Valley RV Resort & Golf Course, in Garberville, only 197 miles north of San Francisco. The week long festival features performances by a professional touring company on an outdoor stage overlooking Benbow Lake — all in the heart of Northern California's Giant Redwood Empire. Recent performances of the festival have included such favorites as *Romeo and Juliet, The Imaginary Invalid,* and *The Taming of The Shrew.* Held during the last week in July to take advantage of the warm days and cool nights, the festival site is situated in a tranquil setting under an ancient redwood tree. Adjacent to the lake is the award winning Benbow Valley RV Resort and Golf Course which features 112 full hookup RV sites and a par 35 9-hole golf course. Also on site is Benbow Inn, a beautifully restored English Tudor Historical Landmark mansion, and visitors are encouraged to make plans for a romantic dinner in the dining room.

Sonoma County's 8th annual **Hot Air Balloon Classic** is held in early July at the Airport Business Center at Shiloh Road and Hwy 101. Visitors will find more than 50 balloons rising above the vineyards, majestic oaks and rolling hills of Sonoma County each of the two mornings of the festival. Other festivities include a pancake breakfast, entertainment, Champagne and wine tastings, and more than 50 booths offering a variety of crafts, games, souvenirs and food products from the area.

Attend southern California's premier outdoor art show, the **Laguna Festival of Artrs and Pageant of the Masters**, held July 10th through August 31. You'll find works from 150 of the area's most accomplished artists, with handcrafted furniture, sculpture, drawings, ceramics, jewelry and much more on display and for sale. After sunset each evening, the festival presents **Pageant of the Masters**, two hours of art re-creations with real people posing to look exactly like their counterparts in the original pieces. Adding to the festivities are art workshops, art tours, musical entertainment, and more. Nearby Newport Dunes Resort, located in Newport Beach, provides a great place to stay while attending the festival. RVers will find a resort that has been described as "The Ritz of RV Parks," with a 10-acre beach, a 7-lane boat launch, and lots of activities for the entire family.

**Fall:**

San Dimas' 29th annual **Western Days** is held in mid-September. The celebration opens with an old fashioned family carnival providing a wide variety of fun including rides, games and entertainment for the whole family. The Western Days Street Faire opens Saturday morning and offers a variety of food, beverages and crafts which are exclusively hand-made, not mass produced. Saturday morning is also time for the parade which includes antique, classic, custom and novelty vehicles; equestrian units and civic youth groups. Continuous entertainment is provided on two stages on Bonita Avenue and varies from year to year. Last year visitors enjoyed the Honky Tonk Wranglers, the Expressions Dance Center Dancers and a fiddling and banjo contest. The city of San Dimas is located approximately 30 miles east of Los Angeles at the base of the San Gabriel Mountains. Though it's close to a big city, the town has adopted a western theme that includes real wooden sidewalks in the downtown area and an integrated network of equestrian trails that keep the western spirit alive year-round.

Plan to attend the world-famous **Monterey Jazz Festival** September 20th through 22nd. The festival began as a dream for founder Jimmy Lyons for a "sylvan setting with the best jazz people in the whole world playing on the same stage, having a whole weekend of jazz." That dream became a reality in 1958 in

*California Festivals continued on page 116*

*California Festivals continued from pg. 114*

Monterey, California when 67 local business people donated $100 each to fund the first ever Monterey Jazz Festival. For that first festival, Lyons brought in entertainers like Dizzy Gillespie, Louis Armstrong, Gerry Mulligan, Ernestine Anderson, Harry James and Billie Holiday, to name just a few. Plan on attending for a weekend filled with entertainment by top name artists, specially commissioned works, photos, jazz workshops, and all the fun, food and festivities of the world's oldest jazz festival.

The **Los Angeles County Fair,** the largest county fair in the United States, is referred to as "America's Fair." Plan to be in the Pomona area beginning early September through early October, and set aside a day or more to visit the fairgrounds which are located approximately 30 miles east of downtown Los Angeles and 10 miles west of Ontario International Airport. The Fairplex grounds cover 487 acres and include a major horse racing facility with grandstand, 12 acres of paved or turf carnival grounds and approximately 200 acres paved for parking 40,000 vehicles. The celebration includes grandstand entertainment, a carnival, horse shows, horse racing, a monorail, professional stage and grounds entertainment, contests, pig races, and much more. The exhibits include fine arts, flowers and gardening, home arts, gems & minerals, dairy products, Wines of the Americas, miniature trains, and livestock of every breed and type.

**Winter:**

**Christmas on the Prado** is a traditional Swedish Christmas presented by the Swedish Women's Educational Association in cooperation with the San Diego Museum of Man. The 18th annual celebration will be held December 6th & 7th serving Swedish meatballs, open-faced sandwiches, baked good, spiced Christmas wine and more. Crafts are sold at the "Christmas mart." A candlelight Santa Lucia procession, folk dancing and a folk costume parade are highlights, and admission is free. Proceeds from this event benefit the Museum's exhibits and educational programs.

"Kids' Laughter & Dreams" is the theme for the 107th **Rose Parade** held in Pasadena on January 1st. The world-famous parade will spotlight thematically designed floral floats, high-stepping equestrian units and spirited marching bands. Following the Rose Parade, the **82nd Rose Bowl Game** will showcase the championship football teams of the Pacific-10 and Big Ten Conferences. The first parade and games were held in 1890 when members of the Valley Hunt Club voted to stage a parade of flower-decorated horse and buggies and an afternoon of public games on the "town lot." This first Tournament was attended by more than 2,000 people. Today, approximately one million spectators view the Rose Parade in person, and it's viewed on television by more than 100 million people in over 90 countries including such far away places as Spain, Zambia, Saudi Arabia and Hong Kong.

## IDAHO FESTIVALS

**Summer:**

On June 27th through the 30th, the **Boise River Festival** will celebrate its 6th anniversary. Since its inception in 1991, the festival has been recognized as one of the "Top 100 Events in North America" as well as several other recognitions. There is truly something for everyone during these four, fun-filled days; in fact, more than 300 entertainment, sports, food, children's and specialty events are all free to spectators. Some highlights from the '95 festival include the new age music of Entertainment Tonight's John Tesh, Peter Noone of Herman's Hermits fame, Jerry Mathers (Leave it to Beaver), and international jazz pianist Gene Harris. The Idaho Statesman River Giants Parade is the largest giant inflatables (Macy's style) parade west of the Mississippi. The giant balloons are joined by floats, musical units and lots of costumed characters.

A slice of cultural heritage comes to Idaho each year during the last week of July through the first week of August — it's the **Idaho International Folk Dance Festival** in Rexburg. During the nine days of the festival, the town (which has a population of about 15,000) transforms itself into an international folk village complete with a spectacular opening ceremony, a parade, street dance, outdoor band concerts, an international food fair and folk dancing performances. A variety of teams perform authentic dances from their native countries. Some previous year's teams came from as far away as India, Malaysia, New Zealand, Slovakia, Denmark, Sweden, Israel, China and Russia. In addition to the folk dancing, the festival also offers American entertainment via a country western concert and rodeo.

The **Ketchum Wagon Days Celebration** takes place on Labor Day weekend August 30th through September 2nd in Ketchum. The main event of the celebration is The Big Hitch Parade, the largest non-motorized parade in the west, displaying more than 100 museum-quality buggies, carriages, hacks, carts, buckboards and wagons of every variety in existence today. Adding interest to the parade is a lively assortment of authentically costumed people and numerous breeds of horses. Other activities include an antique fair, an antique car show, arts & crafts exhibits, live country and jazz music, street dances, Native American dancing, cowboy poetry and song, and a western art show and gallery walk.

## *NEVADA FESTIVALS*

**Las Vegas** is a festival that is celebrated all year long! No other place on earth can offer the non-stop entertainment, excitement and glitter of this glitzy resort city in the desert. The growth of this desert mecca is phenomenal with huge "theme" casinos and resorts being constructed constantly, and the best part is it's not just for grownups anymore. The entire family will enjoy the excitement of nightly entertainment along the famous **Las Vegas Strip.** Visitors are treated to battling pirate ships, a volcano eruption, the Land of Oz, ancient Egypt, and a domed water park. Sporting events are ever popular here, whether major boxing events or tennis and golf tournaments with world-class players. Musical events abound, also, as the many musicians who make their livings in casino showrooms provide additional performances throughout the city.

RV campers will find plenty of first-rate accommodations. **Circusland RV Park** privides visitors with the convenience of a monorail linking the park with a Circul Midway and Grand Slam Canyon, a domed water park featuring lifelike dinosaurs. Just south of the Strip, via Las Vegas Blvd or I-15 (at the Blue Diamond exit), are two wxciting new RV resorts, either of which offers paved sites with lawn and patio areas, as well as telephone and cable service at every site. **Boomtown** prides itself on its "true Western hospitality and friendliness" and offers a 460-space RV park and Western-themed casino. The new **Oasis Las Vegas RV Resort,** a luxurious Casablanca-themed park features over 700 RV spaces and many amenities including an 18-hole professional putting course. Just 40 miles south on I-15, on the California/Nevada border, is an exciting complex of destination casino/resorts. **Whiskey Pete's** and **Primadonna** were joined a couple of years ago by **Buffalo Bill's**, featuring a 6,500-seat special events arena, a water log ride, and *The Desperado*, the world's tallest and fastests roller coaster. Primadonna offers free carousel and ferris wheel rides, bowling lanes, and a 200-space RV park. Western-style trains and a monorail link all three resorts.

Along Boulder Highway, as you travel from Arizona or Lake Mead, plan on a visit to **Sam's Town.** This popular resort complex offers two RV parks and last year completed a major renovation with 400 new hotel rooms, many of which face the Atrium, consisting of a park-like setting complete with waterfalls, walkways, restaurants, a sports bar and virtual reality games. **The California** offers RVers a convenient "heart of downtown" location for enjoying the Fremont Experience, a huge, climate-controlled canopy that covers Fremont Street, creating a pleasant outdoor atmosphere, as well as light shows and fireworks displays.



Other festivals and events throughout Nevada include:

**Summer:**

Celebrating its 10th anniversary this year, **Hot August Nights** runs from July 31st through August 4th. It's one of Reno's most popular events, and is always held the first week in August. Visitors will enjoy thousands of classic cars on display, and fans of the music of the 1950s and '60s make their pilgrimage to the Reno area for concerts, cruises, show-and-shines and much more. There is continuous '50s-style entertainment throughout the city during this nostalgic celebration.

The **Nevada State Fair** will be held in Reno August 21st through 25th. It's a great place to do some shopping, as there are more than 150 commercial booths offering arts and crafts, jewelry, dinnerware, cookware, and much more. Approximately 25 food booths offer Indian tacos, international sausages, philly cheese steak sandwiches, teriyaki steak on a stick, funnel cakes, Chinese food, and something that no fair should be without — cotton candy. Entertainment varies from year to year, but several long-standing and popular events are the Destruction Derby, the fireworks display, lumberjack show, and pig races. There are also blacksmithing competitions, carnival rides, children's games and strolling entertainment such as clowns and jugglers.

*Nevada Festivals continued on pg. 120*



 

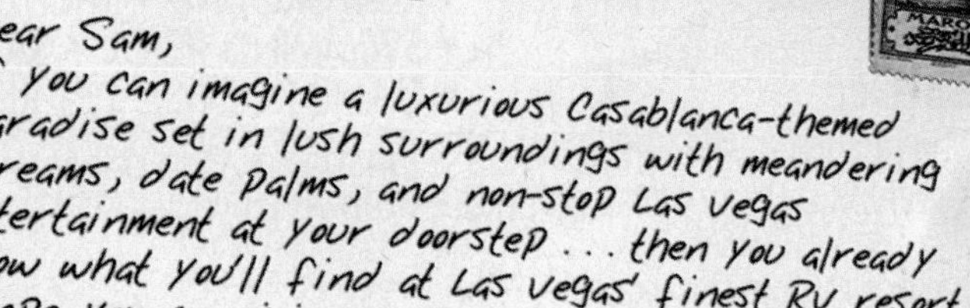
If you can imagine a luxurious Casablanca-themed
Paradise set in lush surroundings with meandering
streams, date palms, and non-stop Las Vegas
entertainment at your doorstep . . . then you already
know what you'll find at Las Vegas' finest RV resort.
I hope you can join us at Oasis Las Vegas.

1•800•566•4707

*Nevada Festivals continued from pg. 118*

**Fall:**

From a small Columbus Day celebration to an extraordinary, week-long festival of food, wine and music, Reno's **Great Italian Festival** has evolved into one of the West's finest events. The festival is highlighted by a grape stomping contest, a European designers fashion show, gourmet Italian buffets, a gelato eating contest and a spaghetti sauce cook-off. While sampling from an array of fine Italian food, festival goers are entertained by singers, dancers, clowns, puppets, stilt walkers, comedians and jugglers. Originated and hosted by the Eldorado Hotel/Casino, the festival is in its 15th year and is an exciting event that all members of the family will enjoy.

The **Las Vegas Jaycees State Fair** is on the calendar September 27th through October 7th, and will mark the 42nd anniversary of the fair. Visitors will find approximately 150 booths in the exhibit hall, with 10 food booths on the baseball field. There are two stages for entertainment such as jugglers, magicians, children's acts and dancers. The small stage is for puppet shows and story telling for the children. In the arts and crafts area you'll find a gem show, photography exhibits, art, home arts and sciences and 4-H exhibits. On the baseball field there's a petting zoo, pony rides, an animal show and special events such as a diaper derby and big wheel races.

*Nevada Festivals continued on page 122*

*Nevada Festivals continued from page 120*

Sunrise has always been a special time of day, but on the 4th weekend in October each year, it becomes even more special as 100 hot air balloons lift off from the Silver Bowl Park in Las Vegas. The **Las Vegas Balloon Classic** held October 25th through the 27th will showcase some of the most beautiful balloons in the world, as some of the world's top balloon pilots take their colorful craft into the skies. Unusual objects amid the round balloons are actually special shaped balloons such as the Korbel Champagne bottle flown by Canadian pilot, Ron Martin. It stands 147 feet tall, and, if you could "pour" in the bubbly, it would hold 283,906 cases of Champagne! There's also a "Witch Craft," piloted by Diane Thomas of Phoenix, Arizona. Activities start on Friday with field demonstrations and tether rides for school and youth groups. Early Christmas shoppers can browse the 150 craft booths and enjoy a vintage auto show and antique machinery on display. With free admission and 14 specialty food booths, visitors should plan on a full day.

**Winter:**

Late January in Elko means it's time for the 12th annual **Cowboy Poetry Gathering.** The week-long event draws thousands of fans of cowboy poetry and music who come to enjoy, close up, real working cowboys who also happen to be poets and musicians. It's no accident that the event is held in January, as that is the only time these working cowboys can take time off from their chores to swap stories, play music and recite poems. Daytime performances are informal, but evening shows are held in the 1,000-seat Elko Convention Center theater. Visitors enjoy open poetry sessions, dances, jamborees, and art exhibits. Hands-on workshops are offered in a range of cowboy artistries including silver engraving, natural Western cooking, songwriting, rawhide braiding and ranch remedies, which are herbal medicines and folk remedies that have been used on ranches for many decades.

# You deserve more than just a parking space!

HOTEL & GAMBLING HALL
Flamingo and Boulder Hwy.

- LOCATED ON THE GROWING BOULDER STRIP OFF I-95 AND FLAMINGO ROAD
- TWO PARKS WITH 500 FULL HOOKUPS
- SWIMMING POOL & SPA
- WESTERN EMPORIUM SPECIALTY STORE
- WESTERN DANCE HALL
- BOWLING CENTER
- ENJOY "SUNSET STAMPEDE" - A LAZER LIGHT AND SOUND EXTRAVAGANZA.
- ALL OF YOUR FAVORITE CASINO GAMES INCLUDING POKER ROOM AND RACE & SPORTS BOOK

FOR RATES AND AVAILABILITY CALL:
**1-800-634-6371**

Sam Boyd's®
**CALIFORNIA**
HOTEL • CASINO • RV PARK
DOWNTOWN

- THE ONLY RV PARK IN THE HEART OF CASINO CENTER - HOME OF THE FREMONT STREET EXPERIENCE, A MUST SEE LIGHT & SOUND EXTRAVAGANZA.
- 222 FULL HOOKUP SPACES
- 60' PULL-THROUGH SPACES AVAILABLE
- CONVENIENCE STORE
- SWIMMING POOL & SPA
- LAUNDRY & SHOWER FACILITIES
- WASTE STATION
- DOG RUN
- ADJACENT TO THE CALIFORNIA HOTEL/CASINO

FOR RATES AND AVAILABILITY CALL:
**1-800-634-6505**

PARK & PLAY IN Las Vegas

**FREE INFO?** Sam's Town, enter #122 on Reader Service Card following page 16.

## *OREGON FESTIVALS*

**Spring:**

Celebrated from late May through mid-July, the **Portland Rose Festival** is the premier civic celebration in the Pacific Northwest, and one of the finest events anywhere! Over 2 million visitors enjoy the events that make up the festival each year, viewing three colorful parades, a waterfront fair and exhibit area, a thrilling airshow, high-speed IndyCar race, concerts and sporting events. In the 1800s, residents discovered that Portland's climate was perfectly suited to growing beautiful roses, and one of the early civic leaders is credited with the original idea of a rose festival. In these early years, the Rose Festival was highlighted by horse-drawn floats in the floral parade, aquatic events in the nearby harbor and fireworks at night. Since then, the Rose Festival has "blossomed" into an extravaganza featuring more than 70 events.

**Summer:**

The weekend after the 4th of July, visit Albany, Oregon for the town's 47th annual **Albany World Championship Timber Carnival.** The 4-day event celebrates the American timber culture with a fireworks display, musical entertainment, a midway and a parade with floats atop log trucks. Over one hundred loggers from every timber growing region of the United States, Canada, Australia, New Zealand, Europe, and Japan compete in the 23 events to test speed, skill, strength and precision. This show of events is the 2nd oldest timber competition in the nation, and the 2nd largest in the world, the largest being held in Sydney, Australia. Many people have seen log rolling contests on television, however there are some events which we aren't as familiar with. The practice of springboard chopping disappeared with the advent of power saws, but is still part of the competition here. Other events include standing block chop, double bucking, ax throwing, women's log rolling, hot power saw and skidder races.

The Bay Area Chamber of Commerce invites visitors to visit the towns of Coos Bay, North Bend and Charleston for fun activities all year long. Summer has some exceptionally exciting celebrations, kicked off with the Shore Acres Historical Formal Gardens' **Father's Day Rose Sunday** and Rose Show. July brings the **Southwestern Oregon Open Amateur Golf Tournament;** the **Oregon Coast Music Festival**; the **City of North Bend July Jubilee**; and the **City of Coos Bay Fourth of July** celebration. In August, there's the **Farwest Lapidary and Gem Show**; the **Coos County Fair and Rodeo**; the **Charleston Seafood and Wine Festival**, and more.

Nestled among giant oak trees in a beautiful historic park setting, the **Salem Art Fair & Festival** is a 3-day celebration of the arts where visitors enjoy superior art and exceptional performing arts each year during the 3rd full weekend in July. This award-winning event is the largest juried fair of its kind in Oregon and maintains a prestigious reputation among participants and visitors. More than 100,000 people visit the festival, where they can enjoy and purchase artwork by approximately 200 artists from across the nation; listen to regional and nationally-known entertainers; enjoy the Kids' Court children's area with performances and hands-on art activities; or watch artists demonstrate their craft. Visitors may take a turn at a potters wheel, try painting, enjoy the variety of folk arts and sample Oregon wines and ale. Take I-5 to exit 253 and head west 2 1/2 miles to Bush's Pasture Park at Mission and High Streets. Parking is limited, but there's a free shuttle service available from South Salem High School parking lot or Pringle Parkade.

Just 14 miles north of Eugene, a rich ethnic heritage comes alive once a year as residents of Junction City transform their city into a Scandinavian village for four days in August. This year marks the 36th year of the **Junction City Scandinavian Festival** with costumes, dance, music, customs and food of the Danish, Swedish, Finnish, Norwegian and Icelandic cultures. The numerous food booths and community dinners are some of the festival's most popular "places to be" as visitors sample everything from aebelskiver (tender, spherical pancakes served sprinkled with powdered sugar and sometimes topped with jam) to a Scandi Delight (a shrimp sandwich with dill and sour cream and a marinated salmon strip). There are also morning and evening meals served at the fire hall, along with a wine terrace. Free entertainment fills the 4-day schedule as traditional folk dancers, polka bands,

choirs and an evening pageant fill the Festival Park stage.

**Fall:**

The **Mt. Angel Oktoberfest** is held September 12th through the 15th, and this year marks the 31st annual harvest festival, held in this small, rural community just 40 miles south of Portland. Begun as a traditional fall festival to celebrate the bounty of the earth, today the celebration features more than 60 arts & crafts booths, a traditional *biergarten, weingarten* and *kindergarten*, and a European style family cabaret. The *biergarten* features a wide variety of costumed bands playing traditional "oompah" music. Delightful free entertainment for children is provided in the *kindergarten*. The cabaret offers lively entertainment in the setting of a European street cafe. Visitors also enjoy the non-stop, free entertainment performed on the Village Bandstand by the local village band, yodelers and folk singers.

Always the 2nd full weekend of September, the **Pendleton Round-Up and Happy Canyon Pageant** is sometimes referred to as "America's Classic Rodeo." There are seven major PRCA events each day on a grass arena, plus pony express, Indian and baton races, wild horse races, wild cow milking and more. Each event is run with clock-like precision with little "down time" between events — it's also called the "fastest moving rodeo in America." The night showing of the Pendleton Round-Up is a colorful evening pageant that takes visitors into the past, beginning with the portrayal of the early American Indian culture and the early pioneers who came to the wild frontier. Following the pageant, guests can head over to the Happy Canyon Dance Hall for live country and western music and other entertainment. A spectacular Westward Ho! parade showcases pack trains, stage coaches, covered wagons, buggies, ox teams, mule teams and hundreds of Native Americans in full costume. This unique parade bills itself as "the way it was," as no motorized vehicles or advertising are allowed.

## *WASHINGTON FESTIVALS*

**Spring:**

In Spokane, May is a big month for festivals, activities and excitement throughout the community. **Bloomsday,** the world's largest timed road race is held the first Sunday in May each year, and this year it'll be on May 6th. This event attracts runners, walkers, and wheel-chair athletes from around the world which gives the race a truly international competitive field. Among the 55,000 to 65,000 participants, many of the top runners will go on to the Olympics. During Bloomsday weekend there are numerous events in Riverfront Park, especially after the race. May also means lilacs for Spokane. It's the month for the annual **Lilac Festival** which begins the Saturday following Bloomsday with the Junior Lilac Parade on May 11th. This parade is for children from throughout the area as schools from as far away as Montana participate by entering home-made floats and featuring marching units.

Leavenworth rolls out the red carpet for spring with its **Maifest** celebration held in mid-May. Visitors will enjoy the beautiful flowers on display, along with oom-pah music and strolling accordian serenades. TheVisitors are welcome to join in the Grand March, and other activities include Art in the Park, a special performance by the Marlin Handbell Ringers, and a popular Saturday evening street dance.

The **Skagit Valley Tulip Festival** is held March 29th through April 14th, with more than a half million visitors attending in recent years. It's a multi-community event which involve cities in Skagit County including Anacortes, La Conner, Mount Vernon, and Burlington. From humble beginnings over 10 years ago, the festival boasts an assortment of events including a golf tournament, running races, fashion shows and more. The Key Bank Flower and Garden Show has flower displays and commercial booths showcasing the latest in gardening products. If you like tulips, but not traffic, or if you don't know your way around, take the Tulip Transit which are buses running every 20 minutes. The vehicles take visitors through the valley's tulip fields with stops at various sites along the way including Tulip Town with its array of cut flowers for sale, Kodak platform, an espresso bar, picnic area, plus a walk-in tulip field with over 60 varieties.

The **Walla Walla Balloon Stampede** was begun over 20 years ago, and continues each May at Howard-Tietan Park. There's a juried arts & crafts show with over 100 exhibits, a car show, golf tournament, volleyball tournament, a fun run, carnival, horse races, a chicken barbecue dinner, and breakfast with the pilots of the more than 50 hot air balloons.

The **Washington State Apple Blossom Festival** is held in Wenatchee at the end of April and beginning of May. The festivities provide 11 days of family-oriented events, including a grand parade, a carnival, food fair, youth day, and arts and crafts.

Grand Coulee Dam offers a nightly laser light show during the summer that is kicked off by the **Laser Light Festival** on Memorial Day weekend. The festival has over 55 arts and crafts booths, and 12 food booths. It's one of the largest entertainment laser projections in the world. The show lasts approximately 40 minutes, during which colorful images created by the lasers move back and forth across the huge surface of the dam. There's a terraced, grassy park adjacent to the east end of the Columbia River Bridge for easy viewing. Other viewing spots are from the parking lot near the dam's Third Power House; from Douglas Park in Coulee Dam; or from Crown Point atop the granite cliffs above Lake Rufus Woods, with access from Highway 174 towards Bridgeport.

**Summer:**

Considered one of the top ten annual festivals in the nation, **Seafair** is truly a Northwest community treasure that has been celebrated for more than 46 years. Residents and visitors of Puget Sound enjoy the community festivals, parades, cultural celebrations and the ever popular Torchlight Night, and hydroplanes and air shows that make Seafair a favorite year after year. Seafair employees and volunteers work year-round to produce this three-week-long festival of over 55 diverse events that take place throughout the Puget Sound area. Cultural festivals include the Japanese Community Bon Odori, the Chinatown/International District Festival, the Seafair Indian Days Pow Wow and other ethnic festivals. The celebrations extend from Seattle to surrounding communities including Maple Valley Days, Silverdale Whaling Days, the Bothell Arts Fair, and many more.

The **Pacific Northwest Arts & Crafts Fair** is a 3-day outdoor arts festival produced by the Bellevue Art Museum, and held in Bellevue Square and Bellevue Place. One of the largest and most prestigious art festivals in the country, the fair is held the last full weekend in July, and will celebrate its 50th anniversary this year. Visitors will find over 300 exceptional juried artists, craft demonstrations, visual art exhibitions, performing arts and an entire fair just for children. Prior to the fair, over 1,200 artists compete to be chosen as one of the 330 exhibitors. The children's fair was added in 1991, and has become a major attraction, featuring family entertainment and craft booths selling merchandise designed especially for children. A popular tradition of the fair is the Demonstration Booth which presents an interactive demonstration area to learn about a featured craft. Past demonstrations have included wood turning, glass blowing and pottery throwing.

The 35th annual **Anacortes Arts & Crafts Festival** is held downtown the 1st weekend in August. The festival offers over 275 craft vendors from Washington, Oregon, California and British Columbia, a juried fine art show and an invitational show comprised of prestigious artists from Anacortes, Guemes Island and western Skagit County. Festival-goers will also enjoy an array of musical and performing arts, hands-on and creative activities, entertainment for children, and an antique/vintage vehicle show. The expanded food booth area offers a variety of ethnic and American favorites.

The annual **Peninsula Saddle Club Rodeo** is held in Long Beach in early August. Held for over 50 years, the event features calf roping, bare back and saddle bronc riding, barrel racing, and America's most dangerous rodeo sport, bull riding. There's a Cowboy Breakfast to start things off, followed by the events. The rodeo grounds are located on Sandridge Road, north of 10th Street. Later this month, Long Beach plays host to the 15th annual **Washington State International Kite Festival** August 19th through the 15th, with lots of fun events such as stunt kites and lighted night flies; a children's and senior citizens' kite day; kite trains and arches, and the Festival of Kites, held in hopes of breaking their Western Hemisphere record for the most kites in the sky at one time.

Mid-August brings the **Omak Stampede and Suicide Race** to Omak, Washington. Almost from its inception, the town was considered a rodeo town, as settlers and Native Americans gathered from miles around to cheer the horse races down a dusty Main Street and the bucking horse contests that were held in a crude canvas arena. For over 60 years the stampede has been held here, followed by the world famous Suicide Race where horses and riders race down a steep embankment and across a river to the finish line. Today, there's also a carnival and midway, shopping in the many concessions, a genuine Native American encampment complete with over 100 teepees, Native American dancing competitions with dancers in full costume, and much more, including plenty of parking and camping nearby.

**Fall:**

When summer draws to a close, September is a big month for Spokane, starting with the annual **Pig Out in the Park Restaurant Fair** over Labor Day weekend. This year Pig Out will run for five days, starting on August 31st. Thousands of people fill Riverfront Park to sample the taste treats offered at more than 40 food booths, including ethnic, exotic and all-American cuisine. The park puts a limit on how much can be charged for a plate of food ($6.00 is the current limit) but you'll receive a heaping plate of goodies for your money. During Pig Out, there's also an arts & crafts fair, special activities throughout the park, and free live entertainment at four different locations in the park. After Pig Out, it's time for the **Spokane County-Interstate Fair,** usually beginning the Friday after Labor Day and continuing for 10 days. This fair features the usual exhibits and displays, but also includes live entertainment throughout the fairgrounds, rodeos, a carnival and a midway.

Lots of food, a family atmosphere, informational exhibits, and more food. That's the perfect formula for a festival, and it's the formula Skookum Rotary Club innovators adopted back in 1982 when they began the **West Coast Oyster Shucking Championship and Washington State Seafood Festival**, now an annual extravanganza permanently set on the first full weekend in October. **OysterFest** is the biggest festival of its kind on the West Coast. Over 20,000 people eat their way throughout the Mason County Fairgrounds, devouring oysters on the half-shell, bacon-wrapped oysters, steamed clams, barbecued salmon, clam linquine, oyster fritters, and lots more. The shucking contest pits professional and amateur shuckers from up and down the coast as all try their hands at oyster shucking and receive certificates to prove their prowess. Entertainment in the past has included Skokomish Indian tribal dances; a jazz ensemble; blues, rock and roll and folk singers; clog dancing, and wandering minstrels. For the children, there's face painting, cartoons, pony rides and more. Evening dances and social activities are planned to entertain overnight RV campers.

**Winter:**

Mark your calendars for the 1st week in December for the **Festival of Lights** held in Chewelah. The festival begins with spectacular lighting displays in the city park and downtown, followed by a variety of events throughout the month of December. The Northeastern Washington Winter Craftfest provides a market of craft items created by regional artisans.

## *BAJA MEXICO FESTIVALS*

**Spring:**

Holy Week (the 3rd week in April) celebrates the approaching Easter holiday, and is second only to Christmas as the most important holiday period of the year in Baja. Called ***Semana Santa*** in Spanish, the week includes a popular custom of breaking *cascarones*, colored eggs stuffed with confetti, over the heads of friends and family.

April also brings a major bicycling event to Baja, the **Rosarito-Ensenada 50-Mile Bicycle Ride.** Taking place the last Saturday in April, this world-class bicycle race is considered one of the largest cycling events in the world. The route of the race follows the coast with an elevation differential of around 1,000 feet. The race is repeated again in the fall, on the last Saturday in September, with even more participants.

May brings **Cinco de Mayo** each May 15th. The celebration commemorates the defeat of an attempted French invasion of Mexico's gulf coast in 1862 and today features dancing, music, food and other cultural celebrations.

**Summer:**

Head to Ensenada for their **Festival of the Grape,** when the best of Baja's wine takes the spotlight August 11th through the 20th. There's dancing in the streets, music, and visitors can sample some of the best wine Baja has to offer. Other entertainment includes grape stomping contests, ballet folklorico and delicious food such as succulent barbequed lamb and authentic Spanish paella.

**Fall:**

The 2nd or 3rd week of November brings the **Baja 1000**, a famous desert race of about 120 motorcycles and over 180 car and trucks. The race, considered the most famous desert race in North America, is a testing ground for many major manufacturers of vehicles and parts, and is considered extremely challenging. The course follows established auto trails to avoid damage to the fragile desert environment, and alternates from year to year between the full 1,000-mile race between Ensenada and La Paz and a 1,000-km course that travels through the northern state only. The race includes several classes from dirt bikes to 4-wheel-drive trucks and an average of 300 drivers compete annually.

Mulege is the site of the **Celebration of Santa Rosalia, Patron Virgin of Mulege,** held September 2nd through 4th. It's a 3-day town-wide party that includes a parade, folk dancing, entertainment, a carnival, an arts and crafts show, horse racing and other sporting events and lots of food.

October brings the **Black and Blue Marlin Jackpot Tournament** to Cabo San Lucas. The 3-day event is the largest sportfishing event of the year, and anglers compete for up to $100,000 in prize money.

One of Ensenada's biggest events is the **Juan Hussong International Chili Cookoff,** held on the 2nd weekend in October. In addition to the chile cooking competitions by various local clubs, individuals and restaurants, there's a daily chile-pepper-eating contest, a tequila "shoot-and-holler" contest, live music and dancing and the selection of Ms. Chile Pepper and Mr. Hot Sauce. Popular Mexican beers and wines are on hand to quench the thirst and put out the fires on festival-goers' palates.

**Winter:**

Beginning each December 16th, Mexicans hold nightly *posadas* in celebration of ***Las Posadas***, candlelight processions that end at elaborate, community-built nativity scenes, all commemorating the Holy Family's search for lodging. Other activities surrounding the celebration include pinata parties for children and ending with the January 6th holiday, Dia de los Santos Reyes (Day of the King-Saints), which refers to the story of the Three Wise Men. This is the day that Mexican children receive their Christmas gifts, and special wreath-shaped fruit cakes are eaten.

**Carnaval** is a pre-Lenten festival held in late February or early March prior to the 40-day lent season preceding Easter. This year it's celebrated during the week of February 22nd through the 27th. In Mexico, the festival traditionally occurs only in port towns, and in Baja, its major celebrations occur in Ensenada, San Felipe and La Paz. Like the Mardi Gras celebrations throughout the southeastern United States' gulf coast, Carnaval is a high-spirited fiesta featuring dancing, music, costumes and parades — a time of wonderful excess and "serious" partying, the Baja way. There are parades, games of skill, mechanical rides, and masquerade costumes. Most streets are blocked off and stands are set up with an intriguing variety of foods such as hot corn coctails, carnitas, churros, tamarindo, jamaica, agua de arroz, tamales, seafood coctails, and much more.

*Guerrero Negro* is held throughout February and celebrates the **Festival of the Whales.** Visitors will enjoy the carnival, music, dancing, films, lectures, food, sporting activities and whale watching excursions.

# Closest Campground to MARINELAND and the FALLS

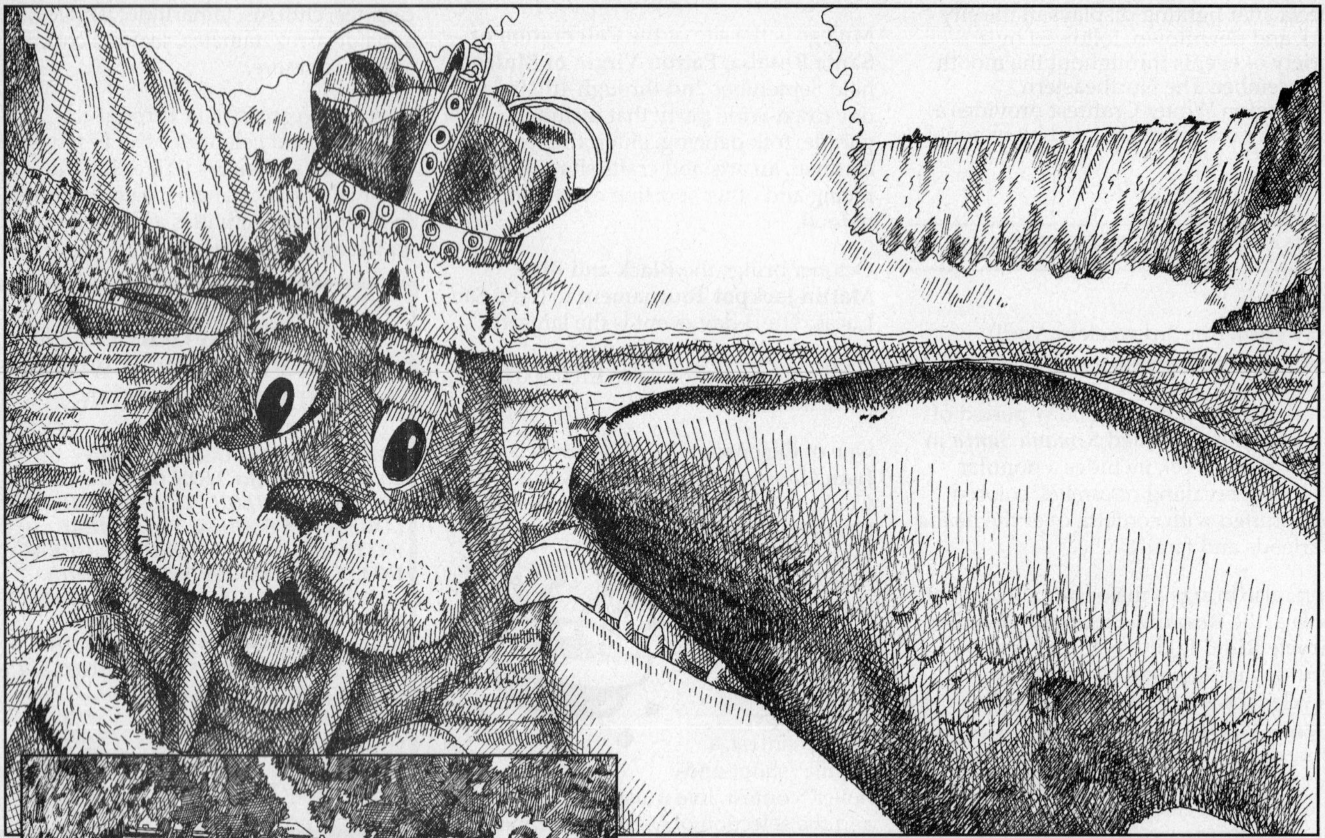

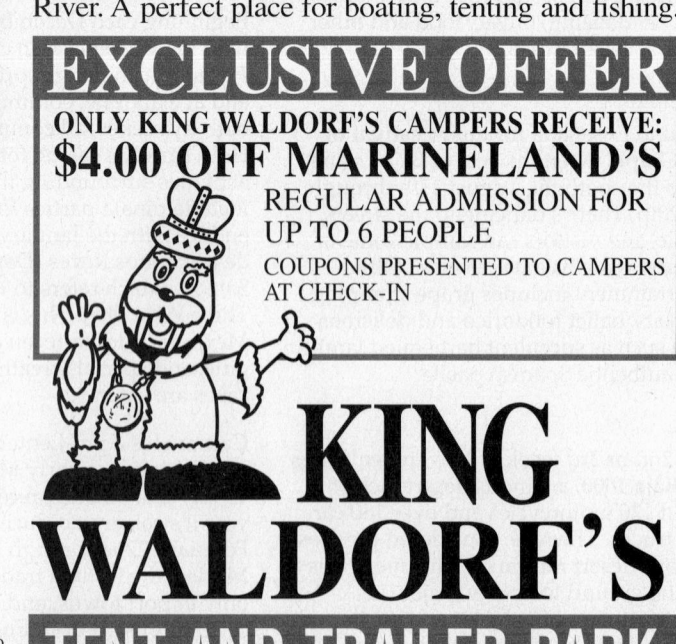

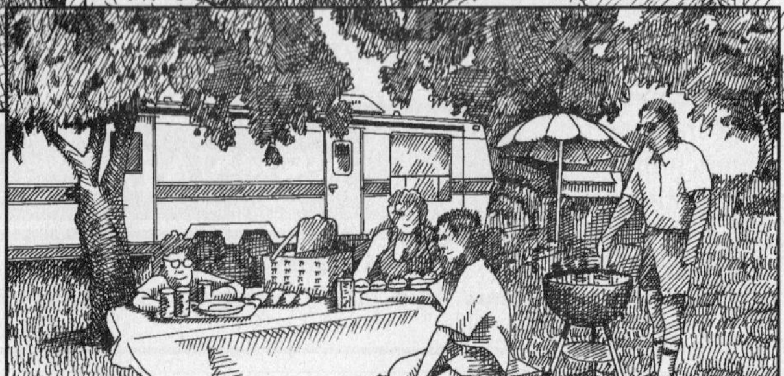

## King Waldorf's offers:

- •Level pull-through trailer sites
- •Large private tent sites
- •Water & electrical hook-ups
- •Full laundry facilities
- •Modern washrooms, showers & tubs
- •Large heated pool & wading pool
- •18-hole golf course
- •Children's playground
- •Gift shop
- •Dump station
- •Fishing
- •Boat ramp

Call: **(905) 295-8191**

Write: 8375 Stanley Ave., Niagara Falls, Ontario, Canada L2E 6X8

Location: 9015 Stanley Ave., Niagara Falls, Ontario, Canada

## AND SAVE UP TO $24

King Waldorf's Tent & Trailer Park offers a delightful country setting with grassy meadows and large shade trees right on the bank of the wide, historical Welland River. A perfect place for boating, tenting and fishing.

## EXCLUSIVE OFFER

**ONLY KING WALDORF'S CAMPERS RECEIVE:**

**$4.00 OFF MARINELAND'S**

REGULAR ADMISSION FOR UP TO 6 PEOPLE

COUPONS PRESENTED TO CAMPERS AT CHECK-IN

# KING WALDORF'S

## TENT AND TRAILER PARK

# DISCOVER THE FESTIVALS *of* Canada

## *ALBERTA FESTIVALS*

**Summer:**

For 10 days in July, the **Calgary Exhibition and Stampede,** held in Calgary, thrills visitors to a city-wide celebration. True western hospitality and a special "stampede spirit" supplies visitors to parades filled with western musicians and dancers, pancake breakfasts on almost every corner, and the bit show itself. As visitors enter Stampede Park, they walk back in time through an authentic Indian village and stroll the streets of a re-created frontier town. There's also the International Stock Show which showcases the world of agriculture. You'll be treated to large, powerful draft horses and to pet-sized miniature horses that are no more than 34 inches tall. Each afternoon brings a 3-hour, ground-shaking rodeo, and each evening, 9 heart-stopping chuckwagon races explode in an all out dash for the finish. An outdoor stage spectacular provides a 2-hour show each evening, as top variety acts from around the world end each exciting day.

Expect non-stop, free-wheeling fun during the 12th annual **Edmonton International Street Performers Festival** held in mid-July. It's a lively community-based celebration of street performance and the city's colorful festival spirit. An international cast performs a dazzling program of high-energy street theater, comedy, music, and dance, as outdoor performances keep downtown hopping from noon 'til night. As one of the founding festivals in "Edmonton, Canada's Festival City," the celebration has gained an international reputation, and is said to be a model for similar festivals throughout the world.

Late July brings **Klondike Days** to Edmonton, as the city celebrates with 10 days of color and excitement, reliving the vibrant Klondike era of the 1890s. Enjoy the King of the Klondike competitions, a parade, World Championship Sourdough raft races, bathtub races, the Exposition, A Taste of Edmonton, and more, as Klondike Days celebrations take place across the city.

The Banff Centre celebrates its **Banff Festival of the Arts** each summer with a variety of art and musical performances including chamber music, jazz, media arts, opera and dance, string quartet competitions, and "digital playgrounds," a festival of electro/acoustic performances.

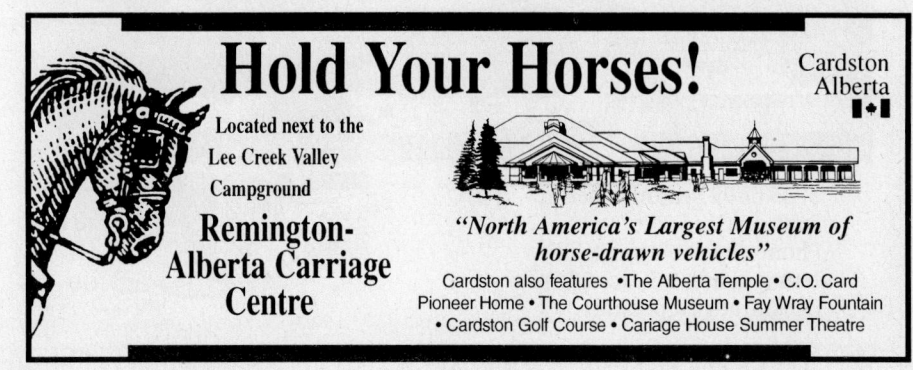

Celebrations, tours and events are held throughout the spring and summer at various historic sites throughout Alberta. **Historic Dunvegan Provincial Park in Fairview** provides guided walks, interpretive programs and a step back in time to when the area was a major fur and provision post. Costumed interpreters provide a personal touch to complete the fun. The **Fort McMurray Oil Sands Interpretive Centre** provides hands-0n interpretive programs including guided tours and science activities for children as they learn the history of the Athabasca oil sands, the world's largest single oil deposit. For a panoramic view of the North Saskatchewan River, **Fort George and Buckingham House Interpretive Centre** provides visitors a view of one of the earliest Alberta trade routes. **Victoria Settlement** provides a glimpse of an 1864 Clerk's Quarters and a 1906 church. Costumed interpreters tell the story of Alberta's past and lead a variety of activities. The **Ukrainian Cultural Heritage Village** near Edmonton, tells the story of the Ukrainian immigrants as role players in period costumes recreate a variety of historic characters who will challenge your family's imagination. Interpretive guides lead visitors through **Father Lacombe Chapel,** the oldest building in Alberta, and around the historic Mission Hill site, in St. Albert, just minutes northwest of Edmonton. The **Provincial Museum of Alberta** in Edmonton showcases the exploration of the province's fascinating history through its galleries, exhibits and special traveling exhibits. **Rutherford House Provincial Historic Site** is a restored residence which was once the home of the first premier of Alberta. It has been restored to its post-Edwardian elegance and is open to the public. The **Reynolds-Alberta Museum** in Wetaskiwin focuses on the air transportation, agriculture and industry in the province from the late 1800s to the 1950s. Stephansson **House Historical Site** is famous for its tours guided by costumed interpreters demonstrating spinning, weaving, baking and household chores. **Cochrane Ranch Historic Site** provides visitors the opportunity to learn about ranching in Alberta in the 1880s. **Royal Tyrrell Museum** in Drumheller has interpretive programs, guided tours and the one of the largest displays of dinosaur specimens anywhere. **Head-Smashed-In Buffalo Jump** is one of the oldest and best preserved buffalo jump sites in North America. **Brooks Aqueduct** is a preserved structure that was a vital link to irrigation in southeastern Alberta for 65 years. **Remington-Alberta Carriage Center** in Cardston, houses one of North America's largest and finest collections of horse-drawn vehicles, and offers 20-minute carriage rides. **Leitch Collieries Provincial Historic Site** in Blairmore offers guided tours of a turn-of-the-century coal mine. The **Frank Slide Interpretive Centre** highlights the rich history of Crowsnest Pass with presentations and special events.

## *BRITISH COLUMBIA FESTIVALS*

**Summer:**

Parksville, on beautiful Vancouver Island, has something for everyone. Scenic attractions include Rhododendron Lake, Englishman River Falls, Little Qualicum Falls, Horne Lake Caves, Cathedral Grove, and the Craig Heritage Museum. Parksville Beach, located in the center of the city, has a large, sandy beach ideal for sunbathing, swimming or beachcombing. The Parksville Community Park has changing rooms, a children's playground and waterspray park, ball park, tennis courts, picnic area and is popular for kite flying. The many artists who live and work in the area attract thousands of visitors who are entertained by several on-going festivals. Two popular events are the **Annual International Sandcastle Competition** and the **Parksville Pageant Days**. Depending upon the tides, the popular Sandcastle Competition is held in middle to late July. The sand at the community beach is favored for its excellent compacting qualities, a most important attribute when it comes to building a prize-winning castle. Thousands of visitors come to view the master builders at work, watch the judging, and then to see the ocean overtake the creations.

Vancouver Island is a wonderful place to escape to. Close to Vancouver, British Columbia, and Seattle, Washington, the island offers all the pleasures of an island retreat, mixed with a variety of fun activities. Special events include the **Luxton Rodeo** held in May in Langford; **Sidney Days** in Sidney held in July; **All Sooke Day** in Sooke in July; and the **Victoria International Festival**, also in July.

Visit Vancouver for the **Canadian International Dragon Boat Festival** held in mid-June at the Plaza of Nations. It's a colorful and spectacular 3-day event featuring dragon boat racing, local and international performers and entertainers, and foods from around the world. It's billed as North America's largest dragon boat festival, celebrating a Chinese tradition dating back over 2,400 years. Join the locals in cheering on more than 120 local and international teams from as far away as the Philippines and Italy as you watch from the north shore of False Creek.



One of the largest agricultural fairs in the province, the **Pacific National Exhibition**, held in Vancouver, attracts more than a million visitors each year for 17 days in late August and early September. In addition to scores of farm and agricultural exhibits and buildings, the fair boasts a giant midway where amusement rides of every type are the attraction for thrill seekers.

Airshows in British Columbia are not competitions, but displays of technology and "daring-do." There are 4 major airshows each year in British Columbia, attracting hundreds of thousands of spectators to view displays of aircraft and flight technology, as well as thrilling aerobatics of daredevils pilots and precision military teams. The **Abbotsford International Airshow**, at the Abbotsford Airport east of Vancouver, takes place every year in early August and claims to be the largest airshow in North America. Its roster of attractions usually includes the Canadian Air Force's Snowbirds or an American aerobatic team, often the Thunderbirds, wing-walkers and military flight equipment.

Logger sports have been a long-standing tradition in British Columbia, and are increasing in popularity. The three largest annual logger sporting events are **All Sooke Days** held in mid-July in Sooke (west of Victoria on Vancouver Island); **Squamish Logger Sports Days** held August 1st through 5th; and the 17-day extravaganza, **Pacific National Exhibition**, held in Vancouver for 17 days in late August and early September. View log rolling, tree climbing, chopping and much more as loggers compete for top honors.

## *MANITOBA FESTIVALS*

**Summer:**

The **Winnipeg Folk Festival** is held July 11th through the 14th, celebrating its 23rd anniversary. With seven continuous daytime stages, an evening main stage, and more than 90 acts playing a variety of musical styles, music abounds everywhere on the site. By combining all this entertainment with the friendly, informal setting of the festival, festival organizers ensure that visitors experience just the right mixture for exciting new

*Manitoba Festivals continued on pg. 132*

*Manitoba Festivals continued from pg. 130*

musical discoveries from all over the world. There's also a craft village featuring more than 60 artisans demonstrating and selling their works, and delicious international cuisine in the food area. The family area provides jugglers, face painting, Origami, kite-making, and lively supervised children's games.

Winnipeg's **Fringe Festival,** said to be the 2nd largest fringe festival in Canada, is held July 12th through the 21st. It's an outrageous, non-stop, noon-to-midnight entertainment odyssey of comedy, drama, dance, music and more, featuring more than 700 performances by more than 120 theater and performing arts companies. Coming from all over Canada and the United States, and some from as far away as Russia, the performers entertain in 10 indoor venues and on the free outdoor stage in Winnipeg's historic Exchange District.

For 4 days of western fun and hospitality, visit Morris in July for "The Big M Stampede." The **Manitoba Stampede** begins with a free family street dance in downtown Morris, followed by an entire evening of games, prizes and entertainment for the whole family. Always scheduled for the 3rd week in July, the stampede and rodeo offers top-rated western-style entertainment. Thursday through Sunday, some of North America's top cowboys try for prize money and championship points in saddle bronc riding, bull riding, steer wrestling, calf roping and more. Evenings bring chuckwagons, pony chuckwagons and chariot races. Visitors also enjoy the agricultural exhibits, livestock shows, and commercial displays.

The **Manitoba Highland Gathering** is held in Selkirk on the first Saturday in July. Guests are able to pay one admission price to gain admission to beautiful Selkirk Park and enjoy the championship Highland dancing competitions, about 10 to 12 individual piping and drumming units and pipe bands, 10 to 12 clan tents where visitors can research their Scottish heritage, and displays and sales of handicrafts by local artists and craftsmen. Heavy games of brawn are held including tossing the caber, and putting the Selkirk Stone of Strength (21-3/4 lbs.!). There is a workshop in the morning with professional athletes, and amateur competitions in the afternoon. Try some Scottish foods such as Scotch pies, pasties, bridies, Scotch eggs, mealie pudding, scones, and shortbread. Or how about a taste of haggis, a traditional Scottish dish consisting of a mixture of the minced liver, lungs, and heart of a sheep or calf, mixed with oatmeal and seasonings, and boiled in the animal's stomach? For the less adventurous, there are hamburgers, hot dogs and french fries.

The Morden Chamber of Commerce invites you to their 30th annual **Corn and Apple Festival** held August 23rd through 25th. The first festival was held to commemorate Canada's 100th birthday in 1967. For the past 29 years, on the last full weekend in August, the tradition of free corn and apple cider has been faithfully carried out. Visitors enjoy free bus tours of the town and of the Canada Agriculture Research Station; a walking tour of historical buildings; a Saturday morning parade; continuous free stage entertainment; and an ever-expanding street area covering 8 full blocks with booths selling everything from homegrown fruit and vegetables, to baked goods, crafts, food, clothing, and household items. There are also children's activities, and three dances to entertain all age groups.

## *NEW BRUNSWICK FESTIVALS*

**Summer:**

Canada Day brings the **Fredericton River Jubilee**, a multi-day event that utilizes the St. John River as its theme. In addition to the Canada Day (July 1st) celebration, Fredericton celebrates with a Little Town Crier Competition, Sunday in the Park, the Carnival of Cultures, the New Brunswick Country Music Hall of Fame induction, flea markets, outdoor concerts, fiddle and step dancing concerts, art exhibits, a parade, and a lovely fireworks display over the river.

Fredericton celebrates the **New Brunswick Highland Games** in late July. The 3-day Scottish cultural event is held on the grounds of the historic Old Government House and includes solo piping and drumming, Highland dancing, pipe bands, Scottish country dancing, Gaelic singing, ancient Scottish heavy events, Ceilidh, clan booths and a Scottish concert.

The **Atlantic Aquaculture Fair** is held June 20th through 23rd in the resort town of St. Andrews. Billed as Canada's largest aquaculture event, the fair provides an opportunity to meet aquaculturalists, attend lectures and learn more about this growing industry. There are boat and aerial tours, a twilight cruise, dinner dance, a sea farmers' market, public information sessions, and tours of New Brunswick Aquaculture sites. Take some time to visit the area, as beautiful St. Andrews by-the-Sea is located on Passamaquoddy Bay, an arm of the Bay of Fundy in an historic resort area. Walking tours and maps are available, but a lovely way to view the town is by taking a horse and carriage tour.

Early July brings the **Lobster Festival** to Shediac, known as "Lobster Capital of the World." Come celebrate the flavor of this popular, deep-sea delicacy with a lobster eating contest, lobster suppers, special days for children and seniors, outdoor entertainment, and a giant parade.

The **Moncton Jazz and Blues Festival** is held in Moncton in early July, usually coinciding with Canada Day. Visit the city and enjoy the sounds from a wide variety of jazz musicians, featuring mainstream to contemporary jazz, classic blues, red hot salsa, and the street music of New Orleans. Local, regional, national and international artists converge upon the city to display their talents and thrill fans who come from far and wide to this fun musical celebration.

Mid-July brings **Canada's Irish Festival on the Miramichi**, when, for 4 days, visitors and locals alike wear their green and experience Ireland in the city of Mirimichi. The four day event includes concerts, pubs, cultural workshops, booths selling Irish wares and local crafts, musical entertainment, puppet shows, a parade, and the Run for the Green, a 6.5km race. Recent performers include Seamus Connolly of County Clare, Ireland, who won the Irish National Fiddle Championship 10 times, and renowned Irish tenor, Frank Patterson.

The **Lameque International Baroque Music Festival** is held July 12th through the 20th in Lameque, often referred to as the "home of baroque," a small fishing village of approximately 1,800 people on the Acadian Peninsula. Held for more than 18 years, this major musical event brings world-class baroque music featuring compositions by Vivaldi and Handel, performed on period instruments and performed by world class musicians and singers from both America and abroad. One of the highlights of the festival is "La Mission Saint-Charles'" concert featuring the festival's choir and orchestra led by a guest conductor.

**Fall:**

Always the 2nd weekend in September, this year, the **Atlantic Balloon Fiesta** will be held September 13th through 15th in Sussex. Visitors will find more than 25 giant hot-air balloons at the event, along with a parade, barbecues, skydivers, and children's events which are held all weekend. The shopping is great, with more than 40 Maritime craftspersons displaying their treasures. Before or after the festival, take some time to tour the area, which provides beautiful countryside, lush valleys, brilliant fall colors and lovely covered bridges.

## *NEWFOUNDLAND FESTIVALS*

**Summer:**

Visitors are greeted with a warm welcome throughout Newfoundland and Labrador, and the province enjoys a rich culture, inspired by Irish, British, French and Scottish ancestry, and by native populations. All year long, festivals and special events celebrate the land and the culture. Summer berry festivals offer up the gifts of the land with wild blueberries, bakeapples, and partridgeberries. Dance and music fill the nights with activity. Fiddles and accordions are favorites here, accompanied by the traditional bodhran drum, the spoons and tapping toes. Outdoor summer pageants bring 500 years of history to life, and seafood festivals tempt visitors with delights from the ocean.

The town of Gander began a 1-day civic celebration in the 1950s, designated "Kin Day." Today, the event has evolved into a 6-day festival called **Festival of Flight,** bringing the town's cultural heritage back to the forefront, as locals and visitors celebrate days gone by. Generally, the festival falls over the 6-day period which ends on the 1st Monday in August, and this year that will be July 31st through August 5th. The festivities begin at the Town Hall with games, prizes, and a bicycle parade. Throughout the weekend, events for young and old include a children's playhouse, derby, antique car show, bingo, games of chance and traditional Newfoundland meals are held daily. Saturday brings parades, an International Picnic, and more. A music festival with regional performers entertains festival-goers at Cobb's Pond Park from noon 'til evening.

Late June brings the **Seafaring Festival** to St. John's. Join the area's residents for 3 days of fun as they celebrate the 499th anniversary of John Cabot's voyage to Newfoundland. You'll be treated to historic re-enactments, parades, races, seafood dinners and parties, as you relive the days of the beginnings of this province. All this is a warm-up to the big celebration in 1997 on the 500th anniversary of John Cabot's landfall. This year-long festival will showcase Newfoundland and Labrador's unique culture and renowned hospitality in events such as: a military reunion of the thousands of military personnel stationed here in the past; a Northern Lights Festival in Labrador; a Squid-Jigging Festival; Bakeapple Festival; an international kayak festival; Viking Days, and a 1,000 kilometer snowmobile race.

Said to be Newfoundland's largest festival, the **Exploits Valley Salmon Festival** is held in mid-July in Grand Falls-Windsor. The event celebrates the great Atlantic salmon with 5 days of musical entertainment and dancing. Visitors are invited to a major concert, a salmon dinner, horse show and Newfoundland night. Sunday brings a craft fair, a salmon derby, Thomas Amusement and a softball tournament. Centennial Field is the site for entertainment by the Fogo Island Accordion Players, children's games and entertainment, and a concert.

The St. John's Arts Council sponsors the annual **Newfoundland & Labrador Folk Festival** in St. John's for three days in early August. The event takes place in historic Bannerman Park, and provides a non-stop parade of about 200 singers, musicians, dancers and storytellers to the stage. Some recent performers include the Irish Descendants, The Codroy Fiddlers and Dermot O'Reilly. The event celebrates the rich cultural heritage of the area, via storytelling, music, song, dance and crafts. Since 1966, folk arts groups have been working to preserve and celebrate these traditions in ways that locals as well as visitors can enjoy.

The 13th annual **Burin Peninsula Festival of Folk Song and Dance** is held in early July at the D.C. Jamieson Academy in Burin. The organizers promise some of the best and most authentic traditional singing, accordion/fiddle music, set-dancing, as well as an abundance of individual step-dancers. Held indoors, so weather is never a problem, the event features an on-going stage show, as well as a children's tent featuring sing-a-longs, face painting and traditional games and activities. Families can teach their children the traditional Newfoundland games of piddley, stilts, bows and arrows, slingshots and the hoop.

Come to Mount Pearl in mid-July for their **Newfoundland International Irish Festival.** The celebration features over 100 local performers and several international performers. You'll enjoy the pub nights, indoor and outdoor concerts, and an Irish Newfoundland breakfast.

Corner Brook holds its **Celebration of Summer** during late July each year. It's a week-long event with activities held throughout the city, and ending with the Annual Corner Brook Triathalon, often referred to as the toughest Olympic distance course in North America.

Mid-July through early August is a perfect time to visit Stephenville, and attend the **Stephenville Festival.** The festival is actually a series of plays — an eclectic celebration that mixes the classical with the brand new, and rollicking music with native legend, Acadian wisdom and fast-paced comedy. Plays are held in the charming Our Lady of Mercy Church in Port au Port, and on a main stage.

## *NOVA SCOTIA FESTIVALS*

**Summer:**

Cape Breton has numerous summer celebrations including ceilidhs, concerts and festivals that serve to preserve the unique traditions and music of the region. Mid-July brings one of the most popular, **The Big Pond Summer Festival**, to Cape Breton Island. The festivities include nature displays, special church services, a strawberry festival, music recitals, children's entertainment and more. Cape Breton fiddlers provide local color as they promote the Island's culture and heritage through their musical performances. The Big Pond Concert features some of the Island's finest musicians including singers, pipers, dancers and fiddlers.

Halifax is the site of the **Nova Scotia International Tattoo**, one of the largest annual indoor shows in the world, with performances by artists from seven countries. Treat the whole family to more than 2 hours of music, comedy, competitions, history and dancing, held in early July at the Halifax Metro Centre.

The **Antigonish Highland Games** originated in 1863 with competitions in archery, foot racing, bagpiping, "heavy events," hurdle races, and the reel and sword dances. Today, the Games are considered one of the foremost events of their kind in North America, as they provide entertainment and maintain the traditions of the Scottish way of life in eastern Nova Scotia and on Cape Breton Island, this year from July 12th through the 14th. The language, traditions, music and dances, and songs of the Gael, along with feats of strength and excellence flourish at the Highland Games in Antigonish, as each July, hundreds of musicians, dancers and athletes perform and compete in this unique festival.

Louisbourg, on Cape Breton Island, provides an on-going festival, considered to be one of the most exciting in North America. The picturesque town with its rugged scenery, beautiful beaches, and historic past, provides a season of celebrations. July's **Summerfest** brings parades, concerts, cances, barbecues, teas and spectacular fireworks. The **Acadian Festival** provides a glimpse into one of the most fascinating cultures in North America by providing the music, food, folklore and crafts of the Acadian culture. The **Grand Encampment** is the largest and most spectacular event of the summer when over 1,000 costumed re-enactors play out the tactical demonstrations, song and dance, musket firings, 18th-century camplife, and much more. The **Annual Crab Fest** held in August provides fresh local seafood and plenty of tradtitional Cape Breton entertainment for the entire family.

July brings the **Lobster Carnival** to Pictou. Originally billed as the "Carnival of Fisherfolk," the carnival was originated by a group of local businessmen in 1934 to recognize the contributions of the local fishermen. Today, visitors will enjoy lobster trap hauling competitions, lobster boat races, top-name Maritime entertainers, a Mardi Gras parade, children's activities, pipe band concerts, and of course, fresh-cooked lobster dinners . . . mmmmm! Put on a bib, and head to Pictou to learn about the area and sample its delicious fruits of the sea.

New Glasgow offers visitors a "Highland welcome" as it celebrates its **Festival of the Tartans** in July. First organized in the 1950s by residents to encourage sports enthusiasts to prepare themselves for the many traditional Scottish competitions, the festival has grown to be considered one of the best events of its kind in Canada. Guest bands from as far away as Australia and Scotland perform annually. Events are held throughout the town of New Glasgow, but most are held on Tartan Field on South Frederick Street. Visitors enjoy the street dancing, a children's parade, sidewalk sales, and a giant parade.

Lunenburg has two charming festivals you won't want to miss. Early July brings the **Lunenburg Craft Festival**, a community celebration featuring 150 of Nova Scotia's finest craftspersons. Enjoy the entire weekend looking for a special treasure to bring home, and enjoy the samplings of local food and entertainment. August brings the **Lunenburg Folk Harbour Festival** to Lunenburg with some of the best traditional and contemporary folk performers anywhere. More than 2 dozen acts entertain visitors and locals alike with their consistently enjoyable music, which is their own special way to preserve their traditions. For centuries, mariners from all corners of the North Atlantic found a snug harbor in Lunenburg. Even though they had few material possessions, they brought their songs and music with them which they share with festival-goers today in this picturesque seaport.

Mahone Bay celebrates its wooden boat building heritage in early August with its **Wooden Boat Festival.** You'll enjoy the harbor filled with the spectacle of wooden boats; workshops on Maritime skills for all ages; tours of boat building yards; waterfront entertainment including schooner races, a sail past, street dance, great food, fireworks, and much more.

Digby, on the Bay of Fundy, home of the famous Digby scallop fleet, celebrates its 21st annual **Digby Scallop Days** in mid-August, with scallop shucking, the parade of scallop draggers, and, of course, plenty of delicious portions of the tasty mollusk.

## *ONTARIO FESTIVALS*

**Spring:**

The area around Windsor in southeastern Ontario provides several events and shows including the **Windsor Quilter's Guild Quilt Show** held in early May at the Roseland Golf and Curling Club. Visitors will enjoy the quilting demonstrations, merchant's mall, a boutique and raffle.

The tulip is a symbol of the special friendship between the Dutch and Canadians, as every year Holland sends tulip bulbs to Ottawa as a gift celebrating their long-lasting friendship. The tradition began during World War II when Canada provided refuge to the Dutch Royal Family while Canadian forces helped liberate Holland. In appreciation, the Dutch have sent a gift of bulbs every year, and today, over 3 million tulips bloom in this region, known as the tulip capital of North America." This year the **Canadian Tulip Festival** will be held May 15th through the 20th, and it includes a juried craft "boulevard" showcasing 40 exhibitors. In addition to the *3 million* tulips, there are floral tapestries, concerts, fireworks, a variety of food booths serving food and drinks including Tulip Julip cocktails!

Milton holds a **Mother's Day Festival** each year, and celebrates with activities for moms and their families. There's a craft show (buy Mom a special gift!), a trout fishing derby, herb demonstration, pony rides, entertainment, farm animals, and a barbecue. Admission is free, and the event is held at Springridge Farm on Bell School Line.

*Ontario Festivals continued on pg. 138*

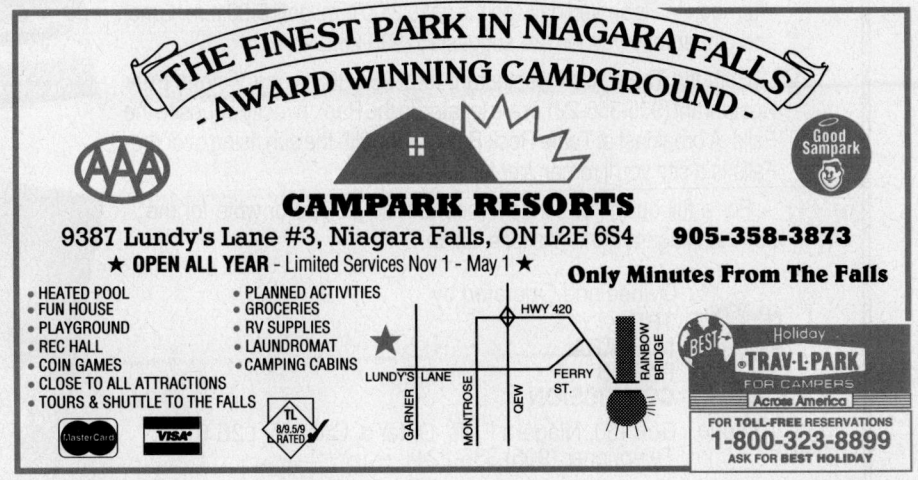

# WELCOME TO NIAGARA FALLS CANADA

In Niagara Falls, Canada you'll find over 2200 fully serviced sites. Check your "Woodall Directory" or the yellow pages of the local telephone book for a full listing.

## Things to Do Along the Route

Once in Niagara, you'll find plenty of things to do. If you wish, you can leave your RV at your Park and visit the nearby attractions and restaurants, of The Niagara Parks system by using the "People Mover" system. These modern green and white buses travel (mid-April to mid-October) along the beautiful Niagara Parkway between Queenston Heights Park and the Falls. One low fee allows you to get off and on different People Movers every twenty minutes. Tickets can be purchased at many stations found along the route (905-357-9340).

If you wish to take your RV near the Falls paid parking is found just beyond the Falls at the main People Mover Terminal (follow the RV signs). After you've parked your unit *all occupants are provided free all day People Mover transportation.*

One of the best and money saving ways to see the sights along the Niagara River is to purchase the Explorer's Passport Plus (see next page).

Another leisurely way is to bicycle, walk, or wheelchair the 56 kilometre (35 mile) Niagara River Recreation Trail. This independent paved pathway runs parallel to the Niagara River from Lake Erie to Lake Ontario.

## Places to Dine Along the Route

Queenston Heights Restaurant is a four star restaurant located in a beautiful Park on the edge of the Niagara Escarpment. Traditional afternoon tea is served daily on the patio 3:00 p.m. until 5:00 p.m. Lunch and dinner reservations are suggested (905-262-4274).

Both the Table Rock Restaurant (905-354-3631) and Victoria Park Restaurant (905-356-2217) are located in the Park, directly opposite the Falls. A breakfast at Table Rock Restaurant with the sun rising over the Falls is a site you'll remember for a lifetime.

For a full outline of things to see and do pick-up or write for the popular Niagara Parks Visitor's Guide.

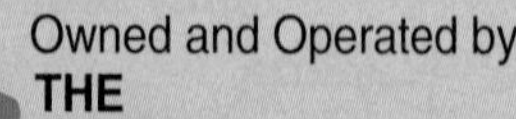

Owned and Operated by

**THE NIAGARA PARKS COMMISSION**

Ontario

Box 150, Niagara Falls, Ontario, Canada L2E 6T2
Telephone: (905) 356-2241

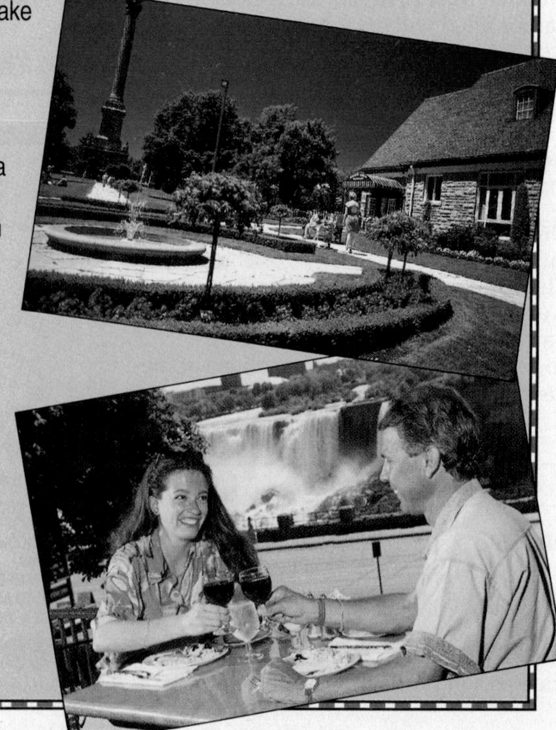

*Ontario Festivals continued from pg. 135*

**Summer:**

Early June in Windsor brings **Day at the River,** an international event focusing on the historical importance of the Detroit River. The festivities include a concert, displays, and river events, all held at Ambassador Park at the bridge. Windsor holds its **International Freedom Festival** mid-June through early July in the downtown waterfront and Dieppe Park areas. Most events are free, and include a midway, church services, fireworks, "Tug-Across-the-River," and Canada Day celebrations.

Amhurstburg holds its **Strawberry Festival** in mid-June at the Park House Museum on Dalhousie Street. The fun includes a strawberry social where visitors can dig into a bowl of fresh strawberries and cream. Games, music and camaraderie are in store for everyone who attends this fun festival.

Early May through mid-October brings many historic celebrations to Peterborough. Visit **Lang Pioneer Village** during these months and you'll be treated to Pioneer Mother's Day, Pioneer Family Day, Pioneer Sheep and Wool Craft Day, Lang Heritage Festival, Pioneer Contests Day, Heritage Canoe Festival, Pioneer Applefest, Pioneer Children's Craft Day, and more.

July 13th, 1953 was the opening night of one of the most improbable ventures in theater history — the **Stratford Festival.** From the first entrance of Alec Guinness, in the title role of *Richard III,* to the last ovations, the event began the history of what has grown to become North America's largest repertory theater, offering world-class drama from early May through the end of October. Recent productions have included performances of *The Merry Wives of Windsor*, *Macbeth*, *The Country Wife*, *Amadeus*, *The Gondoliers*, *The Boy Friend*, *The Comedy of Errors*, *Long Day's Journey Into Night* and *The Stillborn Lover,* held in three beautiful theaters. Visitors to Stratford also enjoy its Music Festival which presents an extensive series of concerts and recitals including jazz, folk, classical, choral and operatic works. Film buffs will enjoy the International Film Festival which shows up to 59 major films in a 2-week period, as well as numerous short subjects, cartoons, documentaries and experimental works. Performances are held Tuesday to Sunday, with matinees on Wednesday, Saturday and Sunday. The Festival is situated in the picturesque city of Stratford, a 90-minute drive southwest of Toronto. In between shows, visitors may enjoy a picnic by the Avon River, browse through the many galleries and shops, go antiqueing in the nearby hamlet of Shakespeare, or stroll through the beautiful Shakespearean gardens.

Mid-June brings **Festival Caravan** to Toronto. It's an international festival with 50 pavilions representing the cultural capitals of the world. Visitors can "take a trip around the world" by visiting the food booths and sampling a variety of ethnic dishes, and by purchasing beautiful crafts representing many nations. More than 200 shows and exhibits make this a truly memorable, not-to-be-missed celebration.

Toronto is also the site of the **Benson and Hedges Symphony of Fire**, an international musical fireworks competition. View magnificent displays of fireworks from far away lands including Italy, Portugal, Spain, United Kingdom and China, followed by the grand finale in early July.

The **Chin International Picnic** held in Toronto in early July is said to be "the largest outdoor free picnic in the world." Begun in 1966 at Toronto's Centre Island as a "spaghetti dig-in," and projected to attract a few picnickers, the event drew 10,000 people. The picnic showcases Toronto's ethnic communities with native folklore presentations, singing, dancing, contests and competitions, beauty pageants, rock groups, marching bands, and special entertainment from all over the world — over 2,000 performers display their varied talents!

Visit Milton on **Canada Day** for their celebration, which includes music, games, live entertainment, an antique car display, and other festivities. The town also holds a **Strawberry Festival** in early July each year at Springridge Farm. Festival-goers will find a craft show, pony rides, entertainment, farm animals, a barbecue, farm demonstrations, and, of course, plenty of delicious fresh strawberries!

For 3 fun-filled days of summertime fun, bring the whole family to Belleville's waterfront for the **Belleville Waterfront Festival** and Folklorama held July 12th through the 14th. From Friday night's parade to Sunday's closing ceremonies, visitors will find fun and entertainment on three sites: Victoria Park, Myer's Pier and Zwicks Park. Folklorama offers a multicultural world of dance, music,

*Ontario Festivals continued on pg. 140*

Closest campground to the Falls, Niagara Glen-View is everyone's favorite.

# YOUR CAMP AND GO PASSPORT

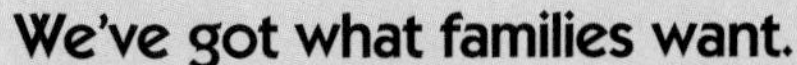

### We've got what families want.

With over 23 years of hospitality, our campground features friendly staff, modern, clean amenities, two pools and cozy, shady sites with a welcoming family atmosphere. We'll make you feel right at home. Enjoy the vacation of a lifetime at Niagara Glen–View.

### Explorer's Passport Plus available here.

It's Niagara's best fun deal. For one low price, you get all day transportation aboard the Niagara Parks air–conditioned People Mover, taking you to all the major attractions. Park your RV, pitch your tent, set up the trailer and go because we're right on the route!

Included in the Passport Plus is admission to Journey Behind the Falls. Tunnels lead you right behind the Falls for an experience you'll never forget. You can't get any closer to the majestic roar.

Also included is admission to the Great Gorge Adventure and the Niagara Spanish Aero Car, two of Niagara's most popular attractions.

### Good food too.

A hearty breakfast is available to get you started before you head out and a full family dinner to finish up your perfect day viewing the spectacular sights of Niagara Falls.

Niagara Glen-View Tent & Trailer Park
3950 Victoria Avenue, PO Box 2087, Niagara Falls, ON Canada L2E 6Z2
(905) 358-8689 Fax (905) 374-4493

**1-800-263-2570**

AAA VISA MasterCard

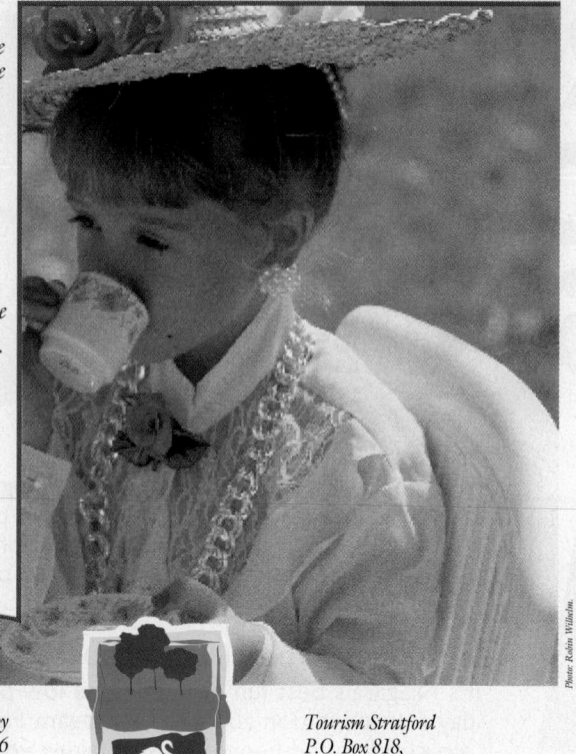

*Ontario Festivals continued from pg. 138*



colorful costumes and delicious food. A children's village provides magicians, artists, a petting zoo, rides and more. Special events include presentations by the International Drum Corps, an International Sail Past, and the show-stopping belly-flop competitions.

No matter where you live, you'll feel right at home in **Sauble Beach** by joining visitors and locals alike in one or all of their many celebrations held during July beginning with July 1st **Canada Day celebrations**. Earl Georgas' Alpha Jazz Band performs at the bandshell, and there are kite flying competitions and fireworks starting at dusk. Sunday, the **Sauble Splash** takes place from 4:00 p.m. 'til 11:00 p.m. when live bands perform at the bandshell. There's a Friday evening **Beef Dinner** at the Sauble Community Centre; an **Open House and Family Fun Day** including a free barbecue, beach volleyball tournament, and sandcastle building. Stop by the Sauble Beach Community Centre for the **Sauble Sandpipers' Annual Arts and Crafts Sale.** Shoppers will find more than 100 vendors inside and outside, displaying a wide variety of beautiful crafts made by local artists. Mid-July brings **Sandfest'**s sand castle and sculpting competitions along with face painting, clowns and Marshall Arts demonstrations, all on the beach, with a street dance later in the evening under the arch. Family Day provides family-oriented activities including a baby pageant, watermelon eating contest, relay races and a dog show. Aqua Day features supervised swimming races for all age groups, canoe races and more at the Sauble River boat ramp.

Head to Vermillion Bay for their **Beach Daze** celebration held in late June. It's a week-long festival that includes volleyball and basketball tournaments, a dance, bathtub race and fireworks display, all held at Fort Vermillion and Eagle River Recreation Centre.

Parkdale holds its **Parkdale Village Festival and Tour of Gardens and Historic Homes** during late June. Visitors enjoy the horse-drawn tours, announcements from the "town crier," a sidewalk sale, steel bands, choir performances, and children's activities, all held in and around the Masaryk-Cowan Community Centre.

Each season in the Niagara Falls area offers its own special qualities, and surrounding local communities provide

*Ontario Festivals continued on pg. 142*

additional shopping, restaurants, and attractions. Millions of vacationers visit Niagara Falls each year, and are captivated by the natural beauty of the Falls, as well as the surrounding parklands that lie parallel to the Niagara River from Lake Erie to Lake Ontario. Encompassing almost 3,000 acres, the **Niagara Parks Commission** offers a variety of on-going events and celebrations throughout the year. Engaging **street performers** will keep the family entertained from July 1st through Labour Day as you stroll through the parklands. **Free band concerts** are held at the Fred Willett Band Shell in Queenston Heights Park from the third week in June through early September, and additional concerts are held Sunday afternoons outside historic Fort Erie. **Traveling bands** also perform at various locations throughout the parks. Fireworks begin on Canada Day, July 1st, and are held Friday evenings at 10:00 p.m. as the parks celebrate **"Falls, Friday, Fireworks."**

The Niagara Parks Greenhouse offers special events throughout the spring and summer. Adjacent to the Canadian Horseshoe Falls, visitors will find the Queen Victoria Park, named after the queen who was the reigning British monarch when the Niagara Parks Commission was established in 1885. From early spring through fall, travelers can enjoy more than a half-million daffodils, the largest mass planting in North America.

Following **"flower festivals"** include the arrival of magnolias, tulips, roses and other annuals, perennials and carpet bedding displays. The Blossom Festival Parade, held in late May, provides a local celebration, and is an ideal time to visit the park.

The Greenhouse is a popular free attraction visited by almost a half million travelers each year. Located on the Niagara Parkway just 1/4 mile south of Horseshoe Falls, the greenhouse is open year-round, daily beginning at 9:a.m. There's a tropical house which features a collection of exotic plants from around the world, along with a gift shop for that special souvenir to take home. Another section features arrangements of fragrant flowers depending upon the season.

Opposite the Maid of the Mist, you'll find the Oakes Garden Theatre, a free architectural and horticultural highlight of your visit to Niagara, Ontario. Opened originally in 1937, the theatre is built to resemble an amphitheater from ancient Greece or Rome. It's fan-shaped, with a podium colonnade and a curved pergols entirely surrounded by a lovely stone wall.

Just 6 miles north of the Niagara Parkway you'll find the Niagara Parks Botanical Gardens, the home of the Niagara Parks School of Horticulture. There are self-guided tours available to stroll the 100 acres of groomed gardens — truly one of North America's most outstanding and beautiful landscapes and botanical collections. Don't miss the Floral Clock, another free horticultural attraction 1-1/2 miles north of the Botanical Gardens. The "floral face" of the clock is changed twice a season to reflect whatever blooms are emerging at the time. Adjacent to the Floral Clock, you'll find the Centennial Lilac Gardens, with more than 250 varieties of these lovely, fragrant flowers, and more than 1,500 individual shrubs.

New this year, and due to open in July, don't miss the Butterfly Conservatory situated on the grounds of the Niagara Parks Botanical Gardens. The permanent exhibit is the home of one of North America's largest and most impressive collections of these lovely insects. You'll find a wide variety of colorful butterflies from around the world displayed throughout a network of pathways, with access for the physically challenged. The conservatory has been designed to allow visitors a rare glimpse of many species of butterflies flitting about as they visit the many varieties of nectar-producing flowers.

Canada's Niagara Falls are a festival in themselves, and a perfect time to enjoy them is at night for the illumination of the Falls. Since 1924, when an agreement was reached between the two cities of Niagara Falls, Ontario and New York, the falls have provided a nightly "light show" of beautiful color. Times vary depending upon the season.

Special events and festivals include the **Conservancy Garden Tour** held in June at Niagara-on-the-Lake. Tour the area's most beautiful gardens with a horticultural expert. Early July brings the **Annual Outdoor Jazz Festival** at the Hillebrand Winery which includes a day of wine, food and music. Fort Erie holds its annual **Living History Weekend** in July, providing a re-enactment of the Seige of Fort Erie complete with period costumes and encampments.

**A Canadian Sunset,** is an Ottawa event which began in 1989, and is normally held during the last week of June up to and including July 1st. It's a display of the equitation program of the Royal Canadian Mounted Police, and the show begins with the guest of honor arriving in a horse-drawn carriage, followed by a Mounted Arms display, a jumping competition, a visit by one of the mares with foal, and a dressage demonstration. The show ends with a performance of The Musical Ride, the origin of which may be traced back to the development of early cavalry formations and their development during battle. Although legend has it that the first Musical Ride was performed as early as 1876, the first recorded Ride was performed in Regina. The highlight of the performance is the "Charge" when the lances with their red and white pennons are lowered and the riders and their mounts launch into the gallop. The conclusion of the performance is the March Past performed to the music of the Force's Regimental March. The horses, considered by many to be the stars of the show, are bred by the Royal Canadian Mounted Police in Pakenham, Ontario. They are 3/4 to 7/8 Thoroughbred, and like most stars, each has his or her own distinct personality, making life around the stables, as well as the performances, especially interesting.

June 20th through the 23rd brings the **Great Balloon Rodeo** to Brockville. Originated in 1991 as a weekend of magic and fun for families by Grenville Christian College and St. Vincent de Paul Hospital, the festival has grown each year. There's a special shape balloon fiesta with 20 of the beautiful balloons launching each morning and evening when the winds are lightest. Evening "balloon glows" add extra beauty to the festival. Visitors also enjoy the artisan and craft sale with 80 artisans displaying their works, and an antique car show. Children's activities have been added each year, and today the Rodeo provides petting zoos, pony rides, old fashioned carnival rides, clowns, puppet shows, story telling, games and more.

**The Great Rendezvous at Old Fort William** in Thunder Bay, Ontario is an exciting spectacle, a colorful, festive celebration of Canada's romantic fur trade history. For 10 days, always the 2nd weekend in July, hundreds of historic re-enactors from across Canada and the United States gather at the Fort to celebrate the spirited camaraderie of a fur trade rendezvous, just like their historic counterparts did centuries ago. Dozens of authentic camps spring up around the Fort's massive palisade. Visitors can meet a seemingly endless array of costumed characters portraying buckskinners, voyagers, mountain men, soldiers and camp followers, Natives and traders. It's a history lesson, brought to life in an enjoyable and entertaining way.

There are boisterous canoe brigade arrivals, salutes with muskets and cannon, distinctive entertainment and music, excellent food, lively demonstrations, spirited games and competitions and much more. Theme days feature a rendezvous picnic, a tribute to period artisans and crafts, and a focus on historic characters of the fur trade. The Fort itself is a sprawling 20-acre site of 42 re-constructed buildings, an exact duplicate of the original fort built by the North West Company of Montreal in 1803. Here, the lifestyles of Ojibwa Natives, French Canadian voyageurs and laborers, as well as Scottish Company partners are portrayed. There's a permanent Native encampment and huge wharf, a working farm, and an historic artisan area for period crafts and much more.

Just 20 minutes from the thunder of Niagara Falls is one of North America's finest cultural attractions — the **Shaw Festival Theatre.** Nestled in the tiny village of Niagara-On-The-Lake, the Shaw Festival's annual array of exciting plays by Bernard Shaw and his contemporaries has been entertaining audiences for over 33 seasons. The Shaw Festival runs from early April through late October with performances held at three theaters, and has become one of the largest and most successful theater festivals in North American, and the only one in the world devoted exclusively to Shaw and his contemporaries. In addition to the festival, historic Niagara-On-The-Lake offers a variety of activites and attractions including one of Canada's oldest golf courses, bicycle trails, historic homes and sites, and beautiful parks and gardens.

The **Friendship Festival** is held in Fort Erie from late June through early July. This major event provides days of fun for the whole family with musical performances including alternative, rock, country, classical, Caribbean and reggae. Recent performers include The Highwaymen, country music's four "outlaws," Willie Nelson, Waylon Jennings, Kris Kristofferson and Johnny Cash. A large midway provides more than 15 rides, including hot-air balloon rides! Hungry festival-goers love the food court with more than 100 vendors cooking up delicacies to suit every palate: clams, crab legs, corn-on-the-cob, sausage-on-a-bun, sugar waffles, ice cream, and much more. Shoppers enjoy the booths that line the Niagara Parkway with an array of crafts and other merchandise for sale. The horse show provides plenty of thrills as visitors view Olympic-caliber athletes competing in a variety of equestrian events. The "sport of kings" is also played here at the Fort Erie Racetrack beginning on Canada Day, July 1st.

Whether or not you have any Scottish heritage in your family, you'll enjoy **Scottish Heritage Day** in Peterborough in early July. The festivities include pipers, highland dancing, tours of historic homes, skills demonstrations, and open hearth cooking, all held at the Hutchinson House Museum on Brock Street.

The community of Thorold holds its **18th annual Arts and Crafts Show** Saturday and Sunday, July 20th and 21st at the Battle of Beaverdams Park, downtown. Visitors will enjoy browsing the more than 150 exhibits displaying jewelry, folk and decorative art, watercolors, country and Victorian flower arrangements, designer baskets, limited edition prints, pen and ink drawings, hand-crafted bird houses and mail boxes, and much more. Hungry after shopping? Community groups offer hot dogs and hamburgers, hot beef on a bun, homemade waffles, freshly made lemonade, and homemade baked goods.

**Fall:**

Labour Day weekend brings the 8th annual **Marshville Heritage Festival Art and Craft Sale.** Stop by the Wainfleet Sports Complex for the show and sale which represents more than 100 juried artists and artisans, displaying their beautiful, hand-crafted merchandise from across Ontario.

The Rotary Club of Niagara Falls Sunrise sponsors their annual fall festival, **Art by the Falls**. Held in Rapidsview Park, Niagara River Parkway, on September 20th through the 22nd, the show celebrates its 5th year with more than 125 vendors displaying pottery, weaving, woodworking, paintings, sculptures, jewelry, clothing, games and much more. In addition to the lovely, hand-made crafts, visitors will find ample free parking, food, drinks (including wine), steel band musical performances, mimes, and face painting.

Mark your calendar for September 20th through 29th with the **Niagara Grape & Wine Festival** held each year for over 44 years. The 10-day celebration was begun to promote the grape and wine industries of the area, and today has grown into one of Niagara's biggest and most popular celebrations. The Grande Parade showcases approximately 150 units consisting of marching bands, floats, majorettes, and more. Other events include gourmet dinners at the more than 20 local wineries, wine tastings, winery and vineyard tours, special family events, concerts featuring internationally-known performers, a large arts and crafts show, and a wine garden with food and entertainment in downtown's Montebello Park.

## *PRINCE EDWARD ISLAND FESTIVALS*

**Summer:**

Come to Cavendish for 3 days of family fun and entertainment in late August at the annual **Lucy Maud Montgomery Festival.** Join in on the tribute to the famous author of Anne of Green Gables. There is a children's festival featuring well-known Maritime entertainers, Kids at Heart, whose versatile and humorous act will please young and old. Enjoy the old-fashioned fun of an ice cream social with strawberries and Cow's homemade ice cream, traditional music and dance, games, and readings from Montgomery's works. Guided tours of the author's Cavendish home are provided, too. Saturday evening brings a fish fest in the beautiful fishing village of North Rustico, just 5 miles from Cavendish, and you'll get to sample from a variety of fresh, local fish prepared "just the way you like it."

The College of Piping holds its **Celtic Festivals** throughout the summer in Summerside. The **Summerside Highland Gathering**, held in late June, offers piping, drumming, Highland dancing, pipe band and athletic competitions. Massed bands, continuous Celtic entertainment, pubs, vendors, fiddling, and activities for the children round out the event. Thursday evenings at 7:00 p.m. bring Scottish performances including drummers, stepdancers, fiddlers, and singers.

Join in on the fun at the **Summerside Lobster Carnival** held in late July for over 40 years. What can you expect by attending this event? Lobster, lobster, and more lobster! There's a seafood fair where visitors can sample a wide variety of Island seafood, along with the enjoyment of a lively parade, a talent contest, nightly entertainment and harness racing.

Late July brings the **PEI Potato Blossom Festival** to O'Leary. A variety of exciting events await guests including a giant parade, horse races, a PEI Potato Blossom Banquet, concerts, dances, a car show, children's day, 5 and 10km runs, pancake breakfasts, and more.

Visit Charlottetown in August for **Old Home Week Provincial Exhibition.** The Charlottetown Driving Park offers 15 racing programs in 8 days, and includes the fastest horses and best drivers in eastern Canada. In addition to action-packed harness racing, the event includes horse shows and livestock exhibitions, a parade, midway, musical entertainment, a 4-H show, and Women's Institute Days. The celebration ends with the running of Eastern Canada's biggest racing spectacular, the $20,000 Gold Cup & Saucer Race.

**Fall:**

Autumn is a wonderful time to visit PEI, and eastern PEI celebrates the season with a variety of events for a wide variety of interests. There are cycling expeditions, windsurfing competitions, and displays of some pretty unusual sports such as "square dancing on horseback!" Theater, birdwatching and gardening competitions are held, also, for a quieter, but equally enjoyable activity.

## *QUEBEC FESTIVALS*

**Spring:**

Come taste the best in maple products at the 38th annual **Maple Festival** held in Plessisville (Coeur-du-Quebec) in late April. You'll be treated to maple treats and festivities of all kinds, including sugaring-off parties with thousands of other maple-syrup lovers, evening festivities, entertainers, horse-pulling contests and lots of great-tasting maple taffy.

**Summer:**

Summertime in Montreal means fireworks, so if you enjoy spectacular fireworks displays, head to Montreal mid-June to early July for the **Benson & Hedges International Fireworks Competition**. Each year's event proves to be more dazzling than before. More than 19 countries have participated since the competition's inception in 1985. It is considered to be the most important competition of its kind in the word with an average of eight shows each year. More than 17 million spectators have enjoyed this unique blend of fireworks and music over the years as competitors launch an average of 3,500 components during each 30-minute competition. Participants utilize more than 3,000 mortars (the "canons" from which the fireworks "bombs" are propelled), 250 tons of sand to bury the mortars, and 250 kilometers of electrical wire to launch all their rockets and bombs.

July 5th through 14th brings the **Festival Mondial De Folklore** to Drummondville. Folk performers come from such far-away countries as Italy, Spain, Russia, Chile, Israel, and many others, and are the highlight of this festival. Welcoming ceremonies begin at a charming park, The Halte Saint-Frederic, where the folk groups visit with festival-goers. Visitors are then invited to join the groups at "The Parc Woodyatt," the heart of the festivities. Other areas of the festival include the Grande Place, an arena seating more than 1,300 guests as they enjoy the music and dancing; Cafe des Traditions, which is a delightful terrace offering exclusive folk shows featuring renowned artists; 35 arts and crafts booths displaying Canadian crafts; and 20 international craft booths displaying works from Africa, Mexico, Asia, and the United States. The Resto du Festival provides a spot where visitors can feast on a variety of tantalizing international and Quebec foods in an area with picnic tables and sunshades. Guests are encouraged to savor the international flavor by trying some Brazilian alligator, Mexican fajitas, or Jamaican pate.

Come join the fun! Montreal is the "humor capital of the world," thanks to the **Just For Laughs Festival** held in July. From its humble beginnings as a 2-night French language comedy show, to the sensational proportions of its current performances, theater shows, open-air venues and television specials, the world's largest comedy event has grown into a very special event. Recent performances have drawn more than 400,000 spectators to this array of international comedians. Artists from as far away as France, Belgium, Iraq, Sri Lanka, Australia, Japan and other countries, as well as the United States and Canada perform in more than 400 shows during the festival. Throughout its history, the event has drawn such international stars as Lily Tomlin, Bob Newhart, Steve Allen, Roseanne and Tom Arnold, Jay Leno, Sandra Bernhard, Penn & Teller, Marcel Marceau, and others.

Come to Trois-Rivieres on the first weekend in August for **Le Grand Prix De Trois-Rivieres,** a series of major professional auto races, including the Player's Ltd/Toyota Atlantic Championship and the Trans-Am Series. Activities surrounding the race include the Pit-Stop Event which takes place in the heart of Trois-Rivieres, bringing thousands of visitors downtown. Spectators can enjoy the sight of competing teams of mechanics working against the clock to make timed wheel changes, exactly as they do during racetrack pit stops. More than 600 people attend a gourmet dinner followed by a dance; and more than 300 guests can be accommodated aboard the *M.S. Jacque Cartier* for a supper and cruise along the Saint-Lawrence River, ending with a magnificent fireworks display.

The 13th celebration of the **Saint-Jean-Sur Richelieu Hot-Air Balloon Festival** will be held during the 3rd week in August. More than 100 hot-air balloons including more than 20 special shapes, some never seen in North America, will enhance the sky of the region for one of the most prestigious hot-air balloon festivals in Canada. The Saint-Jean-sur-Richelieu region offers balloonists and visitors ideal conditions for this growing festival: experienced organizers, attractive and favorable landing grounds, and a welcoming and warm population. Each flight is unique, and only the wind decides the place for landings. The launches take place twice a day, usually at 6:00 a.m. and 6:00 p.m. In addition to the balloons, there are activities, games, entertainment, and an evening outdoor musical concert. If you have always wanted to ride in a hot-air balloon, here's your chance! Rides will be available for a fee.

**Fall:**

The first week of September, the silver screen will once again hold center stage in Quebec City during the 11th edition of the **Quebec International Film Festival.** An exclusive showcase of the most recent trends in filmaking, the festival features about 40 productions, including several comedies, from all over the world. All cinema lovers are invited to this film extravaganza where many types of movies are featured.

## *SASKATCHEWAN FESTIVALS*

**Summer:**

For more than 9 years, the **Regina International Children's Festival** has been providing children with unique art, musical, and cultural shows and exhibits. Performances by world-renowned puppeteers, musicians, comedians, storytellers, and actors provide children with first-class entertainment — just for them! Some recent performances have included: the Cashore Marionettes with characterizations so real you forget they are marionettes; Paul Hann, whose traditional and original songs are showcased in a spirited concert; Beatlemania, featuring the Magical Mystery Tour tribute; and a show featuring acrobatics, magic and comedy by Tom Kubinek.

The **Regina Folk Festival** will be held Saturday, June 22nd and Sunday, June 23, and dedicated to the presentation of folk music in its many variations, performed by talented regional, national and international talent. Recent performances were staged by country-folk-pop quartet, Ranch Romance, and Afro-funk ensemble, Laura Love Band. It's a wonderful, personal event, as artists are given the opportunity to refine new material as well as play along with other festival performers and audience members. There is a popular children's area showcasing musicians, jugglers, face painting, reading/story telling, and craft centers. There are workshops for budding musicians and songwriters, and a variety of food and souvenir booths.

**Folkfest** is a 3-day multicultural festival held on the third weekend in August in Saskatoon. More than 14 cultural groups are located in more than 20 pavilions throughout the city, and each pavilion

***Saskatchewan Festivals con't. on pg. 146***

*Saskatchewan Festivals con't. from pg. 144*

offers its own unique variety of foods, entertainment, souvenirs, displays and demonstrations featuring specific cultures. Inside each pavilion, you'll find something from past festivals, including the folk tales, games, sports, and other celebrations.

The **Big Valley Jamboree** is held in mid-July in Craven, and again in mid-August in Camrose. The event kicks off a summer of country fun, and is billed as Canada's #1 country music festival. It's mostly music with requests from previous year's patrons including more traditional country music in the way of fiddlers and polka fests. As well, the Jamboree has secured some traditional acts to compliment the strong contemporary line-ups. Each main stage features a "corral full" of country music superstars, shared with fans from around the globe. Beginning on a Thursday, the Jamboree provides famous Canadian and international entertainers who sing, dance and entertain folks for four sizzling days and nights of hot country.

Recent performances at Craven include the 1995 best Saskatchewan female country nmusic vocalist, Terri Harris, 1995 best Saskatchewan male vocalist, Scott Kyle King, and 1995 best Saskatchewan group and best Saskatchewan entertainers, the Johner Brothers. Country fans can start their weekend off right at Goodyear's Ribfest. Entertainment starts at 2:p.m. and includes plenty of fine country acts with special performances at 10:p.m. This outdoor cabaret includes a hearty ribs and fixin's dinner for a reasonable price.

At Camrose, there's a great balance between Canadian as well as traditional and contemporary international artists. Recent performances include Canadian performers Ian Tyson, Farmers' Daughter, Sheila Deck, Terry Kelly, and Prescott Brown. The event has been expanded into six action packed days and nights, and country music fans can start their weekend off right at Steakfest. Entertainment begins at 2:p.m. Wednesday, and features plenty of fine country acts and a special 10:p.m. guest appearance.

The **SaskTel Saskatchewan Jazz Festival** takes place June 27th to July 6th, and this year they are celebrating their 10th anniversary. The first event was held in 1987 and attracted 7,000 festival goers. Since those early days, the festival has grown to an attendance of more than 35,000. You'll find the best in jazz from mainstream to contemporary, and blues, gospel and worldbeat music, performed by more than 340 international, Canadian, and Saskatchewan entertainers. The festival is performed on two stages, one an outdoor state set in the spacious Delta Bessborough Hotel gardens. There are also more than 80 free concerts held on "Jazz Street," and 2 stages in Kiwanis Park on the riverbank. The indoor performances are held in Centennial Auditorium & Hall, The Delta Bessborough Hotel, Knox United Church, Mendel Art Gallery and the Broadway Theatre.

Nightly performances are also available at Saskatoon's jazz hotspot, The Bassment, and there are many other shows performed in downtown lounges, restaurants and clubs.

**Winter:**

Late November through early December brings the **Canadian Western Agribition** to Regina. It's billed as Canada's international marketplace, one of the largest livestock shows in the world with around 2,000 exhibitors, 16 different beef cattle breeds, as well as commercial cattle, horses, swine, dairy, sheep and poultry competitions. There's a rodeo that attracts the top cowboys in North America who compete in many exciting events; the National Non-Pro Cutting Horse finals; the Heavy Horse pulls and hitches, and stock dog shows. Attend one of the many livestock auctions and watch the bidding, or take in the sights of the education center, which explains the business of agriculture. Located on more than 19 acres of indoor facilities, the show provides a fun way to learn about the agriculture industry.

## *YUKON FESTIVALS*

**Spring:**

May brings the **Dawson City International Gold Show** to Dawson City. It's an annual exhibit and show featuring placer mining industry exhibits and associates from around the Territory. Activities include seminars, a barbecue, a fashion show and horticultural market, and gold-panning competitions.

The Klondike Visitors Association sponsors its **Thaw-Di-Gras Spring Carnival** to celebrate the arrival of the long-awaited spring thaw. There are themed games, events, entertainment and lots of fun, both indoors and out on the river and around town. The annual Commissioner's Ball is hosted by the Territorial Commission, and this gala event includes a tea party, and a dinner-dance. Visitors delight in seeing guests dressed in period costumes as they enter the Palace Grand Theatre for the evening. The annual Yukon Gold Panning Championship competition is open to amateurs and professionals from the Yukon and around the world. The timed trials and finals create lots of excitement for participants and spectators alike. The annual Yukon Talent Night provides an opportunity for Dawson's stars to compete in Gerties Darts International, a weekend-long dart tournament that draws players from around the world.

**Summer:**

Each year on the last full weekend in June in the city of Whitehorse, the ancient art of storytelling is rekindled via the **Yukon International Storytelling Festival**. In this, the land of northern lights, midnight suns and tall tales, this multicultural event provides an enjoyable tapestry of stories, myths, music and drama. The mission of the festival is to keep alive the art and tradition of storytelling, and to acquaint young people with the art via their active participation in the festival. This unique family event takes place at Rotary Peace Park along the banks of the Yukon River, and is opened with a welcome feast on Thursday evening for performers and volunteers. Public performances begin Friday evening and end with a unifying circle dance and closing ceremony on Sunday night. The celebration is held, rain or shine, in several tents with storytellers performing simultaneously throughout the weekend.

Because so many of the storytellers come from cultures that have always been aware of the critical importance of taking great care of the environment, many of the stories relate to environmental issues. What a wonderful way to teach people of all ages to take gentle care of Planet Earth than by telling them stories about the ways in which to do just that. The festival takes great care in demonstrating respect for the environment in all aspects of its operation.

By its very nature, the festival is suited to children and adults of all ages, and has provided for festival goers with special needs. Most performances are well suited for visitors with visual impairments, and there are special performances for those with hearing problems. In addition, festival organizers make special arrangements for the elderly and physically challenged guests.

There is a special children's tent providing games, children's stories, balloon art, clowns, and more, and shoppers enjoy the festival craft market featuring the works of local artisans including tapes of stories by the performers.

Head to Haines Junction in early June for their **Alsek Music Festival**, an annual 2-day outdoor music event. The fest showcases northern talent at two evening dances, all-day musical performances under a big tent, as well as at performers' workshops in the arena mezzanine. Craft lovers enjoy this festival as well, as there are craft booths located right on the grounds. Bring the children, too, for the children's events include a reading teepee, pony rides, balloons, clowns, and much more.

Mid-August brings the annual **Sourdough Rendezvous Goldrush Bathtub Race** to Whitehorse. Actually, the race begins in Whitehorse with a mandatory overnight stay (for contestants) in Carmacks, and ends in Dawson City. There are plenty of pre- and post-race activities, including a barbecue at Rotary Park with a beer garden, Old Man River Contest and more. Guess the winning time and win a beautiful ivory carving valued at $1,200, and enjoy the wrap-up festivities in Dawson City, in conjunction with their Discovery Days celebration.

**Dawson City's Discovery Days** are held in late August. This annual event commemorates the discovery of gold in 1896 and includes opening day ceremonies, a baseball tournament, parade, pancake breakfasts, horticultural show, canoe and raft race, a barbecue, dance, demolition derby, junior triathlon and gun competitions.

**Dalton Trail Days** in the Village of Haines Junction and the City of Haines, Alaska, offer a 4-day international festival that commemorates the historic Dalton Trail. Events occur between Canada Day (July 1st) and Independence Day (July 4th) in the U.S. The festivities include a parade, birthday party, pancake breakfasts, family events, coffee houses, barbecue dinners and a rodeo in Haines, Alaska.

**Winter:**

If your travels bring you to the Yukon during winter, don't miss the 32nd annual **Yukon Sourdough Rendezvous Festival** held during the last week in February in Whitehorse. For over 30 years, this winter festival has thrilled Yukoners and visitors with events like the Queen's contest, the hairy leg and beard contest, flour packing, and a full schedule of fun, winter activities and sports. It's billed as the true Yukon cure for cabin fever, and the dancing, singing, pubs, and activities are sure to live up to that promise.

Winter in the Yukon also brings the **Gold Rush Games for Special Olympics.** Held in Dawson City in March, (yes, March still offers winter-style activities in the Yukon) the competition qualifies Special Olympic athletes in cross-country and downhill skiing, snowshoeing and figure skating. The event incorporates the discover of gold theme into the opening ceremonies, banquets, sightseeing and cultural activities.

March also brings the **Percy DeWolfe Memorial Mail Race** to Dawson City. The annual sled dog race starts with the transfer of the official race mail from postmaster to R.C.M.P. to the first mushers basket. In a 24-hour time period, mushers and their dogs race from Dawson City to Eagle, Alaska and back. Mushers and race organizers gather together the night after the race for a wind-up banquet. ◆

# DISCOVER THE FESTIVAL

*– that is –*

# NORTH AMERICA

## ALASKA

Chamber of Commerce
Visitor Center – 2550 Mistletoe Drive
P.O. Box 55071–WD
North Pole, AK 99705
(907) 488-2242

## ALASKA

*SKAGWAY CONVENTION & VISITORS BUREAU*
P.O. BOX 415
SKAGWAY, ALASKA 99840

**Come visit Skagway Alaska, "Gateway to the Klondike."**

Stop over and see: • Skagway Arctic Brotherhood Hall • Tour the White Pass and Yukon Route Railroad • Gold Rush Cemetery • Skagway's City Museum in the City Hall

**For More Information Call:**
**(907) 983-2854**

TOUR ALASKA

## CALIFORNIA

**UNIQUE...** ***for Garlic lovers and lovers of...***

- Intriguing gifts
- Gourmet foods
- Fresh farm produce
- Sauces, seasonings & spices

***Also...***
Garlic wreaths, braids, cookbooks
**Call for FREE catalog (800) 537-6122**
4800 Monterey Hwy (Hwy 101) • Gilroy, CA 95020
From Jct Hwy 25 & US 101: Go 1/2 Mi N on US 101

## CALIFORNIA

**PARKWAY LAKES R.V.**
**DAILY • WEEKLY • MONTHLY**

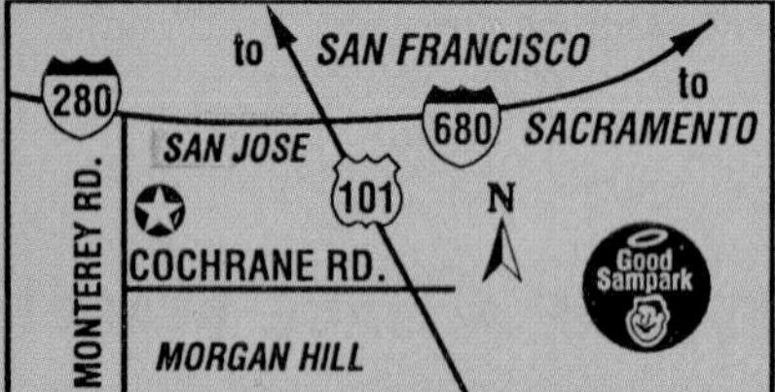


**(408) 779-0244**
100 Ogier Ave., Morgan Hill, CA 95037

## CALIFORNIA

THE
ROY ROGERS-DALE EVANS
MUSEUM

Exhibits depict the complete professional & personal lives of the Rogers.
Gift Shop open 9 am to 5 pm.
**(619)243-4547**
15650 Seneca Rd., Victorville, CA 92392

## KENTUCKY

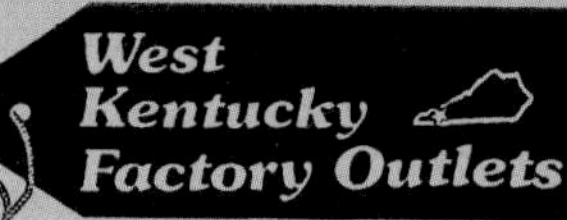


***502-388-7379***
***U.S. 62/641 at KY 93***
46 Stores
**Eddyville, KY**
Fantastic 30% to 70% Savings
On Quality, First-Run Merchandise
**March - Dec.:** 9 a.m. - 9 p.m. Mon-Sat
11 a.m. -7 p.m. Sunday
**January-February:** 9 a.m. - 7 p.m. Mon-Sat
12-7 p.m. Sunday
***NEAR 1-24 & WK PARKWAY***

## LOUISIANA

***VISIT HISTORIC***
***Opelousas!***
Celebrate our
*joie de vivre*
**at our cultural festivals**

Camps in country setting, centrally located in South City Park. Asphalt & grassy sites - Elec. & water hookups, sewer dump station. Picnic shelters, outdoor grills

**5 MINUTES FROM SHOPPING & I-49 –**
**20 MINUTES NORTH I-10**

Ken Vidrine, Supt.
(318) 948-2560

1440 S. Market St.
P.O. Box 712
Opelousas, LA 70570

## OREGON

**NOTHING LIKE IT FOR 2,000 MILES.**

Drive among 600 wild animals from around the world. Open daily just south of Roseburg. Call 1-800-355-4848 for a brochure.

**WILDLIFE SAFARI**
**As close as you'll ever get.**
P.O. Box 1600, Winston, OR 97496

## BRITISH COLUMBIA

**BC RV**
*(Vancouver)*
**DELUXE FACILITIES • INDOOR POOL**
On transit route • Daily tours
8765 Cariboo Place, Burnaby, B.C. V3N 4T2
Phone: (604) 420-1722 Fax: (604) 420-4782
Toll Free Reservation Fax: 1-(800) 667-9901

## BRITISH COLUMBIA

Sponsored by
**CLEARWATER ADVENTURE RESORT**
**GUIDED ACTIVITIES**
• Hiking • Canoeing • Voyager Canoes
• Mountain Biking • Outfitting Packages and Rentals
RESORT
• Serviced Sites • Laundry • Chalets and Cabins
• 2 Restaurants • Canoe Instruction on Our Lake

Adjacent to Clearwater Info Centre
52 Ridge RV Park
**(604) 674-3909**
**Toll Free 1-800-421-3909**

## BRITISH COLUMBIA

To receive your free touring guide:
**Vancouver Island and The Gulf Islands**
Contact:
**The Tourism Association of Vancouver Island**
#302-45 Bastion Square
Victoria, BC V8W 1J1
Ph: (604) 382-3551
FAX: (604) 382-3523
Dept. WC/96

## PROVINCE OF QUEBEC

**Quebec City**
*10 minutes West of Quebec City*
*Six different sight seeing tours daily*

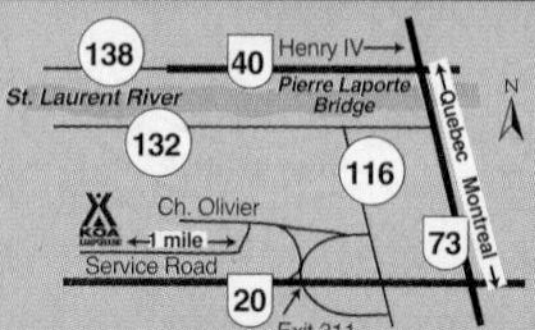


Bernières, Lévis, Qué. G7A 2N6
Tel.: (418) 831-1813 • Fax (418) 836-2406

# how to use this directory

## How the Directory is Organized

Information in **WOODALL'S CAMPGROUND DIRECTORY** is organized alphabetically first by U.S. state, then by Canadian province, followed by Mexico. It is further alphabetized by town, then by campground, RV dealer or attraction under those towns. Each town name is followed by a letter and number (i.e., A-1) which refers to a grid coordinate on the maps found at the beginning of each state or province.

The North American edition is split into Eastern and Western sections, each organized alphabetically starting with Alabama in the East and Alaska in the West. At the end of each section, you'll find an alphabetical index of all facilities listed in this Directory. The "WOODALL Alphabetical Quick Reference" provides the name of each listed campground/RV park, RV service location or tourist attraction — in name order. It's useful when you know the name of the location you want to visit, but don't remember the town it's listed under. Symbols in front of each name indicate ® RV rentals; Δ tent rentals; □ cabin rentals; ★ RV service center; • attraction. **NEW THIS YEAR:** We've added the map coordinate after each town reference for ease in using our maps. Find it quick at the end of the east and the end of the western section. Each state/province begins with travel information and a map, both of which are updated annually. The sole purpose of the state/provincial maps is to show towns where campgrounds (indicated by diamonds ◈), tourist attractions (indicated by flags ⚑), and RV service centers (indicated by gears ✱) are located.

You should NOT use *only* our state maps while traveling. PLEASE use an official state highway map or a full-sized atlas in conjunction with our state maps. We also suggest you check the listing section when planning your itinerary.

## WOODALL Representatives make Personal Inspections

**All privately-owned campgrounds are personally inspected each year by one of our 30 Representative Teams.** Their detailed inspection reports are used to compile the listing information and to recommend the WOODALL ratings. These WOODALL rep teams have years of RV experience before joining WOODALL'S. They are professionally trained in their territory and are brought together each year for additional training. The privately-operated campground listings in this Directory are based upon Reps' personal inspections made in the spring and summer of 1995. In addition to compiling information on a detailed listing form for each park, the Reps also complete an evaluation form (sample shown on pages IV and V) to recommend the ratings.

Our Rep Teams also personally visit and gather information on RV dealers and attractions. Those listed in this Directory are the facilities particularly interested in your business.

The listings for government campgrounds (federal, state, provincial, municipal and military) are based upon information supplied to WOODALL'S from the appropriate government agency.

WOODALL has been publishing RV/camping guides, directories and magazines for nearly 60 years. Each year over 150,000 changes are made to these listings, providing you with the most complete, accurate and up-to-date Campground Directory available on the market today.

## WOODALL'S Dual Rating System

**Ratings Help You Choose The Park You Are Looking For.**

WOODALL'S assigns two ratings to each privately owned campground/RV park. The WOODALL Rating System is shown on pages IV and V with an example of how our representatives complete an evaluation form. One rating is assigned to the facilities at the park (sites, roads, service buildings, restrooms, hookups, etc.). A separate recreation rating is also assigned. Both facilities and recreation ratings range from 1◈ to 5◈. (This ◈ is WOODALL'S copyrighted rating symbol.) Keep in mind the final ratings are a composite of several different areas of interest.

**What do the Woodall Ratings indicate?**

Ratings depend on the quality and quantity of our criteria elements. The more ◈'s a park has generally reflects the presence of more development at the park, and usually more facilities. HOWEVER, THE MAINTENANCE OF THE CAMPGROUND WEIGHS HEAVILY IN ALL RATINGS ASSIGNMENTS. Cleanliness is a major factor in determining if you and your family will have an enjoyable vacation. The maintenance level at a park must meet or exceed the recommended ratings or the rating cannot be assigned at that level.

**Do more ◈'s mean a better park?**

Emphatically, NO! The WOODALL rating system does NOT indicate good, better, best. Each RV/camping family needs to decide how much development is going to make their trip enjoyable. WOODALL lists a wide range of parks from rustic, natural settings to resort-like RV parks. Different factors may make a park attractive: convenience to the Interstate; width of sites; located near a popular attraction; a swim pool, lake or other on-site recreation. Please take the time to understand the WOODALL Rating System and consider the ratings, along with other factors, when choosing the parks you want to stay in. **Be sure to read the listings carefully to make sure they have the facilities and amenities you want, and be sure to let the park owner know you found them in WOODALL'S.**

# special features

## ✔ FREE INFORMATION

Use our Reader Service Card opposite page 16 as an easy way to write for FREE travel and camping information and more information about advertisers' products and services. This card also gives you the opportunity to be a part of WOODALL by sharing with us how far you travel, for how long, and in what type of unit so that we can better meet your needs.

## ✔ TRAVEL SECTIONS

When planning your next trip be sure to refer to the travel sections located at the beginning of each state and province. You'll find loads of information on climate, topography, time zone, travel information sources, recreational information, places to see and things to do, and events.

## ✔ SEASONAL SITE GUIDE

When looking for a park in which to spend a month or an entire season, also refer to WOODALL'S Guide to Seasonal Sites in RV Resorts-Campgrounds (the yellow pages at the back of this directory). Detailed listings include directions, facilities and recreation available on-site, and more, all verified through personal visits by WOODALL'S representatives.

Each facility has purchased advertising in this section to tell you about its unique features, special rates, and nearby attractions. All ads are reader serviced, so you can obtain even more information, FREE!, direct from the parks.

And most important, WOODALL'S 59 dedicated Representatives spent over 5,000 days, traveling half a million miles to update our information by personal inspection. And as a result, our dependable WOODALL ratings for both facilities and recreation have been assigned to privately-operated campgrounds.

## ✔ 100% MONEY BACK GUARANTEE

If for any reason you're not satisfied with this Directory, please return it to us by December 31, 1996, along with your sales receipt, and we will reimburse you for the amount you paid for the Directory. Also please share with us the reason for your dissatisfaction.

# how to use this directory

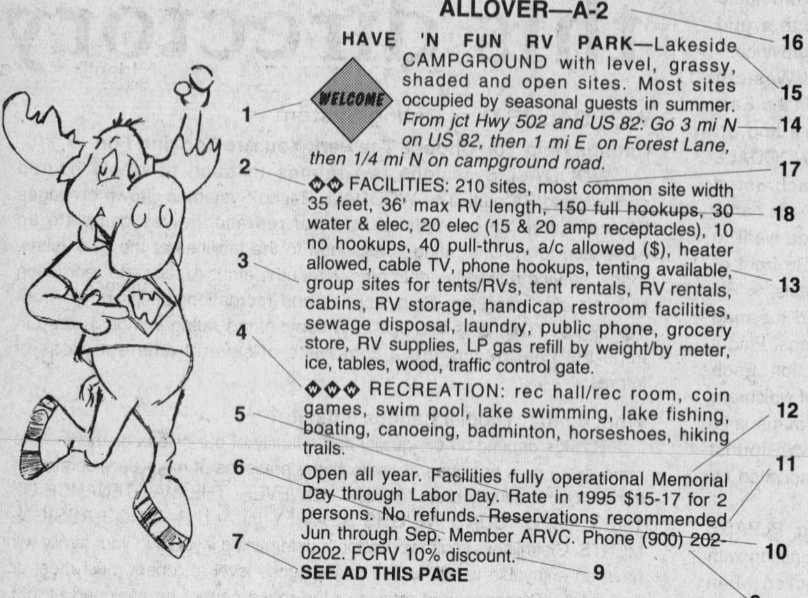

ALLOVER—A-2
HAVE 'N FUN RV PARK—Lakeside CAMPGROUND with level, grassy, shaded and open sites. Most sites occupied by seasonal guests in summer.
WELCOME
*From jct Hwy 502 and US 82: Go 3 mi N on US 82, then 1 mi E on Forest Lane, then 1/4 mi N on campground road.*
◆◆ FACILITIES: 210 sites, most common site width 35 feet, 36' max RV length, 150 full hookups, 30 water & elec, 20 elec (15 & 20 amp receptacles), 10 no hookups, 40 pull-thrus, a/c allowed ($), heater allowed, cable TV, phone hookups, tenting available, group sites for tents/RVs, tent rentals, RV rentals, cabins, RV storage, handicap restroom facilities, sewage disposal, laundry, public phone, grocery store, RV supplies, LP gas refill by weight/by meter, ice, tables, wood, traffic control gate.
◆◆◆ RECREATION: rec hall/rec room, coin games, swim pool, lake swimming, lake fishing, boating, canoeing, badminton, horseshoes, hiking trails.
Open all year. Facilities fully operational Memorial Day through Labor Day. Rate in 1995 $15-17 for 2 persons. No refunds. Reservations recommended Jun through Sep. Member ARVC. Phone (900) 202-0202. FCRV 10% discount.
SEE AD THIS PAGE
1
2
3
4
5
6
7
16
15
14
17
18
13
12
11
10
9
8


1. **WELCOME:** The Welcome symbol before a listing identifies those parks that have purchased an advertisement because they want to tell you more about their business.

2. **FACILITIES:** The ratings range from 1 to 5 ◆'s. All of the facilities listed are available on site.

3. **TENT/RV/CABIN RENTALS:** You may rent a tent or RV or cabin at this park.

4. **RECREATION:** The ratings range from 1 to 5 ◆'s. All recreation listed is available right at the campground. If this same recreation is open to the public, we will tell you in the listing.

5. **RATE INFORMATION:** Most often this will show as a range of rates from low to high which the privately owned campground charged in 1995 (the year in which these inspections were made). THESE ARE NOT GUARANTEED RATES.

6. **PRIVATE CAMPGROUND AFFILIATION:** This directory identifies the privately-owned campgrounds which belong to the National Association of RV Parks & Campgrounds (ARVC) and also those which are members of state private campground associations.

7. **ADV. CROSS-REFERENCE:** This line will refer you to the specific page for this listing's advertisement.

8. **PHONE NUMBER:** Phone numbers are included for ease in calling ahead for a site.

9. **DISCOUNTS:** KOA-10% Value Card Discount & FCRV Discounts are shown.

10. **SPECIAL INFO:** This area includes such information as no pets, age restrictions may apply, and operating season. If the listing doesn't state "No Pets," pets are allowed, however, if you are traveling with a large or unusual pet, please call ahead.

11. **RESERVATIONS:** If reservations are recommended for a certain time of the year, we'll tell you at the end of the listing.

12. **FULLY OPERATIONAL:** This tells you what time of the year you will find all of the facilities in full operation.

13. **TENTING AVAILABLE:** This campground welcomes tenters. NOTE: Tenters are welcome at most campgrounds. If a campground does not have facilities for tenters, its listing will indicate "no tents" or "accepts full hookup units only" in the special info section.

14. **DIRECTIONS:** Detailed, easy-to-read driving directions to guide you right to the park entrance.

15. **DESCRIPTIVE PHRASE:** These descriptions "paint a word picture" about the campground, and include information about the terrain, bodies of water, as well as whether or not most or many sites are seasonally occupied.

16. **MAP COORDINATE:** Matching grids on each state/ provincial map to help you locate the listing town.

17. **MOST COMMON SITE WIDTH:** Most parks have sites of varying sizes. This indicates the most commonly occuring site width at a park.

18. **MAX RV LENGTH:** Indicates the maximum length of RV (excluding tow vehicle) that the campground can accommodate. Factors are turns, access and site sizes, based on the skills of an average RVer.

***• Do all parks qualify for a listing in WOODALL'S Campground Directory?***

No, not all parks are listed. A campground must meet our standards for maintenance, access into the park, and have a minimum of 10 designated sites available for overnight camping. Parks that are deleted are re-visited in three years.

***• Why is a new WOODALL'S Campground Directory needed each year?***

During each inspection season, our representative teams delete several hundred listings because they do not meet our minimum requirements and we think they wouldn't meet yours. Many new parks are added each year, too. Listings that remain in the directory are updated with new phone numbers, different ratings, new open and close dates, new recreation, and much more—important reasons to ALWAYS use a current WOODALL'S Directory.

## special notes

• Unless otherwise noted, all campgrounds have flush toilets and hot showers.

• Use the Alphabetical Quick Reference pages at the end of east and west sections. "Find It Quick" when you don't know the listing town.

• We do list some seasonal ONLY parks (sites at these parks are not available for overnight camping), as well as membership, lots for sale and condominium parks. Each of these types of parks must advertise to be listed, and the type of facility will be indicated after the name of the park.

• WOODALL'S lists "Age Restrictions May Apply" based upon information believed to be correct at the time of WOODALL'S inspections. Some sunbelt area parks cater to senior adults only. Since these classifications may change because of rapidly developing legislation, we suggest that you confirm this status by telephone, if it's important to you.

• You'll find the letters "CPO" in some privately-owned campground listings. These letters indicate the park's management has met the requirements of the Certified Park Operator program. In order to receive this designation, a park operator must obtain 75 credits by attending seminars along with hands-on experience working in a park. The CPO designation is a distinguished honor accorded to campground and RV park operators by the National Association of RV Parks and Campgrounds for their efforts in improving themselves, their parks, and their services for the betterment of the camping & RVing lifestyle.

## DIFFERENT TYPES OF LISTINGS

The top line of every listing identifies the type of listing.
*Only privately-owned campgrounds are rated.*

**✔ ADVERTISER LISTING:** Name is in dark, all capital letters. Also shown with a Welcome diamond at the beginning of the listing.

**HOLIDAY COVE TRAVEL TRAILER RESORT** —RV PARK with level, grassy sites and water access to Gulf. *From jct I-75 (exit 41) & Hwy 70: Go 12 mi W on Hwy 70/53rd Ave, then 4 mi W on Cortez Rd.*

◈◈◈ FACILITIES: 112 sites, 140 full hookups, (20, 30 & 50 amp receptacles), a/c allowed ($), heater not allowed, phone hookups, sewage disposal, laundry, publc phone, RV supplies, LP gas refill by weight/by meter, ice, tables, patios.

**✔ RV SALES/SERVICE LOCATION:** Identified by a gear symbol. Always an advertiser. Also shown with a Welcome diamond at the beginning of the listing.

**✵ QUARTZSITE RV REPAIR**—*From jct Business I-10 & US 95: Go 1 block N on US 95, then 100 feet W on Cowell Lane.* SERVICES: RV appliance mechanic full-time, sells parts/accessories, installs hitches. Open all year. Discover/Master Card/Visa accepted. Phone: (520) 927-6874.

**✔ TOURIST ATTRACTION:** Identified by a flag symbol. Also shown with a Welcome diamond at the beginning of the listing.

**⚑ BLACK BART'S STEAK HOUSE**—*From jct I-17 & I-40: Go 3 mi E on I-40 (exit 198), then 1/4 mi SE on butler Ave.* A western steakhouse with family entertainment including musical revues nightly, in conjunction with an RV Park and antique shop. Open all year. American Express/ Master Card/Visa accepted. Phone: (520) 774-1912.

**✔ PRIVATE CAMPGROUND (NON-ADVERTISER):** Name is in dark type, capital and lower case letters.

**Wagon Wheel RV Park** — RV PARK with grassy sites. *From jct US 17 & Hwy 62: Go 1/2 mi N on US 17, then 1/2 mi W on Bostick Rd.* ◈◈◈◈FACILITIES: 265 sites, accepts full hookup units only, 265 full hookups, (30 & 50 amp receptacles), laundry, public phone, patios. ◈◈◈RECREATION: rec hall/rec room, 6 shuffleboard courts, planned group activities, horseshoes. No tents. Open all year. Rate in 1994 $13 for 2 persons. Phone: (813) 773-3157.

**✔ PUBLICLY OWNED CAMPGROUND:** Operated by a federal, state or local government agency. Name appears in light capital letters.

TONTO NATIONAL FOREST (Burnt Corral Campground) — *From jct Hwy 188 & Hwy 88: Go 6 mi SW on Hwy 88.* FACILITIES: 79 sites, 32 ft. max RV length, 79 no hookups, tenting available, pit toilets, handicap restroom facilities, tables, fire rings, grills. RECREATION: lake swimming, boating, ramp, dock, lake fishing. Recreation open to the public. Open all year. Phone: (602) 467-2236.

**✔ MILITARY CAMPGROUND:** Career-military personnel (active or retired) may camp at these parks. Proper ID is required for admittance. Call ahead to ensure eligibility. Note: use the alphabetical index to locate these parks—look under "M" for MILITARY PARK.

MILITARY PARK (Lake Pippin Rec Area-Maxwell/Gunter AFB AL)—*Off base. Off I-10 on Choctawhatchee Bay.* FACILITIES: 16 sites, 16 water & elec, tenting available, sewage disposal. RECREATION: swimming, boating, fishing. Open all year. Reservations required. Phone: (205) 953-5118.

## TYPES OF NON-RATED LISTINGS.

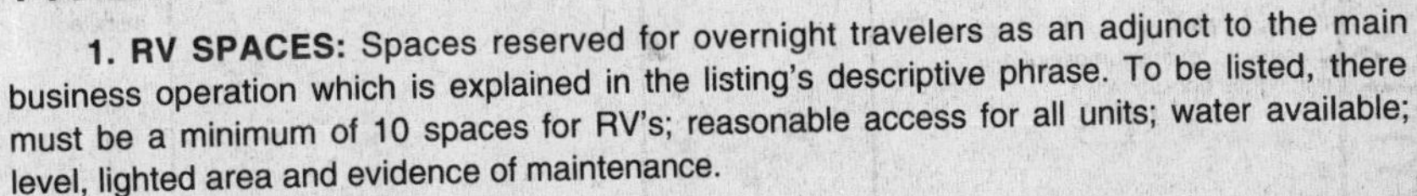

**1. RV SPACES:** Spaces reserved for overnight travelers as an adjunct to the main business operation which is explained in the listing's descriptive phrase. To be listed, there must be a minimum of 10 spaces for RV's; reasonable access for all units; water available; level, lighted area and evidence of maintenance.

**2. TOO NEW TO RATE:** These parks have been inspected by WOODALL and are fully operational, but before a rating is assigned, we want each park to have the opportunity to fully complete its development.

**3. UNDER CONSTRUCTION, PLANNED, REBUILDING, NOT VISITED:** Please write or phone ahead when considering a stay at these parks to confirm their ability to accommodate you.

**4. CAMP RESORT:** Usually fewer than 10 spaces are available to non-members. Phone ahead for site availability, and for more information about purchasing a site.

**5. NUDIST RESORTS:** WOODALL lists a few nudist and clothing optional RV parks/campgrounds.

## a word about camping fees. . .

Neither WOODALL'S nor the campground operator intends the published rate as a guaranteed rate. These rates were gathered by WOODALL Representatives during their inspections in 1995. The rates will almost always be higher by the time you get there because operators' costs have increased just like those of any other business. Rates are provided to give you a comparative overview of the camping fees within a specified area. The fee will most often be shown as a range of rates for either a specific number of persons, a family (2 adults, 2 children) or per vehicle. The range represents the low to high ranges and may or may not include hookups.

## ADVERTISERS WANT YOUR BUSINESS.

The listings in this Directory are provided at no charge to the campground owner. Any campground which meets our minimum criteria requirements receives a listing. Many campground owners want to tell you more about their campground than the listing includes. These campgrounds have purchased advertising for that purpose. These ads can be of great help to you in choosing where to stay—they describe the special features and uniqueness of that campground. They can also tell you about nearby attractions, shopping and restaurants. Remember to "say you saw them in WOODALL'S."

## we'd like to hear from you!

We are always glad to hear from you for any reason and we answer all mail, whether it contains a complaint, a compliment or a suggestion. Use the form at the back of the directory. Your comments will continue to help us improve our Directory. Write to us at: Campground Directory Dept., WOODALL PUBLICATIONS CORPORATION, 13975 W. Polo Trail Drive, P.O. Box 5000, Lake Forest, IL 60045-5000.

CG NAME: Frenz 'N Family Campin' TOWN: Fairplay STATE: ME

| AREAS OF INTEREST | DELETE | 1W | 2W | 3W |
|---|---|---|---|---|
| ENTRANCE<br>Includes an assessment of the following: Sign, Entrance, Access into CG, Entry Roads. | If any of these exist: No Sign, Access or Entry Roads too Dangerous or Difficult — Delete | Requires the following<br>___ Sign<br>___ Reasonable Access — 1 | Requires 2 of the following (in addition to 1W)<br>___ Commercial Quality Sign Lighted<br>___ Developed Entrance<br>___ Wide Easy Access<br>___ All Weather Entry Roads. — 2 | Requires 3 of the following.<br>___ Commercial Quality Sign Lighted<br>___ Developed Entrance<br>___ Wide Easy Access<br>___ All Weather Entry Roads. — 3 |
| SERVICES<br>Includes an assessment of Registration & Laundry | If no registration system — Delete | Requires the following<br>___ Some system of registration (self-service accepted) — 1 | Requires<br>___ Part-time Management (no regular office hours) — 2 | Requires 1 of the following<br>X Management with reg. office hours<br>___ Laundry — 3 (circled) |
| RESTROOMS<br>AFHO/ASCO listings do not require restrooms. If restrooms are provided, numbers can be waived, but construction requirements apply for rating level suggested. If none, assign same level as hookups. | None – unless AFHO/ASCO — Delete | May be crude construction. Pits, chemicals permitted. — 3 | May be non-professional finish. Flush, marine or recirculation toilets. Showers & basins required. — 6 | Over 50% professional finish. Flush toilets, showers & basins required. — 9 (circled) |
| SEWAGE DISPOSAL<br>If park has all Full Hookup Sites or Accepts Self-Contained units only, or if all non-full hookup sites are for *tents only*, No Requirement. If provided, assign the higher of either the dump station or hookups. If none, assign same level as Hookups. | 0 | None. — 1 | Any dumping facility. — 2 | Good quality facility with concrete pad sloped to flush inlet, closure and flushing water. Management provided pump-out service acceptable substitute. — 3 |
| SITES<br>Includes an assessment of Picnic Tables or Patios, Trash Removal, Shade, Plantings, Landscaping<br>CG should have some system of trash collection.<br>Sites must be of reasonable size for intended use. | 0 | Some sites must be level & some sites must have<br>___ picnic table (patio substitute)<br>OR<br>___ shade / plantings / landscaping — 2 | **10% of the sites must:**<br>___ be level<br>___ have reasonable access<br>___ have picnic table (patio substitute)<br>___ have shade / plantings / landscaping — 4 | **25% of the sites must:**<br>___ be level<br>___ have good access<br>___ have picnic table (patio substitute)<br>___ have shade / plantings / landscaping — 6 |
| HOOKUPS<br>If sites for *tents only* exist, disregard those sites for the purpose of determining the hookup rating. | No water available — Delete | Adequate water taps — 2 | 25% electric hookups plus adequate water taps. Wiring may be non-professionally installed. — 4 | 25% electric and water hookups, plus 25% electric hookups. Must be outdoor wiring. — 6 (circled) |
| INTERIOR ROADS<br>An assessment of the predominant road system that exists within Campground | 0 | May be a track through the grass — 1 | Minimum of surfacing with stone, etc. — 2 | All weather roads. Surfacing materials exist. — 3 (circled) |
| GROUNDS<br>This refers to non-camping, non-recreational areas. These are the public & common areas. Include in this element an assessment of the quality of lighting that exists overall in this campground | No lighting — Delete | Little, if any, grounds development. But has a lighted area. — 1 | Some grounds development and outside lighting at central building. — 2 | Some grounds development and outside lighting at more than one building. (if there is more than one.) — 3 |

| RECREATION | 1 major recreation or 3 minors. | 2 major recreations | Minimum 450 sq. ft. Indoor Recreation equipped with 6 items OR swimming |
|---|---|---|---|
| REC HALL (M) MN NC | FISH (M) MN NC | HORSESHOES M (MN) NC | TOTAL REQUIREMENTS 4 |
| REC ROOM/AREA M MN NC | PLAYGROUND (M) MN NC | BADMINTON M MN NC | |
| SWIM (pool) (M) MN NC | BB HOOP M (MN) NC | VOLLEYBALL M (MN) NC | Shuffleboard M (MN) NC |
| BOATING (ramp + dock) (M) MN NC | PGA M MN NC | SPORTS FIELD M MN NC | Tennis (M) MN NC |

Rev. 12/94

- ***The circles shown above indicate the level of each AREA OF INTEREST that exists at this Campground/RV Park.***
- ***The underlined words indicate what is lacking in each AREA OF INTEREST that does not allow it to be shown at the next level.***
- ***Point values are given to the park based on each AREA OF INTEREST circled.***
- ***A 3W Facility Rating would be assigned to the above park. Remember: A park may have particular AREAS OF INTEREST that are at different levels than the rating assigned.***

## MAINTENANCE

| 4W | 5W | TOTAL | unacceptable | minimal | fair | good | very good | superior | 1996 |
|---|---|---|---|---|---|---|---|---|---|
| Requires All of the following: **4**<br>X Commercial Quality Sign Lighted<br>X Landscaped Entrance<br>X Wide Easy Access<br>X All Weather Entry Roads. | Requires All of the following: **5**<br>___ Superior Commercial Quality Sign Lighted<br>___ Superior Landscaped Entrance (Design/Degree)<br>___ Superior Wide Easy Access<br>___ Superior Wide Entry Roads. | 4 | 0 | 1 | 2 | 3 | (4) | 5 | CD |
| Requires both of the following **4**<br>X Management with reg. office hours<br>__ Laundry (Laundry machines set outside with open air ceiling not acceptable) 3 washers & 1 dryer per 100 sites<br>W# _____ D# _____ | Requires both of the following **5**<br>___ Full-time Manager ___ Posted daily office hrs. & separate registration building or area<br>___ Superior Laundry (Commercial Quality Laundromat) 3 washers & 1 dryer per 100 sites | 3 | 0 | 1 | 2 | (3) | 4 | 5 | |
| Only a trace of non-professional finish acceptable. **12**<br>RATIO OF 1:10 NON SEWER SITES PLUS 1:50 SEWER SITES | Full professional finish inside and out. Ceramic tile floors, showers & 4 feet up the walls. Ceramic tile, Formica or Corian counters. Factory built partitions. (Certain quality equivalent materials acceptable as substitute for ceramic tile.) **15**<br>RATIO SAME AS 4W | 9 | 0 | 2 | 4 | (6) | 8 | 10 | |
| | | | (F) | (W) | (C) | (Cn) | S | P | |
| | | | (circle Prof. Items) ← | | | | | | |
| 4' x 6' Concrete pad sloped to flush inlet; self closing cap, flushing water; if drinking water available, it must be at least 30' from dump. **4**<br>Regularly scheduled, daily, Management pump-out service acceptable substitute. | Same as 4W, except must have easy access & be clearly signed. NOTE: Pump-out service is not accepted at this level. **5** | 4 | 0 | 1 | 2 | (3) | 4 | 5 | |
| 50% of the sites must: **8**<br>X be level<br>X have easy access<br>X have picnic table (patio substitute)<br>X have shade / plantings / landscaping<br>X have surface preparation | 75 % of the sites must: **10**<br>X be level<br>X have easy access<br>X have picnic table (patio substitute)<br>X have shade / planting / landscaping<br>100% of the sites must :<br>___ have surface preparation | 8 | 0 | 1 | 2 | 3 | 4 | (5) | |
| 25 % full hookups plus 25% electric & water hookups plus 25% electric plus adequate water taps. Outdoor wiring profess. installed. Logical hookup arrangement. Will accept 2 RVs per full hookup cluster. Will accept 4 RVs per non-full hookup cluster. *Minimum 20 amp receptacles.* **8** | 50% *individual* full hookups plus 50% electric & water hookups with a water tap and electric stanchion for each 4 non-full hookup spaces. Highest possible quality installation & material. Superior hookup relationship 30 amp recep. at all full hookups & 20 amp recep. at all electric hookups. **10** | 6 | 0 | 1 | 2 | 3 | (4) | 5 | |
| All weather roads, surfacing materials exist, shaped. **4** | All weather roads of exceptional quality and width. **5** | 3 | 0 | 1 | 2 | (3) | 4 | 5 | |
| Grounds well-developed AND Lighting at Registration, Restrooms and some activity centers. PLUS some camping area lighting. **4** | Superior Grounds Development AND Lighting at all building and activity areas PLUS GOOD camping area lighting. **5** | 4 | 0 | 1 | 2 | 3 | (4) | 5 | |

41 **FACILITIES TOTALS** 32

| AREAS OF INTEREST | MAINTENANCE |
|---|---|
| | Delete 0-8 |
| 1W 12-21 | 1W 9-15 |
| 2W 22-33 | 2W 16-24 |
| (3W 34-45) | (3W 25-33) |
| 4W 46-57 | 4W 34-42 |
| 5W 58-60 | 5W 43-45 |

| 4W | 5W |
|---|---|
| Minimum 900 sq. ft. Indoor Recreation (with over 50% professional quality finish required) equipped with 12 items AND excellent swimming. PLUS 4 additional Majors.<br>TOTAL REQUIREMENTS (6) | Rec Hall (min. 900 sq. ft. equipped with 12 items and only a trace of non-professional quality finish acceptable) AND superior swimming. Planned Group Activities with full time rec. director PLUS 7 additional Majors.<br>TOTAL REQUIREMENTS 10 |

**REC. LEVEL** 4

**REC. MAINT.** 4

COMMENTS:

F-3-5

*Indicates professional finish. F=floors; W=walls; C=ceilings; Cn=counters; S=showers; P=partitions*

- *The lower portion of the form is used to tally the recreation.*
- *Recreation items are assigned Major (M), Minor (MN) or No Count (NC) value based on the investment and/or quantity and/or usage of that recreation item at the park.*
- *The recreation items shown for the park above yield a 4W Recreation Rating.*
- *The maintenance level at a Campground/RV Park must meet or exceed the recommended rating or the ratings cannot be assigned at that level.*
- *Remember: Ratings are recommended by WOODALL's Field Representatives, and are approved (or declined) by the WOODALL Rating Committee.*

# le guide à l'annuaire

## L'organisation de l'annuaire

Toutes les informations de "WOODALL'S CAMPGROUND DIRECTORY" sont répertoriées en ordre alphabétique. En premier lieu, les Etats Américains, les Provinces Canadiennes et le Mexique, suivent, toujours en ordre alphabétique, les villes, les campings, les concessionnaires de R.V. et finalement, les points d'intéret de ces villes ou régions.

Chaque nom de ville est suivi d'une lettre et d'un chiffre (A-1) qui vous permettent, en vous réferrant à la carte du début de cet Etat ou Province, de situer la ville.

L' Edition "North American" qui comprend les secteurs Est et Ouest, est aussi en ordre alphabétique: Alabama à l Est et Alaska à l'Ouest. A la fin de chaque section, (Est et Ouest), vous trouverez la liste des facilités offertes dans ce Répertoire par lettre Alphabétique. Le "WOODALL Alphabetical Quick Reference" commence par camping/RV parc, service et location d'equipment, attraction touristique — par ordre alphabétique. Cet index est utilisable lorsque vous savez le nom de l'établissement à visiter; et la ville est écrite en dessous. La signification des symboles est indiquée comme ceci: ® location RVs; △ location tentes; ☐ location chalets; ★ réparation d'équipement; • attraction. **NOUVEAU CETTE ANNEE:** Nous avons ajouté après chaque ville une Référence a la carte pour faciliter votre recherche.

A la fin de chaque secteur, vous trouverez, toujours en ordre alphabétique, la liste complète des facilités contenues dans ce bottin.

Chaque Etat ou Province débute par une carte et la liste des "Informations Voyage" qui sont mises a jour annuellement. Cette carte vous permet de situer les villes avec camping (◈) les attractions touristiques (⚑) et les concessionnaires de R.V. (✲).

Attention, ces cartes ne sont pas officielles et doivent être utilisées à titre de supplément aux cartes routières officielles. Nous vous suggérons de jeter un coup d'oeil à la liste des attractions, points d'intérêt lors de la planification de votre voyage.

## Les Représentants de WOODALL: Des campeurs expérimentés

Tous les campings privés listés dans ce bottin, ont été inspectés personnellement par un de nos représentants (qui à chaque année, doit se qualifier.)

La cote d'un terrain est établie suivant le rapport de l'inspection effectuée printemps ou été 95.

En plus d'une liste détaillée pour chaque parc, le représentant complète une formule d'évaluation (voir page 4-5) pour établir la cote.

Ces Représentants font un travail identique pour coter les concessionnaires de R.V. et les points d'intéret (attractions) ceux jugés les plus pertinents sont listés.

La liste des campings publics (féderal, provincial, municipal, et militaire) est basée sur les informations fournies par les agences gouvernementales concernées.

WOODALL CAMPGROUND DIRECTORY existe depuis près de 60 ans. Chaque année, plus de 150,000 modifications sont apportées, et, vous offrent ainsi, le bottin le plus fiable et a jour sur le marché aujourd'hui.

## Le système jumelé d'évaluation

Cette cote d'évaluation vous aide a choisir le terrain désiré. Woodall donne deux cotes a chaque terrain de camping privé (ex. pages VII et VIII). La première cote, considère les facilités offertes (sites, routes, immeubles de services, toilettes, etc.). La deuxième cote considère les activités offertes. Les deux cotes vont de 1◈ a 5◈ (le ◈ est le symbole exclusif à WOODALL). Il ne faut pas oublier que la cote finale est basé sur l'ensemble des éléments présentés.

## Qu'indiquent les ◈ de WOODALLS?

Les cotes varient selon la quantité et la qualité des éléments de base servant à établir nos critères. Le nombre de ◈ obtenus par un parc réflète généralement le nombre de facilités et le développement du parc. Toutefois, la maintenance du terrain est le facteur primordial pour la cotation. La propreté, est un facteur important et déterminant pour assurer à votre famille et à vous même de bonnes vacances. Le niveau de maintenance d'un parc doit être égal ou même dépasser les recommandations pour chaque classification, en cas contraire, le parc ne sera pas coté.

## De nombreux ◈ signifient-ils un meilleur parc?

Définitivement NON! Tous le parcs listés dans ce bottin sont de bons parcs. Le système de cotation, n'en est pas un d'évaluation pour déterminer quel parc est bien, très bien ou parfait. Différents facteurs peuvent faire qu'un parc est plus attrayant: près d'une autoroute; près d'une attraction populaire; piscine, lac ou plusieurs jeux. Prenez bien le temps de comprendre le système d'Evaluation de WOODALL lorsque vous voulez choisir un parc où vous désirez séjourner. **Assurez-vous de lire soigneusement toutes les facilités offertes selon vos besoins et lorsque vous serez sur place le Propriétaire sait que WOODALL a inscrit les bonnes informations.** Chaque famille, doit, selon ses besoins, décider ce qu'elle attend d'un parc. C'est là que WOODALL'S est essentiel avec sa liste détaillée des parcs qui varient de rustiques ou les éléments naturels dominent aux plus luxueux avec beaucoup d'équipements et d'activités.

Prenez donc le temps d'étudier le système de cotation de WOODALL, et, ainsi vous faciliter la tâche, et, trouver le camping qui vous convient.

# Les caractéristiques spéciales

### ✔ L'INFORMATIONS GRATUITES

Pour obtenir de l'information voyage ou plus de renseignements concernant les produits ou services annoncés, il vous suffit d'utiliser la "Reader Service Card" située à la page 16. Cette carte, de plus, nous permet, grâce aux renseignements que vous nous donnez, de connaître: la distance et la durée de votre voyage, le genre de R.V. utilisé, et, ainsi, nous aide à mieux répondre a vos besoins.

### ✔ SECTIONS VOYAGE

Lors de la planification du prochain voyage, en vous réferrant a la "Travel Section" du début de chaque Etat Province, vous trouverez les réponses à vos questions sur: le climat, topographie, horaire, informations voyage, places à voir, choses à faire ainsi que les évènements de ces régions.

### ✔ GUIDE DES SITES SAISONNIERS

Que vous cherchez un parc pour un mois ou pour une saison, consultez notre "WOODALL'S Guide To Seasonal Site in R.V. Resorts–Campgrounds" dans la section des pages jaunes à la fin du bottin. La liste détaillé comprend: les facilités et activités disponibles sur les lieux. Le tout a été vérifié par nos représentants lors de la visite annuelle.

Cette publicité est payé par l'annonceur pour vous informer de ses avantages, prix spéciaux, attractions proches. Vous pouvez obtenir des renseignements supplémentaires gratuits directement de ces parcs. Le plus important, 59 Représentants dévoués de WOODALL ont parcouru plus de 500,000 milles durant plus de 5,000 jours pour permettre la mise à jour de ce bottin, et, suite à leur inspection, établir la cote des parcs tant au niveau facilités qu' activités.

### ✔ SATISFACTION A 100% OU ARGENT REMIS

Si, pour quelque raison, ce bottin ne répond pas a votre attente, retournez le avant le 31 déc. 96 avec votre reçu; nous vous le rembourserons.

S'il vous plait, faites-nous part de la raison de ce retour. Merci.

# le guide à l'annuaire

**ALLOVER—A-2** 16

**HAVE 'N FUN RV PARK**—Lakeside CAMPGROUND with level, grassy, 15
shaded and open sites. Most sites occupied by seasonal guests in summer.
1 WELCOME *From jct Hwy 502 and US 82: Go 3 mi N* 14
*on US 82, then 1 mi E on Forest Lane, then 1/4 mi N on campground road.*
17
2 ◈◈ FACILITIES: 210 sites, most common site width 35 feet, 36' max RV length, 150 full hookups, 30 18
water & elec, 20 elec (15 & 20 amp receptacles), 10 no hookups, 40 pull-thrus, a/c allowed ($), heater 13
allowed, cable TV, phone hookups, tenting available,
3 group sites for tents/RVs, tent rentals, RV rentals, camping cabins, RV storage, handicap restroom facilities, sewage disposal, laundry, public phone, grocery store, RV supplies, LP gas refill by weight/by meter, ice, tables, wood, traffic control gate.
4 ◈◈◈ RECREATION: rec hall/rec room, coin games, swim pool, lake swimming, lake fishing, 12
5 boating, canoeing, badminton, horseshoes, hiking trails.
11
6 Open all year. Facilities fully operational Memorial Day through Labor Day. Rate in 1995 $15-17 for 2 10
persons. No refunds. Reservations recommended Jun through Sep. Member ARVC. Phone (900) 202-0202. FCRV 10% discount. 8
7 **SEE AD THIS PAGE** 9

1. **BIENVENUE:**
   Ce symbole, devant le listing, indentifie les parcs qui ont acheté de la publicité pour mieux faire connaître ce qu' ils ont a vous offrir.

2. **FACILITÉS:**
   Cotés de 1 a 5 ◈. Toutes les facilités listées sont disponibles sur place.

3. **A LOUER: TENTES–R.V.-CABINES:**
   Ce parc fait la locations des équipements de camping.

4. **RÉCRÉATION OU ACTIVITÉS:**
   Cotés de 1 À 5 ◈. Toutes les activités listées sont disponibles directement sur le camping. Si, ces mêmes activités, sont ouvertes au public en général, ce sera mentionné.

5. **INFORMATION TARIF:**
   Les prix indiqués sont du minimum au maximum chargé par le propriétaire en 1995 (année de l'inspection) Attention, ces prix ne sont pas garantis.

6. **L'AFFILIATION DES TERRAINS DE CAMPING PRIVÉS:**
   Ce bottin liste les terrains de camping privés membres de "ARVC" Association Nationale de R.V. Parcs et Campings, ainsi que ceux, membres des Associations de Campings d'état privés.

7. **PUBLICITÉ SUPPLÉMENTAIRE:**
   Cette ligne vous réferre à page spécifique pour publicité plus détaillée de ce terrain.

8. **NUMERO DE TÉLÉPHONE:**
   Le numero de téléphone est donné pour vous permettre de faire réserver votre terrain si vous le désirez.

9. **REMISES OU RABAIS:**
   Sont indiqués: KOA- 10% Avec la carte KOA Ainsi que FCRV.

10. **INFORMATIONS SPÉCIALES:**
    Toutes les restrictions sont dans cette section: l'âge-saison d'opération-si la mention "No Pets" n'apparait pas, les animaux domestiques (chiens ou chats) sont acceptés. Toutefois, si vous possédez un animal de plus de 20 lbs. ou hors de l'ordinaire, il vaut mieux téléphoner d'avance.

11. **RÉSERVATIONS:**
    Il sera mentionné, s'il est préférable de réserver pour une certaine période de l'année.

12. **ENTIÈREMENT OPÉRATIONNEL:**
    Vous indique a quel temps de l'année le camping est complètement opérationnel.

13. **TENTES (TENTING AVAILABLE):**
    Bienvenue aux campeurs avec tentes. Note: Ces campeurs, sont bienvenus dans la plupart des terrains de camping. Si un terrain n'est pas équipé pour ces campeurs, le listing fera mention: "No Tents" ou "Accepts Full Hookups Units Only" dans la section informations spéciales.

14. **DIRECTIONS:**
    Détaillées et faciles à suivre les directions pour vous rendre au parc.

15. **DESCRIPTION DU TERRAIN:**
    Informations sur le terrain: ensoleillé-boisé-bord du lac-pelouse-pavé etc. Combien de sites occupés par les saisonniers.

16. **RÉFERENCE À LA CARTE**
    Indique où la ville est située sur la carte de l'Etat ou Province.

17. **CERTAINS EMPLACEMENTS PLUS LARGE:**
    Certains parcs possède des terrains plus large. Cette information est reportée dans cette case.

18. **LONGUEUR MAXIMUM DU R.V.:**
    Indique la longueur maximale du R.V. (sans le vehicule remorqué) que le terrain peut recevoir. Les facteurs sont: l'accès, la dimension des sites basé sur l'habilité normale d'un conducteur de R.V.

### • *LES PARCS SONT-ILS TOUS QUALIFIÉS POUR UN "LISTING" DANS LE BOTTIN WOODALL?*

Non. Un camping doit rencontrer nos exigences minimales aux niveaux maintenance, accès et offrir un minimum de 10 sites pour les campeurs d'un soir.

### • *Pourquoi UN NOUVEAU BOTTIN À CHAQUE ANNÉE WOODALL?*

A chaque inspection annuelle, des parcs ne satisfaisant pas nos exigences ne sont plus listés, tandis que d'autres les remplacent. Ceux qui sont listés, sont mis à date: no. de téléphone, différentes cotes, nouvelles dates d'ouverture ou de fermeture, nouvelles activités etc. Ce ne sont que quelques raisons pour un nouveau bottin.

## notes spéciales

• A moins d'avis contraire, tous les campings possèdent des toilettes modernes et des douches à l'eau chaude.

• Référez-vous à la section East et Ouest à la fin Lorsque vous ne connaissez pas le nom de la ville "Find It Quick."

• Nous avons des listes de parcs exclusivement pour saisonniers, (Pas de sites pour "overnight" camping d'unsoir) Ainsi que des lots à vendre, Associations (memberships) et parc condominiums. Chacun de ces parcs doit avoir acheté de la publicité pour être listé. Suite au nom du parc, ses facilites seront énumérées.

• "Age Restrictions May Apply" sont listés selon les informations recueuillies lors de l'inspection. Certains parcs dans la "Sunbelt" sont classés " Seniors ou 55 ans et plus." Etant donné les changements apportés par la nouvelle législation, nous vous suggérons de confirmer, par téléphone, le statut du parc.

• Vous trouverez les lettres "CPO" inscrites dans l'information de certains campings privés. Ces lettres signifie que cet établissement faisait parti d'un programme nommé "Certified Park Operator." Pour recevoir, ce certificat, il devait obtenir 75 credits basés sur: leur implication personnelle; leur parc; les services offerts ainsi que le style de vie. Cet honneur leur était remis par National Association de RV parks et campground.

# LISTINGS DIFFÉRENTS

**La première ligne de chaque listing du parc l'identifie. Seuls les campings privés sont évalués.**

# le guide à l'annuaire

✔ **ANNONCEUR:** Le nom du parc en caractères gras noirs et lettres majuscules. Le losange "Welcome" apparait au début du listing.

WELCOME

**HOLIDAY COVE TRAVEL TRAILER RESORT** —RV PARK with level, grassy sites and water access to Gulf. *From jct I-75 (exit 41) & Hwy 70: Go 12 mi W on Hwy 70/53rd Ave, then 4 mi W on Cortez Rd.*

◆◆◆ FACILITIES: 112 sites, 140 full hookups, (20, 30 & 50 amp receptacles), a/c allowed ($), heater not allowed, phone hookups, sewage disposal, laundry, publc phone, RV supplies, LP gas refill by weight/by meter, ice, tables, patios.

✔ **R.V.: VENTES–LOCATIONS–SERVICES:** Identifiés parc un engrenage (✵). Toujours un annonceur, avec le losange de bienvenue.

WELCOME

✵ **QUARTZSITE RV REPAIR**—*From jct Business I-10 & US 95: Go 1 block N on US 95, then 100 feet W on Cowell Lane.* SERVICES: RV appliance mechanic full-time, sells parts/accessories, installs hitches. Open all year. Discover/Master Card/Visa accepted. Phone: (520) 927-6874.

✔ **L'ATTRACTION TOURISTIQUE:** Un fanion (⚑) les identifie, ainsi que le losange de bienvenue.

WELCOME

⚑ **BLACK BART'S STEAK HOUSE**—*From jct I-17 & I-40: Go 3 mi E on I-40 (exit 198), then 1/4 mi SE on butler Ave.* A western steakhouse with family entertainment including musical revues nightly, in conjunction with an RV Park and antique shop. Open all year. American Express/ Master Card/Visa accepted. Phone: (520) 774-1912.

✔ **TERRAIN PRIVE NON ANNONCEUR):** Le nom du parc en caractères gras noirs et lettres minuscules.

**Wagon Wheel RV Park** — RV PARK with grassy sites. *From jct US 17 & Hwy 62: Go 1/2 mi N on US 17, then 1/2 mi W on Bostick Rd.* ◆◆◆◆FACILITIES: 265 sites, accepts full hookup units only, 265 full hookups, (30 & 50 amp receptacles), laundry, public phone, patios. ◆◆◆RECREATION: rec hall/rec room, 6 shuffleboard courts, planned group activities, horseshoes. No tents. Open all year. Rate in 1995 $13 for 2 persons. Phone: (813) 773-3157.

✔ **TERRAIN CAMPING PUBLIC:** Opéré par un agence gouvernementale (Fédérale Provinciale-Municipale-État) le nom en caractères majuscules claires.

TONTO NATIONAL FOREST (Burnt Corral Campground) — *From jct Hwy 188 & Hwy 88: Go 6 mi SW on Hwy 88.* FACILITIES: 79 sites, 32 ft. max RV length, 79 no hookups, tenting available, pit toilets, handicap restroom facilities, tables, fire rings, grills. RECREATION: lake swimming, boating, ramp, dock, lake fishing. Recreation open to the public. Open all year. Phone: (602) 467-2236.

✔ **TERRAIN MILITAIRE:** Le Personnel militaire (actif-retraité) peut camper dans ces parcs. Indentifications officielles requises pour être admis. S'il vous plait, téléphonez d'avance pour vous assurer que vous êtes éligible. Employez l'index alphabétique pour trouver ces parcs. Listés sous la lettre "M" pour Military Park.

MILITARY PARK (Lake Pippin Rec Area-Maxwell/Gunter AFB AL)—*Off base. Off I-10 on Choctawhatchee Bay.* FACILITIES: 16 sites, 16 water & elec, tenting available, sewage disposal. RECREATION: swimming, boating, fishing. Open all year. Reservations required. Phone: (205) 953-5118.

## POURQUOI DES LISTINGS SANS COTES OU EVALUATIONS?

1. **MOINS DE 10 R.V. SITES POUR CAMPEURS D'UNE NUIT:** Terrains ayant des espaces adjacents au parc et décrits dans le listing, mais ne répondants pas a nos exigeances minimales pour être cotés (Minimum 10 sites –facilité d'accès -eau-terrains au niveau-éclairés-bien entretenus.)
2. **TROP RECENT POUR ETRE COTE:** Les Représentents de WOODALL ont inspectés ces parcs qui sont pleinement opérationnels mais, avant de les coter, désirent leur donner l'opportunité de compléter leur rodage.
3. **EN CONSTRUCTION, PROJETE, RECONSTRUIT, PAS VISITE:** S'il vous plait, téléphonez d'advance pour confirmer leur capacité à vous recevoir.
4. **RESORT:** Normalement moins de 10 sites disponibles pour les non-membres. Téléphonez d'avance pour confirmer les disponibilités ou pour autres informations concernant la vente de terrain.
5. **PARC NATURISTE:** Vous trouverez querques parcs inscrits dans le bottin de WOODALL avec leur restriction.

## un mot concernant les tarifs de campings...

Woodall ou les gérants de camping, ne peuvent garantir les prix publiés. Ces prix étaient ceux en vigueur lors de l'inspection de 1995. Il est plus que probable, vu l'inflation générale, que ces prix soient majorés. Ces prix, vous donnent un aperçu des tarifs en vigueur dans ce secteur, pour un nombre spécifique de personnes: une famille (2 adultes - 2 enfants) ou par véhicule. L'éventail des prix ne comprend peut-être pas les 3 services (full hookup).

WELCOME

## LES ANNONCEURS VEULENT VOTRE CLIENTELE

Les propriétaires de camping ne payent pas pour être listés au bottin. Un parc, qui satisfait nos critères minimums est coté. Cependant, certains, propriétaires, dans le but de mieux vous faire connaître leur parc, achètent de la publicité supplémentaire, qui, vous informe des attractions, restaurants proches du parc. N'oubliez pas "Comprendre ce que vous avez vu dans le WOODALL'S."

## nous voulons entendre parler de vous!

Nous sommes toujours contents de recevoir vos commentaires (compliments, plaintes ou suggestions).Employez la formule à la fin de l'annuaire. Avec vos informations, nous améliorerons notre directory. Ecrivez-nous a: Campground Directory Dept., WOODALL PUBLICATIONS CORPORATION, 13975 W. Polo Trail Drive, P.O. Box 5000, Lake Forest, IL 60045-5000.

# RULES of the ROAD

These Rules of the Road are a compilation of the traffic laws obtained by contacting each state's and province's police department. However, laws are never static, but change whenever legislatures enact modifications or new ones.

**ALABAMA:** Children under age 6 yrs. must be in a child restraint safety seat. *RV Safety Requirements:* At 3000 lbs. trailer brakes, flares and breakaway switch required. *Driving Laws*: Headlights must be on if windshield wipers are on. Right turn on red permitted, unless posted otherwise. Riding allowed in truck campers, fifth wheels, and travel trailers. Overnight camping in rest areas is not permitted. Maximum RV width in travel is 102 in. Maximum combined length of 2 vehicles is 57 ft., 3 vehicles would be the size of a tractor, semi trailer, dolly convertor, and trailer combination. *For further information*: Dept. of Public Safety, 500 Dexter Ave., Montgomery, AL 36130. Emergency number: *H.P. on cellular phones.

**ALASKA:** All passengers must wear seat belts. A child restraint safety seat is required for children up to age 4. *Weigh Station Requirements*: Commercially registered trucks, and over 5 tons of unladen weight must stop. *RV Safety Requirements:* Over 5000 lbs., trailer brakes and breakaway switch, are required. On all trailers, safety chains are required. *Driving Laws*: Right turn on red permitted, unless posted otherwise. Riding is allowed only in specifically designed RVs to transport passengers when the vehicle is in motion. Maximum RV width is 102 inches. Overnight parking allowed unless posted. *For further information:* Alaska State Troopers, 5700 E. Tudor, Anchorage, AK 99507. Emergency number: 911.

**ARIZONA:** Children up to 4 yrs./40 lbs. must be in child restraint safety seat. *RV Safety Requirements:* Over 3000 lbs. trailer brakes and breakaway switch, and safety chains are required. *Driving Laws*: Right turn on red permitted, unless posted otherwise. Riding in travel trailers, fifth wheels and truck campers is allowed. Overnight parking allowed unless posted. Maximum RV width is 102 in. Maximum combined length for 2 vehicles is 65 ft. RVs are not permitted in car pool lanes. *For further information*: Motor Vehicle Division, P.O. Box 2100, Mail Drop 530M, Phoenix, AZ 85001. Emergency number: 911.

**ARKANSAS:** Children 5 yrs. and under must be in child restraint safety seat. Front seat passengers are required to wear seat belts. *Weigh Station Requirements*: Commercially registered trucks, and over 10,000 lbs. must stop. *RV Safety Requirements:* Over 3,000 lbs. trailer brakes and breakaway switch, and safety chains are required. *Driving Laws*: Headlights must be on if windshield wipers are on. Right turn on red permitted, unless posted otherwise. Riding allowed in truck campers. Maximum RV width is 102 in. Overnight parking allowed unless posted. *For further information*: Arkansas State Highway and Transportation Dept., P.O. Box 2261, Little Rock, AR 72203. Emergency number: 911 (in some counties) or *55 on cellular phone.

**CALIFORNIA:** Children up to 4 yrs./40 lbs. must be in child restraint safety seat. All passengers are required to wear seat belts. *RV Safety Requirements:* Over 1500 lbs. trailer brakes and safety chains required. All powerbrake systems require breakaway switch. *Driving Laws*: Right turn on red permitted, unless posted otherwise. Overnight parking is not allowed. Maximum RV width is 102 in. Maximum combined length for 2 or 3 vehicles is 65 ft. At least 2 people must be riding in a vehicle to use the car pool lanes. All RVs are required to carry a fire extinguisher. Open propane cylinders are not allowed while traveling on open highways. *For further information:* California Highway Patrol, P.O. Box 942898, Sacramento, CA 94298-0001. Emergency number: 911.

**COLORADO:** Children up to 4 yrs./40 lbs. must wear seat belts. All towed vehicles must stop at ports of entry; smaller trailers may be waived on. *RV Safety Requirements:* Chains required on all RVs; over 3000 lbs. trailer brakes and breakaway switch required. Riding in truck campers allowed. At least 3 people must be riding in a vehicle to use the car pool lanes. *For further information*: Dept. of Trans., Office of Public & Intergovernmental Relations, 4201 E. Arkansas Ave., Rm. 240, Denver, CO 80222. Emergency number: 911.

**CONNECTICUT:** Children up to 4 yrs./40 lbs. must be in child restraint safety seat. Front seat passengers are required to wear seat belts. *Weigh Station Requirements*: Commercially registered trucks must stop. *RV Safety Requirements:* Over 3000 lbs.: trailer brakes, safety chains, and maximum deflection 6" from towing vehicle required. *Driving Laws*: Headlights must be on if windshield wipers are on. Right turn on red is allowed, unless posted otherwise. Riding allowed in truck campers. Maximum RV width is 102 in. Maximum combined length for 2 vehicles is 60 ft. RVs are not allowed in car pool lanes. *For further information*: Dept. of Motor Vehicles, 60 State Street, Wethersfield, CT 06161. Emergency number: 911.

**DELAWARE:** Front seat passengers and all passengers under 16 years of age are required to wear seat belts. Children up to 4 yrs. must be in child restraint safety seats. *Weigh Station Requirements*: Commercially registered trucks must stop. *RV Safety Requirements:* Over 4000 lbs. trailer brakes and safety chains required. *Driving Laws*: Headlights must be on if windshield wipers are on. Right turn on red is allowed, unless posted otherwise. Riding allowed in truck campers. Overnight parking allowed unless posted. Maximum RV width is 102 in. Maximum combined length for 2 or 3 vehicles is 60 ft. *For further information:* Delaware State Police, P.O. Box 430, Dover, DE 19903. Emergency number: 911.

**DISTRICT OF COLUMBIA:** Seat belt requirements not available. *RV Safety Requirements:* At 3000 lbs. trailer brakes required; over 3000 lbs. add breakaway switch and flares; two safety chains required if trailer exceeds 40% of the weight of tow car. Overnight parking allowed. At least 3 people must be riding in a vehicle to use the car pool lanes. Radar detection devices are prohibited. *For further information*: Administrator, DC Dept. of Transportation, 2000 14th Street, NW, Washington, DC 20009. Emergency number: (202) 727-6680.

**FLORIDA:** Front seat passengers must wear seat belts. Children up to 5 yrs. must be in child restraint safety seats. *Weigh Station Requirements*: Commercially registered trucks must stop. At least 2 people must be riding in a vehicle to use the car pool lanes. *RV Safety Requirements:* Brakes not required on trailer of a gross weight not exceeding 3,000 lbs., if the total weight including the wheels of the trailer does not exceed 40% of the gross weight of the towing vehicle when connected to the trailer. Over 3000 lbs. trailer brakes and breakaway switch, and safety chains required. *Driving Laws*: Headlights must be on if windshield wipers are on. Right turn on red allowed, unless posted otherwise. Riding allowed in truck campers. Maximum RV width is 102 in. Maximum combined length for 2 vehicles is 60 ft. *For further information*: FL Dept. of Transportation, Public Information Office MS 54, 605 Suwannee Street, Tallahassee, FL 32399-0450. Emergency number: 911.

**GEORGIA:** Children up to 4 yrs. must wear seat belts. *RV Safety Requirements:* One mirror required on all RVs; over 2500 lbs. trailer brakes required; over 2500 lbs. add breakaway switch and chains; trailers 60' maximum length. *For further information*: Dept. of Transportation, Commissioner, 2 Capitol Square, Atlanta, GA 30334. Emergency number: (404) 656-5267.

**HAWAII:** Children up to 4 yrs. must be restrained. Front seat passengers are required to wear seat belts. *RV Safety Requirements:* Over 3000 lbs. trailer brakes and safety chains are required. *Driving Laws*: Right turn on red allowed, unless posted otherwise. Overnight parking is not allowed. Maximum RV width is 108 in. Maximum combined length for 2 vehicles is 60 ft., for 3 vehicles the length is 65 ft. At least 2 people must be riding in a vehicle to use the car pool lanes. *For further information*: Motor Vehicle Safety Office, 1505 Dillingham Blvd. Room

214, Honolulu, HI 96817. Emergency number: 911.

**IDAHO:** Front seat passengers are required to wear seat belts. Children up to 4 yrs./40 lbs. must be in child restraint safety seats. *RV Safety Requirements:* Over 1500 lbs. trailer brakes and breakaway switch, and safety chains are required. *Driving Laws:* Right turn on red is allowed, unless posted otherwise. Maximum RV width is 102 in. Maximum combined length for 2 vehicles is 48 ft., for 3 vehicles the length is 75 ft. *For further information*: Idaho Transportation Dept., P.O. Box 7129, Boise, ID 83707-1129.

**ILLINOIS**: Children up to 6 yrs. must wear seat belts. *RV Safety Requirements:* Safety chains and flares required on all trailers; over 3000 lbs. trailer brakes required; at 5000 lbs. add breakaway switch. Overnight parking allowed in designated areas only. Illinois Tollway: Rigid hitch and mirror are also required. *Driving Laws:* Headlights must be on if windshield wipers are on. Right turn on red is allowed, unless posted otherwise. Maximum combined length without a permit is 55'. *For further information*: Publ. Info. Off., IL Dept. of Transportation, 2300 S. Dirksen Pkwy, #025, Springfield, IL 62764. Emergency number: 911.

**INDIANA:** Front seat passengers are required to wear seat belts. Children up to 3 yrs. must be in child restraint safety seats. *Weigh Station Requirements*: Commercially registered trucks, and over 5 1/2 tons must stop. *RV Safety Requirements:* Over 3000 lbs. trailer brakes and breakaway switch, and safety chains are required. *Driving Laws*: Headlights must be on if windshield wipers are on. Right turn on red is allowed, unless posted otherwise. Riding in travel trailers, fifth wheels and truck campers is allowed. Overnight parking is not allowed. Maximum RV width is 102 in. Maximum combined length of 2 vehicles is 60 ft., for 3 vehicles the length is 65 ft. Mobile police scanners not permitted. *For further information*: Indiana State Police IGCN RM N-340, 100 N. Senate Ave., Indianapolis, IN 46204. Emergency number: 911 or (317) 232-8250.

**IOWA:** Front seat passengers must wear seat belts.Children up to 6 yrs. must be in a restraint. (Child at least 3 but less than 6 may be secured in a safety belt or harness). *Weigh Station Requirements*: All commercially registered trucks over 3 tons must stop at weigh stations. *RV Safety Requirements:* Over 3000 lbs. trailer brakes and safety chains are required. *Driving Laws*: Right turn on red is allowed, unless posted otherwise. Riding is allowed in truck campers, fifth wheels, and travel trailers. Overnight parking is not allowed. Maximum RV width is 102 in. Maximum combined length for 2 vehicles is 65 ft., for 3 vehicles the length is 60 ft. *For further information*: Iowa Dept. of Transportation Motor Vehicle Enforcement, P.O. Box 10382, Des Moines, IA 50306-0382. Emergency number: (800) 525-5555.

**KANSAS:** Front seat and all passengers under 14 years must wear seat belts. Children under 4 yrs. must be in child restraint safety seats. *Weigh Station Requirements*: All commercially registered trucks must stop at weigh stations. *RV Safety Requirements:* All trailers are required to have safety chains. *Driving Laws*: Right turn on red is allowed, unless posted otherwise. Overnight parking allowed in designated areas only. Maximum RV width is 102 in. Maximum combined length of 2 or 3 vehicles is 65 ft. *For further information*: Kansas Highway Patrol, 122 SW 7th, Topeka, KS 66603. Phone number is (913) 296-6800. Emergency number: 911 or *47 on cellular phone.

**KENTUCKY:** Children up to 40 inches must wear seat belts. Radar detection devices are prohibited. *RV Safety Requirements:* Trailer brakes must be sufficient to stop within legal distance of 40 ft. at 20 mph. *For further information*: KY Dept. of Travel Development, 500 Metro Street, Room 22, Frankfort, KY 40601-1968. Emergency number: 1-800-222-5555.

**LOUISIANA:** Children up to 4 yrs. must wear seat belts. *RV Safety Requirements:* Over 3000 lbs. trailer brakes and breakaway switch, flares, chains, and wheel chocks are required. Maximum combined length for 2 vehicles is 70 ft. Riding in travel trailers, fifth wheels and truck campers is allowed. Overnight parking is allowed when posted. *For further information*: LA Dept. of Public Safety, P.O. Box 64886, Baton Rouge, LA 70896-6614. Emergency number: 911 in metropolitan areas only.

**MAINE:** No mandatory seat belt law for front seat driver or passengers. Children under 19 yrs. must wear seat belts. Children up to 4 yrs. must be in child restraint safety seats. *RV Safety Requirements:* Over 3000 lbs., trailer brakes on all axles and safety chains are required. *Driving Laws*: Right turn on red is allowed, unless posted otherwise. Riding allowed in truck campers. Overnight parking is not allowed. Maximum RV width is 102 in. Maximum combined length for 2 vehicles is 65 ft. *For further information*: Maine State Police, Station 20, Augusta, ME 04333. Emergency number: *77 on cellular phone.

**MARYLAND:** Children up to 4yrs./40 lbs. must be in child restraint safety seats. Front seat passengers are required to wear seat belts. *Weigh Station Requirements*: All commercially registered trucks must stop. *RV Safety Requirements:* Over 3000 lbs. trailer brakes and breakaway switch, safety chains are required. *Driving Laws*: Right turn on red is allowed, unless posted otherwise. Riding is allowed in truck campers. Overnight parking is allowed, unless posted. Maximum RV width is 102 in. At least 2 people must be riding in a vehicle to use the car pool lane. *Tunnel Regulations*: Trailer hitch must be reinforced or braced to frame of towing vehicle. Safety chains must be attached to frame of towing vehicle and not to pintle hook. No vehicle may be more than 13'6" high when loaded. Length of combined vehicles cannot exceed 55'. No Propane tanks allowed through tunnels. *For further information*: State Highway Administration Motor Carrier Division, 7491 Connelley Drive, Hanover, MD 21076. Emergency number: 911 or *77 on cellular phone.

**MASSACHUSETTS:** Children of all ages must wear seat belts. At least 2 people must be riding in a vehicle to use the car pool lanes. *RV Safety Requirements:* Trailer brakes must be sufficient to stop within legal distance. All RVs must have 2 chains and wheel locks. No propane allowed in tunnels (in Boston, I-90, I-93, Rt IA; in Newton, I-90). Check with local government regarding overnight parking restrictions. Massachusetts Turnpike: Rigid hitch required. Maximum combined length without permit is 40'. *For further information*: Executive Office of Transportation & Construction, Attn: Commissioners Office, 10 Park Plaza, Mass Hwy., Boston, MA 02116. Emergency number: 911.

**MICHIGAN:** Front seat passengers must wear seat belts. Children up to 4 yrs. must be secured in child restraint safety seat. *Weigh Station Requirements*: RVs need not stop at weigh stations, but dealers, manufacturers and others using commercially registered trucks and vans as towing vehicles and RVers if their tow vehicles are thus registered, must stop. *RV Safety Requirements:* 2 chains are required on all RVs. Trailers over 3000 lbs., brakes required. *Driving Laws*: Right turn on red is allowed, unless posted. Riding in travel trailers, fifth wheels and truck campers is allowed. Overnight parking is not allowed. Maximum RV width is 96 in. Maximum combined length for 2 vehicles is 80 ft. Mobile police scanners are not allowed. *For further information:* Michigan State Police, 300 N. Clippert, Lansing, MI 48913. Emergency number: 911.

**MINNESOTA:** Children up to 4 yrs. must be in child restraint safety seat. Front seat passengers, and rear passengers up to age 11 are required to wear seat belts. *Weigh Station Requirements*: RVs are required to stop if a truck or combination weighing 12,000 lbs. or more, is being used for commerce. *RV Safety Requirements*: Over 3000 lbs.: trailer brakes, 2 safety chains, glass mirror, and hitch to safety stands required. Over 6000 lbs. add breakaway switch. *Driving Laws*: Right turn on red is allowed, unless posted otherwise. Riding in travel trailers, fifth wheels and truck campers allowed. Maximum RV width is 102 in. Maximum combined length for 2 vehicles is 65 ft., for 3 vehicles the length is 60 ft. (must be a pickup pulling a fifth wheel trailer pulling a watercraft on a trailer). Mobile police scanners are not allowed. At least 2 people must be riding in a vehicle to use the car pool lanes. *For further information*: Minnesota State Patrol, Suite 100A Town Square 444 Cedar Street, St. Paul, MN 55101-2156. Emergency number: 911.

**MISSISSIPPI:** Children up to 4 yrs. must be in child restraint safety seat. Front seat passengers are required to wear seat belts. *RV Safety Requirements:* Trailers over 2,000 lbs. must have trailer brakes and safety chains. *Driving Laws*: Maximum RV width is 102 in. Maximum combined length for 2 vehicles is 30' each. Riding in truck campers, fifth wheels, and travel trailers are allowed. Overnight parking is not allowed. *For further information*: Mississippi Dept. of Public Safety, P.O. Box 958, Jackson, MS 39205-0958. Emergency number: 911.

**MISSOURI:** Children up to 4 yrs must be in child restraint safety seat. Front seat passengers are required to wear seat belts. *Weigh Station Requirements*: All commercially registered vehicles over 6 tons must stop at weigh stations. *RV Safety Requirements:* Trailers over 3,000 lbs., trailer brakes and breakaway switch are required if used commercially. Safety chains are required for bumper hitches. *Driving Laws*: Right turn on red is allowed, unless posted otherwise. Riding is allowed in truck campers, 5th wheels, and travel trailers. Overnight parking is allowed, unless posted. Maximum RV width is 102 in. Maximum combined length for 2 or 3 vehicles are 65 ft. Radar detectors are not allowed in commercial vehicles. *For further information*: Missouri State Highway Patrol, 1510 East Elm St., P.O. Box 568, Jefferson City, MO 65102. Emergency number: 911 or (800) 525-5555.

**MONTANA:** Front seat passengers must wear seat belts. Children up to 4 yrs or less than 40 lbs. are required to be in child restraint safety seats. *Weigh Station Requirements:* All commercially registered trucks must stop. *RV Safety Requirements:* All RVs are required to have flares or reflective signs. Trailers under 3,000 lbs. must have safety chain of a minimum of 1/4" in diameter; over 3,000 lbs. must have trailer brakes and breakaway switch, and safety chains. *Driving Laws*: Right turn on red is allowed, unless posted otherwise. Riding is allowed in truck campers. Overnight parking is allowed. Maximum RV width is 102 in. Maximum combined length for 2 vehicles is 75 ft. *For further information:* Montana Highway Patrol, 303 North Roberts, Helena, MT 59620. Emergency number: (406) 525-5555.

**NEBRASKA:** Children up to 4 yrs./40 lbs. must be in child restraint seats. Front seat passengers are required to wear seat belts. *RV Safety Requirements*: All RVs are required to have flares or reflective signs. Trailers between 3,000 lbs. and 6,500 lbs. must have trailer brakes on at least 2 wheels and breakaway switch, and safety chains. Trailers over 6,500 lbs. must have trailer brakes on each wheel and breakaway switch, and safety chains. *Driving Laws*: Right turn on red is allowed, unless posted otherwise. Riding in travel trailers, fifth wheels and truck campers is allowed. Overnight parking is not allowed. Maximum RV width is 102 in. Maximum combined length for 2 or 3 vehicles is 65'. *For further information*: Nebraska State Hwy. Patrol, P.O. Box 94907, Lincoln, NE 68509-4907. Emergency number: (800) 525-5555.

**NEVADA:** Children up to 5 yrs./40 lbs. must wear seat belts. All passengers in vehicles under 6,000 lbs. must wear seat belts. *RV Safety Requirements:* Tandem length with Class I driver license - unrestricted towing of 2 trailers permitted up to 70'. Chains, and brakes on all wheels are required on all trailers over 1500 lbs. Riding in truck campers is allowed. Overnight parking allowed in designated areas only. *For further information*: Plan. Div. Chief, Dept. of Transportation, 1263 S. Stewart St., Carson City, NV 89712. Emergency number: 911 or (702) ZENITH 1-2000.

**NEW HAMPSHIRE:** All passengers under age12 must wear seat belts. Children up to 4 yrs. must be in child restraint safety seats. *Weigh Station Requirements*: All commercially registered trucks over 10,001 tons must stop. *RV Safety Requirements:* Trailers over 3,000 lbs. must have trailer brakes and breakaway switch, safety chains, and lights. *Driving Laws*: Right turn on red is allowed, unless posted otherwise. Riding in truck campers is allowed. Overnight parking is not allowed. *For further information*: Director, Div. of Motor Vehicles, 10 Hazen Drive, Concord, NH 03305. Emergency number: 911.

**NEW JERSEY:** Children up to 5 yrs. must be in child restraint safety seat. *RV Safety Requirements:* Over 3000 lbs. trailer and breakaway brakes, chains, and safety glass required; or when GVWR of trailer exceeds 40% GVWR of towing vehicle. Maximum length of trailer without special permit is 45'. Riding in travel trailers, fifth wheels and truck campers is allowed as long as seats are anchored. Overnight parking allowed. New Jersey Turnpike: Motorhome may tow vehicle as long as all four wheels are on the ground - no tow dolly or piggybacks. Garden State Parkway: Motorhome may tow another vehicle with tow bars, safety chains and emergency tail lights on both vehicles. Maximum combined length without a permit is 55'. *For further information*: Sec./Asst., Dept. of Law & Public Safety, Div. of Hwy. Traffic Safety, CN 048, Trenton, NJ 08625-0048.

**NEW MEXICO:** Children up to 10 yrs. must wear seat belts. *RV Safety Requirements:* At 3000 lbs. trailer brakes and chains required. Riding in truck campers is allowed. Overnight parking is allowed but not over 24 hrs. in any 3-day period in the same area. *For further information*: NM Transportation, Motor Vehicles Dept., P.O. Box 1028, Santa Fe, NM 87504. Emergency number: (505) 827-5100.

**NEW YORK:** Front seat passengers are required to wear seat belts. Children up to 4 yrs. must be secured in child restraint safety seat. Back seat passengers from 4 yrs. to 9 yrs. must wear seat belts. *Weigh Station Requirements*: All commercially registered trucks must stop. *RV Safety Requirements*: Trailers over a 1,000 lbs. unladen and trailers having a maximum gross weight in excess of 3,000 lbs. must be equipped with brakes. Safety chains are also required. *Driving Laws*: Headlights must be on if windshield wipers are on. Right turn on red is allowed, unless posted otherwise. In New York City, right turn on red is not allowed, unless posted. Riding is allowed in truck campers and fifth wheels. Maximum RV width is 96 in. Maximum combined length for 2 vehicles is 65 ft. Radar detectors and mobile police scanners are not permitted. RVs are not allowed in car pool lanes, unless posted. Open propane cylinders are permitted while traveling on open highways. Bottled gas is prohibited in tunnels, the lower levels of George Washington Bridge and Verrazano-Narrows Bridge, and I-95 through Manhattan.. *For further information*: State of New York Dept. of Motor Vehicles, Empire State Plaza, Albany, NY 12228. Emergency number: 911.

**NORTH CAROLINA:** Children up to 4 yrs. must be in child restraint safety seat. Front seat passengers are required to wear seat belts. *RV Safety Requirements*: All RVs are required to have safety glass. Trailers over 4,000 lbs. must have trailer brakes and safety chains. *Driving Laws*: Headlights must be on if windshield wipers are on. Right turn on red is allowed, unless posted otherwise. Riding is allowed in truck campers. Overnight parking is not allowed. Maximum RV width is 96 in. Maximum combined length for 2 vehicles is 60 ft. Radar detectors are not permitted on commercial vehicles. *For further information*: North Carolina Div. of Motor Vehicles, Enforcement Section, 1100 New Bern Avenue, Raleigh, NC 27697. Emergency number: 911 or (800) 672-4527.

**NORTH DAKOTA:** Children up to 10 yrs. are required to wear seat belts. Front seat passengers are required to wear seat belts. *Weigh Station Requirements*: All commercially registered trucks must stop. *RV Safety Requirements*: All RVs are required to have flares or reflective signs. All trailers must have brakes or safety chains, and breakaway switch. *Driving Laws*: Right turn on red is allowed, unless posted otherwise. Riding in fifth wheels and truck campers is allowed. Maximum RV width is 102 in. Maximum combined length for 2 or 3 vehicles is 75'. *For further information*: North Dakota Highway Patrol, 600 East Boulevard Avenue, Bismarck, ND 58505-0240. Emergency number: 911 or (800) 472-2121.

**OHIO:** Children up to 4 yrs./40 lbs. required to be in child restraint safety seat. *Weigh Station Requirements:* Commercially registered vehicles must stop. *RV Safety Requirements:* Over 2000 lbs. trailer brakes and breakaway switch, chains, and flares required. *Driving Laws:* Roadside parking allowed for a maximum of 3 hours. Ohio Turnpike: Over 2000 lbs. turn signals and brake lights also required. Maximum combined length without a permit is 65'. Overnight parking allowed in 6 service areas, not rest areas. Trailers, etc., may be barred at any time, or tire chains required by authorities due to hazardous road conditions. *For further information*: Director, Dept. of Transportation, 25 S. Front St., Columbus, OH 43266-0578. Emergency number: (800) GRAB-DVL or cellular phone *DVI.

**OKLAHOMA:** Front seat passengers are required to wear seat belts. Children up to 5 yrs. must be in child restraint safety seats. *Weigh Station Requirements*: All commercially registered trucks must stop. *RV Safety Requirements*: Trailers over 3,000 lbs. must have trailer brakes and safety chains. *Driving Laws*: Right turn on red is allowed, unless posted otherwise. Overnight parking is allowed, unless posted. Maximum RV width is 102 in. Maximum combined length for 2 or 3 vehicles is 65 ft. *For further information*: Director, Dept. of Public Safety, 200 NE 21st Street, Oklahoma City, OK 73105. Emergency number: 911 or *55 on cellular phone.

**OREGON:** All passengers are required to wear seat belts. Children up to 4 yrs./40 lbs. must be in child restraint safety seats. *Weigh Station Requirements*: Commercially registered trucks, and over 10 tons must stop. RVs must stop if signaled by an officer. *RV Safety Requirements:* All trailers must have safety chains, and trailer brakes must be sufficient to stop at 20 mph in 35 ft without leaving 12' wide lane. Commercial trailers over 3,000 lbs. must have trailer brakes and breakaway switch, and safety chains. *Driving Laws*: Headlights must be on if windshield wipers are on, and driver can not see a minimum of 1000'. Right turn on red is allowed, unless posted otherwise. Riding in truck campers allowed. Passengers are allowed in fifth-wheel trailers if the trailer is equipped with the following: An auditory or visual signalling device that a passenger can use to gain the attention of the motor vehicle driver towing the vehicle. Maximum RV width is 102 in. Maximum combined length for 2 vehicles is 60 ft. *For further information*: Info. Rep., Dept. of Transportation, Motor Veh. Div., 1905 Lana Ave. NE, Salem, OR 97314. Emergency number: 911.

**PENNSYLVANIA:** Children under 4 yrs. must be secured in child restraint safety seat. Front seat passengers must wear seat belts. *Weigh Station Requirements* : Commercially registered trucks, and over 8 tons must stop. RVs must stop if fifth wheel is over 10,000 lbs. *RV Safety Requirements:* All RVs are required to have flares or reflective signs, and fire extinguisher. Trailers under 3,000 lbs. must have breakaway system, safety chains, and lighting equipment (brakes, turn signals, reflectors). Trailers over 3,000 lbs. must have trailer brakes and breakaway system, safety chains, and lighting. *Driving Laws*: Right turn on red is allowed, unless posted otherwise. Riding is allowed in fifth wheels with electronic communications. Overnight parking is allowed, unless posted. Maximum RV width is 102 in. Maximum combined length for 2 or 3 vehicles is 60'. RVs are not allowed in car pool lanes. *For further information*: PA Dept. of Transportation, Bureau of Highway Safety & Traffic Engineering, 204 Transportation & Safety Building, P.O. Box 2047, Harrisburg, PA 17105-2047. Emergency number: 911.

**RHODE ISLAND:** Children of all ages required to wear seat belts. *RV Safety Requirements:* Over 4000 lbs. trailer brakes and breakaway switch, 2 safety chains, and flares required. Riding allowed in truck campers. Overnight parking allowed unless posted. *For further information*: RI Dept. of Transportation, 210 State Office Bldg.,Two Capitol Hill, Providence, RI 02903. Emergency number: 911.

**SOUTH CAROLINA:** Front seat passengers must wear seat belts. Children must wear seat belts only if they are riding in front. *Weigh Station Requirements*: Commercially registered trucks must stop. RVs must stop only if pulling as classification of a truck. *RV Safety Requirements*: Trailers over 10,001 lbs. or used for commercial enterprise, and other than fifth wheel, must have additional equipment (chains, cable, etc.). *Driving Laws* : Headlights must be on if windshield wipers are on. Right turn on red is allowed, unless posted otherwise. Overnight parking is not allowed. *For further information*: S.C. Dept. of Public Safety, P.O. Box 100178, Columbia, S.C. 29202-3178. Emergency number: 911 or (803) 737-1030.

**SOUTH DAKOTA:** Front seat passengers are required to wear seat belts.Children up to 2 yrs. must be in child restraint safety seats. *Weigh Station Requirements*: All commercially registered trucks must stop. *RV Safety Requirements:* All RVs are required to have flares or reflective signs. Trailers over 3,000 lbs. must have trailer brakes and breakaway switch, and safety chains. *Driving Laws*: Right turn on red is allowed, unless posted otherwise. Riding is allowed in fifth wheels. Overnight parking is not allowed. Maximum RV width is 102 in. Maximum combined length for 3 vehicles is 70 ft. *Mountain Pass Regulations*: On Needles Hwy. 87 in the Black Hills, maximum width is 8'7"; maximum height is 10'8". *For further information*: South Dakota Highway Patrol, 500 E. Capitol Ave., Pierre, SD 57501-5070. Emergency number: 911 or (605) 773-3105.

**TENNESSEE:** Front seat passengers must wear seat belts. Children up to 4 yrs. must be in child restraint safety seat. *Weigh Station Requirements*: All commercially registered trucks must stop. *RV Safety Requirements:* Trailers over 3,000 lbs. must have trailer brakes and breakaway switch, and safety chains. *Driving Laws*: Headlights must be on if windshield wipers are on. Right turn on red is allowed, unless posted otherwise. Riding is allowed in truck campers, fifth wheels, and travel trailers. *Driving Laws:* Overnight parking is allowed, unless posted. Maximum RV width is 102 in. Maximum combined length for 2 or 3 vehicles is 65 ft. *For further information*: Tennessee Highway Patrol, 1150 Foster Avenue, Nashville, TN 37249-1000. Emergency number: 911, (615) 741-2069, or *847 on cellular phone.

**TEXAS:** Children up to 3 yrs. must wear seat belts. *Weigh Station Requirements:* All commercially registered towing trucks and vans are required to stop. *RV Safety Requirements:* Over 4500 lbs. trailer brakes and breakaway switch, flares, and mirrors are required. *Driving Laws:* Overnight parking is allowed. Dallas North Tollway: Over 3000 lbs. trailer brakes and mirror required. Maximum combined length without permit is 65'. There are no rest areas. *For further information*: Chief, TX Dept. of Transportation, Dewitt C. Greer State Hwy. Bldg., 125 E. 11th St., Austin, TX 78701-2483. Emergency number: (800) 424-9393.

**UTAH:** All passengers 8 yrs. and up must wear seat belts. Children from birth to 2 yrs. are required to have a child restraint safety seat. *Weigh Station Requirements*: All commercially registered trucks must stop. *RV Safety Requirements*: Trailers over 2,000 lbs. must have trailer brakes and safety chains. Trailers over 3,000 lbs. must have trailer brakes and breakaway switch and safety chains. *Driving Laws*: Headlights must be on if windshield wipers are on. Right turn on red is allowed, unless posted otherwise. Radar detectors are not permitted. Open propane cylinders are not permitted on open highways.Combined maximum length, 65 ft. Maximum width is 102 in. Maximum height, 14 ft. *For further information*: Director, Utah Dept. of Transportation, 4501 S. 2700 West, Salt Lake City, UT 84119-5998. Emergency number: 911.

**VERMONT:** Children up to 5 yrs. must be in a child restraint safety seat. All passengers must wear seat belts. *Weigh Station Requirements*: RVs must stop if fifth wheel or truck/pickup camper. *RV Safety Requirements:* Trailers over 3,000 lbs. must have safety chains, and brakes on one axle. Trailers over 6,000 lbs. must have trailer brakes on all wheels and breakaway switch, and safety chains. *Driving Laws*: Right turn on red is allowed, unless posted otherwise. Riding is allowed in truck campers. Overnight parking is not allowed. Maximum RV width is 102 in. Maximum combined length for 2 or 3 vehicles is 65 ft. *For further information*: Dept. of Motor Vehicles, 120 State St., Montpelier, VT 05603-0001. Emergency number: posted at rest areas.

**VIRGINIA:** Children up to 4 yrs. must be in child restraint safety seat. Front seat passengers are required to wear seat belts. *RV Safety Requirements:* Trailers 2,999 lbs. or less must have safety chains. Trailers 3,000 lbs. or more must have trailer brakes and breakaway switch, and safety chains. *Driving Laws* : Right turn on red is allowed, unless posted otherwise. Riding is allowed in truck campers. Maximum RV width is 102 in. Maximum combined length for 2 vehicles is 60 ft. Radar detectors are not permitted. RVs are not allowed in car pool lanes. *Tunnel Regulations*: Maximum of 2 approved propane gas tanks of 20 lbs. each. Must be turned off when going through the tunnels. *For further information*: Dept. of State Police, P.O. Box 27472, Richmond, VA 23261-7472. Emergency number: 911 or (804) 674-2026.

**WASHINGTON:** Children up to 3 yrs. must be in child restraint safety seat. All passengers are required to wear seat belts. *Weigh Station Requirements*: Commercially registered trucks, and over 5 tons must stop. Minimum number of 2 riders required to use car pool lanes. *RV Safety Requirements*: All RVs are required to have flares or reflective signs. Trailers over 3,000 lbs. must have trailer brakes and breakaway switch, and safety chains. *Driving Laws*: Right turn on red is allowed, unless posted otherwise. Riding is allowed in truck campers. Maximum RV width is 102 in. Maximum combined length for 2 vehicles is 75 ft. Minimum number of 2 riders required to use car pool lanes. RVs are not allowed in car pool lanes with trailer. Open propane cylinders are not allowed while traveling on open highways. *Mountain Pass Regulations*: All passes: RVs over 10,000 lbs., tire chains are required from November 1 - March 31. *For further information*: Washington State Patrol, P.O. Box 42614, Olympia, WA 98504-2614. Emergency number: 911 or any state patrol office.

**WEST VIRGINIA:** Children up to 9 yrs. must be seat belted. Front seat passengers must wear seat belts. *RV Safety Requirements:* Trailers over 2,000 lbs. the drawbar shall not exceed 15 feet. *Driving Laws*: Headlights must be on if windshield wipers are on. Right turn on red is allowed, unless posted otherwise. Riding is allowed in truck campers, 5th wheels, and travel trailers. Overnight parking is not allowed. Maximum RV width is 96 in.(102 in. on the Interstates). Maximum combined length for 2 vehicles is 60 ft. *For further information*: West Virginia State Police Dept., 710 Central Avenue, Charleston, WV 25302. Emergency numbers: County A-Shinnston (304) 624-7573; County B-South Charleston (304) 746-2222; County C-Elkins (304) 636-3101; County D-Beckley (304) 253-8311 or 911.

**WISCONSIN:** Children up to 4 yrs. must be in a child restraint system. All passengers are required to wear seat belts. *Weigh Station Requirements*: Commercially registered trucks, and over 4 tons must stop. *RV Safety Requirements*: Trailers over 3,000 lbs. must have trailer brakes and safety chains. *Driving Laws*: Right turn on red is allowed, unless posted otherwise. Riding is allowed in fifth wheels. No one under the age of 12 is permitted in a trailer unless accompanied by a person 16 or older and the trailer must be equipped with a two-way voice communication system between driver and trailer. Maximum RV width is 102 in. Maximum combined length for 2 vehicles is 65 ft. Maximum combined length for 3 vehicles is 60 ft (with permit only). *For further information*: Wisconsin State Patrol, 4802 Sheboygan Avenue, Madison, WI 53707-7912. Emergency number: posted at rest areas.

**WYOMING:** Front seat passengers are required to wear seat belts. *RV Safety Requirements*: All RVs are required to have flares or reflective signs if pulling a house trailer. All vehicles or combination of vehicles must have sufficient brakes to be able to stop within 40 ft. from an initial speed of 20 mph on a level, dry, smooth, hard surface. *Driving Laws*: Right turn on red is allowed, unless posted otherwise. Maximum RV width is 102 in. Maximum combined length for 2 or 3 vehicles is 85 ft. No single unit can exceed 60 ft in length. Overnight parking is not allowed. Riding in truck campers is allowed. *For further information*: Wyoming Highway Patrol, P.O. Box 1708, Cheyenne, WY 82003-1708. Emergency number: 911 or (800) 442-9090.

## CANADA

**ALBERTA:** Children up to 6 yrs./40 lbs. must be in child safety restraint seat. All passengers are required to wear seat belts. *Weigh Station Requirements*: Commercially registered trucks, and over 4.95 tons must stop. *RV Safety Requirements:* Trailers over 2,000 lbs. must have trailer brakes and breakaway switch, and safety chains. *Driving Laws* : Right turn on red is allowed, unless posted otherwise. Riding is allowed in truck campers. Maximum RV width is 8'6". Maximum combined length for 2 or 3 vehicles is 20 m. *For further information*: Alberta Transportation and Utilities, Twin Atria Building 4999-98 Avenue, Edmonton, AB T6B 2X3.

**BRITISH COLUMBIA:** Children up to 40 lbs. must be in child restraint safety seat. All passengers must wear seat belts. *Weigh Station Requirements*: Commercially registered trucks, and over 5500 kg must stop. *RV Safety Requirements:* Trailers over 3,000 lbs. must have trailer brakes on all wheels and breakaway switch, and safety chains. Three vehicle combinations are prohibited. *Driving Laws*: Right turn on red is allowed, unless posted otherwise. *For further information*: Motor Vehicle Branch, Commercial Transport and Inspection, 2631 Douglas St., Victoria, BC V8T 5A3.

**MANITOBA:** Children up to age 5 yrs./50 lbs. must be in child restraint safety seat. All passengers are required to wear seat belts. *Driving Laws*: Right turn on red is allowed, unless posted otherwise. Riding is allowed in truck campers. Maximum RV width is 102 in./2.6m. Maximum combined length for 2 vehicles is 70.5 ft/21.5 m. Combined length for 3 vehicles is 75.45 ft/23 m. Radar detectors and mobile scanners are not permitted. Open propane cylinders are not allowed while traveling on open highways. Propane gas is permitted only as a vehicle fuel, and must have shut off to appliances. *For further information*: Royal Canadian Mounted Detachment Division of Driver and Vehicle Licensing, 1075 Portage Avenue, Winnipeg, MB R3G 0S1. Emergency number: (204) 983-5461.

**NEW BRUNSWICK:** Children up to 4 yrs./40 lbs. must be in child restraint safety seat. All passengers must wear seat belts. *Weigh Station Requirements* : Commercially registered trucks, and with gross mass of 10,000 lbs. or more must stop. *RV Safety Requirements:* All RVs are required to have a fire extinguisher. Trailers 3,000 lbs. and over must have trailer brakes and breakaway switch, and safety chains. *Driving Laws*: Right turn on red is allowed, unless posted otherwise. Overnight parking is allowed if posted. Maximum RV width is 102 in./260 cm. Maximum combined length for 2 vehicles is 75'5"/23 m. Radar detectors are not allowed. *Ferry Regulations*: Maximum combined length is 75'5". Maximum width is 102 in. Maximum height is 13'7". Propane tank must be shut off. *For further information*: Dept. of Transportation Motor Vehicle Branch, P.O. Box 6000, Fredericton, NB E3B 5H1. Emergency number:

(800) 442-4900.

**NEWFOUNDLAND:** All passengers are required to wear seat belts. *Weigh Station Requirements*: Commercially registered trucks, and over 3 tons must stop. *RV Safety Requirements*: Trailers 4900 kg must have trailer brakes and breakaway switch, and safety chains. Trailers over 1830 kg must have safety chains. *Driving Laws*: Right turn on red is allowed, unless posted otherwise. Riding is allowed in truck campers, fifth wheels, and travel trailers. Overnight parking is not allowed unless posted. Maximum RV width is 102 in./ 2.6 m. Maximum combined length for 2 vehicles is 74.5 ft/ 23 m. Radar detectors and mobile police scanners are not permitted. *For further information*: Newfoundland Hwy. Div., P.O. Box 8710, St. Johns, NFLD A1B 4J5. Emergency number: 911.

**NOVA SCOTIA:** Children up to 40 lbs. must be in child restraint safety seat. All passengers are required to wear seat belts. *Weigh Station Requirements*: All commercially registered trucks must stop. *RV Safety Requirements:* All RVs are required to have flares or reflective signs (if vehicle registered commercially). Trailers under 3,000 lbs. must have safety chains. Trailers over 3,000 lbs. must have breakaway switch and safety chains. Trailers over 4,000 lbs. must have brakes and breakaway switch, and safety chains. *Driving Laws*: Headlights must be on if windshield wipers are on. Right turn on red is allowed, unless posted otherwise. Riding is allowed in truck campers. Maximum RV width is 2.6 m. Maximum combined length for 2 or 3 vehicles is 23 m. Radar detectors are not allowed. *For further information*: Supervisor Safety Programs, Registry of Motor Vehicles, P.O. Box 2433, Halifax, NS B3J 3E7. Emergency number: (902) 424-4256.

**ONTARIO:** Driver and all passengers in a vehicle are required to wear seat belts. Children up to 9 kg (approx. 20 lbs.) must be secured in a rearward-facing child restraint system secured by the lap belt of a seat belt assembly. Children from 9 kg to 18 kg (approx. 40 lbs.) must be secured in a child restraint system or by the lap belt of a seat belt assembly. Children from 18 kg to 23 kg (approx. 50 lbs.) must be secured by the lap belt of a seat belt assembly. Children over 23 kg must wear the complete, upper torso and lap belt of the seat belt assembly. Radar detection and jamming devices are prohibited. *RV Safety Requirements:* Over 1,360 kg (approx. 3000 lbs.) brakes are required. Safety chains are required unless the trailer is attached by a fifth wheel attachment. *Driving Laws:* Riding in truck campers is allowed. Overnight parking is allowed in restricted areas. Maximum length of car and trailer is 23 meters (approx. 75.5ft.). Maximum height is 4.15 meters (approx. 13.6 ft.). Maximum width of vehicles is 2.6 meters (approx. 102 in.). *For further information*: Min. of Trans. Info., 1201 Wilson Ave., East Bldg., Main Flr., Downsview, ON Canada M3M 1J8. Emergency number: 911.

**PRINCE EDWARD ISLAND:** Children up to 40 lbs. must be in child restraint safety seat. All passengers must wear seat belts. *Weigh Station Requirements*: Commercially registered trucks, and over 4500 kgs must stop. *RV Safety Requirements*: Trailers 1500 kgs and over must have trailer brakes and breakaway switch, and safety chains. *Driving Laws*: Right turn on red is allowed, unless posted otherwise. Riding is allowed in truck campers, 5th wheels, and travel trailers. Maximum RV width is 102 in./ 2.6 m. Maximum combined length for 2 vehicles is 81 ft./ 23 m. 3-vehicle combinations are not permitted. Radar detectors are not allowed. *Ferry Regulations*: Propane tanks must be shut off. *For further information*: Highway Safety Division, P.O. Box 2000, Charlottetown, Prince Edward Island C1A 7N8. Emergency number: (902) 368-5200.

**QUEBEC:** *Weigh Station Requirements:* Commercially registered trucks, and all RV classifications over 3,000 kg must stop. *Driving Laws*: Maximum RV width is 2.6 m. Maximum combined length for 2 or 3 vehicles is 23 m. Maximum height is 4.15 m. *For further information*: Commission des Transports du Quebec, 585 Boul, Charest est, PQ Canada G1K 7W5. Emergency number: 911 or 1-800-461-2131.

**SASKATCHEWAN:** Children up to 40 lbs. must be in child restraint safety seat. All passengers are required to wear seat belts. *Weigh Station Requirements*: Commercially registered trucks, and over 10 tons must stop. *RV Safety Requirements:* Trailers over 3,000 lbs. must have trailer brakes and breakaway switch, and double safety chains. *Driving Laws*: Right turn on red is allowed, unless posted otherwise. Riding is allowed in truck campers. Maximum RV width is 96 in./2.6 m. Maximum combined length for 2 or 3 vehicles is 23 m. *For further information*: Saskatchewan Highways and Transportation, 7th floor, 1855 Victoria Avenue, Regina, SK S4P 3V5. Emergency number: 911.

**YUKON:** Children up to 6 yrs./44 lbs. must be in child restraint safety seat. All passengers are required to wear seat belts. *Weigh Station Requirements*: Commercially registered trucks, and over 10 tons must stop. *RV Safety Requirements*: Trailers over 910 kgs must have trailer brakes and safety chains. *Driving Laws*: Right turn on red is allowed, unless posted. Riding is allowed in truck campers. Overnight parking is allowed unless posted. Maximum RV width is 2.6 m. Maximum combined length for 2 vehicles is 12.5 m. *For further information*: Mktg. Technician, Yukon Tourism, P.O. Box 2703, Whitehorse, YK Canada Y1A 2C6. Emergency number: 911.

## BRIDGE, TUNNEL AND FERRY

***The following will permit units with bottled gas*** provided that equipment is DOT (ICC) approved compressed gas containers not to exceed two in quantity and 45 pounds in LPG capacity for travel trailers, campers and other recreational vehicles, and that in the opinion of the toll collector or police sergeant they are completely shut off and securely attached. No tank of larger size can cross unless a certificate is shown from a recognized gas handling company to the effect that the tank or tanks have been emptied and purged. An exception to the foregoing is that passenger cars using LP gas as a motor fuel are authorized to be equipped with up to 90-pound capacity fuel tanks.

DELAWARE. Cape May - Lewes Ferry - Bottled gas allowed.

VIRGINIA. CHESAPEAKE BAY BRIDGE-TUNNEL - only two 45 lb. bottles allowed. For fixed tanks, the maximum weight is 200 lbs. Same for Hampton Roads Tunnel I-64 & Elizabeth River Tunnel on I-264 between Norfolk & Portsmouth.

TEXAS. HOUSTON SHIP CHANNEL, BAYTOWN-LAPORTE TUNNEL - Permits LP gas as vehicle accessory (fuel, heating, refrigeration, etc.) to a maximum of two 7-1/2 gal. containers (30 lbs. gas ea.) or one 10-gal. container (40 lbs.) gas of DOT (ICC) approved type and with shutoff valve at discharge opening. Valve must be closed when in tunnel. Prohibits LP gas as a vehicle fuel.

WASHINGTON. Washington State Ferry System: Bottled gas is allowed as long as the bottles are connected to the motor home, trailer or camper bottled gas system. This means that the gas bottle must be connected to the piping and/or tubing that connects the bottle to the heater, stove and furnace, etc. Bottles not connected to a system (such as a spare) are not permitted. Gas bottles, including large LPG tanks on motorhomes, must be turned off and tagged. When purchasing a ticket, the ticket seller will provide a tag to be placed on the tank at the shut off valve. LPG appliances must be turned off while on the ferry. Vehicles using LPG/CNG as a primary vehicle fuel are authorized. White gas, for pressurized cook stoves and lanterns such as Coleman or Primus, in cans or appliance containers is not authorized. Up to two Coast Guard approved fuel tanks for boats are authorized. These tanks have a hose which connects them to the boat fuel system. Spare gas cans are not authorized.

***The following will not allow units with bottled gas:***

BALTIMORE HARBOR at Baltimore, MD: Baltimore Harbor and Ft. McHenry Tunnels if exceeds 10 lbs.

BOSTON HARBOR between Boston and East Boston, MA: Sumner and Callahan Tunnels, Prudential Tunnel and Dewey Square Tunnel.

EAST RIVER between Manhattan and Brooklyn, NY: Brooklyn Battery Tunnel. Between Manhattan and Queens, NY: Queens Midtown Tunnel.

HOUSTON SHIP CHANNEL between Pasadena and Galena Park, TX: Washburn Tunnel.

HUDSON RIVER between Manhattan, NY and Jersey City, NJ; Holland Tunnel. Between Manhattan, NY and Fort Lee, NJ; lower levels George Washington Bridge & Verrazano Narrows Bridge or Expressway between Manhattan, NY and Weehawken, NJ; Lincoln Tunnel.

***Trailer restrictions:***

CALIFORNIA. Contact Highway Patrol before entering snow areas; chains may be required by CHP anytime at its discretion. Trailers may be barred due to high winds, blowing sand, etc. Trailers over 20 ft. may experience difficulty in negotiating hairpin turns.

CONNECTICUT. Connecticut River between Chester and Hadlyme, CT; Ferry. The Wilbur Cross and Merrit Parkways do not permit: trailers, all towed vehicles except disabled vehicles, vehicles bearing other than passenger, campers, taxicab, vanpool or hearse registrations and vehicles bearing combination registrations which have a gross weight in excess of 7500 lbs., vehicles whose dimensions including any load exceed one of the following: length - 24 ft., width-7-1/2 ft., height-8 ft.

ILLINOIS. Boulevards in and around Chicago do not permit trailers.

MASSACHUSETTS. Many parkways under M.D.C. control, Memorial Drive and Storrow Drive do not permit trailers.

MONTANA. Vehicles totaling over 30 ft. in length and 96 in. in width are not permitted through Logan Pass at the summit of Going-to-the-Sun Road. The restriction is from Avalanche Campground on the south to Rising Sun Campground on the North.

WISCONSIN. 8 ton load limit on the Merrimac Ferry on State Trunk Highway 113 across the Wisconsin River near Merrimac and Okee in Sauk and Columbia Counties.

# Connecticut TRAVEL SECTION

## Free Information from Travel Section Advertisers

The following business has placed an ad in the Connecticut Travel Section. To receive free information, enter the Reader Service number on the Reader Service Card opposite page 16 in the front of this directory:

| Advertiser | RS # | Ad Pg. |
|---|---|---|
| CT Campground Owners Assn. | 445 | 45 |

## Time Zone/Topography

Eastern (Daylight Savings from the first Sunday in April to the last Sunday in October).

Although the third smallest state in the nation, (5,009 sq. miles) Connecticut's varied landscape offers travelers a wealth of recreation. Between 2,380 foot Mount Frissell (located in the state's northwest corner) and the 253-mile Atlantic coast line, lie fertile meadows and heavily forested uplands. Over half the state is forested, and New England's longest river, the Connecticut, divides the state in half.

## Climate

Taking Hartford as an example, selected average temperatures in Connecticut are as follows:

| | *High* | *Low* |
|---|---|---|
| January | 35° | 18° |
| April | 59 | 38 |
| July | 84 | 63 |
| September | 74 | 53 |
| November | 51 | 43 |

## Travel Information Sources

**State Agency:** Connecticut Department of Economic Development, 865 Brook Street, Rocky Hill, CT 06067 (800-CT-BOUND).

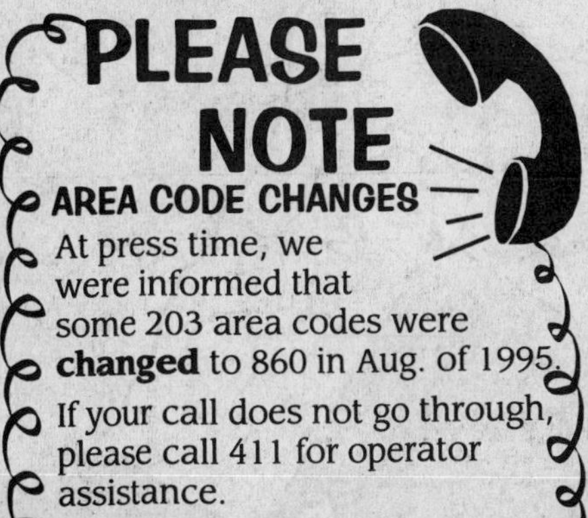
PLEASE
NOTE
AREA CODE CHANGES
At press time, we were informed that some 203 area codes were **changed** to 860 in Aug. of 1995.
If your call does not go through, please call 411 for operator assistance.

**Local Agencies:**

• *Central Connecticut Tourism District,* One Central Park Plaza, Ste. A201, New Britain, CT 06051 (860-225-3901).

• *Connecticut's North Central Tourism Bureau,* 111 Hazard Ave., Enfield, CT 06082 (800-248-8283 or 860-763-2578).

• *Connecticut River Valley & Shoreline Visitors Council,* 393 Main Street, Middletown, CT 06457 (800-486-3346 or 860-347-0028).

• *Coastal Fairfield County District,* 297 West Ave., Gate Lodge-Mathews Park, Norwalk, CT 06850 (800-866-7925 or 203-854-7825).

• *Greater Hartford Tourism District,* One

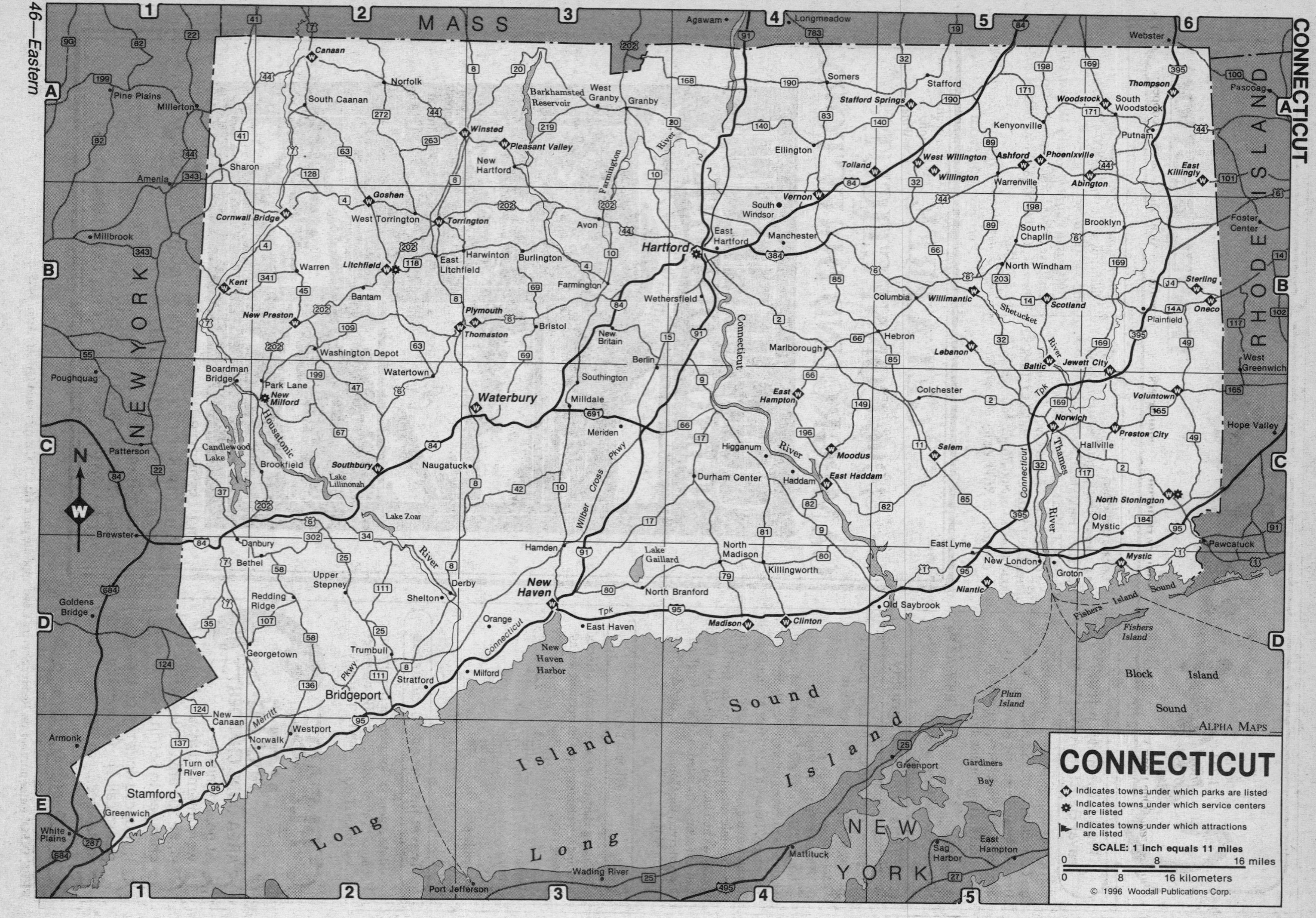
CONNECTICUT
Indicates towns under which parks are listed
Indicates towns under which service centers are listed
Indicates towns under which attractions are listed
SCALE: 1 inch equals 11 miles
0 8 16 miles
0 8 16 kilometers
© 1996 Woodall Publications Corp.
ALPHA MAPS
MASS
RHODE ISLAND
NEW YORK
Long Island Sound
Block Island Sound
Hartford
New Haven
Bridgeport
Waterbury
Stamford
Danbury
Norwich
New London
Connecticut River
Thames River
Housatonic

Civic Center Plaza, Hartford, CT 06103 (800-793-4480 or 860-520-4480).

• *Housatonic Valley Tourism District,* 72 West St., P.O. Box 406, Danbury, CT 06813 (800-841-4488 or 203-743-0546).

• *Litchfield Hills Travel Council,* P.O. Box 968, Litchfield, CT 06759 (860-567-4506).

• *Greater New Haven Convention & Visitors Bureau,* One Long Wharf Dr., New Haven, CT 06511 (800-332-STAY or 203-777-8550).

• *Northeast Connecticut Visitors District,* P.O. Box 598, Putnam, CT 06260 (860-928-1228).

• *Southeastern Connecticut Tourism District,* P.O. Box 89, 27 Masonic St., New London, CT 06320 (800-TO-ENJOY or 860-444-2206).

• *Waterbury Region Convention & Visitors Commission,* P.O. Box 1469, 83 Bank St., 4th Floor, Waterbury, CT 06721 (203-597-9527).

## Recreational Information

*Arts & Culture:* CT Commission on the Arts, 227 Lawrence St., Hartford, CT 06106 (860-566-4770).

*Fishing & Hunting:* For information on fishing licenses, and to receive a free Angler's Guide, contact the Fisheries Div., 79 Elm St., Hartford, CT 06106-5127 (860-424-FISH).

For information on obtaining a hunting licence, contact the Division of Wildlife at 860-424-3011.

*Pick-Your-Own Farms:* For a brochure of farms, send a self-addressed stamped envelope to Connecticut Dept. of Agriculture, Marketing Div., State Office Bldg., Hartford, CT 06106.

## Places to See & Things to Do

### *COASTAL FAIRFIELD*

**Bridgeport.** Local attractions include the *Beardsley Zoological Gardens* (home to hundreds of North American animals as well as exotic creatures), and *The Discovery Museum*–an interactive art and science museum which houses 100 permanent exhibits, a planetarium, art galleries and computer-simulated space missions.

**Connecticut Audubon Society Birdcraft Museum & Sanctuary,** Fairfield. The first privately owned bird sanctuary in the U.S. features wildlife exhibits, children's activity corner, dinosaur footprints, nature trails and pond.

**Norwalk.** Located on Long Island Sound, Norwalk's attractions include: *The Maritime Center at Norwalk* which houses a museum, aquarium, IMAX theater, maritime history hall and interactive exhibits. Catch the ferry (from Hope Dock) and enjoy a scenic ride to a 3-acre park and *Sheffield Island Lighthouse,* with 4 levels and 10 rooms awaiting exploration.

### *CONNECTICUT RIVER VALLEY & SHORELINE*

**Hammonasset Beach State Park,** Madison. 2-mile beach offers swimming, camping, picnicking, saltwater fishing, scuba diving, hiking and boating facilities. Nature center and interpretive programs also available.

**Henry Whitfield State Museum,** Guilford. New England's oldest stone house (1639) contains 17th- and 18th-century furnishings, herb garden and gift shop.

**Military Historians Headquarters Museum,** Westbrook. Contains the country's largest collection of American military uniforms. Also on display are unit crest insignia; restored vehicles from WWII to Desert Storm; research and video library.

### *SOUTHEASTERN CONNECTICUT TOURISM DISTRICT*

**Foxwoods High Stakes Bingo & Casino,** Ledyard. Games of chance (125 tables) include blackjack, roulette, bingo, 45 poker tables and 1,400 slot machines. Also on site is Cinetropolis, an indoor entertainment center and cinema theme park.

**Hungerford Outdoor Center,** Kensington. On site are a pond with an observation station, gardens, exhibits on natural history, geology and agriculture, a trail system and a chance to view Connecticut wildlife.

**Mohegan Park & Memorial Rose Garden,** Norwich. Zoo, swimming, picnic area and gardens which bloom June-Oct. (Roses late June-early July.)

**Mystic.** Attractions around Mystic include: *Haight Vineyard & Winery Wine Education Center,* which offers self-guided tours and tasting room; *Mystic Marinelife Aquarium,* with over 6,000 sealife specimens, Seal Island outdoor exhibit, Penquin Pavilion, and the Marine Theater; *Mystic Seaport,* a nationally acclaimed "living" museum which features 19th century ships, maritime village, historic homes, working craftspeople, planetarium, steamboat cruises and small boat rentals.

### *WATERBURY REGION*

**Catnip Acres Herb Nursery,** Oxford. Features classes and workshops, 400 varieties of herb plants and scented geraniums, formal and informal herb gardens.

**Quassy Amusement Park,** Middlebury. Families enjoy over 30 rides and games, swimming, picnicking, boat rides, petting zoo and free entertainment.

### *THE LITCHFIELD HILLS*

**Flanders Nature Center,** Woodbury. Discover botany, wildlife, geologic sites, woodlands, bog and nut grove at the Van Vleck Farm and Whittemore sanctuaries.

**Housatonic Railroad,** Canaan. Scenic rides along the Housatonic River depart from the nation's oldest train station in continuous use since 1872.

**Lake McDonough,** Barkhamsted. Rowboat and paddleboat rental, fishing, hiking, swimming and picnicking are featured at this popular recreation area.

### *CONNECTICUT'S NORTH CENTRAL*

**Connecticut Trolley Museum,** East Windsor. Antique street cars transport passengers on a three-mile round-trip excursion through the New England countryside.

**New England Air Museum,** Windsor Locks. On display are over 75 aircraft, fighters, bombers, helicopters and gliders from 1909 through WWII to the present.

**Old New-Gate Prison & Copper Mine,** East Granby. National Historic Landmark is North America's first chartered copper mine (1707), and Connecticut's first state prison (1773). Tours of the copper mine's underground caverns are available.

### *NORTHEAST CONNECTICUT*

**Coventry.** Community is home to several older structuress such as the Strong-Porter House Museum which was built around 1730. Other attractions within Coventry include:

*Caprilands Herb Farm.* A rustic 18th century farmhouse is surrounded by 30 herb gardens. Stroll through green-houses, book and gift shop and participate in an herbal lecture/luncheon by reservation.

*Nutmeg Vineyards Farm Winery.* Enjoy wine tastings, vineyard walks, and picnicking.

### *GREATER HARTFORD*

**Day-Lewis Museum,** Farmington. Indian archaeology museum is home to artifacts dating as far back as 10,000-12,000 years.

**Harriet Beecher Stowe House,** Hartford. Victorian cottage was author's home from 1873 to 1896. On display are family and professional memorabilia and period furnishings. On site is a historical garden.

### *HOUSATONIC VALLEY*

**Keeler Tavern Museum,** Ridgefield. Historic tavern features a British cannon ball (circa 1777) embedded in its exterior, guided tours and late 18th-century furnishings.

**McLaughlin Vineyards,** Sandy Hook. Guided tours of the winery and vineyards are available by appointment. Also on the 160-acre estate are hiking and mountain biking traile along the banks of the Housatonic River.

### *GREATER NEW HAVEN*

**Ansonia Nature & Recreation Center,** Ansonia. Interpretive building, over 2 miles of nature trails, hiking, fishing ponds and cross-country skiing are featured at this 104-acre park.

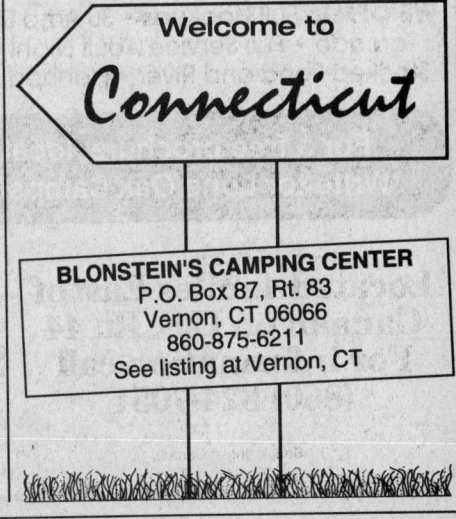

# connecticut

All privately-owned campgrounds personally inspected by Woodall Representatives Charles and Betty Hadlock.

Unless otherwise noted, all listed campgrounds have hot showers & flush toilets.

## ABINGTON—A-6

MASHAMOQUET BROOK STATE PARK—*From jct Hwy 101 & US 44: Go 1 mi E on US 44.* FACILITIES: 55 sites, 55 no hookups, tenting available, sewage disposal, public phone, tables, fire rings. RECREATION: lake swimming, lake fishing, hiking trails. No pets. Open mid Apr through Columbus Day. Phone: (860) 928-6121.

## ASHFORD—A-5

**Brialee RV & Tent Park**—Wooded CAMPGROUND with well spaced sites. *From jct US 44 & Hwy 89: Go 1 mi N on Hwy 89, then 1/2 mi W on Perry Hill Rd. then 3/4 mi N on Laurel Lane.* ◇◇◇FACILITIES: 150 sites, most common site width 40 feet, 16 full hookups, 124 water & elec (20,30 & 50 amp receptacles), 10 no hookups, seasonal sites, tenting available, sewage disposal, laundry, public phone, grocery store, LP gas refill by weight, ice, tables, fire rings, wood. ◇◇◇◇◇RECREATION: rec hall, rec room/area, swim pool (heated), pond

ASHFORD—Continued
BRIALEE RV & TENT PARK—Continued

swimming, boating, no motors, 2 row/2 canoe/2 pedal boat rentals, pond fishing, playground, 3 shuffleboard courts, planned group activities, recreation director, badminton, sports field, horseshoes, hiking trails, volleyball. Open Apr 1 through Dec 1. 3-night minimum holiday weekends by reservation. Rate in 1995 $26-29.50 per family. Member of ARVC;CCOA. Phone: (860) 429-8359.

## BALTIC—B-5

**Salt Rock Family Campground**—Hilly terrain with wooded sites in the pines. *From jct I-395 (exit 83) & Hwy 97: Go 5 mi N on Hwy 97.* ◇◇◇FACILITIES: 128 sites, most common site width 35 feet, 65 full hookups, 33 water & elec, 3 elec (20 & 30 amp receptacles), 27 no hookups, seasonal sites, 29 pull-thrus, tenting available, sewage disposal, laundry, public phone, limited grocery store, LP gas refill by weight/by meter, ice, tables, patios, fire rings, grills, wood. ◇◇◇RECREATION: rec room/area, equipped pavilion, 2 swim pools, river fishing, playground, planned group activities (weekends only), badminton, sports field, horseshoes, hiking trails, volleyball. Open Apr 15 through Oct 15. Rate in 1995 $21-25 per family. No refunds. Member of ARVC; CCOA. Phone: (860) 822-8728.

## CANAAN—A-2

LONE OAK CAMPSITES—Shaded & open sites on rolling hills. *From jct US 7 & US 44: Go 4 mi E on US 44.* ◇◇◇FACILITIES: 500 sites, 340 full hookups, 50 water & elec (20 & 30 amp receptacles), 110 no hookups, seasonal sites, 15 pull-thrus, a/c allowed, cable TV, phone hookups, tenting available, group sites for tents/RVs, RV rentals, cabins, RV storage, sewage disposal,

CANAAN—Continued
LONE OAK CAMPSITES—Continued

laundry, public phone, full service store, RV supplies, LP gas refill by weight/by meter, ice, tables, fire rings, wood, guard.

◇◇◇◇◇RECREATION: rec hall, rec room/area, coin games, 2 swim pools, river/pond/stream fishing, basketball hoop, playground, planned group activities, movies, recreation director, sports field, horseshoes, hiking trails, volleyball.

Open Apr 15 through Oct 15. Rate in 1995 $25-31 for 2 persons. Reservations recommended Memorial Day through Labor Day. Discover/Master Card/Visa accepted. Member of ARVC;CCOA. Phone: (860) 824-7051.

SEE AD THIS PAGE

## CLINTON—D-4

RIVERDALE FARM CAMPSITES—CAMPGROUND with mostly open, grassy sites near ocean. *From jct I-95 (exit 62) & Hammonassett Connector: Go 200 feet N on Hammonasett, then 1/2 mi E on Duck Hole Rd, then E over river, then 1 1/2 mi N on River Rd.*

◇◇◇FACILITIES: 250 sites, most common site width 45 feet, 100 full hookups, 150 water & elec (15,30 & 50 amp receptacles), seasonal sites, 15 pull-thrus, a/c allowed, heater allowed, tenting available, RV rentals, RV storage, sewage disposal, laundry, public phone, limited grocery store, RV supplies, LP gas refill by weight/by meter, ice, tables, patios, fire rings, wood, traffic control gate.

RIVERDALE FARM CAMPSITES—Continued on next page
CLINTON—Continued on next page

CLINTON—Continued
RIVERDALE FARM CAMPSITES—Continued

◆◆◆◆RECREATION: rec hall, rec room/area, equipped pavilion, coin games, river/pond swimming, boating, canoeing, river/pond fishing, basketball hoop, playground, 2 shuffleboard courts, planned group activities, movies, recreation director, tennis court, badminton, sports field, horseshoes, hiking trails, volleyball.

Open Apr 15 through Oct 15. 3 Day Minimum Holiday Weekends by Reservations. Rate in 1995 $23-26 for 5 persons. Reservations recommended Jun 25 through Labor Day. Member of ARVC; CCOA. Phone: (860) 669-5388.

**SEE AD THIS PAGE**

**River Road Campground**—Rustic, hilly, wooded CAMPGROUND. *From jct I-95 (exit 62) & Hammonasset Connector: Go 200 feet N on Hammonasset Connector, then 1/2 mi E on Duck Hole Rd, then E over river, then 1/2 mi N on River Rd.* ◆◆FACILITIES: 50 sites, most common site width 30 feet, 33 ft. max RV length, 50 water & elec (15 & 20 amp receptacles), seasonal sites, 10 pull-thrus, tenting available, sewage disposal, public phone, limited grocery store, ice, tables, fire rings, grills, wood. ◆◆RECREATION: river swimming, canoeing, river fishing, playground, sports field. Open Apr 15 through Oct 15. 3 Day Minimum Holiday Weekends by Reservation. Rate in 1995 $18 per family. No refunds. Member of ARVC; CCOA. Phone: (860) 669-2238.

## CORNWALL BRIDGE—B-2

HOUSATONIC MEADOWS STATE PARK—*From jct US 7 & Hwy 4: Go 1 1/2 mi NE on US 7.* FACILITIES: 95 sites, 35 ft. max RV length, 95 no hookups, tenting available, handicap restroom facilities, sewage disposal, public phone, tables, fire rings. RECREATION: canoeing, river fishing, hiking trails. No pets. Open Apr 19 through Sep 30. Phone: (860) 672-6772.

## EAST HADDAM—C-4

DEVIL'S HOPYARD STATE PARK—*From town: Go 1 mi E on Hwy 82, then continue 8 mi E. On Hopyard Rd.* FACILITIES: 21 sites, 35 ft. max RV length, 21 no hookups, tenting available, non-flush toilets, public phone, tables, grills. RECREATION: stream fishing, hiking trails. Recreation open to the public. No pets. Open mid Apr through Sep 30. No showers. Phone: (860) 873-8566.

**Wolf's Den Family Campground**—A CAMPGROUND on rolling terrain with mostly open, grassy sites. *From jct Hwy 149 & Hwy 82: Go 3 mi E on Hwy 82.* ◆◆FACILITIES: 205 sites, most common site width 30 feet, 205 water & elec (15,30 & 50 amp receptacles), seasonal sites, tenting available, sewage disposal, laundry, public phone, grocery store, LP gas refill by weight/by meter, ice, tables, fire rings, wood. ◆◆◆◆RECREATION: rec hall, rec room/area, pavilion, swim pool, pond fishing, mini-golf ($), playground, 2 shuffleboard courts, planned group activities, tennis court, badminton, sports field, horseshoes, volleyball. Recreation open to the public. Open May 1 through Oct 31. Rate in 1995 $20 per family. CPO. Member of ARVC; CCOA. Phone: (860) 873-9681.

## EAST HAMPTON—C-4

**Markam Meadows Campground**—Wooded and open, grassy sites. *From jct Hwy 196 & Hwy 16: Go 2 mi E on Hwy 16, then 3/4 mi S on Tartia Rd, then 1/4 mi E on Markham Rd.* ◆◆FACILITIES: 72 sites, most common site width 25 feet, 32 ft. max RV length, 72 water & elec (15 amp receptacles), seasonal sites, tenting available, sewage disposal, laundry, public phone, LP gas refill by weight, ice, tables, fire rings, wood. ◆◆◆RECREATION: rec hall, pavilion, pond swimming, pond fishing, planned group activities (weekends only), badminton, horseshoes, volleyball. Open May 1 through Oct 15. Rate in 1995 $21-23 per family. Member of ARVC; CCOA. Phone: (860) 267-9738.

**Nelson's Family Campground**—Rolling terrain with wooded and open, grassy sites. *From jct Hwy 2 (exit 13) & Hwy 66: Go 5 1/2 mi W on Hwy 66, then 1 1/2 mi N on North Main St (follow Lake Rd), then 3/4 mi W on Mott Hill Rd.* ◆◆◆FACILITIES: 260 sites, most common site width 45 feet, 255 water & elec (20,30 & 50 amp receptacles), 5 no hookups, seasonal sites, tenting available, sewage disposal, laundry, public phone, limited grocery store, LP gas refill by weight/by meter, ice, tables, fire rings, wood. ◆◆◆◆RECREATION: rec hall, swim pool, pond swimming, 4 pedal boat rentals, pond fishing, mini-golf ($), playground, planned group activities, recreation director, sports field, horseshoes, volleyball. Open Apr 15 through Columbus Day. 3 day min holiday wkends,2 day min other wkends by res Rate in 1995 $23 per family. CPO. Member of ARVC; CCOA. Phone: (860) 267-5300.

## EAST KILLINGLY—A-6

**Hide-A-Way Cove**—CAMPGROUND with wooded and open, grassy sites. *From jct I-395 (exit 93) & Hwy 101: Go 3 mi E on Hwy 101, then 1/2 mi N on North Rd.* ◆◆◆FACILITIES: 300 sites, most common site width 25 feet, 300 water & elec (20 & 30 amp receptacles), seasonal sites, 35 pull-thrus, tenting available, sewage disposal, laundry, public phone, limited grocery store, LP gas refill by weight/by meter, ice, tables, fire rings, wood. ◆◆◆◆RECREATION: rec hall, rec room/area, swim

EAST KILLINGLY—Continued
HIDE-A-WAY COVE—Continued

pool, lake swimming, boating, 7 hp limit, canoeing, ramp, lake fishing, playground, planned group activities (weekends only), horseshoes, volleyball. Open May 1 through Columbus Day. Rate in 1995 $19 per family. No refunds. Member of ARVC; CCOA. Phone: (860) 774-1128.

**Stateline Campresort**—Membership CAMPGROUND with mostly shaded sites beside a lake. Accepting overnight guests. *From jct I-395 & Hwy 101: Go 5 mi E on Hwy 101.* ◆◆◆FACILITIES: 200 sites, most common site width 25 feet, 200 water & elec (15,20 & 30 amp receptacles), seasonal sites, 8 pull-thrus, tenting available, handicap restroom facilities, sewage disposal, laundry, public phone, limited grocery store, LP gas refill by weight, ice, tables, fire rings, wood. ◆◆◆◆RECREATION: rec hall, rec room/area, swim pool, boating, no motors, canoeing, dock, 6 row boat rentals, lake/pond fishing, playground, planned group activities (weekends only), recreation director, tennis court, badminton, sports field, horseshoes, hiking trails, volleyball. Open Apr 15 through Oct 15. Rate in 1995 $22 per family. Phone: (860) 774-3016.

## FOXWOODS CASINO-LEDYARD—C-6

WELCOME **FRONTIER FAMILY CAMPER PARK**—*From Foxwoods High Stakes Indian Bingo & Casino: Go 5 mi E on Rt 2, then 4 mi E on Rt 184 to Rt 216, turn right, then 3/4 mi N on I-95 N to exit 1, then 1/4 mi S on Hwy 3, then 1/4 mi E on Frontier Rd, then 1/4 mi N on Maxson Hill Rd.*

**SEE PRIMARY LISTING AT ASHAWAY, RI AND AD ASHAWAY, RI PAGE 791**

**HIGHLAND ORCHARDS RESORT PARK**—*From Foxwoods High States Indian Bingo & Casino: Go 7 mi E on Hwy 2, then 1/2 mi E on Hwy 184; then 1/2 mi S on Hwy 49.*

**SEE PRIMARY LISTING AT NORTH STONINGTON AND AD MYSTIC PAGE 52**

WELCOME **SALEM FARMS CAMPGROUND**—*From Foxwood High Stakes Indian Bingo & Casino: Take Hwy 2 W, then W on Hwy 164, then N on I-395 to Hwy 82 (exit 80), then W on Hwy 80, then N on Hwy 11 to exit 5, then 1/2 mi W on Witch Meadow Rd, then 1/4 mi W on Alexander Rd.*

**SEE PRIMARY LISTING AT SALEM AND AD SALEM PAGE 54**

WELCOME **SEAPORT CAMPGROUND**—*From Foxwoods High Stakes Indian Bingo & Casino: Go 5 mi E on Hwy 2, then 4 mi W on Hwy 184.*

**SEE PRIMARY LISTING AT MYSTIC AND AD MYSTIC PAGE 51**

WELCOME **STRAWBERRY PARK RESORT CAMPGROUND**—*From Foxwoods High Stakes Indian Bingo & Casino: Go 2 mi W on Hwy 2, then 2 mi N on Hwy 164, then 1/2 mi E on Hwy 165 to park.*

**SEE PRIMARY LISTING AT PRESTON CITY AND AD MYSTIC NEX PAGE**

## GOSHEN—B-2

**Mohawk Campground**—Semi-shaded, grassy sites. *From jct Hwy 63 & Hwy 4: Go 3 1/2 mi W on Hwy 4.* ◆◆◆FACILITIES: 80 sites, most common site width 50 feet, 9 full hookups, 71 water & elec (20 & 30 amp receptacles), seasonal sites, 48 pull-thrus, tenting available, sewage disposal, public phone, LP gas refill by weight, ice, tables, fire rings, wood. ◆◆◆RECREATION: rec hall, swim pool, playground, badminton, sports field, horseshoes. Open May 4 through Oct 2. Rate in 1995 $20 for 2 persons. No refunds. Phone: (860) 491-2231.

**Valle in the Pines**—Rural CAMPGROUND with wooded sites. *From jct Hwy 63 & US 4: Go 2 1/2 mi W on US 4, then go straight at sharp curve onto Milton Rd, then 2 mi S on Milton Rd.* ◆◆ FACILITIES: 32 sites, most common site width 25 feet, 32 water & elec (30 amp receptacles), seasonal sites, tenting available, sewage disposal, public phone, ice, tables, fire rings, wood. ◆◆RECREATION: rec hall, swim pool, badminton, horseshoes, volleyball. Open Apr 15 through Oct 15. Rate in 1995 $18-26.50 per family. Member of ARVC; CCOA. Phone: (860) 491-2032.

## GROTON—D-5

WELCOME **SEAPORT CAMPGROUND**—*Southbound: From jct I-95 (exit 90) & Hwy 27: Go 1 1/4 mi N on Hwy 27, then 1/2 mi E on Hwy 184. Northbound: From jct I-95 (exit 86) & Hwy 184: Go 6 1/2 mi N on Hwy 184.*

**SEE PRIMARY LISTING AT MYSTIC AND AD MYSTIC PAGE 51**

## HARTFORD—B-4

WELCOME ✽ **RENT N' ROAM RV RENTALS**—*From I-91S (New Britain exit) & Hwy 9: Go W on Hwy 9 (East Berlin exit) & turn left at end of ramp. Go right at first set of lights, then left at next set of lights on to Wilbur Cross Hwy. (Make U-turn at light).* SERVICES: RV rentals, installs hitches. Discover/Master Card/ Visa accepted. Phone: (203) 828-1141.

**SEE AD WORCESTER, MA PAGE 405 AND AD THIS PAGE**

## JEWETT CITY—B-6

HOPEVILLE POND STATE PARK—*From Connecticut Tpk (exit 86): Go 1 mi E on Hwy 201.* FACILITIES: 82 sites, 82 no hookups, tenting available, sewage disposal, public phone, tables, fire rings. RECREATION: pond swimming, boating, canoeing, ramp, pond fishing, hiking trails. No pets. Open Apr 19 through Sep 30. Phone: (860) 376-0313.

**Ross Hill Park**—CAMPGROUND on rolling terrain with wooded and open sites. *From jct I-395 (exit 84) Hwy 12: Go 1/2 mi N on Hwy 12, then 1/2 mi W on Hwy 138, then 1 1/2 mi N on Ross Hill Rd.* ◆◆FACILITIES: 250 sites, most common site width 50 feet, 120 full hookups, 105 water & elec (20 amp receptacles), 25 no hookups, seasonal sites, 30 pull-thrus, tenting available, handicap restroom facilities, sewage disposal, laundry, public phone, grocery store, LP gas refill by weight/by meter, ice, tables, fire rings, wood. ◆◆◆◆RECREATION: rec hall, rec room/area, swim pool, boating, 5 hp limit, canoeing, 10 row/6 canoe/6 pedal boat rentals, river fishing, planned group activities (weekends only), sports field, horseshoes, hiking trails, volleyball. Open all year. Facilities fully operational Apr 1 through Oct 31. Rate in 1995 $18.50-22.50 for 3 persons. Member of ARVC; CCOA. Phone: (860) 376-9606.

## KENT—B-1

**Treetops Campresort**—RV PARK on hilly terrain beside a lake. *From Jct US 7 & Hwy 341: Go 6 mi E on Hwy 341, then 1/2 mi N on Kenico Rd.* ◆◆FACILITIES: 262 sites, most common site width 35 feet, 25 full hookups, 207 water & elec (15,20 & 30 amp receptacles), 30 no hookups, seasonal sites, 10 pull-thrus, tenting available, sewage disposal, laundry, public phone, grocery store, LP gas refill by weight, ice, tables, fire rings, grills, wood. ◆◆◆◆RECREATION: rec room/area, lake swimming, dock, 12 row boat rentals, lake fishing, mini-golf ($), playground, shuffleboard court, planned group activities (weekends only), recreation director, 2 tennis courts, sports field, horseshoes, hiking trails, volleyball. Recreation open to the public. Open May 15 through Oct 15. Rate in 1995 $20-25 per family. Member of ARVC; CCOA. Phone: (860) 927-3555.

## LEBANON—B-5

**Lake Williams Campground**—Lakeside with shaded or open sites. *From jct Hwy 85 & Hwy 207: Go 2 mi E on Hwy 207.* ◆◆FACILITIES: 87 sites, most common site width 25 feet, 62 full hookups, 25 water & elec (30 & 50 amp receptacles), seasonal sites, 2 pull-thrus, tenting available, sewage disposal, laundry, public phone, grocery store, LP gas refill by weight/by meter, ice, tables, fire rings, wood. ◆◆◆RECREATION: rec room/area, equipped pavilion, lake swimming, boating, canoeing, ramp, 13 row/2 canoe boat rentals, lake fishing, planned group activities (weekends only), horseshoes, volleyball. Recreation open to the public. Open Apr 15 through Oct 15. Rate in 1995 $21.95 for 2 persons. Member of ARVC; CCOA. Phone: (860) 642-7761.

**WATERS EDGE CAMPGROUND**—Hilly terrain with wooded & some lakeside sites. *From jct Hwy 87 & Hwy 207: Go 5 mi W on Hwy 207, then 1/2 mi N on Leonard's Bridge Rd.*

WELCOME

◆◆◆FACILITIES: 176 sites, most common site width 40 feet, 170 water & elec (20 & 30 amp receptacles), 6 no hookups, seasonal sites, 5 pull-thrus, a/c allowed ($), heater allowed ($), tenting available, group sites for tents/RVs, RV rentals, RV storage, handicap restroom facilities, sewage disposal, laundry, public phone, grocery store, RV supplies, LP gas refill by weight/by meter, ice, tables, fire rings, wood, traffic control gate.

◆◆◆◆RECREATION: rec hall, rec room/area, coin games, lake swimming, boating, canoeing, 2 row/1 canoe/2 pedal boat rentals, lake fishing, basketball hoop, playground, planned group activities, recreation director, sports field, horseshoes, volleyball.

Open Apr 15 through Oct 15. Rate in 1995 $22-24 for 2 persons. Reservations recommended Jul 1 through Labor Day. Master Card/Visa accepted. CPO. Member of ARVC; CCOA. Phone: (860) 642-7470. FCRV 10% discount.

SEE AD THIS PAGE

## LITCHFIELD—B-2

**HEMLOCK HILL CAMP RESORT**—Hilly terrain with wooded sites. *From jct Hwy 63 & US 202: Go 3/4 mi W on US 202, then 3 mi N on Milton Rd, then 1 mi N on Maple Rd, then 1/2 mi E on Hemlock Hill Rd.*

WELCOME

◆◆◆FACILITIES: 131 sites, most common site width 25 feet, 5 full hookups, 117 water & elec (20 & 30 amp receptacles), 9 no hookups, seasonal sites, 2 pull-thrus, a/c allowed ($), heater not allowed, phone hookups, tenting available, group sites for tents/RVs, RV storage, sewage disposal, laundry, public phone, limited grocery store, RV supplies, LP gas refill by weight, ice, tables, fire rings, wood.

◆◆◆◆RECREATION: rec room/area, equipped pavilion, coin games, 2 swim pools, whirlpool, basketball hoop, playground, planned group activities, recreation director, badminton, horseshoes, volleyball.

Open Apr 28 through Oct 22. Rate in 1995 $19-24 per family. No refunds. Reservations recommended Memorial Day through Labor Day. American Express/Master Card/Visa accepted. CPO. Member of ARVC; CCOA. Phone: (860) 567-2267.

SEE AD THIS PAGE

LITCHFIELD—Continued on next page

LITCHFIELD—Continued

**✲ HEMLOCK HILL RV SALES & SERVICE**—*From jct US 8 & Hwy 118 (exit 42): Go 100 feet W on Hwy 118, then 100 feet N on Old Thomaston Rd.* SALES: travel trailers, park models, 5th wheels, motor homes, mini-motor homes, fold-down camping trailers. SERVICES: Engine/Chassis & RV appliance mechanic full-time, emergency road service business hours, LP gas refill by weight/by meter, RV rentals, RV storage, sells parts/accessories, installs hitches. Open all year. American Express/Discover/Master Card/Visa accepted. Phone: (800) 942-0065.

**SEE AD PAGE 50**

WHITE MEMORIAL FAMILY CAMPGROUND (White Foundation)—*From jct Hwy 63 & US 202: Go 2 1/2 mi SW on Hwy 202, then 1 mi S on North Shore Rd.* FACILITIES: 68 sites, 68 no hookups, tenting available, non-flush toilets, sewage disposal, public phone, limited grocery store, ice, tables, fire rings, wood. RECREATION: rec room/area, lake swimming, boating, canoeing, ramp, dock, lake fishing, hiking trails. Open late Apr through Columbus Day. Facilities fully operational Memorial Day through Labor Day. No showers. Phone: (860) 567-0089.

## MADISON—D-4

HAMMONASET BEACH STATE PARK—*From jct Hwy 79 & US 1: Go 3 mi E on US 1.* FACILITIES: 558 sites, 558 no hookups, tenting available, sewage disposal, public phone, tables, fire rings. RECREATION: salt water swimming, boating, canoeing, salt water fishing. No pets. Open mid May through Oct 31. Phone: (203) 245-1817.

## MOODUS—C-4

**Sunrise Resort**—Grassy CAMPGROUND in conjunction with resort offering American Plan camping. *From jct I-95 (exit 69) & Hwy 9: Go N on Hwy 9 to exit 7, then E on Hwy 82 across East Haddam Bridge, then 3 mi N on Hwy 149, then 1 mi N on Hwy 151.* ◈◈◈FACILITIES: 66 sites, most common site width 30 feet, 16 water & elec (30 amp receptacles), 50 no hookups, tenting available, sewage disposal, laundry, public phone, ice, tables. ◈◈◈◈◈RECREATION: rec hall, rec room/area, equipped pavilion, swim pool, river swimming, boating, no motors, 8 pedal boat rentals, river fishing, mini-golf, playground, 4 shuffleboard courts, planned group activities, recreation director, 4 tennis courts, badminton,

MOODUS—Continued
SUNRISE RESORT—Continued

sports field, horseshoes, hiking trails, volleyball. Open May 25 through Sep 4. Open Memorial Day weekend. Rates available upon request. Phone: (860) 873-8681.

## MYSTIC—D-6

**HIGHLAND ORCHARDS RESORT PARK**—*Southbound: From jct I-95 & Hwy 49: Go 1/4 mi N on Hwy 49. Northbound: From jct I-95 (exit 92) & Hwy 2: Go 1/4 mi N on Hwy 2, then 1 mi NE on service road, then 1/4 mi N on Hwy 49.*

**SEE PRIMARY LISTING AT NORTH STONINGTON AND AD NEXT PAGE**

**SEAPORT CAMPGROUND**—Flat, grassy CAMPGROUND with open sites. *Southbound from jct I-95 (exit 90) & Hwy 27: Go 1 1/4 mi N on Hwy 27, then 1/2 mi E on Hwy 184. Northbound from jct I-95 (exit 86) & Hwy 184: Go 6 1/2 mi N on Hwy 184.*

◈◈◈FACILITIES: 130 sites, most common site width 60 feet, 130 water & elec (20,30 & 50 amp receptacles), seasonal sites, 12 pull-thrus, a/c allowed ($), heater allowed ($), phone hookups, tenting available, group sites for tents/RVs, tent rentals, RV rentals, RV storage, handicap restroom facilities, sewage disposal, laundry, public phone, grocery store, RV supplies, LP gas refill by weight/by meter, ice, tables, fire rings, wood, traffic control gate/guard.

◈◈◈RECREATION: rec room/area, equipped pavilion, coin games, swim pool, pond/stream fishing, mini-golf ($), playground, sports field, horseshoes. Recreation open to the public.

Open Apr through Nov. Rate in 1995 $28.50 per family. Reservations recommended Memorial Day through Labor Day. Master Card/Visa accepted. Member of ARVC; CCOA. Phone: (860) 536-4044.

**SEE AD THIS PAGE**

CT For information of Spooky Hayrides in Connecticut, see Front of Book. CT

MYSTIC—Continued

**STRAWBERRY PARK RESORT CAMPGROUND**—*From jct I-95 (exit 90) & Hwy 27: Go N on Hwy 27 to Hwy 201, follow Hwy 201N to Hwy 2, then 4 mi W on Hwy 2, then 2 mi N on Hwy 164, then 1/2 mi E on Hwy 165, then 1/2 mi N on Pierce Rd.*

**SEE PRIMARY LISTING AT PRESTON CITY AND AD PAGE 50**

## NEW HAVEN—D-3

**PLEASANT ACRES TRAILER PARK**—Flat, graveled open RV SPACES IN A MOBILE HOME PARK. *From jct I-91 (exit 8) & Hwy 80: Go 3 3/4 mi E on Hwy 80 (Totoket Center).*

FACILITIES: 13 sites, most common site width 15 feet, accepts full hookup units only, 13 full hookups, (30 amp receptacles), a/c allowed, heater allowed, tables.

No tents. Open Apr 1 through Nov 1. Rate in 1995 $18 for 2 persons. No refunds. Phone: (203) 484-9681.

**SEE AD THIS PAGE**

CT **STATE BIRD: ROBIN** CT

## NEW MILFORD—C-2

**❖ HEMLOCK HILL RV SALES & SERVICE**—*From jct US 202 & US 7: Go 1/2 mi N on US 7.* SALES: travel trailers, park models, 5th wheels, motor homes, mini-motor homes, fold-down camping trailers. SERVICES: Engine/Chassis & RV appliance mechanic, LP gas refill by weight/by meter, RV rentals, RV storage, sells parts/accessories, installs hitches. Open all year. American Express/Discover/Master Card/Visa accepted. Phone: (800) 354-0350.
**SEE AD LITCHFIELD PAGE 50**

## NEW PRESTON—B-2

LAKE WARAMAUG STATE PARK—*From jct US 202 & Hwy 45: Go 1 1/2 mi N on Hwy 45 to Lake Waramaug Rd, then follow signs around the lake.* FACILITIES: 78 sites, 35 ft. max RV length, 78 no hookups, tenting available, sewage disposal, public phone, tables, fire rings. RECREATION: lake swimming, boating, canoeing, 6 canoe/4 pedal boat rentals, lake fishing. No pets. Open mid May through Sep 30. Phone: (860) 868-0220.

## NIANTIC—D-5

ROCKY NECK STATE PARK—*From jct Hwy 161 & Hwy 156: Go 3 mi W on Hwy 156.* FACILITIES: 160 sites, 160 no hookups, tenting available, sewage disposal, public phone, tables, fire rings. RECREATION: salt water swimming, salt water fishing, hiking trails. No pets. Open Apr 19 through Sep 30. Phone: (860) 739-5471.

## NORTH STONINGTON—C-6

**HIGHLAND ORCHARDS RESORT PARK**—CAMPGROUND with open or shaded grassy sites & wooded tent sites. *Southbound: From jct I-95 & Hwy 49: Go 1/4 mi N on Hwy 49. Northbound: From jct I-95 (exit 92) & Hwy 2: Go 1/4 mi N on Hwy 2, then 1 mi NE on Service Rd, then 1/4 mi N on Hwy 49.*

◆◆◆◆FACILITIES: 260 sites, most common site width 35 feet, 98 full hookups, 144 water & elec (20,30 & 50 amp receptacles), 18 no hookups, seasonal sites, 96 pull-thrus, a/c allowed ($), heater allowed ($), phone hookups, tenting available, group sites for tents/RVs, RV rentals, RV storage, sewage disposal, laundry, public phone, grocery store, RV supplies, LP gas refill by weight/by meter, ice, tables, fire rings, wood, traffic control gate.

◆◆◆◆RECREATION: rec hall, rec room/area, equipped pavilion, coin games, swim pool, pond fishing, mini-golf ($), basketball hoop, playground, 3 shuffleboard courts, planned group activities (weekends only), movies, sports field, horseshoes, volleyball.

Open all year. Rate in 1995 $25.50-32.50 per family. Reservations recommended Memorial Day through Labor Day. American Express/Discover/Master Card/Visa accepted. CPO. Member of ARVC; CCOA. Phone: (800) 624-0829.
**SEE AD MYSTIC THIS PAGE**

**❖ HIGHLAND ORCHARDS TRAILER SALES**—*S'bound: From jct I-95 & Hwy 49: Go 1/4 mi N on Hwy 49. N'bound: From jct I-95 (exit 92) & Hwy 2: Go 1/4 mi N on Hwy 2, then 1 mi NE on service road, then 1/4 mi N on Hwy 49.* SALES: travel trailers, 5th wheels. SERVICES: RV appliance mechanic full-time, emergency road service business hours, LP gas refill by weight/by meter, sewage disposal, RV storage, sells parts/accessories, installs hitches. Open all year. American Express/Discover/Master Card/Visa accepted. Phone: (800) 624-0829.
**SEE AD MYSTIC THIS PAGE**

## NORWICH—C-5

**Acorn Acres Campsites**—Gently rolling, grassy CAMPGROUND with open or wooded sites. *From jct I-395 (exit 80W) & Hwy 82: Go 7 mi W on Hwy 82, then 1 1/2 mi N on Hwy 163, then 1 3/10 mi W on Lake Rd.* ◆◆◆FACILITIES: 225 sites, most common site width 60 feet, 125 full hookups, 100 water & elec (20,30 & 50 amp receptacles), seasonal sites, tenting available, sewage disposal, laundry, public phone, grocery store, LP gas refill by weight, ice, tables, fire rings, grills, wood. ◆◆◆◆◆RECREATION: rec hall, rec room/area, equipped pavilion, swim pool, river/pond fishing, mini-golf ($), playground, 2 shuffleboard courts, planned group activities, recreation director, 2 tennis courts, badminton, sports field, horseshoes, hiking trails, volleyball. Open May 1 through Columbus Day. Rate in 1995 $22-24 per family. Member of ARVC; CCOA. Phone: (860) 859-1020.

**HIDDEN ACRES FAMILY CAMPGROUND**—Riverside with wooded sites. *From jct I-395 (exit 85) & Hwy 164: Go 1 mi S on Hwy 164, then 1 1/2 mi S on Palmer Rd, then 1 1/2 mi S on River Rd.*

◆◆◆FACILITIES: 180 sites, most common site width 40 feet, 125 full hookups, 40 water & elec (30 amp receptacles), 15 no hookups, seasonal sites, 4 pull-thrus, a/c allowed ($), heater not allowed, tenting available, RV rentals, cabins, RV storage, sewage disposal, laundry, public phone, limited grocery store, RV supplies, LP gas refill by weight/by meter, ice, tables, fire rings, wood, traffic control gate.

◆◆◆◆RECREATION: rec hall, rec room/area, equipped pavilion, coin games, swim pool, river/pond swimming, river/pond fishing, basketball hoop, playground, shuffleboard court, planned group activities, badminton, sports field, horseshoes, volleyball.

Open May 1 through Oct 1. 3 day minimum, holiday weekends by reservations. Rate in 1995 $23-25 per family. Reservations recommended Memorial Day through Labor Day. Member of ARVC; CCOA. Phone: (860) 887-9633.

SEE AD THIS PAGE

**ODETAH CAMPGROUND**—Lakeside CAMPGROUND in hilly terrain with leveled sites. *N'bound from I-395 (exit 81W): Go 3 1/2 mi W on Hwy 2 (exit 23), then 100 yards S on Hwy 163, then 1/2 mi E on Bozrah St ext. S'bound from I-395 (exit 82): Go 3 1/2 mi W on Hwy 2 (exit 23), then 100 yards S on Hwy 163, then 1/2 mi E on Bozrah St ext.*

◆◆◆◆FACILITIES: 205 sites, most common site width 40 feet, 25 full hookups, 155 water & elec (15,20 & 30 amp receptacles), 25 no hookups, seasonal sites, a/c allowed ($), heater allowed ($), tenting available, group sites for tents/RVs, cabins, RV storage, handicap restroom facilities, sewage disposal, laundry, public phone, grocery store, RV supplies, LP gas refill by weight, ice, tables, fire rings, wood, traffic control gate/guard.

◆◆◆◆RECREATION: rec hall, rec room/area, coin games, swim pool, lake swimming, boating, no motors, canoeing, ramp, 5 row/4 canoe/6 pedal boat rentals, lake fishing, mini-golf ($), basketball hoop, playground, 3 shuffleboard courts, planned group activities (weekends only), 2 tennis courts, sports field, horseshoes, volleyball.

Open Apr 15 through Oct 15. Rate in 1995 $20-23 for 2 persons. No refunds. Master Card/Visa accepted. Member of ARVC; CCOA. Phone: (860) 889-4144.

SEE AD THIS PAGE

## ONECO—B-6

**River Bend Campground**—Pine shaded or open grassy sites. *From I-395 (exit 88): Go 5 1/2 mi E on 14A, then 1/4 mi S on paved road.* ◆◆◆FACILITIES: 160 sites, most common site width 35 feet, 60 full hookups, 90 water & elec (20,30 & 50 amp receptacles), 10 no hookups, seasonal sites, 70 pull-thrus, tenting available, sewage disposal, laundry, public phone, limited grocery store, LP gas refill by weight, ice, tables, patios, fire rings, grills, wood. ◆◆◆◆◆RECREATION: rec hall, rec room/area, equipped pavilion, swim pool, boating, 3 hp limit, canoeing, ramp, dock, 2 row/15 canoe/2 pedal boat rentals, river/pond fishing, mini-golf, playground, planned group activities (weekends only), recreation director, tennis court, badminton, sports field, horseshoes, volleyball. Open Apr 20 through Columbus Day. Rate in 1995 $23-25 per family. CPO. Member of ARVC; CCOA. Phone: (860) 564-3440.

## PHOENIXVILLE—A-5

**CHARLIE BROWN CAMPGROUND**—Open grassy sites beside river. *From jct US 44 & Hwy 198: Go 1 mi S on Hwy 198.*

◆◆◆FACILITIES: 123 sites, most common site width 50 feet, 14 full hookups, 109 water & elec (20 & 30 amp receptacles), seasonal sites, 8 pull-thrus, a/c allowed,

PHOENIXVILLE—Continued
CHARLIE BROWN CAMPGROUND—Continued

heater allowed, cable TV ($), tenting available, group sites for tents/RVs, handicap restroom facilities, sewage disposal, laundry, public phone, limited grocery store, RV supplies, LP gas refill by weight/by meter, ice, tables, fire rings, wood.

◆◆◆◆RECREATION: rec hall, equipped pavilion, coin games, river swimming, river fishing, basketball hoop, planned group activities (weekends only), badminton, sports field, horseshoes, volleyball.

Open Apr 16 through Oct 15. Rate in 1995 $21-25 per family. Reservations recommended all season. Member of ARVC; CCOA. Phone: (860) 974-0142.

SEE AD THIS PAGE

**Peppertree Camping**—Riverside CAMPGROUND with wooded sites. *From jct US 44 & Hwy 198: Go 1 1/4 mi S on Hwy 198.* ◆◆◆FACILITIES: 55 sites, most common site width 40 feet, 40 full hookups, 15 water & elec (15 & 20 amp receptacles), seasonal sites, tenting available, sewage disposal, laundry, public phone, grocery store, LP gas refill by weight/by meter, ice, tables, fire rings, wood. ◆◆◆RECREATION: river swimming, boating, no motors, canoeing, river fishing, badminton, sports field, horseshoes, volleyball. Open Apr 15 through Oct 12. Rates available upon request. Member of ARVC; CCOA. Phone: (860) 974-1439.

## PLEASANT VALLEY—A-3

AMERICAN LEGION STATE FOREST (Austin F. Hawes Memorial Campground)—*From town: Go N on W River Rd.* FACILITIES: 30 sites, 30 no hookups, tenting available, sewage disposal, tables, fire rings. RECREATION: river fishing, hiking trails. Open Apr 19 through Sep 30. Phone: (860) 379-0922.

## PLYMOUTH—B-3

**Gentiles Campground**—Secluded CAMPGROUND on hilly terrain with wooded sites. *From I-8 (exit 37): Go 3 3/4 mi E on Hwy 262.* ◆◆◆FACILITIES: 150 sites, most common site width 20 feet, 75 full hookups, 75 water & elec (30 amp receptacles), seasonal sites, tenting available, sewage disposal, public phone, LP gas refill by weight, ice, tables, fire rings, wood. ◆◆◆RECREATION: rec hall, rec room/area, mini-golf ($), playground, tennis court, sports field, horseshoes, volleyball. Open Apr 1 through Nov 15. Rates available upon request. Phone: (860) 283-8437.

## PRESTON CITY—C-6

**STRAWBERRY PARK RESORT CAMPGROUND**—Level CAMPGROUND with shaded and open sites. *From jct Hwy 164 & Hwy 165: Go 1 mi E on Hwy 165, then 1/2 mi N on Pierce Rd.*

◆◆◆◆FACILITIES: 430 sites, most common site width 40 feet, 160 full hookups, 270 water & elec (20,30 & 50 amp receptacles), seasonal sites, a/c allowed ($), heater allowed ($), cable TV, phone hookups, tenting available, group sites for tents/RVs, RV rentals, RV storage, handicap restroom facilities, sewage disposal, laundry, public phone, full service store, RV supplies, LP gas refill by weight/by meter, ice, tables, fire rings, grills, wood, traffic control gate/guard.

◆◆◆◆◆RECREATION: rec hall, rec room/area, equipped pavilion, coin games, 3 swim pools, wading pool, sauna, whirlpool, basketball hoop, playground, 3 shuffleboard courts, planned group activities, movies, recreation director, horse riding trails, horse rental, badminton, sports field, horseshoes, hiking trails, volleyball, cross country skiing.

STRAWBERRY PARK RESORT CAMPGROUND—Continued on next page
PRESTON CITY—Continued on next page



CT CONSTITUTION STATE CT





CT *Special tobacco leaves used for the outside of cigars are grown in Connecticut.* CT

PRESTON CITY—Continued
STRAWBERRY PARK RESORT CAMPGROUND—Continued

Open all year. Facilities fully operational Apr 1 through Oct 31. 3 day min. Holiday weekends. Weekend activities Labor Day thru Oct 31. Rate in 1995 $17-39 for 2 persons. No refunds. Reservations recommended Memorial Day through Labor Day. Discover/Master Card/Visa accepted. Member of ARVC; CCOA. Phone: (860) 886-1944.
**SEE AD MYSTIC PAGE 50**

## SALEM—C-5

**SALEM FARMS CAMPGROUND**—Open & shaded sites in a quiet, rural area. *From jct I-11 (exit 5) & Witch Meadow Rd: Go 1/2 mi W on Witch Meadow Rd, then 1/4 mi W on Alexander Rd.*

◆◆◆FACILITIES: 204 sites, most common site width 45 feet, 190 water & elec (30 amp receptacles), 14 no hookups, seasonal sites, 3 pull-thrus, a/c allowed ($), heater allowed ($), tenting available, group sites for tents/RVs, RV rentals, RV storage, sewage disposal, laundry, public phone, limited grocery store, RV supplies, LP gas refill by weight, ice, tables, fire rings, wood, traffic control gate/guard.

◆◆◆◆RECREATION: rec hall, equipped pavilion, coin games, 2 swim pools, mini-golf ($), basketball hoop, playground, 2 shuffleboard courts, planned group activities, movies, recreation director, 2 tennis courts, badminton, sports field, horseshoes, hiking trails, volleyball.

Open May 1 through Oct 1. Rate in 1995 $18-22 for 5 persons. Reservations recommended Memorial Day through Labor Day. Discover/Master Card/Visa accepted. Member of ARVC; CCOA. Phone: (860) 859-2320.
**SEE AD THIS PAGE**

**Witch Meadow Lake Campground**—Hilly CAMPGROUND with mostly shaded sites. *From jct Witch Meadow Rd & Hwy 11 (exit 5): Go 1/8 mi SE on Witch Meadow Rd.* ◆◆◆FACILITIES: 280 sites, most common site width 25 feet, 35 ft. max RV length, 280 water & elec (15,20 & 30 amp receptacles), seasonal sites, tenting available, sewage disposal, laundry, public phone, grocery store, LP gas refill by weight, ice, tables, fire rings, wood. ◆◆◆◆RECREATION: rec hall, rec room/area, equipped pavilion, lake swimming, boating, no motors, canoeing, ramp, dock, 4 canoe/4 pedal boat rentals, lake fishing, mini-golf ($), playground, 2 shuffleboard courts, planned group activities, recreation director, 2 tennis courts, badminton, sports field, horseshoes, hiking trails, volleyball. Open May 1 through Oct 25. Rate in 1995 $22 for 5 persons. No refunds. CPO. Member of ARVC;CCOA. Phone: (860) 859-1542.

## SCOTLAND—B-5

**Highland Campground**—CAMPGROUND with level, wooded sites. *From I-395 (exit 83): Go 7 1/2 mi N on Hwy 97, then 1/8 mi E on Toleration Rd.* ◆◆FACILITIES: 160 sites, most common site width 40 feet, 160 water & elec (20 & 30 amp receptacles), seasonal sites, 100 pull-thrus, tenting available, sewage disposal, laundry, public phone, limited grocery store, LP gas refill by weight/by meter, ice, tables, fire rings, wood. ◆◆◆◆RECREATION: rec hall, rec room/area, swim pool, pond fishing, playground, planned group activities (weekends only), badminton, horseshoes, hiking trails, volleyball. Open all year. Facilities fully operational May 1 through Oct 31. Open weekends only Nov 1 thru Apr 30. Rate in 1995 $20 per family. Member of ARVC; CCOA. Phone: (860) 423-5684.

## SOUTHBURY—C-2

KETTLETOWN STATE PARK—*From jct Hwy 67 & I-84 (exit 15): Go 1/10 mi SE on Hwy 67, then 3 1/2 mi S on Kettletown Rd, then follow sign 3/4 mi W on Georges Hill Rd.* FACILITIES: 72 sites, 26 ft. max RV length, 72 no hookups, tenting available, sewage disposal, public phone, tables, fire rings. RECREATION: lake swimming, boating, canoeing, lake fishing, hiking trails. No pets. Open Apr 19 through Oct 14. Phone: (203) 264-5678.

## STAFFORD SPRINGS—A-5

**MINERAL SPRINGS FAMILY CAMPGROUND**—Rural location with wooded or open sites. *From jct Hwy 190 & Hwy 32: Go 1/4 mi E on 190, then 2 mi N on Hwy 19, then 1 mi W on Leonard Rd.*

◆◆◆FACILITIES: 150 sites, most common site width 30 feet, 10 full hookups, 120 water & elec (15 & 20 amp receptacles), 20 no hookups, seasonal sites, 20 pull-thrus, a/c allowed ($), heater allowed ($), tenting available, group sites for tents/RVs, RV rentals, handicap restroom facilities, sewage disposal, laundry, public phone, limited grocery store, RV supplies, LP gas refill by weight/by meter, ice, tables, fire rings, wood.

◆◆◆RECREATION: rec hall, rec room/area, coin games, swim pool, basketball hoop, playground, planned group activities (weekends only), badminton, horseshoes, volleyball.

Open May 1 through Oct 15. 3 day minimum holiday weekends by reservation. Rate in 1995 $17-18 per family. Reservations recommended Jun through Sep. CPO. Member of ARVC;CCOA. Phone: (860) 684-2993.
**SEE AD THIS PAGE**

## STERLING—B-6

**Sterling Park Campground**—Rural CAMPGROUND with shaded and grassy sites. *From jct I-395 (exit 89) & Hwy 14: Go 6 mi E on Hwy 14, then 1/2 mi N on Gibson Hill Rd.* ◆◆◆FACILITIES: 98 sites, most common site width 25 feet, 48 full hookups, 50 water & elec (20 & 30 amp receptacles), seasonal sites, 4 pull-thrus, tenting available, sewage disposal, laundry, public phone, limited grocery store, LP gas refill by weight/by meter, ice, tables, fire rings, wood. ◆◆◆◆RECREATION: rec hall, rec room/area, swim pool, mini-golf ($), playground, 2 shuffleboard courts, planned group activities (weekends only), badminton, sports field, horseshoes, hiking trails. Open May 1 through Oct 15. Rate in 1995 $22-26 per family. No refunds. Member of ARVC; CCOA. Phone: (860) 564-8777.

## THOMASTON—B-2

BLACK ROCK STATE PARK—*From jct US 6 & Hwy 109: Go 3 mi W on Hwy 109.* FACILITIES: 96 sites, 96 no hookups, tenting available, sewage disposal, public phone, tables, fire rings. RECREATION: pond swimming, lake/stream fishing, hiking trails. No pets. Open Apr 19 through Sep 30. Phone: (860) 283-8088.

**Branch Brook Campground**—Open & shaded sites beside stream. *From jct Hwy 8 (exit 38) & US 6: Go 1 mi W on US 6.* ◆◆FACILITIES: 63 sites, most common site width 30 feet, 55 full hookups, 2 water & elec (15,20,30 & 50 amp receptacles), 6 no hookups, seasonal sites, tenting available, handicap restroom facilities, sewage disposal, laundry, public phone, LP gas refill by weight/by meter, ice, tables, fire rings, wood. ◆◆◆RECREATION: rec room/area, swim pool, river fishing, playground, badminton, sports field, horseshoes, hiking trails, volleyball. Open Apr 1 through Oct 31. 3 day minimum on holiday weekends with reservations. Rate in 1995 $20 per family. Member of ARVC; CCOA. Phone: (860) 283-8144.

## THOMPSON—A-6

WEST THOMPSON LAKE (Corps of Eng. - West Thompson Lake)—*From jct I-395 (exit 99) & Hwy 200: Go 8/10 mi E on Hwy 200, then SW on Hwy 193, then continue W past Hwy 12, follow signs.* FACILITIES: 25 sites, 34 ft. max RV length, 1 water & elec, 24 no hookups, tenting available, handicap restroom facilities, sewage disposal, public phone, tables, fire rings, grills, wood. RECREATION: pavilion, boating, ramp, lake/river fishing, playground, horseshoes, hiking trails. Recreation open to the public. Open Wkend before Memorial Day through Columbus Day Wkend. Phone: (860) 923-2982.

## TOLLAND—A-5

**Del-Air Camp**—Flat CAMPGROUND with wooded or open grassy sites. *From jct I-84 (exit 67) & Hwy 31: Go 1/4 mi N on Hwy 31, then 3 1/2 mi E on Hwy 30, then 3/4 mi N on Browns Bridge Road, then 1/8 mi E on Shenipsit Lake Rd.* ◆◆FACILITIES: 122 sites, most common site width 40 feet, 100 water & elec (15 & 20 amp receptacles), 22 no hookups, seasonal sites, 3 pull-thrus, tenting available, handicap restroom facilities, sewage disposal, public phone, limited grocery store, LP gas refill by weight, ice, tables, fire rings, wood. ◆◆◆RECREATION: rec hall, pond swimming, pond fishing, playground, planned group activities (weekends only), recreation director, tennis court, badminton, sports field, horseshoes, volleyball. Open May 1 through Oct 15. Rate in 1995 $17 per family. Member of ARVC;CCOA. Phone: (860) 875-8325.

## TORRINGTON—B-2

BURR POND STATE PARK - TAYLOR BROOK CAMPGROUND—*From jct Hwy 4 & Hwy 8: Go 6 mi N on Hwy 8, exit 46, then on W Highland Lake Road to Mountain Road.* FACILITIES: 40 sites, 40 no hookups, tenting available, sewage disposal, public phone, tables, fire rings. RECREATION: boating, canoe boat rentals, stream fishing, hiking trails. No pets. Open Apr 19 through Sep 30. Phone: (860) 370-0172.

## VERNON—B-4

✱ **BLONSTEIN'S CAMPING CENTER**—*From jct I-84 (exit 64) & Hwy 83: Go 3 mi N on Hwy 83.* SALES: travel trailers, truck campers, 5th wheels, mini-motor homes, fold-down camping trailers. SERVICES: RV appliance mechanic full-time, emergency road service business hours, RV towing, LP gas refill by weight/by meter, RV rentals, RV storage, sells parts/accessories, installs hitches. Open all year. Discover/Master Card/Visa accepted. Phone: (860) 875-6211.
**SEE AD TRAVEL SECTION PAGE 47**

## VOLUNTOWN—C-6

**CIRCLE C CAMPGROUND**—Pine-shaded or grassy, level sites. *From jct Hwy 138 & Hwy 49: Go 2 1/4 mi N on Hwy 49, then 2 3/4 mi NE on Brown Rd, then 1 mi E on Gallup Homestead Rd, then 3/4 mi S on Bailey Rd.*

◆◆◆FACILITIES: 80 sites, most common site width 35 feet, 76 water & elec (20 & 30 amp receptacles), 4 no hookups, seasonal sites, 55 pull-thrus, a/c allowed ($), heater allowed ($), tenting available, group sites for RVs, RV rentals, cabins, RV storage, sewage disposal, laundry, public phone, limited grocery store, RV supplies, ice, tables, fire rings, grills, wood, traffic control gate.

◆◆◆RECREATION: rec hall, rec room/area, pavilion, pond swimming, boating, 10 hp limit, canoeing,

CIRCLE C CAMPGROUND—Continued on next page
VOLUNTOWN—Continued on next page

VOLUNTOWN—Continued
CIRCLE C CAMPGROUND—Continued

ramp, dock, 5 row/1 canoe boat rentals, pond fishing, basketball hoop, playground, planned group activities (weekends only), badminton, sports field, horseshoes, volleyball.

Open Apr 19 through Columbus Day. Rate in 1995 $20 per family. Reservations recommended Memorial Day through Labor Day. Discover/Master Card/Visa accepted. Member of ARVC; CCOA. Phone: (860) 564-4534.

**SEE AD THIS PAGE**

**Natures Campsites**—Hilly CAMPGROUND with shaded, rustic sites under tall pines. *From jct Hwy 165 & Hwy 49: Go 1/2 mi N on Hwy 49.* ◆◆FACILITIES: 150 sites, most common site width 35 feet, 20 full hookups, 75 water & elec (15 & 20 amp receptacles), 55 no hookups, seasonal sites, 15 pull-thrus, tenting available, sewage disposal, laundry, public phone, LP gas refill by weight, ice, tables, fire rings, wood. ◆◆◆RECREATION: rec room/area, pavilion, swim pool, boating, canoeing, dock, 6 canoe boat rentals, river fishing, playground, 2 shuffleboard courts, badminton, sports field, horseshoes, volleyball. Open May 1 through Oct 15. Rate in 1995 $18-22 per family. No refunds. Member of ARVC; CCOA. Phone: (860) 376-4203. FCRV 10% discount.

PACHAUG STATE FOREST—*From jct Hwy 138E & Hwy 49N: Go 1 mi N on Hwy 49N.* FACILITIES: 40 sites, 40 no hookups, tenting available, non-flush toilets, tables, fire rings. RECREATION: pond swimming, canoeing, pond/stream fishing. Open Apr 19 through Sep 30. No showers. Phone: (860) 376-4075.

**Ye Olde Countryside Campground**—Rural area with sites in a natural setting. *From jct Hwy 138 & Hwy 201: Go 1 mi S on Hwy 201, then 1/3 mi E on Cook Hill Rd.* ◆◆FACILITIES: 68 sites, most common site width 50 feet, 60 water & elec (15,20 & 30 amp receptacles), 8 no hookups, seasonal sites, 4 pull-thrus, tenting available, sewage disposal, ice, tables, fire rings, wood. ◆RECREATION: pond swimming, pond fishing, horseshoes, hiking trails. Open May 1 through Oct 15. Rate in 1995 $17-18 per family. No refunds. Member of ARVC; CCOA. Phone: (860) 376-0029. FCRV 10% discount.

## WATERBURY—C-3

✱ **RV PARTS & ELECTRIC**—*At Hwy 8 (exit 29): Go 100 feet E on S Main St.* SERVICES: RV appliance mechanic full-time, emergency road service business hours, sells parts/accessories, sells camping supplies, installs hitches. Open all year. American Express/Master Card/Visa accepted. Phone: (203) 755-0739.

**SEE AD THIS PAGE**

## WEST WILLINGTON—A-5

**Moosemeadow Camping Resort**—Grassy CAMPGROUND with wooded or open sites. *From jct I-84 (exit 69) & Hwy 74: Go 4 mi E on Hwy 74, then 1 mi N on Moosemeadow Rd.* ◆◆◆FACILITIES: 170 sites, most



WEST WILLINGTON—Continued
MOOSEMEADOW CAMPING RESORT—Continued

common site width 40 feet, 30 full hookups, 63 water & elec, 5 elec (15,20 & 30 amp receptacles), 72 no hookups, seasonal sites, 26 pull-thrus, tenting available, sewage disposal, laundry, public phone, grocery store, LP gas refill by weight, ice, tables, fire rings, grills, wood. ◆◆◆◆RECREATION: rec room/area, pavilion, swim pool, pond swimming, pond fishing, mini-golf ($), playground, 2 shuffleboard courts, planned group activities, recreation director, tennis court, badminton, sports field, horseshoes, volleyball. Open Apr 15 through Oct 17. Rate in 1995 $23-28 per family. No refunds. Phone: (860) 429-7451.

## WILLIMANTIC—B-5

**Nickerson Park**—Wooded CAMPGROUND with sites beside a river. *From jct US 6 & Hwy 198: Go 4 1/2 mi N on Hwy 198.* ◆◆◆FACILITIES: 100 sites, most common site width 30 feet, 60 full hookups, 30 water & elec (20 & 30 amp receptacles), 10 no hookups, seasonal sites, 25 pull-thrus, tenting available, sewage disposal, laundry, public phone, limited grocery store, LP gas refill by weight/by meter, ice, tables, fire rings, wood. ◆◆◆RECREATION: rec room/area, river swimming, canoeing, river fishing, playground, planned group activities (weekends only), badminton, sports field, horseshoes, volleyball. Open all year. 3 Day Minimum Holiday Weekends by Reservation. Rate in 1995 $15-19 per family. Member of ARVC; CCOA. Phone: (860) 455-0007.

## WILLINGTON—A-5

**Rainbow Acres Family Campground**—CAMPGROUND with shaded and open sites beside a lake. *From jct I-84 (exit 70) & Hwy 32: Go 1/10 mi N on Hwy 32, then 1/2 mi E on Village Hill Rd.* ◆◆FACILITIES: 100 sites, most common site width 25 feet, 70 water & elec (30 amp receptacles), 30 no hookups, seasonal sites, 20 pull-thrus, tenting available, sewage disposal, public phone, LP gas refill by weight/by meter, ice, tables, fire rings, wood. ◆◆◆◆RECREATION: rec hall, lake swimming, boating, electric motors only, lake fishing, playground, planned group activities (weekends only), badminton, sports field, horseshoes, hiking trails, volleyball. Open May 1 through Oct 31. Rate in 1995 $18-20 for 2 persons. Phone: (860) 684-5704.

## WINSTED—A-3

**WHITE PINES CAMPSITES**—CAMPGROUND with wooded sites in the pines and open, grassy sites in field. *From jct US 44 & Hwy 8: Go 1 3/4 mi N on Hwy 8, then 1/4 mi E on Hwy 20, then 3/4 mi S on Old North Rd.*

◆◆◆FACILITIES: 206 sites, most common site width 30 feet, 206 water & elec (20 & 30 amp recep-

WINSTED—Continued
WHITE PINES CAMPSITES—Continued

tacles), seasonal sites, 30 pull-thrus, a/c allowed, heater allowed, tenting available, group sites for tents/RVs, RV rentals, RV storage, sewage disposal, public phone, grocery store, RV supplies, LP gas refill by weight/by meter, ice, tables, fire rings, wood, traffic control gate.

◆◆◆◆RECREATION: rec hall, rec room/area, equipped pavilion, coin games, swim pool, 2 pedal boat rentals, pond fishing, basketball hoop, playground, planned group activities (weekends only), movies, recreation director, badminton, sports field, horseshoes, hiking trails, volleyball.

Open Apr 15 through Oct 15. 3 day minimum holiday weekends by reservation. Rate in 1995 $22 for 2 persons. Reservations recommended Memorial Day through Labor Day. Discover/Master Card/Visa accepted. Member of ARVC;CCOA. Phone: (800) 622-6614.

**SEE AD THIS PAGE**

## WOODSTOCK—A-6

**Chamberlain Lake Campground**—Wooded sites beside a lake. *From jct I-84 (exit 73) & Hwy 190: Go 1 9/10 mi E on Hwy 190, then 2 2/10 mi E on Hwy 171, then 3 4/10 mi E on Hwy 197.* ◆◆◆FACILITIES: 150 sites, most common site width 30 feet, 141 water & elec (20 & 30 amp receptacles), 9 no hookups, seasonal sites, tenting available, handicap restroom facilities, sewage disposal, laundry, public phone, grocery store, LP gas refill by weight/by meter, ice, tables, fire rings, wood. ◆◆◆◆RECREATION: rec hall, rec room/area, lake swimming, boating, electric motors only, canoeing, ramp, dock, 5 row/2 canoe boat rentals, lake fishing, playground, planned group activities (weekends only), badminton, sports field, horseshoes, volleyball. Open May 1 through Oct 15. Rate in 1995 $19-22 for 2 persons. Member of ARVC; CCOA. Phone: (860) 974-0567.





## LYME DISEASE

Lyme disease can be cured. See a doctor if you have these symptoms:

- Up to a month after a bite, a bull's-eye rash may appear with a clear center and red circles spreading several inches outward. This symptom occurs in only about 70 percent of cases, however.

- Flu-like symptoms of headache, fever, swollen glands, stiff neck and general malaise also appear.

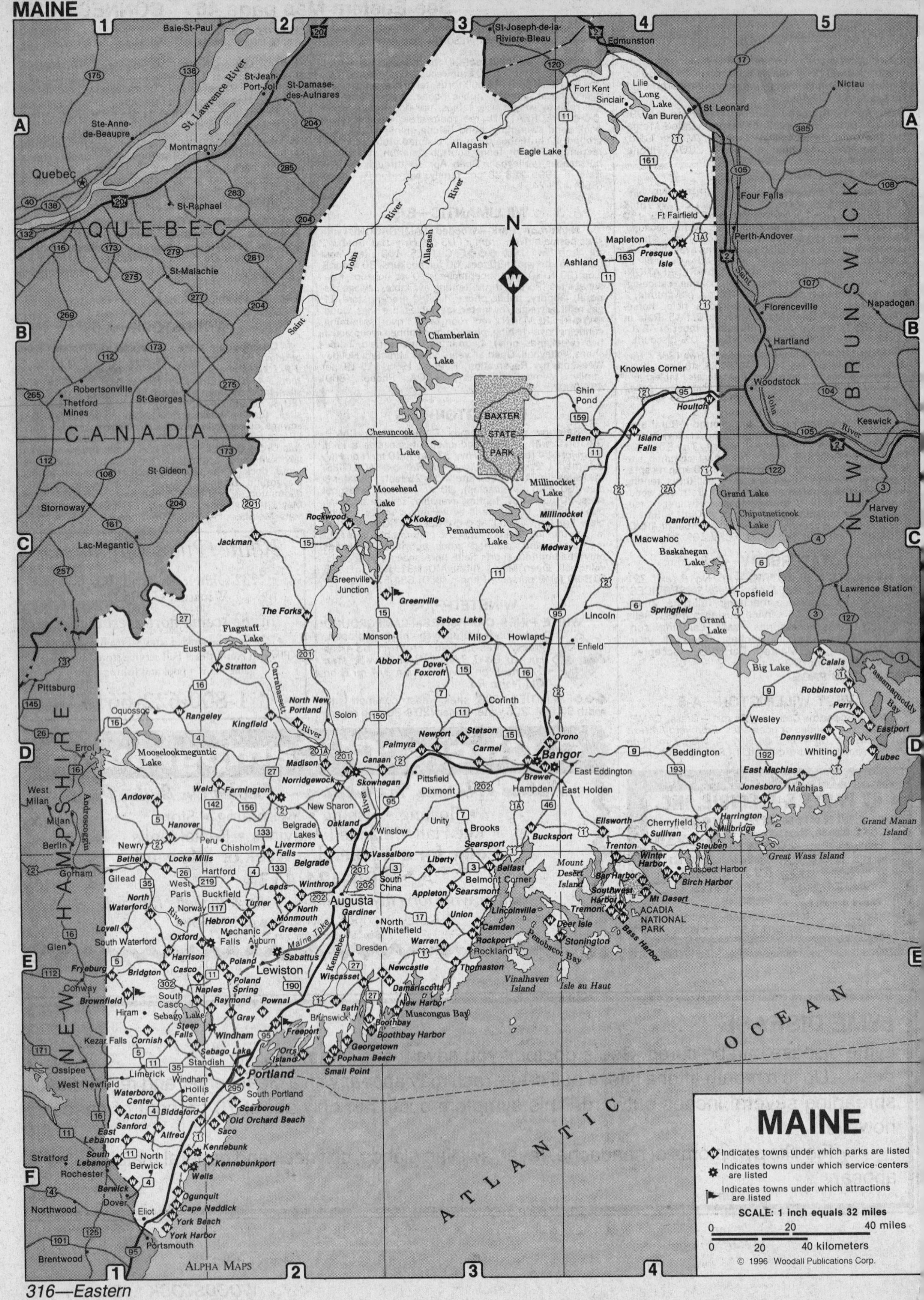
MAINE
Indicates towns under which parks are listed
Indicates towns under which service centers are listed
Indicates towns under which attractions are listed
SCALE: 1 inch equals 32 miles
0 20 40 miles
0 20 40 kilometers
© 1996 Woodall Publications Corp.
ALPHA MAPS
QUEBEC
CANADA
NEW BRUNSWICK
NEW HAMPSHIRE
ATLANTIC OCEAN
St Lawrence River
Quebec
Baie-St-Paul
St-Jean-Port-Joli
St-Damase-des-Aulnares
Ste-Anne-de-Beaupre
Montmagny
St-Raphael
St-Malachie
Robertsonville
Thetford Mines
St-Georges
St-Gideon
Stornoway
Lac-Megantic
St-Joseph-de-la-Riviere-Bleau
Edmunston
Fort Kent
Sinclair
Lille
Long Lake
Van Buren
St Leonard
Allagash
Eagle Lake
Caribou
Ft Fairfield
Four Falls
Nictau
Mapleton
Presque Isle
Ashland
Perth-Andover
Florenceville
Napadogan
Hartland
Woodstock
Keswick
Knowles Corner
Shin Pond
Patten
Island Falls
Houlton
BAXTER STATE PARK
Chamberlain Lake
Chesuncook Lake
Moosehead Lake
Millinocket Lake
Millinocket
Medway
Pemadumcook Lake
Rockwood
Kokadjo
Jackman
Greenville Junction
Greenville
The Forks
Grand Lake
Chiputneticook Lake
Harvey Station
Danforth
Macwahoc
Baskahegan Lake
Topsfield
Lawrence Station
Springfield
Lincoln
Grand Lake
Flagstaff Lake
Eustis
Stratton
Monson
Abbot
Dover-Foxcroft
Sebec Lake
Milo
Howland
Enfield
Big Lake
Calais
Robbinston
Perry
Passamaquoddy Bay
Eastport
Pittsburg
Oquossoc
Rangeley
Kingfield
North New Portland
Solon
Corinth
Wesley
Mooselookmeguntic Lake
Errol
Newport
Palmyra
Stetson
Carmel
Orono
Bangor
Brewer
Beddington
Dennysville
Whiting
Lubec
Madison
Canaan
Norridgewock
Skowhegan
Pittsfield
Dixmont
Hampden
East Eddington
East Holden
East Machias
Jonesboro
Machias
West Milan
Milan
Berlin
Andover
Weld
Farmington
New Sharon
Unity
Hanover
Newry
Peru
Belgrade Lakes
Livermore Falls
Oakland
Winslow
Brooks
Bucksport
Ellsworth
Cherryfield
Harrington
Millbridge
Grand Manan Island
Bethel
Locke Mills
Chisholm
Belgrade
Vassalboro
Liberty
Searsport
Belfast
Trenton
Sullivan
Steuben
Winter Harbor
Prospect Harbor
Great Wass Island
Gorham
Gilead
West Paris
Hartford
Buckfield
Leeds
Winthrop
Augusta
South China
Belmont Corner
Searsmont
Mount Desert Island
Bar Harbor
Birch Harbor
Southwest Harbor
Mt Desert
North Waterford
Norway
Turner
North Monmouth
Gardiner
Appleton
Lincolnville
Tremont
ACADIA NATIONAL PARK
Lovell
Hebron
Mechanic Falls
Greene
North Whitefield
Union
Camden
Deer Isle
Bass Harbor
South Waterford
Oxford
Auburn
Maine Tpke
Warren
Rockport
Stonington
Glen
Harrison
Poland
Sabattus
Lewiston
Dresden
Rockland
Penobscot Bay
Fryeburg
Bridgton
Casco
Kennebec
Thomaston
Conway
Naples
Poland Spring
Wiscasset
Newcastle
Damariscotta
Vinalhaven Island
Isle au Haut
Brownfield
South Casco
Raymond
Pownal
New Harbor
Hiram
Sebago Lake
Gray
Brunswick
Bath
Muscongus Bay
Steep Falls
Boothbay
Boothbay Harbor
Kezar Falls
Cornish
Windham
Freeport
Sebago Lake
Georgetown
Orrs Island
Popham Beach
Small Point
Ossipee
Standish
Limerick
Portland
West Newfield
Windham
Hollis Center
South Portland
Waterboro Center
Scarborough
Acton
Biddeford
Old Orchard Beach
Sanford
Saco
East Lebanon
Alfred
Kennebunk
Kennebunkport
Stratford
South Lebanon
North Berwick
Rochester
Wells
Berwick
Dover
Ogunquit
Cape Neddick
Northwood
Eliot
York Beach
York Harbor
Portsmouth
Brentwood

# TRAVEL SECTION

## Free Information from Travel Section Advertisers

The following businesses have placed an ad in the Maine Travel Section. To receive free information, enter their Reader Service number on the Reader Service Card opposite page 16 in the front of this directory:

| Advertiser | RS # | Ad Pg. |
|---|---|---|
| Acres of Wildlife | 636 | 318 |
| Bayley's Pine Point Resort | 547 | 321 |
| Brake Service & Parts | 548 | 322 |
| Desert of Maine | 635 | 322 |
| Kezar Lake Camping Area | 637 | 317 |
| Maine CG Owners Assn. | 549 | 319 |
| Moosehead Marine Museum | 634 | 322 |
| Timberland Acres RV Park | 473 | 320 |

## Time Zone/Topography

Maine is on Eastern time.

The Pine Tree State has more than 17 million acres of forestland extending over 87 percent of the state's total land area. One-tenth of the state's total area is water, including about 6,000 inland lakes and ponds.

Elevations throughout the southwestern region of the state are usually less than 500 feet; the northeast region is a broad plateau 1,000 to 1,500 feet above sea level. Above this plateau, the Longfellow Mountains of the northern Appalachian chain rise to elevations of 3,000 to 5,000 feet.

Maine's coast consists of 3,478 miles of tidal shoreline with hundreds of islands, bays, coves, beaches and rocky headlands. Southwest of the Kennebec River, the coastal lowlands are relatively level, beaches are sandy and the shoreline is regular. Northeast of the Kennebec, the coast is extremely rugged, with long, narrow promontories jutting out to sea. At the mouth of the river are many small islands.

## Climate

The Northern Interior, which occupies nearly 60 percent of the state's total area, has a continental climate which varies at the extreme northern and southern limits; in the north, the annual average temperature is 37° and in the south it is 43°. The Southern Interior is a longitudinal belt across the southern portion of the state which encompasses about 30 percent of the state's area. While most of the state enjoys peak July temperatures of 70°, temperatures in the Southern Interior may reach 90° for as many as 25 days. On the coast, the annual temperature averages about 46° with summer temperatures reaching 90° for about 2 to 7 days. Temperature variations in the winter are greater, but generally, winters are cold throughout the state.

Average snowfall in Maine is 50-70 inches annually in the Coastal area, 60-90 inches in the Southern Interior and 90-110 inches in the Northern Interior.

## Travel Information Sources

**State Agency:**

• *Maine Publicity Bureau*, P.O. Box 2300, Hallowell, ME 04347 (207-623-0363 or 800-533-9595).

State park central reservation phone



FREE INFO! Enter number on Reader Service Card opposite pg. 16: Kezar Lake Camping #637.

number: in state call 800-332-1501; out-of-state call 207-289-3824.

**Regional Agencies:**

• *Acadia Area Assn.*, P.O. Box 887, Bar Harbor, ME 04609 (207-288-8989; Out-of-state 800-457-1890).

• *Damariscottia Region Chamber of Commerce*, P.O. Box 13, Damariscotta, ME (207-563-8340).

• *Jackman–Moose River Region Chamber of Commerce*, P.O. Box 368, Jackman, ME 04945 (207-668-4171).

• *Moosehead Lake Region Chamber of Commerce*, P.O. Box 581, Greenville, ME 04441 (207-695-2702).

• *Rangeley Lakes Region Chamber of Commerce*, P.O.Box 317, Main St., Rangeley, ME 04970 (207-864-5571).

• *Washington County:* (800-377-9748). (For information on the Sunrise Coast Region.)

**Local Agencies:**

• *Greater Bangor Chamber of Commerce*, P.O. Box 1443, 519 Main St., Bangor, ME 04401 (207-947-0307).

• *Bar Harbor Chamber of Commerce*, P.O. Box 158, 93 Cottage St., Bar Harbor, ME 04609 (207-288-5103).

• *Boothbay Chamber of Commerce*, Box 218, Boothbay, ME 04537 (207-633-4743 seasonal).

• *Bucksport Bay Area Chamber of Commerce*, P.O. Box 1880, Bucksport, ME 04416 (207-469-6818).

• *Ellsworth Area Chamber of Commerce*, P.O. Box 267, 163 High St., Ellsworth, ME 04605 (207-667-2617).

• *Freeport Merchants Assn.*, P.O. Box 452, 10 Morse St., Freeport, ME 04032 (800-865-1994 or 207-865-1212).

• *Kennebunk-Kennebunkport Chamber of Commerce*, P.O. Box 740, Coopers Corner, Rt. 35 & 9, Kennebunk, ME 04043 (207-967-0857).

• *Naples Business Assn.*, P.O. Box 412, Naples, ME 04055 (207-693-3285).

• *Old Orchard Beach Chamber of Commerce*, P.O. Box 600, 1st St., Old Orchard Beach, ME 04064 (207-934-2500).

• *Chamber of Commerce of the Greater Portland Region*, 145 Middle St., Portland, ME 04101 (207-772-2811).

• *Presque Isle Area Chamber of Commerce*, P.O. Box 672, 3 Houlton Rd., Presque Isle, ME 04769 (207-764-6561).

• *Wells Chamber of Commerce*, P.O. Box 356, Wells, ME 04090 (207-646-2451).

## Recreational Information

*Ferry Information:* For general schedule of Maine State Ferry Service call 207-624-7777 or 207-596-2202.

*Fishing and Hunting:* Maine Department of Fisheries and Wildlife, 284 State St., Augusta, ME 04333 (207-289-2571).

*Whitewater Rafting*: For a free copy of the *Consumer's Guide to Whitewater Rafting in Maine*, call 800-664-8911.

## Places to See & Things to Do

***AROOSTOOK REGION***

With more than 6,400 square miles of forests, fields and fresh water, Aroostook County is adventure just waiting to happen. Aroostook is a Maliseet Indian word meaning "phosphorescence," "shining," "bright." Anglers cast their lines into over 2,000 lakes, streams, rivers and ponds and they pull out landlocked salmon, trout, deep fighting squaretail, black bass, brook trout, togue and lake whitefish. The Allagash Wilderness Waterway poses a rushing whitewater challenge to canoeists who think they've seen it all.

**Allagash Wilderness Waterway.** 100-mile-long, northern flowing waterway established in 1996 to "preserve, protect and develop the natural beauty, character and habitat of this unique area." Not for the meek of heart, the Allagash is an area with limited facilities, primative camping, no public transportation, and can be accessed only by a few gravel roads. Those committed to a wilderness experience—a few days or even weeks of solitude amidst great natural beauty—will not be disappointed.

**Aroostook Scenic Highway, Route 11.** Winds its way past Soldier Pond, Wallagrass and Eagle Lake and through some truly beautiful country. Campgrounds and picnic areas can be found along this scenic route.

**Ashland,** south of Portage. One of the largest lumbering communities in Aroostook is home to the *Ashland Logging Museum* which contains tools and photos pertaining to the state's lumber industry.

***SUNRISE COAST REGION***

Maine's (and the nation's) easternmost border is aptly called the Sunrise County of the USA because it's the first place in the country to see the sun rise each morning. Approximately 80% of the nation's wild blueberry crop is grown here and the whole county celebrates the August harvests with blueberry fairs and festivals. Washington County's 2,628 square miles is edged with a rugged 1,000-mile coastline. The interior consists of woods, lakes and streams and contains vast areas of nature seldom seen by man. Those willing to "take a walk on the wild side" thrill to incredible rustic beauty. It remains a notable hunting and fishing territory, with deer, bear, small game and game birds in profusion. Sport fish of unusual size (including Atlantic salmon), can be found in its numerous lakes and streams.

**Calais** is situated in the beautiful St. Croix River Valley, with an international bridge across the river to St. Stephen, New Brunswick. The International Festival (usually the first full week of August) celebrates the friendship between Calais (pronounced "Cal-lay") and St. Stephen.

*Moosehorn National Wildlife Refuge.* Fifty miles of roads and trails delight nature-lovers. Watch for deer, shrew, mole, bear, moose, beaver, mink, geese and eagles. Visitors are invited to accompany wildlife biologists on waterfowl and woodcock banding operations.

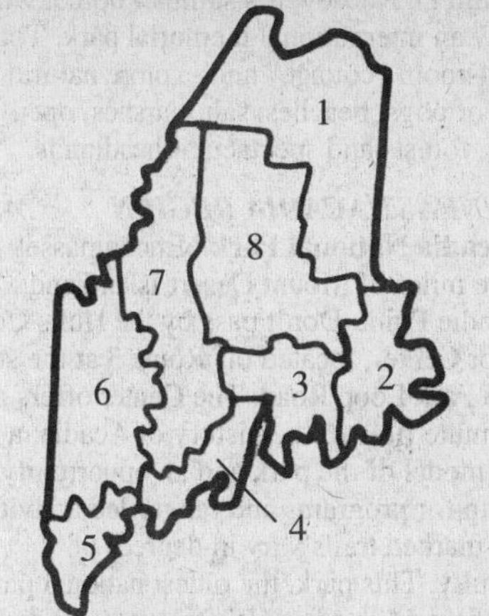


1. — Aroostook
2. — Sunrise Coast
3. — Downeast/Acadia
4. — Mid-Coast
5. — South Coast
6. — Western Lakes and Mountains
7. — Kennebec Valley/Moose River Valley
8. — Katahdin Moosehead

**Eastport,** the most easterly city in the United States, is located on Moose Island which is connected to the mainland by a bridge. The largest whirlpool in the Western Hemisphere lies in view of the car ferry route to Deer Island.

**Roosevelt International Bridge** connects Lubec to Campobello Island, site of the

Franklin D. Roosevelt's summer home, which is now an international memorial park. Tour the 34-room "cottage" and explore natural areas of bogs, beaches, salt marshes, open fields, forests and spectacular headlands.

***DOWNEAST/ACADIA REGION***

**Acadia National Park.** Encompasses 22 square miles of Mount Desert Island and Schoodic Point. Don't pass by the Hulls Cove Visitor Center, located off Route 3 at the start of the Park Loop Road. The Center offers a 15-minute film on the history of Acadia, a scale model of the park and an opportunity to sign up for programs and ranger-led activities. Well-marked trails vary in degrees of difficulty. This park, the oldest national park east of the Mississippi River, is a geological wonder. Ice-age glaciers cut through its existing mountains, carving valleys and fjord-like inlets, leaving the area with islands, bays and peninsulas. Ocean Drive scenic route follows the park's entire eastern perimeter. Sights range from sheer rising cliffs to pounding surf to beaches formed of minute shells as fine as sand. Take the road to the top of Cadillac Mountain (1,530 feet) for an incredible overlook of the surrounding ocean, islands and countryside. *Schoodic Point* lies on the Gouldsboro Peninsula and can be reached from the town of Winter Harbor.

**Bangor**. A farming, industrial, and recreational region bisected by the Penobscot River, Bangor was once an important Indian rendezvous point before Champlain landed here in 1604 in his search for the fabled city of Norumbega. Today the city features boutiques, shopping centers, stately residences and scenic parks and parkways. Sporting, cultural and political events are held at the *Bangor Municipal Auditorium* and Civic Center and the beautiful *Grotto Cascade Park* (opposite the Bangor Salmon Pool) has a forty-five-foot cascade. The *Cole Land Transportation Museum* is a non-profit museum featuring early Maine land transportation vehicles such as vintage automobiles, farm equipment, railroad memorabilia, wagons and sleighs and fire fighting equipment. Hundreds of early Maine photographs are also displayed.

**Black Mansion**, Ellsworth. Donated to the county of Hancock as a historic shrine, the mansion boasts manicured lawns, gardens, a carriage house, and priceless colonial antiques and furniture, rare books, dishes and glassware.

***MID-COAST REGION***

**Bath.** Known as the "City of Ships" due to its vast shipbuilding industries. Located near the mouth of the Kennebec River, the city is rich in maritime history. The downtown area looks much the same as it did 100 years ago—period lighting, original storefronts and brick sidewalks add to the atmosphere.

*Maine Maritime Museum* depicts 300 years of Maine's contribution to American maritime history. Displayed are more than 7,000 items relating to shipbuilding and nautical heritage.

**Boothbay Harbor Area.** A busy summer resort region with excellent facilities for fishing, swimming, antique shows, art exhibits, band concerts, dinner theaters, yachting and boat trips. During the summer, over 30 excursion boats operate from the harbor. Secluded resort communities include Spruce Point, Southport, West Southport and Newagen. (Southport, West Southport and Newagen are on an island connected by a short drawbridge).

*Boothbay Railway Village.* Twenty-four exhibit buildings on eight acres house artifacts, trains and antique cars. Hop aboard the Boothbay Central for a ride around the turn-of-the-century New England village.

**Brunswick Area.** Situated along the Androscoggin River, Brunswick was once a thriving lumber and shipbuilding community. It is now the site of Bowdoin College, Brunswick Naval Air Station and the annual Maine Festival, a celebration of the work of Maine artists and craftsmen. Harpswell, Great Island, Orrs Island and Bailey Island can be reached by highway from Brunswick.

*Bailey Island Bridge.* A 1,200-foot bridge connecting Orrs and Bailey Islands across Will's gut. Built in 1928 of cribstone, no metal or cement was used. It is believed to be the only one of its kind.

*Museum of Art,* Bowdoin College. Contains a permanent collection of Colonial, Federal and American 19th-century paintings, European Old Master drawings, Renaissance and 17th-century paintings.

**Camden** is one of the mid-coast's most popular yachting centers and is known as the town "where mountains meet the sea." The Camden Hills (1,380 feet) provide panoramic views of Penobscot Bay and islands miles out into the Gulf of Maine. Windjammer cruises range from 2 hours to three and six days. Take part in a whitewater rafting excursion on the Penobscot or Kennebec Rivers. Rent a bicycle for a leisurely Sunday afternoon or take to the coast on a mountain bike tour. View the islands of Penobscot Bay, lighthouses, harbor seals and shorefront mansions. Hikers enjoy the network of trails throughout 5,000 acre *Camden State Park.* Fall foliage is beautiful here and winter brings skiing and tobogganing enthusiasts to Camden Snow Bowl.

**Rockport**. Home of the donut hole (dissatisfied with the soggy centers of his mother's dough cakes, 1847 sea captain Hanson Gregory, poked a hole through several cakes), Rockport is a quiet harbor community and an active center for art and music.

**Searsport.** Over 250 sailing vessels have been built in Searsport, once home to 280 sea captains. The *Searsport Antique Mall* has over 70 dealers selling antiques and collectibles. The *Penobscot Marine Museum* houses one of the finest collections of marine paintings and artifacts in the country including historical boat exhibits.

**Thomaston/Rockland Area**. Includes the towns of Thomaston, Rockland, Owl's Head, St. George, Tenants Harbor and Port Clyde. The area is dotted with picturesque resort villages. Rockland is also known as the Lobster and Schooner Capital of the World and celebrates this honor with an annual Lobster Festival (August) and Schooner Days (July).

*Owl's Head Transportation Museum,* Owl's Head. Experience the pioneer era of wheel and wing transportation throught this landmark collection of ground and air vehicles—planes, cars, carriages, bicycles, motorcycles and pioneer engines. Special events include a Foreign Festival, Fall Auto Auction, 50s and 60s Meet and spectacular air shows.

*Shore Village Museum*, Rockland. Marine artifacts, extensive maritime and Civil War memorabilia are displayed.

*William A. Farnsworth Library and Museum,* Rockland. Contains a permanent collection of Andrew Wyeth works, and rotating exhibits by Maine artists.

***SOUTH COAST REGION***

**Freeport.** Often referred to as the "birthplace of Maine", as it is believed that here, in 1820, Maine became a separate state of the Union. Today, the area is known for its distinctive outlet and specialty stores. Popular attractions in the area include:

*Desert of Maine*. Nature trails wind through 50 acres of once fertile land. Beautiful forests surround sand dunes that continue to engulf tall trees and small buildings. Peak touring times are during spring's wildflower season and during autumn's fall foliage color changes.

**Kennebunks.** Kennebunk Beach, Kennebunk and Kennebunkport have long catered to summer residents. Once a shipbuilding town, Kennebunk now provides visitors and residents with a relaxed atmosphere, miles of beautiful beaches and fantastic scenes of rocky coastlines. Fish for striped bass at the mouth of the Kennebunk and Mousam Rivers. Consider taking a reflective walk through the *Shrine of St.*

*Anthony* (Franciscan Monastery). It is within walking distance of the Lower Village and features paths through woods and gardens, past small shrines and statures of saints. Other Kennebunk attractions include:

*Brick Store Museum.* Originally a general store, the museum focuses on local history, both land and sea.

**Kittery.** Boasting a long and prestigious history of shipbuilding, Kittery is Maine's Southern most town and also the state's oldest (settled in 1623). Captain John Paul Jones' sloop *Ranger* and the USS *Raleigh* had their keels laid in Kittery. America's first submarine was launched from Kittery in 1917 and during World War II craftsmen and women built more than 70 submarines. Through displays, models, dioramas, paintings, artifacts and photographs, the *Kittery Historical and Naval Museum* preserves and interprets the history of the Naval Shipyard in Kittery.

Shoppers and bargain hunters delight in an endless array of manufacturer's discount outlet stores, most of them located north of town along Route 1.

**Ogunquit.** What began as an art colony over a century ago is still a painter's and photographer's dream. Rugged cliffs give way to gentle sandy beaches and lobster fishermen haul in their catch for the day. Best viewed by foot or trolley, Ogunquit is certainly a "beautiful place by the sea." Exploring the art galleries and private studios in this small village could take days. The *Ogunquit Playhouse* (opened in 1933) presents 10 weeks of quality summer theater. Seating is only 750 so make reservations early. Deep sea fishing charters and coastal cruises are a wonderful way way to spend the afternoon. You can also sign up for a lobstering trip through *FinestKind* out of Perkins Cove. You'll see lobster traps hauled and learn all you ever wanted to know about lobsters and lobstering.

*Marginal Way.* Famed footpath runs along rocky cliffs from the center of town to Perkins Cove. Mile-long trail offers some of the nation's most outstanding seaside scenery.

**Old Orchard Beach.** Beaches, arcades, amusement rides and nightly entertainment draws visitors by the thousands. This popular resort area is known for its seven-mile-long white sandy beach that stretches from the north of the Saco River to the Scarborough River at Pine Point. Old Orchard Beach was once the landing and take-off point for early trans-Atlantic aviators, including Charles Lindbergh and Wiley Post. Old Orchard's Pier (the center of the recreational activities) extends 475 feet into the Atlantic Ocean and features shops, fast food and games of skill. Frequent fireworks displays add to the fun.

*Palace Playland.* An amusement park with rollercoasters, waterslides, ferris wheels, bumper cars and more.

**Portland**. The town has been destroyed by fire four times, and each time rebuilt. Hence their moto *resurgam* which means "I will rise again." With over 200 stores and 100 restaurants, Portland greets visitors with everything from crafts, antiques and imported goods to lobsters, clams, Indian, Afghani and Vietnamese cuisine. The *Portland Observatory* was built in 1807 and alerted merchants when their ships entered the harbor.

*Casco Bay.* The picturesque islands of Casco Bay extend 20 miles east of Portland and can be reached by ferry boat from Portland Harbor. One of the more popular islands to visit is *Peaks Island*—a resort area offering sandy beaches, a Civil War Museum and the STAR (Solar Technology and Applied Research) facility.

*Children's Museum of Maine.* All ages are mystified and delighted with the hands-on exhibits, Star Lab, Space Shuttle, computer lab and news center.

*Maine Narrow Gauge Railroad Company and Museum.* On display is a 1913 locomotive, seven passenger cars, prints, paintings and restored antique trucks.

*Scarborough Marsh,* located in Scarborough off Pine Point Road. 3,000 acres of nature operated by the Maine Audubon Society. Contact the Scarborough Marsh Nature Center for information on canoe tours through the area. Special programs include Dawn Birding and Full Moon Canoe Tours.

**Saco.** Twin cities of Saco and Biddleford are separated by the lovely Saco River. Enjoy fishing or boating along the river or on Saco Bay. The *Maine Aquarium* is open year-round and features live fish from around the world, exhibits, demonstrations and a touch-pool. The *York Institute Museum* explores the regional cultural and social history of the area.

**Wells.** Bustling beach resort community which features seven miles of wide, flat beaches. Young and old alike play in the tidal pools while sunbather's enjoy the fine, white sand. The *Wells Recreation Area* offers tranquil wooded trails, tennis and basketball courts, horseshoe areas, playground and Hobbs Pond.

*Rachel Carson Wildlife Refuge.* Over 1,600 acres of wetlands set aside to preserve wildlife habitats. More than 250 species of birds call the refuge home during various seasons. Shorebirds, waterfowl, wading birds, gulls, terns and songbirds can be seen from secluded walking paths.

*Wells Auto Museum* supplies fun for the entire family with antique nickelodeons, picture machines to play and rides in antique autos. The collection contains over 70 gas, steam and electric cars.

*Wells National Estuarine Research Reserve.* Seven miles of trails give visitors a view of fields, forest, wetlands and beaches. Programs on coastal ecology and stewardship are offered as well as special events such as Nature Crafts Festivals, Skywatches, Slide Shows, Full Moon Walks, Laudholm Farm Tours, Wildflower Tours, Bird Walks and Estuary Tours. The Visitor Center presents a welcoming slide show and five rooms of exhibits.

**The Yorks**, on route 1A, north of Kittery, consists of York Village, York Harbor, York Beach and Cape Neddick. York was the first chartered city in America (1641). No trip is complete without a photo of *Nubble Light*, located in Cape Neddick. The lighthouse is 41-feet tall and was completed in 1879.

*Old York Historic Sites.* Interpreters recreate life as it was in the 1700s. Tour six historic buildings dating from the Old Gaol (1719) to the John Hancock Warehouse and Wharf (1800). View decorative arts and Colonial-era antiques. Special events throughout the summer include Fourth on the Wharf and Family Day (July). Also on site is a 17-acre nature preserve.

***WESTERN LAKES AND MOUNTAINS REGION***

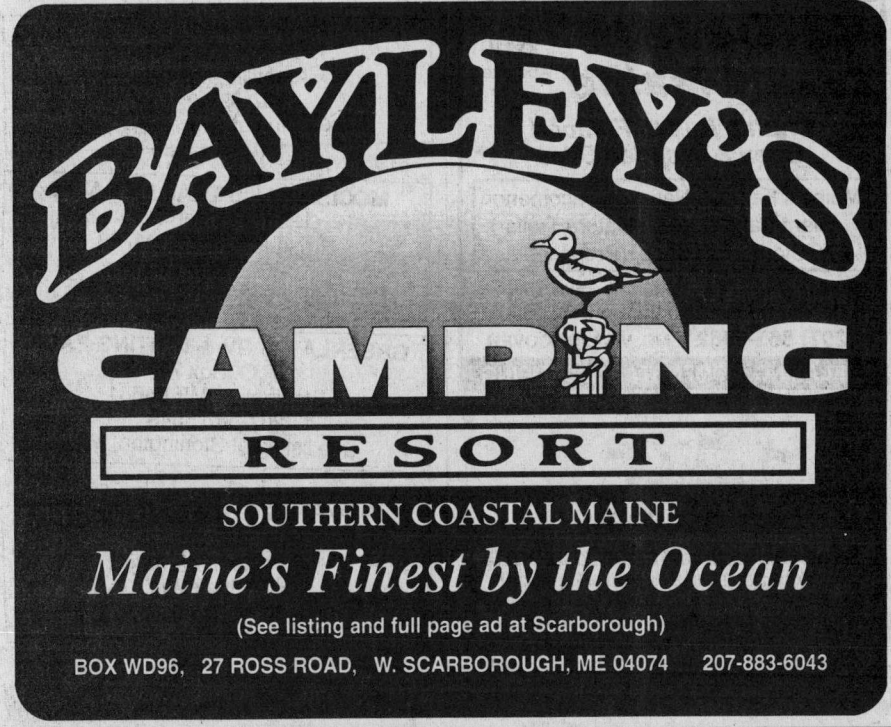

**Carrabassett Valley** is an area rich in forests, outdoor recreation, agriculture and scenery. A marvelous view of Mount Abraham, Saddleback, Spaulding, Sugarloaf and Crocker mountains can be had from the town of Kingfield. (Sugarloaf is Maine's second-highest mountain and offers enclosed four-passenger gondola rides to the summit lodge in summer, fall and winter.)

**Farmington Area.** Consists of small towns and villages nestled among rolling countryside, clear lakes and lush forests. A favorite destination for nordic skiers. Rural roads lead hikers and bikers to views of the Sandy River Valley and distant mountains.

**Lewiston/Auburn Area.** These twin cities, on opposite banks of the Androscoggin River, make important economical, cultural and academic contributions.

*Bates College,* Lewiston. Well known for nearly a century, educators have trained here for service the world over. Also recognized as a pioneer in collegiate and international debating.

**Rangeley Lakes.** Six lakes located in the Longfellow Mountains, bordered to the west the White Mountains of New Hampshire.

**Sebago Lake-Long Lake.** These two inland lakes, plus numerous other smaller lakes, ponds and streams covering an area of hundreds of square miles, offer countless recreational opportunities, including incomparable salmon, trout and black-bass fishing.

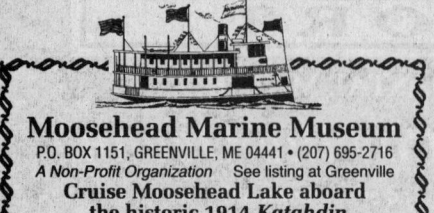

**Shaker Village,** between New Gloucester and Poland Spring, is one of the last representatives of America's oldest denominational sect. Tours are offered of the village shops and meeting house, and the museum has exhibits featuring furniture, crafts, agriculture and manufactured items.

### *KENNEBEC VALLEY/MOOSE RIVER VALLEY*

**Augusta** is the state capital and the dome of the capitol building can be seen for miles up and down the Kennebec River. Visitors can tour the State House, with its Hall of Flags; the Blaine House (governor's residence); and the Maine State Library, Museum and Archive Building. Also within Augusta is *Fort Western,* which contains the original barracks of 20 rooms, built by the Plymouth Company in 1754 during the French and Indian War.

**China Lake Area,** contains the towns of Vassalboro, China, Windsor, Chelsea, Randolph and Pittston. China Lake is the largest of this chain of lakes and ponds and contains some of Maine's most beautiful scenery. Fish for landlocked salmon and small-mouth black bass.

**The Forks.** Small town located at the confluence of the Dead and Kennebec rivers, is home to a number of commercial rafting companies. Outfitters offer a variety of canoe, raft or tube trips geared to various levels of experience. Moxie Falls, located 2 miles east of The Forks, is one of Maine's highest waterfalls.

**Jackman/Moose River.** Located along Highway 201, both towns are surrounded by 250,000 acres of natural, unspoiled wilderness. The area's 60 lakes and ponds keep anglers casting for salmon, brook trout, togue and smelt. Boating, swimming, mountain climbing, backpacking, bicycling and canoeing are also popular during the summer months. Winter tourists enjoy over 200 miles of groomed snowmobile trails, ice fishing, cross-country skiing and snowshoeing.

### *KATAHDIN/MOOSEHEAD REGION*

**Appalachian Trail.** Beginning at Mount Katahdin in Maine and extending to Springer Mountain in Georgia, this 2,000-mile wilderness trail crosses some of Maine's finest peaks through 280 miles of breathtaking scenery.

**Baxter State Park** is a 201,018-acre wilderness and wildlife sanctuary offering mountain climbing, camping, hiking and canoeing opportunities. Mountain trails and shelters harmonize with the unspoiled surroundings. The 5,267-foot Katahdin Mountain and the northern terminus of the Appalachian Trail are located here.

**Grand Canyon of the East**, located on the west branch of the Pleasant River near Brownville and Brownville Junction. Reached only by trail, this secluded area is the site of waterfalls, sheer walls, fantastic shapes and unusual rock formations.

**Greenville**. Located at the foot of Moosehead Lake, this town is the center for recreation in the area—a gateway to the untamed Allagash Wilderness Waterways.

Board the *S/S Katahdin* for a scenic cruise on Lake Moosehead. This restored former steam vessel has been converted into the floating *Moosehead Marine Museum* which displays artifacts and photographs of logging and steamboat operations.

**Moosehead Lake Region** is a centrally-located unspoiled wilderness,with over 20,000 free-roaming moose. The lake itself, surrounded by rugged mountains and dense forests, is forty miles long and ten miles wide and contains several large islands and many bays and inlets.

# maine

All privately-owned campgrounds personally inspected by Woodall Representatives Gary and Sandy Dode.

Unless otherwise noted, all listed campgrounds have hot showers & flush toilets.

## ABBOT—D-3

**Balsam Woods Campground**—Level, open & secluded sites. *From jct Hwy 16 & Hwy 15: Go 1 mi N on Hwy 15, then 3 mi W on Piper Pond Rd.* ◆◆◆FACILITIES: 50 sites, 39 water & elec (20 & 30 amp receptacles), 11 no hookups, tenting available, sewage disposal, laundry, public phone, grocery store, ice, tables, fire rings, wood. ◆◆◆RECREATION: rec room/area, swim pool, playground, badminton, horseshoes, hiking trails, volleyball. Open Memorial Day through mid Nov. Rate in 1995 $17 for 4 persons. Phone: (207) 876-2731. FCRV 10% discount.

## ACADIA NATIONAL PARK—E-4

***See listings at Bar Harbor, Bass Harbor, Ellsworth, Mt. Desert, Southwest Harbor & Tremont***

**THE GATHERINGS FAMILY CAMPGROUND OCEANFRONT CAMPING**—*From entrance of Acadia National Park: Go 17 1/2 mi W on Hwy 3, then 4 mi SW on Hwy 172.*

WELCOME

**SEE PRIMARY LISTING AT ELLSWORTH AND AD THIS PAGE**

## ACTON—F-1

**Apple Valley Campground**—Large wooded sites on a hilly terrain with many seasonals. *From jct Hwy 11 & Hwy 109: Go 2 mi N on Hwy 109.* ◆◆◆FACILITIES: 160 sites, most common site width 40 feet, 32 full hookups, 128 water & elec (20 & 30 amp receptacles), seasonal sites, sewage disposal, laundry, public phone, grocery store, LP gas refill by weight/by meter, ice, tables, grills, wood. ◆◆◆RECREATION: rec hall, rec room/area, swim pool, mini-golf ($), planned group activities (weekends only), sports field, horseshoes. No tents. Open May 15 through Oct 15. Rate in 1995 $18 per family. Phone: (207) 636-2285.

## ALFRED—F-1

**Bunganut Lake Camping Area**—A lakeside CAMPGROUND on a hilly terrain. *From jct Hwy 111 & Hwy 202/4: Go 2 1/2 mi N on Hwy 202/4, then 1 1/2 mi E on Brock Rd, then 1 mi S on Williams Rd.* ◆◆FACILITIES: 110 sites, most common site width 50 feet, 20 ft. max RV length, 110 water & elec (20 amp receptacles), seasonal sites, tenting available, sewage disposal, laundry, public phone, grocery store, ice, tables, fire rings, wood. ◆◆◆◆RECREATION: rec hall, lake swimming, boating, canoeing, ramp, dock, 2 row/4 canoe/2 pedal boat rentals, lake fishing, playground, badminton, horseshoes, volleyball. Open May 1 through Oct 1. Rate in 1995 $18-20 per family. Member of ARVC; MECOA. Phone: (207) 247-3875.

**Scott's Cove Camp Area**—A lakeside, semi-wooded CAMPGROUND. Most sites occupied by seasonal campers. *From jct Hwy 111 & Hwy 202/4: Go 2 1/2 mi N on Hwy 202/4, then 1/2 mi E on Brock Rd.* ◆◆FACILITIES: 50 sites, most common site width 24 feet, 2 full hookups, 48 water & elec (15 & 20 amp receptacles), seasonal sites, tenting available, sewage disposal, limited grocery store, ice, tables, fire rings, wood. ◆◆◆RECREATION: rec room/area, lake swimming, boating, canoeing, dock, 2 row/2 canoe boat rentals, lake fishing, horseshoes, volleyball. No pets. Open May 15 through Sep 30. Rate in 1995 $18-20 for 2 persons. Member of ARVC;MECOA. Phone: (207) 324-6594.

**WALNUT GROVE CAMPGROUND**—Large sites in wooded or grassy setting. *From jct Hwy 111 & Hwy 202/4: Go 1 mi N on Hwy 202/4, then 1 mi NW on Gore Rd, then continue 1 3/4 mi W on Gore Rd.*

WELCOME

◆◆◆FACILITIES: 93 sites, most common site width 36 feet, 93 water & elec (20 & 30 amp receptacles), seasonal sites, a/c allowed ($), tenting available, group sites for tents/RVs, sewage disposal, laundry, public phone, grocery store, RV supplies, ice, tables, fire rings, wood. ◆◆◆RECREATION: rec hall, coin games, swim pool, basketball hoop, playground, planned group activities, sports field, horseshoes, motorbike trails, hiking trails, volleyball.

Open May 1 through mid Oct. Rate in 1995 $16.50 for 4 persons. Phone: (207) 324-1207.

**SEE AD THIS PAGE**

## ANDOVER—D-1

**SOUTH ARM CAMPGROUND**—A secluded CAMPGROUND with modern facilities located within thousands of wilderness acres. *From jct Hwy 5 & Hwy 120: Go 1/2 mi E on Hwy 120, then 11 mi N on South Arm Rd.*

WELCOME

◆◆FACILITIES: 98 sites, most common site width 50 feet, 32 ft. max RV length, 65 water & elec, 33 no hookups, a/c not allowed, heater not allowed, tenting available, sewage disposal, laundry, grocery store, RV supplies, LP gas refill by weight, gasoline, marine gas, ice, tables, fire rings, wood, traffic control gate. ◆◆◆RECREATION: lake swimming, boating, canoeing, ramp, dock, 9 canoe/6 motor boat rentals, lake/river/pond/stream fishing, fishing guides, basketball hoop, planned group activities, badminton, sports field, horseshoes, motorbike trails, hiking trails, volleyball.

SOUTH ARM CAMPGROUND—Continued on next page
ANDOVER—Continued on next page

**FASCINATING FACT**

**The Black-tailed Jack Rabbit will jump higher every 4th or 5th hop so it can get a better view of the surrounding area. They can jump as far as 20 feet.**

ANDOVER—Continued
SOUTH ARM CAMPGROUND—Continued

Open mid May through mid Sep. 10 amp electrical service. Rate in 1995 $12-21 per family. No refunds. Reservations recommended Jul through Aug. Member of MECOA; ARVC. Phone: (207) 364-5155.

SEE AD THIS PAGE

## APPLETON—E-3

**Sennebec Lake Campground**—Lakeside CAMPGROUND. *From west jct Hwy 17 & Hwy 131: Go 3 mi N on Hwy 131.* ◇◇◇FACILITIES: 100 sites, most common site width 28 feet, 11 full hookups, 79 water & elec (15,20 & 30 amp receptacles), 10 no hookups, seasonal sites, 10 pull-thrus, tenting available, sewage disposal, laundry, public phone, limited grocery store, ice, tables, fire rings, wood. ◇◇◇◇RECREATION: rec hall, rec room/area, lake swimming, boating, ramp, dock, 1 row/2 canoe/1 pedal boat rentals, lake fishing, playground, planned group activities (weekends only), badminton, horseshoes, hiking trails, volleyball. Recreation open to the public. Open early May through mid Oct. Rate in 1995 $16-22 per family. Member of ARVC; MECOA. Phone: (207) 785-4250.

## AUBURN—E-2

**POLAND SPRING CAMPGROUND**—*From Maine Turnpike (exit 12) & Hwy 122: Go 5 mi W on Hwy 122, then 2 3/4 mi N on Hwy 26, then 1/2 mi E on campground road.*

SEE PRIMARY LISTING AT POLAND SPRING AND AD POLAND SPRING PAGE 352

## AUGUSTA—E-2

**AUGUSTA-WEST LAKESIDE RESORT KAMPGROUND**—*From jct I-95 (exit 30) & US 202: Go 9 mi W on US 202, then 1 mi S on Highland Ave, then 3/4 mi W on access road.*

SEE PRIMARY LISTING AT WINTHROP AND AD NEXT PAGE

**BEAVER BROOK CAMPING AREA**—*From I-95 (exit 30) & US 202: Go 15 mi W on US 202, then 1 1/2 mi NW on Back Rd, then 1 1/2 mi SW on Wilson Pond Rd.*

SEE PRIMARY LISTING AT NORTH MONMOUTH AND AD NORTH MONMOUTH PAGE 345

AUGUSTA—Continued on next page

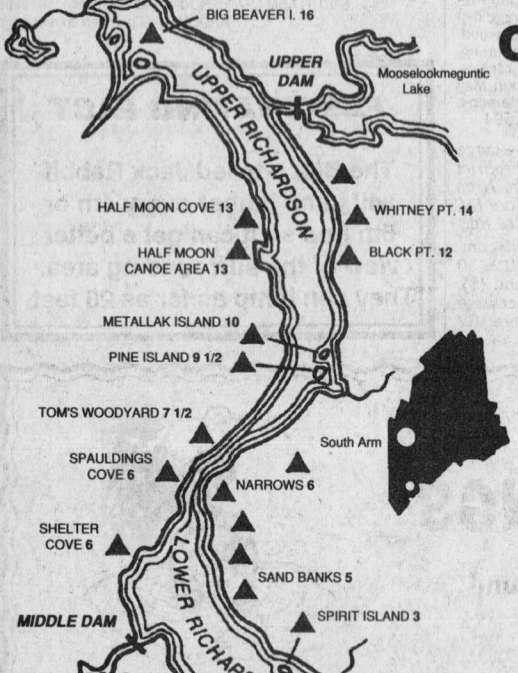

State Tree: White Pine

AUGUSTA—Continued

**KOA-AUGUSTA/GARDINER**—*From jct US 202 & I-95: Go 8 mi S on I-95 (exit 27), then 2 mi S on US 201.* **SEE PRIMARY LISTING AT GARDINER AND AD GARDINER PAGE 339**

## BANGOR—D-3

***See listing at Orono***

**✲ BRAKE SERVICE & PARTS**—*From jct I-95 & I-395 (exit 45): Go 3 mi E on I-395, then 1 mi N on Hwy 9, then 5 blocks N on Washington St (at foot of iron bridge).* SERVICES: Engine/Chassis mechanic full-time. Open all year. Master Card/Visa accepted. Phone: (207) 945-6466.
**SEE AD TRAVEL SECTION PAGE 322**

**KOA-SKOWHEGAN-CANAAN**—*From jct I-395 & I-95: Go 26 mi W on I-95 (exit 39), then 16 mi W on US 2.* **SEE PRIMARY LISTING AT CANAAN AND AD CANAAN PAGE 335**

**PAUL BUNYAN CAMPGROUND**—Spacious, open & shaded sites on a rolling terrain. *S'bound from jct I-95 (exit 47) & Hwy 222 (Union St): Go 2 1/2 mi W on Hwy 222 (Union St). N'bound from exit 47: Go 1 block E on Ohio, then 1 block S on Fifteenth St, then 2 1/2 mi W on Union St (Hwy 222).*

◊◊◊FACILITIES: 52 sites, most common site width 24 feet, 12 full hookups, 40 water & elec (20,30 & 50 amp receptacles), seasonal sites, 10 pull-thrus, a/c allowed, heater allowed, tenting available, sewage disposal, public phone, LP gas refill by meter, ice, tables, fire rings, wood.

◊◊◊RECREATION: rec room/area, equipped pavilion, coin games, swim pool (heated), 2 pedal boat rentals, pond fishing, basketball hoop, playground, planned group activities (weekends only), badminton, sports field, horseshoes, volleyball, cross country skiing, snowmobile trails. Recreation open to the public.

Open all year. Facilities fully operational May 15 through Oct 30. Rate in 1995 $12-18.75 per family. Master Card/Visa accepted. Phone: (207) 941-1177.
**SEE AD THIS PAGE**

ME **Flower: White pine cone & tassel** ME



BANGOR—Continued

**PLEASANT HILL CAMPGROUND**—Family oriented CAMPGROUND with open and shaded sites. *From jct I-95 & Hwy 222 (Union St): S'bound go 2 1/2 mi W on Hwy 222 (Union St). N'bound go 1 block on Ohio, then 1 block S on Fifteenth St, then 2 1/2 mi W on Union St (Hwy 222).*

◊◊◊FACILITIES: 105 sites, most common site width 24 feet, 33 full hookups, 52 water & elec (15,20,30 & 50 amp receptacles), 20 no hookups, seasonal sites, 40 pull-thrus, a/c allowed ($), heater allowed ($), phone hookups, tenting available, group sites for tents/RVs, RV rentals, RV storage, sewage disposal, laundry, public phone, grocery store, RV supplies, LP gas refill by weight/by meter, ice, tables, fire rings, wood.

◊◊◊RECREATION: rec hall, rec room/area, pavilion, coin games, swim pool (heated), mini-golf ($), basketball hoop, playground, sports field, horseshoes, volleyball.

Open May 1 through Columbus Day. Rate in 1995 $13-19 per family. Reservations recommended Jul through Aug. Discover/Master Card/Visa accepted. Member of ARVC; MECOA. Phone: (207) 848-5127.
**SEE AD THIS PAGE**

**Wheeler Stream Camping Area**—Level, shaded CAMPGROUND. *From jct I-95 (exit 45B) & US 2: Go 3 3/4 mi W on US 2.* ◊◊FACILITIES: 25 sites, most common site width 28 feet, 25 water & elec (15 & 30 amp receptacles), tenting available, sewage disposal, laundry, ice, tables, fire rings, wood. Open May 15 through Oct 15. Rate in 1995 $14 per family. Member of ARVC; MECOA. Phone: (207) 848-3713.

## BAR HARBOR—E-4

***All directions start at the foot of Bar Harbor Bridge at jct Hwy 3 & Hwy 102/198. See listings at Bass Harbor, Ellsworth, Mt. Desert & Southwest Harbor***

ACADIA NATIONAL PARK (Blackwoods Campground) —*From jct Hwy 233 & Hwy 3: Go 5 mi S on Hwy 3.* FACILITIES: 306 sites, 35 ft. max RV length, 306 no hookups, 25 pull-thrus, tenting available, handicap restroom facilities, sewage disposal, public phone, tables, fire rings, grills. RECREATION: hiking trails. Open all year. Facilities fully operational mid May through mid Oct. No showers. Phone: (207) 288-3338.

BAR HARBOR—Continued

**BARCADIA CAMPGROUND**—Grassy CAMPGROUND with shaded and open sites directly on the shore. *At jct Hwy 3 & Hwy 102.*

◊◊◊FACILITIES: 200 sites, most common site width 28 feet, 25 full hookups, 150 water & elec (20,30 & 50 amp receptacles), 25 no hookups, seasonal sites, 75 pull-thrus, a/c allowed, heater not allowed, tenting available, group sites for tents/RVs, RV rentals, sewage disposal, laundry, public phone, grocery store, RV supplies, LP gas refill by meter, ice, tables, fire rings, wood.

◊◊◊RECREATION: rec room/area, coin games, salt water swimming, boating, ramp, salt water fishing, basketball hoop, playground, badminton, horseshoes, volleyball, local tours.

Open mid May through mid Oct. Rate in 1995 $16-27.50 for 4 persons. No refunds. Reservations recommended Jul through Aug. Member of ARVC; MECOA. Phone: (207) 288-3520.
**SEE AD NEXT PAGE**

BAR HARBOR—Continued on next page

BAR HARBOR—Continued

**BAR HARBOR CAMPGROUND**—Wooded or open sites with view of ocean bay. *From jct Hwy 102/198 & Hwy 3: Go 5 mi SE on Hwy 3.*

WELCOME

◇◇◇FACILITIES: 300 sites, most common site width 24 feet, 60 full hookups, 100 water & elec (15,20,30 & 50 amp receptacles), 140 no hookups, 60 pull-thrus, a/c allowed, heater allowed, tenting available, sewage disposal, laundry, public phone, LP gas refill by meter, ice, tables, fire rings, grills, wood.

◇◇◇RECREATION: rec room/area, coin games, swim pool (heated), basketball hoop, playground, 2 shuffleboard courts, horseshoes.

Open Memorial Day through Oct 15. Rate in 1995 $17-23 for 4 persons. Phone: (207) 288-5185.
**SEE AD THIS PAGE**

**BASS HARBOR CAMPGROUND**—*From jct Hwy 3 & Hwy 102/198: Go 13 mi S on Hwy 102, then continue 5 mi S on Hwy 102A.*

WELCOME

**SEE PRIMARY LISTING AT BASS HARBOR AND AD THIS PAGE**

**HADLEY'S POINT CAMPGROUND**—Grassy, open and shaded sites near the ocean beach and Acadia National Park. *From jct Hwy 102 & Hwy 3: Go 3 mi SE on Hwy 3, then 1/8 mi N on Hadley Point Rd.*

WELCOME

◇◇◇FACILITIES: 180 sites, most common site width 26 feet, 15 full hookups, 117 water & elec (15,20 & 30 amp receptacles), 48 no hookups, 9 pull-thrus, a/c allowed, heater allowed, tenting available, sewage disposal, laundry, public phone, limited grocery store, LP gas refill by meter, ice, tables, fire rings, wood, church services.

◇◇RECREATION: swim pool (heated), basketball hoop, playground, 2 shuffleboard courts, horseshoes.

Open May 15 through Oct 15. Rate in 1995 $16-20 for 4 persons. No refunds. Reservations recommended Jul 1 through Sep 1. Member of ARVC; MECOA. Phone: (207) 288-4808.
**SEE AD PAGE 329**

**MT. DESERT NARROWS CAMPING RESORT**—An oceanside location with tree-shaded and open sites. *From jct Hwy 102 & Hwy 3: Go 1 1/2 mi SE on Hwy 3.*

WELCOME

◇◇◇FACILITIES: 239 sites, most common site width 24 feet, 50 full hookups, 136 water & elec (20,30 & 50 amp receptacles), 53 no hookups, 61 pull-thrus, a/c allowed ($), heater allowed ($), tenting available, group sites for tents/RVs, handicap restroom facilities, sewage disposal, laundry, public phone, grocery store, RV supplies, LP gas refill by meter, ice, tables, fire rings, wood.

◇◇◇RECREATION: rec hall, rec room/area, coin games, swim pool (heated), canoeing, 4 canoe boat rentals, basketball hoop, playground, planned group activities, movies, recreation director, horseshoes.

MT. DESERT NARROWS CAMPING RESORT—Continued on page 329

BAR HARBOR—Continued on page 329

# Bar Harbor, Maine

***Highest Rated Campground in Bar Harbor***

***1995 Trailer Life***

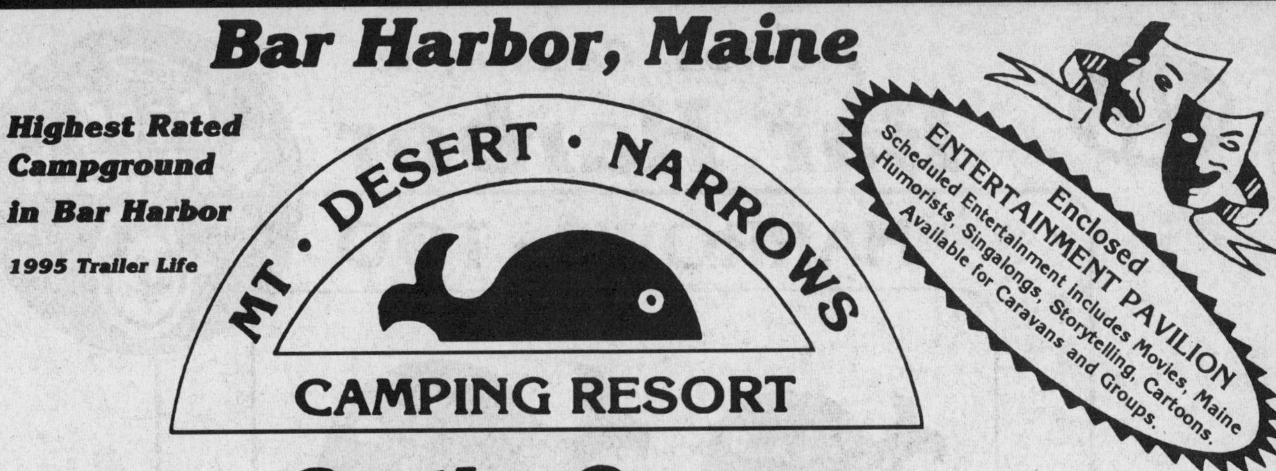

MT • DESERT • NARROWS
CAMPING RESORT
Enclosed
ENTERTAINMENT PAVILION
Scheduled Entertainment includes Movies, Maine Humorists, Singalongs, Storytelling, Cartoons.
Available for Caravans and Groups.


# On the Ocean

## COME TO OUR ISLAND RESORT

Oceanfront and Ocean View Sites on 2100' Shoreline plus 25 Acres of Wilderness Tenting.

***Also Offering...*** Hot Showers (3 locations)
Laundromat • Wood & Ice • Propane
Electric, Water & Sewer Hookups
50 Amp Available • Car Rentals Available

SHUTTLE BUS SERVICE TO...
Bar Harbor's Business District
(Memorial Day to Columbus Day)

Mt. Desert Narrows Camping Resort
Route 3 • Bar Harbor Road
RR 1, Box 2045W
Bar Harbor, ME 04609

MasterCard DISCOVER AAA

*207-288-4782*

Open May 1 to Oct. 25. Low Off-Season Rates

## Outstanding Recreational Facilities

*Your entire family will enjoy our* ***Entertainment Pavilion with Mini Theatre.*** *Relax in our* ***Heated Pool.*** *Visit the* ***Store*** *for RV Supplies, Groceries, Gifts and Souvenir Clothing. The kids will love our* ***Haywagon Rides*** *and want to visit the* ***Playground.*** *The young at heart will enjoy the large* ***Video Game Room with Pool Tables, Horseshoes,*** *and* ***Basketball!*** *The more adventurous will want to try our* ***Canoe Rentals!***

**"Everything for the Smallest Tent to the Largest RV."**

Reservations Accepted Year Round: Recommended for July & August

**NEAR ACADIA NATIONAL PARK AND THE NOVA SCOTIA FERRY**

***Bar Harbor's only Campground on the Ocean with a Heated Pool***

# Trenton, Gateway to
# Bar Harbor

## NARROWS • TOO

## CAMPING RESORT

# On the Ocean

## Breathtaking Ocean Views

**On-Site Trailer Rentals**

**Open Memorial Day to Columbus Day.**
**Low Off-Season Rates.**
**Call or Write for Free Color Brochure**
Reservations Accepted Year Round – Recommended for July & August

**HEATED POOL • SPECTACULAR VIEWS**

Oceanfront & Ocean View Camping
Store with RV Supplies, Groceries,
Gifts, and Souvenir Clothing
Car Rentals Available • Video Game Room
Playground • Basketball Court • Horseshoes
Hot Showers • Laundromat • Propane • Wood • Ice
Water, Electric & Sewer Hookups • Dumping Station

**Near Acadia National Park & Nova Scotia Ferry**

**Narrows Too Camping Resort**
**Route 3 • Bar Harbor Road**
**RR 1 • Box 193W**
**Trenton, ME 04605**
**(207) 667-4300**

**SHUTTLE BUS SERVICE TO...**
**Bar Harbor's Business District**
(From Memorial Day to Columbus Day)

**Whale-in-One Mini Golf**
"Play the Course that Challenges"

BAR HARBOR—Continued
MT. DESERT NARROWS CAMPING RESORT—Continued

Open May 1 through Oct 25. Rate in 1995 $20-37 per family. No refunds. Reservations recommended Jul through Aug. Discover/Master Card/Visa accepted. Member of ARVC; MECOA. Phone: (207) 288-4782.

SEE AD PAGE 327

**NARROWS TOO CAMPING RESORT**—An oceanside CAMPGROUND with open & shaded sites on the shores of Frenchman's Bay. *From Bar Harbor Airport: Go 1/2 mi S on Hwy 3.*

◆◆◆◆FACILITIES: 120 sites, most common site width 24 feet, 50 full hookups, 60 water & elec (20 & 30 amp receptacles), 10 no hookups, seasonal sites, 13 pull-thrus, a/c allowed ($), heater allowed ($), tenting available, group sites for tents/RVs, RV rentals, cabins, sewage disposal, laundry, public phone, grocery store, RV supplies, LP gas refill by meter, ice, tables, fire rings, wood.

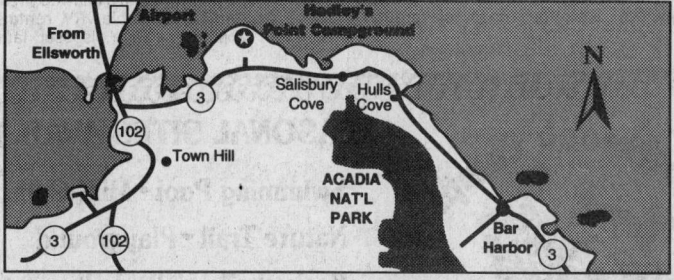

NARROWS TOO CAMPING RESORT—Continued on next page
BAR HARBOR—Continued on next page

BAR HARBOR—Continued
NARROWS TOO CAMPING RESORT—Continued

◊◊◊RECREATION: rec hall, rec room/area, coin games, swim pool (heated), mini-golf ($), basketball hoop, playground, badminton, horseshoes. Recreation open to the public.

Open Memorial Day through Columbus Day. Rate in 1995 $18-35 per family. No refunds. Reservations recommended Jul through Aug. Discover/Master Card/Visa accepted. Member of ARVC;MECOA. Phone: (207) 667-4300.

**SEE AD PAGE 329**

**SPRUCE VALLEY CAMPGROUND**—Family oriented campground with wooded tent and trailer sites. *From jct Hwy 3 & Hwy 102: Go 1 1/2 mi S on Hwy 102.*

◊◊◊FACILITIES: 100 sites, most common site width 35 feet, 10 full hookups, 30 water & elec (20 & 30 amp receptacles), 60 no hookups, seasonal sites, tenting available, group sites for tents, RV rentals, sewage disposal, laundry, public phone, limited grocery store, LP gas refill by meter, ice, tables, fire rings, wood.

◊◊◊RECREATION: rec room/area, coin games, swim pool (heated), basketball hoop, playground, horseshoes, volleyball.

Open mid May through Oct 31. Rate in 1995 $14-20 per family. No refunds. Discover/Master Card/Visa accepted. Member of ARVC: MECOA. Phone: (207) 288-5139.

**SEE AD PAGE 329**

**TIMBERLAND ACRES RV PARK**—*From jct Hwy 102 & Hwy 3: Go 6 1/2 mi N on Hwy 3.*

**SEE PRIMARY LISTING AT ELLSWORTH AND AD PAGE 329**

## BASS HARBOR—E-4

**BASS HARBOR CAMPGROUND**—Level wooded & open sites near Acadia National Park. *From jct Hwy 102 & Hwy 102A: Go 5 mi S on Hwy 102A.*

◊◊◊FACILITIES: 130 sites, most common site width 28 feet, 56 water & elec (15,20 & 30 amp receptacles), 74 no hookups, seasonal sites, 5 pull-thrus, a/c allowed, heater allowed, cable TV, tenting available, RV rentals, handicap restroom facilities, sewage disposal, laundry, public phone, grocery store, ice, tables, fire rings, grills, wood.

◊◊◊RECREATION: rec hall, swim pool (heated), basketball hoop, playground, planned group activities (weekends only), badminton, horseshoes, volleyball. Recreation open to the public.

No pets. Open Jun 15 through Sep 30. Rate in 1995 $18-22 for 2 persons. No refunds. Reservations recommended Jul through Aug. American Express/Discover/Master Card/Visa accepted. CPO. Member of ARVC; MECOA. Phone: (207) 244-5857.

**SEE AD BAR HARBOR PAGE 326**

## BATH—E-2

**MEADOWBROOK CAMPING AREA**—Large shaded and open sites. *From jct US 1 & Hwy 209: Go 2 1/4 mi S on Hwy 209, then 3 mi W on High St.*

◊◊◊FACILITIES: 100 sites, most common site width 26 feet, 55 water & elec (15,20 & 30 amp receptacles), 45 no hookups, seasonal sites, 15 pull-thrus, phone hookups, tenting available, RV storage, sewage disposal, laundry, public phone, grocery store, RV supplies, LP gas refill by weight/by meter, ice, tables, fire rings, wood.

◊◊◊RECREATION: rec hall, rec room/area, coin games, swim pool, mini-golf ($), playground, badminton, sports field, horseshoes, hiking trails, volleyball. Recreation open to the public.

Open all year. Facilities fully operational May 1 through Mid Oct. Winter camping for self-contained RV's only. Rate in 1995 $19 per family. No refunds. Reservations recommended in Winter. American Express/Master Card/Visa accepted. Member of ARVC;MECOA. Phone: (800) 370-CAMP.

**SEE AD THIS PAGE**

## BELFAST—E-3

**THE MOORINGS**—Oceanfront sites in a CAMPGROUND on a major highway. *From jct US 3 & US 1: Go 2 1/2 mi NE on US 1.*

◊◊◊FACILITIES: 50 sites, most common site width 26 feet, 50 water & elec (20 & 30 amp receptacles), a/c allowed ($), heater allowed ($), tenting available, handicap restroom facilities, sewage disposal, laundry, tables.

◊◊◊RECREATION: rec room/area, coin games, salt water swimming, salt water fishing, basketball hoop, playground, badminton, horseshoes, volleyball.

Open mid May through late Oct. Rate in 1995 $22-25 for 2 persons. Master Card/Visa accepted. Phone: (207) 338-6860.

**SEE AD THIS PAGE**

**NORTHPORT TRAVEL PARK**—CAMPGROUND with open and shaded sites convenient to a major highway. *From jct Hwy 3 & US 1: Go 6 mi S on US 1.*

◊◊◊FACILITIES: 77 sites, most common site width 24 feet, 38 full hookups, 22 water & elec (15,20 & 30 amp receptacles), 17 no hookups, seasonal sites, 9 pull-thrus, a/c allowed ($), heater allowed ($), tenting available, sewage disposal, laundry, public phone, limited grocery store, RV supplies, LP gas refill by weight/by meter, ice, tables, grills, wood.

◊◊◊RECREATION: rec hall, coin games, swim pool, pond fishing ($), playground, badminton, horseshoes, hiking trails, volleyball.

Open May 15 through Oct 15. Rate in 1995 $11-16 per family. Reservations recommended Jul through Aug. Member of ARVC;MECOA. Phone: (207) 338-2077.

**SEE AD NEXT PAGE**

BELFAST—Continued on next page

**BELFAST**—Continued

**SEARSPORT SHORES CAMPING RESORT**—*From Hwy 3 & US 1: Go 3 mi NE on US 1.* **SEE PRIMARY LISTING AT SEARSPORT AND AD SEARSPORT PAGE 356**

## BELGRADE—E-2

**Great Pond Campground**—Lakeside sites. *From town centr: Go 1/2 mi S on Hwy 27.* ◆◆◆FACILITIES: 45 sites, most common site width 22 feet, 18 full hookups, 27 water & elec (20 & 30 amp receptacles), seasonal sites, tenting available, sewage disposal, laundry, public phone, limited grocery store, ice, tables, fire rings, wood. ◆◆◆RECREATION: rec room/area, lake swimming, boating, canoeing, ramp, dock, 2 canoe/1 pedal/2 motor boat rentals, lake fishing, playground, horseshoes. Open May 1 through Oct 1. Rate in 1995 $17 per family. Phone: (207) 495-2116.

## BERWICK—F-1

**BEAVER DAM CAMPGROUND**—A lakeside, semi-wooded location. *From jct Hwy 236 & Hwy 9: Go 4 mi NE on Hwy 9.*

◆◆FACILITIES: 60 sites, most common site width 30 feet, 50 water & elec (15 amp receptacles), 10 no hookups, seasonal sites, a/c not allowed, heater not allowed, tenting available, RV rentals, RV storage, sewage disposal, public phone, limited grocery store, RV supplies, ice, tables, fire rings, wood, traffic control gate.

◆◆◆◆RECREATION: rec hall, coin games, swim pool, pond swimming, boating, electric motors only, canoeing, 2 row/2 canoe/3 pedal boat rentals, pond fishing, mini-golf ($), basketball hoop, playground, planned group activities, badminton, sports field, horseshoes, volleyball. Recreation open to the public.

Open mid May through mid Sep. Rate in 1995 $17-22 for 4 persons. No refunds. Reservations recommended during Jul. Master Card/Visa accepted. Member of ARVC; MECOA. Phone: (207) 698-1985.

**SEE AD TRAVEL SECTION PAGE 322**

## BETHEL—E-1

**Pleasant River Campground**—A CAMPGROUND with wooded sites by a river. *From jct Hwy 5 & US 2: Go 4 1/2 mi W on US 2.* ◆◆FACILITIES: 45 sites, 10 water & elec (15 & 30 amp receptacles), 35 no hookups, seasonal sites, tenting available, sewage disposal, laundry, ice, tables, fire rings, wood. ◆◆RECREATION: swim pool, hiking trails, volleyball. Open May 15 through Oct 15. Rate in 1995 $16 for 2 persons. Phone: (800) 847-7786.

**STONY BROOK RECREATION**—*From jct Hwy 26 & US 2/Hwy 5: Go 7 mi E on US 2.* **SEE PRIMARY LISTING AT HANOVER AND AD THIS PAGE**

## BIDDEFORD—F-1

**Shamrock RV Park**—A rustic, wooded CAMPGROUND with level, open sites. *From jct Maine Tpke (exit 4) & Hwy 111: Go 1 mi E on Hwy 111, then go right directly across US 1 and 4 1/2 mi E on West St.* ◆◆◆FACILITIES: 60 sites, most common site width 28 feet, 25 full hookups, 19 water & elec (15 & 30 amp receptacles), 16 no hookups, seasonal sites, 6 pull-thrus, tenting available, sewage disposal, public phone, ice, tables, fire rings, wood. ◆◆RECREATION: rec room/area, swim pool, pond fishing, mini-golf, playground. Open May 1 through Sep 15. Rate in 1995 $14-22 for 2 persons. No refunds. Member of ARVC;MECOA. Phone: (207) 284-4282.

## BIRCH HARBOR—E-4

**OCEAN WOOD CAMPGROUND**—Large wooded sites directly on the open ocean. *From north jct of US 1 & Hwy 186: Go 7 mi S on Hwy 186, then 1/2 mi S on Birch Harbor Rd.*

◆◆FACILITIES: 70 sites, most common site width 55 feet, 20 water & elec (30 amp receptacles), 50 no hookups, 5 pull-thrus, tenting available, sewage disposal, ice, tables, grills, wood.

RECREATION: salt water swimming, salt water fishing.

Open early May through late Oct. Rate in 1995 $14-24 per family. Phone: (207) 963-7194.

**SEE AD THIS PAGE**

## BOOTHBAY—E-2

**Campers Cove Campground**—A rural setting with a saltwater view from all sites. *From jct US 1 & Hwy 27: Go 7 3/4 mi S on Hwy 27, then 3 1/2 mi W on Back River Rd.* ◆◆FACILITIES: 56 sites, most common site width 24 feet, 13 full hookups, 43 water & elec (15 & 20 amp receptacles), seasonal sites, 30 pull-thrus, tenting available, sewage disposal, public phone, ice, tables, fire rings, wood. ◆RECREATION: boating, salt water/river fishing, horseshoes, volleyball. Open May 15 through Oct 15. Rate in 1995 $15.50-16.50 per family. Member of ARVC; MECOA. Phone: (207) 633-5013.

**LITTLE PONDEROSA CAMPGROUND**—A family location in a pine grove on a saltwater inlet. *From jct US 1 & Hwy 27: Go 5 1/4 mi S on Hwy 27.*

◆◆◆◆FACILITIES: 92 sites, most common site width 28 feet, 37 full hookups, 53 water & elec (20 & 30 amp receptacles), 2 no hookups, seasonal sites, 9 pull-thrus, a/c allowed ($), heater allowed, cable TV ($), tenting available, handicap restroom facilities, sewage disposal, laundry, public phone, limited grocery store, RV supplies, LP gas refill by weight/by meter, ice, tables, fire rings, wood, church services.

◆◆◆◆RECREATION: rec room/area, equipped pavilion, coin games, salt water/river swimming, boating, 1 row/2 canoe boat rentals, salt water/river fishing, mini-golf ($), basketball hoop, playground, planned group activities (weekends only), movies, badminton, horseshoes, volleyball, local tours. Recreation open to the public.

Open mid May through Nov 1. Self-contained RV's only after Oct 15. Rate in 1995 $16-20 per family. Reservations recommended Jul through Aug. Master Card/Visa accepted. Member of ARVC; MECOA. Phone: (207) 633-2700.

**SEE AD NEXT PAGE**

**SHORE HILLS CAMPGROUND**—Gravel and grass open & shaded sites on a rural, salt water inlet. *From jct US 1 & Hwy 27: Go 7 1/2 mi S on Hwy 27.*

◆◆◆◆FACILITIES: 150 sites, most common site width 28 feet, 83 full hookups, 52 water & elec (20,30 & 50 amp receptacles), 15 no hookups, seasonal sites, 15 pull-thrus, a/c allowed ($), heater allowed ($), cable TV ($), phone hookups, tenting available, RV storage, sewage disposal, laundry, public phone, grocery store, RV supplies, LP gas refill by weight/by meter, ice, tables, fire rings, wood, traffic control gate.

◆◆◆RECREATION: rec hall, coin games, salt water/river swimming, boating, river fishing, basketball hoop, playground, badminton, horseshoes, volleyball, local tours.

SHORE HILLS CAMPGROUND—Continued on next page
BOOTHBAY—Continued on next page



**The best way to keep camp pests, such as bears, away from your camp is to keep a clean campsite.**

BOOTHBAY—Continued
SHORE HILLS CAMPGROUND—Continued

Open mid Apr through Columbus Day. Rate in 1995 $14-20 per family. Reservations recommended Jul through Aug. Member of ARVC; MECOA. Phone: (207) 633-4782.

SEE AD NEXT PAGE

## BOOTHBAY HARBOR—E-2

**GRAY HOMESTEAD OCEANFRONT CAMPING**—Oceanside, hilly CAMPGROUND. *From jct Hwy 27 & Hwy 238: Go 2 mi S on Hwy 238.*

◊◊◊FACILITIES: 30 sites, most common site width 22 feet, 1 full hookups, 16 water & elec (15,20 & 30 amp receptacles), 13 no hookups, seasonal sites, a/c allowed, heater allowed, tenting available, group sites for tents/RVs, cabins, sewage disposal, laundry, public phone, ice, tables, fire rings, wood.

◊RECREATION: salt water swimming, salt water fishing, basketball hoop, horseshoes, volleyball.

Open May 1 through mid Oct. Rate in 1995 $14-21 per vehicle. Reservations recommended Jun through Aug. Member of ARVC; MECOA. Phone: (207) 633-4612.

SEE AD BOOTHBAY PAGE 331

## BREWER—D-3

✽ **DON'S CAMPERS**—*From jct I-395 & US 1A: Go 1 mi E on US 1A.* SALES: travel trailers, park models, truck campers, 5th wheels, motor homes, mini-motor homes, fold-down camping trailers. SERVICES: Engine/Chassis & RV appliance mechanic full-time, LP gas refill by weight, sells parts/accessories, installs hitches. Open all year. Master Card/Visa accepted. Phone: (207) 989-3851.

SEE AD THIS PAGE

**Greenwood Acres RV Park & Campground**—CAMPGROUND with open and shaded sites near major highway. *From jct US 1A & Hwy 9: Go 4 1/2 mi E on Hwy 9, then 1 mi N on Hwy 178.* ◊◊◊FACILITIES: 50 sites, most common site width 22 feet, 6 full hookups, 26 water & elec (15 & 30 amp receptacles), 18 no hookups, seasonal sites, 8 pull-thrus, tenting available, sewage disposal, laundry, public phone, limited grocery store, ice, tables, fire rings, wood. ◊◊RECREATION: rec hall, rec room/area, swim pool, playground, badminton, volleyball. Open all year. Facilities fully operational Apr 21 through Oct 15. Rate in 1995 $10.50-16.50 per family. Phone: (207) 989-8898.

✽ **MCKAY'S RV CENTER**—*From jct I-395 & US 1A: Go 1 mi E on US 1A.* SALES: travel trailers, truck campers, 5th wheels, motor homes, fold-down camping trailers. SERVICES: RV appliance mechanic full-time, LP gas refill by meter, RV storage, sells parts/accessories, installs hitches. Open all year. Discover/Master Card/Visa accepted. Phone: (800) 924-4309.

SEE AD TRAVEL SECTION PAGE 322

✽ **REC TECH**—*From jct I-395 & Hwy 15: Go 1/2 mi S on Hwy 15.* SERVICES: RV appliance mechanic full-time, LP gas refill by weight/by meter, sells parts/accessories, sells camping supplies, installs hitches. Open all year. Master Card/Visa accepted. Phone: (207) 989-3324.

SEE AD BANGOR PAGE 324

**RED BARN CAMPGROUND**—CAMPGROUND with grassy, open and shaded sites near a major highway. *From jct I-395 & US 1A: Go 3 mi E on US 1A.*

◊◊◊FACILITIES: 126 sites, most common site width 24 feet, 52 full hookups, 49 water & elec (15,20 & 30 amp receptacles), 25 no hookups, seasonal sites, 2 pull-thrus, a/c allowed ($), heater allowed, phone hookups, tenting available, sewage disposal, laundry, public phone, limited grocery store, RV supplies, LP gas refill by weight/by meter, ice, tables, fire rings, wood.

◊◊◊RECREATION: rec room/area, pavilion, coin games, swim pool, basketball hoop, playground, planned group activities, recreation director, badminton, horseshoes, volleyball. Recreation open to the public.

Open May 1 through Oct 31. Rate in 1995 $13-16.50 for 4 persons. No refunds. Discover/Master Card/Visa accepted. Phone: (207) 843-6011.

SEE AD BANGOR PAGE 325

**WEE HOLME CAMPGROUND**—Flat open sites convenient to a major highway and adjacent to an RV dealer. *From jct I-395 & US 1A: Go 1 mi E on US 1A.*

◊◊FACILITIES: 16 sites, most common site width 22 feet, 16 full hookups, (15 & 30 amp receptacles), seasonal sites, 7 pull-thrus, phone hookups, tenting available, RV storage, sewage disposal, RV supplies, LP gas refill by weight, tables, fire rings.

Open May 15 through mid Oct. Rate in 1995 $12 per family. Phone: (207) 989-3851.

SEE AD THIS PAGE

## BRIDGTON—E-1

**LAKESIDE PINES CAMPGROUND**—Heavily wooded CAMPGROUND with a large beach. *From jct US 302 & Hwy 117: Go 2 mi N on Hwy 117.*

◊◊FACILITIES: 185 sites, most common site width 24 feet, 140 full hookups, 45 water & elec (15 amp receptacles), seasonal sites, a/c not allowed, tenting available, RV rentals, cabins, sewage disposal, laundry, public phone, limited grocery store, LP gas refill by weight/by meter, ice, tables, fire rings, wood.

◊◊◊RECREATION: rec room/area, coin games, lake swimming, boating, ramp, dock, 5 canoe/2 pedal boat rentals, lake fishing, basketball hoop, playground, planned group activities (weekends only), movies, horseshoes, volleyball.

Open Memorial Day through Sep 15. Facilities fully operational Jul through Labor Day. Rate in 1995 $23-26 per family. Reservations recommended Jun

LAKESIDE PINES CAMPGROUND—Continued on next page
BRIDGTON—Continued on next page

SEASON MAY 15 to OCTOBER 15

LITTLE Ponderosa CAMPGROUND

*Start a New Tradition-Camp at the Boothbay Harbor Region's Most Complete Family Campground*

**10 Minutes to the Harbor**

***Prettiest pine shaded shore sites in the Region***

***Extremely clean restrooms***

- Cable TV
- Shuttlebus to Harbor
- 32' x 72' Rec Hall
- Swimming - Boating
- Creative Playground
- 18 Hole Mini-Golf
- Metered LP Gas
- Full hook-ups–30 amps
- Up to 40' RV's
- Store - RV Supplies
- Laundry
- Snack Bar

**– JULY AND AUGUST –**

**• Friday Night : Free Family Movie**
**• Saturday: Hayride, Ice Cream Sundaes, Gospel Concert**
**• Sunday: Church Service**

*Come unto me, all ye that labor and are heavy laden, and I will give you rest!*
*— Matt 11:28*

***A unspoiled private campground with a national park flavor in the Boothbay Harbor Region — one of the most beautiful recreation areas on the coast of Maine.***

*Off Season Rates May 15 - June 15 and Labor Day - Oct. 15*

APPROVED CAMPGROUND AAA

FAMILY MOTOR COACH ASSOC.

**Reservations Suggested.**

HC 34, Box 14, BOOTHBAY, MAINE 04537
(207) 633-2700

See listing at Boothbay

Sales & Service
LP Gas

*From I-395, 1 mi SE on Bar Harbor Rd (US 1A)*

**(207) 989-3851**

**Wee Holme Campground Adjacent**
**Donald Goss** See listings at Brewer
**340 Main Road, East Holden, ME 04429**

BRIDGTON—Continued
LAKESIDE PINES CAMPGROUND—Continued

28 through Labor Day. Member of ARVC; MECOA. Phone: (207) 647-3935.
SEE AD NEXT PAGE

**PAPOOSE POND RESORT**—*From jct US 302 & Hwy 117: Go 3 mi N on Hwy 117, then 9 mi N on Hwy 37, then 1 3/4 mi W on Hwy 118.*
**SEE PRIMARY LISTING AT NORTH WATERFORD AND AD NORTH WATERFORD PAGES 346 AND 347**

## BROWNFIELD—E-1

**River Run Canoe & Camping**—Large, secluded, wooded, wilderness sites on the Saco River. *From jct Hwy 5/113 & Hwy 160: Go 1 1/4 mi N on Hwy 160 (over the bridge).* ◆FACILITIES: 22 sites, most common site width 150 feet, 22 no hookups, tenting available, non-flush toilets, tables, fire rings, grills, wood. ◆◆RECREATION: river swimming, canoeing, 100 canoe boat rentals, river/pond fishing, hiking trails. Recreation open to the public. Open mid May through late Sep. No showers. Rate in 1995 $5 for 1 persons. Phone: (207) 452-2500.

**WOODLAND ACRES CAMP 'N CANOE**—*From jct Hwy 5/113 & Hwy 160: Go 1 mi E on Hwy 160.* Canoe rental and shuttle on the Saco River. Open mid May through mid Oct. Master Card/Visa accepted. Phone: (602) 935-2529.
**SEE AD FRONT OF BOOK PAGE 3 AND AD THIS PAGE**

BROWNFIELD—Continued

**WOODLAND ACRES CAMP 'N CANOE**—Riverside CAMPGROUND with wooded and open sites. *From jct Hwy 5/113 & Hwy 160: Go 1 mi E on Hwy 160.*

◆◆◆FACILITIES: 58 sites, most common site width 100 feet, 38 water & elec (15 & 20 amp receptacles), 20 no hookups, a/c allowed ($), heater allowed ($), tenting available, group sites for tents, tent rentals, RV rentals, RV storage, sewage disposal, laundry, public phone, grocery store, LP gas refill by weight/by meter, ice, tables, fire rings, wood.

BROWNFIELD—Continued
WOODLAND ACRES CAMP 'N CANOE—Continued

◆◆◆RECREATION: rec hall, rec room/area, pavilion, coin games, river swimming, boating, canoeing, dock, 100 canoe boat rentals, river fishing, basketball hoop, playground, badminton, horseshoes, volleyball. Recreation open to the public.

Open mid May through mid Oct. Rate in 1995 $17-25 per family. Reservations recommended Jul through Aug. Discover/Master Card/Visa accepted. Member of ARVC; MECOA. Phone: (207) 935-2529.
**SEE AD FRONT OF BOOK PAGE 3 AND AD THIS PAGE**

## BUCKSPORT—D-3

**Balsam Cove Campground**—Lakeside camping on spacious wooded sites. *From south jct Hwy 15 & US 1: Go 7 mi N on US 1, then 1 mi E on county road (follow signs).* ◆◆FACILITIES: 60 sites, 30 water & elec, 20 elec (15 amp receptacles), 10 no hookups, seasonal sites, 3 pull-thrus, tenting available, sewage disposal, laundry, limited grocery store, ice, tables, fire rings, wood. ◆◆◆RECREATION: pavilion, lake swimming, boating, canoeing, ramp, dock, 1 row/2 canoe/1 pedal boat rentals, lake fishing, playground, badminton, horseshoes, volleyball. Open Memorial Day through Sep 30. Rate in 1995 $14.50-19.50 per family. Member of ARVC; MECOA. Phone: (207) 469-7771.

**THE FLYING DUTCHMAN CAMPGROUND**—Wooded and open sites on a scenic river. *From South jct Hwy 15 & US 1: Go 1 mi S on US 1.*

WELCOME

◆◆◆FACILITIES: 35 sites, most common site width 22 feet, 12 full hookups, 13 water & elec (20 amp receptacles), 10 no hookups, seasonal sites, a/c not allowed, heater not allowed, tenting available, group sites for tents, sewage disposal, laundry, public phone, limited grocery store, ice, tables, fire rings, wood.

◆◆◆RECREATION: rec room/area, pavilion, swim pool (heated), whirlpool, boating, salt water fishing, basketball hoop, playground, movies, badminton, horseshoes, volleyball.

Open May 1 through Oct 10. Rate in 1995 $15-18 for 4 persons. Discover/Master Card/Visa accepted. Member of ARVC;MECOA. Phone: (207) 469-6004.
**SEE AD THIS PAGE**





**Masthead Family Campground**—Lakeside, semi-wooded location. *From jct Hwy 15 & US 1: Go 2 mi E on US 1, then 5 1/2 mi N on Hwy 46, then 3/4 mi E on Mast Hill Rd.* ◆◆◆FACILITIES: 38 sites, most common site width 20 feet, 30 ft. max RV length, 38 water & elec (15 & 20 amp receptacles), seasonal sites, tenting available, sewage disposal, laundry, public phone, limited grocery store, ice, tables, fire rings, wood. ◆◆◆RECREATION: pavilion, lake swimming, boating, no motors, canoeing, 1 row/2 canoe boat rentals, lake fishing, playground, badminton, horseshoes, volleyball. Open Memorial Day wknd through mid Sep. Rate in 1995 $12-13 per family. Member of ARVC; MECOA. Phone: (207) 469-3482.

**SHADY OAKS CAMPGROUND**—A family oriented CAMPGROUND. *From jct Hwy 15 & US 1: Go 2 mi E on US 1, then 1/8 mi S on campground road.*

WELCOME

◆◆◆FACILITIES: 50 sites, most common site width 24 feet, 29 full hookups, 21 water & elec (20 amp receptacles), seasonal sites, a/c not allowed, heater not allowed, tenting available, group sites for tents, cabins, sewage disposal, laundry, public phone, limited grocery store, ice, tables, fire rings, wood.

◆◆◆RECREATION: rec room/area, swim pool, basketball hoop, playground, planned group activities, badminton, horseshoes, hiking trails, volleyball.

No pets. Open May 1 through Oct 1. Rate in 1995 $12-14 for 2 persons. Master Card/Visa accepted. Member of ARVC; MECOA. Phone: (207) 469-7739.
**SEE AD THIS PAGE**

**Whispering Pines Campground**—Rural, lakeside campground with shaded sites. *From jct Hwy 15 & US 1: Go 7 1/2 mi NE on US 1.* ◆◆FACILITIES: 50 sites, 40 full hookups, 6 water & elec (15 & 20 amp receptacles), 4 no hookups, seasonal sites, tenting available, sewage disposal, tables, fire rings, wood. ◆◆◆RECREATION: rec room/area, lake swimming, boating, dock, 1 row/2 canoe boat rentals, lake fishing, playground, badminton, horseshoes, volleyball. Open Memorial Day through Sep 30. Rate in 1995 $17 for 2 persons. Member of ARVC; MECOA. Phone: (207) 469-3443.

## CALAIS—D-5

**KEENE'S LAKE CAMPGROUND**—Rural, lakeside CAMPGROUND for active families. *From East city limit: Go 8 mi SE on US 1, then 1 mi W on Shattuck Rd.*

◆◆FACILITIES: 151 sites, most common site width 24 feet, 142 water & elec (15,20 & 30 amp receptacles), 9 no hookups, seasonal sites, 18 pull-thrus, a/c allowed, heater allowed, phone hookups, tenting available, RV storage, sewage disposal, laundry, public phone, limited grocery store, LP gas refill by weight/by meter, ice, tables, fire rings, wood.

◆◆◆RECREATION: rec room/area, coin games, lake swimming, boating, 7.5 hp limit, 2 canoe/6 pedal boat rentals, lake fishing, mini-golf ($), basketball hoop, playground, planned group activities (weekends only), movies, sports field, horseshoes, volleyball. Recreation open to the public.

KEENE'S LAKE CAMPGROUND—Continued on next page
CALAIS—Continued on next page

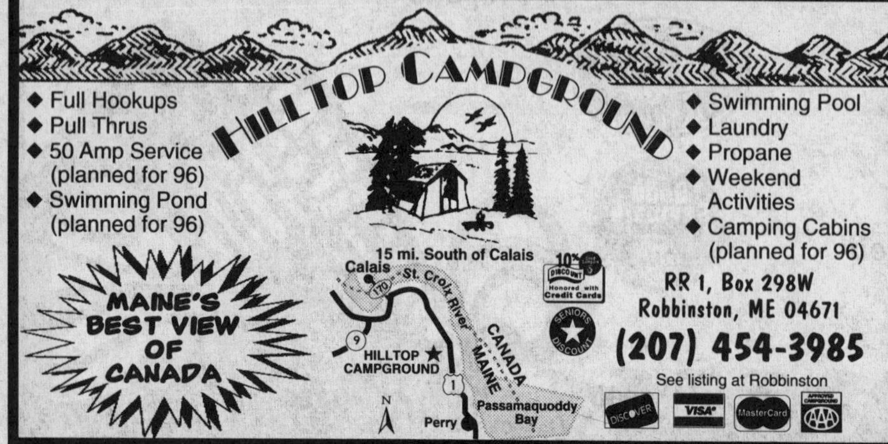

CALAIS—Continued
KEENE'S LAKE CAMPGROUND—Continued

Open May 15 through Oct 1. Rate in 1995 $14 for 5 persons. Reservations recommended Jul through Aug. Master Card/Visa accepted. Member of ARVC; MECOA. Phone: (207) 454-8557.
**SEE AD PAGE 334**

## CAMDEN—E-3

CAMDEN HILLS STATE PARK—*From jct Hwy 105 & US 1: Go 2 mi NE on US 1.* FACILITIES: 112 sites, 31 ft. max RV length, 112 no hookups, tenting available, handicap restroom facilities, sewage disposal, public phone, ice, tables, wood. RECREATION: playground, hiking trails. Open May 15 through Oct 15. Phone: (207) 236-3109.

**MEGUNTICOOK CAMPGROUND BY THE SEA**—*From jct Hwy 105 & US 1: Go 4 mi S on US 1.*
**SEE PRIMARY LISTING AT ROCKPORT AND AD ROCKPORT PAGE 355**

## CANAAN—D-3

**KOA-SKOWHEGAN-CANAAN**—CAMPGROUND with open grassy sites on rolling terrain near a major highway. *From jct Hwy 23 & US 2: Go 1 1/2 mi E on US 2.*

◆◆◆FACILITIES: 120 sites, most common site width 26 feet, 59 full hookups, 43 water & elec (20 & 30 amp receptacles), 18 no hookups, seasonal sites, 60 pull-thrus, a/c allowed ($), heater allowed ($), cable TV ($), tenting available, group sites for tents/RVs, tent rentals, cabins, RV storage, handicap restroom facilities, sewage disposal, laundry, public phone, grocery store, RV supplies, LP gas refill by meter, ice, tables, fire rings, grills, wood.

◆◆◆◆RECREATION: rec room/area, pavilion, coin games, swim pool, 1 canoe boat rentals, basketball hoop, playground, planned group activities, badminton, sports field, horseshoes, hiking trails, volleyball. Recreation open to the public.

Open May 1 through Oct 31. Rate in 1995 $16.50-23.50 for 2 persons. Reservations recommended Jul through Aug. Discover/Master Card/Visa accepted. Phone: (800) 562-3613. KOA 10% value card discount.
**SEE AD THIS PAGE AND AD FRONT OF BOOK PAGES 68 AND 69**

## CAPE NEDDICK—F-1

**Cape Neddick Oceanside Campground**—Oceanside with shaded & open sites. *From jct Hwy 1A & Shore Rd: Go 1/4 m N on Shore Rd.* ◆◆FACILITIES: 80 sites, 28 ft. max RV length, 30 elec (20 & 30 amp receptacles), 50 no hookups, seasonal sites, tenting available, sewage disposal, public phone, ice, tables, fire rings, wood. ◆RECREATION: salt water swimming, boating, salt water fishing. No pets. Open May 1 through Columbus Day. Rate in 1995 $22-25 for 2 persons. No refunds. Member of ARVC;MECOA. Phone: (207) 363-4366.

## CARIBOU—A-4

**AROOSTOOK RIVER CAMPING & RECREATION**—Rural campground on a river with open & wooded sites. *From jct Hwy 161 & US 1: Go 3 1/2 mi S on US 1.*

◆◆FACILITIES: 25 sites, most common site width 20 feet, 4 full hookups, 12 water & elec (15,20 & 30 amp receptacles), 9 no hookups, seasonal sites, a/c allowed ($), heater allowed

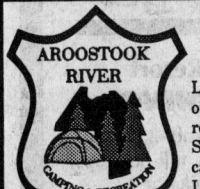

ME For information on ME
**Moosemania**
ME See front of book article. ME

ME **State Bird: Chickadee** ME

CARIBOU—Continued
AROOSTOOK RIVER CAMPING & RECREATION—Continued

($), tenting available, sewage disposal, tables, fire rings, wood.

◆◆RECREATION: river swimming, canoeing, 9 canoe boat rentals, river fishing, fishing guides, hiking trails, cross country skiing, snowmobile trails, local tours. Recreation open to the public.

Open all year. Facilities fully operational mid May through mid Oct. Rate in 1995 $15 for 2 persons. Phone: (207) 498-6969.
**SEE AD THIS PAGE**

✱ **GAGNON'S AUTO & RV SALES**—*From jct US 1 & Hwy 164: Go 2 1/2 mi N on Hwy 164.* SALES: travel trailers, park models, 5th wheels, van conversions, motor homes, fold-down camping trailers. SERVICES: Engine/Chassis & RV appliance mechanic full-time, tent rentals, sells parts/accessories, installs hitches. Open all year. Discover/Master Card/Visa accepted. Phone: (207) 493-3350.
**SEE AD THIS PAGE**

## CARMEL—D-3

**Shady Acres RV & Campground**—Wooded CAMPGROUND with grassy level sites. *From jct I-95 (exit 43): Go 2 1/2 mi W on Hwy 69.* ◆◆FACILITIES: 50 sites, most common site width 24 feet, 27 full hookups, 27 water & elec (20 & 30 amp receptacles), seasonal sites, 18 pull-thrus, tenting available, sewage disposal, laundry, public phone, ice, tables, fire rings, wood. ◆◆RECREATION: rec room/area, swim pool, pond fishing ($), badminton, horseshoes, volleyball. Open May 15 through Oct 15. Rate in 1995 $15-16 per family. Phone: (207) 848-5515.

ME **Our 23rd State** ME

## CASCO—E-1

**POINT SEBAGO**—Lakeside, wooded CAMPGROUND resort with an exceptional recreation program. *From jct Hwy 85 & US 302: Go 5 mi N on US 302.*

◆◆◆FACILITIES: 500 sites, most common site width 30 feet, 244 full hookups, 256 water & elec (15,20 & 30 amp receptacles), seasonal sites, a/c not allowed, heater allowed, phone hookups, tenting available, RV rentals, RV storage, sewage disposal, laundry, public phone, full service store, RV supplies, LP gas refill by weight/by meter, gasoline, marine gas, ice, tables, grills, wood, traffic control gate/guard.

◆◆◆◆◆RECREATION: rec hall, rec room/area, equipped pavilion, coin games, lake swimming, boating, canoeing, ramp, dock, 15 sail/24 canoe/25 pedal/15 motor boat rentals, water skiing, lake fishing, golf ($), mini-golf ($), driving range ($), putting green, basketball hoop, playground, 9 shuffleboard courts, planned group activities, movies, recreation director, 10 tennis courts, sports field, horseshoes, hiking trails, volleyball, local tours.

Open May 1 through Oct 31. Facilities fully operational Memorial Day through Labor Day. Rate in 1995 $22-45 per family. No refunds. Reservations recommended May 30 through Sep 5. Discover/Master Card/Visa accepted. Member of ARVC; MECOA. Phone: (800) 872-7646.
**SEE AD FRONT OF BOOK PAGE 6**

## CORNISH—E-1

**York County Campsite Park**—A family CAMPGROUND with wooded and open grassy sites. *From west jct Hwy 117 & Hwy 25: Go 1 1/2 mi E on Hwy 25.* ◆◆FACILITIES: 60 sites, most common site width 28 feet, 13 full hookups, 47 water & elec (15 & 20 amp receptacles), seasonal sites, tenting available, sewage disposal, grocery store, ice, tables, fire rings, wood.

YORK COUNTY CAMPSITE PARK—Continued on next page
CORNISH—Continued on next page

CORNISH—Continued
YORK COUNTY CAMPSITE PARK—Continued

◆◆◆RECREATION: rec hall, swim pool, river swimming, canoeing, river fishing, playground, badminton, sports field, horseshoes, volleyball. Recreation open to the public. Open May 1 through Oct 1. Facilities fully operational Memorial Day through Labor Day. Rate in 1995 $16-18 per family. No refunds. Phone: (207) 625-8808.

## DAMARISCOTTA—E-3

**DUCK PUDDLE FAMILY CAMPGROUND**—Open & shaded sites on large lake. *From south jct US 1 & Business US 1: Go 6 1/4 mi N on US 1, then 1 1/4 mi E on Duck Puddle Rd.*

◆◆◆FACILITIES: 95 sites, most common site width 24 feet, 35 full hookups, 55 water & elec (15 amp receptacles), 5 no hookups, seasonal sites, 2 pull-thrus, a/c allowed ($), heater allowed ($), phone hookups, tenting available, cabins, RV storage, sewage disposal, laundry, public phone, grocery store, RV supplies, LP gas refill by meter, ice, tables, fire rings, wood.

◆◆◆◆RECREATION: rec hall, coin games, lake swimming, boating, canoeing, ramp, dock, 3 canoe/3 pedal/4 motor boat rentals, lake fishing, basketball hoop, playground, planned group activities, badminton, sports field, horseshoes, volleyball. Recreation open to the public.

Open May 1 through mid Oct. Rate in 1995 $16-25 per family. Reservations recommended Jul through Aug. Discover/Master Card/Visa accepted. Member of ARVC; MECOA. Phone: (207) 563-5608.

**SEE AD THIS PAGE**

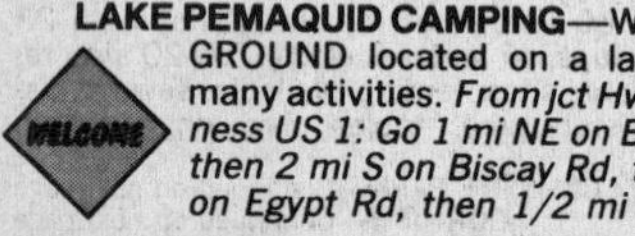


**LAKE PEMAQUID CAMPING**—Wooded CAMPGROUND located on a large lake with many activities. *From jct Hwy 130 & Business US 1: Go 1 mi NE on Business US 1, then 2 mi S on Biscay Rd, then 1/4 mi E on Egypt Rd, then 1/2 mi SE.*

◆◆◆FACILITIES: 250 sites, most common site width 28 feet, 120 full hookups, 130 water & elec (20 & 30 amp receptacles), seasonal sites, 10 pull-thrus, a/c allowed, heater allowed, tenting available, cabins, RV storage, handicap restroom facilities, sewage disposal, laundry, public phone, grocery store, RV supplies, LP gas refill by weight/by meter, marine gas, ice, tables, fire rings, wood, traffic control gate.

◆◆◆◆RECREATION: rec hall, rec room/area, pavilion, coin games, swim pool (heated), lake swimming, sauna, whirlpool, boating, canoeing, ramp, dock, 6 sail/20 canoe/8 pedal/10 motor boat rentals, lake fishing, basketball hoop, playground, planned group activities, movies, 2 tennis courts, horseshoes, volleyball.

Open May 15 through Columbus Day. Rate in 1995 $20-30 per family. No refunds. Reservations recommended Jul through Aug. American Express/Discover/Master Card/Visa accepted. Member of ARVC; MECOA. Phone: (207) 563-5202.

**SEE AD NEXT PAGE**

## DANFORTH—C-4

**Greenland Cove Campground**—Shaded sites on lake with sandy beach. *From jct Hwy 169 & US 1: Go 2 1/4 mi S on US 1, then 2 1/2 mi E on Campground Rd.* ◆◆FACILITIES: 40 sites, most common site width 22 feet, 40 water & elec (30 amp receptacles), seasonal sites, tenting available, sewage disposal, grocery store, ice, tables, fire rings, wood. ◆◆◆RECREATION: rec room/area, lake swimming, boating, ramp, dock, 1 pedal/2 motor boat rentals, lake fishing, playground, badminton, horseshoes, volleyball. Open ice out through Oct 1. Rate in 1995 $16 per family. Member of ARVC; MECOA. Phone: (207) 448-2863.

**Mountain View Campground**—Open, grassy, level sites on a lake with a sandy beach. *From jct Hwy 169 & US 1: Go 8 mi N on US 1.* ◆◆FACILITIES: 60 sites, most common site width 20 feet, 60 water & elec (15 amp receptacles), seasonal sites, tenting available, sewage disposal, laundry, tables, fire rings, wood. ◆◆RECREATION: lake swimming, boating, canoeing, lake fishing, horseshoes. Recreation open to the public. Open Memorial Day through Labor Day. Rate in 1995 $14 per family. Phone: (207) 448-2980.

## DEER ISLE—E-3

**Sunshine Campground**—Wooded sites on a hilly terrain. *From southernmost jct Hwy 175 & Hwy 15: Go 7 3/4 mi S on Hwy 15, then 5 3/4 mi E on Sunshine County Rd.* ◆◆FACILITIES: 22 sites, 15 water & elec (20 amp receptacles), 7 no hookups, tenting available, sewage disposal, laundry, limited grocery store, ice, tables, fire rings, wood. RECREATION: rec room/area, horseshoes. Open Memorial Day through Oct 15. Rate in 1995 $10-14 per family. Member of ARVC; MECOA. Phone: (207) 348-6681.

## DENNYSVILLE—D-5

COBSCOOK BAY STATE PARK—*Southbound, from jct Hwy 86 & US 1: Go 6 mi S on US 1.* FACILITIES: 106 sites, 106 no hookups, tenting available, non-flush toilets, sewage disposal, tables, wood. RECREATION: boating, ramp, fishing, playground, hiking trails. Open May 15 through Oct 15. Phone: (207) 726-4412.

## DOVER-FOXCROFT—D-3

PEAKS-KENNY STATE PARK—*From town: Go 6 mi N on Hwy 153.* FACILITIES: 56 sites, 56 no hookups, tenting available, handicap restroom facilities, sewage disposal, ice, tables, grills, wood. RECREATION: lake swimming, lake fishing, playground, hiking trails. Open May 15 through Sep 30. Phone: (207) 564-2003.

## EAST LEBANON—F-1

**KINGS-QUEENS COURT VACATION RESORT**—A riverside CAMPGROUND with many recreational activities available on site. *In town: From jct US 202 & River Rd: Go 2 mi N on River Rd, then W to campground road.*

◆◆◆FACILITIES: 450 sites, most common site width 34 feet, 200 full hookups, 250 water & elec (20 & 30 amp receptacles), seasonal sites, a/c not allowed, heater not allowed, cable TV, tenting available, group sites for tents/RVs, RV rentals, cabins, RV storage, sewage disposal, laundry, public phone, grocery store, RV supplies, LP gas refill by weight/by meter, ice, tables, fire rings, wood, traffic control gate.

◆◆◆◆◆RECREATION: rec hall, rec room/area, equipped pavilion, coin games, 2 swim pools (heated), wading pool, river/pond swimming, whirlpool, water slide, river fishing, mini-golf ($), basketball hoop, playground, planned group activities, recreation director, badminton, sports field, horseshoes, volleyball.

Open mid May through late Sep. Facilities fully operational Memorial Day through Labor Day. Rate in 1995 $24 for 2 persons. No refunds. Reservations recommended Jul through Aug. Master Card/Visa accepted. Member of ARVC; MECOA. Phone: (207) 339-9465.

**SEE AD THIS PAGE**

## EAST MACHIAS—D-5

MILITARY PARK (Sprague Neck Campsites)—*From jct US 1 & Hwy 191: Go 7 mi S on Hwy 191 to NCTS Cutler Admin. Area, then 6 mi. On base.* FACILITIES: 10 sites, 10 no hookups, seasonal sites, 6 pull-thrus, tenting available, non-flush toilets, public phone, limited grocery store, tables, grills, wood. RECREATION: boating, 2 sail/7 canoe/6 motor boat rentals, salt water/lake/pond fishing, horseshoes, hiking trails. Open May 15 through Oct 31. No showers. Phone: (207) 259-8285.

## EASTPORT—D-5

**THE SEAVIEW**—A CAMPGROUND with open & shaded sites on the ocean. *From jct US 1 & Hwy 190: Go 5 mi S on Hwy 190, then 1/4 mi E on NorwoodRd.*

◆◆◆FACILITIES: 74 sites, most common site width 24 feet, 74 full hookups, (15,20 & 30 amp receptacles), seasonal sites, 23 pull-thrus, a/c allowed ($), heater allowed ($), cable TV, tenting available, group sites for tents/RVs, RV rentals, cabins, sewage disposal, laundry, public phone, grocery store, RV supplies, LP gas refill by meter, ice, tables, fire rings, wood.

◆◆◆RECREATION: rec room/area, boating, dock, salt water fishing, fishing guides, playground, planned group activities (weekends only), horseshoes.

THE SEAVIEW—Continued on next page
EASTPORT—Continued on next page

EASTPORT—Continued
THE SEAVIEW—Continued

Open May 15 through Oct 15. Rate in 1995 $14.50-18.50 for 4 persons. Discover/Master Card/ Visa accepted. Member of ARVC; MECOA. Phone: (207) 853-4471.
SEE AD PAGE 336

## ELLSWORTH—D-4

**THE GATHERINGS FAMILY CAMPGROUND, OCEANFRONT CAMPING**—Oceanside CAMPGROUND with open and shaded sites. *From jct Hwy 1A & US 1: Go 1/2 mi SW on US 1, then 4 mi SW on Hwy 172.*

WELCOME

◆◆◆FACILITIES: 110 sites, most common site width 22 feet, 5 full hookups, 105 water & elec (15 & 20 amp receptacles), seasonal sites, a/c not allowed, heater not allowed, tenting available, group sites for tents, cabins, sewage disposal, laundry, public phone, limited grocery store, RV supplies, ice, tables, fire rings, wood.

◆◆◆RECREATION: rec room/area, coin games, salt water swimming, boating, canoeing, 1 row/2 canoe boat rentals, salt water/pond fishing, basketball hoop, playground, badminton, horseshoes, volleyball.

Open May 1 through Oct 15. Facilities fully operational May 15 through Oct 15. Rate in 1995 $17-23 per family. Reservations recommended Jul through Aug. Master Card/Visa accepted. Member of ARVC; MECOA. Phone: (207) 667-8826.
SEE AD ACADIA NATIONAL PARK PAGE 323

LAMOINE STATE PARK—*From jct US 1 & Hwy 184: Go 10 mi SE on Hwy 184.* FACILITIES: 61 sites, 20 ft. max RV length, 61 no hookups, tenting available, non-flush toilets, tables, fire rings. RECREATION: boating, ramp, dock, salt water fishing, playground, hiking trails. Open May 15 through Oct 15. No showers. Phone: (207) 667-4778.

**Patten Pond Camping Resort**—Lakeside CAMPGROUND with shaded sites near a major highway. *From jct Hwy 3/US 1 & US 1A: Go 7 1/2 mi S on US 1.* ◆◆◆FACILITIES: 145 sites, most common site width 30 feet, 105 water & elec (15,30 & 50 amp receptacles), 40 no hookups, seasonal sites, 35 pull-thrus, tenting available, sewage disposal, laundry, public phone, grocery store, ice, tables, fire rings, wood. ◆◆◆RECREATION: rec room/area, lake swimming, boating, canoeing, ramp, dock, 2 canoe/1 pedal boat rentals, lake/stream fishing, playground, badminton, sports field, horseshoes, hiking trails, volleyball. Open mid May through mid Oct. Rate in 1995 $12-19 per family. Member of ARVC; MECOA. Phone: (207) 667-5745. FCRV 10% discount.

**TIMBERLAND ACRES RV PARK**—Wooded, level sites. *From jct US 1A/US 1 & Hwy 3: Go 3 mi E on Hwy 3.*

WELCOME

◆◆◆FACILITIES: 175 sites, most common site width 24 feet, 87 full hookups, 54 water & elec (20,30 & 50 amp receptacles), 34 no hookups, seasonal sites, 18 pull-thrus, a/c allowed ($), heater allowed ($), tenting available, group sites for tents/RVs, RV storage, handicap restroom facilities, sewage disposal, laundry, public phone, limited grocery store, LP gas refill by weight/ by meter, ice, tables, fire rings, wood.

◆◆◆◆RECREATION: rec room/area, pavilion, coin games, swim pool, basketball hoop, playground, 2 shuffleboard courts, planned group activities, badminton, horseshoes, volleyball.

Open mid May through mid Oct. Rate in 1995 $14-20 for 4 persons. Reservations recommended Jul through Aug. Phone: (207) 667-3600.
SEE AD TRAVEL SECTION PAGE 320 AND AD BAR HARBOR PAGE 329

## FARMINGTON—D-2

✱ **GOOD TIMES UNLIMITED**—*From west jct Hwy 27 & US 2: Go 1 1/2 mi E on US 2.* SALES: travel trailers, park models, truck campers, 5th wheels, fold-down camping trailers. SERVICES: RV appliance mechanic full-time, emergency road service business hours, LP gas refill by weight/by meter, sells parts/accessories, sells camping supplies, installs hitches. Open all year. Discover/Master Card/ Visa accepted. Phone: (207) 778-3482.

WELCOME

SEE AD TRAVEL SECTION PAGE 322

**Nor'-40-Campsite**—Rural, wooded CAMPGROUND with open and shaded sites. *From jct Hwy 27 & US 2: Go 3 mi W on US 2, then 1 mi N on Red School House Rd.* ◆◆FACILITIES: 51 sites, most common site width 26 feet, 40 water & elec, 5 elec (15 amp receptacles), 6 no hookups, seasonal sites, 8 pull-thrus, tenting available, sewage disposal, laundry, public phone, limited grocery store, ice, tables, fire rings, wood. ◆◆◆RECREATION: swim pool, playground, tennis court, badminton, horseshoes, hiking trails, volleyball. Open May 15 through early Oct. Rate in 1995 $15 per family. Phone: (207) 778-6096.

FARMINGTON—Continued on next page

FARMINGTON—Continued

**TWIN POND CAMPGROUND**—Wooded sites next to a family fun center. *From west jct Hwy 27 & US 2: Go 3 mi W on US 2.*

◆◆FACILITIES: 61 sites, most common site width 22 feet, 2 full hookups, 39 water & elec (20 & 30 amp receptacles), 20 no hookups, a/c allowed, heater allowed, tenting available, cabins, sewage disposal, laundry, public phone, ice, tables, fire rings, wood.

◆◆◆◆RECREATION: rec room/area, coin games, swim pool, pond swimming, canoeing, 1 canoe/1 pedal boat rentals, mini-golf ($), basketball hoop, badminton, horseshoes, volleyball. Recreation open to the public.

Open mid May through mid Oct. Rate in 1995 $15-19 for 4 persons. American Express/Discover/ Master Card/Visa accepted. Phone: (207) 778-4977.

**SEE AD THIS PAGE**

## THE FORKS—C-2

**Indian Pond Campground**—Large, wooded, natural sites. *From jct US 201 (Kennebec Bridge) & Indian Pond Rd: Go 13 1/2 mi N on Indian Pond Rd.* ◆◆FACILITIES: 27 sites, most common site width 30 feet, 16 ft. max RV length, 27 no hookups, tenting available, non-flush toilets, sewage disposal, laundry, public phone, tables, fire rings, wood. ◆◆◆RECREATION: pond swimming, boating, canoeing, ramp, 6 canoe boat rentals, pond fishing. Recreation open to the public. Open mid May through mid Oct. Rate in 1995 $14 for 2 persons. Member of ARVC; MECOA. Phone: (800) 371-7774.

## FREEPORT—E-2

**Big Skye Acres Campground**—Open wooded CAMPGROUND in a rural setting. *From jct I-95 (exit 20): Follow signs to Bradbury Mountain State Park on Hwy 9, then continue 2 1/2 mi E on Hwy 9.* ◆◆FACILITIES: 80 sites, most common site width 30 feet, 7 full hookups, 73 water & elec (30 & 50 amp receptacles), seasonal sites, tenting available, sewage disposal, laundry, public phone, limited grocery store, ice, tables, fire rings, grills, wood. ◆◆◆◆RECREATION: rec hall, rec room/area, equipped pavilion, swim pool, playground, badminton, sports field, horseshoes, hiking trails, volleyball. Recreation open to the public. Open May 1 through Oct 1. Rate in 1995 $12-20 for 4 persons. Member of ARVC; MECOA. Phone: (207) 688-4147.

**BLUEBERRY POND CAMPGROUND**—Large, flat, secluded and open sites in a wooded CAMPGROUND. *From I-95 (exit 20) & Hwy 125/136: Go 2 1/2 mi N on Hwy 136, then 1 1/2 mi W on Poland Rd.*

◆◆FACILITIES: 35 sites, most common site width 46 feet, 10 full hookups, 5 water & elec (20 & 30 amp receptacles), 20 no hookups, a/c allowed ($), heater allowed ($), tenting available, group sites for tents, handicap restroom facilities, sewage disposal, public phone, tables, fire rings, wood.

◆◆RECREATION: swim pool, playground, badminton, horseshoes, hiking trails.

Open May 15 through Oct 15. Rate in 1995 $14-17 per vehicle. Member of ARVC; MECOA. Phone: (207) 688-4421.

**SEE AD THIS PAGE**

**CEDAR HAVEN CAMPGROUND**—Family CAMPGROUND with level, open and shaded sites. *From jct I-95 (exit 20) & Hwy 125: Go 1 1/2 mi N on Hwy 125, then 1/4 mi NE on Baker Rd.*

◆◆◆FACILITIES: 58 sites, most common site width 24 feet, 4 full hookups, 44 water & elec (20 & 30 amp receptacles), 10 no hookups, seasonal sites, a/c allowed ($), heater allowed ($), tenting available, RV rentals, sewage disposal, laundry, public phone, grocery store, RV supplies, LP gas refill by meter, ice, tables, grills, wood.

◆◆◆RECREATION: rec room/area, pond swimming, mini-golf ($), basketball hoop, playground, badminton, horseshoes, volleyball.

Open May 1 through late Oct. Rate in 1995 $14-20 per family. No refunds. Reservations recommended Jul through Aug. Master Card/Visa accepted. Member of ARVC; MECOA. Phone: (207) 865-6254.

**SEE AD THIS PAGE**

FREEPORT—Continued

**DESERT DUNES OF MAINE**—CAMPGROUND adjacent to a natural desert surrounded by a forest. *From jct I-95 (exit 19) & Desert Rd: Go 2 mi W on Desert Rd.*

◆◆FACILITIES: 50 sites, most common site width 22 feet, 4 full hookups, 31 water & elec, 6 elec (15,20 & 30 amp receptacles), 9 no hookups, a/c allowed ($), heater allowed ($), tenting available, group sites for RVs, handicap restroom facilities, sewage disposal, laundry, public phone, grocery store, RV supplies, LP gas refill by meter, ice, tables, wood.

◆◆RECREATION: hiking trails, local tours. Recreation open to the public.

Open early May through mid Oct. Rate in 1995 $14-21 for 2 persons. American Express/Discover/ Master Card/Visa accepted. Phone: (207) 865-6962.

**SEE AD TRAVEL SECTION PAGE 322**

**DESERT OF MAINE**—*From jct I-95 (exit 19) & Desert Rd: Go 2 mi W on Desert Rd.* A natural desert surrounded by natural forest. Open early May through mid Oct. Phone: (207) 865-6962.

**SEE AD TRAVEL SECTION PAGE 322**

**Durham Leisure Center & Campground**—Large wooded sites with an indoor recreation area. *From jct I-95 (exit 20) & Hwy 136: Go 5 1/2 mi N on Hwy 136.* ◆◆◆FACILITIES: 38 sites, most common site width 28 feet, 13 full hookups, 25 water & elec (20 & 30 amp receptacles), 6 pull-thrus, tenting available, sewage disposal, laundry, limited grocery store, LP gas refill by weight/by meter, ice, tables, fire rings, wood. ◆◆◆RECREATION: rec room/area, swim pool (indoor) (heated), horseshoes. Recreation open to the public. Open all year. Pool closed Nov 15 through Feb 14. Rate in 1995 $17-20 per family. Phone: (207) 353-4353.

**FLYING POINT CAMPGROUND**—A CAMPGROUND with open sites directly on the ocean. *From jct I-95 (exit 19) & US 1: Go 1 1/2 mi N on US 1, then 3 3/4 mi E on Bow St (Flying Point Rd), then 100 feet S on Lower Flying Point Rd.*

◆◆◆FACILITIES: 42 sites, most common site width 28 feet, 36 water & elec (30 amp receptacles), 6 no hookups, seasonal sites, a/c allowed ($), heater allowed ($), tenting available, sewage disposal, public phone, ice, tables, fire rings, wood.

◆RECREATION: salt water swimming, boating, ramp, salt water fishing, badminton, horseshoes.

Open May 1 through Oct 15. Rate in 1995 $18-20 per family. Reservations recommended Jul through Aug. Master Card/Visa accepted. Member of ARVC; MECOA. Phone: (207) 865-4569.

**SEE AD THIS PAGE**

RECOMPENCE SHORE CAMPSITES (University of Maine)—*From jct I-95 (exit 19) & US 1: Go 1 1/2 mi N on US 1, then 2 1/4 mi E on Bow St (Flying Point Rd), then 2 4/10 mi S on Wolf's Neck Rd.* FACILITIES: 103 sites, 8 water & elec (20 amp receptacles), 95 no hookups, tenting available, sewage disposal, public phone, ice, tables, fire rings, grills, wood. RECREATION: salt water swimming, salt water fishing, playground, badminton, sports field, horseshoes, hiking trails, volleyball. Open mid May through mid Oct. Member of ARVC; MECOA. Phone: (207) 865-9307.

## FRYEBURG—E-1

**Canal Bridge Campground**—A riverside CAMPGROUND with sandy beach. *From jct US 302 & Hwy 5: Go 3 mi N on Hwy 5.* ◆◆FACILITIES: 45 sites, most common site width 40 feet, 20 water & elec (15 & 20 amp receptacles), 25 no hookups, tenting available, sewage disposal, public phone, limited grocery store, ice, tables, fire rings, wood. ◆◆◆RECREATION: river swimming, canoeing, river fishing, playground, badminton,

CANAL BRIDGE CAMPGROUND—Continued on next page
FRYEBURG—Continued on next page

FRYEBURG—Continued
CANAL BRIDGE CAMPGROUND—Continued

horseshoes, hiking trails, volleyball. Open mid May through mid Oct. Rate in 1995 $14-16 for 2 persons. Member of ARVC;MECOA. Phone: (207) 935-2286.

**ZEN FARM RV RESORT** (TOO NEW TO RATE) —Level sites with a resort atmosphere. *From jct US 302 & Hwy 5: Go 4 mi N on Hwy 5, then 1 1/2 mi W on Fish St.*

FACILITIES: 68 sites, 40 water & elec (20,30 & 50 amp receptacles), 28 no hookups, 10 pull-thrus, a/c allowed, heater allowed, tenting available, group sites for tents/RVs, handicap restroom facilities, sewage disposal, public phone, grocery store, RV supplies, ice, tables, fire rings, wood.

RECREATION: rec room/area, river/pond fishing, hiking trails, cross country skiing, snowmobile trails.

Open all year. Facilities fully operational mid Apr through mid Oct. Rate in 1995 $14.95-24.95 per family. Reservations recommended Jul. American Express/Discover/Master Card/Visa accepted. Phone: (207) 697-2000.

**SEE AD THIS PAGE**

## GARDINER—E-2

**KOA-AUGUSTA/GARDINER**—A semi-wooded, family oriented CAMPGROUND. *From jct I-95 (exit 27) & US 201: Go 2 mi S on US 201.*

◆◆◆FACILITIES: 85 sites, most common site width 28 feet, 28 full hookups, 46 water & elec (20,30 & 50 amp receptacles), 11 no hookups, 63 pull-thrus, a/c allowed ($), heater allowed ($), phone hookups, tenting available, cabins, sewage disposal, laundry, public phone, grocery store, RV supplies, LP gas refill by weight/by meter, ice, tables, fire rings, wood.

◆◆◆RECREATION: rec room/area, equipped pavilion, coin games, swim pool, lake swimming, boating, canoeing, 2 row/2 canoe boat rentals, lake fishing, basketball hoop, playground, badminton, sports field, horseshoes, volleyball.

Open May 20 through Oct 15. Rate in 1995 $17.50-23.50 for 2 persons. Reservations recommended Jul through Aug. Discover/Master Card/Visa accepted. Member of ARVC; MECOA. Phone: (800) 562-1496. KOA 10% value card discount.

**SEE AD THIS PAGE AND AD FRONT OF BOOK PAGES 68 AND 69**

## GEORGETOWN—E-2

**Camp Seguin**—Oceanfront, wooded CAMPGROUND. *From south city limits: Go 11 3/4 mi SE on Hwy 127, then 2 mi S on Reid State Park Rd.* ◆◆FACILITIES: 30 sites, most common site width 30 feet, 22 ft. max RV length, 8 water & elec (15 amp receptacles), 22 no hookups, tenting available, sewage disposal, public phone, limited grocery store, ice, tables, fire rings, wood. ◆◆RECREATION: rec room/area, salt water fishing, playground. Open Memorial Day through Columbus Day. Rate in 1995 $15-21 per family. Member of ARVC; MECOA. Phone: (207) 371-2777.

## GRAY—E-2

**TWIN BROOKS CAMPING AREA**—Rural CAMPGROUND on a lake shore with shaded sites. *From jct US 202 & Hwy 26: Go 2 1/2 mi N on Hwy 26, then 1 mi W on Raymond Rd, then 1 mi S on Egypt Rd, then 1/2 mi E on Campground Rd.*

◆◆FACILITIES: 43 sites, most common site width 30 feet, 10 full hookups, 28 water & elec (15 & 20 amp receptacles), 5 no hookups, seasonal sites, a/c allowed ($), heater allowed ($), tenting available, sewage disposal, ice, tables, wood.

◆◆◆RECREATION: lake swimming, boating, ramp, dock, 1 row/6 canoe boat rentals, lake fishing, basketball hoop, badminton, horseshoes, volleyball.

Open Memorial Day through Sep 15. Rate in 1995 $13-18 per family. Master Card/Visa accepted. Member of ARVC; MECOA. Phone: (207) 428-3832.

**SEE AD THIS PAGE**

## GREENE—E-2

**Allen Pond Campground**—Secluded wooded sites on the side of a hill sloping to the pond. *From jct US 202 & Allen Pond Rd: Go 5 mi N on Allen Pond Rd, then 1 mi N on N Mountain Rd.* ◆◆FACILITIES: 65 sites, most common site width 26 feet, 20 ft. max RV length, 55 water & elec (30 amp receptacles), 10 no hookups, seasonal sites, tenting available, sewage disposal, laundry, public phone, grocery store, ice, tables, wood. ◆◆◆RECREATION: pond swimming, boating, canoeing, dock, 2 row/11 canoe/2 pedal boat rentals, pond fishing, mini-golf ($), playground, planned group activities, sports field, horseshoes, hiking trails, volleyball. Recreation open to the public. Open mid May through Sep 30. Rate in 1995 $13.50-17.50 per family. No refunds. Member of ARVC;MECOA. Phone: (207) 946-7439.

## GREENVILLE—C-3

**CASEY'S SPENCER BAY CAMPS**—Wilderness CAMPGROUND on a large lake with waterfront sites for tents and trailers with limited generated electricity. *From Hwy 6/15 & Ripogenus Dam Rd: Go 12 mi N on Ripogenus Dam Rd, then 6 mi W on campground road.*

GREENVILLE—Continued
CASEY'S SPENCER BAY CAMPS—Continued

◆◆FACILITIES: 65 sites, most common site width 30 feet, 10 full hookups, 11 elec (15 & 20 amp receptacles), 44 no hookups, a/c not allowed, heater not allowed, tenting available, cabins, sewage disposal, limited grocery store, marine gas, ice, tables, fire rings, wood.

CASEY'S SPENCER BAY CAMP—Continued on next page
GREENVILLE—Continued on next page

GREENVILLE—Continued
CASEY'S SPENCER BAY CAMPS—Continued

◊◊◊RECREATION: lake swimming, boating, canoeing, ramp, dock, 7 canoe/10 motor boat rentals, lake fishing, fishing guides, 15 bike rentals, horseshoes, hiking trails, volleyball.

Open mid May through mid Oct. Rate in 1995 $14-18 per family. No refunds. Phone: (207) 695-2801.

**SEE AD PAGE 339**

LILY BAY STATE PARK (Moosehead Lake)—*From town: Go 9 mi NE on county road.* FACILITIES: 93 sites, 93 no hookups, tenting available, non-flush toilets, sewage disposal, public phone, tables, wood. RECREATION: lake swimming, boating, ramp, dock, lake fishing, playground, hiking trails. Open May 1 through Oct 15. No showers. Phone: (207) 695-2700.

**MOOSEHEAD FAMILY CAMPGROUND**—Campground located near town. *From town jct Main St & Hwy 6/15: Go 1 mi S on Hwy 6/15.*

◊◊FACILITIES: 40 sites, most common site width 50 feet, 14 water & elec (20,30 & 50 amp receptacles), 26 no hookups, a/c allowed, heater not allowed, tenting available, group sites for tents, marine toilets, sewage disposal, ice, tables, fire rings, wood.

RECREATION: rec room/area, coin games, playground.

Open May 1 through Feb 28. Rate in 1995 $14 for 2 persons. Master Card/Visa accepted. Phone: (207) 695-2210.

**SEE AD TRAVEL SECTION PAGE 322**

**MOOSEHEAD MARINE MUSEUM/KATAHDIN CRUISES**—*From jct Lily Bay Rd & Hwy 6/15: Go 1/2 block N on Lily Bay Rd.* A scenic relaxing voyage on board a historic lake steamer on Moosehead Lake. Open Memorial Day through first weekend Oct. Master Card/Visa accepted. Phone: (207) 695-2716.

**SEE AD TRAVEL SECTION PAGE 322**

## HANOVER—D-1

**STONY BROOK RECREATION**—A CAMPGROUND with large open & wooded sites. *From jct Hwy 26 & US 2: Go 1 mi E on US 2.*

◊◊◊FACILITIES: 33 sites, most common site width 30 feet, 6 full hookups, 16 water & elec (20 & 30 amp receptacles), 11 no hookups, seasonal sites, a/c allowed ($), heater allowed ($), tenting available, group sites for tents/RVs, sewage disposal, laundry, public phone, limited grocery store, ice, tables, fire rings, wood.

◊◊◊RECREATION: rec hall, rec room/area, coin games, swim pool, mini-golf ($), basketball hoop,





HANOVER—Continued
STONY BROOK RECREATION—Continued

playground, 2 shuffleboard courts, badminton, sports field, horseshoes, hiking trails, volleyball, cross country skiing, snowmobile trails.

Open all year. Facilities fully operational mid May through mid Oct. Rate in 1995 $14-18 for 2 persons. Member of ARVC;MECOA. Phone: (207) 824-2836.

**SEE AD BETHEL PAGE 331**

## HARRINGTON—D-4

**Sunset Pointe Campground**—Scenic location with open and grassy sites on a salt river. *From jct US 1A & US 1: Go 3/4 mi N on US 1, then 3 mi E on Marshville Rd.* ◊◊ FACILITIES: 30 sites, most common site width 22 feet, 5 full hookups, 15 water & elec (15 amp receptacles), 10 no hookups, tenting available, sewage disposal, limited grocery store, tables, fire rings, wood. Open May 15 through Oct 15. Rate in 1995 $11-14 for 2 persons. Phone: (207) 483-4412.

## HARRISON—E-1

**Bear Mountain Village Cabins & Campground**—A wooded CAMPGROUND on a lake. *From jct Hwy 117 & Hwy 35: Go 3 mi NW on Hwy 35, then 1/4 mi SW on Hwy 37.* ◊◊FACILITIES: 68 sites, most common site width 28 feet, 65 water & elec (15 amp receptacles), 3 no hookups, tenting available, sewage disposal, laundry, public phone, limited grocery store, ice, tables, fire rings, wood. ◊◊◊RECREATION: rec room/area, lake swimming, boating, canoeing, 3 row/3 canoe/4 pedal boat rentals, lake/river fishing, playground, badminton, sports field, horseshoes, volleyball. Open mid May through Oct 15. Rate in 1995 $10-25 per family. Member of ARVC; MECOA. Phone: (207) 583-2541.

**Vacationland Campsites**—Wooded, lakeside CAMPGROUND with open and shaded sites. *From jct Hwy 35 & Hwy 117: Go 2 mi N on Hwy 117, then 1/2 mi NW on Deer Rd, then 1 mi S on CR.* ◊◊FACILITIES: 125 sites, most common site width 26 feet, 15 full hookups, 110 water & elec (15 & 20 amp receptacles), seasonal sites, tenting available, sewage disposal, laundry, public phone, limited grocery store, LP gas refill by weight, ice, tables, fire rings, wood. ◊◊◊RECREATION: rec room/area, lake swimming, boating, 3 row/1 pedal boat rentals, lake fishing, playground, badminton, sports field, horseshoes, volleyball. Open all year. Facilities fully operational May 15 through Sep 15. Rate in 1995 $20 per family. No refunds. Member of ARVC; MECOA. Phone: (207) 583-4953.

## HEBRON—E-2

**HEBRON PINES CAMPGROUND**—Open and wooded sites on a 400 acre farm. *From Hwy 119 & Hwy 124: Go 2 1/2 mi N on Hwy 124.*

◊◊FACILITIES: 32 sites, most common site width 40 feet, 20 water & elec, 8 elec (20 & 30 amp receptacles), 4 no hookups, seasonal sites, 5 pull-thrus, a/c allowed ($), heater allowed ($), tenting available, group sites for tents/RVs, sewage disposal, public phone, limited grocery store, ice, tables, fire rings, wood.

◊◊◊RECREATION: rec hall, coin games, swim pool, stream fishing, basketball hoop, playground, planned group activities (weekends only), badminton, horseshoes, hiking trails, volleyball.

Open mid May through mid Sep. Rate in 1995 $14 per family. Master Card/Visa accepted. Phone: (207) 966-2179.

**SEE AD AUBURN PAGE 324**

**MAINE**

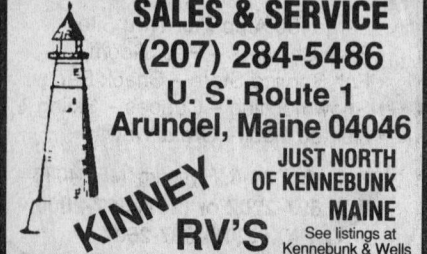

**The entire state of Maine used to belong to just one family! Purchased in 1677 by the Massachusetts Colony for a mere $6000, it remained part of Massachusetts until it became a state in 1820.**

## HOULTON—B-4

**MY BROTHERS PLACE**—A CAMPGROUND with grassy sites. *From jct I-95 (exit 62) & US 1: Go 2 mi N on US 1.*

◊◊FACILITIES: 100 sites, most common site width 28 feet, 21 full hookups, 57 water & elec (15 amp receptacles), 22 no hookups, 31 pull-thrus, a/c allowed, heater not allowed, tenting available, group sites for tents/RVs, sewage disposal, laundry, public phone, ice, tables, fire rings, wood.

◊◊RECREATION: rec hall, coin games, basketball hoop, horseshoes, volleyball.

Open May 15 through Oct 15. Rate in 1995 $14.50-15.50 per family. Master Card/Visa accepted. Phone: (207) 532-6739.

**SEE AD THIS PAGE**

## ISLAND FALLS—B-4

**Birch Point Lodge Campground & Cottage Resort**—Lakeside location with open and shaded sites. *From jct I-95 & Hwy 159: Go 1/2 mi E on Hwy 159, then 3 mi E on US 2, then 1 1/2 mi E on Pleasant Lake Rd.* ◊◊FACILITIES: 65 sites, most common site width 18 feet, 8 full hookups, 57 water & elec (15 & 20 amp receptacles), seasonal sites, 25 pull-thrus, tenting available, sewage disposal, laundry, public phone, limited grocery store, ice, tables, fire rings, wood. ◊◊◊RECREATION: rec room/area, lake swimming, boating, canoeing, ramp, 2 canoe/5 pedal/4 motor boat rentals, lake fishing, playground, horseshoes, volleyball. Recreation open to the public. Open all year. Facilities fully operational May 14 through Oct 1. Rate in 1995 $16-18.25 per family. Member of ARVC; MECOA. Phone: (207) 463-2515.

## JACKMAN—C-2

**Jackman Landing Campground**—Open, level sites on a river. *From jct Hwy 6/15 & US 201: Go 1 1/2 mi N on US 201.* ◊◊◊FACILITIES: 25 sites, most common site width 28 feet, 16 water & elec (20 & 30 amp receptacles), 9 no hookups, tenting available, laundry, tables, fire rings, wood. ◊◊RECREATION: boating, canoeing, ramp, dock, 6 canoe/2 motor boat rentals, lake fishing. Open mid May through Oct 31. Rate in 1995 $15 per family. Phone: (207) 668-3301.

**John's Trailer Park & Four Season Campground**—Wooded private setting in town. *From jct Hwy 6/15 & US 201: Go 1/2 mi N on US 201.* ◊◊FACILITIES: 12 sites, most common site width 20 feet, 6 elec (20 & 30 amp receptacles), 6 no hookups, tenting available, sewage disposal, laundry, tables. ◊RECREATION: rec hall, rec room/area. Open all year. Rate in 1995 $13 per family. Phone: (207) 668-7683.

**Loon Echo Campground**—Wilderness sites on a lake. *From the Forks Bridge & US 201: Go 16 mi N on US 201.* ◊◊FACILITIES: 20 sites, most common site width 30 feet, 30 ft. max RV length, 20 no hookups, tenting available, sewage disposal, ice, tables, fire rings, wood. ◊◊◊RECREATION: river swimming, boating, canoeing, ramp, dock, 4 canoe boat rentals, lake/stream fishing, badminton, horseshoes, hiking trails, volleyball. Open May 1 through early Dec. After Oct 1, by reservation only. Rate in 1995 $12 per family. Member of ARVC; MECOA. Phone: (207) 668-4829.

**Moose River Campground**—Riverside CAMPGROUND near a major highway. *From jct Hwy 6/15 & US 201: Go 2 mi N on US 201/Hwy 6, then 1 1/2 mi E on Nichols Rd.* ◊◊◊FACILITIES: 52 sites, most common site width 22 feet, 11 full hookups, 26 water & elec, 2 elec (15,20 & 30 amp receptacles), 13 no hookups, 6 pull-thrus, tenting available, sewage disposal, laundry, public phone, limited grocery store, ice, tables, fire rings, wood. ◊◊◊RECREATION: rec room/area, swim pool (heated), boating, no motors, canoeing, 6 canoe/2 pedal boat rentals, river/pond fishing ($), playground, badminton, horseshoes, hiking trails, volleyball. Recreation open to the public. Open May 15 through Nov 1. Rate in 1995 $12-17 per family. Member of ARVC; MECOA. Phone: (207) 668-3341.

## JONESBORO—D-5

**Sunkhaze Campground**—An open, grassy location. *From West city limits: Go 1 mi W on US 1.* ◊◊FACILITIES: 30 sites, most common site width 26 feet, 20 water & elec (15 amp receptacles), 10 no hookups, 20 pull-thrus, tenting available, public phone, ice, tables, fire rings, wood. ◊RECREATION: swim pool. Open May 15 through Oct 15. Rate in 1995 $11.50-13.50 for 2 persons. Phone: (207) 434-2542.

## KENNEBUNK—F-1

**Fran-Mort Campground**—Flat, grassy, rural setting with most sites occupied by seasonal campers. *From jct Hwy 35/9A & US 1: Go 1 1/2 mi N on US 1, then 2 1/4 mi E on a blacktop road.* ◊◊◊FACILITIES: 108

FRAN-MORT CAMPGROUND—Continued on next page
**KENNEBUNK**—Continued on next page

ME *Explore the outdoors at the Fall Harvest Camping Festival!* *See article at front of book.* ME

KENNEBUNK—Continued
FRAN-MORT CAMPGROUND—Continued

sites, most common site width 35 feet, 75 full hookups, 33 water & elec (20 & 30 amp receptacles), seasonal sites, 9 pull-thrus, tenting available, sewage disposal, laundry, public phone, tables, fire rings. ◆RECREATION: planned group activities (weekends only), horseshoes. Open May 12 through Oct 12. Rate in 1995 $14. No refunds. Phone: (207) 967-4927.

✽ **KINNEY RV'S SALES & SERVICE**—*From jct I-95 (exit 3) & Hwy 35: Go 1 1/2 mi S on Hwy 35, then 4 3/4 mi N on US 1.* SALES: travel trailers, park models, motor homes, fold-down camping trailers. SERVICES: Engine/Chassis & RV appliance mechanic full-time, emergency road service business hours, LP gas refill by meter, sells parts/accessories, installs hitches. Open all year. Discover/Master Card/Visa accepted. Phone: (207) 284-5486.
**SEE AD PAGE 340**

**Mousam River Campground**—Large, shaded sites. *From jct US 1 & Hwy 35: Go 2 mi NW on Hwy 35 to a fork, bear left after overpass, do not follow Hwy 35, then 1 1/2 mi.* ◆◆◆FACILITIES: 115 sites, most common site width 30 feet, 115 full hookups, (20,30 & 50 amp receptacles), seasonal sites, tenting available, sewage disposal, laundry, limited grocery store, ice, tables, fire rings, wood. ◆◆RECREATION: rec room/area, pavilion, swim pool, badminton, horseshoes. Open May 15 through Oct 15. Rate in 1995 $20 for 2 persons. No refunds. Member of ARVC; MECOA. Phone: (207) 985-2507.

## KENNEBUNKPORT—F-2

**KENNEBUNKPORT CAMPING**—A CAMPGROUND with a natural wooded setting. *From jct Hwy 35/9A & Hwy 9: Go 2 mi E on Hwy 9, then 1/10 mi N on Old Cape Rd.*

◆◆FACILITIES: 82 sites, most common site width 30 feet, 33 full hookups, 26 water & elec (20 & 30 amp receptacles), 23 no hookups, seasonal sites, a/c allowed, heater not allowed, tenting available, group sites for tents, sewage disposal, public phone, limited grocery store, RV supplies, ice, tables, fire rings, wood.

◆◆RECREATION: playground, badminton, horseshoes, volleyball.

Open May 15 through Oct 15. Rate in 1995 $12-20 per family. No refunds. Master Card/Visa accepted. Member of ARVC; MECOA. Phone: (207) 967-2732.
**SEE AD THIS PAGE**

**Salty Acres Camp Grounds**—Spacious, wooded sites. *From jct Hwy 35/9A & Hwy 9: Go 5 mi E on Hwy 9.* ◆◆FACILITIES: 400 sites, 70 full hookups, 90 water & elec (15,20 & 30 amp receptacles), 240 no hookups, seasonal sites, tenting available, sewage disposal, laundry, public phone, limited grocery store, ice, tables, fire rings, wood. ◆◆RECREATION: swim pool, salt water/river fishing, playground, sports field, horseshoes, volleyball. Open May 15 through Oct 15. Rate in 1995 $17-22 for 2 persons. Member of ARVC; MECOA. Phone: (207) 967-8623.

## KINGFIELD—D-2

**DEER FARM CAMPS & CAMPGROUND**—Wooded wilderness sites. *From jct Hwy 27 & Hwy 16: Go 1 mi N on Hwy 16, then 2 1/2 mi W on Tufts Pond Rd.*

◆◆◆FACILITIES: 47 sites, most common site width 30 feet, 47 water & elec (20 & 30 amp receptacles), seasonal sites, a/c allowed ($), heater allowed ($), tenting available, cabins, sewage disposal, laundry, public phone, limited grocery store, ice, tables, grills, wood.

◆◆◆RECREATION: rec room/area, pond swimming, boating, canoeing, dock, 2 row/1 canoe boat rentals, pond fishing, playground, badminton, horseshoes, hiking trails, volleyball.

**KENNEBUNKPORT CAMPING**

MINUTES TO BEACHES
SHADY SITES
FULL FACILITIES

117 Old Cape Rd.
Kennebunkport, ME 04046
(207) 967-2732 • FAX: (207) 967-3519

KINGFIELD—Continued
DEER FARM CAMPS & CAMPGROUND—Continued

Open mid May through Columbus Day. Rate in 1995 $13 per family. Member of ARVC; MECOA. Phone: (207) 265-4599.
**SEE AD THIS PAGE**

## KOKADJO—C-3

**Northern Pride Lodge & Campground**—Spacious, wooded sites on a lake with a rustic atmosphere. *From jct Hwy 6/15 & Kokadjo Rd: Go 18 1/2 mi N on Kokadjo Rd.* ◆◆FACILITIES: 24 sites, most common site width 24 feet, 24 no hookups, tenting available, non-flush toilets, tables, fire rings, wood. ◆◆RECREATION: lake swimming, boating, canoeing, ramp, dock, 4 canoe/5 motor boat rentals, lake fishing. Open May 1 through Nov 1. Rate in 1995 $16 per family. Phone: (207) 695-2890.

## LEEDS—E-2

**Riverbend Campground**—A rural location with large, open and shaded sites on a river. *From jct US 202 & Hwy 106: Go 7 1/2 mi N on Hwy 106.* ◆◆FACILITIES: 80 sites, most common site width 30 feet, 60 water & elec (15,20 & 30 amp receptacles), 20 no hookups, seasonal sites, 12 pull-thrus, tenting available, sewage disposal, public phone, grocery store, LP gas refill by weight/by meter, ice, tables, fire rings, wood. ◆◆◆RECREATION: rec room/area, pavilion, swim pool, river swimming, boating, canoeing, ramp, dock, 1 row/1 canoe/1 motor boat rentals, river fishing, playground, planned group activities (weekends only), badminton, sports field, horseshoes, volleyball. Open May 1 through Sep 30. Rate in 1995 $13.50-18.50 per family. No refunds. Member of ARVC; MECOA. Phone: (207) 524-5711.

## LEWISTON—E-2

**BEAVER BROOK CAMPING AREA**—*From jct Hwy 196 & US 202: Go 15 mi E on US 202, then 3 mi NW on Wilson Pond Rd.*
**SEE PRIMARY LISTING AT NORTH MONMOUTH AND AD NORTH MONMOUTH PAGE 345**

✽ **MOUNTAIN ROAD RV**—*From jct US 202 & Hwy 126: Go 8 1/2 mi E on Hwy 126 (100 feet past Hwy 197), then 1/4 mi N on Dealer Rd.*
**SEE PRIMARY LISTING AT SABATTUS AND AD THIS PAGE**

## LIBERTY—E-3

LAKE ST. GEORGE STATE PARK—*In town on Hwy 3.* FACILITIES: 38 sites, 38 no hookups, tenting available, sewage disposal, grills. RECREATION: lake swimming, boating, ramp, lake fishing. Open May 15 through Sep 30. Phone: (207) 589-4255.

**Pine Ridge Campground & Cabins**◆◆◆—Open & wooded sites convenient to major highway. *From jct Hwy 220 & Hwy 3: Go 1 1/2 mi E on Hwy 3.* ◆◆FACILITIES: 35 sites, most common site width 22 feet, 9 full hookups, 8 water & elec (15 & 20 amp receptacles), 18 no hookups, seasonal sites, tenting available, sewage disposal, laundry, public phone, limited grocery store, ice, tables, fire rings, wood. ◆◆◆RECREATION: rec hall,

**Rol-lin Hills** *A Quiet Family Oriented Lake View Park*

Campground

- 30 Sites
- Water & Electric
- 20 & 30 Amp.
- Tenting Available
- Flush Toilets & Hot Showers
- Laundry
- Swimming Pool
- Volleyball
- Playground
- Hayrides *and more.....*

Near: Norlands Living History Center, Golf, & Shopping

**(207) 897-6394 or (207) 897-3802**
**RR 2, Box 3300, Livermore Falls, ME 04254**
Not visited by Woodall Publications Corp.

LIBERTY—Continued
PINE RIDGE CAMPGROUND & CABINS—Continued

swim pool (heated), 2 canoe boat rentals, playground, planned group activities (weekends only), badminton, sports field, horseshoes, hiking trails, volleyball. Open all year. Facilities fully operational mid May through mid Sep. Rate in 1995 $15 for 4 persons. Phone: (207) 589-4352.

## LINCOLNVILLE—E-3

**Old Massachusetts Homestead**—A wooded CAMPGROUND near the ocean. *From jct Hwy 173 & US 1: Go 2 mi N on US 1.* ◆◆◆FACILITIES: 68 sites, most common site width 40 feet, 10 full hookups, 33 water & elec (20 & 30 amp receptacles), 25 no hookups, seasonal sites, 16 pull-thrus, tenting available, sewage disposal, laundry, public phone, ice, tables, fire rings, wood. ◆◆RECREATION: rec hall, swim pool, horseshoes, hiking trails, volleyball. Open May 1 through Nov 1. Rate in 1995 $17-19 for 4 persons. No refunds. Member of ARVC;MECOA. Phone: (207) 789-5135.

## LIVERMORE FALLS—E-2

**ROL-LIN HILLS CAMPGROUND** (NOT VISITED)—*4 mi S off Hwy 4.*

FACILITIES: 30 sites, 25 water & elec (20 & 30 amp receptacles), 5 no hookups.

Open mid May through mid Sep. Rate in 1995 $13-15 for 4 persons. Phone: (207) 897-6394.
**SEE AD THIS PAGE**

## LOCKE MILLS—E-1

**Littlefield Beaches**—Rural, lakeside CAMPGROUND with a large swimming beach. *From east city limits: Go 1 mi E on Hwy 26.* ◆◆FACILITIES: 130 sites, most common site width 28 feet, 8 full hookups, 118 water & elec (15 amp receptacles), 4 no hookups, seasonal sites, 50 pull-thrus, tenting available, sewage disposal, laundry, public phone, grocery store, LP gas refill by weight, ice, tables, fire rings, wood. ◆◆◆RECREATION: rec hall, lake swimming, boating, ramp, dock, 4 row/5 canoe boat rentals, lake fishing, mini-golf ($), playground, badminton, horseshoes, volleyball. Open late May through Oct 1. Rate in 1995 $14-17 per family. Member of ARVC;MECOA. Phone: (207) 875-3290.

**A Polar Bear can swim without stopping for a 100 miles.**

**Deer Farm**
Camps & Campground
*On Tufts Pond Rd.*

*In The Beautiful Western Mountains, Sugarloaf Area*

- Close to Appalachian Trail and 4,000 foot peaks
- Friendly, relaxed atmosphere
- Log Cabins available year round

**(207) 265-4599** **R.R. 1, Box 2405, Kingfield, ME 04947**

## LOVELL—E-1

**KEZAR LAKE CAMPING AREA**—CAMPGROUND with many lakefront sites and activities. *From jct Hwy 93 & Hwy 5: Go 2 mi N on Hwy 5, then 3 mi W on West Lovell Rd.*

◆◆◆FACILITIES: 120 sites, most common site width 28 feet, 114 water & elec (20 & 30 amp receptacles), 6 no hookups, seasonal sites, 10 pull-thrus, a/c allowed, heater allowed, tenting available, group sites for RVs, RV rentals, RV storage, sewage disposal, laundry, public phone, grocery store, RV supplies, LP gas refill by weight/by meter, marine gas, ice, tables, fire rings, wood.

◆◆◆◆◆RECREATION: rec hall, rec room/area, coin games, lake swimming, boating, canoeing, ramp, dock, 1 row/6 canoe/3 pedal/6 motor boat rentals, float trips, lake fishing, fishing guides, basketball hoop, playground, shuffleboard court, planned group activities, movies, recreation director, badminton, horseshoes, motorbike trails, hiking trails, volleyball, snowmobile trails, local tours.

Open May 1 through Nov 1. Winter reservations required. Rate in 1995 $16-31 per family. Reservations recommended Memorial Day through Labor Day. American Express/Discover/Master Card/Visa accepted. Member of ARVC; MECOA. Phone: (207) 925-1631.

**SEE AD TRAVEL SECTION PAGE 317 AND AD THIS PAGE**

## LUBEC—D-5

**South Bay Campground**—A family oriented park. *From jct US 1 & Hwy 189: Go 6 1/4 mi NE on Hwy 189.* ◆◆FACILITIES: 32 sites, most common site width 24 feet, 17 water & elec (20 & 30 amp receptacles), 15 no hookups, tenting available, sewage disposal, public phone, ice, tables, fire rings, wood. ◆◆RECREATION: rec room/area, playground, horseshoes, volleyball. Open mid May through mid Oct. Rate in 1995 $10-14.50 for 4 persons. Member of ARVC; MECOA. Phone: (207) 733-4359.

**Sunset Point RV Trailer Park**—Oceanview CAMPGROUND with open sites. *From jct US 1 & Hwy 189: Go 9 mi NE on Hwy 189.* ◆◆◆FACILITIES: 40 sites, most common site width 18 feet, 30 water & elec (20 & 30 amp receptacles), 10 no hookups, 12 pull-thrus, tenting available, sewage disposal, laundry, public phone, LP gas refill by weight/by meter, ice, tables, fire rings, wood. ◆RECREATION: salt water swimming, salt water/pond fishing, badminton, horseshoes. Open May 20 through mid Oct. Rate in 1995 $12-16 for 4 persons. Member of ARVC;MECOA. Phone: (207) 733-2150.

## MADISON—D-2

**Sandy Beach Campground**—Wooded sites with a beach. *From jct Hwy 148 & US 201: Go 3 mi N on US 201.* ◆◆◆FACILITIES: 72 sites, most common site width 24 feet, 23 full hookups, 49 water & elec (20 & 30 amp receptacles), seasonal sites, tenting available, sewage disposal, laundry, public phone, grocery store, ice, tables, fire rings, wood. ◆◆◆◆RECREATION: rec hall, rec room/area, lake swimming, boating, canoeing, ramp, dock, 1 row/4 canoe/2 pedal boat rentals, lake/stream fishing, playground, planned group activities, badminton, horseshoes, hiking trails, volleyball. Recreation open to the public. Open Memorial Day through Oct 1. Rate in 1995 $16.50 per family. No refunds. Phone: (207) 474-5975.

**Smitty's Campground**—Level sites in a CAMPGROUND with a huge pool. *From jct US 201A & Hwy 148: Go 1 mi E on Hwy 148, then 1/4 mi S on Shusta Rd.* ◆◆FACILITIES: 35 sites, most common site width 24 feet, 8 full hookups, 27 water & elec (15,20 & 30 amp receptacles), tenting available, sewage disposal, ice, tables, fire rings, wood. ◆◆◆RECREATION: rec hall, rec room/area, swim pool, playground, planned group activities (weekends only), sports field, horseshoes, volleyball. Recreation open to the public. Open May 15 through mid Oct. Rate in 1995 $12-13 per family. Member of ARVC; MECOA. Phone: (207) 696-3360.

## MEDWAY—C-4

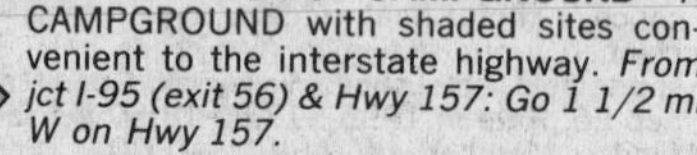

**KATAHDIN SHADOWS CAMPGROUND**—A CAMPGROUND with shaded sites convenient to the interstate highway. *From jct I-95 (exit 56) & Hwy 157: Go 1 1/2 mi W on Hwy 157.*

◆◆◆◆FACILITIES: 125 sites, most common site width 26 feet, 17 full hookups, 81 water & elec (20 & 30 amp receptacles), 27 no hookups, seasonal sites, 12 pull-thrus, a/c allowed ($), heater allowed ($), phone hookups, tenting available, group sites for tents/RVs, tent rentals, RV rentals, cabins, RV storage, handicap restroom facilities, sewage disposal, laundry, public phone, grocery store, RV supplies, LP gas refill by meter, ice, tables, fire rings, wood.

◆◆◆◆RECREATION: rec hall, rec room/area, coin games, swim pool (heated), 10 canoe/1 motor boat rentals, float trips, fishing guides, basketball hoop, playground, planned group activities (weekends only), badminton, horseshoes, hiking trails, volleyball, cross country skiing, snowmobile trails, local tours.

Open May 1 through Thanksgiving. Facilities fully operational Memorial Day through Labor Day. Winter reservations required. Rate in 1995 $15-18 per family. Reservations recommended Jul through Aug.

MEDWAY—Continued
KATAHDIN SHADOWS CAMPGROUND—Continued

Master Card/Visa accepted. Member of ARVC; MECOA. Phone: (800) 794-5267. FCRV 10% discount.

**SEE AD THIS PAGE**

**Pine Grove Campground & Cottages**—A wooded, riverside location. *From jct I-95 & Hwy 157: Go 1 mi W on Hwy 157, then 4 mi N on Hwy 11.* ◆◆FACILITIES: 30 sites, most common site width 24 feet, 4 full hookups, 12 water & elec (20 & 30 amp receptacles), 14 no hookups, seasonal sites, 2 pull-thrus, tenting available, sewage disposal, laundry, public phone, limited grocery store, ice, tables, fire rings, wood. ◆◆RECREATION: rec room/area, river swimming, boating, canoeing, 4 canoe boat rentals, river fishing, playground, horseshoes. Open mid May through Sep 30. Rate in 1995 $13-15 per family. CPO. Member of ARVC; MECOA. Phone: (207) 746-5172.

## MILBRIDGE—D-4

**Bayview Campground**—An oceanside location with open sites. *From jct US 1 & US 1A: Go 1/4 mi N on US 1A, then 1/2 mi E on Bayview St.* ◆◆FACILITIES: 24 sites, most common site width 24 feet, 14 water & elec (20 amp receptacles), 10 no hookups, seasonal sites, tenting available, sewage disposal, tables, fire rings, wood. ◆RECREATION: pavilion, salt water swimming, salt water fishing. Open May 15 through Oct 15. Rate in 1995 $12-15 per family. Phone: (207) 546-2946.

## MILLINOCKET—C-3

**Abol Bridge Campground**—A semi-wooded, riverside CAMPGROUND. *From jct Hwy 11/157 & Baxter State Park Rd: Go 9 3/4 mi NW on Baxter State Park Rd, then 8 1/2 mi W on West Branch Region Rd (Bowater Great Northern Paper Co. Rd).* ◆◆FACILITIES: 37 sites, most common site width 26 feet, 37 no hookups, tenting available, grocery store, LP gas refill by weight, ice, tables, fire rings, wood. ◆◆RECREATION: river swimming, canoeing, 3 canoe boat rentals, river fishing. Open May 15 through Sep 30. Rate in 1995 $13 for 5 persons. Member of ARVC; MECOA.

**Frost Pond Camps**—A wilderness CAMPGROUND with lakeside sites. *From jct Hwy 11/157 & Baxter State Park Rd: Go 9 3/4 mi NW on Baxter State Park Rd, then 17 1/2 mi W on West Branch Region Rd (Bowater Great Northern Paper Co. Rd), then 3 mi N on Frost Pond Rd.* ◆◆FACILITIES: 10 sites, most common site width 60 feet, 18 ft. max RV length, 10 no hookups, tenting available, non-flush toilets, tables, fire rings, wood. ◆◆RECREATION: lake swimming, boating, canoeing, 3 row/25 canoe/3 motor boat rentals, lake fishing, hiking trails. Open May 15 through Sep 30. Rate in 1995 $12 per family. Member of ARVC; MECOA. Phone: (207) 695-2821.

**Pray's Big Eddy Wilderness Campground**—Riverside CAMPGROUND in wilderness area. *From jct Hwy 11/157 & Baxter State Park Rd: Go 9 3/4 mi NW on Baxter State Park Rd, then 17 1/2 mi W on West Branch Region Rd (Bowater Great Northern Paper Co. Rd).* ◆◆FACILITIES: 98 sites, most common site width 22 feet, 26 ft. max RV length, 30 elec (15 amp receptacles), 68 no hookups, seasonal sites, tenting available, sewage disposal, tables, fire rings. ◆◆RECREATION: canoeing, river fishing. Open Apr 1 through mid Nov. Facilities fully operational May 1 through mid Oct. Rate in 1995 $12 for 2 persons.

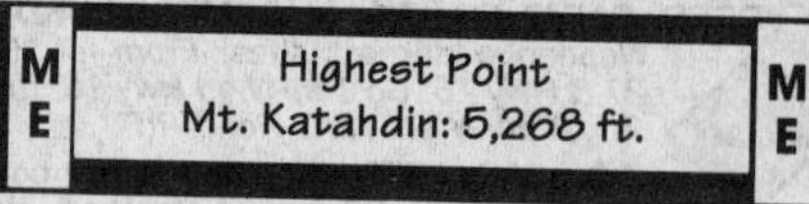

## MOODY—F-1

*See listings at Wells*

## MOUNT DESERT ISLAND—E-4

*See listings at Bar Harbor, Bass Harbor, Ellsworth, Mt. Desert & Southwest Harbor*

## MT. DESERT—E-4

**Mt. Desert Campground**—Traditional camping on saltwater shore in a wooded setting. *From South jct Hwy 102 & Hwy 198: Go 3/4 mi S on Hwy 198.* ◈◈FACILITIES: 153 sites, most common site width 35 feet, 20 ft. max RV length, 35 water & elec, 20 elec (15 amp receptacles), 98 no hookups, tenting available, public phone, limited grocery store, ice, tables, fire rings, wood. ◈RECREATION: salt water swimming, boating, canoeing, ramp, dock, 8 canoe boat rentals. Open Memorial Day through Sep 30. Rate in 1995 $18-25 per family. No refunds. Phone: (207) 244-3710.

**Somes Sound View Camp Ground**—CAMPGROUND on a rocky salt water shore of Somes Sound. *From jct Hwy 198 & Hwy 102: Go 2 mi S on Hwy 102, then 3/4 mi E on Hall Quarry Rd.* ◈◈FACILITIES: 60 sites, most common site width 75 feet, 16 ft. max RV length, 20 water & elec (15 amp receptacles), 40 no hookups, seasonal sites, 1 pull-thrus, tenting available, sewage disposal, public phone, ice, tables, fire rings, grills, wood. ◈◈RECREATION: rec room/area, salt water swimming, boating, canoeing, 1 sail/3 canoe boat rentals. Open Memorial Weekend through mid Oct. Rate in 1995 $15-18 per family. Member of ARVC; MECOA. Phone: (207) 244-3890.

## NAPLES—E-1

**BAY OF NAPLES FAMILY CAMPING**—Lakeside CAMPGROUND with wooded sites. *From jct US 302 & Hwy 11/114: Go 1 mi S on Hwy 11/114.*

◈◈◈FACILITIES: 150 sites, most common site width 36 feet, 61 full hookups, 60 water & elec (15,20 & 30 amp receptacles), 29 no hookups, seasonal sites, 5 pull-thrus, a/c allowed ($), heater not allowed, tenting available, cabins, sewage disposal, laundry, public phone, limited grocery store, LP gas refill by weight, ice, tables, fire rings, wood.

◈◈◈RECREATION: rec room/area, coin games, lake swimming, boating, canoeing, dock, 2 row/3 canoe boat rentals, lake fishing, basketball hoop, playground, badminton, horseshoes, volleyball.

No pets. Open Memorial Day through Columbus Day. Facilities fully operational mid Jun through Labor Day. Rate in 1995 $20-25.50 per family. No refunds. Reservations recommended Jun 15 through Aug 15. Master Card/Visa accepted. Member of ARVC; MECOA. Phone: (800) 348-9750.

**SEE AD THIS PAGE**

**Colonial Mast**—A lakeside CAMPGROUND with open and shaded sites. *From jct Hwy 11/114 & US 302: Go 2 3/4 mi NW on US 302, then 1/4 mi NE on Kansas Rd, then 1/2 mi E on Campground Rd.* ◈◈◈FACILITIES: 79 sites, most common site width 22 feet, 39 full

NAPLES—Continued
COLONIAL MAST—Continued

hookups, 40 water & elec (15 & 20 amp receptacles), seasonal sites, tenting available, handicap restroom facilities, sewage disposal, laundry, public phone, limited grocery store, ice, tables, fire rings, wood. ◈◈◈RECRE-

COLONIAL MAST—Continued on next page
NAPLES—Continued on next page

SAY YOU
SAW IT IN
WOODALL'S!
W

NAPLES—Continued
COLONIAL MAST—Continued

ATION: rec room/area, lake swimming, boating, canoeing, ramp, dock, 2 row/4 canoe/1 pedal boat rentals, lake fishing, playground, 2 shuffleboard courts, planned group activities, badminton, horseshoes, volleyball. Open May 15 through late Sep. Rate in 1995 $19.50-23.50 per family. Member of ARVC; MECOA. Phone: (207) 693-6652.

**FOUR SEASONS CAMPING AREA**—CAMPGROUND with open & shaded sites on a lake. *From jct Hwy 11/114 & US 302: Go 2 1/2 mi NW on US 302.*

♦♦♦FACILITIES: 115 sites, most common site width 30 feet, 11 full hookups, 104 water & elec (20 & 30 amp receptacles), seasonal sites, a/c not allowed, heater not allowed, tenting available, RV rentals, sewage disposal, public phone, grocery store, ice, tables, fire rings, wood, traffic control gate.

♦♦♦RECREATION: rec room/area, coin games, lake swimming, boating, canoeing, ramp, dock, 1 row/3 canoe/1 pedal boat rentals, lake fishing, basketball hoop, playground, badminton, sports field, horseshoes, volleyball.

Open mid May through Columbus Day. Rate in 1995 $19-34 per family. Reservations recommended Jul through Aug. Discover/Master Card/Visa accepted. CPO. Member of ARVC; MECOA. Phone: (207) 693-6797.

**SEE AD PAGE 343**

**K's Family Circle Campground**—A lakeside, wooded location. *From jct US 302 & Hwy 11/114: Go 1 mi S on Hwy 11/114, then 1/4 mi W on Campground Rd.* ♦♦FACILITIES: 125 sites, most common site width 26 feet, 125 water & elec (15 & 20 amp receptacles), seasonal sites, tenting available, sewage disposal, laundry, public phone, limited grocery store, ice, tables, fire rings, wood. ♦♦♦RECREATION: rec room/area, equipped pavilion, lake swimming, boating, canoeing, ramp, dock, 2 row/2 canoe/2 pedal/1 motor boat rentals, lake fishing, playground, planned group activities (weekends only), recreation director, horseshoes, volleyball. Open May 15 through Sep 15. Rate in 1995 $19-23 per family. Member of ARVC; MECOA. Phone: (207) 693-6881.

SEBAGO LAKE STATE PARK—*From jct US 302E & Hwy 11/114: Go 4 mi S on US 302E, then 2 1/2 mi W.* FACILITIES: 250 sites, 30 ft. max RV length, 250 no hookups, tenting available, sewage disposal, public phone, limited grocery store, tables. RECREATION: swimming, boating, ramp, dock, lake fishing, planned group activities, hiking trails. No pets. Open all year. Facilities fully operational May 1 through Oct 15. Open year-round for tenting. Phone: (207) 693-6613.

## NEWCASTLE—E-3

**Sherman Lake View Camping Area**—Open sites at the top of a hill. *From jct Bus US 1 & US 1: Go 5 mi S on US 1.* ♦♦FACILITIES: 30 sites, most common site width 24 feet, 20 ft. max RV length, 8 full hookups, 10 water & elec (15 amp receptacles), 12 no hookups, tenting available, sewage disposal, laundry, public phone, ice, tables, fire rings, wood. ♦RECREATION: swim pool. Open Memorial Day through mid Sep. Rate in 1995 $17-22 for 2 persons. Phone: (207) 563-3239.

## NEW HARBOR—E-3

**Sherwood Forest Campsite**—A wooded CAMPGROUND. *From jct Hwy 32 & Hwy 130: Go 1/4 mi S on Hwy 130, then 3/4 mi W on Pemaquid Beach Rd, then 1/4 mi S on Pemaquid Trail.* ♦♦FACILITIES: 80 sites, most common site width 24 feet, 64 water & elec (15 & 30 amp receptacles), 16 no hookups, seasonal sites, tenting available, sewage disposal, laundry, public phone, grocery store, ice, tables, fire rings, grills, wood. ♦♦♦RECREATION: rec room/area, pavilion, swim pool, playground, badminton, horseshoes, volleyball. Open May 15 through Oct 1. Rate in 1995 $18-20 per family. Member of ARVC; MECOA. Phone: (207) 677-3642.

## NEWPORT—D-3

**CHRISTIE'S CAMPGROUND & COTTAGES**—Lakeside CAMPGROUND with open and shaded sites. *Northbound: From jct I-95 (exit 39) & US 2: Go 3 mi E on US 2. Southbound: From jct I-95 (exit 41) & Hwy 7: Go 1 mi N on Hwy 7, then 1/2 mi W on US 2.*

♦♦♦♦FACILITIES: 50 sites, most common site width 22 feet, 9 full hookups, 27 water & elec (20 & 30 amp receptacles), 15 no hookups, seasonal sites, 10 pull-thrus, a/c allowed ($), heater allowed ($), phone hookups, tenting available, group sites for tents/RVs, cabins, sewage disposal, laundry, public phone, grocery store, LP gas refill by weight/by meter, ice, tables, fire rings, wood.

♦♦♦♦RECREATION: rec hall, rec room/area, coin games, lake swimming, boating, canoeing, ramp, dock, 2 row/2 canoe/3 pedal boat rentals, lake fishing, basketball hoop, 7 bike rentals, playground, planned group activities (weekends only), badminton, horseshoes, volleyball.

Open May 1 through Nov 30. Rate in 1995 $12.50-18.50 for 4 persons. Master Card/Visa accepted. Member of ARVC; MECOA. Phone: (800) 688-5141.

**SEE AD THIS PAGE**

**PALMYRA GOLF COURSE & RV RESORT**—*From jct I-95 (exit 41) & US 2: Go 5 mi W on US 2, then 1/2 mi N on Long Hill Rd.*

**SEE PRIMARY LISTING AT PALMYRA AND AD THIS PAGE**

NEWPORT—Continued

**TENT VILLAGE TRAVEL TRAILER PARK**—Lakeside CAMPGROUND with grassy, open and shaded sites. *From East city limits: Go 1 1/2 mi E on US 2/Hwys 7/100.*

♦♦♦FACILITIES: 54 sites, most common site width 22 feet, 2 full hookups, 52 water & elec (15,20 & 30 amp receptacles), seasonal sites, 16 pull-thrus, a/c allowed, heater allowed, tenting available, cabins, handicap restroom facilities, sewage disposal, public phone, limited grocery store, LP gas refill by weight/by meter, ice, tables, fire rings, wood.

♦♦♦RECREATION: rec hall, rec room/area, coin games, swim pool, lake swimming, boating, canoeing, dock, 3 row/1 canoe/5 pedal/2 motor boat rentals, lake fishing, basketball hoop, playground, badminton, horseshoes, volleyball. Recreation open to the public.

Open May 15 through Oct 15. Rate in 1995 $12-18 for 4 persons. No refunds. Reservations recommended during Jul. Master Card/Visa accepted. Member of ARVC; MECOA. Phone: (207) 368-5047.

**SEE AD THIS PAGE**

## NORRIDGEWOCK—D-2

**Maine Roads Camping**—Grassy, level, open sites on a major highway. *From West city limits: Go 3 mi W on US 2.* ♦♦♦FACILITIES: 44 sites, most common site width 24 feet, 27 full hookups, (20 & 30 amp receptacles), 17 no hookups, 10 pull-thrus, tenting available, sewage disposal, laundry, public phone, grocery store, ice, tables, fire rings, wood. ♦♦♦RECREATION: rec hall, swim pool, playground, badminton, sports field, horseshoes, hiking trails, volleyball. Recreation open to the public. Open May 1 through Oct 3. Rate in 1995 $16 per family. Member of ARVC; MECOA. Phone: (800) 370-MAIN.

## NORTH MONMOUTH—E-2

**BEAVER BROOK CAMPING AREA**—CAMPGROUND with large wooded sites, a pond, a brook and a lake. *From jct Hwy 106 & US 202/Hwy 11/100: Go 2 1/2 mi E on US 202/Hwy 11/100, then 1 1/2 mi NW on Back Rd, then 1 1/2 mi SW on Wilson Pond Rd.*

♦♦♦FACILITIES: 191 sites, most common site width 50 feet, 191 water & elec (20 amp receptacles), seasonal sites, a/c allowed ($), heater allowed ($), tenting available, group sites for tents/RVs, RV storage, sewage disposal, laundry, public phone, grocery store, RV supplies, LP gas refill by weight/by meter, ice, tables, fire rings, wood.

♦♦♦♦RECREATION: rec hall, rec room/area, pavilion, coin games, swim pool, lake swimming, boating, canoeing, ramp, dock, 2 row/3 canoe boat rentals, lake fishing, mini-golf ($), basketball hoop, playground, 4 shuffleboard courts, planned group activities, recreation director, badminton, sports field, horseshoes, hiking trails, volleyball.

Open May 1 through Columbus Day weekend. Rate in 1995 $16-24 per family. No refunds. Reservations recommended Jul through Aug. Master Card/Visa accepted. Member of ARVC; MECOA. Phone: (207) 933-2108.

**SEE AD NEXT PAGE**

## NORTH NEW PORTLAND—D-2

**Happy Horseshoe Campground**—CAMPGROUND in a wilderness location. *From jct Hwy 146 & Hwy 16: Go 1/2 mi E on Hwy 16, then 5 1/4 mi N on Long Falls Dam Rd.* ♦♦♦FACILITIES: 91 sites, most common site width 24 feet, 91 water & elec (20 & 30 amp receptacles), seasonal sites, 6 pull-thrus, tenting available, sewage disposal, laundry, public phone, limited grocery store, ice, tables, fire rings, wood. ♦♦♦RECREATION: rec hall, equipped pavilion, swim

HAPPY HORSESHOE CAMPGROUND—Continued on next page
NORTH NEW PORTLAND—Continued on next page

NORTH NEW PORTLAND—Continued
HAPPY HORSESHOE CAMPGROUND—Continued

pool, playground, shuffleboard court, planned group activities (weekends only), horseshoes, hiking trails, volleyball. Recreation open to the public. Open Memorial Day through mid Sep. Rate in 1995 $17 per family. Member of ARVC;MECOA. Phone: (207) 628-3471.

## NORTH WATERFORD—E-1

**PAPOOSE POND RESORT**—A large CAMPGROUND resort in a pine forest. *From jct Hwy 35 & Hwy 118: Go 3 1/4 mi E on Hwy 118.*

WELCOME

◆◆◆FACILITIES: 170 sites, most common site width 75 feet, 67 full hookups, 89 water & elec (15,20 & 30 amp receptacles), 14 no hookups, tenting available, RV rentals, cabins, sewage disposal, laundry, public phone, full service store, RV supplies, ice, tables, fire rings, grills, wood, guard.

◆◆◆◆◆RECREATION: rec hall, rec room/area, pavilion, coin games, lake swimming, boating, 3 hp limit, canoeing, dock, 9 row/28 canoe/5 pedal boat rentals, river/pond/stream fishing, mini-golf ($), basketball hoop, 16 bike rentals, playground, 3 shuffleboard courts, planned group activities, movies, recreation director, tennis court, badminton, sports field, horseshoes, hiking trails, volleyball.

Open mid May through mid Oct. Facilities fully operational mid Jun through Labor Day. Rate in 1995 $18-44 per family. Reservations recommended Jul through Aug. Master Card/Visa accepted. CPO. Member of ARVC; MECOA. Phone: (207) 583-4470.
**SEE AD PAGES 346 AND 347**

## NORWAY—E-1

**PAPOOSE POND RESORT**—*From jct Hwy 26 & Hwy 118: Go 10 1/2 mi W on Hwy 118.*

WELCOME

**SEE PRIMARY LISTING AT NORTH WATERFORD AND AD NORTH WATERFORD PAGES 346 AND 347**

## OAKLAND—D-2

**Pleasant Point Campground**—Lakeside sites. *From jct I-95 (exit 33) & Hwy 137: Go 4 1/2 mi W on Hwy 137, then 1/4 mi S on McGrath Pond Rd.* ◆◆FACILITIES: 47 sites, most common site width 24 feet, 11 full hookups, 34 water & elec (15 amp receptacles), 2 no hookups, seasonal sites, tenting available, sewage disposal, ice, tables, fire rings, wood. ◆◆RECREATION: rec room/area, lake swimming, boating, canoeing, ramp, lake fishing, volleyball. Open Memorial Day through Labor Day. Rate in 1995 $15 per family. Phone: (207) 465-7265.

## OGUNQUIT—F-1

**DIXON'S CAMPGROUND**—A natural wooded area to enjoy beauty & quiet solitude. *From town center: Go 2 mi S on US 1.*

WELCOME

◆◆◆FACILITIES: 100 sites, most common site width 45 feet, 29 ft. max RV length, 22 water & elec (20 amp receptacles), 78 no hookups, tenting available, sewage disposal, public phone, grocery store, ice, tables, fire rings, traffic control gate/guard.

◆◆RECREATION: playground, local tours.

No pets. Open Memorial Day through mid Sep. Rate in 1995 $20-30 for 2 persons. No refunds. Reservations recommended Jun 20 through Labor Day. Discover/Master Card/Visa accepted. CPO. Member of ARVC; MECOA. Phone: (207) 363-2131.
**SEE AD THIS PAGE**

**Pinederosa Camping Area**—A semi-wooded, riverside CAMPGROUND. *From town center: Go 1 mi N on US 1, then 1 1/2 mi W on Captain Thomas Rd.* ◆◆◆FACILITIES: 100 sites, 8 full hookups, 27 water & elec, 5 elec (15,20 & 30 amp receptacles), 60 no hookups, seasonal sites, tenting available, sewage disposal, laundry, public phone, limited grocery store, ice, tables, fire rings, wood. ◆RECREATION: swim pool. Open May 15 through Sep 30. Rate in 1995 $18 for 2 persons. No refunds. Member of ARVC; MECOA. Phone: (207) 646-2492.

## OLD ORCHARD BEACH—F-2

**BAYLEY'S PINE POINT RESORT**—A flat, semi-wooded CAMPGROUND with a resort atmosphere. *From jct I-95 & I-195 (exit 5): Go 1 3/4 mi E on I-195, then 6 mi N on US 1, then 3 mi E on Hwy 9 to Pine Point (follow signs to campground).*

WELCOME

◆◆◆◆FACILITIES: 470 sites, most common site width 28 feet, 250 full hookups, 100 water & elec, 40 elec (20,30 & 50 amp receptacles), 80 no hookups, seasonal sites, 30 pull-thrus, a/c allowed ($), heater allowed ($), cable TV, phone hookups, tenting available, group sites for tents/RVs, tent rentals, RV rentals, handicap restroom facilities, sewage dis-

BAYLEY'S PINE POINT RESORT—Continued onpage 349
OLD ORCHARD BEACH—Continued on page 349

# Lakeside Camping in the Mountains of Western Maine

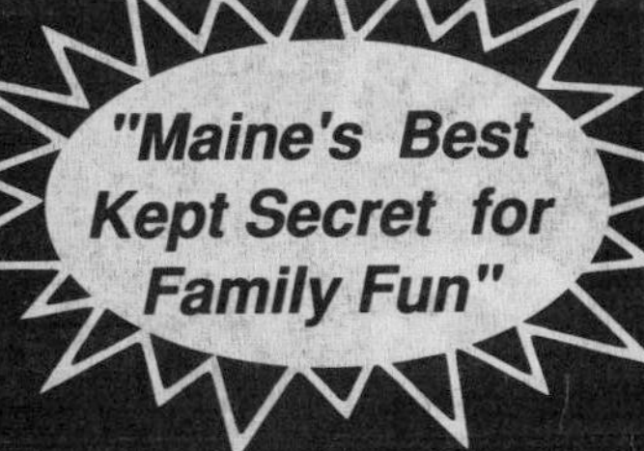


1/2 MILE SANDY BEACH
ACTIVITIES PROGRAM
CANOES · BOATS · FISHING
TRADING POST · CAFE-DELI
MOVIES · ENTERTAINMENT
MERRY-GO-ROUND
18 HOLE MINI GOLF

*Visit Papoose Pond Plaza - home of the Carousel Cafe and our well-stocked Trading Post*

## Family Packages

- One low price for family of 2 adults and 4 children • Discounts on Weekly Stays
- FREE Daily and Nightly Activities
- Off Season Discounts up to 25% PLUS FREE use of Bikes & Boats

## Recreation for All Ages

- FREE Fully Staffed Activities Program with ongoing Daily Schedule in season
- Nightly Entertainment • Feature Movies
- Rec Hall • Game Room • Fishing
- Teen Dances • Square Dances
- Tennis • Basketball • Softball
- Shuffleboard • Ping Pong

Also Available, for a Fee...

- Canoes • Canoe Trips • Paddleboats
- Video Arcade • Bicycles • Hayrides
- Carousel Rides • 18 Hole Mini Golf

## Accommodations

- Lakefront Housekeeping Cottages
- Luxury Travel Trailers & Cabins
- Unbelievably Spacious Secluded Sites - Some Sites with Private Kitchen, Shower and Toilet

*Calling all Kids - For even more fun, join the Waterford Willie Fan Club!*

RECREATION

FACILITIES

3 Hours from Boston

- 2 1/4 hours on 495 to ME Tpke Exit 11, Gray
- 30 minutes from Exit 11 to Norway on Route 26
- 15 minutes from Norway to resort on Route 118

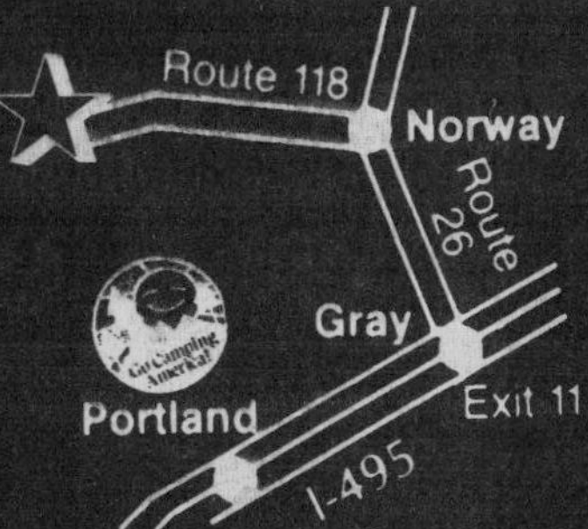


**Call or Write for FREE VIDEO and Vacation Planner Package**

## PAPOOSE POND RESORT & CAMPGROUND

RR1 • Box 2480W • N. Waterford, ME 04267-9600

Early Reservations Suggested

**207-583-4470**

OLD ORCHARD BEACH—Continued
BAYLEY'S PINE POINT RESORT—Continued

posal, laundry, public phone, full service store, RV supplies, LP gas refill by weight/by meter, ice, tables, fire rings, grills, wood, traffic control gate/guard.

◆◆◆◆◆RECREATION: rec hall, rec room/area, equipped pavilion, coin games, 3 swim pools (heated), whirlpool, pond fishing, mini-golf ($), basketball hoop, 10 bike rentals, playground, planned group activities, movies, recreation director, badminton, sports field, horseshoes, hiking trails, volleyball, local tours.

Open May 1 through mid Oct. Rate in 1995 $19-37.50 for 2 persons. Reservations recommended Jul through Aug. Master Card/Visa accepted. Member of ARVC; MECOA. Phone: (207) 883-6043.

**SEE PRIMARY LISTING AT SCARBOROUGH AND AD PAGE 348**

**HID'N PINES**—A CAMPGROUND on rolling terrain with wooded sites. *From jct I-95 & I-195 (exit 5): Go 2 1/2 mi E on I-195, then 2 mi E on Hwy 5, then 1/2 mi N on Hwy 98.*

◆◆◆FACILITIES: 260 sites, most common site width 22 feet, 48 full hookups, 135 water & elec, 15 elec (15 & 20 amp receptacles), 62 no hookups, seasonal sites, a/c allowed, heater allowed, tenting available, handicap restroom facilities, sewage disposal, laundry, public phone, LP gas refill by weight/by meter, ice, tables, patios, fire rings, wood, traffic control gate.

◆◆RECREATION: rec hall, coin games, swim pool (heated), basketball hoop, playground, horseshoes.

Open May 15 through Sep 15. Rate in 1995 $18-22 for 3 persons. No refunds. Reservations recommended during Jul. Master Card/Visa accepted. Member of ARVC; MECOA. Phone: (207) 934-2352.

**SEE AD PAGE 345**

**NE'RE Beach Family Campground**—A flat CAMPGROUND on open terrain. *From jct I-95 & I-195: Go 2 1/2 mi E on I-195, then 1 3/4 mi E on Hwy 5.* ◆◆FACILITIES: 60 sites, most common site width 22 feet, 13 full hookups, 47 water & elec (15,20 & 30 amp receptacles), tenting available, sewage disposal, laundry, public phone, limited grocery store, ice, tables, fire rings, wood. ◆RECREATION: swim pool. Open mid May through mid Sep. Rate in 1995 $18-19 for 2 persons. Member of ARVC; MECOA. Phone: (207) 934-7614.

**Old Orchard Beach Camping**—CAMPGROUND with wooded sites in town. *From jct I-95 & I-195 (exit 5): Go 2 1/2 mi E on I-195, then 100 feet on Hwy 5.* ◆◆FACILITIES: 650 sites, most common site width 22 feet, 125 full hookups, 200 water & elec (15,20 & 30 amp receptacles), 325 no hookups, seasonal sites, tenting available, sewage disposal, laundry, public phone, ice, tables, fire rings, wood. ◆◆◆RECREATION: rec room/area, swim pool, playground, badminton, sports field, horseshoes, volleyball. Open Apr 30 through Columbus Day. Rate in 1995 $16.50-21.50 for 2 persons. No refunds. Member of ARVC; MECOA. Phone: (207) 934-4477.

**Paradise Park Resort Campground**—Wooded CAMPGROUND with sites encircling a pond. *From jct I-95 & I-195 (exit 5): Go 2 1/2 mi E on I-195, then continue on 2 mi E on Hwy 5, then 1/4 mi N on Adelade St.* ◆◆FACILITIES: 200 sites, most common site width 20 feet, 50 full hookups, 100 water & elec (20 & 30 amp receptacles), 50 no hookups, seasonal sites, tenting available, sewage disposal, laundry, public phone, limited grocery store, ice, tables, fire rings, wood. ◆◆RECREATION: rec room/area, swim pool, pond swimming, boating, 4 pedal boat rentals, pond fishing, playground, horseshoes. Open Memorial Day through mid Sep. Rate in 1995 $18.50-25 for 2 persons. No refunds. Member of ARVC; MECOA. Phone: (207) 934-4633.

**POWDER HORN CAMPING**—A family-oriented, semi-wooded CAMPGROUND on open terrain. *From jct I-95 & I-195 (exit 5): Go 1 3/4 mi E on I-195, then 2 1/2 mi N on US 1, then 1 3/4 mi E on Hwy 98.*

◆◆◆FACILITIES: 458 sites, most common site width 24 feet, 217 full hookups, 104 water & elec (20 & 30 amp receptacles), 137 no hookups, seasonal sites, a/c allowed, heater allowed, tenting available, tent rentals, RV storage, handicap restroom facilities, sewage disposal, laundry, public phone, full service store, RV supplies, ice, tables, fire rings, wood, traffic control gate.

◆◆◆◆RECREATION: rec hall, rec room/area, coin games, 3 swim pools, wading pool, whirlpool, mini-golf ($), basketball hoop, playground, 4 shuffleboard courts, planned group activities, badminton, horseshoes, volleyball.

Open Memorial Day through Labor Day. Rate in 1995 $20-28 for 2 persons. Reservations recommended during Jul. Discover/Master Card/Visa accepted. Member of ARVC; MECOA. Phone: (207) 934-4733.

**SEE AD NEXT PAGE**

**SPRUCE LODGE TENT/TRAILER PARK**—A CAMPGROUND with wooded, hilly sites in town. *From jct I-95 & I-195 (exit 5): Go 2 1/2 mi E on I-195, then 1 3/4 mi E on Hwy 5, then 4 blocks S on Union St, then 3 blocks W on Hillside Ave.*

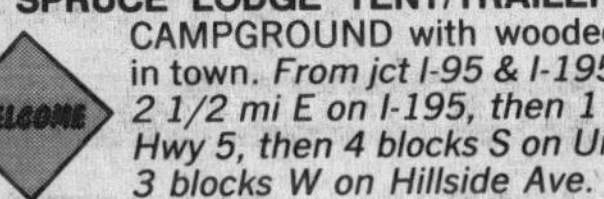

◆◆FACILITIES: 162 sites, 35 ft. max RV length, 47 water & elec (15 amp receptacles), 115 no hookups, seasonal sites, a/c not allowed, heater not allowed, tenting available, group sites for tents, cabins, sewage disposal, public phone, ice, tables, fire rings, wood.

◆RECREATION: badminton, horseshoes, volleyball.

Open late May through mid Sep. Rate in 1995 $17-19 for 4 persons. Discover/Master Card/Visa accepted. Phone: (207) 934-2283.

**SEE AD THIS PAGE**

**VIRGINIA PARK**—A quiet CAMPGROUND with shaded sites. *From jct I-95 & I-195 (exit 5): Go 2 1/2 mi E on I-195, then 1/2 mi E on Hwy 5, then 1/2 mi S on Temple Ave.*

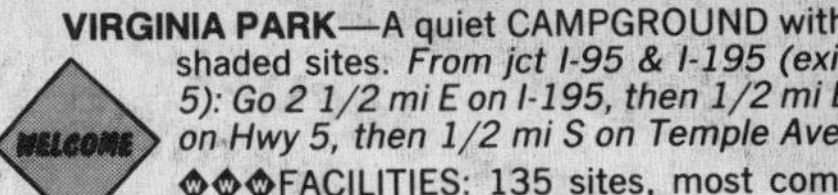

◆◆◆FACILITIES: 135 sites, most common site width 20 feet, 48 full hookups, 50 water & elec (20 & 30 amp receptacles), 37 no hookups, seasonal sites, 20 pull-thrus, a/c allowed, heater allowed, tenting available, RV rentals, sewage disposal, laundry, public phone, limited grocery store, ice, tables, fire rings, wood.

◆◆◆RECREATION: rec room/area, coin games, swim pool, whirlpool, basketball hoop, playground, shuffleboard court, badminton, horseshoes, volleyball.

Open Memorial Day through mid Sep. Rate in 1995 $18-23 for 3 persons. No refunds. Reservations recommended Jul 1 through Aug 15. Master Card/Visa accepted. Member of ARVC; MECOA. Phone: (207) 934-4791.

**SEE AD THIS PAGE**

**Wagon Wheel Camping & Trailer Park**—A CAMPGROUND in a wooded setting. *From jct I-95 & I-195 (exit 5): Go 2 1/2 mi E on I-195, then 1/4 mi E on Hwy 5, then 1/4 mi S on Saco Rd.* ◆◆FACILITIES: 423 sites, 75 full hookups, 75 water & elec (15,20 & 30 amp receptacles), 273 no hookups, seasonal sites, tenting available, sewage disposal, laundry, public phone, limited grocery store, ice, tables, grills, wood. ◆◆◆RECREATION: rec room/area, 2 swim pools, playground, planned group activities, horseshoes, volleyball. Open May 1 through Columbus Day. Facilities fully operational Jun 24 through Labor Day. Rate in 1995 $16.50-21.50 for 2 persons. No refunds. Phone: (207) 934-2160.

**WILD ACRES TENT & TRAILER PARK**—A semi-wooded CAMPGROUND. *From jct I-95 & I-195 (exit 5): Go 2 1/2 mi E on I-195, then 3/4 mi E on Hwy 5.*

◆◆◆FACILITIES: 408 sites, most common site width 30 feet, 199 full hookups, 171 water & elec (15,20 & 30 amp receptacles), 38 no hookups, seasonal sites, 56 pull-thrus, a/c allowed, heater allowed, tenting available, sewage disposal, laundry, public phone, grocery store, RV supplies, ice, tables, fire rings, wood, traffic control gate.

◆◆◆◆RECREATION: rec hall, rec room/area, coin games, 2 swim pools, whirlpool, pond fishing, mini-golf ($), basketball hoop, playground, 4 shuffleboard courts, planned group activities, tennis court, badminton, horseshoes, hiking trails, volleyball, local tours.

Open mid May through Labor Day. Rate in 1995 $20.27 for 2 persons. No refunds. Reservations recommended during Jul. Discover/Master Card/Visa accepted. Member of ARVC; MECOA. Phone: (207) 934-2535.

**SEE AD PAGE 351**

Famous for family camping since 1929... because we care.
A TRADITION FOR 68 YEARS
You'll find everything you'd hoped for and more at
WILD ACRES
For a first class family vacation!
Wild Acres is the oldest family campground in Maine. We offer a fun-filled vacation that sends the whole family home with a new spirit of togetherness. We have the ideal location to enjoy the Atlantic's beautiful beaches and area's many attractions. Stay with us and discover why generations of campers keep returning to Wild Acres year after year, making it a family tradition!
SPACIOUS SITES - YOUR CHOICE OF SHADED OR GRASSY
All sites have picnic tables and fire pots.
• 230 complete hookups
• 120 with water and electricity
• 50 tent sites
Pets Accepted.
57 ACRES OF CAMPING SPACE, JUST 3/4 MILE FROM THE BEACH!
Shuttle service to the beach in season
Good Sampark
APPROVED CAMPGROUND AAA
• 2 pools–large diving pool and large children's pool
• 3 jacuzzis
• Horseshoes, shuffleboard, basketball, volleyball, badminton
• 18 hole miniature golf
• Adult rec room
• Free fishing in stocked fish pond-no license required
• 2 large playgrounds
• Spotless rest rooms with free hot showers - handicap accessible
• Catholic church across the street
• Restaurants next door
• Game room
• Free hayrides Saturday nights
• Tot playground
• Tennis court
• Laundromat
• Grocery store
• Wood and ice
• Dump station
• Seasonal sites
• Security gates
• Night security
• 2 golf courses within 1 mile
Nous parlons Français
EXPLORE THE NATURE TRAIL
EXIT 5
I-95
1
5
5
Saco Ave.
98
WILD ACRES
"World's finest beach"
VISA
MasterCard
DISCOVER
Call for brochure, rates and schedule of events
WILD ACRES
Family Camping Resort
Kenny and Tammy Ahearn-Blow, Your Hosts
179W Saco Avenue
Old Orchard Beach, ME 04064
(207) 934-2535
Fax on same line

## ORONO—D-3

**The Villa Vaughn**—Wooded, lakeside, secluded CAMPGROUND. *From jct I-95 (exit 51-Stillwater Ave): Go 1 mi SW on Stillwater Ave, then 3 mi W on Forest Ave.* ◊◊FACILITIES: 75 sites, most common site width 24 feet, 18 full hookups, 37 water & elec (15 & 30 amp receptacles), 20 no hookups, seasonal sites, 11 pull-thrus, tenting available, sewage disposal, laundry, public phone, limited grocery store, LP gas refill by weight, ice, tables, fire rings, wood. ◊◊◊RECREATION: rec hall, rec room/area, lake swimming, boating, canoeing, ramp, 4 row/2 canoe boat rentals, lake fishing, horseshoes. Open May 15 through Oct 15. Rate in 1995 $13.50-17.50 for 4 persons. Member of ARVC; MECOA. Phone: (207) 945-6796.









## ORR'S ISLAND—E-2

**ORR'S ISLAND CAMPGROUND**—Island CAMPGROUND with shaded & open sites. *From jct US 1 & Hwy 24 (at Cook's Corner): Go 11 1/2 mi S on Hwy 24.*

◊◊FACILITIES: 70 sites, most common site width 24 feet, 35 full hookups, 18 water & elec (20 & 30 amp receptacles), 17 no hookups, seasonal sites, 5 pull-thrus, a/c not allowed, heater not allowed, phone hookups, tenting available, cabins, sewage disposal, laundry, public phone, ice, tables, fire rings, wood.

◊◊RECREATION: salt water swimming, boating, 2 canoe boat rentals, salt water fishing, badminton, horseshoes, hiking trails, volleyball.

Open Memorial Day through mid Sep. Rate in 1995 $15-23 per family. Reservations recommended Jul through Aug. Member of ARVC;MECOA. Phone: (207) 833-5595.

**SEE AD THIS PAGE**

## OXFORD—E-1

✱ **CALL OF THE WILD**—*From jct Hwy 121 & Hwy 26: Go 1 1/2 mi N on Hwy 26.* SALES: travel trailers, truck campers, 5th wheels, motor homes, mini-motor homes, fold-down camping trailers, tents. SERVICES: RV appliance mechanic full-time, LP gas refill by weight, RV rentals, sells parts/accessories, installs hitches. Open all year. Phone: (207) 539-4410.

**SEE AD THIS PAGE**

**Two Lakes Muskegon Camping Area**—CAMPGROUND with wooded sites on a lake. *From south jct Hwy 121 & Hwy 26: Go 1/2 mi S on Hwy 26.* ◊◊FACILITIES: 110 sites, most common site width 28 feet, 16 full hookups, 82 water & elec (15 & 30 amp receptacles), 12 no hookups, seasonal sites, tenting available, sewage disposal, laundry, public phone, grocery store, ice, tables, fire rings, wood. ◊◊◊RECREATION: rec hall, equipped pavilion, lake swimming, boating, canoeing, ramp, 4 row/4 canoe/4 pedal/3 motor boat rentals, lake/river fishing, playground, shuffleboard court, planned group activities, badminton, sports field, horseshoes, hiking trails, volleyball. Open May 1 through Oct 1. Rate in 1995 $18.50-22 per family. Member of ARVC; MECOA. Phone: (207) 539-4851.

## PALMYRA—D-3

**PALMYRA GOLF COURSE & RV RESORT** (UNDER CONSTRUCTION)—A CAMPGROUND with wooded sites. *From jct Hwy 151 & US 2: Go 1/4 mi E on US 2, then 1/2 mi N on Long Hill Rd.*

FACILITIES: 42 sites, most common site width 40 feet, 42 water & elec, sewage disposal.

RECREATION: golf ($), driving range ($), putting green.

No pets. No tents. Open mid Apr through mid Oct. Rates available upon request. Master Card/Visa accepted. Phone: (207) 938-4947.

**SEE AD NEWPORT PAGE 344**

## PATTEN—B-4

**Matagamon Wilderness Campground**—A riverside CAMPGROUND in the wilderness. *From North jct Hwy 11 & Hwy 159: Go 24 mi NW on Hwy 159.* ◊◊FACILITIES: 36 sites, most common site width 50 feet, 36 no hookups, seasonal sites, tenting available, non-flush toilets, sewage disposal, grocery store, LP gas refill by weight, ice, tables, fire rings, wood. ◊◊◊RECREATION: lake/river swimming, boating, canoeing, ramp, 8 canoe/4 motor boat rentals, lake/river fishing, hiking trails. Open all year. Facilities fully operational Apr 15 through Nov 30. Rate in 1995 $12 per family. Member of ARVC;MECOA. Phone: (207) 528-2448.

**Shin Pond Village Camping**—A CAMPGROUND with open & wooded sites in a wilderness location. *From jct Hwy 11 & Hwy 159: Go 10 mi W on Hwy 159.*

PATTEN—Continued
SHIN POND VILLAGE CAMPING—Continued

◊◊◊FACILITIES: 25 sites, most common site width 30 feet, 13 water & elec (20 & 30 amp receptacles), 12 no hookups, tenting available, sewage disposal, laundry, public phone, grocery store, ice, tables, fire rings, wood. ◊◊◊RECREATION: lake/river swimming, 3 canoe boat rentals, lake/river fishing, playground, badminton, sports field, horseshoes, hiking trails, volleyball. Recreation open to the public. Open May 1 through Nov 30. Facilities fully operational May 15 through mid Oct. Rate in 1995 $16.95 per family. Member of ARVC; MECOA. Phone: (207) 528-2900.

## PERRY—D-5

**KNOWLTON'S SEASHORE CAMPGROUND**—Oceanside CAMPGROUND with large tidewater clamming area. *From jct Hwy 190 & US 1: Go 3 mi SW on US 1.*

◊◊FACILITIES: 80 sites, most common site width 24 feet, 50 full hookups, 10 water & elec (15 amp receptacles), 20 no hookups, seasonal sites, 17 pull-thrus, a/c allowed, heater allowed, tenting available, RV rentals, sewage disposal, public phone, ice, tables, fire rings, wood.

◊RECREATION: boating, salt water fishing, playground.

Open May 20 through Oct 15. Rate in 1995 $9-14 per family. No refunds. Reservations recommended Jul through Aug. Phone: (207) 726-4756.

**SEE AD THIS PAGE**

## PHIPPSBURG—E-2

***See listings at Bath, Popham Beach & Small Point Beach***

## POLAND—E-2

**RANGE POND CAMPGROUND**—Level sites in a wooded area. *From jct Hwy 26 & Hwy 122: Go 1 3/10 mi E on Hwy 122, then 1 2/10 mi N on Empire Rd, then 1/2 mi W on Plains Rd.*

◊◊◊FACILITIES: 80 sites, most common site width 24 feet, 62 full hookups, 13 water & elec (30 amp receptacles), 5 no hookups, seasonal sites, 23 pull-thrus, a/c allowed ($), heater not allowed, phone hookups, tenting available, group sites for tents/RVs, RV rentals, RV storage, handicap restroom facilities, sewage disposal, laundry, public phone, grocery store, RV supplies, ice, tables, fire rings, wood.

◊◊◊RECREATION: rec hall, equipped pavilion, coin games, swim pool, basketball hoop, playground, planned group activities, recreation director, badminton, horseshoes, hiking trails, volleyball.

Open mid Apr through mid Oct. Facilities fully operational Memorial Day through Labor Day. Rate in 1995 $13-17 per family. No refunds. Discover/Master Card/Visa accepted. Phone: (207) 998-2624.

**SEE AD AUBURN PAGE 324**

## POLAND SPRING—E-2

**POLAND SPRING CAMPGROUND**—Peaceful, wooded park situated on Lower Range Pond. *From jct Hwy 122 & Hwy 26: Go 2 3/4 mi N on Hwy 26, then 1/2 mi E on campground road.*

◊◊◊FACILITIES: 100 sites, most common site width 35 feet, 42 full hookups, 50 water & elec (20 & 30 amp receptacles), 8 no hookups, seasonal sites, a/c allowed ($), heater not allowed, tenting available, group sites for tents/RVs, handicap restroom facilities, sewage disposal, laundry, public phone, grocery store, RV supplies, ice, tables, fire rings, wood.

POLAND SPRING CAMPGROUND—Continued on next page
POLAND SPRING—Continued on next page

POLAND SPRING—Continued
POLAND SPRING CAMPGROUND—Continued

◆◆◆◆RECREATION: rec hall, rec room/area, coin games, swim pool, lake swimming, boating, 10 hp limit, canoeing, ramp, dock, 1 row/5 canoe boat rentals, lake fishing, basketball hoop, playground, planned group activities, movies, recreation director, badminton, horseshoes, volleyball.

Open Apr 15 through Nov 1. Facilities fully operational Memorial Day through Labor Day. Rate in 1995 $15-19 per family. Reservations recommended Jul through Aug. Master Card/Visa accepted. CPO. Member of ARVC;MECOA. Phone: (207) 998-2151.
**SEE AD PAGE 352**

## POPHAM BEACH—E-2

**Ocean View Park Campground**—Open or shaded sites on the ocean. *From jct US 1 & Hwy 209: Go 13 mi S on Hwy 209.* ◆◆FACILITIES: 48 sites, most common site width 14 feet, 11 full hookups, 31 water & elec, 3 elec (15 amp receptacles), 3 no hookups, seasonal sites, tenting available, sewage disposal, public phone, limited grocery store, ice, tables, wood. ◆RECREATION: salt water swimming, boating, salt water fishing. Open May 1 through Columbus Day weekend. Rate in 1995 $18-22 for 4 persons. Member of ARVC; MECOA. Phone: (207) 389-2564.

## PORTLAND—F-2

**BAYLEY'S PINE POINT RESORT**—*From I-95 (Exit 7): Go 1 3/4 mi E on S Portland Spur, then 5 3/4 mi S on US 1 & Hwy 9, then 2 1/2 mi SE on Hwy 9.*
**SEE PRIMARY LISTING AT SCARBOROUGH AND AD OLD ORCHARD BEACH PAGE 348**

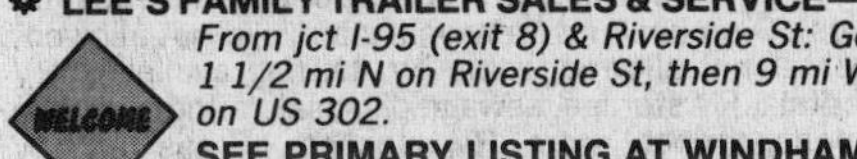

**✱ LEE'S FAMILY TRAILER SALES & SERVICE**—*From jct I-95 (exit 8) & Riverside St: Go 1 1/2 mi N on Riverside St, then 9 mi W on US 302.*
**SEE PRIMARY LISTING AT WINDHAM AND AD WINDHAM PAGE 362**

**WASSAMKI SPRINGS**—A lakeside, semi-wooded CAMPGROUND with lots of activities. *From jct I-95 (exit 7) & Payne Rd: Go 1 mi S on Payne Rd, then 2 1/2 mi N on Hwy 114, then 3/4 mi W on Saco St.* ◆◆◆◆FACILITIES: 170 sites, most common site width 24 feet, 90 full hookups, 50 water & elec (20 & 30 amp receptacles), 30 no hookups, seasonal sites, a/c allowed ($), heater not allowed, phone hookups, tenting available, group sites for tents/RVs, RV storage, sewage disposal, laundry, public phone, limited grocery store, LP gas refill by weight/by meter, ice, tables, fire rings, wood, traffic control gate/guard.

◆◆◆◆RECREATION: rec hall, rec room/area, lake swimming, boating, no motors, canoeing, dock, 6 pedal boat rentals, lake fishing, basketball hoop, playground, planned group activities (weekends only), movies, recreation director, badminton, sports field, horseshoes, volleyball. Recreation open to the public.

Open May 1 through mid Oct. Rate in 1995 $15-26 for 2 persons. Reservations recommended Jul 1 through Aug 15. Master Card/Visa accepted. Member of ARVC; MECOA. Phone: (207) 839-4276.
**SEE AD THIS PAGE**

## POWNAL—E-2

BRADBURG MOUNTAIN STATE PARK—*From town center: Go 1 mi E on Hwy 9.* FACILITIES: 41 sites, 30 ft. max RV length, 41 no hookups, tenting available, non-flush toilets, tables. RECREATION: playground, sports field, hiking trails. Open May 15 through Oct 15. No showers. Phone: (207) 688-4712.



## PRESQUE ISLE—B-4

**ARNDT'S AROOSTOOK RIVER LODGE & CAMPGROUND**—*From jct Hwy 1 & Hwy 167: Go 3 1/2 mi E on Hwy 167, then 3/4 mi N on Hwy 205.* ◆◆FACILITIES: 75 sites, most common site width 40 feet, 10 full hookups, 45 water & elec (30 & 50 amp receptacles), 20 no hookups, seasonal sites, 7 pull-thrus, a/c allowed, heater allowed, tenting available, group sites for tents/RVs, sewage disposal, laundry, grocery store, RV supplies, tables, fire rings, wood.

◆◆◆RECREATION: rec room/area, coin games, swim pool, canoeing, 3 canoe boat rentals, river fishing, fishing guides, basketball hoop, 15 bike rentals, playground, badminton, sports field, hiking trails.

Open May 15 through Oct 15. Rate in 1995 $18-22 for 4 persons. Master Card/Visa accepted. Phone: (207) 764-8677.
**SEE AD THIS PAGE**

AROOSTOOK STATE PARK—*From jct Hwy 163 & US 1: Go 3 3/4 mi S on US 1, then 2 mi SW on Spragueville Rd.* FACILITIES: 30 sites, 24 ft. max RV length, 30 no hookups, tenting available, non-flush toilets, public phone, tables,

PRESQUE ISLE—Continued
AROOSTOOK STATE PARK—Continued

wood. RECREATION: lake swimming, boating, ramp, dock, canoe boat rentals, lake fishing, hiking trails. Open May 15 through Oct 15. No showers. Phone: (207) 768-8341.

**Camper's Paradise**—A rural CAMPGROUND with a magnificent view. *From jct Hwy 163 & US 1: Go 4 3/4 mi S on US 1, then 3 1/4 mi W on Thompkin's Road, then 2 mi W on Simpson's Road.* ◆◆FACILITIES: 102 sites, most common site width 26 feet, 62 water & elec (15 amp receptacles), 40 no hookups, tenting available, handicap restroom facilities, sewage disposal, laundry, ice, tables, fire rings, wood. ◆◆RECREATION: rec room/area, swim pool, horseshoes, hiking trails. Recreation open to the public. Open Memorial Day through Labor Day. Rate in 1995 $11-13 per family. Phone: (207) 429-8178.

PRESQUE ISLE—Continued on next page

ME Leading producer of wooden toothpicks! ME

PRESQUE ISLE—Continued

✱ **MCCLUSKEY'S TRAILER SALES**—*From jct Hwy 163 & US 1: Go 1 mi S on US 1.* SALES: travel trailers, truck campers, 5th wheels, motor homes, mini-motor homes, fold-down camping trailers. SERVICES: RV appliance mechanic full-time, LP gas refill by meter, sells parts/accessories, sells camping supplies, installs hitches. Open all year. Master Card/Visa accepted. Phone: (207) 762-1721.
**SEE AD TRAVEL SECTION PAGE 322**

**NEIL E MICHAUD CAMPGROUND**—Open, wooded, grassy sites convenient to a major highway. *From jct US 1 & Hwy 163: Go 2 1/2 mi S on US 1.*

◆◆FACILITIES: 45 sites, most common site width 28 feet, 6 full hookups, 39 water & elec (15 & 20 amp receptacles), a/c allowed ($), phone hookups, tenting available, RV rentals, sewage disposal, laundry, ice, tables, fire rings, wood.

◆RECREATION: basketball hoop, playground, volleyball.

PRESQUE ISLE—Continued
NEIL E MICHAUD CAMPGROUND—Continued

Open all year. Facilities fully operational May 1 through mid Oct. Rate in 1995 $15 for 4 persons. Member of ARVC; MECOA. Phone: (207) 769-1951.
**SEE AD THIS PAGE**

### RANGELEY—D-1

**BLACK BROOK COVE CAMPGROUND**—A secluded campground with private island sites. *From jct Hwy 4 & Hwy 16: Go 16 mi NW on Hwy 16, then 1/2 mi E on Aziscohos Lake Rd.*

◆◆◆FACILITIES: 73 sites, 28 water & elec (20 amp receptacles), 45 no hookups, a/c allowed ($), tenting available, handicap restroom facili-

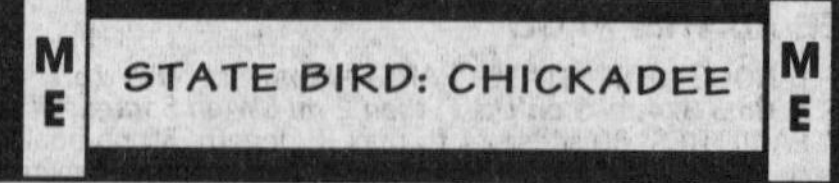


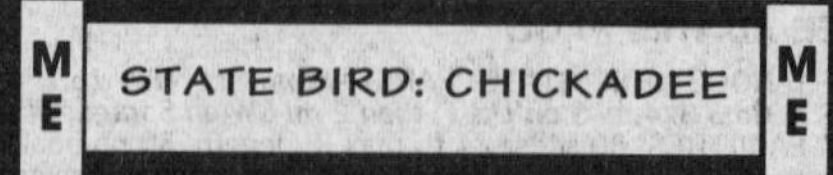

RANGELEY—Continued
BLACK BROOK COVE CAMPGROUND—Continued

ties, sewage disposal, laundry, grocery store, ice, tables, fire rings, wood.

◆◆◆RECREATION: lake swimming, boating, canoeing, ramp, 6 canoe/1 pedal/2 motor boat rentals, lake/river/stream fishing, fishing guides, movies, horseshoes, hiking trails.

Open mid Apr through mid Nov. Rate in 1995 $14. Member of ARVC; MECOA. Phone: (207) 486-3828.
**SEE AD THIS PAGE**

**Cupsuptic Campground**—Lakeside setting in a pine grove. *From jct Hwy 4 & Hwy 16: Go 4 1/2 mi NW on Hwy 16.* ◆◆FACILITIES: 76 sites, most common site width 24 feet, 66 water & elec (15 amp receptacles), 10 no hookups, seasonal sites, tenting available, sewage disposal, public phone, limited grocery store, ice, tables, fire rings, wood. ◆◆◆RECREATION: rec hall, lake swimming, boating, canoeing, 11 canoe/2 motor boat rentals, lake fishing, badminton, horseshoes, hiking trails, volleyball. Recreation open to the public. Open May 1 through Dec 1. Rate in 1995 $12-16 per family. Member of ARVC; MECOA. Phone: (207) 864-5249.

RANGELEY STATE PARK—*From jct Hwy 16 & Hwy 4: Go 4 mi S on Hwy 4, then 5 mi W on S Shore Drive, then 1 mi N.* FACILITIES: 50 sites, 50 no hookups, tenting available, handicap restroom facilities, sewage disposal, public phone, tables, wood. RECREATION: swimming, boating, ramp, dock, lake fishing, playground, hiking trails. Open May 15 through Oct 1. Phone: (207) 864-3858.

### RAYMOND—E-2

**KOKATOSI CAMPGROUND**—Terraced and shaded sites on a lake. *From jct US 302 & Hwy 85: Go 6 mi NE on Hwy 85.*

◆◆◆FACILITIES: 162 sites, most common site width 30 feet, 71 full hookups, 82 water & elec (15 & 20 amp receptacles), 9 no hookups, seasonal sites, a/c not allowed, heater not allowed, cable TV, tenting available, RV rentals, RV storage, sewage disposal, laundry, public phone, grocery store, RV supplies, LP gas refill by weight/by meter, marine gas, ice, tables, patios, grills, wood, traffic control gate.

◆◆◆◆◆RECREATION: rec hall, rec room/area, coin games, lake swimming, boating, canoeing, dock, 7 canoe/4 pedal/5 motor boat rentals, lake fishing, basketball hoop, playground, planned group activities, movies, recreation director, badminton, sports field, horseshoes, volleyball.

Open mid May through mid Oct. Rate in 1995 $22-29 per family. Reservations recommended Jul through Aug. Master Card/Visa accepted. Member of ARVC; MECOA. Phone: (207) 627-4642.
**SEE AD THIS PAGE**

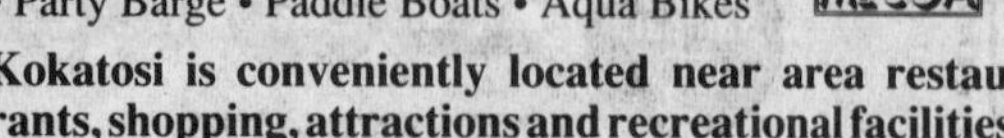



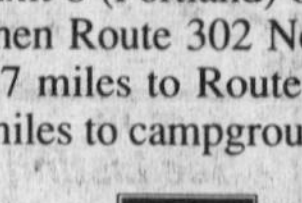

## ROBBINSTON—D-5

**HILLTOP CAMPGROUND**—Rural CAMPGROUND with open and shaded grassy sites. *From South city limits: Go 2 mi S on US 1, then 1 mi W on Ridge Rd.*

◆◆◆FACILITIES: 117 sites, most common site width 24 feet, 34 full hookups, 69 water & elec (15,20 & 30 amp receptacles), 14 no hookups, seasonal sites, 20 pull-thrus, a/c allowed ($), heater not allowed, tenting available, RV storage, sewage disposal, laundry, public phone, grocery store, LP gas refill by meter, ice, tables, fire rings, wood.

◆◆◆RECREATION: rec room/area, coin games, swim pool, basketball hoop, playground, planned group activities (weekends only), recreation director, sports field, horseshoes, hiking trails, volleyball.

Open mid May through late Sep. Rate in 1995 $17-19 for 5 persons. Discover/Master Card/Visa accepted. Phone: (207) 454-3985.

**SEE AD CALAIS PAGE 334**

## ROCKPORT—E-3

**MEGUNTICOOK CAMPGROUND BY THE SEA**—Open & shaded sites with an ocean view. *From jct Hwy 90 & US 1 (in Rockport): Go 2 mi S on US 1.*

◆◆◆FACILITIES: 78 sites, most common site width 26 feet, 56 water & elec (15,20 & 30 amp receptacles), 22 no hookups, 22 pull-thrus, a/c allowed, tenting available, group sites for tents, cabins, sewage disposal, laundry, public phone, grocery store, RV supplies, ice, tables, fire rings, wood.

◆◆◆RECREATION: rec room/area, coin games, swim pool (heated), 12 canoe boat rentals, salt water fishing, playground, sports field, horseshoes, volleyball.

Open early May through late Oct. In Canada: (207) 594-2428. Rate in 1995 $16-20 for 4 persons. Master Card/Visa accepted. Member of ARVC; MECOA. Phone: (800) 884-2428.

**SEE AD THIS PAGE**

**Robert's Roost Campground**—CAMPGROUND near major highway with open and shaded sites. *From jct US 1 & Hwy 90: Go 2 mi SW on Hwy 90.* ◆◆◆FACILITIES: 50 sites, 50 full hookups, (20 & 30 amp receptacles), seasonal sites, tenting available, sewage disposal, laundry, public phone, LP gas refill by weight/by meter, ice, tables, fire rings, wood. ◆RECREATION: badminton, horseshoes, volleyball. Open May 1 through Oct 1. Rate in 1995 $18 for 4 persons. Phone: (207) 236-2498.

ME State Tree: White Pine ME

## ROCKWOOD—C-2

**OLD MILL CAMPGROUND**—Lakeside sites with open & wooded level sites. *From South town limits: Go 2 mi S on Hwy 15.*

◆◆FACILITIES: 50 sites, most common site width 22 feet, 14 full hookups, 36 water & elec (15 amp receptacles), seasonal sites, a/c not allowed, heater not allowed, tenting available, cabins, sewage disposal, laundry, public phone, grocery store, RV supplies, LP gas refill by weight, marine gas, ice, tables, fire rings, wood.

◆◆◆RECREATION: rec room/area, coin games, lake swimming, boating, canoeing, ramp, dock, 7 canoe/2 pedal/15 motor boat rentals, lake fishing, fishing guides, badminton, horseshoes, volleyball.

Open mid May through Columbus Day. Rate in 1995 $13-15 for 2 persons. Discover/Master Card/Visa accepted. Member of ARVC; MECOA. Phone: (207) 534-7333.

**SEE AD THIS PAGE**

**Seboomook Wilderness Campground**—Remote wilderness setting on a lake with open & wooded sites. *From Hwy 15 (in town) & Moose River Bridge (one lane): Go 28 mi NE.* ◆◆FACILITIES: 84 sites, most common site width 26 feet, 35 ft. max RV length, 6 full hookups, (15 amp receptacles), 41 no hookups, seasonal sites, tenting available, sewage disposal, grocery store, LP gas refill by weight, ice, tables, fire rings, wood. ◆◆◆RECREATION: lake swimming, boating, canoeing, ramp, dock, 4 canoe/2 motor boat rentals, lake fishing, badminton, horseshoes, hiking trails, volleyball. Open May 10 through Nov 30. 37 sites have RV hookups for sewer & water only. Rate in 1995 $8-12 per family. Phone: (207) 534-8824.

## SABATTUS—E-2

✲ **MOUNTAIN ROAD RV**—*From jct Hwy 197 & Hwy 126: Go 100 feet E on Hwy 126, then 2/10 mi N on Dealer Rd.* SALES: travel trailers, park models, truck campers, 5th wheels, motor homes, mini-motor homes, fold-down camping trailers. SERVICES: Engine/Chassis & RV appliance mechanic full-time, emergency road service 24 hours, LP gas refill by weight/by meter, sewage disposal, sells parts/accessories, sells camping supplies, installs hitches. Open all year. Discover/Master Card/Visa accepted. Phone: (800) 682-7355.

**SEE AD LEWISTON PAGE 341**

## SACO—F-2

**Cascadia Park**—CAMPGROUND with wooded and open sites. *From jct I-195 & US 1: Go 2 1/2 mi N on US 1.* ◆◆FACILITIES: 100 sites, most common site width

SACO—Continued
CASCADIA PARK—Continued

35 feet, 47 full hookups, 24 water & elec, 2 elec (20 & 30 amp receptacles), 27 no hookups, seasonal sites, 19 pull-thrus, tenting available, laundry, public phone, ice, tables, fire rings, wood. RECREATION: badminton, volleyball. Open May 1 through Oct 30. Rate in 1995 $15-19 for 2 persons. Phone: (207) 282-1666.

**SACO/PORTLAND SOUTH KOA**—A CAMPGROUND with wooded, secluded sites. *From jct I-95 & I-195 (exit 5): Go 1 3/4 mi E on I-195, then 1 1/2 mi N on US 1.*

◆◆◆FACILITIES: 124 sites, most common site width 24 feet, 42 full hookups, 46 water & elec, 4 elec (15 & 30 amp receptacles), 32 no hookups, seasonal sites, 40 pull-thrus, a/c allowed ($), heater allowed ($), tenting available, group sites for tents/RVs, cabins, handicap restroom facilities, sewage disposal, laundry, public phone, grocery store, RV supplies, LP gas refill by weight/by meter, ice, tables, grills, wood.

◆◆◆RECREATION: rec room/area, coin games, swim pool, basketball hoop, playground, planned group activities (weekends only), movies, badminton, horseshoes, volleyball, local tours.

Open early May through mid Oct. Rate in 1995 $19.50-26 for 2 persons. Reservations recom-

SACO/PORTLAND SOUTH KOA—Continued on next page
SACO—Continued on next page

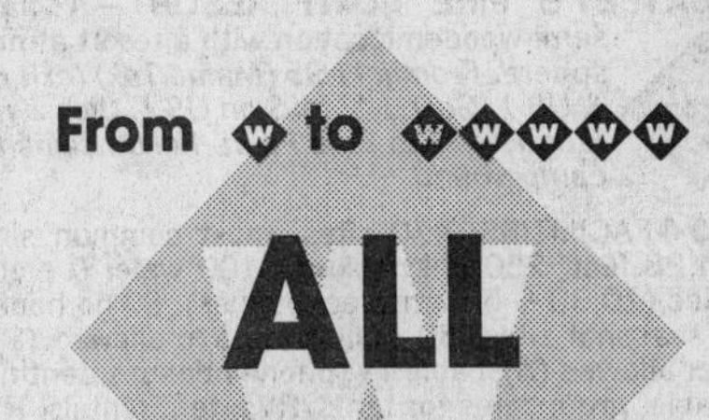
From ◆ to ◆◆◆◆◆
ALL
Woodall Listed Parks
are Quality Parks

mended Jul through Aug. Master Card/Visa accepted. Member of ARVC; MECOA. Phone: (800) 562-1886. KOA 10% value card discount.

**SEE AD PAGE 355 AND AD FRONT OF BOOK PAGES 68 AND 69**

## SANFORD—F-1

**Apache Campground**—Lakeside with large wooded sites. *From jct Hwy 109 & Hwy 4: Go 2 mi N on Hwy 4, then 1 1/2 mi E on New Dam Rd, then 1 mi N on Bernier Rd.* ◇◇◇FACILITIES: 150 sites, most common site width 36 feet, 20 full hookups, 130 water & elec (20 & 30 amp receptacles), seasonal sites, tenting available, sewage disposal, laundry, public phone, grocery store, ice, tables, fire rings, wood. ◇◇◇RECREATION: rec hall, swim pool, lake swimming, boating, 10 hp limit, canoeing, 2 canoe boat rentals, lake fishing, playground, planned group activities, badminton, sports field, horseshoes, volleyball. Open May 15 through Oct 15. Rate in 1995 $14-19 for 2 persons. Phone: (207) 324-5652.

**YOGI BEAR'S JELLYSTONE PARK CAMP RESORT**—*From jct Hwy 4 & Hwy 109: Go 4 mi E on Hwy 109.*

**SEE PRIMARY LISTING AT WELLS AND AD WELLS PAGE 358**

## SCARBOROUGH—F-2

**BAYLEY'S PINE POINT RESORT**—A flat, semi-wooded location with a resort atmosphere. *From jct I-95 (Maine Tpk) (exit 6) & US 1: Go 1 1/2 mi S on US 1, then 3 mi E on Hwy 9 to Pine Point. Follow signs to campground.*

◇◇◇◇FACILITIES: 470 sites, most common site width 28 feet, 250 full hookups, 100 water & elec, 40 elec (20,30 & 50 amp receptacles), 80 no hookups, seasonal sites, 30 pull-thrus, a/c allowed ($), heater allowed ($), cable TV, phone hookups, tenting available, group sites for tents/RVs, tent rentals, RV rentals, handicap restroom facilities, sewage disposal, laundry, public phone, full service store, RV supplies, LP gas refill by weight/by meter, ice, tables, fire rings, grills, wood, traffic control gate/guard.

◇◇◇◇◇RECREATION: rec hall, rec room/area, equipped pavilion, coin games, 3 swim pools (heated), whirlpool, 3 pedal boat rentals, pond fishing, mini-golf ($), basketball hoop, 10 bike rentals, playground, planned group activities, recreation director, badminton, sports field, horseshoes, hiking trails, volleyball, local tours.

Open May 1 through Columbus Day. Rate in 1995 $18-37.50 for 2 persons. Reservations recom-

ME State Motto: I Guide ME



mended Jul through Aug. Master Card/Visa accepted. Member of ARVC; MECOA. Phone: (207) 883-6043.

**SEE AD TRAVEL SECTION PAGE 321 AND AD OLD ORCHARD BEACH PAGE 348**

**Wild Duck Camping Area**—A wooded CAMPGROUND near marshlands. *From I-95 (exit 6) & Paine Rd: Go 2 3/4 mi SE on Paine Rd, then 1/4 mi E on Hwy 9, then 1/2 mi SE on Dunstan Landing Rd.* ◇◇FACILITIES: 60 sites, most common site width 28 feet, 50 full hookups, (20 & 30 amp receptacles), 10 no hookups, seasonal sites, tenting available, sewage disposal, laundry, public phone, ice, tables, fire rings, wood. Open May 1 through Oct 15. Rate in 1995 $12-16 for 2 persons. No refunds. Phone: (207) 883-4432.

## SEARSMONT—E-3

**ALDUS SHORES LAKESIDE CAMPING**—Rural, lakeside CAMPGROUND with open and shaded sites. *From jct US 1 & Hwy 3: Go 6 mi W on Hwy 3, then 3 mi S on Hwy 131, then 1/2 mi W on access road.*

◇◇FACILITIES: 150 sites, most common site width 22 feet, 148 water & elec (15 amp receptacles), 2 no hookups, seasonal sites, 34 pull-thrus, a/c allowed ($), heater not allowed, phone hookups, tenting available, RV storage, sewage disposal, laundry, public phone, limited grocery store, ice, tables, fire rings, wood.

◇◇◇RECREATION: rec hall, rec room/area, coin games, lake swimming, boating, ramp, dock, 1 row/1 canoe/2 pedal boat rentals, lake fishing, playground, planned group activities (weekends only), badminton, sports field, horseshoes, hiking trails, volleyball. Recreation open to the public.

Open mid May through mid Sep. Rate in 1995 $15-17 per family. Member of ARVC; MECOA. Phone: (207) 342-5618.

**SEE AD BELFAST PAGE 330**

## SEARSPORT—E-3

**SEARSPORT SHORES CAMPING RESORT**—Oceanfront CAMPGROUND. *From town center: Go 1 mi S on US 1.*

◇◇◇FACILITIES: 120 sites, 100 water & elec (15 & 30 amp receptacles), 20 no hookups, seasonal sites, 6 pull-thrus, a/c allowed, heater allowed ($), tenting available, group sites for tents/RVs, non-flush/marine toilets, handicap restroom facilities, sewage disposal, laundry, public phone, grocery store, RV supplies, ice, tables, fire rings, wood.

◇◇◇RECREATION: rec hall, equipped pavilion, coin games, salt water swimming, salt water fishing, basketball hoop, playground, horseshoes, hiking trails, volleyball.



Open May 15 through Oct 15. Rate in 1995 $15-25 per family. Discover/Master Card/Visa accepted. Phone: (207) 548-6059.

**SEE AD THIS PAGE**

## SEBAGO LAKE—E-1

**FAMILY-N-FRIENDS CAMPGROUND**—Quiet, wooded sites near Sebago Lake. *From jct Hwy 35 & Hwy 114: Go 3/4 mi NW on Hwy 114.*

◇◇FACILITIES: 39 sites, most common site width 30 feet, 9 full hookups, 27 water & elec (20 & 50 amp receptacles), 3 no hookups, seasonal sites, 4 pull-thrus, a/c allowed, phone hookups, tenting available, sewage disposal, laundry, ice, tables, fire rings, wood.

◇◇◇RECREATION: rec room/area, swim pool (heated), wading pool, whirlpool, playground, planned group activities (weekends only), badminton, horseshoes, volleyball.

Open May 1 through Nov 1. Rate in 1995 $15-21 per family. Member of ARVC; MECOA. Phone: (207) 642-2200.

**SEE AD THIS PAGE**

**SEBAGO LAKE RESORT & CAMPGROUND**—Lakeside setting with large wooded sites. *From jct Hwy 35 & Hwy 114: Go 7 mi N on Hwy 114.*

◇◇◇FACILITIES: 100 sites, most common site width 60 feet, 43 full hookups, 57 water & elec (20 & 30 amp receptacles), seasonal sites, 9 pull-thrus, a/c allowed, heater allowed, cable TV, tenting available, cabins, sewage disposal, laundry, public phone, grocery store, RV supplies, LP gas refill by weight/by meter, ice, tables, fire rings, grills, wood, traffic control gate.

◇◇◇◇RECREATION: rec hall, rec room/area, coin games, lake swimming, boating, canoeing, dock, 3 row/2 pedal boat rentals, lake fishing, mini-golf ($), basketball hoop, playground, badminton, horseshoes, hiking trails, volleyball.

Open May 1 through mid Oct. Rate in 1995 $18-28 per family. Master Card/Visa accepted. Member of ARVC; MECOA. Phone: (207) 787-3671.

**SEE AD THIS PAGE**

## SEBEC LAKE—C-3

**Packard's Moorings Camping Area**—A riverside CAMPGROUND. *In town at end of Hwy 150.* ◇◇FACILITIES: 15 sites, most common site width 22 feet, 12 full hookups, (15 & 30 amp receptacles), 3 no hookups, tenting available, public phone, tables, fire rings, wood. ◇◇◇RECREATION: lake swimming, boating, canoeing, ramp, dock, 20 row/4 canoe/15 motor boat rentals, lake fishing, hiking trails. Open May 1 through Sep 30. No showers. Rate in 1995 $12 per family. Phone: (207) 997-3300.

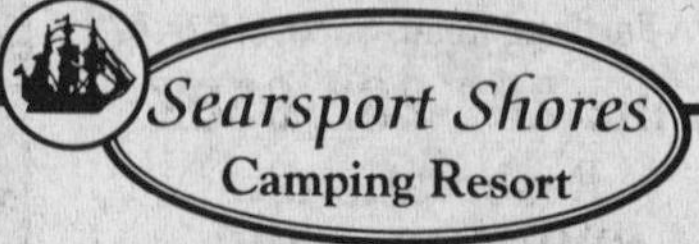

## SKOWHEGAN—D-2

✽ **DON'S TRAILER SALES**—*From jct US 2 & Hwy 150: Go 1 mi N on Hwy 150, then 1 block E on St Marks St, then 1 block N on Parlin St.* SALES: travel trailers, truck campers, 5th wheels, motor homes, mini-motor homes, fold-down camping trailers. SERVICES: RV appliance mechanic full-time, sells parts/accessories, installs hitches. Open all year. Phone: (207) 474-2983.

**SEE AD THIS PAGE**

**TWO RIVERS CAMPGROUND**—CAMPGROUND with riverside sites. *From jct US 201 & US 2: Go 2 1/2 mi E on US 2.*

◆◆◆FACILITIES: 65 sites, most common site width 22 feet, 40 full hookups, 12 water & elec (15,20 & 30 amp receptacles), 13 no hookups, seasonal sites, 24 pull-thrus, a/c allowed ($), heater allowed ($), cable TV ($), phone hookups, tenting available, sewage disposal, laundry, public phone, grocery store, RV supplies, LP gas refill by meter, ice, tables, fire rings, wood.

◆◆◆RECREATION: river swimming, boating, canoeing, dock, 3 row/3 canoe/3 pedal boat rentals, river/stream fishing, 7 bike rentals, playground, badminton, horseshoes, volleyball.

Open May 1 through Oct 31. Rate in 1995 $15-18 per family. Master Card/Visa accepted. Member of ARVC; MECOA. Phone: (207) 474-6482.

**SEE AD THIS PAGE**

**YONDER HILL FAMILY CAMPGROUND**—A family oriented CAMPGROUND with shaded sites. *From jct US 2 & US 201: Go 3 1/2 mi N on US 201.*

◆◆FACILITIES: 80 sites, most common site width 26 feet, 23 full hookups, 57 water & elec (15 & 20 amp receptacles), seasonal sites, a/c not allowed, heater not allowed, phone hookups, tenting available, group sites for tents/RVs, RV storage, sewage disposal, laundry, public phone, limited grocery store, RV supplies, ice, tables, fire rings, wood.

◆◆◆RECREATION: rec hall, coin games, swim pool, basketball hoop, playground, 2 shuffleboard courts, badminton, sports field, horseshoes, volleyball. Recreation open to the public.

Open May 15 through Sep 15. Limited facilities Sep 15 through Oct 1. Rate in 1995 $12-16 per family. Phone: (207) 474-7353.

**SEE AD THIS PAGE**

## SMALL POINT BEACH—E-2

**Hermit Island**—An ocean resort CAMPGROUND for tents, tent trailers and small pickup truck campers. *From jct Hwy 209 & Hwy 216: Go 4 mi S on Hwy 216.* ◆◆FACILITIES: 275 sites, most common site width 250 feet, 275 no hookups, tenting available, public phone, full service store, ice, tables, fire rings, wood. ◆◆◆RECREATION: rec room/area, pavilion, salt water swimming, boating, ramp, dock, 7 row/1 canoe boat rentals, salt water fishing, planned group activities, recreation director, hiking trails, volleyball. Open mid May through mid Oct. Facilities fully operational mid Jun through Labor Day. No visitors allowed-paying guests only. Rate in 1995 $23-33 per family. Member of ARVC; MECOA. Phone: (207) 443-2101.

## SOUTH LEBANON—F-1

**B & B Family Camping**—Wooded sites in a CAMPGROUND convenient to a highway. *From New Hampshire/Maine state border & US 202: Go 1 1/4 mi E on US 202.* ◆◆FACILITIES: 56 sites, most common site width 28 feet, 15 full hookups, 15 water & elec (20 & 30 amp receptacles), 26 no hookups, tenting available, sewage disposal, ice, tables, fire rings, wood. ◆◆RECREATION: rec hall, swim pool, playground, sports field, horseshoes, volleyball. Open May 1 through Oct 31. Rate in 1995 $14-20. Phone: (207) 339-0150.

## SOUTHWEST HARBOR—E-4

ACADIA NATIONAL PARK (Seawall Campground)—*Southbound, from jct Hwy 102 & Hwy 102A: Go 5 mi S on Hwy 102A.* FACILITIES: 218 sites, 35 ft. max RV length, 218 no hookups, tenting available, sewage disposal, public phone, tables, fire rings, grills. RECREATION: fishing. Open late May through late Sep. No showers. Phone: (207) 288-3338.

**Smuggler's Den Campground**—Wooded CAMPGROUND with open and shaded sites. *From jct Hwy 198 & Hwy 102: Go 5 mi S on Hwy 102.* ◆◆◆FACILITIES: 100 sites, most common site width 26 feet, 22 full hookups, 43 water & elec (15,20 & 30 amp receptacles), 35 no hookups, seasonal sites, 5 pull-thrus, tenting available, sewage disposal, laundry, public phone, grocery store, ice, tables, fire rings, wood. ◆◆RECREATION: swim pool (heated), badminton, horseshoes, volleyball. Open Memorial Day through mid Oct. Self-contained units only Sep 15 through mid Oct. Rate in 1995 $18-25 for 4 persons. Member of ARVC; MECOA. Phone: (207) 244-3944.

**White Birches Campground**—Wooded, secluded sites. *From Hwy 198 & Hwy 102: Go 4 mi S on Hwy 102, then 1 mi W on Seal Cove Rd.* ◆◆FACILITIES: 60 sites, most common site width 35 feet, 13 water & elec (15 amp receptacles), 47 no hookups, tenting available, sewage disposal, public phone, ice, tables, fire rings, wood. ◆RECREATION: playground. Open May 15 through Oct 15. Rate in 1995 $18 per family. Phone: (207) 244-3797.

## SPRINGFIELD—C-4

**Maine Wilderness Camps & Campground**—Spacious sites in a wilderness & lake setting with a lodge available. *From jct I-95 (exit 55) & Hwy 6: Go 32 mi E on Hwy 6.* ◆FACILITIES: 19 sites, most common site width 60 feet, 4 water & elec (15 amp receptacles), 15 no hookups, seasonal sites, tenting available, limited grocery store, tables, fire rings, wood. ◆◆◆RECREATION: lake swimming, boating, canoeing, ramp, dock, 29 canoe/6 motor boat rentals, lake fishing, playground, horseshoes, hiking trails, volleyball. Recreation open to the public. Open all year. Facilities fully operational May 15 through Oct 15. Rate in 1995 $8-15. Member of ARVC; MECOA. Phone: (207) 738-5052.

## STEEP FALLS—E-1

**ACRES OF WILDLIFE**—Lakeside CAMPGROUND with miles of natural forest and fishing ponds. *From jct Hwy 113 & Hwy 11: Go 1/2 mi W on Hwy 113/Hwy 11, then 2 1/2 mi N on campground road.*

◆◆◆FACILITIES: 200 sites, most common site width 50 feet, 55 full hookups, 100 water & elec (15,20 & 30 amp receptacles), 45 no hookups, seasonal sites, a/c allowed, heater allowed, phone hookups, tenting available, group sites for tents/RVs, RV rentals, cabins, sewage disposal, laundry, public phone, grocery store, RV supplies, LP gas refill by weight/by meter, ice, tables, fire rings, grills, wood.

◆◆◆◆◆RECREATION: rec hall, rec room/area, equipped pavilion, coin games, lake swimming, boating, electric motors only, canoeing, dock, 10 row/20 canoe/6 pedal boat rentals, lake/pond fishing, mini-golf ($), basketball hoop, 8 bike rentals, playground, planned group activities, movies, recreation director, badminton, sports field, horseshoes, hiking trails, volleyball.

Open mid Apr through Dec 1. Rate in 1995 $15-29 per family. Reservations recommended Jul through Aug. Discover/Master Card/Visa accepted. CPO. Member of ARVC;MECOA. Phone: (207) 675-3211.

**SEE AD TRAVEL SECTION PAGE 318**

## STETSON—D-3

**Stetson Shores Campground**—Rural, wooded sites on a lake. *From jct I-95 (exit 42) & Hwy 143: Go 6 mi N on Hwy 143.* ◆◆FACILITIES: 43 sites, most common site width 26 feet, 40 water & elec (15 amp receptacles), 3 no hookups, seasonal sites, tenting available, sewage disposal, laundry, public phone, limited grocery store, ice, tables, fire rings, wood. ◆◆◆RECREATION: rec hall, lake swimming, boating, canoeing, ramp, dock, 4 canoe/2 pedal boat rentals, lake fishing, badminton, horseshoes, volleyball. Recreation open to the public. Open May 1 through Oct 15. Rate in 1995 $16.50-18.50 per family. CPO. Member of ARVC; MECOA. Phone: (207) 296-2041.

## STEUBEN—D-4

**Mainayr Campground**—Rural oceanside CAMPGROUND with open and shaded sites. *From jct US 1 & Steuben Rd: Go 1/2 mi E on Steuben Rd.* ◆FACILITIES: 32 sites, most common site width 40 feet, 5 full hookups, 5 water & elec, 5 elec (15,20 & 30 amp receptacles), 17 no hookups, seasonal sites, tenting available, sewage disposal, laundry, public phone, limited grocery store, ice, tables, fire rings, wood. ◆RECREATION: salt water swimming, playground, badminton, horseshoes, volleyball. Open Memorial Day through Columbus Day. Rates available upon request. Phone: (207) 546-2690.

## STONINGTON—E-3

**GREENLAW'S RV & TENTING PARK**—Rustic, wooded sites in a CAMPGROUND on a peninsula. *From southernmost jct Hwy 175 & Hwy 15: Go 10 3/4 mi S on Hwy 15, then 1 1/2 mi W on County Rd.*

◆◆FACILITIES: 50 sites, 17 full hookups, 15 water & elec (15 & 20 amp receptacles), 18 no hookups, seasonal sites, a/c allowed ($), heater allowed ($), phone hookups, tenting available, RV rentals, sewage disposal, tables, fire rings, wood.

RECREATION: hiking trails.

Open early Apr through early Dec. Rate in 1995 $10-16 for 2 persons. Phone: (207) 367-5049.

**SEE AD TRAVEL SECTION PAGE 322**

## STRATTON—D-2

CATHEDRAL PINES (Stratton-Eustis Dev. Corp.)—*From jct Hwy 16 & Hwy 27: Go 4 mi N on Hwy 27.* FACILITIES: 115 sites, 98 water & elec (15 & 20 amp receptacles), 17 no hookups, seasonal sites, tenting available, sewage disposal, laundry, public phone, ice, tables, fire rings, wood. RECREATION: rec hall, lake swimming, boating, canoeing, ramp, dock, 8 canoe boat rentals, lake fishing, playground, sports field. Open May 15 through Oct 1. Phone: (207) 246-3491.

## SULLIVAN—D-4

**Mountainview Campground**—A rural, oceanside setting with a mountainview. *From jct Hwy 200 & US 1: Go 3 mi N on US 1.* ◆◆FACILITIES: 50 sites, most common site width 22 feet, 4 full hookups, 46 water & elec (20 & 30 amp receptacles), seasonal sites, 23 pull-thrus, tenting available, sewage disposal, grocery store, ice, tables, fire rings, grills, wood. ◆◆RECREATION: pavilion, salt water fishing, mini-golf ($), horseshoes. Recreation open to the public. Open Memorial Day through Oct 1. Rate in 1995 $12 per family. Member of ARVC; MECOA. Phone: (207) 422-6215.

## THOMASTON—E-3

**SALTWATER FARM CAMPGROUND**—Hilly, open sites overlooking a saltwater river. *From jct Hwy 97 & US 1: Go 1 3/4 mi N on US 1, then 1 1/2 mi E on Prison Store Rd (Wadsworth St).*

◆◆◆FACILITIES: 25 sites, most common site width 26 feet, 25 full hookups, (20 & 30 amp receptacles), seasonal sites, a/c allowed, heater allowed, tenting available, RV rentals, sewage disposal, laundry, public phone, limited grocery store, ice, tables, fire rings, wood.

◆◆◆RECREATION: rec room/area, swim pool, salt water fishing, horseshoes, volleyball, local tours.

Open mid May through mid Oct. Rate in 1995 $15-20 for 4 persons. Master Card/Visa accepted. Phone: (207) 354-6735.

**SEE AD TRAVEL SECTION PAGE 322**

## TREMONT—E-4

**Quietside Campground**—Quiet atmosphere, wooded and well screened private sites with tent platforms or lean to's. *From jct Hwy 102A & Hwy 102: Go 3 1/4 mi S on Hwy 102.* ◆◆FACILITIES: 35 sites, most common site width 35 feet, 6 water & elec (30 amp receptacles), 29 no hookups, seasonal sites, tenting available, sewage disposal, laundry, public phone, ice, tables, fire rings, wood. ◆RECREATION: playground. Open Jun 15 through Columbus Day. Rate in 1995 $18 per family. Member of ARVC; MECOA. Phone: (207) 244-5992.

## TURNER—E-2

**Martin Stream Campsites**—A wooded, rustic, riverside CAMPGROUND. *From jct Hwy 4 & Hwy 117: Go 2 mi S on Hwy 117.* ◆◆FACILITIES: 45 sites, most common site width 35 feet, 35 water & elec (20 & 30 amp receptacles), 10 no hookups, seasonal sites, tenting available, sewage disposal, public phone, grocery store, LP gas refill by weight/by meter, ice, tables, fire rings, wood. ◆◆◆RECREATION: rec room/area, swim pool, river swimming, boating, canoeing, 2 row/7 canoe/2 pedal boat rentals, river/stream fishing, playground, planned group activities (weekends only), recreation director, badminton, horseshoes, volleyball. Open early May through Sep 30. Rate in 1995 $14-16 per family. No refunds. Member of ARVC; MECOA. Phone: (207) 225-3274.

## UNION—E-3

**MIC MAC COVE**—Rural, lakeside CAMPGROUND. *From west jct Hwy 131 & Hwy 17: Go 1 3/4 mi E on Hwy 17.*

WELCOME

◆◆◆FACILITIES: 86 sites, most common site width 24 feet, 8 full hookups, 78 water & elec (15,20 & 30 amp receptacles), seasonal sites, 2 pull-thrus, a/c not allowed, heater not allowed, tenting available, group sites for tents/RVs, cabins, sewage disposal, public phone, limited grocery store, ice, tables, fire rings, wood.

◆◆◆RECREATION: rec hall, rec room/area, coin games, lake swimming, sauna, boating, canoeing, ramp, dock, 2 row/2 canoe/1 pedal boat rentals, lake fishing, basketball hoop, playground, planned group activities (weekends only), badminton, sports field, horseshoes, volleyball.

Open early May through Oct 7. Rate in 1995 $16-18 per family. No refunds. Reservations recommended Jul through Aug. Master Card/Visa accepted. Phone: (207) 785-4100.

SEE AD THIS PAGE



## VASSALBORO—E-2

**Green Valley Campground**—Open & shaded sites on a lake. *From town center: Go 2 mi S on US 201, then 2 mi E on Bog Rd, then 2 3/4 mi S on Crosshill Rd.* ◆FACILITIES: 90 sites, most common site width 22 feet, 18 full hookups, 52 water & elec (15 amp receptacles), 20 no hookups, seasonal sites, tenting available, sewage disposal, laundry, public phone, limited grocery store, LP gas refill by meter, ice, tables, wood. ◆◆◆RECREATION: rec room/area, lake swimming, boating, ramp, dock, 1 row/1 sail/5 canoe/2 pedal/4 motor boat rentals, lake fishing, playground, badminton, horseshoes, volleyball. Open May 15 through Oct 15. Rate in 1995 $18-19. Phone: (207) 923-3000.

## WARREN—E-3

**Loon's Cry Campground**—Lakeside with open & shaded sites. *From jct Hwy 90 & US 1: Go 1 mi S on US 1.* ◆◆◆FACILITIES: 45 sites, most common site width 24 feet, 4 full hookups, 15 water & elec (15,20 & 30 amp receptacles), 26 no hookups, seasonal sites, tenting available, sewage disposal, laundry, public phone, ice, tables, fire rings, wood. ◆◆◆RECREATION: lake swimming, boating, ramp, dock, 6 canoe/2 pedal boat rentals, pond fishing, playground, horseshoes. Recreation open to the public. Open all year. Facilities fully operational May 1 through Thanksgiving. Rate in 1995 $14-22 per family. Phone: (800) 493-2324.

## WATERBORO CENTER—F-1

**Blackburn's Campground**—Grassy CAMPGROUND with open and shaded sites on a scenic lakeshore. *In town on Hwy 5.* ◆◆FACILITIES: 85 sites, most common site width 24 feet, 30 ft. max RV length, 65 full hookups, 20 water & elec (15 amp receptacles), seasonal sites, tenting available, sewage disposal, public phone, ice, tables, fire rings, wood. ◆◆RECREATION: rec room/area, lake swimming, boating, canoeing, dock, 4 canoe/4 pedal boat rentals, lake fishing, badminton, horseshoes, volleyball. Recreation open to the public. Open May 1 through Sep 30. Rate in 1995 $15 for 4 persons. No refunds. Phone: (207) 247-5875.

## WELD—D-2

MOUNT BLUE STATE PARK—*From jct Hwy 156 & Hwy 142: Go 2 1/4 mi N on Hwy 156, then 4 mi W on Shore Road, then 1 mi S.* FACILITIES: 136 sites, 136 no hookups, non-flush toilets, sewage disposal, public phone, ice, tables. RECREATION: lake swimming, boating, ramp, row/canoe boat rentals, fishing, playground, planned group activities, hiking trails. Open May 15 through Oct 1. Phone: (207) 585-2347.

## WELLS—F-1

**BEACH ACRES CAMPGROUND**—Level, open and wooded sites with some seasonal campers. *From jct I-95 (exit 2) & Hwy 109: Go 1 1/2 mi E on Hwy 109, then 2 mi S on US 1, then 1 block E on Eldridge Rd.*

WELCOME

◆◆◆FACILITIES: 400 sites, most common site width 40 feet, 320 full hookups, (20 & 30 amp receptacles), 80 no hookups, seasonal sites, a/c allowed, phone hookups, tenting available, RV storage, sewage disposal, laundry, public phone, limited grocery store, ice, tables, fire rings, traffic control gate/guard.

◆◆◆RECREATION: rec hall, swim pool, basketball hoop, playground, 2 shuffleboard courts, sports field, horseshoes.

No pets. Open Memorial Day through mid Sep. Rate in 1995 $18-24 for 2 persons. No refunds. Reservations recommended Jul through Aug. Member of ARVC;MECOA. Phone: (207) 646-5612.

SEE AD NEXT PAGE

WELLS—Continued

✽ **EAST COAST RV SUPPLY**—*From jct I-95 & Hwy 109: Go 1 1/2 mi E on Hwy 109, then 3 1/4 mi S on US 1.* SERVICES: RV appliance mechanic full-time, emergency road service business hours, LP gas refill by weight/by meter, sells parts/accessories, sells camping supplies. Open Apr through Nov. American Express/Discover/Master Card/Visa accepted. Phone: (207) 646-6285.

WELCOME

SEE AD MOODY PAGE 343

**Gregoire's Campground**—Open and shaded sites on flat terrain. *From jct I-95 (Exit 2) & Hwy 109: Go 1/4 mi W on Hwy 109.* ◆◆◆FACILITIES: 130 sites, 31 full hookups, 62 water & elec (20 & 30 amp receptacles), 37 no hookups, seasonal sites, tenting available, sewage disposal, public phone, limited grocery store, ice, tables, fire rings, wood. ◆RECREATION: rec room/area, playground. Open May 15 through Sep 15. Rate in 1995 $12-17 per family. Phone: (207) 646-3711.

✽ **KINNEY RV'S SALES & SERVICE**—*From jct I-93 (exit 2): Go 6 mi N on I-95 (exit 3), then 1 1/2 mi S on Hwy 35, then 4 3/4 mi N on US 1.*

WELCOME

SEE PRIMARY LISTING AT KENNEBUNK AND AD KENNEBUNK PAGE 340

**Ocean Overlook Campground**—In a resort area within a mile of the ocean. *From jct I-95 (exit 2) & Hwy 109: Go 1 1/2 mi E on Hwy 109, then 1 1/2 mi S on US 1.* ◆◆◆FACILITIES: 50 sites, most common site width 24 feet, 36 full hookups, 14 water & elec (20 & 30 amp receptacles), seasonal sites, 25 pull-thrus, tenting available, sewage disposal, public phone, ice, tables, wood. ◆◆RECREATION: 2 swim pools, playground, badminton, horseshoes, volleyball. No pets. Open mid May through Columbus Day. Rate in 1995 $20-25 for 2 persons. Member of ARVC;MECOA. Phone: (207) 646-3075.

**OCEAN VIEW COTTAGES & CAMPING**—Ocean view, wooded CAMPGROUND with housekeeping cottages. *From jct I-95 (exit 2) & Hwy 109: Go 1 1/2 mi E on Hwy 109, then 100 feet N on US 1, then 1/4 mi E on Lower Landing Rd.*

◆◆◆FACILITIES: 108 sites, most common site width 22 feet, 32 ft. max RV length, 60 full hookups, 30 water & elec, 5 elec (15,20 & 30 amp receptacles), 13 no hookups, seasonal sites, a/c allowed ($), heater not allowed, tenting available, cabins, sewage disposal, laundry, public phone, limited grocery store, ice, tables, fire rings, wood.

◆◆◆RECREATION: rec room/area, coin games, swim pool, basketball hoop, playground, 2 shuffleboard courts, tennis court.

Open May 1 through Columbus Day. Facilities fully operational Memorial Day through Columbus Day. Rate in 1995 $17-25 for 4 persons. Reservations recommended Jul through Aug. Master Card/Visa accepted. Phone: (207) 646-3308.

SEE AD NEXT PAGE

**RIVERSIDE CAMPGROUND**—Flat, grassy, riverside. *From jct I-95 & Hwy 109: Go 1 1/2 mi E on Hwy 109, then 1 3/4 mi N on US 1.*

WELCOME

◆◆◆FACILITIES: 130 sites, most common site width 26 feet, 93 full hookups, 26 water & elec (15,20,30 & 50 amp receptacles), 11 no hookups, seasonal sites, a/c allowed ($), cable TV ($), phone hookups, tenting available, RV storage,

RIVERSIDE CAMPGROUND—Continued on next page
WELLS—Continued on next page

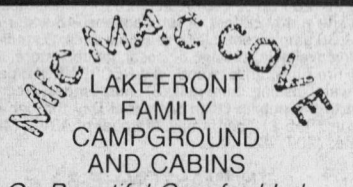

WELLS—Continued
RIVERSIDE CAMPGROUND—Continued

handicap restroom facilities, sewage disposal, public phone, limited grocery store, ice, tables, fire rings, wood.

◆◆RECREATION: rec room/area, swim pool, river fishing, basketball hoop.

Open May 15 through Oct 15. Facilities fully operational Jun 1 through Labor Day. Rate in 1995 $10-16 for 2 persons. Reservations recommended Jul through Aug. Master Card/Visa accepted. Member of ARVC; MECOA. Phone: (207) 646-3145.
**SEE AD THIS PAGE**

**SEA BREEZE CAMPGROUND & MOTEL**—Semi-wooded sites near the beaches. *From jct I-95 (exit 2) & Hwy 109: Go 1 1/2 mi E on Hwy 109, then 1 1/4 mi N on US 1.*

WELCOME

◆◆◆FACILITIES: 56 sites, most common site width 32 feet, 52 full hookups, (20,30 & 50 amp receptacles), 4 no hookups, seasonal sites, a/c allowed ($), cable TV, tenting available, handicap restroom facilities, sewage disposal, laundry, public phone, grocery store, ice, tables, wood.

◆◆RECREATION: rec room/area, swim pool (heated), playground.

WELLS—Continued
SEA BREEZE CAMPGROUND & MOTEL—Continued

Open mid May through mid Oct. Rate in 1995 $24-27 per family. Discover/Master Card/Visa accepted. Phone: (207) 646-4301.
**SEE AD NEXT PAGE**

**SEA VU CAMPGROUND**—Oceanview, semi-wooded, family oriented CAMPGROUND. *From jct I-95 (exit 2) & Hwy 109: Go 1 1/2 mi E on Hwy 109, then 4/10 mi N on US 1.*

WELCOME

◆◆◆◆FACILITIES: 218 sites, most common site width 40 feet, 168 full hookups, 39 water & elec (20 & 30 amp receptacles), 11 no hookups, seasonal sites, a/c allowed ($), cable TV, tenting available, RV storage, sewage disposal, laundry, public phone, grocery store, RV supplies, LP gas refill by weight/by meter, ice, tables, fire rings, wood, traffic control gate.

◆◆◆◆RECREATION: rec hall, rec room/area, coin games, swim pool, mini-golf ($), basketball hoop,

SEA VU CAMPGROUND—Continued on page 361
WELLS—Continued on page 361

WELLS—Continued
SEA VU CAMPGROUND—Continued

playground, planned group activities, badminton, sports field, horseshoes, volleyball. Recreation open to the public.

Open May 15 through Columbus Day. Facilities fully operational Jun 21 through Labor Day. Rate in 1995 $18.50-30 for 2 persons. Reservations recommended Jul through Aug. Discover/Master Card/Visa accepted. Member of ARVC; MECOA. Phone: (207) 646-7732.

SEE AD THIS PAGE

**STADIG CAMPGROUND**—A wooded, flat CAMPGROUND. *From jct I-95 (exit 2) & Hwy 109: Go 1 1/2 mi E on Hwy 109, then 2 mi N on US 1, then 1/4 mi on US 1 Bypass.*

WELCOME

◆◆FACILITIES: 150 sites, most common site width 26 feet, 37 full hookups, 5 water & elec, 11 elec (15,20 & 30 amp receptacles), 97 no hookups, seasonal sites, 22 pull-thrus, tenting available, RV storage, sewage disposal, laundry, public phone, limited grocery store, ice, tables, fire rings, wood.

◆◆RECREATION: rec hall, basketball hoop, playground, shuffleboard court, badminton, sports field, horseshoes, volleyball.

No pets. Open Memorial Day weekend through Oct 1. Rate in 1995 $14-20 for 4 persons. Reservations recommended Jul through Aug. Member of ARVC; MECOA. Phone: (207) 646-2298.

SEE AD PAGE 359

**WELLS BEACH RESORT**—A resort CAMPGROUND with wooded and open sites and an oceanview. *From jct I-95 (exit 2) & Hwy 109: Go 1 1/2 mi E on Hwy 109, then 1 1/4 mi S on US 1.*

WELCOME

◆◆◆◆◆FACILITIES: 212 sites, most common site width 33 feet, 171 full hookups, (20 & 30 amp receptacles), 41 no hookups, seasonal sites, 100 pull-thrus, a/c allowed, heater allowed, cable TV, tenting available, sewage disposal, laundry, public phone, grocery store, RV supplies, ice, tables, fire rings, wood, traffic control gate/guard.

◆◆◆◆RECREATION: rec room/area, coin games, swim pool, mini-golf ($), basketball hoop, playground, badminton, horseshoes, volleyball. Recreation open to the public.

Open mid May through mid Oct. Facilities fully operational Jun 15 through Labor Day. Rate in 1995 $22-34.50 for 2 persons. No refunds. Reservations recommended Jul through Aug. Master Card/Visa accepted. Member of ARVC; MECOA. Phone: (207) 646-7570.

SEE AD FRONT OF BOOK PAGE 8 AND AD PAGE 360

**YOGI BEAR'S JELLYSTONE PARK CAMP-RESORT**—A flat, semi-wooded location. *From jct I-95 (exit 2) & Hwy 109: Go 5 mi NW on Hwy 109.*

WELCOME

◆◆◆FACILITIES: 132 sites, most common site width 24 feet, 35 ft. max RV length, 74 full hookups, 43 water & elec (20,30 & 50 amp receptacles), 15 no hookups, seasonal sites, a/c allowed ($), heater not allowed, tenting available, RV storage, handicap restroom facilities, sewage disposal, laundry, public phone, limited grocery store, ice, tables, fire rings, wood.

◆◆◆RECREATION: rec room/area, coin games, swim pool, basketball hoop, playground, planned group activities, movies, badminton, sports field, horseshoes, volleyball.

Open May 15 through Sep 15. Facilities fully operational Jun 15 through Labor Day. Rate in 1995 $16-21 for 2 persons. No refunds. Reservations recommended Jul through Aug. Master Card/Visa accepted. Member of ARVC; MECOA. Phone: (207) 324-7782.

SEE AD PAGE 358

**Give a man a fish, and you feed him for a day. Teach a man to fish, and you get rid of him on the weekends.**

***Gary Apple***

## WINDHAM—E-2

✽ **CUSTOM LAND YACHTS**—*From jct US 302 & Hwy 115: Go 2 1/4 mi W on Hwy 115.* Custom built bus conversions. Open Apr through Dec. Phone: (207) 892-3885.
**SEE AD FRONT OF BOOK PAGE 3**

✽ **LEE'S FAMILY TRAILER SALES & SERVICE**—*From jct US 202 & US 302 (Fosters Corner): Go 3/4 mi W on US 302.* SALES: travel trailers, truck campers, 5th wheels, motor homes, mini-motor homes, micro-mini motor homes, fold-down camping trailers. SERVICES: Engine/Chassis & RV appliance mechanic full-time, emergency road service business hours, LP gas refill by weight/by meter, RV rentals, tent rentals, sells parts/accessories, sells camping supplies, installs hitches. Open all year. Discover/Master Card/Visa accepted. Phone: (207) 892-8040.
**SEE AD THIS PAGE**

## WINTER HARBOR—E-4

MILITARY PARK (Schoodic Point Rec. Area - Naval Security Campground)—*From jct US 1 & Hwy 186: Go S on Hwy 186, then continue S to Schoodic Point. On base.* FACILITIES: 10 sites, 6 full hookups, (30 amp receptacles), 4 no hookups, tenting available, sewage disposal, tables, grills. RECREATION: equipped pavilion, playground, planned group activities, recreation director, tennis court, badminton, sports field, horseshoes, hiking trails. Open Apr 15 through Oct 15. Phone: (207) 963-5537.

## WINTHROP—E-2

**AUGUSTA-WEST LAKESIDE RESORT KAMPGROUND**—Open or wooded sites on a peninsula on a large lake. *From jct Hwy 41 & US 202: Go 3/4 mi E on US 202, then 1 mi S on Highland Ave, then 3/4 mi W on access road.*

◆◆◆FACILITIES: 81 sites, most common site width 24 feet, 17 full hookups, 52 water & elec (20 & 30 amp receptacles), 12 no hookups, seasonal sites, 20 pull-thrus, a/c allowed ($), heater allowed ($), phone hookups, tenting available, group sites for tents/RVs, RV rentals, RV storage, sewage disposal, laundry, public phone, grocery store, RV supplies, LP gas refill by weight/by meter, gasoline, marine gas, ice, tables, fire rings, wood.

◆◆◆◆RECREATION: rec room/area, equipped pavilion, coin games, swim pool (heated), lake swimming, whirlpool, boating, canoeing, ramp, dock, 1 row/2 canoe/4 pedal/4 motor boat rentals, water skiing, lake fishing, fishing guides, basketball hoop, playground, planned group activities (weekends only), badminton, horseshoes, volleyball.

Open May 15 through Oct 15. Rate in 1995 $13.50-35 for 2 persons. No refunds. Reservations recommended Jul through Aug. Master Card/Visa accepted. Member of ARVC; MECOA. Phone: (207) 377-9993.
**SEE AD AUGUSTA PAGE 325**

**We all admire the wisdom of people who come to us for advice.** ***Jack Herbert***

## WISCASSET—E-2

**Chewonki Campgrounds**—A gently rolling, grassy, riverside location. *From jct Hwy 27 & US 1: Go 3 1/2 mi S on US 1, then 1/4 mi SE on Hwy 144, then 1 mi S on Chewonki Rd.* ◇◇◇FACILITIES: 47 sites, most common site width 30 feet, 8 full hookups, 30 water & elec (15 & 20 amp receptacles), 9 no hookups, seasonal sites, 20 pull-thrus, tenting available, handicap restroom facilities, sewage disposal, grocery store, ice, tables, fire rings, wood. ◇◇◇RECREATION: rec hall, 2 swim pools, salt water swimming, boating, canoeing, dock, 1 row/2 canoe boat rentals, salt water fishing, playground, tennis court, badminton, sports field, horseshoes, hiking trails, volleyball. Recreation open to the public. Open mid May through mid Oct. Rate in 1995 $18-25 per family. Member of ARVC; MECOA. Phone: (207) 882-7426.

**Down East Family Camping**—Northern wilderness CAMPGROUND on Mid Coast Lake catering to tenters, tent trailers and pick-ups. *From south jct US 1 & Hwy 27: Go 4 mi N on Hwy 27.* ◇◇FACILITIES: 40 sites, most common site width 200 feet, 2 water & elec, 6 elec (15 amp receptacles), 32 no hookups, tenting available, ice, tables, fire rings, wood. ◇◇◇RECREATION: lake swimming, boating, electric motors only, canoeing, dock, 2 sail/6 canoe/2 pedal boat rentals, lake fishing, playground, badminton, horseshoes, hiking trails, volleyball. Open Memorial Day through Columbus Day. Rate in 1995 $16-20 per family. Member of ARVC; MECOA. Phone: (207) 882-5431.

## YORK BEACH—F-1

**York Beach Camper Park**—CAMGROUND in a wooded setting near town & beaches. *From jct I-95 (exit 1) & US 1: Go 3 1/4 mi N on US 1, then 1 mi E on US 1A.* ◇◇◇FACILITIES: 46 sites, most common site width 22 feet, 34 full hookups, 5 water & elec (20,30 & 50 amp receptacles), 7 no hookups, tenting available, handicap restroom facilities, sewage disposal, laundry, limited grocery store, ice, tables, grills, wood. Open mid May through mid Oct. Rate in 1995 $18.70-27.50 for 2 persons. Phone: (207) 363-1343.

## YORK HARBOR—F-1

**Camp Eaton**—An open and shaded family-oriented CAMPGROUND adjacent to the ocean. *From I-95 (The Yorks exit): Go 1/4 mi S on US 1, then 3 mi NE on US 1A.* ◇◇◇FACILITIES: 303 sites, 238 full hookups, 18 water & elec, 47 elec (20,30 & 50 amp receptacles), seasonal sites, tenting available, sewage disposal, public phone, ice, tables, fire rings, wood. ◇◇◇◇RECREATION: rec hall, salt water swimming, salt water fishing, playground, 2 shuffleboard courts, planned group activities, recreation director, sports field, horseshoes, volleyball. Open May 1 through Sep 30. Rate in 1995 $19-33 for 2 persons. Member of ARVC; MECOA. Phone: (207) 363-3424.

**LIBBY'S OCEANSIDE CAMP**—An open, grassy, oceanside CAMPGROUND. *From I-95 ("The Yorks" exit): Go 1/4 mi S on US 1, then 3 mi NE on US 1A.*

WELCOME

◇◇◇FACILITIES: 95 sites, most common site width 18 feet, 88 full hookups, 7 water & elec (20 & 30 amp receptacles), seasonal sites, a/c allowed ($), heater allowed ($), tenting available, handicap restroom facilities, public phone, ice, tables.

◇RECREATION: rec room/area, salt water swimming, salt water fishing.

Open May 15 through Oct 15. Rate in 1995 $28-35. Reservations recommended Jul through Aug. Discover/Master Card/Visa accepted. CPO. Member of ARVC; MECOA. Phone: (207) 363-4171.

**SEE AD THIS PAGE**



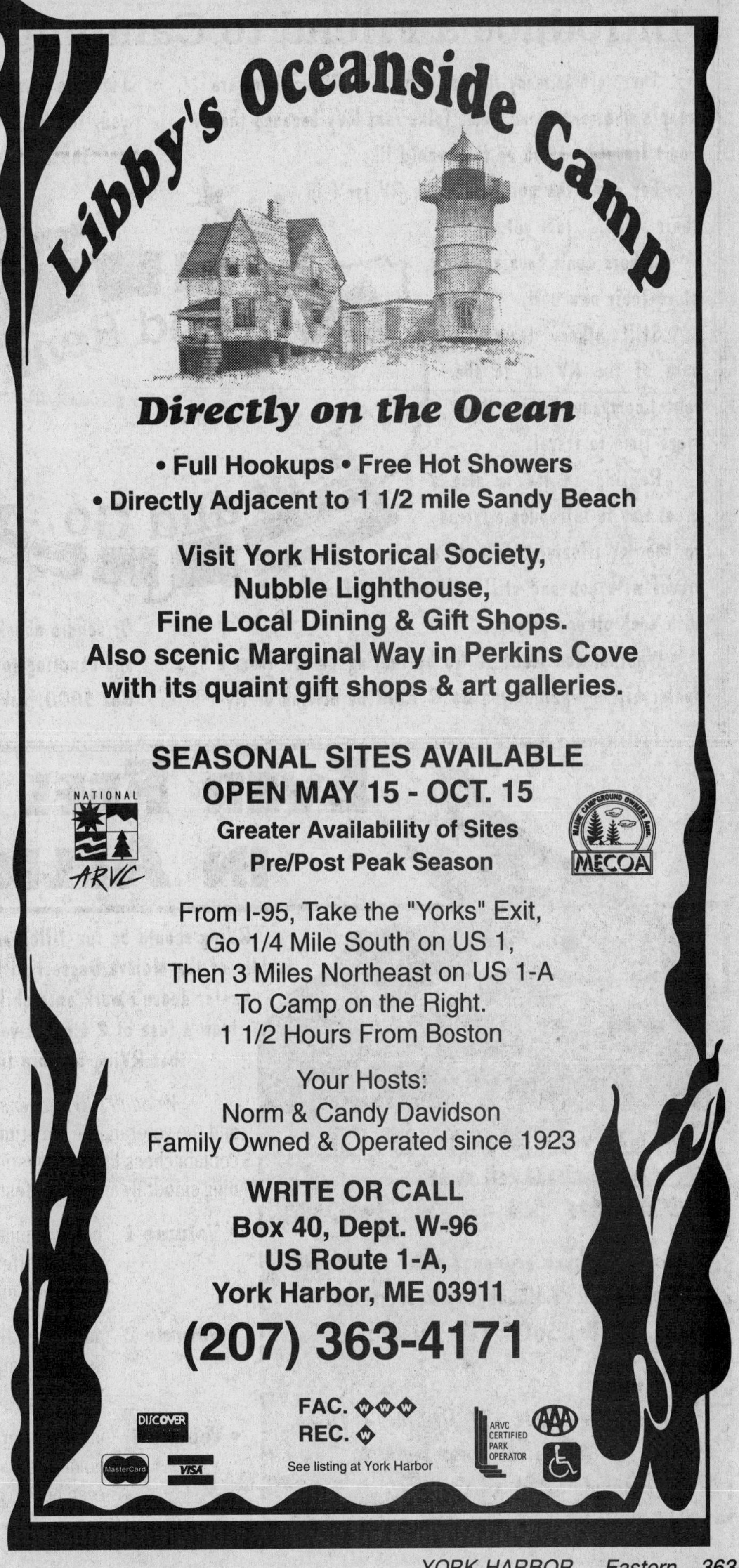

Libby's Oceanside Camp
Directly on the Ocean
• Full Hookups • Free Hot Showers
• Directly Adjacent to 1 1/2 mile Sandy Beach
Visit York Historical Society,
Nubble Lighthouse,
Fine Local Dining & Gift Shops.
Also scenic Marginal Way in Perkins Cove
with its quaint gift shops & art galleries.
SEASONAL SITES AVAILABLE
OPEN MAY 15 - OCT. 15
Greater Availability of Sites
Pre/Post Peak Season
NATIONAL
ARVC
MECOA
From I-95, Take the "Yorks" Exit,
Go 1/4 Mile South on US 1,
Then 3 Miles Northeast on US 1-A
To Camp on the Right.
1 1/2 Hours From Boston
Your Hosts:
Norm & Candy Davidson
Family Owned & Operated since 1923
WRITE OR CALL
Box 40, Dept. W-96
US Route 1-A,
York Harbor, ME 03911
(207) 363-4171
FAC. ◇◇◇
REC. ◇
See listing at York Harbor
DISCOVER
MasterCard
VISA
ARVC CERTIFIED PARK OPERATOR
AAA

# Introduce a Friend to Camping with RV Rentals

There are as many reasons to rent an RV as there are people who rent them. Some folks rent RVs because they don't travel as often as they would like.

For some the purchase of an RV isn't in their plans... just yet.

Others don't have space to store their own unit.

Still others leave the care of the RV up to the rental company, leaving them more time to travel.

Renting an RV is also a great way to introduce a friend to the RV lifestyle. Friends can travel with you and still still not interfer with each other's privacy.

Whether you **Rent & Go** by renting an RV from a dealership or whether you **Go & Rent** by driving or flying to a campsite where your rental unit is waiting for you, the RV lifestyle is now easier than ever to enjoy.

Go and Rent...

Rent and Go...

The excitement of the open road, he warmth of the evening campfire, and the array of activities offered at RV parks will provide memories to last a lifetime.

Don't miss out. Order your copy of *WOODALL'S Go & Rent... Rent & Go...* Today!

To order your copy of *Woodall's Go & Rent... Rent & Go...*, use your Visa or MasterCard and call **800/323-9076.** (Monday-Friday, 8 a.m. to 5 p.m. CST).

Or send a check or money order for $2 U.S. for shipping and handling to: Woodall Publications, Dept. 3036, P.O. Box 5000, Lake Forest IL 60045.

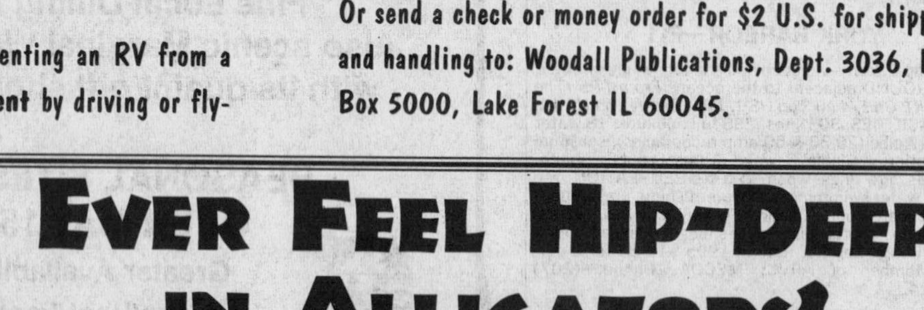


RVing should be fun-filled and fancy-free – but if you're sitting in the middle of the Mojave Dessert with a leaky water system... or find that your heater doesn't work on a chilly fall night in Vermont... or even if you blow a fuse at 2 a.m. at your nearby campground, You just might feel that RVing is more like being in a swampful of alligators.

*Woodall's RV Owner's Handbooks* are written for both the novice and the veteran, the part-time RVer and the full-timer. The Handbooks contain check lists, suggestions and helpful hints to keep your RV running smoothly and your lifestyle uncomplicated.

- **Volume 1** helps familiarize those new to the lifestyle with terminology, different RV categories and basic principles of operation and maintenance procedures.
- **Volume 2** addresses the various systems found on RVs and details specific maintenance and repair procedures to keep your rig in tip-top shape.
- **Volume 3** is for the serious do-it-yourselfer. It details how to repair a holding tank; installing awnings; repair water damage; and even how to establish a master maintenance schedule.

To order any or all of the volumes use your credit card and call us at **800/323-9076.** (Mon.-Fri. 8 a.m.-5 p.m. CST).

Or send check or money order to Woodall's 1995 RV Owner's Handbook, Department 3035, P.O. Box 5000, Lake Forest IL 60045-5000.

One volume costs $10. Or order any two volumes for $19. Or all three for $24. (Prices include S&H)

# Massachusetts

TRAVEL SECTION

## Free Information from Travel Section Advertisers

The following businesses have placed an ad in the Massachusetts Travel Section. To receive free information, enter their Reader Service number on the Reader Service Card opposite page 16 in the front of this directory:

| Advertiser | RS # | Ad Pg. |
|---|---|---|
| MACO | 583 | 377 |
| Plymouth County Attractions | 633 | 379 |
| Springbrook Family Camping | 299 | 377 |

## Time Zone/Topography

Massachusetts is on Eastern Time.

The varied terrain of Massachusetts comprises beaches, farmland, forests and mountains. The highest point in the state is 3,491-foot Mount Greylock.

## Climate

High and low temperature extremes do occasionally occur in certain portions of the state, but temperatures are generally moderate. January averages range from 23° to 36° and July averages 65° to 81°. Annual precipitation is ranges from 40 to 48 inches.

## Travel Information Sources

**State Agency:** Massachusetts Office of Travel and Tourism, 100 Cambridge Street, 13th Floor, Boston, MA 02202 (617-727-3201).

**Regional Agencies:**

- *Berkshire Hills Visitors Bureau*, Berkshire Common Plaza Level, Pittsfield, MA 01201 (800-237-5747 or 413-443-9186).
- *Bristol County Convention & Visitors Bureau*, 70 N. Second St., P.O. Box 976, New Bedford, MA 02741 (800-288-6263 or 508-997-1250).
- *Cape Cod Chamber of Commerce*, Hyannis, MA 02601 (508-362-3225).
- *Franklin County Chamber of Commerce*, 395 Main St., Greenfield, MA 01301 (413-773-5463).
- *Martha's Vineyard Chamber of Commerce*, P.O. Box 1698, Vineyard Haven, MA 02568 (508-693-0085).
- *Greater Merrimack Valley Convention & Visitors Bureau*, 18 Palmer St., Ste. 200, Lowell, MA 01852-1818 (800-443-3332 or 508-459-6150).
- *Mohawk Trail Assn.*, Box 722, Charlemont, MA 01339 (413-664-6256).
- *Nantucket Island Chamber of Commerce*, Main St., Nantucket, MA 02554 (508-228-1700).
- *Plymouth County Development Council*, P.O. Box 1620, Pembroke, MA 02359 (800-231-1620 or 617-826-3136).

**Local Agencies:**

- *Greater Boston Convention & Visitors Bureau*, Prudential Tower, Ste. 400, Box 490, Boston, MA 02199 (800-888-5515 or 617-536-4100).
- *North of Boston Convention & Visitors Bureau*, P.O. Box 642, 248 Cabot St., Beverly, MA 01915 (508-921-4990 or 800-742-5306).
- *Greater Springfield Convention & Visitors Bureau*, 34 Boland Way, Springfield, MA 01103 (800-723-1548).
- *Worcester County Convention & Visitors Bureau*, 33 Waldo St., Worcester, MA 01608 (508-753-2920).

## Recreational Information

*Fall Foliage Hotline:* (800-632-8038 or 617-727-3201).

*Fishing & Hunting:* For information on Sport Fishing call 800-ASK-FISH.

*Golf:* For a free copy of the *Bay State Fairways*, call the Massachusetts Office of Travel and Tourism at 617-727-3201.

*Ski Conditions:* For up-to-date ski conditions call the Massachusetts Office of Travel and Tourism at 800-632-8038 or 617-727-3201.

## Places to See & Things to Do

***WESTERN & CENTRAL MASSACHUSETTS***

**Hancock Shaker Village,** Pittsfield. A restored Shaker settlement dating from 1790

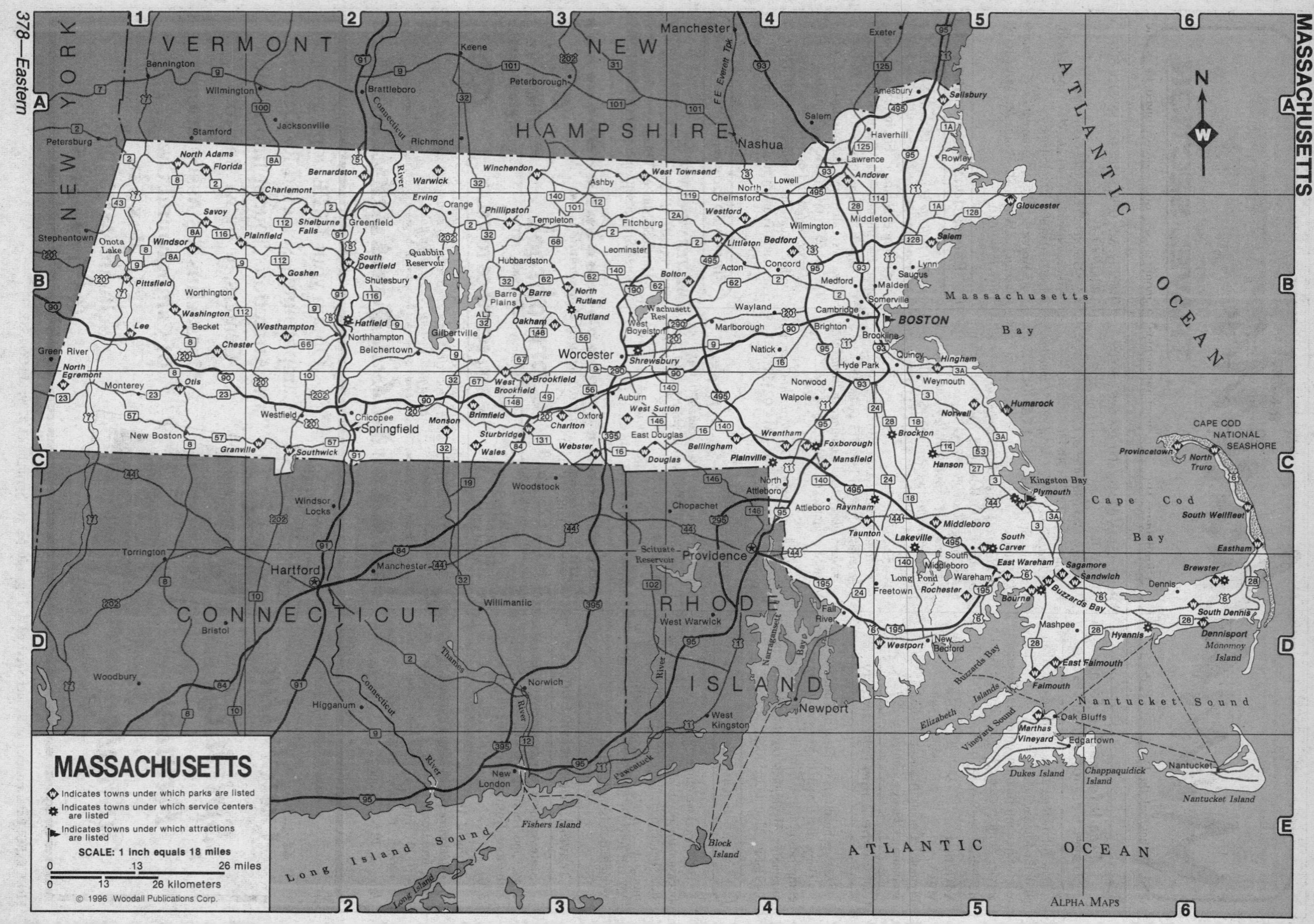
MASSACHUSETTS
Indicates towns under which parks are listed
Indicates towns under which service centers are listed
Indicates towns under which attractions are listed
SCALE: 1 inch equals 18 miles
0 13 26 miles
0 13 26 kilometers
© 1996 Woodall Publications Corp.
ALPHA MAPS
ATLANTIC OCEAN
Massachusetts Bay
Cape Cod Bay
Nantucket Sound
Long Island Sound
NEW YORK
VERMONT
NEW HAMPSHIRE
CONNECTICUT
RHODE ISLAND
CAPE COD NATIONAL SEASHORE
BOSTON
Worcester
Springfield
Providence
Hartford
Pittsfield
Plymouth
Hyannis
Nantucket Island
Dukes Island
Block Island
Fishers Island

interprets the life and industries of the sect. Contains 20 buildings, all furnished with Shaker artifacts, exhibits on the sect's culture, history and philosophy, and shops selling herbs and baked goods.

**Mohawk Trail** follows Route 2 from North Adams east to Orange. A 63-mile natural spectacle that was originally an Indian footpath that took the Deerfield River as its guide. With nearly 100 attractions and over 50,000 acres for recreational enjoyment, the trail moves through woodlands, gorges and mountain peaks.

**The Norman Rockwell Museum,** Stockbridge. View original works of art by one of America's most beloved artists. See the studio, easel, palette, paints and other personal belongings used by the legendary painter.

**Historic Deerfield.** Early settlers first arrived in 1669 and then again in 1682. Both times their village was destroyed by raids. In 1707 Deerfield was finally settled permanently and today, it is a mile-long National Historic Landmark. Twelve homes have been turned into museums which relate a vivid tale of courage, heartache and determination.

**The Quad,** Springfield. Major cultural resource consists of Museum o f Fine Arts, Science Museum, Connecticut Valley Historical Museum, and the George Walter Vincent Smith Art Museum. Enjoy cultural events, exhibitions, special events and activities.

**Old Sturbridge Village,** Sturbridge. This recreated New England country town of homes, shops, mills, schools, meeting houses and general stores illustrates American rural life between 1790 and 1840. Features 40 exhibit buildings, crafts demonstrations, a covered bridge and a tavern that serves refreshments. Open year-round.

### *THE NORTH SHORE*

**Salem.** Among the most popular of Salem's many attractions are the *House of Seven Gables* (built in 1668 and made famous by Nathaniel Hawthorne); the *Peabody & Essex Museum* (founded in 1799 and containing collections of maritime history, ethnology and natural history); the *Witch Museum* (which re-creates through audio-visual techniques, the hysteria of the famous 1692 witch trial).

**Salisbury Beach.** Five miles of clean sand and ocean, miniature golf, waterslide, and go carts are only part of the fun to be had in the northernmost town of Salisbury. Also along the beach is the seaside amusement park, *Pirate's Fun Park*, a wide variety of food concession stands, and video and arcade games.

### *BOSTON & CAMBRIDGE*

**Boston.** The capital of the state of Massachusetts holds many varied attractions for tourists. Among the most popular are the *Freedom Trail* (a self-guided, 2.5-mile walk that begins at the Boston Common and covers the city's most historic landmarks), and the U.S.S. *Constitution,* the oldest commissioned war ship afloat in the world. Visitors can view over 60 miles of breathtaking panorama atop the *John Hancock Observatory*, New England's tallest building.

The *Boston Passport Tourist Pass* offers one, three or seven days of unlimited travel on all MBTA subway and local bus services and over $200 worth of discounts on restaurants, museums & entertainment in Boston. For more information call 617-722-3200.

**Cambridge.** Historical structures include a mansion that served both as George Washington's Revolutionary War headquarters and later as the home of Henry Wadsworth Longfellow. The *Mount Auburn Cemetery* is the resting place of Charles Bulfinch, Winslow Homer, Henry Wadsworth Longfellow and Oliver Wendell Holmes.

**Minuteman National Historic Park,** Concord. This 750-acre park is the site of Battle-Road Visitor Center which features exhibits and orientation programs. Featured are Minuteman Statue and the North Bridge—where the "shot heard around the world" was fired.

### *THE SOUTH SHORE*

**Adams National Historic Site,** Quincy. Built in 1731, this structure was home to four generations of the Adams' family including Presidents John and John Quincy Adams.

**Plymouth.** Known as the original "hometown" in America where 102 passengers from the Mayflower stepped ashore onto Plymouth Rock in December, 1620. A new attraction in Plymouth is the *Whale Discovery Center,* dedicated to the understanding, appreciation and preservation of the whale.

*Cranberry World Visitor Center.* This exhibit of the cranberry industry features outdoor working cranberry bogs and indoor displays of cranberry art, antique and modern picking equipment and various cranberry products. Open daily April–November. Admission is free and so are the samples!

*Mayflower II.* A full-scale reproduction of the ship that carried the Pilgrims to the New World in 1620. Open daily April through November.

*Plimoth Plantation.* A full-scale re-creation of the Pilgrim's Village as it appeared in 1627. Costumed "residents" guide tourists and demonstrate Pilgrim crafts. Open April through November.

*Plymouth National Wax Museum.* Twenty-six life size dioramas portray the Pilgrim story with light, sound and animated effects. Open daily March through November.



**Battleship Cove & Marine Museum,** Fall River. One of the world's largest exhibits of historic fighting ships, including the battleship *Massachusetts*, the destroyer U.S.S. *Joseph P. Kennedy, Jr.*, and the submarine, *Lionfish.*

**New Bedford Whaling Museum,** New Bedford. Museum brings to life the often treacherous lives of fishermen who spent long months at sea. Board a fully rigged, half-scale model of a whaling bark and view a film that takes you on a 19th-century whaling expedition.

### *CAPE COD & THE ISLANDS*

**Cape Cod.** An extremely popular resort area offering a multitude of activities. Featured on this island are many historic homes, lighthouses and museums, as well as a 300-mile coast of pine trees, dunes and surf. *Salt Pond Visitor Center* is the orientation center for Cape Cod National Seashore. Guests enjoy 27,000 acres of beauty, the nature museum, film auditorium and miles of nature and bicycle trails.

*Brewster.* Home to many historic buildings, such as the still functioning Stonybrook Mill. 2,000-acre Nickerson State Park offers eight freshwater kettleponds, four of which are stocked year-round with trout.

*Eastham,* which boasts one of the nation's loveliest coastlines, is the site where the Mayflower shore party met their first Native American. Eastham Windmill, in the town center, is the oldest on the Cape (1680).

**Martha's Vineyard.** Accessable by ferry, this picturesque and popular resort island features sandy beaches, moors, lighthouse, gray-shingled houses, flower-covered cottages, quaint little fishing villages and cruises from Falmouth Harbor, Hyannis and Woods Hole.

**Nantucket Island.** A small, crescent-shaped island that was one of the busiest and most prosperous whaling ports in the world, You can reach Nantucket by ferry (a delightful 3-hour ride).

# massachusetts

All privately-owned campgrounds personally inspected by Woodall Representatives Jerry and Becky Thomas.

Unless otherwise noted, all listed campgrounds have hot showers & flush toilets.

### AMESBURY—A-5

**TUXBURY POND CAMPING AREA**—*From jct I-495 (exit 54) & Hwy 150 (in Massachusetts): Go 3/4 mi N on Hwy 150 to blinking yellow light, then 1/4 mi NW on Highland St, then 1 1/4 mi W on Lions Mouth Rd, then 1 mi N on Newton Rd. Follow signs.*

WELCOME

SEE PRIMARY LISTING AT SOUTH HAMPTON, NH AND AD THIS PAGE

### ANDOVER—A-4

HAROLD PARKER STATE FOREST—*From jct I-495 & Hwy 114: Go 9 mi S on Hwy 114.* FACILITIES: 130 sites, 20 ft. max RV length, 130 no hookups, tenting available, sewage disposal, public phone, ice, tables, fire rings. RECREATION: canoeing, fishing, hiking trails. Recreation open to the public. Open end of Apr through Columbus Day. Phone: (508) 686-3391.

### BEDFORD—B-4

MILITARY PARK (Hanscom AFB FAMCAMP)—*From jct Hwy 128/I-95 (exit 31) & Hwy 4/225: Go NW on Hwy 4/225, then SW on Hartwell Ave, then W on Magyuire Rd, then continue W on Sumner St. Off base.* FACILITIES: 73 sites, 35 full hookups, 21 water & elec (20,30 & 50 amp receptacles), 17 no hookups, 20 pull-thrus, tenting available, handicap restroom facilities, sewage disposal, laundry, public phone, LP gas refill by weight/by meter, ice, tables, grills. RECREATION: rec room/area, pavilion, boating, 15 hp limit, canoeing, row/canoe/pedal boat rentals, river/pond fishing, playground, horseshoes, volleyball. Open May 1 through Oct 30. Reservations not accepted. Phone: (617) 377-4670.

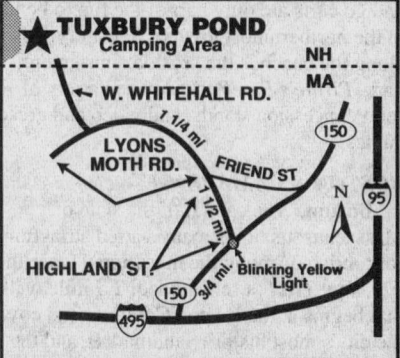

## BELLINGHAM—C-4

**CIRCLE CG FARM ADULT RV PARK**—Level, grassy or graveled, semi-wooded sites in well-developed RV park with western theme. *From jct Hwy 495 & Hwy 126 (exit 18): Go 1 mi S on Hwy 126.*

◆◆◆◆FACILITIES: 151 sites, most common site width 30 feet, 90 full hookups, 61 water & elec (20,30 & 50 amp receptacles), 20 pull-thrus, a/c allowed ($), heater allowed ($), phone hookups, tenting available, group sites for RVs, RV storage, sewage disposal, laundry, public phone, grocery store, RV supplies, LP gas refill by weight/by meter, ice, tables, fire rings, wood, traffic control gate.

◆◆◆◆RECREATION: rec hall, rec room/area, coin games, 2 swim pools, pond fishing, mini-golf ($), basketball hoop, shuffleboard court, planned group activities (weekends only), tennis court, horseshoes, volleyball, local tours.

Age restrictions may apply Oct 15 through Apr 15. Open all year. Facilities fully operational Apr 15 through Oct 15. Monthly rates available. Rate in 1995 $21-23 for 2 persons. No refunds. Reservations recommended Jul 1 through Labor Day. Master Card/Visa accepted. CPO. Member of ARVC;MACO. Phone: (508) 966-1136. FCRV 10% discount.

**SEE AD FRONT OF BOOK PAGE 10 AND AD THIS PAGE**

## BERNARDSTON—A-2

**Purple Meadow Campground**—A secluded CAMPGROUND with large, level, wooded and semi-wooded sites. *From jct I-91 (exit 28A) & Hwy 10: Go 1 1/2 mi E on Hwy 10, then 1 mi N on Purple Meadow Rd.* ◆◆FACILITIES: 40 sites, most common site width 25 feet, 20 full hookups, 20 water & elec (15 & 20 amp receptacles), seasonal sites, tenting available, sewage disposal, public phone, tables, fire rings, wood. Open May 15 through Oct 15. Rate in 1995 $10-13 per family. Phone: (413) 648-9289.

**Travelers Woods of New England**—CAMPGROUND with grassy sites convenient to interstate. *From jct I-91 (exit 28B N'bound, exit 28 S'bound) & Hwy 10: Go 1/4 mi W on Hwy 10, then 1/2 mi SE on River St. (11'6" Underpass. Follow signs for alternative route.)* ◆◆◆FACILITIES: 79 sites, 7 full hookups, 57 water & elec (15,20 & 30 amp receptacles), 15 no hookups, 8 pull-thrus, tenting available, sewage disposal, laundry, public phone, LP gas refill by weight/by meter, ice, tables, wood. ◆◆RECREATION: rec hall, rec room/area, pavilion, stream fishing, playground, badminton, horseshoes, hiking trails, volleyball. Open May 1 through Oct 15. Rate in 1995 $10-16 for 2 persons. No refunds. Member of MACO. Phone: (413) 648-9105.

## BOLTON—B-4

**CRYSTAL SPRINGS CAMPGROUND**—Shaded & open sites in a family-oriented CAMPGROUND in a small town. *From jct I-495 (exit 27) & Hwy 117: Go 1 3/4 mi W on Hwy 117.*

◆◆◆FACILITIES: 219 sites, most common site width 28 feet, 101 full hookups, 114 water & elec (20 & 30 amp receptacles), 4 no hookups, seasonal sites, 12 pull-thrus, a/c allowed ($), heater allowed ($), phone hookups, tenting available, group sites for RVs, RV rentals, sewage disposal, laundry, public phone, grocery store, RV supplies, LP gas refill by weight, ice, tables, fire rings, wood.

◆◆◆◆RECREATION: rec hall, rec room/area, coin games, swim pool, pond swimming, mini-golf ($), basketball hoop, playground, 2 shuffleboard courts, planned group activities, movies, recreation director, 2 tennis courts, badminton, sports field, horseshoes, volleyball.

Open Apr 1 through Oct 15. Rate in 1995 $17-21 for 2 persons. No refunds. Reservations recommended Memorial Day through Labor Day. Member of ARVC; MACO. Phone: (508) 779-2711.

**SEE AD PAGE 380**

## BOSTON—B-5

***See listings at Bellingham, Bolton, Brockton, Foxboro, Gloucester, Hanson, Hingham, Littleton, Mansfield, Middleboro, Norwell, Plainville, Plymouth, Raynham, Salem, Salisbury, South Carver, Westford & Wrentham***

**BLACK BEAR CAMPGROUNDS**—*From Boston: Go 30 minutes N on I-95 to exit 60 (Hwy 286), then go down ramp to first traffic light, take left, for 200 feet to campground entrance.*

**SEE PRIMARY LISTING AT SALISBURY AND AD SALISBURY PAGE 398**

BOSTON—Continued on page 385

# Boston HUB KOA

*Small enough to be friendly, large enough to accommodate*
Exit 15 off I-495, then 200 yds. South on 1A

*For your pleasure, we offer:*
- Private, Wooded Sites
- Boiled Live Lobster Dinners
- Breakfasts
- Shuttle to Public Transportation
- Video Movie Rentals
- Dog Sitting Service
- Large Information Center
- Car Rentals

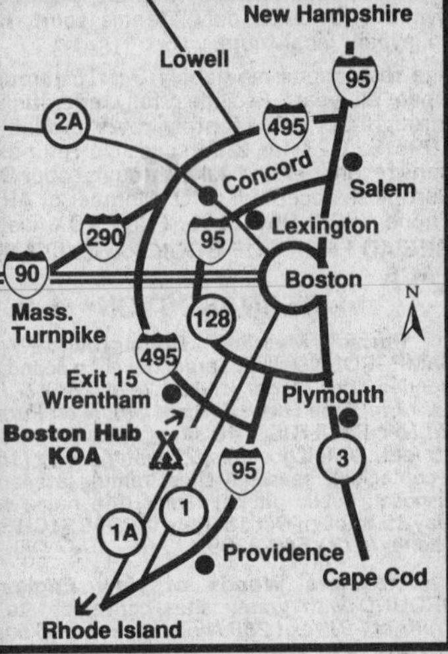


**Camper Tours, Inc.**
Professionally Guided All-Day Tours leave campground daily
May 1—Oct. 31
Boston/Cambridge, Plymouth/Cape Cod
Concord/Salem
Travel Through Centuries of History while leaving the driving to us

ARCADE VIDEO GAMES
MINI-GOLF

**(800) KOA-2173**
US & Canada
**(508) 384-8930**

1095 South Street, PO Box 505
Wrentham, MA 02093

See listings at Wrentham & Boston

40 miles to Boston
20 miles to Cape Cod
15 miles to Plymouth

**Open March 1 to December 1**
**Monthly sites available**

*A great place to check into*

## Plymouth Rock KOA

- Grassy, shaded, wooded RV and Tent Sites
- Swimming Pool · Planned Activities
- Large Play Areas · Bocci Ball
- Ocean Beaches Nearby
- Near Fall River Factory Outlets & Battleship Cove

**BOSTON, PLYMOUTH CAPE COD TOURS**

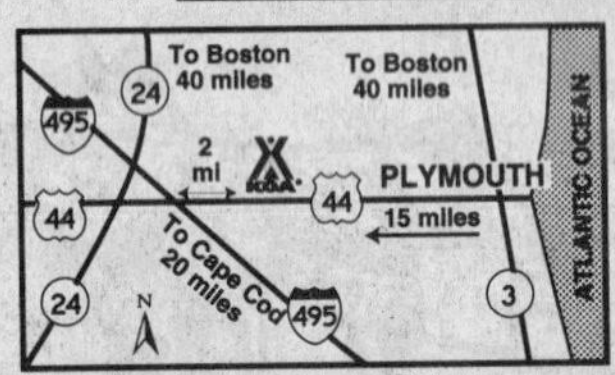


Plymouth Rock KOA
US Hwy. 44
P.O. Box 616, Dept.W
Middleboro, MA 02346
(508) 947-6435

Your Hosts:
The Nicholson Family

For Res.: 1-800-562-3046 · FAX: (508) 947-9844

BOSTON CONCORD LEXINGTON

## MINUTEMAN KOA

**Quiet Family Kampground in New England Pine Forest**

OPEN MAY 1 TO LAST SUNDAY IN OCTOBER

- CLOSEST KAMPGROUND TO MINUTEMAN AND LOWELL NATIONAL PARKS (20 MINUTES)
- ONE HOUR FROM SALEM & GLOUCESTER, MASS.

• Clean Restrooms • Store • 24 Hour Laundry • Heated Swimming Pool
• Rec Hall • 30 & 50 AMP Service • Metered LP Gas • Firewood
• Block Ice • Weekly Rates Available • No Seasonals

Kamping Kabins

Box 2122, Littleton, MA 01460 • (508) 772-0042 See listing at Littleton HOSTS: THE NUSSDORFER FAMILY

Northwest of Boston - From I-495, take Exit 30, Route 2A, 2-1/2 miles west.

**FOR RESERVATIONS, CALL 1-800-562-7606**

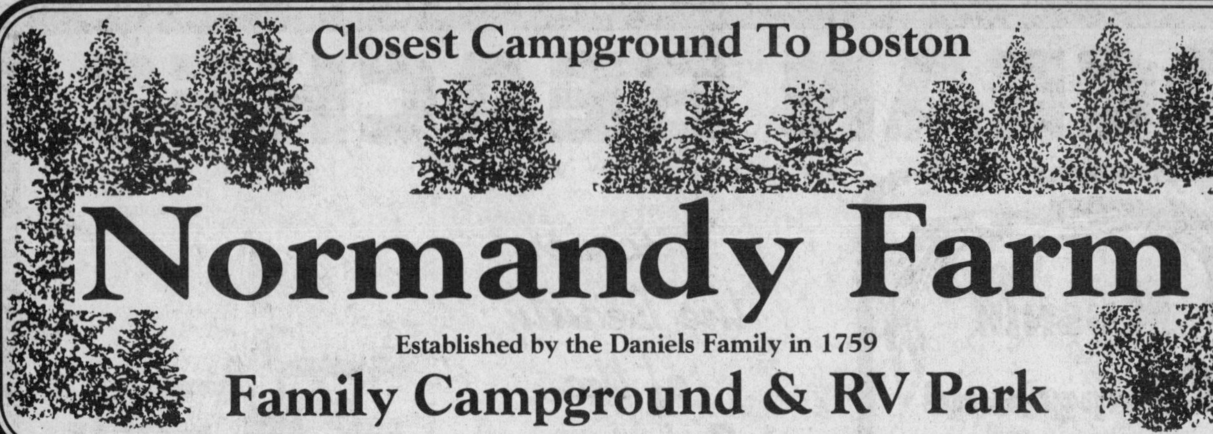


## *A Year Round Vacation Wonderland*

★ We Treat you like we would want to be treated.
★ Extraordinary dedication to our campers.
★ Friendly, down-home atmosphere.
★ Facilities and activities geared to entire family.
★ Personal service and care – beyond the norm.

*"A Restful Place From Which to Visit New England"*

### *Year Round Activities & Recreation Program.*

- Indoor Heated Pool • 2 Whirlpools • 2 Large Playgrounds
- 3 Outdoor Pools, Diving Pool w/ underwater observation area.
- 2 Regulation Softball Fields • Full Court Basketball
- 18-hole Frisbee Golf • Shuffleboard • 8 Horseshoe Courts
- Soccer Field • 2 Volleyball Courts • Tokay Course • Movies
- 60 x 100 2-story Recreation Hall with Air-conditioned Game Room
- Adult Lounge • Group Function Room Available • Campfires 6 p.m. til 12 a.m.

### *Full Time RV Serviceman on Site*

• On site RV Rentals • Escort Service to Sites • Security • Complete Store & Gift Shop
• Car Rentals Available • Free Valet Service to Airport Bus Terminal

*Inquire About Speedy ✔ In*

**PROFESSIONALLY GUIDED DAY-LONG TOURS, LEAVING DIRECTLY FROM CAMPGROUND DAILY TO BOSTON, PLYMOUTH • CAPE COD**

**Boston Area Attractions** The Freedom Trail — USS Constitution — Old North Church — Faneuil Hall and Quincy Market Place
Paul Revere Home — Tea Party Ship — Bunker Hill — Museums — Boston Symphony Hall and Pops
Christian Science Complex — John Hancock Observatory — Kennedy Library

**Convenient Day Trips** Cape Cod — Plymouth — Lexington — Concord — Salem — Glouchester — Sturbridge — Newport, RI
Fall River Factory Outlets — Historic New Bedford — Fine Restaurants — Convention Centers
Great Woods Center for the Performing Arts

AAA

Good Sampark

From Boston, take I-95 S or I-93 then exit I-95S (Providence, RI) to Exit 9 onto Hwy 1, then 6.7 mi S on Hwy 1, then left onto Thurston St. for 1 3/10 mi to Normandy Farm.

From I-495, Exit 14A onto US Hwy 1, N for 1 Mi, then right on Thurston St for 1 3/10 mi to Normandy Farm.

72 West St., Dept. W
Foxboro, MA 02035
**(508) 543-7600**
Reservations: Ext. 5

**Pets on Leash Welcome**
**Deposit accepted with Reservation**
**Your hosts, the Daniels Family**

See listing at Foxboro

**SEND FOR OUR 16-PAGE COLOR BROCHURE**

BOSTON—Continued

▶ **CAMPER TOURS**—*From jct I-93/Hwy 128 & I-95: Go 14 mi SW on I-95, then 5 mi NW on I-495, then 1/4 mi S on Hwy 1A.* Travel through centuries of history on professionally guided all-day tours of Boston, Plymouth and Cape Cod in our deluxe buses. Open May 1 through Oct 31. Master Card/Visa accepted. Phone: (800) 562-2173.
**SEE AD PAGE 382**

**CAPE ANN CAMPSITE**—*From Mystic Tobin Bridge in Boston (US 1): Go 15 mi N on US 1, then 20 mi NE on Hwy 128 to exit 13 (Concord St), then 3/4 mi N on Concord St, then 1/2 mi NE on Atlantic St (Wingaersheek Beach Rd).*
**SEE PRIMARY LISTING AT GLOUCESTER AND AD GLOUCESTER PAGE 392**

**CIRCLE CG FARM ADULT RV PARK**—*From jct I-95 & I-90, Mass. Pike (west of Boston): Go 17 mi W on I-90, then 14 mi SE on I-495, then 1 mi S on Hwy 126.*
**SEE PRIMARY LISTING AT BELLINGHAM AND AD BELLINGHAM PAGE 381**

**KOA-BOSTON HUB**—*From jct I-93/Hwy 128 & I-95: Go 14 mi SW on I-95, then 5 mi NW on I-495, then 1/4 mi S on Hwy 1A.*
**SEE PRIMARY LISTING AT WRENTHAM AND AD PAGE 382**

**KOA-MINUTEMAN**—*30 miles NW of Boston at jct I-495 (exit 30) & Hwy 2A: Go 2 3/4 mi W on Hwy 2A.*
**SEE PRIMARY LISTING AT LITTLETON AND AD PAGE 382**

BOSTON—Continued

**KOA-PLYMOUTH ROCK**—*From jct I-93 & Hwy 24 (south of Boston): Go 21 mi S on Hwy 24, then 4 mi SE on I-495, then 2 3/4 mi E on US 44.*
**SEE PRIMARY LISTING AT MIDDLEBORO AND AD PAGE 382**

**NORMANDY FARM FAMILY CAMPGROUND**—*From jct I-93 & I-95 (south side of Boston): Take exit 95 South (Providence, Rd) to Hwy 1 (exit 9), then 6 7/10 mi S on Hwy 1, then turn left onto Thurston St. 1 3/10 mi to Normandy Farm.*
**SEE PRIMARY LISTING AT FOXBORO AND AD PAGE 384**

**NORWELL CAMPSITES**—*From Boston: Go 20 mi S on Hwy 3 to exit 14, then 1/2 mi NE on Hwy 228, then 1 mi SE on Hwy 53.*
**SEE PRIMARY LISTING AT NORWELL AND AD THIS PAGE**

**RUSNIK CAMPGROUND**—*From Boston: Go 20 minutes NE on US 1 to Danvers, then 20 minutes N on US 95 (exit 58), then 2 1/4 mi E on Hwy 110, then 1 mi N on US 1.*
**SEE PRIMARY LISTING AT SALISBURY AND AD PAGE 383**

**WYMAN'S BEACH**—*Northbound: From jct I-495 (exit 32) & Boston Rd: Go 1 mi NW on Boston Rd, then 1/4 mi N on Lincoln St, then 3 1/2 mi NW on Depot St (follow signs). Southbound: From jct US 3 (exit 33) & Hwy 40: Go 3 mi W on Hwy 40, then 1 mi N on Dunstable Rd.*
**SEE PRIMARY LISTING AT WESTFORD AND AD THIS PAGE**

## BOURNE—D-5

**BAY VIEW CAMPGROUND**—Rustic, semi-wooded sites on a major highway. *From jct Hwy 28 & US 6 South of Bourne Bridge: Go 1 mi S on Hwy 28.*

◆◆◆◆FACILITIES: 415 sites, most common site width 40 feet, 335 full hookups, 80 water & elec (15 & 30 amp receptacles), seasonal sites, a/c allowed ($), heater allowed ($), cable TV ($), phone hookups, tenting available, group sites for tents/RVs, RV storage, sewage disposal, laundry, public phone, grocery store, RV supplies, LP gas refill by weight, ice, tables, fire rings, wood, guard.

BAY VIEW CAMPGROUND—Continued onpage 387
BOURNE—Continued on page 387



MASSACHUSETTS | Feast your eyes on a sea of cranberries at the | MASSACHUSETTS

***See Front of Book for Information on the Festivals of Massachusetts***

MASSACHUSETTS | Massachusetts Cranberry Harvest Festival | MASSACHUSETTS

 See Eastern Map page 378

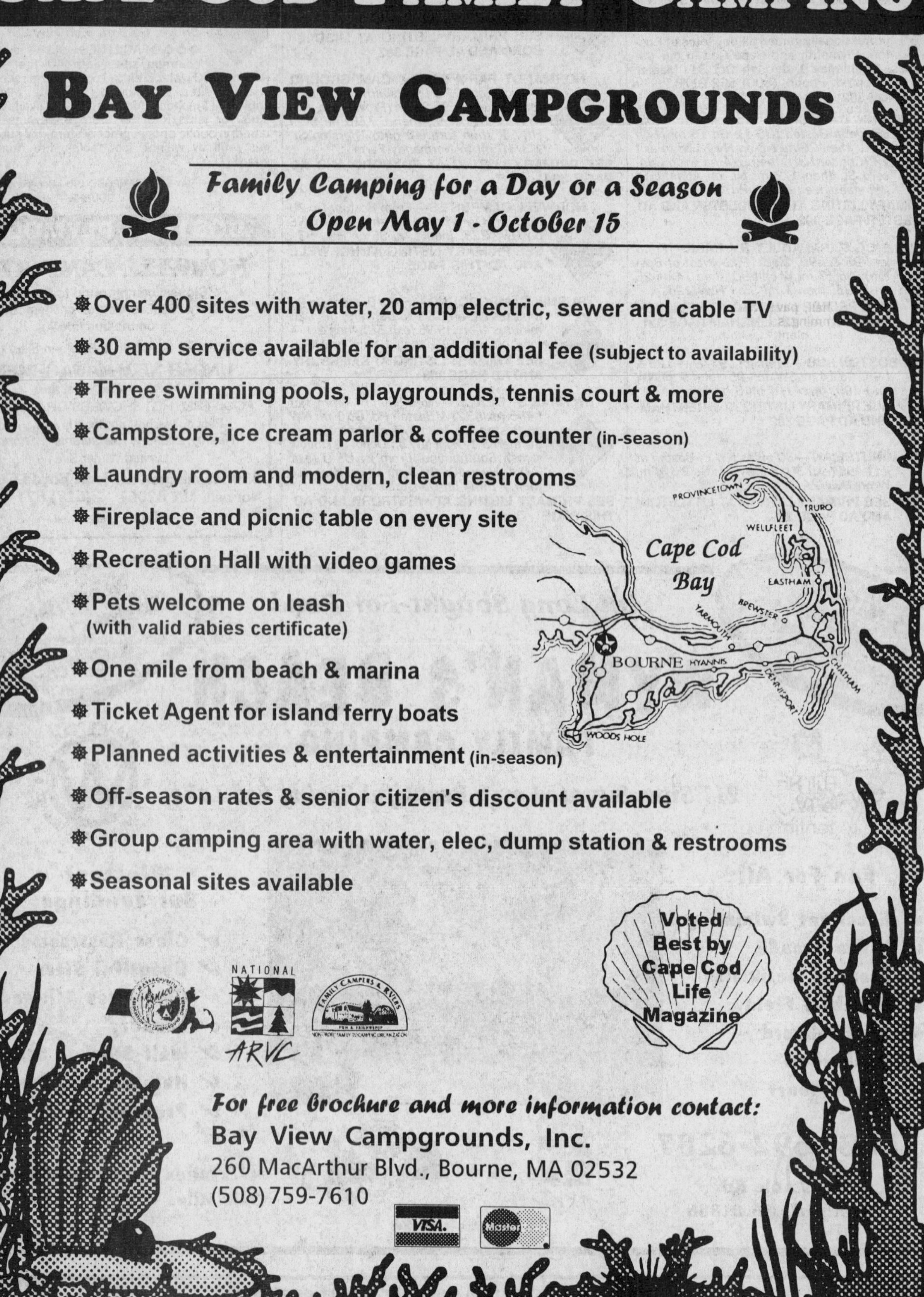

BOURNE—Continued
BAY VIEW CAMPGROUND—Continued

◈◈◈◈RECREATION: rec hall, rec room/area, coin games, 3 swim pools, wading pool, basketball hoop, playground, shuffleboard court, planned group activities, recreation director, tennis court, badminton, sports field, horseshoes, volleyball.

Open May 1 through Oct 15. Rate in 1995 $22-25 for 2 persons. No refunds. Reservations recommended Jul 1 through Labor Day. Master Card/Visa accepted. Member of ARVC; MACO. Phone: (508) 759-7610.

**SEE AD PAGE 386**

**BOURNE SCENIC PARK (Municipal Park)**—*In town on US 6 (Beneath the Bourne Bridge).* FACILITIES: 476 sites, most common site width 40 feet, 437 water & elec (20 amp receptacles), 39 no hookups, tenting available, handicap restroom facilities, sewage disposal, public phone, limited grocery store, RV supplies, ice, tables, patios, fire rings, grills, wood, traffic control gate/guard.

RECREATION: rec hall, pavilion, coin games, swim pool, salt water swimming, salt water fishing, basketball hoop, playground, planned group activities, recreation director, badminton, sports field, horseshoes, hiking trails, volleyball.

Open Apr 1 through mid Oct. Phone: (508) 759-7873.

**SEE AD THIS PAGE**

BOURNE—Continued

**❋ MAJOR'S RV SERVICE CENTER**—*From jct I-495/25 & Hwy 28 (south of Bourne Bridge): Go 1/2 mi S on Hwy 28.* SERVICES: RV appliance mechanic full-time, emergency road service business hours, RV towing, LP gas refill by weight/by meter, sewage disposal, RV storage, sells parts/accessories, installs hitches. Open all year. American Express/Discover/Master Card/Visa accepted. Phone: (508) 759-2833.

**SEE AD CAPE COD PAGE 389**

## BREWSTER—D-6

**Jolly Whaler Trailer Park**—RV SPACES adjacent to a small motel. *From jct US 6 (exit 11) & Hwy 137: Go 4 mi N on Hwy 137, then 1 1/2 mi W on US 6A.* FACILITIES: 28 sites, most common site width 25 feet, 34 ft. max RV length, 23 full hookups, 5 water & elec (15 amp receptacles), seasonal sites. RECREATION: rec hall, 2 shuffleboard courts. No tents. Open May 15 through Oct 1. Rates available upon request. Phone: (508) 896-3474.

ROLAND C NICKERSON STATE PARK—*From jct US 6 (exit 12) & Hwy 6A: Go 3 mi W on Hwy 6A.* FACILITIES: 418 sites, 418 no hookups, tenting available, handicap restroom

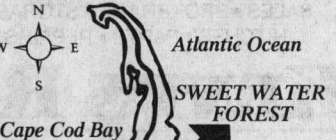

ROLAND C NICKERSON STATE PARK—Continued on next page
BREWSTER—Continued on next page

BREWSTER—Continued
ROLAND C NICKERSON STATE PARK—Continued

facilities, sewage disposal, public phone, tables, grills. RECREATION: pavilion, lake/pond swimming, boating, canoeing, ramp, lake fishing, sports field, hiking trails. Recreation open to the public. Open all year. Facilities fully operational mid Apr through mid Oct. Phone: (508) 896-3491.

**SHADY KNOLL CAMPGROUND**—A CAMPGROUND on the edge of town, with natural sites in the woods and some open grassy sites. *From jct US 6 (exit 11) & Hwy 137: Go 4 mi N on Hwy 137 to jct with US 6 A.*

◆◆◆FACILITIES: 100 sites, most common site width 25 feet, 49 full hookups, 31 water & elec (20 & 30 amp receptacles), 20 no hookups, seasonal sites, 8 pull-thrus, a/c allowed, heater allowed ($), tenting available, RV rentals, cabins, RV storage, sewage disposal, laundry, public phone, RV supplies, ice, tables, fire rings, grills, wood.

◆RECREATION: rec room/area, coin games, basketball hoop, playground.

Open May 15 through Columbus Day. Rate in 1995 $22-28 for 2 persons. No refunds. Reservations recommended late Jun through Labor Day. Discover/Master Card/Visa accepted. Member of ARVC; MACO. Phone: (508) 896-3002.

**SEE AD FRONT OF BOOK PAGE 12 AND AD NEXT PAGE**

**SWEETWATER FOREST**—Spacious, well separated, wooded sites in a family operated lakeside CAMPGROUND. *From jct US 6 (exit 10) & Hwy 124: Go 3 mi N on Hwy 124.*

◆◆◆FACILITIES: 300 sites, most common site width 30 feet, 64 full hookups, 171 water & elec (20 & 30 amp receptacles), 65 no hookups, seasonal sites, cable TV, phone hookups, tenting available, RV storage, handicap restroom facilities, sewage disposal, public phone, limited grocery store, RV supplies, LP gas refill by weight/by meter, ice, tables, traffic control gate.

◆◆◆RECREATION: rec hall, rec room/area, coin games, lake swimming, boating, 3 hp limit, canoeing, dock, 3 row/3 canoe boat rentals, lake fishing, basketball hoop, 10 bike rentals, playground, hiking trails, volleyball, cross country skiing.

Open all year. 3 day minimum reservation on holiday weekends. Rate in 1995 $20-27 for 2 persons. No refunds. Reservations recommended Memorial Day through Labor Day. Member of ARVC;MACO. Phone: (508) 896-3773.

**SEE AD PAGE 387**

✽ **SWEETWATER FOREST RV**—*From jct US 6 (exit 10) & Hwy 124: Go 3 mi N on Hwy 124.* SALES: park models. SERVICES: RV appliance mechanic full-time, LP gas refill by meter, sewage disposal, RV storage, sells parts/accessories, sells camping supplies, installs hitches. Open all year. Master Card/Visa accepted. Phone: (508) 896-3773.

**SEE AD PAGE 387**

## BRIMFIELD—C-3

**QUINEBAUG COVE CAMPSITE**—Shaded, hillside sites in a lakeside CAMPGROUND near a tourism area. *From jct I-84 & US 20: Go 3 1/2 mi W on US 20, then 1/4 mi S on E Brimfield Rd.*

◆◆◆FACILITIES: 125 sites, most common site width 40 feet, 45 full hookups, 65 water & elec (15,20 & 30 amp receptacles), 15 no hookups,

BRIMFIELD—Continued
QUINEBAUG COVE CAMPSITE—Continued

seasonal sites, a/c allowed ($), heater allowed ($), tenting available, RV rentals, RV storage, sewage disposal, laundry, public phone, grocery store, RV supplies, LP gas refill by weight/by meter, ice, tables, wood, traffic control gate/guard.

◆◆◆◆RECREATION: rec hall, rec room/area, coin games, swim pool, lake swimming, boating, canoeing, 3 row/7 canoe boat rentals, water skiing, lake fishing, basketball hoop, playground, shuffleboard court, planned group activities (weekends only), badminton, horseshoes, hiking trails, volleyball.

Open all year. Rate in 1995 $22-28 for 2 persons. Discover/Master Card/Visa accepted. Member of MACO. Phone: (413) 245-9525.

**SEE AD STURBRIDGE PAGE 402**

**VILLAGE GREEN FAMILY CAMPGROUND**—Large wooded and open sites in conjunction with a motel. *From jct I-84 & US 20: Go 4 3/4 mi W on US 20.*

◆◆◆FACILITIES: 120 sites, most common site width 50 feet, 108 water & elec (15 & 20 amp receptacles), 12 no hookups, seasonal sites, a/c allowed ($), heater not allowed, tenting available, group sites for tents/RVs, RV storage, sewage disposal, laundry, public phone, limited grocery store, LP gas refill by weight/by meter, ice, tables, fire rings, wood.

◆◆◆◆RECREATION: rec hall, rec room/area, pavilion, coin games, pond swimming, boating, no motors, canoeing, dock, 1 row/2 pedal boat rentals, pond/stream fishing, basketball hoop, playground, planned group activities (weekends only), badminton, sports field, horseshoes, hiking trails, volleyball.

Open Apr 1 through Oct 30. Winter camping available. Rate in 1995 $19-20 per family. Reservations recommended Jul 1 through Labor Day. Master Card/Visa accepted. Member of ARVC; MACO. Phone: (413) 245-3504.

**SEE AD STURBRIDGE PAGE 402**

## BROCKTON—C-5

✽ **BRADFORD RV CENTER**—*From jct Hwy 24 & E Hwy 106: Go 2 mi E on Hwy 106, then 2 mi N on Hwy 28.* SALES: travel trailers, truck campers, 5th wheels, motor homes, mini-motor homes, fold-down camping trailers. SERVICES: Engine/Chassis & RV appliance mechanic full-time, LP gas refill by weight/by meter, RV storage, sells parts/accessories, installs hitches. Open all year. American Express/Diners Club/Master Card/Visa accepted. Phone: (508) 583-1440.

**SEE AD THIS PAGE**

## BROOKFIELD—C-3

**LAKESIDE RESORT**—Rural CAMPGROUND by Quabog Pond offering open & shaded, grassy sites on an overnight, seasonal, or lots for sale basis. *From jct Hwy 148 & Hwy 9: Go 1 mi E on Hwy 9, then 8/10 mi S on Quabog St, then right 1 block on Hobbs Ave.*

◆◆◆ FACILITIES: 118 sites, most common site width 40 feet,100 full hookups, 18 water & elec (20 & 30 amp receptacles), seasonal sites, 6

BROOKFIELD—Continued
LAKESIDE RESORT—Continued

pull-thrus, a/c allowed, heater not allowed, phone hookups, tenting available, group sites for tents/RVs, RV storage, sewage disposal, laundry, ice, tables, fire rings, wood, guard.

◆◆◆RECREATION: rec hall, swim pool, boating, canoeing, water skiing, lake fishing, basketball hoop, playground, 2 shuffleboard courts, planned group activities, movies, recreation director, horseshoes, hiking trails, volleyball.

Open May 1 through Oct 15. Rate in 1995 $22.50-25 for 2 persons. Reservations recommended Jul through Aug. Phone: (508) 867-2737.

**SEE AD FRONT OF BOOK PAGE 15 AND AD STURBRIDGE PAGE 403**

## BUZZARDS BAY—D-5

✽ **KENT RV SERVICE CENTER**—*From rotary on W side of Bourne Bridge: Go 3 mi W on US 6 & Hwy 28 to 3092 Cranberry Hwy.* SERVICES: Engine/Chassis & RV appliance mechanic full-time, LP gas refill by weight, sewage disposal, RV storage, sells parts/accessories, installs hitches. Open all year. Phone: (508) 295-0250.

**SEE AD THIS PAGE**

## CAPE COD—D-6

***See listings at Bourne, Brewster, Buzzard's Bay, Dennisport, East Falmouth, Eastham, Falmouth, Hyannis, Martha's Vineyard, North Truro, Plymouth, Provincetown, Sandwich, South Carver & South Wellfleet***

**ATLANTIC OAKS**—*From National Seashore Main Visitors Center & Hwy 6: Go 1/2 mi E on Hwy 6.*
**SEE PRIMARY LISTING AT EASTHAM AND AD NEXT PAGE**

**BAY VIEW CAMPGROUND**—*From jct US 6 & Hwy 28 South of Bourne Bridge: Go 1 mi S on Hwy 28.*
**SEE PRIMARY LISTING AT BOURNE AND AD BOURNE PAGE 386**

**CAMPER'S HAVEN**—*From jct US 6 (exit 9) & Hwy 134: Go 2 mi S on Hwy 134, then 1 mi SW on Swan River Rd, then 1/3 mi E on Lower County Rd, then 3/4 mi SE on Old Wharf Rd.*
**SEE PRIMARY LISTING AT DENNISPORT AND AD DENNISPORT PAGE 391**

**DUNROAMIN' TRAILER PARK**—*From jct US 6 (exit 2) & Hwy 130: Go 3 1/10 mi S on Hwy 130, then 3/4 mi E on Quaker Meeting House Rd, then 1 1/10 mi S on Cotuit Rd, then 1/10 mi W on John Ewer Rd.*
**SEE PRIMARY LISTING AT SANDWICH AND AD SANDWICH PAGE 399**

**HORTON'S CAMPING RESORT**—*From jct US 6 & S Highland Rd in N Truro: Go 1 mi E on S Highland Rd.*
**SEE PRIMARY LISTING AT NORTH TRURO AND AD NORTH TRURO PAGE 394**

**MARTHA'S VINEYARD FAMILY CAMPGROUND**—*From Bourne Bridge: Go S on Hwy 28 to Woods Hole, then take ferry to Vineyard Haven.*
**SEE PRIMARY LISTING AT MARTHA'S VINEYARD AND AD MARTHA'S VINEYARD PAGE 393**

CAPE COD—Continued on next page

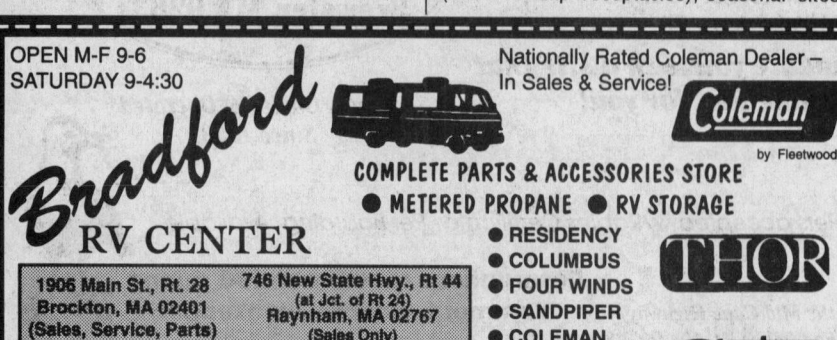

MA State Tree: American Elm MA

CAPE COD—Continued

**PETER'S POND PARK**—*From jct US 6 (exit 2) & Hwy 130: Go 3 1/10 mi S on Hwy 130, then 3/4 mi E on Quaker Meeting House Rd, then 3/4 mi S on Cotuit Rd.*

WELCOME

**SEE PRIMARY LISTING AT SANDWICH AND AD SANDWICH PAGE 399**

**SHADY ACRES CAMPGROUND**—*From Bourne Bridge to Cape Cod: Go 8 mi W on Hwy 25 & I-495 (exit 2), then 2 1/2 mi N on Hwy 58, then 1 1/2 mi N on Tremont St (enter camp at jct Tremont & Mayflower Sts).*

WELCOME

**SEE PRIMARY LISTING AT SOUTH CARVER AND AD PLYMOUTH PAGE 396**

**SHADY KNOLL CAMPGROUND**—*From jct US 6 (exit 11) & Hwy 137: Go 4 mi N on Hwy 137 to jct US 6A.*

WELCOME

**SEE PRIMARY LISTING AT BREWSTER AND AD THIS PAGE**

**SWEETWATER FOREST**—*From jct US 6 (exit 10) & Hwy 124: Go 3 mi N on Hwy 124.*

WELCOME

**SEE PRIMARY LISTING AT BREWSTER AND AD BREWSTER PAGE 387**

**SAFETY TIP**

**If you are treating water with iodine or chlorine, let the water sit at least a half an hour before drinking.**

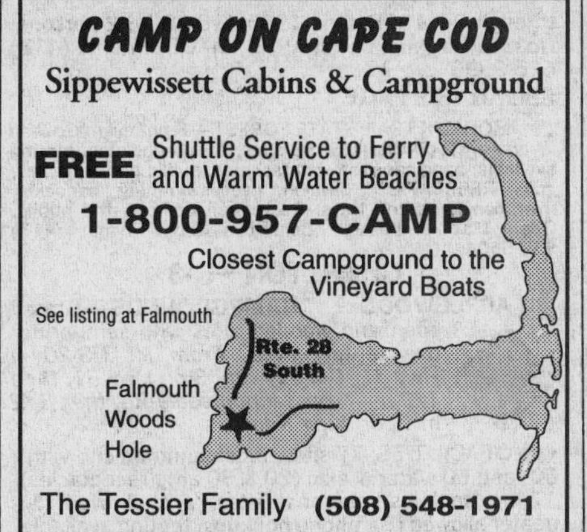

CAMP ON CAPE COD
Sippewissett Cabins & Campground
FREE Shuttle Service to Ferry and Warm Water Beaches
1-800-957-CAMP
Closest Campground to the Vineyard Boats
See listing at Falmouth
Rte. 28 South
Falmouth
Woods Hole
The Tessier Family (508) 548-1971

Your Parts, Accessories & Service Experts

**HITCHES • WIRING • HEATING**
**REFRIGERATION • STORAGE • LP GAS**
**TRAILER TOWING • MOBILE SERVICE**
**WARRANTY CENTER SERVICE**

**(508) 759-2833**
**1-800-287-2833**

**150 MacArthur Blvd. Rte. 28**
**Bourne, MA 02532**

See listing at Bourne

**PAINE'S CAMPGROUND - CAPE COD**

*...In the Heart of the National Seashore*

Large, Private Sites • Quiet "Couples Only" Section
Bike Trails & Canoeing Nearby

**Box 201, South Wellfleet, MA 02663**

**(508) 349-3007** See listing at South Wellfleet **800-479-3017**

**SHADY KNOLL** **ATLANTIC OAKS**

**CAPE COD**

**SHADY KNOLL: 1709 Route 6A, Brewster,MA 02631 (508)896-3002**
**ATLANTIC OAKS: 3700 Route 6, Eastham,MA 02642 (508)255-1437**
**RESERVATIONS:1-800-332-2267**

## RECYCLE-USE RETREADS

According to the Tire Retread Information Bureau, one retreaded truck tire saves 15 gallons of oil, and that adds up. In North America alone, over 400 million gallons of oil are saved annually by retreading tires! The bureau says retreaded tires last as long as new ones, can be driven at the same speeds, and are safe in all driving conditions. The major cause of tire failure is not retreads, but improper maintenance, especially improper inflation, according to the bureau. Among the users of retreads: The Blue Angels, U.S. Postal Service, two major commercial package delivery organizations, and Air Force One.

### CHARLEMONT—B-2

**COUNTRY AIRE CAMPGROUND**—A CAMPGROUND with semi-wooded sites, bordered with pinetrees. *From jct I-91 (exit 26) & Hwy 2: Go 12 1/2 mi W on Hwy 2 (between mileposts 35 & 36).*

◈◈◈FACILITIES: 125 sites, 80 full hookups, 25 water & elec (20 & 30 amp receptacles), 20 no hookups, seasonal sites, 46 pull-thrus, a/c allowed ($), heater allowed ($), phone hookups, tenting available, group sites for tents/RVs, RV storage, sewage disposal, laundry, limited grocery store, RV supplies, LP gas refill by weight/by meter, ice, tables, fire rings, wood.

◈◈◈RECREATION: rec hall, rec room/area, pavilion, coin games, swim pool, stream fishing, basketball hoop, playground, shuffleboard court, horseshoes, hiking trails.

Open all year. Facilities fully operational May 15


See listing at Charlton

CHARLEMONT—Continued
COUNTRY AIRE CAMPGROUND—Continued

through Oct 15. Rate in 1995 $18-20 for 2 persons. No refunds. Member of ARVC; MACO. Phone: (413) 625-2996.

**SEE AD THIS PAGE**

MOHAWK TRAIL STATE FOREST—*From town: Go 3 mi W on Hwy 2.* FACILITIES: 56 sites, 56 no hookups, tenting available, handicap restroom facilities, public phone, tables, grills. RECREATION: pavilion, river swimming, canoeing, river fishing, hiking trails. Recreation open to the public. Open May 1 through Columbus Day. Phone: (413) 339-5504.

### CHARLTON—C-3

**APPLEWOOD CAMPGROUNDS**—Grassy open and wooded sites with semi-primitive tenting area. *From jct US 20 & Hwy 31: Go 4 1/2 mi S on Hwy 31, then 1/2 mi W on Saundersdale Rd, then 1/2 mi S on King Rd.*

◈◈◈FACILITIES: 77 sites, most common site width 60 feet, 60 water & elec (20 & 30 amp receptacles), 17 no hookups, seasonal sites, a/c allowed ($), heater allowed ($), phone hookups, tenting available, group sites for RVs, RV storage, sewage disposal, laundry, public phone, limited grocery store, ice, tables, fire rings, wood.

◈◈◈RECREATION: rec hall, swim pool, wading pool, basketball hoop, playground, sports field, horseshoes, volleyball.

Open May 15 through Columbus Day wknd. Rate in 1995 $18 for 2 persons. No refunds. Reservations recommended Jul 1 through Labor Day. Member of

CHARLTON—Continued
APPLEWOOD CAMPGROUND—Continued

ARVC; MACO. Phone: (508) 248-7017.

**SEE AD THIS PAGE**

**THE WOOD LOT CAMPGROUND**—Large, secluded level sites among oak & pine trees. *From jct US 20 & Hwy 31: Go 1/10 mi N on Hwy 31, then 1/2 mi NE on Stafford St.*

◈◈◈FACILITIES: 91 sites, most common site width 50 feet, 87 water & elec (15,20 & 30 amp receptacles), 4 no hookups, seasonal sites, 2 pull-thrus, a/c allowed ($), heater not allowed, phone hookups, tenting available, RV storage, sewage disposal, laundry, public phone, limited grocery store, RV supplies, LP gas refill by weight, ice, tables, fire rings, wood, traffic control gate.

◈◈◈◈RECREATION: rec hall, rec room/area, equipped pavilion, coin games, swim pool, wading pool, basketball hoop, playground, planned group activities (weekends only), movies, badminton, horseshoes, volleyball.

Open May 1 through Oct 15. Facilities fully operational Memorial Day through Labor Day. Rate in 1995 $20.50 for 2 persons. No refunds. Reservations recommended Jul 1 through Labor Day. Discover/Master Card/Visa accepted. Member of ARVC; MACO. Phone: (508) 248-5141.

**SEE AD STURBRIDGE PAGE 402**

### CHESTER—B-1

**WALKER ISLAND FAMILY CAMPING**—Wooded, natural CAMPGROUND between two streams. *From east jct Hwy 8 & US 20: Go 2 1/4 mi E on US 20.*

◈◈◈FACILITIES: 90 sites, most common site width 35 feet, 27 full hookups, 50 water & elec (30 amp receptacles), 13 no hookups, seasonal sites, a/c allowed ($), heater allowed ($), cable TV ($), phone hookups, tenting available, RV rentals, RV storage, sewage disposal, laundry, public phone, limited grocery store, RV supplies, LP gas refill by weight/by meter, ice, tables, fire rings, grills, wood.

◈◈◈◈RECREATION: rec hall, rec room/area, coin games, swim pool (heated), wading pool, river swimming, stream fishing, mini-golf ($), basketball hoop, playground, shuffleboard court, planned group activities, badminton, horseshoes, hiking trails, volleyball.

Open Apr 15 through Oct 15. Rate in 1995 $18-22 for 2 persons. No refunds. Reservations recommended Jul through Aug. Master Card/Visa accepted. Member of ARVC; MACO. Phone: (413) 354-2295.

**SEE AD THIS PAGE**

### DENNISPORT—D-6

**CAMPER'S HAVEN**—Oceanside RV PARK on Nantucket Sound of Cape Cod. Most sites occupied by seasonal campers. *From jct US 6 (exit 9) & Hwy 134: Go 2 mi S on Hwy 134, then 1 mi SW on Swan River Rd, then 1/3 mi E on Lower County Rd, then 3/4 mi SE on Old Wharf Rd.*

◈◈◈◈FACILITIES: 266 sites, most common site width 25 feet, 240 full hookups, 26 water & elec (20,30 & 50 amp receptacles), seasonal sites, 4 pull-thrus, a/c allowed ($), heater allowed ($), cable TV,

CAMPER'S HAVEN—Continued on next page
DENNISPORT—Continued on next page

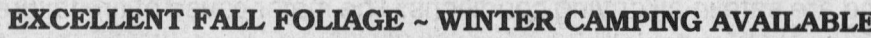

See listing at Chester



See listing at Charlemont

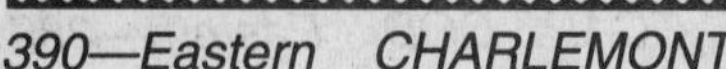

DENNISPORT—Continued
CAMPER'S HAVEN—Continued

phone hookups, RV rentals, sewage disposal, laundry, public phone, grocery store, RV supplies, ice, tables, patios, grills, traffic control gate.

◆◆◆◆RECREATION: rec hall, rec room/area, pavilion, salt water swimming, salt water fishing, mini-golf ($), basketball hoop, playground, 2 shuffleboard courts, planned group activities, recreation director, horseshoes, volleyball.

No tents. Open mid Apr through mid Oct. No pets Jun 25 through Labor Day. Rate in 1995 $30 for 4 persons. No refunds. Reservations recommended Jul through Aug. American Express/Master Card/Visa accepted. CPO. Phone: (508) 398-2811.

SEE AD THIS PAGE

**GRINDELL'S OCEAN VIEW PARK**—Oceanfront RV PARK on Cape Cod. Most sites occupied by seasonal campers. *From jct US 6 (exit 9) & Hwy 134: Go 2 mi S on Hwy 134, then 1 mi SW on Swan River Rd, then 1/3 mi E on Lower County Rd, then 2/10 mi SE on Old Wharf Rd.*

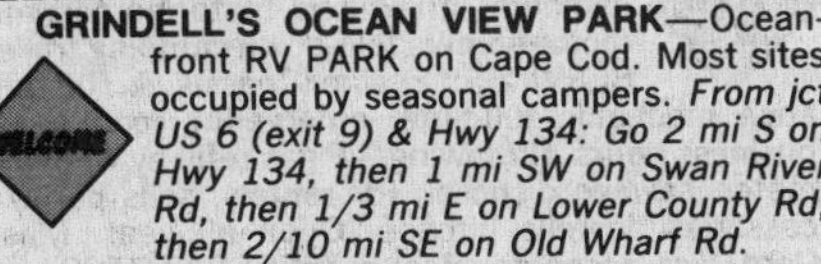

◆◆◆FACILITIES: 160 sites, most common site width 24 feet, 34 ft. max RV length, accepts full hookup units only, 160 full hookups, (20 amp receptacles), seasonal sites, a/c not allowed, heater not allowed, cable TV, phone hookups, cabins, public phone, limited grocery store, RV supplies, LP gas refill by weight/by meter, ice, tables, patios, traffic control gate.

◆RECREATION: salt water swimming, salt water fishing.

No pets. No tents. Open May 1 through Sep 30. Rate in 1995 $30 for 2 persons. Reservations recommended Jul through Aug. Phone: (508) 398-2671.

SEE AD PAGE 390

## DOUGLAS—C-3

**WINDING BROOK CAMPGROUND**—A CAMPGROUND with leveled sites among the pines. *From jct Hwy 16 & Hwy 96: Go 2 1/4 mi S on Hwy 96.*

◆◆FACILITIES: 145 sites, most common site width 50 feet, 80 full hookups, 40 water & elec (15,20 & 30 amp receptacles), 25 no hookups, seasonal sites, a/c allowed ($), heater not allowed, phone hookups, tenting available, RV storage, sewage disposal, public phone, grocery store, LP gas refill by weight, ice, tables, fire rings, wood, church services.

◆◆◆RECREATION: rec hall, rec room/area, coin games, swim pool, pond swimming, pond fishing, basketball hoop, playground, planned group activities, sports field, horseshoes, hiking trails, volleyball.

Open May 15 through Oct 1. Rate in 1995 $18 per family. Reservations recommended Jul 1 through Labor Day. Member of ARVC; MACO. Phone: (508) 476-7549.

SEE AD THIS PAGE

## EAST FALMOUTH—D-5

**Cape Cod Campresort**—CAMPGROUND with sites in a pine forest beside a pond. *From jct Hwy 28 & Thomas Landers Rd: Go 2 1/2 mi E on Thomas Landers Rd.* ◆◆FACILITIES: 185 sites, most common site width 30 feet, 145 water & elec (15,20 & 30 amp receptacles), 40 no hookups, seasonal sites, tenting available, handicap restroom facilities, sewage disposal, public phone, ice, tables. ◆◆◆RECREATION: rec hall, swim pool, pond swimming, boating, 2 pedal boat rentals, pond fishing, playground, planned group activities, badminton, horseshoes, hiking trails. Open Apr 15 through Oct 15. Rate in 1995 $24 per family. Phone: (508) 548-1458.

## EASTHAM—C-6

**ATLANTIC OAKS**—Shaded CAMPGROUND with mostly level sites. *From National Seashore Main Visitors Center and Hwy 6: Go 1/2 mi E on Hwy 6.*

◆◆◆FACILITIES: 100 sites, most common site width 35 feet, 100 full hookups, (30 & 50 amp receptacles), seasonal sites, 100 pull-thrus, a/c allowed, heater allowed ($), cable TV, phone hookups, tenting available, RV rentals, cabins, RV storage, sewage disposal, laundry, public phone, limited grocery store, RV supplies, LP gas refill by weight/by meter, ice, tables.

◆◆RECREATION: basketball hoop, 4 bike rentals, playground, movies, horseshoes, hiking trails.

Open May 1 through Nov 1. Jul & Aug weekends may require minimum length of stay. Winter by reservation. Rate in 1995 $22-29 for 2 persons. No refunds. Reservations recommended Jul 1 through Labor Day. Discover/Master Card/Visa accepted. Member of ARVC;MACO. Phone: (508) 255-1437.

SEE AD FRONT OF BOOK PAGE 12 AND AD CAPE COD PAGE 389

## EAST WAREHAM—D-5

**Maple Park Family Camping**—A secluded, lakeside CAMPGROUND with shaded sites. *From jct Hwy 6 & Hwy 28: Go 2 mi N on Glen Charlie Rd.* ◆◆FACILITIES: 400 sites, most common site width 24 feet, 300 full hookups, (15 amp receptacles), 100 no hookups, seasonal sites, 5 pull-thrus, tenting available, sewage disposal, laundry, public phone, grocery store, LP gas refill by weight, ice, tables, fire rings, wood. ◆◆◆RECREATION: rec hall, rec room/area, lake swimming, boating, no motors, canoeing, 3 pedal boat rentals, lake fishing, playground, planned group activities (weekends only), sports field, horseshoes, hiking trails, volleyball. Open May 1 through Oct 15. Rate in 1995 $18. No refunds. Member of ARVC; MACO. Phone: (508) 295-4945.

## ERVING—B-2

ERVING STATE FOREST—*From town: Go E on Hwy 2, then follow signs on Church St.* FACILITIES: 32 sites, 16 ft. max RV length, 32 no hookups, tenting available, tables, grills. RECREATION: pavilion, lake swimming, boating, 10 hp limit, canoeing, ramp, lake fishing, hiking trails. Recreation open to the public. Open mid May through Columbus Day. No showers. Phone: (508) 544-3939.

## FALMOUTH—D-5

**SIPPEWISSETT CABINS & CAMPGROUND**—A terraced CAMPGROUND with wooded sites near the ocean. *From jct Hwy 28 & Sippewissett Cutoff: Go 200 yards W, then 1/2 mi S on Palmer Ave.*

◆◆◆FACILITIES: 120 sites, most common site width 40 feet, 60 water & elec (20 amp receptacles), 60 no hookups, seasonal sites, a/c not allowed, heater not allowed, phone hookups, tenting available, group sites for tents, cabins, RV storage, sewage disposal, laundry, public phone, ice, tables, fire rings, traffic control gate.

◆◆RECREATION: rec room/area, coin games, playground, volleyball.

No pets. Open May 15 through Oct 15. Rate in 1995 $26-28.50 for 2 persons. No refunds. Reservations recommended Jul 1 through Labor Day. Master Card/Visa accepted. Member of ARVC; MACO. Phone: (508) 548-2542.

SEE AD CAPE COD PAGE 389

## FLORIDA—A-1

SAVOY STATE FOREST—*From town: Go 1 mi W on Hwy 2, then 4 mi S on Central Shaft Rd.* FACILITIES: 45 sites, 16 ft. max RV length, 45 no hookups, tenting available, handicap restroom facilities, public phone, tables, grills. RECREATION: swimming, boating, no motors, canoeing, ramp, fishing, hiking trails. Recreation open to the public. Open Memorial Day through mid Oct. Phone: (413) 663-8469.

## FOXBORO—C-4

**NORMANDY FARM FAMILY CAMPGROUND**—Rolling terrain with mostly wooded, level sites. *From jct I-495 (exit 14A) & US 1: Go 1 mi N on US 1, then 1 1/2 mi E on Thurston-West Sts.*

◆◆◆◆FACILITIES: 355 sites, most common site width 35 feet, 95 full hookups, 260 water & elec (20,30 & 50 amp receptacles), 225 pull-thrus, a/c allowed ($), heater allowed ($), phone hookups, tenting available, group sites for tents/RVs, RV rentals, RV storage, handicap restroom facilities, sewage disposal, laundry, public phone, full service store, RV supplies, LP gas refill by weight/by meter, ice, tables, patios, fire rings, wood, church services, traffic control gate/guard.

◆◆◆◆◆RECREATION: rec hall, rec room/area, coin games, 4 swim pools (indoor) (heated), whirlpool, basketball hoop, playground, 2 shuffleboard courts, planned group activities, movies, recreation director, badminton, sports field, horseshoes, hiking trails, volleyball, cross country skiing, snowmobile trails, local tours.

Open all year. Rate in 1995 $21.60-35 for 2 persons. Reservations recommended Jul 1 through Labor Day. Discover/Master Card/Visa accepted. CPO. Member of ARVC; MACO. Phone: (508) 543-7600.

SEE AD FRONT OF BOOK PAGE 10 AND AD BOSTON 384

FOXBORO—Continued on next page





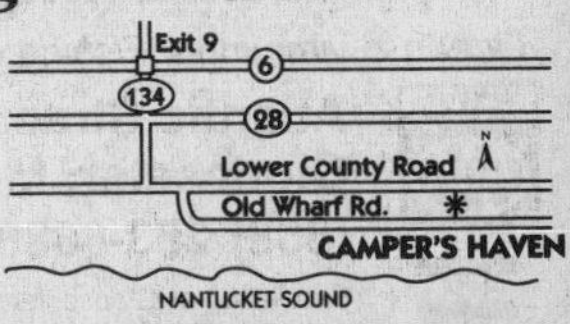

FOXBORO—Continued

✲ **NORMANDY FARM RV SERVICE**—*From jct I-495 (exit 14A) & US 1: Go 1 mi N on US 1, then 1 1/2 mi E on Thurston-West Sts.* SALES: travel trailers. SERVICES: RV appliance mechanic full-time, LP gas refill by meter, sewage disposal, RV storage, sells parts/accessories, installs hitches. Open all year. Phone: (508) 543-7600.

**SEE AD TRAVEL SECTION PAGE 377 AND AD BOSTON PAGE 384**

## GLOUCESTER—B-5

**CAPE ANN CAMP SITE**—CAMPGROUND with shaded sites on hilly terrain overlooking river. *From jct Hwy 128 & Concord St (exit 13): Go 3/4 mi N on Concord St, then 1/2 mi NE on Atlantic St (Wingaersheek Beach Rd).*

◆◆◆FACILITIES: 250 sites, most common site width 40 feet, 42 full hookups, 90 water & elec (15, 20 & 30 amp receptacles), 118 no hookups, seasonal sites, a/c allowed ($), heater allowed ($), tenting available, sewage disposal, laundry, public phone, grocery store, RV supplies, ice, tables, fire rings, wood.

Open May 1 through Nov 1. 3 day minimum Friday arrivals, 2 day minimum Saturday arrivals, June 15 thru Sep 7. Rate in 1995 $15-22 for 2 persons. Reservations recommended Jun 15 through Labor Day. Master Card/Visa accepted. Member of ARVC; MACO. Phone: (508) 283-8683.

**SEE AD THIS PAGE**

## GOSHEN—B-2

D.A.R. STATE FOREST—*From jct Hwy 9 & Hwy 112: Follow signs N on Hwy 112.* FACILITIES: 50 sites, 50 no hookups, tenting available, handicap restroom facilities, tables, grills. RECREATION: pavilion, lake swimming, boating, no motors, canoeing, ramp, lake fishing, hiking trails. Recreation open to the public. Open mid May through Columbus Day. Phone: (413) 268-7098.

## GRANVILLE—C-2

GRANVILLE STATE FOREST—*From town: Go 7 mi W on Hwy 57, then 2 mi S on W Hartland Rd.* FACILITIES: 40 sites, 31 ft. max RV length, 40 no hookups, tenting available, non-flush toilets, tables, grills. RECREATION: river swimming, river fishing, hiking trails. Recreation open to the public. Open mid May through Columbus Day. No showers. Phone: (413) 269-6002.

## GREENFIELD—B-2

*See listing at Shelburne Falls*

## HANSON—C-5

✲ **HUNTER'S RV SALES & SERVICE**—*From jct Hwy 27 & Hwy 14: Go 1 block E on Hwy 14.* SALES: travel trailers, truck campers, 5th wheels, motor homes, mini-motor homes. SERVICES: RV appliance mechanic full-time, emergency road service business hours, RV towing, LP gas refill by weight/by meter, RV storage, sells parts/accessories, installs hitches. Open all year. Discover/Master Card/Visa accepted. Phone: (617) 447-5210.

**SEE AD THIS PAGE**

## HATFIELD—B-2

✲ **DIAMOND RV CENTRE**—*N'bound from jct I-91 (exit 22) & US 5/Hwy 10: Go 3/4 mi S on US 5/Hwy 10. S'bound from jct I-91 (exit 21) & US 5/Hwy 10: Go 2 mi N on US 5/Hwy 10.* SALES: travel trailers, park models, 5th wheels, motor homes, mini-motor homes, fold-down camping trailers. SERVICES: Engine/Chassis & RV appliance mechanic full-time, LP gas refill by weight/by meter, sewage disposal, RV storage, sells parts/accessories, sells camping supplies, installs hitches. Open all year. American Express/Discover/Master Card/Visa accepted. Phone: (413) 247-3144.

**SEE AD NORTHAMPTON PAGE 394**

## HINGHAM—B-5

BOSTON HARBOR ISLANDS STATE PARK—*From Hingham shipyard at 349 Lincoln St/Hwy 3A: Ferry to campsites on 4 islands. (Apply for permit prior to date of camping trip).* FACILITIES: 29 sites, 29 no hookups, tenting available, non-flush toilets, handicap restroom facilities. RECREATION: salt water swimming, boating, canoeing, salt water fishing, planned group activities, hiking trails. Open mid Jun through Labor Day. Reservations required. No showers. Phone: (617) 740-1605.

WOMPATUCK STATE PARK—*From jct Hwy 3A & Hwy 228: Go 1 3/4 mi S on Hwy 228, then 3 mi E on Free St to Union St.* FACILITIES: 400 sites, 30 ft. max RV length, 140 elec, 260 no hookups, tenting available, handicap restroom facilities, sewage disposal, public phone, tables, grills. RECREATION: pavilion, boating, no motors, ramp, fishing, hiking trails. Recreation open to the public. Open mid Apr through mid Oct. Phone: (617) 749-7160.

## HUMAROCK—C-5

MILITARY PARK (Fourth Cliff Rec. Area-Hanscom AFB) —*Off base, 50 mi S of Boston. From jct Hwy 3 & Hwy 139: Go 1 1/2 mi SE on Hwy 139, then continue E on Furnace, then NE on Ferry St, then E on Sea, then N on Central.* FACILITIES: 31 sites, 8 water & elec, 3 elec (30 amp receptacles), 20 no hookups, tenting available, sewage disposal, laundry, public phone, ice, tables, grills. RECREATION: rec hall, pavilion, salt water swimming, boating, salt water fishing, horseshoes. Open May through Oct. Phone: (617) 837-9269.

## HYANNIS—D-6

✲ **MCD RV CENTER**—*From jct US 6 (exit 7) & Willow St/Yarmouth Rd: Go 1 3/4 mi W on Willow St/Yarmouth Rd.* SALES: travel trailers, truck campers, fold-down camping trailers. SERVICES: RV appliance mechanic full-time, RV rentals, sells parts/accessories. Open all year. American Express/Master Card/Visa accepted. Phone: (508) 775-6311.

**SEE AD THIS PAGE**

## LAKEVILLE—C-5

✲ **ROUSSEAU'S RV CENTER**—*From I-495 (exit 5) & Hwy 18: Go 1 3/4 mi S on Hwy 18.* SALES: travel trailers, park models, truck campers, 5th wheels, motor homes, mini-motor homes, fold-down camping trailers. SERVICES: Engine/Chassis & RV appliance mechanic full-time, emergency road service business hours, RV towing, LP gas refill by weight/by meter, sewage disposal, RV rentals, sells parts/accessories, installs hitches. Open all year. Master Card/Visa accepted. Phone: (508) 947-7700.

**SEE AD THIS PAGE**

## LEE—B-1

OCTOBER MOUNTAIN STATE FOREST—*From jct I-90 & US 20: Go 2 mi N on US 20, then 1 mi E on Mill Rd, then N on Washington Mt.* FACILITIES: 50 sites, 30 ft. max RV length, 50 no hookups, tenting available, handicap restroom facilities, sewage disposal, public phone, tables, grills. RECREATION: boating, no motors, canoeing, lake/stream fishing, hiking trails. Recreation open to the public. Open mid May through mid Oct. Phone: (413) 243-1778.

## LENOX—B-1

**WOODLAND HILLS CAMPGROUND**—*About 15 minutes from Lenox: Go W on Hwy 183 to Hwy 102, then turn right on Hwy 102 to Hwy 22, then left on Hwy 22 to Middle Rd, then left on Middle Rd to Fog Hill Rd, follow signs to campground.*

**SEE PRIMARY LISTING AT AUSTERLITZ, NY AND AD AUSTERLITZ, NY PAGE 593**

## LITTLETON—B-4

**KOA-MINUTEMAN**—A CAMPGROUND with wooded sites in a natural setting. *From jct I-495 (exit 30) & Hwy 2A: Go 2 3/4 mi W on Hwy 2A.*

◆◆◆◆FACILITIES: 95 sites, most common site width 40 feet, 30 full hookups, 51 water & elec (20,30 & 50 amp receptacles), 14 no hookups, 18 pull-thrus, a/c allowed, heater allowed, tenting available, cabins, sewage disposal, laundry, public phone, grocery store, RV supplies, LP gas refill by meter, ice, tables, fire rings, wood.

◆◆◆RECREATION: rec hall, rec room/area, coin games, swim pool (heated), basketball hoop, playground, movies, badminton, horseshoes, volleyball.

Open May 1 through last Sun in Oct. Rate in 1995 $22-28 for 2 persons. Reservations recommended peak season. Discover/Master Card/Visa accepted. Member of ARVC; MACO. Phone: (508) 772-0042. KOA 10% value card discount.

**SEE AD BOSTON PAGE 382 AND AD FRONT OF BOOK PAGES 68 AND 69**

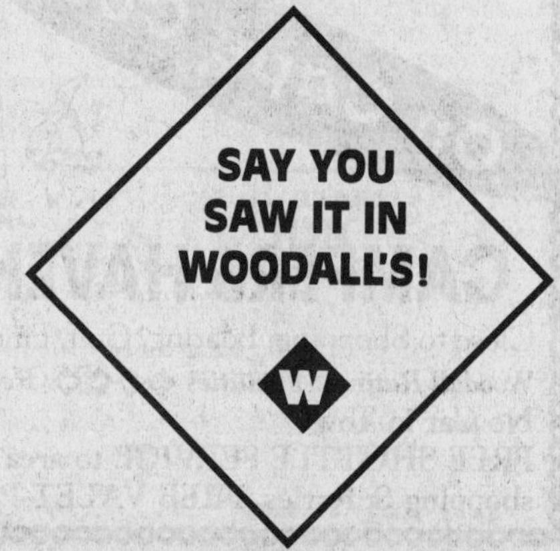
SAY YOU
SAW IT IN
WOODALL'S!
W

## MANSFIELD—C-4

**CANOE RIVER CAMPGROUND**—Level, wooded sites in a family oriented CAMPGROUND. *From jct I-495 (exit 10) & Hwy 123: Go 1 mi E on Hwy 123, then 2 1/4 mi N on Newland St/Mill St.*

◆◆◆FACILITIES: 150 sites, most common site width 24 feet, 150 water & elec (20 & 30 amp receptacles), seasonal sites, a/c allowed ($), heater allowed ($), tenting available, RV storage, handicap restroom facilities, sewage disposal, laundry, public phone, full service store, RV supplies, LP gas refill by weight/by meter, ice, tables, fire rings, wood, traffic control gate.

◆◆◆◆RECREATION: rec hall, rec room/area, pavilion, coin games, 2 swim pools (heated), boating, no motors, canoeing, dock, 3 row/3 canoe/10 pedal boat rentals, pond fishing, basketball hoop, 7 bike rentals, playground, planned group activities, movies, badminton, sports field, horseshoes, hiking trails, volleyball.

Open all year. Facilities fully operational Apr 15 through Oct 15. Rate in 1995 $18-20 per family. No refunds. Reservations recommended Memorial Day through Labor Day. Master Card/Visa accepted. Member of ARVC; MACO. Phone: (508) 339-6462.

**SEE AD THIS PAGE**

## MARTHA'S VINEYARD—D-5

**MARTHA'S VINEYARD FAMILY CAMPGROUND**—Spacious, level, open & shaded sites near beaches on a resort island accessible by ferry. *From Vineyard Haven Ferry: Go 1/4 mi S on Water St, then 1/4 mi SW on Beach St, then 1 mi S on Edgartown Rd.*

◆◆◆FACILITIES: 180 sites, 50 full hookups, 110 water & elec (20 & 30 amp receptacles), 20 no hookups, seasonal sites, 27 pull-thrus, a/c allowed, heater allowed, cable TV ($), phone hookups, tenting available, group sites for tents/RVs, RV rentals, cabins, RV storage, sewage disposal, laundry, public phone, grocery store, RV supplies, ice, tables, fire rings, wood.

◆◆◆RECREATION: rec hall, coin games, 22 bike rentals, playground, badminton, sports field, horseshoes, hiking trails, volleyball.

Open May 15 through Oct 15. No dogs. Rate in 1995 $25-28 for 2 persons. Reservations recommended Jun 15 through Labor Day. Discover/Master Card/Visa accepted. CPO. Member of ARVC; MACO. Phone: (508) 693-3772.

**SEE AD FRONT OF BOOK PAGE 10 AND AD THIS PAGE**

**Webb's Camping Area**—Large, private, waterview sites in a secluded pine forest on a resort island accessible by ferry. *From Oak Bluff Ferry: Go 1/4 mi W on Oak Bluff Rd, then 1/2 mi SW on Circuit Ave, then 1 1/2 mi SW on Barnes Rd.* ◆◆FACILITIES: 166 sites, most common site width 75 feet, 22 ft. max RV length, 26 water & elec (15 & 20 amp receptacles), 140 no hookups, seasonal sites, tenting available, sewage disposal, laundry, public phone, grocery store, ice, tables, fire rings, grills, wood. ◆◆RECREATION: rec room/area, playground, sports field, volleyball. No pets. Open mid May through mid Sep. Rate in 1995 $26-28 for 2 persons. No refunds. Member of ARVC; MACO. Phone: (508) 693-0233.

## MIDDLEBORO—C-5

**KOA-PLYMOUTH ROCK**—A rolling, semi-wooded CAMPGROUND with spacious sites on an Upland Plateau. *From jct I-495 (exit 6) & US 44: Go 2 3/4 mi E on US 44.*

◆◆◆FACILITIES: 274 sites, most common site width 50 feet, 132 full hookups, 122 water & elec (15,20,30 & 50 amp receptacles), 20 no hookups, seasonal sites, 44 pull-thrus, a/c allowed ($), heater allowed ($), phone hookups, tenting available, group sites for tents/RVs, cabins, RV storage, sewage disposal, laundry, public phone, full service



MIDDLEBORO—Continued
KOA-PLYMOUTH ROCK—Continued

store, RV supplies, LP gas refill by meter, ice, tables, fire rings, wood.

◆◆◆RECREATION: rec room/area, coin games, swim pool, basketball hoop, playground, planned group activities, movies, badminton, sports field, horseshoes, hiking trails, volleyball, local tours.

Open Mar 1 through Dec 1. Monthly rates available. Rate in 1995 $20-26.25 for 2 persons. Reservations recommended Memorial Day through Labor Day. Discover/Master Card/Visa accepted. Member of ARVC; MACO. Phone: (508) 947-6435. KOA 10% value card discount.

**SEE AD BOSTON PAGE 382 AND AD TRAVEL SECTION PAGE 379 AND AD FRONT OF BOOK PAGES 68 AND 69**

## MONSON—C-2

**PARTRIDGE HOLLOW CAMPING AREA**—A rural CAMPGROUND on rolling terrain with well-developed sites among young pines and oaks. *From jct I-90 (exit 8) & Hwy 32: Go 3/4 mi S on Hwy 32, then 5 4/10 mi E on US 20, then 3/4 mi SW on Monson Rd, then at Brimfield State Park sign go 2 1/2 mi SE on Dean Pond Rd.*

◆◆◆FACILITIES: 282 sites, most common site width 40 feet, 125 full hookups, 133 water & elec (20 & 30 amp receptacles), 24 no hookups, seasonal sites, 12 pull-thrus, a/c allowed ($), heater not allowed, phone hookups, tenting available, group sites for tents/RVs, RV storage, sewage disposal, laundry, public phone, grocery store, RV supplies, LP gas refill by weight/by meter, ice, tables, fire rings, grills, wood, traffic control gate.

◆◆◆RECREATION: rec hall, rec room/area, coin games, swim pool, basketball hoop, playground, 2 shuffleboard courts, planned group activities (weekends only), badminton, horseshoes, hiking trails, volleyball.

Open all year. Facilities fully operational Apr 15 through Oct 15. Rate in 1995 $18.50-21.95 for 2 persons. Reservations recommended Memorial Day through Labor Day. Master Card/Visa accepted. Member of ARVC; MACO. Phone: (413) 267-5122.

**SEE AD SPRINGFIELD PAGE 400**

**SUNSETVIEW FARM CAMPING AREA**—A CAMPGROUND with sites in an apple orchard and woods, serving many seasonal campers. *From jct I-90 (exit 8) & Hwy 32: Go 1 mi S on Hwy 32/Thorndyke St, then 1 1/2 mi SE on Main St, then 1/2 mi E on Fenton Rd, then 1 1/2 mi S on Town Farm Rd.*

◆◆◆FACILITIES: 120 sites, most common site width 28 feet, 10 full hookups, 70 water & elec (20 & 30 amp receptacles), 40 no hookups, seasonal sites, 10 pull-thrus, a/c allowed ($), heater not allowed, phone hookups, tenting available, group sites for

MONSON—Continued
SUNSETVIEW FARM CAMPING AREA—Continued

tents/RVs, RV storage, sewage disposal, laundry, public phone, grocery store, RV supplies, ice, tables, fire rings, wood, traffic control gate.

◆◆◆◆RECREATION: rec hall, rec room/area, equipped pavilion, coin games, swim pool, pond swimming, pond fishing, basketball hoop, playground, planned group activities (weekends only), badminton, sports field, horseshoes, hiking trails, volleyball.

Open Apr 15 through Oct 15. Rate in 1995 $19-22 for 2 persons. No refunds. Reservations recommended Jul 1 through Labor Day. Master Card/Visa accepted. Member of ARVC; MACO. Phone: (413) 267-9269.

**SEE AD SPRINGFIELD PAGE 400**

## NORTH ADAMS—A-1

CLARKSBURG STATE PARK—*From town: Go N on Hwy 8, then follow signs on Middle Rd.* FACILITIES: 47 sites, 16 ft. max RV length, 47 no hookups, tenting available, non-flush toilets, public phone, tables, grills. RECREATION: swimming, boating, no motors, canoeing, fishing, hiking trails. Recreation open to the public. Open mid May through Labor Day. No showers. Phone: (413) 663-8469.

**HISTORIC VALLEY CAMPGROUND (Municipal Park)**—*From jct Hwy 2 & E Main St: Go 1/4 mi S on E Main St, then 3/4 mi SE on Kemp Ave.*

FACILITIES: 120 sites, most common site width 35 feet, 94 water & elec, 6 elec (20 amp receptacles), 20 no hookups, seasonal sites, a/c allowed ($), heater allowed ($), tenting available, sewage disposal, laundry, public phone, limited grocery store, ice, tables, fire rings, grills, wood, guard.

HISTORIC VALLEY CAMPGROUND (MUNICIPAL PARK)—Continued on next page
NORTH ADAMS—Continued on next page

NORTH ADAMS—Continued
HISTORIC VALLEY CAMPGROUND (MUNICIPAL PARK)—Continued

RECREATION: rec room/area, equipped pavilion, lake swimming, boating, no motors, canoeing, ramp, 2 row/4 canoe boat rentals, lake fishing, playground, planned group activities, badminton, sports field, horseshoes, hiking trails, volleyball, cross country skiing.

Open May 15 through Oct 15. Reservations recommended all season. Phone: (413) 662-3198.

**SEE AD PAGE 393**

MT. GREYLOCKE STATE RESERVATION—*From Hwy 2 W of town: Go 11 mi S on Notch Rd.* FACILITIES: 35 sites, 15 ft. max RV length, 35 no hookups, tenting available, non-flush toilets, handicap restroom facilities, tables, grills. RECREATION: pavilion, hiking trails. Recreation open to the public. Open Memorial Day through mid Oct. No showers. Phone: (413) 499-4262.

## NORTH EGREMONT—C-1

**Prospect Lake Park**—A lakeside CAMPGROUND with some open and some wooded sites. *From jct Hwy 23 & Hwy 71: Go 3 mi W on Hwy 71, then 3/4 mi SW on Prospect Lake Rd.* ◆◆◆FACILITIES: 130 sites, most common site width 40 feet, 15 full hookups, 115 water & elec (15,20 & 30 amp receptacles), seasonal sites, 30 pull-thrus, tenting available, sewage disposal, laundry, public phone, limited grocery store, LP gas refill by weight, ice, tables, fire rings, grills, wood. ◆◆◆◆RECREATION: rec hall, rec room/area, lake swimming, boating, 10 hp limit, canoeing, ramp, dock, 2 row/1 sail/5 canoe/3 pedal boat rentals, lake fishing, playground, planned group activities, 2 tennis courts, badminton, horseshoes, volleyball. Recreation open to the public. Open 1st wkend May through Columbus Day. 3 night minimum holiday weekends. Rate in 1995 $20-27 for 2 persons. No refunds. Member of ARVC; MACO. Phone: (413) 528-4158.

## NORTHAMPTON—B-2

*See listing at Hatfield*

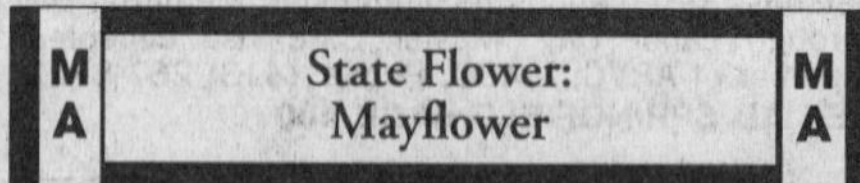


## NORTH RUTLAND—B-3

**POUT & TROUT CAMPGROUND**—A rural setting with wooded or open grassy sites. Most sites occupied by seasonal campers. *From jct Hwy 56 & Hwy 68: Go 1/2 mi N on Hwy 68, then 3/4 mi NE on River Rd.*

◆◆◆FACILITIES: 156 sites, most common site width 35 feet, 70 full hookups, 76 water & elec (15,20 & 30 amp receptacles), 10 no hookups, seasonal sites, a/c allowed ($), heater not allowed, phone hookups, tenting available, group sites for tents/RVs, RV storage, sewage disposal, laundry, public phone, limited grocery store, LP gas refill by weight, ice, tables, fire rings, wood, traffic control gate.

◆◆◆RECREATION: rec hall, pavilion, coin games, swim pool, boating, no motors, canoeing, 3 row/2 pedal boat rentals, river/pond fishing, basketball hoop, playground, planned group activities, sports field, horseshoes.

Open mid Apr through Columbus Day. Rate in 1995 $14-17 per family. No refunds. Reservations recommended Jun 15 through Labor Day. Member of ARVC; MACO. Phone: (508) 886-6677.

**SEE AD THIS PAGE**

## NORTH TRURO—C-6

**HORTON'S CAMPING RESORT**—A CAMPGROUND with wooded and open grassy sites. *From jct US 6 & S Highland Rd (1st right turn after Truro Central School): Go 1 mi E on S Highland Rd.*

◆◆◆FACILITIES: 217 sites, most common site width 35 feet, 42 full hookups, 32 water & elec (20 & 30 amp receptacles), 143 no hookups, seasonal sites, a/c allowed ($), heater allowed ($), tenting available, RV storage, handicap restroom facilities, sewage disposal, laundry, public phone, grocery store, RV supplies, ice, tables, traffic control gate.

◆◆RECREATION: playground, badminton, horseshoes, hiking trails, volleyball.

No pets. Open May 3 through mid Oct. Facilities fully operational late May through Columbus Day. Two week notice required for refunds. Rate in 1995 $16-23 for 2 persons. No refunds. Reservations recommended Memorial Day through Labor Day. Master Card/Visa accepted. Member of ARVC; MACO. Phone: (508) 487-1220.

**SEE AD FRONT OF BOOK PAGE 12 AND AD THIS PAGE**

**North Highland Camping Area**—A secluded CAMPGROUND with wooded sites. Motor homes are excluded. *From jct US 6 & Head of the Meadow Rd: Go 3/4 mi E on Head of the Meadow Rd.* ◆◆ FACILITIES: 237 sites, most common site width 40 feet, 17 ft. max RV length, 237 no hookups, tenting available, laundry, public phone, grocery store, LP gas refill by weight/by meter, ice, tables. ◆RECREATION: rec hall, rec room/area. No pets. Open mid May through mid Sep. Grocery store open late June to Labor Day. Rate in 1995 $18 for 2 persons. Member of ARVC; MACO. Phone: (508) 487-1191.

**North Truro Camping Area**—CAMPGROUND with mostly sandy, level sites. *From jct Hwy 6 & Highland Rd: Go 1/4 mi E on Highland Rd.* ◆◆◆FACILITIES: 332 sites, most common site width 50 feet, 107 full hookups, 125 water & elec (15 amp receptacles), 100 no hookups, seasonal sites, tenting available, sewage disposal, laun-

NORTH TRURO CAMPING AREA—Continued on next page
NORTH TRURO—Continued on next page

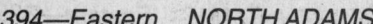

NORTH TRURO—Continued
NORTH TRURO CAMPING AREA—Continued

dry, public phone, grocery store, LP gas refill by weight/by meter, ice, tables, wood. Open all year. Facilities fully operational mid May through mid Oct. No dogs allowed Jun 15-Labor Day. Rate in 1995 $15-21 for 2 persons. No refunds. Member of ARVC; MACO. Phone: (508) 487-1847.

### NORWELL—C-5

**NORWELL CAMPSITES**—A CAMPGROUND with rolling terrain and shaded sites near metro area. *From jct Hwy 3 (exit 13) & Hwy 53: Go 1 1/2 mi N on Hwy 53.*

◆◆FACILITIES: 75 sites, 22 full hookups, 53 water & elec (15 & 20 amp receptacles), seasonal sites, a/c allowed ($), heater allowed ($), phone hookups, sewage disposal, public phone, LP gas refill by weight/by meter, ice.

◆RECREATION: swim pool.

No tents. Open all year. Facilities fully operational Apr 1 through Dec 1. Rate in 1995 $15-19 for 2 persons. Phone: (617) 871-0527.

**SEE AD BOSTON PAGE 385**

### OAKHAM—B-3

**PINE ACRES FAMILY CAMPGROUND**—Shaded, lakeside CAMPGROUND with prepared sites. *From jct Hwy 122 & Hwy 148 (N Brookfield Rd): Go 2 mi SW on N Brookfield Rd, then 1/10 mi S on Spencer Rd, then 4/10 mi E on Bechan Rd.*

◆◆◆◆FACILITIES: 350 sites, most common site width 40 feet, 300 full hookups, (20 & 30 amp receptacles), 50 no hookups, seasonal sites, 3 pull-thrus, a/c allowed ($), heater not allowed, phone hookups, tenting available, group sites for tents/RVs, RV rentals, RV storage, handicap restroom facilities, sewage disposal, laundry, public phone, full service store, RV supplies, LP gas refill by weight/by meter, ice, tables, fire rings, wood, guard.

◆◆◆◆RECREATION: rec hall, rec room/area, coin games, lake swimming, boating, canoeing, ramp, 4 row/3 canoe/1 pedal boat rentals, water skiing, lake fishing, basketball hoop, playground, planned group activities (weekends only), recreation director, tennis court, badminton, sports field, horseshoes, hiking trails, volleyball, cross country skiing, snowmobile trails.

Open all year. Rate in 1995 $17-25 for 2 persons. Reservations recommended Jul weekends. Discover/Master Card/Visa accepted. Member of ARVC; MACO. Phone: (508) 882-9509.

**SEE AD BOSTON PAGE 385**

### OTIS—C-1

TOLLAND STATE FOREST—*From town: Go S on Hwy 8, then E on Reservoir Rd.* FACILITIES: 90 sites, 24 ft. max RV length, 90 no hookups, tenting available, handicap restroom facilities, sewage disposal, public phone, tables, grills. RECREATION: swimming, boating, canoeing, ramp, fishing, hiking trails. Recreation open to the public. Open mid May through mid Oct. Phone: (413) 269-6002.

### PHILLIPSTON—B-3

**Lamb City Campground**—Lakeside CAMPGROUND with shaded, level sites. *E'bound: From jct US 2 (exit 19) & Hwy 2A: Go 400 feet N on Hwy 2A, then 1/2 mi W on Royalston Rd. W'bound: From jct US 2 (exit 19) & Hwy 2A: Go 400 feet S on Hwy 2A, then 1/2 mi W on Royalston Rd.* ◆◆◆FACILITIES: 150 sites, most common site width 44 feet, 130 full hookups, 20 water & elec (20 & 30 amp receptacles), seasonal sites, 17 pull-thrus, tenting available, sewage disposal, laundry, public phone, full service store, LP gas refill by weight/by meter, ice, tables, fire rings, wood. ◆◆◆RECREATION: rec hall, 2 swim pools, pond swimming, boating, electric motors only, ramp, dock, 2 canoe boat rentals, pond fishing, playground, 2 shuffleboard courts, planned group activities (weekends only), sports field, horseshoes, hiking trails, volleyball. Open all year. Rate in 1995 $19-23 per family. Phone: (800) 292-5262.

### PITTSFIELD—B-1

**Bonnie Brae Cabins & Campsites**—Shaded & open grassy sites in an RV PARK near a metro area. *From jct Hwy 9 & Hwy 7: Go 3 mi N on Hwy 7, then 1/4 mi E on Broadway.* ◆◆FACILITIES: 42 sites, most common site width 20 feet, 25 full hookups, 17 water & elec (15,20 & 30 amp receptacles), seasonal sites, 3 pull-thrus, tenting available, sewage disposal, laundry, public phone, tables, fire rings, wood. ◆RECREATION: swim pool. Open May 1 through Oct 31. Facilities fully operational May 1 through Columbus Day. Rate in 1995 $23 for 2 persons. No refunds. Member of ARVC; MACO. Phone: (413) 442-3754.

PITTSFIELD STATE FOREST—*From US 7 N of town: Follow signs.* FACILITIES: 31 sites, 16 ft. max RV length, 31 no hookups, tenting available, handicap restroom facilities, public phone, tables, grills. RECREATION: rec hall, river swimming, boating, no motors, canoeing, river fishing, sports field, hiking trails. Recreation open to the public. Open mid May through mid Oct. No showers. Phone: (413) 442-8992.

### PLAINFIELD—B-1

**BERKSHIRE GREEN ACRES**—CAMPGROUND with open and shaded sites surrounding large, grassy fields. *From jct Hwys 8A/116: Go 4 mi SE on Hwy 116, then 1 mi NE on Bow St.*

◆◆FACILITIES: 190 sites, 180 full hookups, 7 water & elec (15 amp receptacles), 3 no hookups, seasonal sites, 30 pull-thrus, a/c allowed ($), heater allowed ($), tenting available, group sites for tents/RVs, RV storage, sewage disposal, public phone, limited grocery store, LP gas refill by weight, gasoline, ice, tables, patios, fire rings, wood.

◆◆RECREATION: rec hall, rec room/area, coin games, swim pool, basketball hoop, playground, badminton, sports field, horseshoes, hiking trails, volleyball, cross country skiing, snowmobile trails. Recreation open to the public.

Open all year. Facilities fully operational May 1 through Oct 15. Rate in 1995 $18-20 per family. No refunds. Reservations recommended May 20 through Oct 15. Member of ARVC; MCOA. Phone: (413) 634-5385. FCRV 10% discount.

**SEE AD THIS PAGE**

### PLAINVILLE—C-4

✱ **MACDONALD'S RV CENTER**—*From jct I-495 (exit 14B) & US 1: Go 1/2 mi S on US 1.* SALES: travel trailers, truck campers, 5th wheels, motor homes, mini-motor homes, micro-mini motor homes, fold-down camping trailers. SERVICES: RV appliance mechanic full-time, LP gas refill by meter, RV storage, sells parts/accessories, installs hitches. Open all year. Discover/Master Card/Visa accepted. Phone: (508) 695-9241.

**SEE AD THIS PAGE**

MA | See front of book article for info on the Eastern States Exposition | MA



### PLYMOUTH—C-5

***See listings at Bourne, Buzzard's Bay, Lakeville, Middleboro, Norwell & South Carver***

**Ellis Haven**—Open & shaded sites in a mostly seasonal lakeside CAMPGROUND. *From jct Hwy 3 & Hwy 44 (exit 6): Go 1 mi W on Hwy 44, then 2 1/2 mi SW on Seven Hills & Federal Furnace Rd.* ◆◆◆FACILITIES: 420 sites, most common site width 40 feet, 380 water & elec (15,20 & 30 amp receptacles), 40 no hookups, sea-

ELLIS HAVEN—Continued on next page
PLYMOUTH—Continued on next page

PLYMOUTH—Continued
ELLIS HAVEN—Continued

sonal sites, 50 pull-thrus, tenting available, sewage disposal, laundry, public phone, limited grocery store, LP gas refill by weight, ice, tables, wood. ◇◇◇RECREATION: pavilion, lake swimming, boating, no motors, canoeing, 4 pedal boat rentals, lake fishing, mini-golf ($), playground, planned group activities, sports field, horseshoes, volleyball. Recreation open to the public. Open May 1 through Oct 1. Rate in 1995 $17-21 for 4 persons. Member of ARVC; MACO. Phone: (508) 746-0803.

**INDIANHEAD RESORT**—A CAMPGROUND with mostly wooded sites. *From jct Hwy 3 (exit 2) & Hwy 3A: Go 2 mi N on Hwy 3A.*

◇◇◇FACILITIES: 200 sites, most common site width 40 feet, 200 water & elec (15,20,30 & 50 amp receptacles), seasonal sites, a/c allowed, heater allowed, tenting available, group sites for tents/RVs, RV storage, sewage disposal, laundry, public phone, grocery store, RV supplies, LP gas refill by weight, ice, tables, fire rings, grills, wood.

◇◇◇RECREATION: lake swimming, boating, no motors, canoeing, 2 row/3 canoe/4 pedal boat rentals, lake fishing, basketball hoop, playground, badminton, horseshoes, hiking trails, volleyball.

Open mid Apr through Columbus Day. Rate in 1995 $20-26 for 2 persons. No refunds. Reservations recommended Jun 27 through Labor Day. Member of ARVC; MACO. Phone: (508) 888-3688.

**SEE AD PAGE 395**

PLYMOUTH—Continued

**KOA-PLYMOUTH ROCK**—*From jct Hwy 3 & US 44: Go 14 mi W on US 44.*

**SEE PRIMARY LISTING AT MIDDLEBORO AND AD BOSTON PAGE 382**

**NORWELL CAMPSITES**—*From Plymouth: Go 18 mi NW on Hwy 3 to exit 13, then 1 1/2 mi N on Hwy 53.*

**SEE PRIMARY LISTING AT NORWELL AND AD BOSTON PAGE 385**

**PINEWOOD LODGE CAMPGROUND**—A wooded CAMPGROUND above a lake on rolling terrain. *From jct Hwy 3 & Hwy 44 (exit 6): Go 3 mi W on Hwy 44, then 1/2 mi S on Pinewood Rd.*

◇◇◇FACILITIES: 243 sites, 105 full hookups, 100 water & elec (20,30 & 50 amp receptacles), 38 no hookups, seasonal sites, 15 pull-thrus, a/c allowed ($), heater allowed ($), phone hookups, tenting available, group sites for tents/RVs, RV rentals, cabins, RV storage, sewage disposal, laundry, public phone, limited grocery store, RV supplies, LP gas refill by weight, ice, tables, fire rings, wood, traffic control gate/guard.

◇◇◇◇RECREATION: rec room/area, coin games, lake swimming, boating, no motors, canoeing, 5 row/2 canoe boat rentals, lake fishing, playground, planned group activities (weekends only), badminton, sports field, horseshoes, hiking trails, volleyball.

PLYMOUTH—Continued
PINEWOOD LODGE CAMPGROUND—Continued

No pets. Open Apr 1 through Nov 1. Facilities fully operational May 15 through Oct 15. Rate in 1995 $18-25 for 2 persons. No refunds. Reservations recommended Jul 1 through Lab Day. Master Card/Visa accepted. Member of ARVC;MACO. Phone: (508) 746-3548. FCRV 10% discount.

**SEE AD FRONT OF BOOK PAGE 10 AND AD TRAVEL SECTION PAGE 379 AND AD THIS PAGE**

✵ **PINEWOOD LODGE RV SERVICE**—*From jct Hwy 3 & Hwy 44 (exit 6): Go 3 mi W on Hwy 44, then 1/2 mi S on Pinewood Rd.* SERVICES: RV appliance mechanic full-time, LP gas refill by weight, sewage disposal, RV storage, sells parts/accessories. Open May 1 through Nov 1. Phone: (508) 746-3548.

**SEE AD FRONT OF BOOK PAGE 10 AND AD THIS PAGE**

▸ **PLYMOUTH COUNTY ATTRACTIONS**—*At Route 3 (exit 5).* Tourist information office for Plymouth Area attractions. Brochures and information available. Open all year. Phone: (617) 826-3136.

**SEE AD TRAVEL SECTION PAGE 379**

PLYMOUTH—Continued on next page

PLYMOUTH—Continued

**Sandy Pond Campground**—Spacious wooded sites near lake. *From jct I-195 & I-495: Go 12 mi SE on Hwy 25 to exit 2 (Bourne-Sagamore), then 1st right at Rotary to Head of Bay Rd, then 1 1/2 mi NW on Head of Bay Rd, then 1 3/4 mi N on Plymouth Lane (Bourne Rd).* ◆◆◆FACILITIES: 129 sites, most common site width 40 feet, 34 full hookups, 70 water & elec (15,20 & 30 amp receptacles), 25 no hookups, seasonal sites, 50 pull-thrus, tenting available, handicap restroom facilities, sewage disposal, public phone, limited grocery store, LP gas refill by weight/by meter, ice, tables, fire rings, wood. ◆◆◆RECREATION: rec hall, lake swimming, boating, no motors, canoeing, 6 canoe boat rentals, lake fishing, playground, planned group activities (weekends only), sports field, horseshoes, hiking trails, volleyball. Open Apr 15 through Oct 15. Open weekends only in Apr and Oct. Rate in 1995 $17-22 per family. No refunds. Member of ARVC; MACO. Phone: (508) 759-9336.

## PROVINCETOWN—C-6

**COASTAL ACRES CAMPING COURT**—A CAMPGROUND on Cape Cod. *On west Vine St extension on Hwy 6A.*

◆◆◆FACILITIES: 114 sites, most common site width 50 feet, 80 water & elec (15 amp receptacles), 34 no hookups, seasonal sites, a/c not allowed, heater not allowed, tenting available, RV storage, sewage disposal, public phone, grocery store, RV supplies, LP gas refill by weight/by meter, ice, tables, patios.

Open Apr 1 through Nov 1. Rate in 1995 $20-27 for 2 persons. Reservations recommended Jun 15 through Labor Day. Member of ARVC; MACO. Phone: (508) 487-1700.

**SEE AD THIS PAGE**

**DUNES' EDGE CAMPGROUND**—Shaded campsites on rolling terrain at the edge of the sand dunes. *From National Seashore Dunes Parking Area: Go 1 3/4 mi E on Hwy 6 (At milepost 116).*

◆◆◆FACILITIES: 100 sites, most common site width 24 feet, 32 ft. max RV length, 14 water & elec, 8 elec (15 & 20 amp receptacles), 78 no hookups, a/c not allowed, heater not allowed, tenting available, sewage disposal, laundry, public phone, limited grocery store, ice, tables.

◆RECREATION: hiking trails.

Open early May through late Sep. Rate in 1995 $20-25 for 2 persons. No refunds. Reservations recommended Jul through Aug. Member of ARVC; MACO. Phone: (508) 487-9815.

**SEE AD THIS PAGE**

## RAYNHAM—C-4

✽ **BRADFORD RV CENTER**—*From jct Hwy 24 & Hwy 44: Go 500 feet E on Hwy 44.* SALES: travel trailers, park models, truck campers, 5th wheels, motor homes, mini-motor homes, fold-down camping trailers. Open all year. Phone: (508) 822-3800.

**SEE AD BROCKTON PAGE 388**

✽ **SILVER CITY FORD & RV CENTER**—*From jct I-495 (exit 6) & US 44: Go 2 mi W on US 44.* SALES: travel trailers, truck campers, 5th wheels, van conversions, motor homes, mini-motor homes, fold-down camping trailers. SERVICES: Engine/Chassis & RV appliance mechanic full-time, emergency road service 24 hours, RV towing, sells parts/accessories, installs hitches. Open all year. Phone: (508) 822-7161.

**SEE AD THIS PAGE**

## ROCHESTER—D-5

**KNIGHT & LOOK CAMPGROUNDS**—Level, natural sites in a rural setting among tall pines and oaks. *From jct I-195 (exit 20) & Hwy 105: Go 1 1/2 mi NW on Hwy 105.*

◆◆◆FACILITIES: 135 sites, most common site width 40 feet, 20 full hookups,



ROCHESTER—Continued
KNIGHT & LOOK CAMPGROUND—Continued

100 water & elec (15 & 20 amp receptacles), 15 no hookups, seasonal sites, 18 pull-thrus, a/c allowed ($), heater allowed ($), tenting available, group sites for tents/RVs, RV storage, sewage disposal, laundry, public phone, limited grocery store, LP gas refill by weight, ice, tables, fire rings, wood, church services.

◆◆◆RECREATION: rec hall, rec room/area, coin games, swim pool, boating, no motors, canoeing, pond fishing, basketball hoop, playground, planned group activities (weekends only), sports field, horseshoes.

Open Apr 15 through Oct 1. Rate in 1995 $22-25 per family. No refunds. Reservations recommended Jul 1 through Labor Day. Master Card/Visa accepted. Phone: (508) 763-2454.

**SEE AD THIS PAGE**

## RUTLAND—B-3

✽ **MANN'S TRAILER SALES**—*From jct Hwy 56 & Hwy 122A: Take Hwy North 122A to end of road, then 2 1/4 mi SE on Hwy 122.* SALES: travel trailers, truck campers, 5th wheels, mini-motor homes, fold-down camping trailers. SERVICES: RV appliance mechanic full-time, emergency road service business hours, RV towing, LP gas refill by weight/by meter, RV rentals, RV storage, sells parts/accessories, installs hitches. Open all year. Master Card/Visa accepted. Phone:. (508) 886-4821.

**SEE AD TRAVEL SECTION PAGE 379**

## SAGAMORE—D-5

SCUSSET BEACH STATE PARK—*From town: Go N over Sagamore Bridge, then E on Scusset Rd.* FACILITIES: 103 sites, 103 water & elec, tenting available, handicap restroom facilities, sewage disposal, public phone, tables, grills. RECREATION: salt water swimming, salt water fishing, planned group activities, hiking trails. Recreation open to the public. Open all year. Facilities fully operational mid Apr through mid Oct. Phone: (508) 888-0859.

## SALEM—B-5

WINTER ISLAND PARK (City Park)—*From jct Derby St & Fort Ave in town: Go NE on Fort Ave to Winter Island Rd.* FACILITIES: 41 sites, 8 water & elec, 2 elec (20 amp receptacles), 31 no hookups, tenting available, handicap restroom facilities, sewage disposal, public phone, ice, tables, grills, wood. RECREATION: pavilion, salt water swimming, boating, ramp, dock, salt water/pond fishing, sports field, horseshoes, hiking trails, volleyball. Recreation open to the public. Open May 1 through Oct 31. Phone: (508) 745-9430.

**WANT SOMETHING FREE? TURN TO PAGE 16**

MA For information on MA
**Provincetown to Plymouth Race**
MA see front of book article. MA

### SALISBURY—A-5

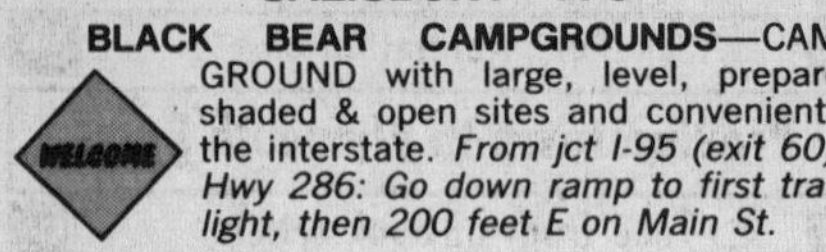

**BLACK BEAR CAMPGROUNDS**—CAMPGROUND with large, level, prepared, shaded & open sites and convenient to the interstate. *From jct I-95 (exit 60) & Hwy 286: Go down ramp to first traffic light, then 200 feet E on Main St.*

◆◆◆◆FACILITIES: 200 sites, most common site width 30 feet, 165 full hookups, 35 water & elec (30 amp receptacles), seasonal sites, 20 pull-thrus, a/c allowed ($), heater not allowed, phone hookups, tenting available, handicap restroom facilities, sewage disposal, laundry, public phone, limited grocery store, ice, tables, fire rings, wood, traffic control gate.



SALISBURY—Continued
BLACK BEAR CAMPGROUND—Continued

◆◆◆RECREATION: rec hall, rec room/area, coin games, swim pool, basketball hoop, playground, 2 shuffleboard courts, horseshoes, volleyball.

Open May 15 through Sep 30. Rate in 1995 $22-25 for 2 persons. Master Card/Visa accepted. Member of ARVC; MACO. Phone: (508) 462-3183.

**SEE AD THIS PAGE**

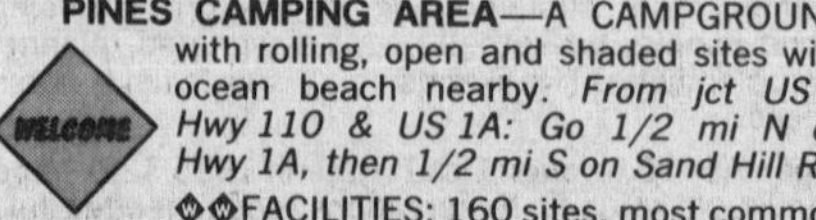

**PINES CAMPING AREA**—A CAMPGROUND with rolling, open and shaded sites with ocean beach nearby. *From jct US 1, Hwy 110 & US 1A: Go 1/2 mi N on Hwy 1A, then 1/2 mi S on Sand Hill Rd.*

◆◆FACILITIES: 160 sites, most common site width 30 feet, 16 full hookups, 115 water & elec (15,20 & 30 amp receptacles), 29 no hookups, seasonal sites, 10 pull-thrus, a/c not allowed, heater not allowed, tenting available, group sites for tents/RVs, RV storage, handicap restroom facilities, sewage disposal, laundry, public phone, limited grocery store, ice, tables, fire rings, wood, traffic control gate.

◆RECREATION: basketball hoop, playground, horseshoes.

Open mid May through Columbus Day. Facilities fully operational mid May through Sep 15. Rate in 1995 $17-21 for 2 persons. No refunds. Discover accepted. Phone: (508) 465-0013.

**SEE AD THIS PAGE**

SALISBURY—Continued

**RUSNIK CAMPGROUND**—Large wooded sites away from highway near ocean beach. *N'bound from I-495 (exit 55): Go 3 1/2 mi E on Hwy 110, then 1 mi N on US 1. From I-95 (S'bound exit 58, N'bound exit 58A): Go 2 1/4 mi E on Hwy 110, then 1 mi N on US 1.*

◆◆◆◆FACILITIES: 150 sites, 141 water & elec (30 amp receptacles), 9 no hookups, seasonal sites, a/c allowed, heater not allowed, tenting available, group sites for tents/RVs, sewage disposal, laundry, public phone, RV supplies, ice, tables, fire rings, wood, traffic control gate/guard.

◆◆◆◆RECREATION: rec room/area, pavilion, coin games, swim pool, mini-golf ($), basketball hoop, playground, 2 shuffleboard courts, sports field, horseshoes, volleyball.

Open May 15 through Oct 1. Rate in 1995 $20-24 for 2 persons. Reservations recommended Memorial Day through Labor Day. Master Card/Visa accepted. Member of ARVC; MACO. Phone: (508) 462-9551.

**SEE AD BOSTON PAGE 383**

SALISBURY BEACH STATE RESERVATION—*From town: Go 2 mi E on Hwy 1A.* FACILITIES: 483 sites, 31 ft. max RV length, 324 water & elec, 159 no hookups, tenting available, handicap restroom facilities, sewage disposal, public phone, tables, grills. RECREATION: pavilion, swimming, boating, canoeing, ramp, fishing, playground, planned group activities, hiking trails. Recreation open to the public. Open mid Apr through mid Oct. Phone: (508) 462-4481.

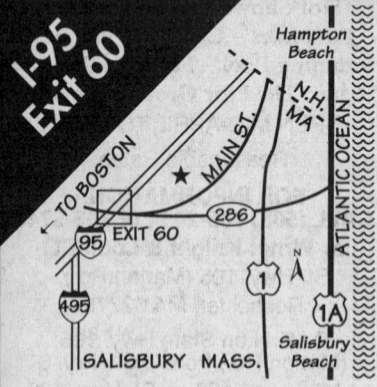

## SANDWICH—D-5

**DUNROAMIN' TRAILER PARK**—RV SPACES in a mostly seasonal park on a 137-acre pond. *From jct US 6 (exit 2) & Hwy 130: Go 3 1/0 mi S on Hwy 130, then 3/4 mi E on Quaker Meeting House Rd, then 1 1/10 mi S on Cotuit Rd, then 1/10 mi W on John Ewer Rd.*

FACILITIES: 60 sites, most common site width 50 feet, 28 ft. max RV length, accepts full hookup units only, 60 full hookups, (15 & 30 amp receptacles), seasonal sites, 15 pull-thrus, a/c allowed, heater allowed, phone hookups, cabins, laundry.

RECREATION: pond swimming, boating, water skiing, pond fishing, basketball hoop, playground, badminton, horseshoes, volleyball.

No tents. Open mid Apr through mid Oct. Rate in 1995 $20 for 4 persons. Master Card/Visa accepted. Phone: (508) 477-0541.
**SEE AD THIS PAGE**

**PETERS POND PARK**—A lakeside wooded CAMPGROUND on a 137-acre pond. *From jct US 6 (exit 2) & Hwy 130: Go 3 1/10 mi S on Hwy 130, then 3/4 mi E on Quaker Meeting House Rd, then 3/4 mi S on Cotuit Rd.*

◇◇◇◇FACILITIES: 407 sites, most common site width 40 feet, 278 full hookups, 100 water & elec (20,30 & 50 amp receptacles), 29 no hookups, seasonal sites, a/c allowed ($), heater allowed ($), cable TV, phone hookups, tenting available, tent rentals, RV rentals, cabins, sewage disposal, laundry, public phone, full service store, RV supplies, LP gas refill by weight, ice, tables, traffic control gate.

◇◇◇◇RECREATION: rec hall, rec room/area, coin games, lake swimming, boating, canoeing, ramp, 10 row boat rentals, lake fishing, basketball hoop, playground, 2 shuffleboard courts, planned group activities, movies, recreation director, badminton, sports field, horseshoes, hiking trails, volleyball.

Open Apr 19 through Oct 15. Pets allowed after Labor Day & before Jul 1. Rate in 1995 $19-32 for 4 persons. Reservations recommended Jul 1 through Labor Day. Master Card/Visa accepted. CPO. Member of ARVC; MACO. Phone: (508) 477-1775.
**SEE AD TRAVEL SECTION PAGE 379 AND AD THIS PAGE**

SHAWME CROWELL STATE FOREST—*From town: Go 1 1/2 mi N on Hwy 6A, then 1 1/2 mi on Hwy 130.* FACILITIES: 280 sites, 30 ft. max RV length, 280 no hookups, tenting available, handicap restroom facilities, sewage disposal, public phone, tables, grills. RECREATION: hiking trails. Open all year. Facilities fully operational mid Apr through mid Oct. Phone: (508) 888-0351.

## SAVOY—B-1

**SHADY PINES CAMPGROUND**—A grassy location with large semi-wooded or open sites. *From West jct Hwy 8A & Hwy 116: Go 3 mi E on Hwy 116.*

◇◇◇◇FACILITIES: 150 sites, most common site width 35 feet, 38 full hookups, 112 water & elec (20 amp receptacles), seasonal sites, 12 pull-thrus, a/c allowed ($), heater allowed ($), tenting available, group sites for tents/RVs, RV rentals, cabins, RV storage, handicap restroom facilities, sewage disposal, laundry, public phone, limited grocery store, ice, tables, fire rings, wood.

◇◇◇◇RECREATION: rec hall, rec room/area, pavilion, coin games, swim pool, basketball hoop, playground, planned group activities (weekends only), badminton, sports field, horseshoes, hiking trails, volleyball, cross country skiing, snowmobile trails. Recreation open to the public.

Open all year. Facilities fully operational May 1 through Nov 1. Rate in 1995 $20 for 2 persons. No refunds. Reservations recommended Jun 1 through Labor Day. Member of ARVC; MACO. Phone: (413) 743-2694.
**SEE AD THIS PAGE**

## SHELBURNE FALLS—B-2

**SPRINGBROOK FAMILY CAMPING AREA**—CAMPGROUND with large, semi-wooded or open grassy sites overlooking hills. *From jct I-91 (exit 26) & Hwy 2: Go 5 1/2 mi W on Hwy 2, then 1 1/2 mi N on Little Mohawk Rd, then 1 mi NW on Patten Rd & Tower Rd.*

◇◇◇FACILITIES: 97 sites, most common site width 40 feet, 85 water & elec (15 & 20 amp receptacles), 12 no hookups, seasonal sites, 10 pull-thrus, phone hookups, tenting available, RV storage, sewage disposal, public phone, limited grocery store, RV sup-

SHELBURNE FALLS—Continued
SPRINGBROOK FAMILY CAMPING AREA—Continued

plies, LP gas refill by weight, ice, tables, fire rings, wood, traffic control gate.

◇◇◇RECREATION: rec room/area, coin games, swim pool, basketball hoop, playground, 2 shuffleboard courts, badminton, sports field, horseshoes, hiking trails, volleyball.

Open May 1 through Oct 15. Rate in 1995 $20-22 for 2 persons. Discover/Master Card/Visa accepted. Member of ARVC; MACO. Phone: (413) 625-6618.
**SEE AD TRAVEL SECTION PAGE 377**

## SHREWSBURY—B-3

✽ **RENT 'N ROAM RV RENTALS**—*From jct Hwy 9 & US 20: Go 1 mi SW on US 20.* SERVICES: Engine/Chassis & RV appliance mechanic full-time, LP gas refill by weight/by meter, RV rentals, RV storage, sells parts/accessories, sells camping supplies, installs hitches. Open all year. Discover/Master Card/Visa accepted. Phone: (508) 842-1400.
**SEE AD HARTFORD, CT PAGE 49 AND AD WORCESTER PAGE 405**

## SOUTH CARVER—C-5

MYLES STANDISH STATE FOREST—*From Federal Furnace Rd in town: Go 3 mi W on Cranberry Rd.* FACILITIES: 475 sites, 32 ft. max RV length, 475 no hookups, tenting available, handicap restroom facilities, sewage disposal, public phone, ice, tables, grills. RECREATION: swimming, boating, canoeing, ramp, fishing, planned group activities, sports field, hiking trails. Recreation open to the public. Open mid Apr through Columbus Day. Self-contained units only Nov 1 thru Apr 15. Phone: (508) 866-2526.

SOUTH CARVER—Continued

**SHADY ACRES CAMPGROUND**—Shaded, rolling terrain beside a pond with many prepared sites. *From jct I-495 (exit 2) & Hwy 58: Go 2 1/2 mi N on Hwy 58, then 1 1/2 mi N on Tremont St (enter camp at jct Tremont & Mayflower Sts).*

◇◇◇FACILITIES: 127 sites, most common site width 50 feet, 57 full hookups, 55 water & elec (15,20,30 & 50 amp receptacles), 15 no hookups, seasonal sites, 10 pull-thrus, a/c allowed ($), heater allowed ($), phone hookups, tenting available, group sites for tents/RVs, RV storage, handicap restroom facilities, sewage disposal, laundry, public phone, limited grocery store, RV supplies, LP gas refill by weight/by meter, ice, tables, fire rings, wood, traffic control gate.

SHADY ACRES CAMPGROUND—Continued on next page
SOUTH CARVER—Continued on next page

SOUTH CARVER—Continued
SHADY ACRES CAMPGROUND—Continued

◆◆◆RECREATION: rec room/area, pavilion, coin games, swim pool, wading pool, boating, no motors, canoeing, pond fishing, basketball hoop, playground, horseshoes, hiking trails, volleyball.

Open Mar 15 through Dec 15. Winter weekends by reservations only. Rate in 1995 $22-29 per family. Reservations recommended Memorial Day through Labor Day. Member of ARVC; MACO. Phone: (508) 866-4040.

**SEE AD PLYMOUTH PAGE 396**

**✲ WESTPORT RV**—*From jct I-495 (exit 2) & Hwy 58: Go 2 1/2 mi N on Hwy 58, then 1 1/2 mi N on Tremont St (enter at jct Tremont & May flower Sts).* SALES: travel trailers, van conversions. SERVICES: RV appliance mechanic full-time, LP gas refill by weight/by meter, sewage disposal, RV storage, sells parts/accessories, installs hitches. Open all year. (by appointment in winter). Phone: (508) 866-4040.

**SEE AD PLYMOUTH PAGE 396**





## SOUTH DEERFIELD—B-2

**WHITE BIRCH CAMPGROUND**—Grassy sites in an open meadow or shaded level sites in the woods. *Southbound: From jct I-91 (exit 25) & Hwy 116: Go 100 yards W on Hwy 116, then 2 mi SW on Whately Rd. Northbound: From jct I-91 (exit 24) & Hwy 116: Go 1 1/2 mi N on Hwy 116, then 100 yards W on Hwy 116, then 2 mi SW on Whately Rd.*

◆◆◆FACILITIES: 80 sites, most common site width 35 feet, 65 water & elec (20 & 30 amp receptacles), 15 no hookups, seasonal sites, 12 pull-thrus, a/c allowed ($), heater allowed ($), phone hookups, tenting available, group sites for tents/RVs, RV storage, sewage disposal, laundry, public phone, limited grocery store, LP gas refill by weight/by meter, ice, tables, fire rings, wood.

◆◆◆RECREATION: rec room/area, pavilion, coin games, swim pool, stream fishing, basketball hoop, playground, sports field, horseshoes, hiking trails, volleyball.

Open May 1 through Nov 1. Facilities fully operational Memorial Day through Columbus Day. Rate in 1995 $18-20 for 2 persons. Reservations recommended Memorial Day through Labor Day. Master Card/Visa accepted. Member of ARVC; MACO. Phone: (413) 665-4941.

**SEE AD THIS PAGE**

## SOUTH DENNIS—D-6

**Airline Mobile Home Park**—RV SPACES in a mobile home park with semi-wooded sites. *From jct US 6 & Hwy 134: Go 1/2 mi N on Hwy 134, then 1/4 NE on Airline Rd, then 1/4 mi SE on Old Chatham Rd.* FACILITIES: 50 sites, most common site width 30 feet, 20 full hookups, 20 water & elec (15 & 20 amp receptacles), 10 no hookups, seasonal sites, tenting available, sewage disposal, public phone, ice, tables. RECREATION: rec hall, swim pool, playground, shuffleboard court, horseshoes, volleyball. No pets. Open May 1 through Oct 1. Rates available upon request. No refunds. Phone: (508) 385-3616.

## SOUTH WELLFLEET—C-6

**Maurice's Campground**—A CAMPGROUND with wooded and semi-wooded sites on level terrain. *From jct US 6 & Entrance to National Seashore Visitors Center: Go 2 1/2 mi N on US 6 (Enter Park at Eastham-Wellfleet Town Line).* ◆◆◆FACILITIES: 240 sites, most common site width 50 feet, 28 ft. max RV length, 127 full hookups, 53 water & elec (20 & 30 amp receptacles), 60 no hookups, seasonal sites, 10 pull-thrus, tenting available, sewage disposal, public phone, full service store, LP gas refill by weight/by meter, ice, tables. RECREATION: hiking trails. No pets. Open Memorial Day through Columbus Day. Rate in 1995 $18-22 for 2 persons. No refunds. Member of ARVC; MACO. Phone: (508) 349-2029.

MA BAY STATE MA

SOUTH WELLFLEET—Continued

**PAINE'S CAMPGROUND**—Ample shaded sites among trees and shrubs catering to tent campers. *From jct US 6 & Old County Rd: Go 3/4 mi E on Old County Rd.*

◆◆FACILITIES: 145 sites, most common site width 50 feet, 25 water & elec (15,20 & 30 amp receptacles), 120 no hookups, seasonal sites, tenting available, group sites for tents, sewage disposal, public phone, ice, tables.

RECREATION: hiking trails.

Open May 15 through late Sep. No pets during Jul & Aug. Rate in 1995 $15-25 for 2 persons. No refunds. Reservations recommended Jul through Aug. Master Card/Visa accepted. Phone: (508) 349-3007.

**SEE AD CAPE COD PAGE 389**

## SOUTHWICK—C-2

**Sodom Mountain Campground**—Mountainside plateau CAMPGROUND with some open and some wooded sites. *From South jct US 202 & Hwy 57: Go 3 1/4 mi W on Hwy 57, then 1/2 mi S on Loomis St.* ◆◆◆FACILITIES: 150 sites, most common site width 40 feet, 20 full hookups, 130 water & elec (20 & 30 amp receptacles), seasonal sites, 10 pull-thrus, tenting available, sewage disposal, laundry, public phone, limited grocery store, LP gas refill by weight/by meter, ice, tables, fire rings, wood. ◆◆◆◆RECREATION: rec hall, rec room/area, swim pool, playground, planned group activities (weekends only), badminton, sports field, horseshoes, hiking trails, volleyball. Open May 1 through Columbus Day. Rate in 1995 $19-23 per family. No refunds. Member of ARVC; MACO. Phone: (413) 569-3930.

**Southwick Acres**—Rustic CAMPGROUND in mountainous area with shaded and open, natural sites. *From jct Hwy 57 & Hwy 202/10: Go 2 mi S on Hwy 202/10.* ◆◆FACILITIES: 80 sites, most common site width 60 feet, 60 water & elec (20 & 30 amp receptacles), 20 no hookups, seasonal sites, tenting available, sewage disposal, laundry, ice, tables, fire rings. ◆◆RECREATION: rec room/area, swim pool, horseshoes, hiking trails. Open May 1 through Oct 1. Rate in 1995 $18-22 for 2 persons. Phone: (413) 569-6339.

## SPRINGFIELD—C-2

***See listings at Hatfield, Monson, Southwick & Westhampton***

**SUNSETVIEW FARM CAMPING AREA**—*From jct I-91 & I-90: Go 18 mi E on I-90 (exit 18), then 1 mi S on Hwy 32/Thorndyke St, then 1 1/2 mi SE on Main St, then 1/2 mi E on Fenton Rd, then 1 1/2 mi S on Town Farm Rd.*

**SEE PRIMARY LISTING AT MONSON AND AD THIS PAGE**

## STURBRIDGE—C-3

***See listings at Brimfield, Brookfield, Charlton, Monson, Wales & West Brookfield***

### STURBRIDGE AREA MAP

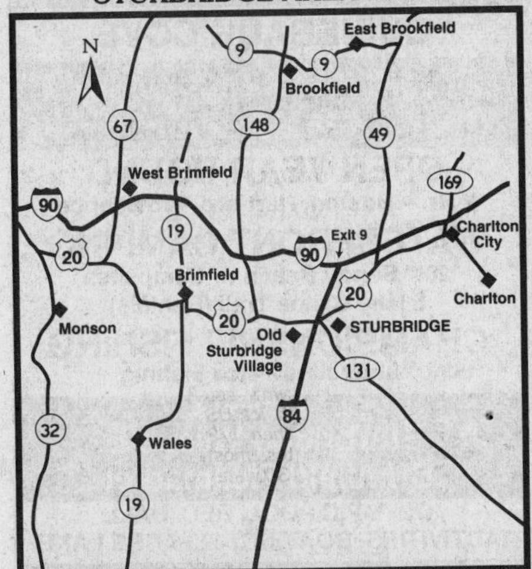


***Symbols on map indicate towns within a 50 mi radius of Sturbridge where campgrounds (diamonds), attractions (flags), & RV service centers & camping supply outlets (gears) are listed. See listings for more information.***

WELCOME

**JELLYSTONE PARK-STURBRIDGE**—A lakeside CAMPGROUND with well developed, wooded sites on rolling terrain. *From jct US 20 & I-84: Go 1 mi W on I-84 to exit 2, then 3/4 mi E on River Rd (follow signs).*

◆◆◆◆FACILITIES: 375 sites, most common site width 28 feet, 53 full hookups, 290 water & elec (20 & 30 amp receptacles), 32 no hookups, seasonal sites, 36 pull-thrus, a/c allowed ($), heater allowed ($), cable TV, tenting available, cabins, RV storage, handicap restroom facilities, sewage disposal, laundry, public phone, grocery store, RV supplies, LP gas refill by weight/by meter, ice, tables, fire rings, wood, traffic control gate/guard.

◆◆◆◆◆RECREATION: rec hall, rec room/area, coin games, 2 swim pools, lake swimming, whirlpool, water slide ($), boating, no motors, canoeing, 2 row/5 canoe/6 pedal boat rentals, lake fishing, mini-golf ($), basketball hoop, playground, 2 shuffleboard courts, planned group activities, movies, recreation director, badminton, horseshoes, hiking trails, volleyball, cross country skiing, snowmobile trails.

Open all year. Facilities fully operational Apr 15 through Oct 31. Pools open Memorial Day-Oct 1. Rate in 1995 $23.75-40.75 for 2 persons. No refunds. Reservations recommended Memorial Day through Labor Day. American Express/Discover/Master Card/Visa accepted. CPO. Member of ARVC; MACO. Phone: (508) 347-2336.

**SEE AD THIS PAGE**

WELCOME

**LAKESIDE RESORT**—*From jct Hwy 148 & Hwy 9: Go 1 mi E on Hwy 9, then 8/10 mi S on Quabog St, then right 1 block on Hobbs Ave.*

**SEE PRIMARY LISTING AT BROOKFIELD AND AD PAGE 403**

WELCOME

**THE OLD SAWMILL CAMPGROUND**—*From jct US 20 & Hwy 148: Go 8 mi N on Hwy 148, then 3 mi W on Hwy 9 to West Brookfield Center (at traffic light), then 1/2 mi S on Central St, then 1/10 mi W on Front St, then 3/4 mi S on Long Hill Rd.*

**SEE PRIMARY LISTING AT WEST BROOKFIELD AND AD NEXT PAGE**

WELCOME

**QUINEBAUG COVE CAMPSITE**—*From jct I-84 & US 20: Go 3 1/2 mi W on US 20, then 1/4 mi S on E Brimfield Rd.*

**SEE PRIMARY LISTING AT BRIMFIELD AND AD NEXT PAGE**

WELCOME

**VILLAGE GREEN FAMILY CAMPGROUND**—*From jct I-84 & US 20: Go 4 1/4 mi W on US 20.*

**SEE PRIMARY LISTING AT BRIMFIELD AND AD NEXT PAGE**

STURBRIDGE—Continued on page 404

## Massachusetts

STATE OF FIRSTS:

First College in the Colonies: Harvard - 1636
First Thanksgiving: 1621
First Battles of the Revolutionary War: 1775
First Public School • First Public Park
First Post Office • First Lighthouse
First Printing Press • First Basketball Game
First Railroad • First Subway



MA Celebrate at the Salem Seaport Festival! See article at front of book. MA

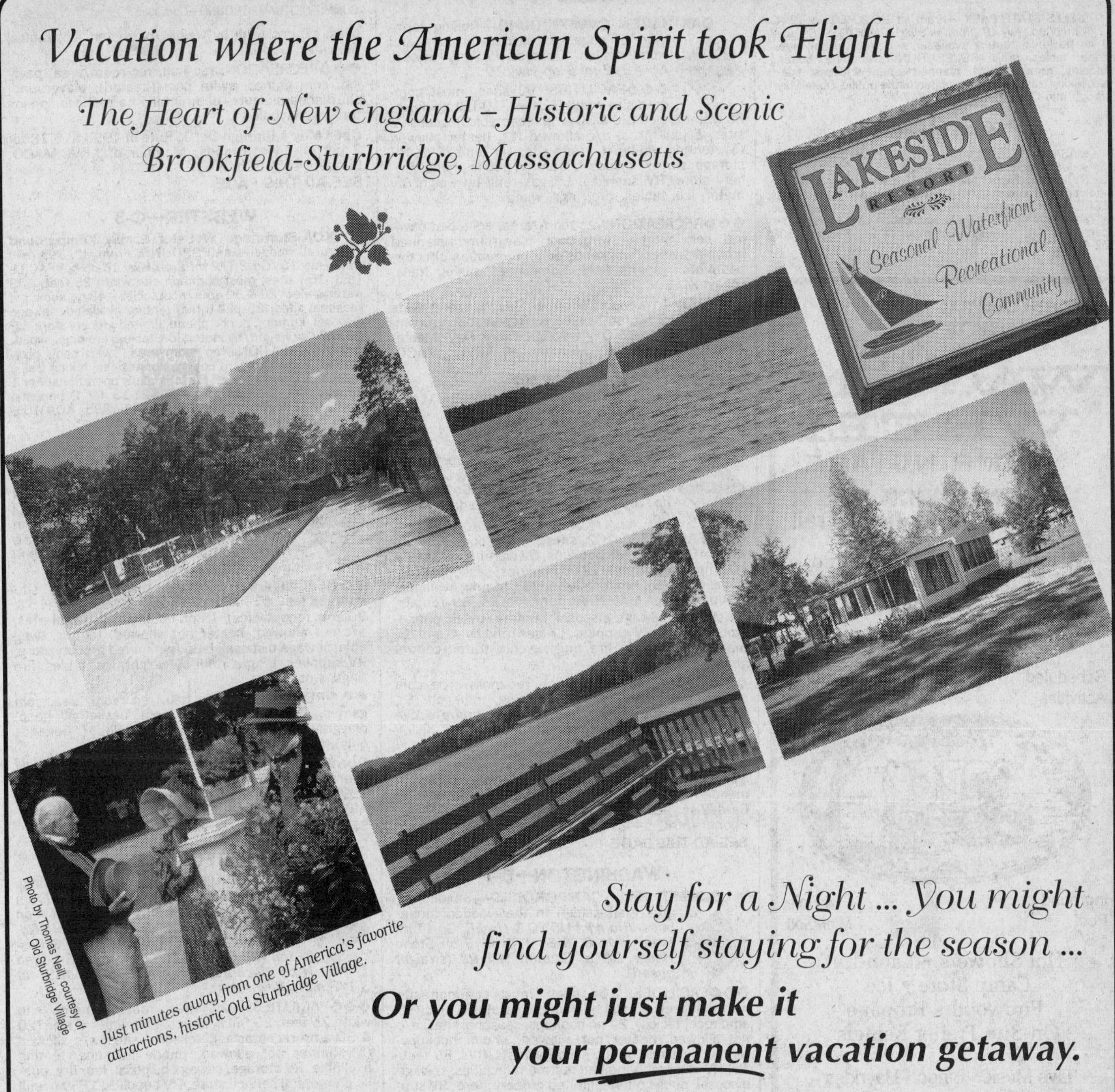


Just minutes away from one of America's favorite attractions, historic Old Sturbridge Village.

Photo by Thomas Neill, courtesy of Old Sturbridge Village

Lakeside Resort is an innovative new camping community specializing in relaxed, vacation home living. Sites will accommodate all types of recreational vehicles ... whether you prefer a travel trailer, fifth-wheel, motor home, park model or cabin. Full hook-ups are available, as are pull-throughs. Come by and see for yourself why our resort park can offer you the finest vacation destination – whether you buy your campsite, stay for the season, or simply enjoy ... a Lakeside weekend.

**LAKESIDE RESORT**

12 Hobbs Avenue, Brookfield, MA 01506
(508) 867-2737 1-800-320-CAMP (2267)

STURBRIDGE—Continued

WELLS STATE PARK—*From jct US 20 & Hwy 49: Go 2 1/4 mi N on Hwy 49 (Podnak Pike).* FACILITIES: 59 sites, 59 no hookups, tenting available, sewage disposal, public phone, tables, grills. RECREATION: swimming, boating, canoeing, ramp, fishing, planned group activities, sports field, hiking trails. Recreation open to the public. Open May 1 through mid Oct. Phone: (508) 347-9257.

## TAUNTON—C-4

MASASOIT STATE PARK—*From jct Hwy 24 (exit 13) & US 44: follow signs E on US 44.* FACILITIES: 126 sites, 21 ft. max RV length, 24 full hookups, 81 elec, tenting available, handicap restroom facilities, sewage disposal, tables, grills. RECREATION: pond swimming, boating, no motors, canoeing, ramp, fishing, hiking trails. Recreation open to the public. Open mid Apr through Columbus Day. Phone: (508) 822-4705.



## WALES—C-3

**OAK HAVEN CAMPGROUND**—Rolling farmland at edge of town, with open and wooded sites. *From jct US 20 & Hwy 19: Go 4 1/2 mi S on Hwy 19.*

◊◊◊FACILITIES: 90 sites, most common site width 32 feet, 10 full hookups, 80 water & elec (20 & 30 amp receptacles), seasonal sites, 5 pull-thrus, a/c allowed ($), heater allowed ($), tenting available, group sites for tents/RVs, RV storage, sewage disposal, laundry, public phone, grocery store, RV supplies, LP gas refill by weight/by meter, ice, tables, fire rings, wood.

◊◊◊RECREATION: rec room/area, equipped pavilion, coin games, swim pool, playground, planned group activities (weekends only), recreation director, badminton, sports field, horseshoes, hiking trails, volleyball.

Open May 1 through Columbus Day Weekend. Rate in 1995 $19.50 for 2 persons. Reservations recommended Memorial Day through Labor Day. Master Card/Visa accepted. Member of ARVC; MACO. Phone: (413) 245-7148.

**SEE AD STURBRIDGE PAGE 402**

## WARWICK—A-2

**WAGON WHEEL CAMPING AREA**—A CAMPGROUND secluded in a pine forest, away from traffic noise. *From jct Hwy 2 & Hwy 2A (Erving State Forest exit): Go 3/4 mi E on Hwy 2A, then 2 mi N on Wendell Depot Rd.*

◊◊◊FACILITIES: 102 sites, most common site width 40 feet, 28 full hookups, 62 water & elec (15 & 20 amp receptacles), 12 no hookups, seasonal sites, a/c allowed ($), heater allowed ($), tenting available, group sites for tents/RVs, tent rentals, RV rentals, RV storage, sewage disposal, laundry, public phone, grocery store, RV supplies, LP gas refill by weight/by meter, ice, tables, fire rings, wood, traffic control gate.

◊◊◊◊RECREATION: rec hall, rec room/area, coin games, swim pool, pond swimming, mini-golf ($), basketball hoop, playground, planned group activities, badminton, sports field, horseshoes, hiking trails, volleyball.

Open May 1 through Columbus Day. Rate in 1995 $17 per family. No refunds. Reservations recommended Jun 15 through Labor Day. Discover/Master Card/Visa accepted. Member of ARVC; MACO. Phone: (508) 544-3425.

**SEE AD THIS PAGE**

## WASHINGTON—B-1

**SUMMIT HILL CAMPGROUND**—Shaded or grassy sites high in the wooded mountains. *From jct US 20 & Hwy 8: Go 11 mi N on Hwy 8, then 1/4 mi E on Stone House Rd to Summit Hill Rd (straight ahead).*

◊◊◊FACILITIES: 104 sites, most common site width 24 feet, 13 full hookups, 67 water & elec (15 amp receptacles), 24 no hookups, seasonal sites, a/c not allowed, heater not allowed, phone hookups, tenting available, group sites for tents/RVs, RV rentals, RV storage, handicap restroom facilities, sewage disposal, public phone, limited grocery store, RV supplies, LP gas refill by weight/by meter, ice, tables, fire rings, wood.



WASHINGTON—Continued
SUMMIT HILL CAMPGROUND—Continued

◊◊◊RECREATION: rec hall, rec room/area, pavilion, coin games, swim pool (heated), playground, shuffleboard court, badminton, horseshoes, hiking trails, volleyball.

Open May 1 through Oct 1. Rate in 1995 $15-18 for 2 persons. No refunds. Member of ARVC;MACO. Phone: (413) 623-5761.

**SEE AD THIS PAGE**

## WEBSTER—C-3

**KOA-Sturbridge Webster Family Kampground**—A rural, wooded CAMPGROUND. *From jct I-395 (exit 2) & Hwy 16: Go 2 1/2 mi E on Hwy 16.* ◊◊◊FACILITIES: 150 sites, most common site width 25 feet, 102 water & elec (20 & 30 amp receptacles), 48 no hookups, seasonal sites, 25 pull-thrus, tenting available, sewage disposal, laundry, public phone, limited grocery store, LP gas refill by weight/by meter, ice, tables, fire rings, wood. ◊◊◊RECREATION: rec room/area, swim pool, playground, 2 shuffleboard courts, horseshoes, hiking trails, volleyball. Open all year. Facilities fully operational Apr 1 through Dec 1. Rate in 1995 $21-23 for 2 persons. Member of ARVC. Phone: (508) 943-1895. KOA 10% value card discount.

## WEST BROOKFIELD—C-3

**THE OLD SAW MILL CAMPGROUND**—A hilly, wooded location in a rural area by a small town. *From jct Hwy 148 & Hwy 9: Go 3 mi W on Hwy 9 to W Brookfield Center (at traffic light), then 1/2 mi S on Central St, then 1/10 mi W on Front St, then 3/4 mi S on Long Hill Rd.*

◊◊◊FACILITIES: 120 sites, most common site width 28 feet, 51 full hookups, 54 water & elec (15 & 20 amp receptacles), 15 no hookups, seasonal sites, a/c not allowed, heater not allowed, tenting available, sewage disposal, laundry, limited grocery store, RV supplies, LP gas refill by weight, ice, tables, fire rings, wood.

◊◊◊RECREATION: rec hall, rec room/area, coin games, swim pool, wading pool, basketball hoop, playground, planned group activities (weekends only), horseshoes, hiking trails.

Open May 1 through Columbus Day. Facilities fully operational Memorial Day through Labor Day. Rate in 1995 $16-20 for 2 persons. No refunds. Member of ARVC;MACO. Phone: (508) 867-2427.

**SEE AD STURBRIDGE PAGE 402**

## WESTFORD—B-4

**WYMAN'S BEACH**—A lakeside, partially shaded CAMPGROUND. *S'bound: From jct US 3 (exit 33) & Hwy 40: Go 3 mi W on Hwy 40, then 1 mi N on Dunstable Rd. N'bound: From jct I-495 (exit 32) & Boston Rd: Go 1 mi NW on Boston Rd, then 1/4 mi N on Lincoln St, then NW on Depot St for 3 1/2 mi (follow signs).*

◊◊◊FACILITIES: 227 sites, most common site width 25 feet, 25 full hookups, 202 water & elec (20 & 30 amp receptacles), seasonal sites, a/c allowed ($), heater not allowed, phone hookups, tenting available, RV storage, sewage disposal, laundry, public phone, full service store, RV supplies, LP gas refill by weight/by meter, ice, tables, fire rings, grills, wood, guard.

◊◊◊◊RECREATION: rec room/area, equipped pavilion, coin games, lake swimming, boating, no motors, canoeing, lake fishing, basketball hoop, playground, 2 shuffleboard courts, planned group activities, movies, recreation director, badminton, sports field, horseshoes, volleyball. Recreation open to the public.

Open early May through early Oct. Rate in 1995 $18-20 for 2 persons. No refunds. Reservations recommended Memorial Day through Labor Day. Discover/Master Card/Visa accepted. Member of ARVC; MACO. Phone: (508) 692-6287.

**SEE AD BOSTON PAGE 385**

MA Discovered MA
**1602**
MA by Bartholomew Gosnold MA

MA *State Motto: "By the Sword We Speak Peace but Peace Only Under Liberty"* MA

## WESTHAMPTON—B-2

**WINDY ACRES CAMPING**—Hillside CAMPGROUND in a rural area. *From jct Hwy 9 & Hwy 66: Go 9 mi W on Hwy 66, then 1 block N on South Rd.*

WELCOME

◆◆FACILITIES: 121 sites, most common site width 40 feet, 18 full hookups, 100 water & elec (15,20 & 30 amp receptacles), 3 no hookups, seasonal sites, 4 pull-thrus, a/c allowed ($), heater not allowed, tenting available, group sites for tents/RVs, RV storage, sewage disposal, laundry, public phone, limited grocery store, RV supplies, LP gas refill by weight/by meter, ice, tables, fire rings, traffic control gate.

◆◆◆RECREATION: rec room/area, equipped pavilion, coin games, pond swimming, playground, planned group activities (weekends only), badminton, sports field, horseshoes, volleyball.

Open May 1 through Oct 15. Rate in 1995 $18-20 per family. Member of ARVC; MACO. Phone: (413) 527-9862.

**SEE AD SPRINGFIELD PAGE 400**

## WESTPORT—D-5

HORSENECK BEACH STATE RESERVATION—*From jct I-195 & Hwy 88: Go 10 mi S on Hwy 88.* FACILITIES: 100 sites, 100 no hookups, tenting available, handicap restroom facilities, sewage disposal, public phone, tables, grills. RECREATION: swimming, boating, canoeing, ramp, fishing. Recreation open to the public. Open Memorial Day through Columbus Day. Phone: (508) 636-8816.

**Westport Camping Grounds**—A wooded, secluded CAMPGROUND. *From jct I-195 (exit 10) & Hwy 88: Go 4 mi S on Hwy 88, then 1/2 mi E on Old County Rd.* ◆◆◆FACILITIES: 110 sites, most common site width 30 feet, 32 ft. max RV length, 40 full hookups, 70 water & elec (15,20 & 30 amp receptacles), seasonal sites, 2 pull-thrus, tenting available, sewage disposal, laundry, public phone, limited grocery store, ice, tables, fire rings, wood. ◆◆◆RECREATION: rec room/area, 2 swim pools, playground, planned group activities (weekends only), sports field, horseshoes, volleyball. No pets. Open Apr 1 through Oct 31. Facilities fully operational Memorial Day through Sep 30. Rate in 1995 $20-21 for 2 persons. No refunds. Member of ARVC; MACO. Phone: (508) 636-2555.

## WEST SUTTON—C-3

**The Old Holbrook Place**—A lakeside CAMPGROUND in a pine grove with open and shaded sites serving many seasonal campers. *From jct I-395 (exit 4A) & Sutton Ave: Go 4 mi E on Sutton Ave, then 1 mi SE on Manchaug Rd.* ◆◆FACILITIES: 66 sites, most common site width 30 feet, 31 ft. max RV length, 35 full hookups, 31 water & elec (20 amp receptacles), seasonal sites, tenting available, public phone, limited grocery store, ice, tables, fire rings, wood. ◆◆◆RECREATION: lake swimming, boating, canoeing, ramp, 4 row boat rentals, lake fishing, hiking trails, volleyball. Recreation open to the public. Open Memorial Day through Labor Day. Rate in 1995 $12-20 per family. Member of ARVC; MACO. Phone: (508) 865-5050.

WEST SUTTON—Continued

**Sutton Falls Camping Area**—A lakeside CAMPGROUND on rolling terrain and semi-wooded sites. Most sites occupied by seasonals. *From jct I-395 (exit 4A) & Sutton Ave: Go 3 1/2 mi E on Sutton Ave, then 3/4 mi SE on Manchaug Rd.* ◆◆◆FACILITIES: 100 sites, most common site width 40 feet, 80 full hookups, 17 water & elec (15 amp receptacles), 3 no hookups, seasonal sites, tenting available, sewage disposal, public phone, limited grocery store, LP gas refill by weight/by meter, ice, tables, fire rings, wood. ◆◆◆RECREATION: equipped pavilion, lake swimming, boating, electric motors only, canoeing, 4 row/2 canoe/1 pedal boat rentals, lake fishing, playground, planned group activities (weekends only), horseshoes, hiking trails. Open mid Apr through Columbus Day wknd.. Rate in 1995 $15-18 per family. Member of ARVC; MACO. Phone: (508) 865-3898.

## WEST TOWNSEND—A-3

PEARL HILL STATE PARK—*From Hwy 119: Go 6 mi S on New Fitchburg Rd.* FACILITIES: 51 sites, 20 ft. max RV length, 51 no hookups, tenting available, public phone, tables, fire rings. RECREATION: swimming, fishing, sports field, hiking trails, volleyball. Recreation open to the public. Open Memorial Day through Labor Day. No showers. Phone: (508) 597-8802.

WILLARD BROOK STATE FOREST—*From town: Go W on Hwy 119.* FACILITIES: 21 sites, 20 ft. max RV length, 21 no hookups, tenting available, tables, grills. RECREATION: pond swimming, lake fishing, hiking trails. Open May 1 through Columbus Day. No showers. Phone: (508) 597-8802.

## WINCHENDON—A-3

LAKE DENNISON STATE RECREATION AREA—*From town: Go 6 mi S on US 202.* FACILITIES: 151 sites, 151 no hookups, tenting available, sewage disposal, tables, grills. RECREATION: swimming, boating, no motors, canoeing, ramp, fishing, planned group activities, hiking trails. Recreation open to the public. Open Memorial Day through Columbus Day. Phone: (508) 939-8962.

OTTER RIVER STATE FOREST—*From town: Go 7 mi S on US 202.* FACILITIES: 100 sites, 100 no hookups, tenting available, public phone, tables, grills, wood. RECREATION: pavilion, lake swimming, stream fishing, planned group activities, sports field, hiking trails. Recreation open to the public. Open Memorial Day through Columbus Day. No showers. Phone: (508) 939-8962.

## WINDSOR—B-1

WINDSOR STATE FOREST—*From town: Go E on Hwy 9, then N on River Rd.* FACILITIES: 24 sites, 24 no hookups, tenting available, non-flush toilets, tables, fire rings. RECREATION: river swimming, canoeing, river/stream fishing, hiking trails. Open Memorial Day through Columbus Day. No showers. Phone: (413) 663-8469.

## WORCESTER—B-3

***See listing at Shrewsbury***

## WRENTHAM—C-4

**KOA-BOSTON HUB**—A CAMPGROUND in the oak trees with rolling terrain. *From jct I-495 (exit 15) & Hwy 1A: Go 1/4 mi S on Hwy 1A.*

WELCOME

◆◆◆FACILITIES: 130 sites, most common site width 40 feet, 40 full hookups, 76 water & elec, 10 elec (30 & 50 amp receptacles), 4 no hookups, seasonal sites, 10 pull-thrus, a/c allowed ($), heater allowed ($), phone hookups, tenting available, cabins, RV storage, handicap restroom facilities, sewage disposal, laundry, public phone, grocery store, RV supplies, LP gas refill by weight/by meter, ice, tables, fire rings, wood.

◆◆◆◆RECREATION: rec room/area, coin games, swim pool, wading pool, mini-golf, basketball hoop, playground, planned group activities, movies, badminton, horseshoes, volleyball, local tours.

Open Apr 15 through Oct 31. Rate in 1995 $23.95-28.45 for 2 persons. Reservations recommended Jun 1 through Labor Day. Discover/Master Card/Visa accepted. Member of ARVC; MACO. Phone: (800) 562-2173. KOA 10% value card discount.

**SEE AD BOSTON PAGE 382 AND AD FRONT OF BOOK PAGES 68 AND 69**

MA *Indian name for Webster Lake* MA

**Chargoggogmanchauggagoggchaubunagungamaugg**

MA *"I fish on my side of the lake, you fish on yours and no one fishes in between."* MA

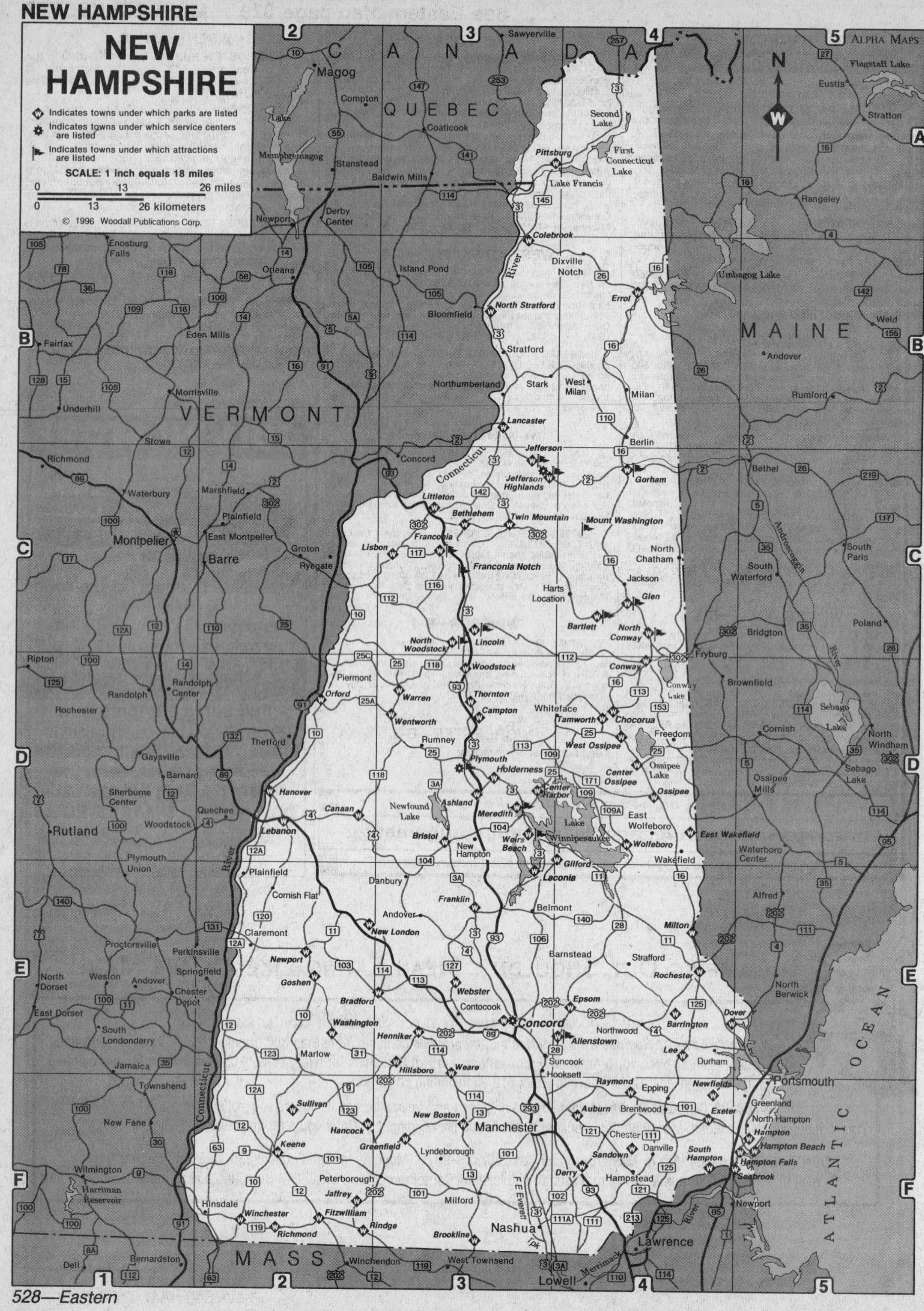
NEW HAMPSHIRE
Indicates towns under which parks are listed
Indicates towns under which service centers are listed
Indicates towns under which attractions are listed
SCALE: 1 inch equals 18 miles
0 13 26 miles
0 13 26 kilometers
© 1996 Woodall Publications Corp.
ALPHA MAPS
N
CANADA
QUEBEC
VERMONT
MAINE
MASS
ATLANTIC OCEAN
Sawyerville
Magog
Compton
Coaticook
Lake Memphremagog
Stanstead
Baldwin Mills
Newport
Derby Center
Second Lake
First Connecticut Lake
Pittsburg
Lake Francis
Colebrook
Dixville Notch
Errol
Umbagog Lake
North Stratford
Bloomfield
Stratford
Island Pond
Orleans
Enosburg Falls
Fairfax
Eden Mills
Morrisville
Underhill
Stowe
Richmond
Waterbury
Marshfield
Plainfield
East Montpelier
Montpelier
Barre
Groton
Ryegate
Northumberland
Stark
West Milan
Milan
Lancaster
Berlin
Jefferson
Jefferson Highlands
Gorham
Concord
Connecticut River
Littleton
Bethlehem
Twin Mountain
Mount Washington
Franconia
Lisbon
Franconia Notch
North Chatham
Jackson
Harts Location
Glen
Bartlett
North Conway
Conway
Conway Lake
Lincoln
North Woodstock
Woodstock
Piermont
Orford
Warren
Thornton
Campton
Wentworth
Whiteface
Tamworth
Chocorua
West Ossipee
Freedom
Rumney
Plymouth
Holderness
Center Ossipee
Ossipee Lake
Ossipee
Center Harbor
Newfound Lake
Ashland
Meredith
Canaan
Hanover
Lebanon
Bristol
New Hampton
Weirs Beach
Lake Winnipesaukee
Wolfeboro
East Wolfeboro
East Wakefield
Wakefield
Gilford
Laconia
Plainfield
Cornish Flat
Danbury
Franklin
Belmont
Andover
New London
Claremont
Newport
Goshen
Bradford
Washington
Henniker
Webster
Contocook
Concord
Epsom
Allenstown
Northwood
Barnstead
Strafford
Milton
Rochester
Barrington
Dover
Lee
Durham
Suncook
Hooksett
Raymond
Epping
Newfields
Portsmouth
Marlow
Hillsboro
Weare
Sullivan
Hancock
New Boston
Manchester
Auburn
Brentwood
Exeter
Greenland
North Hampton
Hampton
Hampton Beach
Hampton Falls
Seabrook
Keene
Greenfield
Lyndeborough
Chester
Danville
Sandown
South Hampton
Derry
Hampstead
Peterborough
Jaffrey
Milford
Hinsdale
Winchester
Fitzwilliam
Rindge
Richmond
Brookline
Nashua
F.E. Everett Tpk
Lawrence
Newport
Winchendon
West Townsend
Lowell
Merrimack
Thetford
Gaysville
Barnard
Sherburne Center
Quechee
Woodstock
Rutland
Plymouth Union
Randolph
Randolph Center
Rochester
Ripton
Proctorsville
Perkinsville
Springfield
Chester Depot
Weston
Andover
North Dorset
East Dorset
South Londonderry
Jamaica
Townshend
New Fane
Wilmington
Harriman Reservoir
Dell
Bernardston
Flagstaff Lake
Eustis
Stratton
Rangeley
Weld
Andover
Rumford
Bethel
Androscoggin River
South Paris
South Waterford
Poland
Bridgton
Fryburg
Brownfield
Sebago Lake
North Windham
Cornish
Ossipee Mills
Waterboro Center
Alfred
North Berwick

# New Hampshire TRAVEL SECTION

## Free Information from Travel Section Advertisers

The following businesses have placed an ad in the New Hampshire Travel Section. To receive free information, enter their Reader Service number on the Reader Service Card opposite page 16 in the front of this directory:

| Advertiser | RS # | Ad Pg. |
|---|---|---|
| Arcadia Campground | 467 | 532 |
| Hart's Turkey Farm | 507 | 533 |
| NH Travel & Tourism | 647 | 531 |
| Terrace Pines | 558 | 529 |
| White Mountain Attractions | 528 | 530 |

## Time Zone/Topography

New Hampshire is on Eastern time.

The area of New Hampshire is 9,304 square miles. Approximately 87 percent is heavily forested and 18 miles is seacoast. Contained within the state are about 1,300 lakes and ponds, 40,000 miles of streams and 182 mountains that are over 3,000 feet high. Mount Washington, at 6,288 feet, is the highest peak in the northeastern United States.

## Climate

In the summer, temperatures range from the 70°s to mid-80°s. During spring and autumn, days range from 50° to 70°. Winter average daytime temperatures vary widely from the teens and 20°s in the far north to the 20°s to 40°s in the south. Along the New Hampshire coast, snowfall averages about 50 inches per year, but in the mountains an annual snowfall of 150 inches is more common.

Travelers flock to New Hampshire for the fall foliage spectacle. About mid-September, colors "peak" in the lowlands and on the mountain tops. In the northern area of the state, changes occur the end of September to the first week in October and the southern portion is brilliant from the first week of October to mid-month. These dates are estimates and peak color can vary as much as two weeks. Fall Foliage conditions updates are available by calling 800-258-3608.

## Travel Information Sources

**State Agency:** State of New Hampshire, Office of Travel & Tourism Development, Box 1856, Concord, NH 03302 (603-271-2343.

**Regional Agencies:**

• *Connecticut Lakes Tourist Assn.*, (603-538-7405).

• *Franconia/Easton/Sugar Hill Chamber of Commerce,* (800-237-9007 or 603-823-5661).

• *Greater Laconia/Weirs Beach Chamber of Commerce,* (800-531-2347 or 603-524-5531).

• *Lakes Region Association,* (603-253-8555).

• *Lake Sunapee Business Assn.,* (800-258-3530 or 603-763-2495).

• *Lincolnwood/Woodstock Chamber of Commerce,* (603-745-6621).

• *Milford-Amherst Chamber of Commerce,* (603-673-4360).

• *Monadnock Travel Council,* (800-432-7864 or 603-352-1308).

• *Mt. Washington Valley Chamber of Commerce,* (800-367-3364 or 603-356-3171).

• *Northern White Mountain Chamber of Commerce,* P.O. Box 298, 164 Main St., Berlin, NH 03570 (603-752-6060; 603-466-3103 or 800-992-7480).

• *Ossipee Area Chamber of Commerce,* (603-539-6201).

• *Seacoast Council on Tourism,* 235 West Rd., Ste. 10, Portsmouth, NH 03801 (603-436-7678; out-of-state and Canada 800-221-5623).

• *Southern New Hampshire Convention & Visitor Bureau,* (800-932-4CVB or 603-635-9000). (Covers the Merrimack Valley Region.)

• *Squam Lake Area Chamber of Commerce,* (603-968-4494).

• *White Mountains Attractions,* Box 10WV, North Woodstock, NH 03262 (800-FIND-MTS or 603-745-8720).

**Local Agencies:**

• *Concord Area Chamber of Commerce,* (603-224-2508).

• *Conway Village Assn.,* (603-447-2639).

• *Dover Chamber of Commerce,* (603-742-2218).

• *Keene Chamber of Commerce,* (603-352-1303).

• *Manchester Chamber of Commerce,* (603-666-6600).

• *Meredith Chamber of Commerce,* (603-279-6121).

• *Nashua Chamber of Commerce,* (603-881-8333).

• *Newport Chamber of Commerce,* (603-863-1510).

• *Plymouth Chamber of Commerce,* (603-536-1001).

• *Greater Rochester Chamber of Commerce,* (603-332-5080).

• *Twin Mountain Chamber of Commerce,* P.O. Box 194, Twin Mountain, NH 03595 (603-846-5407).

## Recreational Information

*Antiquing:* For a free NH Antiques Dealers Assn. Directory wirte to the NH Antique Dealers Assn., c/o Thomas Thompson, RFD 1, Box 305C, Tilton NH 03276.

*Biking:* For information on bicycle rides (of various lengths) throughout New Hampshire contact the Granite State Wheelmen, 2 Townsend Ave., Salem NH 03079.

For free leaflets on mountain biking contact the New Hampshire Division of Parks and Recreation, Trails Bureau, P.O. Box 1856, Concord, NH 03302-1856 (603-271-3254).

*Boating Regulations:* (New Hampshire honors all current, valid, out-of-state registrations for 30 consecutive days.) Contact the Marine Patrol, 31 Dock Rd., Gilford, NH 03246 (603-293-2037).

*Fall Foliage Update*: 800-258-3608.

*Farmer's Markets*: For a listing of pick-your-own fruits and vegetables (available early summer) send a self-addressed envelope

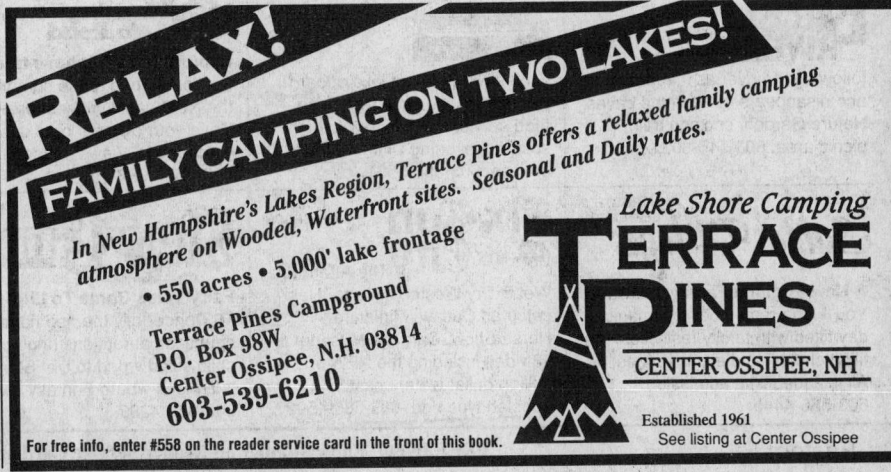

FREE INFO! Enter number on Reader Service Card opposite pg. 16: Terrace Pines #558.

NEW HAMPSHIRE'S WHITE MOUNTAINS

# TravelGuide

P R E V I E W

**The White Mountains:** few areas in the country can match the beauty of its landscape; certainly no area in New England can match its wealth of vacation opportunities…the quality family attractions, campgrounds, lodgings, activities, historic sites, sports and recreation, and tax-free shopping. Preview it all in the FREE White Mountains Travel Guide. Call:

**603-745-8720**

Write: WHITE MOUNTAINS ATTRACTIONS
Box 10WV • North Woodstock, NH 03262

IT'S RIGHT IN
NEW HAMPSHIRE

Distances between attractions are shown in miles, assuming travel along major routes. This mileage is approximate, and should be used as a guide only.

**In the White Mountains, the roads are scenic, the distances between attractions are short, and vacations are long on convenience, value and fun!**

| | ATTITASH BEAR PEAK | CANNON AERIAL TRAMWAY | CLARK'S TRADING POST | MT. WASHINGTON COG RAILWAY | CONWAY SCENIC RAILROAD | FLUME GORGE | HERITAGE-NEW HAMPSHIRE | LOON MOUNTAINPARK | LOST RIVER GORGE | M/S MT. WASHINGTON | MT. WASHINGTON AUTO ROAD | POLAR CAVES PARK | SANTA'S VILLAGE | SIX GUN CITY | STORY LAND | WHALE'S TALE WATERPARK |
|---|---|---|---|---|---|---|---|---|---|---|---|---|---|---|---|---|
| ATTITASH BEAR PEAK | X | 32 | 37 | 24 | 11 | 39 | 4 | 34 | 43 | 55 | 18 | 62 | 47 | 43 | 4 | 40 |
| CANNON AERIAL TRAMWAY | 32 | X | 10 | 18 | 52 | 7 | 37 | 14 | 17 | 53 | 51 | 36 | 26 | 22 | 37 | 8 |
| CLARK'S TRADING POST | 37 | 10 | X | 29 | 41 | 3 | 40 | 3 | 7 | 42 | 57 | 24 | 37 | 33 | 47 | 2 |
| MT. WASHINGTON COG RAILWAY | 24 | 18 | 29 | X | 35 | 25 | 28 | 32 | 36 | 75 | 42 | 54 | 22 | 18 | 28 | 26 |
| CONWAY SCENIC RAILROAD | 11 | 52 | 41 | 35 | X | 45 | 7 | 38 | 47 | 40 | 21 | 65 | 56 | 52 | 7 | 44 |
| FLUME GORGE | 39 | 7 | 3 | 25 | 45 | X | 44 | 7 | 10 | 46 | 58 | 29 | 33 | 29 | 44 | 1 |
| HERITAGE-NEW HAMPSHIRE | 4 | 37 | 40 | 28 | 7 | 44 | X | 37 | 47 | 47 | 14 | 63 | 47 | 43 | 0 | 43 |
| LOON MOUNTAINPARK | 34 | 14 | 3 | 32 | 38 | 7 | 37 | X | 8 | 42 | 52 | 27 | 40 | 36 | 37 | 6 |
| LOST RIVER GORGE | 43 | 17 | 7 | 36 | 47 | 10 | 47 | 8 | X | 50 | 60 | 32 | 45 | 41 | 45 | 9 |
| M/S MT. WASHINGTON | 55 | 53 | 42 | 75 | 40 | 46 | 47 | 42 | 50 | X | 61 | 22 | 79 | 75 | 47 | 45 |
| MT. WASHINGTON AUTO ROAD | 18 | 51 | 57 | 42 | 21 | 58 | 14 | 52 | 60 | 61 | X | 78 | 39 | 35 | 14 | 57 |
| POLAR CAVES PARK | 62 | 36 | 24 | 54 | 65 | 29 | 63 | 27 | 32 | 22 | 78 | X | 63 | 59 | 63 | 28 |
| SANTA'S VILLAGE | 47 | 26 | 37 | 18 | 56 | 33 | 47 | 40 | 45 | 79 | 39 | 63 | X | 4 | 47 | 34 |
| SIX GUN CITY | 43 | 22 | 33 | 18 | 52 | 29 | 43 | 36 | 41 | 75 | 35 | 59 | 4 | X | 43 | 30 |
| STORY LAND | 4 | 46 | 37 | 28 | 7 | 44 | 0 | 37 | 45 | 47 | 14 | 63 | 47 | 43 | X | 43 |
| WHALE'S TALE WATERPARK | 40 | 8 | 2 | 26 | 44 | 1 | 43 | 6 | 9 | 45 | 57 | 28 | 34 | 30 | 43 | X |

**ATTITASH BEAR PEAK & FIELDS OF ATTITASH** — ROUTE 302 BARTLETT

An entire mountain of family fun! Alpine Slide, Waterslides, Scenic Chairlift, Guided Horseback Rides, Golf Driving Range and Mountain Biking. NEW! Buddy Bear's playpool age 2-7. 603-374-2368

I-93, PARKWAY EXIT 2 FRANCONIA NOTCH

80 Passenger Aerial Tramway ride to 4200' elev. summit. New Observation Tower, Summit Cafe & BBQ's, RV sites w/hook-ups & Beach. Canoe & Bike Rental, 8 mile Bike Path, Sandy Beach, Ski Museum. 603-823-5563

**Clark's TRADING POST** — ROUTE 3 LINCOLN

Antique Americana, trained bears, bumper boats, Mystical mansion, 2 1/2 mile train ride. 1890's fire station. Gift, photo, ice cream shops. 603-745-8913

**Mt Washington COG RAILWAY** — ROUTE 302 BRETTON WOODS

Ride the world's first mountain climbing Cog Railway to the top of New England's highest peak. Exciting 3 hr. roundtrip. Gift shop, restaurant, museum. 603-846-5404

**CONWAY SCENIC RAILROAD** — ROUTE 16 -NORTH CONWAY

**Two great trains–three great rides** in NH's White Mountains. Frequent daily departures. Dining car. NEW in 1996–Scenic Train Rides through Crawford Notch. 603-356-5251

**Flume Gorge** — ROUTE 3 FRANCONIA NOTCH

A natural Gorge with granite walls rising 90 feet. See Liberty Gorge, Cascades, Sentinel Pine Covered Bridge & the Pool. Visitor Center with free movie. Gift shop & Cafeteria.. 603-745-8391

ROUTE 16 GLEN

**We're Making History Every Day!** Spend 300 years with us, all in one afternooon as you visit with the people and famous places of New Hampshire's past. 603-383-9776

KANCAMAGUS HWY. LINCOLN

**Outdoor Family Fun & Adventure!** Scenic Gondola Skyride, daily Lumberjack Shows, meet the Mountain Man, wild animal & nature shows, horse & pony rides, mtn. biking, shopping, dining, special events! 603-745-8111

ROUTE 112 NORTH WOODSTOCK

Tour Lost River on boardwalks, following the river as it appears and disappears through the caves. Nature Garden, ecology trail, picnic area. 603-745-8031

ROUTE 3 WEIRS BEACH

Cruise NH's largest lake aboard this 230' cruise ship. Complete food service. Gift shop. Daytime scenic & evening Dinner/Dance cruises. 603-366-5531

ROUTE 16 PINKHAM NOTCH GORHAM

**Explore a world above treeline!** 8 mile toll road to the summit of the Northeast's highest peak. Drive your own car or take a guided tour. Views, museum. 603-466-3988

I-93, EXIT 26 (ROUTE 25) PLYMOUTH

A walking tour of America's most spectacular Glacial Caves. Maple Sugar Museum, 2 distinctive Gift Shops, Nature Trails, Animal Exhibits, more. 603-536-1888

ROUTE 2 JEFFERSON

**A New England Family Tradition!** You'll long remember this magical day filled with family festivities, fun filled shows, and exciting rides. All included with admission. 603-586-4445

ROUTE 2 JEFFERSON

The Affordable Wet & Dry Western Village. Help catch an Outlaw, Miniature Horse Show, Carriage Museum & 13 rides including the NEW 1/2 million dollar water coaster bobsled type ride. 603-586-4592

ROUTE 16 GLEN

**Fairy Tales Come To Life!** 16 wonderfully themed rides and countless attractions bring this child sized world to life! Story Land is a place where Fantasy Lives! 603-383-4293

I-93, EXIT 33 (ROUTE 3) LINCOLN

The White Mountains' only Water Park! Enjoy water slides, Lazy River, Wave Pool, Children's Activity Pool, and more. Gift shop & Snack Bars. Tubes extra. Mid-June til Labor Day. 603-745-8810.



**FREE INFO! Enter number on Reader Service Card opposite pg. 16: White Mountains Attractions #528.**

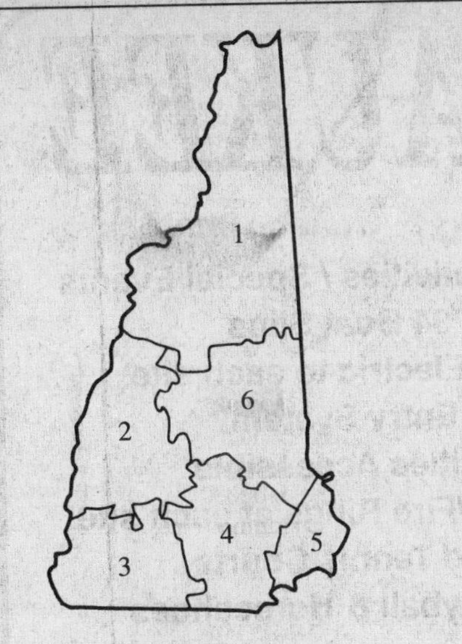


1. — White Mountains
2. — Dartmouth/Lake Sunapee
3. — Monadnock Region
4. — Merrimack Valley
5. — Seacoast Region
6. — Lakes Region

to: "Pick Your Own", New Hampshire Dept. of Agriculture, P.O. Box 2042, Concord, NH 03302.

*Fishing & Hunting:* New Hampshire Fish and Game Department, 2 Hazen Drive, Concord, NH 03301 (603-271-3421).

*Hiking:* For free leaflets on hiking contact the New Hampshire Division of Parks and Recreation, Trails Bureau, P.O. Box 1856, Concord, NH 03302-1856 (603-271-3254).

*Skiing:* For ski conditions (Nov. – March) call 800-262-6660 (cross-country); 800-258-3608 (downhill).

## Places to See & Things to Do

### WHITE MOUNTAINS REGION

**Cog Railway,** Bretton Woods. The world's first mountain climbing railway transports visitors to the top of 6,288-foot Mt. Washington. The 3-mile route is the second steepest railway in world. The *Sherman Adams Observation Center* at the summit affords unsurpassed scenic vistas.

**Conway Scenic Railroad,** North Conway. Antique train takes visitors on an 11-mile, 1-hour scenic ride. Antique steam and diesel locomotives, museum, picnic area and gift shop also on site.

**Franconia Notch State Park,** Franconia & Lincoln. 6,440-acres of adventure lie between the towering peaks of Franconia and Kinsman mountains. Alpine skiing, hiking, biking, camping, swimming, fishing, snowmobiling and cross-country skiing keep visitors busy year-round. A 5-minute ride in the *Cannon Aerial Tramway* brings you to the top of 4,180-foot Cannon Mountain. At the summit, walking trails lead to an observation tower. Don't miss *The Flume,* an 800-foot chasm carved by nature at the base of Mt. Liberty. Walking trails lead to bridges, pools and waterfalls. Alpine flowers bloom seasonally and lush, green mosses adorn moist walls.

**Glen.** Major attractions in Glen include:

*Heritage New Hampshire,* with 30 unique experiences awaiting visitors. Cross the Atlantic on a simulated ocean voyage and take a simulated train ride through Crawford Notch at the height of foliage season.

*Story Land* is a theme park with 15 rides, including: a Victorian-themed river voyage, antique car rides, African Safari, Voyage to the Moon, train rides, antique merry-go-round, pirate ship and swan boat rides. Also, an animated variety show, picnic areas, a chance to feed the animals and meet storybook characters.

**Jackson Village.** Mountain landscapes, Jackson Falls and scenic golf courses lure visitors to this lovely area. Hike the National Forest, fish the Wildcat and Ellis rivers or enjoy an afternoon of biking, swimming or tennis. Winter activities include sleigh rides, ice skating and skiing the Jackson Ski Touring network. Black Mountian and Wildcat are both great for downhill skiing.

**Jefferson.** Home of two major theme parks: *Santa's Village,* where children and adults alike enjoy the Yule Log Flume, the enchanted train ride and the thrilling rollercoaster. Shows include the trained macaw show, electro-animated Jingle Jamboree and the 12 Days of Christmas.

*Six Gun City* offers cowboy skits, frontier show, miniature horse show, Carriage Museum, bumper boats, waterslide and audience participation skits.

**Lincoln.** Places to visit before passing through Lincoln, include:

*Clark's Trading Post* which treats travelers to Antique Americana, trained bears, bumper boats, Mystical Mansion, an 1890s fire station and a 2 1/2 mile train ride.

*Loon Aerial Gondola* whisks riders up 7,000 feet to the summit of Loon Mountain, which features the Summit Cave Walk, 4-story observation tower and self-guided nature trail.

*Whale's Tale Waterpark,* features 8 different waves in a 17,500-square-foot wave pool, speed slides, float trip down the Lazy River, volleyball and horseshoes.

**Lost River,** North Woodstock. Self-guided tours lead explorers through crevasses, caverns, a steep-walled gorge and over breathtaking waterfalls. Nature garden, museum and picnic area also on site.

**Mt Washington Auto Road,** Gorham. Rt. 16 is an 8-mile toll road leading from Gorham, past spectacular mountain views, above the timberline, and to the 6,288-foot summit. Mid-May through mid-October, weathter permitting, drive to the summit of the Northeast's highest peak. No RVs are permitted on the Auto Road, however there is plenty of parking for all vehicles. Take the 1 1/2-hour guided van tour.

**Mt. Washington Valley.** Four season resort area's landscape is dotted with small towns, white-steepled churches, village greens and covered bridges. Recreational opportunities are endless in the valley: hiking, mountain biking, rock climbing and fishing are enjoyed throughout the summer. The *Attitash Alpine Slide* (located in Bartlett) combines a scenic ride up the Attitash skylift and a thrilling 3/4-mile slide down, across mountain meadows and woodland. Skiers relish 5 alpine ski areas offering 125 trails within a 20-mile radius and 2 nordic ski centers with 200 km of trails. Those "Born to Shop" take advantage of over 200 outlet and specialty stores.

**Polar Caves,** West of Plymouth. Visit some of America's greatest glacial caves, maple sugar house, waterfowl exhibit, nature trail and the Rock Garden of the Giants.

**White Mountain National Forest.** 768,000-acres of mountain peaks, wooded valleys, glistening lakes, rushing waters and sparkling waterfalls cover nearly 80% of the

**FREE INFO! Enter number on Reader Service Card opposite pg. 16: NH Travel & Tourism #647.**

# LAKE WINNIPESAUKEE

- Modern Restrooms with Showers
- Convenience Store
- Information / Reservation / Sales Center
- Club House with Screened Porch
- Arcade Room with Video Games
- Wooded, Open and Lakeview Sites
- Modern Laundromat
- Children's Playground
- Open May 1st to October 28th
- Softball Field
- Scheduled Activities / Special Events
- 151 Sites and 34 Boat Slips
- Sewer/Water/Electric to each site
- Security with Entry System
- All Lake Activities Accessible
- Picnic Tables/Fire Rings at each site
- Basketball and Tennis Courts
- Outdoor Volleyball & Horseshoes

**151 sites located on 77 acres with 681 feet of water frontage on Lake Winnipesaukee. The campground offers most all modern conveniences for your vacation spot on the big lake. In addition to renting on a daily, weekly, monthly or seasonal basis — one can also *purchase* a site or boat slip (based on availability).**

**Because of the convenience to all of the Lakes Region's Attractions, Arcadia has always been a well sought after campground for families who appreciate the convenience of shopping and excellent recreational amenities. Aside from the incredible feeling of Arcadia – the key ingredient is being on *LAKE WINNIPESAUKEE***

— Visit Nearby —

- Mill Falls Inn & Marketplace
- Science Center of New Hampshire
- Mt. Washington Lake Cruises
- Surf Coaster
- Lakes Region Greyhound Park
- Polar Caves Park
- Funspot
- Castlesprings
- Annalee's Doll Museum
- Scenic Drives & Hiking Trails

and much more...

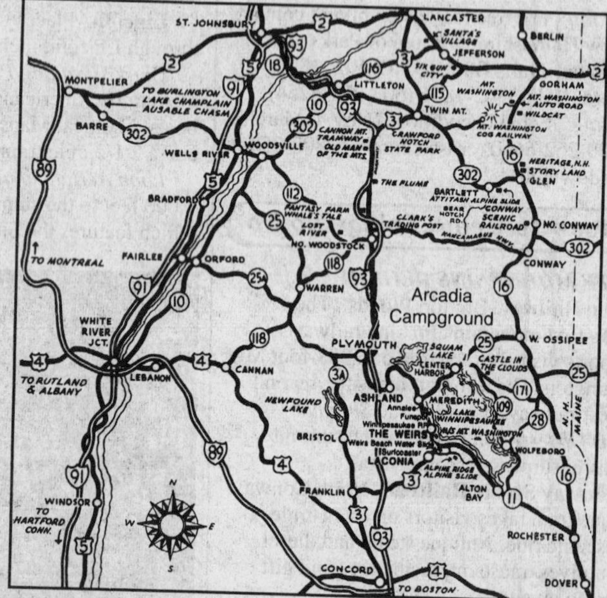


**For reservations, questions or a full color sales package, contact: Arcadia Campground at**

**(603) 253-6759**

See listing at Center Harbor, NH

**DISTANCES**

**70 miles from Manchester, NH +-**
**120 miles from Boston, MA +-**
**110 miles from Portland, ME +-**
**160 miles from Providence, RI +-**
**200 miles from Hartford, CT +-**
**300 miles from New York City +-**
**only 30 minutes off I-93 via exit 23**



**FREE INFO! Enter number on Reader Service Card opposite pg. 16: Arcadia Campground #467.**

White Mountains Region. Recreational amenities include: 360 miles of groomed snowmobile trails, 750 miles of fishing streams, 50 fishing ponds, over 1,300 miles of hiking trails, wildlife viewing, rock climbing, biking, swimming and skiing. Check out the following waterfalls: Upper & Lower Ammonoosuc Falls (Brenton Woods); Arethusa Falls, Flume Cascade and Silver Cascade (all off Route 302 in Crawford Notch); Glen Ellis Falls and Crystal Cascade (off Route 16 in Pinkham Notch); Sabbaday Falls (off the Kancamagus Highway).

***DARTMOUTH/LAKE SUNAPEE REGION***

**Cornish-Windsor Covered Bridge,** Cornish. Now the longest covered bridge in the U.S., it was built in 1866 and is 460 feet long.

**Dartmouth College,** Hanover. Chartered in 1769 by King George III, it is the oldest educational institution in the state. Visitors are welcome to share the joys of its campus, galleries and performing arts center.

**The Fells Historic Site at the John Hay National Wildlife Refuge,** Newbury. Tour the home and formal gardens of John M. Hay's (private secretary to President Lincoln) summer home. Guided weekend tours late May through October.

**Old Fort No. 4,** Charlestown. Authentic reconstruction of a French and Indian War fort. Located on its original site, this fort once guarded New England's western frontier.

**Ruggles Mine,** Grafton. Mineral collecting is permitted at "The Mine in the Sky." This mostly open-pit mine also features giant rooms and tunnels with arched ceilings.

**Saint-Gaudens National Historic Site,** Cornish. Tour the lavish estate, formal gardens and studio of Augustus Saint-Gaudens, one of America's greatest sculptors and the designer of our country's most famous gold coin.

**Samuel Morey House,** Oxford. Visit the home of the inventor of the first paddlewheel steamboat and the internal combustion engine. The house, built in 1773 and remodeled in 1804, contains antique furniture and pictures throughout, as well as paintings by an Oxford native artist, Henry Cheever Pratt (1803-1880).

**Sunapee.** Name of both a spectacular lake and the mountain that rises from its southern shore. The same lift that brings skiers to the summit of Mt. Sunapee in winter affords summer visitors a pleasant ride to a grand view of the region. Hikers enjoy well-marked trails on Mt. Sunapee. Nearly 10 miles long, Lake Sunapee features 3 working lighthouses and clear, cool water for swimmers, sailboaters and anglers fishing for salmon, trout, perch or bass. Boat and windsurf rentals available as well as boat cruises around the lake.

***MONADNOCK REGION***

**Keene.** This attractive city has one of the widest main streets in the world. While in town, stop by *Colony Mill Marketplace*, a beautifully renovated 150-year-old woolen mill which houses over 40 retail stores and restaurants. There's something for everyone here, from unique North East products to quality apparel and accessories. *The Wyman Tavern Museum* is the site of the first meeting of the Dartmouth Trustees in 1770. It's also the rendezvous site of Keene's minutemen before their march to the Battle of Lexington in April, 1775.

**Monadnock State Park,** Jaffrey. Haven for hikers and climbers boasts the most climbed mountain in North America, Grand Monadnock. White Dot Trail is a 2-hr. hike to Mt. Monadnock's summit. Amenities include a visitor center, winter hiking, year-round camping, ski touring and 40 miles of trails which lead to the summit of Mt. Monadnock.

**Pickity Place,** Mason. Handcrafted, early American charm is the theme of the shops and greenhouses at Pickity Place, where fragrant herbs permeate the air. Shop for whimsical handwoven baskets, candle holders, items of tin, wood, ceramics and glass for home decorating.

**Rhododendron State Park,** Fitzwilliam. Over 16 acres of wild rhododendrons burst into bloom mid-July. National Landmark features 1-mile walking trail for views of various peaks including Mt. Monadnock.

**Wapack National Wildlife Refuge,** Greenfield. 1,672 acres of mostly timbered area also contains a bog, swamp, bare rock ledge and cliff. Excellent wildlife observation opportunitites, photography, hiking, ski touring and snowshoeing.

***MERRIMACK VALLEY REGION***

**Bear Brook State Park,** Allenstown. 9,600 heavily-forested acres include swimming, archery ranges, nature center and trails, hiking, hunting, stream/pond fishing, boat rentals and fitness course.

Also within the park is the *Museum of Family Camping*, which houses an extensive display of camping memorabilia, photos, documents and old equipment. The Family Camping Hall of Fame honors those who have contributed significantly to camping, while slides, tape recordings and/or video presentations feature pioneers who recall the "roots" of this recreational lifestyle.

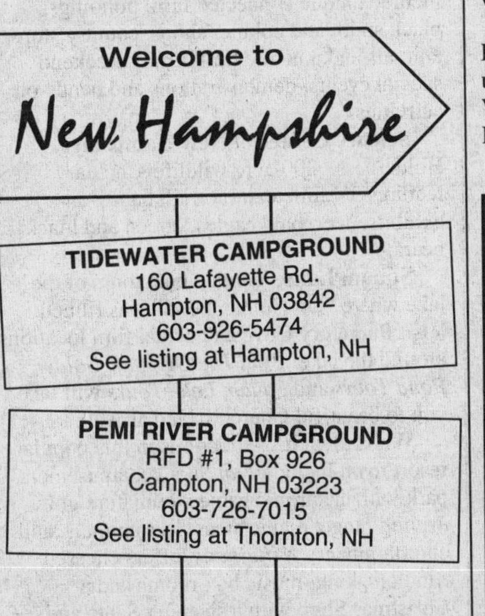

Welcome to
New Hampshire
TIDEWATER CAMPGROUND
160 Lafayette Rd.
Hampton, NH 03842
603-926-5474
See listing at Hampton, NH
PEMI RIVER CAMPGROUND
RFD #1, Box 926
Campton, NH 03223
603-726-7015
See listing at Thornton, NH


**Canobie Lake Park,** Salem. A family amusement park with rides, games, live shows, swimming pool, lake cruises, rollercoaster, fireworks and log flume ride. Open weekends mid-April to Memorial Day; daily Memorial Day-Labor Day 12 p.m. to 10 p.m.

**Canterbury Shaker Village, Inc.,** Canterbury. Experience the Shaker philosophy of "hands to work, hearts to God." Guided tours of restored buildings which include a schoolhouse, sister shop, laundry, bee house, ministry shop and carriage house. Special program, seasonal events and demonstrations highlight the tour.

**Christa McAuliffe Planetarium,** Concord. World's most technologically advanced planetarium transports visitors into the far reaches of the universe. Explore the surface of Jupiter, travel through an exploding star and plunge inside a spiral galaxy.

**New Hampshire International Speedway,** Loudon. From exotic Indy cars to thundering stock cars to super-fast cycles, this "magic mile" has been dubbed "New England's Showcase of Speed."

**New Hampshire Winery,** Henniker. The site of New England's first winery founded in 1969 is presently in operation and also serves as a distillery for New England Spirits, Inc., which manufactures Rock-Maple Liqueur.

**Robert Frost Farm,** Derry. Home of poet Robert Frost from 1901-1909 features a nature-poetry interpretive trail through field and woodland.

***SEACOAST REGION***

**Boat Cruises.** *Isle of Shoals Steamship Company* offers summer cruises from Portsmouth to the Isle of Shoals–nine windswept Atlantic islands ten miles off the east coast. *M.V. Thomas Laighton* offers daytime "whale watches" and evening dinner cruises from Portsmouth.

**Fort Constitution,** New Castle. Band of colonists raided the fort, staging the first aggressive act of the Revolution. First construction was for protection from pirates in the 17th century and later used during every war throughout World War II.

**Fort Stark Historic Site,** New Castle. First used in 1746, this fortification was utilized in every war from the Revolutionary War to World War II. Ten-acre site overlooks Little Harbor and affords terrific ocean views.

**Hampton Beach.** Begin your day with a

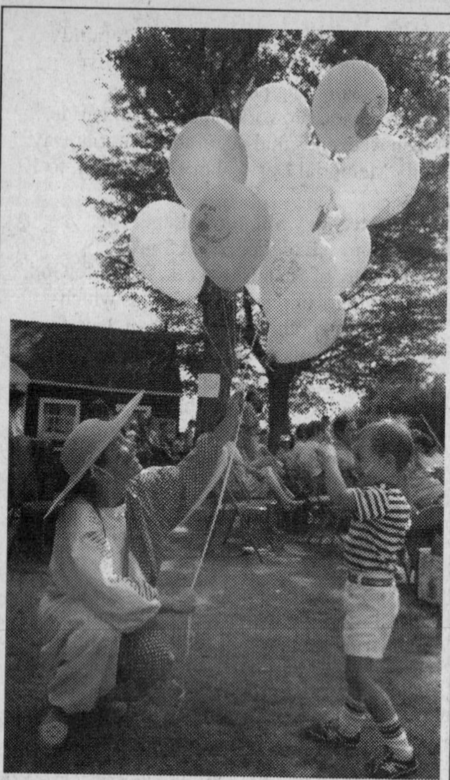

**Children of all ages** delight in festivals and events held throughout the White Mountains. From sugar on snow festivals to craft fairs and music events, nearly every weekend is cause for celebration in the White Mountains. *Photo courtesy of White Mountain Attractions.*

refreshing swim, a parasailing adventure or a stroll down the historic boardwalk—end your day with fireworks, live entertainment and a seafood dinner that can't be beat!

**Old Sandown Depot Railroad Museum,** Sandown. On the National Register of Historic Places, this museum houses railroad memorabilia, telegraph equipment, 2 flanger cars, motorized hand-car and velocipede, hand-pegged shoes and shoe making equipment, old tools, newspapers, magazines, posters, photos and Civil War letters.

**Olde Port Trolley Co.,** Hampton Beach. Public transportation takes a turn (of the century) with this horseless trolley, which is more than just a ride. Travelers are treated to a narrative of local history and happenings on the beach.

**Odiorne Point State Park–Seacoast Science Center,** Rye. Cultural and natural history exhibits on the last stretch of undeveloped New Hampshire coastline. Become acquainted with tide pool animals in the touch tank and watch ocean fish in the 1,000 gallon Gulf of Main tank.

**Portsmouth.** Plenty of fun to be found in this seaside community:

*Port of Portsmouth Maritime Museum & Albacore Park.* A short film and guided tour prepare visitors for the exploration of a U.S. Navy submarine. Walk through Memory Garden and pause to honor those many men who gave their lives for their country in the U.S. Navy Submarine Service. (Handicapped persons may have some difficulty on board submarine.)

*The Science and Nature Center.* More than 30 exhibits and displays focus on the seacoast environment. Touchpool, ocean aquariums, computer quizzes, nature trail and informative videos.

*Strawbery Banke, Inc.* This 10-acre outdoor museum and historic preservation site includes 18th and 19th century homes, period gardens, special events and demonstrations.

*Water Country.* Thrilling water rides include the Black Hole, Warp Eight, Raging Rapids, Geronimo, Polaroid Shoot and the Screamer. Or kick back for a relaxing glide down Adventure River.

### *LAKES REGION*

**Castle Springs/Castle in the Clouds,** Moultonboro. Mountaintop mansion set on 6,000 acres affords fantastic views. Tour the castle overlooking Lake Winnipesaukee or horseback ride along old carriage roads. Natural spring and bottling plant tours also on site.

**Clark House Museum Complex,** Wolfeboro. The first summer resort in America, Clark House contains furniture and furnishings including lace and pewter. The schoolhouse is filled with historic artifacts, old photos and records.

**Meredith.** Attractions within Meredith include:

*Annalee Doll Museum & Gift Shop.* An ever-changing collection of over 1,000 rare, antique felt dolls and an audio-visual slide presentation which traces the history and production of dolls.

*Hart's Turkey Farm.* This restaurant and turkey farm offer dinner guests free transportation from Lake Winnipesaukee.

*Mill Falls Marketplace.* A restored 19th century mill with covered walkway connecting it to a charming country inn which houses 22 distinctive shops, boutiques and restaurants. Arts and crafts gallery overlooks a waterfall and Lake Winnipesaukee.

**New Hampshire Farm Museum,** Milton. Guided tours of this National Historic site include unique connected farm buildings, black smith and cobbler shops, country store, animals and a nature trail. Enjoy weekend special events, demonstrations and hands-on activities.

**Science Center of New Hampshire,** Holderness. 200-acre wildlife sanctuary features 3/4 mile exhibit trail, hands-on exhibits, deer, bald eagles, otters, and black bears.

**Squam Lake.** Guided boat tours of the lake where "On Golden Pond" was filmed. Visit Purgatory Cove and actual film locations around the lake. Both *The Original Golden Pond Tours* and *Squam Lake Tours* will take you to beautiful Church Island as well.

**Weirs Beach.** Attractions in this popular resort town include *Fun Spot*, an amusement park with electronic games, miniature golf, driving range, picnic areas, live animals, and entertainment; *Kellerhaus*, offers cheese, candlemaking, music box rooms and a Christmas Shop with a sleeping Santa and working elves. For a "waterful" afternoon check out *Weirs Beach Water Slide*, with four giant slides, each longer than a football field. *Surf Coaster* water park features the Twin Boomerangs, Crazy River, Spray Ground and Barefoot Action Lagoon or take a relaxing cruise aboard the *M.S. Mt. Washington,* which offers cruises on Lake Winnipesaukee (day or night, dinner and dance cruises).

### Calendar of Events

*April:* Antique Auto Swap & Sell Meet, Amherst; Spring Fling Fly-In, Charlestown; A Wild Affair, Concord; Spring Carnival, Somersworth

*May:* Sheep & Wool Festival, New Boston; Way Out West, Keene; Lilac Time Festival, Lisbon

*June:* Summer Concerts, New London/Nelson; Antique Auto Swap & Sell Meet, Amherst; Chowder Festival, Portsmouth; Market Square Weekend, Portsmouth; Strawberry Moon Festival, Warner; Strawberry Festival, Laconia; Rock Swap, Gilsum; Fiddlers' Contest, Stark; Festival of Myth, Folklore & Story, Milford

*July:* Summer Concerts, New London/ Nelson/Hampton Beach; Prescott Park Arts Festival, Portsmouth; Antique Auto Swap & Sell Meet, Amherst; Cocheco Arts Festival, Dover; Fireworks, Hampton Beach; July-A-Fair, Sunapee; Crafts Festival, Gilford; Summer Sunday Concerts, Concord; Music For Manchester Summer Concert Series, Mancheser; Bow Street Fair, Portsmouth; Flea Market & Craft Sale, Center Harbor; Antiques Show & Sale, Fitzwilliam; Street Festival, Hanover; Market Days & Music Festival, Concord; Antiques Show & Sale, New London; Wildlife Festival, Holderness; Abenaki Music Festival, Wolfeboro; Arts & Crafts Fair, Lincoln; Antiques Fair & Sale, Wolfeboro; Canterbury Fair, Canterbury; Old Home Day & Family Day, Dorchester

*August:* Summer Concerts, New London/ Nelson/Hampton Beach; Antique Auto Swap & Sell Meet, Amherst; Music at the Marketplace, Weirs Beach; Fireworks, Hampton Beach; Prescott Park Arts Festival, Portsmouth; Bluegrass Festival, Campton; Equine Festival, Bartlett; Old Home Week, Freedom; Childrens Fair, New Ipswich; Arts & Crafts Bazaar, Georges Mills; Rodeo, Bartlett; North Country Moose Festival, Pittsburg

*September:* White Mountains Jazz & Blues Festival, Bartlett; Lumberjack Festival, Lincoln; Old Home Day, Pelham; Seafood Festival, Hampton Beach; Mt. Washington Auto Road Bicycle Hillclimb, Gorham; Railfan's Day, North Conway; Shaker Harvest Festival, Enfield; Brewers Festival, Portsmouth

*October:* Juried Art Show, Peterborough; Car Show & Fall Foliage Tour, Charlestown; Handcrafted Furniture Show,Meredith; Octoberfest Arts & Crafts Festival, Concord; Apple Harvest Day, Dover; Chili Cook-Off, Portsmouth; Fall Foliage Festival, Warner; White Mountains Oktoberfest, Bartlett; Harvest Festival, Keene; Craft Bazaar, Weare; Quilt Show, Laconia

# new hampshire

All privately-owned campgrounds personally inspected by Woodall Representatives Les & Barbara Fields.

**Unless otherwise noted, all listed campgrounds have hot showers & flush toilets.**

## ALLENSTOWN—E-4

BEAR BROOK STATE PARK—*From jct US 3 & Hwy 28: Go 8 mi NE on Hwy 28 (Allenstown).* FACILITIES: 81 sites, 81 no hookups, tenting available, sewage disposal, limited grocery store, ice, wood. RECREATION: swimming, boating, no motors, canoeing, row/canoe boat rentals, pond/stream fishing, hiking trails. Open mid May through Columbus Day. Phone: (603) 485-9874.

**Museum of Family Camping**—*From jct US 3 & Hwy 28: Go 3 mi NE on Hwy 28, then 1 1/2 mi NE on entrance road (within Bear Brook State Park).* Exhibits feature early camping gear. Videos & photos depict the history of camping from 1920 to the present. Parking for RVs. Open Memorial Day through Columbus Day. 10 a.m. - 4 p.m. daily. No charge. Donations appreciated. Phone: (603) 239-4768.

## ASHLAND—D-3

**Ames Brook Campground**—Rural CAMPGROUND with mostly open sites. *From jct I-93 (exit 24) & US 3: Go 3/4 mi S on US 3, then 1/4 mi S on Hwy 132, then 1/2 mi S on Winona Rd.* ◆◆◆FACILITIES: 52 sites, most common site width 25 feet, 25 full hookups, 17 water & elec (20 & 30 amp receptacles), 10 no hookups, seasonal sites, 7 pull-thrus, tenting available, sewage disposal, laundry, public phone, grocery store, LP gas refill by weight/by meter, ice, tables, fire rings, wood. ◆◆◆◆RECREATION: rec hall, rec room/area, swim pool, stream fishing, playground, planned group activities (weekends only), badminton, horseshoes, volleyball. Open May 1 through mid Oct. Rate in 1995 $22-26 per family. Member of NE-HA-CA. Phone: (603) 968-7998.

**YOGI BEAR'S JELLYSTONE PARK CAMP RESORT**—CAMPGROUND with grassy, open & shaded sites. Presently accepting overnighters. *From jct I-93 (exit 23): Go 1/4 mi E on Hwy 104, then 4 mi N on Hwy 132N.*

WELCOME

◆◆◆FACILITIES: 228 sites, most common site width 25 feet, 19 full hookups, 204 water & elec (15,20 & 30 amp receptacles), 5 no hookups, seasonal sites, 6 pull-thrus, a/c allowed ($), heater allowed ($), tenting available, group sites for tents/RVs, RV rentals, cabins, RV storage, handicap restroom facilities, sewage disposal, laundry, public phone, full service store, RV supplies, ice, tables, fire rings, wood, guard.

◆◆◆◆◆RECREATION: rec hall, rec room/area, equipped pavilion, coin games, swim pool, river swimming, whirlpool, boating, canoeing, 3 row/11 canoe boat rentals, river fishing, mini-golf ($), basketball hoop, playground, 2 shuffleboard courts, planned group activities, movies, recreation director, badminton, sports field, horseshoes, volleyball.

Open 3rd weekend in May through Mid-Oct. Open weekends only after Labor Day until mid Oct. Rate in 1995 $31-38 for 2 persons. Reservations recommended Memorial Day through Labor Day. Discover/Master Card/Visa accepted. Member of NE-HA-CA. Phone: (603) 968-9000.

SEE AD THIS PAGE

## AUBURN—F-4

**Calef Lake Camping Area**—Rural, rustic, heavily wooded CAMPGROUND. Most sites occupied by seasonal campers. *From jct Bypass Hwy 28 & Hwy 121: Go 5 1/2 mi S on Hwy 121.* ◆◆FACILITIES: 130 sites, most common site width 35 feet, 29 ft. max RV length, 121 water & elec (20 amp receptacles), 9 no hookups, seasonal sites, tenting available, sewage disposal, laundry, public phone, grocery store, LP gas refill by weight, ice, tables, fire rings, grills, wood. ◆◆◆RECREATION: pavilion, lake swimming, boating, electric motors only, canoeing, 3 row/1 canoe/1 pedal boat rentals, lake fishing, playground, badminton, sports field, horseshoes, volleyball. Open mid May through Oct 1. Rate in 1995 $17-20 for 4 persons. Member of ARVC. Phone: (603) 483-8282.

## BARRINGTON—E-4

**Ayer's Lake Farm Campground**—Natural sites in a pine grove and lakeside sites in a rural area. *From jct Spaulding Turnpike & US 202: Go 5 mi SW on US 202.* ◆◆FACILITIES: 50 sites, most common site width 30 feet, 32 ft. max RV length, 44 water & elec (15 & 20 amp receptacles), 6 no hookups, seasonal sites, 4 pull-thrus, tenting available, sewage disposal, public phone, ice, tables, fire rings, wood. ◆◆RECREATION: lake swimming, boating, canoeing, ramp, 3 canoe boat rentals, lake fishing, playground. Open May 20 through Sep 28. Rate in 1995 $15-24 per family. Member of NE-HA-CA. Phone: (603) 332-5940.

**Barrington Shores Campground**—Rural, hilly, wooded, grassy CAMPGROUND by lakeside. *From jct Hwy 4 & Hwy 125: Go 3 mi N on Hwy 125, then 1 mi W on Beauty Hill Rd, then 1 mi S on Hall Rd.* ◆◆FACILITIES: 140 sites, most common site width 35 feet, 70 full hookups, 70 water & elec (15 amp receptacles), seasonal sites, tenting available, sewage disposal, laundry, public phone, limited grocery store, LP gas refill by weight, ice, tables, fire rings, wood. ◆◆◆◆RECREATION: rec hall, rec room/area, lake swimming, boating, canoeing, ramp, dock, 2 row/4 canoe/2 pedal boat rentals, lake fishing, playground, badminton, horseshoes, volleyball. Open May 15 through Sep 17. Rate in 1995 $20-24 per family. Phone: (603) 664-9333.

## BARTLETT—C-4

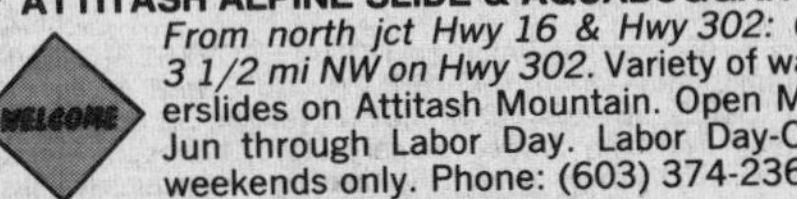

**ATTITASH ALPINE SLIDE & AQUABOGGAN**—*From north jct Hwy 16 & Hwy 302: Go 3 1/2 mi NW on Hwy 302.* Variety of waterslides on Attitash Mountain. Open Mid Jun through Labor Day. Labor Day-Oct weekends only. Phone: (603) 374-2369.

SEE AD TRAVEL SECTION PAGE 530

**Crawford Notch General Store & Campground**—Rustic CAMPGROUND with wooded sites along the Saco River. *From jct US 3 & US 302 (Twin Mt): Go 15 mi S on US 302.* ◆FACILITIES: 75 sites, most common site width 60 feet, 35 ft. max RV length, 23 elec (30 amp receptacles), 52 no hookups, tenting available, non-flush toilets, public phone, full service store, ice, tables, fire rings, grills, wood. ◆◆RECREATION: river swimming, river fishing, hiking trails. Open May 1 through Oct 31. Rate in 1995 $18 for 4 persons. Phone: (603) 374-2779.

CRAWFORD NOTCH STATE PARK (Dry River Campground)—*From town: Go 8 mi NW on US 302.* FACILITIES: 30 sites, 30 no hookups, tenting available, non-flush toilets, tables. RECREATION: river fishing, hiking trails. Open mid May through Columbus Day. No showers. Phone: (603) 374-2272.

**Silver Springs Campground**—Shaded or sunny sites, many riverside. *From Twin Mountain jct US 3 & US 302: Go 21 mi E on US 302.* ◆◆FACILITIES: 58 sites, most common site width 50 feet, 24 water & elec (15 & 20 amp receptacles), 34 no hookups, 1 pull-thrus, tenting available, sewage disposal, public phone, grocery store, ice, tables, fire rings, grills, wood. ◆◆RECREATION: river swimming, river fishing, badminton, horseshoes, volleyball. Open May 16 through Oct 15. Rate in 1995 $15.50-17.50 per family. Member of NE-HA-CA. Phone: (603) 374-2221.

WHITE MOUNTAIN NATIONAL FOREST (Jigger Johnson Campground)—*From jct US 302 & FR 26: Go 9 mi S on FR 26, then 1/4 mi W on Hwy 112.* FACILITIES: 75 sites, 30 ft. max RV length, 75 no hookups, tenting available, tables, fire rings. RECREATION: river fishing, hiking trails. Open late May through mid Oct. No showers. Phone: (603) 447-5448.

## BETHLEHEM—C-3

**Apple Hill Campground**—Rural, wooded with large mostly level sites. *From jct I-93 (exit 40) & Hwy 302: Go 3 mi E on Hwy 302, then 1 mi NE on Hwy 142.* ◆◆FACILITIES: 65 sites, most common site width 35 feet, 20 full hookups, (15,20 & 30 amp receptacles), 45 no hookups, seasonal sites, 18 pull-thrus, tenting available, sewage disposal, laundry, limited grocery store, LP gas refill by weight/by meter, ice, tables, fire rings, wood. ◆◆◆RECREATION: rec room/area, pond swimming, playground, badminton, sports field, horseshoes, hiking trails, volleyball. Open all year. Rate in 1995 $15-18 per family. No refunds. Member of NE-HA-CA. Phone: (800) 284-2238.

**Snowy Mountain Campground**—Shaded, prepared sites in a wooded setting. *From jct I-93 (exit 40) & US 302: Go 1 mi E on US 302.* ◆◆FACILITIES: 40 sites, most common site width 25 feet, 16 water & elec (15 amp receptacles), 24 no hookups, tenting available, sewage disposal, limited grocery store, ice, tables, fire rings,

SNOWY MOUNTAIN CAMPGROUND—Continued on next page
BETHLEHEM—Continued on next page

BETHLEHEM—Continued
SNOWY MOUNTAIN CAMPGROUND—Continued

grills, wood. ◆◆RECREATION: rec room/area, swim pool, badminton, horseshoes, volleyball. Open May 1 through Oct 31. Rate in 1995 $14-16 per family. Member of NE-HA-CA. Phone: (603) 869-2600.

## BRADFORD—E-3

**Lake Massasecum Campground**—Semi-wooded lakeside CAMPGROUND. *From jct US 202 & Hwy 114: Go 6 mi N on Hwy 114, then 1/2 mi E on Massasecum Rd.* ◆◆FACILITIES: 50 sites, most common site width 25 feet, 35 water & elec (15,20 & 30 amp receptacles), 15 no hookups, seasonal sites, 10 pull-thrus, tenting available, sewage disposal, public phone, limited grocery store, ice, tables, grills, wood. ◆◆RECREATION: rec hall, lake swimming, boating, canoeing, ramp, dock, 3 row/2 canoe/1 pedal boat rentals, lake fishing, horseshoes. Recreation open to the public. Open May 15 through Sep 15. Rates available upon request. No refunds. Member of NE-HA-CA. Phone: (603) 938-2571.

## BRISTOL—D-3

**Davidson's Countryside Campground**—Rural, rustic setting with shaded & open, grasssy sites. All full hookups occupied by seasonal campers. *From I-93 (exit 23) & Hwy 104: Go 1 1/2 mi W on Hwy 104, then 1/2 mi N on River Rd.* ◆◆FACILITIES: 130 sites, most common site width 55 feet, 5 full hookups, 110 water & elec (15 & 20 amp receptacles), 15 no hookups, seasonal sites, tenting available, sewage disposal, public phone, limited grocery store, ice, tables, fire rings, grills, wood. ◆◆◆RECREATION: rec hall, river swimming, boating, canoeing, 1 row/5 canoe boat rentals, river fishing, playground, badminton, horseshoes, volleyball. Open Memorial Day through Columbus Day. Rate in 1995 $21-22 per family. Member of NE-HA-CA. Phone: (603) 744-2403.

## BROOKLINE—F-3

**FIELD AND STREAM TRAVEL TRAILER PARK**—Level, grassy sites with some shade in a brookside CAMPGROUND. *From jct US 3 (exit 6) & Hwy 130: Go 12 mi W on Hwy 130, then 1 mi S on Hwy 13, then 1 mi W on Mason Rd, then 1/4 mi N on Dupaw Gould Rd.*

WELCOME

◆◆◆FACILITIES: 54 sites, most common site width 35 feet, 19 full hookups, 35 water & elec (20 & 30 amp receptacles), seasonal sites, 5 pull-thrus, a/c allowed ($), heater allowed ($), phone hookups, tenting available, group sites for RVs, sewage disposal, laundry, public phone, limited grocery store, RV supplies, LP gas refill by weight, ice, tables, fire rings, wood, traffic control gate.

◆◆◆RECREATION: rec room/area, coin games, pond swimming, canoeing, dock, pond/stream fishing, badminton, horseshoes, volleyball.

Open all year. Facilities fully operational May 1 through Oct 31. Open by reservation only Nov 1

BROOKLINE—Continued
FIELD AND STREAM TRAVEL TRAILER PARK—Continued

through May 1. Rate in 1995 $17-20 per family. No refunds. Master Card/Visa accepted. Member of NE-HA-CA. Phone: (603) 673-4677.

SEE AD NASHUA PAGE 547

## CAMPTON—D-3

**BRANCH BROOK CAMPGROUND**—Country CAMPGROUND with many wooded riverside sites. *From jct I-93 (exit 28) & Hwy 49: Go 1 mi W on Hwy 49.*

WELCOME

◆◆◆FACILITIES: 150 sites, most common site width 40 feet, 46 full hookups, 59 water & elec, 45 elec (15 & 20 amp receptacles), seasonal sites, a/c not allowed, heater not allowed, tenting available, group sites for tents/RVs, RV rentals, RV storage, sewage disposal, laundry, public phone, limited grocery store, RV supplies, LP gas refill by weight/by meter, ice, tables, fire rings, wood.

◆◆◆◆RECREATION: rec hall, rec room/area, coin games, river swimming, boating, canoeing, 6 canoe boat rentals, float trips, river/pond fishing, playground, shuffleboard court, badminton, sports field, horseshoes, volleyball, cross country skiing, snowmobile trails.

Open all year. Facilities fully operational May 1 through Nov 1. Rate in 1995 $18-22 per family. No refunds. Reservations recommended Memorial Day through Labor Day. Master Card/Visa accepted. Member of NE-HA-CA. Phone: (603) 726-7001.

SEE AD THIS PAGE

**GOOSE HOLLOW CAMPGROUND**—Grassy and some shaded sites in a meadow surrounded by woods. *From jct I-93 (exit 28) & Hwy 49: Go 3 3/4 mi E on Hwy 49.*

WELCOME

◆◆FACILITIES: 165 sites, 48 full hookups, 17 water & elec (15,20 & 30 amp receptacles), 100 no hookups, seasonal sites, tenting available, group sites for tents/RVs, sewage disposal, public phone, ice, tables, fire rings.

◆◆RECREATION: rec hall, rec room/area, swim pool, river fishing, basketball hoop, horseshoes, volleyball.

Open all year. Rate in 1995 $10-19 for 2 persons. Phone: (800) 204-CAMP.

SEE AD THIS PAGE

WHITE MOUNTAIN NATIONAL FOREST (Campton Campground)—*From I-93 (exit 28): Go 2 mi E on Hwy 49.* FACILITIES: 58 sites, 30 ft. max RV length, 58 no hookups, tenting available, limited grocery store, tables, fire rings. RECREATION: river swimming, boating, canoeing, river fishing, hiking trails. Open mid May through early Sep. Phone: (603) 536-1310.

WHITE MOUNTAIN NATIONAL FOREST (Waterville Campground)—*From town: Go 1/4 mi N on Hwy 175, then 9 mi E on Hwy 49, then 1/4 mi N on FR 30.* FACILITIES: 27 sites, 22 ft. max RV length, 27 no hookups, non-flush toilets, handicap restroom facilities, tables, fire rings. RECREATION: fishing, hiking trails. Open all year. No showers. Phone: (603) 536-1310.

## CANAAN—D-2

**CRESCENT CAMPSITE**—Rustic sites in a rural lakeside CAMPGROUND. *From jct Hwy 118 & US 4: Go 1/10 mi W on US 4 (to blinker), then 1 mi NW on Canaan St, then 1/8 mi N on Fernwood, bear right 1 mi at fork.*

WELCOME

◆◆FACILITIES: 82 sites, most common site width 35 feet, 72 water & elec (15 amp receptacles), 10 no hookups, seasonal sites, a/c not allowed, heater not allowed, tenting available, RV rentals, RV storage, sewage disposal, laundry, public phone, limited grocery store, RV supplies, LP gas refill by weight/by meter, ice, tables, fire rings, wood.

◆◆◆RECREATION: rec hall, coin games, lake swimming, boating, canoeing, ramp, dock, water skiing, lake fishing, basketball hoop, sports field, horseshoes.

Open mid-May through Columbus Day. Rate in 1995 $16-18 per family. No refunds. Member of NE-HA-CA. Phone: (603) 523-9910.

SEE AD THIS PAGE

## CENTER HARBOR—D-3

**ARCADIA CAMPGROUND**—Lakeside CAMPGROUND selling sites and accepting overnight guests. *From jct Hwy 258 & Hwy 25: Go 1 1/2 mi E on Hwy 25, then 2 mi S on Moultonborough Neck Rd, then 1 mi E on Shaker Jerry Rd.*

WELCOME

◆◆◆FACILITIES: 150 sites, most common site width 30 feet, 150 full hookups, (20 & 30 amp receptacles), seasonal sites, a/c allowed, heater allowed, phone hookups, tenting available, laundry, public phone, RV supplies, ice, tables, fire rings, traffic control gate.

◆◆◆◆RECREATION: rec hall, rec room/area, coin games, lake swimming, boating, canoeing, ramp, dock, 2 row/2 canoe boat rentals, lake fishing, basketball hoop, playground, 2 tennis courts, badminton, sports field, horseshoes, volleyball.

Open May 1 through Oct 28. Rate in 1995 $29 per family. Phone: (603) 253-6759.

SEE AD TRAVEL SECTION PAGE 532

**LONG ISLAND BRIDGE CAMPGROUND**—CAMPGROUND with shaded & open sites overlooking a lake. *From jct Hwy 25B & Hwy 25: Go 1 1/2 mi E on Hwy 25, then 6 1/2 mi S on Moultonborough Neck Rd.*

WELCOME

◆◆◆FACILITIES: 112 sites, most common site width 25 feet, 32 ft. max RV length, 76 full hookups, 23 water & elec (20 & 30 amp receptacles), 13 no hookups, seasonal sites, 4 pull-thrus, a/c allowed ($), heater allowed ($), tenting available, sewage disposal, laundry, public phone, ice, tables, fire rings, wood.

◆◆RECREATION: lake swimming, boating, canoeing, ramp, dock, water skiing, lake fishing, basketball hoop, horseshoes, volleyball.

Open May 1 through Oct 1. Rate in 1995 $16-22 for 2 persons. No refunds. Reservations recommended Memorial Day through Labor Day. Member of NE-HA-CA. Phone: (603) 253-6053.

SEE AD THIS PAGE

**Provident Winnipesaukee Campground**—Rural CAMPGROUND with wooded sites. *From jct Hwy 25B & Hwy 25: Go 1 1/2 mi E on Hwy 25, then 4 mi S on Moultonboro Neck Rd.* ◆◆◆FACILITIES: 92 sites, most common site width 25 feet, 80 water & elec (20,30 & 50 amp receptacles), 12 no hookups, seasonal sites, 10 pull-thrus, tenting available, sewage disposal, laundry, public phone, limited grocery store, ice, tables, fire rings, wood. ◆◆◆RECREATION: rec room/area, swim pool, playground, shuffleboard court, badminton, horseshoes, volleyball. Open May 1 through Oct 31. Facilities fully operational Memorial Day through mid Oct. Rate in 1995 $17-20 for 2 persons. Member of NE-HA-CA. Phone: (603) 253-6251.

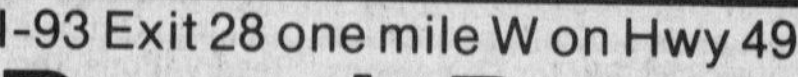

## CENTER OSSIPEE—D-4

**TERRACE PINES**—Level, wooded, prepared sites at a hilly CAMPGROUND on a lake. *From jct Hwy 16 & Center Ossipee Business District Rd: Go 500 feet W & 500 feet S, then 1/2 mi W on Main St to Center Ossipee Village, then 1 1/2 mi SW on Moultinville Rd, then 1 3/4 mi SW on Valley Rd, then 1/2 mi W on Bents Rd.*

◇◇◇FACILITIES: 183 sites, most common site width 45 feet, 29 ft. max RV length, 178 full hookups, 5 water & elec (20 & 30 amp receptacles), seasonal sites, a/c allowed, heater allowed, phone hookups, tenting available, cabins, sewage disposal, laundry, public phone, limited grocery store, LP gas refill by weight/by meter, ice, tables, fire rings, grills, wood, traffic control gate.

◇◇◇◇RECREATION: rec hall, rec room/area, coin games, lake swimming, boating, canoeing, ramp, dock, 2 row/4 canoe/1 pedal boat rentals, water skiing, lake fishing, basketball hoop, playground, badminton, horseshoes, hiking trails, volleyball.

Open May 15 through Columbus Day. Rate in 1995 $22 per family. Reservations recommended Jul through Labor Day. Master Card/Visa accepted. Member of NE-HA-CA. Phone: (603) 539-6210.

SEE AD TRAVEL SECTION PAGE 529

## CHOCORUA—D-4

**CHOCORUA CAMPING VILLAGE**—Lakeside CAMPGROUND on hilly terrain with shaded, prepared sites. *From jct Hwy 113 & Hwy 16: Go 3 mi S on Hwy 16.*

◇◇◇◇FACILITIES: 120 sites, most common site width 80 feet, 53 full hookups, 49 water & elec (15,20 & 30 amp receptacles), 18 no hookups, seasonal sites, 8 pull-thrus, a/c allowed, heater allowed, phone hookups, tenting available, group sites for tents, RV rentals, cabins, RV storage, handicap restroom facilities, sewage disposal, laundry, public phone, grocery store, RV supplies, LP gas refill by weight/by meter, ice, tables, fire rings, grills, wood, traffic control gate.

◇◇◇◇◇RECREATION: rec hall, rec room/area, coin games, lake swimming, boating, electric motors only, canoeing, dock, 2 row/2 canoe/1 pedal boat rentals, lake/river fishing, basketball hoop, playground, planned group activities, movies, recreation director, badminton, sports field, horseshoes, hiking trails, volleyball, cross country skiing, snowmobile trails.

Open all year. Rate in 1995 $18-30 per family. Reservations recommended Jul through Aug. Master Card/Visa accepted. Member of NE-HA-CA. Phone: (603) 323-8536.

SEE AD CONWAY NEXT PAGE

## COLEBROOK—B-3

COLEMAN STATE PARK—*From jct US 3 & Hwy 26: Go 12 mi E on Hwy 26 & Diamond Pond Rd.* FACILITIES: 30 sites, 30 no hookups, tenting available, non-flush toilets, sewage disposal, public phone, limited grocery store, tables. RECREATION: boating, pond fishing, hiking trails. Open mid May through Labor Day. No showers. Phone: (603) 237-4520.

**Mohawk Valley Camping Area**—Rural, partially shaded, grassy CAMPGROUND with mountain view. *From jct US 3 & Hwy 26: Go 5 mi E on Hwy 26, then 1/4 mi S on access road.* ◇◇FACILITIES: 100 sites, most common site width 20 feet, 36 water & elec, 4 elec (20 & 30 amp receptacles), 60 no hookups, seasonal sites, 36 pull-thrus, tenting available, sewage disposal, public phone, ice, tables, fire rings, grills, wood. ◇◇RECREATION: swim pool, river fishing, horseshoes. Open Memorial Day through Oct 12. Rate in 1995 $12-17 for 2 persons. Member of NE-HA-CA. Phone: (603) 237-5756.

## CONCORD—E-3

✲ **GARY'S RTE 4 RV'S**—*From jct I-93 (exit 15E) & I-393: Go 4 mi E on I-393, then 1 1/2 mi E on US 4/Hwy 9/US 202.* SALES: travel trailers, park models, truck campers, 5th wheels, van conversions, motor homes, mini-motor homes, fold-down camping trailers. SERVICES: RV appliance mechanic full-time, LP gas refill by weight/by meter, RV rentals, sells parts/accessories, sells camping supplies, installs hitches. Open all year. American Express/Discover/Master Card/Visa accepted. Phone: (603) 798-4030.

SEE AD THIS PAGE

**HILLCREST CAMPGROUND**—Open and shaded, grassy sites at a wooded location in the country. *From jct I-93 (exit 15E) & I-393: Go 4 mi E on I-393, then 2 mi E on US 4.*

◇◇◇FACILITIES: 123 sites, most common site width 30 feet, 70 full hookups, 44 water & elec (20 & 30 amp receptacles), 9 no hookups, seasonal sites, 6 pull-thrus, a/c allowed ($), heater allowed ($), cable TV, phone hookups, tenting available, group sites for tents/RVs, cabins, RV storage, sewage disposal, laundry, public phone, limited grocery store, RV supplies, ice, tables, fire rings, wood, traffic control gate.

◇◇◇◇RECREATION: rec room/area, equipped pavilion, coin games, swim pool, boating, electric motors only, canoeing, dock, 1 row/3 canoe/2 pedal boat rentals, pond fishing, mini-golf ($), basketball hoop, playground, badminton, horseshoes, hiking trails, volleyball.

Open May 1 through Oct 15. Rate in 1995 $21-24 per family. Master Card/Visa accepted. Member of NE-HA-CA. Phone: (603) 798-5124.

SEE AD THIS PAGE

## CONWAY—D-4

**THE BEACH CAMPING AREA**—Rural CAMPGROUND with shaded sites beside a river. *In town at north jct Hwy 113 & Hwy 16: Go 1 1/2 mi N on Hwy 16.*

◇◇◇FACILITIES: 120 sites, most common site width 30 feet, 87 full hookups, 21 water & elec (15,20 & 30 amp receptacles), 12 no hookups, seasonal sites, a/c allowed ($), heater allowed ($), tenting available, sewage disposal, laundry, public phone, limited grocery store, RV supplies, ice, tables, fire rings, grills, wood.

◇◇◇RECREATION: rec room/area, pavilion, coin games, river swimming, river fishing, basketball hoop, playground, 2 shuffleboard courts, planned group activities, badminton, horseshoes, volleyball.

Open May 17 through Oct 14. Rate in 1995 $19-21.50 per family. Reservations recommended Jul through Columbus Day. Master Card/Visa accepted. Member of NE-HA-CA. Phone: (603) 447-2723. FCRV 10% discount.

SEE AD NEXT PAGE

**Cove Camping Area on Conway Lake**—Rural, wooded, lakeside CAMPGROUND. *From north jct Hwy 16 & Hwy 113: Go 1 mi E on Hwy 113, then 1 3/4 mi S on Stark Rd, then 1 mi E on Cove Rd.* ◇◇FACILITIES: 83 sites, most common site width 30 feet, 32 ft. max RV length, no sites for slide-outs, 5 full hookups, 38 water & elec, 14 elec (15 & 20 amp receptacles), 26 no hookups, seasonal sites, tenting available, sewage disposal, laundry, public phone, grocery store, ice, tables, fire rings, wood. ◇◇◇RECREATION: rec hall, rec room/area, lake swimming, boating, canoeing, ramp, dock, 6 row/8 canoe boat rentals, lake fishing, playground, horseshoes. No pets. Open May 24 through Columbus Day. pets ok after Labor day Rate in 1995 $19-30 per family. Member of NE-HA-CA. Phone: (603) 447-6734.

**Eastern Slope Camping Area**—Wooded, riverside CAMPGROUND with mountain view, and sheltered picnic tables. *From jct US 302 & Hwy 16: Go 1 1/2 mi S on Hwy 16.* ◇◇FACILITIES: 260 sites, most common site width 30 feet, 32 full hookups, 228 water & elec (20 & 30 amp receptacles), tenting available, sewage disposal, public phone, grocery store, ice, tables, fire rings, wood. ◇◇RECREATION: rec room/area, river swimming, canoeing, 12 canoe boat rentals, river fishing, playground, badminton, sports field, horseshoes, volleyball. No pets. Open mid May through Columbus Day. Pets OK after Labor Day Rates available upon request. No refunds. Member of NE-HA-CA. Phone: (603) 447-5092.

CONWAY—Continued on next page

NH State Animal: White-tail Deer NH

CONWAY—Continued

**PINE-KNOLL CAMPGROUND & RV RESORT**—Rural CAMPGROUND with shaded or open sites. *From jct Hwy 112 (Kancamagus Hwy) & Hwy 16: Go 4 1/2 mi S on Hwy 16.*

◆◆FACILITIES: 175 sites, most common site width 50 feet, 40 full hookups, 135 water & elec (15,20 & 30 amp receptacles), seasonal sites, a/c allowed ($), heater allowed ($), phone hookups, tenting available, sewage disposal, laundry, public phone, limited grocery store, ice, tables, fire rings, wood, traffic control gate/guard.

◆◆◆RECREATION: rec room/area, coin games, lake swimming, boating, no motors, canoeing, 5 row boat rentals, lake fishing, basketball hoop, badminton, sports field, horseshoes, volleyball.

Open all year. Rate in 1995 $14 per family. No refunds. Reservations recommended Jul 1 through Labor Day. Master Card/Visa accepted. Member of NE-HA-CA. Phone: (603) 447-3131.
**SEE AD THIS PAGE**

**SACO RIVER CAMPING AREA**—*From center of town: Go 4 mi N on Hwy 16.*
**SEE PRIMARY LISTING AT NORTH CONWAY AND AD NORTH CONWAY PAGE 550**

WHITE MOUNTAIN NATIONAL FOREST (Blackberry Crossing Campground)—*From jct Hwy 16 & Hwy 112: Go 6 1/2 mi W on Hwy 112 (Kancamagus Scenic Hwy).* FACILITIES: 26 sites, 30 ft. max RV length, 26 no hookups, tenting available, non-flush toilets, handicap restroom facilities, tables, fire rings, grills. RECREATION: river swimming, river fishing, hiking trails. Open all year. No showers. Phone: (603) 447-5448.

CONWAY—Continued

WHITE MOUNTAIN NATIONAL FOREST (Covered Bridge Campground)—*From jct Hwy 16 & Hwy 112: Go 6 1/2 mi W on Hwy 112, then 1/3 mi SE on FR 60.* FACILITIES: 49 sites, 30 ft. max RV length, 49 no hookups, tenting available, non-flush toilets, handicap restroom facilities, tables, fire rings, grills. RECREATION: swimming, fishing, hiking trails. Open mid May through late Oct. No showers. Phone: (603) 447-5448.

WHITE MOUNTAIN NATIONAL FOREST (Passaconaway Campground)—*From jct Hwy 16 & Hwy 112: Go 14 1/3 mi W on Hwy 112.* FACILITIES: 33 sites, 30 ft. max RV length, 33 no hookups, tenting available, non-flush toilets, handicap restroom facilities, tables, fire rings. RECREATION: river fishing, hiking trails. Open mid May through late Oct. No showers. Phone: (603) 447-5448.

WHITE MOUNTAIN NATIONAL FOREST (White Ledge Campground)—*From jct Hwy 16 & Hwy 112: Go 5 mi SW on Hwy 16.* FACILITIES: 28 sites, 22 ft. max RV length, 28 no hookups, tenting available, non-flush toilets, handicap restroom facilities, tables, fire rings. RECREATION: hiking trails. Open mid May through mid Oct. No showers. Phone: (603) 447-5448.

## DERRY—F-4

**HIDDEN VALLEY RV & GOLF PARK**—Rural, rolling, wooded CAMPGROUND along large pond. *From jct I-93 (exit 4) & Hwy 102: Go 2 mi E on Hwy 102, then 4 1/2 mi E on East Derry Rd, then 1 mi N on Damren Rd.*

◆◆◆FACILITIES: 280 sites, most common site width 90 feet, 250 full hookups, 10 water & elec (20,30 & 50 amp receptacles), 20 no hookups, seasonal sites, a/c allowed ($), heater allowed ($), phone hookups, tenting available, group sites for tents/RVs, sewage disposal, public phone, limited grocery store, RV supplies, LP gas refill by weight,

DERRY—Continued
HIDDEN VALLEY RV & GOLF PARK—Continued

ice, tables, fire rings, wood, church services, traffic control gate.

◆◆◆RECREATION: rec room/area, coin games, lake/pond swimming, boating, electric motors only, canoeing, lake/pond fishing, golf ($), basketball hoop, playground, 2 shuffleboard courts, planned group activities, recreation director, badminton, horseshoes, hiking trails, volleyball.

Open May through Oct. Rate in 1995 $20-24 per family. Reservations recommended Jul through Aug. Master Card/Visa accepted. Member of ARVC; NE-HA-CA. Phone: (603) 887-3767.
**SEE AD THIS PAGE**

## DOVER—E-4

**OLD STAGE CAMPGROUND**—Rural area with shaded or open sites. *From jct Spaulding Tpk & Hwy 9 (exit 8W): Go 2/10 mi W on Hwy 9, then 1 6/10 mi N on Hwy 9, then 7/10 mi W on Old Stage Rd.*

◆◆◆FACILITIES: 127 sites, most common site width 35 feet, 81 full hookups, 46 water & elec (20 & 30 amp receptacles), seasonal sites, 6 pull-thrus, a/c allowed ($), heater allowed ($), tenting available, group sites for tents/RVs, sewage disposal, laundry, public phone, limited grocery store, RV supplies, ice, tables, fire rings, wood, traffic control gate.

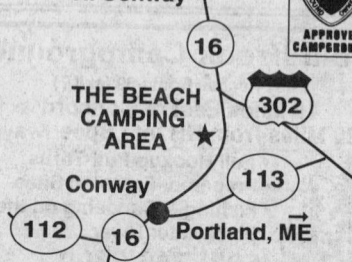

OLD STAGE CAMPGROUND—Continued on next page
DOVER—Continued on next page

DOVER—Continued
OLD STAGE CAMPGROUND—Continued

◆◆◆◆RECREATION: rec hall, rec room/area, coin games, swim pool, pond swimming, river/pond fishing, basketball hoop, 2 shuffleboard courts, planned group activities, movies, recreation director, badminton, sports field, horseshoes, volleyball.

Open May 10 through Oct 14. Rate in 1995 $22 per family. Reservations recommended Jul through Aug. Master Card/Visa accepted. Member of NE-HA-CA. Phone: (603) 742-4050.

**SEE AD THIS PAGE**

## EAST WAKEFIELD—D-4

**BEACHWOOD SHORES CAMPGROUND**—Large, sandy, shaded sites adjacent to a lake. *From jct Hwy 16 & Hwy 153N (Mountain Laurel Rd): Go 12 mi N on Hwy 153, then 2 mi W on Bonnymann Rd.*

◆◆FACILITIES: 87 sites, most common site width 40 feet, 87 full hookups, (20 & 30 amp receptacles), seasonal sites, a/c allowed ($), heater not allowed, phone hookups, tenting available, sewage disposal, laundry, public phone, limited grocery store, RV supplies, LP gas refill by weight, ice, tables, fire rings, grills, wood.

◆◆◆RECREATION: rec room/area, coin games, lake swimming, boating, canoeing, ramp, dock, 2 row/3 canoe boat rentals, water skiing, lake fishing, basketball hoop, planned group activities (weekends only), badminton, horseshoes, hiking trails, volleyball.

Open May 17 through Columbus Day. Rate in 1995 $18-22 per family. Discover/Master Card/Visa accepted. Member of ARVC; NE-HA-CA. Phone: (603) 539-4272.

**SEE AD THIS PAGE**

**LAKE IVANHOE CAMPGROUND**—Shaded sites among tall pines. *N'bound: From jct Hwy 16 & Hwy 153: Go 8 mi N on Hwy 153, then 1 2/10 mi E on Acton Ridge Rd. S'bound: From jct Hwy 16 & Mt. Laurel Rd (opposite Palmers Motel): Go 1/2 mi E on Mt. Laurel Rd, then 2 1/2 mi N on Hwy 153, then 1 2/10 mi E on Acton Ridge Rd.*

◆◆◆FACILITIES: 75 sites, most common site width 48 feet, 49 full hookups, 18 water & elec, 3 elec (15,20 & 30 amp receptacles), 5 no hookups, seasonal sites, 3 pull-thrus, a/c allowed ($), heater allowed ($), tenting available, group sites for tents/RVs, RV rentals, sewage disposal, laundry, public phone, limited grocery store, RV supplies, LP gas refill by weight, ice, tables, fire rings, wood.

◆◆◆◆RECREATION: rec hall, rec room/area, coin games, lake swimming, boating, canoeing, 3 canoe/2 pedal boat rentals, lake fishing, mini-golf ($), basketball hoop, 2 shuffleboard courts, badminton, sports field, horseshoes, volleyball.

Open mid May through Columbus Day. Rate in 1995 $19-25 for 2 persons. Reservations recommended Jul through Aug. Master Card/Visa accepted. Member of NE-HA-CA. Phone: (603) 522-8824.

**SEE AD THIS PAGE**

## EPSOM—E-4

**Blake's Brook Campground**—Wooded, natural sites at a brookside location in a rural area. *From jct Hwy 28 & US 4/202/Hwy 9 (Epsom Traffic Circle): Go 1 1/2 mi E on US 4/202/Hwy 9, then 1 1/2 mi S & 1/4 mi W follow signs.* ◆◆FACILITIES: 50 sites, most common site width 20 feet, 35 ft. max RV length, 33 full hookups, 12 water & elec, 5 elec (15 & 30 amp receptacles), seasonal sites, 3 pull-thrus, tenting available, sewage disposal, ice, tables, fire rings, wood. ◆◆RECREATION: rec room/area, swim pool, playground, horseshoes. Open May 1 through Oct 15. Rate in 1995 $18-20 per family. No refunds. Member of NE-HA-CA. Phone: (603) 736-4793.

**CIRCLE 9 RANCH**—CAMPGROUND with open grassy & shaded sites in a pine grove. *From jct US 4/202/Hwy 9 & Hwy 28 (Epsom Traffic Circle): Go 1/4 mi S on Hwy 28, then 200 yards W on Windymere Dr.*

◆◆◆FACILITIES: 145 sites, most common site width 20 feet, 60 full hookups, 85 water & elec (15,20 & 30 amp receptacles), seasonal sites, a/c allowed ($), heater allowed ($), phone hookups, tenting available, group sites for tents/RVs, RV rentals, sewage disposal, laundry, public phone, limited grocery store, RV supplies, ice, tables, fire rings, wood, traffic control gate.

◆◆◆◆RECREATION: rec hall, rec room/area, coin games, swim pool, whirlpool, pond/stream fishing, basketball hoop, playground, sports field, horseshoes, volleyball, cross country skiing.

Open all year. Rate in 1995 $23 per family. Reservations recommended Jun through Sep. Member of NE-HA-CA. Phone: (603) 736-9656.

**SEE AD THIS PAGE**

**EPSOM VALLEY CAMPGROUND**—Shaded or open, grassy sites beside a river. *From jct US 4/202 & Hwy 28: Go 1/4 mi N on Hwy 28.*

◆◆◆FACILITIES: 65 sites, most common site width 25 feet, 60 water & elec (15,20 & 30 amp receptacles), 5 no hookups, seasonal sites, 3 pull-thrus, a/c allowed ($), heater allowed ($), tenting available, group sites for tents/RVs, sewage disposal, public phone, ice, tables, fire rings, grills, wood.

◆◆RECREATION: river swimming, boating, canoeing, 3 canoe/1 pedal boat rentals, river fishing, basketball hoop, badminton, sports field, horseshoes, volleyball.

Open Memorial Day through Columbus Day. Rate in 1995 $16-18 per family. No refunds. Member of NE-HA-CA. Phone: (603) 736-9758.

**SEE AD THIS PAGE**

**Lazy River Camping Area**—CAMPGROUND with wooded & open sites beside a river. *From jct Hwys 4/202 & Hwy 28: Go 2 mi N on Hwy 28, then 1/2 mi E on Depot Rd.* ◆◆FACILITIES: 112 sites, most common site width 35 feet, 45 full hookups, 67 water & elec (15 & 20 amp receptacles), seasonal sites, 12 pull-thrus, tenting available, sewage disposal, laundry, public phone, ice, tables, fire rings, grills, wood. ◆◆◆RECREATION: rec room/area, swim pool, river swimming, canoeing, river fishing, playground, badminton, horseshoes, volleyball. Open May 1 through Oct 1. Rate in 1995 $20-22 per family. No refunds. Member of NE-HA-CA. Phone: (603) 798-5900.

## ERROL—B-4

MOLLIDGEWOCK STATE PARK—*From jct Hwy 26 & Hwy 16: Go 2 3/4 mi S on Hwy 16.* FACILITIES: 45 sites, 45 no hookups, tenting available, non-flush toilets, limited grocery store, ice, wood. RECREATION: river swimming, canoeing, river fishing. Open late May through mid Oct. Open weekends only May 26-Jun 23. No showers. Phone: (603) 482-3373.

**Umbagog Lake Campground**—CAMPGROUND with shaded, grassy lakeside sites and a separate wilderness area accessible only by boat. *From jct Hwy 16 & Hwy 26: Go 7 mi SE on Hwy 26.* ◆◆FACILITIES: 60 sites, most common site width 25 feet, 30 water & elec (15 amp receptacles), 30 no hookups, tenting available, sewage disposal, public phone, limited grocery store, ice, tables, fire rings, wood. ◆◆RECREATION: lake swimming, boating, canoeing, ramp, dock, 2 row/6 canoe boat rentals, lake fishing. Open Memorial Day through Sep 15. Rate in 1995 $18-22 per family. Member of NE-HA-CA. Phone: (603) 482-7795.

## EXETER—F-4

**THE EXETER ELMS FAMILY CAMPGROUND**—Wooded sites at a riverside location in a rural area. *From jct Hwy 111 & Hwy 108: Go 1 1/2 mi S on Hwy 108.*

◆◆◆FACILITIES: 200 sites, most common site width 50 feet, 81 full hookups, 52 water & elec (15,20 & 30 amp receptacles), 67 no hookups, seasonal sites, a/c allowed, heater allowed, tenting available, sewage disposal, laundry, public phone, grocery store, RV supplies, ice, tables, fire rings, wood, guard.

◆◆◆◆RECREATION: rec room/area, pavilion, coin games, swim pool, boating, no motors, canoeing, 6 canoe boat rentals, river fishing, basketball hoop, playground, shuffleboard court, planned group activities, movies, recreation director, badminton, horseshoes, volleyball.

Open May 15 through Sep 15. Facilities fully operational Memorial Day through Labor Day. Seasonal sites open May 1. Rate in 1995 $15-23 per family. No refunds. Reservations recommended Jul 1 through Aug 15. Master Card/Visa accepted. Member of NE-HA-CA. Phone: (603) 778-7631.

**SEE AD NEXT PAGE**

**The Green Gate Camping Area**—Rural CAMPGROUND with rustic, wooded sites. *From jct Hwy 111 & Hwy 108: Go 1 1/2 mi S on Hwy 108.* ◆◆FACILITIES: 118 sites, most common site width 25 feet, 96 full hookups, 22 water & elec (15 amp receptacles), seasonal

THE GREEN GATE CAMPING AREA—Continued on next page
EXETER—Continued on next page

EXETER—Continued
THE GREEN GATE CAMPING AREA—Continued

sites, tenting available, sewage disposal, laundry, public phone, ice, tables, fire rings, wood. ◆◆◆RECREATION: rec room/area, swim pool, boating, canoeing, 2 canoe boat rentals, river fishing, 2 shuffleboard courts, badminton, sports field, horseshoes, volleyball. No pets. Open May 1 through Oct 1. Facilities fully operational Memorial Day through Labor Day. Rate in 1995 $18.50-20.50 per family. No refunds. Member of NE-HA-CA. Phone: (603) 772-2100.

## FITZWILLIAM—F-2

**LAUREL LAKE CAMPGROUND**—Rural, rustic area near grassy, wooded lakeside. *From jct Hwy 12 & Hwy 119: Go 1 1/2 mi W on Hwy 119, then 1 1/2 mi S on East Lake Rd.*

◆◆FACILITIES: 65 sites, most common site width 40 feet, 32 ft. max RV length, 11 full hookups, 54 water & elec (15 & 20 amp receptacles), seasonal sites, a/c not allowed, heater not allowed, tenting available, group sites for tents, RV storage, sewage disposal, limited grocery store, ice, tables, fire rings, wood.

◆◆◆RECREATION: lake swimming, boating, canoeing, dock, water skiing, lake fishing, basketball hoop, sports field, horseshoes, volleyball.

Open May 15 through Oct 15. Rate in 1995 $17.90-19.90 per family. Reservations recommended Jul 1 through Labor Day. Member of NE-HA-CA. Phone: (603) 585-3304.

**SEE AD THIS PAGE**

NH Green Mountain State NH

**State Nicknames**

NH Granite State NH



## FRANCONIA—C-3

**CANNON AERIAL TRAMWAY/FRANCONIA NOTCH STATE PARK**—*From Franconia: Go 5 mi S on I-93/Franconia Notch Pkwy to exit 3.* Ride an 80-passenger cable car to the summit of 4200-ft Cannon Mountain for panoramic views of neighboring states and Canada. Gift shop, cafeteria and 2000-ft walking trails at the summit. Bike rentals at the base. Open mid May through late Oct. Phone: (603) 823-5563.

**SEE AD TRAVEL SECTION PAGE 530**

FRANCONIA NOTCH STATE PARK (Echo Lake RV Park)—*From Franconia: Go 5 mi S on I-93/Franconia Notch Pkwy to exit 3.* FACILITIES: 7 sites, most common site width 20 feet, accepts full hookup units only, 7 full hookups, (30 amp receptacles), public phone, tables. RECREATION: lake swimming, boating, canoeing, row/canoe/pedal boat rentals, lake fishing, hiking trails. No tents. Open all year. Facilities fully operational mid May through late Oct. Phone: (603) 823-5563.

FRANCONIA NOTCH STATE PARK (Lafayette Campground)—*No N'bound access. N'bound on I-93: turn around at Tramway exit 2, then go back 2 1/2 mi S on I-93. S'bound: At I-93 (Lafayette Place/Campground exit).* FACILITIES: 97 sites, 97 no hookups, tenting available, handicap restroom facilities, public phone, limited grocery store, ice, tables, grills, wood. RECREATION: swimming, boating, no motors, ramp, stream fishing, playground, hiking trails. No pets. Open all year. Facilities fully operational mid May through mid Oct. Phone: (603) 823-9513.

**Fransted Campground**—Rural, wooded & grassy with mountain view. *From jct I-93 (exit 38): Go 50 feet W, then 1 mi S on Hwy 18.* ◆◆FACILITIES: 96 sites, most common site width 30 feet, 26 full hookups, (20 & 30 amp receptacles), 70 no hookups, seasonal sites, tenting available, sewage disposal, laundry, public phone, limited grocery store, LP gas refill by weight, ice, tables, fire rings, wood. ◆◆RECREATION: stream fishing, mini-golf ($), badminton, horseshoes, volleyball. Open May 1 through Columbus Day. Rate in 1995 $15-18 for 2 persons. Member of NE-HA-CA. Phone: (603) 823-5675.

## FRANCONIA NOTCH—C-3

**THE FLUME/FRANCONIA NOTCH STATE PARK**—*Along Franconia Notch Parkway (Hwy 3) beginning at I-93 (exit 33).* Geological wonder- 800 feet chasm. Boardwalks offer closeup views. Souvenirs & cafeteria. Open all year. Phone: (603) 823-5563.

**SEE AD TRAVEL SECTION PAGE 530**

## FRANKLIN—E-3

**Pine Grove Campground**—Rural CAMPGROUND with open grassy sites. *From jct Hwy 11/US 3 & Hwy 3A: Go 5 mi N on Hwy 3A.* ◆◆◆FACILITIES: 29 sites, most common site width 25 feet, 7 full hookups, 11 water & elec (20 & 30 amp receptacles), 11 no hookups, seasonal sites, tenting available, sewage disposal, laundry, ice, tables, fire rings, wood. ◆◆RECREATION: pavilion, swim pool, playground, badminton, horseshoes, volleyball. Open May 15 through Oct 15. Rate in 1995 $14-18 for 2 persons. Member of NE-HA-CA. Phone: (603) 934-4582.

**THOUSAND ACRES FAMILY CAMPGROUND**—Level, wooded, hillside sites and grassy, open sites in a rural area. *S'bound: From jct I-93 (exit 20) & US 3: Go 10 mi S on US 3. N'bound: From jct I-93 (exit 17) & US 3: Go 10 mi N on US 3.*

◆◆◆FACILITIES: 150 sites, most common site width 40 feet, 47 full hookups, 74 water & elec (15,20 & 30 amp receptacles), 29 no hookups, seasonal sites, 7 pull-thrus, a/c allowed ($), heater allowed ($), tenting available, group sites for tents/RVs, sewage disposal, public phone, limited grocery store, ice, tables, wood.

◆◆◆RECREATION: rec hall, rec room/area, coin games, pond swimming, boating, no motors, canoeing, 2 canoe boat rentals, pond fishing, basketball hoop, playground, planned group activities, movies, badminton, sports field, horseshoes, hiking trails, volleyball.

Open May 15 through Oct 2. Rate in 1995 $20-24 for 2 persons. Reservations recommended Jul 1 through Sep 8. Discover/Master Card/Visa accepted. Member of NE-HA-CA. Phone: (603) 934-4440.

**SEE AD THIS PAGE**

## GILFORD—D-4

ELLACOYA STATE PARK—*From north jct Hwy 3 & Hwy 11: Go 5 mi S on Hwy 11.* FACILITIES: 38 sites, most common site width 50 feet, accepts full hookup units only, 38 full hookups, (30 amp receptacles), 5 pull-thrus, handicap restroom facilities, laundry, public phone, limited grocery store, ice, tables. RECREATION: lake swimming, lake fishing. Recreation open to the public. No pets. No tents/tent trailers. Open mid May through mid Oct. Phone: (603) 293-7821.

**GUNSTOCK (Belknap County Park)**—*From North edge of town: Go 1 mi N on Hwy 11B, then 3 1/2 mi E on Hwy 11A.* FACILITIES: 300 sites, most common site width 25 feet, 113 water & elec (20 & 30 amp receptacles), 187 no hookups, seasonal sites, 9 pull-thrus, a/c allowed, heater allowed, tenting available, group sites for tents/RVs, handicap restroom facilities, sewage disposal, laundry, public phone, grocery store, RV supplies, LP gas refill by weight, ice, tables, fire rings, grills, wood, traffic control gate/guard.

RECREATION: rec hall, rec room/area, pavilion, coin games, swim pool, 4 pedal boat rentals, pond fishing, basketball hoop, playground, planned group activities, badminton, sports field, horseshoes, hiking trails, volleyball, cross country skiing. Recreation open to the public.

Open Memorial Day through Columbus Day. Must be 21 to register. Winter camping mid Dec to mid Mar.

GUNSTOCK (BELKNAP COUNTY PARK)—Continued on next page
GILFORD—Continued on next page

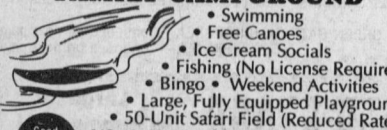

GILFORD—Continued
GUNSTOCK (BELKNAP COUNTY PARK)—Continued

No refunds. American Express/Discover/Master Card/Visa accepted. Member of NE-HA-CA. Phone: (800) GUNSTOCK.

**SEE AD THIS PAGE**

## GLEN—C-4

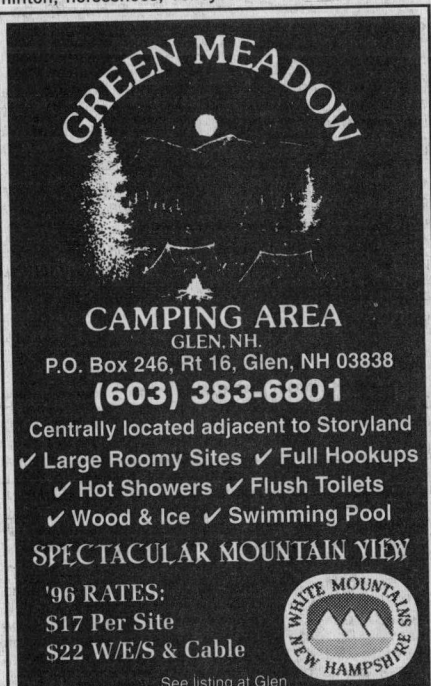

**GLEN ELLIS FAMILY CAMPGROUND**—Grassy & wooded, and some open sites, in a mountain meadow. *From north jct Hwy 16 & US 302: Go 1/4 mi W on US 302.*

WELCOME

◇◇◇FACILITIES: 182 sites, most common site width 50 feet, 99 water & elec (20 & 30 amp receptacles), 83 no hookups, seasonal sites, 15 pull-thrus, a/c allowed ($), heater allowed ($), tenting available, group sites for tents, sewage disposal, public phone, grocery store, RV supplies, ice, tables, fire rings, grills, wood, traffic control gate.

◇◇◇◇RECREATION: rec room/area, pavilion, coin games, swim pool, river swimming, boating, no motors, canoeing, river fishing, basketball hoop, playground, 2 shuffleboard courts, 2 tennis courts, badminton, sports field, horseshoes, volleyball.

Open Memorial Day through Columbus Day. Rate in 1995 $16-20 per family. Member of NE-HE-CA. Phone: (603) 383-4567.

**SEE AD NORTH CONWAY PAGE 548**

**GREEN MEADOW CAMPING AREA**—Grassy CAMPGROUND with mountain view. *From jct Hwy 302 & Hwy 16: Go 1/4 mi N on Hwy 16, then 1/4 mi E.*

WELCOME

◇◇◇FACILITIES: 93 sites, most common site width 25 feet, 31 full hookups, 32 water & elec (15 & 20 amp receptacles), 30 no hookups, seasonal sites, a/c not allowed, heater not allowed, cable TV ($), tenting available, sewage disposal, public phone, RV supplies, ice, tables, fire rings, grills, wood.

◇◇RECREATION: swim pool, basketball hoop, badminton, horseshoes, volleyball.

GLEN—Continued
GREEN MEADOW CAMPING AREA—Continued

Open all year. Rate in 1995 $15-20 for 4 persons. Master Card/Visa accepted. Member of NE-HA-CA. Phone: (603) 383-6801.

**SEE AD THIS PAGE**

**HERITAGE NEW HAMPSHIRE**—*From jct US 302 & Hwy 16: Go 1/2 mi N on Hwy 16.* A 3-Century journey backward tracing New Hampshire's history. Open Memorial Day through Late Oct. Phone: (603) 383-9776.

WELCOME

**SEE AD TRAVEL SECTION PAGE 530**

**STORY LAND**—*From jct US 302 & Hwy 16: Go 1/2 mi N on Hwy 16.* 13 theme rides in a story-book setting. Open Fathers Day through Labor Day. Weekends only Labor Day-Columbus Day. Phone: (603) 383-4293.

WELCOME

**SEE AD TRAVEL SECTION PAGE 530**

## GORHAM—C-4

MOOSE BROOK STATE PARK—*From jct Hwy 16 & US 2: Go 2 mi W off US 2.* FACILITIES: 42 sites, 42 no hookups, tenting available, public phone, limited grocery store, ice, tables, wood. RECREATION: swimming, stream fishing, hiking trails. Open May 28 through Labor Day. Open weekends only late May to mid Jun. Phone: (603) 466-3860.

**MT. WASHINGTON AUTO ROAD**—*Located at Rt 16 Pinkham Notch.* Scenic tollroad leading to the summit of Mt. Washington. Open Mid May through Late Oct. Phone: (603) 466-2222.

WELCOME

**SEE AD TRAVEL SECTION PAGE 530**

GORHAM—Continued

**TIMBERLAND CAMPING AREA**—Semi-wooded CAMPGROUND surrounded by mountains. *From east jct Hwy 16 & US 2: Go 5 mi E on US 2.*

WELCOME

◇◇◇◇FACILITIES: 113 sites, most common site width 20 feet, 41 full hookups, 37 water & elec (20,30 & 50 amp receptacles), 35 no hookups, seasonal sites, 20 pull-thrus, a/c allowed ($), heater allowed ($), cable TV, tenting available, sewage disposal, laundry, public phone, grocery store, RV supplies, ice, tables, fire rings, grills, wood, traffic control gate.

◇◇◇◇RECREATION: rec hall, rec room/area, coin games, swim pool, basketball hoop, playground, badminton, horseshoes, volleyball.

Open May 1 through Oct 25. Facilities fully operational Memorial Day through Oct 1. Rate in 1995 $15-20 for 2 persons. No refunds. Master Card/Visa accepted. Member of NE-HE-CA. Phone: (603) 466-3872.

**SEE AD THIS PAGE**

**WHITE BIRCHES CAMPING PARK**—Grassy, open and wooded CAMPGROUND beside highway in a mountain setting. *From east jct Hwy 16 & US 2: Go 1 1/2 mi E on US 2.*

WELCOME

◇◇◇FACILITIES: 102 sites, most common site width 25 feet, 30 full hookups, 25 water & elec (20 & 30 amp receptacles), 47 no hookups, seasonal sites, 13 pull-thrus, a/c allowed ($), heater allowed ($), tenting available, group sites for tents/

WHITE BIRCHES CAMPING PARK—Continued on next page
GORHAM—Continued on next page

GORHAM—Continued
WHITE BIRCHES CAMPING PARK—Continued

RVs, tent rentals, RV rentals, RV storage, sewage disposal, laundry, public phone, grocery store, RV supplies, LP gas refill by weight/by meter, ice, tables, fire rings, wood.

◆◆◆RECREATION: rec room/area, coin games, swim pool, basketball hoop, badminton, horseshoes, hiking trails, volleyball, snowmobile trails. Recreation open to the public.

Open all year. Facilities fully operational May 1 through Oct 30. Rate in 1995 $14-18 for 2 persons. No refunds. Master Card/Visa accepted. Member of NE-HA-CA. Phone: (603) 466-2022.

**SEE AD PAGE 541**

WHITE MOUNTAIN NATIONAL FOREST (Dolly Copp Campground)—*From jct US 2 & Hwy 16: Go 6 mi SW on Hwy 16.* FACILITIES: 176 sites, 32 ft. max RV length, 176 no hookups, tenting available, tables, fire rings. RECREATION: rec hall, river swimming, river fishing, hiking trails. Open mid May through mid Oct. No showers. Phone: (603) 466-2713.

## GOSHEN—E-2

**Rand Pond Campground**—Open grassy and semi-wooded sites beside a large lake. *From jct Hwy 10 & Hwy 11: Go 5 mi S on Hwy 10, then 2 1/2 mi E on Brook Rd.* ◆◆◆FACILITIES: 100 sites, most common site width 40 feet, 21 full hookups, 79 water & elec (20 amp receptacles), seasonal sites, 6 pull-thrus, tenting available, sewage disposal, laundry, public phone, grocery store, ice, tables, fire rings, grills, wood. ◆◆◆◆RECREATION: rec hall, rec room/area, lake swimming, boating, canoeing, ramp, dock, 6 row/3 canoe/3 pedal boat rentals, lake fishing, playground, 2 shuffleboard courts, badminton, sports field, horseshoes, volleyball. Open all year. Facilities fully operational Apr 30 through Oct 15. Rate in 1995 $17-20 for 2 persons. Member of NE-HA-CA. Phone: (603) 863-3350.

## GREENFIELD—F-3

GREENFIELD STATE PARK—*From jct Hwy 31 & Hwy 136: Go 1 mi W on Hwy 136.* FACILITIES: 252 sites, 252 no hookups, tenting available, sewage disposal, public phone, grocery store, tables. RECREATION: lake swimming, boating, canoeing, row/canoe boat rentals, lake/pond fishing, hiking trails. Open mid May through Columbus Day. Phone: (603) 547-3497.

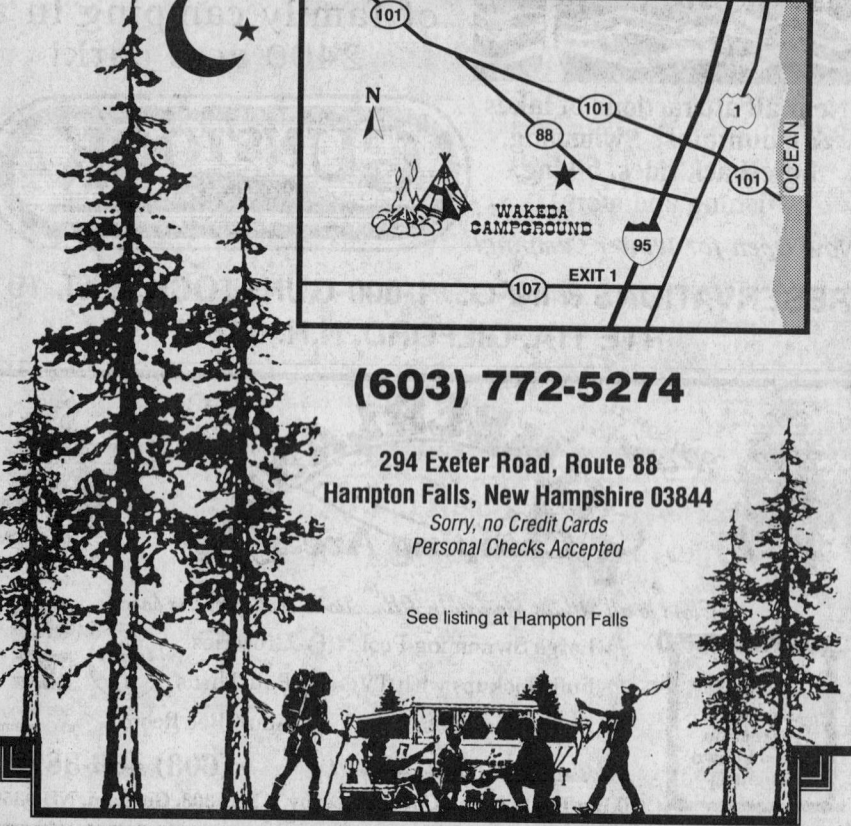



## HAMPTON—F-5

**Shel-Al Campground**—CAMPGROUND with level, open, grassy sites, partially shaded. *From jct Hwy 111 & US 1: Go 1/2 mi N on US 1.* ◆◆◆FACILITIES: 200 sites, most common site width 25 feet, 31 ft. max RV length, 68 full hookups, 66 elec (15 & 30 amp receptacles), 66 no hookups, seasonal sites, tenting available, public phone, limited grocery store, ice, tables, fire rings, grills, wood. ◆RECREATION: playground, shuffleboard court, horseshoes. Open May 15 through Oct 1. Rate in 1995 $12-18 for 2 persons. No refunds. Phone: (603) 964-5730.

**TIDEWATER CAMPGROUND**—Rural, rustic & shaded. *S'bound from jct Hwy 101 & US 1: Go 160 yards S on US 1. N'bound, second light after underpass.*

WELCOME

◆◆◆FACILITIES: 225 sites, most common site width 30 feet, 175 water & elec (15 & 30 amp receptacles), 50 no hookups, seasonal sites, a/c not allowed, heater not allowed, tenting available, sewage disposal, public phone, limited grocery store, RV supplies, ice, tables, fire rings, wood, traffic control gate.

◆◆◆RECREATION: rec room/area, coin games, swim pool, basketball hoop, playground, sports field, horseshoes.

No pets. Open May 15 through Oct 15. Rate in 1995 $20-22 per family. No refunds. Reservations recommended Jun through Aug. Master Card/Visa accepted. Member of NE-HA-CA. Phone: (603) 926-5474.

**SEE AD TRAVEL SECTION PAGE 533**

## HAMPTON BEACH—F-5

HAMPTON BEACH STATE PARK—*From jct I-95 (exit 2) & Hwy 51: Go 3 mi S on Hwy 51, then 1 mi S on Hwy 1A.* FACILITIES: 20 sites, most common site width 50 feet, accepts full hookup units only, 20 full hookups, (30 amp receptacles), handicap restroom facilities, public phone, ice. RECREATION: salt water swimming, salt water fishing. Recreation open to the public. No pets. No tents/tent trailers. Open mid May through mid Oct. Phone: (603) 926-3784.

## HAMPTON FALLS—F-5

**WAKEDA CAMPGROUND**—Level sites shaded by cathedral pines in a hilly, countryside location. *From jct US 1 & Hwy 88: Go 4 mi W on Hwy 88.*

WELCOME

◆◆◆FACILITIES: 320 sites, most common site width 35 feet, 225 water & elec (15,20 & 30 amp receptacles), 95 no hookups, seasonal sites, a/c allowed ($), heater allowed ($), tenting available, RV rentals, RV storage, sewage disposal, laundry, public phone, limited grocery store, ice, tables, fire rings, grills, wood, guard.

◆◆◆RECREATION: rec room/area, pavilion, coin games, mini-golf ($), basketball hoop, playground, badminton, horseshoes, volleyball.

Open May 15 through Oct 1. Rate in 1995 $17-21 per family. No refunds. Reservations recommended Jul 1 through Labor Day. Member of NE-HA-CA. Phone: (603) 772-5274.

**SEE AD THIS PAGE**

## HANCOCK—F-2

**Field 'N Forest Recreation Area**—Wooded, open & grassy sites in a CAMPGROUND near a pond. *From jct Hwy 123 & Hwy 137: Go 3 mi S on Hwy 137.* ◆◆FACILITIES: 40 sites, most common site width 30 feet, 8 water & elec (15 amp receptacles), 32 no hookups, seasonal sites, 8 pull-thrus, tenting available, sewage disposal, ice, tables, fire rings, grills, wood. ◆◆RECREATION: pond swimming, pond fishing, badminton, sports field, horseshoes, hiking trails, volleyball. Open Memorial Day through Labor Day. Rate in 1995 $18-20 for 2 persons. No refunds. Phone: (603) 525-3568.

**Seven Maples Camping Area**—Wooded, shaded CAMPGROUND in a rural area. *From jct Hwy 123 & Hwy 137: Go 1/2 mi N on Hwy 137, then 1/8 mi N on Longview Rd.* ◆◆FACILITIES: 100 sites, most common site width 20 feet, 80 water & elec (15 & 20 amp receptacles), 20 no hookups, seasonal sites, 10 pull-thrus, tenting available, sewage disposal, public phone, grocery store, LP gas refill by weight/by meter, ice, tables, fire rings, grills, wood. ◆◆◆RECREATION: rec hall, rec room/area, swim pool, pond fishing, playground, shuffleboard court, tennis court, badminton, sports field, horseshoes, hiking trails, volleyball. Open May 6 through Oct 12. Rate in 1995 $21-22 per family. No refunds. Member of NE-HA-CA. Phone: (603) 525-3321.

## HANOVER—D-2

**REST N' NEST**—*From jct I-91 (exit 13) & Hwy 10A: Go 9 mi N on I-91 (exit 14), then 200 feet E on Hwy 113, then 1/8 mi N on Latham Rd.*

WELCOME

**SEE PRIMARY LISTING AT THETFORD, VT AND AD TRAVEL SECTION, VT PAGE 847**

HANOVER—Continued on next page

HANOVER—Continued

**STORRS POND RECREATION AREA**—CAMPGROUND with secluded sites located close to Darmouth and the Appalachian Trail. *From jct I-89 & I-91 in VT: Go 5 mi N on I-91 (exit 13-Hanover, NH-Dartmouth College), then turn E and cross the Connecticut River into Hanover, NH (street becomes Wheelock St), 1 mi E on Wheelock St, 1 mi N on Hwy 10, then 1 mi E on Reservoir.*

WELCOME

◆◆◆FACILITIES: 33 sites, most common site width 45 feet, 15 water & elec (15,20 & 30 amp receptacles), 18 no hookups, a/c allowed, heater allowed, tenting available, handicap restroom facilities, sewage disposal, public phone, tables, fire rings, grills, wood.

◆◆◆RECREATION: equipped pavilion, swim pool, pond swimming, boating, no motors, pond fishing, basketball hoop, playground, 4 tennis courts, badminton, sports field, horseshoes, hiking trails, volleyball. Recreation open to the public.

Open May 15 through Sep 30. Facilities fully operational Memorial Day through Labor Day. Rate in 1995 $12-22 per family. Reservations recommended Memorial Day through Labor Day. Member of NE-HA-CA. Phone: (603) 643-2134.

**SEE AD THIS PAGE**

## HENNIKER—E-3

**Keyser Pond Campground**—Wooded CAMPGROUND with terraced sites. *At jct of Hwy 202 & Hwy 127.* ◆◆◆FACILITIES: 116 sites, most common site width 50 feet, 107 water & elec (15 & 20 amp receptacles), 9 no hookups, seasonal sites, tenting available, sewage disposal, laundry, public phone, limited grocery store, LP gas refill by weight, ice, tables, fire rings, wood. ◆◆◆◆RECREATION: rec hall, pond swimming, boating, electric motors only, canoeing, 3 row/6 canoe/4 pedal boat rentals, river/pond fishing, mini-golf ($), playground, 3 shuffleboard courts, badminton, horseshoes, volleyball. Open May 15 through Columbus Day. Rate in 1995 $18-20 per family. No refunds. Member of NE-HA-CA. Phone: (603) 428-7741.

**MILE AWAY CAMPGROUND**—Rural, wooded CAMPGROUND. *From jct I-89 (exit 5) & Hwy 202: Go 5 mi W on Hwy 202, then 1 mi NE on Old West Hopkinton Rd.*

WELCOME

◆◆◆◆FACILITIES: 190 sites, most common site width 35 feet, 53 full hookups, 131 water & elec (20 & 30 amp receptacles), 6 no hookups, seasonal sites, 2 pull-thrus, a/c allowed ($), heater allowed ($), phone hookups, tenting available, group sites for tents/RVs, handicap restroom facilities, sewage disposal, laundry, public phone, limited grocery store, RV supplies, LP gas refill by weight/by meter, ice, tables, fire rings, wood.

◆◆◆◆RECREATION: rec hall, rec room/area, equipped pavilion, coin games, pond swimming, boating, 6 hp limit, canoeing, ramp, dock, 1 row/3

HENNIKER—Continued
MILE AWAY CAMPGROUND—Continued

canoe/3 pedal boat rentals, pond fishing, mini-golf ($), basketball hoop, 2 shuffleboard courts, planned group activities (weekends only), badminton, horseshoes, hiking trails, volleyball, cross country skiing, snowmobile trails.

Open all year. Facilities fully operational May 1 through Oct 31. Rate in 1995 $24-28 per family. Reservations recommended Jul through Aug. Discover/Master Card/Visa accepted. Member of NE-HA-CA. Phone: (603) 428-7616.

**SEE AD THIS PAGE**

## HILLSBORO—E-3

**OXBOW CAMPGROUND**—Rolling terrain with level, wooded or open sites. *From jct US 202 & Hwy 149: Go 3/4 mi S on Hwy 149.*

WELCOME

◆◆◆FACILITIES: 74 sites, most common site width 35 feet, 60 full hookups, 5 elec (20 & 30 amp receptacles), 9 no hookups, seasonal sites, 6 pull-thrus, a/c allowed ($), heater not allowed, cable TV ($), phone hookups, tenting available, RV storage, laundry, public phone, ice, tables, fire rings, grills, wood.

◆◆◆◆RECREATION: rec hall, rec room/area, pavilion, pond swimming, basketball hoop, shuffleboard court, planned group activities (weekends only), badminton, sports field, horseshoes, hiking trails, volleyball.

Open May 15 through Oct 15. Rate in 1995 $16-21 per family. Reservations recommended Jul through Aug. Master Card/Visa accepted. Member of NE-HA-CA. Phone: (603) 464-5952.

**SEE AD THIS PAGE**

## HOLDERNESS—D-3

**BETHEL WOODS CAMPGROUND**—Natural, wooded sites in a rural CAMPGROUND currently accepting overnighters. *From jct Hwy 113 & US 3/Hwy 25: Go 3 mi E & S on US 3/Hwy 25.*

WELCOME

◆◆FACILITIES: 95 sites, most common site width 50 feet, 35 ft. max RV length, 50 water & elec (15 & 30 amp receptacles), 45 no hookups, seasonal sites, a/c allowed, heater allowed, tenting available, group sites for tents/RVs, RV rentals, RV storage, sewage disposal, laundry, public phone, limited grocery store, RV supplies, LP gas refill by weight/by meter, ice, tables, fire rings, wood, church services, traffic control gate.

HOLDERNESS—Continued
BETHEL WOODS CAMPGROUND—Continued

◆◆◆RECREATION: rec room/area, coin games, swim pool, sauna, whirlpool, putting green, basketball hoop, planned group activities (weekends only), badminton, horseshoes, volleyball.

Open May 15 through Oct 15. Rate in 1995 $18 for 2 persons. Reservations recommended all season. Master Card/Visa accepted. Member of ARVC; NE-HA-CA. Phone: (603) 279-6266.

**SEE AD THIS PAGE**

**Squam Lakes Marina & Camp Resort**—Shaded sites on a terraced hillside. *From jct Hwy 113 & US 3/Hwy 25: Go 1/2 mi W & S on US 3/Hwy 25.* ◆◆◆FACILITIES: 119 sites, most common site width 30 feet, 66 full hookups, 41 water & elec (20,30 & 50 amp receptacles), 12 no hookups, seasonal sites, 1 pull-thrus, tenting available, sewage disposal, laundry, public phone, limited grocery store, LP gas refill by weight/by meter, ice, tables, fire rings, grills, wood. ◆◆◆◆RECREATION: rec hall, rec room/area, swim pool, lake swimming, boating, canoeing, dock, 8 canoe/12 motor boat rentals, lake fishing, playground, hiking trails. Open all year. Facilities fully operational May 15 through Oct 15. Rate in 1995 $18-26 for 2 persons. Member of NE-HA-CA. Phone: (603) 968-7227.

NH STATE AMPHIBIAN: RED SPOTTED NEWT NH

## JAFFREY—F-2

MONADNOCK STATE PARK—*From town: Go 4 mi W on Hwy 124.* FACILITIES: 21 sites, 21 no hookups, tenting available, non-flush toilets, tables. RECREATION: hiking trails. No pets. Open all year. No showers. Phone: (603) 532-8862.

## JEFFERSON—C-3

**The Lantern Campground**—CAMPGROUND with open, grassy sites. *From jct Hwy 116 & US 2: Go 1/2 mi W on US 2.* ◊◊FACILITIES: 64 sites, most common site width 20 feet, 23 full hookups, 30 water & elec (15,20 & 30 amp receptacles), 11 no hookups, 7 pull-thrus, tenting available, sewage disposal, laundry, public phone, grocery store, ice, tables, fire rings, grills, wood. ◊◊RECREATION: rec room/area, swim pool, playground, badminton, horseshoes, volleyball. Open May 1 through Oct 15. Rate in 1995 $18-20 for 4 persons. Member of NE-HA-CA. Phone: (603) 586-7151.



▸ **SANTA'S VILLAGE**—*From jct Hwy 116 & US 2: Go 1/2 mi N on US 2.* Visit Santa's summer home & enjoy all his special rides-Reindeer Carousel, Sleigh Ride, Log Flume & more. Rides for all ages. Take in special shows including the Live Tropical Birds. See Santa's elves & reindeer. Also, snack bar, bake shop & 8 gift shops. Open Father's Day through Oct 15. Phone: (603) 586-4445.

**SEE AD TRAVEL SECTION PAGE 530**

## JEFFERSON HIGHLANDS—C-3

**JEFFERSON CAMPGROUND**—Scenic area with mostly open sites away from highway. *From jct Hwy 115 & US 2: Go 1/2 mi NW on US 2.*

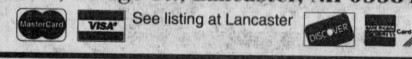

◊◊FACILITIES: 100 sites, most common site width 20 feet, 32 full hookups, 25 water & elec (15,20 & 30 amp receptacles), 43 no hookups, seasonal sites, 83 pull-thrus, a/c allowed ($), heater allowed ($), tenting available, group sites for tents/RVs, handicap restroom facilities, sewage disposal, laundry, limited grocery store, RV supplies, LP gas refill by weight/by meter, ice, tables, fire rings, grills, wood.

◊◊RECREATION: swim pool, basketball hoop, badminton, horseshoes, volleyball.

Open Memorial Day through Labor Day. Rate in 1995 $12-14 for 4 persons. No refunds. Member of NE-HA-CA. Phone: (603) 586-4510.

**SEE AD THIS PAGE**

✲ **JEFFERSON CAMPGROUND RECREATIONAL VEHICLE SALES & SERVICE**—*From jct Hwy 115 & US 2: Go 1/2 mi NW on US 2.* SALES: fold-down camping trailers. SERVICES: RV towing, LP gas refill by weight/by meter, sewage disposal, sells parts/accessories, installs hitches. Open Memorial Day through Labor Day. Phone: (603) 586-4510.

**SEE AD THIS PAGE**

▸ **SIX GUN CITY**—*From jct Hwy 115 & US 2: Go 1/2 mi NW on US 2.* Old West adventure with the Homestead, Fort, Indian Camp, Main St, horse drawn vehicles, antiques and Miniature Ranch animals. Enjoy Cowboy skits, Frontier show, rides (horse, pony or burro) & miniature golf. Also, gift shop, General Store & snack bar. Open May through Oct. Phone: (603) 586-4592.

**SEE AD TRAVEL SECTION PAGE 530**

## KEENE—F-2

**Surry Mountain Camping Area**—Wooded CAMPGROUND in rural area surrounded by Federal recreation land. *From jct Hwy 12 & Hwy 12A: Go 4 mi N on Hwy 12A, then 1/4 mi E & S on entry road.* ◊FACILITIES: 43 sites, most common site width 50 feet, 38 water & elec (20 amp receptacles), 5 no hookups, seasonal sites, 8 pull-thrus, tenting available, portable dump, public phone, ice, tables, fire rings, grills, wood. ◊◊RECREATION: lake swimming, boating, canoeing, ramp, lake fishing, horseshoes, hiking trails, volleyball. Open May 15 through Oct 15. Rate in 1995 $17-19 per family. Phone: (603) 352-9770.



**Swanzey Lake Camping Area**—Mostly wooded CAMPGROUND featuring a crystal clear lake. *From jct Hwys 12 & 32: Go 5 mi S on Hwy 32, then 2 mi SW on Swanzey Lake Rd, then 1/2 mi N on East Shore Rd.* ◊◊FACILITIES: 75 sites, most common site width 75 feet, 35 ft. max RV length, 30 full hookups, 10 water & elec, 5 elec (15,20 & 30 amp receptacles), 30 no hookups, seasonal sites, tenting available, non-flush toilets, sewage disposal, public phone, ice, tables, fire rings, wood. ◊◊RECREATION: lake swimming, boating, canoeing, lake fishing, volleyball. No pets. Open mid May through mid Oct. Pets welcome before Memorial Day & after Labor Day. Rate in 1995 $15-21 for 2 persons. Phone: (603) 352-9880.

## LACONIA—E-3

**SILVER LAKE PARK CAMPGROUND**—CAMPGROUND with terraced sites overlooking beach. *From jct I-93 (exit 20) & US 3: Go 2 mi N on US 3, then 1 mi S on Silver Lake Rd. Alternate directions for longer RV's: exit 20 Route 140E, left on Jamestown Rd.*

◊◊◊FACILITIES: 77 sites, most common site width 25 feet, 30 ft. max RV length, 70 full hookups, 5 water & elec (20 amp receptacles), 2 no hookups, seasonal sites, 4 pull-thrus, a/c allowed ($), heater allowed ($), cable TV ($), tenting available, tent rentals, RV rentals, sewage disposal, laundry, public phone, ice, tables, fire rings, wood, traffic control gate.

◊◊◊RECREATION: rec room/area, coin games, lake swimming, boating, canoeing, ramp, dock, 2 canoe/2 pedal boat rentals, water skiing, lake fishing, badminton, horseshoes, volleyball.

No pets. Open May 7 through Columbus Day. Rate in 1995 $18-23 for 2 persons. Reservations recommended Jul through Labor Day. Master Card/Visa accepted. Member of NE-HA-CA. Phone: (603) 524-6289.

**SEE AD THIS PAGE**

## LANCASTER—B-3

**BEAVER TRAILS CAMPGROUND** (TOO NEW TO RATE)—Partially shaded, grassy sites in a riverside meadow. *From jct US 3 & Hwy 2: Go 3/4 mi W on Hwy 2 (at Vermont state line).*

FACILITIES: 46 sites, 40 full hookups, 6 elec (15,20,30 & 50 amp receptacles), seasonal sites, 10 pull-thrus, a/c allowed, heater allowed, tenting available, RV storage, sewage disposal, public phone, grocery store, LP gas refill by weight/by meter, gasoline, ice, tables, fire rings, wood.

RECREATION: swim pool, boating, canoeing, river fishing, horseshoes, volleyball.

Open May 1 through Oct 31. Rate in 1995 $19.95 per vehicle. American Express/Discover/Master Card/Visa accepted. Phone: (603) 788-3815.

**SEE AD THIS PAGE**

**MOUNTAIN LAKE CAMPGROUND**—CAMPGROUND overlooking mountain lake with sunny and shaded, privately divided sites. *From east jct US 2 & US 3: Go 3 mi S on US 3.*

◊◊◊FACILITIES: 97 sites, most common site width 30 feet, 28 full hookups, 69 water & elec (20 & 30 amp receptacles), seasonal sites, 12 pull-thrus, a/c allowed ($), heater allowed ($), cable TV, tenting available, cabins, sewage disposal, laundry, public phone, grocery store, RV supplies, LP gas refill by weight/by meter, ice, tables, fire rings, wood.

◊◊◊RECREATION: rec hall, coin games, swim pool (heated), lake swimming, boating, canoeing, dock, 2 row/3 canoe/4 pedal boat rentals, lake fishing, basketball hoop, playground, badminton, horseshoes, volleyball.

Open May 1 through Oct 31. Rate in 1995 $16.50-20 per family. No refunds. Master Card/Visa accepted. Member of NE-HA-CA. Phone: (603) 788-4509.

**SEE AD THIS PAGE**

**ROGER'S CAMPGROUND**—Semi-wooded with grassy sites away from main highway. *From jct US 3 & US 2: Go 1 1/2 mi E on US 2.*

◊◊◊◊FACILITIES: 404 sites, most common site width 30 feet, 304 full hookups, 40 water & elec, 20 elec (20 & 30 amp receptacles), 40 no hookups, seasonal sites, 304 pull-thrus, a/c allowed ($), heater allowed ($), phone hookups, tenting available, group sites for tents/RVs, RV storage, handicap restroom facilities, sewage disposal, laundry, public phone, full service store, RV

ROGER'S CAMPGROUND—Continued on next page
LANCASTER—Continued on next page

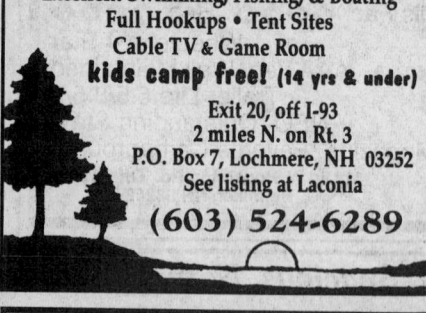

LANCASTER—Continued
ROGER'S CAMPGROUND—Continued

supplies, LP gas refill by weight/by meter, ice, tables, fire rings, grills, wood, traffic control gate.

◆◆◆◆RECREATION: rec hall, rec room/area, equipped pavilion, coin games, 2 swim pools, wading pool, whirlpool, water slide ($), mini-golf ($), basketball hoop, playground, 4 shuffleboard courts, planned group activities (weekends only), tennis court, badminton, sports field, horseshoes, hiking trails, volleyball.

Open Apr 15 through Oct 20. Facilities fully operational Memorial Day through Labor Day. Rate in 1995 $17-19 for 2 persons. Reservations recommended Jul 1 through Labor Day. Member of NE-HA-CA. Phone: (603) 788-4885.
SEE AD THIS PAGE

## LEBANON—D-2

**MASCOMA LAKE CAMPING AREA**—CAMPGROUND with terraced sites overlooking a lake. *From I-89 (exit 17): Go 2 mi E on US 4, then 7/10 mi S on US 4A.*

◆◆◆FACILITIES: 90 sites, most common site width 35 feet, 46 full hookups, 26 water & elec (20 amp receptacles), 18 no hookups, seasonal sites, 2 pull-thrus, a/c allowed ($), heater allowed ($), tenting available, sewage disposal, laundry, public phone, limited grocery store, RV supplies, LP gas refill by weight/by meter, ice, tables, fire rings, wood.

◆◆◆RECREATION: rec hall, rec room/area, coin games, lake swimming, boating, canoeing, dock, 1 row/1 canoe/1 pedal boat rentals, lake fishing, basketball hoop, playground, horseshoes, volleyball.

Open mid May through mid Oct. Rate in 1995 $19-20 per family. Master Card/Visa accepted. Member of NE-HA-CA. Phone: (603) 448-5076.
SEE AD THIS PAGE

**PINE VALLEY RV RESORT**—*From I-89 (exit 18) Lebanon, NH: Go 10 mi N on I-89 to exit 1 (White River Junction, VT), then 1/2 mi W on US 4.*
**SEE PRIMARY LISTING AT QUECHEE, VT AND AD QUECHEE, VT PAGE 855**

## LEE—E-4

**Ferndale Acres Campground**—Rural, riverside, location with wooded sites. *From jct US 4 & Hwy 155: Go 2 1/2 mi S on Hwy 155, then 1 1/2 mi E on Wednesday Hill Rd, then 3/4 mi S on entry road.* ◆◆FACILITIES: 130 sites, most common site width 25 feet, 50 full hookups, 80 water & elec (15 amp receptacles), seasonal sites, 20 pull-thrus, tenting available, handicap restroom facilities, sewage disposal, laundry, public phone, limited grocery store, ice, tables, fire rings, wood. ◆◆◆◆RECREATION: rec hall, rec room/area, swim pool, river swimming, canoeing, river fishing, playground, planned group activities (weekends only), badminton, sports field, horseshoes. Open May 15 through Sep 15. Rates available upon request. No refunds. Member of NE-HA-CA. Phone: (603) 659-5082.

**Forest Glen**—CAMPGROUND with wooded sites. *From jct US 4 & Hwy 155: Go 1 3/4 mi S on Hwy 155.* ◆◆FACILITIES: 130 sites, 130 water & elec (30 amp receptacles), seasonal sites, tenting available, sewage disposal, public phone, LP gas refill by weight/by meter, ice, tables, fire rings, wood. ◆◆◆RECREATION: rec hall, lake swimming, boating, canoeing, lake fishing, badminton, sports field, horseshoes, volleyball. Open May 1 through Oct 1. Rate in 1995 $18 per family. Member of NE-HA-CA. Phone: (603) 659-3416.

**Lamprey River Campground**—Open, grassy & wooded sites at a rustic, rural location. *From jct Hwy 125 & Hwy 152: Go 1 8/10 mi E on Hwy 152, then 2/10 mi S on Campground Rd.* ◆◆FACILITIES: 99 sites, most common site width 30 feet, 89 water & elec (20 amp receptacles), 10 no hookups, seasonal sites, tenting available, sewage disposal, laundry, public phone, limited grocery store, LP gas refill by weight, ice, tables, fire rings, wood. ◆◆◆RECREATION: rec hall, rec room/area, swim pool, river swimming, canoeing, 2 canoe boat rentals, river fishing, planned group activities (weekends only), badminton, sports field, horseshoes, volleyball. Open May 15 through Oct 15. Facilities fully operational Memorial Day through Labor Day. Rate in 1995 $18-20 per family. Member of NE-HA-CA. Phone: (603) 659-3852.

## LINCOLN—C-3

**Cold Spring Camp**—CAMPGROUND with grassy sites. *From jct I-93 (exit 33) & US 3: Go 1/2 mi S on US 3.* ◆◆FACILITIES: 37 sites, most common site width 20 feet, 32 ft. max RV length, 5 full hookups, 12 water & elec (15 amp receptacles), 20 no hookups, seasonal sites, tenting available, tables, fire rings, grills, wood. RECREATION: river fishing. Open Apr 15 through Oct 15. Rate in 1995 $14-17 per family. Phone: (603) 745-8351.

LINCOLN—Continued

**LOON MOUNTAIN PARK**—*From jct I-93 (exit 32) & Kancamagus Hwy: Go 3 mi E on Kancamagus Hwy.* The state's longest aerial ride- 7,000 feet to the summit. Cafeteria, observation tower, nature walks & crafts barn. Open all year. Phone: (603) 745-8111.
**SEE AD TRAVEL SECTION PAGE 530**

**THE WHALE'S TALE WATER PARK**—*From jct I-93 (exit 33) & US 3: Go 1 mi N on US 3.* Whale's Tale Water Park includes wave pool, slides, float rides & special activity pool for your enjoyment. Open Jun 25 through Labor Day. Weekends May 28 thru Jun 19. Phone: (603) 745-8810.
**SEE AD TRAVEL SECTION PAGE 530**

WHITE MOUNTAIN NATIONAL FOREST (Big Rock Campground)—*From jct US 3 & FH 112: Go 8 mi E on FH 112 (Kancamagus Hwy).* FACILITIES: 28 sites, 30 ft. max RV length, 28 no hookups, tenting available, non-flush toilets, tables, fire rings. RECREATION: fishing, hiking trails. Open all year. No showers. Phone: (603) 536-1310.

WHITE MOUNTAIN NATIONAL FOREST (Hancock Campground)—*From jct US 3 & Hwy 112: Go 4 mi E on Hwy 112 (Kancamagus Scenic Hwy).* FACILITIES: 56 sites, 30 ft. max RV length, 56 no hookups, tenting available, non-flush toilets, tables, fire rings, grills. RECREATION: fishing, hiking trails. Open all year. No showers. Campground not plowed in winter. Phone: (603) 536-1310.

## LISBON—C-3

**Mink Brooke Family Campground**—Rural with shaded & open sites. *From jct Hwy 117 & US 302: Go 1 1/4 mi SW on US 302.* ◆◆ FACILITIES: 54 sites, most common site width 15 feet, 26 water & elec (15 amp receptacles), 28 no hookups, 6 pull-thrus, tenting available, sewage disposal, public phone, limited grocery store, ice, tables, fire rings, grills, wood. ◆◆◆RECREATION: rec hall, swim pool, playground, badminton, horseshoes, volleyball. Open May 10 through Oct 12. Pool open Memorial Day thru Labor Day. Rate in 1995 $17-20 for 2 persons. Member of NE-HA-CA. Phone: (603) 838-6658.

## LITTLETON—C-3

**CRAZY HORSE CAMPGROUND**—CAMPGROUND with open & shaded sites in a rural setting. *From jct I-93 (exit 43) & Hwy 135: Go 100 yards E on Hwy 135, then 1 1/4 mi SW on Hwy 135/18, then 1 1/4 mi N on Hilltop Rd.*

◆◆◆FACILITIES: 150 sites, most common site width 24 feet, 17 full hookups, 83 water & elec (20,30 & 50 amp receptacles), 50 no hookups, seasonal sites, 10 pull-thrus, a/c allowed, heater allowed, phone hookups, tenting available, group sites for tents/RVs, RV rentals, RV storage, sewage disposal, laundry, limited grocery store, RV supplies, LP gas refill by weight/by meter, ice, tables, fire rings, grills, wood.

◆◆◆RECREATION: rec room/area, pavilion, coin games, swim pool, boating, canoeing, 6 canoe/1 pedal boat rentals, badminton, sports field, horseshoes, volleyball, cross country skiing, snowmobile trails.

Open all year. Rate in 1995 $16-20 per family. Master Card/Visa accepted. Member of NE-HA-CA. Phone: (800) 639-4107.
SEE AD NEXT PAGE

LITTLETON—Continued on next page

Close to I-89 but Country Quiet
Overlooking the Lake

• New 30 Amps
• Seasonal Sites Available
• Lake Swimming
• Sandy Beach • Store

Close to Shopping & Restaurants

Your Hosts: Jean & Gene Dinsmore

(603) 448-5076
Reservations:
(800) 769-7861

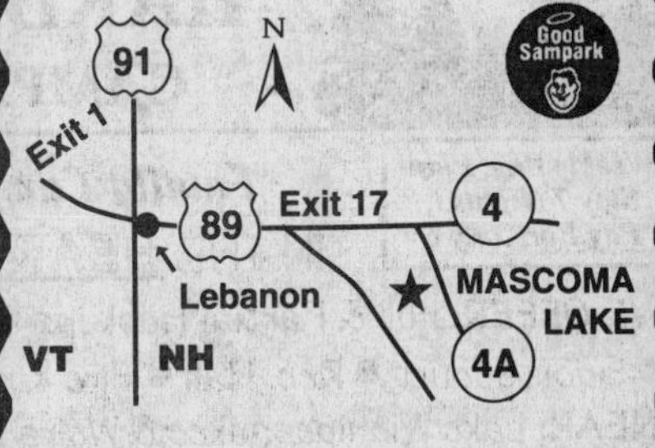


RFD 2, Box 331, Enfield, NH 03748
See listings at Lebanon, NH and Quechee, VT

# ROGER'S CAMPGROUND

YOUR WHITE MOUTAINS FAMILY CAMPING RESORT

• Swimming Pools • Tennis Court • Store • Heated Restroom
• 304 Pull-Thru Sites with Water, Elec. & Sewer • 100 Tent Sites
• Water Slide • Mini-Golf • Laundromat • LP Gas (metered)
• Whirlpool • Rally Pavilion • Large Groups Welcome

Please Call or Write:

RFD #2, BOX 474
LANCASTER, NH 03584

603-788-4885 (SUMMER)
813-368-6741 (WINTER)

FALL FOLIAGE TOURING AT ITS BEST

LITTLETON—Continued

**KOA-Littleton/Lisbon**—Rural, riverside CAMPGROUND with open & shaded, grassy sites. *From jct I-93 (exit 42) & US 302: Go 5 1/2 mi W on Hwy 302.*

◇◇◇◇FACILITIES: 60 sites, most common site width 34 feet, 12 full hookups, 29 water & elec (20 & 30 amp receptacles), 19 no hookups, 20 pull-thrus, tenting available, sewage disposal, laundry, public phone, grocery store, LP gas refill by weight/by meter, ice, tables, fire rings, grills, wood. ◇◇◇RECREATION: rec room/area, swim pool (heated), river fishing, playground, badminton, horseshoes, volleyball. Open May 5 through Oct 14. Facilities fully operational Memorial Day through Labor Day. Rate in 1995 $24-26 for 2 persons. Member of NE-HA-CA. Phone: (603) 838-5525. KOA 10% value card discount.

## LOUDON—E-4

**CIRCLE 9 RANCH**—*About 15 minutes from NH Int'l Speedway: Go 4 mi S on Hwy 106, then left 5 mi on Chichester Rd, then left 3 mi on Hwy 9 to Epsom Traffic Circle, then 1/4 mi S on Hwy 28, then 200 yards W on Windymere Dr.*

WELCOME

**SEE PRIMARY LISTING AT EPSOM AND AD EPSOM PAGE 539**

## MEREDITH—D-3

**CLEARWATER CAMPGROUND**—CAMPGROUND on a lake with wooded sites. *From jct I-93 (exit 23) & Hwy 104: Go 3 mi E on Hwy 104.*

WELCOME

◇◇◇FACILITIES: 153 sites, most common site width 25 feet, 144 water & elec (20 & 30 amp receptacles), 9 no hookups, seasonal sites, 5 pull-thrus, a/c allowed, heater allowed, tenting available, RV rentals, sewage disposal, laundry, public phone, grocery store, RV supplies, ice, tables, fire rings, wood, traffic control gate.

◇◇◇◇◇RECREATION: rec room/area, equipped pavilion, coin games, lake swimming, boating, canoeing, ramp, dock, 2 row/2 canoe/2 pedal boat rentals, water skiing, lake fishing, basketball hoop, playground, 2 shuffleboard courts, planned group activities, recreation director, badminton, sports field, horseshoes, volleyball.

Open May 20 through Oct 11. Rate in 1995 $28-29 per family. Reservations recommended Jul through Aug. American Express/Discover/Master Card/Visa accepted. Member of ARVC; NE-HA-CA. Phone: (603) 279-7761.

**SEE AD THIS PAGE**

**HARBOR HILL CAMPING AREA**—Rural, wooded CAMPGROUND. *From jct US 3 & Hwy 25: Go 2 mi E on Hwy 25.*

WELCOME

◇◇◇FACILITIES: 140 sites, most common site width 25 feet, 81 full hookups, 26 water & elec (15,20 & 30 amp receptacles), 33 no hookups, seasonal sites, 3 pull-thrus, a/c allowed ($), heater not allowed, phone hookups, tenting available, group sites for tents/RVs, RV rentals, cabins, sewage disposal, laundry, public phone, grocery store, RV supplies, LP gas refill by weight/by meter, ice, tables, fire rings, wood, traffic control gate.

◇◇◇RECREATION: rec hall, coin games, swim pool, basketball hoop, playground, shuffleboard court, badminton, horseshoes, volleyball.

Open May 13 through Columbus Day. Rate in 1995 $22-24 for 2 persons. No refunds. Reservations recommended Jun 15 through Labor Day. Discover/Master Card/Visa accepted. Member of ARVC; NE-HA-CA. Phone: (603) 279-6910.

**SEE AD THIS PAGE**

MEREDITH—Continued on next page

MEREDITH—Continued

► **HART'S TURKEY FARM RESTAURANT**—*At jct US 3 & Hwy 104.* Largest lake-region restaurant featuring turkey, prime rib, steaks & seafood. Serving breakfast, lunch & dinner. Open all year. American Express/Diners Club/Discover/Master Card/Visa accepted. Phone: (603) 279-6212.
**SEE AD TRAVEL SECTION PAGE 533**

**MEREDITH WOODS 4 SEASON CAMPING AREA**—RV PARK with large, private treed sites. *From jct I-93 (exit 23) & Hwy 104: Go 3 mi E on Hwy 104.*

◆◆◆FACILITIES: 64 sites, most common site width 30 feet, 64 full hookups, (20,30 & 50 amp receptacles), seasonal sites, a/c allowed, heater allowed, cable TV, phone hookups, tenting available, RV rentals, handicap restroom facilities, laundry, public phone, limited grocery store, RV supplies, ice, tables, fire rings, wood, traffic control gate.

◆◆◆◆RECREATION: rec hall, rec room/area, equipped pavilion, coin games, swim pool (indoor) (heated), lake swimming, whirlpool, boating, canoeing, ramp, dock, 2 row/2 canoe/2 pedal boat rentals, water skiing, lake fishing, basketball hoop, playground, 2 shuffleboard courts, planned group activities, recreation director, badminton, sports field, horseshoes, volleyball, cross country skiing, snowmobile trails.

Open all year. Rate in 1995 $20-32 per family. American Express/Discover/Master Card/Visa accepted. Member of ARVC; NE-HA-CA. Phone: (603) 279-5449.
**SEE AD PAGE 546**

**TWIN TAMARACK FAMILY CAMPING AND RV RESORT**—Lakeside CAMPGROUND with spacious, shaded sites in the countryside. Most full hookups occupied by seasonal campers in summer. *From jct I-93 (exit 23) & Hwy 104: Go 2 1/2 mi E on Hwy 104.*

◆◆◆FACILITIES: 259 sites, most common site width 50 feet, 40 full hookups, 219 water & elec (20,30 & 50 amp receptacles), seasonal sites, 30 pull-thrus, a/c allowed, heater not allowed, phone hookups, tenting available, group sites for tents/RVs, RV rentals, RV storage, handicap restroom facilities, sewage disposal, laundry, public phone, limited grocery store, RV supplies, ice, tables, fire rings, wood, church services.

◆◆◆◆RECREATION: rec room/area, coin games, swim pool, lake swimming, whirlpool, boating, 160 hp limit, canoeing, ramp, dock, 4 row/3 canoe/4 pedal boat rentals, water skiing, lake fishing, basketball hoop, playground, planned group activities, movies, recreation director, badminton, sports field, horseshoes, volleyball.

Open mid May through mid Oct. Rate in 1995 $26 for 2 persons. Discover/Master Card/Visa accepted.

MEREDITH—Continued
TWIN TAMARACK FAMILY CAMPING AND RV RESORT—Continued

Member of NE-HA-CA. Phone: (603) 279-4387.
**SEE AD THIS PAGE**

## MILTON—E-4

**MI-TE-JO CAMPGROUND**—Level, lakeside CAMPGROUND with wooded sites. *From Hwy 16/Spaulding Tpk (exit 17): Go 3/4 mi E on Hwy 75, then 3 1/4 mi N on Hwy 125, then 1 mi E on Townhouse Rd.*

◆◆◆FACILITIES: 179 sites, most common site width 50 feet, 46 full hookups, 133 water & elec (20 & 30 amp receptacles), seasonal sites, a/c allowed ($), heater allowed ($), tenting available, RV rentals, RV storage, handicap restroom facilities, sewage disposal, public phone, limited grocery store, RV supplies, LP gas refill by weight/by meter, ice, tables, fire rings, wood.

◆◆◆◆RECREATION: rec hall, coin games, lake swimming, boating, canoeing, ramp, dock, 1 row/2 canoe boat rentals, lake fishing, basketball hoop, playground, shuffleboard court, badminton, sports field, horseshoes, hiking trails, volleyball.

Open May 15 through Oct 16. Rate in 1995 $20-24 per family. Reservations recommended Jun through Sep. Member of NE-HA-CA. Phone: (603) 652-9022.
**SEE AD THIS PAGE**

## MOUNT WASHINGTON—C-4

► **MT. WASHINGTON COG RAILWAY**—*From jct US 302 & Base Rd (Bretton Woods): Go 6 mi E on Base Rd.* Railway has unique specially built locomotives that climb to the top of Mt Washington. Food service, gift shop, cabins & RV park. Open mid Apr through mid Nov. Phone: (603) 846-5404.
**SEE AD TRAVEL SECTION PAGE 530**

## NASHUA—F-3

**FIELD AND STREAM TRAILER PARK**—*N'bound from US 3 (exit 6): Go 12 mi W on Hwy 130, 1 mi S on Hwy 13, 1 mi W on Mason Rd, then 1/4 mi N on Dupaw Gould Rd. S'bound from I-93 (exit 3) & Hwy 101: Go 17 mi W on Hwy 101, 7 mi S on Hwy 13, 1 mi W on Mason, then 1/4 mi N on Dupaw Gould Rd.*
**SEE PRIMARY LISTING AT BROOKLINE AND AD THIS PAGE**

**Because it pops and blows coals around, the Red Cedar is not a good campfire wood.**

**Field & Stream Travel Trailer Park**

**Closest Campground to Nashua**

**Quiet - Restful - Relaxing**
**Designed for Tents, Tent Trailers and RVs (No Rig Too Big!)**

- Full or Partial Hookups
- Laundry • Dump Station
- Sandy Beach on Private Pond
- Canoe to and Fish Pontanipo Lake from Gould Mill Brook Stocked with Trout

**(603) 673-4677**

*Your Hosts: Daniel & Diana MacLean*
**5 Dupaw Gould Rd., Brookline, NH 03033**
See listings at Nashua & Brookline

**Twin Tamarack**
**FAMILY CAMPING & RV RESORT**
*On Pemigewasset Lake*
ROUTE 104, NEW HAMPTON, NH
(603) 279-4387
See listing at Meredith

- Clean Modern Restrooms & Shower House
- Free Hot Showers
- Crystal Clean Swimming Pool
- Relaxing Hot Tub
- Sandy Beach on Lake
- Recreation Hall with Video Games
- Fishing & Boating
- Boat Launching
- Paddle Boat, Canoe, & Row Boat Rentals
- Maytag Laundromat
- New Factory Outlet Mall - 15 mins

*Designed and operated for families who enjoy the peace and quiet of the natural surroundings*

- 259 Wooded & Sunny Sites
- Facilities for all RVs & Tent Campers
- Pull-Thru Sites for Large & Small RVs
- 30-50 Amp Electric
- Electric & Water Hookups
- Free Honey Wagon Service
- Dumping Station
- RV Clubs & Rally Area
- Seasonal Sites Available

Welcome! Good Neighbor Park — Participating Host — Coast to Coast

Christ is The Answer

NEW HAMPSHIRE APPROVED CAMPGROUND

APPROVED CAMPGROUND AAA

**30 Mins to NH International Speedway**
Directions:
From I-93, Exit 23, 2 1/2 miles East on Rt. 104
*—Open Mid-May to Mid-October—*

**Reservation Suggested**
For more information and a free brochure contact your hosts: Gene & Bev Sands - (603) 279-4387
Twin Tamarack, Rt. 104, Box 121, New Hampton, NH 03256

NH *State Animal: White-Tail Deer* NH

## NEW BOSTON—F-3

**FRIENDLY BEAVER CAMPGROUND**—Wooded CAMPGROUND with some open grassy sites. *From jct Hwy 77 & Hwy 136 & Hwy 13 (Southwest corner): Go 2 mi W on Old Coach Rd.*

◈◈◈FACILITIES: 172 sites, most common site width 20 feet, 131 full hookups, 41 water & elec (15,20 & 30 amp receptacles), seasonal sites, a/c allowed ($), heater not allowed, phone hookups, tenting available, group sites for tents/RVs, RV storage, handicap restroom facilities, sewage disposal, laundry, public phone, limited grocery store, RV supplies, ice, tables, fire rings, wood.

◈◈◈◈◈RECREATION: rec hall, rec room/area, coin games, 3 swim pools (indoor) (heated), wading pool, whirlpool, basketball hoop, playground, planned group activities, recreation director, badminton, sports field, horseshoes, hiking trails, volleyball, snowmobile trails.

Open all year. Rate in 1995 $23-28 per family. Master Card/Visa accepted. Member of NE-HA-CA. Phone: (603) 487-5570.

**SEE AD NEXT PAGE**

**Wildwood Campground**—Open & wooded sites among tall pines. *From jct Hwy 77 & Hwy 136 & Hwy 13 (Southwest corner): Go 3 1/2 mi W on Old Coach Rd.* ◈◈FACILITIES: 100 sites, most common site width 25 feet, 35 full hookups, 62 water & elec (15 & 20 amp receptacles), 3 no hookups, seasonal sites, tenting available, sewage disposal, laundry, grocery store, ice, tables, fire rings, grills, wood. ◈◈RECREATION: rec room/area, swim pool, pond fishing, badminton, horseshoes, hiking trails, volleyball. Open all year. Facilities fully operational May 1 through Oct 15. Rate in 1995 $18-22 per family. No refunds. Member of NE-HA-CA. Phone: (603) 487-3300.

## NEWFIELDS—F-4

**GREAT BAY CAMPING VILLAGE**—CAMPGROUND with wooded sites beside a salt water river. *From I-95 (exit 2) & Hwy 101 W: Go 7 1/2 mi W on Hwy 101 W, then 4 mi N on Hwy 108 (turn E at Citgo gas station).*

NEWFIELDS—Continued
GREAT BAY CAMPING VILLAGE—Continued

◈◈◈FACILITIES: 115 sites, most common site width 40 feet, 69 full hookups, 18 water & elec (20,30 & 50 amp receptacles), 28 no hookups, seasonal sites, 1 pull-thrus, a/c allowed ($), heater allowed ($), tenting available, group sites for tents/RVs, RV rentals, sewage disposal, laundry, public phone, full service store, RV supplies, LP gas refill by weight/by meter, gasoline, ice, tables, fire rings, wood.

◈◈◈RECREATION: rec hall, rec room/area, coin games, swim pool, boating, canoeing, ramp, dock, 6 canoe boat rentals, salt water/river fishing, basketball hoop, badminton, horseshoes, volleyball.

Open May 15 through Oct 15. Rate in 1995 $18.50 per family. American Express/Discover/Master Card/Visa accepted. Member of NE-HA-CA. Phone: (603) 778-0226.

**SEE AD THIS PAGE**

## NEW LONDON—E-2

**Otter Lake Campground**—CAMPGROUND with open & wooded sites near a lake. *From jct I-89 (exit 12) & Hwy 11: Go 3/4 mi W on Hwy 11, then 500 feet N on Otterville Rd.* ◈◈FACILITIES: 28 sites, most common site width 50 feet, 32 ft. max RV length, 12 water & elec (20 & 30 amp receptacles), 16 no hookups, seasonal sites, tenting available, sewage disposal, ice, tables, fire rings, wood. ◈◈RECREATION: lake swimming, boating, canoeing, 2 row/1 canoe/1 pedal boat rentals, horseshoes, hiking trails. Open May 15 through Oct 15. Rate in 1995 $18-22 per family. Member of NE-HA-CA. Phone: (603) 763-5600.

## NEWPORT—E-2

**THE CROW'S NEST CAMPGROUND**—Open, grassy & wooded, level sites on hilly terrain. *From jct Hwy 11 & Hwy 10: Go 2 mi S on Hwy 10.*

◈◈FACILITIES: 94 sites, most common site width 30 feet, 27 full hookups, 47 water & elec (20 & 30 amp receptacles), 20 no hookups, seasonal sites, 15 pull-thrus, a/c allowed ($), heater not allowed, tenting available, group sites for

NEWPORT—Continued
THE CROW'S NEST CAMPGROUND—Continued

tents/RVs, RV storage, sewage disposal, laundry, public phone, limited grocery store, RV supplies, ice, tables, fire rings, wood.

◈◈◈RECREATION: rec hall, coin games, swim pool, wading pool, river/pond swimming, river fishing, mini-golf ($), playground, sports field, horseshoes, volleyball, cross country skiing, snowmobile trails.

Open all year. Rate in 1995 $15-19 for 2 persons. No refunds. Reservations recommended Memorial Day through Labor Day. Master Card/Visa accepted. Member of NE-HA-CA. Phone: (800) 842-6170.

**SEE AD THIS PAGE**

**Northstar Campground**—Rural, wooded riverside CAMPGROUND. *From jct Hwy 10 & Hwy 11: Go 3 1/2 mi S on Hwy 10, then 1/4 mi W on Coon Brook Rd.* ◈◈FACILITIES: 56 sites, most common site width 50 feet, 31 water & elec (20 & 30 amp receptacles), 25 no hookups, seasonal sites, tenting available, sewage disposal, ice, tables, fire rings, wood. ◈◈RECREATION: pavilion, pond swimming, river/stream fishing, horseshoes, hiking trails, volleyball. Open May 15 through Oct 15. Rate in 1995 $12-14 for 2 persons. Member of NE-HA-CA. Phone: (603) 863-4001.

## NORTH CONWAY—C-4

**THE BEACH CAMPING AREA**—*From jct Hwy 302 & Hwy 16: Go 1 mi S on Hwy 16.*
**SEE PRIMARY LISTING AT CONWAY AND AD CONWAY PAGE 538**

▶ **CONWAY SCENIC RAILROAD**—*In town on Hwy 16 & US 302.* An II mile round-trip ride on an antique train. Open all year. Phone: (603) 356-5251.
**SEE AD TRAVEL SECTION PAGE 530**

**SACO RIVER CAMPING AREA**—CAMPGROUND with some shaded sites beside a river. *From south jct US 302 & Hwy 16: Go 1/4 mi N on Hwy 16/US 302.*

◈◈◈FACILITIES: 140 sites, most common site width 40 feet, 71 full hookups, 67 water & elec (20 & 30 amp receptacles), 2 no hookups, seasonal sites, 32 pull-thrus, a/c allowed ($), tenting available, group sites for tents/RVs, sewage disposal, laundry, public phone, limited grocery store, RV supplies, LP gas refill by weight/by meter, ice, tables, fire rings, grills, wood, traffic control gate/guard.

SACO RIVER CAMPING AREA—Continued on page 550
NORTH CONWAY—Continued on page 550

# OPEN ALL YEAR

TAKE A PONY RIDE WITH PEANUTS, OUR LOVABLE PONY

SPECTACULAR PLAYGROUND... YOU HAVE TO SEE IT TO BELIEVE IT

AWESOME POOLS WITH WATER BASKETBALL & KIDDIE POOL

GREAT PATIO

INDOOR HEATED POOL WITH JACUZZI THAT IS OPEN YEAR ROUND

*SUPER ACTIVITIES & RECREATION PROGRAM OFFERED YEAR ROUND WEEKLY & WEEKENDS*

•••

*WE ALSO HAVE 2 REC HALLS: ONE FOR ADULTS AND ONE FOR CHILDREN & TEENS*

•••

*WOODALL'S HIGHEST RATED*
*FOR RECREATION: WWWWW*
*FACILITIES: WWW*

**FRIENDLY BEAVER CAMPGROUND**

Old Coach Road, New Boston, NH 03070

(603) 487-5570

VISA

**NORTH CONWAY**—Continued
SACO RIVER CAMPING AREA—Continued

◆◆◆RECREATION: pavilion, river swimming, canoeing, 4 canoe boat rentals, river fishing, basketball hoop, playground, shuffleboard court, planned group activities, recreation director, badminton, sports field, horseshoes, volleyball.

Open May 1 through Oct 15. Rate in 1995 $16-20 per family. No refunds. Reservations recommended May through Oct. Master Card/Visa accepted. Member of NE-HA-CA. Phone: (603) 356-3360.
**SEE AD THIS PAGE**

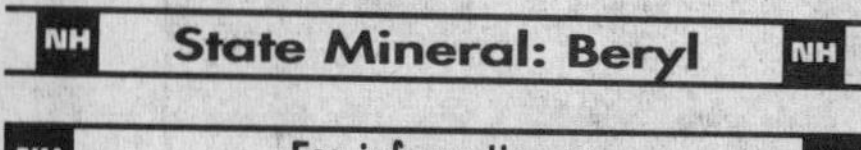


NH For information on NH
**Annual Crafts Festival**
NH see front of book article. NH

## NORTH STRATFORD—B-3

**Scott's Big Rock Camping Area**—Semi-wooded grassy CAMPGROUND away from highway. *From jct Hwy 105 & US 3: Go 5 1/2 mi S on US 3.* ◆◆FACILITIES: 30 sites, most common site width 25 feet, 14 full hookups, 5 water & elec (15 & 20 amp receptacles), 11 no hookups, seasonal sites, 5 pull-thrus, tenting available, sewage disposal, public phone, limited grocery store, ice, tables, fire rings, grills, wood. ◆◆RECREATION: rec room/area, pavilion, swim pool, mini-golf ($), badminton, volleyball. Open all year. Facilities fully operational May 15 through Sep 15. Rate in 1995 $12.50-15.50 per family. Phone: (603) 922-3329.

## NORTH WOODSTOCK—C-3

**CLARK'S TRADING POST**—*From jct Hwy 112 & US 3: Go 1 1/2 mi N on US 3.* Performances by trained bears; 22 mi train ride on standard gauge steam locomotive; visit 1884 replica of Hook & Ladder Fire House with authentic horsedrawn fire equipment; Bumper Boats, Ice Cream Parlor, Peppermint Saloon & antique style photos. Open all year. Phone: (603) 745-8913.
**SEE AD TRAVEL SECTION PAGE 530**

FAMILY CAMPING IN MT. WASHINGTON VALLEY ON THE SACO RIVER

Saco River Camping Area

WALK!!!
- to Factory Outlet Shopping
- to Movies and Entertainment
- to Restaurants
- to Grocery & Drug Store

2000′ of Waterfront Sites
Fifty Acres — 140 Sites
Planned Activities
Metered LP Gas
Group Facilities
Free Hay Wagon Rides

The Scheffler Family

(603) 356-3360

See listing at North Conway

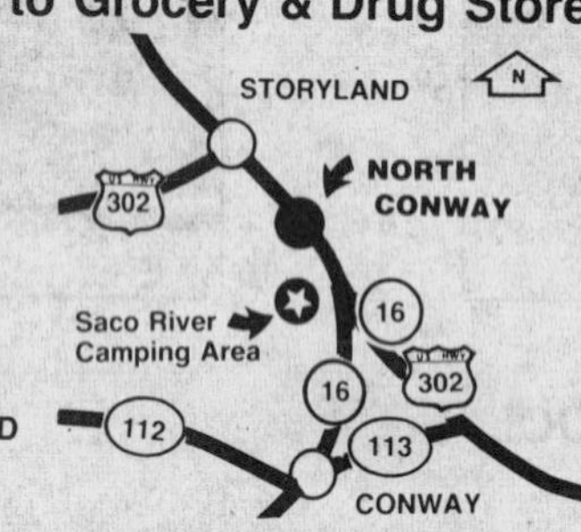


Rt. 16, Box 546W
North Conway, NH 03860

**NORTH WOODSTOCK**—Continued

**LOST RIVER**—*From jct US 3 & Hwy 112: Go 4 1/2 mi W on Hwy 112.* Scenic view of rock formations & waterfalls. Open Mid-May through Mid-Oct. Phone: (603) 745-8031.
**SEE AD TRAVEL SECTION PAGE 530**

**LOST RIVER VALLEY CAMPGROUND**—Spacious, level, wooded sites close to river and brook. *From jct I-93 (exit 32) & Hwy 112: Go 3 1/2 mi W on Hwy 112.*

◆◆◆◆FACILITIES: 130 sites, most common site width 40 feet, 8 full hookups, 51 water & elec (20,30 & 50 amp receptacles), 71 no hookups, 6 pull-thrus, a/c allowed, heater allowed, tenting available, cabins, handicap restroom facilities, sewage disposal, laundry, public phone, grocery store, RV supplies, LP gas refill by weight/by meter, ice, tables, fire rings, wood, traffic control gate.

◆◆◆◆RECREATION: rec hall, rec room/area, coin games, pond swimming, stream fishing, basketball hoop, playground, 2 shuffleboard courts, movies, tennis court, badminton, sports field, horseshoes, hiking trails, volleyball.

Open May 15 through Columbus Day. Rate in 1995 $19.50-27 for 2 persons. No refunds. Reservations recommended Jul through Labor Day. Discover/Master Card/Visa accepted. Member of ARVC; NE-HA-CA. Phone: (800) 370-5678.
**SEE AD THIS PAGE**

**Maple Haven Camping, Cottages & Lodge**—Rural, wooded CAMPGROUND with mountain view. *From jct I-93 & Hwy 112: Go 1 mi W on Hwy 112.* ◆◆FACILITIES: 36 sites, most common site width 20 feet, 22 water & elec (15,20,30 & 50 amp receptacles), 14 no hookups, seasonal sites, 6 pull-thrus, tenting available, sewage disposal, public phone, limited grocery store, ice, tables, fire rings, wood. ◆◆RECREATION: rec room/area, pond swimming, river/pond/stream fishing, badminton, horseshoes, volleyball. Open Mid Apr through Mid Nov. Rate in 1995 $18-23 for 2 persons. Member of NE-HA-CA. Phone: (800) 221-3350.

**MOOSE HILLOCK CAMPGROUND**—*From jct I-93 & Hwy 112: Go 3 mi W on Hwy 112, then 11 mi S on Hwy 118.*
**SEE PRIMARY LISTING AT WARREN AND AD WARREN PAGE 554**

**WHITE MOUNTAIN ATTRACTIONS & CHAMBER OF COMMERCE**—*In the center of town on Kangamagus Hwy.* White Mountain Chamber of Commerce. Phone: (603) 745-8720.
**SEE AD TRAVEL SECTION PAGE 530**

WHITE MOUNTAIN NATIONAL FOREST (Russell Pond Campground)—*From jct US 3 & Hwy 175: Go 2 3/4 mi S on Hwy 175, then 2 mi E on FR 30, then 3 mi N on FR 90.* FACILITIES: 87 sites, 22 ft. max RV length, 87 no hookups, tenting available, tables, fire rings. RECREATION: boating, no motors, ramp, lake fishing, hiking trails. Open May 1 through Oct 15. Phone: (603) 536-1310.

WHITE MOUNTAIN NATIONAL FOREST (Wildwood Campground)—*From jct Hwy 112 & US 3: Go 8 2/3 mi W on Hwy 112.* FACILITIES: 26 sites, 22 ft. max RV length, 26 no hookups, tenting available, non-flush toilets, handicap restroom facilities, tables, fire rings, grills. RECREATION: hiking trails. Open mid May through Dec. No water service in cold weather. No showers. Phone: (603) 869-2626.

## ORFORD—D-2

**JACOBS BROOK CAMPGROUND**—Secluded CAMPGROUND with gravel, shaded sites. *From I-91 (exit 15) in Vermont: Go 100 yards E to US 5, then 3/4 mi N on US 5 to Hwy 25A, then 1/2 mi N on Hwy 10, then 1 mi E on Archertown Rd.*

JACOBS BROOK CAMPGROUND—Continued on next page
ORFORD—Continued on next page

CAMP IN THE NORTH WOODS

LOST RIVER VALLEY

WHITE MOUNTAIN NATIONAL FOREST ON THREE SIDES

FAMILY CAMPGROUND

RD 1 BOX 44W, ROUTE 112 • NORTH WOODSTOCK, N.H. 03262

Spacious, Level, Wooded Sites
Close to River and Brook
Located at Foot of Kinsman Notch in the Heart of White Mts. Recreation Area

REC HALL – PLAYGROUND – TV/READING ROOM
CAMPING CABINS – FISHING – SWIMMING – LARGE REC FIELD – LP GAS
SPORTS COURT – LAUNDRY – HOOKUPS – PETS ON LEASH

Monitoring Ch. 13 **Reservations: 1-800-370-5678**
I-93 To Exit 32, 4 Miles West on Route 112W
See listing at North Woodstock

DISCOVER

**Jacobs Brook Campground**
*a family campground*

*Come and explore our clear brooks, waterfalls & pools tucked in quiet & peace*

- Easy Access from I-91 in Vermont
- Full Hookups with 30 Amp
- Private Wooded Sites • Pool

(603) 353-9210

P.O. Box 167, Orford, NH 03777 See listing at Orford

ORFORD—Continued
JACOBS BROOK CAMPGROUND—Continued

◈◈◈FACILITIES: 75 sites, most common site width 35 feet, 36 ft. max RV length, 15 full hookups, 35 water & elec (20 & 30 amp receptacles), 25 no hookups, seasonal sites, 4 pull-thrus, a/c allowed, heater allowed, tenting available, group sites for tents/RVs, RV rentals, RV storage, sewage disposal, limited grocery store, RV supplies, ice, tables, fire rings, wood.

◈◈RECREATION: swim pool, river swimming, river fishing, basketball hoop, badminton, sports field, horseshoes, hiking trails, volleyball.

Open mid May through mid Oct. Rate in 1995 $14-18 per family. Master Card/Visa accepted. Member of NE-HA-CA. Phone: (603) 353-9210.

SEE AD PAGE 550

WELCOME

**THE PASTURES**—CAMPGROUND with grassy, partially shaded sites adjacent to Connecticut River. *From I-91 (exit 15) Vermont: Go 2 mi E on Hwy 25A, then 1 block S on Hwy 10.*

◈◈FACILITIES: 58 sites, most common site width 50 feet, 58 water & elec (15 & 20 amp receptacles), seasonal sites, a/c not allowed, heater not allowed, tenting available, group sites for tents/RVs, sewage disposal, tables, fire rings, wood.

◈◈RECREATION: boating, canoeing, river fishing, basketball hoop, horseshoes, volleyball.

Open mid May through Oct 15. Rate in 1995 $15 per family. Member of NE-HA-CA. Phone: (603) 353-4579.

SEE AD THIS PAGE

## OSSIPEE—D-4

WELCOME

**BEAVER HOLLOW CAMPGROUND**—Rural, wooded area. *From jct Hwy 28 & Hwy 16: Go 1 mi S on Hwy 16.*

◈◈◈FACILITIES: 120 sites, most common site width 25 feet, 120 water & elec (20 & 30 amp receptacles), seasonal sites, 87 pull-thrus, a/c allowed ($), heater allowed ($), tenting available, group sites for tents/RVs, sewage disposal, laundry, public phone, limited grocery store, RV supplies, ice, tables, fire rings, grills, wood.

◈◈◈RECREATION: rec room/area, equipped pavilion, coin games, swim pool, pond/stream fishing, basketball hoop, 2 shuffleboard courts, planned group activities (weekends only), badminton, sports field, horseshoes, hiking trails, volleyball, cross country skiing, snowmobile trails.

Open all year. Facilities fully operational May 1 through Oct 12. Pool open Memorial Day thru Labor Day Rate in 1995 $15-20 for 4 persons. No refunds. Reservations recommended Memorial Day through Labor Day. Master Card/Visa accepted. Member of NE-HA-CA. Phone: (800) 226-2257.

SEE AD THIS PAGE

## PITTSBURG—A-3

CONNECTICUT LAKES STATE FOREST (Deer Mountain Campground)—*From town: Go 20 mi N on Hwy 3.* FACILITIES: 20 sites, 20 no hookups, non-flush toilets, wood. RECREATION: lake swimming, canoeing, lake fishing, hiking trails. Open late May through early Sep. Open weekends only May 26-Jun 23. No showers. Phone: (603) 538-6965.

LAKE FRANCES STATE PARK—*From town: Go 7 mi N on US 3.* FACILITIES: 40 sites, 40 no hookups, tenting available, sewage disposal, public phone, limited grocery store, tables, wood. RECREATION: boating, canoeing, ramp, lake fishing. Open early may through mid Oct. No showers. Phone: (603) 538-6965.

**NEW HAMPSHIRE**

**"Old Man of the Mountains" is a profile of a man's face "carved" into stone ledges by nature.**

## PLYMOUTH—D-3

WELCOME

✽ **GILMAN'S NH COACH & CAMPER**—*From jct I-93 (exit 26) & Hwy 25: Go 6 mi W on Hwy 25.* SALES: travel trailers, truck campers, 5th wheels, motor homes, mini-motor homes, fold-down camping trailers. SERVICES: Engine/Chassis & RV appliance mechanic full-time, emergency road service business hours, RV towing, sells parts/accessories, sells camping supplies, installs hitches. Open all year. Discover/Master Card/Visa accepted. Phone: (603) 786-2501.

SEE AD THIS PAGE

WELCOME

⚑ **POLAR CAVES PARK**—*From I-93 (exit 26): Go 5 mi W on Hwy 25.* Enjoy tours of Glacial Caves, Rock Gardens of Giants, New Hampshire Minerals exhibit and browse the gift & souvenir shop. Also, feed the animals and enjoy a snack or meal at the full service cafeteria; or plan a cookout in the picnic area. Open mid-May through mid-Oct. Phone: (603) 536-1888.

SEE AD TRAVEL SECTION PAGE 530

## RAYMOND—F-4

PAWTUCKAWAY STATE PARK—*From jct Hwy 101 & Hwy 156: Go 3 1/2 mi N.* FACILITIES: 170 sites, 170 no hookups, tenting available, grocery store, ice, tables, wood. RECREATION: lake swimming, boating, canoeing, ramp, dock, canoe boat rentals, lake fishing, hiking trails. No pets. Open early May through Columbus Day. Phone: (603) 895-3031.

WELCOME

**PINE ACRES FAMILY CAMPGROUND**—Rural, rustic shaded lakeside. *From Hwy 101 (exit 5): Go 3/4 mi S on Hwy 107.*

◈◈◈FACILITIES: 350 sites, most common site width 30 feet, 330 water & elec (15,20 & 30 amp receptacles), 20 no hookups, seasonal sites, tenting available, RV rentals, RV storage, handicap restroom facilities, sewage disposal, laundry, public phone, full service store, RV supplies, LP gas refill by weight/by meter, ice, tables, fire rings, wood, guard.

◈◈◈◈◈RECREATION: rec hall, rec room/area, equipped pavilion, coin games, lake swimming, water slide ($), boating, 7 hp limit, canoeing, 5 row/13 canoe/4 pedal boat rentals, lake fishing, mini-golf ($), basketball hoop, 4 bike rentals, playground, planned group activities, recreation director, badminton, sports field, horseshoes, volleyball, cross country skiing.

Open Apr 15 through Nov 15. Rate in 1995 $24-30 per family. No refunds. Reservations recommended Jul 1 through Labor Day. Discover/Master Card/Visa accepted. Member of NE-HA-CA. Phone: (603) 895-2519.

SEE AD FRONT OF BOOK PAGE 14 AND AD NEXT PAGE

***New Hampshire***

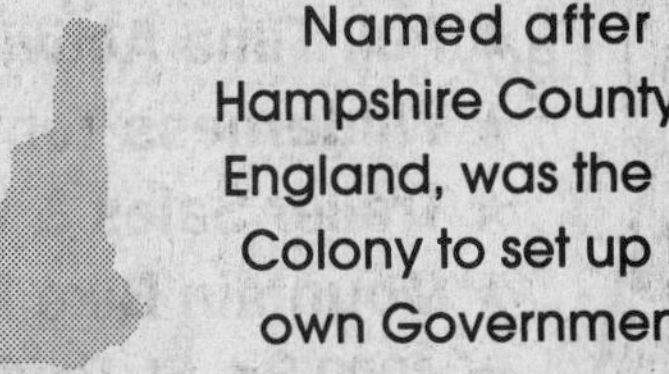

Named after Hampshire County in England, was the 1st Colony to set up its own Government

NH The first railway NH
*The Cog Railway*
NH in North America (1869) NH

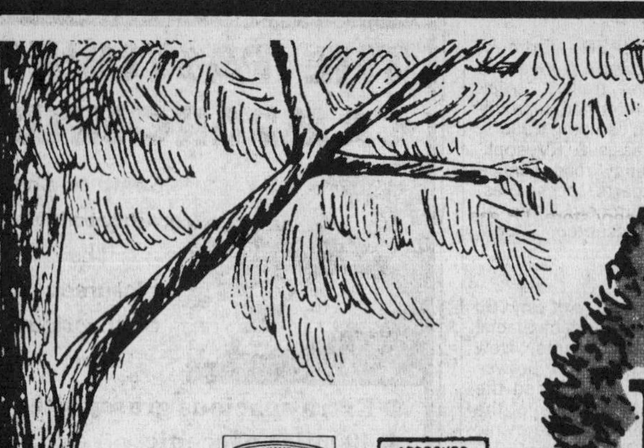

Your New Hampshire Escape

Sea Coast Region

NEW HAMPSHIRE Ne-Ha-Ca CAMPGROUND OWNERS' ASSN. APPROVED CAMPGROUND

APPROVED CAMPGROUND AAA

# Pine Acres

*A Family Camping Resort*

## PINE ACRES

Family Campground
**Jct. Rt. 101 & Rt. 107, 3/4 mi S. on Rt. 107**
Raymond, NH 03077
**(603) 895-2519**

- ★ 150 Acres – 350 Campsites
- ★ Facilities for RV's & Tents
- ★ 19 Hole Miniature Golf Course
- ★ Fully Stocked Camp Store
- ★ Laundromat ★ Live Band ★ Bingo
- ★ LP Gas ★ Canoe & Boat Rentals
- ★ Spectacular Playground ★ Fishing
- ★ Teen Rec Hall ★ Adult Rec Hall
- ★ Full Time Activities Program
- ★ Wilderness Tent Area ★ Snack Bar
- ★ Trailer Sales & Rentals
- ★ Mountain Bike Rentals
- ★ 4000 Sq. Ft. Pavilion

**New & Larger Water Slide**
**3 Large Sandy Beaches**
**2 Swimming Areas**

Fac. WWW
Rec. WWWWW

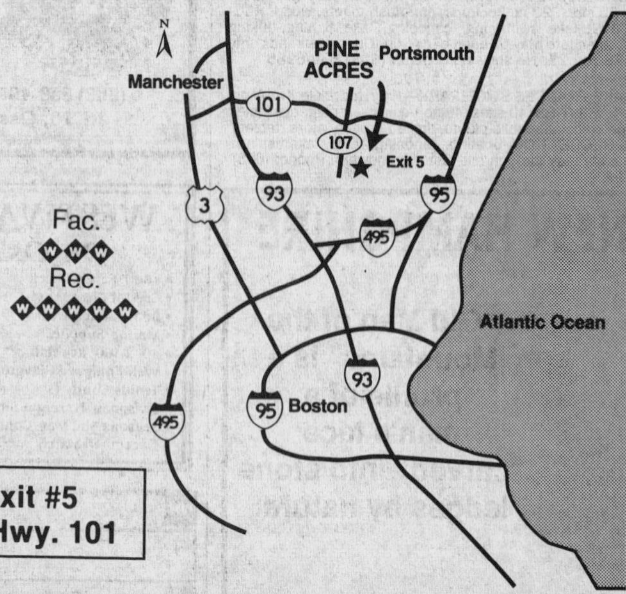

See listing at Raymond

**Exit #5 off Hwy. 101**

## RICHMOND—F-2

**SHIR-ROY CAMPING AREA**—Wooded, lakeside CAMPGROUND in rural area with open, grassy sites also available. *From jct Hwys 119 & 32: Go 1 mi S on Hwy 32.*

◆◆◆FACILITIES: 110 sites, most common site width 30 feet, 107 water & elec (20 & 30 amp receptacles), 3 no hookups, seasonal sites, 10 pull-thrus, a/c allowed ($), heater allowed ($), tenting available, group sites for tents/RVs, RV rentals, RV storage, sewage disposal, laundry, public phone, limited grocery store, RV supplies, ice, tables, fire rings, grills, wood.

◆◆◆◆RECREATION: rec hall, rec room/area, coin games, lake swimming, boating, canoeing, ramp, 4 row/5 canoe/3 pedal boat rentals, lake fishing, playground, badminton, sports field, horseshoes, volleyball.

Open Memorial Day through Columbus Day. Rate in 1995 $16.50-19 per family. Reservations recommended Memorial Day through Labor Day. Member of NE-HA-CA. Phone: (603) 239-4768.

**SEE AD THIS PAGE**

## RINDGE—F-2

**WOODMORE CAMPGROUND**—Shady, grassy, rural area near lakeside. *From west jct Hwy 119 & US 202: Go 1 mi N on US 202, then 1/4 mi E on Davis Crossing Rd, then 1/2 mi N on Woodbound Rd.*

◆FACILITIES: 130 sites, most common site width 50 feet, 90 full hookups, 20 water & elec (20 & 30 amp receptacles), 20 no hookups, seasonal sites, 3 pull-thrus, a/c allowed ($), heater not allowed, tenting available, group sites for tents/RVs, RV storage, sewage disposal, laundry, public phone, limited grocery store, RV supplies, LP gas refill by weight, ice, tables, fire rings, grills, wood, traffic control gate.

◆◆RECREATION: rec room/area, coin games, swim pool, boating, 35 hp limit, canoeing, 1 row/4 canoe/2 pedal boat rentals, water skiing, lake fishing, basketball hoop, playground, shuffleboard court, badminton, horseshoes, volleyball.

Open May 15 through Sep 20. Open weekends only Sep 20 to Columbus Day. Rate in 1995 $14-18 per family. Reservations recommended Memorial Day through Labor Day. Master Card/Visa accepted. Member of NE-HA-CA. Phone: (603) 899-3362.

**SEE AD THIS PAGE**

## ROCHESTER—E-4

**Crown Point Campground**—Hilly, grassy, shady area in country. *From jct Spaulding Tpk & Ten Rod Road (exit 14): Go 2/10 mi S on Hwy 11,then 2/10 mi W on Twombley St, then 4 mi SW on 202A, then 2/10 mi N on FirstCrown Point Road.* ◆◆FACILITIES: 135 sites, most common site width 45 feet, 100 full hookups, 35 water & elec (15,20 & 30 amp receptacles), seasonal sites, tenting available, sewage disposal, public phone, limited grocery store, LP gas refill by weight, ice, tables, fire rings, wood. ◆◆◆RECREATION: rec hall, rec room/area, pond swimming, 2 pedal boat rentals, pond fishing, badminton, horseshoes, volleyball. Recreation open to the public. Open May 15 through Oct 15. Rate in 1995 $18 per family. No refunds. Member of NE-HA-CA. Phone: (603) 332-0405.

**MI-TE-JO-CAMPGROUND**—*From jct Spaulding Tpk (exit 15) & Hwy 11: Go 6 mi N on Spaulding Tpk/US 16 to exit 17, then 3/4 mi E on Hwy 75, then 3 1/4 mi N on Hwy 125, then 1 mi E on Townhouse Rd.*

**SEE PRIMARY LISTING AT MILTON AND AD MILTON PAGE 547**

## SANDOWN—F-4

**ANGLE POND GROVE**—Lakeside CAMPGROUND with wooded sites in a rural area. *From jct Hwy 111 & Hwy 121A: Go 6/10 mi N on Hwy 121A, then 100 yards W on Pillsbury Rd.*

◆◆FACILITIES: 140 sites, most common site width 25 feet, 140 full hookups, (15 & 20 amp receptacles), seasonal sites, 5 pull-thrus, a/c allowed ($), heater not allowed, group sites for RVs, cabins, laundry, public phone, limited grocery store, LP gas refill by weight, ice, tables, fire rings, wood, traffic control gate.

◆◆◆◆RECREATION: rec hall, rec room/area, coin games, lake swimming, basketball hoop, playground, shuffleboard court, tennis court, sports field, horseshoes, volleyball. Recreation open to the public.

No pets. No tents. Open May 15 through Oct 15. Rate in 1995 $16 for 2 persons. No refunds. Reservations recommended Jul through Aug. Member of NE-HA-CA. Phone: (603) 887-4434.

**SEE AD THIS PAGE**

## SEABROOK—F-5

**New Hampshire Seacoast Campground**—Wooded, level CAMPGROUND near beaches. *From I-95 (exit 60 in Mass): Go to 2nd stop light (Hwy 286), then 2 mi E on Hwy 286.* ◆◆FACILITIES: 100 sites, most common site width 50 feet, 35 ft. max RV length, 80 water & elec (15 amp receptacles), 20 no hookups, seasonal sites, 2 pull-thrus, tenting available, sewage disposal, public phone, limited grocery store, ice, tables, fire rings, grills, wood. ◆RECREATION: rec room/area, horseshoes. Open May 15 through Sep 15. Rate in 1995 $15-18 for 2 persons. No refunds. Phone: (603) 474-9813.

## SOUTH HAMPTON—F-4

**TUXBURY POND CAMPING AREA**—A lakeside CAMPGROUND with wooded sites. *From jct I-495 (exit 54) & Hwy 150 (in Massachusetts): Go 3/4 mi N on Hwy 150 to blinking yellow light, then 1/4 mi NW on Highland St, then 1 1/4 mi W on Lions Mouth Rd, then 1 mi N on Newton Rd. Follow signs.*

◆◆FACILITIES: 208 sites, most common site width 50 feet, 149 full hookups, 59 water & elec (15,20 & 30 amp receptacles), seasonal sites, 23 pull-thrus, a/c allowed ($), heater not allowed, tenting available, RV rentals, sewage disposal, laundry, public phone, grocery store, RV supplies, LP gas refill by weight/by meter, ice, tables, fire rings, wood, traffic





SOUTH HAMPTON—Continued
TUXBURY POND CAMPING AREA—Continued

control gate.

◆◆◆◆RECREATION: rec hall, rec room/area, pavilion, coin games, pond swimming, boating, canoeing, 3 row/3 canoe/3 pedal boat rentals, pond fishing, basketball hoop, playground, planned group activities, sports field, horseshoes, volleyball.

Open mid May through mid Oct. Rate in 1995 $20-21 for 4 persons. No refunds. Reservations recommended Memorial Day through Labor Day. Member of NE-HA-CA. Phone: (603) 394-7660.

**SEE AD AMESBURY, MA PAGE 380**

## SULLIVAN—F-2

**Hilltop Campground**—In grassy, rolling country with mountains and shade. *From East jct Hwy 9 & 10: Go 1 mi E on Hwy 9, then 2 mi NE on Sullivan Rd.* ◆◆FACILITIES: 39 sites, most common site width 30 feet, 32 water & elec (20 & 30 amp receptacles), 7 no hookups, seasonal sites, tenting available, sewage disposal, public phone, limited grocery store, ice, tables, wood. ◆◆◆RECREATION: equipped pavilion, swim pool, pond fishing, badminton, horseshoes, hiking trails, volleyball. Open May 1 through Oct 1. Rate in 1995 $15 per family. Member of NE-HA-CA. Phone: (603) 847-3351.

## TAMWORTH—D-4

**The Foothills Campground**—Natural sites shaded by tall pines in a rural setting. *From jct Hwy 25 & Hwy 16: Go 1 1/2 mi N on Hwy 16.* ◆◆FACILITIES: 65 sites, most common site width 35 feet, 53 water & elec (20 & 30 amp receptacles), 12 no hookups, seasonal sites, tenting available, sewage disposal, limited grocery store, LP gas refill by weight/by meter, ice, tables, fire rings, wood. ◆◆RECREATION: rec hall, swim pool, pond fishing, horseshoes. Open May 15 through Columbus Day. Rate in 1995 $16-18 per family. No refunds. Member of NE-HA-CA. Phone: (603) 323-8322.

**TAMWORTH CAMPING AREA**—CAMPGROUND with level, prepared, shaded sites in a meadow. *From jct Hwy 16 & Hwy 25W: Go 3/4 mi N on Hwy 16, then 3 mi W on Depot Rd.*

◆◆◆FACILITIES: 100 sites, most com-

TAMWORTH CAMPING AREA—Continued on next page
TAMWORTH—Continued on next page

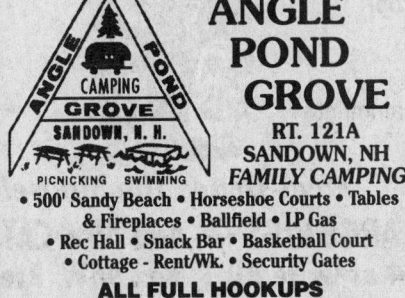

TAMWORTH—Continued
TAMWORTH CAMPING AREA—Continued

mon site width 50 feet, 46 full hookups, 36 water & elec (15,20 & 30 amp receptacles), 18 no hookups, seasonal sites, a/c allowed ($), heater allowed ($), tenting available, group sites for tents/RVs, RV rentals, RV storage, sewage disposal, laundry, public phone, limited grocery store, RV supplies, LP gas refill by weight/by meter, ice, tables, fire rings, grills, wood, traffic control gate.

◆◆◆RECREATION: rec hall, coin games, river swimming, river fishing, mini-golf ($), basketball hoop, bike rental, playground, 2 shuffleboard courts, planned group activities (weekends only), badminton, sports field, horseshoes, volleyball, cross country skiing, snowmobile trails.

Open May 15 through Dec 1. Open Dec 1 to May 15 for seasonal campers only. Rate in 1995 $15-24 per family. No refunds. Reservations recommended Jul through Aug. Master Card/Visa accepted. Member of NE-HA-CA. Phone: (603) 323-8031.

SEE AD PAGE 553

## THORNTON—D-3

**PEMI RIVER CAMPGROUND**—Pine shaded and open grassy sites beside a river. *From jct I-93 (exit 29) & US 3: Go 100 yards E on US 3.*

WELCOME

◆◆◆ FACILITIES: 60 sites, most common site width 40 feet, 34 water & elec (20, 30 & 50 amp receptacles), 26 no hookups, 12 pull-thrus, a/c allowed ($), tenting available, group sites for tents/RVs, sewage disposal, limited grocery store, ice, tables, fire rings, grills, wood.

◆◆◆RECREATION: rec room/area, coin games, river swimming, canoeing, river fishing, playground, badminton, sports field, horseshoes, volleyball. Recreation open to the public. Open Jul 1 through Labor Day. Open weekends in May, Jun, Sep & Oct (through Columbus Day). Rate in 1995 $16-21 per family. Master card/Visa accepted. Member of NE-HA-CA. Phone: (603) 726-7015.

SEE AD TRAVEL SECTION PAGE 533

NH **State Rock: Granite** NH

## TWIN MOUNTAIN—C-3

**Ammonoosuc Campground**—Semi-wooded, grassy area with mountain view. *From jct US 302 & US 3: Go 1/4 mi S on US 3.* ◆◆FACILITIES: 112 sites, most common site width 30 feet, 36 ft. max RV length, 75 full hookups, 13 water & elec (20 amp receptacles), 24 no hookups, seasonal sites, tenting available, sewage disposal, laundry, tables, fire rings, grills, wood. ◆◆RECREATION: swim pool, playground, badminton, horseshoes, volleyball. Open all year. Facilities fully operational May 15 through Columbus Day. Rate in 1995 $18-21 per family. Member of NE-HA-CA. Phone: (603) 846-5527.

**Beech Hill Campground**—Rural, shaded area with mountain view. *From jct US 3 & US 302: Go 2 mi W on US 302.* ◆◆FACILITIES: 87 sites, most common site width 50 feet, 15 full hookups, 33 water & elec (20 & 30 amp receptacles), 39 no hookups, seasonal sites, tenting available, sewage disposal, laundry, public phone, limited grocery store, ice, tables, fire rings, wood. ◆◆◆RECREATION: rec hall, rec room/area, swim pool (indoor), river swimming, river fishing, badminton, horseshoes, volleyball. Open all year. Rate in 1995 $17.50-22 per family. No refunds. Member of NE-HA-CA. Phone: (603) 846-5521.

**KOA-Cherry Mountain**—Open grassy and partially shaded CAMPGROUND with mountain view. *From jct US 302 & US 3: Go 2 mi N on US 3, then 3/4 mi NE on Hwy 115.* ◆◆◆◆FACILITIES: 65 sites, most common site width 25 feet, 35 ft. max RV length, 8 full hookups, 35 water & elec (20,30 & 50 amp receptacles), 22 no hookups, 22 pull-thrus, tenting available, sewage disposal, laundry, public phone, grocery store, ice, tables, fire rings, wood. ◆◆◆RECREATION: rec room/area, swim pool, playground, planned group activities, badminton, horseshoes, hiking trails, volleyball. Open Memorial Day through Columbus Day. Rates available upon request. Member of NE-HA-CA. Phone: (603) 846-5559. KOA 10% value card discount.

**Living Water Campground**—Semi-shaded, grassy, riverside area with a mountain view. *From jct US 3 & US 302: Go 1000 feet E on US 302.* ◆◆◆FACILITIES: 86 sites, most common site width 30 feet, 13 full hookups, 29 water & elec (20 & 30 amp receptacles), 44 no hookups, tenting available, sewage disposal, laundry, public phone, grocery store, ice, tables, fire rings, wood. ◆◆◆RECREATION: rec hall, swim pool, river fishing, playground, badminton, sports field, horseshoes, volleyball. No pets. Open Memorial Day through Columbus Day. Rate in 1995 $20-24 for 2 persons. Member of NE-HA-CA. Phone: (800) 257-0708.

TWIN MOUNTAIN—Continued

**Tarry-Ho Campground**—Grassy meadow with mountain view beside a river. *From jct US 3 & US 302: Go 3/4 mi W on US 302.* ◆◆◆FACILITIES: 67 sites, most common site width 33 feet, 9 full hookups, 53 water & elec (20 amp receptacles), 5 no hookups, seasonal sites, tenting available, sewage disposal, limited grocery store, ice, tables, fire rings, grills, wood. ◆◆◆RECREATION: rec hall, swim pool, river swimming, canoeing, river fishing, badminton, horseshoes, volleyball. Open all year. Rate in 1995 $14-17 for 2 persons. No refunds. Member of NE-HA-CA. Phone: (603) 846-5577.

**Twin Mountain Motor Court & RV Park**—RV PARK with open, level sites and mountain views. *From jct US 302 & US 3: Go 1 mi S on US 3.* ◆◆◆◆FACILITIES: 18 sites, most common site width 30 feet, accepts full hookup units only, 18 full hookups, (15 & 30 amp receptacles), 18 pull-thrus, laundry, limited grocery store, ice, tables. ◆◆RECREATION: swim pool, river fishing, badminton, horseshoes, volleyball. No tents. Open May 20 through Oct 20. Rate in 1995 $25 for 2 persons. Member of NE-HA-CA. Phone: (603) 846-5574.

WHITE MOUNTAIN NATIONAL FOREST (Sugarloaf I Campground)—*From jct US 3 & US 302: Go 2 1/3 mi E on US 302, then at Zealand Recreation Area follow signs 1/2 mi S on FR 16.* FACILITIES: 29 sites, 22 ft. max RV length, 29 no hookups, tenting available, tables, fire rings, grills. RECREATION: fishing, hiking trails. Open mid May through mid Oct. No showers. Phone: (603) 869-2626.

WHITE MOUNTAIN NATIONAL FOREST (Sugarloaf II Campground)—*From jct US 3 & US 302: Go 2 1/4 mi E on US 302, then at Zealand Recreation Area follow signs 1/2 mi S on FR 16.* FACILITIES: 33 sites, 22 ft. max RV length, 33 no hookups, tenting available, non-flush toilets, handicap restroom facilities, tables, fire rings. RECREATION: fishing, hiking trails. Open mid May through mid Oct. No water service in cold weather. No showers. Phone: (603) 869-2626.

## WARREN—D-3

**MOOSE HILLOCK CAMPGROUND**—CAMPGROUND with wooded, brook and pond front sites. *From jct I-93 (exit 26) & Hwy 25W: Go 20 mi W on Hwy 25, then 1 mi N on Hwy 118.*

WELCOME

◆◆◆FACILITIES: 151 sites, most common site width 32 feet, 31 full hookups, 72 water & elec (20 & 30 amp receptacles), 48 no hookups, sea-

MOOSE HILLOCK CAMPGROUND—Continued on next page
WARREN—Continued on next page

WARREN—Continued
MOOSE HILLOCK CAMPGROUND—Continued

sonal sites, a/c allowed, heater allowed, tenting available, group sites for tents, RV rentals, handicap restroom facilities, sewage disposal, laundry, public phone, limited grocery store, RV supplies, LP gas refill by weight/by meter, ice, tables, fire rings, wood.

◆◆◆◆RECREATION: rec hall, coin games, 2 swim pools (heated), wading pool, pond/stream fishing, basketball hoop, playground, planned group activities (weekends only), badminton, sports field, horseshoes, hiking trails, volleyball.

Open May 15 through Columbus Day. Rate in 1995 $23-26 per family. No refunds. Master Card/Visa accepted. Member of NE-HA-CA. Phone: (603) 764-5294.

SEE AD PAGE 554

**SCENIC VIEW CAMPGROUND**—Rural CAMPGROUND with shaded or open sites with most sites along a river & stream. *From jct I-93 (exit 26) & Hwy 25: Go 18 mi W on Hwy 25.*

WELCOME

◆◆◆FACILITIES: 106 sites, most common site width 36 feet, 44 full hookups, 48 water & elec (15,20 & 30 amp receptacles), 14 no hookups, seasonal sites, 5 pull-thrus, a/c allowed ($), heater allowed ($), cable TV ($), tenting available, group sites for tents/RVs, RV storage, handicap restroom facilities, sewage disposal, laundry, public phone, limited grocery store, LP gas refill by weight/by meter, ice, tables, fire rings, wood.

◆◆◆RECREATION: rec hall, rec room/area, coin games, swim pool (heated), river fishing, basketball hoop, playground, badminton, sports field, horseshoes, volleyball.

Open May 1 through Oct 15. Rate in 1995 $16-20 per family. Master Card/Visa accepted. Member of NE-HA-CA. Phone: (603) 764-9380.

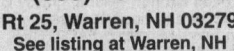

SEE AD THIS PAGE

## WASHINGTON—E-2

PILLSBURY STATE PARK—*From town: Go 2 mi N on Hwy 31.* FACILITIES: 20 sites, 20 no hookups, tenting available, non-flush toilets, tables, fire rings, wood. RECREATION: boating, no motors, canoeing, pond/stream fishing, hiking trails. Recreation open to the public. Open mid May through mid Oct. No showers. Phone: (603) 863-2860.

## WEARE—E-3

**Autumn Hills Campground**—Shaded sites on rolling terrain. *From jct Hwy 149 & Hwy 114: Go 2 1/2 mi E on Hwy 114.* ◆◆FACILITIES: 97 sites, most common site width 25 feet, 76 full hookups, 21 water & elec (15 & 30 amp receptacles), seasonal sites, 5 pull-thrus, tenting available, sewage disposal, public phone, LP gas refill by weight, ice, tables, fire rings, grills, wood. ◆◆◆RECREATION: rec room/area, pavilion, swim pool, pond fishing, playground, badminton, sports field, horseshoes, volleyball. Open Apr 29 through Sep 25. Rate in 1995 $18 per family. Member of NE-HA-CA. Phone: (603) 529-2425.

**Cold Springs Campground**—Rural, wooded area beside a pond. *From jct Hwy 149 & Hwy 114: Go 1 mi S on Hwy 114.* ◆◆◆FACILITIES: 250 sites, most common site width 25 feet, 35 ft. max RV length, 150 full hookups, 90 water & elec (30 amp receptacles), 10 no hookups, seasonal sites, tenting available, sewage disposal, laundry, public phone, grocery store, ice, tables, fire rings, wood. ◆◆◆◆RECREATION: rec hall, rec room/area, equipped pavilion, 2 swim pools (heated), river swimming, playground, planned group activities (weekends only), tennis court, horseshoes, volleyball. Open mid Apr through Columbus Day. Rates available upon request. No refunds. Member of NE-HA-CA. Phone: (603) 529-2528.

## WEBSTER—E-3

**COLD BROOK CAMPGROUND**—Prepared sites along a brook in a forest. *From jct I-89 (exit 7) & Hwy 103: Go 3/4 mi E on Hwy 103, then 3 mi N on Hwy 127.*

WELCOME

◆◆FACILITIES: 60 sites, most common site width 50 feet, 28 full hookups, 32 water & elec (15 & 20 amp receptacles), seasonal sites, 9 pull-thrus, a/c allowed, heater not allowed, tenting available, sewage disposal, laundry, public phone, tables, fire rings, wood.

◆◆RECREATION: canoeing, 4 canoe boat rentals, river/pond fishing, basketball hoop, shuffleboard court, horseshoes.

Open May 1 through Oct 1. Rate in 1995 $12-14 per family. Member of NE-HA-CA. Phone: (603) 746-3390.

SEE AD CONCORD PAGE 537

## WEIRS BEACH—D-3

**Hack-Ma-Tack Family Campground**—CAMPGROUND with some wooded sites. *From jct Hwy 104 & US 3: Go 2 1/2 mi S on US 3.* ◆◆FACILITIES: 75 sites, most common site width 35 feet, 2 full hookups, 68 water & elec (15,20 & 30 amp receptacles), 5 no hookups, seasonal sites, 5 pull-thrus, tenting available, sewage disposal, public phone, limited grocery store, ice, tables, fire rings, wood. ◆◆RECREATION: rec room/area, swim pool, shuffleboard court, horseshoes. Open May 8 through Columbus Day. Facilities fully operational Memorial Day through Labor Day. Rate in 1995 $20-23 for 2 persons. No refunds. Member of NE-HA-CA. Phone: (603) 366-5977.

WEIRS BEACH—Continued on next page

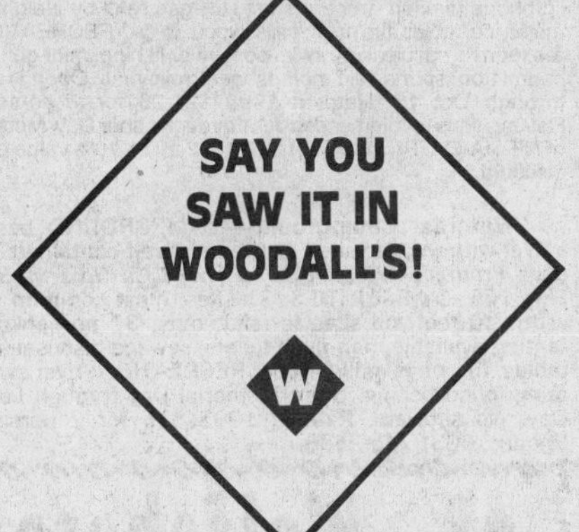
SAY YOU
SAW IT IN
WOODALL'S!
W

**DIVERSITY**

Human beings are more alike than unalike, and what is true anywhere is true everywhere. I encourage travel to as many destinations as possible. Perhaps travel cannot prevent bigotry, but by demonstrating that all people laugh, cry, eat, worry, and die, it can introduce the idea that if we try to understand each other, we may even become friends. *Maya Angelou*

I'm a great believer in luck and I find the harder I work the more I have of it.

WEIRS BEACH—Continued

▶ **MOUNT WASHINGTON CRUISE**—*From jct Hwy 11 & US 3: Go 5 1/2 mi N on US 3, then 1/2 mi NE to Weirs Beach Dock.* Steamship Line offering scenic day and moonlight dinner and dance cruises. Call for port & departure times. Open mid May through late Oct. Discover/Master Card/Visa accepted. Phone: (603) 366-5531.

**SEE AD TRAVEL SECTION PAGE 530**

**Paugus Bay Campground**—Wooded, terraced sites on a hillside. Most full hookups occupied by seasonal campers. *From jct Hwy 104 & US 3: Go 4 mi S on US 3, then 2/10 mi W on Hilliard Rd.* ◆◆◆FACILITIES: 127 sites, most common site width 25 feet, 102 full hookups, 25 water & elec (15,20 & 30 amp receptacles), seasonal sites, tenting available, handicap restroom facilities, sewage disposal, laundry, public phone, limited grocery store, ice, tables, fire rings, wood. ◆◆◆RECREATION: rec hall, pavilion, lake swimming, boating, canoeing, ramp, dock, 5 canoe boat rentals, lake fishing, playground, horseshoes. Open May 15 through Oct 15. Rate in 1995 $25-27 per family. Member of NE-HA-CA. Phone: (603) 366-4757.

**PINE HOLLOW CAMPING WORLD** (CAMP RESORT)—Level, hillside sites in a semi-wooded CAMP RESORT. *From jct Hwy 104 & US 3: Go 2 3/4 mi S on US 3.*

FACILITIES: 31 sites, most common site width 20 feet, 17 full hookups, 12 water & elec (20 & 30 amp receptacles), 2 no hookups, seasonal sites, a/c allowed, heater not allowed, tenting available, tables, fire rings, wood.

RECREATION: swim pool, horseshoes.

Open May 15 through Oct 31. Rate in 1995 $25 per family. Master Card/Visa accepted. Member of NE-HA-CA. Phone: (603) 366-2222.

**SEE AD PAGE 555**

**Weirs Beach Tent and Trailer Park**—CAMPGROUND with some wooded and some grassy sites. *From jct Hwy 104 & US 3: Go 4 mi S on US 3.* ◆◆FACILITIES: 168 sites, most common site width 20 feet, 31 ft. max RV length, 70 full hookups, 70 water & elec (20 amp receptacles), 28 no hookups, seasonal sites, 75 pull-thrus, tenting available, sewage disposal, public phone, ice, tables, fire rings, wood. RECREATION: horseshoes. Open May 15 through Sep 15. Self contained units Sep 16 thru Oct 12 Rate in 1995 $18-20 for 2 persons. No refunds. Phone: (603) 366-4747.



## WENTWORTH—D-3

**PINE HAVEN CAMPGROUND**—Mostly level sites in a pine forest beside river. *From jct I-93 (exit 26) & Hwy 25: Go 12 mi W on Hwy 25.*

◆◆◆FACILITIES: 88 sites, most common site width 25 feet, 19 full hookups, 44 water & elec (15,20 & 30 amp receptacles), 25 no hookups, seasonal sites, 4 pull-thrus, a/c allowed ($), heater not allowed, tenting available, group sites for tents, sewage disposal, laundry, public phone, limited grocery store, RV supplies, LP gas refill by weight, ice, tables, fire rings, grills, wood.

◆◆◆◆RECREATION: rec room/area, coin games, swim pool, river swimming, 4 canoe boat rentals, river fishing, basketball hoop, playground, shuffleboard court, planned group activities, recreation director, badminton, sports field, horseshoes, volleyball.

Open May 15 through Oct 15. Rate in 1995 $17.50-23 per family. American Express/Discover/Master Card/Visa accepted. Member of NE-HA-CA. Phone: (603) 786-9942.

**SEE AD THIS PAGE**

## WEST OSSIPEE—D-4

**WESTWARD SHORES CAMPING AREA**—Level, lakeside CAMPGROUND with wooded sites. *From jct Hwy 25 & Hwy 16: Go 3 1/2 mi S on Hwy 16.*

◆◆◆FACILITIES: 248 sites, most common site width 40 feet, 49 full hookups, 199 water & elec (20 & 30 amp receptacles), seasonal sites, a/c allowed, heater allowed, cable TV, tenting available, RV storage, sewage disposal, public phone, limited grocery store, ice, tables, fire rings, wood, traffic control gate.

◆◆◆◆RECREATION: rec hall, equipped pavilion, coin games, lake swimming, boating, canoeing, ramp, dock, 12 canoe boat rentals, water skiing, lake fishing, basketball hoop, playground, planned group activities, tennis court, badminton, sports field. horseshoes, volleyball, cross country skiing, snowmobile trails.

Open May 15 through Columbus Day. Winter camping Thanksgiving to Mar 15. Rate in 1995 $20 per family. Master Card/Visa accepted. Member of NE-HA-CA. Phone: (603) 539-6445.

**SEE AD OSSIPEE PAGE 551**

WHITE LAKE STATE PARK—*From split of Hwy 16 & Hwy 25: Go N on Hwy 16.* FACILITIES: 200 sites, 200 no hookups, tenting available, public phone, grocery store, ice, tables, wood. RECREATION: lake swimming, boating, canoe boat rentals, lake fishing, hiking trails. No pets. Open mid May through Columbus Day. Phone: (603) 323-7350.



NH **State Gem: Smoky Quartz** NH

## WINCHESTER—F-2

**FOREST LAKE CAMPGROUND**—Scenic, rural area with wooded, lakeside campsites and mountain view. *From jct I-91 (exit 28A, Northfield, Mass. exit): Go 15 mi N on Hwy 10.*

◆◆◆FACILITIES: 150 sites, most common site width 35 feet, 35 ft. max RV length, 85 full hookups, 55 water & elec (20 & 30 amp receptacles), 10 no hookups, seasonal sites, a/c allowed ($), heater not allowed, phone hookups, tenting available, sewage disposal, public phone, LP gas refill by weight/by meter, tables, fire rings, grills, wood, traffic control gate.

◆◆◆◆RECREATION: rec hall, rec room/area, coin games, lake swimming, boating, canoeing, ramp, 3 row/3 canoe/3 pedal boat rentals, water skiing, lake fishing, basketball hoop, playground, shuffleboard court, planned group activities (weekends only), tennis court, sports field, horseshoes.

Open May 1 through Oct 1. Rate in 1995 $15-18 per family. No refunds. Reservations recommended Jun 15 through Labor Day. Member of NE-HA-CA. Phone: (603) 239-4267.

**SEE AD THIS PAGE**

## WOLFEBORO—D-4

**WOLFEBORO CAMPGROUND**—Natural sites shaded by tall trees in a rural setting. *From jct Hwy 109 & Hwy 28 (center of town): Go 4 1/2 mi N on Hwy 28, then 1/4 mi E on Haines Hill Rd.*

◆◆FACILITIES: 50 sites, most common site width 35 feet, 34 ft. max RV length, 40 water & elec (15 & 20 amp receptacles), 10 no hookups, seasonal sites, a/c not allowed, heater not allowed, tenting available, RV storage, sewage disposal, public phone, limited grocery store, LP gas refill by weight/by meter, ice, tables, fire rings, grills, wood.

◆RECREATION: rec hall, badminton, horseshoes, volleyball.

Open May 15 through Oct 15. Rate in 1995 $15-16 for 2 persons. Member of NE-HA-CA. Phone: (603) 569-9881.

**SEE AD THIS PAGE**

## WOODSTOCK—D-3

**KOA-Broken Branch**—Rural, grassy CAMPGROUND with mountain view and mostly level sites. *From I-93 (exit 31): Go 2 mi S on Hwy 175.* ◆◆◆ FACILITIES: 130 sites, most common site width 50 feet, 15 full hookups, 70 water & elec (20 & 30 amp receptacles), 45 no hookups, seasonal sites, 40 pull-thrus, tenting available, sewage disposal, laundry, public phone, limited grocery store, LP gas refill by weight/by meter, ice, tables, fire rings, grills, wood. ◆◆◆RECREATION: rec room/area, pavilion, swim pool, river fishing, mini-golf ($), badminton, sports field, horseshoes, volleyball. Open May 1 through Oct 15. Rate in 1995 $21-26 for 2 persons. Reservations recommended Jul 1 through Labor Day. Member of NE-HA-CA. Phone: (800) 327-1562. KOA 10% value card discount.

**Waterest Campground**—CAMPGROUND beside a river with wooded sites. For tents or self-contained RVs only. *From jct I-93 (exit 31) & Hwy 175: Go 1 mi S on Hwy 175.* ◆◆FACILITIES: 31 sites, most common site width 40 feet, no sites for slide-outs, 31 no hookups, tenting available, non-flush toilets, sewage disposal, ice, tables, fire rings, grills, wood. RECREATION: river swimming, pond fishing. Open Memorial Day through Labor Day. No showers. Rate in 1995 $15 for 2 persons. Phone: (603) 745-2586.



**SAFETY TIP**

***Cottonwood and poplar trees tend to have branches that snap off. Avoid them when pitching your tent.***

# New York

## TRAVEL SECTION

### Free Information from Travel Section Advertisers

The following businesses have placed an ad in the New York Travel Section. To receive free information, enter their Reader Service number on the Reader Service Card opposite page 16 in the front of this directory:

| Advertiser | RS # | Ad Pg. |
|---|---|---|
| Buckridge Nudist Park | 652 | 589 |
| Campark Resorts | 649 | 588 |
| Campground Owners of NY | 553 | 587 |
| Chautauqua-Allegheny | 714 | 585 |
| Fulton Co. Tourism Office | 651 | 583 |
| Kittatinny Campground | 653 | 589 |
| KOA-Niagara Falls | 181 | 586 |
| KOA-Williamsburg | 656 | 588 |
| Leatherstocking Country | 655 | 581 |
| NY State Dept. of Env. Con. | 650 | 582 |
| Oswego County | 705 | 580 |
| Shalamar Lake Niagara | 142 | 586 |
| Sullivan County | 654 | 584 |
| Yogi Bear—Flatrock | 508 | 577 |
| Yogi Bear—Niagara Falls | 244 | 586 |

### Time Zone/Topography

Eastern Standard/Eastern Daylight Savings.

New York covers an area of 49,576 square miles. Of the total area, inland waters account for 1,745 square miles. The state has more than 4,000 lakes and ponds, 3,140 square miles of water in Lakes Ontario and Erie and contains 14 1/2 million acres of forestland.

In the east the state is mountainous, in the western and central parts it is level or hilly, and in the southern section it is rolling and hilly. Highest elevations are in the Adirondack and Catskill Mountains. The highest peak is 5,344-foot Mount Marcy, the largest inland lake is 79.8-square mile Oneida and the longest river is the 315-mile Hudson.

### Climate

Because of its topography and its location between the Atlantic Ocean and the Great Lakes, New York has a varied climate. The average mean annual temperature in the state is about 45°, though it varies from 54° in New York City to about 45° in the Adirondacks. The mountain and plateau regions have heavy snowfalls and extreme changes in temperature; daytime temperature is often high, but nights are quite cool. Long Island, on the other hand, has light snowfall and fairly constant temperatures because of the moderating effect of the Atlantic Ocean. Similarly, the area adjoining the Great Lakes, and to a lesser extent, the Finger Lakes, have long, mild autumns and winters that are much less severe than the uplands a few miles away.

The following are average temperatures and precipitation for various large cities:

| | *Average Temperature* | | *Average Precipitation* | |
|---|---|---|---|---|
| | *Jan.* | *July* | *Jan.* | *July* |
| Albany | 22.7° | 72.1° | 2.47" | 3.49" |
| Binghamton | 23.8 | 68.4 | 2.50 | 3.71 |
| Buffalo | 24.5 | 69.8 | 2.84 | 2.57 |
| NY City | 33.2 | 76.8 | 3.31 | 3.70 |
| Rochester | 25.2 | 71.6 | 2.40 | 2.84 |
| Syracuse | 24.0 | 72.2 | 3.15 | 3.09 |

### Travel Information Sources

**State Agency:** New York State Dept. of Economic Development, Division of Tourism, 1 Commerce Plaza, Albany, NY 12245 (800-CALL-NYS or 518-474-4116).

State park central reservation phone number: 800-456-CAMP.

The hours of operation for New York state parks and historic sites are subject to change. For up-to-date information, please contact New York State Parks, 518-474-0456.

**Regional Agencies:**

• *Adirondack Regional Information:* (800-487-6867).

• *Central Adirondack Assn.:* (315-369-6983).

• *Allegany County Tourism,* Rm. 208, City Office Bldg., Belmont, NY 14815 (800-836-1869 or 716-268-9229).

• *Broome County Chamber of Commerce,* Box 995, Binghamton, NY 13902 (800-836-6740 or 607-772-8860).

• *Catskills Region:* (800-882-2287).

• *Cattaraugus County Tourism Bureau,* 303 Court St., Little Valley, NY 14755 (800-331-0543 or 716-938-9111).

• *Delaware County Chamber of Commerce,* 97 Main St., Delhi, NY 13753 (800-642-4443 or 607-746-2281).

• *Dutchess County Tourism,* 3 Neptune Rd., Poughkeepsie, NY 12601 (800-445-3131 or 914-463-4000).

• *Essex County Info. Center,* RD 1, Box 230, Crown Point, NY 12928 (518-597-4646).

• *Finger Lakes Assn.,* 309 Lake St., Penn Yan, NY 14527 (800-KIT-4-FUN or 315-536-7488).

• *Franklin County Tourism,* 63 W. Main St., Malone, NY 12953 (518-483-6788).

• *Fulton County Chamber of Commerce,* 18 Cayadutta St., Gloversville, NY 12078 (800-676-3858 or 518-725-0641).

• *Greene County Promotion Dept.,* Box 527, Catskill, NY 12414 (800-542-2414 or 518-943-3223).

• *Herkimer County Chamber of Commerce,* Box 129, Mohawk, NY 13407 (315-866-7820).

• *Leatherstocking Country,* 327 N. Main St., P.O. Box 447, Herkimer, NY 13350 (800-233-8778 or 315-866-1500).

• *Livingston County Chamber of Commerce,* 53 Main St., Mount Morris, NY 14510 (716-346-6690).

• *Long Island Convention & Visitor's*



**FREE INFO! Enter number on Reader Service Card opposite pg. 16: Yogi Bear's Jellystone–Flatrock #508.**

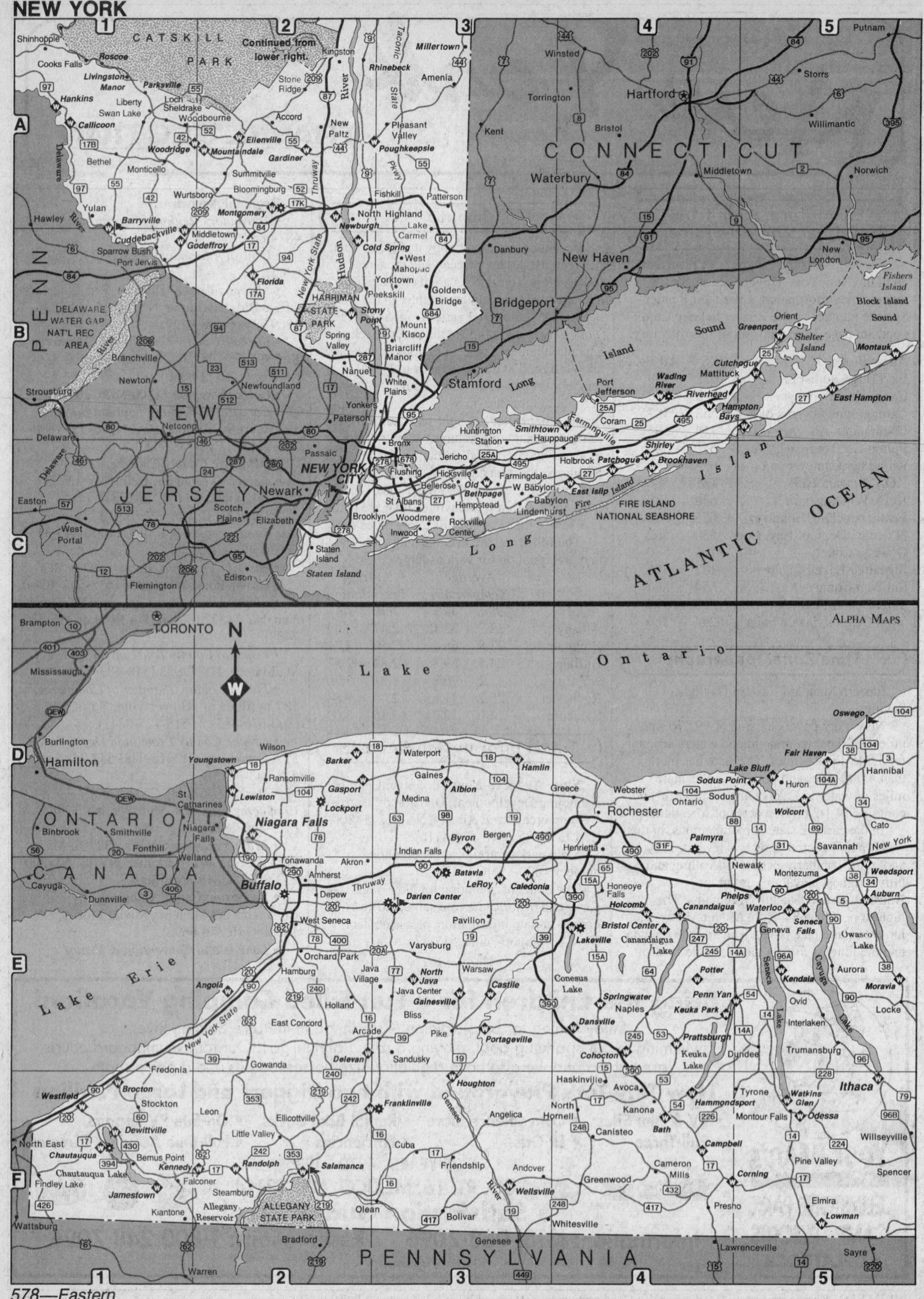

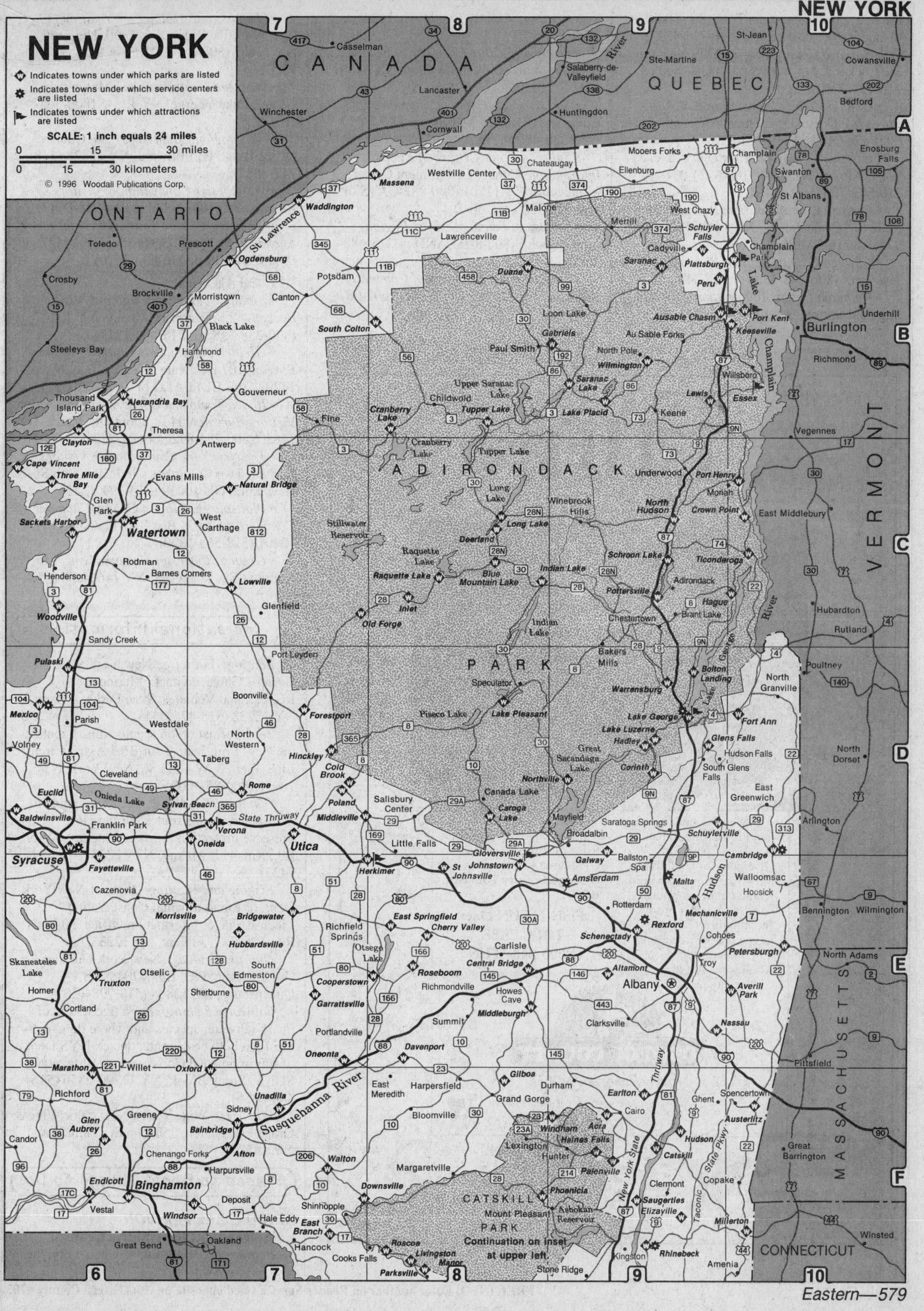
NEW YORK
Indicates towns under which parks are listed
Indicates towns under which service centers are listed
Indicates towns under which attractions are listed
SCALE: 1 inch equals 24 miles
0 15 30 miles
0 15 30 kilometers
© 1996 Woodall Publications Corp.
CANADA
QUEBEC
ONTARIO
ADIRONDACK PARK
VERMONT
MASSACHUSETTS
CONNECTICUT
CATSKILL PARK
Continuation on inset at upper left.
Casselman
Lancaster
Winchester
Cornwall
Salaberry-de-Valleyfield
Huntingdon
Ste-Martine
St-Jean
Cowansville
Bedford
Enosburg Falls
Swanton
St Albans
Champlain
Mooers Forks
Chateaugay
Ellenburg
Westville Center
Massena
Malone
West Chazy
Schuyler Falls
Merrill
Cadyville
Saranac
Plattsburgh
Peru
Champlain Park
Waddington
St Lawrence
Lawrenceville
Toledo
Prescott
Ogdensburg
Potsdam
Duane
Crosby
Brockville
Morristown
Canton
Loon Lake
Ausable Chasm
Port Kent
Keeseville
Burlington
Underhill
South Colton
Gabriels
Au Sable Forks
Black Lake
Paul Smith
North Pole
Wilmington
Steeleys Bay
Hammond
Richmond
Saranac Lake
Upper Saranac Lake
Willsboro
Gouverneur
Childwold
Tupper Lake
Lake Placid
Lewis
Essex
Thousand Island Park
Alexandria Bay
Cranberry Lake
Fine
Keene
Theresa
Vegennes
Clayton
Antwerp
Tupper Lake
Cape Vincent
Three Mile Bay
Evans Mills
Natural Bridge
Long Lake
Underwood
Port Henry
Moriah
Glen Park
North Hudson
Crown Point
East Middlebury
Sackets Harbor
Watertown
West Carthage
Winebrook Hills
Stillwater Reservoir
Deerland
Long Lake
Rodman
Raquette Lake
Schroon Lake
Ticonderoga
Henderson
Barnes Corners
Blue Mountain Lake
Indian Lake
Adirondack
Lowville
Pottersville
Hague
Inlet
Glenfield
Brant Lake
Hubardton
Woodville
Old Forge
Chestertown
Sandy Creek
Rutland
Port Leyden
Bakers Mills
Pulaski
Bolton Landing
Poultney
North Granville
Speculator
Warrensburg
Boonville
Mexico
Parish
Forestport
Lake Pleasant
Piseco Lake
Lake George
Fort Ann
Westdale
Lake Luzerne
Hadley
Glens Falls
Volney
North Western
Hinckley
Great Sacandaga Lake
Hudson Falls
North Dorset
Taberg
Cold Brook
South Glens Falls
Cleveland
Northville
Corinth
Euclid
Oneida Lake
Sylvan Beach
Rome
Canada Lake
East Greenwich
Baldwinsville
Poland
Salisbury Center
Caroga Lake
Franklin Park
State Thruway
Verona
Middleville
Mayfield
Saratoga Springs
Schuylerville
Arlington
Oneida
Utica
Little Falls
Broadalbin
Syracuse
Fayetteville
Herkimer
St Johnsville
Gloversville
Johnstown
Galway
Ballston Spa
Cambridge
Amsterdam
Malta
Walloomsac
Hoosick
Cazenovia
Rotterdam
Hudson
Bennington
Wilmington
Morrisville
Bridgewater
East Springfield
Cherry Valley
Rexford
Mechanicville
Richfield Springs
Carlisle
Schenectady
Cohoes
Hubbardsville
Otsego Lake
Petersburgh
Skaneateles Lake
Otselic
South Edmeston
Central Bridge
Altamont
Troy
North Adams
Truxton
Cooperstown
Roseboom
Albany
Homer
Sherburne
Richmondville
Howes Cave
Averill Park
Cortland
Garrattsville
Middleburgh
Summit
Clarksville
Portlandville
Nassau
Marathon
Willet
Oxford
Oneonta
Davenport
Pittsfield
Gilboa
Richford
Unadilla
East Meredith
Harpersfield
Durham
Earlton
Thruway
Ghent
Spencertown
Sidney
Grand Gorge
Cairo
Glen Aubrey
Greene
Susquehanna River
Bloomville
Windham
Acra
Austerlitz
Candor
Bainbridge
Lexington
Haines Falls
Hudson
Chenango Forks
Afton
Hunter
Catskill
Great Barrington
Harpursville
Walton
Margaretville
Palenville
New York State
Taconic State Pkwy
Copake
Endicott
Binghamton
Downsville
Phoenicia
Clermont
Vestal
Deposit
Shinhopple
Mount Pleasant
Ashokan Reservoir
Saugerties
Elizaville
Windsor
Hale Eddy
East Branch
Millerton
Oakland
Great Bend
Hancock
Roscoe
Livingston Manor
Kingston
Rhinebeck
Winsted
Cooks Falls
Parksville
Stone Ridge
Amenia
Lake Champlain
Lake George
Hudson River
A
B
C
D
E
F
6
7
8
9
10

*Bureau,* 1899 Hempstead Tpke, Ste. 500, East Meadow, NY 11554-1042 (516-794-4222).

• *Niagara County Tourism,* 139 Niagara St., Lockport, NY 14094 (800-338-7890 or 716-439-7300).

• *Oneida County Convention & Vistiors Bureau,* P.O. Box 551, Utica, NY 13503 (800-426-3132 or 315-724-7221).

• *Orleans County Tourism Office,* Rte. 31 West, Albion, NY 14411 (800-724-0314 or 716-589-7004).

• *Ontario County Tourism Bureau,* 248 S. Main St., Canandaigua, NY 14424 (800-654-9798 or 716-394-3915).

• *Oswego County Dept. of Promotion & Tourism:* (800-248-4386 or 315-349-8322).

• *Puthnam County Information,* 76 Main St., Cold Spring, NY 10516.

• *Saratoga County Promotion Agency:* (800-526-8970).

• *Schuyler County Chamber of Commerce,* 1000 Franklin St., Watkins Glen, NY 14891 (607-535-4300).

• *St. Lawrence County Chamber of Commerce,* Drawer A., Canton, NY 13617 (315-386-4000).

• *Sullivan County Office of Public Information,* County Government Center, Monticello, NY 12701 (800-882-CATS or 914-793-3000 ext. 5010).

• *Thousand Islands-Seaway Region Information:* (800-8-ISLAND or 315-482-2520).

• *Tioga County Chamber of Commerce,* 188 Front St., Owego, NY 13827 (607-687-2020).

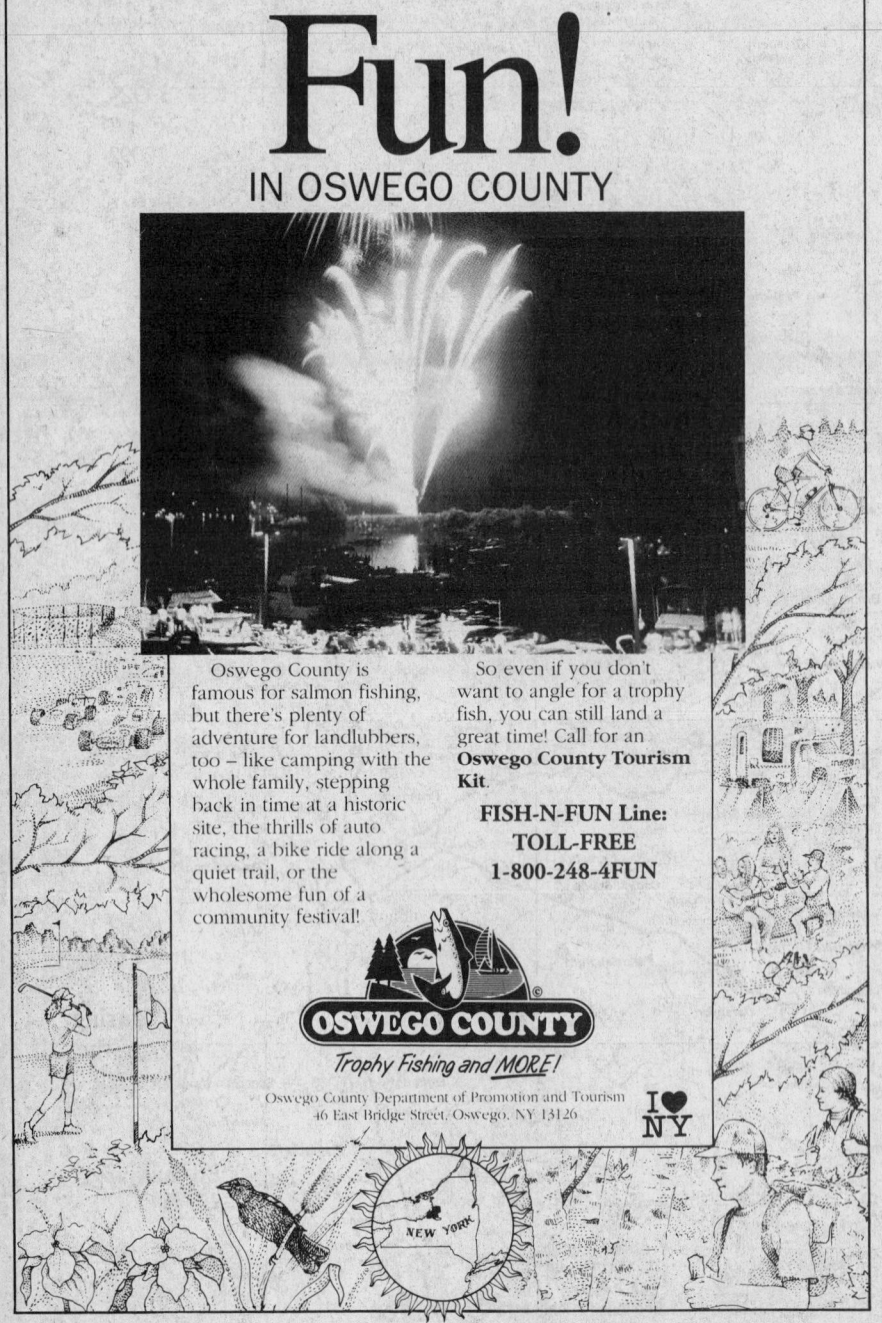



• *Ulster County Public Information Office,* County Office Bldg., Box 1800, Kingston, NY 12401 (800-DIAL-UCO or 914-331-9300).

• *Warren County Tourism,* Municipal Center, Lake George, NY 12845 (800-365-1050).

• *Washington County Tourism,* County Office Bldg., Fort Edward, NY 12828 (518-747-4687).

• *Westchester Convention & Visitors Bureau:* (800-833-9282 or 914-948-0047).

• *Wyoming County Tourism Promotion Agency,* P.O. Box 502, Castile, NY 14427 (800-839-3919 or 716-493-3190).

**Local Agencies:**

• *Albany County Convention & Visitors Bureau,* 52 S. Pearl St., Albany, NY 12207 (800-258-3582 or 518-434-1217).

• *Greater Buffalo Convention & Visitors Bureau,* 107 Delaware Ave., Buffalo, NY 14202 (800-BUFFALO or 716-852-0511).

• *Ithaca/Tompkins County Convention & Visitors Bureau,* 904 E. Shore Dr., Ithaca, NY 14850 (800-284-8422 or 607-272-1313).

• *The New York Convention & Visitors Bureau,* Two Columbus Circle and 59th St., New York, NY 10019 (212-397-8222).

• *Plattsburgh, Clinton County Chamber of Commerce,* Chazy, Box 310, Plattsburgh, NY 12901 (518-563-1000).

• *Greater Rochester Visitors Assn.,* 126 Andrews St., Rochester, NY 14604 (716-546-6810).

## Recreational Information

*Boating:* For a free New York State Boater's Guide, contact: Marine & Recreational Vehicles, State Parks, Albany, NY 12238 (518-474-0445).

For information on scenic cruises contact the New York State Tour Boat Assn., Circle Line, Pier 83, W 42nd St., New York, NY 10036 (800-852-0095).

*Canoeing/Kayaking:* For a free guide to Adirondack canoe routes, write: DEC Preserve Protection & Management, 50 Wolf Rd., Rm. 412, Albany, NY 12233 (518-457-7433).

*Fishing and Hunting:* State of New York Dept. of Environmental Conservation, License Sale & Information Office, 50 Wolf Rd., Rm. 111, Albany, NY 12233.

*Outfitters/guides:* New York Outdoor Guides Assn., P.O. Box 4704 NYS, Queensbury, NY 12804 (518-798-1253).

*Saltwater Fishing:* For a free listing of many saltwater species and where they're most likely to be caught, contact: NYS Dept. of Environmental Conservation, Bldg. 40 SUNY, Stony Brook, NY 11790-2356 (516-444-0435).

*Wineries:* Wine Trails, New York Wine & Grape Foundation, 350 Elm St., Penn Yan, NY 14527.

## Places to See & Things to Do

### *ADIRONDACKS REGION*

**Adirondacks Interpretive Centers,** Newcomb and Paul Smiths. Open daily, these

FREE INFO! Enter number on Reader Service Card opposite pg. 16: Leatherstocking Country #655.

informative centers provide visitors with interpretive trails, exhibit halls, theater and classroom presentations, demonstrations and festival programs.

**Ausable Chasm.** Walking tour and boat ride through 1 1/2-mile long natural scenic wonder. When Major John Howe first discovered the Chasm, he made a perilous descent suspended on ropes. Today visitors proceed along stone galleries by way of stairs and steel bridges at various levels, or by boat.

**Crown Point State Historic Site,** Crown Point. Ruins of Fort St. Frederic, "His Majesty's Fort of Crown Point," and surrounding lands. Original 18th-century structures. Modern visitor center features exhibits interpreting the French, British and American chapters of Crown Point's history.

**Fort Ticonderoga,** Ticonderoga. Built by the French in 1755 and called "Carillon." Then it was captured by the British in 1759 and renamed "Ticonderoga." In 1775, Ethan Allen seized it in the first victory of the American Revolution. This "Gibraltar of the North" played a key role in the wars for Empire and Freedom in the New World. Today, the Fort houses a great museum collection of 18th-century artifacts and the largest collection of cannons in the New World defends the walls.

**Glens Falls.** "Hometown USA," is home to the Adirondack Red Wings Hockey Team (farm team of the Detroit Red Wings) and the Glens Falls Red Birds Baseball Team, affiliate of the St. Louis Cardinals. Local festivities and attractions include programs by the

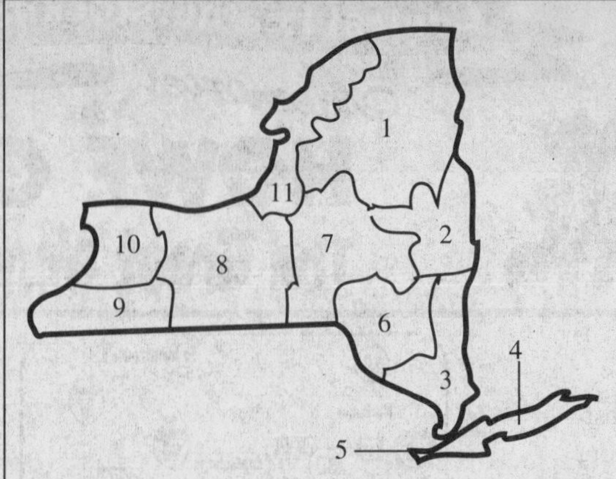


International Arts & Cultural Association, LARAC arts and crafts festivals, the Adirondack Hot Air Balloon Festival and an 8 1/2 mile Warren County Bikeway extending from Glens Falls to Lake George. Other special attractions include:

**High Falls Gorge,** Wilmington. The gorge offers spectacular view of falls and rock formations from modern steel walks. The Ausable River spills 100 feet over High Falls and over three falls down 600 more feet.

**Lake Champlain Ferries.** Visitors can enjoy an auto ferry ride across scenic Lake Champlain. Three crossings: Essex, NY/ Charlotte, VT; Plattsburgh, NY/Grand Isle, VT; and Port Kent, NY/Burlington, VT.

**Lake George.** A resort area of breathtaking beauty, it is an ideal destination during all four seasons. The area offers an array of campgrounds and RV parks, dinner theatres, arcades, water parks, fine restaurants, steamboat cruises and the factory outlets of Lake George on the "Million Dollar Half-Mile." Outdoor sports opportunities abound–from cross-country skiing to sailboating. Lake George is 32 miles long with an excellent beach and features every water sport imaginable from parasailing and scuba diving (some depths are 200 feet) to fishing and leisurely cruises.

*Fort William Henry* is a restored colonial fortress where American history was made during the French and Indian War. It is the site of the history and heritage that inspired the clasic novel "The Last of the Mohicans." Audio-visuals, tours, military drills and

musket and cannon firing.

*Lake George Historical Museum.* Canada St. at Old Warren County Courthouse (1845). Local history, art displays, preservation of original courtroom and jail cells, historical maps and prints.

*Lake George Steamboat Co.* 13 cruises daily in season on Lake George on 3 ships, including an authentic steamboat paddlewheeler. Dinner, jazz and moonlight cruises.

**Lake Placid.** Site of the 1980 Winter Olympic Games has nature trails, boat trips, boat regattas and winter sports museum. Tour Olympic sites by self-guided motor tours or packaged guide tours.

*Olympic Sports Complex*, the only bobsled run in the United States. Take the trolley car ride up Mt. Van Hoevenberg and get a close look at the mile-long Olympic track. Olympic luge run and displays of bobsledding and luge equipment. (Ride the runs in winter.)

*Whiteface Mt. Highway and Chairlift.* The eight-mile drive to the 4,867 foot summit offers the most spectacular views in the northeast.

**Old Forge.** Boat liveries, seaplane tour and horseback rides are available. Boat trips include a 28-mile historical lake cruise.

**Split Rock Falls,** Split Rock. The Boquet River drops significantly in a beautiful series of waterfalls and deep pools. Site of the Bishop Iron Forge, ca. 1825 which, by the unique "trompe" method, used falling water to provide a constant flow of air to feed the smelting fires.



**Warrensburg.** Historic river mill town at the confluence of the the Hudson and Schroon Rivers, both of which are noted for fishing, rafting and canoeing. Post-Colonial through Victorian homes are memorials to yesteryear. The antiques capital of the Adirondacks proudly hosts the "World's Largest Garage Sale" where 500 dealers and private sellers provide a treasure hunt each fall.

### CAPITAL-SARATOGA REGION

**Albany.** The state capital city boasts 300 years of history, making it one of the oldest cities in the United States. It was founded by Dutch settlers and in 1797, was chosen the capital of New York State because of its riverside location and system of turnpikes that fanned out from the city making it a transportation hub. Albany attractions include:

*Governor Nelson A. Rockefeller Empire State Plaza.* Free tours are offered of this government complex which encompasses a convention center, performing arts center, the NYS Museum, world's largest contemporary art collection, reflecting pools and more.

*Urban Cultural Park Visitors Center* and recently opened *Henry Hudson Planetarium* explains history of the city as a business, government, and financial leader since the 1600s.

**Fulton County Museum,** Gloversville. Located at 237 Kingsboro Avenue, the museum contains the only glove making exhibit in New York State. It has specialized in the most stylish ladies gloves over the past two centuries. There are collections and displays of historic equipment and methods used to manufacture gloves, as well as a leather tanning exhibit, country store, old candy making shop, and Indian artifacts.

**Saratoga Springs.** A resort city with over 60 restaurants featuring everything from French cuisine to Bavarian delicacies. Lots to see and do–sidewalk cafes, boutiques, U.S.'s longest running coffee house, factory outlets and amusement parks. Points of interest include:

*National Museum of Dance*, which features three large exhibition galleries, Hall of Fame, and a shop dedicated to American dance.

*Saratoga Performing Arts Center.* A summer music and dance festival offering plays, operas, ballet, symphonies, pop music, internationally known modern dance companies and special events.

**Tryon County Court House,** Johnstown. The only Colonial courthouse standing in New York State, perhaps in the country. Located on West Main Street.

**Watervliet Arsenal Museum,** Watervliet. Depicts the story of the Arsenal's service to the U.S. Armed Forces. It traces cannon development from the earliest times to the present day.

### HUDSON VALLEY REGION

**Alice and Hamilton Fish Library,** Garrison. $3 million library emphasizes Revolutionary War period by displaying original documents signed by Washington, Jefferson, Hamilton and others.

**Brotherhood Winery,** Washingtonville.

# CHAUTAUQUA-ALLEGHENY

I ♥ NY. CAMPING

Campers will welcome the variety and beauty of the Chautauqua-Allegheny region. Your options are open when it comes to your desired mode of camping - from full RV hook-ups to primitive tent camping - from cool running springs to heated swimming pools, your family will love the challenges of outdoor living and the advantages of the many amenities offered.

Forests and waterways provide ample opportunities for hiking, scenic tours, fishing, canoeing and boating. There's Lake Erie, Chautauqua Lake, the Allegheny Reservoir, Genesee River and other small lakes and streams in the area.

A buffalo ranch is an unexpected treat to visitors to western New York. A ride on a paddle-wheeled steamboat conjures up visions of Mark Twain or ride the rails on an old-time train. Visit Amish shops and an Indian museum. Enjoy historic sites and quaint little villages, festivals and fairs.

Each of the seasons offers something to enjoy and many campgrounds are open year around. Nature puts on its own show from colorful spring flowers to autumn's special attire of reds, yellows and earth tones. Winter's charm is the backdrop for alpine and nordic skiing, ice skating and snowmobiling.

For additional information or a free Chautauqua-Allegheny Travel Packet:
CHAUTAUQUA-ALLEGHENY REGION: 4 NORTH ERIE STREET,
MAYVILLE, NY 14757-1095 (716) 753-4304

**800-242-4569**

**CAMPING RESORT**

HIGHEST RATED CAMPGROUND IN AREA

**LOCATED RIGHT ON BEAUTIFUL CHAUTAUQUA LAKE**

- TRAVELERS RATE - In after 7 PM, out by 9 AM
- NEAR INTERSTATE HIGHWAY
- ALWAYS OPEN
- ALL CONVENIENCES
- 24 HR. SECURITY
- CHURCH SERVICES (P & C)

ONLY 5 MINUTES FROM THE WORLD FAMOUS **CHAUTAUQUA INSTITUTION**

**CAMP CHAUTAUQUA**
P.O. BOX 100 - STOW, NY 14785
716/789-3435

FULL AMENITIES, SEE LISTING UNDER **CHAUTAUQUA** FOR FURTHER INFO.

Large, Level Sites • Log Cabin Rentals
Mid-Week Rates • Full Service Park
R.V. Service & Parts • Playground
2 In-Ground Pools • Mini-Golf
Pond Fishing • Hiking Trails
Video Arcade • Volleyball
Basketball • Horseshoes

TRIPLE•R CAMPGROUND

REST • RELAXATION • RECREATION •

**3491 Bryant Hill Road • Franklinville, NY**
**716-676-3856**

**CAMPING AREA**

Water & Electric
Primitive
Seasonal Camping Available
Exceptionally Scenic & Active
200 Acres
Swimming • Fishing • Boating • Trails
• Store • Recreation Building

**OPEN MAY 15 THRU COLUMBUS DAY**

Rt. 16, Delevan, NY 14042 492-3715

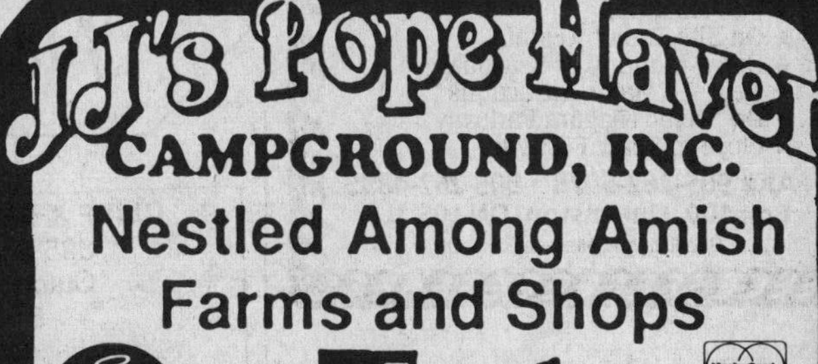


**CAMPGROUND, INC.**

**Nestled Among Amish Farms and Shops**

**"CLEAN, QUIET, SPACIOUS SITES COME FOR ACTIVE FUN OR RELAXATION"**

**30 amp Pull-thru Sites**
**Open May 1st - October 15th**
**Rt. 241 Pope Road, Randolph, NY 14772**
(5 miles from Rt. 17 Expressway, Exit 16)
**Reservations (716) 358-4900**
See listing at Randolph

CHAUTAUQUA • CATTARAUGUS • ALLEGANY COUNTIES

America's oldest winery offers free guided tours and wine tasting, cafe and shops.

**Caramoor Center of Music and the Arts,** Katonah. Mediterranean-style villa and home of the Rosens on 117 wooded acres houses 9 centuries of imported collectibles. Summer outdoor music performances.

**Franklin D. Roosevelt National Historic Site,** Hyde Park. Home of the 32nd President, still maintained as it was in 1945, is now the burial place of Franklin and his wife Eleanor.

**Greenburgh Nature Center,** located on Dromore Road, Scarsdale. Nature museum contains more than 145 exotic and local animals, outdoor nature trails, art exhibits in the manor house and special events.

**Hammond Museum & Oriental Stroll Gardens,** North Salem. Museum of the Humanities plus gardens on 3 1/2-acre site. 15 of these gardens provide the tranquility of the Stroll Garden, which originated in Japan to refresh the spirit.

**Martin Van Buren National Historic Site,** Kinderhook. Restored home of the 8th president contains cartoons about "Old Kinderhook," from whom the positive response, "OK" was derived.

**Museum of the Hudson Highlands,** Cornwall-on-Hudson. Over 60 exhibits of live animals indigenous to Hudson Highlands. Hiking trails and cultural exhibits also on site.

**Museum Village in Orange County,** Monroe. This rural 19th-century village features 30 working exhibits including a blacksmith shop, log cabin and one-room schoolhouse. Live farm animals fill the barn and the general store offers the same items found in a typical 1800s store. Sheep shearing, wool spinning, open hearth cooking and more are demonstrated.

**Newburgh.** One-hour tours of historic homes and points of interest. *Knox Headquarters*, an 18th-century stone house, was the center for several of Washington's commanding officers; *Washington's Headquarters*, was Washington's headquarters during the Revolutionary War; and the *New Windsor Cantonment* which was the last encampment of Washington's Revolutionary Army 1782-83.

**Olana,** Hudson. A 250-acre landscaped estate of artist Frederic Edwin Church, complete with visitor center, walking paths, restoration gardens and home-museum tours. Overlooking the Hudson River, it offers a majestic view of the valley with living scenes of the landscapes Church made famous.

**Rhinebeck.** Site of the oldest hotel in the U.S., circa 1700. Old Rhinebeck Aerodome has a world-famous display of vintage WWI and earlier air craft. Air show Saturday and Sunday, mid-May through October.

**Shaker Museum,** Old Chatham. Finest collection of Shaker-made artifacts in the world depicts over 200 years of Shaker history and culture. Walking trails and herb garden also on premises.

**Tarrytown.** Sleepy Hollow country made famous by Washington Irving. Features include *Sunnyside*, the author's delightful home (built in 1835) on the banks of the Hudson. *Union Church of Pocantico Hills* boasts stained glass windows by modern masters Henri Matisse and Marc Chagall which create a joyful experience in light and color at this small country church.

**Widmark Honey Farms**, Gardiner. One of the largest comb honey producers in the state. Demonstrations every Saturday May-October.

**United States Military Academy,** West Point. Founded in 1802 to train officers for the Army. Parades of cadets in spring, late summer and fall; Military Museum, new Visitors' Center, self-driving tours to the cemetery, old and new chapels, Trophy Point and Fort Putnam.

*LONG ISLAND REGION*

**African-American Museum,** Hempstead. Traces history, culture and contributions of African-American Long Islanders.

**Fire Island.** Fire Island Ferry supplies visitors with easy access to fishing, clamming, swimming, beach walks, guided nature walks and view of Sunken Forest on the Island.

**Greenport.** "New England" on Long Island has everything from boat rentals, charters and seafood restaurants to country yard sales and auctions.

**Long Beach.** This resort island has a 3-mile boardwalk, 5-mile beach and recreation to supply hours of fun.

**Montauk Point Lighthouse,** Montauk. 197-year-old lighthouse, now a museum. Climb 138 steps to the top and walk the grounds.

**Museums at Stony Brook.** History museum features costumes, dolls, toys, textiles and housewares. Carriage Museum has over 100 horsedrawn vehicles and the Art Museum contains works by 19th-century artists.

**Old Bethpage Village Restoration,** Old Bethpage. Pre-Civil War farm village includes inn, store & church. Witness first-hand, craft demonstrations and farm activities.

**Old Westbury Gardens and Mansion,** Old Westbury. Stuart-style mansion surrounded by 100 acres of formal gardens, fields and woods. Summer lawn concerts.

**Planting Fields Arboretum and Coe Mansion,** Oyster Bay. Labeled trees, shrubs, bulbs, plants and greenhouse displays. Visit Coe Mansion, a 75-room, Elizabethan Tudor home of marine-insurance magnate William Robertson Coe. Arboretum open year-round.

**Sagamore Hill,** Oyster Bay. The first summer White House, home of President Theodore Roosevelt and his family. TR Nature Sanctuary nearby contains his grave.

**Vanderbilt Museum and Planetarium,** Centerport. Estate of the late William K. Vanderbilt, gardens, marine museum and mansion.

**Walt Whitman House,** Huntington. The 1810 farmhouse is the boyhod home of America's poet. Exhibits include manuscripts and pictures.

*CATSKILLS REGION*

**Athens Lighthouse,** Athens. This architectural gem that was built in 1874 is visable from Riverfront Park.

**Auto Memories,** Arkville. Vintage automobiles are on display daily throughout the summer.

**Bronck House Museum,** Coxsackie. Early Dutch house of stone contains elegant furniture, silver, glass and china, Dutch and 13-sided barns, cemetery and trading post.

**Catskill Game Farm,** Cairo. African animals, exotic birds, amusement park and special animal shows entertain visitors.

**Catskill Reptile Institute,** Catskill. Visitors tour the grounds and encounter meek garden creatures as well as the king cobra in this collection which features some of the world's most dangerous snakes.

**Delaware County Historical Association.** Six restored buildings in Delhi feature exhibits and weekend demonstrations of domestic farm tasks.

**Delaware & Ulster Rail Ride,** Arkville. Relive the golden age of railroading along the Catskill Scenic Trail, a network of country roads and trails suitable for hiking, biking and driving. Enjoy magnificent mountain scenery and pastoral landscapes from the vintage coach or open air car.

**Hanford Mills Museum,** East Meredith. More than 10 authentic 19th-century machines have been made operational: a shingle maker and step saw are powered by the giant Fitz waterwheel, the force of which makes the entire mill seem to throb. Listed in both the New York and National Registers of Historic Places, the museum is also engaged in the business of custom woodworking. If you are having trouble matching wood in an older house you are restoring, Hanford Mills can probably solve your problem.

**Hunter Mountain,** Hunter. Hosts major ethnic music festivals during the summer and fall, and features fantastic views of the Northeast from the longest, highest chairlift in the Catskills.

**Kittatinny Canoes,** Barryville. Exciting Delaware River canoeing and whitewater rafting for beginner through experienced adventurers.

**Mohonk Mountain House,** located in New Paltz, on Lake Mohonk. A turreted architectural delight, reaching seven stories skyward and stretching for nearly an eighth of a mile along Lake Mohonk. Walking, horseback or carriage tours of the forest and gardens, restaurant, theme programs, summer festival of the arts.

**Roscoe.** Called "Trout Town" because of its excellent trout fishing on the Beaverkill, which is famous for its brown trout and dry fly fishing. This stocked trout stream also contains fair numbers of wild browns, an occasional rainbow, and beautiful native brookies.

**Woodstock**. Long-established art colony of artists, writers and musicians. Famed world performers are featured July through September in the 78-year-old, hand-built, *Maverick Concert Hall.*

**Zoom Flume Aquamusement Park**, East Durham. Waterslides, bumper boats, Mountain Coaster and other fun rides for the entire family.

*CENTRAL-LEATHERSTOCKING REGION*

**Americana Village.** Just outside Hamilton on the crest of a hill, this collection of more than 20 original and replicated 19th-century structures circles a miniature village which serves as the setting for a variety of special events. Operated by the Central New York Village Artists and Craftsmen.

**Binghamton.** Highlights include the Anderson Center for the Performing Arts, Roberson Center for the Arts & Sciences, Kopernik Observatory and Ross Park Zoo.

**Canajoharie Art Gallery,** Canajoharie. Outstanding art collection of American paintings plus full-size replica of Rembrandt's "Night Watch".

**Cherry Valley Museum,** Cherry Valley. 250-year-old village was the scene of one of the most memorable battles of the American Revolution and the site of the Cherry Valley Massacre, where British troops and a Mohawk legion attacked the settlement. Fifteen rooms of memorabilia including 1800s ladies apparel, early fire fighting equipment, melodeons and household and farm tools of yesteryear.

**Chittenango.** "Oztown USA," complete with a yellow brick sidewalk, honors Frank Baum, author of "The Wizard of Oz", who was born here in 1856. Scenic Chittenango Falls is located within the State Park.

**Cooperstown.** Explore America's past and enjoy recreation on picturesque Otsego Lake in the village of Cooperstown. The town offers charm as it graciously shares its history. Flower baskets hang from street lamps, and window boxes brighten the well-kept store fronts. Visitors enjoy museums, golf courses, water recreation, antiquing and performances by the Glimmerglass Opera. The attractions within the Cooperstown area are many:

*Farmers' Museum and Village Crossroads.* Inside authentically restored buildings, working craftsmen demonstrate the ingenuity of the people who settled in Upstate New York between the Revolutionary and Civil Wars. The housewife, blacksmith, spinner, broommaker, printer and weaver explain as they work and are eager to answer questions. Exhibits of household objects, personal possessions, tools and art bring history to life.

*Fenimore House.* One of Cooperstown's best kept secrets is the extensive art collection maintained by the New York State Historical Association. Inside Fenimore House, there's a collection of American folk art, characterized by strong design and vigorous colors. Many pieces are the highly imaginative work of unknown 19th century craftsmen. James Fenimore Cooper admirers can see the extensive collection of Cooper memorabilia which is on permanent display.

*Glimmerglass Opera*, Route 80, eight miles north. During past seasons the company has presented classics from operatic literature, modern operas, light operas and American operas to packed houses. Reviews of these productions, which are performed in their original language (with English subtitles) have been universally excellent. The Glimmerglass' Alice Busch Opera Theatre is widely regarded as one of the best regional opera houses in the country.

*Lake Otsego*. Boat tours, fishing, swimming and boat liveries are just a few of the recreational opportunities.

*National Baseball Hall of Fame and Museum.* Since its dedication in 1939, millions of baseball fans from around the world have made the pilgrimage to Cooperstown to relive the great moments of the game's colorful past. The museum, displays over 8,000 artifacts. The Hall of Fame Gallery honors the giants of the game while the Great Moments Room portrays the game's milestones with television monitors, films and the theater show "Memories & Dreams."

**Erie Canal Village,** Rome. An 1840s canal village with church, horsedrawn packet boat, steam engine train, tavern, museums, stable, ice house, hotels and more.

**Fort Plain Museum,** Fort Plain. Housed in an 1848 Greek Revival home, the museum features exhibits on the mid-Mohawk Valley and the village of Fort Plain with a special emphasis on the American Revolution. Located on the property is the site of Fort Plain dating from the American Revolution.

**Herkimer Diamond Mine,** Herkimer. These diamonds are beautifully doubly-terminated quartz crystals already faceted by nature. This special treat for rockhounds also offers a rock shop, gift shop, geological museum and prospecting.

**Herkimer Home,** Little Falls. Residence of General Herkimer of the Revolutionary War has programs and tours. Also, maple syrup gatherings and sheepshearing displays in season.

**Howes Cave,** located on route 7, just east of Cobleskill. Attractions within Howes Cave include:

*Howe Caverns.* Time marches on in this geological wonder 200 feet below ground. Within this live cave are stalactites, stalagmites and other formations still being created by water. Take a boat ride on an underground lake–a remnant of the ancient glacial ocean which once covered upstate New York. Guided tours available all year and a gift shop, picnic grove, snack bar, restaurant and lounge are on the premises.

*Iroquois Indian Museum.* Features exhibits, arts and crafts of historic and contemporary Iroquois culture. Storytelling and demonstrations. Annual Iroquois Festival Labor Day weekend with lacrosse tournament.

**Middlefield.** This entire hamlet is in the National Register of Historic Places. Only three buildings in town were built after the Civil War. The Old Middlefield Schoolhouse Museum has original desks and teaching materials dating back to 1875. Open on Saturdays during July and August.

**Musical Museum,** Deansboro. See fully restored music boxes, nickelodeons, organs and melodeons. Also on site is The Old Lamplighter Shop, with hundreds of antique lamps and lamp parts, and Morgan's Bar Room, featuring "roaring twenties" music.

**National Shrine of North American Martyrs,** Auriesville. Site of St. Isaac Jogues martyrdom and birthplace of Indian maiden Kateri Tekakwitha, expected to be the first native American to reach sainthood in the Roman Catholic Church.

**Oneonta.** Attractions within Oneonta include:

*Doll Artisan Guild.* This international organization is dedicated to the art of porcelain dollmaking. The museum is located on Main Street.

*National Soccer Hall of Fame.* Experience the personalities, the plays and the history of "America's original football." Photos and artifacts offer a look at this fast-paced sport, past and present.

*Orpheus Theatre.* Regional theatre company stages professional and semi-professional musical and dramatic productions.

**Schoharie Crossing,** Fort Hunter. Only existing site with visable remains of all three stages of Erie Canal development, with 7 arches and Schoharie Aqueduct, an engineering marvel of the 1800s built to carry the canal over the creek.

**Stone Fort Museum Complex,** Schoharie. Originally, The Reformed Protestant High Dutch Church Society house of worship, built in 1772, and then enclosed by a stockade and blockhouses for protection during the revolution. Museum houses two floors of exhibits and a fine historical and genealogical library.

**Sylvan Beach.** A 4-mile beach on Oneida Lake. Amusement park adjacent, band concerts, fishing boats, helicopter rides, lake cruises and swimming.

**Utica.** History buffs will delight in the areas Revolutionary and Colonial folklore. Highlights of Utica include: *Children's Museum of History, Natural History and Science* has hands-on exhibits for youngsters; *Munson-Williams-Proctor Institute* contains one of the finest collections of 18th-20th century American and European works of art in the Northeast; *F.X. Matt Brewing Co.*, demonstrates the entire process of beer manufacturing and gives trolley rides to 1888 tavern where samples are served; *Utica Zoo* has over 300 animals and a children's zoo.

### *FINGER LAKES REGION*

**Beaver Lake Nature Center,** Baldwinsville. A 560-acre preserve with 8 miles of nature trails, guided walks and canoe tours.

**Champagne Trail Excursion Train.** Hop aboard one of the area's newest attractions for a ride through the scenic hills of the Finger Lakes wine country. The train runs from Bath to Cohocton and stops at the *Taylor Winery* and at the *Cohocton Valley Farm Museum.* Riders will enjoy wine tours and tastings as well as a tour of the museum which features a unique collection of farm equipment and antiques and dioramas that depict farming and life from as far back as 1790.

**Corning.** Gateway to the southern Finger Lakes region is home to the *Corning Glass Center*, a unique complex depicting the art, history, science and industry of glass, complete with a tour of the museum, Technology Gallery, Hall of Science and Industry and Steuben Glass Factory. Also within Corning is the *Rockwell Museum* which holds the largest collection of Western American art, Indian artifacts and Steuben glass. The *Rockwell Gallery* contains the world's largest collection of Carder Steuben Glass.

**Curtiss Museum,** Hammondsport. Interesting aeronautical museum revolves around Glenn H. Curtiss, inventor, designer, and pilot. Planes on site include a 1907 Chanute glider, 1912 Curtiss "Pusher" and the 1949 OHM Special Racer. View turn-of-the-century collectibles such as china dolls, cameras, radios, and woodworking tools.

**Electronic Communication Museum,** East Bloomfield. One of only two public museums in the nation devoted exclusively to radio and electronic's origins, history and today's achievements.

**Elmira.** Home of the *National Soaring Museum*, is also the final resting place of author Mark Twain. Catch the *Mark Twain Musical Drama*, hike the trails of the *Tanglewood Nature Center*, or dig up some interesting local history at the *Chemung County Historical Society.*

**Hornell.** Scenic route to the Finger Lakes at Southern Tier Expressway has bike and physical fitness trails, railroad-themed shopping mall and a variety of recreation.

**Letchworth State Park,** Castile. Site of the Grand Canyon of the East, 17-mile long, 600-foot deep Genesee River Gorge. Three waterfalls, scenic roads and overlooks.

**Rochester.** State's third largest city has blend of metropolitan atmosphere and historic attractions:

*Center at High Falls.* On site are hands-on exhibits, a simulated open raceway of running water, the Pont de Rennes pedestrian bridge, an archaelogical site and seasonal laser, light and sound shows in the Gorge at High Falls.

*George Eastman House* includes the International Museum of Photography which is dedicated to the art and science of photography spanning 130 years. Also on site is Kodak founder's renovated mansion and gardens.

*Margaret Woodbury Strong Museum* is the nation's only major museum whose collection centers on decorative arts, toys and history of the Industrial Revolution. Western World's most extensive doll collection, miniatures and doll houses.

**Sonnenburg Gardens and Mansion,** Canandaigua. A 50-acre estate complete with Victorian mansion, 9 historical gardens, garden cafe, wine tasting room and conservatory.

**Syracuse.** The "Salt City" has 10 enclosed malls plus factory outlets. Museums include the Salt Museum (a reconstructed 1856 salt factory); the *Milton J. Rubenstein Museum of Science and Technology*; the *Onondaga Historical Assn. Museum*; *Erie Canal Museum* and the *Everson Museum of Art*. Syracuse is also home to the *Burnet Park Zoo* which houses over 1,000 animals in 9 complexes.

**Watkins Glen.** Highlight is *Seneca Market* on the historic and picturesque lakefront. Over 30 shops, cafes and pushcarts of pleasures set in a 19th century aura.

*Captain Bill's Seneca Lake Cruises* offers shoreline cruises on Seneca Lake with lunch, dinner and cocktail cruises by appointment.

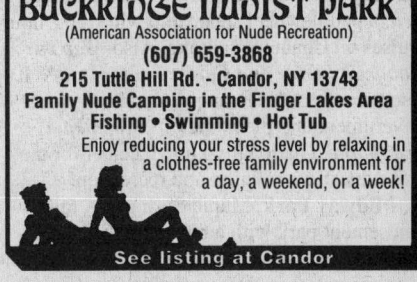

*International Race Track.* World-class

circuit auto racing is tops in the nation.

*Timespell,* in Watkins Glen State Park, recreates the evolution of the world through an extensive light and sound show.

**Wineries.** Fine wines comparable in taste and quality to any in the world are produced in the Finger Lakes region. Wineries such as *Taylor Gold Seal* are located in Bluff Point, Branchport, Conesus, Dundee, Hammondsport, Hector, Lodi, Naples, Burdett, Fairport, Himrod, Interlaken, Romulus and Valois.

**Ye Olde Wood Shoppe Village,** Waterloo. Watch woodworkers and sawmillers skillfully perform their craft or visit early American gift, candy and craft shops, made of hand-hewn trees. Homecooking and bakery goods in the log cabin Feed Bag Restaurant.

### *CHAUTAUQUA-ALLEGHENY REGION*

**Bemus Point.** 181-year-old Bemus Point-Stow Ferry is a cable-drawn wooden ferry which carries passengers, cars, vans and cows, back and forth to each community located in the middle of Chautauqua Lake. Visit the Casino where you can still hear the "big band" sound–it's also popular for its chicken wings. Nearby, Long Point State Park has a marina, hiking, picnicking, swimming, but no camping.

**Cattaraugus County Memorial and Historical Museum,** Little Valley. Houses many fine examples of folk art, Indian artifacts, mementos from the American Revolution and the Civil War, household items, tools, music, jewelry and toys.

**Chautauqaua.** Home of Chautauqua Institution, a National Historic Landmark founded in 1874. Accommodations are available at this internationally-known center for the arts, education, philosophy, politics and outdoor recreation programs. Chautauqua Lake provides excellent fishing, boating and water-skiing.

**Dunkirk.** The largest regional community on Lake Erie is in the heart of the Concord grape-growing area. *The Woodbury Winery* is open for wine tasting tours. Also visit the *Historic Lighthouse & Veteran's Museum,* where each one of the seven rooms is dedicated to a branch of military service. There's also a replica of a lightkeeper's quarters.

**Jamestown.** Birthplace of Lucille Ball hosts a Lucyfest, Lucille Ball Festival of Comedy, each May. Also, walking tours of historic buildings. At the *Audubon Nature Center,* 1600 Riverside Rd., the Interpretive Building houses a large collection of exhibits and children's hands-on Discovery Room, an arboretum, lectures and special programs.

**Mayville** is home port for the *Chautauqua Bell,* a paddlewheel steamship with 1-1/2 hour cruises on Chautauqua Lake. Also, *Webb's Goatmilk Fudge and Candy Factory* tours. It's also the seat of Chautauqua County government and the home of *Chautauqua Institution,* a nationally known center for the arts, education, religion and recreation.

**Midway Park,** Maple Springs. A family amusement park with a beach on the lake, rides and refreshments, splash-n-bash bumper boats, paddle boats, rides, mini-golf, go-karts, penny arcade, roller rink, covered pavilions, and docking facilities. Open Memorial Day through Labor Day.

**Molly World,** Lakewood. On site is a fully-lighted miniature golf course, batting cages, go-karts, mini-go-carts, bumper and mini-bumper boats, and an arcade room.

**Nannen Arboretum,** Ellicottville, the only arboretum in western New York houses over 250 species, Chapman's Chapel, Ryoanji meditation and ancient Japanese gardens.

**New York and Lake Erie Railroad,** Gowanda. Ride through scenic countryside, dine or indulge in a murder mystery train and bring back the good old days.

**Panama Rocks,** Panama. The world's most extensive outcrop of glacially cut ocean quartz–a conglomerate of cliffs, crevices, cavernous dens, and caves. *The Trail's End Gallery* has limited editions and originals, hand-carved Indian pottery, secondary market prints, wildlife art and custom framing.

**Salamanca**. The only city in the world located on an Indian reservation. *The Seneca-Iroquois National Museum* serves the Seneca Nation of Indians as an education center and holding center for cultural treasures. The Seneca Indians lived in New York over 10,000 years ago. Their culture developed into the Iroquoian speaking people who inhabited western New York.

*Allegany State Park*, the largest state park in New York State, covers over 64,000 acres and offers a wide variety of recreation including 75 miles of hiking trails, fishing, nature education, swimming, boating and bicycling.

*The Salamanca Rail Museum* has a restored 1912 passenger rail depot, exhibits and slide presentations on the history of western New York's railroads, as well as scenic rail excursions during summer and fall.

**Westfield.** *The McClurg Museum*, home of *The Chautauqua County Historical Society,* has 16 restored period rooms, as well as changing exhibits, a carriage house converted to a library, photographs, genealogical records, and archival collections.

### *NIAGARA FRONTIER*

**Artpark,** Lewiston. A 200-acre state park with nature trails, bicycle paths and a 2,400-seat theatre offering major dance, musical productions and shows.

**Buffalo.** The state's second largest city has such outstanding attractions as the *Albright-Knox Art Gallery,* which has one of the foremost art collections in the world dating back to 3,000 BC; *Allentown,* one of the largest historic preservation sites in the U.S.; *Broadway Market*, an Old World market where farmers sell fresh field grown products; *Buffalo & Erie County Naval & Servicemen's Park*, the only inland naval park in the nation; and *Buffalo Museum of Science*, which has such unique exhibits as two dinosaurs, mummies and Chinese jades.

**Herschell Carrousel Factory Museum,** North Tonawanda. Located in a factory building which has been nominated to the National Register of Historic Places. Exhibits of early carousel memorabilia, wood carving demonstrations and rides on fine antique carousels.

**Niagara Falls.** A haven not exclusively for honeymooners. Site of the natural wonder of Niagara's thundering waters. Other points of interest include: *Aquarium of Niagara Falls* with hourly dolphin and sea lion performances; *Niagara's Wax Museum of History* with life-size figures; *Rainbow Centre* is a one-stop fashion, shopping, dining and entertainment experience just a block from the Falls; *Wintergarden*, connected to Niagara Falls Convention Center, is a majestic, glass-enclosed year-round tropical park with ponds, waterfalls and 7,000 trees. The whole family will enjoy *Niagara Splash Water Park* with its water slides, wave pool and kiddie pool.

**Old Fort Niagara,** Youngstown. Military drills and demonstrations by costumed soliders.

### *1000 ISLANDS—SEAWAY REGION*

**Boldt Castle,** Heart Island, near Alexandria Bay. Tours of the planned full-sized replica of a Rhineland Castle with eleven buildings and over 120 rooms. George Boldt, the proprietor of the Waldorf Astoria, spent $2.5 million to build the castle for his wife, but after she died suddenly, he lost all ambition and never finished his splendorous dream. The castle is now operated by the Thousand Islands Bridge Authority and is undergoing restoration

**Clayton.** On the shores of the St. Lawrence River, Clayton offers many recreational activities, historical attractions and annual events, including annual consumer shows at Clayton Recreation Park Arena.

*The Antique Boat Museum.* The largest freshwater maritime museum in North America is dedicated to preserving the boating heritage of the St. Lawrence River. The museum has exhibits of antique boats, motors, boat building tools and a restoration shop. The oldest outboard motor on display in the U.S. is the *Grant Skiff,* made in 1875 for Ulysses S. Grant.

**Ogdensburg**. Oldest settlement in northern New York, it is the site of the *Ogdensburg-Prescott International Bridge,* a scenic suspension bridge and the most direct route from Ottawa, Canada. Also in Ogdensburg is the *Frederick Remington Art Museum,* which houses the largest single collection of paintings, bronzes and sketches. by the foremost artist of the Old West. Also collections of other masterful paintings, cut glass and Dresden china, Victorian home furnishings.

**Oswego.** Town of Oswego offers attractions such as *Fort Ontario*—a 1750s fort which features demonstrations and tours; the *H. Lee White Marine Museum*, with its intriguing look into the 300-year history of the Oswego Harbor and Eastern Lake Ontario; the *Oswego County Historical Society,* home of the Richardson-Bates House Museum which displays 1860-80 period rooms and a permanent county history exhibit; and the *Oswego Speedway*—a 3/4-mile supermodified race track, one of three raceways in the county.

# new york

All privately-owned campgrounds personally inspected by Woodall Representatives John and Jean Everett.

Unless otherwise noted, all listed campgrounds have hot showers & flush toilets.

## ACRA—F-9

**WHIP-O-WILL CAMPSITE**—CAMPGROUND with wooded and open sites. *From jct Hwy 145 & Hwy 23: Go 2 1/4 mi W on Hwy 23, then 2 mi S on CR 31.*

WELCOME

◆◆FACILITIES: 257 sites, most common site width 50 feet, 58 full hookups, 100 water & elec (20,30 & 50 amp receptacles), 99 no hookups, seasonal sites, 29 pull-thrus, a/c allowed ($), heater not allowed, tenting available, group sites for tents/RVs, RV storage, sewage disposal, laundry, public phone, limited grocery store, RV supplies, ice, tables, fire rings, wood.

◆◆◆RECREATION: rec hall, pavilion, coin games, swim pool, wading pool, boating, no motors, canoeing, 4 row/2 pedal boat rentals, lake fishing, playground, sports field, horseshoes.

Open Apr 15 through Oct 15. Rate in 1995 $19-23 for 2 persons. Master Card/Visa accepted. Member of ARVC; CONY. Phone: (518) 622-3277.
**SEE AD THIS PAGE**

## AFTON—F-7

**KELLYSTONE PARK CAMPSITE**—Mountainview CAMPGROUND with open and shaded sites. *From I-88 (Afton exit 7) & Hwy 41: Go 5 mi S on Hwy 41, then 1/4 mi E on Hawkins Rd.*

WELCOME

◆◆◆FACILITIES: 70 sites, 50 full hookups, 10 water & elec (15,20 & 30 amp receptacles), 10 no hookups, seasonal sites, a/c allowed ($), heater allowed ($), phone hookups, tenting available, group sites for tents/RVs, RV storage, sewage disposal, laundry, public phone, limited grocery store, RV supplies, ice, tables, fire rings, wood.

◆◆◆RECREATION: rec hall, rec room/area, pavilion, coin games, swim pool, boating, no motors, pond fishing, golf, basketball hoop, playground, shuffleboard court, tennis court, badminton, sports field, horseshoes, hiking trails, volleyball.

Open Apr 1 through Nov 1. Facilities fully operational May 1 through Oct 15. Rate in 1995 $15-21 per family. Discover accepted. Member of ARVC; CONY. Phone: (607) 639-1090. FCRV 10% discount.
**SEE AD BINGHAMTON PAGE 595**

## ALBANY—E-9

✲ **HYDE'S RV AND BOATS**—*From Albany area: Go N on I-87 to exit 9, then 6 mi W on Hwy 146, then 3/4 mi N on Blue Barns Rd.*

WELCOME

**SEE PRIMARY LISTING AT REXFORD AND AD SARATOGA SPRINGS PAGE 631**

## ALBION—D-3

LAKESIDE BEACH STATE PARK—*From town: Go 10 mi N on Hwy 98, then 2 mi W on Lake Ontario Pkwy.* FACILITIES: 268 sites, 268 elec, tenting available, handicap restroom facilities, sewage disposal, laundry, public phone, grocery store, ice, tables, wood. RECREATION: rec hall, boating, canoeing, lake fishing, playground, hiking trails. Open late Apr through late Oct. Phone: (716) 682-5246.

## ALEXANDRIA BAY—B-6

GRASS POINT STATE PARK—*From business center: Go 5 mi S on Hwy 12.* FACILITIES: 75 sites, 18 elec, 57 no hookups, tenting available, handicap restroom facilities, sewage disposal, public phone, ice, tables. RECREATION: swimming, boating, canoeing, river fishing, playground. Open early May through Sep 10. Phone: (315) 686-4472.

KEEWAYDIN STATE PARK—*From business center: Go 1/2 mi W on Hwy 12.* FACILITIES: 41 sites, 41 no hookups, tenting available, handicap restroom facilities, public phone, tables, wood. RECREATION: swim pool, boating, canoeing, ramp, river fishing, playground. Open late May through early Sep. Phone: (315) 482-3331.

KRING POINT STATE PARK—*From town: Go 6 mi NE on Hwy 12.* FACILITIES: 146 sites, 34 elec, 112 no hookups, handicap restroom facilities, sewage disposal, ice, tables. RECREATION: rec hall, river swimming, boating, canoeing, ramp, river fishing, playground, hiking trails. Open early May through Oct 8. Phone: (315) 482-2444.

WELLESLEY ISLAND STATE PARK—*From business center: Go 6 mi N on Hwy 12, then cross 1000 Island Bridge (Toll).* FACILITIES: 438 sites, 57 full hookups, 74 elec, 307 no hookups, tenting available, handicap restroom facilities, sewage disposal, public phone, grocery store, tables. RECREATION: rec hall, swimming, boating, canoeing, ramp, dock, river fishing, playground, hiking trails. Open late Apr through Oct 8. Phone: (315) 482-2722.

## ALTAMONT—E-9

THOMPSON'S LAKE STATE PARK—*From business center: Go 4 mi S on 156, then 1 mi SE on Hwy 157.* FACILITIES: 137 sites, 30 ft. max RV length, 137 no hookups, tenting available, handicap restroom facilities, public phone, ice, tables, wood. RECREATION: lake swimming, boating, no motors, canoeing, lake fishing, playground, hiking trails. Open mid May through mid Oct. Phone: (518) 872-1674.



## AMSTERDAM—E-9

✲ **ALPIN HAUS**—*From jct I-90 (exit 27) & Hwy 30: Go 3 mi N on Hwy 30.* SALES: travel trailers, park models, truck campers, 5th wheels, van conversions, motor homes, mini-motor homes, micro-mini motor homes, fold-down camping trailers. SERVICES: Engine/Chassis & RV appliance mechanic full-time, LP gas refill by weight, sewage disposal, sells parts/accessories, installs hitches. Open all year. Discover/Master Card/Visa accepted. Phone: (518) 843-4400.

WELCOME

**SEE AD NEXT PAGE**

## ANGOLA—E-2

EVANGOLA STATE PARK—*From business center: Go 4 mi W on Hwy 5 (Silver Creek exit for NY thruway).* FACILITIES: 80 sites, 33 elec (20 amp receptacles), 47 no hookups, tenting available, handicap restroom facilities, sewage disposal, laundry, public phone, tables, fire rings. RECREATION: rec hall, lake swimming, lake fishing, playground, planned group activities, tennis court, sports field, hiking trails. Open late Apr through early Oct. Phone: (716) 549-1802.

## AUBURN—E-5

**Yawger Brook Family Campsites**—Campground with open & shaded sites in a rural setting. *From jct Hwy 34 & US 20/Hwy 5: Go 6 mi W on US 20/Hwy 5, then 1 mi S on Blanchard Rd to blinking light, then 50 feet W on Genessee Rd, then 1 mi S on Benham Rd.* ◆◆FACILITIES: 60 sites, 50 water & elec (15 & 20 amp receptacles), 10 no hookups, seasonal sites, 8 pull-thrus, tenting available, sewage disposal, ice, tables, fire rings, grills, wood. ◆◆◆RECREATION: pavilion, swim pool, pond fishing, sports field, hiking trails, volleyball. Recreation open to the public. Open May 1 through Oct 31. Rates available upon request. Phone: (315) 252-8969.

## AUSABLE CHASM—B-10

***See listings at Keeseville & Peru***

**AUSABLE CHASM**—*From jct Hwy 373 & US 9: Go 800 feet S on US 9.* Walking & boat tour of Ausable Chasm with picnic grounds & amusement park. Open Memorial Day through Columbus Day. American Express/Master Card/Visa accepted. Phone: (518) 834-7454.

WELCOME

**SEE AD THIS PAGE**

**AUSABLE RIVER CAMPSITE**—*From Ausable Chasm: Go 2 1/4 mi SW on Hwy 9N, then 3/4 mi S on entry road.*

WELCOME

**SEE PRIMARY LISTING AT KEESEVILLE AND AD THIS PAGE**

**Holiday Travel Park**—Wooded sites in a CAMPGROUND convenient to a major highway. *From jct Hwy 373 & Hwy 9: Go 1 1/4 mi E on Hwy 373.* ◆◆◆FACILITIES: 48 sites, most common site width 35 feet, 30 full hookups, 3 water & elec (20 & 30 amp receptacles), 15 no hookups, seasonal sites, tenting available, sewage disposal, public phone, ice, tables, fire rings, wood. ◆◆RECREATION: rec room/area, swim pool, playground. Open Apr 15 through Oct 15. Rate in 1995 $14-16 for 2 persons. Phone: (518) 834-9216.

**KOA-AUSABLE CHASM**—Wooded CAMPGROUND near Ausable Chasm. *From jct US 9 & Hwy 373: Go 800 feet E on Hwy 373.*

WELCOME

◆◆◆FACILITIES: 145 sites, most common site width 25 feet, 27 full hookups, 63 water & elec (20 & 30 amp receptacles), 55 no hookups, seasonal sites, 80 pull-thrus, a/c allowed, heater allowed, phone hookups, tenting available, group sites for tents/RVs, cabins, RV storage, handicap restroom facilities, sewage disposal, laundry, public phone, limited grocery store, RV supplies, LP gas refill by weight/by meter, ice, tables, wood.

◆◆◆◆RECREATION: rec room/area, coin games, swim pool, mini-golf ($), basketball hoop, playground, shuffleboard court, movies, tennis court, badminton, sports field, horseshoes, hiking trails, volleyball, local tours.

Open mid May through mid Oct. Rate in 1995 $19-22 for 2 persons. American Express/Master Card/Visa accepted. Member of ARVC; CONY. Phone: (518) 834-9990. KOA 10% value card discount.

**SEE AD THIS PAGE AND AD FRONT OF BOOK PAGES 68 AND 69**



## AUSTERLITZ—F-10

**WOODLAND HILLS CAMPGROUND**—Semi-wooded park with open and shaded sites. *From jct I-90 (exit B-3) & Hwy 22: Go 2 mi S on Hwy 22, then 1/2 mi W onMiddle Rd, then 3/4 mi N on Fog Hill Rd.*

WELCOME

◆◆◆FACILITIES: 202 sites, most common site width 40 feet, 149 full hookups, 39 water & elec (20 & 30 amp receptacles), 14 no hookups, seasonal sites, a/c allowed ($), heater not allowed, tenting available, group sites for tents/RVs, RV rentals, RV storage, sewage disposal, laundry, public phone, limited grocery store, RV supplies, LP gas refill by weight/by meter, ice, tables, fire rings, wood.

◆◆◆◆RECREATION: rec hall, rec room/area, coin games, lake swimming, boating, no motors, canoeing, 2 pedal boat rentals, pond fishing, basketball hoop, playground, planned group activities (weekends only), recreation director, badminton, sports field, horseshoes, hiking trails, volleyball. Recreation open to the public.

Open May 1 through Columbus Day. Rate in 1995 $18-21 per family. Discover/Master Card/Visa accepted. Member of ARVC; CONY. Phone: (518) 392-3557.

**SEE AD THIS PAGE**

## AVERILL PARK—E-10

**ALPS FAMILY CAMPGROUND**—Shaded sites in a country setting. *From jct Hwy 66 & Hwy 43: Go 3 mi SE on Hwy 66/Hwy 43, then 1 1/2 mi SE on Hwy 43.*

WELCOME

◆◆◆◆FACILITIES: 94 sites, most common site width 40 feet, 40 full hookups, 41 water & elec (20 & 30 amp receptacles), 13 no hookups, seasonal sites, 3 pull-thrus, a/c allowed ($), heater not allowed, phone hookups, tenting available, group sites for tents/RVs, RV storage, sewage disposal, laundry, public phone, grocery store, RV supplies, LP gas refill by weight/by meter, ice, tables, fire rings, grills, wood.

◆◆◆◆RECREATION: rec hall, rec room/area, coin games, swim pool, 1 pedal boat rentals, pond/stream fishing, basketball hoop, playground, shuffleboard court, planned group activities (weekends only), badminton, sports field, horseshoes, hiking trails, volleyball.

Open all year. Facilities fully operational May 1 through Oct 15. Rate in 1995 $18-25 per family. Master Card/Visa accepted. Member of ARVC; CONY. Phone: (518) 674-5565.

**SEE AD ALBANY PAGE 591**

## BAINBRIDGE—F-7

OQUAGA CREEK STATE PARK—*From jct I-88 & Hwy 206: Go 6 mi SE on Hwy 206, then S on Beech Hill Rd.* FACILITIES: 94 sites, 94 no hookups, tenting available, handicap restroom facilities, sewage disposal, ice, tables. RECREATION: swimming, boating, canoeing, river fishing, playground, hiking trails. Open mid May through mid Oct. Phone: (607) 467-4160.

**Riverside RV Camping**—Grassy RV SPACES behind a motel. *From jct I-88 (exit 8) & Hwy 206: Go 500 feet W on Hwy 206, then 100 feet S on CR 39 (behind*

BAINBRIDGE—Continued
RIVERSIDE RV CAMPING—Continued

*Susquehanna Motor Lodge).* FACILITIES: 18 sites, 11 full hookups, 1 water & elec (20 & 30 amp receptacles), 6 no hookups, 9 pull-thrus, tenting available, handicap restroom facilities, sewage disposal, public phone, ice, tables. RECREATION: canoeing, river fishing. Open Apr 15 through Oct 15. Rate in 1995 $15 for 2 persons. Phone: (607) 967-2102.

## BALDWINSVILLE—D-6

**KOA-Syracuse**—CAMPGROUND with level, grassy, terraced sites. *From jct Hwy 690 & Hwy 370: Go 4 1/2 mi W on Hwy 370, then 1 1/2 mi S on Plainville-Jack's Reef Rd.* ◆◆FACILITIES: 94 sites, 29 full hookups, 60 water & elec (15,20 & 30 amp receptacles), 5 no hookups, seasonal sites, 17 pull-thrus, tenting available, sewage disposal, laundry, public phone, limited grocery store, LP gas refill by weight, ice, tables, fire rings, grills, wood. ◆◆◆RECREATION: rec room/area, swim pool, boating, canoeing, ramp, river fishing, playground, badminton, horseshoes, hiking trails, volleyball. Open May 1 through Oct 15. Rate in 1995 $18-24 for 2 persons. Phone: (315) 635-6405. KOA 10% value card discount.

BALDWINSVILLE—Continued on next page

BALDWINSVILLE—Continued

**Sunset Park**—Lakeside CAMPGROUND with shaded and open sites. *From jct Hwy 690 & Hwy 370: Go 4 1/2 mi W on Hwy 370, then 1 3/4 mi S on Plainville-Jacks Reef Rd, then 1 3/4 mi W on Sprague Rd.* ◆◆FACILITIES: 233 sites, 170 water & elec, 8 elec (20 amp receptacles), 55 no hookups, seasonal sites, tenting available, sewage disposal, public phone, limited grocery store, LP gas refill by weight, ice, tables, fire rings, wood. ◆◆◆RECREATION: rec room/area, lake swimming, boating, canoeing, ramp, lake fishing, playground, planned group activities (weekends only), sports field, volleyball. Open May 1 through Oct 1. Rate in 1995 $15-17 for 2 persons. Member of ARVC; CONY. Phone: (315) 635-6450.

## BARKER—D-2

GOLDEN HILL STATE PARK—*From business center: Go 6 mi NE on Lower Lake Rd.* FACILITIES: 50 sites, 18 water & elec, 4 elec (15 amp receptacles), 28 no hookups, tenting available, sewage disposal, public phone, tables, grills. RECREATION: rec hall, boating, canoeing, ramp, lake fishing, playground, planned group activities, badminton, sports field, horseshoes, hiking trails, volleyball. Open late Apr through early Oct. Phone: (716) 795-3885.

## BARRYVILLE—A-1

**KITTATINNY CAMPGROUNDS**—Level, shaded sites with grass. *From jct Hwy 55 & Hwy 97: Go 2 mi NW on Hwy 97.*

◆◆◆FACILITIES: 352 sites, most common site width 25 feet, 100 water & elec (15 & 20 amp receptacles), 252 no hookups, seasonal sites, a/c allowed, heater not allowed, tenting available, group sites for tents, sewage disposal, laundry, public phone, grocery store, RV supplies, ice, tables, fire rings, wood, traffic control gate.

◆◆◆◆RECREATION: rec hall, rec room/area, pavilion, coin games, swim pool, boating, canoeing, 1000 canoe boat rentals, float trips, river/stream fishing, basketball hoop, playground, badminton, sports field, horseshoes, hiking trails, volleyball.

Open Apr 15 through Oct 15. Rate in 1995 $22-25 for 2 persons. Discover/Master Card/Visa accepted. Member of ARVC; CONY. Phone: (914) 557-8611.

**SEE AD FRONT OF BOOK PAGE 40 AND AD TRAVEL SECTION PAGE 589**



BARRYVILLE—Continued

**KITTATINNY CANOES**—*From jct Hwy 55 & Hwy 97: Go 2 mi NW on Hwy 97.* Delaware River canoeing and whitewater rafting. Open Apr 1 through Oct 31. Discover/Master Card/Visa accepted. Phone: (914) 557-6213.

**SEE AD FRONT OF BOOK PAGE 40 AND AD TRAVEL SECTION PAGE 589**

## BATAVIA—E-3

WELCOME

**LEI-TI CAMPGROUND**—A CAMPGROUND with open & shaded sites in a country atmosphere. *From jct Hwy 5 and Hwy 63: Go 2 1/2 mi SE on Hwy 63, then 1/2 mi S on Shepherd Rd, then 3/4 mi W on Putnam Rd, then 2 mi S on Francis Rd.*

◆◆◆FACILITIES: 203 sites, most common site width 40 feet, 60 full hookups, 127 water & elec (20 & 30 amp receptacles), 16 no hookups, seasonal sites, 7 pull-thrus, a/c allowed ($), heater allowed ($), phone hookups, tenting available, group sites for tents/RVs, RV rentals, cabins, RV storage, sewage disposal, laundry, public phone, limited grocery store, RV supplies, LP gas refill by weight/by meter, ice, tables, fire rings, wood, traffic control gate/guard.

◆◆◆◆RECREATION: rec hall, equipped pavilion, coin games, lake swimming, boating, no motors, canoeing, 2 row/1 pedal boat rentals, lake fishing, mini-golf ($), basketball hoop, 3 bike rentals, playground, 2 shuffleboard courts, planned group activities (weekends only), tennis court, badminton, sports field, horseshoes, hiking trails, volleyball, cross country skiing. Recreation open to the public.

Open all year. Facilities fully operational May 1 through Columbus Day. Rate in 1995 $17-23 for 2 persons. No refunds. Discover/Master Card/Visa accepted. Member of ARVC; CONY. Phone: (800) HI-LEITI.

**SEE AD DARIEN CENTER PAGE 601 AND AD NIAGARA FALLS PAGE 623**

WELCOME

✱ **LEI-TI RV SALES & SERVICE**—*From jct Hwy 5 & Hwy 63: Go 2 1/2 mi SE on Hwy 63, then 1/2 mi S on Shepherd Rd, then 3/4 mi W on Putnam Rd, then 2 mi S on Francis Rd.* SALES: travel trailers, park models, 5th wheels, fold-down camping trailers. SERVICES: RV appliance mechanic full-time, LP gas refill by weight/by meter, sewage disposal, RV storage, sells parts/accessories, sells camping supplies, installs hitches. Open all year. Discover/Master Card/Visa accepted. Phone: (716) 343-8600.

**SEE AD DARIEN CENTER PAGE 601 AND AD NIAGARA FALLS PAGE 623**

## BATH—F-4

**BABCOCK HOLLOW CAMPGROUND**—Grassy, open & shaded sites in a lakeside location. *From jct Hwy 17 (exit 39) & Hwy 415/CR 11: Go 2 mi S on CR 11.*

◆◆◆FACILITIES: 93 sites, most common site width 30 feet, 32 full hookups, 61 water & elec (20 & 30 amp receptacles), seasonal sites, a/c allowed ($), heater allowed ($), phone hookups, tenting available, group sites for tents, RV rentals, cabins, RV storage, sewage disposal, laundry, public phone, limited grocery store, RV supplies, LP gas refill by weight/by meter, ice, tables, fire rings, wood.

◆◆◆◆RECREATION: rec hall, rec room/area, coin games, swim pool, boating, electric motors only, canoeing, 2 pedal boat rentals, lake fishing, driving range ($), basketball hoop, playground, badminton, volleyball.

Open all year. Facilities fully operational Apr 15 through Oct 15. Rate in 1995 $18 for 4 persons. Phone: (607) 776-7185.

**SEE AD THIS PAGE**

BATH—Continued on next page

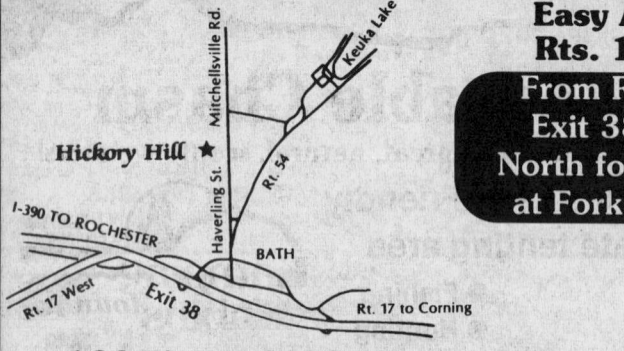

BATH—Continued

**HICKORY HILL CAMPING RESORT**—CAMPGROUND with shaded and open sites in country area. *From jct Hwy 17 (exit 38) & Hwy 54: Go 1 mi E & N following Hwy 54, then 2 mi N on Haverling St.*

◆◆◆FACILITIES: 185 sites, most common site width 35 feet, 93 full hookups, 82 water & elec (15,20 & 30 amp receptacles), 10 no hookups, seasonal sites, 40 pull-thrus, a/c allowed ($), heater allowed ($), cable TV ($), phone hookups, tenting available, group sites for tents/RVs, RV rentals, cabins, RV storage, sewage disposal, laundry, public phone, grocery store, RV supplies, LP gas refill by weight/by meter, ice, tables, fire rings, wood.

◆◆◆◆RECREATION: rec hall, pavilion, coin games, 2 swim pools, wading pool, pond fishing, mini-golf ($), basketball hoop, playground, shuffleboard court, planned group activities (weekends only), recreation director, badminton, sports field, horseshoes, hiking trails, volleyball.

Open May 1 through Oct 23. Rate in 1995 $19-23 for 2 persons. Reservations recommended weekends Jul & Aug. Discover/Master Card/Visa accepted. Member of ARVC; CONY. Phone: (607) 776-4345. FCRV 10% discount.

**SEE AD PAGE 594**

## BINGHAMTON—F-6

CHENANGO VALLEY STATE PARK—*E'bound from I-88 (exit 3): Go 5 mi N on Hwy 369. S'bound from I-81 (exit 8): Go 12 mi E on Hwy 79, cross Chenango River, then right 4 mi on Pigeon Hill Rd.* FACILITIES: 216 sites, 51 elec, 165 no hookups, tenting available, handicap restroom facilities, sewage disposal, public phone, tables. RECREATION: pavilion, lake swimming, boating, no motors, canoeing, row boat rentals, lake fishing, playground, hiking trails. Open early Apr through late Oct. Phone: (607) 648-5251.

**KELLYSTONE PARK CAMPSITE**—*About 25 mi E of Binghamton. From jct I-81 & I-88: Go E on I-88 to exit 7 (Hwy 41), then 5 mi S on Hwy 41, then 1/4 mi E on Hawkins Rd.*

**SEE PRIMARY LISTING AT AFTON AND AD THIS PAGE**

**PINE VALLEY CAMPGROUND**—*From jct I-81 & Hwy 17: Go W on Hwy 17 to exit 67 N (Hwy 26), then 6 mi N on Hwy 26, then 1 block NW on Maple Dr, then 1 mi W on Boswell Hill Rd.*

**SEE PRIMARY LISTING AT ENDICOTT AND AD THIS PAGE**

## BLUE MOUNTAIN LAKE—C-8

LAKE DURANT (Adirondack State Forest)—*From jct Hwy 30 & Hwy 28: Go 3 mi E on Hwy 28.* FACILITIES: 61 sites, 30 ft. max RV length, 61 no hookups, tenting available, sewage disposal, public phone, tables, fire rings. RECREATION: lake swimming, boating, ramp, lake fishing, hiking trails. Facilities fully operational mid May through early Oct. Phone: (518) 352-7797.





## BOLTON LANDING—D-9

**SCENIC VIEW CAMPGROUND**—Terraced, wooded & open grassy sites convenient to a lake. *From jct I-87 (Northway exit 24): Go 4 3/4 mi E on Bolton Landing Rd, then 1/2 mi S on Hwy 9N.*

◆◆FACILITIES: 100 sites, 44 full hookups, 50 water & elec (20 & 30 amp receptacles), 6 no hookups, seasonal sites, a/c allowed ($), heater not allowed, phone hookups, tenting available, RV rentals, sewage disposal, public phone, limited grocery store, RV supplies, LP gas refill by weight, ice, tables, fire rings, wood.

◆◆◆RECREATION: rec room/area, coin games, swim pool (heated), basketball hoop, badminton, horseshoes, volleyball.

Open May 1 through Oct 15. Rate in 1995 $19-22.50 for 2 persons. No refunds. Master Card/Visa accepted. Member of ARVC; CONY. Phone: (518) 644-2115.

**SEE AD LAKE GEORGE PAGE 610**

## BRIDGEWATER—E-7

**Lake Chalet Campground & Motel**—Lakeside with grassy open & shaded sites. *From jct US 20 & Hwy 8: Go 1 mi N on Hwy 8.* ◆◆◆FACILITIES: 50 sites, most common site width 30 feet, 22 water & elec (20,30 & 50 amp receptacles), 28 no hookups, seasonal sites, tenting available, sewage disposal, laundry, public phone, limited grocery store, ice, tables, fire rings, grills, wood. ◆◆◆RECREATION: pavilion, lake swimming, boating, no motors, canoeing, dock, 6 pedal boat rentals, lake/river fishing, playground, badminton, horseshoes, volleyball. Recreation open to the public. Open Apr 15 through Oct 31. Rate in 1995 $17.50-20 for 2 persons. Member of ARVC;CONY. Phone: (315) 822-6074.

## BRISTOL CENTER—E-4

**Bristol Woodlands Campground**—Open & shaded sites in a hilltop CAMPGROUND. *From jct Hwy 64 & CR 32 in the center of the village: Go 1 1/2 mi W on CR 32, then 1 mi S on South Hill Rd (unpaved road).* ◆◆FACILITIES: 120 sites, 43 full hookups, 15 water & elec (30 amp receptacles), 62 no hookups, seasonal sites, tenting available, sewage disposal, tables, fire rings, wood. ◆◆RECREATION: pond fishing, horseshoes, hiking trails, volleyball. Open May 1 through Oct 30. Rate in 1995 $13-20 for 4 persons. Member of ARVC; CONY. Phone: (716) 229-2290.

## BROCTON—F-1

LAKE ERIE STATE PARK—*From New York Thruway (Exit 59-Dunkirk): Go S on Hwy 5.* FACILITIES: 95 sites, 33 elec, 62 no hookups, tenting available, handicap restroom facilities, sewage disposal, tables. RECREATION: lake swimming, boating, canoeing, lake fishing, playground, hiking trails. Open late Apr through Oct 9. Phone: (716) 792-9214.



## BROOKHAVEN—C-4

SOUTHAVEN (Suffolk County Park)—*From Long Island Expwy (I-495, exit 68S): Go S on William Floyd Pkwy to 4th traffic light, then W on Victory Ave, then 1/2 mi N on River Rd.* FACILITIES: 200 sites, 200 no hookups, tenting available, handicap restroom facilities, sewage disposal, public phone, tables. RECREATION: boating, electric motors only, 35 row boat rentals, lake/stream fishing ($), playground, sports field, hiking trails. Open Apr 1 through Sep 11. Facilities fully operational May 19 through Sep 11. Open weekends only in Apr. Phone: (516) 854-1414.

## BUFFALO—E-2

**✱ ALL-SEASON RV SERVICE CENTER**—*From jct I-90 (exit 49) & Hwy 78: Go 1/2 mi S on Hwy 78, then 1/4 mi W on Hwy 33 (Genesee St).* SALES: travel trailers, 5th wheels, motor homes, mini-motor homes. SERVICES: RV appliance mechanic full-time, emergency road service business hours, RV rentals, RV storage, sells parts/accessories, installs hitches. Open all year. Phone: (716) 684-3003.

**SEE AD THIS PAGE**

**SHERKSTON SHORES**—*From toll bridge in Buffalo: Go approximately 25 mi W on Hwy 3, then 1 1/2 mi S on Empire Rd (Regional Rd 98).*

**SEE PRIMARY LISTING AT PORT COLBORNE, ON AND AD FRONT OF BOOK PAGE 142**

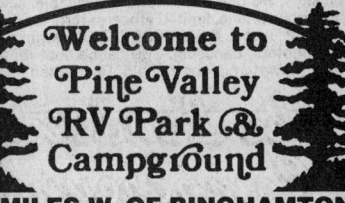

## BYRON—D-3

**SOUTHWOODS RV RESORT**—A CAMPGROUND in the country with open, grassy and wooded sites. *From jct I-90 (exit 47) & Hwy 19: Go 3 1/2 mi N on Hwy 19, then 4 1/2 mi W on Hwy 262.*

◆◆◆FACILITIES: 160 sites, 80 full hookups, 60 water & elec (20,30 & 50 amp receptacles), 20 no hookups, seasonal sites, a/c allowed ($), heater allowed ($), tenting available, group sites for tents/RVs, RV storage, handicap restroom facilities, sewage disposal, public phone, limited grocery store, LP gas refill by weight, ice, tables, fire rings, wood.

◆◆◆RECREATION: rec room/area, pavilion, coin games, swim pool, basketball hoop, playground, planned group activities (weekends only), badminton, sports field, horseshoes, hiking trails, volleyball.

Open May 1 through Nov 1. Rate in 1995 $16.50-17.50 for 2 persons. Member of ARVC; CONY. Phone: (716) 548-9002.
**SEE AD ROCHESTER PAGE 629**

## CALEDONIA—E-3

**GENESEE COUNTRY CAMPGROUND**—Wooded, prepared sites & sunny, grassy sites in a rural area. *From jct Hwy 36 N (center of town) & Hwy 5: Go 3 mi W on Hwy 5, then 1/2 mi NE on Flint Hill Rd.*

◆◆◆FACILITIES: 100 sites, most common site width 30 feet, 50 water & elec (20 & 30 amp receptacles), 50 no hookups, seasonal sites, 30 pull-thrus, a/c allowed ($), heater allowed ($), phone hookups, tenting available, cabins, RV storage, sewage disposal, laundry, public phone, limited grocery store, RV supplies, LP gas refill by weight/by meter, ice, tables, fire rings, wood.

◆◆◆RECREATION: rec hall, rec room/area, pavilion, coin games, basketball hoop, playground, planned group activities (weekends only), badminton, sports field, horseshoes, hiking trails, volleyball.

Open May 1 through Oct 31. Rate in 1995 $14-18 for 2 persons. Master Card/Visa accepted. Member of ARVC; CONY. Phone: (716) 538-4200.
**SEE AD ROCHESTER PAGE 630**

## CALLICOON—A-1

**Upper Delaware Campgrounds**—Riverside with grassy open & shaded sites. *From jct Hwy 97 & Hwy 17B: Go 1 block W on Hwy 17B (under bridge), then follow signs 2 blocks S.* ◆◆FACILITIES: 250 sites, 100 water & elec (15 & 20 amp receptacles), 150 no hookups, seasonal sites, 50 pull-thrus, tenting available, sewage disposal, public phone, limited grocery store, ice, tables, fire rings, grills, wood. ◆◆◆RECREATION: swim pool, boating, no motors, canoeing, 300 canoe boat rentals, river fishing, playground, sports field. Recreation open to the



CALLICOON—Continued
UPPER DELAWARE CAMPGROUNDS—Continued

public. Open all year. Facilities fully operational May 1 through Nov 1. Rate in 1995 $20-25 for 2 persons. No refunds. Member of ARVC;CONY. Phone: (914) 887-5344.

## CAMBRIDGE—D-10

**Battenkill Sports Quarters**—Grassy, open & shaded sites in a rustic CAMPGROUND along the river. *From jct Hwy 22 & Hwy 313: Go 3 1/2 mi NE on Hwy 313.* ◆◆FACILITIES: 60 sites, 20 water & elec (15 amp receptacles), 40 no hookups, tenting available, sewage disposal, ice, tables, fire rings, grills, wood. ◆◆◆RECREATION: canoeing, 40 canoe boat rentals, river fishing, playground, sports field, horseshoes. Recreation open to the public. No pets. Open May 15 through Columbus Day. Rate in 1995 $18 for 2 persons. Member of ARVC; CONY. Phone: (518) 677-8868.

✱ **DOUG GORDON RV REPAIRS**—*From jct Hwy 372 & Hwy 22: Go 4 1/2 mi N on Hwy 22, then 3/4 mi E on CR 61 (Shushan Rd).* SERVICES: Engine/Chassis & RV appliance mechanic full-time, sewage disposal, RV storage, sells parts/accessories, sells camping supplies, installs hitches. Open May 1 through Oct 15. Phone: (518) 677-8855.
**SEE AD THIS PAGE**

**LAKE LAUDERDALE CAMPGROUND**—Sunny and wooded sites on a hilltop in a country setting. *From jct Hwy 372 & Hwy 22: Go 4 1/2 mi N on Hwy 22, then 3/4 mi E on CR 61 (Shushan Rd).*

◆◆FACILITIES: 75 sites, most common site width 40 feet, 17 full hookups, 43 water & elec (20 amp receptacles), 15 no hookups, seasonal sites, a/c allowed ($), heater allowed ($), tenting available, group sites for tents, RV rentals, RV storage, sewage disposal, laundry, limited grocery store, RV supplies, LP gas refill by weight/by meter, ice, tables, fire rings, wood.

◆◆◆RECREATION: equipped pavilion, coin games, basketball hoop, playground, 2 shuffleboard courts, planned group activities (weekends only), badminton, sports field, horseshoes, hiking trails, volleyball.

Open May 1 through Oct 15. Rate in 1995 $14-18.50 for 2 persons. Member of ARVC; CONY. Phone: (518) 677-8855.
**SEE AD THIS PAGE**

## CAMPBELL—F-4

**CAMP BELL CAMPGROUND**—CAMPGROUND with open and shaded sites. *From jct Hwy 17 (exit 41) & Hwy 333: Go 1/2 mi E on Hwy 333, then 3/4 mi NW on Hwy 415.*

◆◆◆FACILITIES: 111 sites, most common site width 40 feet, 111 water & elec (20 & 30 amp receptacles), seasonal sites, 5 pull-thrus, a/c allowed ($), heater allowed ($), cable TV ($), phone hookups, tenting available, group sites for tents/RVs, sewage disposal, laundry, public phone, limited grocery store, RV supplies, LP gas refill by weight/by meter, ice, tables, patios, fire rings, wood.

◆◆◆RECREATION: rec hall, rec room/area, pavilion, coin games, swim pool, basketball hoop, playground, sports field, horseshoes.

Open May 1 through Oct 15. Rate in 1995 $19-23 for 2 persons. Master Card/Visa accepted. Member of ARVC;CONY. Phone: (607) 527-3301.
**SEE AD CORNING PAGE 600**

## CANANDAIGUA—E-4

**CANANDAIGUA-ROCHESTER KOA**—Grassy CAMPGROUND with shaded & open sites. *From jct I-90 (exit 44) & Hwy 332: Go 4 mi S on Hwy 332, then 1 mi E on Farmington/Town Line Rd.*

◆◆◆◆FACILITIES: 120 sites, most common site width 20 feet, 26 full hookups, 64 water & elec (20,30 & 50 amp receptacles), 30 no hookups, seasonal sites, 36 pull-thrus, a/c allowed ($), heater allowed ($), tenting available, group sites for tents/RVs, cabins, RV storage, sewage disposal, laundry, public phone, grocery store, RV supplies, LP gas refill by weight/by meter, ice, tables, wood.

◆◆◆◆RECREATION: rec hall, coin games, swim pool, 2 pedal boat rentals, pond fishing, mini-golf ($), basketball hoop, playground, 2 shuffleboard courts, planned group activities (weekends only), movies, sports field, horseshoes.

Open Apr 1 through Nov 1. Rate in 1995 $26-29 for 2 persons. Master Card/Visa accepted. Member of ARVC;CONY. Phone: (716) 398-3582. KOA 10% value card discount.
**SEE AD THIS PAGE AND AD FRONT OF BOOK PAGES 68 AND 69**

**Creek Side Campsite**—Grassy, sunny sites & wooded sites in a rural CAMPGROUND. *From east jct Hwy 64 & Hwy 5/20: Go 1/2 mi E on Hwy 5/20, then 1 1/2 mi N on Wheeler Station Rd.* ◆◆FACILITIES: 40 sites, 5 full hookups, 20 water & elec (20 & 30 amp receptacles), 15 no hookups, seasonal sites, tenting available, non-flush toilets, sewage disposal, limited grocery store, LP gas refill by weight/by meter, ice, tables, fire rings, wood. ◆◆RECREATION: pavilion, stream fishing, playground, horseshoes. Open May 15 through Oct 15. Rate in 1995 $11-16 for 2 persons. Phone: (716) 657-7746.

## CANDOR—F-6

**BUCKRIDGE NUDIST PARK** (NUDIST PARK)—Wooded and open sites on a terraced hillside in a rural CAMP RESORT. *From jct Hwy 96 Truck/Hwy 96B & Hwy 96: Go 2 mi W on Hwy 96, then 1 mi S on Tuttle Hill Rd.*

FACILITIES: 50 sites, 40 water & elec (20 amp receptacles), 10 no hookups, seasonal sites, a/c not allowed, heater not allowed, tenting available, group sites for tents/RVs, tent rentals, RV rentals, RV storage, sewage disposal.

RECREATION: rec room/area, lake swimming, whirlpool, boating, no motors, canoeing, 1 row boat rentals, lake fishing, planned group activities (weekends only), horseshoes, hiking trails, volleyball.

Open May 15 through Sep 30. Rates available upon request. Master Card/Visa accepted. CPO. Member of ARVC; CONY. Phone: (607) 659-3868.
**SEE AD TRAVEL SECTION PAGE 589**

## CAPE VINCENT—C-6

BURNHAM POINT STATE PARK—*From business center: Go 3 mi E on Hwy 12E.* FACILITIES: 50 sites, 19 elec, 31 no hookups, tenting available, sewage disposal, public phone, ice, tables. RECREATION: boating, canoeing, ramp, river fishing, playground. Open mid May through early Sep. No showers. Phone: (315) 654-2324.

CAPE VINCENT—Continued on next page

CAPE VINCENT—Continued

**HI LO HICKORY FAMILY CAMPGROUND**—*Take south shore ferry service (Horn's Ferry Co.) to Wolfe Island (CN), then 11.2 km/7 mi N on Hwy 95, then 11.2 km/7 mi E on Hwy 96, then 1.6 km/1 mi E on Hogan Rd.*

WELCOME

**SEE PRIMARY LISTING AT WOLFE ISLAND, ON AND AD TRAVEL SECTION, ON PAGE 976**

## CAROGA LAKE—D-8

CAROGA LAKE CAMPGROUND (Adirondack State Forest)—*From jct Hwy 10 & Hwy 29A: Go 1 mi S on Hwy 29A (Campground on E Caroga Lake).* FACILITIES: 161 sites, 161 no hookups, tenting available, handicap restroom facilities, sewage disposal, tables. RECREATION: lake swimming, boating, canoeing, ramp, fishing, hiking trails. Open mid May through Labor day. Phone: (518) 835-4241.

## CASTILE—E-3

**FOUR WINDS CAMPGROUND**—*From the south entrance of Letchworth State Park (Portageville): Turn opposite park entrance onto Griffith Rd, then 1 3/4 mi w on Griffith Rd, then left on Tenefly Rd 1 1/4 mi to Campground.*

WELCOME

**SEE PRIMARY LISTING AT PORTAGEVILLE AND AD THIS PAGE**

LETCHWORTH STATE PARK—*From the center of town: Go 1 1/2 mi SW on Hwy 39, then 3 mi S on Hwy 19A.* FACILITIES: 270 sites, 270 elec, tenting available, handicap restroom facilities, sewage disposal, laundry, public phone, grocery store, ice, tables. RECREATION: rec hall, swim pool, playground, planned group activities, hiking trails. Open May through Oct. Phone: (716) 237-3303.

## CATSKILL—F-9

**Cedar Grove Campgrounds**—Rolling, semi-wooded CAMPGROUND with grassy, wooded & some open sites. *From I-87 (NY Thruway exit 21): Go 1 1/4 mi E on Hwy 23, then 4 1/2 mi N on US 9W, then 1 mi W on Schoharie Tpk.* ◈◈FACILITIES: 50 sites, 30 water & elec (15 amp receptacles), 20 no hookups, seasonal sites, 9

CATSKILL—Continued
CEDAR GROVE CAMPGROUNDS—Continued

pull-thrus, tenting available, sewage disposal, limited grocery store, ice, tables, fire rings, wood. ◈◈◈RECREATION: pavilion, lake swimming, boating, no motors, canoeing, 1 row/1 pedal boat rentals, pond fishing, sports field, horseshoes, hiking trails, volleyball. Recreation open to the public. Open May 15 through Oct 15. Rate in 1995 $18-21. Member of ARVC; CONY. Phone: (518) 945-1451.

**INDIAN RIDGE CAMPSITES**—Semi-wooded CAMPGROUND with mostly wooded & some open sites. *From NY Thruway (exit 21): Go 1/4 mi W on Hwy 23B, then 1/2 mi N on Forest Hill Ave.*

WELCOME

◈◈◈FACILITIES: 70 sites, most common site width 30 feet, 44 water & elec (20 & 30 amp receptacles), 26 no hookups, seasonal sites, 10 pull-thrus, a/c allowed ($), heater allowed ($), tenting available, tent rentals, cabins, sewage disposal, laundry, public phone, limited grocery store, RV supplies, ice, tables, fire rings, wood.

◈◈◈RECREATION: rec room/area, coin games, swim pool, pond fishing, playground, badminton, horseshoes, volleyball.

Open May 1 through Oct 25. Rate in 1995 $18-20 per family. American Express/Master Card/Visa accepted. Member of ARVC;CONY. Phone: (518) 943-3516.

**SEE AD THIS PAGE**

**Woods Road Campsites**—CAMPGROUND with open & shaded sites. *From NY Thruway (exit 21): Go 2 1/2 mi W on Hwy 23, then 25 feet S on Five Mile Woods Rd, then 1/4 mi E on Vedder Rd.* ◈◈◈FACILITIES: 90 sites, most common site width 30 feet, 4 full hookups, 66 water & elec (15,20 & 30 amp receptacles),

CATSKILL—Continued
WOODS ROAD CAMPSITES—Continued

20 no hookups, seasonal sites, 10 pull-thrus, tenting available, sewage disposal, laundry, public phone, limited grocery store, ice, tables, fire rings, wood. ◈◈◈RECREATION: rec room/area, pavilion, swim pool, mini-golf ($), playground, horseshoes, volleyball. Open May 1 through Oct 31. Rate in 1995 $18-23 for 2 persons. Member of ARVC; CONY. Phone: (518) 943-9118.

## CATSKILL MOUNTAINS—F-8

***See listings at Catskill, Downsville, East Branch, Livingston Manor, Palenville, Parksville, Phoenicia, Roscoe, Saugerties & Windham***

## CENTRAL BRIDGE—E-8

**HIDE-A-WAY CAMPSITES**—CAMPGROUND with grassy, open & shaded sites. *From jct I-88 (Central Bridge exit 23) & Hwy 7/30A: Go 1 1/4 mi W on Hwy 7/30A, then 3/4 mi W & N on Hwy 30A, then 1/4 mi N on Pine Hill Rd, then 1 1/4 mi W on State Rd, then follow signs 1/2 mi N.*

WELCOME

◈◈FACILITIES: 50 sites, 39 water & elec (15,20 & 30 amp receptacles), 11 no hookups, seasonal sites, a/c allowed ($), heater not allowed, tenting available, RV rentals, RV storage, sewage disposal, laundry, public phone, limited grocery store, RV supplies, LP gas refill by weight/by meter, ice, tables, fire rings, wood.

◈◈RECREATION: rec room/area, coin games, swim pool, pond fishing, basketball hoop, horseshoes.

HIDE-A-WAY CAMPSITES—Continued on next page
CENTRAL BRIDGE—Continued on next page

CENTRAL BRIDGE—Continued
HIDE-A-WAY CAMPSITES—Continued

Open May 15 through Oct 15. Rate in 1995 $16 for 4 persons. Master Card/Visa accepted. Member of ARVC; CONY. Phone: (518) 868-9975.
**SEE AD PAGE 597**

**LOCUST PARK**—CAMPGROUND with grassy open & some shaded sites. *From jct I-88 (Central Bridge exit) & Hwy 7/Hwy 30A: Go 1 mi W on Hwy 7/Hwy 30A.*

WELCOME

◈◈◈FACILITIES: 32 sites, most common site width 30 feet, 20 full hookups, 12 water & elec (20 & 30 amp receptacles), seasonal sites, 14 pull-thrus, a/c allowed ($), heater not allowed, tenting available, sewage disposal, tables.

RECREATION: pavilion, horseshoes.



CENTRAL BRIDGE—Continued
LOCUST PARK—Continued

Open May 1 through Nov 1. Rate in 1995 $13-16 for 4 persons. Phone: (518) 868-9927.
**SEE AD PAGE 597**

## CHATEAUGAY—A-9

**High Falls Park**—*From village: Go 1/2 mi W on US 11, then 1/4 mi S on Cemetery Rd.* FACILITIES: 41 sites, 18 full hookups, 11 water & elec (30 amp receptacles), 12 no hookups, tenting available, sewage disposal, public phone, ice, tables, fire rings, wood. RECREATION: rec hall, swim pool, sports field, horseshoes, volleyball. Open May 1 through Oct 15. No showers. Rate in 1995 $14-16 for 2 persons. Member of ARVC; CONY. Phone: (518) 497-3156.

## CHAUTAUQUA—F-1

**CAMP CHAUTAUQUA CAMPING RESORT**—Lakeside CAMPGROUND with open & shaded sites. *E'bound: From southeast town limits: Go 2 3/4 mi SE on Hwy 394. W'bound: From Expressway 17 (exit 8) & Hwy 394: Go 3 mi N on Hwy 394.*

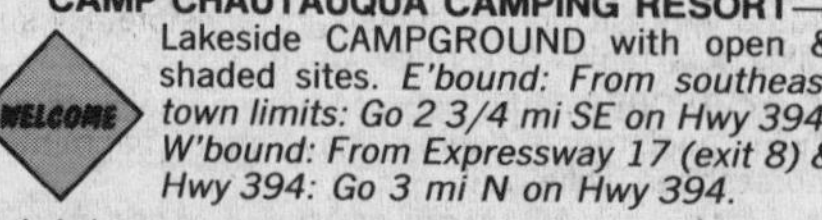

WELCOME

◈◈◈◈FACILITIES: 300 sites, most common site width 50 feet, 125 full hookups, 165 water & elec (20,30 & 50 amp receptacles), 10 no hookups, seasonal sites, 114 pull-thrus, a/c allowed, heater allowed, cable TV, tenting available, group sites for tents/RVs, RV storage, sewage disposal, laundry, public phone, full service store, RV supplies, LP gas refill by weight/by meter, gasoline, marine gas, ice, tables, patios, fire rings, wood, church services, traffic control gate/guard.

◈◈◈◈◈RECREATION: rec hall, rec room/area, equipped pavilion, coin games, swim pool (heated), wading pool, lake swimming, boating, canoeing, ramp, dock, 12 row/3 canoe/2 pedal boat rentals, water skiing, lake/pond fishing, basketball hoop, playground, planned group activities (weekends only), recreation director, tennis court, badminton, sports field, horseshoes, volleyball, cross country skiing, snowmobile trails.

Open all year. Facilities fully operational Apr 15 through Oct 15. Special traveler's rate of $20: arrival after 7 p.m.: departure before 9 a.m. Rate in 1995 $20-33 per family. Discover/Master Card/Visa accepted. Member of ARVC;CONY. Phone: (716) 789-3435. FCRV 10% discount.
**SEE AD TRAVEL SECTION PAGE 585 AND AD THIS PAGE**

✱ **CAMP CHAUTAUQUA RV**—*From southeast town limits: Go 2 3/4 mi SE on Hwy 394.* SERVICES: RV appliance mechanic full-time, emergency road service 24 hours, LP gas refill by weight/by meter, sewage disposal, RV storage, sells parts/accessories. Open all year. Discover/Master Card/Visa accepted. Phone: (716) 789-3435.

WELCOME

**SEE AD TRAVEL SECTION PAGE 585 AND AD THIS PAGE**

## CHERRY VALLEY—E-8

**Mohawk Campground**—Grassy, open and shaded sites convenient to a major highway. *From jct Hwy 166 & US 20: Go 2 1/2 mi E on US 20, then 1/4 mi SE on Chestnut St.* ◈◈FACILITIES: 50 sites, most common site width 35 feet, 40 water & elec (15,20 & 30 amp receptacles), 10 no hookups, seasonal sites, tenting available, sewage disposal, laundry, public phone, limited grocery store, LP gas refill by weight/by meter, ice, tables, fire rings, wood. ◈◈◈RECREATION: rec hall, rec room/area, swim pool (heated), boating, no motors, canoeing, 1 row/1 pedal boat rentals, pond fishing, playground, planned group activities (weekends only), badminton, sports field, horseshoes, hiking trails, volleyball. Open May 1 through Oct 15. Rate in 1995 $16-20 for 2 persons. Member of ARVC; CONY. Phone: (607) 264-3241.



## CLAYTON—B-6

CEDAR POINT STATE PARK—*From business center: Go 6 mi W on Hwy 12E.* FACILITIES: 182 sites, 17 full hookups, 68 elec, 97 no hookups, tenting available, handicap restroom facilities, sewage disposal, public phone, ice, tables. RECREATION: rec hall, swimming, boating, canoeing, ramp, river fishing, playground. Open early May through Oct 8. Phone: (315) 654-2522.

**MERRY KNOLL 1000 ISLANDS CAMPGROUND**—Riverside CAMPGROUND with open & shaded sites. *From jct Hwy 12 & Hwy 12 E: Go 2 1/2 mi SW on Hwy 12E.*

WELCOME

◈◈◈FACILITIES: 87 sites, most common site width 30 feet, 77 full hookups, 10 water & elec (20,30 & 50 amp receptacles), seasonal sites, 12 pull-thrus, a/c allowed ($), heater allowed ($), phone hookups, tenting available, RV rentals, RV storage, sewage disposal, laundry, public phone, limited grocery store, RV supplies, ice, tables, fire rings, wood.

◈◈◈RECREATION: rec room/area, coin games, swim pool, boating, canoeing, dock, 4 row/4 motor boat rentals, water skiing, river fishing, fishing guides, playground, badminton, volleyball.

Open May 15 through Oct 15. Rate in 1995 $19-20 for 2 persons. Member of ARVC; CONY. Phone: (315) 686-3055.
**SEE AD THIS PAGE**

## COHOCTON—E-4

**TUMBLE HILL CAMPGROUND**—Level, hilltop sites with shade & grass in rural area. *From jct I-390 (exit 2) & Hwy 415: Go 1 mi SE on Hwy 415, then 1/2 mi N on Hwy 371, then 1/2 mi W on Atlanta Back Rd.*

WELCOME

◈◈FACILITIES: 50 sites, most common site width 35 feet, 32 full hookups, (15,20,30 & 50 amp receptacles), 18 no hookups, seasonal sites, a/c allowed ($), heater allowed ($), cable TV ($), tenting available, group sites for tents, RV storage, laundry, LP gas refill by weight/by meter, tables, fire rings, wood.

◈◈RECREATION: rec hall, playground, 2 shuffleboard courts, hiking trails.

Open Memorial Day through Labor Day. Rate in 1995 $16-18 per family. CPO. Member of ARVC; CONY. Phone: (716) 384-5248.
**SEE AD CORNING PAGE 600**

## COLD BROOK—D-7

**Adirondack Gateway Campground (Not Visited)**—Grassy, shaded sites in the countryside. *From jct Hwy 28 & Hwy 8: Go 5 mi NE on Hwy 8, then 1/2 mi E on Hall Rd, then 1/4 mi N on Burt Rd.* FACILITIES: 57 sites, most common site width 30 feet, 35 water & elec (15,20,30 & 50 amp receptacles), 22 no hookups, tenting available, sewage disposal, laundry, public phone, limited grocery store, ice, tables, fire rings. RECREATION: rec room/area, swim pool, pond fishing, sports field, horseshoes, hiking trails, volleyball. Open May 1 through Oct 15. Rate in 1995 $19 for 2 persons. Phone: (315) 826-7619.

## COLD SPRING—B-2

CLARENCE FAHNESTOCK MEMORIAL STATE PARK—*From jct Hwy 9 & Hwy 301: Go 8 mi E on Hwy 301.* FACILITIES: 81 sites, 81 no hookups, tenting available, public phone, tables. RECREATION: lake swimming, boating, no motors, canoeing, ramp, lake fishing, playground, hiking trails. Recreation open to the public. No pets. Open mid May through late Oct. Phone: (914) 225-7207.

## COOPERSTOWN—E-8

**COOPERSTOWN BEAVER VALLEY CAMPGROUND**—Open & shaded sites in a CAMPGROUND with a view of wooded hills. *From jct Hwy 80 & Hwy 28 in town: Go 4 mi S on Hwy 28, then follow signs 2 1/4 mi W (Seminary Rd).*

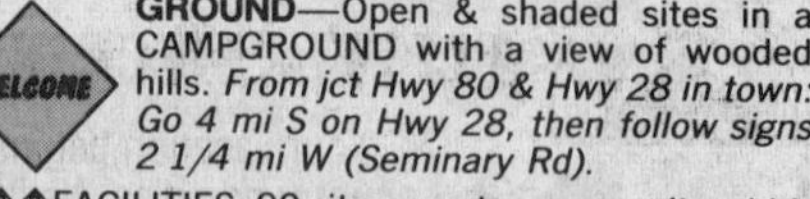

WELCOME

◈◈◈FACILITIES: 90 sites, most common site width 35 feet, 70 water & elec (15 & 30 amp receptacles), 20 no hookups, seasonal sites, 7 pull-thrus, a/c allowed ($), heater not allowed, tenting available, group sites for tents/RVs, RV rentals, cabins, RV storage, sewage disposal, laundry, public phone, limited grocery store, RV supplies, LP gas refill by weight/by meter, ice, tables, fire rings, wood.

◈◈◈RECREATION: rec hall, rec room/area, pavilion, coin games, swim pool, wading pool, boating, no motors, canoeing, dock, 1 row/1 canoe/2 pedal boat rentals, pond fishing, basketball hoop, 7 bike rentals, playground, planned group activities, recreation director, badminton, sports field, horseshoes, hiking trails, volleyball. Recreation open to the public.

COOPERSTOWN BEAVER VALLEY CAMPGROUND—Continued on next page
COOPERSTOWN—Continued on next page

COOPERSTOWN—Continued
COOPERSTOWN BEAVER VALLEY CAMPGROUND—Continued

Open May 15 through Oct 15. Rate in 1995 $20-23 per family. Master Card/Visa accepted. Member of ARVC;CONY. Phone: (800) 726-7314. FCRV 10% discount.
**SEE AD PAGE 598**

**Cooperstown Ringwood Farms Campground**—Open, grassy and wooded sites in a rural area. *From jct Hwy 28 & Hwy 80: Go 9 mi NE on Hwy 80.* ◊◊FACILITIES: 86 sites, most common site width 30 feet, 47 full hookups, 39 water & elec (20 & 30 amp receptacles), seasonal sites, tenting available, sewage disposal, laundry, public phone, limited grocery store, ice, tables, fire rings, grills, wood. ◊◊◊RECREATION: rec hall, pavilion, swim pool, pond fishing, playground, sports field, horseshoes, hiking trails, volleyball. Recreation open to the public. Open all year. Facilities fully operational Apr 15 through Oct 15. Rate in 1995 $16-21 for 2 persons. Member of ARVC; CONY. Phone: (800) 231-9114.

WELCOME

**COOPERSTOWN SHADOW BROOK CAMPGROUND**—Semi-wooded with grassy, shaded & open sites. *From center of town at jct Hwy 80 & Main St: Go 3/4 mi SE on Main St, then 10 mi N on CR 31.*

◊◊◊◊FACILITIES: 100 sites, most common site width 30 feet, 15 full hookups, 75 water & elec (20 & 30 amp receptacles), 10 no hookups, seasonal sites, 20 pull-thrus, a/c allowed ($), heater allowed ($), tenting available, RV rentals, RV storage, handicap restroom facilities, sewage disposal, laundry, public phone, limited grocery store, RV supplies, LP gas refill by weight/by meter, ice, tables, fire rings, wood.

◊◊◊◊RECREATION: rec hall, rec room/area, coin games, swim pool (heated), boating, no motors, canoeing, 4 pedal boat rentals, pond fishing, basketball hoop, playground, planned group activities (weekends only), badminton, horseshoes, volleyball.

Open May 1 through Oct 1. Rate in 1995 $19-24 for 2 persons. Discover/Master Card/Visa accepted. Member of ARVC; CONY. Phone: (607) 264-8431.
**SEE AD THIS PAGE**

WELCOME

**KOA-COOPERSTOWN**—CAMPGROUND with shaded & open sites. *From jct Hwy 28 & Hwy 80: Go 11 mi N on Hwy 80 East, then 1/2 mi W on US 20, then 1 mi N & W on a blacktop road (follow signs).*

◊◊◊◊FACILITIES: 117 sites, most common site width 30 feet, 32 full hookups, 57 water & elec (20 & 30 amp receptacles), 28 no hookups, 58 pull-thrus, a/c allowed, heater allowed, phone hookups, tenting available, group sites for tents/RVs, cabins, handicap restroom facilities, sewage disposal, laundry, public phone, limited grocery store, RV supplies, LP gas refill by weight/by meter, ice, tables, fire rings, grills, wood.

◊◊◊RECREATION: rec room/area, pavilion, coin games, swim pool, basketball hoop, playground, planned group activities (weekends only), movies, badminton, sports field, horseshoes, hiking trails, volleyball.

COOPERSTOWN—Continued
KOA-COOPERSTOWN—Continued

Open Apr 15 through Nov 1. Rate in 1995 $20-25 for 2 persons. American Express/Master Card/Visa accepted. Member of ARVC; CONY. Phone: (800) 562-3402. KOA 10% value card discount.
**SEE AD THIS PAGE AND AD FRONT OF BOOK PAGES 68 AND 69**

WELCOME

**MEADOW-VALE CAMPSITES**—Semi-wooded, mountainview CAMPGROUND with wooded & open sites. *From jct Hwy 80 & Hwy 28: Go 2 1/2 mi S on Hwy 28, then 7 1/2 mi W onCR 11, then 4 mi SW on CR 14, then 1/4 mi S on Gilbert Lake Rd.*

◊◊◊FACILITIES: 110 sites, most common site width 35 feet, 96 water & elec (15,20 & 30 amp receptacles), 14 no hookups, seasonal sites, a/c allowed ($), heater not allowed, tenting available,

MEADOW-VALE CAMPSITES—Continued on next page
COOPERSTOWN—Continued on next page

COOPERSTOWN—Continued
MEADOW-VALE CAMPSITES—Continued

group sites for tents/RVs, RV rentals, RV storage, sewage disposal, laundry, public phone, grocery store, RV supplies, LP gas refill by weight, ice, tables, fire rings, wood.

◈◈◈RECREATION: equipped pavilion, coin games, swim pool (heated), boating, no motors, canoeing, dock, 1 canoe/2 pedal boat rentals, pond fishing, mini-golf ($), basketball hoop, playground, planned group activities (weekends only), movies, badminton, sports field, horseshoes, hiking trails, volleyball.

Open May 15 through Oct 15. Rate in 1995 $18-22 for 4 persons. Master Card/Visa accepted. Member of ARVC; CONY. Phone: (607) 293-8802.
**SEE AD PAGE 599**

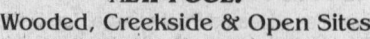

## CORINTH—D-9

**ALPINE LAKE CAMPING RESORT**—Developed RV PARK with lakeside and wooded sites. *From south village limits: Go 1 1/4 mi S on Hwy 9N, then 1 1/4 mi E on Heath Rd.*

◈◈◈FACILITIES: 450 sites, most common site width 60 feet, 450 full hookups, (30 & 50 amp receptacles), seasonal sites, 250 pull-thrus, a/c allowed ($), heater not allowed, cable TV ($), phone hookups, tenting available, RV rentals, RV storage, sewage disposal, laundry, public phone, grocery store, RV supplies, LP gas refill by weight/by meter, ice, tables, patios, fire rings, wood, church services.

◈◈◈◈RECREATION: rec hall, rec room/area, equipped pavilion, coin games, 2 swim pools (heated), lake swimming, boating, electric motors only, canoeing, 20 row/5 canoe/8 pedal boat rentals, lake fishing, basketball hoop, playground, planned group activities, movies, recreation director, 2 tennis courts, badminton, sports field, horseshoes, hiking trails, volleyball.

Open May 1 through Sep 30. Rate in 1995 $27-29 for 2 persons. No refunds. Member of ARVC; CONY. Phone: (518) 654-6260.
**SEE AD FRONT OF BOOK PAGE 26 AND AD LAKE GEORGE PAGES 612 AND 613**

**River Road Campground**—Rustic, wooded sites in a seculded, riverside location. *From north village limits: Go 2 mi N on Hwy 9N.* ◈◈FACILITIES: 80 sites, most common site width 30 feet, 35 full hookups, 22 water & elec (20 & 30 amp receptacles), 23 no hookups, seasonal sites, 6 pull-thrus, tenting available, sewage disposal, public phone, limited grocery store, ice, tables, fire rings, wood. ◈◈◈RECREATION: equipped pavilion, swim pool, river swimming, boating, canoeing, ramp, dock, 4 row boat rentals, river/stream fishing, playground, shuffleboard court, planned group activities (weekends only), badminton, horseshoes, volleyball. Open Memorial Day through Sep 15. Rate in 1995 $20-23 for 2 persons. Member of ARVC; CONY. Phone: (518) 654-6630.

## CORNING—F-4

**CAMP AT FERENBAUGH**—CAMPGROUND with level, wooded & open sites. *From center of the city at jct Hwy 17 & Hwy 414: Go 6 mi N on Hwy 414.*

◈◈◈FACILITIES: 166 sites, most common site width 50 feet, 36 full hookups, 110 water & elec (15,20,30 & 50 amp receptacles), 20 no hookups, seasonal sites, 40 pull-thrus, a/c allowed, heater allowed, cable TV, phone hookups, tenting available, group sites for tents/RVs, RV storage, sewage disposal, laundry, public phone, limited grocery store, RV supplies, LP gas refill by weight/by meter, ice, tables, fire rings, wood.

◈◈◈◈RECREATION: rec room/area, coin games, swim pool, pond/stream fishing, mini-golf ($), play-

CORNING—Continued
CAMP AT FERENBAUGH—Continued

ground, badminton, sports field, horseshoes, hiking trails, volleyball. Recreation open to the public.

Open Apr 15 through Oct 20. Facilities fully operational May 1 through Oct 15. Rate in 1995 $16-25 for 2 persons. American Express/Discover/Master Card/Visa accepted. Member of ARVC;CONY. Phone: (607) 962-6193.
**SEE AD FRONT OF BOOK PAGE 26 AND AD THIS PAGE**

**CAMP BELL CAMPGROUND**—*From jct Hwy 414 & Hwy 17 (Southern Tier Expressway): Go 9 mi W on Hwy 17 (exit 41), then 1/2 mi E on Hwy 333, then 3/4 mi NW on Hwy 415.*
**SEE PRIMARY LISTING AT CAMPBELL AND AD THIS PAGE**

**HICKORY HILL CAMPING RESORT**—*About 20 min NW of Corning. From jct Hwy 17 (exit 38) & Hwy 54: Go 1 mi E & N following Hwy 54, then 2 mi N on Haverling St.*
**SEE PRIMARY LISTING AT BATH AND AD BATH PAGE 594**

## CRANBERRY LAKE—B-8

CRANBERRY LAKE CAMPGROUND (Adirondack State Forest)—*From town: Go 1 1/2 mi off Hwy 3.* FACILITIES: 173 sites, 173 no hookups, tenting available, handicap restroom facilities, sewage disposal, tables. RECREATION: lake swimming, boating, canoeing, lake fishing, hiking trails. Open mid May through late Oct. Phone: (315) 848-2315.

## CROWN POINT—C-10

CROWN POINT RESERVATION CAMPGROUND (Adirondack State Forest)—*From town: Go 8 mi N on Hwy 9N.* FACILITIES: 66 sites, 66 no hookups, tenting available, handicap restroom facilities, sewage disposal, tables. RECREATION: boating, canoeing, ramp, lake fishing. Open mid Apr through mid Oct. Phone: (518) 597-3603.

## CUDDEBACKVILLE—B-1

**OAKLAND VALLEY CAMPGROUND**—A CAMPGROUND with mostly wooded sites beside a river. *From jct Hwy 211 & US 209: Go 100 feet N on US 209, then 1 3/4 mi W on CR 7.*

◈◈FACILITIES: 120 sites, most common site width 50 feet, 56 water & elec (15 & 30 amp receptacles), 64 no hookups, seasonal sites, a/c allowed ($), heater not allowed, cable TV ($), tenting available, RV storage, handicap restroom facilities, sewage disposal, laundry, public phone, limited grocery store, RV supplies, LP gas refill by weight, ice, tables, fire rings, wood.

◈◈◈RECREATION: rec hall, rec room/area, coin games, river swimming, river fishing, playground, sports field, horseshoes, volleyball.

Open Apr 19 through Oct 20. Rate in 1995 $18-22 for 2 persons. Discover/Master Card/Visa accepted. Member of ARVC; CONY. Phone: (914) 754-8732.
**SEE AD PORT JERVIS PAGE 627**

## CUTCHOGUE—B-5

**CLIFF & ED'S TRAILER PARK** (NOT VISITED) —*From jct I-495 (exit 73) & CR 58: Continue 15 1/4 mi E, then 1 block N on Depot Lane, then 1 block W on Schoolhouse Rd.*

FACILITIES: 23 sites, 23 full hookups, (20 & 30 amp receptacles).

Open Apr 1 through Nov 1. Rate in 1995 $20 for 4 persons. Phone: (516) 298-4091.
**SEE AD TRAVEL SECTION PAGE 586**

## DANSVILLE—E-4

**Skybrook Campground**—A hilltop locatin in a country setting with level, sunny & shaded sites. Most

SKYBROOK CAMPGROUND—Continued on next page
DANSVILLE—Continued on next page

**DANSVILLE**—Continued
SKYBROOK CAMPGROUND—Continued

full hookup sites occupied by seasonal campers. *From jct I-390 (exit 4) & Hwy 36: Go 1 1/2 mi N on Hwy 36, then 1/2 mi W on Hwy 436, then 1 mi S on Ossian Hill Rd, then 2 3/4 mi SE on McCurdy Rd.* ◆◆FACILITIES: 470 sites, most common site width 40 feet, 20 full hookups, 350 water & elec (15 & 20 amp receptacles), 100 no hookups, seasonal sites, tenting available, sewage disposal, laundry, public phone, limited grocery store, LP gas refill by weight/by meter, ice, tables, fire rings, wood. ◆◆◆RECREATION: rec hall, rec room/area, pavilion, swim pool, 4 pedal boat rentals, pond fishing, playground, 2 shuffleboard courts, planned group activities (weekends only), badminton, sports field, horseshoes, hiking trails, volleyball. Open May 1 through Oct 1. Rate in 1995 $15-19 for 2 persons. Phone: (716) 335-6880.

STONY BROOK STATE PARK—*From business center: Go 3 mi S on Hwy 36.* FACILITIES: 130 sites, 130 no hookups, tenting available, handicap restroom facilities, sewage disposal, public phone, tables. RECREATION: swimming, tennis court, hiking trails. Open early May through Oct 9. Phone: (716) 335-8111.

**SUGAR CREEK GLEN CAMPGROUND**—A wooded creekside location with shaded sites. *From jct I-390 (exit 4) & Hwy 36: Go 500 feet S on Hwy 36, then 5 mi SW on Poag's Hole Rd.*

◆◆◆FACILITIES: 135 sites, most common site width 40 feet, 100 water & elec (15 & 30 amp receptacles), 35 no hookups, seasonal sites, a/c allowed ($), heater not allowed, tenting available, group sites for tents/RVs, cabins, sewage disposal, public phone, limited grocery store, RV supplies, ice, tables, fire rings, grills, wood.

◆◆◆◆RECREATION: rec hall, coin games, river swimming, stream fishing, basketball hoop, playground, planned group activities (weekends only), recreation director, badminton, hiking trails, volleyball.

Open Apr 21 through Oct 13. Rate in 1995 $15-18 for 1 persons. Master Card/Visa accepted. CPO. Member of ARVC;CONY. Phone: (716) 335-6294.

**SEE AD THIS PAGE**

## DARIEN CENTER—E-3

**Darien Lake Camping Resort**—Lakeside, open, grassy or wooded sites on rolling terrain. *From jct I-90 (exit 48A) & Hwy 77: Go 5 mi S on Hwy 77.* ◆◆◆FACILITIES: 1500 sites, most common site width 30 feet, 275 full hookups, 1058 water & elec (20 & 30 amp receptacles), 167 no hookups, seasonal sites, tenting available, sewage disposal, laundry, public phone, full service store, LP gas refill by weight/by meter, ice, tables. ◆◆◆◆◆RECREATION: swim pool (heated), 100 pedal boat rentals, lake/pond fishing, mini-golf ($), playground, volleyball. Open Memorial Day through Labor Day. Rates available upon request for 2 persons. Member of ARVC; CONY. Phone: (716) 599-2211.

DARIEN LAKE STATE PARK—*From business center: Go 1/4 mi N of Hwy 20 on Harlow Rd.* FACILITIES: 150 sites, 150 no hookups, tenting available, handicap restroom facilities, tables, wood. RECREATION: rec hall, lake swimming, boating, no motors, canoeing, lake fishing, playground, hiking trails. Open early Jun through early Sep. Open weekends in May. Phone: (716) 547-9242.

**LEI-TI CAMPGROUND**—A CAMPGROUND with open & shaded sites in a country atmosphere. *From I-90 (exti 48A): Go 12 mi E on I-90 to exit 48, then 1 mi S on Hwy 98, then 2 1/2 mi SE on Hwy 63, then 1/2 mi S on Shepherd Rd, then 3/4 mi W on Putnam Rd, then 2 mi S on Francis Rd.*

◆◆◆FACILITIES: 203 sites, most common site width 40 feet, 60 full hookups, 127 water & elec (20 & 30 amp receptacles), 16 no hookups, seasonal sites, 7 pull-thrus, a/c allowed ($), heater allowed ($), phone hookups, tenting available, group sites for tents/RVs, RV rentals, cabins, RV storage, sewage disposal, laundry, public phone, limited grocery store, RV supplies, LP gas refill by weight/by meter, ice, tables, fire rings, wood, traffic control gate/guard.

◆◆◆◆RECREATION: rec hall, equipped pavilion, coin games, lake swimming, boating, no motors, canoeing, 2 row/1 pedal boat rentals, lake fishing, mini-golf ($), basketball hoop, 3 bike rentals, playground, 2 shuffleboard courts, planned group activities (weekends only), tennis court, badminton, sports field, horseshoes, hiking trails, volleyball, cross country skiing. Recreation open to the public.

Open all year. Facilities fully operational May 1 through Columbus Day. Rate in 1995 $17-23 for 2 persons. No refunds. Discover/Master Card/Visa accepted. Phone: (800) HI-LEITI.

**SEE PRIMARY LISTING AT BATAVIA AND AD NIAGARA FALLS PAGE 623**

**DARIEN CENTER**—Continued

**SKYLINE RESORT CAMPGROUND**—Lakeside semi-wooded park with shaded or open sites. *From jct Hwy 77 & US 20: Go 4 mi E on US 20, then 1 mi S on Townline Rd.*

◆◆◆FACILITIES: 225 sites, 225 water & elec (20 & 30 amp receptacles), seasonal sites, a/c allowed ($), heater allowed ($), tenting available, group sites for tents/RVs, RV storage, sewage disposal, public phone, limited grocery store, RV supplies, LP gas refill by weight, ice, tables, wood, guard.

◆◆◆◆RECREATION: rec hall, rec room/area, coin games, 2 swim pools (heated), wading pool, lake fishing, mini-golf ($), basketball hoop, playground, 2 shuffleboard courts, planned group activities, recreation director, tennis court, badminton, sports field, horseshoes, volleyball.

Open Apr 15 through Oct 15. Pool open mid Jun through Labor Day. Rate in 1995 $20 per family. Master Card/Visa accepted. Member of ARVC; CONY. Phone: (716) 591-2021.

**SEE AD BUFFALO PAGE 595**

✽ **SKYLINE RV SALES & SERVICE**—*From jct Hwy 77 & US 20: Go 4 mi E on US 20, then 1 mi S on Town Line Rd.* SALES: travel trailers, park models, 5th wheels, fold-down camping trailers. SERVICES: RV appliance mechanic full-time, LP gas refill by weight, sewage disposal, RV storage, sells parts/accessories, installs hitches. Open all year. Master Card/Visa accepted. Phone: (716) 591-2021.

**SEE AD BUFFALO PAGE 595**

## DAVENPORT—E-8

**CHRISTY'S BEAVER SPRING LAKE CAMPSITES**—Grassy open and shaded sites. *At east village limits on Hwy 23.*

◆◆◆FACILITIES: 122 sites, most common site width 40 feet, 65 full hookups, 38 water & elec (15,20 & 30 amp receptacles), 19 no hookups, seasonal sites, 12 pull-thrus, a/c allowed ($), heater allowed ($), tenting available, group sites for RVs, RV rentals, RV storage, sewage disposal, laundry, public phone, limited grocery store, RV supplies, LP gas refill by weight/by meter, ice, tables, fire rings, wood.

◆◆◆RECREATION: rec room/area, equipped pavilion, coin games, swim pool, boating, electric motors only, canoeing, 5 row/2 canoe/4 pedal boat rentals, lake/stream fishing, basketball hoop, playground, planned group activities (weekends only), badminton, sports field, horseshoes, volleyball. Recreation open to the public.

Open Apr 15 through Dec 10. Rate in 1995 $15-17 per family. Member of ARVC; CONY. Phone: (607) 278-5293.

**SEE AD ONEONTA PAGE 626**

## DEERLAND—C-8

FORKED LAKE CAMPGROUND (Adirondack State Forest)—*From business center: Go 3 mi W off Hwy 30 (access by foot or boat only).* FACILITIES: 80 sites, 80 no hookups, tenting available, non-flush toilets, tables. RECREATION: boating, canoeing, ramp, canoe boat rentals, lake fishing, hiking trails. Open mid May through Labor Day. No showers. Phone: (518) 624-6646.



## DELEVAN—E-2

**ARROWHEAD CAMPING AREA**—Secluded CAMPGROUND with wooded & grassy open sites. *From south village limits: Go 1 1/2 mi S on Hwy 16.*

◆◆FACILITIES: 250 sites, most common site width 50 feet, 35 ft. max RV length, 200 water & elec (20 & 30 amp receptacles), 50 no hookups, seasonal sites, 10 pull-thrus, a/c allowed ($), heater allowed ($), tenting available, sewage disposal, limited grocery store, RV supplies, ice, tables, fire rings, wood.

◆◆◆RECREATION: rec room/area, pavilion, coin games, pond swimming, boating, no motors, canoeing, 6 row/3 canoe/4 pedal boat rentals, pond/stream fishing, playground, sports field, horseshoes, volleyball.

Open May 15 through Columbus Day Weekend. Rate in 1995 $14-16 per family. No refunds. Discover/Master Card/Visa accepted. Member of ARVC; CONY. Phone: (716) 492-3715.

**SEE AD TRAVEL SECTION PAGE 585**

## DEWITTVILLE—F-1

**Chautauqua Heights Campground**—Grassy sites in a wooded CAMPGROUND. *From the center of the village: Go 1/2 mi E on Hwy 430.* ◆◆◆FACILITIES: 100 sites, 66 full hookups, 16 water & elec (20 & 30 amp receptacles), 18 no hookups, seasonal sites, 40 pull-thrus, tenting available, sewage disposal, laundry, public phone, limited grocery store, LP gas refill by weight, ice, tables, fire rings, wood. ◆◆◆RECREATION: rec room/area, pavilion, swim pool, playground, horseshoes, hiking trails, volleyball. Open Apr 15 through Oct 15. Rate in 1995 $12-22.50 per family. Member of ARVC; CONY. Phone: (716) 386-3804.

## DOWNSVILLE—F-7

**Catskill Mtn. Kampground**—Riverside CAMPGROUND with level, grassy & shaded sites. *From center of the village at jct Hwy 206 & Hwy 30: Go 2 3/4 mi S on Hwy 30.* ◆◆◆FACILITIES: 100 sites, most common site width 30 feet, 64 full hookups, 18 water & elec (15 & 30 amp receptacles), 18 no hookups, seasonal sites, 5 pull-thrus, tenting available, sewage disposal, laundry, public phone, limited grocery store, ice, tables, fire rings, grills, wood. ◆◆◆RECREATION: rec room/area, pavilion, swim pool, boating, canoeing, river fishing, playground, badminton, sports field, horseshoes, volleyball. Open Apr 1 through Columbus Day. Facilities fully operational May 1 through Oct 10. Rate in 1995 $16-21 for 2 persons. Member of ARVC; CONY. Phone: (607) 363-2599.

**Delaware Valley Campsite**—Riverside CAMPGROUND with shaded sites. *From center of the village at jct Hwy 206 & Hwy 30: Go 3 3/4 mi S on Hwy 30.* ◆◆FACILITIES: 88 sites, most common site width 30 feet, 80 full hookups, (15 & 20 amp receptacles), 8 no hookups, seasonal sites, 5 pull-thrus, tenting available, laundry, public phone, limited grocery store, ice, tables, fire rings, grills, wood. ◆◆RECREATION: river fishing, sports field, horseshoes, volleyball. Open May 1 through Oct 15. Rate in 1995 $18.50 for 2 persons. Member of ARVC;CONY. Phone: (607) 363-2306.

## DUANE—B-8

**DEER RIVER CAMPSITE**—Wooded & lake-front sites in forested CAMPGROUND. *From jct Hwy 30, CR 26 & CR 14: Go 1 1/2 mi W on CR 14 (Red Tavern Rd).*

◊◊◊FACILITIES: 83 sites, most common site width 35 feet, 6 full hookups, 71 water & elec (20 & 30 amp receptacles), 6 no hookups, seasonal sites, 3 pull-thrus, a/c allowed ($), heater allowed ($), tenting available, cabins, RV storage, sewage disposal, laundry, public phone, limited grocery store, RV supplies, LP gas refill by weight/by meter, ice, tables, fire rings, wood, traffic control gate.

◊◊◊RECREATION: rec room/area, coin games, lake swimming, boating, 9.5 hp limit, canoeing, dock, 5 row/4 canoe/1 pedal boat rentals, lake fishing, basketball hoop, playground, badminton, sports field, horseshoes, hiking trails, volleyball.

Open May 1 through Oct 7. Rate in 1995 $18-19.50 for 2 persons. Discover/Master Card/Visa accepted. Member of ARVC; CONY. Phone: (518) 483-0060.

**SEE AD THIS PAGE**

MEACHAM LAKE CAMPGROUND (Adirondack State Forest)—*From jct Hwy 99 & Hwy 30: Go 10 mi S on Hwy 30.* FACILITIES: 224 sites, 224 no hookups, tenting available, handicap restroom facilities, sewage disposal, tables. RECREATION: lake swimming, boating, canoeing, ramp, canoe boat rentals, lake fishing, playground, hiking trails. Open mid May through mid Oct. Phone: (518) 483-5116.

## EARLTON—F-9

**Earlton Hill Campsites/Ministries (Not Visited)**—Christian CAMPGROUND with open and shaded grassy sites. *From jct I-87 (NY State Thruway) (Coxackie exit 21 B) & US 9W: Go 2 mi S on US 9W, then 4 mi W on Hwy 81, then 1 1/2 mi N on Medway-Earlton Rd.* FACILITIES: 182 sites, 35 full hookups, 119 water & elec (15,20 & 30 amp receptacles), 28 no hookups, seasonal sites, 55 pull-thrus, tenting available, sewage disposal, public phone, limited grocery store, LP gas refill by weight, tables, fire rings. RECREATION: pavilion, lake swimming, boating, no motors, canoeing, 1 pedal boat rentals, lake fishing, playground, planned group activities (weekends only), recreation director, badminton, sports field, volleyball. Recreation open to the public. Open Memorial Day through Sep. Rate in 1995 $16-20 for 2 persons. Phone: (518) 731-2751.

## EAST BRANCH—F-7

**Ox-Bow Campsites**—Riverside CAMPGROUND with level grassy sites. *From jct Hwy 17 (exit 90) & Hwy 30: Go 3 mi N on Hwy 30.* ◊◊FACILITIES: 113 sites, most common site width 30 feet, 8 full hookups, 83 water & elec (15 & 20 amp receptacles), 22 no hookups, seasonal sites, 40 pull-thrus, tenting available, sewage disposal, laundry, public phone, ice, tables, fire rings, wood. ◊◊◊RECREATION: rec room/area, pavilion, river swimming, boating, no motors, canoeing, river fishing, playground, badminton, sports field, horseshoes, volleyball. Open May 1 through Oct 15. Rate in 1995 $17-20 for 2 persons. Member of ARVC;CONY. Phone: (607) 363-7141.

## EAST HAMPTON—B-5

CEDAR POINT (Suffolk County Park)—*From town: Go E on Hwy 27 (Montauk Hwy), then N on Stephens Hands Path to Old Northwest Rd, then follow signs to Alewive Brook Rd.* FACILITIES: 190 sites, 190 no hookups, tenting available, handicap restroom facilities, sewage disposal, public phone, full service store, ice, tables. RECREATION: boating, 8 row boat rentals, salt water fishing, playground, sports field, hiking trails. Open Apr 1 through Oct 16. Facilities fully operational May 19 through Sep 11. Weekends only Apr 1-May 15 & Sep 15-Oct 16. Phone: (516) 852-7620.

## EAST ISLIP—C-4

HECKSCHER STATE PARK—*From jct Hwy 27A & Southern State Pkwy (exit 45): Go 1 1/2 mi S on Southern State Pkwy.* FACILITIES: 69 sites, 69 no hookups, tenting available, handicap restroom facilities, sewage disposal, public phone, tables, grills. RECREATION: swim pool, salt water swimming ($), boating, canoeing, ramp, salt water fishing, playground, sports field, hiking trails. Recreation open to the public. No pets. Open mid May through early Sep. Phone: (516) 581-2100.

## EAST SPRINGFIELD—E-8

GLIMMERGLASS STATE PARK—*From town: Go 4 mi S of US 20, on E Lake Rd.* FACILITIES: 36 sites, 36 no hookups, tenting available, sewage disposal, tables, grills. RECREATION: lake swimming, boating, canoeing, lake fishing, playground, hiking trails. Open mid May through mid Oct. Phone: (607) 547-8662.

## ELIZABETH TOWN—B-9

***See listing at Lewis***

## ELIZAVILLE—F-9

**Brook-N-Wood Family Campground**—Open and shaded sites in a rual CAMPGROUND. *From jct CR 199 & US 9: Go 9 mi N on US 9, then 2 mi E on CR 8.* ◊◊◊FACILITIES: 135 sites, 80 full hookups, 31 water & elec (15 & 30 amp receptacles), 24 no hookups, seasonal sites, tenting available, sewage disposal, laundry, public phone, limited grocery store, LP gas refill by weight/by meter, ice, tables, fire rings, wood. ◊◊◊RECREATION: rec hall, swim pool, stream fishing, playground, planned group activities (weekends only), badminton, sports field, horseshoes, hiking trails, volleyball. Open all year. Facilities fully operational Apr 1 through Oct 31. Rate in 1995 $18-20 for 4 persons. Phone: (518) 537-6896.

## ELLENVILLE—A-2

**SKYWAY CAMPING RESORT**—Mountainview PARK with open or shady sites. *From jct US 209 & Hwy 52: Go 5 mi W on Hwy 52, then 1 mi S on Skyway RV Rd (immediate right fork).*

◊◊◊◊FACILITIES: 147 sites, most common site width 30 feet, 140 full hookups, (20 & 30 amp receptacles), 7 no hookups, seasonal sites, a/c allowed, heater not allowed, cable TV, phone hookups, tenting available, group sites for tents/RVs, RV rentals, RV storage, handicap restroom facilities, laundry, public phone, limited grocery store, RV supplies, LP gas refill by weight/by meter, ice, tables, fire rings, wood.

◊◊◊◊RECREATION: rec hall, rec room/area, coin games, swim pool (heated), whirlpool, boating, no motors, 3 row boat rentals, lake fishing, basketball hoop, playground, planned group activities, movies, recreation director, tennis court, badminton, sports field, horseshoes, hiking trails, volleyball.

Open May 1 through Columbus Day. Rates available upon request for 2 persons. Master Card/Visa accepted. Member of ARVC; CONY. Phone: (914) 647-5747.

**SEE AD PAGE 603**

✲ **SKYWAY RV SALES**—*From jct US 209 & Hwy 52: Go 5 mi W on Hwy 52.* SALES: travel trailers, 5th wheels. SERVICES: LP gas refill by weight/by meter, sells parts/accessories. Open all year. Master Card/Visa accepted. Phone: (914) 647-5747.

**SEE AD PAGE 603**

**YOGI BEAR'S JELLYSTONE PARK AT BIRCHWOOD ACRES**—Semi-wooded, well developed CAMPGROUND in a country atmosphere. *From jct US 209 & Hwy 52: Go 8 mi W on Hwy 52, then 1/2 mi S on Martinfeld Rd.*

◊◊◊◊FACILITIES: 252 sites, most common site width 40 feet, 136 full hookups, 91 water & elec (20 & 30 amp receptacles), 25 no hookups, seasonal sites, a/c allowed, heater not allowed, phone hookups, tenting available, group sites for tents/RVs, RV rentals, cabins, RV storage, sewage disposal, laundry, public phone, grocery store, RV supplies, LP gas refill by weight, ice, tables, fire rings, wood, guard.

◊◊◊◊RECREATION: rec hall, rec room/area, coin games, swim pool, whirlpool, boating, no mo-



ELLENVILLE—Continued
YOGI BEAR'S JELLYSTONE PARK AT BIRCHWOOD ACRES—Continued

tors, canoeing, 3 row/3 pedal boat rentals, lake fishing, basketball hoop, playground, 3 shuffleboard courts, planned group activities, movies, recreation director, tennis court, badminton, sports field, horseshoes, hiking trails, volleyball.

Open May 1 through Columbus Day. Rate in 1995 $26-29 for 2 persons. Master Card/Visa accepted. Member of ARVC; CONY. Phone: (914) 434-4743.

**SEE AD PAGE 604 AND AD FRONT OF BOOK PAGE 26**

## ELLICOTTVILLE—D-4

**TRIPLE-R CAMPGROUND**—*15 minutes from downtown. Go NE on Hwy 242 to CR 17, turn right on CR 17 to Bryant Hill Rd, then 1/2 mi to campground.*

**SEE PRIMARY LISTING AT FRANKLINVILLE AND AD TRAVEL SECTION PAGE 585**

## ELMIRA—F-5

***See listings at Lowman***

## ENDICOTT—F-6

**PINE VALLEY CAMPGROUND**—Lakeside with open & shaded sites. *From jct Hwy 17 (exit 67N) & Hwy 26: Go 6 mi N on Hwy 26, then 1 block NW on Maple Dr, then 1 mi W on Boswell Hill Rd.*

◊◊◊FACILITIES: 118 sites, most common site width 45 feet, 47 full hookups, 56 water & elec (20,30 & 50 amp receptacles), 15 no hookups, seasonal sites, a/c allowed ($), heater allowed ($), phone hookups, tenting available, RV storage, sewage disposal, laundry, public phone, limited grocery store, RV supplies, LP gas refill by weight, ice, tables, fire rings, wood.

◊◊◊◊RECREATION: rec hall, rec room/area, coin games, lake swimming, boating, no motors, canoeing, 3 row/3 pedal boat rentals, lake fishing, mini-golf ($), basketball hoop, playground, planned group activities (weekends only), sports field, horseshoes, hiking trails, volleyball.

Open May 1 through Oct 15. Rate in 1995 $15.95-20.95 for 2 persons. No refunds. Master Card/Visa accepted. Member of ARVC;CONY. Phone: (607) 785-6868.

**SEE AD BINGHAMTON PAGE 595**

## ESSEX—B-10

⚑ **LAKE CHAMPLAIN FERRIES**—*N'bound: From I-87 (exit 31): Go 10 mi E on paved road (follow Essex signs). S'bound: From I-87 (exit 33): Go 12 mi S on Hwy 22 (follow Essex signs).* Auto ferries cross scenic Lake Champlain between Essex, NY & Charlotte, VT. Open Apr through early Jan. Phone: (802) 864-9804.

**SEE AD LAKE CHAMPLAIN, VT PAGE 853**

## EUCLID—D-6

**Wigwam Campground**—Lakeside location with shaded sites. *From jct I-81 & Hwy 49: Go 1 mi W on Hwy 49, then 1 block S on Hwy 11, then 7 mi W on CR 12, then 1/2 mi S on CR 10.* ◊◊FACILITIES: 110 sites, most common site width 35 feet, 91 full hookups, 9 water & elec (20 & 30 amp receptacles), 10 no hookups, seasonal sites, tenting available, sewage disposal, public phone, limited grocery store, LP gas refill by weight/by meter, ice, tables, fire rings, wood. ◊◊◊RECREATION: rec hall, lake swimming, boating, no motors, canoeing, lake fishing, playground, badminton, volleyball. Open May 1 through Sep 30. Rate in 1995 $17-23 for 2 persons. Member of ARVC; CONY. Phone: (315) 668-2074.

## FAIR HAVEN—D-5

FAIR HAVEN BEACH STATE PARK—*From business center: Go 2 mi N on Hwy 104A.* FACILITIES: 195 sites, 44 elec, 151 no hookups, tenting available, handicap restroom facilities, sewage disposal, public phone, tables. RECREATION: rec hall, pavilion, lake swimming, boating, canoeing, ramp, lake fishing, playground, hiking trails. Open mid Apr through Oct 9. Phone: (315) 947-5205.

## FAYETTEVILLE—E-6

GREEN LAKES STATE PARK—*From business center: Go 3 mi E on Hwy 5.* FACILITIES: 137 sites, 42 elec, 95 no hookups, tenting available, handicap restroom facilities, sewage disposal, public phone, ice, tables. RECREATION: lake swimming, boating, canoeing, lake fishing, playground, hiking trails. Open mid May through Oct 9. Phone: (315) 637-6111.

# *Live the Dream . . .*

## At New York State's Famous Catskill Mountains Camping Resort

### New 9,000 Sq. Foot Recreation Building with Workout Room

- Scenic Sites
- Full Hookups
- 20/30 Amps
- Sparkling New Laundry Facilities
- Picnic Tables
- Fire Rings
- Wood
- Groceries & Gifts
- On-Site Luxury RV Rentals
- RV Supplies
- Propane by Weight & Meter
- Tennis
- Basketball
- Handball
- Bocce
- Toddler's Romper Room
- Volleyball
- Planned Activities
- Lake with Row Boats
- Fishing
- **Free Cable TV**
- Playground
- Regulation Horseshoe Court
- Softball Field
- Large Meeting Room
- Hiking Trails
- Teen Center with Coin Games & Billiards

**Olympic-Size Heated Pool with Sun Deck, Hot Tub Spa**

## Full Service RV Center Featuring Newmar, Carriage & Layton

**RESERVATIONS: (800) 44-SKYWAY**
**INFORMATION: (914) 647-5747**

WOODALL RATINGS: FACILITIES WWWWW RECREATION WWWWW

See listings at Ellenville

*5 Miles West of Ellenville off Route 52*
Box 194, Greenfield Park, NY 12435

NEW YORK For information on festivals in New York NEW YORK

SHOP FOR THAT SPECIAL SOMETHING AT THE LETCHWORTH ARTS & CRAFTS SHOW & SALE

NEW YORK see front of book article. NEW YORK

## FLORIDA—B-2

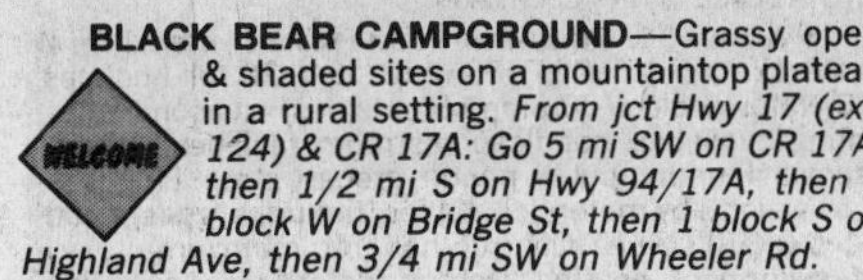

**BLACK BEAR CAMPGROUND**—Grassy open & shaded sites on a mountaintop plateau in a rural setting. *From jct Hwy 17 (exit 124) & CR 17A: Go 5 mi SW on CR 17A, then 1/2 mi S on Hwy 94/17A, then 1 block W on Bridge St, then 1 block S on Highland Ave, then 3/4 mi SW on Wheeler Rd.*

◇◇◇FACILITIES: 160 sites, most common site width 30 feet, 70 full hookups, 61 water & elec (20,30 & 50 amp receptacles), 29 no hookups, seasonal sites, 10 pull-thrus, a/c allowed, heater allowed, cable TV, phone hookups, tenting available, cabins, RV storage, handicap restroom facilities, sewage disposal, laundry, public phone, limited grocery store, RV supplies, LP gas refill by weight/by meter, ice, tables, fire rings, grills, wood.

◇◇◇RECREATION: rec room/area, pavilion, coin games, swim pool, pond fishing, mini-golf, basketball hoop, playground, planned group activities (weekends only), recreation director, badminton, sports field, horseshoes, volleyball.

Open all year. Facilities fully operational Apr 19 through Oct 25. Rate in 1995 $18-24 for 2 persons. Discover/Master Card/Visa accepted. CPO. Member of ARVC; CONY. Phone: (914) 651-7717.

SEE AD THIS PAGE

## FORESTPORT—D-7

**Kayuta Lake Campground**—Lakeside CAMPGROUND with level, shaded sites. Most full-hookup sites occupied by seasonal campers. *From jct Hwy 12 & Hwy 28: Go 2 mi NE on Hwy 28, then 1 3/10 mi S to Forestport Station, then take right fork in road 2 mi S, then 1/2 mi E, follow sign.* ◇◇◇FACILITIES: 138 sites, 85 full hookups, 45 water & elec (20,30 & 50 amp receptacles), 8 no hookups, seasonal sites, 10 pull-thrus, tenting available, sewage disposal, laundry, public phone, limited grocery store, LP gas refill by weight/by meter, ice, tables, fire rings, grills, wood. ◇◇◇◇RECREATION: rec hall, pavilion, lake swimming, boating, canoeing, ramp, dock, 3 row/3 canoe boat rentals, lake/stream fishing, mini-golf ($), playground, 2 shuffleboard courts, planned group activities (weekends only), tennis court, badminton, sports field, horseshoes, hiking trails, volleyball. Open May 15 through Oct 15. Rate in 1995 $16.50-18.50 for 2 persons. No refunds. Phone: (315) 831-5077.

## FORT ANN—D-10

**Fort Ann Campground**—Rural countryside CAMPGROUND with mostly shaded sites. *From jct Hwy 149 & Hwy 4 in village of Fort Ann: Follow signs.* ◇◇FACILITIES: 50 sites, most common site width 30 feet, 15 full hookups, 35 water & elec (15,20 & 30 amp receptacles), seasonal sites, 3 pull-thrus, tenting available, sewage disposal, laundry, ice, tables, fire rings, wood. ◇◇◇RECREATION: rec room/area, swim pool, playground, badminton, horseshoes, hiking trails, volleyball. Open May 15 through Oct 15. Rate in 1995 $17-19 for 2 persons. Member of ARVC; CONY. Phone: (518) 639-8840.

## FRANKLINVILLE—F-3

**Shangri-La Camping Sites**—Country CAMPGROUND on rolling hills with level, open & wooded sites. *From south jct Hwy 16 & Hwy 98: Go 3 mi SW on Hwy 98, then 1/4 mi W on Jarecki Rd.* ◇◇FACILITIES: 150 sites, most common site width 50 feet, 72 full hookups, (20 & 30 amp receptacles), 78 no hookups, seasonal sites, tenting available, public phone, ice, tables, fire rings, wood. ◇◇◇RECREATION: rec hall, rec room/area, pond swimming, boating, no motors, canoeing, pond fishing, playground, horseshoes, hiking trails, volleyball. Open May 1 through Oct 1. Rate in 1995 $18 for 2 persons. Member of ARVC; CONY. Phone: (716) 676-2413.

**TRIPLE-R CAMPGROUND**—Semi-wooded park with open & shaded sites. *From south jct Hwy 98 & Hwy 16: Go 1 mi N on Hwy 16/98, then 1 /1/2 mi W on Elm St, then 1/3 mi SW on Bryant Hill Rd.*

◇◇◇FACILITIES: 130 sites, most common site width 50 feet, 92 full hookups, 26 water & elec (20 & 30 amp receptacles), 12 no hookups, seasonal sites, 14 pull-thrus, a/c allowed ($), heater allowed ($), tenting available, group sites for tents/RVs, cabins, RV storage, sewage disposal, laundry, public phone, grocery store, RV supplies, LP gas refill by weight/by meter, ice, tables, fire rings, wood.

◇◇◇◇RECREATION: rec room/area, coin games, 2 swim pools, pond fishing, mini-golf ($), basketball hoop, playground, planned group activities (weekends only), horse riding trails, sports field, horseshoes, hiking trails, volleyball.

Open Apr 15 through Oct 15. Rate in 1995 $15-20 for 2 persons. Discover/Master Card/Visa accepted. Member of ARVC;CONY. Phone: (716) 676-3856.

SEE AD TRAVEL SECTION PAGE 585

FRANKLINVILLE—Continued

✱ **TRIPLE-R CAMPGROUND**—*From south jct Hwy 98 & Hwy 16: Go 1 mi N on Hwy 16/98, then 1 1/2 mi W on Elm St, then 1/3 mi SW on Bryant Hill Rd.* SERVICES: Engine/Chassis & RV appliance mechanic full-time. Open all year. Discover/Master Card/Visa accepted. Phone: (716) 676-3856.

SEE AD TRAVEL SECTION PAGE 585

## GABRIELS—B-9

BUCK POND (Adirondack State Forest)—*From jct Hwy 86 & CR 30: Go 6 mi N on CR 30.* FACILITIES: 116 sites, 116 no hookups, tenting available, sewage disposal. RECREATION: pond swimming, boating, canoeing, 4 row/6 canoe boat rentals, pond fishing, hiking trails. Open mid May through Labor Day. Phone: (518) 891-3449.

## GAINESVILLE—E-3

**Woodstream Campsite**—CAMPGROUND with shaded & open sites. *From jct Hwy 78 & Hwy 19: Go 1 1/2 mi S on Hwy 19, then 1/2 mi E on School Rd.* ◇◇◇FACILITIES: 200 sites, most common site width 30 feet, 190 water & elec (15,20,30 & 50 amp receptacles), 10 no hookups, seasonal sites, 10 pull-thrus, tenting available, sewage disposal, laundry, public phone, limited grocery store, LP gas refill by weight/by meter, ice, tables, fire rings, wood. ◇◇◇◇RECREATION: rec hall, rec room/area, pavilion, pond swimming, stream fishing, playground, badminton, horseshoes, hiking trails, volleyball. Open all year. Facilities fully operational May 1 through Oct 15. Rate in 1995 $15-20 for 4 persons. Member of ARVC;CONY. Phone: (716) 493-5643.

## GALWAY—D-9

**McConchies Heritage Acres**—CAMPGROUND with shaded and open sites. *From jct Hwy 147 & Hwy 67: Go 1 1/2 mi E on Hwy 67, then 1 mi N on Division St.* ◇◇FACILITIES: 190 sites, most common site width 50 feet, 170 water & elec (15,20 & 30 amp receptacles), 20 no hookups, seasonal sites, tenting available, sewage disposal, public phone, limited grocery store, LP gas refill by weight/by meter, ice, tables, fire rings, wood. ◇◇◇RECREATION: rec room/area, equipped pavilion, swim pool, pond fishing, playground, planned group activities (weekends only), badminton, sports field, horseshoes, hiking trails, volleyball. Open May 1 through Oct 1. Rate in 1995 $12-17 for 2 persons. Member of ARVC; CONY. Phone: (518) 882-6605.

GALWAY—Continued on next page

GALWAY—Continued

**Pop's Lake Campground**—Rustic, heavily wooded sites in a secluded location. *From jct Hwy 147 & Hwy 29: Go 2 mi W on Hwy 29, then 1 3/4 mi N on Fishhouse Rd, then 3/4 mi NE on Centerline Rd, then 1/4 mi W on entry road.* ◇◇FACILITIES: 60 sites, most common site width 20 feet, 30 ft. max RV length, 20 full hookups, 25 water & elec (15 amp receptacles), 15 no hookups, seasonal sites, tenting available, sewage disposal, limited grocery store, ice, tables, fire rings, wood. ◇◇RECREATION: rec room/area, lake swimming, 1 row/1 canoe/1 pedal boat rentals, lake fishing, playground, badminton, sports field, horseshoes, hiking trails, volleyball. Recreation open to the public. Open May 15 through Sep 30. Rate in 1995 $14.50 for 2 persons. Member of ARVC;CONY. Phone: (518) 883-8678.

## GARDINER—A-2

**YOGI BEAR'S JELLYSTONE PARK CAMP-RESORT AT LAZY RIVER**—Riverside CAMPGROUND with grassy open & shaded sites. *From jct Hwy 208 & Hwy 44/55: Go 2 1/2 mi W on Hwy 44/55, then 2/10 mi S on Albany Post Rd, then 1/2 mi E on Bevier Rd.*

◇◇◇◇FACILITIES: 145 sites, most common site width 40 feet, 30 full hookups, 63 water & elec (20,30 & 50 amp receptacles), 52 no hookups, seasonal sites, 30 pull-thrus, a/c allowed ($), heater allowed ($), tenting available, group sites for RVs, RV rentals, cabins, RV storage, handicap restroom facilities, sewage disposal, laundry, public phone, grocery store, RV supplies, LP gas refill by weight/by meter, ice, tables, fire rings, wood, traffic control gate.

◇◇◇◇◇RECREATION: rec hall, rec room/area, pavilion, coin games, swim pool, river swimming, boating, no motors, canoeing, dock, 1 canoe boat rentals, river fishing, mini-golf ($), basketball hoop, playground, 2 shuffleboard courts, planned group activities, movies, recreation director, badminton, sports field, horseshoes, volleyball.

Open Apr 15 through Oct 30. Rate in 1995 $23-28 for 2 persons. Discover/Master Card/Visa accepted. Member of ARVC; CONY. Phone: (914) 255-5193. FCRV 10% discount.

SEE AD THIS PAGE

## GARRATTSVILLE—E-7

**Crystal Lake Park**—Rolling, semi-wooded, lakeside CAMPGROUND with shaded & open sites. *From jct CR 16 & Hwy 51: Go 3/4 mi N on Hwy 51, then 1 mi W on CR 17.* ◇◇◇FACILITIES: 250 sites, 30 full hookups, 220 water & elec (30 amp receptacles), seasonal sites, tenting available, handicap restroom facilities, sewage disposal, laundry, public phone, grocery store, LP gas refill by weight/by meter, ice, tables, fire rings, grills, wood. ◇◇◇◇RECREATION: rec hall, rec room/area, pavilion, swim pool, boating, electric motors only, canoeing, dock, 10 row/6 pedal boat rentals, lake fishing, playground, planned group activities, recreation director, 2 tennis courts, badminton, sports field, horseshoes, hiking trails, volleyball. Recreation open to the public. Open May 1 through Oct 1. Rate in 1995 $15-25 for 2 persons. Member of ARVC;CONY. Phone: (607) 965-8265.

## GASPORT—D-2

**Niagara Hartland Campgrounds**—Grassy sites with young trees in the countryside. *From the center of the village at jct Hwy 31 & Hartland Rd: Go 6 1/2 mi N on Hartland Rd.* ◇◇◇FACILITIES: 100 sites, most common site width 30 feet, 75 full hookups, 15 water & elec (20 & 30 amp receptacles), 10 no hookups, seasonal sites, 14 pull-thrus, tenting available, sewage disposal, laundry, public phone, limited grocery store, ice, tables, fire rings, wood. ◇◇RECREATION: rec room/area, pavilion, boating, no motors, canoeing, 2 pedal boat rentals, lake/pond fishing, playground, badminton, horseshoes, volleyball. Open May 15 through Oct 15. Rate in 1995 $12.50-16 for 2 persons. Phone: (716) 795-3812.

## GILBOA—F-8

**BLENHEIN GILBOA POWER PROJECT**—*From jct Hwy 23 & Hwy 30: Go 7 mi N on Hwy 30.* Visitors center inside a converted 19th century dairy barn includes displays and a multi-media shows which explain the world of electricity and the pumped power project. Open all year. Phone: (518) 827-6121.

SEE AD TRAVEL SECTION PAGE 581

**COUNTRY ROADS CAMPSITES**—Hilltop CAMPGROUND with level, open and shaded sites. *From jct Hwy 23 & Hwy 30: Go 3 mi N on Hwy 30, then 1 3/4 mi E on Hwy 990V toward Gilboa (across bridge), then follow signs 3 1/4 mi N.*

◇◇◇FACILITIES: 85 sites, most common site width 30 feet, 21 full hookups, 41 water & elec (15,20 &

COUNTRY ROADS CAMPSITES—Continued on next page
GILBOA—Continued on next page

GILBOA—Continued
COUNTRY ROADS CAMPSITES—Continued

30 amp receptacles), 23 no hookups, seasonal sites, 15 pull-thrus, a/c allowed ($), heater allowed ($), tenting available, group sites for tents/RVs, RV rentals, RV storage, sewage disposal, laundry, public phone, limited grocery store, RV supplies, ice, tables, fire rings, wood, traffic control gate.

◇◇◇RECREATION: rec room/area, pavilion, coin games, swim pool (heated), whirlpool, playground, planned group activities (weekends only), badminton, sports field, horseshoes, volleyball.

Open May 15 through Columbus Day. Rate in 1995 $16.50-18.50 for 2 persons. Discover/Master Card/Visa accepted. CPO. Member of ARVC;CONY. Phone: (518) 827-6397.
**SEE AD PAGE 606**

**NICKERSON PARK CAMPGROUND**—CAMPGROUND with shaded and open sites. *From jct Hwy 23 & Hwy 30: Go 5 mi N on Hwy 30, then 1 mi E on Stryker Rd (CR 13).*

◇◇FACILITIES: 200 sites, most common site width 50 feet, 170 full hookups, 30 water & elec (15 & 20 amp receptacles), seasonal sites, a/c allowed ($), heater allowed ($), phone hookups, tenting available, group sites for tents/RVs, RV storage, sewage disposal, laundry, public phone, limited grocery store, RV supplies, LP gas refill by weight, ice, tables, fire rings, wood, traffic control gate.

◇◇◇RECREATION: rec hall, equipped pavilion, coin games, swim pool, wading pool, river fishing, basketball hoop, playground, planned group activities (weekends only), badminton, sports field, horseshoes, volleyball.

Open May 1 through Columbus Day. Open by reservation only Oct 15 to May 1. Tenters not allowed to bring dogs. Rate in 1995 $15-19 per family. Member of ARVC;CONY. Phone: (607) 588-7327.
**SEE AD THIS PAGE**

## GLEN AUBREY—F-6

**Fire Fox Resorts**—Wooded sites in a rural CAMPGROUND. *From the center of the village: Go 3 mi N on Hwy 26, then 1/4 mi W on Cherry Valley Hill Rd, then 1 mi SW on Rabbit Path Rd.* ◇◇FACILITIES: 78 sites, 68 water & elec (30 amp receptacles), 10 no hookups, seasonal sites, 4 pull-thrus, non-flush toilets, sewage disposal, public phone, ice, tables, fire rings, wood. ◇◇◇RECREATION: rec room/area, swim pool, boating, no motors, canoeing, ramp, 2 canoe boat rentals, lake fishing, badminton, sports field, horseshoes, hiking trails, volleyball. Recreation open to the public. Open May through Oct 31. Rate in 1995 $12 for 2 persons. Phone: (607) 692-4440.

## GLENS FALLS—D-9

MOREAU LAKE STATE PARK—*From business center: Go 5 mi S on US 9.* FACILITIES: 146 sites, 146 no hookups, tenting available, handicap restroom facilities, sewage disposal, public phone, tables, fire rings, wood. RECREATION: lake swimming, boating, no motors, canoeing, ramp, dock, lake fishing, playground, hiking trails. Open mid May through Oct 8. Phone: (518) 793-0511.

## GLOVERSVILLE—D-8

**FULTON COUNTY TOURISM OFFICE**—*From jct Hwy 30A & Hwy 29A: Go 1 1/4 mi NW on Hwy 29A (Fulton St), then 1 block W on Caydautta St.* Tourist information on Fulton County, a world of outdoor recreation with 44 lakes, including the beautiful Sacandaga. Many restored historical buildings, outlet stores, and golf courses. Open all year. Open 8:00 a.m.- 5:00 p.m., Mon.-Fri. Phone: (518) 725-0641.
**SEE AD TRAVEL SECTION PAGE 583**

## GODEFFROY—B-1

**American Family Campground**—Wooded and open, grassy sites at the edge of a small town. Most full hookups occupied by seasonals. *From center of town at jct US 209 & Guymard Tpk: Go 1/2 mi E on Guymard Tpk.* ◇◇◇FACILITIES: 135 sites, most common site width 40 feet, 58 full hookups, 34 water & elec (20 & 30 amp receptacles), 43 no hookups, seasonal sites, 2 pull-thrus, tenting available, sewage disposal, laundry, public phone, limited grocery store, LP gas refill by weight/by meter, ice, tables, fire rings, wood. ◇◇◇RECREATION: rec hall, rec room/area, swim pool, 3 pedal boat rentals, river/pond/stream fishing, mini-golf ($), playground, planned group activities (weekends only), badminton, sports field, horseshoes, volleyball. Open Apr 1 through Oct 31. Rate in 1995 $23-28 for 2 persons. No refunds. Member of ARVC; CONY. Phone: (914) 754-8388.

## GREENPORT—B-5

**EASTERN LONG ISLAND KAMPGROUND**—CAMPGROUND with grassy, level, open & some wooded sites. *From jct Hwy 25 & CR 48/Old 27: Go 1 mi W on CR 48/Old 27 (North Rd). From jct L.I. Expressway (Hwy 495 exit 73) at Riverhead &*

GREENPORT—Continued
EASTERN LONG ISLAND KAMPGROUND—Continued

*Hwy 58: Go 4 mi E on Hwy 58, then 2 mi N on 105 to deadend, then 18 mi E on Sound Ave.*

◇◇◇FACILITIES: 148 sites, most common site width 25 feet, 33 full hookups, 71 water & elec (15,20 & 30 amp receptacles), 44 no hookups, seasonal sites, a/c allowed ($), heater not allowed, tenting available, RV rentals, RV storage, sewage disposal, laundry, public phone, limited grocery store, RV supplies, ice, tables, fire rings, wood, traffic control gate.

◇◇◇RECREATION: rec hall, rec room/area, coin games, swim pool, 12 bike rentals, playground, planned group activities, badminton, sports field, horseshoes, volleyball.

Open Apr 15 through Oct 13. Rate in 1995 $21.50-25.50 per family. American Express/Discover/Master Card/Visa accepted. Member of ARVC; CONY. Phone: (516) 477-0022.
**SEE AD THIS PAGE**

GREENPORT—Continued

**MC CANN'S TRAILER PARK (NOT VISITED)**—*From jct I-495 (Long Island Expwy-exit 73) & CR 58: Go 6 mi E on CR 58, then 20 mi E on Hwy 25, then 3/4 mi N on Moore's Lane.*

FACILITIES: water & elec hookups, no hookups.

Open Apr 1 through Nov 1. Rate in 1995 $15-22 per family. Phone: (516) 477-1487.
**SEE AD TRAVEL SECTION PAGE 586**

## HADLEY—D-9

**Stewart's Pond Campsite**—Lakeside CAMPGROUND with wooded sites. Water & sewer sites available. *From jct Hwy 9N & Antone Rd: Go 4 3/4 mi W on Antone Rd.* ◇◇FACILITIES: 60 sites, 25 ft. max RV length, seasonal sites, tenting available, tables, fire rings, wood. ◇◇◇RECREATION: rec hall, lake swimming, boating, canoeing, ramp, lake fishing, sports field, hiking trails. Open Memorial Day through Labor Day. Rate in 1995 $14 for 2 persons. Phone: (518) 696-2779.

## HAGUE—C-10

**Green Acres by the Brook**—Shaded, grassy sites in a streamside CAMPGROUND at the edge of the village. *From jct Hwy 9N & Hwy 8: Go 1/2 mi W on Hwy 8.* ◆◆FACILITIES: 64 sites, 42 full hookups, 7 water & elec (20 & 30 amp receptacles), 15 no hookups, seasonal sites, tenting available, sewage disposal, public phone, tables, fire rings, grills. ◆◆RECREATION: stream fishing, playground, horseshoes, volleyball. Open May 1 through Oct 15. Rates available upon request. Phone: (518) 543-6645.

## HAINES FALLS—F-9

NORTH/SOUTH LAKE CAMPGROUND (Catskills State Forest)—*From town: Go 3 mi NE on Hwy 23A.* FACILITIES: 219 sites, 219 no hookups, tenting available, handicap restroom facilities, sewage disposal, tables. RECREATION: lake swimming, boating, no motors, canoeing, ramp, canoe boat rentals, lake fishing, hiking trails. Open early May through late Oct. Phone: (518) 589-5058.

## HAMLIN—D-3

HAMLIN BEACH STATE PARK—*From business center: Go 3 mi W on Lake Ontario Pkwy.* FACILITIES: 250 sites, 250 elec, tenting available, handicap restroom facilities, sewage disposal, laundry, public phone, grocery store, ice, tables. RECREATION: rec hall, lake swimming, lake fishing, playground, planned group activities, hiking trails. Open late Apr through mid Oct. Phone: (716) 964-2462.

## HAMMONDSPORT—F-4

**Hill 'N Hollow Campsites**—A rural, rolling CAMPGROUND with level, open & shaded grassy sites. *From jct Hwy 54A & Hwy 54: Go 1/2 mi N on Hwy 54, then 1 mi NE on CR 87, then 3 mi S on CR 113, then follow signs 1/2 mi SE.* ◆◆◆FACILITIES: 40 sites, most common site width 40 feet, 25 water & elec (15,20 & 30 amp receptacles), 15 no hookups, tenting available, marine toilets, sewage disposal, public phone, ice, tables, fire rings, wood. ◆◆◆RECREATION: rec room/area, pond fishing, playground, badminton, sports field, horseshoes, hiking trails, volleyball. Open May 15 through Oct 15. Rate in 1995 $18-20 for 2 persons. Member of ARVC; CONY. Phone: (607) 569-2711.

## HAMPTON BAYS—B-5

SEARS BELLOWS (Suffolk County Park)—*From Sunrise Hwy (Hwy 27, exit 65N): Go N on Bellows Pond Rd.* FACILITIES: 70 sites, 70 no hookups, tenting available, handicap restroom facilities, sewage disposal, public phone, tables. RECREATION: pond swimming, boating, electric motors only, 10 row boat rentals, pond fishing, playground, hiking trails. Open Apr 1 through Sep 11. Facilities fully operational May 19 through Sep 11. Open Thurs, Fri, Sat only Apr 1-May 15. Phone: (516) 852-8290.

## HANKINS—A-1

**Red Barn Family Campground**—Riverside CAMPGROUND with open & shaded grassy sites. *In town on Hwy 97.* ◆◆FACILITIES: 92 sites, most common site width 45 feet, 19 full hookups, 35 water & elec (15,20 & 30 amp receptacles), 38 no hookups, seasonal sites, tenting available, laundry, limited grocery store, ice, tables, fire rings, wood. ◆◆◆RECREATION: rec room/area, river swimming, boating, no motors, canoeing, 2 row/20 canoe boat rentals, river fishing, playground, badminton, sports field, horseshoes, volleyball. Open May 1 through Oct 15. Rate in 1995 $18-20 for 2 persons. Member of ARVC; CONY. Phone: (914) 887-4995.

## HERKIMER—E-7

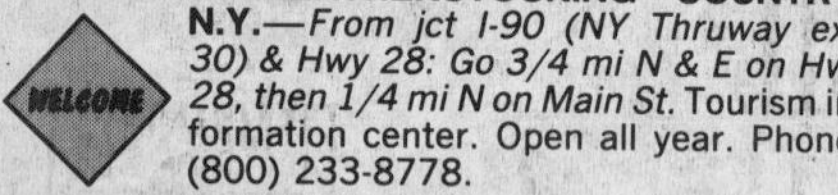

**CENTRAL LEATHERSTOCKING COUNTRY, N.Y.**—*From jct I-90 (NY Thruway exit 30) & Hwy 28: Go 3/4 mi N & E on Hwy 28, then 1/4 mi N on Main St.* Tourism information center. Open all year. Phone: (800) 233-8778.

**SEE AD TRAVEL SECTION PAGE 581**

HERKIMER—Continued

**CRYSTAL CHANDELIER RESTAURANT**—*From NE jct Hwy 5 & Hwy 28: Go 7 mi N on Hwy 28.* Restaurant specializing in ribs. Open Apr 1 through Jan 1. Wed-Thurs 5-9 p.m.; Fri-Sat 5-10 p.m.; Sun 1-8 p.m. American Express/Diners Club/Master Card/Visa accepted. Phone: (315) 891-3366.

**SEE AD THIS PAGE**

**ELMTREE CAMPSITES**—*From Herkimer I-90 (exit 30): About 10 minutes W on Hwy 5 (not 5 S), halfway between Herkimer & Utica.*

**SEE PRIMARY LISTING AT UTICA AND AD UTICA PAGE 633**

**HERKIMER DIAMOND MINE**—*From NE jct Hwy 5 & Hwy 28: Go 7 mi N on Hwy 28.* Rock shop, gift shop, geological museum, prospecting for Herkimer diamonds. Open Apr 1 through Dec 1. Hours: 9-5, 7 days a week. Master Card/Visa accepted. Phone: (315) 891-7355.

**SEE AD THIS PAGE**

**KOA-HERKIMER DIAMOND CAMPGROUND**—Riverside CAMPGROUND with level, open & shaded sites. *From northeast jct Hwy 5 & Hwy 28: Go 7 mi N on Hwy 28.*

◆◆◆◆FACILITIES: 127 sites, most common site width 35 feet, 22 full hookups, 57 water & elec (20,30 & 50 amp receptacles), 48 no hookups, 18 pull-thrus, a/c allowed, heater allowed, tenting available, group sites for tents/RVs, cabins, RV storage, sewage disposal, laundry, public phone, limited grocery store, RV supplies, LP gas refill by weight/by meter, ice, tables, fire rings, grills, wood.

◆◆◆RECREATION: rec room/area, equipped pavilion, coin games, swim pool, canoeing, river fishing, mini-golf ($), basketball hoop, playground, movies, badminton, sports field, horseshoes, hiking trails, volleyball.

Open Apr 15 through Nov 1. Rate in 1995 $20-25 for 2 persons. American Express/Master Card/Visa accepted. Member of ARVC;CONY. Phone: (800) 562-0897. KOA 10% value card discount.

**SEE AD THIS PAGE AND AD FRONT OF BOOK PAGES 68 AND 69**

## HINCKLEY—D-7

**Trail's End Campsite (Not Visited)**—Lakeside CAMPGROUND with open & shaded sites. *From jct Hwy 12 & Hwy 365: Go 4 mi E on Hwy 365, then 3 mi SE on Southside (CR 151). Follow signs.* FACILITIES: 84 sites, most common site width 30 feet, 25 full hookups, 46 water & elec (15,20 & 30 amp receptacles), 13 no hookups, seasonal sites, 1 pull-thrus, tenting available, sewage disposal, laundry, public phone, limited grocery store, ice, tables, fire rings, grills, wood. RECREATION: rec room/area, lake swimming, boating, canoeing, ramp, 4 canoe boat rentals, lake/pond fishing, playground, shuffleboard court, badminton, sports field, horseshoes, hiking trails, volleyball. Recreation open to the public. Open May 1 through Oct 15. Rate in 1995 $17-21 for 2 persons. No refunds. Member of ARVC;CONY. Phone: (315) 826-7220.

## HOUGHTON—F-3

**Hickory Lake Campground**—Wooded park with open & shaded sites. *From jct Hwy 243 & Hwy 19: Go 3 mi N on Hwy 19, then 1/4 mi W on Houghton College Rd (CR 35), then 1 mi W on Centerville Rd.* ◆◆FACILITIES: 100 sites, 74 water & elec (30 amp receptacles), 26 no

HOUGHTON—Continued
HICKORY LAKE CAMPGROUND—Continued

hookups, seasonal sites, 2 pull-thrus, tenting available, sewage disposal, public phone, limited grocery store, LP gas refill by weight, ice, tables, fire rings, wood. ◆◆◆RECREATION: rec hall, swim pool (indoor), pond fishing, badminton, sports field, hiking trails, volleyball. Open May 1 through Oct 20. Rate in 1995 $12-15 for 2 persons. Member of ARVC; CONY. Phone: (716) 567-4211. FCRV 10% discount.

## HOWES CAVE—E-8

**HOWE CAVERNS**—*From jct I-88 (exit 22) & Hwy 145: Go 500 feet N on Hwy 145, then 1 1/4 mi E on Hwy 7, then follow signs 2 mi N & E on paved roads.* Enter caverns via elevator for an approximately 1 hour 20 minute tour that includes a boat ride on a subterranean lake. Free parking & picnic area. Open all year. Closed Thanksgiving, Christmas & New Year's Day. Phone: (518) 296-8990.

**SEE AD TRAVEL SECTION PAGE 581**

## HUBBARDSVILLE—E-7

**Canaan Campground**—Open, grassy sites in a rural setting. *From north village limits at jct Hwy 12 & Green Rd: Go 3/4 mi W on Green Rd.* ◆◆FACILITIES: 32 sites, most common site width 30 feet, 28 water & elec (15 & 30 amp receptacles), 4 no hookups, seasonal sites, 5 pull-thrus, tenting available, sewage disposal, limited grocery store, ice, tables, fire rings, wood. ◆◆◆RECREATION: rec room/area, pavilion, river fishing, mini-golf ($), horseshoes, volleyball. Recreation open to the public. Open May 15 through Oct 1. Rate in 1995 $10-18 for 4 persons. Member of ARVC; CONY. Phone: (315) 691-2005.

## HUDSON—F-9

LAKE TAGHKANIC STATE PARK—*From business center: Go 11 mi S on Hwy 82.* FACILITIES: 51 sites, 51 no hookups, tenting available, sewage disposal, public phone, grocery store, ice, tables. RECREATION: rec hall, lake swimming, boating, no motors, canoeing, ramp, lake fishing, playground, hiking trails. No pets. Open mid May through late Oct. Phone: (518) 851-3631.

## INDIAN LAKE—C-8

LEWEY LAKE PUBLIC CAMPGROUND (Adirondack State Forest)—*From business center: Go 12 mi S on Hwy 30.* FACILITIES: 209 sites, 209 no hookups, tenting available, handicap restroom facilities, sewage disposal, tables. RECREATION: lake swimming, boating, canoeing, ramp, lake fishing, hiking trails. Open mid May through mid Nov. Phone: (518) 648-5266.

## INLET—C-8

LIMEKILN LAKE (Adirondack State Forest)—*From business center: Go 1 mi E on Hwy 28, then 2 mi S.* FACILITIES: 271 sites, 271 no hookups, tenting available, sewage disposal, public phone, tables. RECREATION: lake swimming, boating, canoeing, ramp, lake fishing, hiking trails. Open mid May through Labor Day. Phone: (315) 357-4401.

## ITHACA—F-5

BUTTERMILK FALLS STATE PARK—*From business center: Go 2 mi S on Hwy 13.* FACILITIES: 61 sites, 61 no hookups, tenting available, handicap restroom facilities, sewage disposal, public phone, tables. RECREATION: pavilion, lake swimming, lake/stream fishing, playground, planned group activities, hiking trails. Open mid May through Oct 9. Phone: (607) 273-5761.

ROBERT H TREMAN STATE PARK—*From business center: Go 5 mi S on Hwy 13, then E on 327.* FACILITIES: 70 sites, 11 elec, 59 no hookups, tenting available, handicap restroom facilities, sewage disposal, public phone, tables, wood. RECREATION: river swimming, river fishing, playground, planned group activities, hiking trails. Open mid May through Nov 30. Phone: (607) 273-3440.

**SPRUCE ROW CAMPSITE & RV RESORT**—CAMPGROUND with grassy, level open & shaded sites in a quiet country area. *From north jct Hwy 13 & Hwy 96: Go 7 mi NW on Hwy 96, then 1/2 mi N on Jacksonville Rd, then 1 1/4 mi E on Kraft Rd.*

◆◆◆FACILITIES: 202 sites, most common site width 40 feet, 10 full hookups, 162 water & elec (20 & 30 amp receptacles), 30 no hookups, seasonal sites, 30 pull-thrus, a/c allowed ($), heater not allowed, tenting available, group sites for tents/RVs, RV rentals, cabins, RV storage, sewage disposal, public phone, limited grocery store, RV supplies, LP gas refill by weight/by meter, ice, tables, fire rings, wood.

◆◆◆◆RECREATION: equipped pavilion, coin games, swim pool, 2 pedal boat rentals, pond fishing, mini-golf ($), basketball hoop, playground, shuffleboard court, planned group activities (weekends only), badminton, sports field, horseshoes, hiking trails, volleyball.

SPRUCE ROW CAMPSITE & RV RESORT—Continued on next page
ITHACA—Continued on next page

**ITHACA**—Continued
SPRUCE ROW CAMPSITE & RV RESORT—Continued

Open May 1 through Columbus Day. Rate in 1995 $17-21 for 2 persons. Discover/Master Card/Visa accepted. CPO. Member of ARVC;CONY. Phone: (607) 387-9225.
**SEE AD THIS PAGE**

TAUGHANNOCK FALLS STATE PARK—*From business center: Go 8 mi N on Hwy 89.* FACILITIES: 75 sites, 16 elec, 59 no hookups, tenting available, handicap restroom facilities, sewage disposal, public phone, tables. RECREATION: lake swimming, boating, canoeing, ramp, dock, fishing, playground, hiking trails. Open late Mar through Oct 9. Phone: (607) 387-6739.

## JAMESTOWN—F-1

**Hidden Valley Camping Area**—A rural CAMPGROUND with wooded and grassy, open sites. *From jct Hwy 60 & US 62: Go 3 1/4 mi S on US 62, then 1/2 mi W on Riverside Rd, then 1 block S on Kiantone Rd.* ◆◆FACILITIES: 164 sites, most common site width 40 feet, 164 water & elec (20 & 30 amp receptacles), seasonal sites, 17 pull-thrus, tenting available, sewage disposal, laundry, public phone, limited grocery store, LP gas refill by weight/by meter, ice, tables, fire rings, wood. ◆◆◆RECREATION: rec hall, rec room/area, swim pool, stream fishing, playground, planned group activities (weekends only), tennis court, badminton, sports field, horseshoes, volleyball. Open Apr 15 through Oct 15. Rate in 1995 $16 per vehicle. Member of ARVC;CONY. Phone: (716) 569-5433.

## JOHNSTOWN—E-8

**Royal Mountain Campsite**—Shaded sites in a rural CAMPGROUND convenient to a major highway. *From west jct Hwy 67 & Hwy 29: Go 9 mi NW on Hwy 29.* ◆◆FACILITIES: 65 sites, most common site width 30 feet, 65 water & elec (15 & 20 amp receptacles), seasonal sites, tenting available, sewage disposal, public phone, ice, tables, fire rings, wood. ◆◆RECREATION: equipped pavilion, pond fishing, badminton, horseshoes, hiking trails, volleyball. Open Apr 1 through Nov 1. Rate in 1995 $15-17 for 2 persons. Phone: (518) 762-1946. FCRV 10% discount.

## KEESEVILLE—B-10

**AUSABLE RIVER CAMPSITE**—Grassy CAMPGROUND with mostly open sites on the AuSable River. *From jct I-87 (exit 34) & Hwy 9N: Go 1/4 mi W on Hwy 9N, then 3/4 mi S on entry road.*
◆◆◆FACILITIES: 106 sites, 94 full hookups, 3 water & elec (20 & 30 amp receptacles), 9 no hookups, seasonal sites, 12 pull-thrus, a/c allowed, heater allowed, cable TV, phone hookups, tenting available, RV rentals, laundry, public phone, limited grocery store, RV supplies, ice, tables, fire rings, wood.
◆◆◆RECREATION: rec room/area, coin games, swim pool, canoeing, river/pond fishing, basketball hoop, 2 bike rentals, playground, shuffleboard court, planned group activities (weekends only), movies, sports field, horseshoes, volleyball.

**KEESEVILLE**—Continued
AUSABLE RIVER CAMPSITE—Continued

Open May 15 through Oct 15. Rate in 1995 $18-20 for 2 persons. Phone: (518) 834-9379.
**SEE AD AUSABLE CHASM PAGE 593**

POKE-O-MOONSHINE CAMPGROUND (Adirondack State Forest)—*From town: Go 6 mi S on Hwy 9.* FACILITIES: 25 sites, 30 ft. max RV length, 25 no hookups, tenting available, tables. RECREATION: playground, hiking trails. Open mid May through Labor Day. Phone: (518) 834-9045.

## KENDAIA—E-5

SAMPSON STATE PARK—*In town off Hwy 96A.* FACILITIES: 245 sites, 35 ft. max RV length, 245 elec, tenting available, handicap restroom facilities, sewage disposal, public phone, tables, fire rings. RECREATION: rec hall, lake swimming, boating, canoeing, ramp, lake fishing, playground, tennis court, hiking trails. Open early Apr through late Nov. Phone: (315) 585-6392.

## KENNEDY—F-2

**Forest Haven Campground**—Level, grassy sites in rural area. *From jct Hwy 17 (exit 14) & US 62: Go 1 1/2 mi S on US 62, then 2 mi E on Mud Creek Rd, then 1/2 mi S on Page Rd.* ◆◆FACILITIES: 122 sites, most common site width 40 feet, 9 full hookups, 88 water & elec (20 & 30 amp receptacles), 25 no hookups, seasonal sites, 4 pull-thrus, tenting available, sewage disposal, laundry, public phone, limited grocery store, LP gas refill by weight/by meter, ice, tables, fire rings, wood. ◆◆◆RECREATION: rec room/area, swim pool (heated), playground, sports field, horseshoes, hiking trails. Open Apr 1 through Nov 30. Facilities fully operational May 1 through Nov 1. Rate in 1995 $14-15 for 2 persons. Member of ARVC; CONY. Phone: (716) 267-5902. FCRV 10% discount.

## KEUKA PARK—E-4

KEUKA LAKE STATE PARK—*From west town limits: Go 1 mi SW on Hwy 54A.* FACILITIES: 150 sites, 150 no hookups, tenting available, handicap restroom facilities, sewage disposal, tables, wood. RECREATION: lake swimming, boating, canoeing, ramp, lake fishing, playground, hiking trails. Open mid May through Oct 9. Phone: (315) 536-3666.

## KINGSTON—F-9

✽ **CAMPERS BARN OF KINGSTON**—*From jct NY Thruway I-87 (exit 19) & Hwy 28: Go 1/4 mi W on Hwy 28 (behind Johnson Ford).* SALES: travel trailers, park models, truck campers, 5th wheels, van conversions, motor homes, mini-motor homes, fold-down camping trailers, tents. SERVICES: Engine/Chassis & RV appliance mechanic full-time, emergency road service business hours, RV towing, LP gas refill by weight/by meter, RV storage, sells parts/accessories, sells camping supplies, installs hitches. Open all year. Discover/Master Card/Visa accepted. Phone: (914) 338-8200.
**SEE AD THIS PAGE**

## LAKE BLUFF—D-5

**Lake Bluff Campground**—Open and shaded, grassy sites in the countryside. All full hookup sites occupied by seasonal campers. *From jct Hwy 104 & Hwy 414: Go 4 mi N on Hwy 414.* ◆◆◆FACILITIES: 100 sites, most common site width 40 feet, 40 full hookups, 49 water & elec (20 & 30 amp receptacles), 11 no hookups, seasonal sites, tenting available, sewage disposal, public phone, limited grocery store, LP gas refill by weight, ice, tables, fire rings, wood. ◆◆◆RECREATION: equipped pavilion, swim pool, pond fishing, playground, 2 shuffleboard courts, planned group activities (weekends only), badminton, horseshoes, volleyball. Open Apr 15 through Oct 15. Rate in 1995 $16 for 2 persons. Member of ARVC; CONY. Phone: (315) 587-4517.

## LAKE GEORGE—D-9

**Adirondack Camping Village**—Level, terraced hillside sites in a wooded CAMPGROUND at the north edge of the village. *From jct I-87 (Northway exit 22) & Hwy 9N/US 9: Go 1 1/2 mi N on US 9.* ◆◆◆FACILITIES: 150 sites, most common site width 35 feet, 50 full hookups, 70 water & elec (15 & 20 amp receptacles), 30 no hookups, seasonal sites, 4 pull-thrus, tenting available, sewage disposal, laundry, public phone, limited grocery store, ice, tables, fire rings, wood. ◆◆◆◆RECREATION: rec hall, pavilion, swim pool, pond fishing, playground, 2 shuffleboard courts, planned group activities (weekends only), badminton, sports field, horseshoes, hiking trails, volleyball. Open May 15 through Sep 15. Rate in 1995 $22-24 for 2 persons. No refunds. Member of ARVC; CONY. Phone: (518) 668-5226.

**ALPINE LAKE CAMPING RESORT**—*From jct I-87 (Northway exit 21) & Hwy 9N: Continue south on Hwy 9N to 1 1/2 mi below Corinth, then turn left on Heath Rd.*
**SEE PRIMARY LISTING AT CORINTH AND AD PAGES 612 AND 613**

**EVERGREEN CAMPING RESORT**—Wooded, riverside CAMPGROUND with sites open to the public on a daily or weekly basis. Memberships available. *From jct I-87 (exit 23) & Diamond Point Rd: Go 1/4 mi E on Diamond Point Rd, then 3/4 mi N on East Schroon River Rd.*
◆◆◆◆FACILITIES: 257 sites, 116 full hookups, 141 water & elec (15 & 30 amp receptacles), a/c not allowed, heater not allowed, cable TV ($), tenting available, RV rentals, sewage disposal, laundry, public phone, limited grocery store, RV supplies, LP gas refill by weight/by meter, ice, tables, patios, fire rings, wood, traffic control gate/guard.
◆◆◆◆◆RECREATION: rec hall, pavilion, coin games, 2 swim pools, river swimming, boating, 10 hp limit, canoeing, 12 row/20 canoe boat rentals, river/pond fishing, golf, mini-golf ($), putting green, basketball hoop, playground, planned group activities, movies, recreation director, 2 tennis courts, badminton, sports field, horseshoes, hiking trails, volleyball. Recreation open to the public.

EVERGREEN CAMPING RESORT—Continued on next page
LAKE GEORGE—Continued on next page

LAKE GEORGE—Continued
EVERGREEN CAMPING RESORT—Continued

Open May 1 through Oct 10. Rate in 1995 $28-31 for 2 persons. American Express/Discover/Master Card/Visa accepted. CPO. Member of ARVC; CONY. Phone: (518) 623-3207.

**SEE AD PAGE 611**

HEARTHSTONE POINT CAMPGROUND (Adirondack State Forest)—*From business center: Go 2 mi N on Hwy 9N.* FACILITIES: 251 sites, 251 no hookups, tenting available, handicap restroom facilities, sewage disposal, public phone. RECREATION: swimming, canoeing, lake fishing. Open mid May through Labor Day. Phone: (518) 668-5193.

**KOA-LAKE GEORGE**—*From jct I-87 (exit 21) & Hwy 9N: Go 8 1/2 mi SW on Hwy 9N.*

**SEE PRIMARY LISTING AT LAKE LUZERNE AND AD THIS PAGE**

LAKE GEORGE—Continued

LAKE GEORGE BATTLEGROUND CAMPGROUND (Adirondack State Forest)—*From town: Go 1/4 mi S on US 9.* FACILITIES: 68 sites, 68 no hookups, tenting available, handicap restroom facilities, sewage disposal, tables. Open early May through mid Oct. Phone: (518) 668-3348.

**LAKE GEORGE CAMPSITE**—Semi-wooded CAMPGROUND with wooded & some open grassy sites. *Southbound: From jct I-87 (exit 20) & US 9: Go 1 mi S on US 9. Northbound: From jct I-87 (exit 19) & US 9: Go 1 mi N on US 9.*

◆◆◆FACILITIES: 238 sites, most common site width 75 feet, 59 full hookups, 85 water & elec (15 & 30 amp receptacles), 94 no hookups, seasonal sites, 45 pull-thrus, a/c allowed, heater not allowed, cable TV ($), tenting available, group sites for tents/RVs, RV rentals, RV storage, sewage disposal, laundry, public phone, limited grocery store, RV supplies, LP gas refill by weight/by meter, ice, tables, fire rings, wood, guard.

◆◆◆RECREATION: rec room/area, coin games, swim pool, basketball hoop, playground, badminton, horseshoes, volleyball.

Open all year. Facilities fully operational May 1 through Oct 31. Rate in 1995 $15-26 for 2 persons. No refunds. Discover/Master Card/Visa accepted. Member of ARVC. Phone: (800) 542-2292.

**SEE AD FRONT OF BOOK PAGE 28 AND AD PAGE 616**

LAKE GEORGE—Continued

✽ **LAKE GEORGE CAMPSITE RV SALES**—*From jct I-89 (exit 20) & US 9: Go 1 mi S on US 9.* SALES: travel trailers, 5th wheels, fold-down camping trailers, tents. SERVICES: RV appliance mechanic full-time, emergency road service business hours, LP gas refill by weight/by meter, sewage disposal, RV storage, sells parts/accessories, installs hitches. Open all year. Discover/Master Card/Visa accepted. Phone: (800) 542-2292.

**SEE AD FRONT OF BOOK PAGE 28 AND AD PAGE 616**

**LAKE GEORGE RV PARK**—Well developed RV PARK with wooded, level sites. *From jct I-87 (Exit 20-Northway) & Hwy 149/US 9: Go 3/4 mi N on Hwy 149/US 9, then 1/2 mi E on Hwy 149.*

◆◆◆◆◆FACILITIES: 350 sites, most common site width 40 feet, 350 full hookups, (20 & 30 amp receptacles), seasonal sites, 250 pull-thrus, a/c allowed, heater allowed, cable TV, group sites for RVs, RV rentals, RV storage, handicap restroom facilities, sewage disposal, laundry, public phone, full service store, RV supplies, LP gas refill by weight/by meter, ice, tables, patios, fire rings, grills, wood, guard.

◆◆◆◆◆RECREATION: rec hall, rec room/area, pavilion, coin games, 3 swim pools (indoor) (heated), wading pool, 6 pedal boat rentals, pond/stream fishing, basketball hoop, playground, planned group activities, movies, recreation director, 8 tennis courts, badminton, sports field, horseshoes, hiking trails, volleyball, local tours.

No tents. Open May 15 through Oct 13. Rate in 1995 $35 for 2 persons. Reservations recommended Jul through Aug. Discover/Master Card/Visa accepted. Phone: (518) 792-3775.

**SEE AD FRONT OF BOOK PAGE 26 AND AD PAGE 614**

⚑ **LAKE GEORGE STEAMBOAT COMPANY**—*From jct I-87 (exit 21) & Hwy 9N: Go 1 mi NE on Hwy 9N North, then 1/4 mi E on Beach Rd to Steel Pier.* Daily lunch, dinner and cruise only. Moonlight cruises with entertainment. Open May through Oct. Discover/Master Card/Visa accepted. Phone: (518) 668-5777.

**SEE AD THIS PAGE**

**LEDGEVIEW VILLAGE RV PARK**—RV PARK with large, level wooded sites. *From jct I-87 (exit 20-Northway) & Hwy 149/US 9: Go 3/4 mi N on Hwy 149/US 9, then 1 1/2 mi E on Hwy 149.*

◆◆◆FACILITIES: 103 sites, most common site width 20 feet, 103 full hookups, (30 & 50 amp receptacles), seasonal sites, 17 pull-thrus, a/c allowed, heater allowed, cable TV, RV storage, laundry, public phone, limited grocery store, RV supplies, ice, tables, fire rings, wood, traffic control gate.

◆◆◆RECREATION: rec hall, pavilion, coin games, swim pool, playground, 2 shuffleboard courts, horseshoes.

No pets. No tents. Open Apr 27 through Oct 15. Rate in 1995 $25 for 2 persons. Member of ARVC; CONY. Phone: (518) 798-6621.

**SEE AD PAGE 617**

**Mohawk Camping on Lake George**—Heavily wooded, lakeside CAMPGROUND with terraced sites. *From jct I-87 (Northway exit 22) & Hwy 9N/US 9: Go 1 mi N on Hwy 9N.* ◆◆◆FACILITIES: 75 sites, most common site width 20 feet, 30 ft. max RV length, 17 full hookups, 58 water & elec (20 amp receptacles), tenting available, laundry, public phone, limited grocery store,

MOHAWK CAMPING ON LAKE GEORGE—Continued on page 616
LAKE GEORGE—Continued on page 616

See listing at Lake George

# Alpine Lake Camping Resort

***Nearby are all the attractions and amenities of the beautiful Adirondacks region.***

## Minutes from Lake George and Saratoga

Alpine Lake Offers You

- 2 Swimming Pools
- Sandy Beach • Fishing
- Boat Rentals:
  Rowboats
  Paddleboats
  Canoes
- Lighted Tennis Courts
- Playgrounds • Church Service
- Gift Shop • Pool Tables
- Video Games
- Activities Director

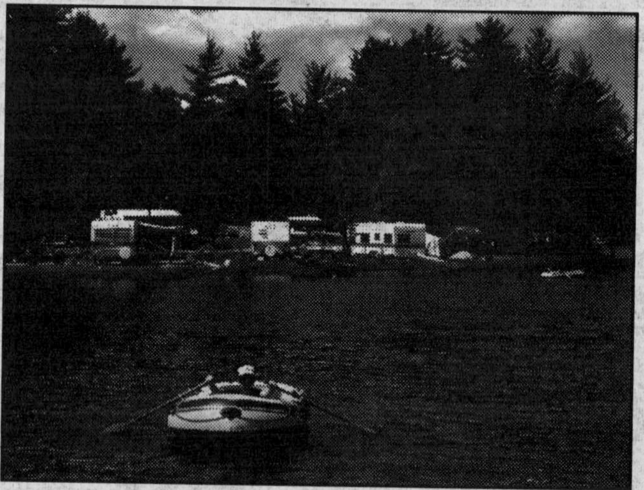

*Two spring-fed lakes with sites directly on the water.*

Near:

Horseback Riding - Golf - Shopping
Saratoga Performing Arts Center
Facilities to Accommodate Large Groups (Up to 800)

*Alpine Lake Camping Resort is centrally located, between Lake George and Saratoga Springs, in the beautiful Adirondack forest preserve.*

400 Sites with:

- Full Hookups
- Lakefront Sites
- Laundromat
- Hot Showers
- Flush Toilets
- Paved Roads
- Two Pavilions
- Sandy Beach
- Basketball
- Volleyball
- Softball Field
- Trailer Storage Area
- Hiking Trails

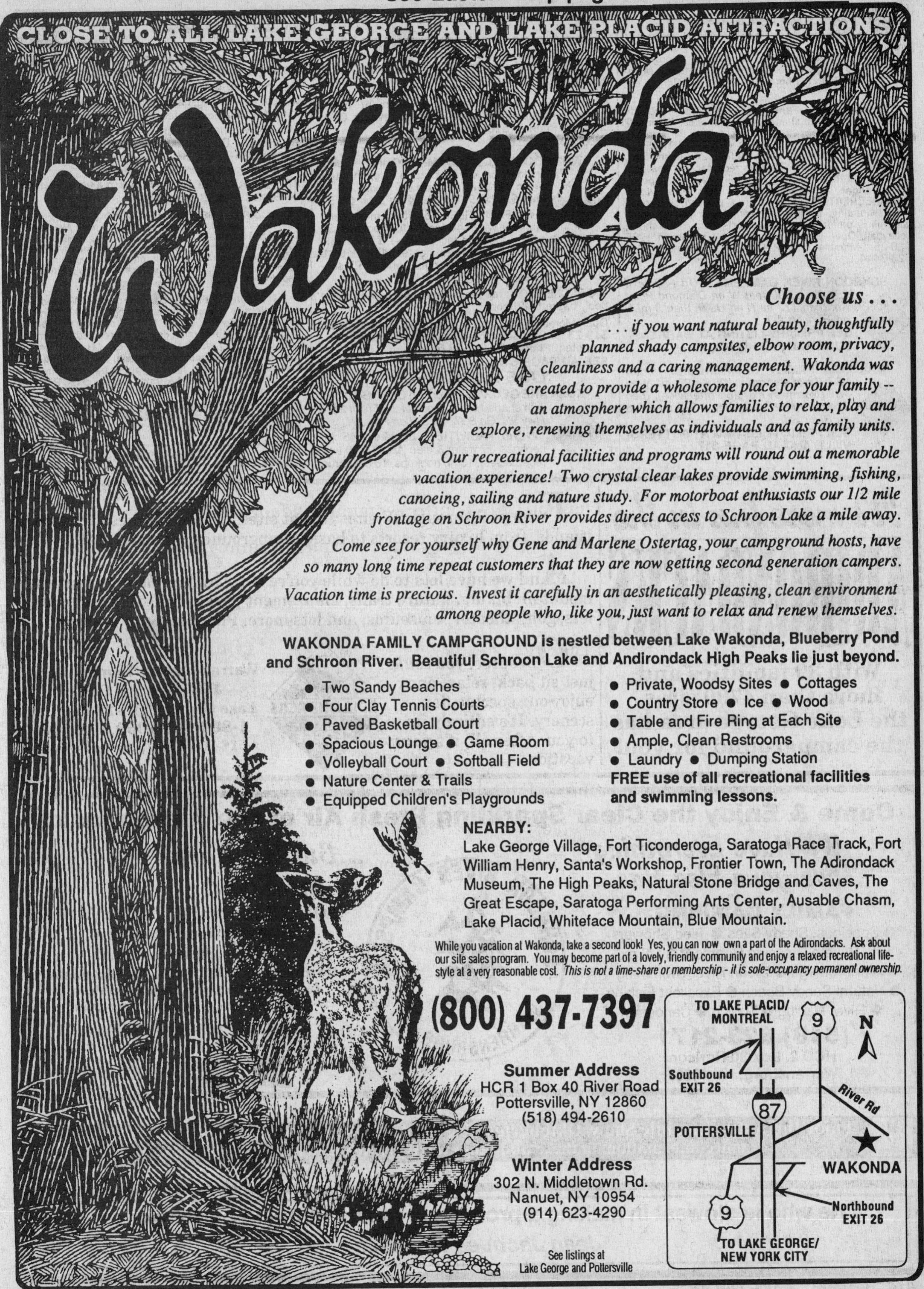

CLOSE TO ALL LAKE GEORGE AND LAKE PLACID ATTRACTIONS
Wakonda
Choose us . . .
. . . if you want natural beauty, thoughtfully planned shady campsites, elbow room, privacy, cleanliness and a caring management. Wakonda was created to provide a wholesome place for your family -- an atmosphere which allows families to relax, play and explore, renewing themselves as individuals and as family units.
Our recreational facilities and programs will round out a memorable vacation experience! Two crystal clear lakes provide swimming, fishing, canoeing, sailing and nature study. For motorboat enthusiasts our 1/2 mile frontage on Schroon River provides direct access to Schroon Lake a mile away.
Come see for yourself why Gene and Marlene Ostertag, your campground hosts, have so many long time repeat customers that they are now getting second generation campers.
Vacation time is precious. Invest it carefully in an aesthetically pleasing, clean environment among people who, like you, just want to relax and renew themselves.
WAKONDA FAMILY CAMPGROUND is nestled between Lake Wakonda, Blueberry Pond and Schroon River. Beautiful Schroon Lake and Andirondack High Peaks lie just beyond.
• Two Sandy Beaches
• Four Clay Tennis Courts
• Paved Basketball Court
• Spacious Lounge • Game Room
• Volleyball Court • Softball Field
• Nature Center & Trails
• Equipped Children's Playgrounds
• Private, Woodsy Sites • Cottages
• Country Store • Ice • Wood
• Table and Fire Ring at Each Site
• Ample, Clean Restrooms
• Laundry • Dumping Station
FREE use of all recreational facilities and swimming lessons.
NEARBY:
Lake George Village, Fort Ticonderoga, Saratoga Race Track, Fort William Henry, Santa's Workshop, Frontier Town, The Adirondack Museum, The High Peaks, Natural Stone Bridge and Caves, The Great Escape, Saratoga Performing Arts Center, Ausable Chasm, Lake Placid, Whiteface Mountain, Blue Mountain.
While you vacation at Wakonda, take a second look! Yes, you can now own a part of the Adirondacks. Ask about our site sales program. You may become part of a lovely, friendly community and enjoy a relaxed recreational life-style at a very reasonable cost. This is not a time-share or membership - it is sole-occupancy permanent ownership.
(800) 437-7397
Summer Address
HCR 1 Box 40 River Road
Pottersville, NY 12860
(518) 494-2610
Winter Address
302 N. Middletown Rd.
Nanuet, NY 10954
(914) 623-4290
See listings at
Lake George and Pottersville
TO LAKE PLACID/
MONTREAL
9
N
Southbound
EXIT 26
River Rd
87
POTTERSVILLE
WAKONDA
9
Northbound
EXIT 26
TO LAKE GEORGE/
NEW YORK CITY

**LAKE GEORGE**—Continued
MOHAWK CAMPING ON LAKE GEORGE—Continued

ice, tables, grills, wood. ◆◆◆RECREATION: rec room/area, lake swimming, canoeing, 2 row boat rentals, lake fishing, playground. No pets. Open May 23 through Sep 4. Rate in 1995 $24-29 for 2 persons. No refunds. Member of ARVC; CONY. Phone: (518) 668-2760.

**Rainbow View Family Campground**—Riverside CAMPGROUND with shaded and open sites. *From I-87 (exit 23-Warrensburg exit): Go 200 feet W on Diamond Point Rd, then 1/4 mi N on US 9.* ◆◆◆FACILITIES: 97 sites, most common site width 35 feet, 20 full hookups, 77 water & elec (20 & 30 amp receptacles), seasonal sites, 6 pull-thrus, tenting available, sewage disposal, public phone, ice, tables, fire rings, grills, wood. ◆◆◆RECREATION: rec room/area, pavilion, swim pool, river swimming, boating, canoeing, river fishing, mini-golf, playground, badminton, sports field, horseshoes, volleyball. Open May 1 through Oct 15. Rate in 1995 $20-25. Member of ARVC; CONY. Phone: (518) 623-9444.

WELCOME

**SCHROON RIVER CAMPSITE**—*Off I-87 (exit 23), then 200 feet W on Diamond Point Rd, then 1/2 mi N on US 9, then 3 mi N on Horicon Ave.*
**SEE PRIMARY LISTING AT WARRENSBURG AND AD THIS PAGE**

WELCOME

**WAKONDA FAMILY CAMPGROUND**—*From I-87 (Lake George exit): Go 25 mi N on I-87 (Northway exit 26-Pottersville), then 3/4 mi N on Hwy 9, then 1 3/4 mi E & S on River Rd.*
**SEE PRIMARY LISTING AT POTTERSVILLE AND AD PAGE 617**

**LAKE GEORGE**—Continued

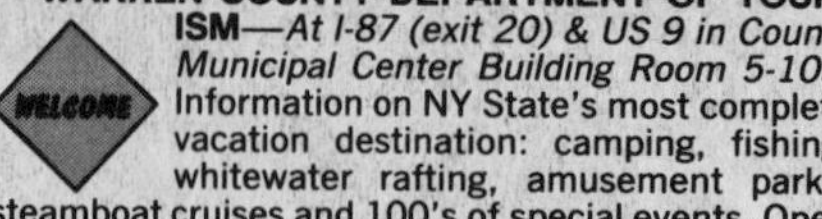

WELCOME

**WARREN COUNTY DEPARTMENT OF TOURISM**—*At I-87 (exit 20) & US 9 in County Municipal Center Building Room 5-105.* Information on NY State's most complete vacation destination: camping, fishing, whitewater rafting, amusement parks, steamboat cruises and 100's of special events. Open all year. Phone: (518) 761-6366.
**SEE AD PAGE 616**

WELCOME

**WHIPPOORWILL CAMPGROUND**—Semi-wooded park with shaded & open sites. *From jct I-87 (Northway exit 21) & Hwy 9N/US 9: Go 1 1/4 mi S on US 9.*
◆◆◆FACILITIES: 45 sites, most common site width 40 feet, 3 full hookups, 31 water & elec (20 & 30 amp receptacles), 11 no hookups, 12 pull-thrus, a/c allowed, heater allowed, tenting available, sewage disposal, public phone, RV supplies, ice, tables, fire rings, wood.

◆◆RECREATION: rec room/area, coin games, swim pool, basketball hoop.

Open Memorial Day through Labor Day. Rate in 1995 $19-23 for 2 persons. No refunds. Master Card/Visa accepted. Phone: (518) 668-5565.
**SEE AD PAGE 610**

## LAKE LUZERNE—D-9

WELCOME

**KOA-LAKE GEORGE**—Wooded CAMPGROUND with shaded sites. *From jct I-87 (exit 21) & Hwy 9N: Go 8 1/2 mi SW on Hwy 9N.*
◆◆◆ FACILITIES: 85 sites, 45 full hookups, 27 water & elec (15,20 & 30 amp receptacles), 13 no hookups, 16 pull-thrus,

**LAKE LUZERNE**—Continued
KOA-LAKE GEORGE—Continued

a/c allowed ($), heater allowed, cabins, tenting available, sewage disposal, laundry, public phone, limited grocery store, RV supplies, ice, tables, fire rings, wood.

◆◆◆RECREATION: rec room/area, coin games, swim pool, stream fishing, basketball hoop, playground, badminton, sports field, horseshoes, volleyball.

Open May 1 through Sep 15. Rate in 1995 $21-25 for 2 persons. Discover/Master Card/Visa accepted. Member of ARVC; CONY. Phone: (518) 696-2615. KOA 10% value card discount.
**SEE AD LAKE GEORGE PAGE 610 AND AD FRONT OF BOOK PAGES 68 AND 69**

LUZERNE PUBLIC CAMPGROUND (Adirondack State Forest)—*From business center: Go 2 mi N on Hwy 9N.* FACILITIES: 174 sites, 174 no hookups, tenting available, handicap restroom facilities, sewage disposal, tables. RECREATION: lake swimming, boating, no motors, canoeing, ramp, canoe boat rentals, lake fishing. Open mid May through mid Sep. Phone: (518) 696-2031.

**Mt. Kenyon Family Campground**—Wooded sites convenient to a major highway. *From jct I-87 (Northway exit 21) & Hwy 9N: Go 3 3/4 mi S on Hwy 9N.* ◆◆FACILITIES: 110 sites, most common site width 25 feet, 21 full hookups, 57 water & elec, 14 elec (15 & 20 amp receptacles), 18 no hookups, seasonal sites, tenting available, sewage disposal, laundry, public phone, limited grocery store, ice, tables, fire rings, wood. ◆◆◆RECREATION: rec room/area, swim pool, stream fishing, playground, horseshoes, hiking trails. Open May 15 through Sep 30. Rate in 1995 $15-22 for 2 persons. Phone: (518) 696-2905.

NY **State Tree: Sugar Maple** NY





N Y Enjoy the Autumnmobile Show, Oktoberfest & Craft Expo Weekends at Hunter Mountain. For more information on these and other festivals, see article at front of book.

**He who is slowest in making a promise is most faithful in performance.**

***Jean Jacques Rousseau***

# LEDGEVIEW VILLAGE

## R.V. PARK

LAKE GEORGE'S NEWEST AND FINEST
"More than a breath of fresh air"

— *One Price Covers All* —

Large Level Wooded Sites W/ Full Hookups
Wide Paved Roads ♦ Excellent Maintenance
Tiled Rest Rooms W/ Private Dressing Rooms
Laundromat ♦ Recreation Hall ♦ Pavilion
Store ♦ Ice ♦ Firewood ♦ Cable TV
Shuffleboard ♦ Bocce Ball ♦ Horseshoes
Swimming Pool ♦ Playground
Near All The Best Attractions

♦ NO PETS ♦

ASK ABOUT OUR SPECIAL OFF-SEASON RATES
CALL OR WRITE FOR RESERVATIONS AND / OR OUR COLOR BROCHURE
Rt. 149, Box 3293-2, Lake George, NY 12845
Phone (518) 798-6621

# LAKE GEORGE

## CAMPSITE & RV SALES

*In the Heart of the Lake George Region*

**OPEN ALL YEAR**

*Discount Tickets to Area Attractions Available to our Campers*

- 238 Wooded & Open Sites
- Modern Restrooms & Showers
- Pool ▪ Playground ▪ Recreation Room
- Laundry ▪ Cable TV at some Sites
- Propane ▪ Dump Station ▪ Ice
- Fully Stocked Store
- On Site Trailer Rentals

**WALK TO AREA ATTRACTIONS**

- The Great Escape Fun Park
- Lake George Zoo ▪ Go Karts
- Roller Skating ▪ Waterslides
- Laser Storm ▪ Five Theater Cinema
- Restaurants

**NEARBY**

- Bike and Hiking Trails

**HOP A BUS**

Right at our door and in a few minutes hit the thrill of Lake George. Bargain shopping at over **50 Factory Outlet Stores** or shop an 80 Store Mall.

**RV REPAIR · SERVICE · SALES**
**Service all makes and models**
**Parts and accessories**

**ASK ABOUT OUR SPECIAL ★ OFF SEASON RATES ★**

**Write or call for our free brochure:**
**1053 Rt. 9, Queensbury, NY 12804**
**1-800-542-2292**
**(518) 798-6218**

See listings at Lake George

"The family suggests that memorial contributions be made to the American Heart Association."

When people want to honor a loved one and fight heart disease.

American Heart Association℠
*Fighting Heart Disease and Stroke*

AMERICAN HEART ASSOCIATION MEMORIALS & TRIBUTES

1-800-AHA-USA1

This space provided as a public service.

## LAKE PLACID—B-9

**KOA-LAKE PLACID-WHITEFACE MOUNTAIN**—*From jct Hwy 73 & Hwy 86 in Lake Placid: Go 9 mi NE on Hwy 86, then follow signs 1/4 mi E.*

**SEE PRIMARY LISTING AT WILMINGTON AND AD PAGE 619**

**NORTH POLE CAMPGROUND**—*From Lake Placid Village: Go 12 3/4 mi NW on Hwy 86.*

**SEE PRIMARY LISTING AT WILMINGTON AND AD THIS PAGE**

**Whispering Pines Campground**—Open & shaded sites in a resort area. *From jct Hwy 86 & Hwy 73: Go 6 mi S on Hwy 73.* ◆◆FACILITIES: 80 sites, most common site width 35 feet, 9 full hookups, 42 water & elec, 2 elec (15 & 30 amp receptacles), 27 no hookups, 35 pull-thrus, tenting available, sewage disposal, public phone, grocery store, LP gas refill by weight/by meter, ice, tables, fire rings, wood. ◆◆RECREATION: playground, badminton, horseshoes, volleyball. Open May 1 through Oct 15. Rate in 1995 $15-20 for 2 persons. Phone: (518) 523-9322.

## LAKE PLEASANT—D-8

LITTLE SAND POINT (Adirondack State Forest)—*From business center: Go 7 mi SW on Hwy 8.* FACILITIES: 78 sites, 78 no hookups, tenting available, non-flush toilets, sewage disposal, tables, wood. RECREATION: swimming, boating, canoeing, ramp, lake fishing, hiking trails. Open mid May through Labor Day. No showers. Phone: (518) 548-7585.

MOFFITT BEACH CAMPGROUND (Adirondack State Forest)—*From business center: Go 4 mi NE on Hwy 8.* FACILITIES: 260 sites, 260 no hookups, tenting available, handicap restroom facilities, sewage disposal, tables. RECREATION: lake swimming, boating, canoeing, ramp, lake fishing, playground, hiking trails. Open mid May through mid Oct. Phone: (518) 548-7102.

## LAKEVILLE—E-4

**CONESUS LAKE CAMPGROUND**—Terraced, hillside sites with grass and shade. *From jct I-390 (exit 8) & US 20A: Go 2 1/2 mi E on US 20A, then 5 3/4 mi S on E Lake Rd.*

◆◆◆FACILITIES: 125 sites, most common site width 35 feet, 85 full hookups, 35 water & elec (15 & 20 amp receptacles), 5 no hookups, seasonal sites, a/c not allowed, heater not allowed, phone hookups, tenting available, RV rentals, RV storage, sewage disposal, laundry, public phone, grocery store, RV supplies, LP gas refill by weight, ice, tables, fire rings, wood, traffic control gate.

◆◆◆◆RECREATION: rec hall, rec room/area, coin games, swim pool (indoor) (heated), lake swimming, boating, canoeing, dock, 2 row boat rentals, water skiing, lake fishing, basketball hoop, playground, planned group activities (weekends only), badminton, horseshoes, hiking trails, volleyball.

Open May 15 through Oct 15. Rate in 1995 $18-23 for 2 persons. No refunds. Master Card/Visa accepted. Member of ARVC;CONY. Phone: (716) 346-5472.

**SEE AD ROCHESTER PAGE 630**

✽ **LEISURE TRAILER SALES**—*From jct I-390 (exit 8) & US 20A: Go 2 1/2 mi E on US 20A, then 5 3/4 mi S on E Lake Rd.* SALES: travel trailers, park models. SERVICES: LP gas refill by weight, sewage disposal, RV rentals, RV storage, sells parts/accessories. Open May 15 through Oct 15. Master Card/Visa accepted. Phone: (716) 346-5472.

**SEE AD ROCHESTER PAGE 630**

## LEROY—E-3

**FROST RIDGE CAMPGROUND**—Grassy sites among apple trees and at the edge of the woods. *From jct I-90 (exit 47) & Hwy 19: Go 1/2 mi S on Hwy 19, then 1 mi east on North Rd, then 1/2 mi S on Conlon Rd.*

◆◆◆FACILITIES: 116 sites, most common site width 50 feet, 16 full hookups, 85 water & elec (15,20 & 30 amp receptacles), 15 no hookups, seasonal sites, 10 pull-thrus, a/c allowed ($), heater allowed ($), phone hookups, tenting available, RV storage, sewage disposal, public phone, LP gas refill by weight, ice, tables, fire rings, wood.

◆◆◆RECREATION: rec hall, coin games, basketball hoop, playground, badminton, sports field, horseshoes, hiking trails, volleyball, cross country skiing. Recreation open to the public.

Open all year. Rate in 1995 $10-12 per family. Phone: (716) 768-4883.

**SEE AD ROCHESTER PAGE 629**

**TIMBERLINE LAKE PARK**—CAMPGROUND with grassy open & shaded sites. *From jct I-90 (exit 47), Hwy 19 & I-490: Go 1/10 mi N on I-490 (exit 1), then 1/10 mi SW on Hwy 19, then 1 mi E on Vallance Rd. Westbound I-490 (exit 1): Go 1/10 mi NE on county road, then 1 mi E on Vallance Rd.*

◆◆◆FACILITIES: 200 sites, most common site width 35 feet, 80 full hookups, 95 water & elec (20 & 30 amp receptacles), 25 no hookups, seasonal sites, a/c allowed, heater not allowed, phone hookups, tenting available, group sites for tents/RVs, sewage disposal, laundry, public phone, limited grocery store, RV supplies, LP gas refill by weight/by meter, ice, tables, fire rings, wood.

◆◆◆RECREATION: rec room/area, pavilion, coin games, lake swimming, lake fishing, basketball hoop, playground, sports field, horseshoes.

Open May 1 through Oct 15. Rate in 1995 $14-16 per family. Phone: (716) 768-6635.

**SEE AD ROCHESTER PAGE 630**

## LEWIS—B-9

**MAGIC PINES FAMILY CAMPGROUND**—CAMPGROUND with pine shaded sites. *From I-87 (exit 32 Lewis exit): Go 1 1/2 mi W on Stoverville Rd, then 3 mi N on US 9.*

◆◆FACILITIES: 90 sites, 37 full hookups, 32 water & elec (15,20 & 30 amp receptacles), 21 no hookups, seasonal sites, a/c allowed ($), heater allowed ($), tenting available, RV storage, sewage disposal, laundry, LP gas refill by weight/by meter, ice, tables, fire rings, wood.

◆◆◆RECREATION: rec hall, rec room/area, coin games, swim pool, mini-golf, basketball hoop, playground, tennis court, horseshoes.

Open May 15 through Oct 15. Rate in 1995 $15-20 for 2 persons. Phone: (518) 873-2288.

**SEE AD ELIZABETHTOWN PAGE 602**

## LEWISTON—D-2

**KOA-NIAGARA FALLS NORTH**—CAMPGROUND with open and shaded sites. *From north jct I-190 (exit 25B) & Robert Moses Pkwy: Go 3 mi N on Robert Moses Pkwy, then 1 3/4 mi E on Pletcher Rd.*

◆◆◆◆FACILITIES: 112 sites, most common site width 24 feet, 18 full hookups, 69 water & elec (20 & 30 amp receptacles), 25 no hook-

LEWISTON—Continued
KOA-NIAGARA FALLS NORTH—Continued

ups, 40 pull-thrus, a/c allowed ($), heater allowed ($), tenting available, cabins, sewage disposal, laundry, public phone, grocery store, RV supplies, LP gas refill by weight/by meter, ice, tables, fire rings, wood.

◆◆◆RECREATION: rec room/area, coin games, swim pool, playground, horseshoes, volleyball, local tours.

Open Apr 1 through Oct 15. Rate in 1995 $21-29 for 2 persons. Discover/Master Card/Visa accepted. Member of ARVC;CONY. Phone: (716) 754-8013. KOA 10% value card discount.

**SEE ADS FRONT OF BOOK PAGES 26, 68 AND 69 AND AD NIAGARA FALLS PAGE 624**

## LIVINGSTON MANOR—F-8

BEAVERKILL CAMPGROUND (Catskills State Forest)—*From business center: Go 6 mi NE on county road.* FACILITIES: 115 sites, 30 ft. max RV length, 115 no hookups, tenting available, handicap restroom facilities, sewage disposal, tables. RECREATION: river swimming, river fishing, hiking trails. Open mid May through Labor Day. Phone: (914) 439-4281.

**Covered Bridge Campsite**—Rustic, streamside CAMPGROUND with wooded sites. *From Hwy 17 (exit 96): Go 7 1/2 mi N on Debruce/Willowemoc Rd (Hwy 82), then 1/4 mi E on Conklin Rd.* ◆◆FACILITIES: 100 sites, 50 water & elec (20 amp receptacles), 50 no hookups, seasonal sites, tenting available, sewage disposal, public phone, limited grocery store, LP gas refill by weight, ice, tables, fire rings, wood. ◆◆RECREATION: rec room/area, stream fishing, playground, badminton, horseshoes, hiking trails, volleyball. Open Apr 1 through mid Dec. Rate in 1995 $21 for 2 persons. Member of ARVC; CONY. Phone: (914) 439-5093.

## LOCKPORT—D-2

✽ **MANTELLI TRAILER SALES**—*From jct Hwy 31 & Hwy 78: Go 5 mi S on Hwy 78.* SALES: travel trailers, truck campers, 5th wheels, mini-motor homes, fold-down camping trailers. SERVICES: RV appliance mechanic full-time, LP gas refill by weight/by meter, RV storage, sells parts/accessories, sells camping supplies, installs hitches. Open all year. American Express/Discover/Master Card/Visa accepted. Phone: (716) 625-8877.

**SEE AD NIAGARA FALLS PAGE 623**

**Niagara County Camping Resort**—A country CAMPGROUND with grassy, shaded and open sites. *From jct Hwy 31 & Hwy 78: Go 4 mi N on Hwy 78, then 1/4 mi N on Hwy 78/104, then 2 1/2 mi E on Wheeler Rd.* ◆◆FACILITIES: 260 sites, 15 full hookups, 115 water & elec (30 amp receptacles), 130 no hookups, seasonal sites, 14 pull-thrus, tenting available, sewage disposal, public phone, limited grocery store, LP gas refill by weight, ice, tables, fire rings, wood. ◆◆◆RECREATION: rec room/area, pavilion, lake swimming, boating, no motors, canoeing, 2 pedal boat rentals, lake fishing, mini-golf, playground, planned group activitie (weekends only), volleyball. Open May 1 through Nov 1. Rate in 1995 $17 per family. Member of ARVC; CONY. Phone: (716) 434-3991.

## LONG ISLAND—B-3

**EASTERN LONG ISLAND KAMPGROUND**—*From Eastern end of Long Island Expressway (Hwy 495, exit 73) & Hwy 58: Go 5 mi E on Hwy 58, then 2 mi N on 105 to dead end, then 20 mi E on Sound Ave.*

**SEE PRIMARY LISTING AT GREENPORT AND AD GREENPORT PAGE 607**

LONG ISLAND—Continued on next page

LONG ISLAND—Continued

✱ **W.E.S. TRAILER SALES**—*From I-495 (Long Island Expy) (exit 68) & Hwy 46: Go 4 mi N on Hwy 46, then 3 mi E on Hwy 25.*

WELCOME

**SEE PRIMARY LISTING AT WADING RIVER AND AD WADING RIVER PAGE 634**

## LONG LAKE—C-8

LAKE EATON CAMPGROUND (Adirondack State Forest)—*From business center: Go 2 mi NW on Hwy 30.* FACILITIES: 135 sites, 30 ft. max RV length, 135 no hookups, tenting available, sewage disposal, tables. RECREATION: lake swimming, boating, canoeing, ramp, canoe boat rentals, lake fishing, hiking trails. Open mid May through Labor Day. Phone: (518) 624-2641.

LAKE HARRIS CAMPGROUND (Adirondack State Forest)—*From business center: Go 14 mi E on Hwy 28N to Newcomb then 3 mi N.* FACILITIES: 89 sites, 89 no hookups, tenting available, sewage disposal, tables. RECREATION: lake swimming, boating, canoeing, ramp, canoe boat rentals, lake fishing, hiking trails. Open mid May through Labor Day. Phone: (518) 582-2503.

## LOWMAN—F-5

**GARDNER HILL CAMPGROUND**—Open and shaded sites on a hilltop with mountain views. *From jct Hwy 17 & Old Lowman Rd (CR 2): Go 1/2 mi N on Old Lowman Rd (CR 2), then 1 3/4 mi NE on Hoffman Hollow Rd, then 1 mi N on Norway Rd.*

WELCOME

◈◈◈FACILITIES: 150 sites, most common site width 20 feet, 104 full hookups, 16 water & elec, 20 elec (20,30 & 50 amp receptacles), 10 no hookups, seasonal sites, 44 pull-thrus, a/c allowed ($), heater allowed ($), phone hookups, tenting available, RV rentals, RV storage, sewage disposal, laundry, public phone, limited grocery store, ice, tables, fire rings, wood.

◈◈◈RECREATION: rec hall, swim pool, pond fishing, basketball hoop, playground, planned group activities, badminton, horseshoes, hiking trails, volleyball.

Open all year. Rate in 1995 $13-16 for 2 persons. Member of ARVC;CONY. Phone: (607) 732-9827.

**SEE AD ELMIRA PAGE 604**

## LOWVILLE—C-7

WHETSTONE GULF STATE PARK—*From business center: Go 8 mi S on Hwy 12D.* FACILITIES: 56 sites, 56 no hookups, tenting available, handicap restroom facilities, sewage disposal, tables. RECREATION: rec hall, lake swimming, canoeing, lake fishing, hiking trails. Open late May through mid Sep. Phone: (315) 376-6630.

## MALTA—E-9

✱ **NORTHWAY TRAVEL TRAILERS**—*From jct I-87 (exit 12) & Hwy 67: Go 1/4 mi E on Hwy 67, then 1/2 mi N on US 9.* SALES: travel trailers, 5th wheels, motor homes, mini-motor homes. SERVICES: RV appliance mechanic full-time, LP gas refill by weight/by meter, RV storage, sells parts/accessories, installs hitches. Open all year. Discover/Master Card/Visa accepted. Phone: (518) 899-2526.

WELCOME

**SEE AD THIS PAGE**

## MARATHON—F-6

**COUNTRY HILLS CAMPGROUND**—Lakeside CAMPGROUND with open & shaded sites. *From jct I-81 (exit 9) & Hwy 221: Go 1 mi W on Hwy 221, then 2 mi N on Highland Rd, then 1/4 mi E on Muckey Rd.*

WELCOME

◈◈◈FACILITIES: 119 sites, most common site width 50 feet, 28 full hookups, 80 water & elec (20 & 30 amp receptacles), 11 no hookups, seasonal sites, a/c allowed ($), heater allowed ($), tenting available, group sites for tents/RVs, RV storage, sewage disposal, public phone, ice, tables, fire rings, wood.

◈◈◈RECREATION: lake swimming, boating, no motors, canoeing, 1 row/1 canoe/1 pedal boat rentals, lake fishing, playground, badminton, sports field, horseshoes, hiking trails, volleyball.

Open May 1 through Oct 1. Rate in 1995 $13-17 per family. Phone: (607) 849-3300.

**SEE AD THIS PAGE**

## MASSENA—A-8

**KOA-Massena**—Riverview CAMPGROUND with shaded, grassy & open sites. *From jct Hwy 56 & Hwy 37: Go 6 mi E on Hwy 37, then follow signs 1/2 mi NE.* ◈◈◈◈FACILITIES: 131 sites, most common site width 35 feet, 68 full hookups, 47 water & elec (20 & 30 amp receptacles), 16 no hookups, seasonal sites, tenting available, sewage disposal, laundry, public phone, limited grocery store, LP gas refill by weight/by meter, ice, tables, grills, wood. ◈◈◈◈RECREATION: rec hall, rec room/area, swim pool, canoeing, river fishing, playground, badminton, sports field, horseshoes, volleyball. Open May 1 through Oct 15. Rate in 1995 $19-24 for 2 persons. Member of ARVC; CONY. Phone: (315) 769-9483. KOA 10% value card discount.

ROBERT MOSES STATE PARK—*From town: Go 9 mi NE on Hwy 37, then 3 mi N.* FACILITIES: 173 sites, 26 elec, 147 no hookups, tenting available, sewage disposal, ice, tables. RECREATION: river swimming, boating, canoeing, ramp, river fishing, playground, hiking trails. Open mid May through Oct 8. Phone: (315) 769-8663.

## MAYVILLE—F-1

⚑ **CHAUTAUQUA COUNTY TOURIST INFORMATION CENTER**—*At jct Hwy 394 & Hwy 430 (at 4 North Erie).* Information center for Chautauqua area, home of world-famous Chautauqua Institution. Area is noted for matchless natural beauty, top-notch recreational activites & unique attractions. Open all year. Open Mon-Fri 8:00 a.m. - 4:00 p.m. Phone: (716) 753-4306.

WELCOME

**SEE AD TRAVEL SECTION PAGE 585**

MAYVILLE—Continued on next page

MAYVILLE—Continued

**CHAUTAUQUA COUNTY VISITORS BUREAU**—*In center of town on Hwy 394 at traffic light (across from courthouse).* Tourist information center. Open Jun 15 through Oct 15. Open 9 a.m. - 5 p.m. 7 days a week. Phone: (716) 753-4304.

SEE AD TRAVEL SECTION PAGE 585

## MECHANICVILLE—E-9

**DEER RUN CAMPGROUNDS**—Developed CAMPGROUND with level, wooded sites. *From jct I-87 (Northway exit 9E) & Hwy 146: Go 5 mi NE on Hwy 146, then 2 1/4 mi N on Hwy 4/Hwy 32, then 1 1/4 mi E on Hwy 67, then 1 1/2 mi N on Deer Run Dr.*

◊◊◊◊FACILITIES: 369 sites, most common site width 40 feet, 369 full hookups, (30 amp receptacles), seasonal sites, 230 pull-thrus, a/c allowed ($), heater not allowed, RV rentals, RV storage, sewage disposal, laundry, public phone, limited grocery store, RV supplies, ice, tables, fire rings, wood.

◊◊◊◊◊RECREATION: rec hall, rec room/area, coin games, 3 swim pools (heated), wading pool, pond fishing, mini-golf ($), basketball hoop, playground, planned group activities, movies, recreation director, badminton, sports field, horseshoes, hiking trails, volleyball.

No tents. Open May 1 through Oct 15. Rate in 1995 $28 per family. Member of ARVC; CONY. Phone: (518) 664-2804.

SEE AD THIS PAGE

## MEXICO—D-6

**KOA-Mexico**—CAMPGROUND with open & shaded sites. *From jct I-81 (exit 34) & Hwy 104: Go 1 mi W on Hwy 104, then 1/2 mi N on US 11, then 1 1/4 mi W on Tubbs Rd.* ◊◊FACILITIES: 77 sites, most common site width 40 feet, 36 full hookups, 29 water & elec (20 & 30 amp receptacles), 12 no hookups, seasonal sites, 44 pull-thrus, tenting available, sewage disposal, laundry, public phone, limited grocery store, LP gas refill by meter, ice, tables, fire rings, wood. ◊◊◊RECREATION: rec room/area, swim pool, playground, shuffleboard court, planned group activities (weekends only), volleyball. Open Mar 15 through Dec 1. Rate in 1995 $18-25 for 2 persons. Member of ARVC; CONY. Phone: (315) 963-3509. KOA 10% value card discount.

**YOGI BEAR'S JELLYSTONE PARK/FLATROCK**—Streamside CAMPGROUND with open & shaded sites. *From west jct Hwy 3 & Hwy 104 & CR 16 (Academy St): Go 2 3/4 mi N on CR 16.*

◊◊◊FACILITIES: 119 sites, most common site width 50 feet, 22 full hookups, 82 water & elec (20 & 30 amp receptacles), 15 no hookups, seasonal sites, 15 pull-thrus, a/c allowed, heater allowed, phone hookups, tenting available, tent rentals, RV rentals, cabins, RV storage, handicap restroom facilities, sewage disposal, laundry, public phone, grocery store, RV supplies, LP gas refill by weight/by meter, ice, tables, fire rings, wood, traffic control gate.

◊◊◊RECREATION: rec room/area, pavilion, coin games, swim pool (heated), river fishing, fishing guides, mini-golf ($), basketball hoop, playground, 4 shuffleboard courts, planned group activities, movies, recreation director, sports field, horseshoes, volleyball.

Open all year. Facilities fully operational Apr 15 through Nov 1. Rate in 1995 $19-23 for 2 persons. Discover/Master Card/Visa accepted. CPO. Member of ARVC; CONY. Phone: (800) 248-7096.

SEE AD TRAVEL SECTION PAGE 577 AND AD NEXT PAGE

✱ **YOGI BEAR'S JELLYSTONE PARK/FLATROCK**—*From west jct Hwy 3 & Hwy 104 & CR 16: Go 2 3/4 mi N on CR 16.* SALES: park models, tents. SERVICES: RV appliance mechanic full-time, LP gas refill by weight/by meter, sewage disposal, RV storage, sells parts/accessories, sells camping supplies. Open all year. Discover/Master Card/Visa accepted. Phone: (315) 963-7096.

SEE AD THIS PAGE

## MIDDLEBURGH—E-8

MAX V. SHAUL STATE PARK—*From business Center: Go 5 mi S on Hwy 30.* FACILITIES: 30 sites, 30 no hookups, tenting available, public phone, tables, wood. RECREATION: fishing, playground, hiking trails. Open mid May through Oct 8. Phone: (518) 827-4711.

## MIDDLEVILLE—D-7

**Ace of Diamonds**—Shaded RV SPACES in town. *From jct Hwy 29/Hwy 169 & Hwy 28: Go 1/2 mi S on Hwy 28 (approach entry from north only).* FACILITIES: 27 sites, 15 water & elec (15 amp receptacles), 12 no hookups, tenting available. Open Apr 1 through Nov 1. Rate in 1995 $10-13 for 2 persons. Phone: (315) 891-3855.

## MILLERTON—F-10

COPAKE FALLS AREA (Taconic State Park)—*From business center: Go 13 mi NE on Hwy 22 & Hwy 344.* FACILITIES: 112 sites, 22 ft. max RV length, 112 no hookups, tenting available, sewage disposal, tables. RECREATION: river swimming, boating, canoeing, river fishing, playground, hiking trails. No pets. Open mid May through mid Dec. Phone: (518) 329-3993.

## MONTAUK—B-5

HITHER HILLS STATE PARK—*From town: Go 8 mi W on Hwy 27A (Old Montauk Hwy).* FACILITIES: 168 sites, 168 no hookups, tenting available, handicap restroom facilities, sewage disposal, grocery store, ice, tables. RECREATION: salt water swimming, salt water fishing, playground, hiking trails. No pets. Open late Apr through mid Nov. Facilities fully operational mid May through late Oct. Phone: (516) 668-2554.

## MONTGOMERY—A-2

✱ **PRICE RITE TRAILER SALES**—*From jct I-84 (exit 5) & Hwy 208: Go 1 mi N on Hwy 208, then 1/2 mi W on Hwy 17K.* SALES: travel trailers, park models, truck campers, 5th wheels, motor homes, mini-motor homes, fold-down camping trailers. SERVICES: RV appliance mechanic full-time, LP gas refill by weight/by meter, sells parts/accessories, installs hitches. Open all year. Discover/Master Card/Visa accepted. Phone: (914) 457-3127.

SEE AD THIS PAGE



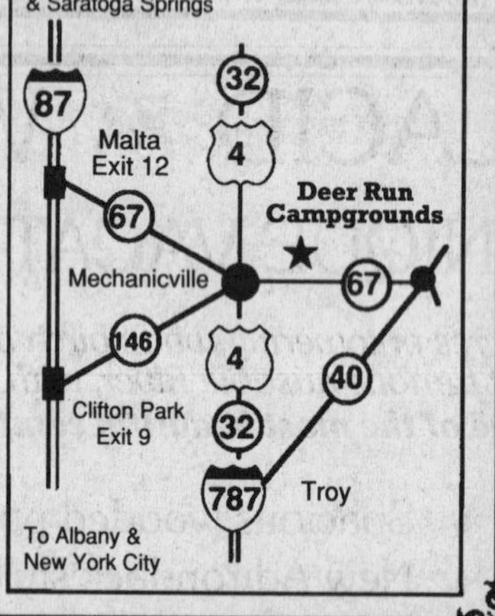

## MONTICELLO—A-1

**SULLIVAN COUNTY-OFFICE OF PUBLIC INFORMATION**—*From jct Hwy 17 (exit 106B) & Hwy 42: Go 3/4 mi S on Hwy 42, then 3/4 mi W on High St. County Government Center (corner of High & Liberty Sts).* Tourist information center for the Sullivan County Catskills and the magnificent Delaware River. Long known as a quiet & scenic resort area, it is also an action-packed playground for adults and children. Open all year. Phone: (914) 794-3000.

**SEE AD TRAVEL SECTION PAGE 584**

## MORAVIA—E-5

FILLMORE GLEN STATE PARK—*From business center: Go 1 mi S on Hwy 38.* FACILITIES: 70 sites, 70 no hookups, tenting available, handicap restroom facilities, sewage disposal, public phone, tables. RECREATION: swim pool, playground, hiking trails. Open mid May through Oct 9. Phone: (315) 497-0130.

## MORRISVILLE—E-7

**Buck's Woods Campsites**—CAMPGROUND with grassy sites. *From west village limits: Go 3 mi W on US 20.* ◆◆FACILITIES: 27 sites, 20 full hookups, 7 water & elec (20 & 30 amp receptacles), seasonal sites, 20 pull-thrus, tenting available, sewage disposal, laundry, tables, fire rings. RECREATION: horseshoes. Open May 15 through Nov 1. Rate in 1995 $15 for 4 persons. Member of ARVC; CONY. Phone: (315) 684-3286.

**Lebanon Reservoir Campground**—Open and shaded, grassy sites in a secluded area. *From jct US 20 & Eaton St (CR 105): Go 4 mi S on Eaton St, then 1 block E on Hwy 26, then 3 mi S on River Rd (CR 73), then 1 1/4 W on Reservoir Rd.* ◆◆FACILITIES: 120 sites, most common site width 50 feet, 11 full hookups, 56 water & elec, 53 elec (15,20 & 30 amp receptacles), seasonal sites, tenting available, sewage disposal, public phone, limited grocery store, ice, tables, fire rings, grills, wood. ◆◆◆RECREATION: rec hall, rec room/area, lake swimming, boating, canoeing, lake fishing, playground, horseshoes, hiking trails, volleyball. Open May 15 through Oct 1. Rate in 1995 $18-22 for 2 persons. Member of ARVC; CONY. Phone: (315) 824-2278.

## MOUNTAINDALE—A-2

MOUNTAINDALE PARK (City Park)—*From Hwy 17 (exit 112) & Old Hwy 17: Go 1 mi W on Old Hwy 17, then 8 mi N on New Rd (CR 56), then 1/4 mi E on CR 54, then 1 mi N on Post Hill Rd. Caution: Steep, winding entrance road.* FACILITIES: 150 sites, 56 full hookups, 60 water & elec (20 & 30 amp receptacles), 34 no hookups, seasonal sites, 15 pull-thrus, sewage disposal, laundry, public phone, ice, tables, fire rings, wood. RECREATION: pavilion, swim pool, boating, no motors, ramp, 6 row boat rentals, lake fishing, playground, 2 tennis courts, sports field, volleyball. Open May 1 through Oct 15. Phone: (914) 434-7337.

## NASSAU—E-9

**DINGMANS FAMILY CAMPGROUND**—Riverside with grassy shaded & open sites. *E'bound: From jct I-90 (exit 11E) & US 20: Go 8 1/2 mi E on US 20, then 1/3 mi S on Hwy 66. W'bound: From jct I-90 (exit 3B) & Hwy 22: Go 5 mi N on Hwy 22, then 8 mi W on Hwy 20, then 1/3 mi S on Hwy 66.*

◆◆◆FACILITIES: 60 sites, most common site width 30 feet, 36 water & elec (15,20 & 30 amp receptacles), 24 no hookups, 1 pull-thrus, a/c allowed ($), heater not allowed, tenting available, sewage disposal, limited grocery store, ice, tables, fire rings, wood.

◆◆◆RECREATION: rec room/area, pavilion, coin games, river fishing, basketball hoop, playground, badminton, sports field, horseshoes, volleyball.

No pets. Open May 1 through Oct 1. Rate in 1995 $18 for 2 persons. Phone: (518) 766-2310.

**SEE AD ALBANY PAGE 591**

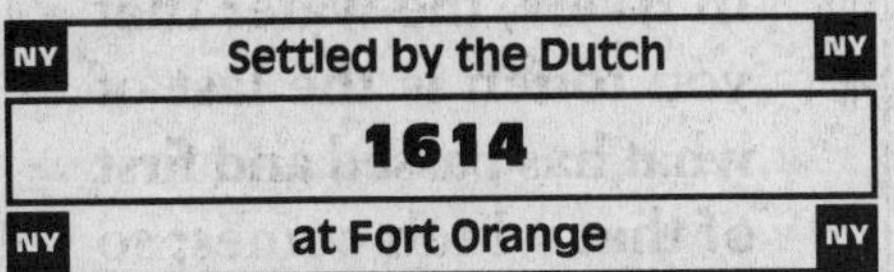

NY Settled by the Dutch NY
1614
NY at Fort Orange NY


## NATURAL BRIDGE—C-7

**KOA-Natural Bridge/Watertown**—Semi-wooded CAMPGROUND with shaded & some open sites. *From east jct Hwy 3A & Hwy 3: Go 6 mi E on Hwy 3.* ◆◆◆◆FACILITIES: 95 sites, 35 full hookups, 48 water & elec (20,30 & 50 amp receptacles), 12 no hookups, 37 pull-thrus, tenting available, sewage disposal, laundry, public phone, grocery store, LP gas refill by weight/by meter, ice, tables, fire rings, grills, wood. ◆◆◆◆RECREATION: rec hall, rec room/area, swim pool (indoor) (heated), playground, planned group activities (weekends only), badminton, sports field, horseshoes, hiking trails, volleyball. Recreation open to the public. Open Apr 1 through Nov 1. Rate in 1995 $19-24 for 2 persons. Member of ARVC;CONY. Phone: (315) 644-4880. KOA 10% value card discount.

## NEWBURGH—A-2

**KOA-NEWBURGH/NEW PALTZ**—Wooded CAMPGROUND with spacious sites. *From jct I-84 (exit 7N) & I-87 (exit 17): Go 4 mi N on Hwy 300, then 5 mi N on Hwy 32, then 1/2 mi NE on Freetown Hwy.*

◆◆◆◆FACILITIES: 140 sites, most common site width 32 feet, 90 full hookups, 41 water & elec (20,30 & 50 amp receptacles), 9 no hookups, seasonal sites, 20 pull-thrus, a/c allowed ($), heater allowed ($), cable TV, tenting available, group sites for tents/RVs, cabins, RV storage, sewage disposal, laundry, public phone, grocery store, RV supplies, LP gas refill by weight/by meter, ice, tables, fire rings, wood.

◆◆◆◆◆RECREATION: rec hall, rec room/area, coin games, 2 swim pools, pond fishing, mini-golf ($), basketball hoop, playground, 2 shuffleboard courts, planned group activities, movies, recreation director, badminton, sports field, horseshoes, hiking trails, volleyball, local tours.

KOA-NEWBURGH/NEW PALTZ—Continued on next page
NEWBURGH—Continued on next page

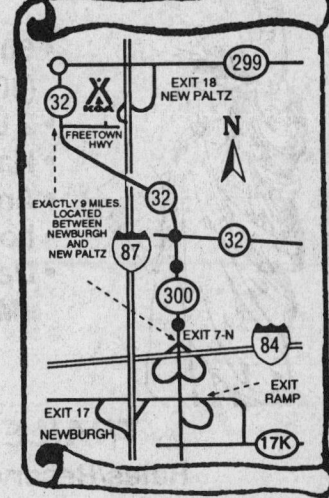

NEW YORK — INTERESTING PLACES TO VISIT — NEW YORK

**Hayden Planetarium, Bronx Zoo, Empire State Building, Statue of Liberty**

NEW YORK — IN NEW YORK — NEW YORK

- Only 15 minutes to Times Square

GRAY LINE

- New York City Bus Tours
- 150 full hookup, paved pull-thru sites
- Grassy, Shaded Tent Sites
- Free Hot Showers
- Laundry Room
- Ice & Propane
- Public transportation to NY City
- Easy access from New Jersey Tpk. I-95 & Garden State Parkway
- Free Campground brochure with map

**1-(800)-688-5080**

New Yorker RV Park & Campground

4901 Tonnelle Ave • North Bergen, NJ 07047

NEWBURGH—Continued
KOA-NEWBURGH/NEW PALTZ—Continued

Open Apr 1 through Oct 31. Rate in 1995 $27.50-31 for 2 persons. Reservations recommended May through Oct 15. Discover/Master Card/Visa accepted. Member of ARVC; CONY. Phone: (914) 564-2836. KOA 10% value card discount.

**SEE ADS FRONT OF BOOK PAGES 30, 68 AND 69 AND AD PAGE 621**

MILITARY CAMPGROUND (Round Pond Recreation Area-West Point USMA)—*Off I-87 & US 9W. On base.* FACILITIES: 43 sites, 23 water & elec (30 amp receptacles), 20 no hookups, seasonal sites, tenting available, sewage disposal, public phone, LP gas refill by weight/by meter, ice, tables, grills. RECREATION: equipped pavilion, lake swimming ($), boating, electric motors only, dock, 30 row/10 pedal boat rentals, lake fishing, playground, horseshoes, hiking trails, volleyball. Open Apr 15 through Nov 15. Facilities fully operational Apr 15 through Oct 15. Phone: (914) 938-2503.

WELCOME **NEW YORK CITY TOURS - KOA-NEWBURGH/NEW PALTZ**—*From I-84 (exit 7N) & I-87 (exit 17): Go 4 mi N on Hwy 300, then 5 mi N on Hwy 32, then 1/2 mi NE on Freetown Hwy.* Guided bus or van tours of New York City. Individual & groups. Reservations recommended. Open mid May through mid Oct. Discover/Master Card/Visa accepted. Phone: (914) 564-2836.

**SEE AD FRONT OF BOOK PAGE 30 AND AD PAGE 621**

> In rivers, the water that you touch is the last of what has passed and first of that which comes; so with time present.
>
> Leonardo da Vinci

## NEW PALTZ—A-2

WELCOME **YOGI BEAR'S JELLYSTONE PARK CAMP-RESORT AT LAZY RIVER**—*From New York State Thruway (I-87 exit 18) at New Paltz: Go 3/10 mi W on Hwy 299, then 3 mi S on South Putt Corners Rd, then 4 1/2 mi S on Hwy 32, then 3 1/2 mi W on US 44/Hwy 55, then 2/10 mi S on Albany Post Rd & follow signs to campground.*

**SEE PRIMARY LISTING AT GARDINER AND AD GARDINER PAGE 606**

## NEW YORK CITY—C-2

WELCOME **BLACK BEAR CAMPGROUND**—*About 1-hr NW via I-87 to exit 16 (US 17W), then 13 mi W on US 17 to exit 124, then SW on Hwy 17A, then follow signs to campground.*

**SEE PRIMARY LISTING AT FLORIDA, NY AND AD FLORIDA PAGE 605**

WELCOME **NEW YORK CITY TOURS-KOA NEWBURGH/NEW PALTZ**—*About 60 mi N to Newburgh. From jct I-84 (exit 7N) & I-87 (exit 17): Go 4 mi N on Hwy 300, then 5 mi N on Hwy 32, then 1/2 mi NE on Freetown Hwy.*

**AND AD NEWBURGH PAGE 621**

WELCOME **NEW YORKER RV PARK & CAMPGROUND**—*15 minutes from New York City in New Jersey.*

**SEE PRIMARY LISTING AT NORTH BERGEN, NJ AND AD THIS PAGE**

**New York**

Sample
TASTE OF BUFFALO
where more than 55 restaurants & wineries represent many ethnic food specialties.

For more information on this and other New York Festivals, see article at front of book.

# Liberty Harbor RV Park

**View Statue of Liberty, Liberty State Park and other New York attractions from campground.**

- 60 Sites w/water & electric hook-ups (30 & 50 Amp),
- 2 Dump Stations
- Handicapped Restroom/Shower Facilities
- Arcade • Laundry facilities
- Located at full service Marina
- Daily Bus Tours from Park (May 1 - Oct. 31)

***OPEN ALL YEAR***

***TRAILERS/TENTS WELCOME***

**Rates/Reservations available upon request:**

**(201) 451-1000 • 1-800-646-2066**

5 min. walk to PATH (subway)
5 min. Drive to NJ Turnpike, Holland Tunnel & Liberty State Park
11 Marin Blvd., Jersey City, NJ 07302

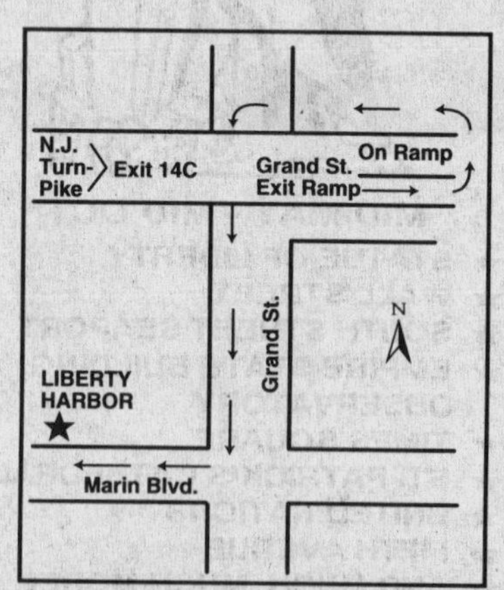


**Liberty Harbor RV Park - NJ Tpke to Exit 14C - Grand Street Exit - (3 Lefts in a row), onto Grand Street - to Marin Blvd. Make Right Turn - Go 1/4 mi. to the waterfront.**

See listing at Jersey City, NJ

## NIAGARA FALLS—D-2

**Cinderella Campsite & Motel**—Prepared and grassy RV SPACES in a metro area. *From jct I-190 (exit N 19) & Whitehaven Rd: Go 1 1/2 mi E on Whitehaven Rd, then 1 1/4 mi N on Hwy 324 (Grand Island Blvd).* FACILITIES: 90 sites, most common site width 18 feet, 30 full hookups, 30 elec (15,30 & 50 amp receptacles), 30 no hookups, seasonal sites, tenting available, sewage disposal, laundry, public phone, tables, grills. RECREATION: pavilion. Open all year. Rate in 1995 $23-27 for 2 persons. Phone: (716) 773-2872.

WELCOME

**KOA-NIAGARA FALLS**—Metro CAMPGROUND with sunny & shaded sites. *From jct I-190 (exit N-19) & Whitehaven Rd: Go 1/2 mi E on Whitehaven Rd, then 3/4 mi N on Hwy 324 (Grand Island Blvd).*

◆◆◆FACILITIES: 462 sites, most common site width 32 feet, 162 full hookups, 200 water & elec (20,30 & 50 amp receptacles), 100 no hookups, 58 pull-thrus, a/c allowed, heater allowed, tenting available, group sites for tents/RVs, cabins, sewage disposal, laundry, public phone, grocery store, RV supplies, LP gas refill by weight/by meter, ice, tables, fire rings, grills, wood, church services.

◆◆◆◆RECREATION: rec hall, rec room/area, coin games, 2 swim pools (indoor) (heated), 5 pedal boat rentals, pond fishing, mini-golf ($), basketball hoop, playground, planned group activities, movies, badminton, horseshoes, volleyball, local tours.

Open Apr 1 through Nov 15. Rate in 1995 $20.95-28.95 for 2 persons. Master Card/Visa accepted. Member of ARVC;CONY. Phone: (716) 773-7583. KOA 10% value card discount.

**SEE AD NEXT PAGE AND AD FRONT OF BOOK PAGE 68 AND 69**

WELCOME

**KOA-NIAGARA FALLS NORTH**—*From Niagara Falls: Take either Robert Moses Pkwy north toward Ft Niagara to Pletcher Rd exit, turn right on Pletcher 2 mi. Or, take Hwy 104E to Hwy 18 East (not 18F) to Pletcher Rd, turn right on Pletcher 1 1/2 mi.*

**SEE PRIMARY LISTING AT LEWISTON AND AD NEXT PAGE**



NIAGARA FALLS—Continued

WELCOME

**LEI-TI CAMPGROUND**—A CAMPGROUND with open & shaded sites in a country atmosphere. *From Niagara Falls: Take I-90 E to exit 48 (Hwy 98-Batavia), then 2 1/4 mi S to Hwy 5 & Hwy 36, then 2 1/2 mi SE on Hwy 63, then 1/2 mi S on Shepherd Rd, then 3/4 mi W on Putnam Rd, then 2 mi S on Francis Rd.*

◆◆◆FACILITIES: 203 sites, most common site width 40 feet, 60 full hookups, 127 water & elec (20 & 30 amp receptacles), 16 no hookups, seasonal sites, 7 pull-thrus, a/c allowed ($), heater allowed ($), phone hookups, tenting available, group sites for tents/RVs, RV rentals, cabins, RV storage, sewage disposal, laundry, public phone, limited grocery store, RV supplies, LP gas refill by weight/by meter, ice, tables, fire rings, wood, traffic control gate/guard.

◆◆◆◆RECREATION: rec hall, equipped pavilion, coin games, lake swimming, boating, no motors, canoeing, 2 row/1 pedal boat rentals, lake fishing, mini-golf ($), basketball hoop, 3 bike rentals, playground, 2 shuffleboard courts, planned group activities (weekends only), tennis court, badminton, sports field, horseshoes, hiking trails, volleyball, cross country skiing. Recreation open to the public.

Open all year. Facilities fully operational May 1 through Columbus Day. Rate in 1995 $17-23 for 2 persons. Discover/Master Card/Visa accepted. Phone: (800) HI-LEITI.

**SEE PRIMARY LISTING AT BATAVIA AND AD PAGE 623**

WELCOME

✱ **MANTELLI TRAILER SALES**—*30 minutes east of Niagara Falls on Rt 78.*

**SEE PRIMARY LISTING AT LOCKPORT AND AD THIS PAGE**

NIAGARA FALLS—Continued

WELCOME

**NIAGARA FALLS CAMPGROUND & MOTEL**—Prepared sites with shade & grass in a metro area. *N'bound: From jct I-290 (exit 3) & US 62: Go 9 mi N on US 62. S'bound: From jct I-190 (exit 22) & US 62: Go 4 1/2 mi S on US 62.*

◆◆◆FACILITIES: 72 sites, most common site width 22 feet, 15 full hookups, 14 water & elec, 13 elec (20 & 30 amp receptacles), 30 no hookups, a/c allowed, heater allowed, tenting available, sewage disposal, laundry, public phone, ice, tables, fire rings, grills, wood.

◆◆RECREATION: rec room/area, coin games, swim pool (heated), horseshoes, local tours.

NIAGARA FALLS CAMPGROUND & MOTEL—Continued on next page

NIAGARA FALLS—Continued on next page





NY *Enjoy the spectacle of the Adirondack Balloon Festival! See Front of Book Article.* NY

# Niagara Falls KOA

*7 mi. to Falls along scenic Niagara River. Ten minutes from downtown Buffalo. GRAYLINE GUIDED TOURS direct from the campground 3 times daily.*

- * Indoor & outdoor heated pool * 50 cabins
- * Kid's Club & Free movies July & August
- * Pond with paddle boats & mini-golf
- * Meeting hall for reunions & conventions
- * All aboard at KOA Train Station to FANTASY ISLAND Fun & Water Park!

Kamping Kabins™

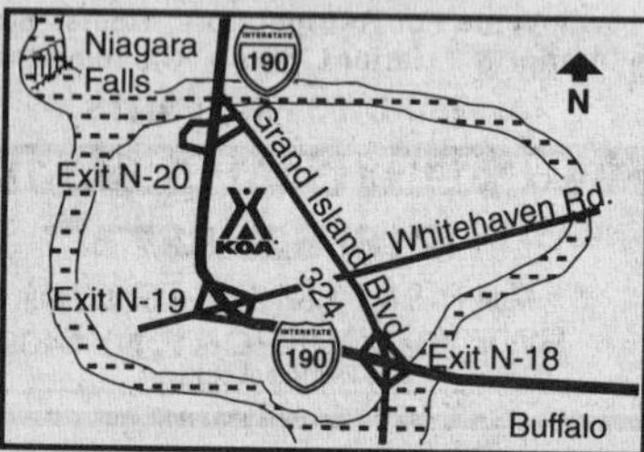


*Campground is on St. Hwy. 324 (2570 Grand Island Blvd.) Taking I-190 from Buffalo, take Exits 18A or 19; From Niagara Falls, take Exits 20B or 19, and follow signs.*

**For reservations write: P.O. Box 509, Grand Island, NY 14072 • Or call: 1-800-KOA-0787 or (716) 773-7583**

NIAGARA FALLS—Continued
NIAGARA FALLS CAMPGROUND & MOTEL—Continued

Open Apr 1 through Nov 15. Rate in 1995 $18-22 for 2 persons. American Express/Master Card/Visa accepted. Member of ARVC; CONY. Phone: (716) 731-3434.
**SEE AD THIS PAGE**

**NIAGARA GLEN-VIEW TENT & TRAILER PARK**—*From Rainbow Bridge: Go 2 1/2 mi N on Niagara Parkway, then 300 feet W on Victoria Ave.*
**SEE PRIMARY LISTING AT NIAGARA FALLS, ON AND AD NIAGARA FALLS, ON PAGE 1005**

**PLAZA COURT MOTEL CAMPGROUND**—Level, gravel RV SPACES with young trees behind a motel. *Southbound: From jct I-190 (exit 22) & US 62: Go 1/2 mi S on US 62 South. Northbound: From jct I-290 (exit 3) & US 62: Go 12 mi N on US 62.*

FACILITIES: 24 sites, 8 full hookups, 4 water & elec, 12 elec (15 & 30 amp receptacles), 24 pull-thrus, a/c allowed ($), heater allowed ($), tenting available, sewage disposal, laundry, ice.

RECREATION: local tours.

Open all year. Facilities fully operational Apr 1 through Oct 31. Rate in 1995 $16-20 for 2 persons. American Express/Discover/Master Card/Visa accepted. Member of ARVC; CONY. Phone: (716) 283-2638.
**SEE AD THIS PAGE**

**SCOTTS TENT & TRAILER PARK**—*From Rainbow Bridge: Go 2 1/2 mi W on Hwy 20 (Lundys Lane).*
**SEE PRIMARY LISTING AT NIAGARA FALLS, ON AND AD NIAGARA FALLS, ON PAGE 1004**

**SHALAMAR LAKE NIAGARA**—*From the Queenston-Lewiston Bridge Canadian Toll Booth: Go 4.8 km/3 mi N on Niagara Parkway (River Rd), then .25 km/1/4 mi W on Line 8 Rd.*
**SEE PRIMARY LISTING NIAGARA FALLS, ON AND AD NIAGARA FALLS, ON PAGE 1008**

NIAGARA FALLS—Continued on next page

## PLAZA COURT MOTEL CAMPGROUND

*"The Only Campground In The City Of Niagara Falls"*

- Motel Rooms, Family Units
- Full Hook-ups
- Dump Station
- Clean Restrooms
- Tent Sites
- Guided Tours
- Pull Thrus
- Showers
- Laundry
- City Bus Stop
- Swimming Pool Available

**15% OFF WITH THIS AD**

**(716) 283-2638 or (716) 283-3151**

**7680 Niagara Falls Blvd.
Niagara Falls, NY 14304**

See listing for directions

## NIAGARA FALLS CAMPGROUND & MOTEL

**The Shadiest Campground in Niagara Falls**

**Minutes Away From The Falls
Three Guided Tours Daily
Near All Attractions**

● Prepared, Shaded Sites ● 30 Amps ● A/C Motel Rooms
● Laundry ● New Swimming Pool ● Free Showers
● Dump Station ● Grassy Picnic Areas ● Game Room

**FAMILY OWNED AND OPERATED**

**For Reservations (716) 731-3434**

**2405 Niagara Falls Blvd., Niagara Falls, NY 14304**

See listing at Niagara Falls

## NIAGARA FALLS NORTH

**Guided Tours to Niagara Falls**

See listings at Lewiston & Niagara Falls

**Highest Rated Campground in Niagara Falls Area**

**2 Miles East of Robert Moses Pkwy. on Pletcher Rd.**

*A quiet, wooded campground in a rural area, within 15 Minutes of Niagara Falls. Fantasy Island, Aquarium, Fort Niagara, Golfing, Fatima Shrine, Canada, Artpark, Outlet Mall, Niagara Splash nearby.*

● Full Hookups ● Pull-Thrus ● Shaded, Grassy Tent Sites ● Hiking Areas
● Well-Equipped Laundry ● Very Clean Restrooms ● Sparkling Pool
● Kamping Kabins (1 & 2 rooms available) ● Guided Tours Available ● Breakfasts in Season

**For information: (716) 754-8013**

**For Reservations (only): 1-800-562-8715**

**1250 Pletcher Road – Box 71, Lewiston, NY 14092**

NIAGARA FALLS—Continued

**SHERKSTON SHORES**—*From Rainbow Bridge: Go 4 mi W on Hwy 20, then 9 1/2 mi S on QEW, then 10 mi S on Regional Rd 116, then 3 mi W on Hwy 3, then 1 1/2 mi S on Reg. Rd 98.*

**SEE PRIMARY LISTING AT PORT COLBORNE, ON AND AD FRONT OF BOOK PAGE 142**

## NORTH HUDSON—C-9

**PARADISE PINES CAMPING RESORT**—CAMPGROUND on the Schroon River with open and shaded, grassy sites. *From jct I-87 (exit 29-North Hudson) & Blue Ridge Rd: Go 750 feet E on Blue Ridge Rd (across from McDonald's).*

◆◆◆FACILITIES: 101 sites, most common site width 30 feet, 55 full hookups, 36 water & elec (20,30 & 50 amp receptacles), 10 no hookups, seasonal sites, 8 pull-thrus, a/c allowed ($), heater allowed ($), tenting available, group sites for tents/RVs, RV rentals, cabins, RV storage, sewage disposal, laundry, public phone, grocery store, RV supplies, LP gas refill by weight/by meter, ice, tables, fire rings, grills, wood.

◆◆◆RECREATION: rec room/area, pavilion, coin games, swim pool, wading pool, river swimming, whirlpool, 2 pedal boat rentals, river fishing, mini-golf ($), basketball hoop, playground, 2 shuffleboard courts, planned group activities, movies, sports field, horseshoes, volleyball. Recreation open to the public.

Open May 1 through Oct 20. Rate in 1995 $17-21 for 2 persons. Discover/Master Card/Visa accepted. Member of ARVC; CONY. Phone: (518) 532-7493.

**SEE AD THIS PAGE**

## NORTH JAVA—E-3

**Yogi Bear's Jellystone Park Camp Resort**—Rolling, rural CAMPGROUND with level, shaded sites. *From the center of the village: Go 2 1/4 mi S on Hwy 98, then 1 1/2 mi E on Pee Dee Rd, then 3/4 mi S on Youngers Rd.* ◆◆◆FACILITIES: 200 sites, most common site width 24 feet, 40 full hookups, 160 water & elec (15,20 & 30 amp receptacles), seasonal sites, 20 pull-thrus, tenting available, sewage disposal, laundry, public phone, limited grocery store, LP gas refill by weight, ice, tables, fire rings, wood. ◆◆◆RECREATION: rec room/area, pavilion, swim pool, boating, no motors, canoeing, 2 pedal boat rentals, lake fishing, mini-golf ($), playground, planned group activities, badminton, sports field, horseshoes, hiking trails, volleyball. Recreation open to the public. Open May 15 through Oct 31. Rate in 1995 $20-23 for 2 persons. Member of ARVC; CONY. Phone: (716) 457-9644.

## NORTHVILLE—D-9

SACANDAGA CAMPGROUND (Adirondack State Forest)—*From town: Go 8 mi N on Hwy 30.* FACILITIES: 143 sites, 143 no hookups, tenting available, sewage disposal, tables. RECREATION: fishing, hiking trails. Open mid May through Labor Day. Phone: (518) 924-4121.

## ODESSA—F-5

**Cool-Lea Camp**—Open and shaded, grassy sites in a lakeside CAMPGROUND. *From jct Hwy 14 & Hwy 224: Go 3 1/2 mi E on Hwy 224, then 2 1/2 mi N on Hwy 228.* ◆◆FACILITIES: 59 sites, most common site width 30 feet, 44 water & elec (15,20 & 30 amp receptacles), 15 no hookups, seasonal sites, tenting available, handicap restroom facilities, sewage disposal, public phone, ice, tables, fire rings, wood. ◆◆◆RECREATION: rec room/area, pavilion, lake swimming, boating, canoeing, ramp, dock, 3 row/2 canoe boat rentals, lake fishing, planned group activities (weekends only), sports field, horseshoes, hiking trails. Open May 15 through Oct 1. Rate in 1995 $16-18 for 2 persons. Member of ARVC; CONY. Phone: (607) 594-3500.

## OGDENSBURG—B-7

JACQUES CARTIER STATE PARK—*From business center: Go 12 mi SW on Hwy 37, then 3 mi W on River Rd (Morristown).* FACILITIES: 98 sites, 22 elec, 76 no hookups, tenting available, handicap restroom facilities, sewage disposal, public phone, grocery store, tables. RECREATION: river swimming, boating, canoeing, river fishing, playground. Open mid May through Oct 8. Phone: (315) 375-8980.

**KOA-THOUSAND ISLANDS**—Wooded sites in a riverside CAMPGROUND convenient to a major highway. *From south jct of Hwy 812 & Hwy 37: Go 7 mi SW on Hwy 37.*

◆◆◆FACILITIES: 105 sites, most common site width 30 feet, 20 full hookups, 63 water & elec (15 & 20 amp receptacles), 22 no hookups, seasonal sites, 16 pull-thrus, a/c allowed, heater allowed, tenting available, RV rentals, cabins, RV storage, sewage disposal, laundry, public phone, grocery store, RV supplies, ice, tables, fire rings, grills, wood.

◆◆◆RECREATION: rec room/area, pavilion, coin games, swim pool, canoeing, river fishing, playground, planned group activities (weekends only), badminton, horseshoes, volleyball.

Open May 1 through Oct 15. Rate in 1995 $19-25 for 2 persons. No refunds. Discover/Master Card/Visa accepted. Phone: (315) 393-3951. KOA 10% value card discount.

**SEE AD THIS PAGE AND AD FRONT OF BOOK PAGES 68 AND 69**

## OLD BETHPAGE—C-3

BATTLE ROW CAMPGROUND (Nassau County Park)—*From jct I-495 (exit 48) & Round Swamp Rd: Go 1 3/4 mi SE on Round Swamp Rd, then 1 block E on Bethpage-Sweetholow Rd, then 1 block S on Claremont Rd.* FACILITIES: 60 sites, 30 water & elec (30 amp receptacles), 30 no hookups, tenting available, handicap restroom facilities, sewage disposal, public phone, tables, fire rings, grills, wood. RECREATION: playground, sports field, horseshoes, volleyball. Open 1st Fri in Apr through last Sun in Nov. Phone: (516) 293-7120.

## OLD FORGE—C-7

**KOA-OLD FORGE**—Lakeside CAMPGROUND with wooded sites at the edge of the village. *From north village limits: Go 1/2 mi N on Hwy 28.*

◆◆◆FACILITIES: 198 sites, most common site width 40 feet, 57 full hookups, 96 water & elec (20 & 30 amp receptacles), 45 no hookups, seasonal sites, 2 pull-thrus, tenting available, cabins, RV storage, sewage disposal, laundry, public phone, grocery store, RV supplies, LP gas refill by weight/by meter, ice, tables, fire rings, wood.

◆◆◆RECREATION: rec room/area, pavilion, coin games, lake swimming, boating, no motors, canoeing, 2 row/4 canoe boat rentals, lake fishing, basketball hoop, playground, movies, sports field, horseshoes, hiking trails, cross country skiing, snowmobile trails, local tours.

OLD FORGE—Continued

Open all year. Facilities fully operational May 1 through Oct 15. Rate in 1995 $20-24.50 for 2 persons. Discover/Master Card/Visa accepted. Member of ARVC;CONY. Phone: (315) 369-6011. KOA 10% value card discount.

**SEE AD THIS PAGE AND AD FRONT OF BOOK PAGES 68 AND 69**

**Singing Waters Campground**—Riverside, semi-wooded with wooded & open sites. *From south town limits: Go 5 3/4 mi S on Hwy 28.* ◆◆FACILITIES: 142 sites, most common site width 25 feet, 64 full hookups, 53 water & elec (15 & 20 amp receptacles), 25 no hookups, seasonal sites, tenting available, sewage disposal, public phone, limited grocery store, ice, tables, fire rings, grills, wood. ◆◆◆RECREATION: rec room/area, river swimming, canoeing, river fishing, playground, 2 tennis courts, badminton, sports field, horseshoes, volleyball. Open all year. Facilities fully operational May 15 through Nov 15. Rate in 1995 $17-25 for 2 persons. No refunds. Phone: (315) 369-6618.

NY **State Flower: Rose** NY

*Easy-On Easy Off Right at Exit 29*

**PARADISE PINES CAMPING RESORT**

**Enjoy Camping In The Adirondacks**

*Halfway Between Lake George & Lake Placid*

**BIG RIGS ACCOMMODATED**

*With us, you're "more than just a number"*

● Sites on the Schroon River ●
● Personal Service ● Escorted Parking ●
● Clean Restrooms ● Mini-Mart ●
● Laundry ● Pool ● Kiddie Pool ● Spa ●
● Shuffleboard ● Movies ● Pavilion ●
● Fishing ● Mini Golf ● Paddleboats ●

**ACROSS FROM FRONTIER TOWN & MCDONALDS**

**(518) 532-7493**

*Free Brochure*

Mike & Gina Lenhard

**Box 180, Blue Ridge Road North Hudson, NY 12855**

See listing at North Hudson, NY

KOA **THOUSAND ISLANDS**

On The St. Lawrence River, 9 Miles From International Bridge To Canada

**(315) 393-3951**

Rt 2, Box 64 Ogdensburg, NY 13669

See Listing at Ogdensburg

# OLD FORGE, NY

**1/2 mi. North of Old Forge on Rt. 28**

**Year 'Round Camping - 198 Wooded Sites on Lake Serene.**

**SWIM, FISH, CANOE, HIKE ON 115 ACRES**

- Full Hookups ● Tent Sites ● Laundry
- Groceries ● Free Nightly Movies
- Nature Trails ● X-C Skiing
- Winter Snowmobiling ● Over 20 Cabins
- Shuttle Service to Enchanted Forest Water Safari

P.O. BOX 51
OLD FORGE, NY 13420
(315) 369-6011

RESERVATIONS ONLY:
800-562-3251

**NEAR ALL ATTRACTIONS:**
Water Safari/
Enchanted Forest
(NY's Largest Water Park)
Adirondack Museum
Mt. McCauley Chair Lift
Fulton Chain of Lakes
Championship Golf Course

See listing at Old Forge

## ONEIDA—D-7

VERONA BEACH STATE PARK—*From jct I-90 & Hwy 13: Go 7 mi NW on Hwy 13.* FACILITIES: 35 sites, 35 no hookups, tenting available, handicap restroom facilities, sewage disposal, tables. RECREATION: lake swimming, canoeing, lake fishing, playground, hiking trails. Open early May through mid Oct. Phone: (315) 762-4463.

## ONEONTA—E-7

GILBERT LAKE STATE PARK—*From business center: Go 12 mi NW on Hwy 205.* FACILITIES: 221 sites, 25 ft. max RV length, 17 elec, 204 no hookups, tenting available, sewage disposal, public phone, grocery store, tables. RECREATION: rec hall, lake swimming, boating, canoeing, row boat rentals, lake fishing, playground, hiking trails. Open early May through Oct 9. Phone: (607) 432-2114.

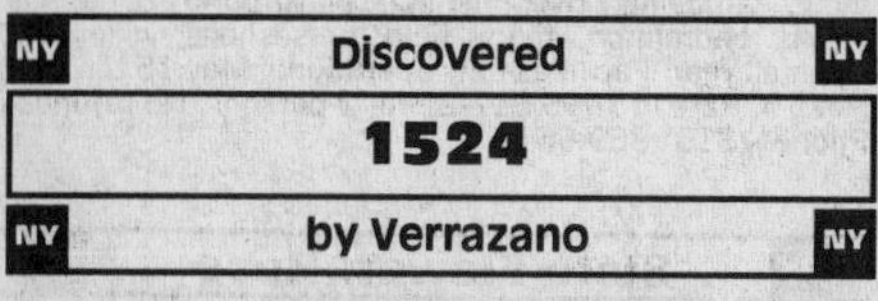

NY Discovered NY
1524
NY by Verrazano NY




## OSWEGO—D-5

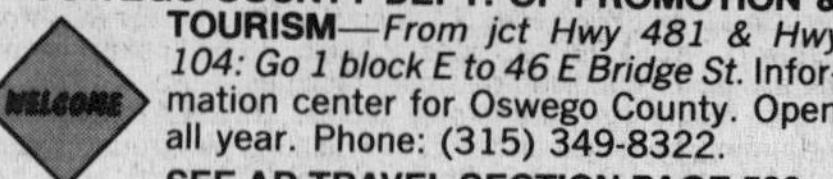

**OSWEGO COUNTY DEPT. OF PROMOTION & TOURISM**—*From jct Hwy 481 & Hwy 104: Go 1 block E to 46 E Bridge St.* Information center for Oswego County. Open all year. Phone: (315) 349-8322.

**SEE AD TRAVEL SECTION PAGE 580**

## OXFORD—F-7

BOWMAN LAKE STATE PARK—*From business center: Go 8 mi NW on Hwy 220.* FACILITIES: 198 sites, 30 ft. max RV length, 198 no hookups, tenting available, handicap restroom facilities, sewage disposal, limited grocery store, ice, tables. RECREATION: rec hall, lake swimming, boating, canoeing, lake fishing, playground, hiking trails. Open early May through Oct 10. Phone: (607) 334-2718.

## PALENVILLE—F-9

**Pine Hollow Campground**—Rustic CAMPGROUND with pine shaded sites. *From jct Hwy 23A & Hwy 32A: Go 1 mi SE on Hwy 32A.* ◆◆◆FACILITIES: 31 sites, most common site width 40 feet, 17 water & elec (20 & 30 amp receptacles), 14 no hookups, seasonal sites, tenting available, sewage disposal, laundry, ice, tables, fire rings, wood. ◆◆RECREATION: rec hall, playground, badminton, horseshoes, hiking trails, volleyball. Open May 15 through Oct 15. Rate in 1995 $18-21 for 2 persons. Member of ARVC; CONY. Phone: (518) 678-2245.

## PALMYRA—D-4

**GARY JOHNSTON'S RV CENTER**—*From jct Hwy 31 & Hwy 21: Go 2 mi N on Hwy 21.* SALES: travel trailers, truck campers, 5th wheels, motor homes, mini-motor homes, fold-down camping trailers. SERVICES: Engine/Chassis & RV appliance mechanic full-time, LP gas refill by weight/by meter, RV rentals, RV storage, sells parts/accessories, installs hitches. Open all year. Master Card/Visa accepted. Phone: (800) 698-5388.

**SEE AD ROCHESTER PAGE 629**



## PARKSVILLE—F-8

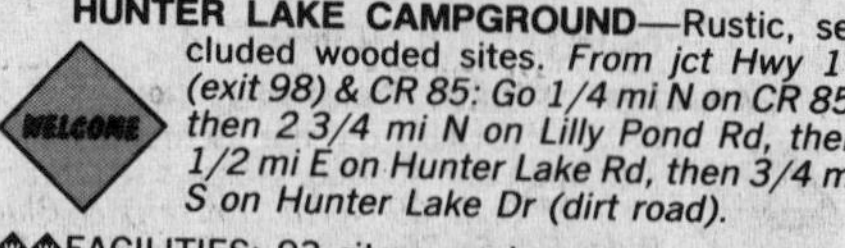

**HUNTER LAKE CAMPGROUND**—Rustic, secluded wooded sites. *From jct Hwy 17 (exit 98) & CR 85: Go 1/4 mi N on CR 85, then 2 3/4 mi N on Lilly Pond Rd, then 1/2 mi E on Hunter Lake Rd, then 3/4 mi S on Hunter Lake Dr (dirt road).*

◆◆FACILITIES: 93 sites, most common site width 50 feet, 45 full hookups, 48 water & elec (30 amp receptacles), seasonal sites, 12 pull-thrus, a/c allowed ($), heater allowed ($), tenting available, sewage disposal, laundry, public phone, limited grocery store, RV supplies, ice, tables, fire rings, wood, traffic control gate.

◆◆◆RECREATION: rec hall, coin games, lake swimming, boating, electric motors only, canoeing, dock, 4 row/4 canoe boat rentals, lake fishing, basketball hoop, shuffleboard court, badminton, sports field, horseshoes, volleyball.

Open Memorial Day through Labor Day weekend. Rate in 1995 $22-23.50 for 2 persons. No refunds. Member of ARVC; CONY. Phone: (914) 292-3629.

**SEE AD THIS PAGE**

## PATCHOGUE—C-4

FIRE ISLAND NATIONAL SEASHORE (Watch Hill Campground)—*Access by private boat or passenger ferry only (Fire Island).* FACILITIES: 25 sites, 25 no hookups, tenting available, cold showers, handicap restroom facilities, public phone, limited grocery store, tables, grills. RECREATION: salt water swimming, boating, dock, motor boat rentals, salt water fishing, hiking trails, volleyball. Recreation open to the public. Open mid May through mid Oct. Reservations required Phone: (516) 597-6633.

## PATTERSON—A-3

**HOLIDAY ON WHEELS**—*From jct I-684 & I-84: Go 6 mi N on Hwy 22, then 1 block W into Robin Hill Corp Park.* SALES: motor homes, mini-motor homes, fold-down camping trailers. SERVICES: Engine/Chassis & RV appliance mechanic full-time, emergency road service business hours, LP gas refill by meter, sells parts/accessories. Open all year. Discover/Master Card/Visa accepted. Phone: (914) 878-9400.

**SEE AD THIS PAGE**

## PENN YAN—E-4

**Wigwam Keuka Lake Campground**—CAMPGROUND with open & shaded, grassy sites. *From jct Hwy 14 A & Hwy 54 A (Penn Yan): Go 5 3/4 mi SW on Hwy 54 A, then 1/2 mi W on James Rd, then 1/4 mi N on Esperanza Rd.* ◆◆FACILITIES: 49 sites, 38 water & elec, 2 elec (30 amp receptacles), 9 no hookups, seasonal sites, 3 pull-thrus, tenting available, non-flush toilets, sewage disposal, public phone, limited grocery store, ice, tables, fire rings, wood. ◆◆◆RECREATION: swim pool, pond fishing, playground, planned group activities (weekends only), sports field, horseshoes, volleyball. Open May 15 through Oct 15. Rate in 1995 $12-17 for 4 persons. Member of CONY. Phone: (315) 536-6352.

## PERU—B-9

**Ausable Pines Campground**—A secluded, riverside location with shaded sites convenient to an interstate. *From jct I-87 (exit 35) & Hwy 442: Go 3 mi E on Hwy 442, then 300 yards N on US 9.* ◆◆◆FACILITIES: 130 sites, most common site width 35 feet, 76 full hookups, 3 water & elec (30 amp receptacles), 51 no hookups, seasonal sites, tenting available, sewage disposal, laundry, public phone, LP gas refill by weight/by meter, tables, patios, fire rings, grills, wood. ◆◆◆RECREATION: rec room/area, swim pool, boating, canoeing, dock, 1 row/2 pedal boat rentals, river fishing, playground, badminton, sports field, horseshoes, hiking trails, volleyball. Open May 15 through Oct 15. Rate in 1995 $17-19 for 4 persons. No refunds. Member of ARVC; CONY. Phone: (518) 561-1188.

AUSABLE POINT CAMPGROUND (Adirondack State Forest)—*From jct I-87 & Hwy 442: Go 3 mi E on Hwy 422, then 1/2 mi S on US 9.* FACILITIES: 123 sites, 43 elec, 80 no hookups, tenting available, handicap restroom facilities, sewage disposal, public phone, tables. RECREATION: lake swimming, boating, canoeing, ramp, lake fishing. Open early May through mid Oct. Phone: (518) 561-7080.

**Iroquois RV Park & Campground**—Semi-wooded sites in a rural area convenient to an interstate. *From jct I-87 (exit 35) & Hwy 442: Go 1 1/2 mi E on Hwy 442.*

IROQUOIS RV PARK & CAMPGROUND—Continued on next page
PERU—Continued on next page

◆◆◆FACILITIES: 200 sites, most common site width 25 feet, 180 full hookups, 20 water & elec (20 & 30 amp receptacles), seasonal sites, 50 pull-thrus, tenting available, sewage disposal, laundry, public phone, limited grocery store, LP gas refill by weight/by meter, ice, tables, fire rings, wood. ◆◆◆◆RECREATION: rec room/area, pavilion, swim pool, 3 pedal boat rentals, pond fishing, playground, 2 shuffleboard courts, planned group activities (weekends only), tennis court, badminton, sports field, horseshoes, volleyball. Open May 1 through Oct 1. Rate in 1995 $20 for 2 persons. No refunds. Member of ARVC; CONY. Phone: (518) 643-9057.

## PETERSBURGH—E-10

**AQUA VISTA VALLEY CAMPGROUND**—Riverside mountainview park with grassy, shaded & wooded sites. *From jct Hwy 2 & Hwy 22: Go 1/4 mi N on Hwy 22, then 1/4 mi NE on Armsby Rd.*

WELCOME

◆◆FACILITIES: 160 sites, most common site width 30 feet, 130 water & elec (20 amp receptacles), 30 no hookups, seasonal sites, a/c not allowed, heater not allowed, tenting available, RV storage, sewage disposal, laundry, public phone, limited grocery store, ice, tables, fire rings, wood.

◆◆◆◆RECREATION: rec room/area, coin games, swim pool, wading pool, river fishing, basketball hoop, playground, planned group activities (weekends only), sports field, horseshoes, volleyball.

Open May 1 through Oct 15. Rate in 1995 $18-20 per family. Member of ARVC;CONY. Phone: (518) 658-3659.

**SEE AD THIS PAGE**

**BROKEN WHEEL CAMPGROUND**—Sunny and shaded sites with mountain views in a country setting. *From jct Hwy 2 and Hwy 22: Go 2 mi S on Hwy 22.*

WELCOME

◆◆◆FACILITIES: 75 sites, most common site width 30 feet, 65 water & elec (15 & 20 amp receptacles), 10 no hookups, seasonal sites, a/c not allowed, heater not allowed, tenting available, RV storage, sewage disposal, public phone, grocery store, LP gas refill by weight, ice, tables, fire rings, wood.

◆◆◆◆RECREATION: rec room/area, equipped pavilion, coin games, swim pool, river fishing, basketball hoop, playground, planned group activities (weekends only), badminton, sports field, horseshoes, volleyball.

Open May 1 through Oct 15. Rate in 1995 $13-16 for 2 persons. Member of ARVC;CONY. Phone: (518) 658-2925.

**SEE AD ALBANY PAGE 591**

## PHELPS—E-5

**CHEERFUL VALLEY CAMPGROUND**—Rolling, grassy location with level, sunny and shaded sites. *From jct I-90 (exit 42) & Hwy 14: Go 1/2 mi N on Hwy 14.*

WELCOME

◆◆◆◆FACILITIES: 160 sites, most common site width 35 feet, 65 full hookups, 80 water & elec (20 & 30 amp receptacles), 15 no hookups, 35 pull-thrus, a/c allowed ($), heater allowed ($), tenting available, group sites for tents/RVs, RV storage, sewage disposal, laundry, public phone, limited grocery store, RV supplies, LP gas refill by weight/by meter, ice, tables, fire rings, wood.

◆◆◆◆RECREATION: rec room/area, pavilion, coin games, swim pool ($), canoeing, river fishing, basketball hoop, playground, 2 shuffleboard courts,





planned group activities (weekends only), badminton, sports field, horseshoes, volleyball.

Open Apr 15 through Oct 15. Rate in 1995 $19-25 for 2 persons. No refunds. Master Card/Visa accepted. CPO. Member of ARVC; CONY. Phone: (315) 781-1222.

**SEE AD ROCHESTER PAGE 629**

## PHOENICIA—F-8

KENNETH L. WILSON CAMPGROUND (Catskills State Forest)—*From jct Hwy 28 & Hwy 212: Go 1/2 mi E on Hwy 212, then 4 mi SE on CR 40.* FACILITIES: 76 sites, 76 no hookups, tenting available, handicap restroom facilities, sewage disposal, tables, fire rings. RECREATION: swimming, boating, no motors, canoeing, ramp, fishing, playground, hiking trails. Open mid May through mid Oct. Phone: (914) 679-7020.

WOODLAND VALLEY CAMPGROUND (Catskill State Forest)—*From town: Go 6 mi SW off Hwy 28.* FACILITIES: 72 sites, 72 no hookups, tenting available, sewage disposal, tables. RECREATION: river fishing, hiking trails. Open mid May through mid Oct. Phone: (914) 688-7647.

## PLATTSBURGH—B-10

CUMBERLAND BAY STATE PARK—*From town: Go 1 mi E on Hwy 314.* FACILITIES: 200 sites, 200 no hookups, tenting available, handicap restroom facilities, tables. RECREATION: lake swimming, boating, playground. Open May 1 through Oct 8. Phone: (518) 563-5240.

⚑ **LAKE CHAMPLAIN FERRIES**—*From jct I-87 (exit 39) & Hwy 314: Go 5 mi E on Hwy 314 to ferry dock.* Auto ferries cross scenic Lake Champlain between Plattsburgh, NY & Grand Isle, VT. Open all year. Phone: (802) 864-9804.

WELCOME

**SEE AD LAKE CHAMPLAIN, VT PAGE 853**

✱ **WALTON H BULL RECREATION BARN**—*From jct I-87 (exit 38 N) & Hwy 374: Go 11 mi W on Hwy 374.* SALES: travel trailers, park models, truck campers, 5th wheels, motor homes, mini-motor homes, fold-down camping trailers. SERVICES: RV appliance mechanic full-time, emergency road service business hours, LP gas refill by weight, sewage disposal, RV storage, sells parts/accessories, installs hitches. Open all year. Master Card/Visa accepted. Phone: (518) 492-7007.

WELCOME

**SEE AD THIS PAGE**

## POLAND—D-7

**WEST CANADA CREEK CAMPSITES**—Developed CAMPGROUND on rolling terrain with level, open & shaded sites. *From east jct Hwy 28 & Hwy 8: Go 1 mi W on Hwy 8 South/Hwy 28 North.*

WELCOME

◆◆◆◆FACILITIES: 74 sites, 30 full hookups, 30 water & elec (20,30 & 50 amp receptacles), 14 no hookups, seasonal sites, 10 pull-thrus, a/c allowed ($), heater allowed ($), phone hookups, group sites for tents/RVs, RV rentals, cabins, RV storage, handicap restroom facilities, sewage disposal, laundry, public phone, limited grocery store, RV supplies, LP gas refill by weight/by meter, ice, tables, fire rings, grills, wood.

◆◆◆RECREATION: rec room/area, pavilion, coin games, swim pool, river swimming, boating, canoeing, 2 row/6 canoe boat rentals, river fishing, basketball hoop, playground, planned group activities (weekends only), badminton, sports field, horse-



shoes, hiking trails, volleyball.

Open Apr 15 through Oct 15. Rate in 1995 $24-28 for 2 persons. Master Card/Visa accepted. Member of ARVC; CONY. Phone: (315) 826-7390.

**SEE AD UTICA PAGE 633**

## PORTAGEVILLE—E-3

**FOUR WINDS CAMPGROUND**—CAMPGROUND with open & shaded sites. *From south jct Hwy 436 & Hwy 19A: Go 1/4 mi N on Hwy 19A to state park entrance, then 1 3/4 mi W on Griffith Rd, then 1 1/4 mi S on Tenefly Rd.*

WELCOME

◆◆◆FACILITIES: 145 sites, 85 full hookups, 28 water & elec (20,30 & 50 amp receptacles), 32 no hookups, seasonal sites, 10 pull-thrus, a/c allowed, heater allowed, tenting available, group sites for RVs, RV storage, sewage disposal, laundry, public phone, limited grocery store, RV supplies, LP gas refill by weight/by meter, ice, tables, fire rings, wood.

◆◆◆RECREATION: rec room/area, equipped pavilion, coin games, pond swimming, stream fishing, basketball hoop, playground, shuffleboard court, sports field, horseshoes, hiking trails, volleyball.

Open May 3 through Oct 19. Rate in 1995 $17.50-19.50 for 2 persons. Master Card/Visa accepted. Member of ARVC;CONY. Phone: (716) 493-2794. FCRV 10% discount.

**SEE AD CASTILE PAGE 597**

## PORT HENRY—C-10

BULWAGGA BAY CAMPSITE (City Park)—*1/2 mile south of town on Hwy 9N-22.* FACILITIES: 175 sites, 40 ft. max RV length, 125 water & elec (20 amp receptacles), 50 no hookups, seasonal sites, tenting available, sewage disposal, tables, fire rings. RECREATION: pavilion, lake swimming, boating, canoeing, ramp, lake fishing, playground, horseshoes. Recreation open to the public. Open May 20 through Labor Day. Phone: (518) 546-7500.

## PORT JERVIS—B-1

***See listing at Cuddebackville***

## PORT KENT—B-10

⚑ **LAKE CHAMPLAIN FERRIES**—*N'bound: From jct I-87 (exit 34) & Hwy 9N: Go 1 mi NE on Hwy 9N, then 2 mi N on Hwy 9, then 3 mi E on Hwy 373 to ferry dock. S'bound: From jct I-87 (exit 35): Go 2 1/2 mi E on Bear Swamp Rd, then 3 1/2 mi S on US 9, then 3 mi E on Hwy 373 to ferry dock.* Auto ferries cross scenic Lake Champlain between Port Kent, NY & Burlington, VT. Open mid-May through mid-Oct. Phone: (802) 864-9804.

WELCOME

**SEE AD LAKE CHAMPLAIN, VT PAGE 853**

PORT KENT—Continued on next page

PORT KENT—Continued

**Yogi Bear's Jellystone Park**—Secluded CAMPGROUND with rustic, shaded sites. *From Port Kent: Go 1/2 mi W on Hwy 373.* ◇◇FACILITIES: 127 sites, 97 full hookups, 10 water & elec (15 & 30 amp receptacles), 20 no hookups, seasonal sites, tenting available, sewage disposal, laundry, public phone, limited grocery store, LP gas refill by weight, ice, fire rings, wood. ◇◇◇RECREATION: rec room/area, pavilion, swim pool, playground, 2 shuffleboard courts, planned group activities (weekends only), hiking trails, volleyball. Open May 15 through Oct 15. Rates available upon request. No refunds. Phone: (518) 834-9011.

## POTTER—E-4

**Flint Creek Campgrounds**—CAMPGROUND with some shady, mostly open, level sites in a rural area. *From jct Hwy 247 & Hwy 364: Go 1/2 mi SE on Hwy 364, then 1 1/2 mi W on Phelps Rd.* ◇◇FACILITIES: 133 sites, most common site width 50 feet, 110 full hookups, 7 water & elec (20 & 30 amp receptacles), 16 no hookups, seasonal sites, 22 pull-thrus, tenting available, sewage disposal, laundry, public phone, ice, tables, fire rings, wood. ◇◇◇RECREATION: rec hall, swim pool, pond/stream fishing, mini-golf ($), playground, planned group activities (weekends only), recreation director, badminton, sports field, horseshoes, hiking trails, volleyball. Open May 1 through Sep 30. Rate in 1995 $14-15 for 4 persons. Phone: (716) 554-3567.

## POTTERSVILLE—C-9

EAGLE POINT CAMPGROUND (Adirondack State Forest)—*From town: Go 2 mi N on Hwy 9.* FACILITIES: 72 sites, 72 no hookups, tenting available, handicap restroom facilities, sewage disposal, tables. RECREATION: lake swimming, boating, canoeing, ramp, lake fishing. Open mid May through Labor Day. Phone: (518) 494-2220.

**Ideal Campground**—Riverside with grassy, level, open & shaded sites. *N'bound: From I-87 (Northway exit 26): Go 1/4 mi S on Valley Farm Rd. S'bound From I-87 (Northway exit 26): Go 1 1/4 mi S on Hwy 9, then 1/4 mi E & S on Valley Farm Rd.* ◇◇◇FACILITIES: 68 sites, most common site width 30 feet, 30 full hookups, 25 water & elec (20 & 30 amp receptacles), 13 no hookups, seasonal sites, 56 pull-thrus, tenting available, sewage disposal, public phone, ice, tables, fire rings, wood. ◇◇RECREATION: rec hall, river swimming, boating, canoeing, ramp, dock, 2 row/2 canoe boat rentals, river/stream fishing, playground, horseshoes, volleyball. Open May 15 through Oct 15. Rate in 1995 $17 for 2 persons. Member of ARVC; CONY. Phone: (518) 494-2096.

POTTERSVILLE—Continued

**WAKONDA FAMILY CAMPGROUND**—Wooded sites at a lakeside location in a mountain setting. *From jct I-87 (Northway exit 26 Pottersville): Northbound: Go 3/4 mi N onHwy 9, then 1 3/4 mi E & S on River Rd. Southbound: Go 800 feet S on Hwy 9,then 1 3/4 mi E & S on River Rd.*

◇◇◇FACILITIES: 140 sites, most common site width 30 feet, 12 full hookups, 128 water & elec (15,20 & 30 amp receptacles), seasonal sites, 24 pull-thrus, a/c allowed ($), heater allowed ($), tenting available, cabins, RV storage, sewage disposal, laundry, public phone, limited grocery store, RV supplies, ice, tables, fire rings, grills, wood.

◇◇◇◇◇RECREATION: rec hall, rec room/area, coin games, lake swimming, boating, canoeing, dock, 6 row/9 canoe boat rentals, lake/river fishing, basketball hoop, playground, planned group activities, movies, recreation director, 4 tennis courts, sports field, horseshoes, hiking trails, volleyball.

Open Memorial Day through Oct 15. Rate in 1995 $23-26 for 2 persons. Discover/Master Card/Visa accepted. Phone: (518) 494-2610.

**SEE AD LAKE GEORGE PAGE 615**

## POUGHKEEPSIE—A-2

MILLS-NORRIE STATE PARK—*From town: Go 9 mi N on US 9.* FACILITIES: 56 sites, 56 no hookups, tenting available, sewage disposal, tables. RECREATION: boating, canoeing, ramp, river fishing, playground, hiking trails. No pets. Open mid May through late Oct. Phone: (914) 889-4646.

## PRATTSBURGH—E-4

**Wagon Wheel Campground**—Rolling, mountain-view CAMPGROUND with level, grassy sites. *From center of the village at jct Hwy 53 & CR 74: Go 1 3/4 mi E on CR 74, then 1/4 mi S on gravel road.* ◇◇FACILITIES: 95 sites, most common site width 35 feet, 95 water & elec (15 amp receptacles), seasonal sites, 12 pull-thrus, tenting available, sewage disposal, laundry, public phone, limited grocery store, LP gas refill by weight, ice, tables, fire rings, wood. ◇◇◇RECREATION: rec hall, rec room/area, swim pool, pond fishing, playground, planned group activities (weekends only), badminton, sports field, horseshoes, hiking trails, volleyball. Open May 1 through Oct 15. Rate in 1995 $15-17 for 2 persons. Member of ARVC; CONY. Phone: (607) 522-3270. FCRV 10% discount.

## PULASKI—D-6

**Bear's Sleepy Hollow RV Park**—Sunny & shaded, grassy sites at a streamside CAMPGROUND. *From jct Hwy 13 & Hwy 3: Go 1 1/2 mi S on Hwy 3.* ◇◇FACILITIES: 66 sites, most common site width 40 feet, 31 full hookups, 3 water & elec (20 & 30 amp receptacles), 20 no hookups, seasonal sites, tenting available, sewage disposal, laundry, public phone, ice, tables, fire rings, wood. ◇◇RECREATION: canoeing, stream fishing, horseshoes, volleyball. Open Apr 15 through Oct 27. Rate in 1995 $14-18 for 2 persons. Phone: (315) 298-5560.

**BRENNAN BEACH RV PARK**—CAMPGROUND on Lake Ontario with lakeside, wooded and open sites. *From jct Hwy 13 & Hwy 3: Go 1 mi N on Hwy 3, then follow signs 1/2 mi W on entry road.*

◇◇◇FACILITIES: 1400 sites, most common site width 40 feet, 1380 full hookups, 20 water & elec (20 & 30 amp receptacles), seasonal sites, 150 pull-thrus, a/c allowed, heater allowed, phone hookups, tenting available, RV rentals, handicap restroom facilities, sewage disposal, public phone, limited grocery store, RV supplies, LP gas refill by weight/by meter, ice, tables, patios, fire rings, wood, traffic control gate.

◇◇◇◇◇RECREATION: rec hall, rec room/area, coin games, 2 swim pools, wading pool, lake swimming, boating, canoeing, water skiing, lake/stream fishing, fishing guides, mini-golf ($), basketball hoop, playground, 4 shuffleboard courts, planned group activities, recreation director, 2 tennis courts, sports field, horseshoes, volleyball.

Open May 1 through Oct 15. Rate in 1995 $20-25 for 2 persons. Discover/Master Card/Visa accepted. Member of ARVC; CONY. Phone: (315) 298-2242.

**SEE AD THIS PAGE**

SELKIRK SHORES STATE PARK—*From town: Go 3 mi W on Hwy 3.* FACILITIES: 149 sites, 92 elec, 57 no hookups, tenting available, handicap restroom facilities, sewage disposal, public phone, grocery store, ice, tables. RECREATION: rec hall, lake swimming, boating, canoeing, ramp, lake fishing, playground, hiking trails. Open late Apr through mid Oct. Phone: (315) 298-5737.

## RANDOLPH—F-2

**JJ'S POPE HAVEN CAMPGROUND**—Level, open & shaded sites with grass at a hilltop location. *From jct Hwy 17 (exit 16) & Hwy 394: Go 1 1/2 mi NE on Hwy 394, then 3 1/2 mi N on Hwy 241.*

◇◇◇FACILITIES: 130 sites, most common site width 45 feet, 130 water & elec (20 & 30 amp receptacles), seasonal sites, 10 pull-thrus, a/c allowed ($), heater allowed ($), tenting available, group sites for tents/RVs, RV storage, marine toilets, sewage disposal, laundry, public phone, limited grocery store, RV supplies, LP gas refill by weight/by meter, ice, tables, fire rings, wood.

◇◇◇RECREATION: rec room/area, pavilion, coin games, pond swimming, pond fishing, playground, planned group activities (weekends only), badminton, sports field, horseshoes, hiking trails, volleyball.

Open May 1 through Columbus Day. Rate in 1995 $16 for 2 persons. No refunds. Master Card/Visa accepted. Member of ARVC;CONY. Phone: (716) 358-4900.

**SEE AD TRAVEL SECTION PAGE 585**

## RAQUETTE LAKE—C-8

BROWN TRACT POND CAMPGROUND (Adirondack State Forest)—*From business center: Go 2 mi NW on Town Rd.* FACILITIES: 90 sites, 30 ft. max RV length, 90 no hookups, tenting available, sewage disposal, tables. RECREATION: pond swimming, boating, no motors, canoeing, ramp, pond fishing, hiking trails. Open mid May through Labor Day. No showers. Phone: (315) 354-4412.

EIGHTH LAKE (Adirondack State Forest)—*From town: Go 5 mi W on Hwy 28.* FACILITIES: 126 sites, 126 no hookups, tenting available, handicap restroom facilities, sewage disposal, tables. RECREATION: lake swimming, boating, canoeing, ramp, lake fishing, hiking trails. Open mid Apr through mid Nov. Phone: (315) 354-4120.

GOLDEN BEACH (Adirondack State Forest)—*From town: Go 3 mi N on Hwy 28.* FACILITIES: 205 sites, 30 ft. max RV length, 205 no hookups, tenting available, handicap restroom facilities, sewage disposal, tables. RECREATION: lake swimming, boating, canoeing, ramp, lake fishing, hiking trails. Open mid May through Labor Day. Phone: (315) 354-4230.

## REXFORD—E-9

✱ **HYDE'S RV AND BOATS**—*From jct I-87 (exit 9) & Hwy 146: Go 6 mi W on Hwy 146, then 3/4 mi N on Blue Barns Rd.* SALES: travel trailers, park models, truck campers, 5th wheels, fold-down camping trailers. SERVICES: RV appliance mechanic full-time, LP gas refill by weight/by meter, RV rentals, RV storage, sells parts/accessories, installs hitches. Open all year. Discover/Master Card/Visa accepted. Phone: (518) 399-2880.

**SEE AD SARATOGA SPRINGS PAGE 631**

## RHINEBECK—F-9

**INTERLAKE FARM CAMPGROUND & TRAILER SALES**—Rural mountainview park with wooded and open sites. *From jct US 9 & Hwy 9G in Rhinebeck: Go 3 1/2 mi S on Hwy 9G, then 3 1/2 mi E on Slate Quarry Hill Rd (CR 19), then 3/10 mi S on Lake Drive.*

◈◈◈FACILITIES: 159 sites, most common site width 30 feet, 27 full hookups, 116 water & elec, 3 elec (15,20 & 30 amp receptacles), 13 no hookups, seasonal sites, 5 pull-thrus, a/c allowed ($), heater allowed ($), phone hookups, tenting available, group sites for tents/RVs, RV rentals, RV storage, sewage disposal, laundry, public phone, limited grocery store, RV supplies, ice, tables, fire rings, wood.

◈◈◈◈RECREATION: rec hall, coin games, swim pool, wading pool, boating, electric motors only, canoeing, 6 row boat rentals, lake/pond fishing, basketball hoop, playground, planned group activities (weekends only), badminton, horseshoes, volleyball.

Open Apr 15 through Oct 15. Rate in 1995 $20-25.50 for 2 persons. Discover/Master Card/Visa accepted. Member of ARVC; CONY. Phone: (914) 266-5387.

**SEE AD THIS PAGE**

✲ **INTERLAKE TRAILER SALES**—*From jct US 9 & Hwy 9G in Rhinebeck: Go 3 1/2 mi S on HWy 9G, then 3 1/2 mi E on Slate Quarry Hill Rd (CR 19), then 3/10 mi S on Lake Dr.* SALES: travel trailers, 5th wheels. SERVICES: RV appliance mechanic full-time, RV storage. Open all year. Discover/Master Card/Visa accepted. Phone: (914) 266-5387.

**SEE AD THIS PAGE**

## RIVERHEAD—B-4

INDIAN ISLAND PARK (Suffolk County Park)—*From jct Hwy 24 & CR 105: Go E on CR 105 past golf course.* FACILITIES: 100 sites, 100 no hookups, tenting available, handicap restroom facilities, sewage disposal, public phone, tables. RECREATION: salt water fishing, playground, sports field, hiking trails. Open all year. Facilities fully operational Apr 21 through Sep 18. Open weekends only Sep 22-Apr 17. Phone: (516) 852-3232.

## ROCHESTER—D-4

**CHEERFUL VALLEY CAMPGROUND**—*From Rochester: Take I-90 (Thruway) east to exit 42, then turn left (north on Hwy 14) for 1/2 mi.*
**SEE PRIMARY LISTING AT PHELPS AND AD THIS PAGE**

**FROST RIDGE CAMPGROUND**—*From Rochester 490W to Rt 19, then 1/2 mi S on Hwy 19, then 1 mi E on North Rd, then 1/2 mi S on Conlon Rd.*
**SEE PRIMARY LISTING AT LEROY AND AD THIS PAGE**

✲ **GARY JOHNSTON'S RV CENTER**—*From Rochester: Take Hwy 31 E to Route 21N, or take Hwy 104 E to Route 21 S.*
**SEE PRIMARY LISTING AT PALMYRA AND AD THIS PAGE**

**SOUTHWOODS RV RESORT**—*From jct Rochester I-490 W (exit 2) & Hwy 262: Go 5 mi W on Hwy 262.*
**SEE PRIMARY LISTING AT BYRON AND AD THIS PAGE**

**SUGAR CREEK GLEN CAMPGROUND**—*Just 1 hour from Rochester. Take I-390 S to exit 4, then 500 feet S on Hwy 36, then 5 mi SW on Poag's Hole Rd.*
**SEE PRIMARY LISTING AT DANSVILLE AND AD DANSVILLE PAGE 601**

ROCHESTER—Continued on next page

**He who is slowest in making a promise is most faithful in performance.**

***Jean Jacques Rousseau***

**My grandfather once told me that there were two kinds of people: those who do the work and those who take the credit. He told me to try to be in the first group; there was much less competition.** ***Indira Gandhi***

ROCHESTER—Continued

**TUMBLE HILL CAMPGROUND**—*From jct I-90 & I-390: Go about 50 mi S on I-390 (exit 2), then 1 mi SE on Hwy 415, then 1/2 mi N on Hwy 371, then 1/2 mi W on Atlanta Back Rd.*

WELCOME

**SEE PRIMARY LISTING AT COHOCTON AND AD CORNING PAGE 600**

## ROME—D-7

DELTA LAKE STATE PARK—*From town: Go 6 mi N on Hwy 46.* FACILITIES: 101 sites, 101 no hookups, tenting available, handicap restroom facilities, sewage disposal, tables, wood. RECREATION: lake swimming, boating, canoeing, ramp, lake fishing, playground, hiking trails. Open May 1 through Oct 9. Phone: (315) 337-4670.

MILITARY PARK (Griffiss AFB FAMCAMP)—*Off jct Hwy 46 & Hwy 365. On base.* FACILITIES: 10 sites, 10 water & elec, tenting available, sewage disposal, public phone, LP gas refill by weight/by meter, tables, grills. RECREATION: pavilion, swim pool (indoor) (heated) ($), river fishing, playground, planned group activities, recreation director, sports field, horseshoes, hiking trails, volleyball. Open May 1 through Oct 15. Reservations not accepted. No showers. Phone: (315) 330-2848.

## ROSCOE—F-8

**RUSSELL BROOK CAMPSITE**—CAMPGROUND with wooded & semi-shaded sites. *WESTBOUND: From Hwy 17 (Quickway) take exit 93 Cooks Falls: Go 1/10 mi W on Old Hwy 17, then 3/4 mi N on Russell Brook Rd. EASTBOUND: From Hwy 17 (Quickway) take exit 92: Go 1 1/2 mi SE on Old Hwy 17, then 3/4 mi N on Russell Brook Rd.*

WELCOME

◆◆◆FACILITIES: 140 sites, most common site width 40 feet, 140 water & elec (20 amp receptacles), seasonal sites, a/c not allowed, heater not allowed, tenting available, group sites for tents, RV rentals, sewage disposal, laundry, public phone, grocery store, RV supplies, LP gas refill by weight, ice, tables, fire rings, wood.

◆◆◆◆RECREATION: rec hall, rec room/area, coin games, swim pool, pond/stream fishing, basketball hoop, playground, planned group activities (weekends only), horseshoes, hiking trails.

Open May 1 through Dec 3. RV's over 30 feet by reservations only. Rate in 1995 $20-21 for 2 persons. Master Card/Visa accepted. Member of ARVC; CONY. Phone: (607) 498-5416.
**SEE AD THIS PAGE**

## ROSEBOOM—E-8

**Belvedere Lake Campground**—Open, grassy sites and prepared, shaded sites in a rural area. *From jct Hwy 166 & Hwy 165: Go 1/2 mi SE on Hwy 165, then 1/8 mi E on paved road, then 3/4 mi N following signs.* ◆◆◆FACILITIES: 160 sites, most common site width 35 feet, 160 full hookups, (20 & 30 amp receptacles), seasonal sites, tenting available, handicap restroom facilities, sewage disposal, laundry, public phone, limited grocery store, ice, tables, fire rings, wood. ◆◆◆◆RECREATION: rec hall, rec room/area, lake swimming, 8 row/2 pedal boat rentals, lake fishing, mini-golf ($), 2 tennis courts, badminton, sports field, horseshoes, hiking trails, volleyball. Recreation open to the public. Open May 1 through Nov 1. Rate in 1995 $18-20 for 2 persons. Member of ARVC; CONY. Phone: (607) 264-8182.

**If you think Woodall Ratings mean Good, Better, Best . . .**
***THINK AGAIN***
**See the "How to Use" pages (following the glossy pages) in the front of this Directory for an explanation of our Rating System**

NY **STATE BIRD: BLUEBIRD** NY

## SACKETS HARBOR—C-6

**ALLEN'S BOAT LIVERY MARINA AND CAMPGROUND**—Sunny, grassy sites and wooded sites in a lakeside setting. *From jct I-81 (exit 45) & Hwy 3: Go 9 1/2 mi W on Hwy 3.*

◆◆FACILITIES: 215 sites, most common site width 30 feet, 155 full hookups, 35 water & elec (15,20 & 30 amp receptacles), 25 no hookups, seasonal sites, a/c allowed ($), heater allowed ($), phone hookups, tenting available, RV rentals, sewage disposal, public phone, grocery store, RV supplies, LP gas refill by weight/by meter, marine gas, ice, tables, fire rings, wood.

◆◆◆RECREATION: lake swimming, boating, canoeing, ramp, dock, 6 row/2 canoe/6 motor boat rentals, water skiing, lake/stream fishing, fishing guides, basketball hoop, playground, volleyball. Recreation open to the public.

Open May 1 through Oct 15. Rate in 1995 $14-16 for 4 persons. Master Card/Visa accepted. Phone: (315) 646-2486.

**SEE AD WATERTOWN PAGE 635**

WESCOTT BEACH STATE PARK—*From town: Go 2 mi W on Hwy 3.* FACILITIES: 209 sites, 85 elec, 124 no hookups, tenting available, handicap restroom facilities, sewage disposal, ice, tables. RECREATION: lake swimming, boating, canoeing, ramp, lake fishing, playground, hiking trails. Recreation open to the public. Open early May through Oct 6. Phone: (315) 646-2239.

## ST. JOHNSVILLE—E-8

**Crystal Grove Campsite**—Wooded, streamside CAMPGROUND with wooded sites. *From center of village at jct Hwy 5 & Division St: Go 3/4 mi N on Division St, then 3 3/4 mi NE on Lassellville Rd (CR 114).* ◆◆◆FACILITIES: 33 sites, most common site width 40 feet, 23 water & elec (15 & 30 amp receptacles), 10 no hookups, tenting available, sewage disposal, public phone, limited grocery store, ice, tables, fire rings, grills, wood. ◆◆RECREATION: pavilion, stream fishing, playground, badminton, sports field, horseshoes, volleyball. Open Apr 15 through Oct 15. Rate in 1995 $16-18 for 4 persons. Phone: (518) 568-2914.

## SALAMANCA—F-2

ALLEGANY STATE PARK (Quaker Area)—*From Hwy 17 (Exit 18): Go S on Hwy 280, then E on Park Rd 3.* FACILITIES: 189 sites, 94 elec, 95 no hookups, tenting available, handicap restroom facilities, sewage disposal, limited grocery store, ice, tables, wood. RECREATION: lake swimming, canoeing, ramp, fishing, playground, tennis court, hiking trails. Open late May through early Sep. Phone: (716) 354-2182.

ALLEGANY STATE PARK (Red House Area)—*From Hwy 17 (Exit 19): Go E on Hwy 2, then S on Hwy 1.* FACILITIES: 134 sites, 67 elec, 67 no hookups, tenting available, handicap restroom facilities, sewage disposal, laundry, grocery store, ice, tables, wood. RECREATION: lake swimming, boating, no motors, canoeing, ramp, lake fishing, playground, tennis court, hiking trails. Open late Mar through early Dec. Phone: (716) 354-9121.

**CATTARAUGUS-ALLEGANY COUNTY TOURIST BUREAU**—*From jct Hwy 17 & Hwy 417: Go 1/2 mi N on Hwy 417 (at the caboose).* Tourist information center for Cattaraugus & Allegany counties. In the foothills of the Allegany Mountains, outdoor recreation flourishes in all seasons. Open all year. Mon-Fri 10 a.m. - 5 p.m. Sat & Sun 10 a.m. - 3 p.m. Phone: (714) 938-9111.

**SEE AD TRAVEL SECTION PAGE 585**

## SARANAC—B-9

**Baker's Acres**—CAMPGROUND with grassy, riverside sites. *From jct I-87 (Adirondack Northway exit 37) & Hwy 3: Go 14 mi W on Hwy 3.* ◆◆FACILITIES: 53 sites, 30 full hookups, 20 water & elec (15 amp receptacles), 3 no hookups, seasonal sites, 20 pull-thrus, tenting available, sewage disposal, tables, fire rings, wood.

◆◆◆RECREATION: swim pool (heated), boating, canoeing, river fishing, playground. Open May 1 through Oct 1. Rate in 1995 $15 for 2 persons. Member of ARVC; CONY. Phone: (518) 293-6471.



## SARANAC LAKE—B-9

**Junction Campsite**—Open and shaded, grassy sites in a secluded CAMPGROUND in the Adirondack Mountains. *From west jct Hwy 3 & Hwy 86: Go 4 1/2 mi W on Hwy 86, then 4 mi SW on Hwy 186, then 1/4 mi N on Hwy 30, then 1/4 mi E on private road.* ◆◆◆FACILITIES: 31 sites, most common site width 50 feet, 24 full hookups, (20 & 30 amp receptacles), 7 no hookups, tenting available, sewage disposal, laundry, public phone, ice, tables, fire rings, wood. ◆◆RECREATION: badminton, horseshoes, hiking trails, volleyball. Open all year. Facilities fully operational May 1 through Oct 31. Rate in 1995 $15-18 for 4 persons. Phone: (518) 891-1819.

MEADOWBROOK CAMPGROUND (Adirondack State Forest)—*From town: Go 4 mi E on Hwy 86.* FACILITIES: 62 sites, 25 ft. max RV length, 62 no hookups, tenting available, handicap restroom facilities, sewage disposal, tables. RECREATION: fishing, playground. Open mid May through Labor Day. Phone: (518) 891-4351.

## SARATOGA SPRINGS—D-9

***See listings at Albany and Rex Pond***

## SAUGERTIES—F-9

**Blue Mountain Campground**—Wooded sites convenient to a major highway. *From jct I-87 & Hwy 32: Go 5 mi N on Hwy 32.* ◆◆FACILITIES: 55 sites, most common site width 20 feet, 35 ft. max RV length, 15 full hookups, 15 water & elec (15 amp receptacles), 25 no hookups, seasonal sites, 4 pull-thrus, tenting available, sewage disposal, public phone, ice, tables, fire rings, wood. ◆RECREATION: sports field, horseshoes, volleyball. Open May 15 through Oct 15. Rate in 1995 $18-24 for 2 persons. Phone: (914) 246-5208.

**KOA-SAUGERTIES/WOODSTOCK**—Mountainview CAMPGROUND with wooded sites. *N'bound: From I-87 (Thruway exit 20): Go 2 1/2 mi W on Hwy 212. S'bound: From jct I-87 (exit 20-Saugerties) & Hwy 32: Go 1/8 mi S on Hwy 32, then 2 1/2 mi W on Hwy 212.*

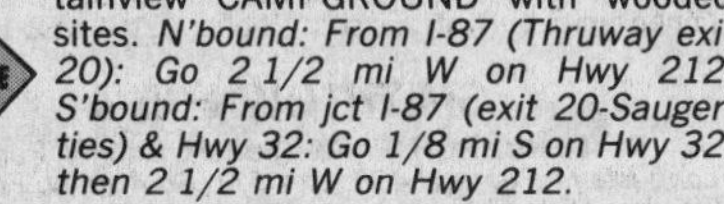

◆◆◆FACILITIES: 75 sites, most common site width 25 feet, 14 full hookups, 41 water & elec (15 & 30 amp receptacles), 20 no hookups, 11 pull-thrus, a/c allowed ($), heater allowed ($), cable TV, tenting available, cabins, RV storage, sewage disposal, laundry, public phone, grocery store, RV supplies, LP gas refill by weight/by meter, ice, tables, fire rings, wood.

◆◆◆RECREATION: rec room/area, pavilion, coin games, swim pool, pond fishing, basketball hoop, playground, planned group activities (weekends only), movies.

Open Apr 1 through Nov 1. Rate in 1995 $21-26 for 2 persons. Reservations recommended all year.



SAUGERTIES—Continued
KOA-SAUGERTIES/WOODSTOCK—Continued

American Express/Discover/Master Card/Visa accepted. Member of ARVC; CONY. Phone: (914) 246-4089. KOA 10% value card discount.

**SEE AD THIS PAGE AND AD FRONT OF BOOK PAGES 68 AND 69**

**RIP VAN WINKLE CAMPGROUND**—Wooded sites in a rural area. *S'bound from I-87 (exit 20-Saugerties) & Hwy 32: Go 1/8 mi S on Hwy 32, 2 mi W on Hwy 212, then 1/2 mi N at Centerville Fork on CR 35. N'bound from jct I-87 (exit 20-Saugerties) & Hwy 212: Go 2 mi W on Hwy 212, then 1/2 mi N at Centerville Fork on CR 35.*

◆◆◆FACILITIES: 125 sites, most common site width 60 feet, 33 full hookups, 50 water & elec (20 & 30 amp receptacles), 42 no hookups, seasonal sites, 37 pull-thrus, a/c allowed ($), heater allowed ($), tenting available, RV storage, sewage disposal, laundry, public phone, limited grocery store, RV supplies, LP gas refill by weight/by meter, ice, tables, fire rings, wood, traffic control gate.

◆◆◆RECREATION: river swimming, river fishing, basketball hoop, playground, badminton, sports field, horseshoes, hiking trails, volleyball.

Open mid May through Sep 30. Rate in 1995 $20.50-24.90 for 2 persons. Reservations recommended on weekends. Master Card/Visa accepted. Member of ARVC; CONY. Phone: (914) 246-8114.

**SEE AD THIS PAGE**

NY Named in honor of the Duke of York NY

## SCHENECTADY—E-9

**ARROWHEAD MARINA & RV PARK**—Developed CAMPGROUND on the Mohawk River with sunny & shaded sites. *From jct I-90 (exit 26) & Hwy 5S: Go 3 mi W on Hwy 5S, then 1/4 mi N on Hwy 103, then 2 1/2 mi E on Hwy 5, then 1/4 mi S on Van Buren Lane (follow signs).*

◆◆◆◆FACILITIES: 68 sites, most common site width 35 feet, 34 full hookups, 31 water & elec (20 & 30 amp receptacles), 3 no hookups, seasonal sites, 10 pull-thrus, a/c allowed ($), heater allowed ($), phone hookups, tenting available, sewage disposal, laundry, public phone, RV supplies, marine gas, ice, tables, patios, fire rings, wood.

◆◆RECREATION: boating, canoeing, ramp, dock, water skiing, river fishing, fishing guides, badminton, horseshoes, volleyball. Recreation open to the public.

Open May 15 through Oct 15. Rate in 1995 $12-14 per family. Member of ARVC; CONY. Phone: (518) 382-8966.

**SEE AD THIS PAGE**

## SCHROON LAKE—C-9

SHARP BRIDGE CAMPGROUND (Adirondack State Forest)—*From town: Go 15 mi N on Hwy 9.* FACILITIES: 40 sites, 40 no hookups, tenting available, non-flush toilets, handicap restroom facilities, sewage disposal, tables. RECREATION: river fishing, playground, hiking trails. Open mid May through Labor Day. Phone: (518) 532-7538.

## SCHUYLER FALLS—B-9

MACOMB RESERVATION STATE PARK—*From the center of the village at jct Hwy 22B & Norrisville Rd: Go 2 mi W on Norrisville Rd.* FACILITIES: 175 sites, 175 no hookups, tenting available, handicap restroom facilities, sewage disposal, public phone, tables. RECREATION: rec hall, river swimming, canoeing, river fishing, playground, hiking trails. Open late May through early Sep. Phone: (518) 643-9952.

## SCHUYLERVILLE—D-9

**SCHUYLER YACHT BASIN**—Open & shaded, grassy sites on the Hudson River. *From I-87 (exit 15): Go 1/4 mi E on Hwy 50, then 1 1/4 mi S on Weibel, then 9 mi E on Hwy 29 (west side of river).*

FACILITIES: 23 sites, 8 water & elec (15 amp receptacles), 15 no hookups, a/c not allowed, heater not allowed, tenting available, group sites for tents, laundry, public phone, marine gas, ice, grills.

RECREATION: river swimming, boating, canoeing, dock, water skiing.

Open Apr 15 through Oct 31. Rate in 1995 $12 for 2 persons. American Express/Discover/Master Card/Visa accepted. Phone: (518) 695-3193.

**SEE AD SARATOGA SPRINGS PAGE 631**



## SENECA FALLS—E-5

CAYUGA LAKE STATE PARK—*From town: Go 3 mi E on Bayard St, then S on Hwy 89.* FACILITIES: 286 sites, 36 elec, 250 no hookups, tenting available, handicap restroom facilities, sewage disposal, public phone, tables. RECREATION: pavilion, lake swimming, boating, canoeing, ramp, lake fishing, playground, hiking trails. Open early May through late Oct. Phone: (315) 568-5163.

**OAK ORCHARD MARINA & CAMPGROUND**—Grassy sites in a wooded, riverside location. *From jct Hwy 5/US 20 & Hwy 89: Go 4 mi N on Hwy 89.*

◆◆FACILITIES: 75 sites, most common site width 40 feet, 8 full hookups, 62 water & elec (15,20 & 30 amp receptacles), 5 no hookups, seasonal sites, a/c allowed ($), heater allowed ($), phone hookups, tenting available, group sites for tents, cabins, sewage disposal, laundry, limited grocery store, RV supplies, LP gas refill by weight, ice, tables, fire rings, wood.

◆◆RECREATION: rec room/area, coin games, boating, canoeing, 3 row boat rentals, river fishing, badminton, horseshoes, hiking trails, volleyball.

Open May 1 through Oct 1. Rate in 1995 $12.50-20 for 4 persons. Member of ARVC; CONY. Phone: (315) 365-3000.

**SEE AD THIS PAGE**

## SHIRLEY—C-4

SMITH POINT PARK (Suffolk County Park)—*From Long Island Expwy (I-495, exit 68): Go S on William Floyd Pkwy to the end on Fire Island.* FACILITIES: 145 sites, 145 no hookups, tenting available, handicap restroom facilities, sewage disposal, public phone, tables. RECREATION: salt water swimming, salt water fishing, playground, hiking trails. Open all year. Facilities fully operational Apr through Oct. Self-contained units only off season. Phone: (516) 852-1315.

## SMITHTOWN—B-4

BLYDENBURGH PARK (Suffolk County Park)—*From Long Island Expwy (I-495, exit 57): Go 4 mi N.* FACILITIES: 50 sites, 50 no hookups, tenting available, handicap restroom facilities, sewage disposal, tables. RECREATION: boating, electric motors only, dock, row boat rentals, pond fishing, playground, sports field, hiking trails. Open all year. Facilities fully operational Apr 21 through Sep 18. Open weekends only Sep 22-Apr 17. Phone: (516) 854-3713.

## SODUS POINT—D-5

**Idlewood on the Lake**—Lakeside CAMPGROUND with shaded sites. *From south town limits: Go 1 1/4 mi N on Hwy 14, then 1 mi on Bay St (Lake Rd).* ◆FACILITIES: 68 sites, 50 full hookups, 18 water & elec (20 & 30 amp receptacles), seasonal sites, 7 pull-thrus, tenting available, laundry, public phone, limited grocery store, LP gas refill by weight/by meter, ice, tables, fire rings, wood. ◆RECREATION: rec room/area, lake fishing. Open all year. Facilities fully operational Mar 15 through Oct 15. Rate in 1995 $18-22 for 4 persons. Phone: (315) 483-8649.

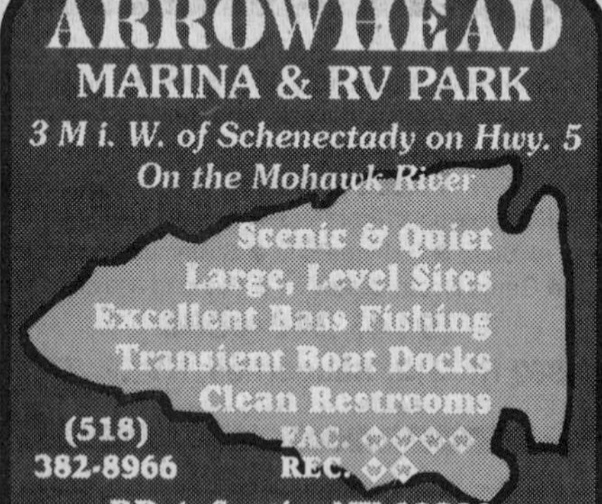

## SOUTH COLTON—B-8

HIGBEY FLOW STATE PARK—*From town: Go 1 1/2 mi W of Hwy 56 on Coldbrook.* FACILITIES: 143 sites, 43 elec, 100 no hookups, tenting available, handicap restroom facilities, sewage disposal, public phone, tables. RECREATION: lake swimming, boating, canoeing, ramp, river fishing, playground, hiking trails. Open late May through early Sep. Phone: (315) 262-2880.

## SPRINGWATER—E-4

**Holiday Hill Campground**—Semi-wooded park with shaded & open sites. *From jct I-390 (exit 3) & Hwy 15: Go 4 mi N on Hwy 15, then 1/2 mi E on Walker Rd, then 3 mi NW on Strutt St, then 1/2 mi S on Marvin Hill Rd.* ◆◆◆FACILITIES: 160 sites, most common site width 40 feet, 151 water & elec (15,20 & 30 amp receptacles), 9 no hookups, seasonal sites, tenting available, sewage disposal, laundry, public phone, grocery store, ice, tables, fire rings, wood. ◆◆◆◆RECREATION: rec hall, rec room/area, pavilion, swim pool, pond fishing, mini-golf ($), playground, planned group activities (weekends only), recreation director, badminton, sports field, horseshoes, hiking trails, volleyball. Open May 1 through Columbus Day. Rate in 1995 $19-22 per family. Member of ARVC;CONY. Phone: (716) 669-2600.

## STONY POINT—B-2

BEAVER POND CAMPGROUND (Harriman State Park)—*5 mi W of town on Gate Hill Rd.* FACILITIES: 52 sites, 17 ft. max RV length, 52 no hookups, tenting available, handicap restroom facilities, sewage disposal, public phone, tables. RECREATION: lake swimming, boating, no motors, canoeing, ramp, fishing, hiking trails. No pets. Open mid Apr through early Oct. Phone: (914) 947-2792.

## SYLVAN BEACH—D-6

**The Landing Campground**—Riverside park with shaded and open sites. *From jct Hwy 49 & Hwy 13: Go 2 1/4 mi S on Hwy 13, then 2 1/4 mi NE on Vienna Rd, then 100 feet E on Kellogg Rd.* ◆◆◆FACILITIES: 94 sites, most common site width 30 feet, 74 full hookups, 20 water & elec (15,20 & 30 amp receptacles), seasonal sites, tenting available, sewage disposal, laundry, public phone, limited grocery store, ice, tables, fire rings, wood. ◆◆◆RECREATION: rec room/area, pavilion, river swimming, boating, canoeing, ramp, 2 row/4 canoe/2 pedal boat rentals, river fishing, mini-golf ($), playground, planned group activities (weekends only), badminton, horseshoes, volleyball. Open May 1 through Oct 1. Rate in 1995 $24 for 2 persons. Member of ARVC; CONY. Phone: (315) 762-5572.

**TA-GA-SOKE CAMPGROUNDS**—Riverside with open or shaded sites. *From jct I-90 (exit 34) & Hwy 13 N: Go 9 mi N, then 2 1/2 mi NE on Vienna Rd, then 100 feet E on Higginsville Rd.*

◆◆◆FACILITIES: 150 sites, most common site width 30 feet, 135 water & elec (15 & 30 amp receptacles), 15 no hookups, seasonal sites, 20 pull-thrus, a/c allowed, heater allowed, tenting available, group sites for tents/RVs, cabins, non-flush/marine toilets, sewage disposal, laundry, limited grocery store, RV supplies, LP gas refill by weight/by meter, ice, tables, fire rings, wood, traffic control gate.

◆◆◆RECREATION: rec hall, pavilion, coin games, river swimming, boating, canoeing, ramp, dock, 2 row/1 canoe/4 pedal boat rentals, river fishing, basketball hoop, playground, planned group activities (weekends only), movies, sports field, horseshoes, volleyball.

Open May 1 through mid Oct. Rate in 1995 $17-20 per family. No refunds. Discover/Master Card/Visa accepted. Member of ARVC; CONY. Phone: (800) 831-1744.

**SEE AD THIS PAGE**

## SYRACUSE—D-6

✱ **FOLAND SALES**—*From jct I-690 & Hwy 635: Go 2 mi N on Hwy 635 (Thompson Rd), then 1/4 mi W on Hwy 298 (around Carrier Circle), then 1/2 mi SW on Court St, then 500 feet S on Midler Ave.* SERVICES: RV appliance mechanic full-time, LP gas refill by weight/by meter, sewage disposal, RV storage, sells parts/accessories. Open all year. Master Card/Visa accepted. Phone: (315) 463-1892.

**SEE AD THIS PAGE**

SYRACUSE—Continued on next page

SYRACUSE—Continued

**FOLAND'S TRAILER PARK**—RV SPACES in a mobile home park, adjacent to a dealership. *From jct I-690 & Hwy 635: Go 2 mi N on Hwy 635 (Thompson Rd), then 1/4 mi W on Hwy 298 (around Carrier Circle), then 1/2 mi SW on Court St, then 500 feet S on Midler Ave.*

WELCOME

FACILITIES: 15 sites, accepts full hookup units only, 15 full hookups, (15,20 & 30 amp receptacles), a/c allowed ($), heater allowed ($), RV storage, sewage disposal, LP gas refill by weight/by meter.

No tents. Open all year. Rates available upon request. Phone: (315) 463-1892.

**SEE AD PAGE 632**

**THE VILLAGE OF TURNING STONE RV PARK** —*From Syracuse jct I-481 & I-90 (exit 35): Go 23 mi E on I-90 to exit 33 (I-90 & Hwy 365), then 1 1/2 mi S on Hwy 365.* **SEE PRIMARY LISTING AT VERONA AND AD FRONT OF BOOK PAGE 28**

WELCOME

## THREE MILE BAY—C-6

LONG POINT STATE PARK (Thousand Islands Region) —*From town: Go 2 mi W on Hwy 12E, then 9 mi S on access road.* FACILITIES: 87 sites, 18 elec, 69 no hookups, tenting available, ice, tables. RECREATION: boating, canoeing, ramp, lake fishing. Open late May through mid Sep. Phone: (315) 649-5258.

## TICONDEROGA—C-10

PARADOX LAKE CAMPGROUND (Adirondack State Forest)—*From town: Go 8 mi W on Hwy 74.* FACILITIES: 58 sites, 58 no hookups, tenting available, handicap restroom facilities, sewage disposal, tables. RECREATION: lake swimming, boating, canoeing, ramp, canoe boat rentals, lake fishing, playground, hiking trails. Open mid May through mid Oct. Phone: (518) 532-7451.

PUTNAM POND CAMPSITE (Adirondack State Forest) —*From town: Go 6 mi SW on Hwy 74 & FR.* FACILITIES: 72 sites, 72 no hookups, tenting available, handicap restroom facilities, sewage disposal, tables. RECREATION: pond swimming, boating, canoeing, ramp, pond fishing, playground, hiking trails. Open mid May through Labor Day. Phone: (518) 585-7280.

ROGERS ROCK CAMPGROUND (Adirondack State Forest)—*From town: Go 7 mi SW on Hwy 9N.* FACILITIES: 321 sites, 321 no hookups, tenting available, handicap restroom facilities, sewage disposal, tables. RECREATION: lake swimming, boating, canoeing, ramp, lake fishing, playground. Open early May through mid Oct. Phone: (518) 585-6746.

## TUPPER LAKE—B-8

FISH CREEK PONDS CAMPGROUND (Adirondack State Forest)—*From town: Go 12 mi E on Hwy 30.* FACILITIES: 355 sites, 355 no hookups, tenting available, handicap restroom facilities, sewage disposal, tables. RECREATION: swimming, boating, canoeing, ramp, fishing, playground, hiking trails. Open late Apr through mid Nov. Phone: (518) 891-4560.

ROLLINS POND CAMPGROUND (Adirondack State Forest)—*From town: Go 12 mi NE on Hwy 30.* FACILITIES: 288 sites, 288 no hookups, tenting available, handicap restroom facilities, sewage disposal. RECREATION: boating, canoeing, ramp, fishing, hiking trails. Open mid May through Labor Day. Phone: (518) 891-3239.

## UNADILLA—F-7

**KOA-Unadilla/I-88/Oneonta**—Creekside CAMPGROUND with grassy, open & some shaded sites. *From jct I-88 (exit 11) & Hwy 357: Go 1/4 mi W on Hwy 357, then 2 mi NE on Covered Bridge Rd, then 1 mi S on CR 44, then 1/4 mi W on Union Church Rd.* ◆◆◆◆FACILITIES: 72 sites, most common site width 30 feet, 63 water & elec (20,30 & 50 amp receptacles), 9 no hookups, seasonal sites, 21 pull-thrus, tenting available, sewage disposal, laundry, public phone, limited grocery store, LP gas refill by weight, ice, tables, fire rings, grills, wood. ◆◆◆RECREATION: rec room/area, swim pool, 2 pedal boat rentals, pond/stream fishing, playground, badminton, sports field, horseshoes, hiking trails, volleyball. Open May 1 through Oct 15. Rate in 1995 $22-25 for 2 persons. Member of ARVC; CONY. Phone: (607) 369-9030. KOA 10% value card discount.

## UTICA—D-7

**ELMTREE CAMPSITES**—Shaded CAMPGROUND with level, grassy sites. *From I-90 (NY Thruway exit 31): Go 1 block N on Genesee St., then 5 1/2 mi E on Hwy 5.*

WELCOME

◆◆◆FACILITIES: 36 sites, most common site width 30 feet, 12 full hookups, 17 water & elec (20,30 & 50 amp receptacles), 7 no hookups, seasonal sites, 10 pull-thrus, a/c allowed ($), heater allowed ($), cable TV ($), phone hookups, tenting available, RV storage, sewage disposal, laundry, public phone, limited grocery store, RV supplies, LP gas refill by weight/by meter, ice, tables, fire rings, grills, wood.

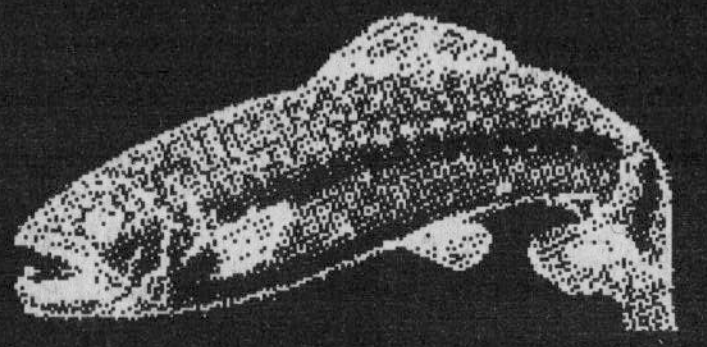

◆◆RECREATION: rec room/area, playground.

UTICA—Continued
ELM TREE CAMPSITES—Continued

Open Apr 15 through Nov 1. Rate in 1995 $15-20 for 2 persons. Member of ARVC;CONY. Phone: (315) 724-6678.

**SEE AD THIS PAGE**

**WEST CANADA CREEK CAMPSITES**—*From Utica, take Hwy 12 N, then Hwy 8 N.* **SEE PRIMARY LISTING AT POLAND AND AD THIS PAGE**

WELCOME

## VERONA—D-7

**KOA-ROME/VERONA**—Developed CAMPGROUND in a rural setting with open and shaded sites. *From jct I-90 (exit 33) & Hwy 365: Go 3 1/2 mi NE on Hwy 365, then 1 1/2 mi N on Blackman's Corner Rd.*

◆◆◆◆FACILITIES: 93 sites, 38 full hookups, 55 water & elec (20,30 & 50 amp receptacles), 25 pull-thrus, a/c allowed ($), heater allowed ($), tenting available, cabins, handicap restroom facilities, sewage disposal, laundry, public phone, grocery store, RV supplies, LP gas refill by weight/by meter, ice, tables, fire rings, grills, wood.

◆◆◆◆RECREATION: rec hall, rec room/area, pavilion, coin games, swim pool, wading pool, stream fishing, basketball hoop, playground, 2 shuffleboard courts, movies, badminton, sports field, horseshoes, hiking trails, volleyball.

Open Apr 20 through Oct 20. Rate in 1995 $21-26 for 2 persons. Discover/Master Card/Visa accepted. Member of ARVC;CONY. Phone: (315) 336-7318. KOA 10% value card discount.

**SEE AD THIS PAGE AND AD FRONT OF BOOK PAGES 68 AND 69**

**TURNING STONE CASINO**—*From jct I-90 (NY Thruway-exit 33) & Hwy 365: Go 1 mi S on Hwy 365.* Round the clock casino action with exciting table games, three restaurants, gift and smoke shop. Phone: (315) 361-7711.

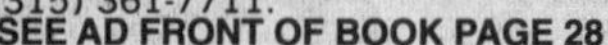

**SEE AD FRONT OF BOOK PAGE 28**

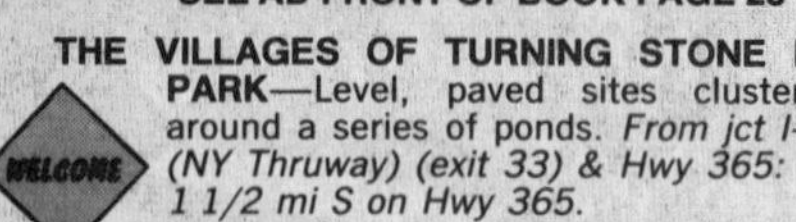

**THE VILLAGES OF TURNING STONE RV PARK**—Level, paved sites clustered around a series of ponds. *From jct I-90 (NY Thruway) (exit 33) & Hwy 365: Go 1 1/2 mi S on Hwy 365.*

◆◆◆FACILITIES: 175 sites, most common site width 40 feet, 175 full hookups, (20,30 & 50 amp receptacles), 50 pull-thrus, a/c allowed, heater allowed, cable TV, phone hookups, group sites for RVs, RV storage, handicap restroom facilities, sewage disposal, laundry, public phone, grocery store, RV supplies, LP gas refill by weight/by meter, ice, tables, fire rings, grills, wood, traffic control gate.

◆◆◆◆◆RECREATION: rec hall, rec room/area, pavilion, coin games, pond swimming, 10 pedal boat rentals, pond fishing, basketball hoop, playground, planned group activities (weekends only), movies, recreation director, tennis court, horseshoes, motorbike trails, hiking trails, volleyball, local tours.



VERONA—Continued
THE VILLAGES OF TURNING STONE RV PARK—Continued

No tents. Open May 1 through Oct 31. Rate in 1995 $25 per family. Reservations recommended all season. American Express/Master Card/Visa accepted. Phone: (800) 771-7711.

**SEE AD FRONT OF BOOK PAGE 28**

## WADDINGTON—A-7

COLES CREEK STATE PARK—*From town: Go 5 mi N on Hwy 37.* FACILITIES: 235 sites, 154 elec, 81 no hookups, tenting available, handicap restroom facilities, sewage disposal, laundry, public phone, ice, tables. RECREATION: swimming, boating, canoeing, ramp, fishing, playground. Open mid May through early Sep. Phone: (315) 388-5636.

## WADING RIVER—B-4

**W.E.S. TRAILER SALES**—*From jct Hwy 46 & Hwy 25: Go 3 mi E on Hwy 25.* SALES: travel trailers, 5th wheels, motor homes, mini-motor homes, fold-down camping trailers. SERVICES: RV appliance mechanic full-time, LP gas refill by weight/by meter, sewage disposal, RV storage, sells parts/accessories, installs hitches. Open all year. Master Card/Visa accepted. Phone: (516) 727-5852.

**SEE AD THIS PAGE**

WILDWOOD STATE PARK—*From jct I-495 (Long Island Expwy) (Exit 68) & Hwy 46: Go 7 mi N on Hwy 46, then 4 mi E on Hwy 25A (follow signs).* FACILITIES: 320 sites, 80 full hookups, (15 amp receptacles), 240 no hookups, tenting available, handicap restroom facilities, sewage disposal, ice, tables. RECREATION: salt water swimming, salt water fishing, playground, sports field, hiking trails. No pets. Open early Apr through mid Oct. Facilities fully operational Memorial Day through Labor Day. Phone: (516) 929-4314.

## WALTON—F-7

BEAR SPRING MOUNTAIN (Catskill State Forest)—*From town: Go 5 mi SE on Hwy 206.* FACILITIES: 41 sites, 41 no hookups, tenting available, non-flush toilets, sewage disposal, public phone, tables, fire rings, wood. RECREATION: pond swimming, boating, no motors, canoeing, 3 row/4 canoe boat rentals, pond fishing, hiking trails. Open late Apr through early Dec. No showers. Phone: (607) 865-6989.

**HERMAN'S TRAILER SALES**—*From jct Hwy 10 & Hwy 206: Go 1 mi E on Hwy 206, then 3/4 mi E on River Rd.* SALES: travel trailers, park models, truck campers, 5th wheels, motor homes, mini-motor homes, fold-down camping trailers. SERVICES: Engine/Chassis & RV appliance mechanic full-time, emergency road service business hours, RV towing, LP gas refill by weight/by meter, RV rentals, RV storage, sells parts/accessories, installs hitches. Open all year. Master Card/Visa accepted. Phone: (607) 865-6191.

**SEE AD TRAVEL SECTION PAGE 586**

## WARRENSBURG—D-9

**Daggett Lake Campsites (Not Visited)**—Lakeside CAMPGROUND with wooded sites. Most full hookup sites occupied by seasonal campers. *From I-87 (exit 23-Warrensburg): Go 200 feet W on Diamond Point Rd, then 4 mi N on US 9, then 5 mi NW on Hwy 28, then 3 mi S on Glen-Athol Rd.* FACILITIES: 62 sites, most common site width 30 feet, 28 full hookups, 22 water & elec (15 & 20 amp receptacles), 12 no hookups, tenting available, sewage disposal, laundry, public phone, limited grocery store, ice, tables, fire rings, grills, wood. RECREATION: equipped pavilion, lake swimming, boating, electric motors only, canoeing, 3 row/3 canoe boat rentals, lake fishing, playground, badminton, horseshoes, hiking trails, volleyball. Open Apr 15 through Oct 15. Open date weather permitting. Rate in 1995 $18-23 for 2 persons. Member of ARVC; CONY. Phone: (518) 623-2198.

WARRENSBURG—Continued

**LAKE GEORGE/SCHROON VALLEY RESORT**—Riverside CAMPGROUND with grassy, shaded & open sites. *From I-87 (exit 24/ Bolton Landing): Go 50 yards E, then 3/4 mi S on Schroon River Rd.*

◆◆◆FACILITIES: 140 sites, 37 full hookups, 103 water & elec (15,20 & 30 amp receptacles), seasonal sites, 26 pull-thrus, a/c allowed ($), heater allowed ($), tenting available, group sites for tents/RVs, RV rentals, sewage disposal, laundry, public phone, limited grocery store, RV supplies, LP gas refill by weight/by meter, ice, tables, fire rings, wood, traffic control gate.

◆◆◆◆RECREATION: rec room/area, equipped pavilion, coin games, 2 swim pools (heated), canoeing, river fishing, basketball hoop, playground, planned group activities (weekends only), movies, recreation director, badminton, sports field, horseshoes, volleyball.

Open May 15 through Oct 15. Rate in 1995 $18-25 for 2 persons. Master Card/Visa accepted. Phone: (800) 958-2267.

**SEE AD LAKE GEORGE PAGE 610**

**SCHROON RIVER CAMPSITE**—Riverside CAMPGROUND with open & shaded sites. *From I-87 (exit 23-Warrensburg): Go 200 feet W on Diamond Point Rd, then 1/2 mi N on US 9, then 3 mi N on Horicon Ave.*

◆◆FACILITIES: 300 sites, most common site width 30 feet, 200 full hookups, 100 water & elec (15,20 & 30 amp receptacles), seasonal sites, a/c allowed ($), heater not allowed, tenting available, cabins, sewage disposal, laundry, public phone, grocery store, RV supplies, LP gas refill by weight, ice, tables, fire rings, wood.

◆◆◆RECREATION: rec room/area, coin games, swim pool (heated), river swimming, boating, 5 hp limit, canoeing, ramp, 4 row/6 canoe boat rentals, river fishing, basketball hoop, 4 bike rentals, playground, planned group activities, movies, badminton, sports field, horseshoes, hiking trails, volleyball.

Open May 15 through Sep 30. Rate in 1995 $21-23 for 2 persons. Master Card/Visa accepted. Member of ARVC; CONY. Phone: (518) 623-2171.

**SEE AD LAKE GEORGE PAGE 616**

**Warrensburg Travel Park**—Riverside CAMPGROUND with open & wooded sites. *From I-87 (exit 23-Warrensburg): Go 1,000 feet W on Diamond Point Rd, then 1/2 mi N on US 9, then 1/2 mi NE on Horicon Rd.* ◆◆FACILITIES: 150 sites, most common site width 28 feet, 66 full hookups, 74 water & elec (15 & 20 amp receptacles), 10 no hookups, seasonal sites, 77 pull-thrus, tenting available, sewage disposal, laundry, public phone, limited grocery store, ice, tables, fire rings, wood. ◆◆◆◆RECREATION: rec room/area, pavilion, swim pool, boating, 5 hp limit, canoeing, 6 row/6 canoe boat rentals, river fishing, playground, planned group activities (weekends only), tennis court, badminton, sports field, horseshoes, hiking trails, volleyball. Open May 5 through Oct 15. Rate in 1995 $17-20 for 2 persons. No refunds. Member of ARVC; CONY. Phone: (518) 623-9833.

## WATERLOO—E-5

**Welcome Traveler Trailer Court**—Level, grassy sites, many occupied by seasonal campers. *From jct I-90 (exit 42) & Hwy 14: Go 3 mi S on Hwy 14, then 3 mi E on Packwood Rd.* ◆◆FACILITIES: 32 sites, most common site width 18 feet, 37 ft. max RV length, 18 full hookups, 4 elec (30 amp receptacles), 10 no hookups, seasonal sites, tenting available, tables, patios, fire rings, grills, wood. RECREATION: rec hall, planned group activities. Open Apr 15 through Oct 15. Rate in 1995 $12-14 for 2 persons. Phone: (315) 789-2102.

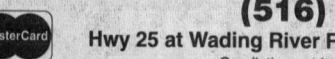

*When I hear somebody sigh that "Life is hard," I am always tempted to ask, "Compared to what?"*

## WATERTOWN—C-6

**ALLEN'S BOAT LIVERY MARINA AND CAMPGROUND**—*From Watertown: Go 10 mi SW on Hwy 3.*

WELCOME **SEE PRIMARY LISTING AT SACKETS HARBOR AND AD THIS PAGE**

❀ **DAVE FOSTER'S RV CENTER**—*From jct I-81 (exit 47) & Hwy 12: Go 1 1/2 mi SE on Hwy 12, then 3/4 mi NE on US 11.*

WELCOME SALES: travel trailers, truck campers, 5th wheels, fold-down camping trailers. SERVICES: sells parts/accessories. Open all year. American Express/Discover/Master Card/Visa accepted. Phone: (315) 788-6666.

**SEE AD THIS PAGE**

**Kelley's RV Park**—Level, grassy RV SPACES at the edge of town. *From jct I-81 (exit 45) & Hwy 3: Go 3 mi E on Hwy 3, then 200 feet SW on Marble after bridge, then 500 feet N on Eastern Blvd.* FACILITIES: 16 sites, accepts full hookup units only, 16 full hookups (30 amp receptacles). No tents.Open May 15 through Oct 15. Rate in 1995 $15 per vehicle. Phone: (315) 782-5317.

**KOA-Natural Bridge/Watertown**—Semi-wooded CAMPGROUND with shaded & some open sites. *From east jct Hwy 3A & Hwy 3: Go 6 mi E on Hwy 3.* ◇◇◇FACILITIES: 95 sites, 35 full hookups, 48 water & elec (20,30 & 50 amp receptacles), 12 no hookups, 37 pull-thrus, tenting available, sewage disposal, laundry, public phone, grocery store, LP gas refill by weight/by meter, ice, tables, fire rings, grills, wood. ◇◇◇◇RECREATION: rec hall, rec room/area, swim pool (indoor) (heated), playground, planned group activities (weekends only), badminton, sports field, horseshoes, hiking trails, volleyball. Recreation open to the public. Open Apr 1 through Nov 1. Rate in 1995 $19-24 for 2 persons. Member of ARVC; CONY. Phone: (315) 644-4880. KOA 10% value card discount.

## WATKINS GLEN—F-5

**KOA-WATKINS GLEN/CORNING**—Semi-wooded CAMPGROUND with wooded and open sites. *From South jct Hwy 14 & Hwy 414: Go 4 1/2 mi S on Hwy 414.*

WELCOME ◇◇◇◇FACILITIES: 102 sites, most common site width 35 feet, 40 full hookups, 51 water & elec (20 & 30 amp receptacles), 11 no hookups, 30 pull-thrus, a/c allowed ($), heater allowed ($), tenting available, group sites for tents, cabins, sewage disposal, laundry, public phone, grocery store, RV supplies, LP gas refill by weight/by meter, ice, tables, fire rings, grills, wood.

◇◇◇◇RECREATION: rec room/area, coin games, swim pool, 1 canoe/3 pedal boat rentals, pond/stream fishing, mini-golf ($), playground, movies, badminton, sports field, horseshoes, hiking trails, volleyball.

Open Apr 20 through Oct 20. Rate in 1995 $20-25 for 2 persons. Discover/Master Card/Visa accepted. Member of ARVC;CONY. Phone: (607) 535-7404. KOA 10% value card discount.

**SEE AD THIS PAGE AND AD FRONT OF BOOK PAGES 68 AND 69**

**Paradise Park Campground**—Semi-wooded & open, grassy sites in a rural location. *From North jct Hwy 414 & Hwy 14: Go 3 1/2 mi N on Hwy 14, then 1 1/2 mi NW on Hwy 14A, then 1 mi W on Church Rd, then 1/4 mi N on Cross Rd.* ◇◇FACILITIES: 160 sites, most common site width 35 feet, 140 water & elec (20 & 30 amp receptacles), 20 no hookups, seasonal sites, 25 pull-thrus, tenting available, sewage disposal, laundry, public phone, grocery store, LP gas refill by weight/by meter, ice, tables, fire rings, wood. ◇◇◇RECREATION: rec hall, rec room/area, swim pool, pond fishing, mini-golf ($), playground, planned group activities (weekends only), badminton, sports field, horseshoes, hiking trails, volleyball. Recreation open to the public. Open May 1 through Oct 15. Rate in 1995 $15-18.50 for 4 persons. Member of ARVC;CONY. Phone: (607) 535-6600. FCRV 10% discount.



WATKINS GLEN—Continued

**SPRUCE ROW CAMPSITES & RV RESORT**—*From Watkins Glen (25 min): Go E on Hwy 79 to Hwy 227, then NE to Trumansburg, then SE on Hwy 96, then 1/2 mi N on Jacksonville Rd, then 1 1/4 mi E on Kraft Rd.*

WELCOME **SEE PRIMARY LISTING AT ITHACA AND AD ITHACA PAGE 609**

**Vickio's Deerfield Park**—Countryside RV PARK with level, grassy sites on a hilltop meadow. *From jct Hwy 14/414 & Hwy 329: Go 1 1/2 mi SW on Hwy 329.* ◇◇◇FACILITIES: 43 sites, most common site width 30 feet, 43 water & elec (20 & 30 amp receptacles), 43 pull-thrus, tenting available, sewage disposal, tables, fire rings, wood. RECREATION: rec room/area. Open May 1 through Oct 1. Rate in 1995 $16.50 for 2 persons. Phone: (800) 298-1340.

WATKINS GLEN STATE PARK—*At jct Hwy 14 & Hwy 414.* FACILITIES: 303 sites, 20 ft. max RV length, 303 no hookups, tenting available, handicap restroom facilities, sewage disposal, public phone, limited grocery store, ice, tables. RECREATION: swim pool, canoeing, fishing, planned group activities, hiking trails. Open mid May through Oct 9. Phone: (607) 535-4511.

## WEEDSPORT—E-5

**Riverforest Park**—Riverside CAMPGROUND with shaded and open sites. *From jct I-90 (exit 40) & Hwy 34: Go 1/4 mi N on Hwy 34, then follow signs 3/4 mi NW.* ◇◇FACILITIES: 250 sites, 250 water & elec (20 & 30 amp receptacles), seasonal sites, tenting available, sewage disposal, laundry, public phone, limited grocery store, LP gas refill by weight/by meter, ice, tables, fire rings, grills, wood. ◇◇◇◇RECREATION: rec hall, rec room/area, pavilion, swim pool, boating, canoeing, ramp, dock, 4 row/4 canoe/3 pedal boat rentals, river/pond fishing, playground, badminton, sports field, horseshoes, hiking trails, volleyball. Open Apr 1 through Oct 15. Rate in 1995 $17 for 2 persons. No refunds. Member of ARVC; CONY. Phone: (315) 834-9458.

## WELLSVILLE—F-3

**Breezy Point Campsite**—CAMPGROUND in the country with open and shaded grassy sites. Most full hookup sites occupied by seasonal campers. *From jct Hwy 19 & Hwy 417: Go 4 3/4 mi W on Hwy 417, then 2 mi NW on Wolf Spring Rd.* ◇◇FACILITIES: 245 sites, 175 full hookups, 70 water & elec (15 amp receptacles), seasonal sites, tenting available, sewage disposal, laundry, public phone, LP gas refill by weight/by meter, ice, tables, fire rings, wood. ◇◇RECREATION: rec hall, pond swimming, boating, no motors, canoeing, pond fishing, mini-golf ($), playground, horseshoes. Open May 1 through Oct 15. Rate in 1995 $15-16 for 2 persons. Member of ARVC; CONY. Phone: (716) 593-3085.

## WESTFIELD—F-1

**KOA-Westfield-Lake Erie**—CAMPGROUND with shaded & open sites. *From jct I-90 (exit 60) & Hwy 394: Go 1/4 mi N on Hwy 394, then 1 mi NE on Hwy 5.* ◇◇◇FACILITIES: 121 sites, most common site width 35 feet, 52 full hookups, 50 water & elec (20 & 30 amp receptacles), 19 no hookups, seasonal sites, 80 pull-thrus, tenting available, sewage disposal, laundry, public

WESTFIELD—Continued
KOA-WESTFIELD-LAKE ERIE—Continued

phone, grocery store, LP gas refill by weight/by meter, ice, tables, fire rings, wood. ◇◇◇RECREATION: rec room/area, 2 swim pools, pond fishing, playground, horseshoes. Open Apr 15 through Oct 15. Rate in 1995 $20-23 for 2 persons. Member of ARVC;CONY. Phone: (716) 326-3573. KOA 10% value card discount.

## WILMINGTON—B-9

**KOA-LAKE PLACID-WHITEFACE MOUNTAIN**—CAMPGROUND with shaded sites. *From jct Hwy 441 & Hwy 86: Go 2 mi SW on Hwy 86, then 1/4 mi E on Fox Farm Rd.*

WELCOME ◇◇◇◇FACILITIES: 200 sites, most common site width 50 feet, 48 full hookups, 49 water & elec, 26 elec (20,30 & 50 amp receptacles), 77 no hookups, seasonal sites, 82 pull-thrus, a/c allowed ($), heater allowed ($), tenting available, group sites for tents, cabins, RV storage, sewage disposal, laundry, public phone, limited grocery store, RV supplies, LP gas refill by weight/by meter, ice, tables, fire rings, wood.

◇◇◇◇RECREATION: rec hall, rec room/area, coin games, 2 swim pools (heated), wading pool, canoeing, 8 canoe boat rentals, river fishing, mini-golf ($), basketball hoop, playground, planned group activities, movies, recreation director, tennis court, horseshoes, hiking trails, cross country skiing, local tours.

Open Feb 1 through Nov 1. Facilities fully operational May 1 through Nov 1. Open weekends during ski season. Rate in 1995 $20-28 for 2 persons. Discover/Master Card/Visa accepted. Phone: (518) 946-7878. KOA 10% value card discount.

**SEE ADS FRONT OF BOOK PAGES 30, 68 AND 69 AND AD LAKE PLACID PAGE 619**

WILMINGTON—Continued on next page

WILMINGTON—Continued

**NORTH POLE CAMPGROUND**—Shaded, grassy sites in a riverside location. *From jct Hwy 431 & Hwy 86: Go 1/4 mi SW on Hwy 86.*

WELCOME

◇◇◇◇FACILITIES: 77 sites, most common site width 30 feet, 33 full hookups, 24 water & elec (20,30 & 50 amp receptacles), 20 no hookups, 1 pull-thrus, a/c allowed ($), heater allowed ($), cable TV ($), phone hookups, tenting available, cabins, RV storage, sewage disposal, laundry, public phone, limited grocery store, RV supplies, LP gas refill by weight/by meter, ice, tables, fire rings, wood.

◇◇◇◇RECREATION: rec hall, rec room/area, coin games, swim pool, boating, 10 hp limit, canoeing, 5 row/3 canoe/1 pedal boat rentals, lake/river fishing, fishing guides, mini-golf ($), basketball hoop, playground, planned group activities (weekends only), movies, badminton, sports field, horseshoes, volleyball, cross country skiing, local tours.

Open all year. Facilities fully operational Apr 15 through Oct 15. Rate in 1995 $18-22 for 2 persons. No refunds. Diners Club/Master Card/Visa accepted. Member of ARVC; CONY. Phone: (800) 245-0228.

**SEE AD LAKE PLACID PAGE 618**

**Whiteface Terrace Campsite**—Rustic, wooded CAMPGROUND with open and shaded sites. *From jct Hwy 431 & Hwy 86: Go 1/2 mi SW on Hwy 86.* ◇◇FACILITIES: 51 sites, most common site width 35 feet, 8 full hookups, 20 water & elec (15,20 & 30 amp receptacles), 23 no hookups, seasonal sites, tenting available, sewage disposal, laundry, public phone, ice, tables, fire rings, wood. ◇◇RECREATION: rec room/area, badminton, horseshoes, hiking trails, volleyball. Open May 15 through Sep 15. Rate in 1995 $15-18 for 2 persons. Phone: (518) 946-2576.

WILMINGTON NOTCH CAMPGROUND (Adirondack State Forest)—*From town: Go 4 mi W on Hwy 86.* FACILITIES: 54 sites, 30 ft. max RV length, 54 no hookups, tenting available, handicap restroom facilities, sewage disposal, tables. RECREATION: river fishing, hiking trails. Open late Apr through mid Oct. Phone: (518) 946-7172.

## WINDHAM—F-9

**White Birches Campsites**—Wooded sites in a rural CAMPGROUND. *From jct Hwy 296 & Hwy 23: Go 500 yards W on Hwy 23, then 1/4 mi N on Old Rd, then 2 1/4 mi NW on Nauvoo Rd.* ◇◇FACILITIES: 130 sites, 126 water & elec (15 & 20 amp receptacles), 4 no hookups, seasonal sites, tenting available, sewage disposal, public phone, limited grocery store, tables, fire rings, wood. ◇◇◇◇RECREATION: rec hall, lake swimming, boating, no motors, canoeing, lake fishing, playground, planned group activities, sports field, horseshoes, hiking trails. Open all year. Facilities fully operational Memorial Day through Columbus Day. Rate in 1995 $18-20 per family. Phone: (518) 734-3266.

## WINDSOR—F-7

**Forest Hill Lake Park**—CAMPGROUND with open & shaded sites. Most sites occupied by seasonals. *From jct Hwy 17 (exit 80) & Damascus Rd: Go 3/4 mi NE on Old Rt 17, then 2 3/4 mi NW on Ostrander Rd (caution: narrow, steep road).* ◇◇FACILITIES: 75 sites, 61 full hookups, 4 water & elec (20 & 30 amp receptacles), 10 no hookups, seasonal sites, 4 pull-thrus, tenting available, laundry, tables, fire rings, wood. ◇◇◇RECREATION: pavilion, lake swimming, boating, electric motors only, canoeing, 1 row/2 canoe/1 pedal boat rentals, lake fishing, playground, badminton, sports field, horseshoes, hiking trails, volleyball. Open May 1 through Oct 15. Rate in 1995 $15-19 per family. Member of ARVC; CONY. Phone: (607) 655-1444.

**Lakeside Campground**—Wooded, lakeside campsites. *From jct Hwy 17 (exit 79) & Hwy 79: Go 3 1/2 mi S on Hwy 79, then 2 1/2 mi W on Edson Rd (CR 16), then 1 mi SW on Hargrave Rd.* ◇◇◇FACILITIES: 52 sites, 39 full hookups, 8 water & elec (15 & 30 amp receptacles), 5 no hookups, seasonal sites, 2 pull-thrus, tenting available, sewage disposal, laundry, public phone, limited grocery store, LP gas refill by weight, ice, tables, fire rings, wood. ◇◇◇RECREATION: rec room/area, pavilion, lake swimming, boating, electric motors only, canoeing, 3 row/4 canoe/2 pedal boat rentals, lake fishing, playground, badminton, horseshoes, volleyball. Open May 1 through Oct 1. Rate in 1995 $17.50-18.50 for 2 persons. Member of ARVC; CONY. Phone: (607) 655-2694.

**Pine Crest Camping**—Open, grassy sites in a CAMPGROUND. Most sites occupied by seasonals. *From jct Hwy 17 (exit 79) & Hwy 79: Go 5 mi S on Hwy 79, then 1/2 mi E on dirt road. Follow signs.* ◇◇FACILITIES: 70 sites, 55 full hookups, 15 water & elec (15 amp receptacles), seasonal sites, 7 pull-thrus, tenting available, sewage disposal, ice, tables, fire rings, wood. ◇◇◇RECREATION: rec hall, pavilion, swim pool, boating, canoeing, ramp, 3 row/1 pedal boat rentals, river/pond fishing, playground, badminton, sports field, horseshoes, volleyball. Recreation open to the public. Open May 15 through Oct 1. Rate in 1995 $16-17 for 4 persons. Phone: (607) 655-1515.

## WOLCOTT—D-5

**CHERRY GROVE CAMPGROUND**—Semi-wooded with level, grassy open & shaded sites. *From jct Hwy 89 & Hwy 104: Go 1 mi E on Hwy 104, then 300 feet N on Ridge Rd.*

WELCOME

◇◇◇FACILITIES: 90 sites, most common site width 40 feet, 58 full hookups, 12 water & elec (20 & 30 amp receptacles), 20 no hookups, seasonal sites, 16 pull-thrus, a/c allowed ($), heater allowed ($), phone hookups, tenting available, group sites for tents, RV rentals, RV storage, sewage disposal, laundry, public phone, limited grocery store, RV supplies, LP gas refill by weight/by meter, ice, tables, fire rings, wood.

WOLCOTT—Continued
CHERRY GROVE CAMPGROUND—Continued

◇◇◇RECREATION: rec room/area, coin games, fishing guides, playground, planned group activities (weekends only), badminton, sports field, horseshoes, volleyball.

Open Apr 15 through Oct 15. Rate in 1995 $17-20 for 2 persons. Member of ARVC; CONY. Phone: (315) 594-8320.

**SEE AD SODUS POINT PAGE 632**

## WOODRIDGE—A-1

**Lazy "G" Campground**—Open, grassy & shaded, wooded sites in the country. *From jct Hwy 17 (exit 109) & Glen Wild Rd: Go 6 mi N on Glen Wild Rd, then 2 mi NE on Greenfield Rd/Rosemond Rd.* ◇◇FACILITIES: 35 sites, most common site width 50 feet, 35 full hookups, (20 & 30 amp receptacles), seasonal sites, tenting available, handicap restroom facilities, sewage disposal, laundry, public phone, limited grocery store, LP gas refill by weight, ice, tables, fire rings, wood. ◇◇◇RECREATION: rec hall, rec room/area, pond fishing, mini-golf ($), playground, 2 shuffleboard courts, volleyball. Open May 15 through Oct 1. Rate in 1995 $20 for 2 persons. Member of ARVC; CONY. Phone: (914) 434-3390.

**ROSEMOND CAMPGROUND & MOTEL**—Hilly, semi-wooded with shaded & open sites. *From jct Hwy 17 (exit 109) & Glen Wild Rd: Go 6 mi N on Glen Wild Rd, then 1 mi NE on Greenfield Rd/Rosemond Rd.*

WELCOME

◇◇FACILITIES: 225 sites, most common site width 40 feet, 180 full hookups, 45 water & elec (15,20 & 30 amp receptacles), seasonal sites, a/c allowed ($), heater allowed ($), tenting available, group sites for tents/RVs, cabins, RV storage, sewage disposal, laundry, public phone, limited grocery store, ice, tables, fire rings, wood.

◇◇◇RECREATION: rec hall, rec room/area, pavilion, coin games, swim pool, boating, electric motors only, canoeing, lake fishing, basketball hoop, playground, planned group activities (weekends only), tennis court, badminton, horseshoes, hiking trails, volleyball.

Open May 15 through Oct 15. Rate in 1995 $19 for 2 persons. Member of ARVC; CONY. Phone: (914) 434-7433.

**SEE AD THIS PAGE**

**YOGI BEAR'S JELLYSTONE PARK AT BIRCHWOOD ACRES**—*From jct US 209 & Hwy 52: Go 8 mi W on Hwy 52, then 1/2 mi S on Martinfeld Rd.*

WELCOME

**SEE PRIMARY LISTING AT ELLENVILLE AND AD ELLENVILLE PAGE 603**

## WOODVILLE—C-6

SOUTHWICK BEACH STATE PARK—*From town: Go 3 mi W on Hwy 3.* FACILITIES: 110 sites, 44 elec, 66 no hookups, tenting available, handicap restroom facilities, sewage disposal, public phone, grocery store, ice, tables, wood. RECREATION: rec hall, lake swimming, canoeing, lake fishing, playground, planned group activities, hiking trails. Open early May through Oct 8. Phone: (315) 846-5338.

## YOUNGSTOWN—D-2

FOUR MILE CAMPSITE (Fort Niagara State Park)—*From town: Go 4 mi E on Hwy 18.* FACILITIES: 266 sites, 102 elec (15 amp receptacles), 164 no hookups, tenting available, sewage disposal, fire rings, grills. RECREATION: rec hall, lake/stream fishing, playground, planned group activities, sports field, hiking trails. Open mid Apr through Oct 10. Phone: (716) 745-3802.



In a calm sea every man is a pilot. *John Ray*

# Rhode Island

TRAVEL SECTION

## Time Zone/Topography

Rhode Island is on Eastern time.

Rhode Island, the smallest state in the United States, has a total area of 1,214 square miles, maximum length of 48 miles and maximum width of 37 miles. In addition to the 156 square miles of inland waters included in its area, the state has 400 miles of coastline, including Narragansett Bay. Elevation in the state ranges from sea level along the coast to 812 feet above sea level at Jerimoth Hill in the northwestern area. Other physical features include five major bays, several "saltwater rivers" (actually arms of Narragansett Bay), 5 major rivers and half a dozen major lakes, ponds and reservoirs. High, rocky cliffs dominate the Atlantic southeast coastline.

## Climate

The warming influence of Narragansett Bay makes the climate of Rhode Island milder—and with fewer high and low extremes—than that of the other New England states. Average annual precipitation is about 40 inches in the north and about 50 inches on the coast.

| | *High* | *Low* |
|---|---|---|
| January | 36.9° | 21.3° |
| April | 55.8 | 38.6 |
| June | 76.6 | 57.3 |
| August | 80.1 | 61.8 |
| October | 63.2 | 44.5 |
| December | 40.0 | 25.0 |

## Travel Information Sources

**State Agency:** Rhode Island Tourism Division, 7 Jackson Walkway, Providence, RI 02903 (401-277-2601 in state; or 800-556-2484 U.S. and Canada).

**Local Agencies:**

• *Blackstone Valley Tourism Council,* P.O. Box 7663, Cumberland, RI 02864 (401-334-7773).

• *Greater Providence Convention & Visitors Bureau,* 30 Exchange Terrace, Providence, RI 02903 (800-233-1636 or 401-274-1636).

• *Newport County Convention & Visitor's Bureau,* Newport Gateway Center, 23 America's Cup Avenue, Newport, RI 02840 (800-326-6030 or 401-849-8048).

• *South County Tourism Council,* 4808 Tower Hill Rd., Wakefield, RI 02879 (800-548-4662 or 401-789-4422 ).

• *Warwick Dept. of Economic & Community Development,* Warwick City Hall, 3275 Post Rd., Warwick, RI 02886 (800-4-WARWIC or 401-738-2000 ext. 6402).

## Recreational Information

*Fishing & Hunting:* Rhode Island Department of Environmental Management, Licensing Division, 22 Hayes St., Providence, RI 02908 (401-277-3576).

## Places to See & Things to Do

**Adventureland,** Narragansett. Features include: a unique miniature golf course featuring waterfalls, caves, streams and island; bumper boats; batting cages; and a driving range.

**Beach Pond State Park,** near West Greenwich, is a hilly, wooded, 1,000-acre recreation area with a beach, picnic facilities, waterfall and unusual rock formations.

**Blackstone Valley.** The valley is 40-minutes south of Boston, 3 hours north of New York, and 45 minutes north of historic Newport. Blackstone Valley, with the mighty Blackstone River, offers an abundance of scenic vistas, historic homes, factory outlets and special events.

**Block Island.** A popular resort area with many recreational opportunities and historic sites, as well as spectacular 200-foot cliffs which stretch for several miles along the southeast shore. Popular attractions include *Mohegan Bluffs* which rise abruptly about 200 feet above the sea and stretch for several miles along the southeast shore, and *Southeast Lighthouse* which has the most powerful beacon on the eastern U.S. coast.

**Bristol.** Popular attractions include *Blithewold Mansion and Gardens*, 45 room mansion and 33 acres of landscaped grounds and gardens bordering Bristol Harbor; the *Bristol Art Museum*; *Coggeshall Farm Museum,* an 18th century working farm restoration featuring a colonial orchard, herb garden, farm animals and crafts demonstrations; *Colt State Park,* featuring playing fields, picnic areas, saltwater fishing and a scenic drive around the shoreline of the former Colt family estate on the east side of Narragansett Bay.

**Brown & Hopkins Country Store,** Glocester. Home of the nation's oldest operating country store, dating from 1809. Antiques, country furnishings, gourmet food and penny candy.

**Burlingame State Park,** Charlestown. A 3,100-acre recreation area surrounding Watchaug Pond. Adjacent to the recreation area is a bird sanctuary.

**Crescent Park Carousel,** East Providence. Designed by Charles I.D. Looff and built in 1895, this carousel features 66 beautifully carved figures, no two alike.

**George B. Parker Woodland,** Coventry. Wildlife refuge headquartered at 18th century Isaac Bowen House offers hiking, natural history programs and a self-guided historical archeology trail.

**Green Animals Topiary Garden,** Portsmouth. Eighty sculptured trees and shrubs shaped into animal forms: giraffe, elephant, lion, etc. Espaliered fruit trees, rose arbor and formal flower beds.

**Kimball Wildlife Refuge,** Charlestown. Nature trails provide excellent opportunities for viewing a wide variety of wildlife.

**Newport.** Famous for its fine beaches and swimming facilities, Newport has been a popular resort center since the pre-Revolutionary War era, when wealthy southerners spent their summers here. Stroll along the beautiful "cliff walk" (three miles) and view the rocky coast on one side and several outstanding estates on the other.

Additional Newport attractions include *Touro Synagogue,* the oldest in America; *Trinity Church*, an Episcopal church of colonial times; *Friends Meeting House,* the oldest Quaker meeting house in America; *Old Stone Mill*, built either by Viking voyagers around 1,000 A.D. or by colonists before 1677. *Fort Adams State Park*, built in the 1700s, was designed to garrison 2,400 troups. Today the park offers picnicking, swimming, boating and fishing.

The *Newport Jazz Festival* features outstanding music by legendary performers as well as rising stars. Internationall renowned event occurs in August.

**Providence.** The capital is known as the site of Brown University, as well as for countless other educational and historic attractions. Among them are the *First Baptist Meeting House,* built in 1774-75; and *The Arcade*, which is the oldest indoor shopping center in the U.S.;Stroll down Benefit Street's "Mile of History," said to be the most impressive concentration of original Colonial homes in America. The *Roger Williams Park and Zoo* affords a relaxing retreat on 430 acres of woodlands waterway and winding drives.

**Pawtucket.** Attractions within Pawtucket include the *Slater Mill Historic Site* which dates back to 1793 and is the birthplace of the American Revolution, and the *Children's Museum of Rhode Island* with its "hands-on" approach to science.

**Rocky Point Park,** Warwick. A family recreation area featuring Rhode Island shore dinners, amusement rides and games, and free midway entertainment.

**Ruecker Wildlife Refuge,** Tiverton. Sanctuary offers 1.5-mile trail through woodland, meadow, salt marsh and open water. Watch for herons, egrets and osprey.

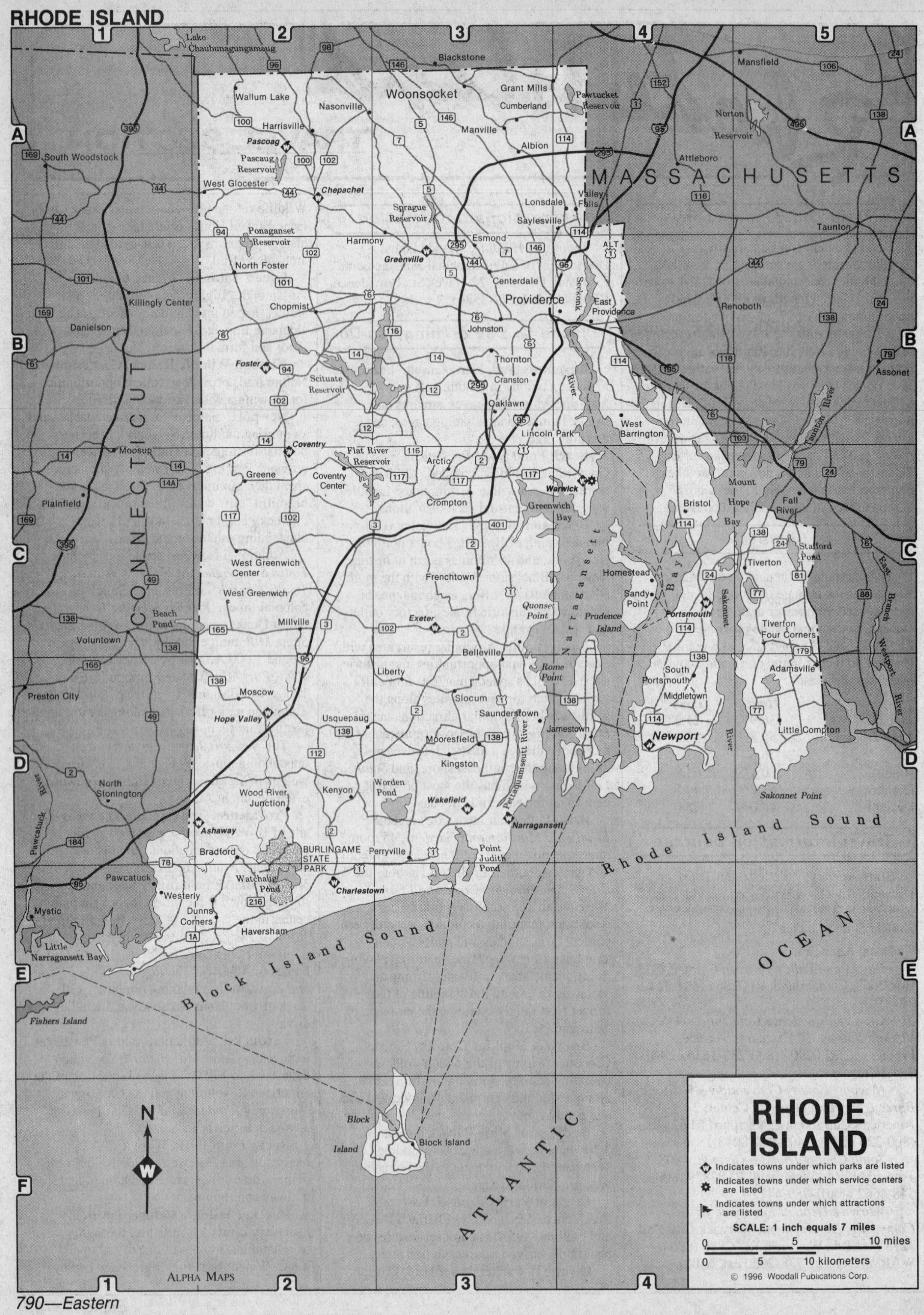
RHODE ISLAND
Indicates towns under which parks are listed
Indicates towns under which service centers are listed
Indicates towns under which attractions are listed
SCALE: 1 inch equals 7 miles
0 5 10 miles
0 5 10 kilometers
© 1996 Woodall Publications Corp.
ALPHA MAPS
MASSACHUSETTS
CONNECTICUT
Rhode Island Sound
Block Island Sound
ATLANTIC
OCEAN
Narragansett Bay
Lake Chaubunagungamaug
Blackstone
Mansfield
Woonsocket
Grant Mills
Cumberland
Pawtucket Reservoir
Wallum Lake
Nasonville
Norton Reservoir
Harrisville
Manville
Pascoag
Pascoag Reservoir
Albion
Attleboro
South Woodstock
West Glocester
Chepachet
Sprague Reservoir
Lonsdale
Valley Falls
Saylesville
Taunton
Ponaganset Reservoir
Harmony
Esmond
Greenville
North Foster
Centerdale
Providence
East Providence
Killingly Center
Chopmist
Seekonk River
Rehoboth
Danielson
Johnston
Foster
Scituate Reservoir
Thornton
Cranston
Assonet
Oaklawn
Lincoln Park
West Barrington
Taunton River
Moosup
Coventry
Flat River Reservoir
Arctic
Greene
Coventry Center
Warwick
Mount Hope Bay
Plainfield
Crompton
Greenwich Bay
Bristol
Fall River
West Greenwich Center
Stafford Pond
Tiverton
West Greenwich
Frenchtown
Homestead
Sandy Point
Beach Pond
Millville
Quonset Point
Prudence Island
Portsmouth
Sakonnet
Voluntown
Exeter
Tiverton Four Corners
East Branch Westport River
Belleville
Rome Point
South Portsmouth
Adamsville
Liberty
Middletown
Preston City
Moscow
Slocum
Saunderstown
Hope Valley
Usquepaug
Jamestown
Newport
Little Compton
Pettaquamscutt River
Mooresfield
Kingston
Sakonnet River
North Stonington
Wood River Junction
Kenyon
Worden Pond
Wakefield
Sakonnet Point
Pawcatuck River
Ashaway
Narragansett
Bradford
BURLINGAME STATE PARK
Perryville
Point Judith Pond
Pawcatuck
Watchaug Pond
Charlestown
Westerly
Mystic
Dunns Corners
Haversham
Little Narragansett Bay
Fishers Island
Block Island
N

# rhode island

All privately-owned campgrounds personally inspected by Woodall Representatives Charles & Betty Hadlock.

Unless otherwise noted, all listed campgrounds have hot showers & flush toilets.

## ASHAWAY—D-2

**FRONTIER FAMILY CAMPER PARK**—A CAMPGROUND with flat, shaded sites. *From jct I-95 (exit 1) & Hwy 3: Go 1/4 mi S on Hwy 3, then 1/4 mi E on Frontier Rd, then 1/4 mi N on Maxson Hill Rd.*

WELCOME

◆◆◆FACILITIES: 217 sites, most common site width 40 feet, 100 water & elec (15 & 20 amp receptacles), 117 no hookups, seasonal sites, 15 pull-thrus, a/c not allowed, heater not allowed, tenting available, handicap restroom facilities, sewage disposal, public phone, limited grocery store, RV supplies, ice, tables, fire rings, wood.

◆◆RECREATION: equipped pavilion, swim pool, badminton, volleyball.

Open May 1 through Oct 1. Minimum 3-day stay on holiday weekends. Rates available upon request. Reservations recommended Jul 1 through Labor Day. Phone: (401) 377-4510.

**SEE AD THIS PAGE**

## CHARLESTOWN—E-2

BURLINGAME STATE PARK—*From town: Go 4 mi W on US 1, then N on CR.* FACILITIES: 755 sites, 755 no hookups, tenting available, sewage disposal, public phone, grocery store, ice, tables, grills, wood. RECREATION: rec hall, pond swimming, boating, ramp, pond fishing, hiking trails. No pets. Open Apr 15 through Oct 31. Phone: (401) 322-7337.

CHARLESTOWN BREACHWAY (State Camping Area)—*From town: Go S on Charlestown Beach Rd.* FACILITIES: 75 sites, 75 no hookups. RECREATION: salt water swimming, boating, ramp, salt water fishing. No pets. No tents. Open Apr 15 through Oct 31. For self-contained units only. No showers. Phone: (401) 364-7000.

## CHEPACHET—A-2

**Bowdish Lake Camping Area**—Large, heavily wooded CAMPGROUND adjacent to a lake. *From jct Hwy 102 & US 44: Go 5 1/2 mi W on US 44.* ◆◆FACILITIES: 350 sites, most common site width 40 feet, 350 water & elec (20 & 30 amp receptacles), seasonal sites, 10 pull-thrus, tenting available, sewage disposal, public phone, limited grocery store, ice, tables, fire rings, wood. ◆◆◆◆RECREATION: rec hall, rec room/area, lake swimming, boating, 10 hp limit, canoeing, dock, 4 row/6 canoe/6 pedal boat rentals, lake/pond fishing, planned group activities (weekends only), sports field, horseshoes, hiking trails. Open Apr 30 through Oct 15. Rate in 1995 $14-30 per family. No refunds. Phone: (401) 568-8890.

GEORGE WASHINGTON MANAGEMENT AREA (State Park)—*From jct US 44 & Hwy 102: Go 6 mi W on US 44.* FACILITIES: 72 sites, 72 no hookups, tenting available, tables.



CHEPACHET—Continued
GEORGE WASHINGTON MANAGEMENT AREA (STATE PARK)—Continued

RECREATION: lake swimming, boating, lake fishing, playground, hiking trails. No pets. Open Apr 9 through Oct 15. Phone: (401) 568-2013.

## COVENTRY—C-2

**Hickory Ridge Campground**—CAMPGROUND with open & shaded sites. Most full hookup sites occupied by seasonal campers. *From jct Hwy 117 & Hwy 102: Go 1 1/4 mi N on Hwy 102.* ◆◆FACILITIES: 200 sites, most common site width 20 feet, 60 full hookups, 140 water & elec (15 & 20 amp receptacles), seasonal sites, 50 pull-thrus, tenting available, sewage disposal, laundry, public phone, limited grocery store, LP gas refill by weight, ice, tables, fire rings, wood. ◆◆◆RECREATION: rec hall, swim pool, pond fishing, badminton, sports field, horseshoes, volleyball. Open May 1 through Oct 10. Rate in 1995 $14 per family. No refunds. Phone: (401) 397-7474.

## EXETER—C-3

**Oak Embers Campground**—Shaded CAMPGROUND with graded sites in peaceful rural area. *From jct Hwy 3 & Hwy 165: Go 5 1/4 mi W on Hwy 165, then 1 1/2 mi N on Escoheag Hill Rd.* ◆◆◆FACILITIES: 61 sites, most common site width 30 feet, 37 water & elec (20 & 30 amp receptacles), 24 no hookups, seasonal sites, 10 pull-thrus, tenting available, sewage disposal, laundry, public phone, limited grocery store, LP gas refill by weight/by meter, ice, tables, fire rings, wood. ◆◆RECREATION: rec room/area, pavilion, swim pool, badminton, horseshoes, volleyball. Open Nov 1 through Sep 30. Rate in 1995 $16-18 for 2 persons. Member of ARVC. Phone: (401) 397-4042.

**Peeper Pond Campground**—Secluded CAMPGROUND with wooded sites. *From jct Hwy 102 & Hwy 2: Go 3 1/2 mi S on Hwy 2, then 1 1/2 mi W on Mail Rd, then 8/10 mi N on Liberty Church Rd.* ◆◆FACILITIES: 31 sites, most common site width 30 feet, 28 water & elec (30 amp receptacles), 3 no hookups, seasonal sites, 10 pull-thrus, tenting available, sewage disposal, public phone, ice, tables, fire rings, wood. ◆RECREATION: badminton, horseshoes, volleyball. Open May 1 through Sep 30. Rate in 1995 $10-16 per family. Phone: (401) 294-5540.

**Wawaloam Campground**—Rolling terrain with open and wooded sites. *From jct I-95 (exit 5A) & Hwy 102: Go 3 mi S on Hwy 102, then 1/2 mi SW on Town Hall Rd, then 2 mi S on Gardiner Rd.* ◆◆FACILITIES: 250 sites, most common site width 50 feet, 70 full hookups, 180 water & elec (20 & 30 amp receptacles), seasonal sites, tenting available, sewage disposal, laundry, public phone, grocery store, LP gas refill by weight, ice, tables, fire rings, wood. ◆◆◆◆RECREATION: rec hall, rec room/area, pavilion, swim pool, mini-golf ($), planned group activities, badminton, sports field, horseshoes, volleyball. Open all year. Facilities fully operational Apr 30 through Oct 31. Minimum 3-day stay on holiday weekends by reservation. Rate in 1995 $20-21 per family. No refunds. Phone: (401) 294-3039.

## FOSTER—B-2

**GINNY-B FAMILY CAMPGROUND**—CAMPGROUND with large, grassy sites adjacent to a golf course. *From jct Hwy 94 & US 6: Go 3 1/4 mi W on US 6, then 3 1/2 mi S on Cucumber Hill Rd, then 1/2 mi E on Harrington Rd.*

WELCOME

◆◆FACILITIES: 275 sites, most common site width 35 feet, 50 full hookups, 225 water & elec (15 & 20 amp receptacles), seasonal sites, 35 pull-thrus, a/c not allowed, heater not allowed, phone hookups, tenting available, group sites for tents/RVs, RV storage, sewage disposal, laundry, public phone, limited grocery store, ice, tables, fire rings, wood.

◆◆◆RECREATION: rec hall, pavilion, pond swimming, pond/stream fishing, basketball hoop, planned group activities (weekends only), sports field, horseshoes, volleyball.

Open May 1 through Sep 30. Rate in 1995 $14.50-15.50 for 2 persons. Reservations recommended Jul 1 through Labor Day. Member of ARVC. Phone: (401) 397-9477.

**SEE AD THIS PAGE**

**Whippoorwill Hill Family Campground**—CAMPGROUND with shaded sites among tall pines. *From jct I-95 (exit 5B): Go 9 mi N on Hwy 102 to jct Hwy 14 & Hwy 102, then 2 mi E on Old Plainfield Pike.* ◆◆FACILITIES: 155 sites, most common site width 35 feet, 70 full hookups, 75 water & elec (15,20,30 & 50 amp receptacles), 10 no hookups, seasonal sites, 10 pull-thrus, tenting available, sewage disposal, laundry, public phone, limited grocery store, ice, tables, fire rings, wood. ◆◆◆RECREATION: rec hall, rec room/area, pond swimming, pond fishing, mini-golf ($), planned group activities, recreation director, badminton, sports field, horseshoes, volleyball. Open Apr 15 through Sep 30. Rate in 1995 $14-16 per family. Member of ARVC. Phone: (401) 397-7256.

## GREENVILLE—B-3

**Holiday Acres Campground**—Hilly terrain with open & wooded sites. *From jct I-295 & Hwy 44: Go 1 3/4 mi W on Hwy 44, then 1 1/2 mi S on Hwy 116 (Smith Ave), then at Knight's Farm go straight on Snake Hill Rd for 2 3/4 mi.* ◆◆◆FACILITIES: 225 sites, most common site width 40 feet, 200 full hookups, (15 & 20 amp receptacles), 25 no hookups, seasonal sites, 30 pull-thrus, tenting available, sewage disposal, laundry, public phone, limited grocery store, LP gas refill by weight/by meter, ice, tables, fire rings, wood. ◆◆◆◆RECREATION: rec hall, rec room/area, pavilion, lake swimming, boating, no motors, canoeing, 5 row/7 canoe/4 pedal boat rentals, lake fishing, mini-golf ($), playground, planned group activities (weekends only), recreation director, badminton, sports field, horseshoes, volleyball. Open all year. Facilities fully operational May 1 through Oct 30. Rate in 1995 $15-25 per family. No refunds. Phone: (401) 934-0780.



RI *Green Animals Topiary Gardens contains many shrubs & trees shaped like animals.* RI

## HOPE VALLEY—D-2

**GREENWOOD HILL FAMILY CAMPGROUND**—Rolling terrain with wooded sites. *From jct I-95 (exit 3B) & Hwy 138: Go 3 1/2 mi W on Hwy 138.*

WELCOME

◈◈◈FACILITIES: 50 sites, most common site width 35 feet, 13 full hookups, 37 water & elec (15,20 & 30 amp receptacles), seasonal sites, 4 pull-thrus, a/c allowed ($), heater allowed ($), tenting available, group sites for tents/RVs, RV rentals, cabins, RV storage, sewage disposal, public phone, limited grocery store, RV supplies, ice, tables, fire rings, wood.

◈◈◈RECREATION: rec hall, coin games, pond swimming, basketball hoop, badminton, sports field, horseshoes, hiking trails, volleyball.

Open May 1 through Oct 15. Rate in 1995 $17-20 per family. No refunds. Discover/Master Card/Visa accepted. Phone: (800) 232-7154.
**SEE AD THIS PAGE**

HOPE VALLEY—Continued

**WHISPERING PINES**—Rolling terrain with natural wooded sites in a CAMPGROUND. *From jct I-95 (exit 3B) & Hwy 138: Go 3 mi W on Hwy 138, then 1/2 mi N on Saw Mill Rd.*

WELCOME

◈◈◈FACILITIES: 200 sites, most common site width 25 feet, 60 full hookups, 105 water & elec (15,20 & 30 amp receptacles), 35 no hookups, seasonal sites, 20 pull-thrus, a/c allowed ($), heater allowed ($), tenting available, RV rentals, RV storage, sewage disposal, laundry, public phone, limited grocery store, RV supplies, LP gas refill by weight/by meter, ice, tables, fire rings, wood, guard.

◈◈◈◈RECREATION: rec hall, equipped pavilion, coin games, pond swimming, canoeing, 4 canoe boat rentals, river/pond fishing, mini-golf ($), basketball hoop, playground, 2 shuffleboard courts, planned group activities, movies, tennis court, badminton, sports field, horseshoes, volleyball.

HOPE VALLEY—Continued
WHISPERING PINES—Continued

Open Mar 1 through Dec 31. Facilities fully operational Memorial Day through Labor Day. 3 day minimum on holiday weekends Rate in 1995 $22-27 per family. Reservations recommended Jul 1 through Labor Day. Member of ARVC. Phone: (401) 539-7011.
**SEE AD THIS PAGE**

## NARRAGANSETT—D-3

FISHERMEN'S MEMORIAL STATE PARK—*From town: Go S on Hwy 108 (Point Judith Rd), then E.* FACILITIES: 182 sites, 40 full hookups, 107 water & elec, 35 no hookups, tenting available, sewage disposal. RECREATION: playground, tennis court, horseshoes. No pets. Open all year. Facilities fully operational Apr 15 through Oct 31. Phone: (401) 789-8374.

**LONG COVE MARINA & CAMPSITES**—A coveside CAMPGROUND with mostly open, grassy sites near the ocean. *From jct US 1 & Hwy 108: Go 1 mi S on Hwy 108.*

WELCOME

◈◈◈FACILITIES: 150 sites, most common site width 35 feet, 32 ft. max RV length, 125 water & elec (15 & 20 amp receptacles), 25 no hookups, seasonal sites, 15 pull-thrus, a/c not allowed, heater not allowed, tenting available, sewage disposal, public phone, ice, tables, fire rings, wood.

◈◈RECREATION: boating, canoeing, ramp, dock, salt water fishing.

LONG COVE MARINA—Continued on next page
NARRAGANSETT—Continued on next page



RI Last of the 13 colonies to become a state RI

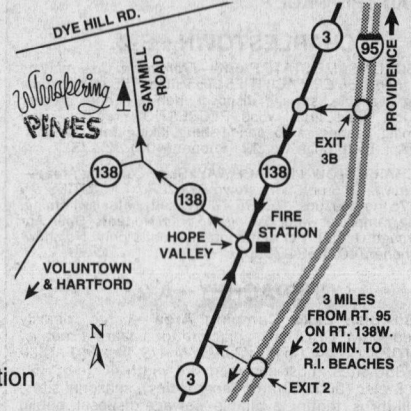

## THE POISON IVY TEST

Poison Ivy can appear as a plant, bush or a vine. In summer the leaves are green, but young leaves may be reddish. Pyramid-shaped clusters of flowers appear and tiny berries develop on female plants later. If you have a plant you suspect is a member of this poisonous family, here is a way to test it, as described in the *Prevention Total Health Care System:* Grasp a leaf with a folded piece of paper and crush it with a rock. If the plant is poison ivy, the sap released will turn dark brown in 10 minutes and black in a day. If it is poison ivy, spray it with a commercial weed killer. After the plant is dead, remove it while wearing heavy gloves. If you burn the dried vine, you can get an allergic reaction from inhaling the smoke. Burying the dried plant is one solution to disposal.

NARRAGANSETT—Continued
LONG COVE MARINA—Continued

Open May 1 through Oct 15. Rate in 1995 $17-19 per family. No refunds. Member of ARVC. Phone: (401) 783-4902.

SEE AD THIS PAGE

## NEWPORT—D-4

**MEADOWLARK**—RV SPACES in a mobile home park with open, grassy sites in a resort area. *From Hwy 138 (end of bridge): Go 2 1/2 mi N on Hwy 138, then 2 mi S on Admiral Kalbfus Rd (Green End Ave), then 1/2 mi E on Prospect Ave.*

FACILITIES: 40 sites, most common site width 22 feet, accepts full hookup units only, 40 full hookups, (20 & 30 amp receptacles), seasonal sites, a/c allowed ($), heater allowed ($), group sites for RVs, RV storage, sewage disposal, public phone, RV supplies, LP gas refill by weight, tables.

No tents. Open Apr 15 through Oct 30. Rate in 1995 $22 for 2 persons. No refunds. Reservations recommended Apr 15 through Labor Day. Phone: (401) 846-9455.

SEE AD THIS PAGE

## PASCOAG—A-2

**Echo Lakes Campground**—Lakeside CAMPGROUND with wooded sites and many seasonal campers. *From jct Hwy 102 & US 44: Go 2 mi W on US 44, then 1 mi N on Jackson School House Rd, then 1/2 mi NE on Moroney Rd.* ◆◆ FACILITIES: 200 sites, most common site width 30 feet, 110 full hookups, 65 water & elec (15 & 20 amp receptacles), 25 no hookups, seasonal sites, 10 pull-thrus, tenting available, sewage disposal, public phone, limited grocery store, ice, tables, fire rings, wood. ◆◆RECREATION: pavilion, lake swimming, boating, canoeing, ramp, lake fishing, badminton, sports field, horseshoes, volleyball. No pets. Open May 1 through Sep 30. Rate in 1995 $20 for 2 persons. No refunds. Phone: (401) 568-7109.

## PORTSMOUTH—C-4

MELVILLE POND CAMP GROUND (City Park)—*N'bound from jct Hwy 138 & Hwy 114: Go 4 3/4 mi N on Hwy 114, then 1/2 mi W on Stringham Rd, then 1/2 mi N on Sullivan Rd. S'bound from jct Hwy 24 & Hwy 114: Go 1 1/2 mi S on Hwy 114, then 1/2*

PORTSMOUTH—Continued
MELVILLE PONDS CAMPGROUND—Continued

*mi W on Stringham, then N on Sullivan.* FACILITIES: 123 sites, 33 full hookups, 33 water & elec (30 amp receptacles), 57 no hookups, seasonal sites, tenting available, handicap restroom facilities, sewage disposal, public phone, ice, tables, fire rings, wood. RECREATION: boating, electric motors only, canoeing, pond fishing, playground, sports field, horseshoes, hiking trails, volleyball. Recreation open to the public. Open Apr 1 through Oct 31. Phone: (401) 849-8212.

## WAKEFIELD—D-3

**WORDEN POND FAMILY CAMPGROUND**—Flat terrain with open, grassy sites & shaded, wooded sites. *From jct US 1 & Hwy 110: Go 2 mi N on Hwy 110, then 1 mi W on Worden Pond Road.*

◆◆◆FACILITIES: 250 sites, most common site width 25 feet, 195 water & elec (20 & 30 amp receptacles), 55 no hookups, seasonal sites, a/c not allowed, heater not allowed, tenting available, group sites for tents/RVs, RV storage, sewage disposal, public phone, ice, tables, fire rings, wood, traffic control gate.

◆◆◆RECREATION: equipped pavilion, lake swimming, boating, canoeing, water skiing, lake fishing, basketball hoop, playground, horseshoes, volleyball.

Open May 1 through Oct 15. Rate in 1995 $17-20 per family. No refunds. Reservations recommended Jun through Sep. Phone: (401) 789-9113.

SEE AD THIS PAGE

## WARWICK—C-4

**ARLINGTON RV SUPERCENTER**—RV SPACES beside a dealership with one night maximum stay at no charge. *N'bound: From jct I-95 (exit 8B) & Hwy 2: Go 1/4 mi N on Hwy 2. S'bound: At I-95 (exit 8A).*

FACILITIES: 10 sites, most common site width 15 feet, 10 water & elec (20 & 30 amp receptacles),

WARWICK—Continued
ARLINGTON RV SUPERCENTER—Continued

sewage disposal, LP gas refill by weight/by meter.

No tents. Open all year. Rates available upon request. Phone: (401) 884-7550.

SEE AD THIS PAGE

✲ **ARLINGTON RV SUPERCENTER**—*N'bound: From jct I-95 (exit 8B) & Hwy 2: Go 1/4 mi N on Hwy 2. S'bound: At I-95 (exit 8A).* SALES: travel trailers, 5th wheels, van conversions, motor homes, mini-motor homes, fold-down camping trailers. SERVICES: Engine/Chassis & RV appliance mechanic full-time, LP gas refill by weight/by meter, sewage disposal, RV rentals, RV storage, sells parts/accessories, sells camping supplies, installs hitches. Open all year. American Express/Discover/Master Card/Visa accepted. Phone: (401) 884-7550.

SEE AD THIS PAGE

# TRAVEL SECTION

## Free Information from Travel Section Advertisers

The following businesses have placed an ad in the Vermont Travel Section. To receive free information, enter their Reader Service number on the Reader Service Card opposite page 16 in the front of this directory:

| Advertiser | RS # | Ad Pg. |
|---|---|---|
| Rest 'N Nest | 487 | 847 |

## Time Zone/Topography

Vermont is on Eastern time.

Although small in total area (9,609 sq. miles), Vermont's geography affords plenty of recreational opportunities, from "sugaring off" parties in spring to spectacular fall foliage colors and snow skiing that can't be beat. Two-thirds of the state is forestland with hilly to mountainous terrain, including Mt. Mansfield at 4,393 ft. Extending the length of the state are the Green Mountains, with many peaks over 3,000 feet.

## Climate

Vermont enjoys four distinct seasons. During the summer months, daytime temperatures average in the mid-70s and during the winter dip into the low 20s. Snowfall averages between 100" to more than 250", depending on elevation.

Below are average monthly temperatures in Burlington.

| | *Max Avg.* | *Min. Avg.* |
|---|---|---|
| January | 25° | 8° |
| March | 38 | 21 |
| June | 76 | 54 |
| July | 80 | 59 |
| August | 78 | 57 |
| October | 57 | 39 |

## Travel Information Sources

**State Agency:** Vermont Dept. of Travel & Tourism, 134 State St., Montpelier, VT 05602 (802-828-3236).

**Regional Agencies:**

- *Addison County Chamber of Commerce,* 2 Court St., Middlebury, VT 05753 (802-388-7951).
- *Central Vermont Chamber of Commerce,* P.O. Box 336, Barre, VT 05641 (802-229-4619).
- *Lake Champlain Regional Chamber of Commerce,* 60 Main St., Ste. 100, Burlington, VT 05401-8418 (802-863-3489).
- *Northeast Kingdom Travel & Tourism Assn.,* 30 Western Ave., St. Johnsbury, VT 05819 (800-639-6379).
- *Smugglers' Notch Area Chamber of Commerce,* P.O. Box 364, Jeffersonville, VT 05464 (802-644-2239).

**Local Agencies:**

- *Arlington Chamber of Commerce,* Rte. 7A, Box 245, Arlington, VT 05250 (802-375-2800).
- *Brattleboro Area Chamber of Commerce,* 180 Main St., Brattleboro, VT 05301 (802-254-4565).
- *Quechee Chamber of Commerce,* P.O. Box 106, 15 Main St., Quechee, VT 05059 (800-295-5451 or 802-295-7900).
- *Stowe Area Assn.*, Main St., P.O. Box 1320, Main St., Stowe, VT 05672 (802-253-7321).
- *White River Chamber of Commerce,* P.O. Box 697, 15 Main St., Gates-Briggs Bldg., Ste. 311, White River Junction, VT 05001 (802-295-6200).

## Recreational Information

*Antiquing:* For information about antiquing in Vermont, send a self-addressed, stamped #10 envelope to: Muriel McKirryher, 55 Allen St., Rutland, VT 05701.

*Fall Foliage Hot Line:* Early Sept. - late Oct., (802-828-3239).

*Fishing& Hunting*: Vermont Dept. of Fish & Wildlife, 103 S. Main St., Waterbury, VT 05671 (802-241-3700).

## Places to See & Things to Do

### *THE LAKES AND THE KINGDOM*

**Church Street Marketplace**, Burlington. The heart of downtown Burlington offers over 100 specialty shops, over 20 restaurants and 30 unique vendors. Live entertainment and festivals are featured throughout the year.

**Jay Peak Scenic Tram,** Jay Peak Resort. Breathtaking ride to the summit (3,861 ft.) of Jays Peak.

**Lake Champlain.** Located in the northwestern corner of Vermont, this recreational paradise is surrounded by mountain vistas and boasts 250 miles of shoreline. Hopping a ferry saves travelers 50 to 85 miles.

**Shelburne Museum,** Shelburne. Billed as New England's Smithsonian, this museum is comprised of 37 exhibit buildings on 45 scenic acres. Discover American folk art, artifacts and architecture.

**Stowe Mountain Resort,** *Stowe.* Take the ride of your life on this 2,300-foot alpine slide. You control the speed so your ride can be as relaxing or as thrilling as you like! Another terrific ride is aboard the 8-passenger gondola that whisks you to the top of Vermont's highest peak—Mt. Mansfield.

### *THE HEART OF VERMONT*

**Ben & Jerry's,** located just north of Waterbury. Visitors are treated with a slideshow on the beginnings of this very successful ice cream company. Top off the tour with a fresh-made sample of the Flavor of the Day!

**Killington.** There's plenty to do and see in the Killington area. Bird watchers won't want to miss The Birds of Killington—a unique program for early-risers who enjoy having breakfast with the birds. Transportation and binoculars are provided. The Hiking Center (at Killington Resort) offers guided interpretive tours, self-guided hiking trails, descriptive maps and rental hiking boots. Ride the chairlift to the top of Killington Peak (4,241 ft.).

**Morse Farm,** Montpelier. Four-season farm affords tours of the rustic sugarhouse and Maple Museum. Maple syrup samples and slide show.

**Vermont Marble Exhibit,** Proctor. Reputed to be the world's largest marble museum, it features working sculptors, historical displays, Hall of Presidents, marble chapel, outdoor marble market and gift shop.

### *PLACES IN HISTORY*

**Norman Rockwell Exhibition,** Arlington. The tour guides who lead viewers through this extensive display of Rockwell's works were once models for the famous artist. Hundreds of *Saturday Evening Post* covers, illustrations, ads and large prints are housed in a historic 1880s church.

**North River Winery,** located in Jacksonville, 6 miles south of Wilmington. One of the east's most scenic wineries offers tours and tastings late May-December.

**The Westminster MG Car Museum,** Westminster. World's largest private exhibit of a single make of car. Facility features 29MG models and an extensive motor car library.

**Wilson Castle,** located near Rutland in the heart of the Green Mountains. Three floors and 32 rooms are filled with stained-glass windows, fireplaces, European and Far Eastern antiques and museum pieces, Chinese scrolls and oriental rugs.

**FREE INFO! Enter number on Reader Service Card opposite pg. 16: Rest 'N Nest #487.**

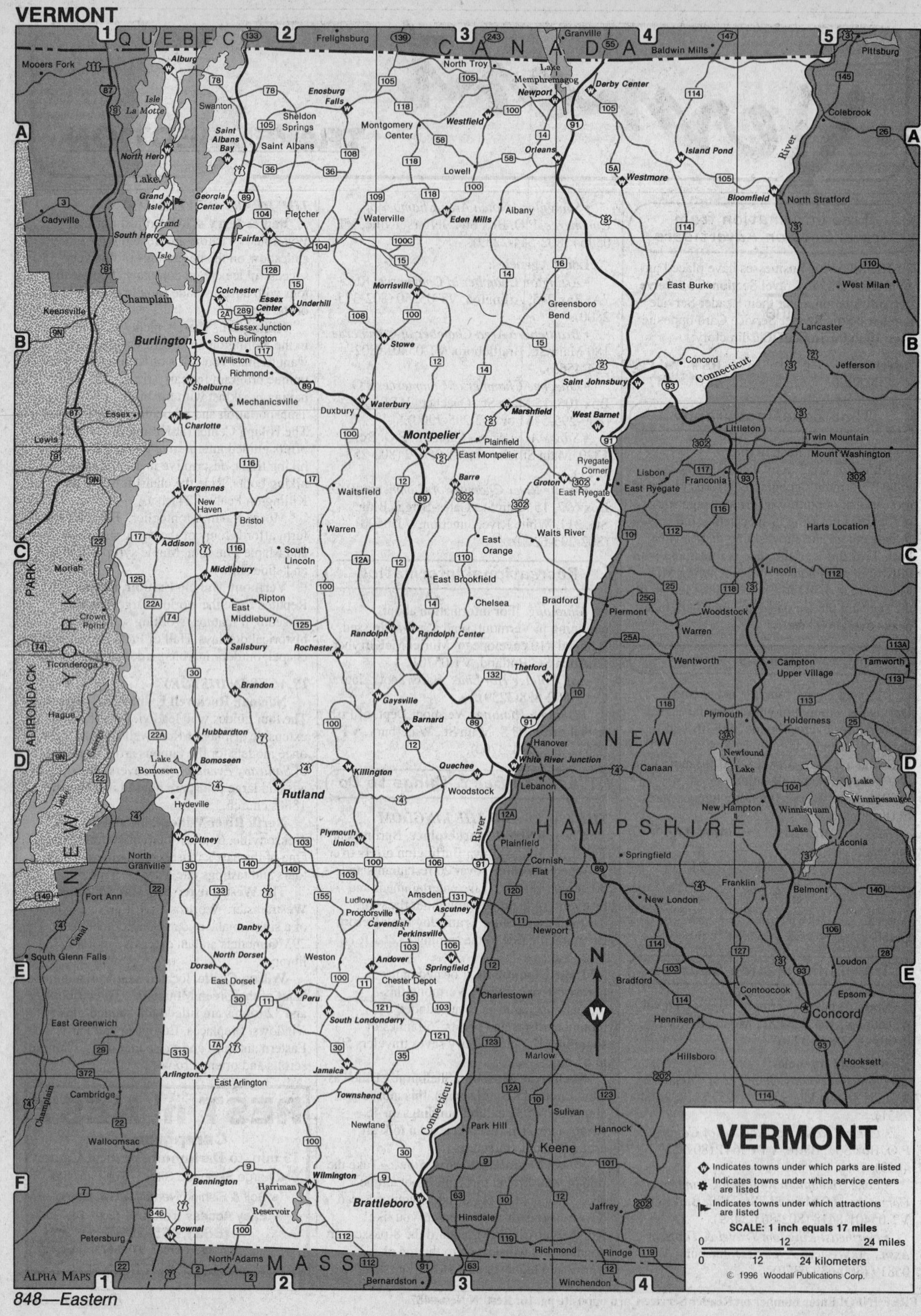
VERMONT
Indicates towns under which parks are listed
Indicates towns under which service centers are listed
Indicates towns under which attractions are listed
SCALE: 1 inch equals 17 miles
0 12 24 miles
0 12 24 kilometers
© 1996 Woodall Publications Corp.
ALPHA MAPS
QUEBEC
CANADA
NEW YORK
NEW HAMPSHIRE
MASS
ADIRONDACK PARK
Lake Champlain
Lake Memphremagog
Connecticut River
Lake George
Champlain Canal
Lake Bomoseen
Harriman Reservoir
Newfound Lake
Lake Winnipesaukee
Winnisquam Lake
Isle La Motte
Grand Isle
Alburg
Swanton
Sheldon Springs
Saint Albans Bay
Saint Albans
North Hero
Georgia Center
South Hero
Fairfax
Fletcher
Colchester
Essex Center
Essex Junction
Underhill
Burlington
South Burlington
Williston
Richmond
Shelburne
Mechanicsville
Charlotte
Vergennes
New Haven
Bristol
Addison
Middlebury
East Middlebury
Ripton
South Lincoln
Warren
Salisbury
Rochester
Brandon
Hubbardton
Bomoseen
Rutland
Hydeville
Poultney
Killington
Gaysville
Barnard
Quechee
Woodstock
Plymouth Union
Ludlow
Proctorsville
Cavendish
Amsden
Ascutney
Perkinsville
Springfield
Andover
Chester Depot
Weston
Danby
North Dorset
Dorset
East Dorset
Peru
South Londonderry
Jamaica
Townshend
Newfane
Arlington
East Arlington
Bennington
Wilmington
Brattleboro
Pownal
Frelighsburg
North Troy
Newport
Derby Center
Enosburg Falls
Montgomery Center
Westfield
Orleans
Lowell
Albany
Eden Mills
Waterville
Morrisville
Stowe
Island Pond
Westmore
Bloomfield
North Stratford
East Burke
Greensboro Bend
Concord
Saint Johnsbury
Marshfield
West Barnet
Plainfield
Montpelier
East Montpelier
Waterbury
Duxbury
Waitsfield
Barre
Groton
Ryegate Corner
East Ryegate
Waits River
East Orange
East Brookfield
Chelsea
Bradford
Randolph
Randolph Center
Thetford
White River Junction
Hanover
Lebanon
Granville
Baldwin Mills
Pittsburg
Colebrook
West Milan
Lancaster
Jefferson
Littleton
Twin Mountain
Mount Washington
Lisbon
Franconia
Harts Location
Lincoln
Piermont
Woodstock
Warren
Wentworth
Campton Upper Village
Tamworth
Plymouth
Holderness
Canaan
New Hampton
Laconia
Springfield
Franklin
Belmont
New London
Newport
Plainfield
Cornish Flat
Charlestown
Bradford
Henniker
Contoocook
Concord
Loudon
Epsom
Hooksett
Hillsboro
Marlow
Sulivan
Hannock
Park Hill
Keene
Canaan
Jaffrey
Hinsdale
Richmond
Rindge
Winchendon
Bernardston
North Adams
Mooers Fork
Cadyville
Keensville
Essex
Lewis
Moriah
Crown Point
Ticonderoga
Hague
Lake Bomoseen
North Granville
Fort Ann
South Glenn Falls
East Greenwich
Cambridge
Walloomsac
Petersburg

# vermont

All privately-owned campgrounds personally inspected by Woodall Representatives Fred & Peg Strout.

**Unless otherwise noted, all listed campgrounds have hot showers & flush toilets.**

## ADDISON—C-1

DAR STATE PARK—*From jct Hwy 22A & Hwy 17: Go 7 mi SW on Hwy 17.* FACILITIES: 71 sites, 71 no hookups, tenting available, handicap restroom facilities, sewage disposal, public phone, tables, fire rings, wood. RECREATION: lake swimming, boating, lake fishing, playground. Open mid May through early Sep. Phone: (802) 759-2354.

## ALBURG—A-1

**ALBURG RV RESORT & TRAILER SALES**—Lakeside location with grassy shaded sites. *From jct US 2 & Hwy 78: Go 2 mi E on Hwy 78, then 1/2 mi S on Blue Rock Rd.*

◆◆◆FACILITIES: 185 sites, most common site width 50 feet, 150 full hookups, 25 water & elec (15,20 & 30 amp receptacles), 10 no hookups, seasonal sites, a/c allowed ($), heater not allowed, tenting available, RV storage, sewage disposal, laundry, public phone, grocery store, RV supplies, LP gas refill by weight, ice, tables, fire rings, wood.

◆◆◆◆RECREATION: rec hall, swim pool, lake swimming, boating, canoeing, lake fishing, basketball hoop, playground, 2 shuffleboard courts, badminton, sports field, horseshoes, volleyball.

Open May 1 through Oct 1. Rate in 1995 $22 per family. No refunds. Reservations recommended Jul 1 through Labor Day. Member of VAPCOO. Phone: (802) 796-3733.
**SEE AD THIS PAGE**

**Goose Point Campground**—Open rolling, grassy terrain overlooking lake. *From jct Hwy 78 & US 2: Go 3 mi SE on US 2.* ◆◆FACILITIES: 140 sites, most common site width 25 feet, 80 full hookups, 60 water & elec (20 & 30 amp receptacles), seasonal sites, 38 pull-thrus, tenting available, sewage disposal, laundry, grocery store, LP gas refill by weight, ice, tables, fire rings, wood. ◆◆◆RECREATION: rec hall, swim pool, lake swimming, boating, canoeing, ramp, dock, 1 canoe boat rentals, lake fishing, 2 shuffleboard courts, badminton, horseshoes, volleyball. Recreation open to the public. Open May 1 through Oct 15. Rate in 1995 $16-18 for 4 persons. No refunds. Member of VAPCOO. Phone: (802) 796-3711.

## ANDOVER—E-3

**Horseshoe Acres**—Rural CAMPGROUND with wooded or open sites. *From west jct Hwy 103 & Hwy 11: Go 3 mi W on Hwy 11, then 4 mi NW on Andover-Weston Rd.* ◆◆◆FACILITIES: 135 sites, most common site width 40 feet, 17 full hookups, 98 water & elec (20 & 30 amp receptacles), 20 no hookups, seasonal sites, 74 pull-thrus, tenting available, sewage disposal, laundry, public phone, limited grocery store, LP gas refill by weight/by meter, ice, tables, fire rings, grills, wood. ◆◆◆RECREATION: rec hall, rec room/area, pavilion, swim pool, pond swimming, river/stream fishing, playground, badminton, sports field, horseshoes, hiking trails, volleyball. Open all year. Facilities fully operational May 1 through Columbus Day. Rate in 1995 $17-19 per family. Member of VAPCOO. Phone: (802) 875-2960.

## ARLINGTON—E-2

**CAMPING ON THE BATTENKILL**—Grassy wooded CAMPGROUND on rushing river. *From north jct US 7A & Hwy 313: Go 3/4 mi N on US 7A.*

◆◆◆FACILITIES: 95 sites, most common site width 25 feet, 45 full hookups, 41 water & elec, 3 elec (30 & 50 amp receptacles), 6

ARLINGTON—Continued
CAMPING ON THE BATTENKILL—Continued

no hookups, seasonal sites, 15 pull-thrus, a/c allowed ($), heater not allowed, tenting available, sewage disposal, public phone, LP gas refill by weight/by meter, ice, tables, fire rings, wood.

◆◆RECREATION: river swimming, river fishing, playground, sports field.

Open Apr 15 through Oct 20. Rate in 1995 $15-18.50 for 2 persons. Reservations recommended Jul through Labor Day. Member of VAPCOO. Phone: (802) 375-6663.
**SEE AD THIS PAGE**

**Howell's Camping Area**—Wooded CAMPGROUND beside a pond. *From new Hwy 7 (exit 3): Go 2 mi W, then 1 mi N on Historic 7A, then 200feet W on Hwy 313, then S on School Street to end.* ◆◆FACILITIES: 73 sites, most common site width 25 feet, 40 full hookups, 33 water & elec (30 amp receptacles), seasonal sites, 8 pull-thrus, tenting available, sewage disposal, laundry, LP gas refill by weight/by meter, tables, fire rings, wood. ◆◆RECREATION: rec room/area, pond swimming, boating, electric motors only, canoeing, dock, 3 canoe/2 pedal boat rentals, pond fishing, horseshoes. Open mid Apr through mid Oct. Rate in 1995 $16 for 4 persons. Phone: (802) 375-6469.

**LAKE LAUDERDALE CAMPGROUND**—*Less than 1/2 hr from Arlington: Go W on Hwy 313, then turn right on CR 61.*
**SEE PRIMARY LISTING AT CAMBRIDGE, NY AND AD CAMBRIDGE, NY PAGE 596**

## ASCUTNEY—E-3

ASCUTNEY STATE PARK—*From I-91 (exit 8): Go 2 mi N on US 5, then 1 mi NW on Hwy 44A.* FACILITIES: 49 sites, 49 no hookups, tenting available, handicap restroom facilities, sewage disposal, fire rings, wood. RECREATION: playground, hiking trails. Open mid May through Oct 9. Phone: (802) 674-2060.

**Running Bear Camping Area**—Rural, wooded, hilly terrain convenient to a major highway. *From jct I-91 (exit 8) & US 5: Go 1 mi N on US 5.* ◆◆FACILITIES: 101 sites, most common site width 25 feet, 43 full hookups, 38 water & elec (20 & 30 amp receptacles), 20 no hookups, seasonal sites, tenting available, sewage disposal, public phone, limited grocery store, LP gas refill by weight/by meter, ice, tables, fire rings, grills, wood. ◆◆◆RECREATION: rec hall, swim pool, badminton, sports field, horseshoes, volleyball. Open May 1 through Oct 15. Rate in 1995 $18-20 per family. Member of VAPCOO. Phone: (802) 674-6417.

WILGUS STATE PARK—*From jct I-91 (exit 8) & US 5: Go 1 1/2 mi S on US 5.* FACILITIES: 29 sites, 29 no hookups, tenting available, handicap restroom facilities, sewage disposal, tables, fire rings, wood. RECREATION: boating, canoeing, 2 canoe boat rentals, river fishing, playground, horseshoes, hiking trails. Recreation open to the public. Open mid May through Oct 9. Phone: (802) 674-5422.

**SILVER LAKE**
**Family Campground**
*In the Picturesque Village of Barnard overlooking Beautiful Silver Lake*
**Complete Camping Facilities**
**Camping Cabin Rentals**
Offering clean restrooms,
quiet surroundings,
and relaxation
Visit Central Vermont's finest attractions
**Out of State Reservations Call:**
**1-800-898-9974 code 94**
**For Information Call:**
**(802) 234-9974**
Box 111, Barnard VT 05031 See listing at Barnard

## BARNARD—D-3

**SILVER LAKE FAMILY CAMPGROUND**—CAMPGROUND with grassy, open and shaded sites. *From center of town on Hwy 12: Go 1/4 mi S at General Store to park located opposite post office.*

◆◆FACILITIES: 67 sites, most common site width 20 feet, 26 full hookups, 12 water & elec (15 & 20 amp receptacles), 29 no hookups, seasonal sites, 4 pull-thrus, a/c allowed ($), heater not allowed, tenting available, cabins, sewage disposal, public phone, LP gas refill by weight, ice, tables, fire rings, grills, wood.

◆◆RECREATION: rec hall, coin games, lake swimming, canoeing, 3 canoe boat rentals, lake fishing, badminton, horseshoes, volleyball.

Open May 15 through mid Oct. Rate in 1995 $19-20 per family. No refunds. Master Card/Visa accepted. Member of VAPCOO. Phone: (802) 234-9974.
**SEE AD THIS PAGE**

SILVER LAKE STATE PARK—*From town: Go 1/4 mi N on Town Rd.* FACILITIES: 47 sites, 47 no hookups, tenting available, handicap restroom facilities, sewage disposal, pub-

SILVER LAKE STATE PARK—Continued on next page
BARNARD—Continued on next page

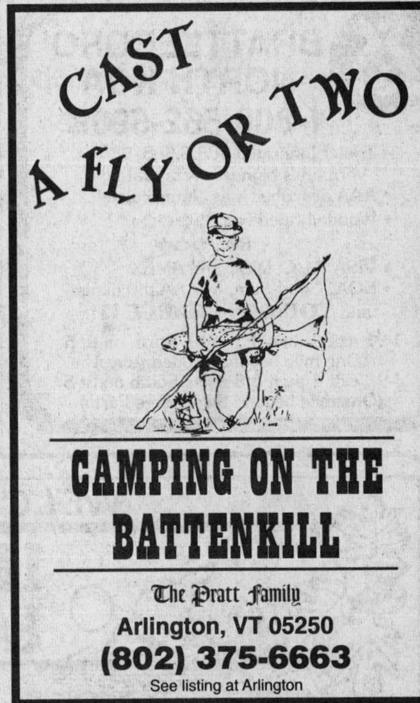

*On beautiful Lake Champlain*

**1500' OF SANDY BEACH**
**L-Shaped Pool with Diving Area**
**Excellent Fishing, Swimming and Boating**
**Our Site Is Reputed Among Windsailing Enthusiasts**
**Call (802) 796-3733 or write**
**P.O. Box 50, Alburg, VT 05440-0050**
**55 MILES FROM MONTREAL'S NEW CASINO**

BARNARD—Continued
SILVER LAKE STATE PARK—Continued

lic phone, tables, fire rings, grills, wood. RECREATION: lake swimming, boating, no motors, 4 row/4 canoe/2 pedal boat rentals, lake fishing, playground. Open mid May through early Sep. Phone: (802) 234-9451.

## BARRE—C-3

**Lazy Lions Campground**—CAMPGROUND with wooded grassy sites. *From I-89 (exit 6): Go 4 mi E on Hwy 63 to Hwy 14, then 1 mi straight ahead from stop light.* ◆◆◆FACILITIES: 35 sites, most common site width 30 feet, 21 full hookups, (30 amp receptacles), 14 no hookups, seasonal sites, 3 pull-thrus, tenting available, handicap restroom facilities, sewage disposal, laundry, public phone, ice, tables, fire rings, grills, wood. RECREATION: horseshoes. Open May 15 through Nov 1. Rate in 1995 $17-20 per family. Member of VAPCOO. Phone: (802) 479-2823.

**LIMEHURST LAKE CAMPGROUND**—Open partially shaded terrain, with grassy sites beside a lake. *From jct I-89 (exit 6) & Hwy 63: Go 4 mi E on Hwy 63, then 6 mi S on Hwy 14.*

WELCOME

◆◆◆◆FACILITIES: 71 sites, most common site width 35 feet, 25 full hookups, 26 water & elec (20 & 30 amp receptacles), 20 no hookups, seasonal sites, 8 pull-thrus, a/c allowed ($), heater allowed ($), cable TV, phone hookups, tenting available, group sites for tents/RVs, RV rentals, cabins, RV storage, sewage disposal, laundry, public phone, limited grocery store, RV supplies, LP gas refill by meter, ice, tables, fire rings, grills, wood.

◆◆◆RECREATION: rec room/area, equipped pavilion, coin games, lake swimming, water slide ($), boating, canoeing, 3 row/3 canoe/5 pedal boat rentals, lake fishing, playground, planned group activities (weekends only), horseshoes, hiking trails, volleyball. Recreation open to the public.

Open Apr 1 through Nov 30. Facilities fully operational May 1 through Oct 30. Rate in 1995 $16.50-20 per family. Reservations recommended Jul through Oct 15. Master Card/Visa accepted. Member of VAPCOO. Phone: (802) 433-6662. FCRV 10% discount.

**SEE AD THIS PAGE**

## BENNINGTON—F-1

**Greenwood Lodge and Campsites**—Spacious CAMPGROUND with, wooded mountaintop sites. *From jct US 7 & Hwy 9: Go 8 mi E on Hwy 9 (enter at Prospect Ski Mountain sign).* ◆◆FACILITIES: 26 sites, most common site width 25 feet, 30 ft. max RV length, 6 water & elec (20 amp receptacles), 20 no hookups, tenting available, ice, tables, fire rings, grills, wood. ◆◆◆RECREATION: rec room/area, pond swimming, boating, canoeing, 2 row/2 canoe boat rentals, pond fishing, badminton, sports field, horseshoes, hiking trails, volleyball. Open May through Nov. Rate in 1995 $13-15 for 2 persons. Member of VAPCOO. Phone: (802) 442-2547.

WOODFORD STATE PARK—*From town: Go 10 mi E on Hwy 9.* FACILITIES: 102 sites, 102 no hookups, tenting available, handicap restroom facilities, sewage disposal, public phone, tables, fire rings, wood. RECREATION: lake swimming, boating, no motors, row/canoe boat rentals, lake fishing, playground, hiking trails. Open mid May through Oct 9. Phone: (802) 447-7169.

## BLOOMFIELD—A-5

MAIDSTONE STATE PARK—*From town: Go 5 mi S on Hwy 102, then 5 mi SW on State Forest highway.* FACILITIES: 83 sites, 83 no hookups, tenting available, sewage disposal, public phone, tables, fire rings, wood. RECREATION: lake swimming, boating, ramp, row/canoe boat rentals, lake fishing, playground, hiking trails. Open mid May through early Sep. Phone: (802) 676-3930.

## BOMOSEEN—D-2

BOMOSEEN STATE PARK—*From jct US 4 (exit 4) & Hwy 30: Go 1 mi S on Hwy 30, then 2 mi W on US 4, then 4 mi N on West Shore Rd.* FACILITIES: 66 sites, 19 ft. max RV length, 66 no hookups, tenting available, handicap restroom facilities, sewage disposal, public phone, tables, fire rings, wood. RECREATION: pavilion, lake swimming, boating, ramp, dock, 6 row/2 canoe boat rentals, lake fishing, playground, horseshoes, hiking trails, volleyball. Open mid May through early Sep. Phone: (802) 265-4242.

**LAKE BOMOSEEN CAMPGROUND**—A lakeside location with shaded sites. *From jct US 4 & Hwy 30 (Exit 4): Go 5 mi N on Hwy 30.*

WELCOME

◆◆◆FACILITIES: 131 sites, most common site width 50 feet, 40 full hookups, 34 water & elec, 5 elec (20 & 30 amp receptacles), 52 no hookups, seasonal sites, a/c allowed ($), heater allowed ($), cable TV, tenting available, group sites for tents/RVs, tent rentals, RV rentals, RV storage, sewage disposal, laundry, public phone, full service store, RV supplies, LP gas refill by weight/by meter, gasoline, marine gas, ice, tables, fire rings, wood, traffic control gate.

◆◆◆◆RECREATION: rec hall, rec room/area, coin games, swim pool, boating, canoeing, ramp, dock, 2 row/4 canoe/4 pedal/10 motor boat rentals, lake/stream fishing, mini-golf ($), basketball hoop, playground, shuffleboard court, movies, tennis court, badminton, sports field, horseshoes, hiking trails, volleyball.

Open late Apr through mid Oct. Rate in 1995 $20.50-23.50 per family. No refunds. Discover/Master Card/Visa accepted. Member of VAPCOO. Phone: (802) 273-2061.

**SEE AD RUTLAND PAGE 856**

## BRANDON—D-2

**Country Village Campground**—Rural park with open meadow and wooded sites. *From jct US 7 & Hwy 73: Go 3 mi N on US 7.* ◆◆◆FACILITIES: 44 sites, most common site width 30 feet, 37 water & elec (20 & 30 amp receptacles), 7 no hookups, seasonal sites, 5 pull-thrus, tenting available, sewage disposal, limited grocery store, ice, tables, fire rings, grills, wood. ◆◆RECREATION: swim pool, mini-golf ($), 2 shuffleboard courts, badminton, horseshoes, volleyball. Open May 15 through Oct 15. Rate in 1995 $11.50-13.25 per family. Phone: (802) 247-3333.

**Smoke Rise Diner and Campground**—Rural, open, grassy sites. *From jct US 7 & Hwy 73: Go 2 mi N on US 7.* ◆◆FACILITIES: 45 sites, most common site width 25 feet, 21 full hookups, 24 water & elec (20 & 30 amp receptacles), seasonal sites, 23 pull-thrus, tenting available, sewage disposal, laundry, public phone, LP gas refill by weight/by meter, ice, tables, fire rings, wood. ◆◆RECREATION: pavilion, swim pool, badminton, sports field, horseshoes, volleyball. Open May 15 through Oct 15. Rate in 1995 $14-16 for 2 persons. No refunds. Member of VAPCOO. Phone: (802) 247-6472.

## BRATTLEBORO—F-3

**BALD MOUNTAIN CAMPGROUND**—*From I-91 (exit 2): Go E on Rt 9 to Rt 30, then 15 mi N on Rt 30, then 3/4 mi W on CR (State Forest TH 4), then 1 1/4 mi NW on State Park Rd.*

WELCOME

**SEE PRIMARY LISTING AT TOWNSHEND AND AD TOWNSHEND PAGE 857**

FORT DUMMER STATE PARK—*From jct I-91 (exit 1) & US 5: Go 1/10 mi N on US 5, then 1/2 mi E on Fairground Rd, then 1 mi S on Main St & Old Guilford Rd.* FACILITIES: 61 sites, 61 no hookups, tenting available, sewage disposal, public phone, tables, fire rings, wood. RECREATION: playground, hiking trails. Open mid May through early Sep. Phone: (802) 254-2610.

**HIDDEN ACRES RV PARK & CAMPGROUND**—An RV PARK with open & partially shaded sites. *From jct I-91 (exit 3) Hwy 9E & US 5: Go 2 1/2 mi N on US 5.*

WELCOME

◆◆◆FACILITIES: 87 sites, most common site width 40 feet, 11 full hookups, 44 water & elec, 12 elec (20 & 30 amp receptacles), 20 no hookups, 26 pull-thrus, a/c allowed ($), heater allowed ($), tenting available, group sites for tents/RVs, RV storage, handicap restroom facilities, sewage disposal, laundry, public phone, limited grocery store, RV supplies, ice, tables, fire rings, wood, church services.

◆◆◆RECREATION: rec hall, rec room/area, coin games, swim pool, mini-golf ($), basketball hoop,

HIDDEN ACRES RV PARK & CAMPGROUND—Continued on next page
BRATTLEBORO—Continued on next page







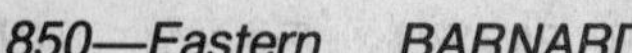

**BRATTLEBORO**—Continued
HIDDEN ACRES RV PARK & CAMPGROUND—Continued

playground, 2 shuffleboard courts, badminton, horseshoes, volleyball.

Open May 1 through Oct 15. Rate in 1995 $17-23 for 2 persons. Master Card/Visa accepted. Member of VAPCOO. Phone: (802) 254-2098.

**SEE AD PAGE 850**

**KOA-BRATTLEBORO NORTH**—Open, grassy flat CAMPGROUND with gravel pull-thru sites and shade trees. *Northbound: From jct I-91 (exit 3), Hwy 9 East & US 5: Go 3 1/2 mi N on US 5. Southbound: From jct I-91 (exit 4): Go 2 3/4 mi S on US 5.*

◆◆◆◆FACILITIES: 42 sites, most common site width 50 feet, 12 full hookups, 29 water & elec (20 & 30 amp receptacles), 1 no hookups, 34 pull-thrus, a/c allowed, heater allowed, tenting available, sewage disposal, laundry, public phone, limited grocery store, ice, tables, grills.

◆◆◆RECREATION: rec hall, rec room/area, coin games, swim pool, basketball hoop, playground, badminton, horseshoes, volleyball.

Open Apr 19 through Oct 26. Rate in 1995 $18-26 for 2 persons. Reservations recommended Jul 1 through Columbus Day. American Express/Discover/Master Card/Visa accepted. Member of VAPCOO. Phone: (802) 254-5908. KOA 10% value card discount.

**SEE AD PAGE 850 AND AD FRONT OF BOOK PAGES 68 AND 69**

**VERMONT TRAVELER**—*From jct I-91 (exit 2) & Hwy 9: Go 2 mi W on Hwy 9.* SALES: travel trailers, truck campers, 5th wheels, motor homes, mini-motor homes, fold-down camping trailers. SERVICES: RV appliance mechanic full-time, LP gas refill by weight/by meter, RV rentals, RV storage, sells parts/accessories, installs hitches. Open all year. Master Card/Visa accepted. Phone: (802) 254-4881.

**SEE AD THIS PAGE**

## BURLINGTON—B-2

**LAKE CHAMPLAIN FERRIES**—*From jct I-89 (exit 14W) & US 2: Go 2 mi W on US 2 (Main St), then 1 block S on Battery St to the King St Dock.* Auto ferries cross scenic Lake Champlain between Burlington, VT & Port Kent, NY. Open Mid May through Mid Oct. Phone: (802) 864-9804.

**SEE AD LAKE CHAMPLAIN PAGE 853**

## CAVENDISH—E-3

**Catton Place Campground**—Wooded and open, grassy sites nestled in the foothills. *From jct Hwy 103 & Hwy 131: Go 4 1/2 mi E on Hwy 131, then 1 1/2 mi NE on Tarbell Rd, then 1/4 mi W on East Rd.* ◆◆ FACILITIES: 81 sites, most common site width 33 feet, 30 ft. max RV length, 38 full hookups, 28 water & elec, 15 elec (15 amp receptacles), seasonal sites, 22 pull-thrus, tenting available, sewage disposal, laundry, public phone, ice, tables, fire rings, grills, wood. ◆◆RECREATION: swim pool ($), shuffleboard court, badminton, horseshoes, volleyball. Open Memorial Day through Nov 1. Rate in 1995 $13-14 for 4 persons. Member of VAPCOO. Phone: (802) 226-7767.

## CHARLOTTE—B-1

**LAKE CHAMPLAIN FERRIES**—*From jct US 7 & Hwy F5: Go 2 1/2 mi W on F5.* Auto ferries cross scenic Lake Champlain between Charlotte, VT & Essex, NY. Open Apr through Dec. Phone: (802) 864-9804.

**SEE AD LAKE CHAMPLAIN PAGE 853**

**OLD LANTERN CAMPGROUND**—Rolling terrain with grassy, open or wooded sites in rural area. *From jct US 7 & Hwy F5: Go 1/2 mi W on Hwy F5, then 1/2 mi S on Green Bush Rd.*

◆◆FACILITIES: 95 sites, most common site width 40 feet, 28 full hookups, 47 water & elec (30 amp receptacles), 20 no hookups, seasonal sites, 10 pull-thrus, a/c allowed ($), heater allowed, phone hookups, tenting available, group sites for tents, sewage disposal, laundry, public phone, limited grocery store, LP gas refill by weight/by meter, ice, tables, fire rings, grills, wood.

◆◆RECREATION: rec hall, swim pool, badminton, horseshoes, hiking trails, volleyball.

Open May 1 through Oct 15. Rate in 1995 $15-22 for 4 persons. No refunds. Member of VAPCOO. Phone: (802) 425-2120.

**SEE AD THIS PAGE**

## COLCHESTER—B-2

**LONE PINE CAMPSITES**—CAMPGROUND with paved roads & level, grassy sites. *N'bound from jct I-89 (exit 16) & US 2/7: Go 3 1/2 mi N on US 2/7, then 1 mi left on Bay Rd. S'bound from jct I-89 (exit 17) & US 2/7: Go 3 1/2 mi S on US 2/7, then 1 mi right on Bay Rd.*

◆◆◆◆FACILITIES: 260 sites, most common site width 30 feet, 165 full hookups, 95 water & elec (15 & 30 amp receptacles), seasonal sites, a/c allowed ($), phone hookups, tenting available, RV rentals, RV storage, handicap restroom facilities, sewage disposal, laundry, public phone, grocery store, RV supplies, LP gas refill by weight/by meter, ice, tables, fire rings, grills, wood.

◆◆◆◆RECREATION: rec room/area, equipped pavilion, coin games, 2 swim pools, mini-golf ($), basketball hoop, playground, shuffleboard court, planned group activities, 4 tennis courts, horseshoes, volleyball.

Open May 1 through Oct 15. 3 day minimum stay holiday weekends. Rate in 1995 $17-25 for 4 persons. No refunds. Reservations recommended Jul 1 through Labor Day. Master Card/Visa accepted. Member of VAPCOO. Phone: (802) 878-5447.

**SEE AD THIS PAGE**

**Malletts Bay Camp Ground**—A CAMPGROUND with wooded & open sites close by Lake Champlain. *From jct I-89 (exit 16) & US 2/7: Go 2 mi N on US 2/7, then 3 mi W on Hwy 127.* ◆◆◆FACILITIES: 112 sites, most common site width 25 feet, 78 full hookups, 34 water & elec (20 & 30 amp receptacles), seasonal sites, tenting available, laundry, public phone, limited grocery store, ice, tables, fire rings, wood. ◆◆RECREATION: rec hall, swim pool, horseshoes, volleyball. Open May 1 through Oct 15. Rate in 1995 $17-22 per family. No refunds. Member of VAPCOO. Phone: (802) 863-6980.

## DANBY—E-2

**Otter Creek Campground**—Grassy, partially shaded sites beside river. *From US 7 & north town limits: Go 3/4 mi N on US 7.* ◆◆FACILITIES: 50 sites, most common site width 20 feet, 35 water & elec (15 & 20 amp receptacles), 15 no hookups, seasonal sites, 5 pull-thrus, tenting available, sewage disposal, laundry, public phone, grocery store, LP gas refill by weight/by meter, ice, tables, fire rings, grills, wood. ◆◆RECREATION: rec room/area, swim pool, river swimming, canoeing, 3 canoe boat rentals, river fishing, badminton, sports field, horseshoes, volleyball. Open all year. Facilities fully operational May 1 through Oct 1. Rate in 1995 $14 per family. No refunds. Phone: (802) 293-5041.

VT Discovered VT
1609
VT by Champlain VT

## DERBY CENTER—A-4

**CHAR-BO CAMPGROUND**—Rural, rolling, grassy plateau on hilltop overlooking lake. *From jct I-91 (exit 28) & Hwy 105: Go 4 mi E on Hwy 105, then 1/2 mi N on Haywood Rd TH 50.*

◆◆◆FACILITIES: 45 sites, most common site width 28 feet, 18 full hookups, 15 water & elec (20 & 30 amp receptacles), 12 no hookups, seasonal sites, 19 pull-thrus, a/c allowed ($), heater not allowed, tenting available, RV rentals, RV storage, sewage disposal, laundry, public phone, limited grocery store, RV supplies, ice, tables, fire rings, grills, wood.

◆◆◆RECREATION: rec room/area, coin games, swim pool, lake swimming, boating, canoeing, 2 row/2 canoe/2 pedal boat rentals, lake fishing, basketball hoop, badminton, horseshoes.

Open May 15 through Oct 8. Rate in 1995 $15-17 for 2 persons. Master Card/Visa accepted. Phone: (802) 766-8807.

**SEE AD THIS PAGE**

## DORSET—E-2

**DORSET RV PARK**—An RV PARK with mostly shaded sites. *From jct US 7A & Hwy 30 (in Manchester): Go 4 mi N on Hwy 30.*

◆◆◆◆FACILITIES: 40 sites, most common site width 25 feet, 6 full hookups, 21 water & elec (30 amp receptacles), 13 no hookups, 6 pull-thrus, a/c allowed ($), heater allowed ($), tenting available, sewage disposal, laundry, public phone, ice, tables, fire rings, grills, wood.

◆◆RECREATION: rec room/area, playground, horseshoes.

Open Apr 15 through Oct 31. Rate in 1995 $15-17 per family. Member of VAPCOO. Phone: (802) 867-5754.

**SEE AD THIS PAGE**

## EDEN MILLS—A-3

**Lakeview Camping Area**—CAMPGROUND with open grassy sites, overlooking lake. *From jct Hwy 118 & Hwy 100: Go 2 mi N on Hwy 100.* ◆◆FACILITIES: 68 sites, most common site width 30 feet, 68 water & elec (20 & 30 amp receptacles), seasonal sites, 6 pull-thrus, tenting available, sewage disposal, limited grocery store, ice, tables, fire rings, grills, wood. ◆◆RECREATION: rec hall, lake swimming, lake fishing, 2 shuffleboard courts, badminton, horseshoes, volleyball. Open May 15 through Sep 15. Rate in 1995 $12-16 for 2 persons. No refunds. Phone: (802) 635-2255.

## ENOSBURG FALLS—A-2

LAKE CARMI STATE PARK—*From town: Go 3 mi W on Hwy 105, then 3 mi N on Hwy 236.* FACILITIES: 178 sites, 178 no hookups, tenting available, sewage disposal, public phone, tables, fire rings, wood. RECREATION: lake swimming, boating, ramp, row boat rentals, lake fishing, playground. Open mid May through early Sep. Phone: (802) 933-8383.

## ESSEX CENTER—B-2

**EHLER'S RV**—*From jct I-289 & Hwy 15: Go 100 yards N on Hwy 15.* SALES: travel trailers, park models, truck campers, 5th wheels, motor homes, mini-motor homes, fold-down camping trailers. SERVICES: Engine/Chassis & RV appliance mechanic full-time, LP gas refill by meter, RV storage, sells parts/accessories, installs hitches. Open all year. Discover/Master Card/Visa accepted. Phone: (802) 878-4907.

**SEE AD THIS PAGE**

## FAIRFAX—A-2

**MAPLE GROVE CAMPGROUND**—Rural setting with shaded, level sites. *N'bound from jct I-89 (exit 18) & Hwy 104A: Go 4 3/4 mi E on Hwy 104A, then 3/4 mi W on Hwy 104. S'bound from jct I-89 (exit 19) & Hwy 104: Go 8 mi S on Hwy 104.*

◆◆◆FACILITIES: 24 sites, most common site width 20 feet, 12 full hookups, 12 water & elec (30 & 50 amp receptacles), seasonal sites, 2 pull-thrus, a/c allowed ($), heater not allowed, tenting available, sewage disposal, laundry, public phone, limited grocery store, RV supplies, ice, tables, fire rings, grills, wood.

◆RECREATION: basketball hoop, badminton, horseshoes, volleyball.

Open May 1 through Oct 15. Rate in 1995 $14-16 per family. Master Card/Visa accepted. Member of VAPCOO. Phone: (802) 849-6439.

**SEE AD THIS PAGE**

## GAYSVILLE—D-3

**WHITE RIVER VALLEY CAMPING**—Partially shaded CAMPGROUND beside a river. *From jct I-89 (exit 3) & Hwy 107: Go 8 mi W on Hwy 107.*

◆◆◆FACILITIES: 102 sites, most common site width 30 feet, 19 full hookups, 39 water & elec, 8 elec (15 & 30 amp receptacles), 36 no hookups, seasonal sites, 11 pull-thrus, a/c allowed, heater allowed, tenting available, RV storage, laundry, public phone, grocery store, RV supplies, LP gas refill by weight/by meter, ice, tables, fire rings, wood.

◆◆◆RECREATION: rec hall, coin games, river swimming, whirlpool, canoeing, river fishing, basketball hoop, playground, shuffleboard court, badminton, horseshoes, volleyball.

Open May 1 through Oct 14. Rate in 1995 $17-22 for 2 persons. Discover/Master Card/Visa accepted. Member of VAPCOO. Phone: (802) 234-9115.

**SEE AD THIS PAGE**

## GEORGIA CENTER—A-2

**HOMESTEAD CAMPGROUNDS**—Wooded, grassy park with level sites. *From jct I-89 (exit 18) & Hwy 7: Go 1/4 mi S on Hwy 7.*

◆◆FACILITIES: 160 sites, most common site width 25 feet, 160 water & elec (15,20,30 & 50 amp receptacles), seasonal sites, 53 pull-thrus, a/c allowed ($), heater not allowed, cable TV ($), tenting available, group sites for tents/RVs, RV rentals, RV storage, sewage disposal, laundry, public phone, grocery store, RV supplies, LP gas refill by weight/by meter, ice, tables, fire rings, grills, wood.

◆◆◆RECREATION: rec hall, equipped pavilion, coin games, swim pool, wading pool, basketball hoop, playground, 2 shuffleboard courts, planned group activities (weekends only), badminton, horseshoes, volleyball.

Open May 1 through Oct 15. Rate in 1995 $18 per family. Master Card/Visa accepted. Member of VAPCOO. Phone: (802) 524-2356.

**SEE AD FAIRFAX THIS PAGE**

## GRAND ISLE—A-1

GRAND ISLE STATE PARK—*From town: Go 1 mi S on US 2.* FACILITIES: 156 sites, 156 no hookups, tenting available, handicap restroom facilities, sewage disposal, public phone, ice, tables, fire rings, wood. RECREATION: rec hall, lake swimming, boating, ramp, row boat rentals, lake fishing, playground. Open mid May through Oct 9. Phone: (802) 372-4300.

**LAKE CHAMPLAIN FERRIES**—*From jct US 2 & Hwy 314: Go 3 mi W on Hwy 314.* Auto ferries cross scenic Lake Champlain between Grand Isle, VT & Plattsburgh, NY. Open all year. Phone: (802) 864-9804.

**SEE AD LAKE CHAMPLAIN NEXT PAGE**

## GROTON—C-4

NEW DISCOVERY CAMPGROUND (Groton State Forest)—*From town: Go 2 mi W on US 302, then 9 1/2 mi N on Hwy 232.* FACILITIES: 61 sites, 61 no hookups, tenting available, sewage disposal, tables, fire rings, wood. RECREATION: lake fishing, playground, hiking trails. Open mid May through early Sep. Phone: (802) 584-3820.

RICKER CAMPGROUND (Groton State Forest)—*From town: Go 2 mi W on US 302, then 2 1/2 mi N on Hwy 232.* FACILITIES: 58 sites, 58 no hookups, tenting available, sewage disposal, tables, fire rings, wood. RECREATION: pond swimming, boating, ramp, row boat rentals, pond fishing, hiking trails. Open mid May through early Sep. Phone: (802) 584-3821.

STILLWATER CAMPGROUND (Groton State Forest)—*From town: Go 2 mi W on US 302, then 6 mi N on Hwy 232, then 1/2 mi E on Boulder Beach Rd.* FACILITIES: 79 sites, 79 no hookups, tenting available, sewage disposal, tables, fire rings, wood. RECREATION: lake swimming, boating, ramp, row boat rentals, fishing, playground, hiking trails. Open mid May through Oct 9. Phone: (802) 584-3822.

## HUBBARDTON—D-2

HALF MOON POND STATE PARK—*From town: Go 2 mi N on Hwy 30, then 2 mi W on Town Rd, then 1 1/2 mi S on Town Rd.* FACILITIES: 69 sites, 69 no hookups, tenting available, handicap restroom facilities, sewage disposal, public phone, tables, fire rings, wood. RECREATION: pond swimming, boating, no motors, canoeing, ramp, 3 row/3 canoe/2 pedal boat rentals, pond fishing, playground, sports field, horseshoes, hiking trails, volleyball. Open mid May through early Sep. Phone: (802) 273-2848.

## ISLAND POND—A-4

BRIGHTON STATE PARK—*From town: Go 2 mi E on Hwy 105, then 3/4 mi S on local road.* FACILITIES: 84 sites, 84 no hookups, tenting available, handicap restroom facilities, sewage disposal, public phone, tables, fire rings, wood. RECREATION: lake/pond swimming, boating, no motors, 4 row/4 canoe boat rentals, lake/pond fishing, playground, horseshoes, hiking trails. Recreation open to the public. Open mid May through Oct 9. Phone: (802) 723-4360.

## JAMAICA—E-2

JAMAICA STATE PARK—*From Hwy 30 in town: Go 1/2 mi N on town road.* FACILITIES: 59 sites, 59 no hookups, tenting available, handicap restroom facilities, sewage disposal, public phone, tables, fire rings, grills, wood. RECREATION: river swimming, river fishing, playground, horseshoes, hiking trails. Recreation open to the public. Open late Apr through Oct 9. Phone: (802) 874-4600.

## KILLINGTON—D-2

GIFFORD WOODS STATE PARK—*From jct US 4 & Hwy 100: Go 1/2 mi N on Hwy 100.* FACILITIES: 48 sites, 48 no hookups, tenting available, handicap restroom facilities, sewage disposal, public phone, tables, fire rings, wood. RECREATION: pond fishing, playground, hiking trails. Open mid May through Oct 9. Phone: (802) 775-5354.

**KILLINGTON CAMPGROUND AT ALPENHOF LODGE**—RV SPACES behind ski lodge. *From jct US 4 & Killington Rd: Go 2 1/2 mi S on Killington Rd.*

WELCOME

FACILITIES: 8 sites, 5 water & elec (30 amp receptacles), 3 no hookups, a/c allowed ($), tenting available, public phone, tables, fire rings, wood.

Rate in 1995 $16-20 for 2 persons. Master Card/Visa accepted. Phone: (802) 422-9787.

**SEE AD THIS PAGE**

## LAKE CHAMPLAIN—B-2

***See listings at Alburg, Burlington, Charlotte, Grand Isle, North Hero, South Hero VT & Plattsburg, NY***

## MARSHFIELD—B-3

**Groton Forest Road Campground**—Open CAMPGROUND with grassy sites. *From jct US 2 & Hwy 232: Go 3 mi S on Hwy 232.* ◆◆FACILITIES: 35 sites, most common site width 25 feet, 35 water & elec (20 & 30 amp receptacles), tenting available, sewage disposal, ice, tables, fire rings, wood. ◆◆RECREATION: swim pool, playground. Open May 1 through Oct 15. Rate in 1995 $14 per family. Member of VAPCOO. Phone: (802) 426-3231.

**Onion River Camping Area**—Grassy, hilly, riverside CAMPGROUND. *From jct Hwy 14 & US 2: Go 5 1/4 mi E on US 2.* ◆◆FACILITIES: 33 sites, most common site width 20 feet, 6 full hookups, 11 water & elec, 5 elec (15 & 30 amp receptacles), 11 no hookups, seasonal sites, tenting available, sewage disposal, laundry, public phone, limited grocery store, LP gas refill by weight/by meter, ice, tables, fire rings, grills, wood. ◆◆RECREATION: river fishing, badminton, horseshoes, hiking trails, volleyball. Open early May through mid Oct. Rate in 1995 $10-16 per family. Member of VAPCOO. Phone: (802) 426-3232.

## MIDDLEBURY—C-2

**LAKE DUNMORE KAMPERSVILLE**—Wooded CAMPGROUND beside a lake. *From jct Hwy 125 & Hwy 30, & US 7: Go 6 mi S on US 7, then 1 1/2 mi S on Hwy 53.*

WELCOME

◆◆◆◆FACILITIES: 210 sites, most common site width 35 feet, 119 full hookups, 67 water & elec (30 amp receptacles), 24 no hookups, seasonal sites, a/c allowed ($), heater allowed ($), cable TV ($), phone hookups, tenting available, cabins, RV storage, sewage disposal, laundry, public phone, full service store, RV supplies, LP gas refill by weight, gasoline, ice, tables, fire rings, grills, wood.

◆◆◆◆◆RECREATION: rec hall, rec room/area, equipped pavilion, coin games, 2 swim pools (heated), wading pool, lake swimming, boating, canoeing, ramp, dock, 6 row/4 canoe/5 pedal/4 motor boat rentals, water skiing, lake fishing, mini-golf ($), basketball hoop, playground, 4 shuffleboard courts, planned group activities, movies, recreation director, badminton, sports field, horseshoes, hiking trails, volleyball, cross country skiing, snowmobile trails.

Open all year. Pools open Memorial Day thru Labor Day. Rate in 1995 $23-25 per family. No refunds. Reservations recommended Jul 1 through Labor Day. Master Card/Visa accepted. Member of VAPCOO. Phone: (802) 352-4501.

**SEE AD TRAVEL SECTION PAGE 847 AND AD NEXT PAGE**

**RIVERS BEND CAMPGROUND**—CAMPGROUND with sites along a river bank. *From jct Hwy 125 & US 7: Go 4 mi N on US 7.*

WELCOME

◆◆FACILITIES: 57 sites, 53 water & elec (20 & 30 amp receptacles), 4 no hookups, 10 pull-thrus, a/c allowed, phone hookups, tenting available, RV rentals, sewage disposal, laundry, public phone, LP gas refill by weight, ice, tables, fire rings, wood.

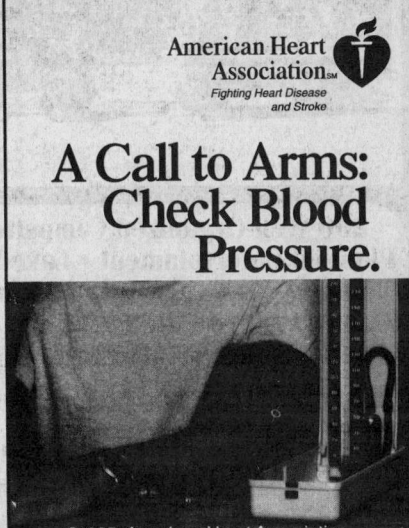

RIVERS BEND CAMPGROUND—Continued on next page
MIDDLEBURY—Continued on next page

MIDDLEBURY—Continued
RIVERS BEND CAMPGROUND—Continued

◊◊◊RECREATION: pavilion, river swimming, canoeing, float trips, river fishing, playground, horseshoes, hiking trails, volleyball.

Open May 1 through Oct 15. Rate in 1995 $18 for 4 persons. Reservations recommended all season. Master Card/Visa accepted. Member of VAPCO. Phone: (802) 388-9092.
**SEE AD PAGE 853**

## MONTPELIER—B-3

**GREEN VALLEY CAMPGROUND**—Grassy, level sites convenient to a major highway. *From jct I-89 (exit 8) & US 2: Go 6 mi E on US 2.*

◊◊◊FACILITIES: 45 sites, most common site width 25 feet, 23 full hookups, 12 water & elec (20 & 30 amp receptacles), 10 no hookups, seasonal sites, a/c allowed ($), heater not allowed, cable TV ($), tenting available, group sites for tents/RVs, sewage disposal, laundry, public phone, limited grocery store, LP gas refill by weight/by meter, ice, tables.

◊RECREATION: swim pool, playground, horseshoes.

Open May 1 through Oct 30. Rate in 1995 $14-18 for 2 persons. Member of VAPCOO. Phone: (802) 223-6217.
**SEE AD THIS PAGE**



## MORRISVILLE—B-3

ELMORE STATE PARK—*From town: Go 5 mi S on Hwy 12 (Lake Elmore).* FACILITIES: 60 sites, 60 no hookups, tenting available, handicap restroom facilities, sewage disposal, public phone, ice, tables, fire rings, wood. RECREATION: lake swimming, boating, ramp, row boat rentals, lake fishing, playground, hiking trails. Open mid May through Oct 9. Phone: (802) 888-2982.

**MOUNTAIN VIEW CAMPGROUND AND COTTAGES**—Country, semi-shaded grassy CAMPGROUND. *From jct Hwy 100 & Hwy 15: Go 3 mi E on Hwy 15.*

◊◊◊◊FACILITIES: 60 sites, most common site width 25 feet, 8 full hookups, 27 water & elec (20 & 30 amp receptacles), 25 no hookups, a/c allowed ($), heater not allowed, phone hookups, tenting available, group sites for tents/RVs, cabins, handicap restroom facilities, sewage disposal, laundry, public phone, ice, tables, fire rings, wood.

◊◊◊RECREATION: 2 swim pools, river swimming, whirlpool, canoeing, river fishing, mini-golf, playground, badminton, horseshoes, volleyball.

Open May 1 through Oct 15. Rate in 1995 $18-20 for 4 persons. No refunds. Master Card/Visa accepted. Member of VAPCOO. Phone: (802) 888-2178.
**SEE AD STOWE PAGE 857**

## NEWPORT—A-4

PROUTY BEACH CAMPGROUND (City Park)—*From jct I-91 (exit 27) & Hwy 191: Go 3 mi NW on Hwy 191, then W on Freeman St, then S on Veterans Ave.* FACILITIES: 50 sites, 18 full hookups, 28 water & elec, 4 no hookups, seasonal sites, tenting available, handicap restroom facilities, sewage disposal, laundry, public phone, tables, fire rings, grills, wood. RECREATION: lake swimming, boating, canoeing, 1 canoe/1 pedal boat rentals, lake fishing, playground, shuffleboard court, 4 tennis courts, sports field, horseshoes, hiking trails, volleyball. Recreation open to the public. Open May 10 through Oct 12. Phone: (802) 334-7951.

## NORTH DORSET—E-2

EMERALD LAKE STATE PARK—*In town on US 7.* FACILITIES: 105 sites, 105 no hookups, tenting available, handicap restroom facilities, sewage disposal, public phone, tables, fire rings, wood. RECREATION: lake swimming, boating, no motors, ramp, row/canoe boat rentals, lake fishing, playground, hiking trails. Open mid May through Oct 9. Phone: (802) 362-1655.

## NORTH HERO—A-1

**CARRY BAY CAMPGROUND**—Partially shaded, level, grassy, lakeside CAMPGROUND. *From North Hero Post Office: Go 1 3/4 mi N on US 2.*

◊◊◊FACILITIES: 68 sites, most common site width 25 feet, 8 full hookups, 30 water & elec (15,20 & 30 amp receptacles), 30 no hookups, seasonal sites, a/c allowed ($), heater allowed ($), tenting available, group sites for tents/RVs, cabins, sewage disposal, limited grocery store, ice, tables, fire rings, wood.

◊◊◊RECREATION: swim pool, boating, canoeing, ramp, dock, 1 canoe/2 pedal/5 motor boat rentals, lake fishing, basketball hoop, playground, badminton, horseshoes, volleyball. Recreation open to the public.

Open May 15 through Oct 15. Rate in 1995 $15-18 for 2 persons. No refunds. Member of VAPCOO. Phone: (802) 372-8233.
**SEE AD LAKE CHAMPLAIN PAGE 853**

NORTH HERO STATE PARK—*From town: Go 4 mi N on US 2, then 4 mi E on town road.* FACILITIES: 117 sites, 117 no hookups, tenting available, handicap restroom facilities, sewage disposal, public phone, ice, tables, fire rings, wood. RECREATION: lake swimming, boating, ramp, 4 row boat rentals, lake fishing, playground, sports field, hiking trails. Open mid May through early Sep. Phone: (802) 372-8727.

## ORLEANS—A-4

**WILL-O-WOOD CAMPGROUND**—Rural, partially shaded, grassy, mountainview overlooking lake. *From jct I-91 (exit 26) & Hwy 58: Go 6 1/4 mi E on Hwy 58, then 1/2 mi S on Hwy 5A.*

◊◊◊FACILITIES: 115 sites, most common site width 30 feet, 55 full hookups, 31 water & elec (20 & 30 amp receptacles), 29 no hookups, seasonal sites, 8 pull-thrus, a/c allowed ($), heater allowed ($), tenting available, RV rentals, RV storage, sewage disposal, laundry, public phone, grocery store, RV supplies, LP gas refill by weight/by meter, ice, tables, fire rings, grills, wood.

WILL-O-WOOD CAMPGROUND—Continued on next page
**ORLEANS**—Continued on next page

ORLEANS—Continued
WILL-O-WOOD CAMPGROUND—Continued

◆◆◆RECREATION: rec hall, coin games, swim pool, basketball hoop, shuffleboard court, badminton, horseshoes, volleyball.

Open May 1 through Oct 15. Rate in 1995 $17-19 per family. No refunds. Master Card/Visa accepted. Member of VAPCOO. Phone: (802) 525-3575. FCRV 10% discount.

**SEE AD THIS PAGE**

## PERKINSVILLE—E-3

**Crown Point Camping Area**—CAMPGROUND in a pine grove. *Southbound: From jct Hwy 131 & Hwy 106: Go 2 mi S on Hwy 106, then 1 mi E on Stoughton Pond Rd. Northbound: From jct I-91 (exit 7): Go 10 mi N on Hwy 106, then 1 mi E on Stoughton Pond Rd.* ◆◆FACILITIES: 140 sites, most common site width 35 feet, 74 full hookups, 46 water & elec (15 & 20 amp receptacles), 20 no hookups, seasonal sites, 11 pull-thrus, tenting available, sewage disposal, laundry, public phone, ice, tables, fire rings, grills, wood. ◆◆RECREATION: pavilion, boating, electric motors only, canoeing, 2 row/2 canoe/1 pedal boat rentals, lake fishing, playground, horseshoes, hiking trails. Open May 1 through Nov 1. Facilities fully operational May 1 through Columbus Day. Rate in 1995 $15-17 per family. No refunds. Member of VAPCOO. Phone: (802) 263-5555.

## PERU—E-2

GREEN MOUNTAIN NATIONAL FOREST (Hapgood Pond Campground)—*From town: Go 1 3/4 mi NE on Hapgood Pond Rd (FR 3).* FACILITIES: 28 sites, 32 ft. max RV length, 28 no hookups, tenting available, non-flush toilets, handicap restroom facilities, tables, fire rings, grills, wood. RECREATION: pond swimming, boating, electric motors only, canoeing, pond/stream fishing, hiking trails. Open Memorial Day through mid Oct. No showers. Phone: (802) 824-6456.

## PLYMOUTH UNION—D-2

COOLIDGE STATE PARK—*From jct Hwy 100 & Hwy 100A: Go 3 mi N on Hwy 100A.* FACILITIES: 60 sites, 60 no hookups, tenting available, handicap restroom facilities, sewage disposal, public phone, ice, tables, fire rings, wood. RECREATION: pavilion, playground, hiking trails. Open mid May through Oct 9. Phone: (802) 672-3612.

## POULTNEY—D-1

LAKE ST. CATHARINE STATE PARK—*From town: Go 3 mi S on Hwy 30.* FACILITIES: 61 sites, 61 no hookups, tenting available, handicap restroom facilities, sewage disposal, public phone, limited grocery store, tables, fire rings, wood. RECREATION: lake swimming, boating, ramp, dock, 6 row boat rentals, lake fishing, playground, sport field. Open mid May through Oct 9. Phone: (802) 287-9158.

## POWNAL—F-1

**Pine Hollow Camping**—Rural, semi-wooded, grassy, CAMPGROUND. *N'bound from MA state line & US 7: Go 6 1/2 mi N on US 7, then 1 1/2 mi E on Barbers Pond Rd, then 3/4 mi S on Old Military Rd, then 1/4 mi W on camp road. S'bound from jct Hwy 9 & US 7: Go 6 mi S on US 7, then follow northbound directions.* ◆◆◆FACILITIES: 58 sites, most common site width 25 feet, 19 full hookups, 34 water & elec (15, 20 & 30 amp receptacles), 5 no hookups, seasonal sites, 1 pull-thrus, tenting available, sewage disposal, public phone, ice, tables, fire rings, grills, wood. ◆◆RECREATION: pond swimming, canoeing, 1 canoe/2 pedal boat rentals, pond fishing, shuffleboard court, badminton, sports field, horseshoes, volleyball. Open May 15 through Oct 15. Rate in 1995 $12-16 for 2 persons. No refunds. Member of VAPCOO. Phone: (802) 823-5569.

## QUECHEE—D-3

WELCOME

**MASCOMA LAKE CAMPING AREA**—*From jct I-89 (exit 1) in VT: Go 10 mi S on I-89 into NH to exit 17, then 2 mi E on US 4, then 7/10 mi S on US 4A.*

**SEE PRIMARY LISTING AT LEBANON, NH AND AD LEBANON, NH PAGE 545**

WELCOME

**PINE VALLEY RV RESORT**—A wooded campground near tourist attractions. *From jct I-89 (exit 1) & US 4: Go 1/2 mi W on US 4.*

◆◆◆◆FACILITIES: 72 sites, most common site width 30 feet, 49 full hookups, 21 water & elec (20,30 & 50 amp receptacles), 2 no hookups, 13 pull-thrus, a/c allowed ($), heater allowed ($), tenting available, sewage disposal, laundry, public phone, limited grocery store, LP gas refill by weight/by meter, ice, tables, fire rings, wood.

◆◆◆RECREATION: rec hall, rec room/area, coin games, swim pool, boating, 2 canoe/1 pedal boat rentals, pond fishing ($), playground.

Open May 1 through Oct 15. Rate in 1995 $17-24 for 2 persons. Master Card/Visa accepted. Member of VAPCOO. Phone: (802) 296-6711.

**SEE AD FRONT OF BOOK PAGE 31 AND AD THIS PAGE**

QUECHEE—Continued

QUECHEE GORGE STATE PARK—*From jct I-89 (exit 1) & US 4: Go 3 mi W on US 4.* FACILITIES: 54 sites, 54 no hookups, tenting available, handicap restroom facilities, sewage disposal, tables, fire rings, wood. RECREATION: river fishing, playground, sports field, hiking trails. Open mid May through Oct 9. Phone: (802) 295-2990.

## RANDOLPH—C-3

ALLIS STATE PARK—*From town: Go 12 mi N on Hwy 12, then 1 1/2 mi E on Hwy 65.* FACILITIES: 27 sites, 27 no hookups, tenting available, handicap restroom facilities, sewage disposal, tables, fire rings, wood. RECREATION: pavilion, playground, horseshoes, hiking trails. Recreation open to the public. Open mid May through early Sep. Phone: (802) 276-3175.

**Mobile Acres**—Grassy, mostly level RV AREA in a mobile home park. *From jct I-89 (exit 4) & Hwy 66: Go 2 1/2 mi W on Hwy 66, then 2 mi N on Hwy 12A.* ◆◆◆FACILITIES: 93 sites, most common site width 25 feet, 78 full hookups, 15 water & elec (20 amp receptacles), seasonal sites, 10 pull-thrus, tenting available, sewage disposal, laundry, public phone, LP gas refill by weight/by meter, ice, tables, fire rings, wood. ◆◆RECREATION: swim pool, playground, planned group activities (weekends only), sports field, horseshoes. Open May 15 through Oct 15. Rate in 1995 $15-17 for 2 persons. No refunds. Member of VAPCOO. Phone: (802) 728-5548.

## RANDOLPH CENTER—C-3

**Lake Champagne Campground**—Open grassy terrain, overlooking a small lake. *From jct I-89 (exit 4) & Hwy 66: Go 1 mi E on Hwy 66, then 1/10 mi N on Hwy 66.* ◆◆◆FACILITIES: 131 sites, most common site width 30 feet, 68 full hookups, 44 water & elec (20,30 & 50 amp receptacles), 19 no hookups, seasonal sites, 36 pull-thrus, tenting available, handicap restroom facilities, sewage disposal, laundry, public phone, LP gas refill by weight/by meter, ice, tables, fire rings, grills, wood. ◆◆◆RECREATION: rec hall, equipped pavilion, lake swimming, playground, 2 shuffleboard courts, horseshoes, volleyball. Open May 24 through Oct 15. Rate in 1995 $18-20 for 2 persons. No refunds. Member of VAPCOO. Phone: (802) 728-5293.

## ROCHESTER—C-2

**Mountain Trails**—CAMPGROUND with hillside, shaded & open sites. *From jct Hwy 73 & Hwy 100: Go 2 3/4 mi N on Hwy 100, then 1 1/2 mi E on Quarry Rd.* ◆FACILITIES: 27 sites, most common site width 30 feet, 20 ft. max RV length, 5 full hookups, 9 water & elec (15 & 20 amp receptacles), 13 no hookups, seasonal sites, tenting available, sewage disposal, tables, fire rings, grills, wood. ◆RECREATION: badminton, horseshoes, hiking trails. Open May 1 through end of Nov. Rate in 1995 $10.50-13.50 for 2 persons. Member of VAPCOO. Phone: (802) 767-3352.

## RUTLAND—D-2

**Iroquois Land Family Camping**—Semi-shaded, open & wooded sites with a mountain view. *From south jct US 7 & US 4: Go 1/2 mi S on US 7, then 1 mi E towards North Shrewsbury, then 3/4 mi S on East Rd.* ◆◆FACILITIES: 50 sites, most common site width 25 feet, 12 full hookups, 38 water & elec (20 & 30 amp receptacles), 12 pull-thrus, tenting available, sewage disposal, public phone, limited grocery store, ice, tables, fire rings, wood. ◆◆RECREATION: rec hall, swim pool, badminton, horseshoes, volleyball. Open May 1 through Oct 15. Pool open Memorial Day to Labor Day. Rate in 1995 $20-22 for 2 persons. No refunds. Member of VAPCOO. Phone: (802) 773-2832.

## ST. ALBANS BAY—A-2

BURTON ISLAND STATE PARK—*From town: Go 2 1/2 mi SW on town road, Lake Rd & Point Rd to Kill Kare Area. Then take passenger ferry or private boat to Burton Island.* FACILITIES: 42 sites, 42 no hookups, tenting available, sewage disposal, public phone, ice, tables, fire rings, wood. RECREATION: lake swimming, boating, ramp, row/canoe boat rentals, lake fishing, playground, hiking trails. Open mid May through early Sep. For tent or boat camping only. No vehicles. Phone: (802) 524-6353.

## ST. JOHNSBURY—B-4

**MOOSE RIVER CAMPGROUND**—Semi-shaded, grassy, riverside CAMPGROUND. *From jct I-91 (exit 19) & I-93: Go 2 mi S on I-93 (exit 1), then 1/3 mi N on Hwy 18, then 200 ft W on US 2.*

WELCOME

◆◆◆FACILITIES: 50 sites, most common site width 25 feet, 20 full hookups, 20 water & elec (20 & 30 amp receptacles), 10 no hookups, 8 pull-thrus, a/c allowed ($), tenting available, group sites for tents/RVs, sewage disposal, public phone, ice, tables, fire rings, grills, wood.

◆RECREATION: river fishing, badminton, horseshoes.

VT See the beauty of LILAC SUNDAY! See article at front of book for details. VT

ST. JOHNSBURY—Continued
MOOSE RIVER CAMPGROUND—Continued

Open May 1 through Oct 15. Rate in 1995 $17-18 for 2 persons. Master Card/Visa accepted. Member of VAPCOO. Phone: (802) 748-4334.

**SEE AD THIS PAGE**

## SALISBURY—C-2

BRANBURY STATE PARK—*From jct US 7 & Hwy 53: Go 2 mi S on Hwy 53.* FACILITIES: 44 sites, 44 no hookups, tenting available, handicap restroom facilities, sewage disposal, public phone, tables, fire rings, wood. RECREATION: lake swimming, boating, lake fishing, playground, hiking trails. Open mid May through Oct 9. Phone: (802) 247-5925.

**LAKE DUNMORE KAMPERSVILLE**—*From jct US 7 & Hwy 53: Go 2 mi S on Hwy 53.*

WELCOME

**SEE PRIMARY LISTING AT MIDDLEBURY AND AD MIDDLEBURY PAGE 854**

## SHELBURNE—B-1

**SHELBURNE CAMPING AREA**—Partially shaded, grassy CAMPGROUND adjacent to a motel and family restaurant. *From Shelburne village: Go 1 mi N on US 7 (behind Dutch Mill Motel).*

WELCOME

◆◆◆FACILITIES: 78 sites, most common site width 40 feet, 28 full hookups, 40 water & elec (20 & 30 amp receptacles), 10 no hookups, 5 pull-thrus, a/c allowed ($), heater allowed ($), cable TV, phone hookups, tenting available, sewage disposal, laundry, public phone, limited grocery store, RV supplies, LP gas refill by weight/by meter, ice, tables, fire rings, grills, wood.

◆◆RECREATION: rec room/area, coin games, 2 swim pools, basketball hoop, badminton, horseshoes, volleyball.

Open May 1 through Nov 1. Rate in 1995 $20-24 for 2 persons. Reservations recommended Jul 1 through Oct 15. Member of VAPCOO. Phone: (802) 985-2540.

**SEE AD THIS PAGE**

## SOUTH HERO—B-1

**APPLE TREE BAY RESORT**—Mostly open, rolling grassy terrain adjacent to lake and marina. *From I-89 (exit 17) & US 2: Go 6 mi NW on US 2.*

WELCOME

◆◆◆FACILITIES: 300 sites, most common site width 25 feet, 200 full hookups, 100 water & elec (30 amp receptacles), seasonal sites, 20 pull-thrus, a/c allowed, phone hookups, tenting available, group sites for tents/RVs, RV rentals, RV storage, sewage disposal, laundry, public phone, full service store, RV supplies, LP gas refill by weight/by meter, gasoline, marine gas, ice, tables, fire rings, grills, wood.

◆◆◆◆◆RECREATION: rec hall, rec room/area, coin games, swim pool (heated), lake swimming, boating, canoeing, ramp, dock, 3 row/4 sail/4 canoe/4 motor boat rentals, water skiing, lake/pond fishing, fishing guides, golf ($), basketball hoop, 4 bike rentals, playground, planned group activities, recreation director, badminton, horseshoes, volleyball. Recreation open to the public.

Open May 1 through Oct 25. Rate in 1995 $22-25 per family. Reservations recommended Memorial Day through Labor Day. American Express/Master Card/Visa accepted. Member of VAPCOO. Phone: (802) 372-5398.

**SEE AD LAKE CHAMPLAIN PAGE 853**

**Camp Skyland**—Semi-wooded, grassy, lakeside CAMPGROUND. *From jct US 2 & South St: Go 3 1/2 mi S on South St.* ◆◆FACILITIES: 32 sites, most common site width 30 feet, 30 ft. max RV length, 12 full hookups, 9 water & elec (15 amp receptacles), 11 no hookups, seasonal sites, tenting available, laundry, public phone, ice, tables, fire rings, grills, wood. ◆◆RECREATION: rec hall, lake swimming, boating, canoeing, ramp, 5 row/1 canoe boat rentals, lake fishing, horseshoes. Open Jun 15 through Labor Day. Rate in 1995 $15-17 for 4 persons. No refunds. Member of VAPCOO. Phone: (802) 372-4200.

## SOUTH LONDONDERRY—E-2

WINHALL BROOK CAMPING AREA (Corps of Engineers-Ball Mountain Lake)—*From town: Go 2 1/2 mi S on Hwy 100.* FACILITIES: 108 sites, 108 no hookups, tenting available, handicap restroom facilities, sewage disposal, public phone, tables, grills, wood. RECREATION: river fishing, planned group activities, horseshoes, hiking trails. Open May 21 through Sep 6. Phone: (802) 824-9509.

## SPRINGFIELD—E-3

**Tree Farm Campground**—Rural, wooded, mostly level CAMPGROUND. *From jct Hwy 11 & Hwy 143: Go 1 1/4 mi E on Hwy 143.* ◆◆FACILITIES: 105 sites, most common site width 35 feet, 80 full hookups, 25 water & elec (20 & 30 amp receptacles), seasonal sites, 16 pull-thrus, tenting available, sewage disposal, public phone, LP gas refill by weight, ice, tables, fire rings, grills, wood. ◆◆RECREATION: rec room/area, planned group activities (weekends only), badminton, horseshoes, volleyball. Open all year. Facilities fully operational May 1 through Columbus Day. Rate in 1995 $15-16 per family. Member of VAPCOO. Phone: (802) 885-2889.



VERMONT was the first state that allowed all men the vote.

In 1777, Vermont's first constitution was written, making it a separate country. (It did not become our 14th state until 1791.) This constitution outlawed slavery and said men did not need to own property to vote.



VT STATE VT
MORGAN HORSE
VT ANIMAL VT

## STOWE—B-3

**Gold Brook Campground**—Partially shaded, riverside CAMPGROUND. *From jct I-89 (exit 10) & Hwy 100: Go 7 1/2 mi N on Hwy 100.* ◆◆◆FACILITIES: 79 sites, most common site width 35 feet, 26 full hookups, 24 water & elec (20,30 & 50 amp receptacles), 29 no hookups, seasonal sites, tenting available, sewage disposal, laundry, public phone, ice, tables, fire rings, grills, wood. ◆◆◆RECREATION: rec room/area, swim pool, river swimming, river fishing, playground, shuffleboard court, badminton, horseshoes, volleyball. Open all year. Rate in 1995 $20-25 for 2 persons. No refunds. Member of VAPCOO. Phone: (802) 253-7683.

SMUGGLERS NOTCH CAMPGROUND (Mount Mansfield State Forest)—*From jct Hwy 100 & Hwy 108: Go 10 mi NW on Hwy 108.* FACILITIES: 38 sites, 38 no hookups, tenting available, handicap restroom facilities, sewage disposal, public phone, ice, tables, fire rings, wood. RECREATION: playground, hiking trails. Open mid May through Oct 9. Phone: (802) 253-4014.

## THETFORD—D-3

**REST N' NEST**—Rural shaded CAMPGROUND convenient to a major highway. *From jct I-91 (exit 14) & Hwy 113: Go 200 feet E on Hwy 113, then 1/8 mi N on Latham Rd.*

◆◆◆FACILITIES: 90 sites, most common site width 50 feet, 46 full hookups, 29 water & elec (20 & 30 amp receptacles), 15 no hookups, seasonal sites, 6 pull-thrus, a/c allowed ($), heater allowed ($), phone hookups, tenting available, group sites for tents/RVs, RV storage, sewage disposal, laundry, public phone, limited grocery store, ice, tables, fire rings, grills, wood.

◆◆◆RECREATION: rec hall, rec room/area, coin games, pond swimming, basketball hoop, playground, badminton, horseshoes, volleyball.

Open Apr 1 through Nov 1. Rate in 1995 $20 per family. No refunds. Reservations recommended 2nd week in Aug. Master Card/Visa accepted. Member of VAPCOO. Phone: (802) 785-2997.

SEE AD TRAVEL SECTION PAGE 847

## TOWNSHEND—F-3

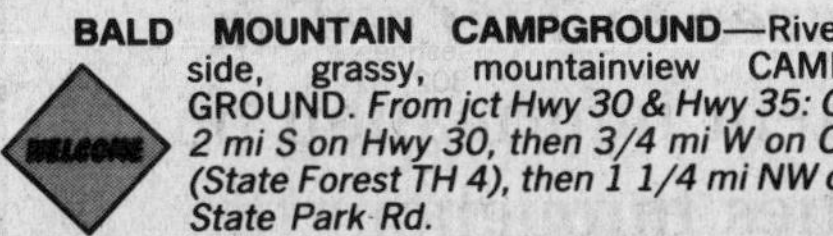

**BALD MOUNTAIN CAMPGROUND**—Riverside, grassy, mountainview CAMPGROUND. *From jct Hwy 30 & Hwy 35: Go 2 mi S on Hwy 30, then 3/4 mi W on CR (State Forest TH 4), then 1 1/4 mi NW on State Park Rd.*

◆◆◆FACILITIES: 210 sites, most common site width 25 feet, 16 full hookups, 184 water & elec (15, 20 & 30 amp receptacles), 10 no hookups, seasonal sites, 56 pull-thrus, a/c allowed, heater not allowed, tenting available, group sites for tents/RVs, RV storage, sewage disposal, laundry, public phone, limited grocery store, RV supplies, ice, tables, fire rings, wood.

◆◆◆RECREATION: rec hall, rec room/area, pavilion, coin games, river swimming, river fishing, basketball hoop, playground, badminton, sports field, horseshoes, hiking trails, volleyball.

Open May 1 through Columbus Day. Rate in 1995 $17 per family. Master Card/Visa accepted. Phone: (802) 365-7510.

SEE AD THIS PAGE

**CAMPERAMA FAMILY CAMPGROUND**—Semi-wooded, flat, grassy, riverside with mountain view. *From jct Hwy 30 & Hwy 35: Go 3/4 mi S on Hwy 30, then 1/4 mi W on Depot St.*

◆◆◆FACILITIES: 218 sites, most common site width 30 feet, 52 full hookups, 166 water & elec (20 & 30 amp receptacles), seasonal sites, 3 pull-thrus, a/c allowed ($), cable TV ($), phone hookups, tenting available, group sites for RVs, RV storage, sewage disposal, laundry, public phone, limited grocery store, RV supplies, LP gas refill by weight/by meter, ice, tables, fire rings, wood.

◆◆RECREATION: rec hall, swim pool, river swimming, river fishing, basketball hoop, 2 shuffleboard courts, badminton, sports field, horseshoes, volleyball.

Open May 15 through Oct 15. Rate in 1995 $18-20 for 3 persons. Member of VAPCOO. Phone: (802) 365-4315.

SEE AD THIS PAGE

TOWNSEND—Continued

TOWNSHEND STATE FOREST—*From jct Hwy 30 & Town Rd: Go 3 mi N on Town Rd.* FACILITIES: 34 sites, 16 ft. max RV length, 34 no hookups, tenting available, tables, fire rings, wood. RECREATION: boating, hiking trails. Open mid May through Oct 9. Phone: (802) 365-7500.

## UNDERHILL—B-2

**South-Hill Riverside Campground**—Level grassy, partially shaded sites beside river near mountains. *From jct Hwy 128 & Hwy 15: Go 6 mi E on Hwy 15.* ◆◆FACILITIES: 50 sites, most common site width 25 feet, 32 ft. max RV length, 42 full hookups, (15 amp receptacles), 8 no hookups, seasonal sites, tenting available, laundry, tables, fire rings. ◆RECREATION: river swimming, river/pond fishing, hiking trails. Open May 15 through Oct 15. Rate in 1995 $16.50-17.50 per family. Member of VAPCOO. Phone: (802) 899-2232.

## VERGENNES—C-1

BUTTON BAY STATE PARK—*From town: Go 1/2 mi S on Hwy 22A, then 6 1/2 mi NW on local roads.* FACILITIES: 72 sites, 72 no hookups, tenting available, handicap restroom facilities, sewage disposal, public phone, tables, fire rings, wood. RECREATION: pavilion, swim pool, lake swimming, boating, ramp, dock, 4 row boat rentals, lake fishing, playground, planned group activities, hiking trails, volleyball. Open mid May through Oct 9. Phone: (802) 475-2377.

## WATERBURY—B-2

LITTLE RIVER STATE PARK—*From jct Hwy 100 & US 2: Go 1 1/2 mi W on US 2, then 3 1/2 mi N on Little River Rd.* FACILITIES: 101 sites, 101 no hookups, tenting available, handicap restroom facilities, sewage disposal, public phone, tables, fire rings, wood. RECREATION: lake swimming, lake/stream fishing, playground, hiking trails. Open mid May through Oct 9. Phone: (802) 244-7103.

## WEST BARNET—B-4

**Harvey's Lake Cabins & Campground**—Lakeside CAMPGROUND with wooded sites. *From I-91 (exit 18): Go 5 mi W to W Barnet, then 100 yards S over bridge beside white church following signs.* ◆◆FACILITIES: 45 sites, most common site width 20 feet, 30 ft. max RV length, 15 full hookups, 26 water & elec (20,30 & 50 amp receptacles), 4 no hookups, seasonal sites, tenting available, sewage disposal, public phone, ice, tables, fire rings, wood. ◆◆RECREATION: rec hall, lake swimming, boating, canoeing, ramp, 3 row/5 canoe/1 pedal boat rentals, lake fishing, horseshoes. Open May 15 through Oct 15. Rate in 1995 $16-20 per family. Member of VAPCOO. Phone: (802) 633-2213.

## WESTFIELD—A-3

**Barrewood Campground**—CAMPGROUND with open, level, grassy sites. *From jct Hwy 87 (North Hill Rd) & Hwy 100: Go 1 1/2 mi S on Hwy 100.* ◆◆FACILITIES: 45 sites, most common site width 30 feet, 6 full hookups, 39 water & elec (20 & 30 amp receptacles), seasonal sites, 10 pull-thrus, tenting available, laundry, public phone, ice, tables, fire rings, wood. ◆◆RECREATION: pavilion, swim pool, stream fishing, playground, badminton, horseshoes, hiking trails, volleyball. Open May 15 through Oct 15. Rate in 1995 $15-17 per family. Member of VAPCOO. Phone: (802) 744-6340.

## WESTMORE—A-4

**White Caps Campground**—Grassy CAMPGROUND with most sites occupied by seasonal campers. *From I-91 (exit 23 North): Go N on US 5, then 6 mi N on Hwy 5A.* ◆◆◆FACILITIES: 50 sites, 35 full hookups, 7 water & elec (30 amp receptacles), 8 no hookups, seasonal sites, 10 pull-thrus, tenting available, laundry, public phone, limited grocery store, ice, tables, fire rings, wood. Open May 15 through Oct 15. Rate in 1995 $15 for 4 persons. Member of VAPCOO. Phone: (802) 467-3345.

## WHITE RIVER JUNCTION—D-3

**Maple Leaf Motel and Campground**—Grassy, partially shaded sites in conjunction with a motel. *From jct I-91 & I-89 interchange & US 5: Go 2 mi S on US 5.* ◆◆FACILITIES: 20 sites, most common site width 25 feet, 4 full hookups, 10 water & elec (30 amp receptacles), 6 no hookups, 4 pull-thrus, tenting available, sewage disposal, public phone, ice, tables, fire rings, grills, wood. RECREATION: playground, badminton, horseshoes. Open May 15 through Oct 20. Rate in 1995 $13-19 per family. Phone: (802) 295-2817.

**PINE VALLEY RV RESORT**—*From jct I-89 (exit 1) & US 4: Go 1/2 mi W on US 4.* **SEE PRIMARY LISTING AT QUECHEE AND AD QUECHEE PAGE 855**

## WILMINGTON—F-2

MOLLY STARK STATE PARK—*From jct Hwy 100 & Hwy 9: Go 3 mi E on Hwy 9.* FACILITIES: 34 sites, 30 ft. max RV length, 34 no hookups, tenting available, handicap restroom facilities, sewage disposal, public phone, ice, tables, fire rings, wood. RECREATION: pavilion, playground, hiking trails. Open mid May through Oct 9. Phone: (802) 464-5460.

# Crossing into Canada!

So...You're planning a visit to our neighbors up north. Good idea! From the rugged sea-swept coastlines of British Columbia and Newfoundland, to the indescribably beautiful Canadian Rockies that tumble along the Alberta border, you'll find unlimited avenues of adventure awaiting your discovery.

Cosmopolitan cities greet visitors with an evening of fine dining and dancing—a relaxing finish to a day of unsurpassed fly fishing. Herds of caribou cross miles of wilderness and charming homespun villages sell intricate arts and crafts particular to their cultural heritage.

It is indeed, a whole different country. One certainly worth exploration. But before you and your rig hit the road, we'd like to clarify a few of the requirements associated with traveling to another country.

### Is identification required?

Yes. Any one of the following will do:

- Birth or baptismal certificate
- Voter's registration card
- Draft card
- Passport

Permanent U.S. residents who are not citizens are advised to bring their Alien Registration Receipt Card.

Persons under 18 who are not accompanied by their parents should have a letter of authorization from a parent or guardian.

### Is insurance required? Will I need a vehicle permit?

Car insurance (and proof of insurance) is mandatory. Many visitors choose to carry a Canadian Non-Resident Inter-Province Motor Vehicle Liability Insurance Card. This card is valid anywhere in Canada, is proof of financial responsibility, and is available only in the U.S. through insurance companies.

Motor vehicle and RV registration cards should be carried with you. If the vehicle is registered to someone else, you should have a letter from that person stating authorization of use.

If you plan to leave your vacation trailer in Canada to return home, ask Canada Customs for an E99 permit. Notice the expiration date and post the permit in the window of the trailer so it can be easily seen. Keep in mind, you can not store a vacation trailer in Canada during the off-season.

If you need to leave your boat, motor and/or boat trailer during the off-season, be prepared to prove that maintenance work is being undertaken by a bona fide marina or service depot. Customs will require a copy of a work order from the establishment handling the repairs. This work order must contain a description of the article, owner's name and address, type of work to be done and the time and location at which the work will be effected.

### Are there any restrictions as to what I can bring across the border?

Personal baggage (in reasonable quantities) is duty-free, provided all items are declared upon entry and are for your own personal use (that is, not intended for resale). Personal items include camping, fishing and other recreational equipment, boats & motors, cameras, typewriters, musical instruments and consumable goods. You are allowed up to 44 pounds of meat products. Any gasoline or oil imported, beyond the normal capacity of your vehicle, is dutiable.

*Alcohol:*

If you're 19 or over, you can bring, duty-free, either: 40 ounces of liquor or wine; or 24 12-ounce cans or bottles of beer or ale. With the exception of the Northwest Territories, additional quantities may be imported (up to 2 gallons) but are subject to duty and taxes, plus provincial fees.

*Tobacco:*

If you're 16 or over, you can transport, duty-free: 50 cigars, 200 cigarettes and 2.2 pounds of manufactured tobacco.

Additional quantities are subject to duty and tax.

*Fireworks:*

All fireworks need authorization to be imported into Canada. An Explosives Importation Permit can be acquired by contacting:

Chief Inspector of Explosives
Explosives Branch
Energy, Mines & Resources Canada
580 Booth St.
Ottawa, Ontario
Canada
K1A 0E4

### What is "duty" and "GST"?

"Duty" is the same as tax. Duty-free means you won't be taxed on the items.

GST stands for Goods and Services Tax. This is a 7% federal tax (in addition to varying provincial taxes) which applies to most goods and services sold or provided in Canada. Rebates to foreign visitors apply as follows:

- Rebates apply when the GST paid is $7 or more. (Minimum of $100 worth of goods or services purchased and removed from Canada within 60 days.)
- Rebates apply to accommodations (except on camping and trailer-park fees) of up to 30 nights per visit and on goods purchased in Canada for export.
- Up to four (4) rebate claims per year are allowed or you can accumulate purchases over several visits to Canada and submit one large claim.

When you enter Canada, you'll be given information on the GST visitor rebate. It's a good idea to request a copy of the booklet "GST Rebate for Visitors," which contains a rebate application form. For more information, call 800-668-4748 (in Canada), or 613-991-3346 (outside Canada).

### What about firearms?

Fully automatic firearms and handguns are prohibited. Long guns (rifles or shotguns with a barrel over 18.5") may be imported provided the visitor is 16 years of age or older, and the firearm is for competition or sporting use. If you're not going to use it in competition or for hunting, don't bring it. Basically, you can import 5,000 rounds of ammunition. Two hundred rounds will be duty-free, but the remainder is subject to tax.

Hunting is prohibited in Canada's national parks and firearms are not allowed entry unless dismantled or wrapped and tied securely so that no part of the firearm is exposed.

### Am I allowed to bring my pet?

Sure. If Spot or Kitty is over 3 months old, you'll need to have certification (signed by a licensed veterinarian) stating that they have been vaccinated against rabies during the preceding 36 months. This certificate must provide a legible description of your pet and the date of vaccination.

You can also bring pet monkeys, small pet mammals, fish and reptiles (other than turtles and tortoises) and up to 2 birds, without certification or restriction.

Pet dogs and cats entering Newfoundland need an entry permit from:

Provincial Veterinary Service
Government of Newfoundland
P.O. Box 7400
St. John's West, Newfoundland
Canada
AIE 3Y5

### Could you explain the Metric System?

We'll try. For those who are mathematically minded, following are the formulas for metric conversion. The rest of us will appreciate the charts:

*Distance & Speed Limits (Kilometers):*

Kilometers refer to both distance and speed. A kilometer is approximately 5/8 mile. To convert miles to kilometers: number of miles x 1.6 = kilometers; and number of kilometers x 0.62 = miles.

| | | |
|---|---|---|
| 9 mph | = | 15 km/h |
| 12 mph | = | 20 km/h |
| 18 mph | = | 30 km/h |
| 25 mph | = | 40 km/h |
| 31 mph | = | 50 km/h |
| 37 mph | = | 60 km/h |
| 43 mph | = | 70 km/h |
| 50 mph | = | 80 km/h |
| 56 mph | = | 90 km/h |
| 62 mph | = | 100 km/h |

*Temperature (Celsius):*
9/5 x 0C + 32 = Fahrenheit.
F - 32 x 5/9 = Celsius.

| | | |
|---|---|---|
| -22°F | = | -30°C |
| -13°F | = | -25°C |
| 5°F | = | -15°C |
| 14°F | = | -10°C |
| 23°F | = | -5°C |
| 32°F | = | 0°C |
| 43°F | = | 6°C |
| 50°F | = | 10°C |
| 61°F | = | 16°C |
| 70°F | = | 21°C |
| 86°F | = | 30°C |
| 95°F | = | 35°C |

*Gasoline:*
Gas and oil are sold in Canada by the litre. One U.S. gallon is approx. 3.8 litres. (One Imperial gallon is approx. 4.5 litres.) Number of gallons x 3.79 = litres. Number of litres x 0.26 = gallons.

| | | |
|---|---|---|
| 10 gal. | = | 37 litres |
| 15 gal. | = | 56 litres |
| 25 gal. | = | 94 litres |
| 30 gal. | = | 113 litres |
| 40 gal. | = | 151 litres |
| 49 gal. | = | 189 litres |
| 59 gal. | = | 227 litres |
| 69 gal. | = | 265 litres |
| 79 gal. | = | 303 litres |
| 89 gal. | = | 341 litres |

### Is money the same in Canada as in the U.S.?

The unit of currency is the Canadian dollar, which amounts to 100 cents. Monetary units are a one dollar coin, 2, 5, 10, 20, 50 and 100 bill denominations. Banking hours vary from bank to bank but are generally Monday-Friday, 10 a.m. to 4 p.m. with some being open on Saturday. Banks are not open on the following official Canadian holidays:

| Occasion | Date |
|---|---|
| New Year's Day | Jan. 1 |
| Good Friday | April 5 |
| Easter Monday | April 8 |
| Victoria Day | May 20 |
| Canada Day | July 1 |
| Labor Day | Sept. 2 |
| Thanksgiving | Oct. 14 |
| Remembrance Day | Nov. 11 |
| Christmas | Dec. 25 |
| Boxing Day | Dec. 26 |

To get the best rate of exchange, change your travelers checks into Canadian currency at a Canadian bank just after you cross the border.

### Are traffic rules the same?

Yes and No. In some provinces, the *use* of radar warning devices is illegal. In some provinces, even the *possession* of radar warning devices is illegal. Police officers can confiscate such devices and fine violators.

Seat belt use is mandatory for all drivers and passengers in Canada, except in Yukon. (Don't forget car seats for youngsters! In Yukon, children under 48 lbs. or 6 years, must use an approved child restraint device.) While traveling on Yukon highways, the law requires use of headlights at all times.

### Do the RV parks in Canada differ from those in the U.S.?

Not really. Canada has an extensive system of RV parks and campgrounds ranging from rustic fishing and hunting camps to fully-equipped resorts.

Where available, electrical hookups are usually of the 15-amp, two-wire type furnishing 115 volt, 60 cycle AC. Newer parks offer full 30-amp electrical service and some offer 50-amp. Water taps are standard thread and sewer drops will usually accept the standard 3-inch hose, although a cushion seal or a threaded adapter may be required in some instances.

### What about sending gifts to our friends in the States?

Mark the package "Unsolicited Gift" and list the contents and fair retail value. If the retail value isn't over $50, you can send it tax-free. If it's over $50, it's subject to a tax, to be collected by the U.S. Postal Service, plus a handling fee.

### Are there limitations as to what I can bring home?

When re-entering the U.S., just be sure to list your purchases, have your sales receipts handy and pack your purchases separately for convenience of inspection.

If you've been in Canada more than 48 hours, you may bring back, free of duty, $400 (based on fair retail value in Canada) worth of articles for personal or household use. Also considered duty-free: 100 non-Cuban cigars, one liter of alcohol and one carton of cigarettes.

If you've run up a tab larger than $400, a flat duty rate of 2% will be applied to the next $1,000 worth of merchandise. This flat duty rate applies only to goods legally marked "made in Canada" or "made in USA."

Anything over $1,400 is subject to varying taxes.

There are restrictions on exporting objects over 50 years old that are of historical, cultural or scientific significance. Items subject to export permit requirements include: fossils, archaeological artifacts, fine and decorative art, technological objects, books and archival material.

Cut flowers, fresh fruit and vegetables (except in certain cases) purchased in Canada can be brought back without restriction. Most house plants can be brought into the U.S. without restriction, but certain other plants may require a phytosanitary certificate, which can be obtained from offices of the Agricultural Inspection Directorate, located throughout Canada.

### We live in Canada and are returning home from a visit to the States. What are we allowed to bring back?

That depends on how long you've been gone. If you've been out of Canada for 24 hours you may bring back goods worth up to $50 duty-free. If you've been away for 48 hours you can bring back up to $200 and after seven days away you can bring in duty-free goods worth up to $500. (The once-a-year restriction on the above mentioned seven-day exemption has been eliminated.)

### We're just passing through on our way to Alaska. Does all this still apply?

You bet. Plus, goods that are in transit (not for use in Canada) require a temporary admission permit, form E29B. You won't be taxed on these items, but a refundable security deposit may be required at the time of entry. This deposit is usually nominal, but may be as high as the tax that would normally apply. Your refund will be sent to your home as soon as the items are taken out of Canada. Be sure you have a list of the goods you're transporting (in triplicate). This list should indicate respective values and serial numbers when applicable. Food and alcoholic beverages should be boxed so that they can be corded and sealed by Canadian Customs at the time of entry.

### Anything else?

You might want to check your health insurance policy as some plans do not extend coverage outside the country of residence.

### Where can I write for more information?

For information on joining a Canadian auto club (or whether or not your current club is an affiliate member–qualifying you for membership services):

Canadian Automobile Assn.
1775 Courtwood Crescent
Ottawa, Ontario
Canada
K2C 3J2

For information on the importation of firearms:

Revenue Canada, Customs & Excise
Commercial Verification & Enforcement
Connaught Bldg., Mackenzie Ave.
Ottawa, Ontario
Canada K1A 0L5

For information on hunting and fishing licenses contact the appropriate provincial tourism agency. Addresses and phone numbers are located in this directory in the Travel Section editorial preceding each province.

**RV Width Regulation**

**The maximum width of any RV (with a regular vehicle license) traveling on Canadian highways is not to exceed 102 inches–including an awning rolled up in travel mode.**

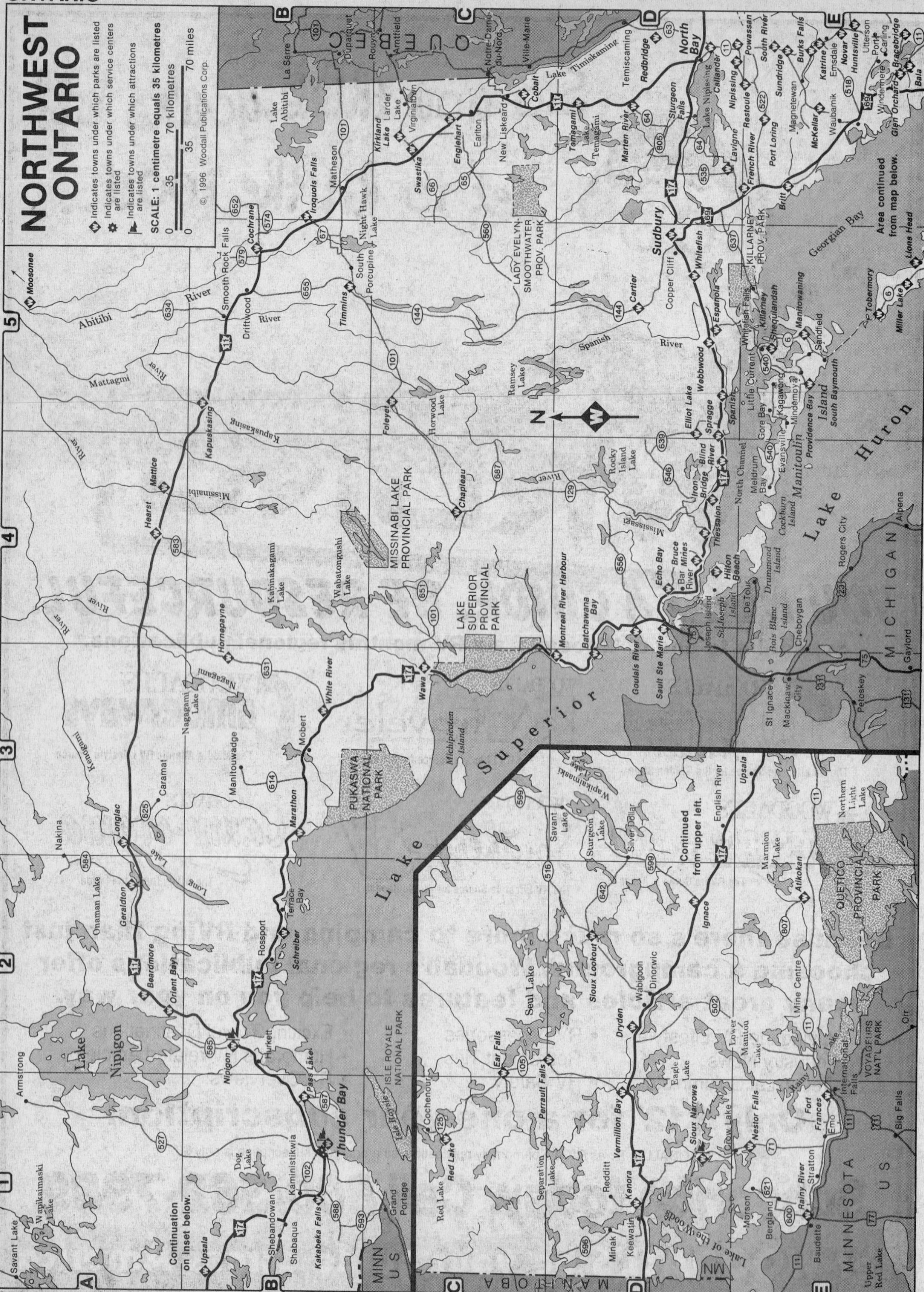

# NORTHWEST ONTARIO

- Indicates towns under which parks are listed
- Indicates towns under which service centers are listed
- Indicates towns under which attractions are listed

**SCALE: 1 centimetre equals 35 kilometres**

0 35 70 kilometres

0 35 70 miles



Continuation on inset below.

Continued from upper left.

Area continued from map below.

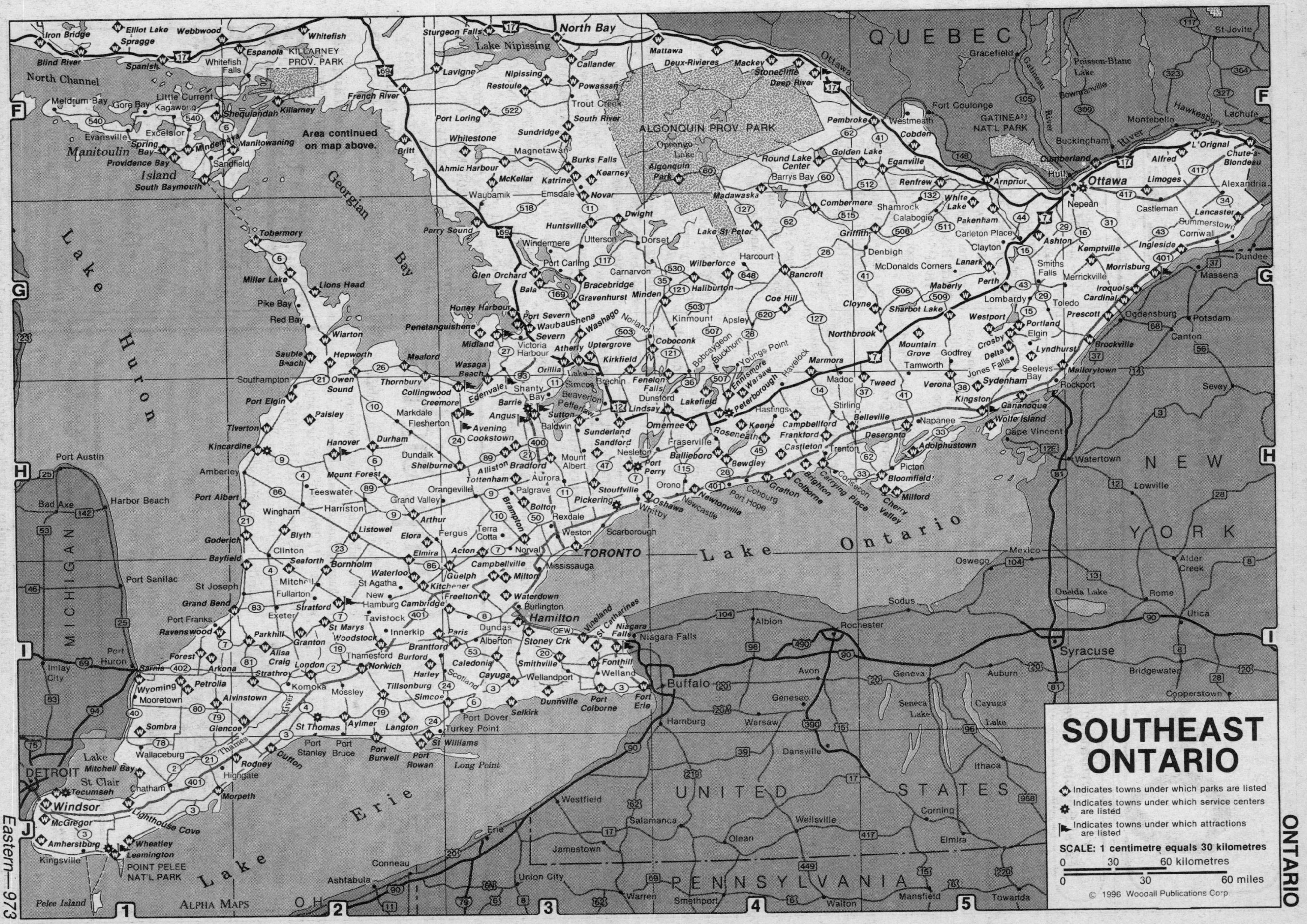
SOUTHEAST ONTARIO
Indicates towns under which parks are listed
Indicates towns under which service centers are listed
Indicates towns under which attractions are listed
SCALE: 1 centimetre equals 30 kilometres
0 30 60 kilometres
0 30 60 miles
© 1996 Woodall Publications Corp
Area continued on map above.
ALPHA MAPS

# Ontario

## TRAVEL SECTION

### Free Information from Travel Section Advertisers

The following businesses have placed an ad in the Ontario Travel Section. To receive free information, enter their Reader Service number on the Reader Service Card opposite page 16, in the front of this directory:

| Advertiser | RS # | Ad Pg. |
|---|---|---|
| Birchwood Cottages | 440 | 974 |
| Campark Resorts | 689 | 982 |
| Cedar Valley Resort | 500 | 984 |
| The Dunes Oakridge Park | 311 | 982 |
| Glenrock Cottages/Trailer Pk. | 501 | 981 |
| Grand River Conservation | 249 | 978 |
| Huronia Historical Park | 469 | 980 |
| Knight's Hide-Away Park | 250 | 984 |
| Lafontaine Campground | 502 | 979 |
| Little Austria Family CG | 312 | 983 |
| Narrows Lock Campground | 503 | 984 |
| Nighthawk Retreat | 504 | 981 |
| Nottawasaga Valley Conserv. | 561 | 980 |
| Ontario Gem Mining | 471 | 983 |
| ON Private CG Owners | 852 | 984 |
| Roth Park | 438 | 982 |
| St. Lawrence Parks Comm. | 690 | 974 |
| Sand Hill Park | 251 | 983 |
| SaugeenValley Conservation | 313 | 979 |
| Stratford Tourism Dept. | 314 | 978 |
| West Lake Willows | 505 | 981 |

### Camping Fees

Camping fees in Ontario listings are stated in Canadian dollars.

### Time Zone/Topography

Most of Ontario is on Eastern time. About one-quarter of the province, at the western end, is on Central time.

Ontario extends for 1,000 miles from east to west, and 1,050 miles from north to south. Almost 17 percent of the province–68,490 square miles–is water. The southern boundary runs almost entirely through waterways, and the freshwater shoreline on the Great Lakes extends for 2,362 miles.

In the central and northern parts of Ontario, there are literally thousands of lakes. The northern area bordering on Hudson Bay is low and flat; going southward, the elevation gradually increases up to about 1,500 feet. North-central Ontario is noted for its many small lakes and tree-covered terrain. Southern Ontario is the most populated and industrialized section in the province and its highest elevation is around 1,700 feet. Ontario's physiographic divisions are marked by wide variations, the most remarkable of which is the famous Niagara Escarpment.

### Travel Information Sources

**Provincial Agency**: Ministry of Economic Development, Trade & Tourism, Queen's Park, Toronto, Ontario M7A 2R9. From Canada and U.S. (800-ONTARIO, in English); from Canada (800-268-3736, in French). From Toronto calling area – English (416-314-0944), French (416-314-0956).

**Regional Agencies:**

• *Algoma Kinniwabi Travel Assn.*, 553 Queen St., Ste 1, Sault Ste. Marie, ON P6A 2A3 (705-254-4293).

• *Almaguin Nipissing Travel Assn.*, Regional Information Centre, Seymour St. & North Bay Bypass, Box 351, North Bay, ON P1B 8H5 (800-387-0516 or 705-474-6634). (Incorporates Ontario's Near North region.)

• *Cochrane Timiskaming Travel Assn.*, P.O. Bag 920, 76 McIntyre Rd., Schumacher, ON P0N 1G0 (800-461-3766 or 705-360-1989). (Incorporates the James Bay Frontier region.)

• *Eastern Ontario Travel Assn.*, 1040 Gardiners Rd., Ste. B, Kingston, ON K7P 1R7 (613-384-3682 or 800-567-3278 from Eastern Canada and Eastern U.S.)

• *Central Ontario Travel Assn.*, c/o 1040 Gardiners Rd., Ste. B, Kingston, ON K7P 1R7 (613-384-3682). (Incorporates the Getaway Country travel region.)

• *Lakeland Region:* HTA–Simcoe County Building, Midhurst, ON L0L 1X0 (800-487-6642 or 705-726-9300 ext. 220).

• *Niagara and Mid-Western Ontario Travel Assn.*, 38 Darling St., Ste. 102, Brantford, ON N3T 6A8 (800-267-3399 or 519-756-3230). (Incorporates Ontario's Festival Country region).

• *North of Superior Tourism,* 1119 Victoria Ave. E., Thunder Bay, ON P7C 1B7 (800-265-3951 or 807-626-9420).

• *Ontario's Sunset Country Travel Assn.*, 102 Main St., Ste 201, Kenora, ON P9N 3X6 (800-665-0730 from Canada; 800-665-7567 from U.S.; 807-468-5853).

• *Rainbow Country Travel Assn.*, 1984 Regent St. South, Cedar Pointe Mall, Sudbury, ON P3E 5S1 (800-465-6655 or 705-522-0104).

• *Southwestern Ontario Travel Assn.*, 920 Commissioner's Rd. East, Main Floor,





FREE INFO! Enter number on Reader Service Card opposite pg. 16: St. Lawrence Parks #690; Birchwood #440.

# ONTARIO

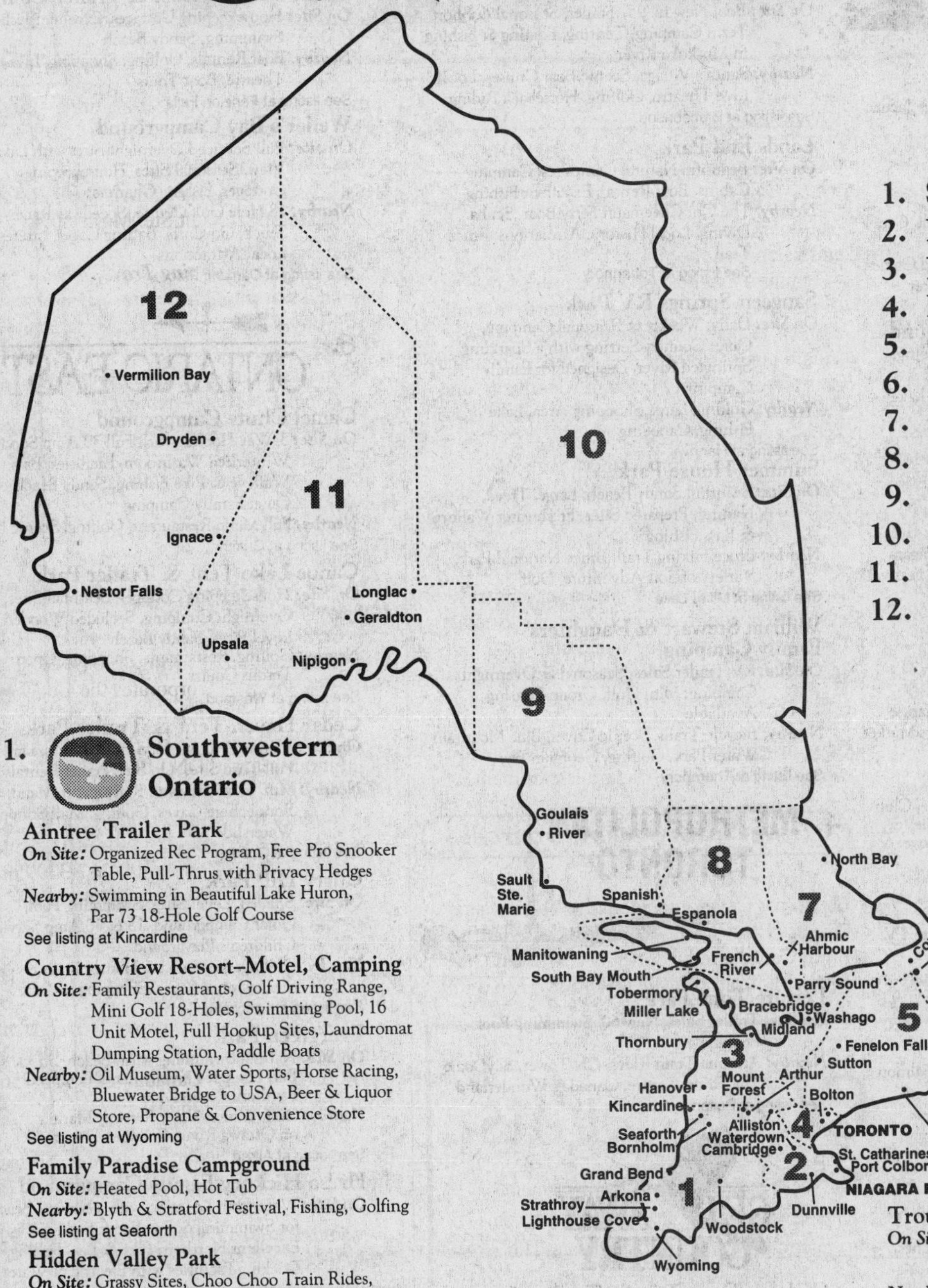

12
Vermilion Bay
Dryden
11
Ignace
Nestor Falls
Upsala
Nipigon
Longlac
Geraldton
10
9
Goulais River
Sault Ste. Marie
8
Spanish
Espanola
North Bay
7
Manitowaning
South Bay Mouth
Tobermory
Miller Lake
French River
Ahmic Harbour
Parry Sound
Bracebridge
Washago
Midland
Thornbury
3
Hanover
Mount Forest
Arthur
Kincardine
Seaforth
Bornholm
Alliston
Waterdown
Cambridge
Bolton
Sutton
Fenelon Falls
5
4
TORONTO
2
St. Catharines
Port Colborne
NIAGARA FALLS
Dunnville
Grand Bend
Arkona
Strathroy
Lighthouse Cove
1
Woodstock
Wyoming
Combermere
Griffith
Cobden
Renfrew
Pakenham
OTTAWA
Alfred
6
Perth
Lancaster
Westport
McDonald's Corners
Wolfe Island
Belleville
Carrying Place

1. Southwestern Ontario
2. Festival Country
3. Lakelands
4. Metropolitan Toronto
5. Getaway Country
6. Ontario East
7. Near North
8. Rainbow Country
9. Algoma Country
10. James Bay Frontier
11. North of Superior
12. Ontario's Sunset Country

## 1. Southwestern Ontario

**Aintree Trailer Park**
*On Site:* Organized Rec Program, Free Pro Snooker Table, Pull-Thrus with Privacy Hedges
*Nearby:* Swimming in Beautiful Lake Huron, Par 73 18-Hole Golf Course
See listing at Kincardine

**Country View Resort–Motel, Camping**
*On Site:* Family Restaurants, Golf Driving Range, Mini Golf 18-Holes, Swimming Pool, 16 Unit Motel, Full Hookup Sites, Laundromat Dumping Station, Paddle Boats
*Nearby:* Oil Museum, Water Sports, Horse Racing, Bluewater Bridge to USA, Beer & Liquor Store, Propane & Convenience Store
See listing at Wyoming

**Family Paradise Campground**
*On Site:* Heated Pool, Hot Tub
*Nearby:* Blyth & Stratford Festival, Fishing, Golfing
See listing at Seaforth

**Hidden Valley Park**
*On Site:* Grassy Sites, Choo Choo Train Rides, Lots of Nature
*Nearby:* Flea Markets, Stratford Festival, Golfing
See listing at Woodstock

**Rus-Ton Family Campground**
*On Site:* Family Camping Overnight & Seasonal, RV Rentals & Sales, New Extended Stay Area
*Nearby:* Sandy Beaches, Golfing, Local Attractions
See listing at Grand Bend

**Thames River Trailer Park**
*On Site:* Excellent Fishing of Numerous Varieties of Fish on Lake St. Clair, 15 & 30 Amp Available
*Nearby:* Bird Watching, Golfing, Local Attractions
See listing at Lighthouse Cove

**Trout Haven**
*On Site:* Fishing in Stocked Rainbow Trout Ponds Shuffleboard & Horseshoe Tournaments Seasonal & Overnight Camping
*Nearby:* Local Attractions, Farmers Market & Golf Course
See listing at Strathroy

**Woodland Lake Camp & RV Resort**
*On Site:* Friendly Family Camping, New Activity Centre Built in '95
*Nearby:* Stratford Shakespearean Festival, Golfing, Blyth Summer Festival
See listing at Bornholm

**Be Sure to Tell the Ontario Campground Owners You Found Them in Woodall's**

# FOR THE

## 2. FESTIVAL COUNTRY

### Blue Heron Trailer Park
***On Site:*** New Heated Swimming Pool, Large Jacuzzi Pull Thru Sites, Full Rec Program
***Nearby:*** Golfing, Local Tours, Theatre
See listing at Dunnville

### Conestoga Family Campgrounds
***On Site:*** Fishing in Stocked Pond, Mini Golf, Canoe & Paddleboat Rentals
***Nearby:*** Drayton Theatre Festival, Highland Games, Jamborees, Waterloo Farmers Market
See listing at Arthur

### Dressel's Jordan Valley Campground
***On Site:*** Overnight & Seasonal Sites, Canoeing, Quiet Family Camping
***Nearby:*** Local Winery Tours, Water Sports-Lake Ontario, Golfing, Balls Falls, Major Attractions
See listing at St. Catharines

### Dressel's Still Acres
***On Site:*** Seasonal-Overnight Tenting Sites, Swimming Pool, Friendly Folk
***Nearby:*** Boating & Fishing on Lake Erie, Niagara Falls, Major Attractions, Showboat Festival Live Theatre
See listing at Port Colborne

### Olympia Village Trailer Park
***On Site:*** Best Rates, Best Pool, Best Location, Friendly Staff
***Nearby:*** Min. to Hamilton, African Lion Safari, Flamboro Downs, Kitchener Farmers Market
See listing at Waterdown

### Pike Lake Campground & Resort
***On Site:*** 18-Hole Championship Golf Course, Club House Dining & Lounge, Trailer Sales & Rentals, Fishing in Stocked Lake, Boat Rentals
See listing at Mount Forest

### Pine Valley Park
***On Site:*** Overnight & Seasonal Sites, Satellite TV, Olympic Size Pool
***Nearby:*** African Lion Safari, Flamboro Downs, Flamboro Speedway
See listing at Cambridge

### Rolling Acres Farm Campground
***On Site:*** Canoe Rentals, Excellent Trout & Salmon Fishing, Riverside Camping Sites
***Nearby:*** Golfing, Live Theatre, Canada's Wonderland, Antique Shopping
See listing at Alliston

### Spring Valley Park
***On Site:*** Trailer Sales & Rentals, 18-Hole Mini Golf, Boat Rentals, Pre-School Playground
***Nearby:*** Stock Car Races, Flea Market, Churches, Golfing
See listing at Mount Forest

## 3. Lakelands

### Bayfort Camp
***On Site:*** Sandy Beach, Overnight & Large Seasonal Lots, Tenting
***Nearby:*** Martyr's Shrine, Ste. Marie Among the Hurons, Wye Marsh, Full Service Marina
See listing at Midland

### Black River Wilderness Park
***On Site:*** 180 Acres of Wilderness Camping, Hiking, Fishing, Swimming, Canoeing
***Nearby:*** Golfing, Boating, Shopping, Boat Tours, Summer Theatre
See listing at Washago

### Bracebridge Camping & Trailer Park
***On Site:*** Pool New in '95, Trailer, Seasonal & Short Term Camping, Tenting, Boating & Fishing in Muskoka River
***Nearby:*** Santa's Village, Scenic Boat Cruises, Local Live Theatre, Golfing, Horseback Riding
See listing at Bracebridge

### Lands End Park
***On Site:*** Beautiful Natural Campsites, Camping Cabins, Boat Rental, Excellent Fishing
***Nearby:*** The Chi Cheemaun Ferry Boat, Scuba Diving, Local Historic Attractions, Bruce Trail
See listing at Tobermory

### Saugeen Springs RV Park
***On Site:*** Daily, Weekly & Seasonal Camping, Quiet Country Setting with a Sparkling Springfed River, Designed for Family Camping
***Nearby:*** Golfing, Large Shopping Area, Lake Fishing, Canoeing
See listing at Hanover

### Summer House Park
***On Site:*** Beautiful Sandy Beach, Large, Treed, Natural, Prepared Sites, Freshwater Walleye & Bass Fishing
***Nearby:*** Bruce Hiking Trail, Bruce National Park, Variety of Soft Adventure, Golf
See listing at Miller Lake

### William Stewart & Daughters Family Camping
***On Site:*** RV Trailer Sales, Seasonal & Overnight Camping, Mini Golf, Group Tenting Available
***Nearby:*** Bicycle Trails, Scenic Caves, Blue Mountain Water Park, Golfing, Georgian Bay
See listing at Thornbury

## 4. METROPOLITAN TORONTO

### Leisure Time Park
***On Site:*** Trailer Sales, New 60' Swimming Pool, Propane
***Nearby:*** Antique Train Rides, CN Tower, SkyDome The Eaton Centre, Canada's Wonderland
See listing at Bolton

## 5. GETAWAY COUNTRY

### Carleton Cove Tourist Trailer Park & Camping-New Management
***On Site:*** On Site Trailer Rentals, Fishing-Pickerel, Bass & Muskie, Boat Rentals, Large Pull Thru Sites, Closest Campground to Hwy 401
***Nearby:*** Excellent Pickerel Fishing in the Bay of Quinte, Kingston Heritage Attractions, Belleville Shopping & Local Attractions, Horse Racing, Golfing
See listing at Belleville

### Elm Grove Trailer Park
***On Site:*** Large Treed Sites, Serviced Tent Sites, Large Pull Thru Sites
***Nearby:*** Red Barn Theatre, Golf Courses, Fishing & Boating on Lake Simcoe
See listing at Sutton

### Sandy Beach Resort & Trailer Court
***On Site:*** Housekeeping Cottages, Excellent Fishing Swimming, Sandy Beach
***Nearby:*** Boat Rentals, Golfing, Shopping, Live Theatre, Boat Tours
See listing at Fenelon Falls

### Weller's Bay Campground
***On Site:*** Full Serviced Overnight Sites with Lake View, Seasonal Sites, Housekeeping Cottages, Fishing Charters
***Nearby:*** 18 Hole Golf Course, Speedway Race Track, Go-Carts, Batting Cages, Interesting Local Attractions
See listing at Carrying Place

## 6. ONTARIO EAST

### Camel Chute Campground
***On Site:*** 3-Way Hookup with Full 30 Amp Service, Winterized Washroom, Facilities, Bass, Walleye & Pike Fishing, Sandy Beach, Quiet Family Camping
***Nearby:*** Full Menu Restaurant, Golfing, Scenic Drive
See listing at Griffith

### Canoe Lake Tent & Trailer Park
***On Site:*** Housekeeping Cottages, Seasonal Sites, Overnight Camping, Secluded Wooded Level Sites, Sandy Beach
***Nearby:*** Golfing, Restaurants, Shopping, Open Tennis Courts
See listing at Westport

### Cedar Haven Tent & Trailer Park
***On Site:*** Planned Activities, Seasonal Sites, Large Pull Thru Sites, On Site Trailer Rentals
***Nearby:*** Min. to Whitewater Rafting, Storyland, Bonnechere Caves, Golfing, Mall Shopping, Waterslide
See listing at Cobden

### Curry Hill Park
***On Site:*** Shaded, Level Sites, Swimming Pool, Quiet Campground, 15 & 30 Amp Service, Children's Playground
***Nearby:*** Golfing, Restaurants, Hiking Trails, St. Lawrence River, Shopping
See listing at Lancaster

### Evergreen Park
***On Site:*** Natural Swimming with Beach, Snack Bar, Equipped Kiddie Land, Equipped Pavilion, Petting Zoo
***Nearby:*** Golf, White Water Rafting, Marina on Ottawa River, Summer Theatre
See listing at Alfred

### Hi Lo Hickory Family Campground
***On Site:*** Waterfront Location with a Natural Beach for Swimming & Smallcraft Sailing, Excellent Northern Pike & Bass Fishing, Docking Facilities with Electric & Water Hookups, Evening Campfires Permitted
***Nearby:*** Free 52-Car Ferry Leaving from Historic Kingston, Boat Tours, Use Wolfe Island as a Port of Entry to and from the USA (Cape Vincent, NY)
See listing at Wolfe Island

### Paul's Creek Campsite
***On Site:*** Heated Swimming Pool, Seasonal Sites, Serviced Overnight Sites, Snack Bar
***Nearby:*** Dalhousie Lake, Sandy Beach, Golfing, Balderson Cheese Factory, Local Shopping
See listing at Mc Donald's Corners

### Pine Cliff Resort
***On Site:*** 4 Season Retirement Campground, Family Camping, Modern H.K. Cottages, Sandy Beach, Seasonal Sites, New & Used Trailer Sales

# Excitement!

**Nearby:** Algonguin Park, Whitewater Rafting, Storyland, Great Golfing, Rock Hounding
See listing at Combermere

### Riverbend Park
**On Site:** Quiet Family Campground, Large Sites, Boating on Mississippi River
**Nearby:** Golfing, Antique & Craft Shopping, Oldest 5 Span Stone Bridge
See listing at Pakenham

### Sand Bay Camp
**On Site:** Seasonal Sites, HK Cabins, Boat Rentals, Sandy Beach
**Nearby:** Annual Rockhound Gemboree, Bonnechere Caves, Storyland
See listing at Combermere

### Tay River Tent & Trailer Camp
**On Site:** Quiet Relaxing Family Campground, Level, Open Seasonal Sites, Fishing, Boating
**Nearby:** Canada's Capital, Golfing, Rideau Canal System
See listing at Perth

### Timberland Campground
**On Site:** Friendly Relaxing Camping, Large 20' x 50' Swimming Pool, Picnic Facilities for Large Groups
**Nearby:** Ottawa & Local Attractions, Golfing, Water Slides, Excellent Walleye, Bass & Pike Fishing
See listing at Renfrew

### Yonder Hill Campground
**On Site:** Seasonal Sites, Beautiful Sandy Beach, Snack Bar
**Nearby:** White Water Rafting, Bonnechere Caves, Fine Restaurants, Museums
See listing at Cobden

## 7.

### Franklin Motel Tent & Trailer Park
**On Site:** Nous Parlons Francais, Heated Pool, Cable TV, Full Hookups
**Nearby:** Sandy Beach (across the road), (walk to) North Bay & Nipissing Shopping Centre, Access to Snowmobile Trails
See listing at North Bay

## 8.

RAINBOW COUNTRY

### Ahmic Lake Resort
**On Site:** Full Service Marina, Excellent Walleye Fishing, Beautiful Sand Beach, Open Year Round, Cottage Rentals
**Nearby:** Scenic Drives, Museums & Local Attractions Golfing, Churches
See listing at Ahmic Harbour

### Holiday Haven Trailer Park & Resort
**On Site:** Lakeshore Sites Available, Excellent Lake Trout, Bass & Perch Fishing, Fishing Guide Service, Sandy Bottom Lake Swimming, Housekeeping Cottages
**Nearby:** Golfing, Hiking, Horseback Riding, Museum
See listing at Manitowaning

### Horseshoe Lake Camp & Cottages
**On Site:** Friendly Family Camping, Large Seasonal Sites Available, Winterized H.K. Cottages
**Nearby:** Scenic Georgian Bay Cruise, Live Theatre, Santa's Village
See listing at Parry Sound

### Riverside Campground
**On Site:** Large Pull Thru Sites, Seasonal & Overnight Camping, Boat Docks & Launching, Great Fishing on the Spanish River
**Nearby:** Golfing, Shopping Mall, E.B. Eddy Forest and Mill Tours, Antique Shops
See listing at Espanola

### Schell's Camp & Park
**On Site:** Marina - Live Bait, Fishing Guides, Housekeeping Cottages, Full Grocery Store
**Nearby:** Sudbury, Shopping & Attractions, Science North & Big Nickel
See listing at French River

### South Bay Resort
**On Site:** Pull Thru Sites, Overnight & Seasonal Sites, Lakeside Tenting, Great Salmon & Lake Trout Fishing, Housekeeping Cottages
**Nearby:** Chi-Cheeman Ferry, Pow-Wow, Hawberry Festival, Hiking Trails, Golfing, Horseback Riding, Fishing Charters
See listing at South Baymouth

## 9.

Algoma COUNTRY

### Bell's Point Beach
**On Site:** Swimming, Fishing, Boating, Playground
**Nearby:** Agawa Canyon, Lock Tours, Local Shopping
See listing at Sault Ste. Marie

### Blueberry Hill Motel & Campground
**On Site:** 104 Acres of Natural Beauty, Indoor Heated Pool, Motel Accommodations, Wagon Rides, River Canoeing & Rentals
**Nearby:** 1/2 Hour from Sault Ste. Marie., MI., Sault Ste. Marie Shopping, Agawa Canyon Train Tour, Area Beaches, Sault Lock Boat Tours
See listing at Goulais River

### Glenview Vacation Homes & Campground
**On Site:** Large Pull Thru Sites, Group Camping, Spectacular 6K Groomed Hiking Trail, Year Round Recreation
**Nearby:** Golfing, Agawa Canyon Train Rides, Soo Lock Tours
See listing at Sault Ste. Marie

### Vance's Cottages-Campground & Marina
**On Site:** Transient Dock Service for the North Channel-Lake Huron, Open Level Pull Thrus, Live Bait, Excellent Fishing, Housekeeping Cottages
**Nearby:** Elliot Lake, Golfing, World Famous Benjamin Island, " A Sailor's Paradise"
See listing at Spanish

### Woody's Restaurant & Trailer Park
**On Site:** RV Spaces Handy to the Highway, Grassy Tent Sites, Restaurant, Home Cooked, Full Menu Meals
**Nearby:** Vegas Kewadin Casino, Algoma Lock Tours, Agawa Canyon Train Tours, Golfing, Local Shopping
See listings at Sault Ste. Marie

## 11.

### Open Bay Cottages & Campground
**On Site:** Beautiful Tranquil Setting on Lac Des Mille Lacs, Excellent Fishing, Lakeside RV Sites, Housekeeping Cabins
**Nearby:** Fly in Fishing, Restaurant
See listing at Upsala

### Sky-View Trailer Park
**On Site:** New Heated Pool, Something Different– Private Bathrooms Available at Your Site, Large Pull Thru Sites, Privacy Barriers
**Nearby:** Golfing, Hunting, Fishing, Hiking
See listing at Longlac

### Stillwater Trailer Park
**On Site:** Exotic Amethyst Rock & Gift Shop, Pull Thru Sites, Special Live Entertainment
**Nearby:** Swimming, Boating, 9 Hole Golf Course, Mini Putt, Marina
See listings at Nipigon

### Wild Goose Lake Trailer Park
**On Site:** Boating & Fishing on Wild Goose Lake, Fishing Licenses, Lakeside Camping, Secluded Wooded Sites, Seasonal Sites Available, Laundry & Limited Groceries, Housekeeping Cabins
**Nearby:** Golfing, Hiking, Moose Hunting, Local Shopping & Restaurants
See listing at Geraldton

## 12.

Ontario's Sunset Country

### Blue Bird Trailer & Campsite
**On Site:** Lakefront Camping, Fishing Boat Rentals, Mini Golf, We Honor All Camping Discount Cards
**Nearby:** Golfing, Fly Out Fishing, Paper Mill Tours, Local Tours
See listing at Vermillion Bay

### Davy Lake Campground
**On Site:** Clean & Quiet, Large Well Groomed Pull Thru Sites, Fresh Water Lake Swimming, Playground, Mini Store, Rallies & Caravans Welcome
**Nearby:** Golfing, Excellent Fishing, Local Shopping, White Otter Castle Tours Available, Fly Out Fishing
See listing at Ignace

### Huber's Lone Pine Lodge
**On Site:** Fly Out Fishing Packages, H.K. Cottages, Fishing, Adventure Tours, Well Maintained RV Sites
**Nearby:** Golfing, Shopping
See listings at Dryden

### The Northwestern Tent & Trailer Park
**On Site:** In Town The Campground with a Heart, We Honor All Camping Club Discounts, RV Pull Thru Sites All Full Hookup, Modern, Clean Facilities, New Owners
**Nearby:** Fishing, Boating, Golfing, Restaurants, Town Shopping
See listings at Dryden

### Parkview R.V. Resort & Cottage Rental
**On Site:** 60 ft RV Drive Thrus, Choice of Walleye, Northern Pike, Crappies & Bass, Sandy Beach for Sun, Play & Relaxing, Surrounded by Pristine Crown Land, with over 1200' of Natural Shoreline, Fly In Fishing Trips
**Nearby:** Lake of the Woods & Crow Lake Launching & Docking Facilities, Hiking Trails, Horseback Riding, Golfing
See listing at Nestor Falls

**Remember to Tell Your Campground Owner You Saw It In Woodall's**

London, ON N5Z 3J1 (800-661-6804 or 519-649-7075). (For information on the following travel regions: Southwestern Ontario, Festival Country, Lakelands, Metropolitan Toronto.)

**Local Agencies:**

• *Tourism Stratford,* City of Stratford, P.O. Box 818, 88 Wellington St., Stratford, ON N5A 6W1 (800-561-SWAN or 519-271-5140).

• *Metropolitan Toronto Convention & Visitors Assn.*, 207 Queen's Quay West, Ste. 509, P.O. Box 126, Toronto, ON M5J 1A7 (800-363-1990 or 416-203-2600).

## Climate

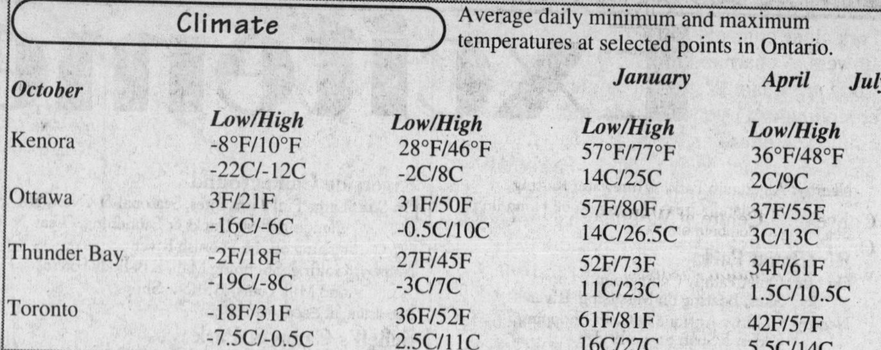

Average daily minimum and maximum temperatures at selected points in Ontario.

| October | | | January | April July |
|---|---|---|---|---|
| | Low/High | Low/High | Low/High | Low/High |
| Kenora | -8°F/10°F<br>-22C/-12C | 28°F/46°F<br>-2C/8C | 57°F/77°F<br>14C/25C | 36°F/48°F<br>2C/9C |
| Ottawa | 3F/21F<br>-16C/-6C | 31F/50F<br>-0.5C/10C | 57F/80F<br>14C/26.5C | 37F/55F<br>3C/13C |
| Thunder Bay | -2F/18F<br>-19C/-8C | 27F/45F<br>-3C/7C | 52F/73F<br>11C/23C | 34F/61F<br>1.5C/10.5C |
| Toronto | -18F/31F<br>-7.5C/-0.5C | 36F/52F<br>2.5C/11C | 61F/81F<br>16C/27C | 42F/57F<br>5.5C/14C |

## Recreational Information

*Bicycling:* Ontario Cycling Assn., 1220 Sheppard Ave. E., Willowdale, ON M2K 2X1 (416-4426-7242).

*Canoeing & Kayaking:* Canoe Ontario, 1220 Sheppard Ave. E., Ste 323, Willowdale, ON M2K 2X1 (416-426-7170).

*Charter Fishing:* For a list of charter fishing companies, contact the Ontario Sportfishing Guides Assn., 40 Sherwood Rd. E., Ajax, ON L1T 2Y9 (905-683-3214)

*Fishing & Hunting:* Natural Resources Information Centre, Mcdonald Block, Room M1-73, 900 Bay St., Toronto, ON M7A 2C1 (416-314-2000).

*Pick-Your-Own Farms:* Ontario boasts several hundred Pick-Your-Own farms and orchards. The Ministry of Agriculture, Food and Rural Affairs produces a terrific book which contains farm locations and directions, produce to be acquired and a variety of recipes. You can obtain a copy of this booklet by calling 800-ONTARIO.

*Sailing:* Ontario Sailing Assn., 1220 Sheppard Ave. E., Ste. 301, Willowdale, ON M2K 2X1 (416-426-7271).

*Skiing:* Recorded winter ski reports, 24-hour taped message: alpine (416-314-0998); cross country (416-314-0960).

## Places to See & Things to Do

***SOUTHWESTERN ONTARIO***

**Amherstburg.** One of the oldest settlements of southwestern Ontario with numerous historic sites and buildings. Among these places are the *North American Black Historical Museum* tracing the history of black people from Africa to slavery and finally to their emancipation. *The Fort Malden National Historic Site* contains several stone buildings which display artifacts of Indians, French, British and Americans who all controlled the area at various times. Also featured are British military demonstrations. *The Park House Museum*, the oldest house in Amherstburg, dating back to colonial times, is restored and furnished.

**Chatham.** Located near the mouth of the Thames River, just as its counterpart in England. Chatham's First Baptist Church was the site of a meeting held by abolitionist John Brown to plan the raid on Harper's Ferry, West Virginia. Highlights within Chatham include the site of a major battle in the War of 1812; establishment of an underground railroad to secretly route slaves to their freedom from the United States; London Winery with wine tours and tastings; and Chatham-Kent Museum.

**Goderich.** Historic town features museums, parks, beaches, marinas and old town square. Also located here is the unique *Marine Museum,* which is actually a wheelhouse from a Great Lakes freighter. Steamboat artifacts of lifeboat, anchors and chains, as well as nautical photos are exhibited.

**Grand Bend.** View rare birds and animal amid 20 acres of natural foliage and trails at the *Pine Ridge Zoo.* Also in Grand Bend is the *Lambton Heritage Museum* which features a Slaughterhouse, chapel, working blacksmith's shop and pioneer home and artifacts which trace Indian and pioneer history of area.

*Pinery Provincial Park.* One of the busiest provincial parks in Ontario, it includes 50 miles of roadways, nine hiking and skiing trails, six miles of Lake Huron beaches and a free year-round interpretive center that looks at the 700 species of plants, 29 species of mammals and 200 species of birds attracted to its unique environment.

**Kingsville.** Noted as Canada's most southerly town, Kingsville attracts birdwatchers with the following attractions:

*Jack Miner Bird Sanctuary.* Located on the migration path of the Canada goose. The best times to visit are the last 20 days in March and late October/early November.

*Point Pelee National Park.* More than half a million visitors flock to this national park in search of 347 species of birds. You can also find turtles, deer and Canada's only lizard, the five-lined skink. Best time to visit the park is for the spring bird migrations and in the autumn for the hawk and monarch butterfly migrations.

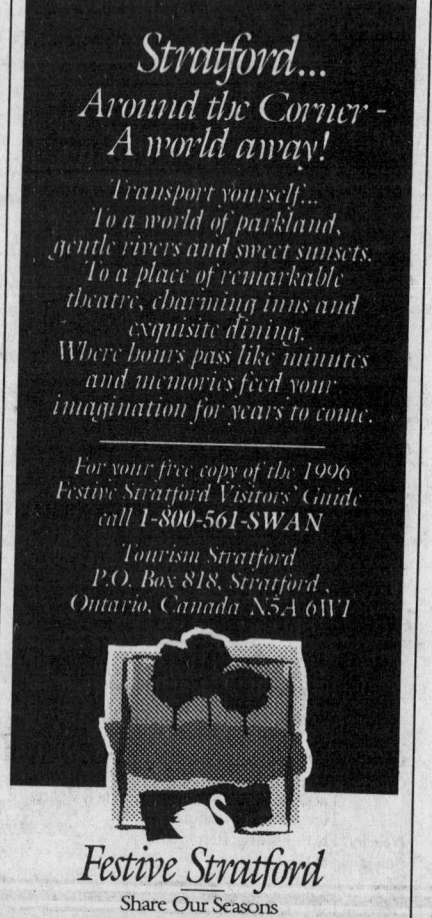

**London.** Growing town on the River Thames boasts 1,500 acres of parks and has been called the Forest City. The Springbank Park alone contains 350 acres of lawns and flowers. A charming mix of old and new, London's quaint Victorian neighborhoods are complimented by modern shopping facilities, cultural activities and special events and a major university. Hop a double-decker bus for a fun tour of London (departs from the Convention Centre at Wellington and York.) Or, if you'd like to see the city from the water, the *London Princess* sets sail from Storybook Landing in Springbank Park.

*Fanshawe Pioneer Village.* Complex of 22 restored buildings bring to life Ontario's rural origins. Costumed interpreters show visitors what it was like to live in the pioneer era.

*Storybook Gardens* is a family-oriented park (located in Springbank Park) featuring children's petting zoo, children's playworld, a mysterious tree house, wading pool, merry-go-round and picnic grounds.

**Rock Glen Conservation Area,** Arkona. Cool off under scenic falls, or just admire their beauty via handicap accessible trails. Includes limited hunting of fossils, some dating back 350 million years, and museum with fossils and Indian artifacts.

**St. Clair Parkway**, Sarnia. Follows the shores of the St. Clair River from the Blue Water Bridge at Sarnia, along the waterway to Chatham. Eighteen parks along the parkway feature picnic areas, Great Lakes ship viewing, camping, golfing, boating, fishing, swimming and museums.

**Stratford.** Consists of picturesque parks and gardens, fine dining restaurants and boutiques filled with crafts and handiworks. Quaint, tree-lined streets and historic century-old homes add to the city's charm. *The Gallery Stratford* features international art, sculpture and film exhibits, lectures and concerts. The *Stratford Festival* is a major world theatrical event which runs from May to October.More than a dozen different plays (in three theaters) are presented throughout the festival.

**"Uncle Tom's Cabin" Historic Site,** Dresden. Six museum buildings and Rev. Josiah Henson's burial site. Rev. Henson escaped slavery and established refuge and rehabilitation centers in Canada for runaway slaves. Inspired by Harriet Beecher Stowe's famous abolitionist novel, *Uncle Tom's Cabin.*

**Wineries.** Many of the following wineries offer tours of their wine-making facilities and tastings of the finished product: London Winery-Cedar Springs Vineyard (Blenheim); Pelee Island Winery (Kingsville); Colio Wines (Harrow); LeBlanc Estate Winery (Harrow); D'Angelo Estate Winery (Amherstburg); Hiram Walker & Sons (Windsor).

**Windsor.** City of Roses welcomes visitors with the *Rose Test Garden* (over 12,000 roses and 500 varieties), *Ojiby Park and Nature Center* (the largest protected tall-grass prairies in eastern North America), and *Windsor Casino* (with over 1,700 slot machines and over 60 gaming tables).

***FESTIVAL COUNTRY***

**African Lion Safari and Game Farm,** Hamilton-Wentworth. Drive through this wildlife park and view 750 exotic animals and birds amidst their natural habitat. Game reserves, scenic railway, daily animal and bird shows and children's playground are additional features.

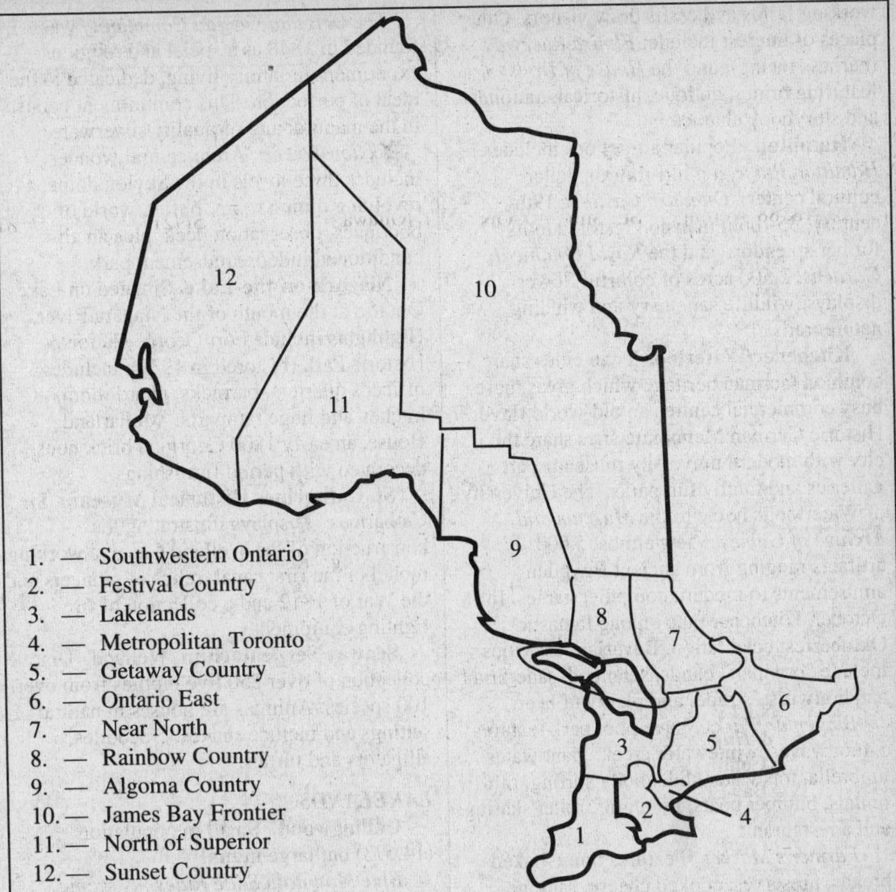


1. — Southwestern Ontario
2. — Festival Country
3. — Lakelands
4. — Metropolitan Toronto
5. — Getaway Country
6. — Ontario East
7. — Near North
8. — Rainbow Country
9. — Algoma Country
10. — James Bay Frontier
11. — North of Superior
12. — Sunset Country

**Brantford.** Hometown of Alexander Graham Bell is the site of the *Bell Homestead,* furnished just as it was when he lived there—inventions and all. Also in Brantford is the *Canadian Military Heritage Museum* which explores Canada's military heritage; The *Waterfront Park* with mini-golf, go karts, leisure pool, waterslide and Lazy River ride; and the *Woodland Cultural Centre* which preserves and promotes the Aboriginal culture and heritage of the First Nations.

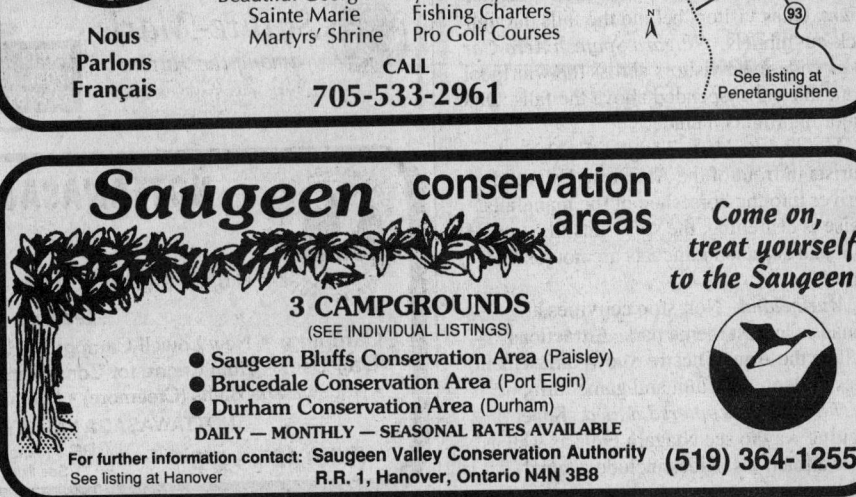

**Elmira.** Located in the heart of Ontario's German country, Elmira was settled in the early 1880s by the Mennonites. Mennonite working farms and crafts draw visitors. Other places of interest include: *Elmira Raceway* (harness racing); and the *House of Dolls* featuring brides, antique, historical, national and storybook characters.

**Hamilton.** Popular attractions include *Hamilton Place,* a multi-million dollar cultural center; *Dundurn Castle*, a 19th-century, 35-room mansion restored to its former splendor; and the *Royal Botanical Gardens,* 2,500 acres of colorful flower displays, wildlife sanctuary and winding nature trails.

**Kitchener/Waterloo.** Twin cities share a common German heritage which gives these busy commercial centres an old-world flavor. Historic German Mennonite sites share the city with modern university museums, art galleries and family fun parks. The University of Waterloo is home to the *Museum and Archive of Games.* View almost 5,000 artifacts ranging from ancient Egyptian amusements to modern computer games. In October, Kitchener puts on one fantastic Oktoberfest celebration. Bavarian festivities include "oompah" bands, schnitzel, sauerkraut and bratwurst, strudel and plenty of beer.

*Bingeman Park.* Wave pool park features 5-foot waves, whitewater creek, giant water umbrella, tots water slide, body surfing, raft rentals, bumper boats, mini golf, roller skating and a restaurant.

*Farmer's Market.* Features home-baked breads, preserves, cooked cheese, sausage, fresh vegetables, and handicrafts of the Amish and Mennonites.

*Seagram Museum.* The history and technology of the spirits and wine industry is depicted through artifacts from around the world. Housed in the original Seagram distillery barrel warehouse.

*Sportsworld.* 30-acres water park features a wave pool, tube slide, amusement rides, mini-golf, indoor driving range and more.

**The Meeting Place,** St. Jacobs. A unique museum which tells the history of the Mennonite people through displays and audio visuals.

**Niagara Falls.** A bustling tourist town featuring one of the natural wonders of the world as well as countless man-made attractions: *Niagara Falls Museum*, North America's oldest museum displaying over 700,000 exhibits; *Table Rock Scenic Tunnel Tours,* takes visitors behind the falls through rock-cut tunnels; *Niagara Spanish Aero Car* takes wide-eyed visitors across the whirlpool in a cable car suspended above the falls. Other major highlights include:

*Maid of the Mist.* Tough little ship takes tourists in front of the American Falls and upriver into the horseshoe of the main falls. Noise is deafening, the spray hits like tropical rain, and supplied raincoats are not just for show!

*Marineland.* Non-stop activities at Canada's largest theme park. Attractions include the Aqua Theatre Show, amusement rides, indoor aquarium and game farm.

*Niagara Helicopters Limited.* Super exciting way to see Niagara Falls as well as other attractions. Rides include a taped commentary.

*The Original Oneida Community* was founded in 1848 as a social and religious experiment in family living, dedicated to the ideal of perfection. This commitment persists in the manufacture of quality silverware.

*Skylon Tower.* Architectural wonder includes three levels in the Skylon dome, a revolving dining room, buffet, world of boutiques, observation deck, plus an air-conditioned indoor amusement park.

**Niagara-on-the-Lake.** Situated on Lake Ontario at the mouth of the Niagara River. Highlights include Fort George National Historic Park (restored in 1939), includes officer's quarters, barracks, guard room, kitchen and huge ramparts; McFarland House, an early 1800 Georgian brick house decorated with period furnishings.

**St. Catharines Historical Museum,** St. Catharines. Displays illustrating the construction of the Welland Canal, a working model of the first canal, relics of pioneers and the War of 1812 and a collection of fire-fighting equipment.

**Seaway Serpentarium,** Welland. Unique collection of over 250 live reptiles from over 100 species. Animals are houses in natural settings and include snakes, crocodiles, alligators and turtles.

### *LAKELANDS*

**Collingwood.** Small in population (14,673) but large in fun!

*Blue Mountain Slide Rides.* A scenic chairlift ride with a 3,000-foot descent through woods and ski trails via mini bob sled. Other features include the giant Slipper Dipper waterslide and the Tube Ride.

*Candy Factory.* The child in all of us enjoys watching sweet delectables being created by old-time tried and true receipes.

*Collingwood Air & Sightseeing Tours.* View the beautiful area of Bruce Peninsula and Georgian Bay from the air. 1/2 hour to two-hour tours available.

*Collingwood Scenic Caves Nature Preserve.* Located on the top of Blue Mountain, these caves plunge hundreds of feet into the depths. Above ground, nature trails feature rare and exotic plants.

**Discovery Harbor**, Penetanguishene. Recreated 19th-centry British naval and military base houses 15 reconstructed buildings. Costumed interpreters and musketry demonstrations bring back the sights and sounds of days long past. Explore the facilities by horse-drawn wagon or take a sailing excursion aboard *HMS Bee* and *Tecumseth*.

**Fathom Five National Marine Park,** Tobermory. Canada's only underwater park is explored by scuba divers and passengers on glass-bottom boats. The park boasts 19 islands, beautiful rock formations, sea caves and shipwrecks.

**Midland.** Southern gateway to the 30,000 Islands is located in the heart of the Lakelands region known as Huronia. First settled by French Jesuits (1639) and later occupied by the British military, Midland certainly has its share of history to tell.

*Huron Indian Village.* Full-scale replica of a 16th-centry Huron village recreates life 500 years ago.

*Martyrs' Shrine.* Honors the Canadian martyrs John Brebeuf and companions and the Christian Hurons of the 17th century. Shrine Church 1926. Daily religious devotions, cafeteria, religious articles and souvenir shop, picnic grounds and gardens.

*Sainte-Marie Among the Hurons.* 22 structures comprise this accurate recreation of the 17th-century Jesuit mission to the Huron people. The settlement became the first European community in what is now Ontario. Costumed interpreters, audio-visual presentation and museum.

*30,000 Island Cruises.* Three-hour cruises following the route of French explorers through the inside passage to Georgian Bay. 2 1/2-hour cruises show passengers the largest concentration of islands in the world.

*RMS Segwun Cruises,* Gravenhurst. Elegant Victorian steamship offers a variety of cruises exploring the landmarks of the beautiful Muskoka Lakes.

*Wye Marsh Wildlife Centre.* Learn the secrets of the marshland via boardwalks, trails, observation tower, underwater window, guides and movies. Canoe trips through the marsh are available.

**Waterworld** and **Wasaga Landing,** Wasaga Beach. Water theme amusement parks featuring water slides, wave pool, bumper boats, children's adventure playground and mini-golf.

### *METROPOLITAN TORONTO*

One of Canada's most cosmopolitan cities is a joy to explore. From the parks, gardens and lakefront boardwalks to the soaring glass towers of the commercial area, Toronto features fun around every corner. Cultural enthusiasts browse through galleries such as the *Art Gallery of Ontario and the Grange*, and the *McMichael Canadian Art Collection.* Canada's largest public museum is the *Royal Ontario Museum* with a vast collection of objects and specimens—everything from dinosaurs to totem poles, insects and Egyptian mummies to one of the greatest Chinese collections in the western world. Rich in ethnic diversity, the neighborhoods of Toronto portray authentic old world charm. Shop for herbal remedies at a Chinese pharmacy. Make your way through the bustling Kensington Market. On College Street between Ossington and Euclid and on St. Clair Avenue West between Dufferin and Lansdowne you'll encounter one of the world's largest Italian communities outside of Italy. In Greektown (on Danforth) savor Saganaki and baklava.

*Art Gallery of Ontario.* Houses a collection of 15,000 works including Oldenburg's "Hamburger," over 600 works of Henry Moore's sculptures and over 40 special exhibitions throughout the year.

*Black Creek Pioneer Village.* Living history village re-creates rural pioneer community of 100 years ago. Among over 35 buildings are a flour mill, blacksmith shop and craft shops.

*Casa Loma.* Fairytale castle in the heart of the city, this amazing creation of Sir Henry Pellat took $3 million in 1911 to build, housed numerous luxuries and ingenious inventions and entertained much royalty.

*CN Tower.* World's tallest free-standing structure (533 metres or 1,815 feet) with indoor/out-door observation decks, revolving restaurant, and the EcoDek and interactive environmental attraction featuring state-of-the-art muliti-media and computer technology. At the base of CN Tower is *Q-Zar Laser Game*. The world's most advanced laser equipment creates for the player, a futureistic live-action laser game not for the faint of heart.

*Harbourfront.* From York Street west to Bathurst Street, a unique waterfront indoor/out-door entertainment complex offers antique market, art gallery, craft shop, playgrounds, boutiques and theater.

*Historic Fort York.* Restored with eight original log, stone and brick buildings, the fort is highlighted by the Fort York Guard which marches, fires musket volleys and artillery salutes to the strain of the fife and drum.

*Metro Toronto Zoo.* 710-acre establishment that is so huge it sports its own silent monorail system which transports visitors to exotic setups and free-form pavilions.

*Ontario Place.* Built on three man-made islands, this beautifuly landscaped urban retreat boasts lagoons, canals and lookout points. Attractions such as *Haida,* WWII destroyer, a marina, a Cinesphere, a six-story movie theater, Forum outdoor amphitheatre, Children's Village, a playground, bumper and peddel boats, roller rink and water slide make Ontario Place a place you'll want to stay!

*Ontario Science Centre.* Part museum, part fun fair, the centre uses participation to illustrate how science and technology affect everyday life. Visitors are encouraged to touch and experiment with exhibits.

*Paramount Canada's Wonderland,* (technically located in Maple). Fun and fantasty combine to make a wonderland for the whole family. Amusement rides including nine roller coasters and Top Gun (an inverted jetcoaster), a waterpark with whitewater rafting, an aquarium and live entertainment provide a day of joy.

*Tours. Gray Line Tours* offers narrated bus tours of downtown Toronto, from April through November. *Old Town Toronto Tours* offers two-hour, narrated tours (within an old-fashioned trolley-style bus) covering 100 points of interest.

### *GETAWAY COUNTRY*

**Cullen Gardens & Miniature Village,** Whitby. Reproductions in miniature of over 100 historic buildings, all from southern Ontario, in a garden setting. Entertainment and dining facilities.

**Lang Pioneer Village,** Keene. Over 20 restored buildings where pioneer crafts, arts and festivals are in progress all summer.

**Picton.** The hub of Prince Edward County is an attractive and historic small town with a natural deepwater harbour.

*The Exotarium* is home to over 100 species of rare reptiles and amphibians from around the world.



*Mariners' Museum Lighthouse Park.* Features a collection of marine artifacts salvaged from local waters highlighting the period of steam and sail power on the Bay of Quinte.

**Presqu'ile Provincial Park,** Brighton. Contains 2,000 acres of marsh, woodlands, fields, wide swimming beaches, a marsh boardwalk, historic lighthouse, visitor center and camping. During summer, there are morning canoe trips through the marsh and in the spring, an annual waterfowl viewing weekend.

**Trent Severn Waterway.** System of 240 miles (348 kilometers) allows watercraft to pass on this sheltered water highway from Trenton on Lake Ontario to Port Severn on Georgian Bay. Boaters pass 1,006 miles of shoreline and 160 major islands, numerous cities, fields and forests through 44 locks in all.

### *ONTARIO EAST*

**Kingston.** Lovely city at the confluence of the St. Lawrence and Lake Ontario. Architecturally unique due to the concentration of 19th-century limestone buildings. Flourishing theatrical community boasts a dozen legitimate theater groups. Known to be the birthplace of organized hockey, the first league game was played in 1885. The *International Hockey Hall of Fame and Museum* follows the games development. At Confederation Park (opposite City Hall) you can hop on a tour train for a 50-minute ride through Kingston. Or take to the water aboard the *Island Queen* or the *Island Belle* for a cruise past Kingston's historic waterfront.

*Fort Henry.* Once Canada's mightiest fortress is today a living museum of military life in the 1800s. Contains an extensive display of 19th-century military equipment.

**Morrisburg.** One of the earliest settled parts of Canada is home to the following attractions:

*Prehistoric World.* Meet full-sized reproductions of dinosaurs and other prehistoric creatures as you walk the nature trail.

*Upper Canada Village.* Re-creation of a pre-1867 town. Contains 35 buildings including an inn, an operating woolen mill, sawmill and blacksmith's shop. Can be explored on foot, by ox cart or boat.

**Ottawa.** The capital of Canada features acres of greenery which create a park-like setting anytime of year. Don't miss the changing of the guard on Parliment Hill (10 a.m. daily). Here on Parliment Hill stand the *Parliment Buildings* (Gothic stone buildings with green copper roofs), the *Royal Canadian Mint* and the *Superme Court of Canada.* Museums in Ottawa are many and include the *National Museum of Science and Technology* (with hands-on exhibits and an observatory), the *National Aviation Museum* (housing over 100 aircraft), the *Canadian Museum of Nature* (featuring hands-on exhibits, live animals and mini-theater presentations) and the *Canadian Museum of Civilization* (with an IMAX/ OMNIMAX theater and children's museum.) For shopping check out the *Bayward Market* (Rideau St. Walkway). Farmers have brought their produce here since 1830. Sparks Street Mall is closed to vehicles and contains exclusive shops and boutiques, illuminated fountains, sidewalk cafes and open-air displays.

**Playing to a packed house** at the Stratford Festival. *The Gondoliers,* by W.S. Gilbert and Arthur Sullivan, is one of many theatrical productions brought to the stage during the summer-long festival. *Photo courtesy of Cylla von Tiedemann.*

**Rideau Canal and Locks.** The system spans 49 locks and 125 miles (200 km) connecting Ottawa and Kingston. Operating May to October, the water system's corridor has been preserved to include the cultural, historical and environmental character of the Rideau system. Used by Canadian and American cruising yachtsmen, boaters and vacationers, the system offers a series of interpretive programs and presentations enroute. And in winter, where the Rideau cuts through downtown Ottawa, the Capital's executives and civil servants commute to work on ice skates.

**Thousand Islands,** Gananoque. This town is the center of the Thousand Islands tourist area and host/boarding point for numerous tours through the islands by boat and plane. Gananoque Boat Lines offers 1 1/2 or 3 hour cruises with stopovers at the famous Boldt Castle.

**Whitewater Float Trips,** Pembroke. Thrilling roller coaster rides running the rapids of two of eastern Ontario's wildest rivers—the Ottawa and the Madawaska. Advance reservations are necessary.

### *NEAR NORTH*

**Algonquin Provincial Park.** One through-road (Hwy. 60), cuts across the southwest corner of this 3,000 square-mile park. Leaveing your vehicle behind allows you to experience excellent fishing and unpopulated canoeing areas. Explore two over-nigh hiking trails (47 miles and 22 miles) or stroll along one of two short nature trails. Canoe into the heart of the wilderness and watch for moose, bears, beavers and wolves.

***Chief Commanda II* Cruises,** North Bay. Six and 3 1/2-hour trips following the route of the voyageurs across Lake Nipissing to the Upper French River.

**Maple Syrup Museum,** Sundridge. Attractive log cabin atmosphere is backdrop for maple syrup demonstrations in late March-early April when sap is running.

**Nature Trails,** Canadore College, North Bay. Miles of good walking and cross country trails on campus. Also accessible from campus or from Highway 17 is Duchesnay Falls and Hiking Trails which offer restful scenery, roaring waterfalls, picnic sites and spectacular lookouts.

### *RAINBOW COUNTRY*

**The French River.** This 70 mile (112 km) shallow, swift-moving, freshwater river connects Lake Nipissing with Georgian Bay. The shores of the French River are the source for numerous water sports. A monument on the south shore commemorates Samuel de Champlain's passage in 1615.

***Island Queen* Cruises,** Parry Sound. Three-hour cruises on a 3-deck cruise ship through the largest concentration of islands in the world.

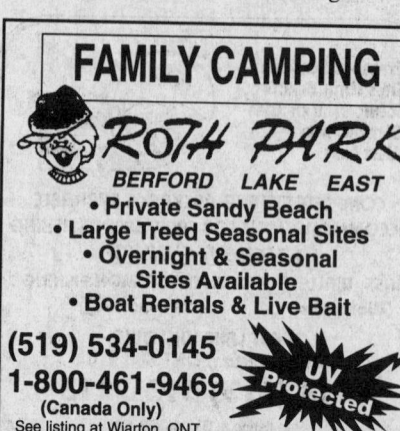

**Manitoulin Isand.** The world's largest fresh-water island offers nearly 1,000 miles of picturesque coastline, numerous lakes and bays, fine sandy beaches and serene little towns and villages. *Bridal Veil Falls* is a delicate, lacy cascade in a pastoral wooded setting east of Gore Bay.

**Sudbury.** City boasts 30 sparkling lakes and 6,000 acres of protected woodland. Visit 4 museums, *Theatre Center*, or *Science North* and *Big Nickel Mine* where you can see the erection of a mining headframe and expansion of the mineshaft. Sudbury contains the largest known concentration of nickel in the world, and to commemorate this feat, a huge 30-foot replica of a Canadian nickel can be seen at the mine.

### ALGOMA COUNTRY

**Aubrey Falls.** Mid-point between Chapleau and Thessalon, the falls are a spectacular attraction on the Mississagi River, just one mile off Highway 129.

**Fort St. Joseph National Historic Site,** St. Joseph Island. Guided tours through ruins of original fort (1800), plus large wilderness area, bird santuary and reception center displaying artifacts.

**Lake Superior Provincial Park,** Wawa. A natural environment park with camping and picnicking facilities along the beaches and headlands of Lake Superior shores. Indian pictographs and guided nature walks.

**Sault Ste. Marie.** Pronounced "soo-saint-marie", the city has one of the most active canals on the St. Lawrence Seaway. Old brick and stone buildings grace this city, established by French missionaries in 1699. Canal and lock tours allow a glimpse into the workings of one of the world's busiest locks.

*Agawa Canyon* can be reached via the Algoma Central Railway, which allows visitors a two-hour stop to view waterfalls, mountains and ravines, or to explore, hill climb, rockhound, picnic or fish. Catch the train at Station Mall, on Bay Street., early June to mid-October.

**Timber Village Museum,** Blind River. Relics of pioneer agriculture and lumbering fill this museum. Full-scale replica of logging camp, blacksmith shop, riverboats, steam engines, and operating press of the 1800s.

### JAMES BAY FRONTIER

**Cobalt's Northern Ontario Mining Museum & Tours,** Cobalt. Seven rooms of mining exhibits and what may be the world's finest display of native silver. Tours can be taken by bus (advance notice required) and maps are available for self-guided tours of the surface mine.

**Moose Factory Island,** Moosonee. 15-minute boat trip brings visitors to the island which was the original site of the Hudson's Bay Post. Several early 19th-century buildings remain as well as a blacksmith shop built in 1740. Museum devoted to fur trade and early community. The Wilderness Excursion, a 6-hour cruise, takes in James Bay, the Ship Sands Island Bird Sanctuary. Bus tours of Moose Factory Island are also available.

**Pioneer Museum,** Iroquois Falls. Housed in the Ontario Northwest Railway station, it displays tools, housewares and small family treasures depicting the life of early settlers. The Shay, a restored locomotive engine used by Abitibi in the early days to haul wood, now rests next to the museum.

**Polar Bear Express,** Cochrane. An exciting day trip (186 miles) by rail to the Arctic tidewater of James Bay, port of Hudson Bay. The train operates from the end of June to Labour Day.

**Timmins.** Productive city boasts the richest silver-zinc mine in the world and is also a centre for the lumber industry.

*Timmins Underground Gold Mine Tour.* See quartz veins, ore shutes, drills and a mock explosion. Guided tours take visitors 200 feet below ground.



*Ukranian Museum.* The culture and customs of the Ukranians (the first immigrants that arrived in Canada in 1891), are displayed through literature, arts and crafts.

### NORTH OF SUPERIOR

**Nipigon.** A popular tourist center on Lake Superior at the mouth of the Nipigon River, it is an excellent area for trout fishing. Once the home of the ancient Ojibwa Indians, Nipigon was also the site of the first white settlement on the North Shore. *Kama Lookout* offers a wide, majestic panorama of the Lake Superior shore and *Ouimet Canyon,* 500 feet wide and 350 feet deep, is an impressive chasm carved from solid rock.

**Thunder Bay.** Canada's third largest port. Highlights of the city include Amethyst mines where visitors can mine for the gems in open pits; *Old Fort William,* the reconstructed 19th-century fort looks just as it did 170 years ago; *The Sleeping Giant Legend*, an Ojibwa Indian legend explaining the existence of a giant stone structure; and *Thunder Bay Historical Museum* which houses Indian artifacts, pioneer, marine and military material as well as photographs, maps and authentic documents. Other attractions in the Thunder Bay area include:

*Centennial Park.* Contains a 1910 logging camp and museum, plus 12 miles (19 km) of nature/cross country ski trails.

*International Friendship Garden.* Nine nations are represented in separate floral tributes.

*Kakabeka Falls.* Magnificent cascades located west of town are extremely impressive

due to the great volume of water tumbling over the sheer drop.

*Mt. McKay.* View the town and surroundings from a 600-foot bridge, located south on Hwy. 61B.

*Welcome Cruise Ships.* Two-hour cruises viewing shoreline docks, industries and offshore islands, plus upriver cruise available to Old Fort William.

***SUNSET COUNTRY***

**Aviation and Fire Management Centre,** Dryden. Tour the command centre for fire supression strategy and see the fleet of fire detection aircraft, including the CL-215, the only aircraft in the world designed specifically for firefighting.

**Fort Vermilion,** Vermilion Bay. Replica of an early log fort houses an information center and hosts a variety of special summer events.

**Kenora.** Picturesque hub of the northwest is also the headquarters for the Lake of the Woods area. Tour *Boise Cascade's* pulp and paper mill (June-Aug.), or charter a boat to take you through the islands of Lake of the Woods. Kenora's colorful history is brought to life at the *Lake of the Woods Museum*.

**Lake of the Woods.** Explore nearly 15,000 islands and 65,000 miles of jagged shoreline at Ontario's second largest inland lake. Beautiful in all seasons, Lake of the Woods provides ample fishing (especially for muskie), wildlife watching (keep an eye out for bald eagles, moose and pelicans), and miles of hiking trails.

**Quetico Provincial Park,** Atikokan. Enormous wilderness park with 930 miles of canoe routes.

## Calendar of Events

*May:* Good Food Festival, Toronto; Folklore Festival, Thunder Bay; Antique Shows, St. Jacobs/Belleville/Peterborough/Aberfoyle/Richards Landing/Shakespeare; Art & Craft Sales and Shows, Lion's Head/Sarnia/Toronto/Whitby/Jarratt/Elora/Brampton/Windsor/Barrie/Ottawa/Buckhorn/Southampton/Port Colborne; Festival of the Arts, Dunnville

*June:* Antique Shows, Beaverton/Westport/Niagara Falls/Picton; Stratford Festival, Stratford; Art & Craft Sales and Shows, Stratford/Burlington/Waterloo/Toronto (Scarborough); Automotive Flea Market, Barrie; Multicultural Festival, Brockville; Bread & Honey Festival, Streetsville; Festival of the Arts, Brampton; Mudcat Festival, Dunnville; Rosy Rhubarb Days, Shedden; Sound of Music Festival, Burlington; International Freedom Festival, Windsor; Festival Caravan, Toronto; Symphony of Fire, Toronto; Fiesta Week, Oshawa; Friendship Festival, Fort Erie

*July:* Canada Day Celebrations, Province-wide; Antique Shows, Owen Sound/Barrie/Port Carling; Art & Craft Shows, Fenelon Falls/Buckhorn/Goderich/Toronto/Kitchener/Bracebridge/Markham/Collingwood/Thorold/Port Carling/Owen Sound/Port Elgin; Stratford Festival, Stratford; Country Fest, Kitchener; Flea Market & Car Show, Huntsville; Antique Car Show, London; Auto Show, Ridgetown; Balloon Festival, Barrie; International Villages Festival, Brantford; International Picnic, Toronto; Waterfront Festival & Folklorama, Belleville; Square Dance Festival, Thunder Bay; Norseman Festival, Red Lake; Aquafest, Hamilton; Lumber Baron Festival, Renfrew

*August:* Antique Shows, Odessa/Burk's Falls/Bracebridge/Bayfield/Stratford/St. Thomas/Whitby; Art & Craft Sales and Shows, Collingwood/Bancroft/Richards Landing/Port Elgin/Cannington/Buckhorn/Brighton/Campbellford/Colchester/Port Dover; Stratford Festival, Stratford; Boat Show, Merrickville; Rodeo, Bancroft; Classic Car Shows, Bowmanville/Fenelon Falls; Summer Festival, Barrie; Busker Festival, Ottawa; Balloon Fiesta, London; Celtic Roots Festival, Goderich; Festival of the Islands, Gananoque; Peach Festival, Harrow; Festival of the Arts, Gravenhurst; Winnie's Hometown Festival, White River; Iron Horse Festival; Heritage Days Weekend, Gananoque

*September:* Air Shows, Toronto/Muirkirk; Antique Shows, Dundas/Sarnia/Windsor/Barrie; Art & Craft Sales and Shows, Oakville/Bewdley/Toronto (East York)/Elora/Niagara Falls/Burlington/Grand Bend/St. Catharines; Stratford Festival, Stratford; Auto Shows, Barrie/Perry/New Hamburg/Huntsville; Tomatofest, Rowan; Festival by the Bay, Sarnia; International Film Festival, Toronto; Apple Days, Brantford; Harvest Festival, Delhi; Grape & Wine Festival, St. Catharines; Old Sandwich Towne Festival, Windsor; Applefest, Brighton

# ontario

All privately-owned campgrounds personally inspected by Woodall Representatives Phil and Pat Douglas.

Unless otherwise noted, all listed campgrounds have hot showers & flush toilets.

## ACTON—H-3

**NOR-HALTON PARK**—Secluded, semi-wooded CAMPGROUND. *From south jct Hwy 7 & Hwy 25: Go 1.6 km/1 mi S on Hwy 25, then 2 km/1 1/4 mi W on Regional Rd 12.*

WELCOME

◆◆◆FACILITIES: 150 sites, 86 full hookups, 39 water & elec (15 & 30 amp receptacles), 25 no hookups, seasonal sites, 14 pull-thrus, tenting available, group sites for tents, RV storage, handicap restroom facilities, sewage disposal, laundry, public phone, limited grocery store, ice, tables, fire rings, wood, traffic control gate.

◆◆◆◆RECREATION: rec hall, rec room/area, swim pool (heated), basketball hoop, playground, 2 shuffleboard courts, planned group activities (weekends only), sports field, horseshoes, volleyball.

Open Apr 15 through mid Oct. Facilities fully operational May 1 through Thanksgiving. Rate in 1995 $18-22 per family. Member of OPCA. Phone: (519) 853-2959.

**SEE AD TORONTO PAGE 1022**

## ADOLPHUSTOWN—H-5

**Adolphustown Park**—CAMPGROUND with large, open & shaded sites on Adolphustown Lake. *In town on Hwy 33.* ◆◆◆FACILITIES: 124 sites, most common site width 50 feet, 49 elec (15 & 30 amp receptacles), 75 no hookups, seasonal sites, 11 pull-thrus, tenting available, handicap restroom facilities, sewage disposal, public phone, tables, fire rings. ◆◆◆RECREATION: lake swimming, boating, canoeing, ramp, dock, lake fishing, playground, badminton, sports field, horseshoes, volleyball. Open May 5 through mid Oct. Rate in 1995 $15-18 per family. Phone: (613) 373-2632.

**Bass Cove Park**—CAMPGROUND on Bass Cove. *From east city limits: Go .4 km/1/4 mi E on Hwy 33, then 1.2 km/3/4 mi N on CR 8.* ◆◆FACILITIES: 96 sites, most common site width 30 feet, 7 full hookups, 89 water & elec (15 amp receptacles), seasonal sites, tenting available, sewage disposal, laundry, ice, tables, fire rings, wood. ◆◆RECREATION: rec room/area, swim pool, boating, canoeing, ramp, dock, lake fishing. Open May 1 through Oct 15. Rate in 1995 $15-18. Phone: (613) 373-2651. FCRV 10% discount.

**Pickerel Park**—CAMPGROUND on south shore of Hay Bay. *From east city limits: Go .4 km/1/4 mi E on Hwy 33, then 13.2 km/8 mi N on CR 8.* ◆◆FACILITIES: 240 sites, most common site width 40 feet, 160 water & elec (15 & 30 amp receptacles), 80 no hookups, seasonal sites, tenting available, sewage disposal, laundry, public phone, grocery store, ice, tables, fire rings, wood. ◆◆◆RECREATION: rec hall, pavilion, lake swimming, boating, canoeing, ramp, dock, 7 motor boat rentals, lake fishing, mini-golf ($), playground, planned group activities (weekends only), horseshoes, volleyball. Recreation open to the public. Open May 1 through Sep 30. Rate in 1995 $16-19 per family. Member of OPCA. Phone: (613) 373-2812.

## AHMIC HARBOUR—F-3

**AHMIC LAKE RESORT**—Secluded, lakeside CAMPGROUND. *From east jct Hwy 520 & Hwy 124: Go 6.5 km/4 mi W on Hwy 124.*

WELCOME

◆◆◆FACILITIES: 70 sites, most common site width 12 feet, 29 full hookups, 18 water & elec, 21 elec (15 & 30 amp receptacles), 2 no hookups, seasonal sites, 4 pull-thrus, a/c not allowed, tenting available, cabins, sewage disposal,

**AHMIC HARBOUR**—Continued
AHMIC LAKE RESORT—Continued

laundry, public phone, limited grocery store, RV supplies, LP gas refill by weight, gasoline, marine gas, ice, tables, fire rings, wood.

◆◆◆RECREATION: lake swimming, boating, canoeing, ramp, dock, 2 row/12 canoe/1 pedal/8 motor boat rentals, water skiing, lake fishing, playground, planned group activities (weekends only), badminton, sports field, horseshoes, hiking trails, volleyball.

Open all year. Facilities fully operational May 15 through Oct 15. Rate in 1995 $18-26 per family. Master Card/Visa accepted. Member of OPCA. Phone: (705) 387-3853.

**SEE AD TRAVEL SECTION PAGES 975, 976 AND 977**

## AILSA CRAIG—I-2

**Shady Pines Campground**—A CAMPGROUND in a grassy wooded area. *From jct Hwy 7 & CR 19 (business centre of town): Go 3.2 km/2 mi S on CR 19.* ◆◆◆FACILITIES: 275 sites, most common site width 39 feet, 248 water & elec (15 & 30 amp receptacles), 27 no hookups, seasonal sites, tenting available, sewage disposal, laundry, public phone, grocery store, LP gas refill by weight, ice, tables, fire rings, wood. ◆◆◆◆RECREATION: rec hall, rec room/area, pavilion, 2 swim pools, canoeing, river/pond fishing, playground, 2 shuffleboard courts, planned group activities (weekends only), badminton, sports field, horseshoes, hiking trails, volleyball. Recreation open to the public. Open May 1 through mid Oct. Rate in 1995 $15-18 for 2 persons. Member of OPCA. Phone: (519) 232-4210.

## ALFRED—F-6

**EVERGREEN PARK**—Wooded CAMPGROUND with grassy sites convenient to a major highway. *From west side of town: Go 3.2 km/2 mi W on Hwy 17.*

WELCOME

◆◆◆FACILITIES: 150 sites, most common site width 60 feet, 60 full hookups, 20 water & elec (15 & 30 amp receptacles), 70 no hookups, seasonal sites, 12 pull-thrus, a/c allowed ($), heater not allowed, tenting available, group sites for tents, sewage disposal, laundry, limited grocery store, ice, tables, fire rings, wood.

◆◆◆RECREATION: equipped pavilion, lake swimming, playground, 2 shuffleboard courts, planned group activities (weekends only), badminton, sports field, horseshoes, hiking trails, volleyball.

Open May 1 through Oct 1. Rate in 1995 $16-20 per family. Phone: (613) 679-4059.

**SEE AD TRAVEL SECTION PAGES 975, 976 AND 977**

## ALGONQUIN PARK—F-4

CANISBAY LAKE CAMPGROUND (Algonquin Provincial Park)—*From town: Go 24 km/15 mi E of west park gate on Hwy 60, then 1 1/2 km/1 mi N.* FACILITIES: 248 sites, 248 no hookups, tenting available, sewage disposal, laundry, tables, wood. RECREATION: swimming, boating, canoeing, lake fishing, hiking trails. Open late Jun through early Sep. No showers. Phone: (705) 633-5572.

KEARNEY LAKE CAMPGROUND (Algonquin Provincial Park)—*From town: Go 38 1/2 km/24 1/2 mi E of west park gate on Hwy 60.* FACILITIES: 104 sites, 104 no hookups, tenting available, sewage disposal, tables, wood. RECREATION: swimming, boating, canoeing, lake fishing, hiking trails. Open late Jun through early Sep. Phone: (705) 633-5572.

LAKE OF TWO RIVERS CAMPGROUND (Algonquin Provincial Park)—*From town: Go 33 1/2 km/21 mi E of west park gate on Hwy 60.* FACILITIES: 241 sites, 241 no hookups, tenting available, sewage disposal, laundry, limited grocery store, ice, tables, wood. RECREATION: swimming, boating, canoeing, lake fishing, hiking trails. Open mid May through mid Oct. Phone: (705) 633-5572.

MEW LAKE CAMPGROUND (Algonquin Provincial Park)—*From town: Go 32 km/20 mi E of west park gate on Hwy 60.* FACILITIES: 131 sites, 131 no hookups, tenting available, sewage disposal, laundry, tables, wood. RECREATION: swimming, boating, no motors, canoeing, lake fishing, hiking trails. Open May through Mar. Facilities fully operational May through Sep. Open for winter camping Oct thru Mar. Phone: (705) 633-5572.

POG LAKE CAMPGROUND (Algonquin Provincial Park)—*From town: Go 36 3/4 km/23 mi E of west park gate on Hwy 60.* FACILITIES: 281 sites, 281 no hookups, tenting available, sewage disposal, laundry, tables, wood. RECREATION: swimming, boating, no motors, canoeing, lake fishing, hiking trails. Open late Jun through early Sep. Phone: (705) 633-5572.

**ALGONQUIN PARK**—Continued

ROCK LAKE CAMPGROUND (Algonquin Provincial Park)—*From town: Go 48 km/30 mi E of west park gate on Hwy 60.* FACILITIES: 124 sites, 72 elec, 52 no hookups, tenting available, non-flush toilets, sewage disposal, tables, wood. RECREATION: swimming, boating, canoeing, ramp, lake fishing, hiking trails. Open late Apr through mid Oct. No showers. Phone: (705) 633-5572.

TEA LAKE CAMPGROUND (Algonquin Provincial Park)—*From town: Go 12 km/7 1/2 mi E of west park gate on Hwy 60.* FACILITIES: 43 sites, 43 no hookups, tenting available, non-flush toilets, sewage disposal, tables, wood. RECREATION: swimming, boating, canoeing, ramp, lake fishing, hiking trails. Open late Apr through mid Oct. No showers. Phone: (705) 633-5572.

## ALLISTON—H-3

EARL ROWE PROVINCIAL PARK—*From town: Go 3 1/4 km/2 mi W on Hwy 89, then 3/4 km/1/2 mi N on Concession 1.* FACILITIES: 370 sites, 83 elec, 287 no hookups, tenting available, handicap restroom facilities, sewage disposal, limited grocery store, ice, tables, wood. RECREATION: swimming, boating, no motors, canoeing, lake fishing, playground, hiking trails. Open May through early Sep. Phone: (705) 435-4331.

**ROLLING ACRES FARM CAMPGROUND**—Family oriented CAMPGROUND. *From jct Hwy 400 & Hwy 89: Go 14 km/8 3/4 mi W on Hwy 89.*

WELCOME

◆◆◆FACILITIES: 90 sites, most common site width 40 feet, 30 ft. max RV length, 83 water & elec (15 & 30 amp receptacles), 7 no hookups, seasonal sites, 4 pull-thrus, a/c allowed ($), heater allowed, tenting available, sewage disposal, tables, wood, traffic control gate.

◆◆◆RECREATION: swim pool, boating, canoeing, 2 canoe/2 pedal boat rentals, river fishing, playground, planned group activities (weekends only), horseshoes, hiking trails.

Open mid May through mid Oct. Rate in 1995 $16-23 per family. Phone: (705) 435-7860.

**SEE AD TRAVEL SECTION PAGES 975, 976 AND 977**

## ALVINSTON—I-1

A.W. CAMPBELL (St. Clair Region Conservation Auth.)—*From north city limits: Go 3/4 km/1/2 mi N on Hwy 79, then 3 1/4 km/2 mi E on Concession 1.* FACILITIES: 155 sites, 95 water & elec (15 & 30 amp receptacles), 60 no hookups, seasonal sites, tenting available, sewage disposal, laundry, public phone, tables, fire rings, wood. RECREATION: rec hall, pond swimming, boating, no motors, canoeing, lake fishing, playground, sports field, horseshoes, hiking trails, volleyball. Recreation open to the public. Open Victoria Day through Thanksgiving. Phone: (519) 847-5357.

## AMHERSTBURG—J-1

HOLIDAY BEACH CONSERVATION AREA (Essex Region Conservation Auth.)—*From town: Go 12 km/7 1/2 mi SE on Hwy 18, then 3 1/4 km/2 mi S on CR 50.* FACILITIES: 85 sites, 85 no hookups, tenting available, handicap restroom facilities, sewage disposal, limited grocery store, ice, fire rings, wood. RECREATION: lake swimming, boating, lake fishing, playground. Open May 9 through Sep 1. Phone: (519) 736-3772.

**JELLYSTONE PARK**—Semi-wooded, grassy CAMPGROUND with many activities. *From east city limits: Go 3.2 km/2 mi E on Pike Rd (CR 18, Simcoe St).*

WELCOME

◆◆◆FACILITIES: 315 sites, most common site width 50 feet, 22 full hookups, 293 water & elec (15 & 30 amp receptacles), seasonal sites, a/c allowed, tenting available, group sites for tents/RVs, RV rentals, RV storage, sewage disposal, laundry, public phone, full service store, RV supplies, LP gas refill by weight/by meter, ice, tables, fire rings, wood, church services, guard.

◆◆◆◆◆RECREATION: rec hall, rec room/area, equipped pavilion, coin games, swim pool, wading pool, mini-golf ($), basketball hoop, playground, 2 shuffleboard courts, planned group activities, movies, recreation director, sports field, horseshoes, volleyball.

Open Apr 15 through Oct 15. Rate in 1995 $23 for 2 persons. Master Card/Visa accepted. Member of OPCA. Phone: (519) 736-3201.

**SEE AD FRONT OF BOOK PAGE 142 AND AD TRAVEL SECTION, MI PAGE 413A AND AD WINDSOR PAGE 1025**

## ANGUS—H-3

⚑ **NOTTAWASAGA VALLEY CONSERVATION AUTHORITY**—*From jct Hwy 400 & Hwy 90: Go 19 km/12 mi W on Hwy 90.* Administrator over 2 campgrounds and 9 day-use parks. Open all year. Phone: (705) 424-1479.

**SEE AD TRAVEL SECTION PAGE 980**

## ARNPRIOR—F-5

FITZROY PROVINCIAL PARK—*From Hwy 17 in town: Go 17 1/2 km/11 mi NE on paved, local roads to Fitzroy Harbour.* FACILITIES: 235 sites, 32 elec, 203 no hookups, 20 pull-thrus, tenting available, handicap restroom facilities, laundry, wood. RECREATION: lake swimming, boating, ramp, lake fishing, playground, hiking trails. Open mid May through early Sep. Phone: (613) 623-5159.

**Grainger's Tent & Trailer Park**—Grassy, level CAMPGROUND on Trans-Canada highway. *From south town limits: Go 16 km/10 mi E on Hwy 17, then .4 km/1/4 mi S on Grainger Park Rd.* ◆◆◆FACILITIES: 145 sites, most common site width 35 feet, 95 water & elec (15 & 30 amp receptacles), 50 no hookups, seasonal sites, 30 pull-thrus, tenting available, sewage disposal, public phone, ice, tables, fire rings, wood. ◆◆◆RECREATION: rec room/area, pavilion, swim pool, pond swimming, planned group activities (weekends only), horseshoes, hiking trails, volleyball. Recreation open to the public. Open May 15 through Oct 15. Rate in 1995 $17.50-19 per family. Phone: (613) 839-5202.

## ARTHUR—H-2

**CONESTOGA FAMILY CAMPGROUNDS**—CAMPGROUND with open & shaded area & springfed lake. *From jct Hwy 6 & Hwy 9: Go 11.2 km/7 mi W on Hwy 9, then 2.4 km/1.5 mi N on Con 9.*

◆◆◆FACILITIES: 298 sites, most common site width 30 feet, 168 full hookups, 80 water & elec (15 & 30 amp receptacles), 50 no hookups, seasonal sites, 10 pull-thrus, heater allowed, tenting available, RV rentals, RV storage, handicap restroom facilities, sewage disposal, laundry, public phone, limited grocery store, RV supplies, LP gas refill by weight, ice, tables, fire rings, wood, guard.

◆◆◆◆RECREATION: rec hall, swim pool (heated), lake swimming, boating, electric motors only, canoeing, dock, 1 row/2 canoe/3 pedal boat rentals, pond fishing, mini-golf ($), basketball hoop, playground, planned group activities (weekends only), movies, sports field, horseshoes, hiking trails, volleyball.

Open May 15 through Oct 15. Rate in 1995 $18.50 per family. Reservations recommended May 15 through Aug 15. Member of OPCA. Phone: (519) 848-3640.

**SEE AD TRAVEL SECTION PAGES 975, 976 AND 977**

## ASHTON—G-5

**DWYER HILL RV RESORT**—Grassy, level private sites in a metro area CAMPGROUND with a rural setting. *At jct Hwy 7 & CR 3 (Dwyer Hill Rd).*

◆◆◆◆FACILITIES: 140 sites, 80 full hookups, 30 water & elec (15 & 30 amp receptacles), 30 no hookups, seasonal sites, 3 pull-thrus, a/c allowed ($), heater allowed ($), tenting available, group sites for tents/RVs, sewage disposal, laundry, public phone, limited grocery store, RV supplies, LP gas refill by weight, ice, tables, fire rings, wood.

◆◆◆RECREATION: rec room/area, swim pool, playground, badminton, sports field, horseshoes, volleyball, cross country skiing.



ASHTON—Continued
DWYER HILL RV RESORT—Continued

Open all year. Reservations must be made during winter months. Rate in 1995 $18-19 per family. Master Card/Visa accepted. Phone: (613) 257-2568.

**SEE AD OTTAWA PAGE 1010**

## ATHERLEY—G-3

MARA PROVINCIAL PARK—*From town: Go 4 3/4 km/3 mi E on Hwy 12, then 1 1/2 km/1 mi S on Courtland St.* FACILITIES: 106 sites, 106 no hookups, tenting available, sewage disposal, tables, wood. RECREATION: swimming, boating, canoeing, fishing, playground. Open mid Jun through Sep. No showers. Phone: (705) 326-4451.

## ATIKOKAN—E-2

QUETICO PROVINCIAL PARK—*From town: Go 40 km/25 mi E on Hwy 17.* FACILITIES: 156 sites, 28 elec, 128 no hookups, tenting available, handicap restroom facilities, sewage disposal, tables, wood. RECREATION: swimming, boating, no motors, canoeing, ramp, fishing, playground, hiking trails. Open all year. Facilities fully operational late May through early Oct. No showers. Phone: (807) 597-2430.

## AVENING—H-3

⚑ **CARRUTHER'S MEMORIAL CONSERVATION AREA**—*In town on CR 42.* Picnicking, fishing or just relaxing along the banks of The Mad River in a spacious day-use park. Open May 1 through end of Sep. Phone: (705) 424-1479.

**SEE AD TRAVEL SECTION PAGE 980**

## AYLMER—I-2

SPRINGWATER CONSERVATION AREA (Catfish Creek Conservation Auth.)—*From town: Go 4 km/2 1/2 mi W on Hwy 3, then 3 1/4 km/2 mi S on CR 35.* FACILITIES: 155 sites, 140 water & elec (15 & 30 amp receptacles), 15 no hookups, tenting available, handicap restroom facilities, sewage disposal, laundry, public phone, limited grocery store, ice, tables, fire rings, grills, wood. RECREATION: pavilion, lake swimming, boating, no motors, canoeing, ramp, dock, lake/stream fishing, playground, planned group activities (weekends only), sports field, horseshoes, hiking trails, volleyball. Recreation open to the public. Open mid May through mid Oct. Phone: (519) 773-9037.

## BAILIEBORO—H-4

**BENSFORT BRIDGE RESORT**—Rustic CAMPGROUND on the Otonabee River. *From jct Hwy 28 & CR 2: Go 6.4 km/4 mi E on CR 2, then 6.4 km/4 mi N to park.*

◆◆◆FACILITIES: 63 sites, most common site width 40 feet, 51 full hookups, 7 water & elec (30 amp receptacles), 5 no hookups, seasonal sites, a/c allowed ($), heater allowed, phone hookups, tenting available, cabins, sewage disposal, laundry, public phone, limited grocery store, marine gas, ice, tables, fire rings, wood, traffic control gate.

◆◆◆RECREATION: rec hall, lake swimming, boating, canoeing, ramp, dock, 2 row/2 canoe/5 motor boat rentals, water skiing, river fishing, planned group activities (weekends only), badminton, horseshoes, volleyball.

Open May 5 through Oct 15. Rate in 1995 $17-22. Master Card/Visa accepted. Member of OPCA. Phone: (705) 939-6515.

**SEE AD PETERBOROUGH PAGE 1012**

## BALA—G-3

**Bala Woodlands**—A lakeside CAMPGROUND. *From jct Muskoka Rd 38 & Hwy 169: Go 4 km/2 1/2 mi N on Hwy 169, then 3.2 km/2 mi W on Medora Lake Rd.* ◆◆◆FACILITIES: 105 sites, 65 water & elec (15 amp receptacles), 40 no hookups, seasonal sites, tenting available, sewage disposal, public phone, limited grocery store, ice, tables, fire rings, grills, wood. ◆◆◆RECREATION: lake swimming, boating, canoeing, ramp, dock, 4 row/2 canoe boat rentals, lake fishing, playground, sports field, horseshoes, hiking trails. Open May 24 through Oct 15. Rate in 1995 $20-24 per family. Phone: (705) 762-3332.

**Gullwing Lake Tent & Trailer Park**—Lakeside CAMPGROUND with grassy, shaded and open sites. *From east city limits: Go 4 km/2 1/2 mi E on Hwy 169, then 2.4 km/1 1/2 mi S on Clear Lake Rd (Southwood Rd exit).* ◆◆◆FACILITIES: 100 sites, most common site width 35 feet, 70 full hookups, (15 & 30 amp receptacles), 30 no hookups, seasonal sites, tenting available, handicap restroom facilities, sewage disposal, laundry, public phone, limited grocery store, ice, tables, fire rings, grills, wood. ◆◆◆RECREATION: rec room/area, pavilion, lake swimming, boating, canoeing, ramp, dock, 2 row/1 canoe boat rentals, lake fishing, playground, planned group activities (weekends only), sports field, horseshoes, volleyball. Open May 15 through Oct 15. Rate in 1995 $16-20 per family. Member of OPCA. Phone: (705) 762-3737.

## BANCROFT—G-4

**Bancroft Campground**—Secluded, grassy lakeside CAMPGROUND with open & shaded sites. *From jct Hwy 28 & Hwy 62: Go 6.4 km/4 mi N on Hwy 62, then .4 km/1/4 mi W on S Baptiste Lake Rd, then .4 km/1/4 mi N on Bird Lake Rd.* ◆◆◆FACILITIES: 100 sites, most common site width 50 feet, 28 full hookups, 16 water & elec (15 amp receptacles), 56 no hookups, 29 pull-thrus, tenting available, sewage disposal, public phone, LP gas refill by weight, ice, tables, fire rings, wood. ◆◆◆RECREATION: rec room/area, swim pool, boating, no motors, canoeing, dock, 3 row/1 canoe boat rentals, lake fishing, hiking trails. Open May 15 through Oct 15. Rate in 1995 $16-19.50 for 2 persons. Member of OPCA. Phone: (613) 332-3673.

**Bancroft Tent & Trailer Camp**—CAMPGROUND on Marble Lake. Most full hookup sites occupied by seasonal campers. *From jct Hwy 28 & Hwy 62: Go 3.2 km/2 mi S on Hwy 62.* ◆◆◆FACILITIES: 69 sites, most common site width 30 feet, 30 full hookups, 30 water & elec (15 & 30 amp receptacles), 9 no hookups, seasonal sites, tenting available, sewage disposal, laundry, limited grocery store, ice, tables, fire rings. ◆◆◆RECREATION: lake swimming, boating, 10 hp limit, canoeing, ramp, 3 row/6 pedal boat rentals, lake fishing, playground, planned group activities, horseshoes. Open May 1 through Oct 31. Rate in 1995 $13.50-15 per family. Phone: (613) 332-2183.

**Birch Cliff Lodge**—Lakeside CAMPGROUND with grassy sites. *From jct Hwy 28 & Hwy 62: Go 6.4 km/4 mi N on Hwy 62, then 8.8 km/5 1/2 mi W on S Baptiste Lake Rd.* ◆◆FACILITIES: 31 sites, most common site width 30 feet, 15 full hookups, 14 water & elec (15 amp receptacles), 2 no hookups, seasonal sites, tenting available, sewage disposal, laundry, public phone, limited grocery store, ice, tables, fire rings, wood. ◆◆RECREATION: lake swimming, boating, canoeing, ramp, dock, 1 canoe/8 motor boat rentals, lake fishing, playground, planned group activities, badminton, horseshoes, hiking trails. Open all year. Facilities fully operational mid May through mid Oct. Rate in 1995 $16-19 per family. Phone: (613) 332-3316.

**The Homestead Trailer Park**—Secluded lakeside CAMPGROUND with wooded & open sites. Most sites occupied by seasonal campers. *From south city limits: Go 29 km/18 mi S on Hwy 28, then 3.6 km/2 1/4 mi W on Dyno Rd, then 1.6 km/1 mi S on Road 10.* ◆◆◆FACILITIES: 150 sites, most common site width 40 feet, 150 full hookups, (15 & 30 amp receptacles), seasonal sites, 2 pull-thrus, tenting available, laundry, public phone, full service store, ice, tables, fire rings, wood. ◆◆◆◆RECREATION: rec hall, rec room/area, lake swimming, boating, canoeing, ramp, dock, 3 canoe/2 pedal/2 motor boat rentals, lake fishing, playground, planned group activities (weekends only), badminton, sports field, horseshoes, volleyball. Open May 1 through Oct 15. Rate in 1995 $20 per family. Member of OPCA. Phone: (613) 339-2500.

**Jolly Roger Campsite**—A CAMPGROUND with level, forested sites on a lake. *From town centre: Go 9.6 km/6 mi N on Hwy 62, then 6.4 km/4 mi E on Hybla Rd.* ◆◆FACILITIES: 14 sites, most common site width 35 feet, 14 no hookups, tenting available, non-flush toilets, tables, fire rings, grills. ◆RECREATION: lake swimming, boating, canoeing, lake fishing. Open mid May through mid Oct. No showers. Rate in 1995 $13. Phone: (613) 332-2900.

SILENT LAKE PROVINCIAL PARK—*From town: Go 22 1/2 km/14 mi S on Hwy 28.* FACILITIES: 167 sites, 167 no hookups, tenting available, handicap restroom facilities, sewage disposal, laundry, tables, fire rings, wood. RECREATION: lake swimming, boating, no motors, canoeing, ramp, lake fishing, hiking trails. Open early May through mid Sep. Phone: (613) 339-2807.

## BARRIE—H-3

**HEIDIS' CAMPGROUND**—CAMPGROUND with open & shaded area in alpine surroundings and fitness trails. *From jct Hwy 400 & Hwy 11: Go 14.4 km/9 mi N on Hwy 11 (exit CR 11 Hawkstone).*

◆◆◆◆FACILITIES: 180 sites, 160 full hookups, 20 water & elec (15 & 30 amp receptacles), seasonal sites, a/c allowed ($), heater allowed, phone hookups, tenting available, RV storage, handicap restroom facilities, laundry, public phone, grocery store, ice, tables, fire rings, wood, traffic control gate.

◆◆◆◆RECREATION: rec hall, rec room/area, coin games, swim pool (indoor) (heated), whirlpool, stream fishing, mini-golf ($), playground, planned group activities (weekends only), sports field, horseshoes, hiking trails, volleyball. Recreation open to the public.

Open all year. Facilities fully operational May 1 through Oct 15. Rate in 1995 $19.95-21.95 per family. Reservations recommended Jul through Aug. American Express/Master Card/Visa accepted. Member of OPCA. Phone: (705) 487-3311. FCRV 10% discount.

**SEE AD NEXT PAGE**

BARRIE—Continued on next page

BARRIE—Continued

**✽ HEIDIS' CAMPGROUND & RV TRAILER SALES** —*From jct hwy 400 & Hwy 11: Go 14.4 km/9 mi N on Hwy 11 (exit CR 11).* SALES: travel trailers, park models, 5th wheels. SERVICES: RV appliance mechanic part-time, sewage disposal, RV storage, sells parts/accessories, installs hitches. Open all year. American Express/Master Card/Visa accepted. Phone: (705) 487-2214.

**SEE AD THIS PAGE**

**KOA-BARRIE**—Rolling, grassy CAMPGROUND. *From jct Hwy 11 & Hwy 93: Go 11.2 km/7 mi N on Hwy 93.*

◆◆◆◆FACILITIES: 103 sites, most common site width 32 feet, 51 full hookups, 47 water & elec (15 & 30 amp receptacles), 5 no hookups, seasonal sites, 24 pull-thrus, a/c allowed ($), heater allowed ($), tenting available, group sites for tents/RVs, cabins, RV storage, sewage disposal, laundry, public phone, limited grocery store, RV supplies, LP gas refill by weight/by meter, ice, tables, fire rings, wood, traffic control gate.

◆◆◆◆RECREATION: rec hall, rec room/area, coin games, 2 swim pools (heated), boating, no motors, canoeing, pond fishing, mini-golf ($), playground, planned group activities, movies, recreation director, badminton, horseshoes, hiking trails, volleyball. Recreation open to the public.

Open May 15 through Oct 15. Rate in 1995 $20-24 for 2 persons. Master Card/Visa accepted. Member of OPCA. Phone: (705) 726-6128. KOA 10% value card discount. FCRV 10% discount.

**SEE AD PAGE 986 AND AD FRONT OF BOOK PAGES 68 AND 69**

**⚑ TIFFIN CENTRE FOR CONSERVATION**—*From jct Hwy 400 & Hwy 90: Go 11.2 km/7 mi W on Hwy 90, then 4 km/2 1/2 mi S on Con 8 of Essa Twp.* A day-use educational learning centre for enviromental purposes. Open mid May through mid Oct. Phone: (705) 424-1479.

**SEE AD TRAVEL SECTION PAGE 980**

**UTOPIA (Nottawasaga Vly. Conservation Area)**—*From jct Hwy 400 & Hwy 90: Go 16 km/10 mi W on Hwy 90, then 4 km/2 1/2 mi S on Con Rd 6 of Essa Twp.*

FACILITIES: 80 sites, 10 full hookups, (30 amp receptacles), 70 no hookups, seasonal sites, a/c allowed, heater allowed, tenting available, RV storage, non-flush toilets, sewage disposal, tables, fire rings, grills, wood, guard.

RECREATION: equipped pavilion, lake swimming, boating, no motors, canoeing, pond fishing, sports field, horseshoes, hiking trails, cross country skiing. Recreation open to the public.

Open all year. Facilities fully operational May 1 through end Sep. No showers. Master Card/Visa accepted. Phone: (705) 424-6908.

**SEE AD TRAVEL SECTION PAGE 980**

## BATCHAWANA BAY—D-3

PANCAKE BAY PROVINCIAL PARK—*From town: Go 6 1/2 km/4 mi W on Hwy 60.* FACILITIES: 329 sites, 69 elec, 260 no hookups, tenting available, handicap restroom facilities, sewage disposal, limited grocery store, ice, tables, wood. RECREATION: swimming, lake fishing, playground, hiking trails. Open early May through early Oct. Phone: (705) 882-2209.

## BAYFIELD—I-2

**THE OLD HOMESTEAD LIMITED**—Level CAMPGROUND with pioneer motif. *From north city limits at Bayfield River Bridge: Go 90 m/100 yards N on Hwy 21, then 1.6 km/1 mi E on Old River Rd.*

◆◆◆FACILITIES: 246 sites, most common site width 40 feet, 212 full hookups, 29 water & elec (15 & 30 amp receptacles), 5 no hookups, seasonal sites, a/c allowed, phone hookups, tenting available, RV storage, sewage disposal, laundry, public phone, RV supplies, ice, tables, fire rings, wood.

◆◆◆◆RECREATION: rec hall, coin games, swim pool, wading pool, basketball hoop, playground, planned group activities (weekends only), sports field, horseshoes.

Open mid Apr through mid Oct. Pool open mid Jun thru Sep 15. Rate in 1995 $21-23 per family. Reservations recommended Jul through Aug. Phone: (519) 482-9256.

**SEE AD THIS PAGE**

## BEARDMORE—A-2

LAKE NIPIGON PROVINCIAL PARK—*From town: Go 16 km/10 mi S on Hwy 11, then 4 3/4 km/3 mi W.* FACILITIES: 60 sites, 60 no hookups, tenting available, handicap restroom facilities, sewage disposal, laundry, tables, wood. RECREATION: swimming, boating, canoeing, ramp, lake fishing, hiking trails. Open early Jun through early Sep. Phone: (807) 885-3181.

## BELLEVILLE—H-5

**CARLETON'S COVE TOURIST TRAILER PARK AND CAMPING** (REBUILDING)—Grassy, riverside CAMPGROUND. *From jct Hwy 401 (exit 543B) & Hwy 62: Go 4 km/2 1/2 mi N on Hwy 62, then .4 km/1/4 mi E on Carleton's Cove Rd.*

FACILITIES: 75 sites, most common site width 40 feet, 75 water & elec (15 amp receptacles), seasonal sites, 4 pull-thrus, a/c allowed ($), heater not allowed, tenting available, sewage disposal, ice, tables.

RECREATION: pavilion, river swimming, boating, canoeing, river fishing, sports field, horseshoes.

Open May 15 through Oct 15. Rate in 1995 $15-20 per family. Phone: (613) 962-6344.

**SEE AD TRAVEL SECTION PAGES 975, 976 AND 977**

## BEWDLEY—H-4

**SUNRISE TOURIST TRAILER PARK**—CAMPGROUND on Rice Lake. *From jct Hwy 28 & Rice Lake Dr: Go 4.8 km/3 mi E on Rice Lake Dr.*

◆◆◆FACILITIES: 59 sites, most common site width 30 feet, 53 full hookups, 6 water & elec (30 amp receptacles), seasonal sites, a/c allowed ($), tenting available, RV rentals, cabins, RV storage, sewage disposal, public phone, grocery store, RV supplies, ice, tables, patios, wood, traffic control gate.

◆◆◆◆RECREATION: rec hall, coin games, swim pool, boating, canoeing, ramp, dock, 1 row/1 canoe/1 pedal/10 motor boat rentals, lake fishing, playground, planned group activities (weekends only), movies, badminton, horseshoes.

Open May 1 through mid Oct. Rate in 1995 $24 for 4 persons. Member of OPCA. Phone: (905) 797-2456.

**SEE AD FRONT OF BOOK PAGE 140 AND AD RICE LAKE PAGE 1015**

## BLIND RIVER—F-1

**Leisure Bay Campground & Marina**—Lakeside CAMPGROUND with grassy sites. *From jct Hwy 17 & CR 557: Go 3.2 km/2 mi N on CR 557, then 2 km/1 1/4 mi NE on CR 555, then 2 km/1 1/4 mi NW on Lake Duborne Rd.* ◆◆FACILITIES: 25 sites, most common site width 25 feet, 8 full hookups, 11 water & elec (15 amp receptacles), 6 no hookups, seasonal sites, tenting available, sewage disposal, public phone, limited grocery store, LP gas refill by weight, ice, tables, fire rings, grills, wood. ◆◆◆RECREATION: lake swimming, boating, canoeing, ramp, dock, 1 canoe/1 pedal/4 motor boat rentals, lake fishing, badminton, horseshoes, volleyball. Open May 1 through Sep 30. Rate in 1995 $12.50-16.50 per family. Phone: (705) 356-7028.

## BLOOMFIELD—H-5

**Edgewater Park**—CAMPGROUND with terraced sites at West Lake, facing the sandbanks. *From jct Hwy 33 & CR 12: Go 8 km/5 mi S on CR 12, then 1.2 km/3/4 mi W on Sheba Island Rd.* ◆◆◆FACILITIES: 130 sites, most common site width 30 feet, 88 full hookups, 19 water & elec (15 amp receptacles), 23 no hookups, seasonal sites, 2 pull-thrus, tenting available, laundry, public phone, ice, tables, fire rings, wood. ◆◆◆RECREATION: rec room/area, swim pool, lake swimming, boating, canoeing, ramp, dock, 1 canoe/1 pedal boat rentals, lake fishing, planned group activities (weekends only), badminton, horseshoes, volleyball. Open May 15 through Oct 15. Rate in 1995 $15-20 per family. Phone: (613) 393-2831. FCRV 10% discount.

**Hideaway Trailer Park**—Lakeside CAMPGROUND. *From jct Hwy 33 & CR 12: Go 6.4 km/4 mi S on CR 12.* ◆◆◆FACILITIES: 233 sites, most common site width 50 feet, 143 full hookups, 40 water & elec (15 & 30 amp receptacles), 50 no hookups, seasonal sites, tenting available, sewage disposal, limited grocery store, ice, tables, fire rings, wood. ◆◆◆RECREATION: pavilion, lake swimming, boating, canoeing, ramp, lake fishing, playground, planned group activities (weekends only), badminton, horseshoes, volleyball. Open mid May through mid Oct. Rate in 1995 $18-22 per family. Phone: (613) 393-2267.

SANDBANKS PROVINCIAL PARK—*From town: Go 12 3/4 km/8 mi S on West Lake Rd (CR 12), follow signs.* FACILITIES: 411 sites, 411 no hookups, tenting available, handicap restroom facilities, tables, wood. RECREATION: lake swimming, boating, canoeing, ramp, lake fishing, hiking trails. Open mid May through mid Oct. Phone: (613) 393-3319.

**Sandview Campground**—Campground with RV & tenting spaces. *From jct Hwy 33 & CR 12: Go 8.8 km/5 1/2 mi S on CR 12.* ◆◆FACILITIES: 30 sites, most common site width 40 feet, 15 full hookups, (15 & 30 amp receptacles), 15 no hookups, seasonal sites, tenting available, sewage disposal, ice, tables, wood. ◆◆RECREATION: lake swimming, boating, canoeing, ramp, dock, lake fishing, playground. Open May 15 through Oct 15. Rate in 1995 $20-26. Phone: (613) 393-3014.

**WEST LAKE WILLOWS**—Level, grassy sites overlooking the sandbanks on the south shore of West Lake. *From jct Hwy 33 & CR 12: Go 9.6 km/6 mi S on CR 12.*

◆◆◆FACILITIES: 110 sites, most common site width 35 feet, 110 full hookups, (15 & 30 amp receptacles), seasonal sites, 8 pull-thrus, a/c allowed ($), heater not allowed, tenting available, group sites for tents/RVs, sewage disposal, laundry, public phone, limited grocery store, ice, tables, wood.

◆◆◆RECREATION: lake swimming, boating, canoeing, ramp, dock, 3 row/3 motor boat rentals, water skiing, lake fishing, basketball hoop, badminton, horseshoes, volleyball.

Open mid May through mid Oct. Rate in 1995 $23-28 per family. Member of OPCA. Phone: (613) 393-3213.

**SEE AD TRAVEL SECTION PAGE 981**

## BLYTH—H-2

WAWANOSH PARK (Maitland Valley Conservation Authority)—*From jct Hwy 4 & CR 25: Go 6 1/2 km/4 mi W on CR 25, then 6 km/3 3/4 mi N on CR 22, then 2 km/1 1/4 mi E on Concession Rd 6/7.* FACILITIES: 25 sites, 25 no hookups, tenting available, non-flush toilets, tables, fire rings, grills, wood. RECREATION: pavilion, river/pond swimming, river/pond fishing, playground, hiking trails. Recreation open to the public. Open May 15 through Oct 15. No showers. Phone: (519) 335-3357.

## BOLTON—H-3

ALBION HILLS CONSERVATION AREA (Metro Toronto & Region Cons. Auth.)—*From town: Go 8 km/5 mi N on Hwy 50.* FACILITIES: 173 sites, most common site width 35 feet, 65 water & elec (15 & 30 amp receptacles), 108 no hookups, seasonal sites, 60 pull-thrus, tenting available, handicap restroom facilities, sewage disposal, laundry, public phone, limited grocery store, ice, tables, fire rings, grills, wood. RECREATION: lake swimming, river/pond fishing, playground, badminton, horseshoes, hiking trails, volleyball. Open May 12 through Oct 9. Phone: (905) 880-4855.

**LEISURE TIME PARK**—Rolling, grassy CAMPGROUND in scenic area. *From north end of town: Go 17 km/10.6 mi N on Hwy 50, then 1.6 km/1 mi W on Hwy 9.*

◆◆◆◆FACILITIES: 222 sites, most common site width 50 feet, 213 water & elec (15 & 30 amp receptacles), 9 no hookups, seasonal sites, 2 pull-thrus, a/c allowed, heater allowed, tenting available, group sites for RVs, RV storage, sewage disposal, laundry, public phone, limited grocery store, RV supplies, LP gas refill by weight, ice, tables, fire rings, wood, traffic control gate.

◆◆◆◆RECREATION: rec hall, rec room/area, coin games, swim pool, lake swimming, boating, no motors, canoeing, pond fishing, basketball hoop, playground, shuffleboard court, planned group activities (weekends only), movies, tennis court, sports field, horseshoes, volleyball.

Open May 1 through Oct 15. Rate in 1995 $20-24 per family. Master Card/Visa accepted. Member of OPCA. Phone: (416) 880-4921. FCRV 10% discount.

**SEE AD TRAVEL SECTION PAGES 975, 976 AND 977**

## BORNHOLM—I-2

**WOODLAND LAKE CAMP & RV RESORT**—A CAMPGROUND with open and shaded sites overlooking a woodland lake. *From jct Hwy 8 & Hwy 23: Go 8 km/5 mi N on Hwy 23, then 4.8 km/3 mi W on Logan Concession Rd 10-11 to park.*

◆◆◆FACILITIES: 160 sites, most common site width 40 feet, 139 full hookups, 5 water & elec (15 & 30 amp receptacles), 16 no hookups, seasonal sites, a/c allowed ($), heater allowed ($), tenting available, laundry, public phone, limited grocery store, LP gas refill by weight, ice, tables, fire rings, wood, traffic control gate.

◆◆◆RECREATION: rec hall, rec room/area, lake swimming, boating, no motors, canoeing, 4 pedal

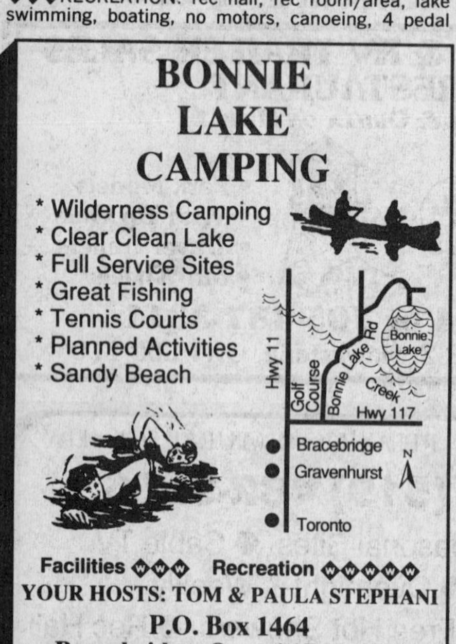


BORNHOLM—Continued
WOODLAND LAKE CAMP & RV RESORT—Continued

boat rentals, lake fishing, basketball hoop, playground, planned group activities (weekends only), horse riding trails, sports field, horseshoes, hiking trails.

Open May 1 through mid Oct. Rate in 1995 $16-19 per family. Visa accepted. Member of OPCA. Phone: (519) 347-2315.

**SEE AD TRAVEL SECTION PAGES 975, 976 AND 977**

## BRACEBRIDGE—G-3

**BONNIE LAKE CAMPING**—Secluded wooded CAMPGROUND on private lake. *From jct Hwy 11 & Hwy 117: Go 3.2 km/2 mi E on Hwy 117, then 4.5 km/2 3/4 mi N on Bonnie Lake Rd, then 1.6 km/1 mi E on gravel road.*

◆◆◆FACILITIES: 450 sites, most common site width 35 feet, 260 water & elec (15 & 20 amp receptacles), 190 no hookups, seasonal sites, 50 pull-thrus, tenting available, RV storage, sewage disposal, laundry, public phone, full service store, RV supplies, LP gas refill by weight, marine gas, ice, tables, fire rings, wood, guard.

◆◆◆◆◆RECREATION: rec room/area, equipped pavilion, coin games, lake swimming, boating, 10 hp limit, canoeing, ramp, dock, 10 row/6 canoe/2 pedal/3 motor boat rentals, lake/pond fishing ($), basketball hoop, playground, 2 shuffleboard courts, planned group activities, movies, recreation director, 2 tennis courts, badminton, sports field, horseshoes, hiking trails, volleyball.

Open May 1 through Oct 15. Rate in 1995 $17.50-23.75 per family. Reservations recommended Jul through Aug. Master Card/Visa accepted. Member of OPCA. Phone: (705) 645-4511.

**SEE AD THIS PAGE**

**BRACEBRIDGE CAMPING & TRAILER PARK**—CAMPGROUND by the Muskoka River. *From jct Hwy 11 & Muskoka Rd 4: Go 4.5 km/2 3/4 mi N on Muskoka Rd 4, then 2.5 km/1 1/2 mi W on Muskoka Rd 16.*

◆◆◆FACILITIES: 124 sites, most common site width 35 feet, 29 full hookups, 76 water & elec (15 amp receptacles), 19 no hookups, seasonal sites, 26 pull-thrus, tenting available, group sites for tents/RVs, RV storage, sewage disposal, laundry, public phone, grocery store, RV supplies, ice, tables, fire rings, grills, wood, traffic control gate.

◆◆◆RECREATION: rec room/area, swim pool, river swimming, boating, canoeing, dock, river fishing, planned group activities (weekends only), badminton, sports field, horseshoes, hiking trails, volleyball, local tours.

Open May 15 through Oct 15. Rate in 1995 $18-20 per family. Master Card/Visa accepted. Member of OPCA. Phone: (705) 645-2174.

**SEE AD TRAVEL SECTION PAGES 975, 976 AND 977**

**Whispering Pines Family Camping**—CAMPGROUND on Muskoka River. Adjacent to Santa's Village complex. *From west city limits: Go 4.8 km/3 mi W on CR 15 (the river road).* ◆◆◆FACILITIES: 70 sites, most common site width 35 feet, 42 full hookups, 28 water & elec (15 & 30 amp receptacles), seasonal sites, 6 pull-thrus, tenting available, sewage disposal, public phone, limited grocery store, ice, tables, fire rings, wood. ◆◆RECREATION: boating, canoeing, ramp, dock, river fishing, playground, planned group activities (weekends only), horseshoes. Open May 15 through Oct 15. Rates available upon request. No refunds. Member of OPCA. Phone: (705) 645-5682.

## BRADFORD—H-3

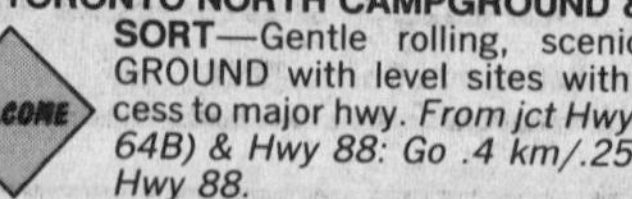

**TORONTO NORTH CAMPGROUND & RV RESORT**—Gentle rolling, scenic CAMPGROUND with level sites with easy access to major hwy. *From jct Hwy 400 (exit 64B) & Hwy 88: Go .4 km/.25 mi W on Hwy 88.*

◆◆◆◆FACILITIES: 112 sites, 28 full hookups, 58 water & elec (30 amp receptacles), 26 no hookups, 54 pull-thrus, a/c allowed ($), heater allowed, tenting available, group sites for tents/RVs, sewage disposal, laundry, public phone, limited grocery store, ice, tables, fire rings, wood.

◆◆◆RECREATION: rec hall, rec room/area, coin games, swim pool (heated), mini-golf ($), basketball hoop, sports field, hiking trails, volleyball.

Open mid May through Sep 30. Rate in 1995 $27-31 for 2 persons. Diners Club/Master Card/Visa accepted. Member of OPCA. Phone: (905) 859-0026.

**SEE AD TORONTO PAGE 1022**

## BRAMPTON—H-3

TERRA COTTA CONSERVATION AREA (Credit Valley Cons. Auth.)—*From jct Hwy 10 & King St in town: Go 8 km/5 mi W on King St, then 2 km/1 1/4 mi N on Winston Churchill*

BRAMPTON—Continued
TERRA COTTA CONSERVATION AREA (CREDIT VALLEY CONS. AUTH.)—Continued

*Blvd.* FACILITIES: 137 sites, 25 ft. max RV length, 137 no hookups, tenting available, handicap restroom facilities, sewage disposal, public phone, limited grocery store, ice, tables, fire rings, grills, wood. RECREATION: pavilion, swim pool ($), pond fishing, mini-golf ($), playground, planned group activities, hiking trails. Recreation open to the public. Open mid May through mid Oct. Phone: (905) 877-9650.

## BRANTFORD—I-3

**BRANT CONSERVATION AREA (Grand River Conservation Authority)**—*From town: Go 1 1/2 km/1 mi W on Hwy 53, follow signs.*

FACILITIES: 530 sites, 30 full hookups, 100 water & elec (15 & 30 amp receptacles), 400 no hookups, seasonal sites, tenting available, group sites for tents, sewage disposal, public phone, limited grocery store, ice, tables, wood, guard.

RECREATION: swim pool, boating, no motors, canoeing, 30 canoe boat rentals, river fishing, playground, sports field, hiking trails. Recreation open to the public.

Open May 1 through Oct 15. Phone: (519) 752-2040.

**SEE AD TRAVEL SECTION PAGE 978**

## BRIGHTON—H-4

**Cedar Creek Campground**—Semi-wooded CAMPGROUND convenient to the highways. *From jct Hwy 401 (exit 509) & Hwy 30: Go 3.2 km/2 mi N on Hwy 30.* ◆◆◆FACILITIES: 75 sites, most common site width 35 feet, 45 full hookups, 30 water & elec (15 amp receptacles), seasonal sites, tenting available, sewage disposal, public phone, limited grocery store, ice, tables, fire rings, wood. ◆◆◆RECREATION: rec room/area, swim pool (heated), playground, planned group activities (weekends only), badminton, horseshoes, hiking trails, volleyball. Open May 1 through Oct 15. Rate in 1995 $17-20 per family. Member of OPCA. Phone: (613) 475-0640.

**KOA-Brighton/401**—Hilltop CAMPGROUND with scenic view. *From jct Hwy 401 (exit 509) & Hwy 30: Go 152 m/500 feet N of Hwy 401 on Hwy 30, then 1.6 km/1 mi W on Telephone Rd.* ◆◆◆FACILITIES: 127 sites, most common site width 40 feet, 32 full hookups, 65 water & elec, 8 elec (15 & 30 amp receptacles), 22 no hookups, seasonal sites, 90 pull-thrus, tenting available, sewage disposal, laundry, public phone, grocery store, ice, tables, fire rings, wood. ◆◆◆RECREATION: rec room/area, swim pool, playground, horseshoes, volleyball. Recreation open to the public. Open May 1 through Oct 15. Pool open Jun 1-Sep 15. Rate in 1995 $18-21 for 2 persons. Phone: (613) 475-2186. KOA 10% value card discount.

PRESQU'ILE PROVINCIAL PARK—*From town: Go 3/4 km/1/2 mi W on Hwy 2, then 3 1/4 km/2 mi S on Ontario St.* FACILITIES: 393 sites, 24 elec, 369 no hookups, tenting available, handicap restroom facilities, sewage disposal, laundry, limited grocery store, ice, tables, wood. RECREATION: lake swimming, boating, canoeing, ramp, lake fishing, hiking trails. Open May through mid Oct. Phone: (613) 475-2204.

## BRITT—F-2

GRUNDY LAKE PROVINCIAL PARK—*From town: Go 14 1/2 km/9 mi N on Hwy 69.* FACILITIES: 460 sites, 37 elec, 423 no hookups, tenting available, handicap restroom facilities, sewage disposal, tables, wood. RECREATION: swimming, boating, no motors, canoeing, ramp, lake fishing, hiking trails. Open mid May through mid Oct. Phone: (705) 383-2286.

KILLBEAR PROVINCIAL PARK—*From town: Go 12 3/4 km/8 mi N on Hwy 69, then 19 1/4 km/12 mi W on Hwy 559, then 9 1/2 km/6 mi W on Dillon Rd.* FACILITIES: 882 sites, 882 no hookups, tenting available, handicap restroom facilities, sewage disposal, tables, wood. RECREATION: swimming, boating, canoeing, ramp, fishing, hiking trails. Open mid May through mid Oct. Phone: (705) 342-5492.

STURGEON BAY PROVINCIAL PARK—*From town: Go 27 1/4 km/17 mi S on Hwy 69, then 1 1/2 km/1 mi on Hwy 644 (Pointe au Baril).* FACILITIES: 82 sites, 82 no hookups, tenting available, non-flush toilets, sewage disposal, tables, wood. RECREATION: swimming, boating, canoeing, ramp, lake fishing. Open early May through mid Oct. No showers. Phone: (705) 366-2521.

## BROCKVILLE—G-6

**Graham Lake Campground**—Lakeside campground. *From jct Hwy 401 & Hwy 29: Go 10.4 km/6 1/2 mi N on Hwy 29, then 1.2 km/3/4 mi W on CR 32, then 4.8 km/3 mi on Graham Lake Rd.* ◆◆FACILITIES: 123 sites, most common site width 40 feet, 93 water & elec (15 amp receptacles), 30 no hookups, seasonal sites, 2 pull-thrus, tenting available, sewage disposal, laundry, public phone, limited grocery store, ice, tables, fire rings, wood. ◆◆◆RECREATION: rec room/area, lake swimming, boating, canoeing, ramp, dock, lake fishing, mini-golf ($), playground, planned group activities (weekends only), badminton, sports field, horseshoes,

GRAHAM LAKE CAMPGROUND—Continued on next page
BROCKVILLE—Continued on next page

BROCKVILLE—Continued
GRAHAM LAKE CAMPGROUND—Continued

volleyball. Open May 15 through Sep 15. Rate in 1995 $13-15 per family. Member of OPCA. Phone: (613) 923-5449.

**Happy Green Acres Tent & Trailer Park**—Grassy, level CAMPGROUND near a major highway. *From jct Hwy 401 (exit 687) & Hwy 2: Go 1.6 km/1 mi W on Hwy 2.* ◆◆◆FACILITIES: 150 sites, most common site width 25 feet, 100 full hookups, 50 water & elec (15 & 30 amp receptacles), seasonal sites, 40 pull-thrus, tenting available, laundry, public phone, limited grocery store, ice, tables, fire rings, wood. ◆◆RECREATION: swim pool, sports field, horseshoes, hiking trails. Open all year. Facilities fully operational Apr 15 through Nov 1. Rate in 1995 $18-22 per family. Phone: (613) 342-9646.

**Pleasure Park**—Lakeside CAMPGROUND with grassy sites. *From jct Hwy 401 & Hwy 29: Go 10.4 km/6 1/2 mi N on Hwy 29, then 1.2 km/3/4 mi W on CR 32, then 4 km/2 1/2 mi N on Graham Lake Rd.* ◆◆◆FACILITIES: 250 sites, most common site width 35 feet, 200 water & elec (15 & 30 amp receptacles), 50 no hookups, seasonal sites, 40 pull-thrus, tenting available, handicap restroom facilities, sewage disposal, laundry, public phone, grocery store, ice, tables, fire rings, wood. ◆◆◆◆RECREATION: rec room/area, equipped pavilion, lake swimming, boating, canoeing, ramp, dock, 5 row/3 canoe/2 pedal/7 motor boat rentals, lake fishing, playground, planned group activities, recreation director, badminton, horseshoes. Recreation open to the public. Open May 15 through Sep 15. Rate in 1995 $14-18 for 2 persons. Member of OPCA. Phone: (613) 923-5490.

SAINT LAWRENCE PARK (City Park)—*From town: Go 3.2 km/2 mi W on Hwy 2.* FACILITIES: 30 sites, 10 water & elec, 20 no hookups, seasonal sites, 20 pull-thrus, tenting available, handicap restroom facilities, sewage disposal, public phone, tables. RECREATION: pavilion, river swimming, boating, river fishing, playground, horseshoes. Recreation open to the public. Open mid May through mid Sep. Phone: (613) 345-1341.

## BRUCE MINES—D-4

BRUCE MINES MUNICIPAL PARK—*In town on Hwy 17.* FACILITIES: 38 sites, 28 ft. max RV length, 18 water & elec (15 amp receptacles), 20 no hookups, 8 pull-thrus, tenting available, sewage disposal, tables, grills, wood. RECREATION: lake swimming, boating, canoeing, ramp, lake fishing, playground, hiking trails. Open Jun 1 through Sep 15. Phone: (705) 785-3300.

## BURFORD—I-2

**LITTLE AUSTRIA FAMILY CAMPGROUND**—Secluded, grassy location with open or shaded sites. *From west jct Hwy 24 & Hwy 53: Go 8 km/5 mi W on Hwy 53, then 1.2 km/3/4 mi N on E .4 km/1/4 Townline Rd.*

WELCOME

◆◆◆FACILITIES: 264 sites, most common site width 35 feet, 194 full hookups, 16 water & elec (15 & 30 amp receptacles), 54 no hookups, seasonal sites, 4 pull-thrus, tenting available, RV storage, sewage disposal, public phone, limited grocery store, ice, tables, fire rings, wood.

◆◆◆◆RECREATION: rec hall, rec room/area, pavilion, coin games, swim pool, wading pool, canoeing, stream fishing, playground, planned group activities, sports field, horseshoes, hiking trails, volleyball.

Open May 1 through mid Oct. Rate in 1995 $15-18 per family. Member of OPCA. Phone: (519) 449-5612. FCRV 10% discount.
SEE AD TRAVEL SECTION PAGE 983

## BURK'S FALLS—F-3

**Russ Haven Resort**—Lakeside CAMPGROUND amidst gently rolling hills. *From jct Hwy 11 & Pickerel & Jack Lake Rd: Go 10.4 km/6 1/2 mi E on Pickerel & Jack Lake Rd.* ◆◆◆FACILITIES: 110 sites, 45 full hookups, 34 water & elec (15 amp receptacles), 31 no hookups, seasonal sites, tenting available, sewage disposal, laundry, public phone, grocery store, ice, tables, fire rings, grills, wood. ◆◆◆◆RECREATION: rec room/area, lake swimming, boating, canoeing, ramp, dock, 2 row/2 canoe/1 pedal/5 motor boat rentals, lake fishing, playground, planned group activities, badminton, sports field, horseshoes, hiking trails, volleyball. Open all year. Rate in 1995 $20-25 per family. Member of OPCA. Phone: (705) 382-2027.

## CALEDONIA—I-3

LA FORTUNE (Town of Haldimand)—*From north town limits: Go 1 1/2 km/1 mi N on Hwy 54.* FACILITIES: 130 sites, 80 water & elec (15 & 30 amp receptacles), 50 no hookups, tenting available, sewage disposal, tables, wood. RECREATION: swim pool, boating, canoeing, ramp, river fishing, playground, sports field. Recreation open to the public. Open May 1 through Oct 15. Phone: (905) 772-3324.

## CALLANDER—F-3

**BAYVIEW CAMP & COTTAGES**—CAMPGROUND on south shore of Callander Bay. *From jct Hwy 11 & Hwy 654: Go 4.4 km/2 3/4 mi W on Hwy 654, then .8 km/1/2 mi N on Lighthouse Rd.*

WELCOME

◆◆◆◆FACILITIES: 50 sites, most common site width 30 feet, 50 full hookups, (15 & 30 amp receptacles), seasonal sites, a/c allowed, tenting available, cabins, RV storage, laundry, public phone, limited grocery store, gasoline, marine gas, ice, tables, fire rings, wood.

◆◆◆◆RECREATION: rec hall, lake swimming, boating, canoeing, ramp, dock, 1 canoe/1 pedal/5 motor boat rentals, water skiing, lake fishing, basketball hoop, playground, planned group activities (weekends only), movies, sports field, horseshoes.

Open mid May through Oct 15. Rate in 1995 $18.69 per family. Visa accepted. Member of OPCA. Phone: (705) 752-2095.
SEE AD TRAVEL SECTION PAGE 983

**Link's Camping Grounds**—Treed grassy sites. *From jct Hwy 11 & Hwy 654: Go 12.5 km/7 3/4 mi W on Hwy 654, then 5.5 km/3 1/2 mi on Sunset Cove Rd, then follow signs.* ◆◆FACILITIES: 50 sites, most common site width 40 feet, 26 water & elec (20 amp receptacles), 24 no hookups, seasonal sites, tenting available, non-flush toilets, sewage disposal, public phone, limited grocery store, ice, tables, fire rings, wood. ◆◆◆RECREATION: rec room/area, lake swimming, boating, canoeing, ramp, 1 motor boat rentals, lake fishing, horseshoes, hiking trails. Open all year. Facilities fully operational May 15 through Oct 15. No showers. Rate in 1995 $15-16.25 per family. Phone: (705) 752-1266.

## CAMBRIDGE—I-3

**PINE VALLEY PARK**—CAMPGROUND in rustic location. *From jct Hwy 5 & Hwy 8: Go 4.8 km/3 mi NW on Hwy 8, then 3.2 km/2 mi N on Valens Rd.*

WELCOME

◆◆◆FACILITIES: 190 sites, most common site width 30 feet, 190 water & elec (30 amp receptacles), seasonal sites, a/c allowed, heater allowed, cable TV, portable dump, laundry, public phone, limited grocery store, ice, tables, fire rings, wood, traffic control gate.

◆◆◆◆RECREATION: rec hall, swim pool, pond fishing, playground, planned group activities (weekends only), badminton, sports field, horseshoes, hiking trails, volleyball.

No tents. Open mid May through mid Oct. Pool open Jun thru Sep. Rate in 1995 $20 per family. Member of OPCA. Phone: (519) 623-4998.
SEE AD TRAVEL SECTION PAGES 975, 976 AND 977

VALENS (Hamilton Reg. Conservation Authority)—*From town: Go 14 1/2 km/9 mi E on Hwy 97.* FACILITIES: 154 sites, 16 elec (30 amp receptacles), 138 no hookups, tenting available, handicap restroom facilities, sewage disposal, laundry, ice. RECREATION: pavilion, lake swimming, boating, electric motors only, canoeing, ramp, row/canoe boat rentals, lake fishing, playground, sports field, hiking trails. Open all year. Phone: (905) 659-7715.

## CAMPBELLFORD—H-4

FERRIS PROVINCIAL PARK—*From town: Go 6 1/2 km/4 mi S on CR.* FACILITIES: 163 sites, 163 no hookups, tenting available, handicap restroom facilities, limited grocery store, ice. RECREATION: boating, canoeing, ramp, fishing. Open mid Jun through early Sep. Phone: (705) 653-2330.

**Percy Boom Lodge**—Lakeside CAMPGROUND with grassy sites. *From south city limits: Go 4 km/2 1/2 mi S on Hwy 30, then 1.6 km/1 mi E on Percy Boom Rd.* ◆◆◆FACILITIES: 57 sites, most common site width 40 feet, 30 water & elec (15 amp receptacles), 27 no hookups, seasonal sites, tenting available, sewage disposal, public phone, limited grocery store, ice, tables, fire rings, wood. ◆◆RECREATION: rec room/area, lake swimming, boating, canoeing, ramp, dock, 2 canoe/1 pedal/8

CAMPBELLFORD—Continued
PERCY BOOM LODGE—Continued

motor boat rentals, lake fishing, horseshoes. Open May 1 through Oct 15. Rate in 1995 $16 per family. Phone: (705) 653-5601.

## CAMPBELLVILLE—I-3

**KOA-TORONTO WEST**—CAMPGROUND with easy access to major highway and all Toronto attractions. *From jct Hwy 401 (exit 312) & Guelph Line: Go 1.6 km/1 mi N on Guelph Line, then 1.6 km/1 mi W on 10th Side Rd, then 1.6 km/1 mi S on Second Line Rd.*

WELCOME

◆◆◆FACILITIES: 132 sites, most common site width 30 feet, 44 full hookups, 40 water & elec (15 & 30 amp receptacles), 48 no hookups, seasonal sites, 42 pull-thrus, a/c allowed ($), heater allowed ($), tenting available, group sites for tents/RVs, RV rentals, cabins, RV storage, handicap restroom facilities, sewage disposal, laundry, public phone, grocery store, RV supplies, LP gas refill by weight/by meter, ice, tables, fire rings, grills, wood.

◆◆◆RECREATION: rec room/area, coin games, swim pool, horseshoes, hiking trails, local tours.

Open Apr 1 through Oct 31. Facilities fully operational May 1 through Oct 15. Rate in 1995 $22-27 for 2 persons. Master Card/Visa accepted. Member of OPCA. Phone: (905) 854-2495. KOA 10% value card discount. FCRV 10% discount.
SEE AD TORONTO PAGE 1022 AND AD FRONT OF BOOK PAGES 68 AND 69

## CARDINAL—G-6

**KOA-Cardinal**—Semi-wooded CAMPGROUND with open & shaded sites. *From jct Hwy 401 (exit 730) & Shanly Rd (CR 22): Go 6.4 km/4 mi N on CR 22, then .4 km/1/4 mi E on paved road.* ◆◆◆FACILITIES: 85 sites, most common site width 40 feet, 72 water & elec (15,30 & 50 amp receptacles), 13 no hookups, seasonal sites, 40 pull-thrus, tenting available, handicap restroom facilities, sewage disposal, laundry, public phone, grocery store, ice, tables, fire rings, wood. ◆◆◆RECREATION: rec room/area, swim pool, mini-golf ($), playground, planned group activities (weekends only), badminton, sports field, horseshoes, volleyball. Open mid Apr through Oct 31. Rate in 1995 $15-20 for 2 persons. Phone: (613) 657-4536. KOA 10% value card discount.

Use the Alphabetical Quick Reference Index At The End Of Book

From ◆ to ◆◆◆◆◆
ALL
Woodall Listed Parks
are Quality Parks

## CARRYING PLACE—H-4

**CAMP BARCOVAN**—CAMPGROUND with grassy, open & shaded sites on Wellers Bay. *From jct Hwy 401 (exit 522): Go 6.4 km/4 mi S on CR 40 (Wooler Rd), then 3.2 km/2 mi S on Hwy 33, then 5.6 km/3 1/2 mi W on CR 64 to Barcovan Rd, then follow signs.*

◊◊◊FACILITIES: 141 sites, most common site width 40 feet, 125 full hookups, 16 water & elec (15 & 30 amp receptacles), seasonal sites, 20 pull-thrus, a/c allowed, heater allowed, tenting available, group sites for tents/RVs, RV rentals, cabins, laundry, public phone, grocery store, RV supplies, LP gas refill by weight, ice, tables, fire rings, wood, traffic control gate.

◊◊◊◊RECREATION: rec hall, rec room/area, coin games, swim pool, boating, canoeing, ramp, dock, 4 motor boat rentals, water skiing, lake fishing, basketball hoop, playground, planned group activities (weekends only), movies, badminton, horseshoes, volleyball. Recreation open to the public.

Open May 1 through Oct 15. Rate in 1995 $20-22 per family. Master Card/Visa accepted. Member of OPCA. Phone: (613) 475-1355.

**SEE AD THIS PAGE**

**WELLERS BAY CAMPGROUND**—CAMPGROUND with grassy, open & wooded sites on Wellers Bay. *From jct Hwy 33 & CR 64: Go 5.6 km/3 1/2 mi W on CR 64, then 1.2 km/3/4 mi S on Barcovan Rd.*

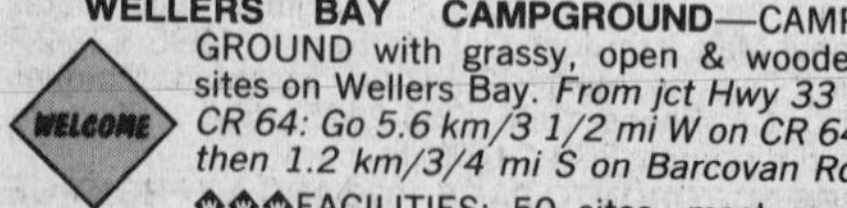


◊◊◊FACILITIES: 50 sites, most common site width 35 feet, 47 full hookups, (15 amp receptacles), 3 no hookups, seasonal sites, a/c allowed ($), heater not allowed, tenting available, RV rentals, cabins, laundry, public phone, grocery store, RV supplies, LP gas refill by weight, gasoline, marine gas, ice, tables, fire rings, wood.

◊◊◊RECREATION: rec room/area, lake swimming, boating, canoeing, ramp, dock, 2 canoe/12 motor boat rentals, water skiing, lake fishing, basketball hoop, playground, planned group activities (weekends only), movies, badminton, horseshoes, volleyball.

Open May 1 through Oct 15. Rate in 1995 $14-17 per family. Master Card/Visa accepted. Member of OPCA. Phone: (613) 475-3113.

**SEE AD TRAVEL SECTION PAGES 975, 976 AND 977**

## CARTIER—D-5

HALFWAY LAKE PROVINCIAL PARK—*From town: Go 25 1/2 km/16 mi N on Hwy 144.* FACILITIES: 215 sites, 215 no hookups, tenting available, handicap restroom facilities, laundry, tables, grills, wood. RECREATION: lake swimming, boating, canoeing, ramp, lake fishing, playground, hiking trails. Open mid May through late Sep. Phone: (705) 965-2702.

## CASTLETON—H-4

**Castleton Hills Trailer Park**—Secluded CAMPGROUND. *From jct Hwy 401 & Interchange 497: Go 9.6 km/6 mi N, then follow signs.* ◊◊◊FACILITIES: 82 sites, most common site width 40 feet, 60 full hookups, 12 water & elec (15 amp receptacles), 10 no hookups, seasonal sites, 8 pull-thrus, tenting available, sewage disposal, laundry, public phone, limited grocery store, LP gas refill by weight, ice, tables, wood. ◊◊◊RECREATION: rec room/area, pond swimming, boating, canoeing, 2 pedal boat rentals, mini-golf, playground, planned group activities (weekends only), horseshoes, hiking trails, volleyball. Open mid May through mid Oct. Rate in 1995 $17 per family. Member of OPCA. Phone: (905) 344-7838.

## CAYUGA—I-3

**Grand Oaks Park**—Secluded, well treed family CAMPGROUND with level sites. *From town center: Go 1.6 km/1 mi N on Hwy 54 to park.* ◊◊FACILITIES: 290 sites, most common site width 40 feet, 240 full hookups, 25 water & elec (15 amp receptacles), 25 no hookups, seasonal sites, tenting available, sewage disposal, laundry, public phone, limited grocery store, LP gas refill by weight, ice, tables, fire rings, grills, wood. ◊◊RECREATION: rec room/area, equipped pavilion, swim pool, river fishing, playground, 2 shuffleboard courts, planned group activities (weekends only), horseshoes, volleyball. Recreation open to the public. Open mid May through mid Oct. Rate in 1995 $16-20. Phone: (905) 772-3713.

## CHAPLEAU—C-4

MISSINAIBI LAKE PROVINCIAL PARK—*From town: Go 56 km/35 mi N on local road.* FACILITIES: 36 sites, 36 no hookups, tenting available, non-flush toilets, sewage disposal, tables, fire rings, wood. RECREATION: lake swimming, boating, canoeing, ramp, lake fishing, hiking trails. Open mid May through mid Sep. No showers. Phone: (705) 864-1710.

THE SHOALS PROVINCIAL PARK—*From jct Hwy 129 & Hwy 101: Go 51 1/4 km/32 mi W on Hwy 101.* FACILITIES: 44 sites, 44 no hookups, tenting available, non-flush toilets, wood. RECREATION: lake swimming, boating, canoeing, ramp, lake fishing, hiking trails. Open early Jun through early Sep. No showers. Phone: (705) 864-1710.

WAKAMI LAKE PROVINCIAL PARK—*From jct Hwy 129 & FR 667 (Forest Access Rd): Go 32 km/20 mi E on FR 667.* FACILITIES: 65 sites, 65 no hookups, tenting available, non-flush toilets, tables, wood. RECREATION: lake swimming, boating, canoeing, ramp, lake fishing, hiking trails. Open mid May through late Sep. No showers. Phone: (705) 864-1710.

## CHERRY VALLEY—H-5

**Fairfield's Resort & Family Camping**—CAMPGROUND at East Lake on Quinte's Isle. *From town at jct CR 10 & CR 18: Go 2.4 km/1 1/2 mi S on CR 18.* ◊◊◊FACILITIES: 300 sites, most common site width 40 feet, 200 full hookups, 100 water & elec (20 & 30 amp receptacles), seasonal sites, 10 pull-thrus, tenting available, sewage disposal, laundry, public phone, ice, tables, fire rings, wood. ◊◊◊RECREATION: rec hall, rec room/area, swim pool, lake swimming, boating, ramp, dock, lake fishing, playground, planned group activities, sports field, horseshoes, volleyball. Open May 15 through Oct 15. Rate in 1995 $17.50-23.50 per family. Member of OPCA. Phone: (613) 476-2810.

**Lake Avenue Park**—Lakeside CAMPGROUND with shaded, grassy sites. *In town from jct CR 10 & CR 18: Go 4.8 km/3 mi W on CR 18.* ◊◊◊FACILITIES: 116 sites, most common site width 35 feet, 22 full hookups, 75 water & elec (15 & 30 amp receptacles), 19 no hookups, seasonal sites, 32 pull-thrus, tenting available, handicap restroom facilities, portable dump, laundry, public phone, grocery store, ice, tables, fire rings, wood. ◊◊◊RECREATION: rec room/area, swim pool, lake swimming, boating, ramp, dock, 4 row/1 canoe/4 motor boat rentals, lake fishing, playground, planned group activities (weekends only), recreation director, badminton, sports field, horseshoes, volleyball. Open May 1 through Oct 15. Rate in 1995 $18-22 per family. Member of OPCA. Phone: (613) 476-4990.

**Log Cabin Point**—CAMPGROUND on East Lake. *From town at jct CR 10 & CR 18: Go 8.8 km/5 1/2 mi S on CR 18, then .4 km/1/4 mi W on Outlet Rd.* ◊◊FACILITIES: 34 sites, most common site width 25 feet, 17 full hookups, 5 water & elec (15 & 30 amp receptacles), 12 no hookups, seasonal sites, tenting available, sewage disposal, laundry, public phone, limited grocery store, ice, tables, fire rings, wood. ◊◊RECREATION: rec room/area, lake swimming, boating, canoeing, ramp, dock, 3 canoe/1 pedal/9 motor boat rentals, lake fishing, badminton, horseshoes, volleyball. Recreation open to the public. Open May 1 through Oct 15. Rate in 1995 $16-22 per family. Phone: (613) 393-5255.

**Martin's Outlet Park**—CAMPGROUND on the Outlet River with serviced sites occupied by seasonal campers. *From town at jct CR 10 & CR 18: Go 9.6 km/6 mi S on CR 18.* ◊FACILITIES: 140 sites, most common site width 40 feet, 50 full hookups, 10 water & elec, 5 elec (15 & 30 amp receptacles), 75 no hookups, seasonal sites, tenting available, laundry, public phone, limited grocery store, LP gas refill by weight, ice, tables, fire rings, wood. ◊◊RECREATION: rec hall, rec room/area, river swimming, boating, canoeing, ramp, dock, 8 row/5 canoe/5 pedal/motor boat rentals, lake/river fishing, planned group activities, badminton, horseshoes, volleyball. Recreation open to the public. Open May 1 through Sep 15. Rate in 1995 $17-25 per family. Phone: (613) 393-5645.

**QUINTE'S ISLE CAMPARK**—Recreation oriented CAMPGROUND with open & shaded sites. *From town at jct CR 10 (Lake St) & CR 18: Go 9.6 km/6 mi S on CR 18, then .4 km/1/4 mi E on Salmon Point Rd.*

WELCOME

◊◊◊FACILITIES: 225 sites, most common site width 50 feet, 139 full hookups, 36 water & elec (15 & 30 amp receptacles), 50 no hookups, seasonal sites, a/c allowed ($), phone hookups, tenting available, group sites for RVs, RV rentals, RV storage, sewage disposal, laundry, public phone, grocery store, LP gas refill by weight, ice, tables, fire rings, wood, traffic control gate.

CHERRY VALLEY—Continued
QUINTE'S ISLE CAMPARK—Continued

◊◊◊◊◊RECREATION: rec hall, rec room/area, coin games, swim pool, wading pool, lake swimming, boating, canoeing, lake fishing, mini-golf ($), basketball hoop, playground, 2 shuffleboard courts, planned group activities, movies, recreation director, tennis court, horse riding trails, horse rental, badminton, sports field, horseshoes, hiking trails, volleyball. Recreation open to the public.

Open Apr 15 through Oct 31. Rate in 1995 $18-24.75 per family. Reservations recommended all season. Master Card/Visa accepted. Member of OPCA. Phone: (613) 476-6310. FCRV 10% discount.

**SEE AD KINGSTON PAGE 999**

**Salmon Point Campground**—Lakeside CAMPGROUND with grassy, shaded sites. *From town at jct CR 10 & CR 12: Go 9.6 km/6 mi S on CR 12, then .8 km/1/2 mi E on Salmon Point Rd.* ◊◊FACILITIES: 105 sites, most common site width 30 feet, 55 water & elec (15 amp receptacles), 50 no hookups, seasonal sites, tenting available, sewage disposal, ice, tables, fire rings. ◊◊RECREATION: lake swimming, boating, ramp, dock, lake fishing. Open mid May through mid Oct. Rate in 1995 $16-18. Phone: (613) 476-4868.

## CHUTE-A-BLONDEAU—F-6

VOYAGEUR PROVINCIAL PARK—*From town: Go 8 km/5 mi E on Hwy 17.* FACILITIES: 416 sites, 110 elec, 306 no hookups, tenting available, handicap restroom facilities, sewage disposal, laundry, tables, wood. RECREATION: river swimming, boating, canoeing, ramp, river fishing, playground, hiking trails. Open mid May through early Oct. Phone: (613) 674-2825.

## CLOYNE—G-5

BON ECHO PROVINCIAL PARK—*From town: Go 9 1/2 km/6 mi N on Hwy 41.* FACILITIES: 500 sites, 42 elec, 458 no hookups, tenting available, handicap restroom facilities, sewage disposal, laundry, tables, wood. RECREATION: swimming, boating, canoeing, ramp, fishing, playground, hiking trails. Open mid May through mid Oct. Phone: (613) 336-2228.

**GLENCANNON RESORT**—CAMPGROUND is part of a resort complex. *From jct Hwy 41 & Hwy 506: Go 8 km/5 mi E on Hwy 506, then 2 km/1 1/4 mi N on Perrys Rd.*

WELCOME

◊◊FACILITIES: 48 sites, 28 ft. max RV length, 28 water & elec (15 amp receptacles), 20 no hookups, seasonal sites, tenting available, cabins, sewage disposal, laundry, public phone, limited grocery store, gasoline, marine gas, ice, tables, fire rings, grills, wood.

◊◊◊RECREATION: rec hall, rec room/area, equipped pavilion, coin games, swim pool (indoor) (heated), lake swimming, sauna, whirlpool, boating, canoeing, ramp, dock, 15 row/2 sail/5 canoe/2 pedal/motor boat rentals, water skiing, lake/pond fishing ($), fishing guides, mini-golf ($), basketball hoop, planned group activities, recreation director, 2 tennis courts, badminton, sports field, horseshoes, hiking trails, volleyball, cross country skiing, snowmobile trails. Recreation open to the public.

Open all year. Facilities fully operational May 15 through Oct 30. Rate in 1995 $18-21 per family. Master Card/Visa accepted. Member of OPCA. Phone: (613) 336-2425.

**SEE AD KINGSTON PAGE 999**

**Sherwood Park Campground**—Level, semi-wooded CAMPGROUND on Story Lake. *From jct Hwy 41 & Hwy 506: Go .4 km/1/4 mi E on Hwy 506.* ◊◊FACILITIES: 100 sites, most common site width 45 feet, 75 water & elec (15 & 30 amp receptacles), 25 no hookups, seasonal sites, tenting available, sewage disposal, laundry, limited grocery store, ice, tables, fire rings, wood. ◊◊◊RECREATION: rec room/area, lake swimming, boating, canoeing, ramp, dock, 3 row/2 canoe boat rentals, lake fishing, mini-golf ($), playground, horseshoes, volleyball. Open May 1 through Oct 31. Rate in 1995 $14-17 per family. Phone: (613) 336-8844.

## COBALT—C-6

**Marsh Bay Resort Tent & Trailer Park**—Guest family CAMPGROUND with open and shaded lots on Montreal River. *From jct Hwy 11B & Hwy 11: Go 90 m/100 yards S on Hwy 11, then 2.4 km/1 1/2 mi E on Marsh Bay Rd.* ◊◊◊FACILITIES: 30 sites, most common site width 30 feet, 19 full hookups, 4 water & elec, 2 elec (15 amp receptacles), 5 no hookups, seasonal sites, 25 pull-thrus, tenting available, limited grocery store, ice, tables, fire rings, wood. ◊◊◊RECREATION: pavilion, river swimming, boating, canoeing, ramp, dock, 3 row/3 canoe/1 pedal/6 motor boat rentals, river fishing, playground, badminton, sports field, horseshoes. Open May 1 through Oct 31. Rate in 1995 $14-18 per family. Phone: (705) 679-8810.

## COBDEN—F-5

**CEDAR HAVEN TENT & TRAILER PARK**—Terraced CAMPGROUND on Muskrat Lake. *From town: Go 1.6 km/1 mi E on Hwy 17, then 4 km/2 1/2 mi N on CR 2 (Cedar Haven Park Rd).*

◆◆◆FACILITIES: 150 sites, most common site width 40 feet, 100 full hookups, 30 water & elec (15 & 30 amp receptacles), 20 no hookups, seasonal sites, a/c allowed, heater allowed, tenting available, sewage disposal, laundry, public phone, limited grocery store, ice, tables, fire rings, wood.

◆◆◆RECREATION: rec room/area, coin games, lake swimming, boating, ramp, dock, 1 row/2 motor boat rentals, lake fishing, playground, planned group activities (weekends only), movies, sports field, horseshoes, volleyball.

Open mid May through early Oct. Rate in 1995 $13.50-16.50 per family. Phone: (613) 646-7989.

**SEE AD TRAVEL SECTION PAGES 975, 976 AND 977**

COBDEN MUNICIPAL PARK—*In town on Hwy 417.* FACILITIES: 46 sites, 12 water & elec, 12 elec, 22 no hookups, tenting available, ice, tables, fire rings, wood. RECREATION: lake swimming, boating, canoeing, ramp, dock, lake fishing. Open May 24 through Oct. No showers. Phone: (613) 646-2282.

**YONDER HILL CAMPGROUND**—CAMPGROUND with large, wooded sites. *From east town limits: Go 11.2 km/7 mi E on Hwy 17.*

◆◆◆FACILITIES: 127 sites, most common site width 35 feet, 115 water & elec (15 & 30 amp receptacles), 12 no hookups, seasonal sites, 3 pull-thrus, tenting available, group sites for tents, handicap restroom facilities, sewage disposal, laundry, public phone, limited grocery store, ice, tables, fire rings, wood, traffic control gate.

◆◆◆RECREATION: coin games, lake swimming, boating, canoeing, ramp, dock, 3 row/1 pedal boat rentals, lake fishing, planned group activities (weekends only), badminton, horseshoes, volleyball.

Open May 15 through Sep 30. Rate in 1995 $15-18 per family. Master Card/Visa accepted. Phone: (613) 432-6584.

**SEE AD TRAVEL SECTION PAGES 975, 976 AND 977**

## COBOCONK—G-4

BALSAM LAKE PROVINCIAL PARK—*From town: Go 9 1/2 km/6 mi W on Hwy 46.* FACILITIES: 489 sites, 112 elec, 377 no hookups, tenting available, handicap restroom facilities, sewage disposal, laundry, tables, wood. RECREATION: swimming, boating, canoeing, ramp, fishing, playground, hiking trails. Open mid May through mid Oct. Phone: (705) 454-1077.

## COCHRANE—B-5

DRURY PARK (Municipal Park)—*From town: Go 1/2 km/1/4 mi N of Hwy 11 & 3/4 km/1/2 mi E on Second St.* FACILITIES: 140 sites, 60 elec (15 amp receptacles), 80 no hookups, tenting available, sewage disposal, public phone, tables, wood. RECREATION: canoeing, playground, hiking trails. Open Jun 15 through Sep 15. Phone: (705) 272-4361.

GREENWATER PROVINCIAL PARK—*From town: Go 36 3/4 km/23 mi W on Hwy 11, then 12 3/4 km/8 mi N on Old Hwy 11.* FACILITIES: 90 sites, 35 elec, 55 no hookups, tenting available, handicap restroom facilities, sewage disposal, laundry, tables, wood. RECREATION: swimming, boating, canoeing, ramp, fishing, hiking trails. Open mid May through mid Sep. Phone: (705) 272-6335.

## COE HILL—G-4

**Island View Cottages & Campground**—Lakeside CAMPGROUND set in rolling, grassy terrain. *From east city limits: Go 3.2 km/2 mi S on Ridge Rd.* ◆◆◆FACILITIES: 40 sites, most common site width 35 feet, 30 full hookups, (15 amp receptacles), 10 no hookups, seasonal sites, tenting available, public phone, limited grocery store, ice, tables, fire rings, wood. ◆◆◆RECREATION: rec room/area, lake swimming, boating, canoeing, ramp, dock, 4 row/3 canoe/1 pedal/3 motor boat rentals, lake/pond fishing ($), horseshoes, hiking trails, volleyball. Open all year. Facilities fully operational Apr 1 through Oct 31. Rate in 1995 $16 per vehicle. Member of OPCA. Phone: (613) 337-5533.

## COLBORNE—H-4

**The Big Apple RV Park**—RV SPACES at a theme park with bakery and restaurant. *From Hwy 401 (exit 497): Go S on Orchard Dr, then follow signs.* FACILITIES: 13 sites, accepts full hookup units only, 13 full hookups, (30 amp receptacles), public phone, tables. RECREATION: mini-golf ($), playground. Recreation open to the public. No tents. Open all year. Facilities fully operational mid May through mid Oct. Rate in 1995 $15 per family. Phone: (416) 355-2574.

**Blythwood Acres Trailer Park** (REBUILDING)—Level, grassy sites among maple trees. *From jct Hwy 401 (exit 497) & Percy St: Go 3.2 km/2 mi S on Percy St, then 3.2 km/2 mi E on Hwy 2, then .4 km/1/4 mi S on Blyth Park Rd, then .4 km/1/4 mi W on gravel road.* FACILITIES: 50 sites, 30 full hookups, 10 water & seasonal elec (15 & 30 amp receptacles), 10 no hookups, seasonal sites, 6

**COLBORNE**—Continued
BLYTHWOOD ACRES TRAILER PARK—Continued

pull-thrus, tenting available, sewage disposal, public phone, tables, fire rings, wood. RECREATION: pond swimming, boating, no motors, canoeing, dock, 1 pedal boat rentals, pond fishing, shuffleboard court, sports field, horseshoes. Recreation open to the public. Open mid Apr through mid Oct. Rate in 1995 $18-20 per family. Phone: (416) 355-3826.

## COLLINGWOOD—H-3

CRAIGLEITH PROVINCIAL PARK—*From town: Go 12 3/4 km/8 mi W on Hwy 26.* FACILITIES: 172 sites, 42 elec, 130 no hookups, tenting available, handicap restroom facilities, sewage disposal, limited grocery store, tables, wood. RECREATION: swimming, fishing, playground. Open mid Apr through late Oct. No showers. Phone: (705) 445-4467.

⚑ **PETUN CONSERVATION AREA**—*From jct Hwy 24 & Poplar Sideroad: Go 4.8 km/3 mi W on Poplar Sideroad, then 152.50 m/500 feet N on CR 19, then 2.4 km/1 1/2 mi W on New Mountain Rd.* A day-use facility with an educational outdoor program. Open all year. Phone: (705) 424-1479.

**SEE AD TRAVEL SECTION PAGE 980**

## COMBERMERE—G-4

**PINE CLIFF RESORT**—CAMPGROUND with open & shaded sites on a river. *From north city limits: Go 3.2 km/2 mi N on Hwy 62, then .4 km/1/4 mi W on Pine Cliff Rd.*

◆◆◆FACILITIES: 95 sites, most common site width 30 feet, 85 full hookups, 10 water & elec (30 amp receptacles), seasonal sites, tenting available, cabins, RV storage, laundry, public phone, RV supplies, marine gas, ice, tables, fire rings, wood.

◆◆◆RECREATION: rec room/area, coin games, river swimming, boating, canoeing, ramp, dock, 2 row/2 canoe/9 motor boat rentals, lake/river fishing, basketball hoop, shuffleboard court, planned group activities, movies, recreation director, horseshoes, hiking trails, volleyball.

Open all year. Facilities fully operational May 1 through Oct 15. Rate in 1995 $20 per family. Master Card/Visa accepted. Member of OPCA. Phone: (613) 756-3014.

**SEE AD TRAVEL SECTION PAGES 975, 976 AND 977**

**SAND BAY CAMP**—Lakeside CAMPGROUND in a forested area. *From Combermere: Go 4.8 km/3 mi S on Hwy 62, then .8 km/1/2 mi W on Sand Bay Rd.*

◆◆◆FACILITIES: 50 sites, most common site width 30 feet, 25 full hookups, 15 water & elec (15 amp receptacles), 10 no hookups, seasonal sites, tenting available, cabins, public phone, grocery store, gasoline, marine gas, ice, tables, fire rings, wood.

◆◆◆RECREATION: lake swimming, boating, canoeing, ramp, dock, 2 canoe/1 pedal/6 motor boat rentals, water skiing, lake fishing, fishing guides, basketball hoop, horseshoes, hiking trails, volleyball, cross country skiing, snowmobile trails.

Open all year. Facilities fully operational May 1 through Oct 15. Rate in 1995 $16-17 per family. Master Card/Visa accepted. Phone: (613) 756-5060.

**SEE AD TRAVEL SECTION PAGES 975, 976 AND 977**

## COOKSTOWN—H-3

**Cookstown Toronto North KOA** (TOO NEW TO RATE)—*From jct Hwy 400 & Hwy 89: Go 61 m/200 feet E, then .4 km/1/4 mi N on Rieve Blvd.* FACILITIES: 113 sites, 52 full hookups, 54 water & elec (30 & 50 amp receptacles), 7 no hookups, tenting available, sewage disposal, laundry, public phone, limited grocery store, LP gas refill by weight, ice, tables, fire rings, grills, wood. RECREATION: rec room/area, swim pool, playground. Open May 1 through Oct 9. Rate in 1995 $20-24 for 2 persons. Phone: (705) 458-2267. KOA 10% value card discount.

## CREEMORE—H-3

⚑ **NOTTAWASAGA BLUFFS CONSERVATION AREA**—*From jct Hwy 24 & SR 12 (Nottawasaga Twp): Go 2.4 km/1 1/2 mi E on SR 12.* Camping, hiking and spelunking along the Bruce Trail. Open all year. Phone: (705) 424-1479.

**SEE AD TRAVEL SECTION PAGE 980**

## CROSBY—G-5

**NARROWS LOCK CAMPGROUND**—Wooded, lakeside CAMPGROUND with open & shaded sites. *From jct Hwy 15 & Hwy 42: Go 45 m/50 yards W on Hwy 42, then 6.4 km/4 mi N on Narrows Lock Rd (CR 14).*

◆◆◆FACILITIES: 95 sites, most common site width 50 feet, 80 full hookups, 10 water & elec (15 & 30 amp receptacles), 5 no hookups, seasonal sites, tenting available, sewage disposal, laundry, public phone, limited grocery store, RV supplies, ice, tables, fire rings, wood.

◆◆◆◆RECREATION: rec room/area, coin games, lake swimming, boating, canoeing, ramp, dock, 5 motor boat rentals, water skiing, lake fishing, basketball hoop, playground, planned group activities (weekends only), sports field, horseshoes, volleyball.

Open May 15 through Oct 15. Rate in 1995 $16-20 per family. Member of OPCA. Phone: (613) 272-3401.

**SEE AD TRAVEL SECTION PAGE 984**

## CUMBERLAND—F-6

**RECREATIONLAND TENT & TRAILER PARK**—Grassy CAMPGROUND near a main highway. *From jct Hwy 417 & Hwy 17: Go 26.5 km/16 1/2 mi E on Hwy 17, then .4 km/1/4 mi S on Canaan Rd.*

◆◆◆FACILITIES: 100 sites, most common site width 35 feet, 50 full hookups, 26 water & elec (15,30 & 50 amp receptacles), 24 no hookups, seasonal sites, 26 pull-thrus, a/c allowed, heater allowed ($), cable TV, phone hookups, tenting available, group sites for tents/RVs, RV storage, handicap restroom facilities, sewage disposal, laundry, public phone, limited grocery store, RV supplies, ice, tables, fire rings, wood.

◆◆◆RECREATION: rec room/area, swim pool, playground, sports field, horseshoes, volleyball.

Open May 1 through Oct 15. Rate in 1995 $14-21 for 2 persons. Master Card/Visa accepted. Member of OPCA. Phone: (613) 833-2974.

**SEE AD OTTAWA PAGE 1010**

## DEEP RIVER—F-4

DRIFTWOOD PROVINCIAL PARK—*From town: Go 27 1/4 km/17 mi W on Hwy 17 (Stonecliffe).* FACILITIES: 79 sites, 79 no hookups, tenting available, non-flush toilets, sewage disposal, tables, wood. RECREATION: swimming, boating, canoeing, ramp, fishing, hiking trails. Open mid May through early Sep. No showers. Phone: (613) 586-2553.

**Ryan's Campsite**—CAMPGROUND on the Ottawa River. *From west city limits: Go 4.8 km/3 mi W on Hwy 17.* ◆◆FACILITIES: 100 sites, most common site width 50 feet, 2 full hookups, 98 water & elec (15 amp receptacles), seasonal sites, 6 pull-thrus, tenting available, sewage disposal, laundry, public phone, limited grocery store, ice, tables, fire rings, wood. ◆◆◆RECREATION: river swimming, boating, canoeing, ramp, dock, 1 row/1 sail/6 canoe/2 motor boat rentals, river/pond fishing ($), playground, hiking trails, volleyball. Recreation open to the public. Open all year. Facilities fully operational May 15 through Oct 15. Rate in 1995 $18.70 for 2 persons. Member of OPCA. Phone: (613) 584-3453.

⚑ **Ryan's Gifts**—*From west city limits: Go 4.8 km/3 mi W on Hwy 17.* Extensive selection of Canadian gifts, Eskimo art, furs, Indian crafts, wood carvings, etc. Also scenic float plane rides, wildlife museum & coffee bar. Open all year. Master Card/Visa accepted. Phone: (613) 584-3453.

## DELTA—G-5

LOWER BEVERLEY LAKE TOWNSHIP PARK—*In town on Lower Beverley Lake Rd.* FACILITIES: 180 sites, 135 water & elec, 45 no hookups, tenting available, sewage disposal, laundry, public phone, limited grocery store, ice, tables, wood. RECREATION: lake swimming, boating, canoeing, ramp, dock, 4 row/6 motor boat rentals, fishing, playground, badminton, sports field, horseshoes, hiking trails, volleyball. Open May 15 through Oct 15. Phone: (613) 928-2881.

## DEUX RIVIERES—F-4

**Antler's Kingfisher Lodge**—Riverside CAMPGROUND with shaded sites in conjunction with RV SPACES. *In town on Hwy 17.* ◆◆◆FACILITIES: 43 sites, most common site width 50 feet, 19 full hookups, 24 water & elec (30 amp receptacles), seasonal sites, 18 pull-thrus, tenting available, sewage disposal, public phone, grocery store, LP gas refill by weight, ice, tables, fire rings, wood. ◆◆◆RECREATION: river swimming, boating, canoeing, ramp, dock, 2 row/2 canoe/1 pedal/9 motor boat rentals, river fishing, horseshoes, hiking trails. Open May 1 through Nov 1. Rate in 1995 $19-22 per family. Member of OPCA. Phone: (705) 747-0851.

## DRYDEN—D-2

**Birchland Trailer Park**—CAMPGROUND convenient to highway. *From jct Hwy 665 & Hwy 17: Go 1.2 km/3/4 mi W on Hwy 17.* ◆◆◆FACILITIES: 60 sites, most common site width 35 feet, 33 full hookups, 9 water & elec, 5 elec (15 amp receptacles), 13 no hookups, seasonal sites, 4 pull-thrus, tenting available, sewage disposal, laundry, public phone, ice, tables, fire rings, wood. ◆◆RECREATION: mini-golf ($), playground. Open all year. Facilities fully operational May 1 through Oct 30. Rates available upon request. Phone: (807) 937-4938.

**Claybanks Marina & Trailer Park**—Campground & Marina located on Lake Wabigoon. *From jct Hwy 17 & Hwy 594 (Duke St): Go 1.2 km/3/4 mi S & W on Hwy 594, then .8 km/1/2 mi S on VanHorn Ave (adjacent to government dock).* ◆◆◆FACILITIES: 34 sites, 34 full hookups, (30 amp receptacles), 12 pull-thrus, tenting available, public phone, limited grocery store, ice, tables, wood. ◆◆RECREATION: lake swimming, boating, canoeing, ramp, dock, lake fishing. Open May 15 through Oct 15. Rate in 1995 $15 for 2 persons. Phone: (807) 223-3085.

**HUBER'S LONE PINE LODGE**—CAMPGROUND in conjunction with resort cabins, marina & restaurant. *From jct Hwy 72 & Hwy 17: Go 5.6 km/3 1/2 mi W on Hwy 17, then 2.4 km/1 1/2 mi S on Bear Paw Lone Pine Rd.*

◆◆◆FACILITIES: 20 sites, 20 full hookups, (15 & 30 amp receptacles), a/c allowed, heater allowed, tenting available, cabins, sewage disposal, laundry, public phone, limited grocery store, gasoline, marine gas, ice, tables, fire rings, wood.

◆◆◆RECREATION: lake swimming, boating, canoeing, ramp, dock, 50 motor boat rentals, water skiing, lake fishing, fishing guides, horseshoes.

Open May 17 through Sep 30. Rate in 1995 $18 per vehicle. Master Card/Visa accepted. Phone: (807) 938-6474.

**SEE AD TRAVEL SECTION PAGES 975, 976 AND 977**

**THE NORTHWESTERN TENT & TRAILER PARK**—Wooded and open sites in a CAMPGROUND in town. *Located at the east end of town on Hwy 17.*

◆◆◆FACILITIES: 65 sites, most common site width 20 feet, 65 full hookups, (15 & 30 amp receptacles), seasonal sites, 5 pull-thrus, a/c allowed, heater allowed, cable TV, tenting available, group sites for tents/RVs, RV storage, sewage disposal, laundry, public phone, tables, wood.

◆RECREATION: playground.

Open mid Apr through mid Oct. Rate in 1995 $19 per family. Phone: (807) 223-4945.

**SEE AD TRAVEL SECTION PAGES 975, 976 AND 977**

**Twin Towers Trailer Park**—RV SPACES behind a restaurant & gas station on a major highway. *From east jct Hwy 601 & Hwy 17: Go 6.5 km/4 mi E on Hwy 17.* FACILITIES: 10 sites, most common site width 25 feet, 10 full hookups (15 amp receptacles), 2 pull-thrus, tenting available, public phone, grocery store, ice, tables. Open mid May through Oct. No showers. Rate in 1995 $15 per vehicle. Phone: (807) 938-6569.

## DUNNVILLE—I-3

**BLUE HERON TRAILER PARK**—Level CAMPGROUND across road from Lake Erie. *From bridge in business center: Go 11 km/7 mi W on Regional Rd 3, then 1.6 km/1 mi S on Regional Rd 50, then 1.6 km/1 mi W on Lakeshore Rd.*

◆◆◆FACILITIES: 110 sites, most common site width 35 feet, 40 full hookups, 10 water & elec (15 amp receptacles), 60 no hookups, seasonal sites, a/c allowed ($), heater not allowed, tenting available, group sites for tents/RVs, RV rentals, RV storage, sewage disposal, ice, tables, patios, fire rings, grills, wood, traffic control gate.

◆◆◆◆RECREATION: rec hall, swim pool (heated), lake swimming, whirlpool, boating, canoeing, ramp, 3 sail boat rentals, lake fishing, shuffleboard court, planned group activities (weekends only), sports field, horseshoes, hiking trails, volleyball, local tours.

Open mid May through Oct 15. Rate in 1995 $25-30 per family. Phone: (905) 774-3800.

**SEE AD TRAVEL SECTION PAGES 975, 976 AND 977**

**BYNG ISLAND (Grand River Conservation Authority)**—*From town: Go 1/2 km/1/4 mi W across bridge.*

FACILITIES: 400 sites, 100 water & elec (15 & 30 amp receptacles), 300 no hookups, seasonal sites, tenting available, group sites for tents, sewage disposal, public phone, limited grocery store, ice, tables, wood, guard.

RECREATION: swim pool, boating, canoeing, ramp, 30 canoe boat rentals, water skiing, river fishing, playground, sports field, hiking trails. Recreation open to the public.

Open May 1 through Oct 15. Phone: (905) 774-5755.

**SEE AD TRAVEL SECTION PAGE 978**

CHIPPAWA CREEK (Niagara Peninsula Conservation Auth.)—*From east city limits: Go 9 1/2 km/6 mi E on Hwy 3, then 4 3/4 km/3 mi N on Wellandport Rd.* FACILITIES: 95 sites, 61 water & elec (15 amp receptacles), 34 no hookups, seasonal sites, 95 pull-thrus, tenting available, handicap restroom facilities, sewage disposal, public phone, ice, tables, wood. RECREATION: pavilion, lake/river swimming, boating, ramp, lake/river fishing, playground, sports field, horseshoes, hiking trails. Recreation open to the public. Open May 24 through Sep 15. Phone: (905) 227-1013.

**GRAND RIVER RV RESORT**—Open & shaded sites in a CAMPGROUND on the Grand River. *From Hwy 3 in town center: Go .8 km/1/2 mi W on Hwy 3, then 9.6 km/6 mi S on Regional Rd 17.*

◆◆◆◆FACILITIES: 263 sites, 263 full hookups, (15 & 30 amp receptacles), seasonal sites, 12 pull-thrus, a/c allowed ($), heater not allowed, phone hookups, RV rentals, handicap restroom facilities, portable dump, public phone, limited grocery store, RV supplies, LP gas refill by weight, gasoline, marine gas, ice, tables, fire rings, wood, traffic control gate.

◆◆◆◆RECREATION: rec room/area, coin games, swim pool, wading pool, boating, canoeing, ramp, dock, water skiing, river fishing, mini-golf, basketball hoop, playground, shuffleboard court, planned group activities, movies, sports field, horseshoes, volleyball, local tours.

No tents. Open May 1 through Oct 31. Rate in 1995 $22 per family. Master Card/Visa accepted. Phone: (905) 774-4257.

**SEE AD HAMILTON PAGE 996**

**Highland Tent & Trailer Park**—CAMPGROUND on Lake Erie with open & treed sites. *From jct Main St & CR 3: Go 11 km/7 mi E on CR 3 (Lakeshore Rd) to park.* ◆◆◆FACILITIES: 100 sites, most common site width 35 feet, 100 full hookups, (15 amp receptacles), seasonal sites, 6 pull-thrus, sewage disposal, laundry, public phone, limited grocery store, ice, tables, fire rings, wood. ◆◆◆RECREATION: rec hall, swim pool, lake swimming, boating, lake fishing, playground, planned group activities (weekends only), sports field, horseshoes. No tents. Open May 1 through Oct 31. Rate in 1995 $18-20 for 2 persons. Phone: (905) 774-8082.

**Knight's Beach**—Lakeside CAMPGROUND at Evans Point. *From bridge in business center: Go 14.5 km/9 mi W on Regional Rd 3, then 1.6 km/1 mi S on Regional Rd 50, then 1.2 km/3/4 mi W on Lakeshore Rd.* ◆◆◆FACILITIES: 280 sites, most common site width 35 feet, 268 full hookups, 12 water & elec (15 & 30 amp receptacles), seasonal sites, tenting available, sewage disposal, laundry, public phone, limited grocery store, ice, tables, wood. ◆◆◆◆RECREATION: rec hall, rec room/area, lake swimming, boating, canoeing, ramp, dock, lake fishing, playground, planned group activities, recreation director, sports field, horseshoes, hiking trails, volleyball. Recreation open to the public. Open May 1 through Sep 30. Rate in 1995 $27.75-38.50 per family. Member of OPCA. Phone: (905) 774-4566. FCRV 10% discount.

ROCK POINT PROVINCIAL PARK—*From town: Go 3/4 km/1/2 mi E on Hwy 3, then 12 3/4 km/8 mi S on Haldimand Rd 20.* FACILITIES: 135 sites, 40 elec, 95 no hookups, tenting available, handicap restroom facilities, sewage disposal, laundry, tables, wood. RECREATION: lake swimming, lake fishing, playground, hiking trails. Open mid May through early Sep. Phone: (905) 774-6642.

**Sunnibank Park**—Open, shaded and level sites. *From Hwy 3 in the town centre: Go .8 km/1/2 mi W on Hwy 3, then 8 km/5 mi S on Regional Rd 17.* ◆◆◆FACILITIES: 100 sites, 15 full hookups, 85 water & elec (15 amp receptacles), seasonal sites, 6 pull-thrus, tenting available, sewage disposal, public phone, limited grocery store, LP gas refill by weight, ice, tables, patios, fire rings, wood. ◆◆◆RECREATION: river swimming, boating, canoeing, ramp, dock, 2 row/2 pedal boat rentals, river fishing, playground, sports field, horseshoes, hiking trails. Open May 1 through Oct 1. Rate in 1995 $15 per family. Phone: (905) 774-7052.

## DURHAM—H-2

**DURHAM CONSERVATION AREA (Saugeen Valley Conservation Auth.)**—*From jct Hwy 4 & Hwy 6: Go .8 km/1/2 mi N on Hwy 6, then 1.6 km/1 mi E on Old Durham Rd.*

FACILITIES: 195 sites, 66 water & elec (15 & 30 amp receptacles), 129 no hookups, seasonal sites, tenting available, sewage disposal, public phone, tables, fire rings, wood, guard.

RECREATION: river swimming, boating, canoeing, ramp, river fishing, playground, badminton, sports field, horseshoes, hiking trails, volleyball.

Open late Apr through Oct 15. Phone: (519) 364-1255.

**SEE AD TRAVEL SECTION PAGE 979**

## DUTTON—J-2

**DUTTONA TRAILER PARK**—CAMPGROUND overlooking Lake Erie with shaded and open sites. *From Hwy 401 (exit 149): Go 4.8 km/3 mi S at exit 149, then 3.2 km/2 mi W on Hwy 3, then S on Coyne Rd.*

◆◆◆FACILITIES: 250 sites, most common site width 35 feet, 250 full hookups, (15 & 30 amp receptacles), seasonal sites, 4 pull-thrus, tenting available, RV storage, laundry, public phone, limited grocery store, RV supplies, LP gas refill by weight, ice, tables, patios, fire rings, wood, traffic control gate.

◆◆◆◆RECREATION: rec hall, rec room/area, coin games, swim pool, lake swimming, lake fishing, playground, 2 shuffleboard courts, planned group activities (weekends only), horseshoes, volleyball.

Open mid May through mid Oct. Rate in 1995 $17.50 per family. Reservations recommended Jul through Aug. Visa accepted. Phone: (519) 762-3643.

**SEE AD THIS PAGE**

## DWIGHT—G-3

**ALGONQUIN TRAILS RESORT**—Semi-wooded, level, CAMPGROUND with open & shaded sites. *From jct Hwy 60 & 35: Go .8 km/1/2 mi E on Hwy 60.*

◆◆◆FACILITIES: 100 sites, 47 water & elec (30 amp receptacles), 53 no hookups, seasonal sites, 42 pull-thrus, a/c allowed, heater allowed, tenting available, group sites for tents/RVs, RV storage, sewage disposal, laundry, public phone, limited grocery store, RV supplies, ice, tables, fire rings, grills, wood.

◆◆◆◆RECREATION: rec room/area, swim pool (indoor) (heated), mini-golf ($), basketball hoop, playground, planned group activities, movies, badminton, sports field, horseshoes, hiking trails, volleyball.

Open mid May through mid Oct. Rate in 1995 $18-20 per family. Master Card/Visa accepted. Phone: (705) 635-1262.

**SEE AD THIS PAGE**

VISA

## EAR FALLS—C-2

**Goff's Pakwash Camp**—A CAMPGROUND with campsites on Chukuni River. *From jct Hwy 657 & Hwy 105: Go 31.2 km/19 1/2 mi N on Hwy 105, then 1.2 km/3/4 mi W on Snake Falls Rd.* ◆◆FACILITIES: 18 sites, most common site width 30 feet, 5 full hookups, 13 water & elec (15 amp receptacles), seasonal sites, 18 pull-thrus, tenting available, non-flush toilets, public phone, limited grocery store, ice, tables, fire rings, wood. ◆◆◆RECREATION: rec hall, river swimming, boating, canoeing, ramp, dock, 14 motor boat rentals, lake/river fishing, badminton, horseshoes, volleyball. Recreation open to the public. Open May 15 through Oct 15. Rate in 1995 $10.70-13.85 for 2 persons. Phone: (807) 222-3300.

PAKWASH PROVINCIAL PARK—*From town: Go 20 3/4 km/13 mi N on Hwy 105.* FACILITIES: 40 sites, 16 elec, 24 no hookups, tenting available, sewage disposal, tables, wood. RECREATION: swimming, boating, canoeing, ramp, fishing, playground, hiking trails. Open early Jun through early Sep. No showers. Phone: (807) 727-2253.

**Whitewing Resort**—Level RV SPACES in conjuction with housekeeping cabins. *From town: Go 8 km/5 mi S on Hwy 105, then .8 km/1/2 mi E on Whitewing Rd.* FACILITIES: 27 sites, 7 water & elec (15 & 30 amp receptacles), 20 no hookups, tenting available, public phone, ice, fire rings, wood. RECREATION: lake swimming, boating, canoeing, ramp, dock, 1 pedal/12 motor boat rentals, lake fishing, badminton, horseshoes. Open mid May through mid Oct. Rate in 1995 $18 for 2 persons. Phone: (800) 265-1764.

## ECHO BAY—D-4

**DOWN HOME CAMPGROUNDS**—RV SPACES behind a restaurant on a major highway. *On Hwy 17 (4.8 km/3 mi E of town limits).*

WELCOME

FACILITIES: 30 sites, most common site width 30 feet, 22 water & elec (15 amp receptacles), 8 no hookups, seasonal sites, 11 pull-thrus, a/c allowed, tenting available, cabins, sewage disposal, limited grocery store, ice, tables, fire rings, wood.

RECREATION: playground, sports field.

Open May 1 through Oct 15. Rate in 1995 $12-14 per vehicle. Phone: (705) 248-2745.

**SEE AD SAULT STE. MARIE PAGE 1016**

## EDENVALE—H-3

**EDENVALE CONSERVATION AREA**—*In town on Hwy 26.* Picnic, hiking, fishing and boating area on the Nottawasaga River. Open all year. Phone: (705) 424-1479.

WELCOME

**SEE AD TRAVEL SECTION PAGE 980**

## EGANVILLE—F-5

**Lake Dore Tent & Trailer Park**—Grassy, lakeside CAMPGROUND on Lake Dore. *From jct Hwy 60 & Hwy 41 (4.8 km/3 mi NW of town): Go 2.4 km/1 1/2 mi W on Germanicus Rd.* ◆◆◆FACILITIES: 146 sites, most common site width 35 feet, 108 full hookups, 22 water & elec (15 amp receptacles), 16 no hookups, seasonal sites, 3 pull-thrus, tenting available, sewage disposal, public phone, limited grocery store, LP gas refill by weight, ice, tables, fire rings, wood. ◆◆◆◆RECREATION: rec room/area, lake swimming, boating, canoeing, ramp, dock, 2 row/3 canoe/2 pedal/3 motor boat rentals, lake fishing, playground, planned group activities, badminton, sports field, horseshoes, hiking trails, volleyball. Open May 15 through Oct 2. Rate in 1995 $14-17 per family. Phone: (613) 628-2615.

## ELLIOT LAKE—F-1

MISSISSAGI PROVINCIAL PARK—*From town: Go 17 1/2 km/11 mi N on Hwy 639.* FACILITIES: 90 sites, 21 ft. max RV length, 90 no hookups, tenting available, non-flush toilets, sewage disposal, tables, wood. RECREATION: swimming, boating, canoeing, ramp, fishing, playground, hiking trails. Open mid May through early Sep. No showers. Phone: (705) 848-2806.

WESTVIEW TRAILER PARK (City Park)—*From town: Go 1 1/2 km/1 mi N on Hwy 108.* FACILITIES: 30 sites, 30 water & elec, 20 pull-thrus, tenting available, sewage disposal, tables, fire rings, grills, wood. RECREATION: lake swimming, boating, ramp, dock, lake fishing, playground, hiking trails. Open May 1 through Oct 15. No showers. Phone: (705) 848-2871.

## ELMIRA—I-2

**CONESTOGO LAKE (Grand River Conservation Authority)**—*From town: Go 16 km/10 mi W on Hwy 86, follow signs.*

WELCOME

FACILITIES: 205 sites, 70 water & elec (15 & 30 amp receptacles), 135 no hookups, seasonal sites, tenting available, group sites for tents, sewage disposal, public phone, LP gas refill by weight, tables, wood, guard.

RECREATION: lake swimming, boating, canoeing, ramp, water skiing, lake/river fishing, playground, sports field, hiking trails. Recreation open to the public.

ELMIRA—Continued
CONESTOGO LAKE (GRAND RIVER CONSERVATION AUTHORITY)—Continued

Open May 1 through Oct 15. Phone: (519) 638-2873.

**SEE AD TRAVEL SECTION PAGE 978**

## ELORA—H-2

**ELORA GORGE (Grand River Conservation Authority)**—*From west town limits: Go 1/2 km/1/4 mi W.*

WELCOME

FACILITIES: 550 sites, 50 full hookups, 150 water & elec (15 & 30 amp receptacles), 350 no hookups, seasonal sites, tenting available, group sites for tents, sewage disposal, public phone, limited grocery store, ice, tables, wood, guard.

RECREATION: lake swimming, boating, no motors, canoeing, 15 pedal boat rentals, lake fishing, playground, sports field, hiking trails, cross country skiing. Recreation open to the public.

Open all year. Facilities fully operational May 1 through Oct 15. Day use only for winter sports. Phone: (519) 846-9742.

**SEE AD TRAVEL SECTION PAGE 978**

## ENGLEHART—C-6

KAP-KIG-IWAN PROVINCIAL PARK—*From town: Go 3/4 km/1/2 mi W on Hwy 11, then 2 1/2 km/1 1/2 mi S on 5th St.* FACILITIES: 64 sites, 32 elec, 32 no hookups, tenting available, sewage disposal, laundry, limited grocery store, ice, tables, wood. RECREATION: playground, hiking trails. Open early Jun through early Sep. Phone: (705) 544-2050.

## ENNISMORE—H-4

**Anchor Bay Camp**—Secluded, grassy, lakeside CAMPGROUND. *From business centre: Go 11.2 km/7 mi N on CR 16.* ◆◆◆FACILITIES: 165 sites, most common site width 50 feet, 135 full hookups, 17 water & elec (30 amp receptacles), 13 no hookups, seasonal sites, tenting available, handicap restroom facilities, sewage disposal, laundry, public phone, limited grocery store, ice, tables, fire rings, wood. ◆◆◆RECREATION: rec room/area, equipped pavilion, lake swimming, boating, canoeing, ramp, dock, 4 canoe/2 pedal/8 motor boat rentals, lake fishing, playground, planned group activities, sports field, horseshoes, volleyball. No pets. Open May 1 through Oct 30. Rate in 1995 $15-20. Member of OPCA. Phone: (705) 657-8439.

**Woodland Camp Site**—Rustic CAMPGROUND beside a lake. *From business centre: Go 16 km/10 mi N on CR 16, then follow signs for .4 km/1/4 mi E.* ◆◆◆FACILITIES: 175 sites, most common site width 30 feet, 150 water & elec (15 & 30 amp receptacles), 25 no hookups, seasonal sites, tenting available, sewage disposal, public phone, tables, fire rings, wood. ◆◆◆RECREATION: lake swimming, boating, canoeing, ramp, dock, 8 row/3 canoe boat rentals, lake fishing, playground, tennis court, sports field, horseshoes, volleyball. No pets. Open May 1 through Oct 31. Rate in 1995 $18-20 per family. Member of OPCA. Phone: (705) 657-8946.

## ESPANOLA—F-2

**Lake Apsey Resort & Trailer Park**—A lakeside CAMPGROUND. *From jct Hwy 17 & Hwy 6: Go 9.6 km/6 mi S on Hwy 6, then .8 km/1/2 mi W on Lake Apsey Rd.* ◆◆◆FACILITIES: 30 sites, most common site width 30 feet, 20 water & elec (15 amp receptacles), 10 no hookups, tenting available, sewage disposal, public phone, limited grocery store, ice, tables, fire rings, grills, wood. ◆◆◆RECREATION: lake swimming, boating, canoeing, ramp, dock, 1 row/1 sail/2 canoe/2 pedal/6 motor boat rentals, lake fishing, playground, horseshoes. Open mid May through mid Oct. Rate in 1995 $14.02-15.89 per family. Phone: (800) 559-6583.

**RIVERSIDE CAMPGROUND**—CAMPGROUND in wooded area on Spanish River. *From jct Hwy 6 & Hwy 17: Go 9.6 km/6 mi E on Hwy 17.*

WELCOME

◆◆FACILITIES: 40 sites, most common site width 30 feet, 28 water & elec (15 & 30 amp receptacles), 12 no hookups, seasonal sites, 3 pull-thrus, a/c allowed, tenting available, RV storage, non-flush toilets, sewage disposal, limited grocery store, ice, tables, fire rings, wood.

◆◆RECREATION: river swimming, boating, canoeing, dock, river fishing, horseshoes.

Open May 1 through end of Sep. Rate in 1995 $12-16 per family. Phone: (705) 869-2049.

**SEE AD TRAVEL SECTION PAGES 975, 976 AND 977**

## FENELON FALLS—H-4

**SANDY BEACH RESORT & TRAILER COURT**—CAMPGROUND on Balsam Lake. *From jct Hwy 35A & Hwy 35: Go 4.8 km/3 mi N, follow signs.*

WELCOME

◆◆◆◆FACILITIES: 171 sites, most common site width 50 feet, 171 full hookups, (15 & 30 amp receptacles), seasonal sites,

FENELON FALLS—Continued
SANDY BEACH RESORT & TRAILER COURT—Continued

2 pull-thrus, a/c allowed, heater not allowed, cabins, tables, fire rings.

◆◆◆RECREATION: lake swimming, boating, canoeing, ramp, dock, 1 motor boat rentals, lake fishing, playground, sports field.

No tents. Open mid May through mid OCt. Rate in 1995 $22 per family. Master Card/Visa accepted. Member of OPCA. Phone: (705) 887-2550.

**SEE AD TRAVEL SECTION PAGES 975, 976 AND 977**

**SUNNY ACRES**—CAMPGROUND with many sites occupied by seasonal campers. *From jct Hwy 35A & Hwy 35: Go 1.2 km/3/4 mi N on Hwy 35.*

WELCOME

◆◆◆FACILITIES: 100 sites, most common site width 40 feet, 52 full hookups, 30 water & elec (15 & 30 amp receptacles), 18 no hookups, seasonal sites, tenting available, cabins, sewage disposal, public phone, limited grocery store, marine gas, ice, tables, fire rings, wood.

◆◆◆RECREATION: lake swimming, boating, canoeing, ramp, dock, 3 motor boat rentals, lake fishing, basketball hoop, horseshoes, volleyball.

Open May 10 through Oct 30. Rate in 1995 $20-22 per family. Member of OPCA. Phone: (705) 887-3416.

**SEE AD TRAVEL SECTION PAGE 983**

## FOLEYET—C-5

IVANHOE LAKE PROVINCIAL PARK—*From town: Go 12 3/4 km/8 mi NW on Hwy 101, then 4 3/4 km/3 mi S on Park Rd.* FACILITIES: 120 sites, 63 elec, 57 no hookups, tenting available, handicap restroom facilities, sewage disposal, public phone. RECREATION: lake swimming, boating, canoeing, ramp, lake fishing, hiking trails. Open mid May through early Sep. Phone: (705) 899-2644.

**Red Pine Lodge**—Open & shaded, level sites in a CAMPGROUND on Ivanhoe Lake. *From jct Younge St & Hwy 101: Go 7.2 km/4 1/2 mi W on Hwy 101, then .4 km/1/4 mi S on Ivanhoe Lake Rd.* ◆◆◆FACILITIES: 75 sites, most common site width 30 feet, 71 full hookups, 4 water & elec (15 amp receptacles), seasonal sites, 3 pull-thrus, tenting available, sewage disposal, laundry, public phone, limited grocery store, LP gas refill by weight, ice, tables, fire rings, wood. ◆◆◆◆RECREATION: rec room/area, lake swimming, boating, canoeing, ramp, dock, 3 canoe/5 pedal/20 motor boat rentals, lake fishing, horseshoes. Open all year. Facilities fully operational mid May through mid Oct. Rate in 1995 $17.50 per family. Member of OPCA. Phone: (705) 899-2875.

## FONTHILL—I-3

**BISSELL'S HIDEAWAY RESORT**—CAMPGROUND on rolling terrain with wild fruit trees & evergreens. *From west city limits: Go .4 km/1/4 mi W on Hwy 20, then 2.4 km/1 1/2 mi N on Effingham Rd, then .8 km/1/2 mi E on Metler Rd.*

WELCOME

◆◆◆◆FACILITIES: 350 sites, most common site width 40 feet, 250 full hookups, (15 & 30 amp receptacles), 100 no hookups, seasonal sites, a/c allowed, heater allowed, tenting available, RV rentals, RV storage, sewage disposal, laundry, public phone, limited grocery store, LP gas refill by weight, ice, tables, wood, traffic control gate.

◆◆◆◆◆RECREATION: rec hall, rec room/area, equipped pavilion, coin games, swim pool, water slide, boating, no motors, 6 pedal boat rentals, mini-golf ($), basketball hoop, playground, 2 shuffleboard courts, planned group activities, recreation director, badminton, sports field, horseshoes, hiking trails, volleyball. Recreation open to the public.

Open May 15 through Oct 15. Rate in 1995 $22-25 for 2 persons. Reservations recommended Jul through Aug. Member of OPCA. Phone: (905) 892-5706.

**SEE AD NIAGARA FALLS PAGE 1006**

## FOREST—I-1

**Happy Holiday Family Campground**—Open & treed lots in a quiet CAMPGROUND. *From jct Hwy 21 & Ipperwash Rd: Go 1.6 km/1 mi W on Ipperwash Rd.* ◆◆◆FACILITIES: 171 sites, most common site width 55 feet, 171 full hookups, (15 & 30 amp receptacles), seasonal sites, 3 pull-thrus, tenting available, handicap restroom facilities, sewage disposal, laundry, limited grocery store, LP gas refill by weight, ice, tables, fire rings, wood. ◆◆◆RECREATION: rec hall, rec room/area, pavilion, playground, planned group activities (weekends only), badminton, sports field, horseshoes, hiking trails, volleyball. Open mid May through mid Oct. Rate in 1995 $19-24 per family. Member of OPCA. Phone: (519) 243-2258.

FOREST—Continued on next page

FOREST—Continued

**OUR PONDEROSA FAMILY CAMPGROUND & GOLF RESORT**—Grassy, level CAMPGROUND near Ipperwash Beach with open & shaded sites. *From town: Go 9.6 km/6 mi N on Hwy 21, then 90 m/100 yards W on Lambton CR 7, then 1.6 km/1 mi N on West Ipperwash Rd.*

◆◆◆◆FACILITIES: 396 sites, most common site width 40 feet, 331 full hookups, 51 water & elec (15 & 30 amp receptacles), 14 no hookups, seasonal sites, 5 pull-thrus, a/c allowed, heater allowed, tenting available, group sites for tents/RVs, RV rentals, RV storage, handicap restroom facilities, sewage disposal, laundry, public phone, limited grocery store, RV supplies, LP gas refill by weight/by meter, ice, tables, patios, fire rings, wood, traffic control gate/guard.

◆◆◆◆◆RECREATION: rec hall, rec room/area, pavilion, coin games, 2 swim pools, whirlpool, water slide, boating, 7 pedal boat rentals, golf ($), mini-golf ($), basketball hoop, playground, 3 shuffleboard courts, planned group activities, movies, recreation director, badminton, sports field, horseshoes, hiking trails, volleyball, snowmobile trails.

Open all year. Facilities fully operational May 15 through Oct 15. Rate in 1995 $20-22.50 per family. Reservations recommended summer months. Master Card/Visa accepted. Member of OPCA. Phone: (519) 786-2031.

**SEE AD THIS PAGE**

## FORT ERIE—I-3

**Windmill Point Park**—Secluded, grassy CAMPGROUND around spring fed quarry. *From jct QEW (at Peace Bridge) & Hwy 3: Go 7.2 km/4 1/2 mi W on Hwy 3, then 2 km/1 1/4 mi S on Stonemill Rd (Reg Rd 120), then .4 km/1/4 mi W on Dominion Rd, then .4 km/1/4 mi S on paved road.* ◆◆FACILITIES: 199 sites, most common site width 35 feet, 27 water & elec, 12 elec (15 amp receptacles), 160 no hookups, seasonal sites, tenting available, sewage disposal, public phone, ice, tables, wood. ◆◆◆RECREATION: rec room/area, lake swimming, boating, no motors, canoeing, ramp, 1 canoe/8 pedal boat rentals, lake fishing, playground, planned group activities (weekends only), sports field, horseshoes, volleyball. Open May 15 through mid Oct. Rate in 1995 $23-25 per family. Phone: (905) 894-2809.

## FORT FRANCES—E-1

**The Fisheries Resort**—CAMPGROUND on Rainy Lake. *From jct Hwy 502 & Hwy 11: Go 10 km/6 1/4 mi E on Hwy 11, then 3.6 km/2 1/4 mi N on Armstrong Rd.* ◆◆◆FACILITIES: 35 sites, most common site width 25 feet, 35 ft. max RV length, 25 full hookups, (15 amp receptacles), 10 no hookups, seasonal sites, tenting available, laundry, public phone, limited grocery store, ice, tables, fire rings, wood. ◆◆◆RECREATION: lake swimming, boating, canoeing, ramp, dock, 1 canoe/1 pedal/8 motor boat rentals, lake fishing, horseshoes. Open May 1 through Oct 1. Rate in 1995 $15-18.70. Phone: (807) 481-2534.

**Holiday Village Campground**—Grassy CAMPGROUND on east edge of town. *From business center: Go 1.6 km/1 mi E on Hwy 111.* ◆◆FACILITIES: 42 sites, most common site width 40 feet, 17 full hookups, 20 water & elec, 5 elec (15 amp receptacles), 3 pull-thrus, tenting available, sewage disposal, laundry, public phone, ice, tables, wood. ◆RECREATION: sports field, horseshoes. Open mid May through mid Oct. Rate in 1995 $13-15 per family. Phone: (807) 274-7374.

**Taylor's Cove**—Lakeside CAMPGROUND & marina. *From jct Hwy 502 & Hwy 11: Go 8.8 km/5 1/2 mi E on Hwy 11, then .4 km/1/4 mi N on Taylor's Rd.* ◆◆◆FACILITIES: 25 sites, most common site width 30 feet, 8 water & elec, 5 elec (15 amp receptacles), 12 no hookups, tenting available, sewage disposal, public phone, limited grocery store, ice, tables, fire rings, wood. ◆◆◆RECREATION: lake swimming, boating, canoeing, ramp, dock, 2 canoe/1 pedal/5 motor boat rentals, lake fishing. Open May 1 through Oct 1. Rate in 1995 $13-15 for 2 persons. Phone: (807) 481-2526.



## FRANKFORD—H-4

FRANKFORD TOURIST PARK (Village Park)—*In Frankford at east end of bridge on Hwy 33.* FACILITIES: 64 sites, 24 water & elec (15 amp receptacles), 40 no hookups, tenting available, sewage disposal, tables, fire rings, grills. RECREATION: river swimming, boating, canoeing, ramp, dock, river fishing, playground, sports field. Open all year. Facilities fully operational May 1 through Sep 30. Phone: (613) 398-6200.

## FREELTON—I-3

**Lawson Park**—A semi-wooded CAMPGROUND with level sites. Most sites occupied by seasonal campers. *From jct CR 97 & Hwy 6: Go .4 km/1/4 mi N on Hwy 6, then 3.2 km/2 mi E on Concession 11.* ◆◆◆FACILITIES: 325 sites, most common site width 45 feet, 300 full hookups, 25 water & elec, 13 elec (15 & 30 amp receptacles), seasonal sites, 9 pull-thrus, sewage disposal, public phone, limited grocery store, ice, tables, fire rings, wood. ◆◆◆RECREATION: swim pool (heated), boating, no motors, canoeing, lake fishing, playground, 2 shuffleboard courts, planned group activities (weekends only), 2 tennis courts, sports field. No tents. Open May 1 through Sep 30. Rate in 1995 $22-25 per family. Phone: (905) 659-3395.

## FRENCH RIVER—F-2

**Loon's Landing**—Treed, riverside CAMPGROUND & boat landing. *From jct Hwy 69 & Hwy 607/607A: Go .4 km/1/4 mi E on Hwy 607/607A, then S to Hass Rd, follow signs.* ◆◆◆FACILITIES: 40 sites, most common site width 35 feet, 22 full hookups, 8 water & elec (15 & 30 amp receptacles), 10 no hookups, seasonal sites, 5 pull-thrus, tenting available, sewage disposal, public phone, limited grocery store, ice, tables, fire rings, grills, wood. ◆◆◆RECREATION: river swimming, boating, canoeing, ramp, dock, 4 canoe/12 motor boat rentals, river fishing, planned group activities, horseshoes, volleyball. Recreation open to the public. Open May 15 through Oct 15. Rate in 1995 $13-15 per family. Phone: (705) 857-2175.

**Martins Camp**—CAMPGROUND with grassy and wooded sites by the river. *From jct Hwy 69 & Hwy 64: Go 4.8 km/3 mi E on Hwy 64, then 3.2 km/2 mi S on Hwy 607, and follow signs.* ◆◆FACILITIES: 40 sites, most common site width 35 feet, 20 full hookups, 20 water & elec (15 amp receptacles), seasonal sites, tenting available, sewage disposal, laundry, public phone, limited grocery store, ice, tables, fire rings, grills, wood. ◆◆◆RECREATION: rec room/area, river swimming, boating, canoeing, ramp, dock, 1 pedal/9 motor boat rentals, river fishing, sports field, horseshoes. Recreation open to the public. Open May 15 through Oct 15. Rate in 1995 $13-16 per family. Phone: (705) 857-5477.

**SCHELL'S CAMP AND PARK**—Secluded CAMPGROUND by the riverside. *From jct Hwy 69 & Hwy 607 & 607A: Go .4 km/1/4 mi E on Hwy 607 & 607A, then 4 km/2 1/2 mi S on Hwy 607A.*

◆◆◆FACILITIES: 100 sites, most common site width 35 feet, 15 full hookups, 60 water & elec (15 & 30 amp receptacles), 25 no hookups, seasonal sites, a/c allowed ($), heater allowed ($), tenting available, group sites for tents, cabins, sewage disposal, laundry, public phone, grocery store, gasoline, marine gas, ice, tables, fire rings, wood.

◆◆◆RECREATION: river swimming, boating, canoeing, ramp, dock, 5 canoe/18 motor boat rentals, water skiing, river fishing, fishing guides, playground, badminton, horseshoes, hiking trails.

Open May 15 through Oct 15. Rate in 1995 $14.25-17.35 per family. Master Card/Visa accepted. Member of OPCA. Phone: (705) 857-2031.

**SEE AD TRAVEL SECTION PAGES 975, 976 AND 977**

## GANANOQUE—H-5

**IVY LEA CAMPSITE (Parks of the St. Lawrence)**—*From east city limits: Go 12 3/4 km/8 mi E on Thousand Islands Pkwy. Just west of the Ivy Lea Bridge.*

FACILITIES: 157 sites, 11 water & elec, 33 elec (15 & 30 amp receptacles), 113 no hookups, tenting available, handicap restroom facilities, portable dump, public phone, tables.

RECREATION: river swimming, boating, canoeing, ramp, dock, river fishing, playground, planned group activities, badminton, horseshoes, hiking trails, volleyball. Open May 19 through Sep 24. Phone: (613) 659-3057.

**SEE AD TRAVEL SECTION PAGE 974**

**KOA-Ivy Lea**—Grassy, semi-wooded CAMPGROUND. *From jct Hwy 401 (exit 659) & Reynolds Rd: Go 2.4 km/1 1/2 mi S on Reynolds Rd, then 3.2 km/2 mi W on Thousand Island Pkwy.* ◆◆◆FACILITIES: 120 sites, most common site width 30 feet, 95 water & elec (15 & 30 amp receptacles), 25 no hookups, seasonal sites, 40 pull-thrus, tenting available, sewage disposal, laundry, public phone, grocery store, LP gas refill by weight/by meter, ice, tables, fire rings, wood. ◆◆◆◆RECREATION: rec hall, rec room/area, swim pool, playground, planned group activities, badminton, sports field, horseshoes, hiking trails, volleyball. Open May 1 through Oct 15. Rate in 1995 $17-20 for 2 persons. Phone: (613) 659-2817. KOA 10% value card discount.

**The Landon Bay Centre**—CAMPGROUND in a tourist area in conjunction with extensive nature trails marked by a Canadian biologist. *From Hwy 401 (exit 659): Go 2.4 km/1 1/2 mi S, then 8 km/5 mi W on the 1000 Islands Pkwy.* ◆◆FACILITIES: 125 sites, most common site width 35 feet, 75 water & elec (15 amp receptacles), 50 no hookups, tenting available, handicap restroom facilities, sewage disposal, public phone, limited grocery store, ice, tables, wood. ◆◆◆RECREATION: swim pool, planned group activities (weekends only), horseshoes, hiking trails, volleyball. Open mid May through mid Sep. Rate in 1995 $12-14 per family. Phone: (613) 382-2719.

**Pinecrest Resort**—Grassy, riverside CAMPGROUND. *From jct Hwy 401 (exit 632) & Joyceville Rd: Go 3.6 km/2 1/4 mi S on Joyceville Rd (CR 16), then 6.8 km/4 1/4 mi E on Hwy 2, then .8 km/1/2 mi S on Resort Rd.* ◆◆FACILITIES: 60 sites, most common site width 30 feet, 50 water & elec (15 amp receptacles), 10 no hookups, seasonal sites, tenting available, sewage disposal, public phone, ice, tables, fire rings, wood. ◆◆◆RECREATION: river swimming, boating, canoeing, ramp, dock, 2 canoe/12 motor boat rentals, river fishing, playground. Open Apr 15 through Oct 31. Rate in 1995 $13-16 per family. Phone: (613) 382-2836.

**1000 Islands Camping Resort**—Rolling, grassy CAMPGROUND in a tourist area. *From jct Hwy 401 (exit 659) & Reynolds Rd: Go 2.4 km/1 1/2 mi S on Reynolds Rd, then 6.4 km/4 mi W on the 1000 Islands Pkwy.* ◆◆◆FACILITIES: 164 sites, most common site width 40 feet, 35 full hookups, 80 water & elec (15,30 & 50 amp receptacles), 49 no hookups, seasonal sites, 3 pull-thrus, tenting available, handicap restroom facilities, sewage disposal, laundry, public phone, grocery store, ice, tables, fire rings, wood. ◆◆◆◆RECREATION: rec hall, rec room/area, swim pool, mini-golf ($), playground, planned group activities (weekends only), horseshoes, hiking trails, volleyball. Recreation open to the public. Open May 15 through Oct 15. Rate in 1995 $16-21 per family. Phone: (613) 659-3058.

## GERALDTON—A-2

MACLEOD PROVINCIAL PARK—*From jct Hwy 584 & Hwy 11: Go 2 3/4 km/1 3/4 mi E on Hwy 11.* FACILITIES: 85 sites, 28 elec, 57 no hookups, 28 pull-thrus, tenting available, laundry, tables, wood. RECREATION: lake swimming, boating, canoeing, ramp, lake fishing, playground, hiking trails. Open mid Jun through early Sep. Phone: (807) 854-1030.

**WILD GOOSE LAKE TRAILER PARK**—Lakeside CAMPGROUND. *From west city limits: Go 19.3 km/12 mi W on Hwy 11, then 1.2 km/3/4 mi N on Kuengs Rd.*

◆◆FACILITIES: 50 sites, most common site width 30 feet, 50 full hookups, (30 amp receptacles), seasonal sites, a/c allowed ($), tenting available, cabins, laundry, public phone, limited grocery store, marine gas, ice, tables, fire rings, grills, wood.

◆◆RECREATION: lake swimming, boating, canoeing, ramp, dock, 5 canoe/5 motor boat rentals, water skiing, lake fishing, badminton, horseshoes, volleyball.

Open May 15 through Oct 15. Rate in 1995 $10-15.25. Phone: (807) 854-0836.

**SEE AD TRAVEL SECTION PAGES 975, 976 AND 977**

## GLENCOE—I-2

**VALLEY VIEW CAMPGROUND**—Rustic grassy sites in a country club setting. *From jct Hwy 80 & Hwy 2: Go 6.4 km/4 mi E on Hwy 2, then 1.2 km/3/4 mi S on Middlesex Rd 8, then 1.6 km/1 mi W on Ekfrid Rd (R1-S).*

◆◆◆FACILITIES: 200 sites, most common site width 40 feet, 105 full hookups, 14 water & elec (15 & 30 amp receptacles), 81 no hookups, seasonal sites, 2 pull-thrus, a/c allowed, heater allowed, tenting available, group sites for tents/RVs, RV rentals, sewage disposal, public phone, limited grocery store, RV supplies, LP gas refill by weight/by meter, ice, tables, fire rings, wood.

◆◆◆RECREATION: rec hall, rec room/area, coin games, swim pool, pond fishing, mini-golf ($), basketball hoop, playground, shuffleboard court, planned group activities (weekends only), movies, 2 tennis courts, badminton, sports field, horseshoes, hiking trails, volleyball.

VALLEY VIEW CAMPGROUND—Continued on next page
GLENCOE—Continued on next page

GLENCOE—Continued
VALLEY VIEW CAMPGROUND—Continued

Open May 1 through mid Oct. Rate in 1995 $17-22 per family. Reservations recommended Jul through Aug. Phone: (519) 289-2100.

SEE AD THIS PAGE

### GODERICH—H-2

**BRANDY'S HIDEAWAY CAMPGROUND**—CAMPGROUND on the Maitland River with open & shaded sites. *From town: Go 3.2 km/2 mi N on Hwy 21, then 12.8 km/8 mi E on CR 25 to park.*

◆◆◆FACILITIES: 74 sites, most common site width 35 feet, 47 full hookups, 9 water & elec, 12 elec (15 & 30 amp receptacles), 6 no hookups, seasonal sites, 4 pull-thrus, a/c allowed ($), heater not allowed, tenting available, group sites for tents/RVs, RV storage, sewage disposal, laundry, public phone, limited grocery store, ice, tables, fire rings, wood.

◆◆◆RECREATION: rec hall, swim pool, boating, canoeing, river fishing, basketball hoop, playground, shuffleboard court, planned group activities (weekends only), horseshoes, volleyball.

Open May 15 through mid Oct. Rate in 1995 $15.50-18 per family. Member of OPCA. Phone: (519) 526-7238.

SEE AD THIS PAGE

FALLS RESERVE (Maitland Valley Conservation Auth.) —*From town: Go 6 1/2 km/4 mi S on Hwy 8, then 4 3/4 km/3 mi E on CR 31.* FACILITIES: 160 sites, 60 water & elec (15 amp receptacles), 100 no hookups, tenting available, sewage disposal, limited grocery store, ice. RECREATION: pavilion, river swimming, river/pond fishing, playground, sports field, horseshoes, hiking trails, volleyball. Open May 24 through Oct 15.

POINT FARMS PROVINCIAL PARK—*From town: Go 4 3/4 km/3 mi N on Hwy 21.* FACILITIES: 200 sites, 74 elec, 126 no hookups, tenting available, handicap restroom facilities, sewage disposal, tables. RECREATION: lake swimming, river fishing, playground, hiking trails. Open mid May through early Oct. Phone: (519) 524-7124.

**SHELTER VALLEY TENT & TRAILER PARK**—Level, grassy sites in a CAMPGROUND nestled in a valley by a river. *From center of town at jct Hwy 21 & Hwy 8: Go 8 km/5 mi SE on Hwy 8.*

◆◆◆FACILITIES: 152 sites, most common site width 40 feet, 72 full hookups, 73 water & elec (15 & 30 amp receptacles), 7 no hookups, seasonal sites, 4 pull-thrus, a/c allowed ($), heater allowed ($), tenting available, group sites for tents/RVs, RV storage, sewage disposal, laundry, public phone, limited grocery store, RV supplies, LP gas refill by weight, ice, tables, fire rings, wood, traffic control gate.

◆◆◆◆RECREATION: rec hall, coin games, swim pool (heated), canoeing, river fishing, playground, 2 shuffleboard courts, planned group activities (weekends only), movies, badminton, sports field, horseshoes, volleyball.

Open mid May through mid Oct. Rate in 1995 $15-17 per family. Master Card/Visa accepted. Member of OPCA. Phone: (519) 524-4141. FCRV 10% discount.

SEE AD THIS PAGE

### GOLDEN LAKE—F-5

**GOLDEN LAKE CAMP GROUND & MARINA** (REBUILDING)—Grassy, lakeside CAMPGROUND with open & shaded sites. *From west city limits: Go 12.8 km/8 mi W on Hwy 60.*

FACILITIES: 500 sites, most common site width 40 feet, 150 full hookups, 350 water & elec (15 amp receptacles), seasonal sites, 20 pull-thrus, a/c allowed, heater allowed, tenting available, group sites for tents/RVs, cabins, RV storage, sewage disposal, laundry, public phone, limited grocery store, LP gas refill by weight, marine gas, ice, tables, fire rings, wood.

RECREATION: rec room/area, coin games, wading pool, lake swimming, boating, canoeing, ramp, dock, 9 row/2 canoe/2 pedal boat rentals, water skiing, lake fishing, playground, planned group activities, movies, badminton, sports field, horseshoes, volleyball.

GOLDEN LAKE—Continued
GOLDEN LAKE CAMP GROUND & MARINA—Continued

Open all year. Facilities fully operational mid May through mid Oct. Rate in 1995 $15 per family. Master Card accepted. Phone: (613) 757-0390.

SEE AD THIS PAGE

### GOULAIS RIVER—D-4

**BLUEBERRY HILL MOTEL & CAMPGROUND**—A level CAMPGROUND in a wooded area. *From jct Hwy 552 & Hwy 17: Go 3.6 km/2 1/4 mi S on Hwy 17.*

◆◆◆FACILITIES: 100 sites, most common site width 25 feet, 12 full hookups, 42 water & elec, 6 elec (15 amp receptacles), 40 no hookups, 28 pull-thrus, a/c allowed, heater allowed, tenting available, sewage disposal, laundry, public phone, limited grocery store, RV supplies, LP gas refill by weight, ice, tables, fire rings, wood.

◆◆◆◆RECREATION: rec hall, rec room/area, coin games, swim pool (indoor) (heated), sauna, boating, canoeing, 10 canoe boat rentals, river fishing, playground, planned group activities, recreation director, sports field, horseshoes, volleyball.

Open all year. Facilities fully operational May 1 through Oct 15. Rate in 1995 $12-17 for 2 persons. Master Card/Visa accepted. Member of OPCA. Phone: (800) 811-4411.

SEE AD TRAVEL SECTION PAGES 975, 976 AND 977

### GRAFTON—H-4

**Cobourg East Campground**—Grassy, semi-wooded CAMPGROUND near a major highway. *From jct Hwy 401 (exit 487) & Aird St: Go S on Aird St, then 1.6 km/1 mi E on Hwy 2, then .8 km/1/2 mi S on Benlock Rd.* ◆◆◆◆FACILITIES: 160 sites, most common site width 40 feet, 17 full hookups, 108 water & elec (15 & 30 amp receptacles), 35 no hookups, seasonal sites, 26 pull-thrus, tenting available, sewage disposal, laundry, public phone, limited grocery store, LP gas refill by weight, ice, tables, fire rings, wood. ◆◆◆◆RECREATION: rec room/area, equipped pavilion, swim pool, stream fishing, playground, planned group activities (weekends only), badminton, sports field, horseshoes, volleyball. Open May 1 through mid Oct. Rate in 1995 $14.50-19 for 2 persons. Member of OPCA. Phone: (905) 349-2594. FCRV 10% discount.

**Jubalee Beach Park**—CAMPGROUND on Lake Ontario. *From jct Hwy 401 (exit 487) & Aird St: Go 1.6 km/1 mi S on Aird St, then 2.4 km/1 1/2 mi E on Hwy 2, then 2.4 km/1 1/2 mi S on Wicklow Beach Rd.* ◆◆FACILITIES: 140 sites, most common site width 45 feet, 110 full hookups, 30 water & elec (15 & 30 amp receptacles), seasonal sites, 15 pull-thrus, tenting available, sewage disposal, public phone, limited grocery store, LP gas refill by weight, ice, tables, fire rings, wood. ◆◆RECREATION: swim pool, lake swimming, boating, canoeing, lake fishing, playground, planned group activities (weekends only), sports field, horseshoes, hiking trails, volleyball. Recreation open to the public. Open May 1 through Oct 26. Pool open Jul 1-Sep 30. Rate in 1995 $17.50-22.50 per vehicle. Phone: (905) 349-2670.

### GRAND BEND—I-2

**Birch Bark Tent & Trailer Park**—Level, grassy CAMPGROUND with open and shaded sites. *From jct Hwy 21 & 83: Go 3.2 km/2 mi E on Hwy 83.* ◆◆◆FACILITIES: 100 sites, most common site width 35 feet, 35 ft. max RV length, 88 full hookups, 12 water & elec (15 & 30 amp receptacles), seasonal sites, 4 pull-thrus, tenting available, sewage disposal, laundry, public phone, limited grocery store, LP gas refill by weight, ice, tables, fire rings, wood. ◆◆◆RECREATION: rec room/area, swim pool, playground, planned group activities (weekends only), sports field, horseshoes. Open mid May through may Oct. Rate in 1995 $19 per family. Member of OPCA. Phone: (519) 238-8256.

**THE DUNES OAKRIDGE PARK**—Open, shaded and level sites in a CAMPGROUND. Most sites occupied by seasonal campers. *From jct Hwy 81 & Hwy 21: Go 11 km/7 mi S on Hwy 21, then .4 km/1/4 mi W on Northville Crescent.*

◆◆◆◆FACILITIES: 208 sites, most common site width 40 feet, 119 full hookups, 9 water & elec (15 & 30 amp receptacles), 80 no hookups, seasonal sites, a/c allowed, heater not allowed, phone hookups, tenting available, group sites for tents, RV rentals, RV storage, sewage disposal, laundry, public phone, limited grocery store, RV supplies, LP gas refill by weight, ice, tables, fire rings, wood, traffic control gate.

◆◆◆◆RECREATION: rec hall, rec room/area, coin games, 2 swim pools, wading pool, basketball hoop, playground, planned group activities, movies, recreation director, horseshoes, hiking trails. Recreation open to the public.

Open all year. Facilities fully operational mid May through mid Oct. Rate in 1995 $20-25 per family. Reservations recommended Jul through Aug. Master Card/Visa accepted. Member of OPCA. Phone: (519) 243-2500.

SEE AD TRAVEL SECTION PAGE 982

PINERY PROVINCIAL PARK—*From town: Go 8 km/5 mi S on Hwy 21.* FACILITIES: 1000 sites, 126 elec, 874 no hookups, tenting available, handicap restroom facilities, sewage disposal, laundry, limited grocery store, ice, tables, wood. RECREATION: swimming, boating, no motors, canoeing, fishing, hiking trails. Open early Apr through late Oct. Phone: (519) 243-2220.

**RUS-TON VILLAGE FAMILY CAMPGROUND**—Semi-wooded location with open & shaded sites. Most sites occupied by seasonal campers. *From jct Hwy 81 & Hwy 21: Go 6.4 km/4 mi S on Hwy 21.*

◆◆◆◆FACILITIES: 220 sites, most common site width 40 feet, 204 full hookups, (15 & 30 amp receptacles), 16 no hookups, seasonal sites, tenting available, RV rentals, RV storage, sewage disposal, laundry, public phone, limited grocery store, RV supplies, LP gas refill by weight, ice, tables, fire rings, wood, traffic control gate.

RUS-TON VILLAGE FAMILY CAMPGROUND—Continued on next page
GRAND BEND—Continued on next page

GRAND BEND—Continued
RUS-TON VILLAGE FAMILY CAMPGROUND—Continued

◇◇◇◇RECREATION: rec hall, coin games, swim pool (heated), wading pool, whirlpool, basketball hoop, playground, 2 shuffleboard courts, planned group activities, movies, recreation director, badminton, sports field, horseshoes, volleyball.

Open May 1 through Oct 1. Rate in 1995 $25 per family. Reservations recommended during summer. Master Card/Visa accepted. Member of OPCA. Phone: (519) 243-2424.

SEE AD TRAVEL SECTION PAGES 975, 976 AND 977

## GRANTON—I-2

**Prospect Hill Camping Grounds**—Riverside CAMPGROUND. *From jct Hwy 4 & Hwy 7: Go 10 km/6 1/4 mi E on Hwy 7, then 2.8 km/1 3/4 mi N on Middlesex CR 50.* ◇◇◇FACILITIES: 218 sites, most common site width 30 feet, 182 water & elec (15 & 30 amp receptacles), 36 no hookups, seasonal sites, tenting available, sewage disposal, public phone, limited grocery store, LP gas refill by weight, ice, tables, patios, fire rings, wood. ◇◇◇◇RECREATION: rec hall, rec room/area, pavilion, swim pool (heated), canoeing, stream fishing, playground, planned group activities (weekends only), sports field, horseshoes, volleyball. Open mid May through mid Oct. Rate in 1995 $18-22 per family. Member of OPCA. Phone: (519) 225-2405.

## GRAVENHURST—G-3

**KOA-Gravenhurst Muskoka**—Semi-wooded CAMPGROUND at Duck Lake. *From north jct Hwy 169 & Hwy 11: Go 6.5 km/4 mi N on Hwy 11, then .4 km/1/4 mi E on Reay Rd.* ◇◇◇FACILITIES: 184 sites, most common site width 35 feet, 40 full hookups, 123 water & elec, 5 elec (15 & 30 amp receptacles), 16 no hookups, seasonal sites, 30 pull-thrus, tenting available, sewage disposal, laundry, public phone, grocery store, LP gas refill by weight, ice, tables, fire rings, grills, wood. ◇◇◇◇RECREATION: rec hall, rec room/area, swim pool (indoor) (heated), pond swimming, boating, no motors, canoeing, 2 row/4 canoe boat rentals, lake/pond fishing ($), mini-golf ($), playground, planned group activities, sports field, horseshoes, hiking trails, volleyball. Open all year. Facilities fully operational May 1 through Oct 31. Rate in 1995 $18-26 for 2 persons. Member of OPCA. Phone: (705) 687-2333. KOA 10% value card discount.

## GRIFFITH—G-5

**CAMEL CHUTE CAMPGROUND**—Terraced, grassy, open & shaded sites along the Madawaska River. *From jct Hwy 41 & Matawatchan Rd: Go 9 km/5 1/2 mi E on Matawatchan Rd.*

WELCOME

◇◇FACILITIES: 38 sites, most common site width 50 feet, 38 full hookups, (30 amp receptacles), seasonal sites, a/c allowed ($), heater allowed ($), tenting available, marine gas, ice, tables, fire rings, wood.

◇◇RECREATION: lake swimming, boating, canoeing, ramp, dock, lake fishing.

Open all year. Facilities fully operational mid May through mid Oct. Rate in 1995 $17 per family. Member of OPCA. Phone: (613) 333-2980.

SEE AD TRAVEL SECTION PAGES 975, 976 AND 977

## GUELPH—I-3

***See listings at Acton, Cambridge, Campbellville, Freelton, Kitchener, Milton and Waterloo***

**GUELPH LAKE (Grand River Conservation Authority)**—*From north town limits: Go 1 1/2 km/1 mi N on Hwy 6, then 1 1/2 km/1 mi E on CR 6.*

WELCOME

FACILITIES: 500 sites, 100 water & elec (15 & 30 amp receptacles), 400 no hookups, seasonal sites, tenting available, group sites for tents, sewage disposal, public phone, tables, wood, guard.

GUELPH—Continued
GUELPH LAKE (GRAND RIVER CONSERVATION AUTHORITY)—Continued

RECREATION: lake swimming, boating, no motors, canoeing, ramp, 20 canoe boat rentals, lake fishing, playground, sports field, hiking trails. Recreation open to the public.

Open May 1 through Oct 15. Phone: (519) 824-5061.

SEE AD TRAVEL SECTION PAGE 978

GUELPH TOWNSHIP RECREATIONAL PARK—*From jct Hwy 401 (exit 295) & Hwy 6: Go 19 1/4 km/12 mi E on Hwy 6, then W on Wellington Rd 30, follow signs.* FACILITIES: 173 sites, 153 water & elec (15 amp receptacles), 20 no hookups, tenting available, handicap restroom facilities, sewage disposal, public phone, limited grocery store, ice, tables, wood. RECREATION: pavilion, lake swimming, lake fishing, playground, sports field, horseshoes, hiking trails, volleyball. Open Victoria Day through Thanksgiving. Phone: (519) 824-4470. FCRV 10% discount.

**ROCKWOOD (Grand River Conservation Authority)**—*From town: Go 11 1/4 km/7 mi E on Hwy 7.*

WELCOME

FACILITIES: 110 sites, 50 water & elec (15 & 30 amp receptacles), 60 no hookups, seasonal sites, tenting available, group sites for tents, sewage disposal, public phone, ice, tables, wood, guard.

RECREATION: lake swimming, boating, no motors, canoeing, 30 canoe boat rentals, lake fishing, minigolf, playground, sports field, hiking trails. Recreation open to the public.

Open May 1 through Oct 15. Phone: (519) 856-9543.

SEE AD TRAVEL SECTION PAGE 978

## HALIBURTON—G-4

**RIP'S SLEEPY HOLLOW RESORT**—Terraced, grassy CAMPGROUND by a lake. *From jct Hwy 121 & Hwy 118: Go 11 km/7 mi W on Hwy 118, then .8 km/1/2 mi N on Kennisis Lake Rd. (Follow signs)*

WELCOME

◇◇FACILITIES: 250 sites, most common site width 40 feet, 150 full hookups, (30 amp receptacles), 100 no hookups, seasonal sites, tenting available, group sites for RVs, cabins, RV storage, handicap restroom facilities, sewage disposal, public phone, limited grocery store, ice, tables, fire rings, wood.

◇◇◇RECREATION: pavilion, lake swimming, boating, canoeing, dock, 6 row/5 canoe/1 pedal boat rentals, water skiing, lake fishing, basketball hoop, playground, badminton, sports field, horseshoes, volleyball, cross country skiing, snowmobile trails. Recreation open to the public.

Open all year. Facilities fully operational May 1 through Oct 15. Rate in 1995 $15-18 per family. Master Card/Visa accepted. Phone: (705) 754-2057.

SEE AD TRAVEL SECTION PAGE 983

## HAMILTON—I-3

CONFEDERATION PARK (Hamilton Reg. Conservation Auth.)—*From jct Queen Elizabeth Way & Hwy 20: Go 1/2 km/1/4 mi N on Hwy 20, then 1/2 km/1/4 mi W on Confederation Park Dr.* FACILITIES: 142 sites, 66 water & elec (20 amp receptacles), 76 no hookups, tenting available, sewage disposal, laundry, public phone, limited grocery store, ice, tables. RECREATION: swim pool (heated), lake swimming, boating, ramp, lake/pond fishing, playground, horseshoes. Recreation open to the public. Open May through Oct. Phone: (905) 547-6141.

## HANOVER—H-2

**Saugeen Cedars Campground**—Riverside CAMPGROUND. *From jct Hwy 6 & Hwy 4: Go 14.5 km/9 mi W on Hwy 4 to campground on N.* ◇◇◇FACILITIES: 104 sites, most common site width 40 feet, 75 water & elec (15 & 30 amp receptacles), 29 no hookups, seasonal sites, 4 pull-thrus, tenting available, sewage dis-



HANOVER—Continued
SAUGEEN CEDARS CAMPGROUND—Continued

posal, laundry, limited grocery store, ice, tables, fire rings, wood. ◇◇◇RECREATION: rec hall, river swimming, boating, no motors, canoeing, 1 canoe boat rentals, river fishing, playground, planned group activities (weekends only), badminton, sports field, horseshoes, hiking trails, volleyball. Open May 1 through Oct 15. Rate in 1995 $17-19 per family. Member of OPCA. Phone: (519) 364-2069.

**SAUGEEN SPRINGS RV PARK**—CAMPGROUND on the Saugeen River. *From east city limits: Go 10.8 km/6 3/4 mi E on Hwy 4, then 4.8 km/3 mi N on Mulock Rd.*

WELCOME

◇FACILITIES: 105 sites, most common site width 50 feet, 12 full hookups, 65 water & elec (15 & 30 amp receptacles), 28 no hookups, seasonal sites, a/c allowed, heater allowed, tenting available, cabins, RV storage, non-flush toilets, sewage disposal, public phone, ice, tables, fire rings, wood.

◇◇◇RECREATION: rec room/area, river swimming, boating, canoeing, 1 canoe boat rentals, river fishing, basketball hoop, playground, sports field, horseshoes, hiking trails, volleyball.

Open May 1 through Oct 15. No showers. Rate in 1995 $17-19 per family. Member of OPCA. Phone: (519) 369-5136.

SEE AD TRAVEL SECTION PAGES 975, 976 AND 977

► **SAUGEEN VALLEY CONSERVATION AUTHORITY (Headquarters)**—*From jct Hwy 4 & 7th Ave (CR 10): Go 4.8 km/3 mi S on CR 10, then .8 km/1/2 mi E on local road.* Visitors center for information and brochures on Saugeen Conservation areas campground, Brucedale Conservation Area, Saugeen Bluffs and Durham Conservation Area. Open all year. Phone: (519) 364-1255.

WELCOME

SEE AD TRAVEL SECTION PAGE 979

## HAVELOCK—H-4

**RED SETTER RESORT**—Grassy, level sites in a lakeside CAMPGROUND. *From town: Go 3.2 km/2 mi S on Hwy 30, then 3.6 km/2 1/4 mi E on Trent River Rd E.*

WELCOME

◇◇FACILITIES: 87 sites, most common site width 35 feet, 68 full hookups, 14 water & elec (15 & 30 amp receptacles), 5 no hookups, seasonal sites, 2 pull-thrus, a/c allowed, heater allowed, tenting available, cabins, sewage disposal, public phone, limited grocery store, ice, tables, fire rings, wood.

◇◇◇RECREATION: equipped pavilion, swim pool, boating, ramp, dock, 4 row/8 motor boat rentals, lake fishing, playground, planned group activities, badminton, horseshoes, volleyball.

Open mid May through mid Oct. Rate in 1995 $20-23 per family. Visa accepted. Member of OPCA. Phone: (705) 778-3096.

SEE AD CAMPBELLFORD PAGE 989

## HEARST—A-4

**Cecile's Campsite**—RV SPACES in front of a mobile home park. *From east jct Hwy 583 & Hwy 11: Go 2.4 km/1 1/2 mi E on Hwy 11.* FACILITIES: 55 sites, most common site width 30 feet, 30 full hookups, (15 amp receptacles), 25 no hookups, 18 pull-thrus, tenting available, laundry, ice, tables, fire rings, grills, wood. Open May 1 through Oct 30. Rate in 1995 $11.50-12.50 for 3 persons. Phone: (705) 362-8118.

FUSHIMI LAKE PROVINCIAL PARK—*From town: Go 24 km/15 mi W on Hwy 11, then 12 3/4 km/8 mi N on Fushimi Forest access road.* FACILITIES: 44 sites, 24 elec, 20 no hookups, 8 pull-thrus, tenting available, handicap restroom facilities, wood. RECREATION: lake swimming, boating, canoeing, ramp, lake fishing, hiking trails. Open mid May through late Sep. Phone: (705) 362-4346.

## HEPWORTH—G-2

**Whispering Pines Recreational Park**—Wooded, level sites in a CAMPGROUND. *From jct Hwy 6 & Hwy 70: Go .8 km/1/2 mi E on Hwy 70.* ◇◇◇FACILITIES: 225 sites, most common site width 60 feet, 210 water & elec (15 & 30 amp receptacles), 15 no hookups, seasonal sites, 12 pull-thrus, tenting available, handicap restroom facilities, sewage disposal, laundry, public phone, limited grocery store, ice, tables, fire rings, wood. ◇◇◇RECREATION: pavilion, swim pool (heated), playground, sports field, horseshoes, hiking trails, volleyball. Open May 1 through Sep 15. Rate in 1995 $18-21. Phone: (519) 935-2571.

## HILTON BEACH—D-4

**Busy Beaver Campground**—Open and shaded, level sites on the banks of Hilton Lake. *From jct Hwy 17 & Hwy 548: Go 4.8 km/3 mi S on Hwy 548, then 9.6 km/6 mi E on Hwy 548 E, then 4.8 km/3 mi W on Hilton*

BUSY BEAVER CAMPGROUND—Continued on next page
HILTON BEACH—Continued on next page

HILTON BEACH—Continued
BUSY BEAVER CAMPGROUND—Continued

Rd. ◇◇◇FACILITIES: 62 sites, most common site width 30 feet, 24 full hookups, 38 water & elec (15 & 30 amp receptacles), seasonal sites, 1 pull-thrus, tenting available, sewage disposal, laundry, public phone, limited grocery store, ice, tables, fire rings, wood. ◇◇◇RECREATION: lake swimming, boating, canoeing, ramp, dock, lake fishing, 2 shuffleboard courts, horseshoes, volleyball. Open mid May through mid Oct. Rate in 1995 $14 per family. Phone: (705) 246-2636.

## HONEY HARBOUR—G-3

GEORGIAN BAY ISLANDS NATIONAL PARK (Cedar Spring)—*Take water taxi or private boat to Beausoleil Island. Info available at mainland park office on Muskoka Rd #5 off Hwy 69.* FACILITIES: 85 sites, 85 no hookups, tenting available, handicap restroom facilities, public phone, tables. RECREATION: lake swimming, boating, dock, lake fishing, hiking trails. Recreation open to the public. Open all year. Facilities fully operational Spring through Fall. For tent camping only. No tent trailers or RVs. Phone: (705) 756-2415.

## HORNEPAYNE—B-3

NAGAGAMISIS PROVINCIAL PARK—*From town: Go 25 1/2 km/16 mi N on Hwy 631.* FACILITIES: 86 sites, 86 no hookups, tenting available, sewage disposal, tables, grills, wood. RECREATION: lake swimming, boating, canoeing, ramp, dock, lake fishing, hiking trails. Open mid May through late Sep. Phone: (807) 868-2254.

## HUNTSVILLE—G-3

ARROWHEAD PROVINCIAL PARK—*From town: Go 4 3/4 km/3 mi N on Hwy 11.* FACILITIES: 388 sites, 115 elec, 273 no hookups, tenting available, handicap restroom facilities, sewage disposal, tables, wood. RECREATION: swimming, boating, no motors, canoeing, ramp, fishing, hiking trails. Open mid May through mid Oct. Phone: (705) 789-5105.

**LAGOON TENT & TRAILER PARK**—CAMPGROUND with grassy sites beside Big East River. *From jct Hwy 60 & Hwy 11: Go 4 km/2 1/2 mi N on Hwy 11, then .8 km/1/2 mi E on Muskoka Rd 3.*

◇◇◇FACILITIES: 70 sites, 27 full hookups, 24 water & elec (15 amp receptacles), 19 no hookups, seasonal sites, 50 pull-thrus, phone hookups, tenting available, cabins, sewage disposal, laundry, public phone, grocery store, gasoline, ice, tables, fire rings, wood.

◇◇◇RECREATION: river swimming, boating, no motors, canoeing, 9 canoe boat rentals, river fishing, basketball hoop, playground, sports field, horseshoes, hiking trails, volleyball.

Open May 15 through Oct 15. Rate in 1995 $14-17 per family. Phone: (705) 789-5011.

**SEE AD THIS PAGE**

**Silver Sands Tent & Trailer Park**—Semi-wooded CAMPGROUND on Big East River. *From jct Hwy 60 & Hwy 11: Go 1.6 km/1 mi N on Hwy 11, then .4 km/1/4 mi W on Old North Rd.* ◇◇◇FACILITIES: 142 sites, most common site width 35 feet, 30 ft. max RV length, 8 full hookups, 113 water & elec (15 & 30 amp receptacles), 21 no hookups, seasonal sites, tenting available, sewage disposal, laundry, public phone, limited grocery store, ice, tables, fire rings, grills, wood. ◇◇◇◇RECREATION: rec room/area, swim pool, river swimming, boating, no motors, canoeing, dock, 1 row/16 canoe/1 motor boat rentals, river fishing, playground, shuffleboard court, planned group activities, recreation director, sports field, horseshoes, hiking trails, volleyball. Open May 15 through Oct 15. Rate in 1995 $16-18 per family. Member of OPCA. Phone: (705) 789-5383.

## IGNACE—D-2

**Agimac's Lakeview Cabins & RV Park**—RV SPACES in conjunction with cabins beside Lake Agimac. *From west town limits: Go 1.6 km/1 mi W on Hwy 17.* FACILITIES: 12 sites, most common site width 30 feet, 12 full hookups, (30 amp receptacles), tenting available, sewage disposal, laundry, public phone, ice, tables, fire rings, wood. RECREATION: lake swimming, boating, canoeing, ramp, dock, 2 pedal/10 motor boat rentals, lake fishing. Open mid May through mid Oct. Rate in 1995 $16 for 2 persons. Phone: (807) 934-2891.

**Cobblestone Lodge**—RV SPACES in conjuction with a tourist resort. *From jct Hwy 599 & Hwy 17: Go 28.8 km/18 mi W on Hwy 17, then .8 km/1/2 mi S on Raleigh Lake Rd.* FACILITIES: 10 sites, most common site width 20 feet, 6 full hookups, 4 water & elec (15 amp receptacles), tenting available, sewage disposal, limited grocery store, ice, tables, fire rings. RECREATION: rec room/area, lake swimming, boating, canoeing, ramp, dock, 15 motor boat rentals, lake fishing. Open mid May through Sep 30. Rate in 1995 $14-16 for 2 persons. Phone: (807) 934-2345.

**DAVY LAKE CAMPGROUND**—Open, level sites on Davy Lake in a park-like setting. *In town on Davy Lake Rd.*

◇◇◇FACILITIES: 50 sites, 29 full hookups, 15 water & elec (15 amp receptacles), 6 no hookups, 33 pull-thrus, a/c allowed ($), heater allowed ($), tenting available,

IGNACE—Continued
DAVY LAKE CAMPGROUND—Continued

group sites for tents/RVs, sewage disposal, laundry, public phone, limited grocery store, ice, tables, grills.

◇RECREATION: lake swimming, playground.

Open mid May through mid Oct. Rate in 1995 $12-16 for 2 persons. Phone: (807) 934-2817.

**SEE AD TRAVEL SECTION PAGES 975, 976 AND 977**

**Greenpines Campground & RV Park**—Level CAMPGROUND with open & shaded sites convenient to a major highway. *From east town limits: Go 17.7 km/11 mi E on Hwy 17.* ◇◇◇FACILITIES: 16 sites, 6 full hookups, 5 water & elec (15 amp receptacles), 5 no hookups, 7 pull-thrus, tenting available, sewage disposal, ice, tables, fire rings, wood. RECREATION: horseshoes. Open mid May through mid Oct. Rate in 1995 $12-15 per family. Phone: (807) 934-2945.

SANDBAR LAKE PROVINCIAL PARK—*From town: Go 1 1/2 km/1 mi E on Hwy 17, then 11 1/4 km/7 mi N on Hwy 599.* FACILITIES: 75 sites, 17 elec, 58 no hookups, tenting available, tables, wood. RECREATION: swimming, boating, canoeing, lake fishing, hiking trails. Open mid May through mid Sep. Phone: (807) 934-2233.

## INGLESIDE—G-6

**MCLAREN CAMPSITE (Parks of the St. Lawrence)**—*From east town limits: Go 3/4 km/1/2 mi E on Hwy 2, then 3/4 km/1/2 mi E on Long Sault Pkwy.*

FACILITIES: 205 sites, 14 water & elec, 51 elec (15 & 30 amp receptacles), 140 no hookups, tenting available, handicap restroom facilities, sewage disposal, public phone, tables, wood.

RECREATION: lake swimming, boating, canoeing, ramp, lake fishing, playground, planned group activities, badminton, sports field, horseshoes, hiking trails, volleyball.

Open May 19 through Sep 24. Phone: (613) 537-2708.

**SEE AD TRAVEL SECTION PAGE 974**

**MILLE ROCHES CAMPSITE (Parks of the St. Lawrence)**—*From east town limits: Go 3/4 km/1/2 mi E on Hwy 2, then 8 km/5 mi E on Long Sault Pkwy.*

FACILITIES: 244 sites, 46 elec (15 & 30 amp receptacles), 208 no hookups, tenting available, handicap restroom facilities, sewage disposal, public phone, ice, tables, wood.

RECREATION: lake swimming, boating, canoeing, ramp, canoe/pedal boat rentals, lake fishing, playground, planned group activities, badminton, sports field, horseshoes, hiking trails, volleyball.

Open May 19 through Sep 4. Phone: (613) 534-2129.

**SEE AD TRAVEL SECTION PAGE 974**

**UPPER CANADA MIGRATORY BIRD SANCTUARY CAMPSITE (Parks of the St. Lawrence)**—*From west town limits: Go 3 1/4 km/2 mi W on Hwy 2.*

FACILITIES: 50 sites, 30 elec (15 amp receptacles), 20 no hookups, tenting available, handicap restroom facilities, sewage disposal, public phone, tables, wood.

RECREATION: river swimming, boating, canoeing, river fishing, cross country skiing.

Open Jul 1 through Aug 25. No showers. Phone: (613) 537-2024.

**SEE AD TRAVEL SECTION PAGE 974**

**WOODLAND'S CAMPSITE (Parks of the St. Lawrence)**—*From east town limits: Go 3/4 km/1/2 mi E on Hwy 2, then 1 1/2 km/1 mi E on Long Sault Pkwy.*

FACILITIES: 210 sites, 45 elec (15 amp receptacles), 165 no hookups, tenting available, sewage disposal, public phone, ice, tables,wood.

RECREATION: lake swimming, boating, canoeing, ramp, canoe/pedal boat rentals, lake fishing, playground, planned group activities, badminton, sports field, horseshoes, hiking trails, volleyball.

Open May 19 through Aug 7. Phone: (613) 537-2616.

**SEE AD TRAVEL SECTION PAGE 974**

## IRON BRIDGE—F-1

**Delmar Campground**—CAMPGROUND on a major highway with shaded & grassy sites. *From east city limits: Go 6.4 km/4 mi W on Hwy 17.* ◇◇◇FACILITIES: 35 sites, most common site width 45 feet, 4 full hookups, 17 water & elec (15 amp receptacles), 14 no hookups, seasonal sites, 6 pull-thrus, tenting available, sewage disposal, laundry, public phone, limited grocery store, ice, tables, fire rings, wood. ◇◇◇RECREATION: rec hall, swim pool, mini-golf, badminton, horseshoes. Open Apr through Sep. Rate in 1995 $12.50-20 for 2 persons. Phone: (705) 843-2098.

IRON BRIDGE—Continued

**VIKING TENT & TRAILER PARK**—Level CAMPGROUND convenient to a major highway. *From east city limits: Go 2.4 km/1 1/2 mi W on Hwy 17.*

◇◇◇FACILITIES: 50 sites, most common site width 40 feet, 13 full hookups, 10 water & elec, 8 elec (15 & 30 amp receptacles), 19 no hookups, seasonal sites, a/c allowed ($), heater allowed ($), tenting available, group sites for tents, sewage disposal, laundry, public phone, limited grocery store, ice, tables, fire rings, grills, wood.

◇◇RECREATION: swim pool, sauna, sports field. Recreation open to the public.

Open May 1 through Oct 15. Rate in 1995 $8-13 per vehicle. Phone: (705) 843-2834.

**SEE AD THIS PAGE**

## IROQUOIS—G-6

IROQUOIS MUNICIPAL PARK—*From jct Hwy 401 & Hwy 2 (Carman Rd): Go 3/4 km/1/2 mi S on Hwy 2.* FACILITIES: 100 sites, 55 elec (20 amp receptacles), 45 no hookups, tenting available, tables, wood. RECREATION: pavilion, river swimming, boating, canoeing, ramp, dock, sail/canoe boat rentals, river fishing, playground, horseshoes, hiking trails. Open May 24 through Oct. Phone: (613) 652-2121.

## IROQUOIS FALLS—B-6

KETTLE LAKES PROVINCIAL PARK—*From town: Go 19 1/4 km/12 mi W on Hwy 67.* FACILITIES: 165 sites, 83 elec, 82 no hookups, tenting available, handicap restroom facilities, sewage disposal, laundry, tables, wood. RECREATION: swimming, boating, no motors, canoeing, fishing, playground, hiking trails. Open mid May through early Oct. Phone: (705) 363-3511.

## KAKABEKA FALLS—B-1

KAKABEKA FALLS PROVINCIAL PARK—*In town on Hwy 17.* FACILITIES: 166 sites, 50 elec, 116 no hookups, tenting available, handicap restroom facilities, sewage disposal, laundry, limited grocery store, tables, wood. RECREATION: swimming, fishing, playground, hiking trails. Open mid May through early Oct. Phone: (807) 473-9231.

## KAPUSKASING—B-5

RENE BRUNELLE PROVINCIAL PARK—*From town: Go 20 3/4 km/13 mi E on Hwy 11, then 9 1/2 km/6 mi N on Hwy 581.* FACILITIES: 90 sites, 60 elec, 30 no hookups, tenting available, handicap restroom facilities, sewage disposal, laundry, tables, wood. RECREATION: swimming, boating, canoeing, ramp, fishing, playground, hiking trails. Open mid May through late Sep. Phone: (705) 367-2692.

**Two Bridges Motel & Campground**—RV SPACES in conjunction with a motel. *From business centre: Go .4 km/1/4 mi W on Hwy 11.* FACILITIES: 25 sites, 20 full hookups, 5 elec (15 amp receptacles), public phone, ice, tables. RECREATION: mini-golf ($). No tents. Open all year. Facilities fully operational May 1 through Sep 30. Rate in 1995 $16 for 2 persons. Phone: (705) 335-2281.

## KATRINE—F-3

**Almaguin Parklands Campground**—Semi-wooded location by a lake. *From jct Hwy 11 & 3 Mile Lake Rd: Go .4 km/1/4 mi E on 3 Mile Lake Rd, then 2 km/1 1/4 mi S on gravel road.* ◇◇◇◇FACILITIES: 219 sites, most common site width 35 feet, 95 full hookups, 56 water & elec (15 & 30 amp receptacles), 68 no hookups, seasonal sites, 20 pull-thrus, tenting available, sew-

ALMAGUIN PARKLANDS CAMPGROUND—Continued on next page
KATRINE—Continued on next page

KATRINE—Continued
ALMAGUIN PARKLANDS CAMPGROUND—Continued

age disposal, laundry, public phone, limited grocery store, ice, tables, fire rings, grills, wood. ◆◆◆◆RECREATION: rec room/area, swim pool (heated), lake swimming, boating, no motors, canoeing, dock, 2 row/3 canoe boat rentals, lake fishing, mini-golf, playground, planned group activities (weekends only), badminton, sports field, horseshoes, hiking trails, volleyball. Open all year. Facilities fully operational May 15 through Oct 15. Rate in 1995 $16-20 per family. Phone: (705) 382-3802.

**Lillie Kup Kamp**—Grassy, riverside CAMPGROUND. Most sites occupied by seasonal campers. *From jct Hwy 11 & Doe Lake Rd: Go .4 km/1/4 mi W on Doe Lake Rd.* ◆◆FACILITIES: 85 sites, most common site width 30 feet, 85 water & elec (15 & 30 amp receptacles), seasonal sites, tenting available, sewage disposal, laundry, public phone, ice, tables, fire rings, wood. ◆◆◆RECREATION: rec hall, river swimming, boating, canoeing, ramp, dock, 6 row/4 canoe/motor boat rentals, river fishing, playground, badminton, sports field, horseshoes, volleyball. Open May 1 through Oct 31. Rate in 1995 $16 per family. Phone: (705) 382-3410. FCRV 10% discount.

**Old Mill Camp**—Riverside CAMPGROUND with grassy sites. *At jct Hwy 11 & 3 Mile Lake Rd.* ◆◆FACILITIES: 36 sites, most common site width 60 feet, 30 ft. max RV length, 27 full hookups, 9 water & elec (15 & 30 amp receptacles), seasonal sites, tenting available, sewage disposal, laundry, public phone, limited grocery store, LP gas refill by weight, ice, tables, fire rings, wood. ◆◆◆RECREATION: pavilion, river swimming, boating, canoeing, ramp, dock, 4 motor boat rentals, river fishing, playground, sports field, horseshoes, hiking trails. Open all year. Facilities fully operational May 1 through Oct 30. Rate in 1995 $12-18 per family. Phone: (705) 382-3346.

## KEARNEY—F-3

**Kel-Mac Family Camping Resort**—Secluded, lakeside CAMPGROUND. *From jct Hwy 11 & Hwy 518E: Go 6.4 km/4 mi E on Hwy 518, then follow signs for 4 km/2 1/2 mi.* ◆◆◆FACILITIES: 50 sites, most common site width 40 feet, 30 water & elec (15 amp receptacles), 20 no hookups, seasonal sites, tenting available, handicap restroom facilities, sewage disposal, ice, tables, fire rings, wood. ◆◆◆RECREATION: rec hall, lake swimming, boating, no motors, canoeing, 1 row/4 canoe/2 pedal boat rentals, lake fishing, playground, badminton, sports field, horseshoes, volleyball. Open mid May through mid Oct. Rate in 1995 $15.50-17.50 per family. Phone: (705) 636-7818.

**Sandhurst**—Wooded CAMPGROUND with a sandy beach. *From jct Hwy 11 & Hwy 518: Go 20 km/12 1/2 mi E on Hwy 518.* ◆◆FACILITIES: 150 sites, most common site width 50 feet, 120 full hookups, 30 water & elec (15 amp receptacles), seasonal sites, tenting available, sewage disposal, laundry, public phone, grocery store, LP gas refill by weight, ice, tables, fire rings, wood. ◆◆◆◆RECREATION: rec hall, rec room/area, lake swimming, boating, canoeing, ramp, dock, 6 canoe/2 pedal/4 motor boat rentals, lake/stream fishing, playground, planned group activities, recreation director, badminton, sports field, horseshoes, hiking trails, volleyball. Recreation open to the public. Open May 15 through Oct 15. Rate in 1995 $18.70 per family. Phone: (705) 636-7705.

**Silversands Family Resort**—Open and shaded sites in a CAMPGROUND. *From jct Hwy 11 & Hwy 518: Go 22.4 km/14 mi E on Hwy 518.* ◆◆FACILITIES: 25 sites, most common site width 50 feet, 25 full hookups, (15 amp receptacles), seasonal sites, tenting available, sewage disposal, laundry, public phone, limited grocery store, ice, tables, fire rings, grills, wood. ◆◆◆RECREATION: lake swimming, boating, canoeing, dock, 3 canoe/1 pedal/3 motor boat rentals, lake fishing, playground, planned group activities (weekends only), badminton, horseshoes, hiking trails, volleyball. Open all year. Facilities fully operational mid May through mid Oct. Rate in 1995 $12-15 per family. Phone: (705) 636-5380.

## KEENE—H-4

HOPE MILL (Otonabee Region Conservation Authority) —*From town: Go 3 1/4 km/2 mi N on CR 34.* FACILITIES: 65 sites, 20 elec (15 & 30 amp receptacles), 45 no hookups,

KEENE—Continued
HOPE MILL (OTONABEE REGION CONSERVATION AUTHORITY) —Continued

tenting available, non-flush toilets, tables, wood. RECREATION: river swimming, canoeing, 2 canoe boat rentals, river/pond fishing. Open Jul 1 through Sep 4. No showers. Phone: (705) 295-6250.

SERPENT MOUNDS PROVINCIAL PARK—*From town: Go 4 3/4 km/3 mi S on Serpent Mounds Rd.* FACILITIES: 113 sites, 113 no hookups, tenting available, handicap restroom facilities, sewage disposal, laundry, tables, wood. RECREATION: swimming, boating, canoeing, ramp, fishing, playground, hiking trails. Open mid May through early Sep. Phone: (705) 295-6879.

## KEMPTVILLE—G-6

RIDEAU RIVER PROVINCIAL PARK—*From town: Go 6 1/2 km/4 mi N on Hwy 16.* FACILITIES: 186 sites, 30 elec, 156 no hookups, tenting available, handicap restroom facilities, sewage disposal, limited grocery store, ice, tables, wood. RECREATION: swimming, boating, canoeing, ramp, river fishing, playground. Open early May through early Sep. Phone: (613) 258-2740.

**WILDWOOD CAMPGROUND**—CAMPGROUND with grassy, shaded & open sites. *From jct Hwy 43 & Hwy 16: Go 15.2 km/9 1/2 mi S on Hwy 16, then 1.2 km/3/4 mi E on Jochems Rd, then 91 m/100 yards N on CR 44.*

◆◆◆FACILITIES: 115 sites, most common site width 51 feet, 5 full hookups, 110 water & elec (15 & 30 amp receptacles), seasonal sites, 10 pull-thrus, a/c allowed ($), heater allowed ($), tenting available, group sites for RVs, sewage disposal, laundry, public phone, limited grocery store, ice, tables, fire rings, wood, traffic control gate.

◆◆◆◆RECREATION: rec hall, equipped pavilion, coin games, swim pool, playground, planned group activities (weekends only), badminton, sports field, horseshoes, hiking trails, volleyball.

Open May 15 through Oct 15. Rate in 1995 $17.66 per family. Visa accepted. Phone: (613) 258-2940.
**SEE AD OTTAWA PAGE 1010**

## KENORA—D-1

***See listings at Nestor Falls, Sioux Narrows & Vermilion Bay***

**KOA-Heritage Place**—CAMPGROUND beside major highway. *From jct Hwy 71 & Hwy 17: Go 2 1/4 mi W on Hwy 17.* ◆◆◆FACILITIES: 84 sites, most common site width 30 feet, 65 full hookups, 15 water & elec (15,30 & 50 amp receptacles), 4 no hookups, 14 pull-thrus, tenting available, sewage disposal, laundry, public phone, limited grocery store, ice, tables, fire rings, wood. ◆◆RECREATION: rec room/area, pavilion, pond swimming, sports field, volleyball. Open May 15 through Sep 30. Rate in 1995 $14-20 for 2 persons. Phone: (807) 548-4380. KOA 10% value card discount.

**Longbow Lake Camp & Trailer Park**—A CAMPGROUND on Longbow Lake with wooded sites. *From jct Hwy 71 & Hwy 17: Go 6 km/3 3/4 mi W on Hwy 17.* ◆◆◆◆FACILITIES: 61 sites, most common site width 30 feet, 47 full hookups, 14 water & elec (15 & 30 amp receptacles), seasonal sites, 34 pull-thrus, tenting available, sewage disposal, laundry, public phone, ice, tables, fire rings, wood. ◆◆◆RECREATION: lake swimming, boating, canoeing, ramp, dock, 3 motor boat rentals, lake fishing, playground, badminton. Open May 15 through Oct 1. Rate in 1995 $16.50-19.75 for 2 persons. Phone: (807) 548-5444.

**Redden's Trailer Park**—A semi-wooded CAMPGROUND on Longbow Lake. *From jct Hwy 71 & Hwy 17: Go 6 km/3 3/4 mi W on Hwy 17.* ◆◆◆FACILITIES: 25 sites, most common site width 25 feet, 23 full hookups, 2 water & elec (15 & 30 amp receptacles), seasonal sites, tenting available, laundry, public phone, grocery store, ice, tables, grills, wood. ◆◆◆RECREATION: lake swimming, boating, canoeing, ramp, dock, 1 canoe/2 pedal/25 motor boat rentals, lake fishing, horseshoes. Open May 1 through Oct 15. Rate in 1995 $17-18 per family. Phone: (807) 548-4066.

RUSHING RIVER PROVINCIAL PARK—*From town: Go 25 1/2 km/16 mi E on Hwy 17, then 6 1/2 km/4 mi S on Hwy 71.* FACILITIES: 191 sites, 38 elec, 153 no hookups, tenting available, handicap restroom facilities, sewage disposal, tables, wood. RECREATION: swimming, boating, canoeing, ramp, dock, fishing, playground, hiking trails. Open mid May through mid Sep. Phone: (807) 548-4351.

## KILLARNEY—F-2

KILLARNEY PROVINCIAL PARK—*From jct Hwy 69 & Hwy 637: Go 61 1/2 km/38 1/2 mi W on Hwy 637.* FACILITIES: 122 sites, 122 no hookups, 11 pull-thrus, tenting available, non-flush toilets, wood. RECREATION: lake swimming, boating, canoeing, fishing, hiking trails. Open mid May through mid Mar. No showers. Phone: (705) 287-2900.

## KINCARDINE—H-2

**AINTREE TRAILER PARK**—CAMPGROUND adjacent to Lake Huron with open & shaded sites. *From jct Hwy 9 & Hwy 21: Go 3.2 km/2 mi S on Hwy 21, then 2.4 km1 1/2 mi W on Huron Con 12.*

◆◆◆FACILITIES: 165 sites, most common site width 30 feet, 35 ft. max RV length, 160 full hookups, 5 water & elec (15 & 30 amp receptacles), seasonal sites, 6 pull-thrus, a/c allowed, heater allowed, tenting available, RV storage, sewage disposal, laundry, public phone, LP gas refill by weight, tables, patios, fire rings, wood.

◆◆◆RECREATION: rec hall, rec room/area, basketball hoop, playground, 2 shuffleboard courts, planned group activities (weekends only), badminton, sports field, horseshoes, volleyball.

Open mid Apr through mid Oct. Rate in 1995 $18-21 per family. Master Card/Visa accepted. Member of OPCA. Phone: (519) 396-8533.
**SEE AD TRAVEL SECTION PAGES 975, 976 AND 977**
BLUEWATER TRAILER PARK (City Park)—*From jct Hwy 9 & Hwy 21: Go 1/2 km/1/4 mi S on Hwy 21, then 1/2 km/1/4 mi W on Durham St.* FACILITIES: 50 sites, 32 ft. max RV length, 50 full hookups, seasonal sites, tenting available, sewage disposal, public phone, tables. RECREATION: lake swimming, boating, canoeing, ramp, dock, lake fishing, playground, sports field. Open May 15 through Oct 15. Phone: (519) 396-3468.

**FISHERMAN'S COVE TENT & TRAILER PARK**—CAMPGROUND on Otter Lake. *From jct Hwy 21 & Hwy 9: Go 18 km/11 1/4 mi E on Hwy 9, then 1.6 km/1 mi S on Bruce Rd 1.*

◆◆◆◆FACILITIES: 400 sites, most common site width 40 feet, 400 full hookups, (15 & 30 amp receptacles), seasonal sites, a/c allowed, heater allowed, tenting available, RV storage, sewage disposal, laundry, public phone, limited grocery store, RV supplies, LP gas refill by weight, ice, tables, fire rings, wood, traffic control gate.

◆◆◆◆RECREATION: rec hall, swim pool (indoor) (heated), lake swimming, whirlpool, boating, 10 hp limit, canoeing, dock, 1 row/3 canoe/4 pedal/5 motor boat rentals, water skiing, lake fishing, basketball hoop, playground, planned group activities, movies, recreation director, badminton, sports field, horseshoes, hiking trails, volleyball.

Open May 15 through Oct 1. Rate in 1995 $23 for 2 persons. No refunds. Master Card/Visa accepted. Member of OPCA. Phone: (519) 395-2757.
**SEE AD THIS PAGE**

**Green Acres Family Camp**—Level CAMPGROUND with open & shaded sites. *From jct Hwy 9 & Hwy 21: Go 3.2 km/2 mi S on Hwy 21, then .4 km/1/4 mi W on 12 Cone Rd.* ◆◆◆FACILITIES: 115 sites, most common site width 30 feet, 90 full hookups, (15 & 30 amp receptacles), 25 no hookups, seasonal sites, tenting available, sewage disposal, laundry, ice, tables, fire rings, wood. ◆◆◆RECREATION: rec hall, swim pool (heated), playground, 2 shuffleboard courts, planned group activities (weekends only), badminton, sports field, horseshoes, hiking trails. Open all year. Facilities fully operational May 1 through mid Oct. Rate in 1995 $20-22. Member of OPCA. Phone: (519) 395-2808.

✽ **RICK TRAILER SALES**—*From jct Hwy 21 & Hwy 9: Go 18 km/11 1/4 mi E on Hwy 9, then 1.6 km/1 mi S on Bruce Rd 1.* SALES: travel trailers, park models, truck campers, 5th wheels, motor homes, mini-motor homes, fold-down camping trailers. SERVICES: RV storage, sells parts/accessories, sells camping supplies. Open Apr 1 through Dec 1. Phone: (519) 395-2757.
**SEE AD THIS PAGE**

## KINGSTON—H-5

***See listings at Sydenham & Wolfe Island***

⚑ **FORT HENRY**—*At jct Hwy 2 & Hwy 15.* Restored British garrison, built in early 1800s, features the Fort Henry Guard recreating battle tactics drills with cannon & rifle fire. A living history attraction of everyday life with Queen Victoria's Army's stirring music. Open all year. American Express/Master Card/Visa accepted. Phone: (613) 543-3704.
**SEE AD TRAVEL SECTION PAGE 974**

**KOA-KINGSTON**—Rolling, grassy CAMPGROUND near major highway. *From jct Hwy 401 (exit 611) & Hwy 38: Go .8 km/1/2 mi N on Hwy 38, then .8 km/1/2 mi E on Cordukes Rd.*

◆◆◆FACILITIES: 112 sites, most common site width 40 feet, 76 water & elec (15 & 30 amp receptacles), 36 no hookups, seasonal sites, 40 pull-thrus, a/c allowed ($), heater allowed ($), tent-

KOA-KINGSTON—Continued on next page
KINGSTON—Continued on next page

KINGSTON—Continued
KOA-KINGSTON—Continued

ing available, group sites for tents/RVs, cabins, RV storage, sewage disposal, laundry, public phone, grocery store, ice, tables, fire rings, wood.

◆◆◆RECREATION: rec room/area, coin games, swim pool, basketball hoop, playground, planned group activities, movies, badminton, sports field, horseshoes, volleyball.

Open May 1 through Oct 15. Rate in 1995 $16-21 for 2 persons. Master Card/Visa accepted. Phone: (613) 546-6140. KOA 10% value card discount.

**SEE AD THIS PAGE AND AD FRONT OF BOOK PAGES 68 AND 69**

**LAKE ONTARIO PARK (City Park)**—*From town: Go 4.8 km/3 mi W on King St.*

WELCOME

FACILITIES: 250 sites, 6 full hookups, 112 water & elec (20 amp receptacles), 132 no hookups, tenting available, handicap restroom facilities, sewage disposal, public phone, ice, tables.

RECREATION: rec room/area, lake swimming, boating, ramp, dock, lake fishing, mini-golf, playground, hiking trails.

Open May 1 through Sep 30. Facilities fully operational May 15 through Sep 30. Phone: (613) 542-6574.

**SEE AD THIS PAGE**

**RIDEAU ACRES CAMPGROUND**—Grassy, lakeside CAMPGROUND near a major highway. *From jct Hwy 401 (exit 623) & Hwy 15: Go 1.6 km/1 mi N on Hwy 15, then .4 km/1/4 mi W on Cunningham Rd.*

WELCOME

◆◆◆FACILITIES: 341 sites, most common site width 40 feet, 122 full hookups, 194 water & elec (15 & 30 amp receptacles), 25 no hookups, seasonal sites, 52 pull-thrus, a/c allowed, heater allowed ($), phone hookups, tenting available, group sites for tents/RVs, RV storage, sewage disposal, laundry, public phone, grocery store, RV supplies, LP gas refill by weight/by meter, ice, tables, wood, church services, traffic control gate.

◆◆◆◆◆RECREATION: rec hall, rec room/area, coin games, swim pool (heated), lake swimming, boating, canoeing, ramp, dock, 9 row/3 canoe/4 pedal boat rentals, water skiing, lake fishing, mini-golf ($), playground, 3 shuffleboard courts, planned group activities, movies, recreation director, badminton, sports field, horseshoes, volleyball, local tours. Recreation open to the public.

Open May 1 through Nov 1. Pool open Jun 1 thru Sep 30 Rate in 1995 $17.50-23.40 per family. Master Card/Visa accepted. Member of OPCA. Phone: (613) 546-2711. FCRV 10% discount.

**SEE AD THIS PAGE**

## KIRKFIELD—G-3

VICTORIA COUNTY CENTENNIAL PARK—*From town: Go 8 km/5 mi W on Hwy 48, then 1 1/2 km/1 mi N.* FACILITIES: 170 sites, 98 water & elec, 72 no hookups, tenting available, handicap restroom facilities, laundry, public phone, limited grocery store, ice, tables, wood. RECREATION: pavilion, lake swimming, lake fishing, playground. Recreation open to the public. Open May 24 through Oct 15. Phone: (705) 438-3251.

## KIRKLAND LAKE—C-6

ESKER LAKES PROVINCIAL PARK—*From town: Go 20 3/4 km/13 mi NE on Provincial Rd.* FACILITIES: 100 sites, 63 elec, 37 no hookups, tenting available, handicap restroom facilities, sewage disposal, laundry, limited grocery store, ice, tables. RECREATION: lake swimming, boating, no motors, canoeing, ramp, fishing, playground, hiking trails. Open mid May through mid Sep. Phone: (705) 567-4849.

## KITCHENER—I-2

***See listings at Cambridge, Guelph & Waterloo***

**Bingemans Park**—CAMPGROUND is part of a large resort complex with wave pool, go-karts, roller skating, six water slides, batting cages, golf driving range & daily smorgasbord. *From jct Hwy 86 & Hwy 7: Go 3.2 km/2 mi E on Hwy 7, then .8 km/1/2 mi N on Bingeman Park Rd.* ◆◆◆◆FACILITIES: 473 sites, most common site width 35 feet, 117 full hookups, 284 water & elec (15 & 30 amp receptacles), 72 no hookups, seasonal sites, tenting available, sewage disposal, laundry, public phone, limited grocery store, ice, tables, wood.

◆◆◆◆◆RECREATION: rec hall, rec room/area, pavilion, 2 swim pools (heated), boating, no motors, canoeing, 4 canoe/4 pedal boat rentals, river fishing, mini-golf ($), playground, 2 shuffleboard courts, planned group activities, recreation director, sports field, horseshoes, hiking trails, volleyball. Recreation open to the public. Open all year. Facilities fully operational May 15 through Oct 31. Rate in 1995 $20-27 per family. Member of OPCA. Phone: (519) 744-1555.

**CAMPARK RESORTS**—*From jct Hwy 401 & Hwy 8: Go 80 km/50 mi S on Hwy 8, then 64 km/40 mi SE on QEW, then .4 km/1/4 mi W on Hwy 20 (Lundy's Lane).* **SEE PRIMARY LISTING AT NIAGARA FALLS AND AD NIAGARA FALLS PAGE 1004**

WELCOME

KITCHENER—Continued on next page

KITCHENER—Continued

**LAUREL CREEK (Grand River Conservation Authority)**—*From town: Go 8 km/5 mi N on Conestogo Pkwy, then 3 1/4 km/2 mi W on Northfield Dr.*

FACILITIES: 100 sites, 50 water & elec (15 & 30 amp receptacles), 50 no hookups, seasonal sites, tenting available, group sites for tents, sewage disposal, public phone, tables, wood, guard.

RECREATION: lake swimming, boating, no motors, canoeing, ramp, 30 canoe boat rentals, lake fishing, playground, sports field, hiking trails, cross country skiing. Recreation open to the public.

Open May 1 through Oct 15. Phone: (519) 885-0160.

**SEE AD TRAVEL SECTION PAGE 978**

## LAKEFIELD—H-4

LAKEFIELD PARK (City Park)—*From jct Hwy 7 & Hwy 28: Go 12 3/4 km/8 mi N on Hwy 28.* FACILITIES: 150 sites, 37 ft. max RV length, 48 full hookups, 82 water & elec (15 & 30 amp receptacles), 20 no hookups, seasonal sites, 40 pull-thrus, tenting available, handicap restroom facilities, sewage disposal, laundry, public phone, limited grocery store, ice, tables, wood. RECREATION: lake/river swimming, boating, canoeing, ramp, 2 canoe/2 pedal boat rentals, lake/river fishing, playground, 2 tennis courts, sports field, horseshoes, volleyball. Recreation open to the public. Open May through Oct. Phone: (705) 652-8610.

## LAKE ST. PETER—G-4

LAKE SAINT PETER PROVINCIAL PARK—*From town: Go 1 1/2 km/1 mi N on Hwy 127, then 1 1/2 km/1 mi E on North Rd.* FACILITIES: 62 sites, 62 no hookups, tenting available, sewage disposal, laundry, tables, wood. RECREATION: swimming, boating, canoeing, ramp, fishing, hiking trails. Open mid Jun through early Sep. Phone: (613) 338-5312.

## LANARK—G-5

**Mal's Camping**—Riverside CAMPGROUND with grassy, open & shaded sites. *At south edge of town on Hwy 511: Go 2.4 km/1 1/2 mi E on CR 15.* ◆◆◆FACILITIES: 145 sites, most common site width 35 feet, 120 water & elec (15 amp receptacles), 25 no hookups, seasonal sites, tenting available, sewage disposal, laundry, public phone, full service store, LP gas refill by weight, ice, tables, fire rings, wood. ◆◆◆RECREATION: river swimming, boating, 20 hp limit, canoeing, ramp, dock, 3 row/2 canoe boat rentals, river fishing, playground, badminton, horseshoes, hiking trails, volleyball. Open May 1 through Oct 1. Rate in 1995 $15-17 per family. Member of OPCA. Phone: (613) 259-5636.

## LANCASTER—G-6

**CURRY HILL PARK**—CAMPGROUND with most sites occupied by seasonals. *From jct Hwy 401 (exit 825) & Curry Hill Rd: Go 3.2 km/2 mi N on Curry Hill Rd (CR 23).*

◆◆FACILITIES: 80 sites, most common site width 50 feet, 60 full hookups, 10 water & elec (15 & 30 amp receptacles), 10 no hookups, seasonal sites, tenting available, group sites for tents, RV storage, sewage disposal, laundry, public phone, limited grocery store, ice, tables, fire rings, wood.

◆◆◆RECREATION: rec room/area, coin games, swim pool, basketball hoop, playground, badminton, horseshoes.

Open May 1 through Oct 31. Rate in 1995 $16-19.50 for 2 persons. Phone: (613) 347-2130. FCRV 10% discount.

**SEE AD TRAVEL SECTION PAGES 975, 976 AND 977**

**GLENGARRY PARK (Parks of the St. Lawrence)**—*From jct Hwy 401 (exit 814) & Hwy 2: Go 3 1/4 km/2 mi E on S service road.*

FACILITIES: 234 sites, 14 water & elec, 55 elec (15 & 30 amp receptacles), 165 no

LANCASTER—Continued
GLENGARRY PARK (PARKS OF THE ST. LAWRENCE)—Continued

hookups, tenting available, handicap restroom facilities, sewage disposal, public phone, tables, wood.

RECREATION: lake swimming, boating, canoeing, ramp, lake fishing, playground, planned group activities, badminton, sports field, horseshoes, hiking trails, volleyball.

Open May 19 through Sep 4. Phone: (613) 347-2595.

**SEE AD TRAVEL SECTION PAGE 974**

**LANCASTER PARK OUTDOOR RESORT**—CAMPGROUND on Lake St. Francis. Full hookup sites occupied by seasonal campers. *From jct Hwy 401 (exit 814) & Hwy 2: Go 3.2 km/2 mi E on S Service Rd.*

◆◆◆FACILITIES: 360 sites, most common site width 40 feet, 90 full hookups, 223 water & elec (15 amp receptacles), 47 no hookups, seasonal sites, 15 pull-thrus, a/c allowed ($), heater not allowed, tenting available, group sites for RVs, sewage disposal, laundry, public phone, limited grocery store, ice, tables, fire rings, wood, traffic control gate.

◆◆◆◆◆RECREATION: rec hall, rec room/area, coin games, lake swimming, boating, canoeing, ramp, dock, water skiing, lake fishing, playground, 2 shuffleboard courts, planned group activities, movies, recreation director, sports field, horseshoes, volleyball.

No pets. Open May 15 through Oct 15. Facilities fully operational Jun 25 through Sep 5. Rate in 1995 $19-21 for 4 persons. Phone: (613) 347-3452.

**SEE AD MONTREAL, PQ PAGE 1047**

## LANGTON—I-2

DEER CREEK AREA (Long Point Region Conservation Auth.)—*From town: Go 4 3/4 km/3 mi S on Hwy 59, then 1/2 km/1/4 mi W on Regional Rd 45.* FACILITIES: 35 sites, 35 no hookups, tenting available, non-flush toilets, sewage disposal, tables, wood. RECREATION: pavilion, lake swimming, boating, no motors, ramp, dock, lake fishing, volleyball. Recreation open to the public. Open Jun through Labour Day. No showers. Phone: (519) 428-4623.

## LAVIGNE—F-3

**Panorama Camp**—Open and shaded sites on the northwest shore of Lake Nipissing. *From jct Hwy 17 & Hwy 64: Go 11.2 km/7 mi S on Hwy 64, then 1.6 km/1 mi E on Avenue Du Lac Rd.* ◆◆◆FACILITIES: 60 sites, most common site width 40 feet, 35 full hookups, 17 water & elec (15 & 30 amp receptacles), 8 no hookups, seasonal sites, tenting available, sewage disposal, public phone, ice, tables, fire rings, wood. ◆◆◆RECREATION: lake swimming, boating, canoeing, dock, 2 canoe/1 pedal/4 motor boat rentals, lake fishing, sports field, horseshoes. Recreation open to the public. Open May 15 through Oct 15. Rate in 1995 $13-20 per family. Member of OPCA. Phone: (705) 594-2509.

## LEAMINGTON—J-1

**LEISURE LAKE CAMPGROUND**—Level, grassy, lakeside location. *From jct Hwys 3 & 77: Go 3.6 km/2 1/4 mi N on Hwy 77, then 3.6 km/2 1/4 mi W on Mersea Rd 5, then 90 m/100 yards N on Albuna Side Rd.*

◆◆◆FACILITIES: 495 sites, most common site width 35 feet, 365 full hookups, 80 water & elec (15 & 30 amp receptacles), 50 no hookups, seasonal sites, a/c allowed ($), tenting available, group sites for tents/RVs, RV rentals, RV storage, sewage disposal, laundry, public phone, grocery store, RV supplies, LP gas refill by weight/by meter, ice, tables, patios, fire rings, wood, traffic control gate/guard.

◆◆◆◆◆RECREATION: rec hall, coin games, lake swimming, boating, electric motors only, canoeing, 1 row/1 canoe/4 pedal boat rentals, lake fishing, mini-golf ($), basketball hoop, playground, planned group activities, movies, recreation director, 2 tennis courts, badminton, sports field, horseshoes, volleyball. Recreation open to the public.

Open Apr 1 through Oct 15. Facilities fully operational May 1 through Oct 15. Rate in 1995 $18-27 per family. American Express/Master Card/Visa accepted. Member of OPCA. Phone: (519) 326-1255.

**SEE AD WINDSOR PAGE 1025**

✱ **LEISURE LAKE TRAILER SALES**—*From jct Hwy 3 & Hwy 77: Go 3.6 km/2 1/4 mi N on Hwy 77, then 3.6 km/2 1/4 mi W on Mersea Rd 5, then 90 m/100 yards N on Albuna Side Rd.* SALES: park models. SERVICES: LP gas refill by weight/by meter, sewage disposal, RV rentals, sells parts/accessories. Open all year. Master Card/Visa accepted. Phone: (519) 326-1171.

**SEE AD WINDSOR PAGE 1025**

LEAMINGTON—Continued

⚑ **STURGEON WOODS TRAILER PARK & MARINA**—*From jct Hwys 3, 77 & 18: Go 2 km/1 1/4 mi S on Hwy 18, then 1.2 km/3/4 mi E on Seacliff Dr (CR 20), then 3.2 km/2 mi SE on Essex CR 33 to Point Pelee, then 180 m/200 yards E on a paved road.* Marina on the western basin of Lake Erie and Point Pelee Peninsula. Open Apr 15 through Oct 15. Phone: (519) 326-1156.

**SEE AD WINDSOR PAGE 1026**

**STURGEON WOODS TRAILER PARK & MARINA**—Level, grassy CAMPGROUND near Point Pelee. *From jct Hwys 3, 77 & 18: Go 2 km/1 1/4 mi S on Hwy 18, then 1.2 km/3/4 mi E on Seacliff Dr (CR 20), then 3.2 km/2 mi SE on (Essex CR 33) to Point Pelee, then 180 m/200 yards E on a paved road.*

◆◆◆FACILITIES: 395 sites, 200 full hookups, 160 water & elec (15 & 30 amp receptacles), 35 no hookups, seasonal sites, 20 pull-thrus, a/c allowed, heater not allowed, tenting available, group sites for tents/RVs, RV storage, sewage disposal, laundry, public phone, limited grocery store, LP gas refill by weight, ice, tables, fire rings, wood.

◆◆◆◆RECREATION: rec hall, pavilion, coin games, swim pool, lake swimming, boating, canoeing, ramp, dock, pedal boat rentals, water skiing, lake fishing, basketball hoop, playground, planned group activities, movies, recreation director, sports field, horseshoes, volleyball, local tours.

Open all year. Facilities fully operational Apr 15 through Oct 15. Rate in 1995 $19.50-21.50 per family. Member of OPCA. Phone: (519) 326-1156.

**SEE AD WINDSOR PAGE 1026**

## LIGHTHOUSE COVE—J-1

**THAMES RIVER TRAILER PARK**—CAMPGROUND with level sites on the Thames River. *From jct Hwy 401 (exit 48) & CR 35: Go 2.8 km/1 3/4 mi N on CR 35, then 3.6 km/2 1/4 mi E on Hwy 2, then 2.8 km/1 3/4 mi N on CR 37, then 2.8 km/1 3/4 mi E on CR 2, then 3.6 km/2 1/4 mi N on CR 39, then 1 block S at center of town. Follow camp signs.*

◆◆FACILITIES: 50 sites, most common site width 30 feet, 50 water & elec (15 & 30 amp receptacles), seasonal sites, a/c allowed ($), heater allowed ($), tenting available, sewage disposal, limited grocery store, ice, tables.

◆RECREATION: boating, dock, lake/river fishing.

Open May 1 through Oct 15. Rate in 1995 $15-25 per family. Member of OPCA. Phone: (519) 682-2482.

**SEE AD TRAVEL SECTION PAGES 975, 976 AND 977**

## LIMOGES—G-6

**Kittawa Camping**—Grassy CAMPGROUND near a major highway. Most sites occupied by seasonal campers. *From jct Hwy 417 (exit 79) & Limoges Rd: Go 1.2 km/3/4 mi N on Limoges Rd.* ◆◆◆◆FACILITIES: 256 sites, most common site width 40 feet, 225 full hookups, 6 water & elec (20 & 30 amp receptacles), 25 no hookups, seasonal sites, 11 pull-thrus, tenting available, sewage disposal, laundry, public phone, limited grocery store, ice, tables, fire rings, wood. ◆◆◆◆RECREATION: rec hall, rec room/area, swim pool (heated), lake swimming, boating, no motors, 6 canoe/7 pedal boat rentals, pond fishing, playground, planned group activities (weekends only), sports field, horseshoes, hiking trails. Recreation open to the public. Open all year. Facilities fully operational May 1 through Oct 15. Rate in 1995 $15.50-21.50 per family. Phone: (613) 443-3040.

## LINDSAY—H-4

**ALPINE RV RESORT - CAMPSITE**—Located on the Scugog River. Most sites occupied by seasonal campers. *From north jct Hwy 7 & Hwy 35: Go 4.8 km/3 mi N on Hwy 35, then 3.2 km/2 mi E on Kenrei Park Rd.*

◆◆◆◆FACILITIES: 122 sites, most common site width 50 feet, 102 full hookups, 20 water & elec (15 & 30 amp receptacles), seasonal sites, 11 pull-thrus, a/c allowed, heater allowed ($), phone hookups, tenting available, RV rentals, RV storage, handicap restroom facilities, sewage disposal, laundry, public phone, grocery store, ice, tables, fire rings, wood, traffic control gate.

◆◆◆◆◆RECREATION: rec hall, rec room/area, coin games, swim pool, boating, canoeing, ramp, dock, 2 canoe/1 pedal/3 motor boat rentals, water skiing, river fishing, basketball hoop, playground,

ALPINE RV RESORT - CAMPSITE—Continued on next page
LINDSAY—Continued on next page

LINDSAY—Continued
ALPINE RV RESORT - CAMPSITE—Continued

planned group activities, movies, recreation director, badminton, sports field, horseshoes, volleyball.

Open May 12 through Oct 15. Rate in 1995 $16-21 per family. Reservations recommended May through Sep. Master Card/Visa accepted. Member of OPCA. Phone: (705) 324-6447.
**SEE AD PAGE 1000**

**DOUBLE "M" RV PARK & CAMPGROUND**—CAMPGROUND on the Scugog River. *From south jct Hwy 35 & Hwy 7: Go 1.2 km/3/4 mi W on Hwy 7, then .4 km/1/4 mi S on Victoria Rd 4.*

WELCOME

◊◊◊◊FACILITIES: 191 sites, most common site width 40 feet, 170 full hookups, 21 water & elec (15 & 30 amp receptacles), seasonal sites, a/c allowed ($), heater not allowed, tenting available, group sites for tents/RVs, RV storage, sewage disposal, laundry, public phone, limited grocery store, RV supplies, LP gas refill by weight, ice, tables, fire rings, wood, traffic control gate.

◊◊◊◊RECREATION: rec hall, rec room/area, coin games, river swimming, boating, canoeing, ramp, dock, river fishing, basketball hoop, playground, planned group activities (weekends only), movies, sports field, horseshoes, volleyball.

Open May 15 through mid Oct. Rate in 1995 $20 per family. Member of OPCA. Phone: (705) 324-9317.
**SEE AD THIS PAGE**

**Riverwood Park**—Secluded grassy sites alongside a river. *From jct Hwy 7 & Hwy 35: Go .4 km/1/4 mi S on Hwy 35, then .8 km/1/2 mi W on Riverwood Rd.* ◊◊◊FACILITIES: 296 sites, most common site width 40 feet, 244 full hookups, 52 water & elec (15 & 30 amp receptacles), seasonal sites, tenting available, sewage disposal, laundry, public phone, limited grocery store, ice, tables, fire rings, wood. ◊◊◊RECREATION: rec hall, pavilion, river swimming, boating, canoeing, ramp, dock, 2 row boat rentals, river/stream fishing, playground, planned group activities, recreation director, sports field, horseshoes, hiking trails, volleyball. Open May 20 through Oct 15. Rate in 1995 $20 per family. Member of OPCA. Phone: (705) 324-1655.

**TROUT WATER FAMILY CAMPING**—*From jct Hwy 35 & Hwy 7: Go 24.8 km/15 1/2 mi W on Hwy 7.*

WELCOME

**SEE PRIMARY LISTING AT SUNDERLAND AND AD PAGE 1019**

## LION'S HEAD—G-2

LION'S HEAD BEACH PARK—*From jct Hwy 6 & CR 9A (Lions Head Rd at Ferndale): Go 4 km/2 1/2 mi E on CR 9A, then 1/2 km/1/4 mi N on Main St, then 1 block E on Webster St.* FACILITIES: 51 sites, 37 full hookups, 4 water & elec (15 amp receptacles), 10 no hookups, seasonal sites, tenting available, sewage disposal, public phone, tables, fire rings, wood. RECREATION: lake swimming, boating, canoeing, ramp, dock, lake fishing, playground, horseshoes, volleyball. Open May 15 through Thanksgiving. Phone: (519) 793-4090.

## LISTOWEL—H-2

GALBRAITH CONSERVATION AREA (Maitland Valley Conservation Authority)—*From jct Hwy 86 & Hwy 23: Go 6 km/3 3/4 mi S on Hwy 23, then 8 km/5 mi E on Concession Rd 5/6.* FACILITIES: 20 sites, 20 water & elec (15 amp receptacles), tenting available, non-flush toilets, sewage disposal, tables, fire rings, wood. RECREATION: pond swimming, canoeing, sports field, hiking trails. Open May 15 through Oct 15. No showers..

## LONDON—I-2

***See listings at Ailsa Craig, Granton, St. Marys, St. Thomas & Strathroy***

FANSHAWE CONSERVATION AREA (Upper Thames River Conservation Authority)—*From jct Hwy 401 & Hwy 100: Go N on Hwy 100, then W on Oxford St, then 2 km/1 1/4 mi N on Clarke Sideroad.* FACILITIES: 650 sites, 450 water & elec (15 & 30 amp receptacles), 200 no hookups, tenting available, handicap restroom facilities, sewage disposal, laundry, public phone, limited grocery store, ice, tables, fire rings, wood. RECREATION: pavilion, swim pool (heated), lake swimming, boating, no motors, canoeing, ramp, dock, row/15 pedal boat rentals, lake fishing, playground, planned group activities (weekends only), recreation director, sports field, horseshoes, hiking trails, volleyball. Recreation open to the public. Open May through Oct 10. Day use only for winter sports. Phone: (519) 451-2800.

**Elk will often try to outrun a storm**

LONDON—Continued

**KOA-LONDON/401**—Level, shaded grassy CAMPGROUND near major highway. *From jct Hwy 401 (exit 195) & Hwy 74: Go .4 km/1/4 mi E on Concession Rd 2.*

WELCOME

◊◊◊◊FACILITIES: 120 sites, most common site width 35 feet, 24 full hookups, 78 water & elec (15 & 30 amp receptacles), 18 no hookups, seasonal sites, 55 pull-thrus, a/c allowed ($), heater allowed ($), tenting available, cabins, sewage disposal, laundry, public phone, limited grocery store, RV supplies, LP gas refill by weight/by meter, ice, tables, fire rings, wood.

◊◊◊RECREATION: rec room/area, coin games, swim pool (indoor) (heated), whirlpool, mini-golf ($), playground, badminton, sports field, horseshoes, volleyball.

Open May 1 through Oct 19. Rate in 1995 $20-27 for 2 persons. Master Card/Visa accepted. Phone: (519) 644-0222. KOA 10% value card discount.
**SEE AD THIS PAGE AND AD FRONT OF BOOK PAGES 68 AND 69**

**Oriole Park Resort**—Family CAMPGROUND with sunny & shaded sites. *From jct Hwy 402 (exit 82 Mt. Brydges Komoka) & CR 14 (Commissioners Rd): Go 2.4 km/1 1/2 mi E on CR 14, then 1.2 km/3/4 mi N on Lobo-Caradoc Townline. (Caution: low bridge 3.7 m/12 feet max clearance).* ◊◊◊FACILITIES: 210 sites, most common site width 35 feet, 180 full hookups, (15 & 30 amp receptacles), 30 no hookups, seasonal sites, tenting available, handicap restroom facilities, sewage disposal, public phone, limited grocery store, LP gas refill by weight, ice, tables, fire rings, wood. ◊◊◊◊RECREATION: rec hall, rec room/area, swim pool, playground, planned group activities, recreation director, sports field, horseshoes, hiking trails, volleyball. Recreation open to the public. Open all year. Facilities fully operational May 1 through mid Oct. Winter camping available. Rate in 1995 $17-23 per family. Member of OPCA. Phone: (519) 471-2720.

## LONGLAC—A-3

**SKY-VIEW TRAILER PARK**—Semi-wooded CAMPGROUND on Phipps Lake. *From business center: Go 10 km/6 1/4 mi E on Hwy 11.*

WELCOME

◊◊◊◊FACILITIES: 31 sites, most common site width 35 feet, 23 full hookups, 7 water & elec (15 & 30 amp receptacles), 1 no hookups, seasonal sites, 6 pull-thrus, tenting available, group sites for tents, cabins, RV storage, laundry, public phone, limited grocery store, gasoline, marine gas, ice, tables, fire rings, wood.

◊◊◊RECREATION: swim pool (heated), lake swimming, boating, canoeing, ramp, 1 pedal/2 motor boat rentals, water skiing, lake fishing, playground, horseshoes, volleyball.

Open May 1 through mid Oct. Rate in 1995 $15-17 per family. Visa accepted. Phone: (807) 876-2755.
**SEE AD TRAVEL SECTION PAGES 975, 976 AND 977**

## L'ORIGNAL—F-6

L'ORIGNAL PARK (City Park)—*From town: Go 1 1/2 km/1 mi N of Hwy 17 on St John St.* FACILITIES: 48 sites, 30 full hookups, 18 water & elec, tenting available, sewage disposal, laundry, grocery store, ice, tables, wood. RECREATION: river swimming, boating, ramp, fishing, playground. Open May 15 through Sep 15. Phone: (613) 675-4524.

## LYNDHURST—G-5

CHARLESTON LAKE PROVINCIAL PARK—*From town: Go 11 1/4 km/7 mi S on CR 3 (outlet).* FACILITIES: 236 sites, 26 elec, 210 no hookups, tenting available, handicap restroom facilities, sewage disposal, laundry, tables, wood. RECREATION: lake swimming, boating, canoeing, ramp, lake fishing, playground, hiking trails. Open mid Jun through early Oct. Phone: (613) 659-2065.

**Wilson's Tent & Trailer Camp**—CAMPGROUND at edge of town on Lyndhurst Lake. *From jct Hwy 15 & CR 33: Go 10 km/6 1/4 mi E on CR 33.* ◊◊◊FACILITIES: 170 sites, most common site width 40 feet, 130 water & elec (15 amp receptacles), 40 no hookups, seasonal sites, tenting available, sewage disposal, laundry, public phone, ice, tables, fire rings, wood. ◊◊◊RECREATION: rec room/area, lake swimming, boating, canoeing, ramp, dock, 5 row/1 canoe boat rentals, lake fishing, playground, horseshoes. Open May 15 through Oct 15. Rate in 1995 $13-15 per vehicle. Phone: (613) 928-2557.

LYNDHURST—Continued
WILSON'S TENT & TRAILER CAMP—Continued

## MABERLY—G-5

**McGowan Lake Campground**—A lakeside setting. *From east town limits: Go 3.2 km/2 mi E on Hwy 7.* ◊◊◊FACILITIES: 218 sites, most common site width 25 feet, 30 ft. max RV length, 196 water & elec (15 amp receptacles), 22 no hookups, seasonal sites, 8 pull-thrus, tenting available, sewage disposal, laundry, public phone, grocery store, LP gas refill by weight, ice, tables, fire rings, wood. ◊◊◊RECREATION: rec room/area, lake swimming, boating, 10 hp limit, canoeing, ramp, dock, 3 row/1 canoe/1 pedal boat rentals, lake fishing, playground, planned group activities (weekends only), sports field, horseshoes, hiking trails, volleyball. Recreation open to the public. Open May 1 through Oct 15. Rate in 1995 $14-18 per family. Member of OPCA. Phone: (613) 268-2234.

SILVER LAKE PROVINCIAL PARK—*In town on Hwy 7.* FACILITIES: 148 sites, 148 no hookups, tenting available, handicap restroom facilities, sewage disposal, tables, wood. RECREATION: swimming, boating, canoeing, ramp, lake fishing, playground. Open mid May through early Sep. Phone: (613) 268-2000.

## MACKEY—F-4

**Camelot Tent & Trailer Park**—Lakeside CAMPGROUND with open and shaded sites. *From west city limits: Go 1.6 km/1 mi W on Hwy 17, then 1.6 km/1 mi S on a gravel road.* ◊◊FACILITIES: 87 sites, most common site width 35 feet, 77 water & elec (15 & 30 amp receptacles), 10 no hookups, seasonal sites, tenting available, sewage disposal, laundry, limited grocery store, ice, tables, fire rings, wood. ◊◊◊RECREATION: pavilion, lake swimming, boating, canoeing, ramp, dock, lake fishing, planned group activities (weekends only), horseshoes. Open all year. Facilities fully operational mid May through mid Oct. Rate in 1995 $15 per vehicle. Phone: (613) 586-2342.

## MADAWASKA—F-4

**All Star Resort Tent & Trailer Park**—Level, open & shaded sites along the Madawaska River. *From jct Hwy 523 & Hwy 60: Go .4 km/1/4 mi N on Major Lake Rd.* ◊◊◊FACILITIES: 72 sites, most common site width 60 feet, 57 water & elec (15 amp receptacles), 15 no hook-

ALL STAR RESORT TENT & TRAILER PARK—Continued on next page
MADAWASKA—Continued on next page





**There are more than a 100 species of birds in North America.**

MADAWASKA—Continued
ALL STAR RESORT TENT & TRAILER PARK—Continued

ups, seasonal sites, 10 pull-thrus, tenting available, sewage disposal, tables, fire rings, wood. ◆◆◆RECREATION: lake swimming, boating, canoeing, ramp, dock, 2 row/2 canoe/1 pedal/2 motor boat rentals, lake fishing, horseshoes, hiking trails. Open all year. Facilities fully operational mid May through mid Oct. Rate in 1995 $18 per family. Phone: (613) 637-5592.

**Riverland Camp and Outfitters**—Grassy, level, riverside CAMPGROUND with open & shaded sites. *At jct Hwy 60 & Hwy 523.* ◆◆◆FACILITIES: 175 sites, most common site width 40 feet, 140 water & elec (15 amp receptacles), 35 no hookups, seasonal sites, 25 pull-thrus, tenting available, sewage disposal, laundry, public phone, limited grocery store, LP gas refill by weight, ice, tables, fire rings, grills, wood. ◆◆◆RECREATION: rec room/area, river swimming, boating, canoeing, ramp, dock, 6 row/20 canoe/4 motor boat rentals, river fishing, playground, horseshoes, hiking trails. Open all year. Facilities fully operational May 1 through mid Oct. Rate in 1995 $18.50-19 per family. Member of OPCA. Phone: (613) 637-5338.

## MALLORYTOWN—G-6

**KOA-Thousand Islands**—Grassy CAMPGROUND near a major highway. *From jct Hwy 401 (exit 675) & Mallorytown Rd: Go .8 km/1/2 mi N on Mallorytown Rd, then .8 km/1/2 mi W on Hwy 2.* ◆◆◆FACILITIES: 200 sites, most common site width 35 feet, 24 full hookups, 126 water & elec (15,30 & 50 amp receptacles), 50 no hookups, seasonal sites, 24 pull-thrus, tenting available, sewage disposal, laundry, public phone, grocery store, ice, tables, fire rings, wood. ◆◆◆◆RECREATION: rec room/area, swim pool (heated), mini-golf ($), playground, planned group activities (weekends only), sports field, horseshoes, volleyball. Open May 1 through Oct 15. Rate in 1995 $16-23 for 2 persons. Phone: (613) 923-5339. KOA 10% value card discount.

ST. LAWRENCE ISLANDS NATIONAL PARK (Mallorytown Landing)—*From Hwy 401 (exit 675): Go S on Leeds CR 5. At jct CR 5 & 1000 Islands Pkwy.* FACILITIES: 50 sites, 50 no hookups, tenting available, handicap restroom facilities, public phone, tables, grills, wood. RECREATION: river swimming, boating, canoeing, ramp, dock, river fishing, playground, hiking trails. Recreation open to the public. Open mid May through mid Oct. No showers. Phone: (613) 923-5261.

## MANITOULIN ISLAND—F-1

***See listings at Manitowaning, Mindemoya, Providence Bay, Sheguiandah, South Baymouth & Spring Bay***

## MANITOWANING—F-2

**Black Rock Resort**—Rustic, level sites overlooking South Bay. *9.6 km/6 mi S on Hwy 6, then 1.6 km/1 mi W on Black Rock Rd.* ◆◆FACILITIES: 20 sites, most common site width 20 feet, 32 ft. max RV length, 12 water & elec (15 amp receptacles), 8 no hookups, seasonal sites, tenting available, sewage disposal, laundry, limited grocery store, ice, tables, fire rings, wood. ◆◆◆RECREATION: rec room/area, lake swimming, boating, canoeing, ramp, dock, 1 canoe/6 motor boat rentals, lake fishing, horseshoes. No pets. Open all year. Facilities fully operational mid May through mid Oct. Rate in 1995 $15-25 per family. Phone: (705) 859-3262.

**Camp Bragmore**—Lakeside CAMPGROUND with shady sites. *From jct Hwy 6 & Bidwell Rd (north of town): Go 8 km/5 mi W on Bidwell Rd.* ◆◆FACILITIES: 46 sites, most common site width 30 feet, 26 water & elec (15 & 30 amp receptacles), 20 no hookups, seasonal sites, 3 pull-thrus, tenting available, portable dump, laundry, limited grocery store, ice, tables, fire rings, grills, wood. ◆◆◆RECREATION: rec room/area, lake swimming, boating, canoeing, ramp, dock, 1 canoe/1 pedal/7 motor boat rentals, lake fishing, badminton, horseshoes, hiking trails, volleyball. Recreation open to the public. Open May 1 through mid Oct. Rate in 1995 $12.50-15 for 4 persons. Phone: (705) 859-3488.

**HOLIDAY HAVEN TRAILER PARK & RESORT**—A semi-wooded, lakeside CAMPGROUND. *From jct Hwy 6 & Bidwell Rd (north of town): Go .8 km/1/2 mi W on Bidwell Rd, then .8 km/1/2 mi W on Lake Manitou Rd.*

WELCOME

◆◆◆FACILITIES: 110 sites, most common site width 40 feet, 90 water & elec (15 & 30 amp receptacles), 20 no hookups, seasonal sites, a/c allowed, heater not allowed, tenting available, cabins, RV storage, sewage disposal, laundry, limited grocery store, marine gas, ice, tables, fire rings, grills, wood, traffic control gate.

◆◆◆RECREATION: lake swimming, boating, canoeing, ramp, dock, 2 canoe/2 pedal/10 motor boat rentals, water skiing, lake fishing, fishing guides, playground, shuffleboard court, planned group activities (weekends only), horseshoes, volleyball.

Open mid May through Oct 1. Rate in 1995 $16-19 for 4 persons. Master Card/Visa accepted. Member of OPCA. Phone: (705) 859-3550.



SEE AD TRAVEL SECTION PAGES 975, 976 AND 977

## MARATHON—B-3

NEYS PROVINCIAL PARK—*From town: Go 30 1/2 km/19 mi W on Hwy 17.* FACILITIES: 144 sites, 27 elec, 117 no hookups, tenting available, handicap restroom facilities, sewage disposal, laundry, tables, wood. RECREATION: swimming, boating, canoeing, ramp, fishing, hiking trails. Open mid May through mid Sep. Phone: (807) 229-1624.

## MARMORA—H-4

BOOSTER PARK (City Park)—*From town: Go 2 1/2 km/1 1/2 mi W on Hwy 7, then 1 1/2 km/1 mi N on Crowe Lake Rd.* FACILITIES: 60 sites, 30 full hookups, 10 water & elec (15 amp receptacles), 20 no hookups, seasonal sites, 6 pull-thrus, tenting available, non-flush/marine toilets, sewage disposal, public phone, limited grocery store, ice, tables, fire rings, wood. RECREATION: lake swimming, boating, canoeing, ramp, dock, lake fishing, playground, horseshoes, hiking trails. Open Victoria Day through Thanksgiving. Phone: (613) 472-3127.

**Glen Allan Park**—CAMPGROUND on Crowe Lake. *From jct Hwy 7 & Hwy 14: Go 1 block N on McGill St, then 4.8 km/3 mi W & N on CR 3, then 2 km/1 1/4 mi W on Glen Allan Rd.* ◆◆◆FACILITIES: 235 sites, most common site width 30 feet, 110 full hookups, 115 water & elec (15 & 30 amp receptacles), 10 no hookups, seasonal sites, 6 pull-thrus, tenting available, sewage disposal, laundry, public phone, limited grocery store, LP gas refill by weight, ice, tables, fire rings, wood. ◆◆◆◆RECREATION: rec hall, rec room/area, lake swimming, boating, canoeing, ramp, dock, 5 row/2 canoe/1 pedal/2 motor boat rentals, lake fishing, playground, 2 shuffleboard courts, planned group activities, recreation director, badminton, horseshoes, hiking trails, volleyball. Open May 10 through Oct 15. Rate in 1995 $19-23 per family. Member of OPCA. Phone: (613) 472-2415.

**KOA-Marmora**—Secluded, grassy CAMPGROUND near a major highway with most serviced sites occupied by seasonal campers. *From business center: Go 3.2 km/2 mi E on Hwy 7, then .8 km/1/2 mi S on KOA Campground Rd.* ◆◆◆FACILITIES: 125 sites, most common site width 40 feet, 120 water & elec (15 & 30 amp receptacles), 5 no hookups, seasonal sites, 10 pull-thrus, tenting available, sewage disposal, laundry, public phone, limited grocery store, ice, tables, fire rings, wood. ◆◆◆RECREATION: rec hall, rec room/area, swim pool (indoor) (heated), no motors, canoeing, dock, 2 canoe boat rentals, mini-golf ($), playground, planned group activities (weekends only), horseshoes, hiking trails, volleyball. Recreation open to the public. Open May 1 through Oct 15. Rate in 1995 $16-19 for 2 persons. Member of OPCA. Phone: (613) 472-2233. KOA 10% value card discount. FCRV 10% discount.

## MARTEN RIVER—D-6

MARTEN RIVER PROVINCIAL PARK—*From town: Go on Hwy 11.* FACILITIES: 190 sites, 190 no hookups, tenting available, handicap restroom facilities, sewage disposal, public phone, limited grocery store, ice, tables, wood. RECREATION: lake swimming, boating, canoeing, ramp, dock, fishing, playground, hiking trails. Open mid May through late Sep. No showers. Phone: (705) 892-2200.

## MATTAWA—F-4

SAMUEL DE CHAMPLAIN PROVINCIAL PARK—*From town: Go 14 1/2 km/9 mi W on Hwy 17.* FACILITIES: 215 sites, 215 no hookups, tenting available, sewage disposal, laundry, tables, grills, wood. RECREATION: swimming, boating, canoeing, ramp, fishing, playground, hiking trails. Open mid May through late Sep. No showers. Phone: (705) 744-2276.

**Sid Turcotte Park**—A riverside CAMPGROUND. *From business center: Go 1.6 km/1 mi W on Hwy 17, then .4 km/1/4 mi N on Turcotte Pk Rd.* ◆◆◆FACILITIES: 310 sites, most common site width 20 feet, 135 full hookups, 140 water & elec (15 & 30 amp receptacles), 35 no hookups, seasonal sites, 40 pull-thrus, tenting available, sewage disposal, laundry, public phone, limited grocery store, LP gas refill by weight, ice, tables, fire rings, wood. ◆◆◆RECREATION: rec hall, river swimming, boating, canoeing, ramp, dock, 6 row/4 canoe boat rentals, river fishing, playground, horseshoes, volleyball. Open all year. Facilities fully operational May 15 through Oct 15. Rate in 1995 $15.75-19.50 for 4 persons. Phone: (705) 744-5375.

## MATTICE—A-4

**Missinaibi Outfitters**—Level CAMPGROUND with lakeside sites in conjunction with an outfitter with complete services. *From west town limits: Go .4 km/1/4 mi W on Hwy 11, then 2.4 km/1 1/2 mi N on Shallow Lake Rd.* ◆◆FACILITIES: 40 sites, most common site width 30 feet, 40 full hookups, (15 & 20 amp receptacles), seasonal sites, tenting available, laundry, limited grocery store, ice, tables, fire rings, wood. ◆◆◆RECREATION: lake swimming, boating, canoeing, ramp, 17 canoe/1 pedal/7 motor boat rentals, lake fishing, horseshoes. Open all year. Facilities fully operational mid May through mid Sep. Rate in 1995 $13.50 for 4 persons. Phone: (705) 364-7312.

## MCDONALD'S CORNERS—G-5

**PAUL'S CREEK CAMPSITE**—CAMPGROUND on a wooded hillside. *From town: Go 5.6 km/3 1/2 mi W on CR 12.*

WELCOME

◆◆◆FACILITIES: 62 sites, most common site width 35 feet, 62 water & elec (15 amp receptacles), seasonal sites, a/c allowed ($), heater allowed ($), tenting available, group sites for tents, sewage disposal, laundry, limited grocery store, ice, tables, fire rings, wood.

◆◆◆RECREATION: rec room/area, swim pool (heated), stream fishing, basketball hoop, playground, movies, badminton, horseshoes, hiking trails, volleyball. Recreation open to the public.

Open May 1 through Oct 15. Rate in 1995 $5-6 for 1 persons. Member of OPCA. Phone: (613) 278-2770.

SEE AD TRAVEL SECTION PAGES 975, 976 AND 977

## MCGREGOR—J-1

**Wildwood Golf & RV Resort**—Level, open sites in a manicured park on an 18-hole executive par 3 golf course. *From jct Hwy 401 (exit 14) & CR 46: Go 153 m/500 feet W on CR 46, then 8 km/5 mi S on Walker Rd (CR 11), then 1.6 km/1 mi E on Con 11 (McGregor).* ◆◆◆◆FACILITIES: 301 sites, most common site width 35 feet, 301 full hookups, (30 amp receptacles), seasonal sites, 83 pull-thrus, tenting available, handicap restroom facilities, laundry, public phone, LP gas refill by weight/by meter, ice, tables, patios, fire rings, wood. ◆◆◆◆RECREATION: rec hall, 2 swim pools (heated), playground, planned group activities, tennis court, badminton, sports field, horseshoes, volleyball. Open May 1 through Oct 31. Rate in 1995 $23.50 for 2 persons. Member of OPCA. Phone: (519) 726-6176.

## MEAFORD—G-2

MEAFORD MEMORIAL PARK (City Park)—*From jct Hwy 26 (Sykes) & Edwin St: Go 2 km/1 1/4 mi E on Edwin, continuing on Aiken & Grant.* FACILITIES: 140 sites, 30 full hookups, 110 water & elec (15 & 30 amp receptacles), 24 pull-thrus, tenting available, handicap restroom facilities, sewage disposal, laundry, public phone, limited grocery store, ice, tables, patios, fire rings, wood. RECREATION: pavilion, lake swimming, boating, canoeing, lake/river fishing, mini-golf ($), playground, 2 shuffleboard courts, horseshoes, hiking trails. Recreation open to the public. Open May through Oct. Phone: (519) 538-2530.

## MIDLAND—G-3

**BAYFORT CAMP**—Grassy, level, lakeside CAMPGROUND. *From east town limits: Go 1.6 km/1 mi E on Hwy 12, then 2.4 km/1 1/2 mi N on Ogdens Beach Rd.*

WELCOME

◆◆◆FACILITIES: 150 sites, most common site width 40 feet, 120 water & elec (15 amp receptacles), 30 no hookups, seasonal sites, a/c allowed, tenting available, cabins, sewage disposal, public phone, limited grocery store, ice, tables, fire rings, wood.

◆◆◆RECREATION: rec hall, coin games, lake swimming, boating, canoeing, lake fishing, mini-golf ($), basketball hoop, playground, planned group activities (weekends only), horseshoes, volleyball.

Open mid May through mid Oct. Rate in 1995 $14-17 per family. Member of OPCA. Phone: (705) 526-8704.

SEE AD TRAVEL SECTION PAGES 975, 976 AND 977

▶ **HURONIA HISTORICAL PARKS**—*East of town on Hwy 12.* Administator of 2 of the largest historical attractions in Midland Saint Marie Among The Hurons (1639-1649) & Discovery Harbour (1817-1856). Phone: (705) 526-7838.

WELCOME

SEE AD TRAVEL SECTION PAGE 980

**SMITH'S CAMP**—CAMPGROUND in Mobile Home Park with open & shaded areas. *From jct Hwy 93 & Hwy 12: Go 3.2 km/2 mi E on Hwy 12, then .8 km/1/2 mi N on King St.*

WELCOME

◆◆◆FACILITIES: 150 sites, most common site width 40 feet, 100 full hookups, 20 water & elec (15 & 30 amp receptacles), 30 no hookups, seasonal sites, a/c allowed, heater allowed, tenting

SMITH'S CAMP—Continued on next page
MIDLAND—Continued on next page

MIDLAND—Continued
SMITH'S CAMP—Continued

available, RV storage, sewage disposal, public phone, grocery store, ice, tables, fire rings, grills, wood.

◆◆RECREATION: rec room/area, coin games, lake swimming, boating, 10 hp limit, canoeing, ramp, dock, lake fishing, basketball hoop, playground, 2 shuffleboard courts, sports field, horseshoes, volleyball.

Open mid May through mid Oct. Rate in 1995 $15 per family. Reservations recommended Jul through Aug. Member of OPCA. Phone: (705) 526-4339.

**SEE AD PAGE 1002**

## MILFORD—H-5

**Smugglers Cove Campground**—Lakeside CAMPGROUND with grassy sites. *From town at jct CR 10 & CR 9: Go 9.6 km/6 mi S on CR 9.* ◆◆◆FACILITIES: 104 sites, most common site width 45 feet, 12 full hookups, 50 water & elec (15 & 30 amp receptacles), 42 no hookups, seasonal sites, tenting available, sewage disposal, laundry, limited grocery store, ice, tables, fire rings, wood. ◆◆◆RECREATION: lake swimming, boating, canoeing, ramp, dock, 2 motor boat rentals, lake fishing, playground, badminton, horseshoes, volleyball. Open May 15 through Oct 15. Rate in 1995 $13-16. Phone: (613) 476-4125. FCRV 10% discount.

## MILLER LAKE—G-2

**SUMMER HOUSE PARK**—Semi-wooded, Lakeside CAMPGROUND with open & shaded sites. *From jct Hwy 6 & Miller Lake Rd: Go 3.2 km/2 mi E on Miller Lake Rd.*

◆◆◆FACILITIES: 201 sites, most common site width 30 feet, 56 full hookups, 115 water & elec (15 & 30 amp receptacles), 30 no hookups, seasonal sites, 12 pull-thrus, a/c allowed, heater allowed ($), tenting available, group sites for tents/RVs, RV rentals, cabins, RV storage, sewage disposal, laundry, public phone, grocery store, RV supplies, LP gas refill by weight, gasoline, ice, tables, fire rings, grills, wood, traffic control gate.

◆◆◆◆RECREATION: rec hall, rec room/area, coin games, lake swimming, boating, canoeing, ramp, dock, 9 row/1 sail/6 canoe/4 pedal/7 motor boat rentals, water skiing, lake fishing, basketball hoop, 6 bike rentals, playground, 2 shuffleboard courts, planned group activities, movies, recreation director, 2 tennis courts, badminton, horseshoes, hiking trails, volleyball.

Open May 1 through Oct 12. Rate in 1995 $19.50-23.50 for 2 persons. No refunds. Master Card/Visa accepted. Member of OPCA. Phone: (519) 795-7712.

**SEE AD TRAVEL SECTION PAGES 975, 976 AND 977**

## MILTON—I-3

**MILTON HEIGHTS CAMPGROUND**—Open and shaded grassy sites. *From jct Hwy 401 (exit 320) & Hwy 25: Go 1.6 km/1 mi N on Hwy 25, then 2.4 km/1 1/2 mi W on Campbellville Rd, then 90 m/100 yards S on Townline Rd 22.*

◆◆◆◆FACILITIES: 450 sites, most common site width 40 feet, 110 full hookups, 90 water & elec (15 & 30 amp receptacles), 250 no hookups, seasonal sites, 24 pull-thrus, a/c allowed ($), heater allowed ($), phone hookups, tenting available, group sites for tents/RVs, RV storage, sewage disposal, laundry, public phone, grocery store, RV supplies, LP gas refill by weight/by meter, ice, tables, fire rings, wood, traffic control gate.

◆◆◆◆RECREATION: rec hall, rec room/area, equipped pavilion, coin games, swim pool (heated), basketball hoop, playground, planned group activities, badminton, sports field, horseshoes, volleyball.

Open all year. Rate in 1995 $18-22 for 2 persons. Master Card/Visa accepted. Member of OPCA. Phone: (905) 878-6781

**SEE AD FRONT OF BOOK PAGE 138 AND AD TORONTO PAGE 1022**

## MINDEMOYA—F-1

**Mindemoya Court Cottages & Campground**—Shaded, level campsites overlooking Lake Mindemoya. *From town at jct CR 542 & CR 551: Go 1.2 km/3/4 mi N, then 1.6 km/1 mi W on Ketchankookum Trail.* ◆◆◆FACILITIES: 15 sites, most common site width 25 feet, 15 full hookups, (15 amp receptacles), seasonal sites, tenting available, laundry, limited grocery store, ice, tables, fire rings, grills, wood. ◆◆◆RECREATION: lake swimming, boating, canoeing, dock, 2 row/7 motor boat rentals, lake fishing, shuffleboard court, planned group activities, recreation director, sports field, horseshoes, hiking trails, volleyball. No pets. Open mid May through mid Oct. Rate in 1995 $17-20 for 2 persons. Phone: (705) 377-5778.

## MINDEN—G-4

**Jay Lake Campground & RV Park**—CAMPGROUND on Jay Lake. *From jct Hwy 35 & Hwy 121 (Haliburton): Go 4 km/2 1/2 mi E on Hwy 121.* ◆◆◆FACILITIES: 80 sites, 42 full hookups, 18 water & elec (15 & 30 amp receptacles), 20 no hookups, seasonal sites, tenting available, sewage disposal, laundry, public phone, limited grocery store, ice, tables, fire rings, wood. ◆◆◆◆RECREATION: rec hall, swim pool, lake swimming, boating, electric motors only, canoeing, dock, 1 sail/3 canoe/2 pedal boat rentals, lake fishing, playground, planned group activities (weekends only), recreation director, badminton, horseshoes, hiking trails, volleyball. Open May 15 through Oct 15. Rate in 1995 $18-24 per family. Member of OPCA. Phone: (705) 286-1233.

**South Lake Trailer Park**—Lakeside CAMPGROUND with open, grassy sites. *From jct Hwy 121 (Kinmount) & CR 16 at south city limits: Go 3.6 km/2 1/4 mi E on CR 16, then 2.4 km/1 1/2 mi S on Hospitality Rd, then .4 km/1/4 mi E on gravel road.* ◆◆FACILITIES: 153 sites, most common site width 35 feet, 25 ft. max RV length, 70 full hookups, 25 water & elec (15 & 30 amp receptacles), 58 no hookups, seasonal sites, tenting available, sewage disposal, laundry, grocery store, ice, tables, fire rings, wood. ◆◆◆RECREATION: rec room/area, lake swimming, boating, canoeing, ramp, dock, 3 row/2 canoe boat rentals, lake fishing, playground, planned group activities (weekends only), sports field, horseshoes, volleyball. Open May 15 through Oct 15. Rate in 1995 $15.50-19.50 per family. Member of OPCA. Phone: (705) 286-2555.

## MITCHELL BAY—J-1

MARINE PARK (St. Clair Parkway Commission)—*From jct Hwy 40 & Mitchell Bay Rd: Go 8 km/5 mi W on Mitchell Bay Rd.* FACILITIES: 80 sites, 80 water & elec, tenting available, sewage disposal, public phone, ice, tables, fire rings, grills. RECREATION: lake swimming, boating, ramp, motor boat rentals, lake fishing, playground. Open May 24 through Oct 15. Phone: (519) 354-8423.

## MONTREAL RIVER HARBOUR—D-3

**Twilight Resort**—CAMPGROUND with sites by Lake Superior. *In town on Hwy 17.* ◆◆FACILITIES: 45 sites, most common site width 25 feet, 6 full hookups, 17 water & elec (15 amp receptacles), 22 no hookups, tenting available, sewage disposal, laundry, public phone, limited grocery store, ice, tables, fire rings, wood. ◆◆◆RECREATION: lake swimming, 13 canoe/1 motor boat rentals, lake fishing, badminton, sports field, horseshoes, hiking trails, volleyball. Open Apr 15 through Oct 31. Rate in 1995 $14-16 for 2 persons. Phone: (705) 882-2183.

## MOOSONEE—A-5

TIDEWATER PROVINCIAL PARK—*From Polar Bear Express: Take a water-taxi from town across theMoose River to Charles Island.* FACILITIES: 30 sites, 30 no hookups, tenting available, non-flush toilets, tables, grills, wood. RECREATION: boating, canoeing, lake fishing, hiking trails. Open mid Jun through early Sep. No showers. Phone: (705) 336-2987.

## MORPETH—J-1

**RONDEAU SHORES TRAILER PARK**—Level CAMPGROUND on lakefront. *From jct Hwy 3, Hwy 21 & CR 17 (Kent Rd): Go 2 km/1 1/4 mi S on CR 17, then .8 km/1/2 mi E on gravel road.*

◆◆◆FACILITIES: 123 sites, most common site width 30 feet, 109 full hookups, 14 water & elec (15 amp receptacles), seasonal sites, tenting available, RV rentals, cabins, sewage disposal, laundry, public phone, grocery store, RV supplies, LP gas refill by weight, ice, tables, fire rings.

◆◆◆RECREATION: rec hall, rec room/area, swim pool, lake swimming, lake fishing, playground, planned group activities (weekends only), movies, horseshoes.

Open May 15 through Oct 15. Rate in 1995 $18 per family. Reservations recommended Jul & Aug. Master Card/Visa accepted. Member of OPCA. Phone: (519) 674-3330.

**SEE AD TRAVEL SECTION PAGE 983**

## MORRISBURG—G-6

**RIVERSIDE/CEDAR CAMPSITE (Parks of the St. Lawrence)**—*From jct Hwy 401 (exit 750) & Hwy 31: Go 1 1/2 km/1 mi S on Hwy 31, then 6 1/2 km/4 mi E on Hwy 2.*

FACILITIES: 298 sites, 15 water & elec, 113 elec (15 & 30 amp receptacles), 170 no hookups, tenting available, handicap restroom facilities, sewage disposal, public phone, tables, wood.

RECREATION: lake swimming, boating, canoeing, ramp, lake fishing, playground, planned group activities, badminton, sports field, horseshoes, hiking trails, volleyball.

Open May 19 through Sep 4. Phone: (613) 543-3287.

**SEE AD TRAVEL SECTION PAGE 974**

MORRISBURG—Continued

⚑ **ST. LAWRENCE PARKS COMMISSION**—*From jct Hwy 401 (exit 758) & Upper Canada Rd: Go 1.6 km/1 mi S on Upper Canada Rd, then 2.4 km/1 1/2 mi E on Hwy 2.* Administrator of Upper Canada Village, Ft. Henry, Upper Canada Golf Course attractions and day-use parks & campgrounds. Visitors Information Centre with activity centre & scenic garden walks. Open all year. American Express/Master Card/Visa accepted. Phone: (613) 543-3704.

**SEE AD TRAVEL SECTION PAGE 974**

**Upper Canada Campground**—Family oriented CAMPGROUND. *From jct Hwy 401 (exit 758) & Upper Canada Rd: Go 100 yards N on Upper Canada Rd.* ◆◆◆FACILITIES: 100 sites, most common site width 40 feet, 90 water & elec (15 & 30 amp receptacles), 10 no hookups, seasonal sites, 5 pull-thrus, tenting available, sewage disposal, laundry, public phone, limited grocery store, ice, tables, fire rings, wood. ◆◆◆RECREATION: rec room/area, swim pool, pond swimming, boating, no motors, dock, 2 pedal boat rentals, pond fishing, playground, planned group activities, horseshoes, volleyball. Recreation open to the public. Open May 1 through Nov 1. Rate in 1995 $15.50-19.50 for 2 persons. Member of OPCA. Phone: (613) 543-2201. FCRV 10% discount.

⚑ **UPPER CANADA GOLF COURSE**—*From jct Hwy 401 (exit 758) & Upper Canada Rd: Go 1.6 km/1 mi S on Upper Canada Rd, then 2.4 km/1 1/2 mi E on Hwy 2.* A golf course designed by C.E. (Roby) Robinson. The 6922 (Blue) yard course offers a degree of challenge for both experienced and novice golfers. Driving range, pro-shop, PGA lessons, restaurant & lounge. American Express/Master Card/Visa accepted. Phone: (613) 543-3704.

**SEE AD TRAVEL SECTION PAGE 974**

⚑ **UPPER CANADA VILLAGE**—*From jct Hwy 401 (exit 758) & Upper Canada Rd: Go 1.6 km/1 mi S on Upper Canada Rd, then 2.4 km/1 1/2 mi E on Hwy 2.* Re-creation of a pre-1867 town. Costumed interpreters recreate the daily routine life of Ontario, circa 1865, with daily demonstrations of their skills from the past. Open all year. Phone: (613) 543-3704.

**SEE AD TRAVEL SECTION PAGE 974**

## MOUNTAIN GROVE—G-5

**O'Reilly Lake Family Campground**—Secluded, rustic, lakeside location with open & shady sites. *From jct Mt Grove Rd & Hwy 7: Go 1.6 km/1 mi E on Hwy 7, then 6.4 km/4 mi S on Frontenac Rd (gravel road).* ◆◆FACILITIES: 215 sites, most common site width 20 feet, 24 ft. max RV length, 160 water & elec (15 amp receptacles), 55 no hookups, seasonal sites, 5 pull-thrus, tenting available, sewage disposal, laundry, public phone, limited grocery store, LP gas refill by weight, ice, tables, fire rings, wood. ◆◆◆RECREATION: rec hall, rec room/area, lake swimming, boating, electric motors only, canoeing, dock, 8 canoe boat rentals, lake fishing, mini-golf, playground, planned group activities (weekends only), sports field, horseshoes, hiking trails, volleyball. Open mid May through mid Oct. Rate in 1995 $15-18.50 per family. Phone: (613) 335-5643.

## MOUNT FOREST—H-2

**PIKE LAKE CAMPGROUND & RESORT**—Part of a resort complex on a private lake. *From jct Hwy 6 & Hwy 89: Go 7 km/4.5 mi W on Hwy 89, then .4 km/.25 mi S on Pike Lake Rd.*

◆◆◆◆FACILITIES: 550 sites, most common site width 40 feet, 500 full hookups, (15 & 30 amp receptacles), 50 no hookups, seasonal sites, a/c allowed ($), heater allowed ($), tenting available, group sites for tents, RV rentals, cabins, RV storage, sewage disposal, laundry, public phone, limited grocery store, RV supplies, LP gas refill by weight/by meter, ice, tables, fire rings, wood, traffic control gate.

◆◆◆◆◆RECREATION: rec hall, rec room/area, lake swimming, boating, no motors, canoeing, ramp, dock, 10 row/10 canoe/10 pedal boat rentals, lake fishing, golf ($), driving range ($), putting green, basketball hoop, playground, 6 shuffleboard courts, planned group activities, movies, recreation director, 3 tennis courts, sports field, horseshoes, volleyball. Recreation open to the public.

Open May 1 through Oct 15. Rate in 1995 $17 per family. Master Card/Visa accepted. Member of OPCA. Phone: (519) 338-3010.

**SEE AD TRAVEL SECTION PAGES 975, 976 AND 977**

**River Place Park**—A CAMPGROUND on rolling terrain overlooking a river valley. *From jct Hwy 89 & Hwy 6: Go 13.6 km/8.5 mi N on Hwy 6, then 2.5 km/1.5 mi W on Normanby Concession Rd 11-12.* ◆◆◆FACILI-

RIVER PLACE PARK—Continued on next page
MOUNT FOREST—Continued on next page

**MOUNT FOREST**—Continued
RIVER PLACE PARK—Continued

TIES: 267 sites, most common site width 35 feet, 152 full hookups, 50 water & elec (15 & 30 amp receptacles), 65 no hookups, seasonal sites, tenting available, handicap restroom facilities, sewage disposal, laundry, public phone, limited grocery store, LP gas refill by weight, ice, tables, fire rings, wood. ◆◆◆RECREATION: swim pool (heated), river fishing, mini-golf ($), playground, sports field, horseshoes, hiking trails, volleyball. Recreation open to the public. Open May 15 through Oct 15. Rate in 1995 $19-23 per family. Member of OPCA. Phone: (519) 665-2228.

**SPRING VALLEY PARK**—Secluded, grassy, lakeside CAMPGROUND. *From jct Hwy 89 & Hwy 6: Go 8 km/5 mi S on Hwy 6, then 3 1/4 km/2 mi E on Sideroad 5.*

WELCOME

◆◆◆◆FACILITIES: 235 sites, most common site width 35 feet, 235 full hookups, (15 & 30 amp receptacles), seasonal sites, a/c allowed ($), heater allowed ($), tenting available, group sites for RVs, cabins, RV storage, portable dump, laundry, public phone, limited grocery store, RV supplies, LP gas refill by weight, ice, tables, fire rings, wood, traffic control gate.

◆◆◆◆◆RECREATION: rec hall, rec room/area, coin games, swim pool (heated), lake swimming, boating, no motors, canoeing, dock, 2 row/4 canoe/2 pedal boat rentals, lake fishing, mini-golf ($), basketball hoop, playground, planned group activities, movies, recreation director, sports field, horseshoes, hiking trails, volleyball. Recreation open to the public.

Open May 15 through Oct 15. Rate in 1995 $22-25 per family. Master Card/Visa accepted. Member of OPCA. Phone: (519) 323-2581.

**SEE AD TRAVEL SECTION PAGES 975, 976 AND 977**

## NESTOR FALLS—E-1

CALIPER LAKE PROVINCIAL PARK—*From town: Go 6 1/2 km/4 mi S on Hwy 71, then 1 1/2 km/1 mi W on Park Rd.* FACILITIES: 92 sites, 26 elec, 66 no hookups, tenting available, handicap restroom facilities, sewage disposal, ice, tables, grills, wood. RECREATION: lake swimming, boating, canoeing, ramp, lake fishing, playground, hiking trails. Open mid May through mid Sep. Phone: (807) 484-2181.

**Clark & Crombie Camps**—RV SPACES in conjunction with a motel and Lake of the Woods. *At south edge of town on Hwy 71.* FACILITIES: 45 sites, most common site width 20 feet, 30 full hookups, (15 & 30 amp receptacles), 15 no hookups, 8 pull-thrus, tenting available, laundry, public phone, grocery store, ice, tables, fire rings, wood. RECREATION: rec room/area, lake swimming, boating, canoeing, ramp, dock, 25 motor boat rentals, lake fishing. Open all year. Facilities

**NESTOR FALLS**—Continued
CLARK & CROMBIE CAMPS—Continued

fully operational May 1 through Nov 1. Rate in 1995 $15 for 2 persons. Phone: (807) 484-2114.

**Crawford's Crow Lake Resort**—A wooded, lakeside CAMPGROUND. *From north city limits: Go 11 km/7 mi N on Hwy 71.* ◆◆FACILITIES: 24 sites, most common site width 30 feet, 20 full hookups, 4 water & elec (15 amp receptacles), tenting available, laundry, public phone, limited grocery store, ice, tables. ◆◆RECREATION: lake swimming, boating, canoeing, ramp, dock, 1 canoe/1 pedal/27 motor boat rentals, lake fishing. Open May 1 through Oct 1. Rate in 1995 $16.50 for 2 persons. Phone: (807) 484-2183.

**Lecuyer's Tru-Tail Lodge**—A wooded, lakeside CAMPGROUND. *From jct Hwy 71 & Airport Rd at north edge of town: Go 1.2 km/3/4 mi W on Sabaskong Rd.* ◆◆◆FACILITIES: 60 sites, most common site width 16 feet, 29 full hookups, 20 water & elec (15 & 30 amp receptacles), 11 no hookups, 18 pull-thrus, tenting available, sewage disposal, public phone, ice, tables, fire rings, grills, wood. ◆◆◆RECREATION: lake swimming, boating, canoeing, ramp, dock, 2 canoe/1 pedal/20 motor boat rentals, lake fishing, horseshoes, hiking trails. Open May 1 through Oct 1. Rate in 1995 $17 for 2 persons. Phone: (807) 484-2448.

**Little Pine Lake Campground**—Open & shaded level sites. *From town: Go 24 km/15 mi S on Hwy 71.* ◆◆◆FACILITIES: 24 sites, most common site width 40 feet, 12 full hookups, 6 water & elec (15 & 30 amp receptacles), 6 no hookups, 1 pull-thrus, tenting available, laundry, public phone, limited grocery store, ice, tables, fire rings, wood. ◆◆RECREATION: lake swimming, boating, canoeing, ramp, dock, 8 row/1 canoe/2 pedal/5 motor boat rentals, lake fishing. Open May 1 through Sep 15. Rate in 1995 $13-15 for 2 persons. Phone: (807) 487-2252.

**PARKVIEW RV RESORT & COTTAGE RENTAL**—CAMPGROUND on Caliper Lake. *From south city limits: Go 6.4 km/4 mi S on Hwy 71.*

WELCOME

◆◆◆FACILITIES: 39 sites, most common site width 25 feet, 22 full hookups, 11 water & elec (15 & 30 amp receptacles), 6 no hookups, seasonal sites, 12 pull-thrus, tenting available, group sites for tents, RV rentals, cabins, sewage disposal, laundry, public phone, marine gas, ice, tables, fire rings, grills, wood.

◆◆◆RECREATION: lake swimming, boating, canoeing, ramp, dock, 1 canoe/1 pedal/4 motor boat rentals, water skiing, lake fishing, playground, horseshoes.

**NESTOR FALLS**—Continued
PARKVIEW RV RESORT & COTTAGE RENTAL—Continued

Open May 1 through Oct 1. Rate in 1995 $16-17 per family. Phone: (807) 484-2337.

**SEE AD TRAVEL SECTION PAGES 975, 976 AND 977**

## NEW LOWELL—H-3

**NEW LOWELL (Nottawasaga Vly. Conservation Area)**—*From town center: Go 2 km/1.2 mi S on Mill St.*

WELCOME

FACILITIES: 98 sites, 49 water & elec (15 & 30 amp receptacles), 49 no hookups, seasonal sites, tenting available, group sites for tents/RVs, RV storage, handicap restroom facilities, sewage disposal, public phone, limited grocery store, ice, tables, fire rings, grills, wood, guard.

RECREATION: equipped pavilion, pond swimming, boating, no motors, canoeing, pond fishing, basketball hoop, playground, sports field, horseshoes, hiking trails, volleyball, cross country skiing, snowmobile trails. Recreation open to the public.

Open all year. Facilities fully operational May 1 through end Sep. Phone: (705) 424-1479.

**SEE AD TRAVEL SECTION PAGE 980**

## NEWTONVILLE—H-4

**Marydale Estates**—CAMPGROUND in a natural setting. *From jct Hwy 401 (exit 448) & Reg. Rd 18: Go .8 km/1/2 mi S to 1st Concession Rd, then follow signs 3.2 km/2 mi E .* ◆◆FACILITIES: 180 sites, most common site width 33 feet, 180 full hookups, (15 & 30 amp receptacles), seasonal sites, tenting available, handicap restroom facilities, public phone, tables, fire rings, wood. ◆◆RECREATION: rec hall, swim pool, 2 shuffleboard courts, sports field, horseshoes, hiking trails. Open all year. Pool open May 15 thru Oct 15. Rate in 1995 $15 per vehicle. Phone: (905) 786-2345. FCRV 10% discount.

## NIAGARA FALLS—I-3

### NIAGARA FALLS AREA MAP

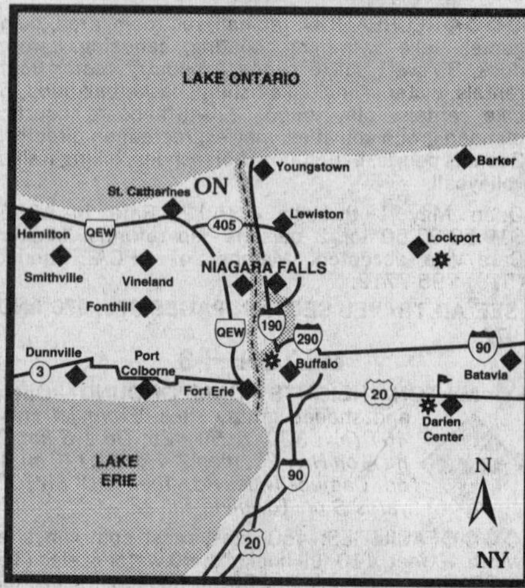


*Symbols on map indicate towns within a 64 km/40 mi radius of Niagara Falls where campgrounds (diamonds), attractions (flags), & RV service centers & camping supply outlets (gears) are listed. Check listings for more information.*

NIAGARA FALLS—Continued on page 1006

Closest campground to the Falls

# no small wonder

we're your favorite site.

With over 23 years of hospitality, we offer a welcoming family atmosphere.

Whether you plan to stay for a day or a week, choose Niagara Glen–View for a fabulous vacation in Niagara Falls, Ontario.

## What a site!

Whether you've got an RV, trailer or tent, Niagara Glen–View has cozy, shady sites with city water, 15, 30 and 50 amp electrical and sewer hook–ups. Situated on 20 wooded acres, we've got special areas especially for tents and connected sites for families travelling together.

- 15, 30 and 50 amp electrical sites
- Sewer hook-ups
- Extremely clean restrooms
- Large grocery and souvenir store
- Firewood available on-site
- Paved, all-weather roads
- Playground area, pool and wading pool
- Paved and concrete RV sites

## Close to all major attractions.

We're minutes away from all your favorite Niagara fun spots and offer package prices to major attractions.

Getting there is fast and easy. Hop on the Niagara People Mover. It stops every 15 minutes and we're right on the route! If you like more activity, bring your helmets and bikes or in-line skates and follow the scenic Niagara River on a 32 mile paved fitness trail.

Niagara Glen-view Tent & Trailer Park
3950 Victoria Avenue, PO Box 2087, Niagara Falls, ON Canada L2E 6Z2
(905) 358-8689 Fax (905) 374-4493

# 1-800-263-2570

**Woodall Rated:**
**Fac.** ◆◆◆
**Rec.** ◆◆◆

NIAGARA FALLS—Continued

**BISSELL'S HIDEAWAY RESORT**—*From jct Hwy QEW & Hwy 20 (Lundy Lane): Go 24 km/15 mi W on Hwy 20 (Lundy Lane), then 2.4 km/1 1/2 mi N on Effingham Rd, then .8 km/1/2 mi E on Metler Rd.*

**SEE PRIMARY LISTING AT FONTHILL AND AD THIS PAGE**

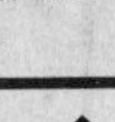

**CAMPARK RESORTS**—Quiet, level CAMPGROUND near tourist attractions. *From jct Queen Elizabeth Way & Hwy 420 (exit Lundy's Lane, Hwy 20): Go 2.4 km/1 1/2 mi W on Lundy's Lane.*

◊◊◊◊FACILITIES: 250 sites, most common site width 36 feet, 160 full hookups, 26 water & elec (15 & 30 amp receptacles), 64 no hookups, seasonal sites, 7 pull-thrus, a/c allowed ($), heater allowed ($), phone hookups, tenting available, group sites for tents/RVs, cabins, RV storage, sewage disposal, laundry, public phone, limited grocery store, RV supplies, ice, tables, fire rings, wood, traffic control gate.

◊◊◊◊RECREATION: rec hall, rec room/area, pavilion, coin games, swim pool (heated), basketball hoop, playground, planned group activities (weekends only), movies, recreation director, badminton, sports field, horseshoes, volleyball, local tours.

Open all year. Facilities fully operational May 1 through Oct 31. Rate in 1995 $20-25 per family. Master Card/Visa accepted. Member of OPCA. Phone: (905) 358-3873.

**SEE AD FRONT OF BOOK PAGE 135 AND AD TRAVEL SECTION, NY PAGE 588 AND AD TRAVEL SECTION PAGE 982 AND AD PAGE 1004**



NIAGARA FALLS—Continued

**KING WALDORF'S TENT & TRAILER PARK**—CAMPGROUND located on the Welland River in a tourist area. *From jct Hwy 420 & Queen Elizabeth Way: Go 7.2 km/4 1/2 mi S on QEW (exit 21), then 2.4 km/1 1/2 mi E on Lyons Creek Rd, then .8 km/1/2 mi N on Stanley Ave.*

◊◊◊FACILITIES: 220 sites, most common site width 30 feet, 186 water & elec (15 & 20 amp receptacles), 34 no hookups, seasonal sites, 83 pull-thrus, a/c allowed, heater allowed, tenting available, group sites for tents/RVs, sewage disposal, laundry, public phone, limited grocery store, ice, tables, fire rings, wood, traffic control gate.

◊◊◊RECREATION: swim pool (heated), wading pool, boating, canoeing, ramp, dock, water skiing, river fishing, golf ($), playground, sports field.

Open May 18 through Sep 29. Rate in 1995 $22.43-24.30 for 4 persons. Reservations recommended Jul through Aug. Master Card/Visa accepted. Member of OPCA. Phone: (905) 295-8191.

**SEE AD FRONT OF BOOK PAGE 128 AND AD NEXT PAGE**

**KNIGHT'S HIDE-AWAY PARK**—A semi-wooded CAMPGROUND in a tourist area. *From jct QEW (at Peace Bridge) & Hwy 3: Go 10.4 km/6 1/2 mi W on Hwy 3, then .4 km/1/4 mi N on Regional Rd 116.*

◊◊◊FACILITIES: 185 sites, most common site width 35 feet, 140 water & elec (15 & 30 amp receptacles), 45 no hookups, seasonal sites, 50 pull-thrus, a/c allowed ($), heater allowed ($), tenting available, group sites for tents, RV storage, sewage disposal, laundry, public phone, limited grocery store, RV supplies, LP gas refill by weight, ice, tables, fire rings, wood, traffic control gate/guard.

◊◊◊RECREATION: rec room/area, coin games, swim pool (heated), basketball hoop, playground, planned group activities (weekends only), sports field, horseshoes, volleyball.

Open May 1 through Oct 15. Rate in 1995 $19-21 per family. Visa accepted. Member of OPCA. Phone: (905) 894-1911.

**SEE AD TRAVEL SECTION PAGE 984**

**KOA-NIAGARA FALLS**—A grassy, level CAMPGROUND in a tourist area. *From jct Queen Elizabeth Way & Hwy 20 (Lundys Lane): Go 2 km/1 1/4 mi W on Hwy 20.*

◊◊◊◊FACILITIES: 340 sites, most common site width 35 feet, 100 full hookups, 215 water & elec (15 & 30 amp receptacles), 25 no hookups, 37 pull-thrus, a/c allowed ($), heater allowed ($), cable TV, tenting available, group sites for tents, cabins, handicap restroom facilities, sewage disposal, laundry, public phone, grocery store, RV supplies, LP gas refill by weight/by meter, ice, tables, fire rings, wood, guard.

◊◊◊◊RECREATION: rec hall, rec room/area, equipped pavilion, coin games, swim pool (indoor) (heated), wading pool, sauna, whirlpool, mini-golf ($), basketball hoop, 20 bike rentals, playground, 2 shuffleboard courts, planned group activities, movies, recreation director, sports field, horseshoes, volleyball, local tours.

Open Apr 1 through Nov 1. 2 outdoor heated pools. Rate in 1995 $25-31 for 2 persons. Reservations recommended all season. Master Card/Visa accepted. Member of OPCA. Phone: (905) 356-2267. KOA 10% value card discount.

**SEE AD TRAVEL SECTION, NY PAGE 586 AND AD THIS PAGE AND AD FRONT OF BOOK PAGES 68 AND 69**

**MARINELAND**—*From jct Hwy 420 & Queen Elizabeth Way: Go 3.2 km/2 mi S on QEW, then 3.2 km/2 mi E on McLeod Rd, then .8 km/1/2 mi S on Portage Rd.* Marineland plus a wild & domestic animal farm with special shows. Open early Apr through end Oct. Amusement rides open mid May to mid Oct. Phone to confirm. Phone: (905) 356-8250.

**SEE AD FRONT OF BOOK PAGE 128 AND AD NEXT PAGE**

**NIAGARA GLEN-VIEW TENT & TRAILER PARK**—CAMPGROUND convenient to tourist attractions. *From jct the Rainbow Bridge & Niagara River Pkwy (River Rd): Go 3.2 km/2 mi N on River Rd, then 90 m/100 yards S on Victoria Ave.*

◊◊◊FACILITIES: 277 sites, most common site width 35 feet, 96 full hookups, 53 water & elec (15,30 & 50 amp receptacles), 128 no hookups, 60 pull-thrus, a/c allowed, heater allowed, tenting available, group sites for tents/RVs, sewage disposal,

NIAGARA GLEN-VIEW TENT & TRAILER PARK—Continued on page 1008

NIAGARA FALLS—Continued on page 1008

# Closest Campground to MARINELAND and the FALLS

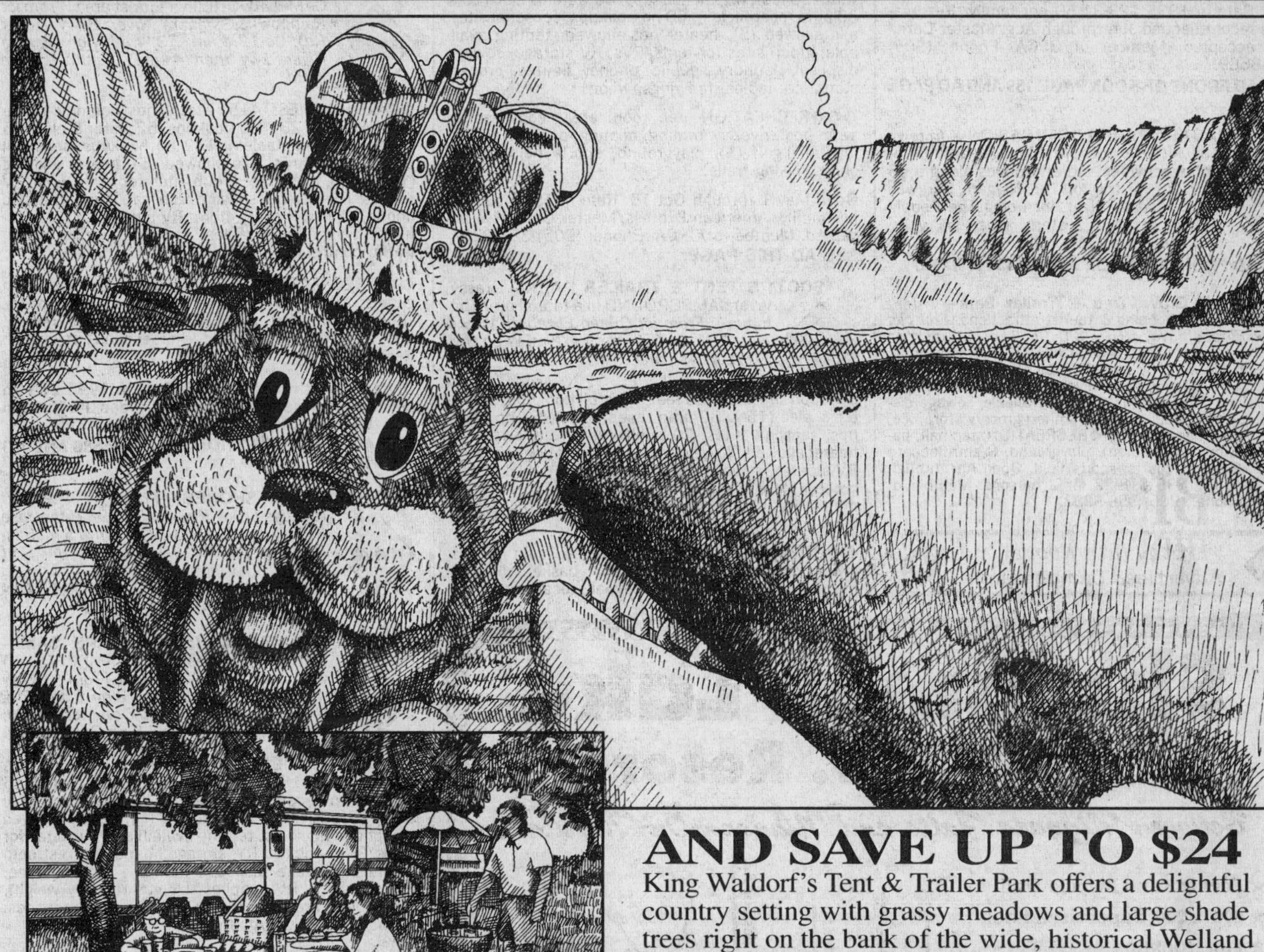

## AND SAVE UP TO $24

King Waldorf's Tent & Trailer Park offers a delightful country setting with grassy meadows and large shade trees right on the bank of the wide, historical Welland River. A perfect place for boating, tenting and fishing.

## EXCLUSIVE OFFER

**ONLY KING WALDORF'S CAMPERS RECEIVE:**

**$4.00 OFF MARINELAND'S**

REGULAR ADMISSION FOR UP TO 6 PEOPLE

COUPONS PRESENTED TO CAMPERS AT CHECK-IN

## King Waldorf's offers:

- Level pull-through trailer sites
- Large private tent sites
- Water & electrical hook-ups
- Full laundry facilities
- Modern washrooms, showers & tubs
- Large heated pool & wading pool
- 18-hole golf course
- Children's playground
- Gift shop
- Dump station
- Fishing
- Boat ramp

Call: **(905) 295-8191**

Write: 8375 Stanley Ave., Niagara Falls, Ontario, Canada L2E 6X8

Location: 9015 Stanley Ave., Niagara Falls, Ontario, Canada

# KING WALDORF'S

## TENT AND TRAILER PARK

NIAGARA FALLS—Continued
NIAGARA GLEN-VIEW TENT & TRAILER PARK—Continued

laundry, public phone, grocery store, RV supplies, ice, tables, patios, grills, wood, guard.

◆◆◆RECREATION: rec room/area, coin games, swim pool, wading pool, playground, badminton, sports field, horseshoes, volleyball, local tours.

Open May 1 through Oct 12. Large rec hall for groups only. Rate in 1995 $23-31.50 per family. Reservations recommended Jun through Aug. Master Card/Visa accepted. Member of OPCA. Phone: (905) 358-8689.

**SEE AD FRONT OF BOOK PAGE 139 AND AD PAGE 1005**

**THE NIAGARA PARKS COMMISSION**—*In town at 7400 Portage Rd.* Manages and promotes activities and attractions along a 56 km/35 mi trek of The Niagara Parkway and Niagara River, including The People Mover Transit System. Open all year. Phone: (905) 356-2241.

**SEE AD FRONT OF BOOK PAGES 136 AND 137**

**Orchard Grove Tent & Trailer Park**—CAMPGROUND near shopping & tourist attractions. *From jct Queen Elizabeth Way & Hwy 420: Go .8 km/1/2 mi W on Hwy 20 (Lundys Lane).* ◆◆FACILITIES: 395 sites, most common site width 30 feet, 171 full hookups, 124 water & elec (15 & 30 amp receptacles), 100 no hookups, seasonal sites, 70 pull-thrus, tenting available, sewage disposal, laundry, public phone, limited grocery store, ice, tables, fire rings, wood. ◆◆RECREATION: rec hall, pavilion, swim pool (heated), playground, 3 shuffleboard courts, 2 tennis courts, sports field. Open Apr through Oct. Rate in 1995 $18-22 for 2 persons. Member of OPCA. Phone: (905) 358-9883.

Stay With Woodall Advertised Campgrounds

NIAGARA FALLS—Continued

**RIVERSIDE PARK MOTEL & CAMPGROUND**

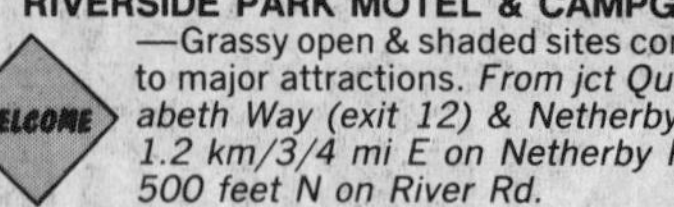

—Grassy open & shaded sites convenient to major attractions. *From jct Queen Elizabeth Way (exit 12) & Netherby Rd: Go 1.2 km/3/4 mi E on Netherby Rd, then 500 feet N on River Rd.*

◆◆◆FACILITIES: 185 sites, most common site width 30 feet, 45 full hookups, 80 water & elec (15 & 30 amp receptacles), 60 no hookups, seasonal sites, a/c allowed ($), heater not allowed, tenting available, group sites for tents/RVs, RV storage, sewage disposal, laundry, public phone, limited grocery store, ice, tables, fire rings, wood.

◆◆◆RECREATION: rec room/area, coin games, swim pool, river swimming, boating, dock, river fishing, mini-golf ($), playground, sports field, horseshoes, hiking trails.

Open May 1 through Oct 15. Rate in 1995 $21-24 per family. American Express/Master Card/Visa accepted. Member of OPCA. Phone: (905) 382-2204.

**SEE AD THIS PAGE**

**SCOTT'S TENT & TRAILER PARK**—Grassy, level CAMPGROUND in a tourist area (bilingual). *From jct Queen Elizabeth Way & Hwy 420: Go 2.4 km/1 1/2 mi W on Hwy 20 (Lundys Lane).*

◆◆◆◆FACILITIES: 270 sites, most common site width 30 feet, 168 full hookups, 50 water & elec (15 & 30 amp receptacles), 52 no hookups, seasonal sites, 20 pull-thrus, a/c allowed ($), heater allowed ($), phone hookups, tenting available, RV storage, sewage disposal, laundry, public phone, grocery store, RV supplies, LP gas refill by weight/by meter, ice, tables, fire rings, wood, traffic control gate/guard.

◆◆◆RECREATION: rec room/area, coin games, swim pool (heated), wading pool, basketball hoop, playground, horseshoes, volleyball, local tours.

NIAGARA FALLS—Continued
SCOTT'S TENT & TRAILER PARK—Continued

Open Apr 1 through Nov 1. Rate in 1995 $21-23 for 4 persons. Reservations recommended Jul through Aug. Master Card/Visa accepted. Member of OPCA. Phone: (905) 356-6988.

**SEE AD PAGE 1004**

**SHALAMAR LAKE NIAGARA**—A grassy CAMPGROUND in a tourist area. *From jct Rainbow & Niagara River Pkwy (River Rd): Go 12.4 km/7 3/4 mi N on Niagara River Pkwy, then .4 km/1/4 mi W on Line 8 Rd.*

◆◆◆FACILITIES: 415 sites, most common site width 35 feet, 231 full hookups, 52 water & elec (15 & 30 amp receptacles), 132 no hookups, seasonal sites, 6 pull-thrus, a/c allowed ($), heater allowed ($), tenting available, group sites for tents/RVs, RV rentals, RV storage, sewage disposal, laundry, public phone, limited grocery store, RV supplies, LP gas refill by weight, ice, tables, fire rings, grills, wood, traffic control gate.

◆◆◆RECREATION: rec room/area, pavilion, coin games, swim pool, basketball hoop, playground, shuffleboard court, planned group activities, recreation director, sports field, horseshoes, volleyball. Recreation open to the public.

Open May 1 through Oct 15. Rate in 1995 $19-25 per family. Reservations recommended Jul through Aug. Visa accepted. Phone: (905) 262-4895.

**SEE AD TRAVEL SECTION, NY PAGE 586 AND AD THIS PAGE**

**SHERKSTON SHORES**—*From jct Hwy 20 (Lundys Ln) & Regional Rd 98 (Montrose Rd): Go approximately 24 km/15 mi S on Regional Rd 98. 2.4 km/1 1/2 mi S of Hwy 3.*

**SEE PRIMARY LISTING AT PORT COLBORNE AND AD THIS PAGE**

**YOGI BEAR'S JELLYSTONE PARK CAMP-RESORT**—Grassy, level CAMPGROUND with open & shaded sites. *From jct Hwy 420 & QEW: Go 3.2 km/2 mi S on QEW, then 183 m/200 yards E on McLeod Rd, then 2.4 km/1 1/2 mi S on Oakwood Dr.*

◆◆◆◆FACILITIES: 304 sites, most common site width 35 feet, 167 full hookups, 73 water & elec (15 & 30 amp receptacles), 64 no hookups, seasonal sites, 22 pull-thrus, a/c allowed ($), heater allowed ($), phone hookups, tenting available, group sites for tents/RVs, cabins, RV storage, handicap restroom facilities, sewage disposal, laundry, public phone, grocery store, RV supplies, LP gas refill by weight, ice, tables, fire rings, grills, wood, church services, traffic control gate/guard.

◆◆◆◆◆RECREATION: rec hall, rec room/area, equipped pavilion, coin games, swim pool (heated), wading pool, river fishing, mini-golf, basketball hoop, playground, planned group activities, movies, recreation director, badminton, sports field, horseshoes, volleyball, local tours.

YOGI BEAR'S JELLYSTONE PARK CAMP-RESORT—Continued on next page
NIAGARA FALLS—Continued on next page

Open May 15 through mid Oct. Rate in 1995 $21-27 for 2 persons. Reservations recommended Jul through Aug. Master Card/Visa accepted. Member of OPCA. Phone: (905) 354-1432.

**SEE AD FRONT OF BOOK PAGE 135 AND AD TRAVEL SECTION, NY PAGE 586 AND AD THIS PAGE**

## NIAGARA-ON-THE-LAKE—I-3

**CAMPARK RESORTS**—*From jct Hwy 55 & QEW: Go 16 km/10 mi SE on QEW, then .4 km/1/4 mi W on Hwy 20 (Lundy's Lane).*

**SEE PRIMARY LISTING AT NIAGARA FALLS AND AD FRONT OF BOOK PAGE 135**

## NIPIGON—B-2

**Birchwood Gift House and RV Park**—Open & shaded, level RV SPACES. *From west city limits: Go 12.8 km/8 mi W on Hwy 17.* FACILITIES: 50 sites, most common site width 15 feet, 12 full hookups, 4 water & elec, 4 elec (15 & 30 amp receptacles), 30 no hookups, tenting available, sewage disposal, public phone, tables, fire rings, wood. Open Apr 15 through Oct 15. Rate in 1995 $10-12 per family. Phone: (807) 886-2440.

**STILLWATER GIFT SHOP**—*From jct Hwy 11 & Hwy 17: Go 4.8 km/3 mi W on Hwy 11/17.* Exotic amethyst rock & gift shop. Open May 15 through Oct 15. Master Card/Visa accepted. Phone: (807) 887-3701.

**SEE AD TRAVEL SECTION PAGES 975, 976 AND 977**

**STILLWATER TRAILER PARK**—CAMPGROUND connected with a rock shop. *From jct Hwy 11 & Hwy 17: Go 4.8 km/3 mi W on Hwy 11/17.*

◆◆◆FACILITIES: 77 sites, most common site width 20 feet, 17 full hookups, 54 water & elec (15 & 30 amp receptacles), 6 no hookups, seasonal sites, 43 pull-thrus, a/c allowed, heater allowed, phone hookups, tenting available, group sites for tents/RVs, RV storage, sewage disposal, laundry, public phone, limited grocery store, ice, tables, fire rings, grills, wood.

◆◆RECREATION: stream fishing, playground, sports field, horseshoes, hiking trails.

Open May 15 through Oct 15. Rate in 1995 $12-15 for 2 persons. Master Card/Visa accepted. Phone: (807) 887-3701.

**SEE AD TRAVEL SECTION PAGES 975, 976 AND 977**

## NIPISSING—F-3

**BIRCHWOOD COTTAGES TENT & TRAILER PARK**—Secluded CAMPGROUND on South River. *From jct CR 534 & CR 654: Go 1.6 km/1 mi E on CR 654, then 1.6 km/1 mi N on Lake Nipissing Rd, then follow signs for 2.8 km/1 3/4 mi.*

◆◆◆FACILITIES: 36 sites, most common site width 35 feet, 7 full hookups, 9 water & elec (15 amp receptacles), 20 no hookups, a/c allowed ($), tenting available, cabins, limited grocery store, gasoline, marine gas, ice, tables, fire rings, wood.

◆◆◆RECREATION: equipped pavilion, river swimming, boating, canoeing, dock, 7 motor boat rentals, river fishing, fishing guides, basketball hoop, badminton, horseshoes, hiking trails, volleyball.

Open May 1 through Oct 31. Rate in 1995 $16-18 for 4 persons. Visa accepted. Phone: (705) 724-2935.

**SEE AD TRAVEL SECTION PAGE 974**

**Fish Bay Yacht Club & Marina**—Lakeside RV SPACES in conjunction with full marina facilities. *From jct CR 534 & CR 654: Go 1.6 km/1 mi E on CR 654, then N on Lake Nipissing Rd.* FACILITIES: 14 sites, most common site width 15 feet, 14 water & elec (30 amp receptacles), seasonal sites, tenting available, sewage disposal, laundry, public phone, limited grocery store, LP gas refill by weight/by meter, ice, tables, fire rings. RECREATION: lake swimming, boating, canoeing, ramp, dock, 12 row/1 sail/1 canoe/1 pedal/7 motor boat rentals, lake fishing,





horseshoes. Recreation open to the public. Open mid May through mid Oct. Rate in 1995 $12-15 for 4 persons. Phone: (705) 724-3130.

## NORTH BAY—F-3

***See listings at Callander, Nipissing, Powassan, Restoule & Sturgeon Falls***

**Champlain Tent & Trailer Park**—CAMPGROUND in town near beaches. *From jct Hwys 11, 17 & 11-B: Go 8.8 km/5 1/2 mi S on Hwy 11-B, then 1.6 km/1 mi S on Premier Rd.* ◆◆FACILITIES: 55 sites, most common site width 30 feet, 35 ft. max RV length, 31 full hookups, 11 water & elec (15 & 30 amp receptacles), 13 no hookups, seasonal sites, 8 pull-thrus, tenting available, sewage disposal, laundry, public phone, limited grocery store, ice, tables, wood. ◆RECREATION: rec room/area, canoeing, 2 canoe boat rentals, river fishing, horseshoes. Open May 1 through Oct 31. Rate in 1995 $15-19 per family. Phone: (705) 474-4669.

**Dreany Haven Campground**—Grassy, lakeside CAMPGROUND. *From south jct Hwy 11 & Hwy 17: Go 6.4 km/4 mi E on Hwy 17.* ◆◆◆FACILITIES: 75 sites, 20 full hookups, 35 water & elec (15 & 30 amp receptacles), 20 no hookups, seasonal sites, 10 pull-thrus, tenting available, sewage disposal, public phone, limited grocery store, ice, tables, fire rings, wood. ◆◆◆RECREATION: swim pool, boating, canoeing, ramp, dock, 2 row boat rentals, lake fishing, mini-golf ($), playground, horseshoes, hiking trails, volleyball. Open May 1 through Sep 30. Rate in 1995 $14.01-17.75 per family. Phone: (705) 752-2800.

**Fairview Park Camping & Marina**—Level CAMPGROUND on the historic LaVase River. *From jct Hwy 11 & 11B (South) Lakeshore Rd exit: Go .8 km/1/2 mi W on 11B (Lakeshore Dr), then .8 km/1/2 mi S on Riverbend Rd.* ◆◆◆FACILITIES: 36 sites, most common site width 35 feet, 17 full hookups, 19 water & elec (15 & 30 amp receptacles), seasonal sites, 8 pull-thrus, tenting available, laundry, public phone, limited grocery store, ice, tables, fire rings, wood. ◆◆RECREATION: swim pool (heated), boating, ramp, dock, 1 pedal/4 motor boat rentals, river fishing, horseshoes. Open May 1 through Oct 30. Rate in 1995 $18-20 per family. Phone: (705) 474-0903.

**FRANKLIN MOTEL TENT & TRAILER PARK**—CAMPGROUND in town across from the lake. *From jct Hwys 11, 17 & 11-B: Go 6.4 km/4 mi S on Hwy 11-B.*

◆◆◆FACILITIES: 52 sites, most common site width 35 feet, 30 full hookups, 22 water & elec (15 & 30 amp receptacles), seasonal sites, 5 pull-thrus, cable TV, tenting available, sewage disposal, laundry, public phone, ice, tables.

◆◆◆RECREATION: swim pool (heated), boating, canoeing, 2 pedal boat rentals, playground, 2 shuffleboard courts, horseshoes.

Open mid May through mid Oct. Rate in 1995 $18-19 for 2 persons. Master Card/Visa accepted. Phone: (705) 472-1360.

**SEE AD TRAVEL SECTION PAGES 975, 976 AND 977**

## NORTHBROOK—G-5

**Woodcrest Resort Park**—A wooded all-season waterfront CAMPGROUND. *From jct Hwy 7 & Hwy 41: Go 16 km/10 mi N on Hwy 41, then 6.4 km/4 mi E on Harlowe Rd and follow signs.* ◆◆◆FACILITIES: 96 sites, most common site width 25 feet, 65 water & elec (15 & 30 amp receptacles), 31 no hookups, seasonal sites, 12 pull-thrus, tenting available, handicap restroom facilities, sewage disposal, laundry, limited grocery store, LP gas refill by weight, ice, tables, fire rings, wood. ◆◆◆RECREATION: lake swimming, boating, canoeing, ramp, dock, 2 row/7 canoe/2 pedal/4 motor boat rentals, lake fishing, mini-golf ($), sports field, horseshoes, volleyball. Open all year. Facilities fully operational May 1 through Oct 31. Rate in 1995 $15-19.50 per family. Member of OPCA. Phone: (613) 336-2966.

## NORWICH—I-2

LITTLE LAKE AREA (Long Point Conservation Region)—*From town: Go 4 3/4 km/3 mi S on Hwy 59, then 9 1/2 km/6 mi E on CR 19.* FACILITIES: 50 sites, 30 water & elec (15 amp receptacles), 20 no hookups, non-flush toilets, sewage disposal, tables, wood. RECREATION: pavilion, lake swimming, boating, 10 hp limit, ramp, dock, fishing, hiking trails. Recreation open to the public. Open Victoria Day through Labour Day. Phone: (519) 428-4623.

## NOVAR—G-3

**Tea Kettle Campground**—Secluded, lakeside CAMPGROUND on Fish lake. *From jct Hwy 11 & Fish Lake Rd: Go 1.6 km/1 mi E on Fish Lake Rd and follow signs.* ◆◆◆FACILITIES: 36 sites, most common site width 35 feet, 6 full hookups, 18 water & elec (15 amp receptacles), 12 no hookups, seasonal sites, tenting available, sewage disposal, ice, tables, fire rings, grills, wood. ◆◆◆RECREATION: rec hall, lake swimming, boating, 5 hp limit, canoeing, dock, 2 row/1 canoe boat rentals, lake fishing, planned group activities (weekends only), badminton, sports field, horseshoes, hiking trails, volleyball. Open mid May through mid Oct. Rate in 1995 $13-16 per family. Phone: (705) 789-9793.

## OMEMEE—H-4

EMIL PROVINCIAL PARK—*From town: Go 4 km/2 1/2 mi E on Hwy 7, then 3 1/4 km/2 mi N on Emily Park Rd.* FACILITIES: 299 sites, 107 elec, 192 no hookups, tenting available, handicap restroom facilities, sewage disposal, laundry, limited grocery store, ice, tables, wood. RECREATION: swimming, boating, canoeing, ramp, fishing, playground, hiking trails. Open mid May through early Oct. Phone: (705) 799-5170.

## ORIENT BAY—A-2

**Royal Windsor**—CAMPGROUND at Orient Bay on Lake Nipigon. *In town on Hwy 11.* ◆◆FACILITIES: 30 sites, most common site width 30 feet, 30 full hookups, (15 amp receptacles), 24 pull-thrus, tenting available, public phone, ice, tables, fire rings, wood. ◆◆◆RECREATION: rec hall, lake swimming, boating, canoeing, ramp, dock, 6 canoe/14 motor boat rentals, lake fishing, horseshoes. Open May 15 through Sep 15. No showers. Rate in 1995 $16-18 for 2 persons. Phone: (807) 885-5291.

### ORILLIA—G-3

BASS LAKE PROVINCIAL PARK—*From jct Hwy 12 & Concession 2: Go 6 1/2 km/4 mi W on Concession 2.* FACILITIES: 92 sites, 92 no hookups, 10 pull-thrus, tenting available, handicap restroom facilities. RECREATION: lake swimming, boating, canoeing, ramp, lake fishing, hiking trails. Open mid May through early Sep. Phone: (705) 326-7054.

**Layzee Acres RV Park**—Lakeside CAMPGROUND with grassy sites. *From jct Hwy 11 & Hwy 12: Go 11 km/7 mi S on Hwy 12, then 11 km/7 mi E on Simcoe Rd 46, then 1.6 km/1 mi N on Hwy 503 following signs.* ◈◈◈FACILITIES: 155 sites, most common site width 30 feet, 106 full hookups, 30 water & elec (15 & 30 amp receptacles), 19 no hookups, seasonal sites, tenting available, sewage disposal, laundry, public phone, limited grocery store, ice, tables, fire rings, wood. ◈◈◈RECREATION: rec hall, lake swimming, boating, ramp, dock, lake fishing, playground, planned group activities (weekends only), sports field, horseshoes, volleyball. Open May 8 through Oct 15. Rate in 1995 $19-23 for 2 persons. Member of OPCA. Phone: (705) 833-2539.

### ORONO—H-4

WELCOME

**CEDAR VALLEY RESORT**—Secluded wooded CAMPGROUND. *From jct Hwy 401 (exit 436) & Hwys 35/115: Go 6.4 km/4 mi N on Hwys 35/115, then 7.2 km/4 1/2 mi E on 4th Conc., then 1.6 km/1 mi N on local road.*

◈◈◈FACILITIES: 175 sites, 175 full hookups, (15 amp receptacles), seasonal sites, 5 pull-thrus, a/c allowed ($), heater allowed ($), tenting available, RV storage, sewage disposal, public phone, LP gas refill by weight, ice, tables, fire rings, wood.

◈◈◈RECREATION: equipped pavilion, pond swimming, pond fishing ($), sports field, horseshoes, hiking trails.

Open May 10 through Oct 15. Rate in 1995 $18.70 for 4 persons. Member of OPCA. Phone: (905) 786-2562.

**SEE AD TRAVEL SECTION PAGE 984**

### OSHAWA—H-4

DARLINGTON PROVINCIAL PARK—*From Hwy 401 (exit 425): Go 3/4 km/1/2 mi S on Courtice Rd.* FACILITIES: 300 sites, 100 elec, 200 no hookups, 102 pull-thrus, tenting available, handicap restroom facilities, sewage disposal, public phone, limited grocery store, ice, tables, wood. RECREATION: lake swimming, boating, canoeing, ramp, canoe/pedal boat rentals, lake fishing, playground, hiking trails. Open mid May through mid Oct. Phone: (905) 436-2036.

HEBER DOWN CONSERVATION AREA (Central Lake Cons. Auth.)—*From jct Hwy 401 & Hwy 12 (Interchange 410): Go 11 1/4 km/7 mi N on Hwy 12, then 3 1/4 km/2 mi W on Hwy 7, then follow signs.* FACILITIES: 50 sites, 50 water & elec (15 & 30 amp receptacles), tenting available, sewage disposal, laundry, public phone, ice, tables, grills, wood. RECREATION: stream fishing, playground, hiking trails. Recreation open to the public. Open May 1 through Oct 31. Phone: (905) 655-4843.

### OTTAWA—G-6

***See listings at Alfred, Ashton, Cumberland, Kemptville, Limoges & Nepean***

**OTTAWA AREA MAP**

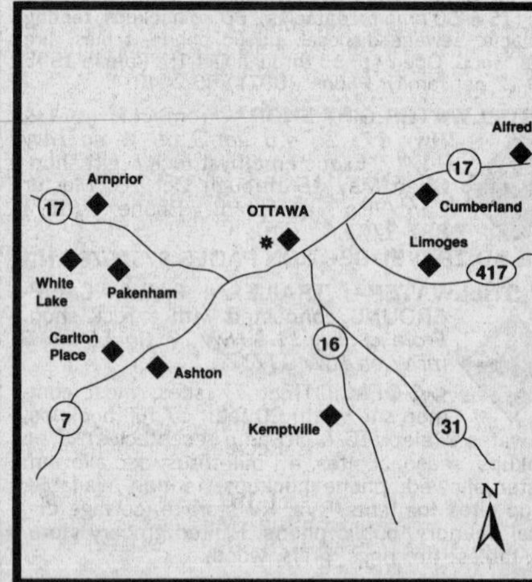


***Symbols on map indicate towns within a 50 mi radius of Ottawa where campgrounds (diamonds), attractions (flags) & RV service centers & camping supply outlets (gears) are listed. Check listings for more information.***

OTTAWA—Continued on next page



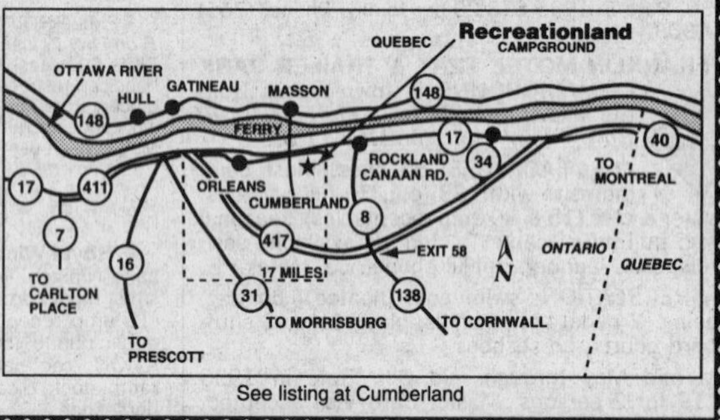


See listing at Cumberland

OTTAWA—Continued

**CAMP HITHER HILLS**—A semi-wooded CAMPGROUND on the outskirts of Ottawa. *From south city limits: Go 9.6 km/6 mi S on Hwy 31.*

◆◆◆FACILITIES: 186 sites, most common site width 30 feet, 60 full hookups, 50 water & elec (15 & 30 amp receptacles), 76 no hookups, seasonal sites, 17 pull-thrus, a/c allowed, tenting available, group sites for tents/RVs, RV storage, sewage disposal, ice, tables, fire rings, wood.

◆RECREATION: swim pool (heated), sports field.

Open Mar 15 through Nov 15. Facilities fully operational Apr 1 through Nov 15. pool open Jun 1 thru Sep 15 Rate in 1995 $15-22 for 4 persons. Phone: (613) 822-0509.

**SEE AD PAGE 1010**

**✱ OTTAWA CAMPING TRAILERS**—*From south city limits: Go 6.4 km/4 mi S on Hwy 31.* SALES: travel trailers, park models, truck campers, 5th wheels, van conversions, motor homes, mini-motor homes, fold-down camping trailers. SERVICES: RV appliance mechanic full-time, LP gas refill by weight, RV rentals, RV storage, sells parts/accessories, installs hitches. Open all year. Master Card/Visa accepted. Phone: (613) 822-2268.

**SEE AD THIS PAGE**

**OTTAWA-NEPEAN MUNICIPAL TENT & TRAILER PARK**—*From jct Hwy 417 (Queensway-exit 134) & Moodie Dr: Go .4 km/1/4 mi N on Moodie Dr, then 3.2 km/2 mi W on CR 18.*

FACILITIES: 153 sites, most common site width 60 feet, 103 water & elec, 50 elec (15 & 30 amp receptacles), a/c allowed, heater allowed, tenting available, group sites for tents/RVs, sewage disposal, laundry, public phone, limited grocery store, ice, tables, fire rings, wood.

RECREATION: pavilion, wading pool, playground, sports field, hiking trails. Recreation open to the public.

Open May 1 through Oct 15. Reservations recommended Jul through Aug. Master Card/Visa accepted. Phone: (613) 828-6632.

**SEE AD THIS PAGE**

**POPLAR GROVE TOURIST CAMP**—Rolling, grassy CAMPGROUND. *From jct Hwy 417 & Hwy 31: Go 20.8 km/13 mi S on Hwy 31, then .4 km/1/4 mi W on Poplar Grove Camp Rd.*

◆◆◆FACILITIES: 260 sites, most common site width 50 feet, 120 full hookups, 110 water & elec (15 & 30 amp receptacles), 30 no hookups, seasonal sites, 70 pull-thrus, a/c allowed, heater allowed ($), phone hookups, tenting available, group sites for tents/RVs, RV storage, sewage disposal, laundry, public phone, limited grocery store, RV supplies, ice, tables, fire rings, wood, traffic control gate.

◆◆◆◆RECREATION: rec hall, pavilion, coin games, swim pool (indoor) (heated), whirlpool, water slide ($), mini-golf ($), playground, planned group activities, 2 tennis courts, sports field, horseshoes, hiking trails. Recreation open to the public.

Open all year. Facilities fully operational May 1 through Oct 31. Rate in 1995 $14-19.50 for 2 persons. Reservations recommended Jul through Aug. Master Card/Visa accepted. Member of OPCA. Phone: (613) 821-2973.

**SEE AD THIS PAGE**

## OWEN SOUND—G-2

HARRISON PARK (City Park)—*From jct Hwy 6 & 2nd Ave E: Go 3/4 km/1/2 mi S on 2nd Ave E.* FACILITIES: 114 sites, 114 water & elec (15 & 30 amp receptacles), 10 pull-thrus, tenting available, handicap restroom facilities, sewage disposal, public phone, limited grocery store, ice, tables, fire rings, grills, wood. RECREATION: pavilion, swim pool (heated), river swimming, boating, no motors, canoe/pedal boat rentals, river fishing ($), mini-golf, playground, shuffleboard court, 2 tennis courts, sports field, horseshoes, hiking trails. Recreation open to the public. Open May 1 through Sep 30. Phone: (519) 371-9734.

**SAFETY TIP**

**Fires can create their own wind. Practice fire safety while camping. Before starting a fire, clean a 10-foot circle clear of forest debris.**

OWEN SOUND—Continued

KELSO BEACH (City Park)—*From town: Go 3/4 km/1/2 mi W on Hwy 21, then 2 1/2 km/1 1/2 mi N on 4th Ave West.* FACILITIES: 40 sites, 40 water & elec, tenting available. RECREATION: lake swimming, lake fishing, playground. Open Jun through Sep. Phone: (519) 376-1440.

**KOA-Owen Sound**—CAMPGROUND in rustic natural area on the Bruce Trail. *From jct Hwy 26 & Hwy 6 & 10: Go .4 km/1/4 mi S on Hwy 6 & 10, then 3.2 km/2 mi E on 8th St, then .4 km/1/4 mi S on gravel road.* ◆◆◆FACILITIES: 139 sites, most common site width 35 feet, 108 water & elec (15 amp receptacles), 31 no hookups, seasonal sites, tenting available, sewage disposal, laundry, public phone, grocery store, ice, tables, fire rings, wood. ◆◆◆RECREATION: rec room/area, swim pool (heated), stream fishing, mini-golf ($), playground, sports field, horseshoes, hiking trails, volleyball. Open May 1 through Sep 30. Rate in 1995 $20-23 for 2 persons. Phone: (519) 371-1331. KOA 10% value card discount.

## PAISLEY—H-2

**SAUGEEN BLUFFS (Saugeen Valley Conservation Auth.)**—*From town: Go 4 km/2 1/2 mi N on CR 3, follow signs.*

FACILITIES: 172 sites, 60 water & elec (15 & 30 amp receptacles), 112 no hookups, seasonal sites, tenting available, sewage disposal, laundry, public phone, limited grocery store, ice, tables, fire rings, grills, wood, guard.

RECREATION: wading pool, river swimming, boating, canoeing, dock, 4 canoe boat rentals, river fishing, playground, shuffleboard court, badminton, sports field, horseshoes, hiking trails.

Open mid May through Oct 15. Phone: (519) 364-1255.

**SEE AD TRAVEL SECTION PAGE 979**

## PAKENHAM—G-5

**RIVERBEND PARK**—Riverside CAMPGROUND with mostly seasonal sites. *From south city limits: Go 1.6 km/1 mi S on Hwy 15.*

◆◆FACILITIES: 112 sites, most common site width 40 feet, 107 full hookups, (15 amp receptacles), 5 no hookups, seasonal sites, a/c not allowed, heater not allowed, tenting available, group sites for tents/RVs, sewage disposal, public phone, limited grocery store, ice, tables, fire rings, wood.

◆◆◆RECREATION: river swimming, boating, canoeing, dock, river fishing, basketball hoop, planned group activities (weekends only), horseshoes.

Open May 15 through Oct 1. Rate in 1995 $17.50 per family. Member of OPCA. Phone: (613) 624-5426.

**SEE AD TRAVEL SECTION PAGES 975, 976 AND 977**



## PARIS—I-2

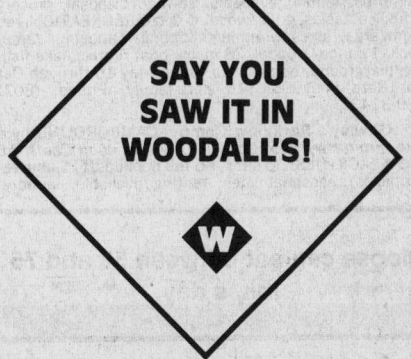

**PINEHURST LAKE (Grand River Conservation Authority)**—*From north town limits: Go 9 1/2 km/6 mi N on Hwy 24A.*

FACILITIES: 300 sites, 175 water & elec (15 & 30 amp receptacles), 125 no hookups, seasonal sites, tenting available, group sites for tents, sewage disposal, public phone, limited grocery store, ice, tables, wood, guard.

RECREATION: lake swimming, boating, no motors, canoeing, 5 row/30 canoe boat rentals, lake fishing, playground, sports field, hiking trails, cross country skiing. Recreation open to the public.

Open all year. Facilities fully operational May 1 through Oct 15. Day use only for winter sports. Phone: (519) 442-4721.

**SEE AD TRAVEL SECTION PAGE 978**

## PARKHILL—I-2

PARKHILL CONSERVATION AREA (Ausable-Bayfield Conservation Auth.)—*From jct Hwy 7 & Hwy 81: Go 1 1/2 km/1 mi N on Centre Rd.* FACILITIES: 117 sites, 86 water & elec (15 amp receptacles), 31 no hookups, seasonal sites, sewage disposal, public phone, ice, tables, fire rings, wood. RECREATION: pavilion, lake swimming, boating, electric motors only, canoeing, lake/river fishing, playground, sports field, hiking trails. Recreation open to the public. Open mid May through mid Oct. Phone: (519) 294-0114.

## PARRY SOUND—G-3

**HORSESHOE LAKE CAMP & COTTAGES**—Quiet, wooded CAMPGROUND on Horseshoe Lake. *From jct Hwy 69 & Hwy 141: Go 1.6 km/1 mi E on Hwy 141, then 1.6 km/1 mi N on North Sandy Plains Rd.*

◆◆◆FACILITIES: 74 sites, most common site width 60 feet, 9 full hookups, 55 water & elec (15 & 30 amp receptacles), 10 no hookups, seasonal sites, a/c allowed ($), heater allowed ($), tenting available, cabins, RV storage, sewage disposal, laundry, limited grocery store, ice, tables, fire rings, wood.

◆◆◆RECREATION: rec room/area, coin games, lake swimming, sauna, boating, canoeing, ramp, dock, 5 row/2 canoe/2 pedal/3 motor boat rentals, lake fishing, basketball hoop, playground, lanned group activities (weekends only), sports field, horseshoes, hiking trails, volleyball, cross country skiing, snowmobile trails.

Open all year. Facilities fully operational May 1 through mid Oct. Rate in 1995 $15-19 per family. Master Card/Visa accepted. Member of OPCA. Phone: (705) 732-4928.

**SEE AD TRAVEL SECTION PAGES 975, 976 AND 977**

OASTLER LAKE PROVINCIAL PARK—*From town: Go 8 km/5 mi S on Hwy 69.* FACILITIES: 145 sites, 22 elec, 123

OASTLER LAKE PROVINCIAL PARK—Continued on next page
PARRY SOUND—Continued on next page

PARRY SOUND—Continued
OASTLER LAKE PROVINCIAL PARK—Continued

no hookups, tenting available, handicap restroom facilities, sewage disposal, tables, wood. RECREATION: swimming, boating, canoeing, ramp, lake fishing. Open mid May through mid Oct. Phone: (705) 378-2401.

**PARRY SOUND-KOA KAMPGROUND**—CAMPGROUND in a wooded, natural setting with open, shaded and secluded sites. *From jct Hwy 518 & Hwy 69: Go 4.8 km/3 mi S on Hwy 69, then 2.4 km/1 1/2 mi W on Rankin Lake Rd.*

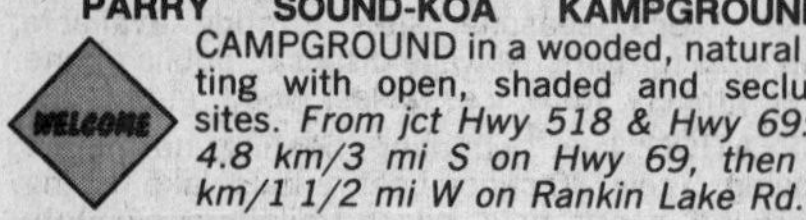


◆◆◆◆FACILITIES: 100 sites, most common site width 35 feet, 55 water & elec (15 & 30 amp receptacles), 45 no hookups, seasonal sites, 12 pull-thrus, a/c allowed ($), heater allowed ($), tenting available, group sites for tents/RVs, cabins, RV storage, sewage disposal, laundry, public phone, limited grocery store, RV supplies, LP gas refill by weight, ice, tables, fire rings, wood.

◆◆◆RECREATION: rec room/area, swim pool (heated), 5 canoe boat rentals, mini-golf ($), 8 bike rentals, playground, badminton, sports field, horseshoes, hiking trails.

Open May 1 through Oct 15. Rate in 1995 $19-23 for 2 persons. Master Card/Visa accepted. Member of OPCA. Phone: (705) 378-2721. KOA 10% value card discount.

**SEE AD THIS PAGE AND AD FRONT OF BOOK PAGES 68 AND 69**

**Roll-in-G Campsite**—Shaded CAMPGROUND on Tucker Lake. *From jct Hwy 518 & Hwy 69: Go 16 km/10 mi S on Hwy 69, then .4 km/1/4 mi E on Clear Lake Rd.* ◆◆FACILITIES: 50 sites, most common site width 30 feet, 30 water & elec (15 amp receptacles), 20 no hookups, seasonal sites, tenting available, limited grocery store, ice, tables, fire rings, wood. ◆◆◆RECREATION: rec room/area, lake swimming, boating, no motors, canoeing, 2 row/3 canoe boat rentals, lake fishing, sports field, horseshoes. Open May 24 through Oct 15. Rates available upon request. Member of OPCA. Phone: (705) 375-2518.

**Terrawoods on Horseshoe Lake** (REBUILDING)—CAMPGROUND on Horseshoe Lake. *From jct Hwy 141 & Hwy 69: Go 1.6 km/1 mi N on Hwy 69, then .8 km/1/2 mi E on Horseshoe Lake Rd.* FACILITIES: 39 sites, 32 water & elec (15 amp receptacles), 7 no hookups, seasonal sites, tenting available, sewage disposal, laundry, limited grocery store, ice, tables, fire rings, wood. RECREATION: lake swimming, boating, canoeing, ramp, dock, 3 canoe/4 pedal/4 motor boat rentals, lake fishing, playground, horseshoes. Open all year. Facilities fully operational mid May through mid Oct. Rates available upon request. Member of OPCA. Phone: (705) 378-2762.

## PASS LAKE—B-1

SLEEPING GIANT PROVINCIAL PARK—*From town: Go 19 1/4 km/12 mi S on Hwy 587.* FACILITIES: 168 sites, 168 no hookups, tenting available, handicap restroom facilities, sewage disposal, tables, fire rings, wood. RECREATION: lake

PASS LAKE—Continued
SLEEPING GIANT PROVINCIAL PARK—Continued

swimming, boating, canoeing, ramp, lake fishing, playground, hiking trails. Open mid May through mid Oct. Phone: (807) 977-2526.

## PEMBROKE—F-5

***See listings at Cobden, Eganville, Golden Lake & Round Lake Centre***

**Pine Ridge Park & Resort**—Riverside CAMPGROUND. *From jct Hwy 17 & Hwy 62: Go 7.2 km/4 1/2 mi W on Hwy 17, then 1.6 km/1 mi NE on CR 26, then 2.4 km/1 1/2 mi N on CR 44 (Airport Rd), then 2.4 km/1 1/2 mi N on Radke Rd, then 15 m/50 feet E on River Rd.* ◆◆◆FACILITIES: 50 sites, most common site width 30 feet, 26 full hookups, 16 water & elec (15 & 30 amp receptacles), 8 no hookups, seasonal sites, 7 pull-thrus, tenting available, sewage disposal, laundry, public phone, limited grocery store, ice, tables, fire rings, wood. ◆◆◆RECREATION: river swimming, boating, canoeing, ramp, dock, 2 row/4 canoe/1 pedal/6 motor boat rentals, river fishing, playground, shuffleboard court, badminton, horseshoes, hiking trails, volleyball. Recreation open to the public. Open all year. Facilities fully operational May 1 through mid Oct. Rate in 1995 $18-22 for 2 persons. Phone: (613) 732-9891.

RIVERSIDE PARK (City Park)—*From jct Hwy 417 & Hwy 62: Go 8 km/5 mi N on Hwy 62, then 3/4 km/1/2 mi W on Pembroke St.* FACILITIES: 75 sites, 50 water & elec, 25 no hookups, 28 pull-thrus, tenting available, handicap restroom facilities, sewage disposal, laundry, public phone, ice, tables, fire rings, wood. RECREATION: river swimming, river fishing, mini-golf ($), playground, sports field, horseshoes. Recreation open to the public. Open May 8 through Thanksgiving. Facilities fully operational Victoria Day through Labour Day. Phone: (613) 735-2251.

## PENETANGUISHENE—G-3

AWENDA PROVINCIAL PARK—*From town: Go N on Hwy 35, then W.* FACILITIES: 200 sites, 200 no hookups, tenting available, handicap restroom facilities, sewage disposal, laundry, tables, fire rings, wood. RECREATION: lake swimming, lake fishing, hiking trails. Open mid May through mid Sep. Phone: (705) 549-2231.

**LAFONTAINE CAMPGROUND & RV PARK**—Rustic CAMPGROUND in connection with winter skiing. *From jct Hwy 93 & CR 25: Go 6.4 km/4 mi W on CR 25, then 9.6 km/6 mi N on CR 6, then 1.6 km/1 mi E on CR 26.*

◆◆◆FACILITIES: 150 sites, most common site width 45 feet, 26 full hookups, 124 water & elec (15 & 30 amp receptacles), seasonal sites, a/c allowed, heater allowed, tenting available, group sites for tents/RVs, RV rentals, sewage disposal, laundry, public phone, limited grocery store, ice, tables, fire rings, wood, guard.

◆◆◆RECREATION: rec hall, rec room/area, swim pool, sauna, whirlpool, basketball hoop, 20 bike rentals, playground, planned group activities (weekends only), movies, badminton, sports field, horseshoes, hiking trails, volleyball, cross country skiing. Recreation open to the public.

Open all year. Facilities fully operational May 1 through Oct 15. Rate in 1995 $16-18 per family. Reservations recommended Jul through Aug. Master Card/Visa accepted. Member of OPCA. Phone: (705) 533-2961.

**SEE AD TRAVEL SECTION PAGE 979**

OJIBWA LANDING PARK (City Park)—*From jct Hwy 93 & Robert St W (in center of town): Go 1 1/2 km/1 mi W on Robert St.* FACILITIES: 85 sites, 16 full hookups, 40 water & elec (15 amp receptacles), 29 no hookups, seasonal sites, tenting available, sewage disposal, tables, wood. RECREATION: lake swimming, boating, canoeing, lake fishing, playground, horseshoes. Recreation open to the public. Open May 1 through Sep 6. Phone: (705) 549-2531.

## PERRAULT FALLS—D-2

**Bob & Gale's Rainbow Camp & Trailer Park**—CAMPGROUND with cabins on Perrault Lake. *From Hwy 105: Go .4 km/1/4 mi E on Rainbow Point Rd.* ◆◆FACILITIES: 15 sites, most common site width 20 feet, 13 full hookups, 2 water & elec (15 amp receptacles), 10 pull-thrus, tenting available, sewage disposal, grocery store, ice, tables, grills, wood. ◆◆◆◆RECREATION: rec room/area, lake swimming, boating, canoeing, ramp, dock, 1 canoe/1 pedal/28 motor boat rentals, lake fishing, playground, horseshoes. Open May 15 through Oct 15. Rate in 1995 $15 per family. Phone: (807) 529-3143.

**Gawley's Parkview Camp**—CAMPGROUND by a lake. *From Hwy 105: Go .4 km/1/4 mi W on Camp Rd.* ◆◆FACILITIES: 36 sites, 36 full hookups, (15 amp receptacles), seasonal sites, tenting available, laundry,

**Moose can eat between 50 and 75 lbs. a day.**

PERRAULT FALLS—Continued
GAWLEY'S PARKVIEW CAMP—Continued

public phone, ice, tables, fire rings, wood. ◆◆RECREATION: lake swimming, boating, canoeing, ramp, dock, 25 motor boat rentals, lake fishing, horseshoes. Open mid May through mid Sep. Rate in 1995 $19 for 2 persons. Phone: (807) 529-3147.

## PERTH—G-5

LAST DUEL PARK (City Park)—*In town on Hwy 43.* FACILITIES: 150 sites, 42 water & elec (15 & 30 amp receptacles), 108 no hookups, 20 pull-thrus, tenting available, sewage disposal, laundry, public phone, ice, tables, grills, wood. RECREATION: river swimming, boating, canoeing, ramp, dock, river fishing, playground, volleyball. Recreation open to the public. Open May through Oct. Phone: (613) 267-3311.

**McCreary's Beach Vacation Resort**—CAMPGROUND on Mississippi Lake. *From jct Hwy 43 & Hwy 7: Go 12 km/7 1/2 mi N on Hwy 7, then 1.6 km/1 mi E on Mississippi Lake W Shore Dr.* ◆◆◆FACILITIES: 180 sites, most common site width 35 feet, 150 full hookups, 30 water & elec (15 & 30 amp receptacles), seasonal sites, tenting available, sewage disposal, laundry, public phone, limited grocery store, LP gas refill by weight, ice, tables, fire rings, wood. ◆◆◆◆RECREATION: rec hall, rec room/area, swim pool (indoor) (heated), lake swimming ($), boating, canoeing, ramp, dock, 6 row/2 canoe/6 motor boat rentals, lake fishing, playground, planned group activities, tennis court, horseshoes, volleyball. Recreation open to the public. Open all year. Facilities fully operational Apr 1 through Oct 15. Rate in 1995 $18-20 for 4 persons. Member of OPCA. Phone: (613) 267-4450.

**McCullough's Landing**—Grassy, lakeside CAMPGROUND. *From jct Hwy 43 & Hwy 7: Go 12 km/7 1/2 mi N on Hwy 7, then 1.6 km/1 mi E on Mississippi Lake W Shore Dr.* ◆◆◆FACILITIES: 200 sites, most common site width 30 feet, 180 water & elec (15 & 30 amp receptacles), 20 no hookups, seasonal sites, 6 pull-thrus, tenting available, sewage disposal, public phone, limited grocery store, ice, tables, fire rings, wood. ◆◆◆◆RECREATION: rec room/area, lake swimming, boating, canoeing, ramp, dock, 18 row/2 pedal/3 motor boat rentals, lake fishing, mini-golf ($), playground, 2 shuffleboard courts, planned group activities, badminton, sports field, horseshoes, volleyball. Recreation open to the public. Open May 1 through Sep 30. Rate in 1995 $16.50-18.50 per family. Phone: (613) 267-4310.

MURPHY'S POINT PROVINCIAL PARK—*From town: Go 16 km/10 mi S on Hwy 10, then 4 3/4 km/3 mi SE on Hwy 14.* FACILITIES: 167 sites, 30 elec, 137 no hookups, tenting available, handicap restroom facilities, sewage disposal, laundry, tables, fire rings, wood. RECREATION: lake swimming, boating, canoeing, ramp, lake fishing, playground, hiking trails. Open mid May through mid Oct. Phone: (613) 267-5060.

**TAY RIVER TENT & TRAILER CAMP**—CAMPGROUND on the Tay River with open grassy sites. *From jct Hwy 43 & Christie Lake Rd (CR 6) in town: Go 14.4 km/9 mi W on Christie Lake Rd (CR 6).*

WELCOME

◆◆◆FACILITIES: 100 sites, most common site width 50 feet, 50 water & elec (15 & 30 amp receptacles), 50 no hookups, seasonal sites, a/c allowed ($), heater allowed ($), tenting available, group sites for tents/RVs, sewage disposal, ice, tables, fire rings, wood.

◆◆◆RECREATION: rec hall, river swimming, boating, ramp, dock, river fishing, basketball hoop, horseshoes. Recreation open to the public.

Open mid May through mid Oct. Rate in 1995 $12-15 per family. Member of OPCA. Phone: (613) 267-3955.

**SEE AD TRAVEL SECTION PAGES 975, 976 AND 977**

## PETERBOROUGH—H-4

***See listings at Bailieboro, Bewdley & Ennismore***

**Bailey's Bay Resort**—A terraced CAMPGROUND with open and shaded sites. *From jct Hwy 7 & Hwy 7B: Go 305 m/1000 feet E on Hwy 7B.* ◆◆FACILITIES: 234 sites, most common site width 50 feet, 234 full hookups, (30 amp receptacles), seasonal sites, sewage disposal, laundry, public phone, LP gas refill by weight, tables, fire rings, wood. ◆◆◆◆RECREATION: rec hall, swim pool, lake swimming, boating, ramp, dock, lake fishing, playground, planned group activities (weekends only), tennis court, badminton, sports field, horseshoes, volleyball. No tents. Open May 5 through Oct 29. Rate in 1995 $20 per family. Member of OPCA. Phone: (705) 748-9656.

BEAVERMEAD (City Park)—*From jct Hwy 115 & Hwy 7: Go 4 3/4 km/3 mi E on Hwy 7, then 1 1/2 km/1 mi N on Ashburnham Dr.* FACILITIES: 381 sites, 96 water & elec (15 amp receptacles), 285 no hookups, tenting available, sewage disposal, public phone, limited grocery store, ice, tables, fire rings, wood. RECREATION: pavilion, lake swimming, boating, canoeing, ramp, 5 canoe/10 pedal boat rentals, mini-golf ($), playground, sports field. Open May 11 through Oct 8. Phone: (705) 742-9712.

PETERBOROUGH—Continued on next page

PETERBOROUGH—Continued

❋ **PETERBOROUGH RV CENTRE**—*From jct Hwy 115 & Hwy 7: Go E on Hwy 7.* SALES: travel trailers, park models, truck campers, 5th wheels. SERVICES: RV appliance mechanic full-time, emergency road service business hours, sewage disposal, RV storage, sells parts/accessories, installs hitches. Open all year. Master Card/Visa accepted. Phone: (705) 745-4313.

**SEE AD THIS PAGE**

## PETROLIA—I-1

LORNE C. HENDERSON AREA (St. Clair Region Conservation Auth.)—*From town: Go 2 km/1 1/4 mi W on CR 4.* FACILITIES: 90 sites, 90 water & elec (30 amp receptacles), seasonal sites, tenting available, sewage disposal, public phone, tables, fire rings, wood. RECREATION: equipped pavilion, swim pool, boating, no motors, canoeing, stream fishing, playground, sports field, horseshoes, hiking trails, volleyball. Recreation open to the public. Open late May through mid Oct. Phone: (519) 882-2280.

## PICKERING—H-3

❋ **PICKERING MOTORHOMES**—*From Brock Rd & Hwy 7: Go 5.6 km/3 1/2 mi W on Hwy 7.* SALES: motor homes, mini-motor homes. SERVICES: Engine/Chassis & RV appliance mechanic full-time, emergency road service business hours, RV towing, LP gas refill by weight/by meter, sewage disposal, sells parts/accessories, installs hitches. Open all year. Master Card/Visa accepted. Phone: (905) 686-5874.

**SEE AD THIS PAGE**

## PICTON—H-5

***See listings at Adolphustown, Bloomfield, Cherry Valley & Milford***

## PORT ALBERT—H-2

**MacKenzie's Trailer Park**—Grassy, level CAMPGROUND with a lake view. *From jct Concession Rd 4 & 5 & Hwy 21: Go 7.2 km/4 1/2 mi N on Hwy 21 (to Kintail), then 1.6 km/1 mi W on Mackenzie Rd.* ◊◊◊FACILITIES: 115 sites, most common site width 35 feet, 30 ft. max RV length, 94 full hookups, 9 elec (15 & 20 amp receptacles), 12 no hookups, seasonal sites, 3 pull-thrus, tenting available, sewage disposal, ice, tables, fire rings, wood. ◊◊RECREATION: pavilion, playground, shuffleboard court, sports field, horseshoes. Open mid May through mid Oct. Rate in 1995 $15-18 per family. Phone: (519) 529-7536.

## PORT BURWELL—J-2

**Big Otter Marina & Campgrounds**—Open & wooded sites along a river flowing into Lake Erie. *From north end of town & Bridge St (CR 42): Go 500 feet N on CR 42.* ◊◊◊FACILITIES: 62 sites, most common site width 35 feet, 28 full hookups, 20 water & elec (15 amp receptacles), 14 no hookups, seasonal sites, tenting available, portable dump, public phone, ice, tables, fire rings, wood. ◊◊◊RECREATION: rec hall, river swimming, boating, ramp, dock, 4 canoe/2 pedal boat rentals, lake/river fishing, playground, planned group activities (weekends only), horseshoes. Open mid May through mid Oct. Rate in 1995 $16-19 per family. Member of OPCA. Phone: (519) 874-4034.

PORT BURWELL PROVINCIAL PARK—*From town: Go 4 3/4 km/3 mi W on Lakeshore Rd.* FACILITIES: 232 sites, 232 no hookups, tenting available, sewage disposal, laundry, tables, wood. RECREATION: swimming, boating, canoeing, ramp, fishing, playground, hiking trails. Open mid May through early Sep. Phone: (519) 874-4691.

**SAND HILL PARK**—CAMPGROUND on the north shore of Lake Erie. *From east town limits: Go 14.4 km/9 mi E on Lakeshore Rd (CR 42).*

◊◊◊FACILITIES: 300 sites, most common site width 30 feet, 48 full hookups, 75 elec (15 & 30 amp receptacles), 177 no hookups, seasonal sites, a/c allowed, heater not allowed, tenting available, RV storage, sewage disposal, public phone, limited grocery store, ice, tables, wood, traffic control gate.

◊◊◊RECREATION: rec hall, lake swimming, boating, canoeing, lake fishing, planned group activities (weekends only), movies, sports field, horseshoes, hiking trails, volleyball. Recreation open to the public.

Open May 1 through mid Oct. Rate in 1995 $16-24 per family. Member of OPCA. Phone: (519) 586-3891.

**SEE AD TRAVEL SECTION PAGE 983**

## PORT COLBORNE—I-3

**DRESSEL'S STILL ACRES** (REBUILDING)—CAMPGROUND with grassy, open and shaded sites. *From west town limits: Go 3.2 km/2 mi W on Hwy 3, then 1.6 km/1 mi S on Bessey Rd.*

FACILITIES: 91 sites, most common site width 30 feet, 81 water & elec (15 amp receptacles), 10 no hookups, seasonal sites, 4 pull-thrus, a/c not allowed, heater not allowed, phone hookups, tenting available, group sites for tents/RVs, RV rentals, RV storage, sewage disposal, ice, tables, fire rings, grills, wood.

RECREATION: rec hall, coin games, swim pool, lake swimming, basketball hoop, playground, planned group activities (weekends only), horseshoes, volleyball.

Open May 24 through Oct 31. Rate in 1995 $15-17 per family. Reservations recommended Jun through Aug. Phone: (905) 834-0724.

**SEE AD TRAVEL SECTION PAGES 975, 976 AND 977**

LONG BEACH (Niagara Peninsula Conservation Auth.)—*From town: Go 16 km/10 mi W on Hwy 3 to Lake Shore Rd.* FACILITIES: 275 sites, 110 water & elec (15 amp receptacles), 165 no hookups, seasonal sites, 275 pull-thrus, tenting available, handicap restroom facilities, sewage disposal, public phone, limited grocery store, ice, tables, wood. RECREATION: pavilion, lake swimming, boating, canoeing, ramp, lake fishing, playground, sports field, horseshoes, hiking trails. Recreation open to the public. Open May 24 through Sep 15. Phone: (905) 227-1013.

**Pleasant Beach Trailer Park** (REBUILDING)—Level, shaded, grassy sites with a half mile walk to sandy beach. *From Peace Bridge: Go 19 km/12 mi W on Hwy 3, then 4.8 km/3 mi S on Pleasant Beach Rd to park.* FACILITIES: 45 sites, 45 water & elec (15 amp receptacles), seasonal sites, 5 pull-thrus, sewage disposal, public phone, ice, tables, wood. RECREATION: rec room/area, sports field, horseshoes. No tents. Open mid May through Sep 30. Rate in 1995 $20 per family. Phone: (905) 894-4249.

**SHERKSTON SHORES**—Beachfront resort complex with a number of CAMPGROUND areas. Recreational complex. *From jct Hwy 140 & Hwy 3: Go 8 km/5 mi E on Hwy 3, then 2.4 km/1 1/2 mi S on Empire Rd (Regional Rd 98).*

◊◊◊◊FACILITIES: 1840 sites, most common site width 35 feet, 770 full hookups, 150 water & elec (15,30 & 50 amp receptacles), 920 no hookups, seasonal sites, 42 pull-thrus, a/c allowed, heater allowed, tenting available, RV rentals, sewage disposal, laundry, public phone, grocery store, LP gas refill by weight/by meter, ice, tables, fire rings, wood, church services, traffic control gate/guard.

◊◊◊◊RECREATION: rec hall, rec room/area, coin games, swim pool (heated), lake/pond swimming, whirlpool, water slide ($), boating, canoeing, ramp, water skiing, lake fishing, mini-golf ($), basketball hoop, playground, planned group activities, movies, recreation director, 4 tennis courts, horse riding trails, horse rental, sports field, horseshoes, volleyball, local tours. Recreation open to the public.

Open all year. Facilities fully operational May 1 through Oct 31. Rate in 1995 $20-25 per family. No refunds. Reservations recommended May 1 through Oct 31. American Express/Master Card/Visa accepted. Member of ARVC; OPCA. Phone: (800) 263-8121.

**SEE AD FRONT OF BOOK PAGE 142 AND AD NIAGARA FALLS PAGE 1008**

## PORT ELGIN—H-2

**BRUCEDALE CONSERVATION AREA (Saugeen Valley Conservation Area)**—*From town: Go 13 km/8 mi S on Hwy 21, then 8 km/5 mi W on Concession Rd 10.*

FACILITIES: 54 sites, 54 no hookups, seasonal sites, tenting available, non-flush toilets, tables, fire rings, wood, guard.

RECREATION: lake swimming, boating, canoeing, dock, lake fishing, playground, badminton, horseshoes, volleyball.

Open mid May through Sep 1. Phone: (519) 364-1255.

**SEE AD TRAVEL SECTION PAGE 979**

**KENORUS QUIET RV RESORT**—Grassy, shaded level CAMPGROUND convenient to a major highway. *From north city limits: Go 2.4 km/1 1/2 mi N on Hwy 21.*

◊◊◊FACILITIES: 247 sites, most common site width 30 feet, 241 full hookups, 6 water & elec (15 & 30 amp receptacles), seasonal sites, 85 pull-thrus, a/c allowed ($), heater allowed ($), tenting available, group sites for RVs, RV storage, handicap restroom facilities, sewage disposal, laundry, public phone, limited grocery store, RV supplies, LP gas refill by weight/by meter, ice, tables, patios, fire rings, wood, traffic control gate.

◊◊◊RECREATION: rec room/area, coin games, swim pool (heated), whirlpool, basketball hoop, playground, planned group activities (weekends only), sports field, horseshoes, volleyball.

Open May 1 through Oct 15. Rate in 1995 $19 for 2 persons. Master Card/Visa accepted. Member of OPCA. Phone: (519) 832-5183.

**SEE AD TRAVEL SECTION PAGE 983**

MACGREGOR POINT PROVINCIAL PARK—*From town: Go 4 3/4 km/3 mi S on Hwy 21.* FACILITIES: 360 sites, 50 elec, 310 no hookups, tenting available, handicap restroom facilities, sewage disposal, laundry, tables, wood. RECREATION: lake swimming, playground, hiking trails. Open mid May through mid Oct. Phone: (519) 389-9056.

PORT ELGIN MUNICIPAL TOURIST CAMP—*In town at corner of Bruce St & Johnson Ave.* FACILITIES: 341 sites, 40 full hookups, 301 water & elec (15 & 30 amp receptacles), seasonal sites, tenting available, sewage disposal, public phone, tables, wood. RECREATION: lake swimming, boating, ramp, dock, lake/river fishing, mini-golf, playground, sports field. Open May 15 through Oct 15. Phone: (519) 832-2512.





Forty is the old age of youth; fifty is the youth of old age. *Victor Hugo*

## PORTLAND—G-5

**Waterways Campground**—Lakeside CAMPGROUND with grassy, open & shaded sites. Most sites occupied by seasonals. *From jct Hwy 42 & Hwy 15 (Crosby): Go 4 km/2 1/2 mi N on Hwy 15, then W on Big Rideau Lake Rd following signs.* ◆◆◆FACILITIES: 150 sites, most common site width 50 feet, 138 full hookups, 9 water & elec (15 & 30 amp receptacles), 3 no hookups, seasonal sites, 60 pull-thrus, tenting available, sewage disposal, laundry, public phone, limited grocery store, ice, tables, fire rings, wood. ◆◆◆RECREATION: lake swimming, boating, canoeing, ramp, dock, 5 row/2 pedal boat rentals, lake fishing, horseshoes. Recreation open to the public. Open May 15 through Oct 15. Rate in 1995 $13.75-20 per family. Member of OPCA. Phone: (613) 272-2791.

## PORT LORING—F-3

**Minnehaha Camp Resort**—CAMPGROUND on Wilson Lake with open, grassy sites. *From east city limits: Go 2.4 km/1 1/2 mi S on Duck Lake Rd.* ◆◆◆FACILITIES: 25 sites, most common site width 50 feet, 30 ft. max RV length, 25 full hookups, (15 & 30 amp receptacles), seasonal sites, 4 pull-thrus, tenting available, laundry, public phone, limited grocery store, ice, tables, fire rings, wood. ◆◆◆◆RECREATION: rec hall, lake swimming, boating, canoeing, ramp, dock, 8 canoe/4 pedal/30 motor boat rentals, lake fishing, planned group activities, badminton, horseshoes, hiking trails, volleyball. Open May 10 through Oct 20. Rate in 1995 $16 for 2 persons. Member of OPCA. Phone: (705) 757-2004.

## PORT PERRY—H-3

**BROCK RV CENTRE**—*From jct Hwy 401 & Hwy 12: Go 28.8 km/18 mi N on Hwy 12.* SALES: travel trailers, park models, 5th wheels. SERVICES: RV appliance mechanic full-time, LP gas refill by weight/by meter, sells parts/accessories, installs hitches. Open all year. Visa accepted. Phone: (905) 985-0390.

**SEE AD THIS PAGE**

## PORT ROWAN—J-2

BACKUS HERITAGE CONSERVATION AREA (Long Point Region Conservation Auth.)—*From town: Go 2 1/2 km/1 1/2 mi N on Regional Rd 42.* FACILITIES: 150 sites, 60 water & elec (15 amp receptacles), 90 no hookups, tenting available, handicap restroom facilities, sewage disposal, laundry, public phone, ice, tables, wood. RECREATION: pavilion, swim pool, boating, no motors, dock, pond fishing, hiking trails. Recreation open to the public. Open Victoria Day through Oct 9. Phone: (519) 586-2201.

LONG POINT PROVINCIAL PARK—*From town: Go 4 3/4 km/3 mi S on Hwy 59.* FACILITIES: 258 sites, 53 elec, 205 no hookups, tenting available, handicap restroom facilities, sewage disposal, laundry, limited grocery store, tables, wood. RECREATION: swimming, boating, canoeing, ramp, fishing, playground. Open early May through early Oct. Phone: (519) 586-2133.



## PORT SEVERN—G-3

**Hidden Glen Trailer Park** (REBUILDING)—Wooded CAMPGROUND on Georgian Bay. *From north city limits: Go 11 km/7 mi N on Hwy 69, then 1.2 km/3/4 mi W on Hidden Glen Rd.* FACILITIES: 160 sites, most common site width 35 feet, 150 water & elec (15 & 30 amp receptacles), 10 no hookups, seasonal sites, 2 pull-thrus, tenting available, sewage disposal, laundry, public phone, limited grocery store, ice, tables, fire rings, wood. RECREATION: lake swimming, boating, canoeing, ramp, dock, 3 row/2 canoe/1 pedal/3 motor boat rentals, lake fishing, playground, badminton, sports field, horseshoes, volleyball. Open all year. Facilities fully operational May 15 through Oct 15. Rate in 1995 $16-21 per family. Member of OPCA. Phone: (705) 756-2675.

SIX MILE LAKE PROVINCIAL PARK—*From town: Go 9 1/2 km/6 mi N on Hwy 103.* FACILITIES: 190 sites, 190 no hookups, tenting available, handicap restroom facilities, sewage disposal, tables, wood. RECREATION: lake swimming, boating, canoeing, ramp, fishing, playground, hiking trails. Open mid May through mid Oct. Phone: (705) 756-2746.

## POWASSAN—F-3

**Munro Tent & Trailer Park**—CAMPGROUND on the South River *From jct Hwy 11 & Hwy 534: Go 4.8 km/3 mi W on Hwy 534, then 2 km/1 1/4 mi S on Alsace Rd, then .8 km/1/2 mi E on gravel road.* ◆◆FACILITIES: 65 sites, most common site width 35 feet, 28 ft. max RV length, 40 water & elec (15 amp receptacles), 25 no hookups, seasonal sites, tenting available, sewage disposal, public phone, limited grocery store, ice, tables, fire rings, wood. ◆◆RECREATION: pavilion, river swimming, boating, canoeing, ramp, dock, river fishing, planned group activities (weekends only), badminton, sports field, horseshoes, hiking trails, volleyball. Open May 15 through Oct 15. Rate in 1995 $13-15 per family. Member of OPCA. Phone: (705) 724-2539.

## PRESCOTT—G-6

**GRENVILLE PARK**—Campground on the St. Lawrence River. *From jct 401 (exit 721) & Hwy 16: Go .8 km/1/2 mi S on Hwy 16, then .4 km/1/4 mi E on Hwy 2.*

◆◆◆FACILITIES: 160 sites, most common site width 40 feet, 160 water & elec (15 & 30 amp receptacles), seasonal sites, 8 pull-thrus, tenting available, group sites for tents/RVs, RV rentals, cabins, sewage disposal, public phone, limited grocery store, ice, tables, fire rings, grills, wood.

◆◆◆RECREATION: equipped pavilion, river swimming, boating, canoeing, ramp, 2 pedal/1 motor boat rentals, water skiing, river fishing, basketball hoop, playground, planned group activities (weekends only), movies, badminton, sports field, horseshoes, volleyball. Recreation open to the public.

Open Apr 1 through Oct 31. Rate in 1995 $14-18 per family. Master Card/Visa accepted. Member of OPCA. Phone: (613) 925-2000.

**SEE AD THIS PAGE**

## PROVIDENCE BAY—F-1

**PROVIDENCE BAY TENT & TRAILER PARK**—A wooded, lakeside CAMPGROUND on Manitoulin Island. *From town: Go .8 km/1/2 mi E on Hwy 551.*

◆◆◆FACILITIES: 200 sites, most common site width 40 feet, 150 water & elec (15 & 30 amp receptacles), 50 no hookups, seasonal sites, 2 pull-thrus, a/c allowed, tenting available, group sites for tents/RVs, RV rentals, cabins, sewage disposal, public phone, limited grocery store, RV supplies, ice, tables, fire rings, grills, wood, church services.

◆◆◆RECREATION: lake swimming, lake/river fishing, fishing guides, basketball hoop, badminton, sports field, horseshoes, hiking trails, volleyball.

Open May 1 through mid Oct. Rate in 1995 $16-19 per family. Reservations recommended Jul through Aug. American Express/Master Card/Visa accepted. Phone: (705) 377-4650.

**SEE AD THIS PAGE**



## RAINY RIVER—E-1

LAKE OF THE WOODS PROVINCIAL PARK—*From town: Go 8 km/5 mi E on Hwy 11, then 32 km/20 mi N on Hwy 621.* FACILITIES: 99 sites, 16 elec, 83 no hookups, tenting available, handicap restroom facilities, sewage disposal, laundry, tables, wood. RECREATION: lake swimming, boating, canoeing, ramp, fishing, playground, hiking trails. Open mid May through early Sep. Phone: (807) 274-5337.

## RAVENSWOOD—I-1

IPPERWASH PROVINCIAL PARK—*From town: Go 3 1/4 km/2 mi N on Hwy 21, then 1 1/2 km/1 mi W on Ipperwash Rd.* FACILITIES: 266 sites, 114 elec, 152 no hookups, tenting available, handicap restroom facilities, sewage disposal, laundry, limited grocery store, ice, tables, wood. RECREATION: swimming, boating, canoeing, ramp, fishing. Open mid May through early Sep. Phone: (519) 243-2220.

## RED LAKE—C-1

**Golden Hook Camp**—Open, level RV SPACES in resort on Gull Rock Lake. *From south city limits: Go 14.4 km/9 mi S on Hwy 105.* FACILITIES: 13 sites, 13 water & elec (15 amp receptacles), tenting available, sewage disposal, limited grocery store, ice, tables. RECREATION: lake swimming, boating, canoeing, ramp, dock, pedal/20 motor boat rentals, lake fishing, hiking trails. No pets. Open mid May through mid Oct. Rate in 1995 $12 for 2 persons. Phone: (807) 727-2708.

**Poplar Point Resort**—Open, level RV SPACES in conjuction with a lodge. *From south city limits: Go 12 km/7 1/2 mi S on Hwy 105.* FACILITIES: 10 sites, 6 water & elec (15 amp receptacles), 4 no hookups, tenting available, sewage disposal, limited grocery store, ice, tables, fire rings. RECREATION: boating, canoeing, ramp, dock, 10 motor boat rentals, lake fishing, horseshoes. Open mid May through end Sep. Rate in 1995 $14 for 2 persons. Phone: (807) 727-3154.

**Snowshoe Dam Tent & Trailer Park**—A CAMPGROUND with open, grassy sites and trees in a rustic setting beside the Chukuni River. *From south city limits: Go 34 km/21 mi S on Hwy 105, then 3.2 km/2 mi E on Snowshoe Dam Rd.* ◆FACILITIES: 20 sites, most common site width 50 feet, 3 water & elec (15 amp receptacles), 17 no hookups, tenting available, non-flush toilets, ice, tables. ◆◆RECREATION: river swimming, boating, canoeing, ramp, dock, 3 motor boat rentals, river fishing, horseshoes, hiking trails. Open mid May through mid Oct. Rates available upon request. Phone: (807) 749-3531.

**South Bay on Gullrock**—Semi-wooded CAMPGROUND beside a lake. *From south city limits: Go 13 km/8 mi S on Hwy 105, then .8 km/1/2 mi E on Hopperstad Rd.* ◆◆◆FACILITIES: 20 sites, most common site width 50 feet, 15 full hookups, 5 water & elec (30 amp receptacles), 15 pull-thrus, tenting available, sewage disposal, laundry, limited grocery store, ice, tables, fire rings, wood. ◆◆◆RECREATION: rec room/area, lake swimming, boating, canoeing, ramp, dock, 2 pedal/6 motor boat rentals, lake fishing, horseshoes. Open May 1 through Oct 1. Rate in 1995 $17.50 for 2 persons. Phone: (807) 727-2830.

## RENFREW—F-5

**KOA-RENFREW**—Lakeside grassy CAMPGROUND near a major highway. *From jct Hwy 17 & Hwy 60: Go 9.6 km/6 mi W on Hwy 17, then .4 km/1/4 mi N on Storyland Rd.*

◆◆◆FACILITIES: 110 sites, most common site width 35 feet, 85 full hookups, 10 water & elec (15 & 30 amp receptacles), 15 no hookups, seasonal sites, 40 pull-thrus, a/c allowed ($), tenting available, cabins, RV storage, sewage disposal, laundry, public phone, grocery store, RV supplies, ice, tables, fire rings, wood.

◆◆◆RECREATION: rec room/area, coin games, lake swimming, boating, no motors, canoeing, 2 row/2 canoe/2 pedal boat rentals, lake fishing, driving range ($), basketball hoop, playground, planned group activities, movies, sports field, horseshoes, hiking trails, volleyball.

Open May 1 through Oct 15. Rate in 1995 $16-22 for 2 persons. Master Card/Visa accepted. Member of OPCA. Phone: (613) 432-6280. KOA 10% value card discount.

**SEE AD OTTAWA PAGE 1010 AND AD FRONT OF BOOK PAGES 68 AND 69**

**TIMBERLAND CAMPGROUND**—Secluded sites in a natural setting. *From jct Hwy 17 & CR 20: Go 5.6 km/3 1/2 mi N on CR 20.*

◆◆◆FACILITIES: 98 sites, most common site width 30 feet, 35 full hookups, 62 water & elec (15 & 30 amp receptacles), 1 no hookups, seasonal sites, 10 pull-thrus, tenting available, group sites for tents/RVs, RV storage, sewage disposal, laundry, public phone, limited grocery store, RV supplies, ice, tables, fire rings, grills, wood, traffic control gate.

TIMBERLAND CAMPGROUND—Continued on next page
RENFREW—Continued on next page

RENFREW—Continued
TIMBERLAND CAMPGROUND—Continued

◆◆◆RECREATION: rec hall, swim pool, basketball hoop, playground, badminton, horseshoes, hiking trails, volleyball.

Open May 15 through Oct 15. Rate in 1995 $14-18 per family. Member of OPCA. Phone: (613) 432-5767.

**SEE AD TRAVEL SECTION PAGES 975, 976 AND 977**

## RESTOULE—F-3

RESTOULE PROVINCIAL PARK—*From town: Go 4 3/4 km/3 mi W on Hwy 534.* FACILITIES: 275 sites, 97 elec, 178 no hookups, tenting available, sewage disposal, tables, wood. RECREATION: swimming, boating, canoeing, ramp, fishing, playground, hiking trails. Open mid May through late Sep. Phone: (705) 729-2010.

## RICE LAKE—H-4

***See listings at Bailieboro, Bewdley & Roseneath***

## RODNEY—J-2

PORT GLASGOW TENT & TRAILER PARK (Township Park)—*From jct Hwy 3 & Elgin CR 3: Go 2 km/1 1/4 mi S on CR 3.* FACILITIES: 145 sites, 125 full hookups, 20 water & elec, seasonal sites, tenting available, sewage disposal, public phone, limited grocery store, ice, tables, fire rings, wood. RECREATION: rec hall, pavilion, lake swimming, boating, lake fishing, playground, shuffleboard court, sports field. Open May 15 through Oct 15. Phone: (519) 785-0069.

## ROSENEATH—H-4

**Golden Beach Resort and Trailer Park**—CAMPGROUND within a lakeside resort. *From jct Hwy 401 (exit 464) & Hwy 28: Go 12 km/7 1/2 mi N on Hwy 28, then 15.2 km/9 1/2 mi E on CR 9, then 1.6 km/1 mi N on Lilac Valley Rd (gravel road).* ◆◆◆◆FACILITIES: 289 sites, most common site width 40 feet, 289 full hookups, (30 amp receptacles), seasonal sites, 40 pull-thrus, tenting available, laundry, full service store, LP gas refill by weight, ice, tables, fire rings, wood. ◆◆◆◆◆RECREATION: rec room/area, equipped pavilion, swim pool, boating, canoeing, 2 canoe/2 pedal/60 motor boat rentals, lake fishing, playground, 2 shuffleboard courts, planned group activities, recreation director, 2 tennis courts, sports field, horseshoes, hiking trails, volleyball. Open May 1 through Oct 15. Rate in 1995 $30 for 2 persons. Member of OPCA. Phone: (905) 342-5366.

## ROUND LAKE CENTRE—F-4

BONNECHERE PROVINCIAL PARK—*From town: Go 6 1/2 km/4 mi N on Hwy 62.* FACILITIES: 114 sites, 114 no hookups, tenting available, handicap restroom facilities, sewage disposal, laundry, tables, wood. RECREATION: swimming, boating, canoeing, ramp, fishing, playground. Open mid May through early Sep. Phone: (613) 757-2103.

**Pine Cone Park**—CAMPGROUND on Round Lake with grassy sites. *From north town limits: Go 4 km/2 1/2 mi N on Hwy 62.* ◆◆◆FACILITIES: 100 sites, most common site width 40 feet, 60 full hookups, 40 water & elec (15 amp receptacles), seasonal sites, tenting available, sewage disposal, laundry, public phone, ice, tables, fire rings, wood. ◆◆◆RECREATION: lake swimming, boating, ramp, dock, lake fishing, playground, sports field, horseshoes. Open May 15 through Sep 15. Rate in 1995 $14-18 per family. Member of OPCA. Phone: (613) 757-2560.

**Tramore's Covered Bridge Park**—A riverside CAMPGROUND with a covered bridge at the entrance (12 foot overhead clearance). *From town center: Go 6.4 km/4 mi S on Hwy 62.* ◆◆◆FACILITIES: 31 sites, most common site width 35 feet, 31 full hookups, (15 & 30 amp receptacles), seasonal sites, 8 pull-thrus, tenting available, handicap restroom facilities, sewage disposal, laundry, tables, fire rings, wood. ◆◆◆RECREATION: rec hall, lake/river swimming, boating, canoeing, ramp, dock, 2 pedal boat rentals, lake/river fishing, planned group activities (weekends only), horseshoes, hiking trails. Open mid May through Oct 1. Rate in 1995 $11.50-14.75 per family. Phone: (613) 757-3444.

## ST. CATHARINES—I-3

**DRESSEL'S JORDON VALLEY CAMPGROUND**—Open, shaded & grassy sites on Twenty Mile Creek. *From jct QEW (exit 57) & Regional Rd 24: Go 2.4 km/1 1/2 mi S on Regional Rd 24, then 1.2 km/3/4 mi E on Culp, then .8 km/1/2 mi S on 21st St.*

◆◆◆FACILITIES: 90 sites, most common site width 40 feet, 28 full hookups, 12 water & elec (15 & 30 amp receptacles), 50 no hookups, seasonal sites, a/c allowed, heater allowed, phone hookups, tenting available, group sites for tents, RV storage, sewage disposal, ice, tables, fire rings, wood.

◆◆◆RECREATION: river swimming, boating, canoeing, river fishing, basketball hoop, playground, badminton, sports field, horseshoes, hiking trails, volleyball.

Open mid May through mid Oct. Rate in 1995 $18-25 per family. Phone: (905) 562-7816.

**SEE AD TRAVEL SECTION PAGES 975, 976 AND 977**

ST. CATHARINES—Continued

**SHANGRI-LA PARK CAMPGROUND**—CAMPGROUND with open and shaded sites on the Bruce Trail. *From jct QEW (exit 55) & Jordan Rd: Go 4.8 km/3 mi S on Jordan Rd, then 500 feet E on Regional Rd 81, then 1.6 km/1 mi S on 17th St.*

◆◆◆FACILITIES: 300 sites, most common site width 40 feet, 200 water & elec, 50 elec (15 & 30 amp receptacles), 50 no hookups, seasonal sites, a/c allowed ($), heater allowed ($), phone hookups, tenting available, group sites for tents/RVs, RV storage, sewage disposal, public phone, limited grocery store, LP gas refill by weight/by meter, ice, tables, fire rings, wood.

◆◆◆◆RECREATION: rec hall, swim pool, wading pool, mini-golf ($), playground, planned group activities (weekends only), sports field, horseshoes, hiking trails, volleyball.

Open May 1 through Oct 1. Rate in 1995 $19-21 for 2 persons. Reservations recommended Jul through Aug. Member of OPCA. Phone: (905) 562-5851.

**SEE AD NIAGARA FALLS PAGE 1006**

## ST. JOSEPH'S ISLAND—D-4

***See listings at Hilton Beach***

## ST. MARY'S—I-2

**Lakeside Summer Resort**—Lakeside CAMPGROUND with sandy beach. *From jct Hwy 7 & Hwy 19: Go 8 km/5 mi S on Hwy 19, then 2.8 km/1 3/4 mi E on Oxford CR 25, then 1.2 km/3/4 mi S on Brock St.* ◆◆◆FACILITIES: 135 sites, most common site width 35 feet, 67 full hookups, 68 water & elec (15 & 30 amp receptacles), seasonal sites, tenting available, sewage disposal, laundry, public phone, ice, tables, fire rings, wood. ◆◆◆◆RECREATION: rec hall, lake swimming, boating, canoeing, 1 row/3 canoe/4 pedal boat rentals, lake fishing, planned group activities (weekends only), badminton, horseshoes, volleyball. Open May 1 through Oct 1. Rate in 1995 $20-22.50 per family. Member of OPCA. Phone: (519) 349-2820.

## ST. THOMAS—I-2

✽ **RV WORLD**—*Located at east city limits on Hwy 3 (Talbot St).* SALES: travel trailers, truck campers, 5th wheels, van conversions, motor homes, mini-motor homes, fold-down camping trailers. SERVICES: mechanic full-time, emergency road service business hours, RV towing, RV storage, sells parts/accessories, installs hitches. Open all year. American Express/Master Card/Visa accepted. Phone: (519) 631-1092.

**SEE AD THIS PAGE**

## ST. WILLIAMS—J-2

**Woodland Park**—Level CAMPGROUND in a country setting. *From jct Hwy 59 & Hwy 24: Go 6.4 km/4 mi E on Hwy 24, then 4.8 km/3 mi S on Regional Rd 16.* ◆◆◆FACILITIES: 90 sites, most common site width 30 feet, 62 full hookups, 12 water & elec (15 & 30 amp receptacles), 16 no hookups, seasonal sites, tenting available, sewage disposal, public phone, limited grocery store, ice, tables, fire rings, wood. ◆◆◆◆RECREATION: swim pool (heated), playground, planned group activities (weekends only), sports field, horseshoes, hiking trails. Open May 1 through mid Oct. Rate in 1995 $20-23 per family. Member of OPCA. Phone: (519) 586-2957. FCRV 10% discount.

## SANDFORD—H-3

**Grangeways Trailer Park**—CAMPGROUND with open, grassy sites. Most sites occupied by seasonal campers. *From jct Hwy 48 & Reg Rd 31: Go 2.8 km/1 3/4 mi E on Reg Rd 31, then 1.6 km/1 mi N on Reg Rd 30, then follow signs.* ◆◆◆FACILITIES: 300 sites, most common site width 40 feet, 300 full hookups, (15 & 30 amp receptacles), seasonal sites, tenting available, sewage disposal, laundry, public phone, limited grocery store, LP gas refill by weight, ice, tables, fire rings, wood. ◆◆◆◆RECREATION: rec hall, rec room/area, pavilion, swim pool, river/pond swimming, boating, canoeing, river/pond fishing, mini-golf, playground,

SANDFORD—Continued
GRANGEWAYS TRAILER PARK—Continued

planned group activities (weekends only), badminton, sports field, horseshoes, volleyball. Open May 15 through Oct 15. Rate in 1995 $20 per family. Member of OPCA. Phone: (905) 852-3260.

## SARNIA—I-1

WARWICK AREA (St. Clair Region Conservation Auth.) —*From east city limits: Go 28 3/4 km/18 mi E on Hwy 7.* FACILITIES: 144 sites, 95 water & elec (15 & 30 amp receptacles), 49 no hookups, seasonal sites, tenting available, sewage disposal, laundry, public phone, tables, fire rings, wood. RECREATION: swim pool, boating, no motors, canoeing, lake fishing, playground, sports field, horseshoes, hiking trails, volleyball. Recreation open to the public. Open mid May through mid Oct. Phone: (519) 849-6770.

## SAUBLE BEACH—G-2

**CARSON'S CAMP**—CAMPGROUND with many sites occupied by seasonal campers. *From south city limits: Go .4 km/1/4 mi S on CR 21 (Southampton Pkwy).*

◆◆◆◆◆FACILITIES: 700 sites, most common site width 38 feet, 700 full hookups, (15 & 30 amp receptacles), seasonal sites, a/c allowed, heater allowed, tenting available, group sites for RVs, RV storage, laundry, public phone, limited grocery store, RV supplies, LP gas refill by weight, ice, tables, fire rings, wood, traffic control gate/guard.

◆◆◆◆RECREATION: rec hall, rec room/area, swim pool (indoor) (heated), lake swimming, whirlpool, boating, no motors, canoeing, basketball hoop, playground, planned group activities, movies, recreation director, badminton, sports field, horseshoes, volleyball.

Open May 1 through mid Oct. Rate in 1995 $21 for 2 persons. Reservations recommended Jul through Aug. Member of OPCA. Phone: (519) 422-1143.

**SEE AD NEXT PAGE**

**Fiddlehead Resort**—Family CAMPGROUND with cottages close to Lake Huron. *From jct Hwy 6 & CR 21: Go 10.5 km/6 1/2 mi W on CR 21.* ◆◆◆FACILITIES: 34 sites, most common site width 50 feet, 11 full hookups, 12 water & elec (15 & 30 amp receptacles), 11 no hookups, seasonal sites, tenting available, sewage disposal, ice, tables, fire rings, wood. ◆◆RECREATION: playground, badminton, sports field, horseshoes, volleyball. Open May 1 through Oct 30. Rate in 1995 $20-24 per family. Member of OPCA. Phone: (519) 534-0405.

**ROTH PARK**—*From jct CR 8-Hwy 70 & Hwy 6: Go 12 km/7.5 mi N on Hwy 6, then 152 m/500 feet E on CR 9, then 4.8 km/3 mi N on Berford Lake Rd, then follow signs.*

**SEE PRIMARY LISTING AT WIARTON AND AD TRAVEL SECTION PAGE 982**

**SAUBLE BEACH RESORT CAMP**—Grassy, level CAMPGROUND with many activities. *From east city limits: Go 1.6 km/1 mi E on CR 8.*

◆◆◆◆FACILITIES: 275 sites, most common site width 35 feet, 200 full hookups, 69 water & elec (15 & 30 amp receptacles), 6 no hookups, seasonal sites, 20 pull-thrus, a/c allowed, heater allowed, tenting available, group sites for RVs, RV storage, sewage disposal, laundry, public phone, limited grocery store, RV supplies, LP gas refill by weight, ice, tables, wood, traffic control gate.

◆◆◆RECREATION: rec hall, rec room/area, coin games, 2 swim pools (indoor) (heated), whirlpool,

SAUBLE BEACH RESORT CAMP—Continued on next page
SAUBLE BEACH—Continued on next page

SAUBLE BEACH—Continued
SAUBLE BEACH RESORT CAMP—Continued

basketball hoop, playground, planned group activities, movies, recreation director, sports field, horseshoes, volleyball.

Open May 15 through Sep 15. Rate in 1995 $22 for 2 persons. Reservations recommended Jul through Aug. Master Card/Visa accepted. Member of OPCA. Phone: (519) 422-1101.
**SEE AD THIS PAGE**

SAUBLE FALLS PROVINCIAL PARK—*From town: Go 4 km/2 1/2 mi N on CR 21.* FACILITIES: 152 sites, 21 elec, 131 no hookups, tenting available, handicap restroom facilities, sewage disposal, tables, wood. RECREATION: fishing, hiking trails. Open late Apr through late Oct. Phone: (519) 422-1952.

**WOODLAND PARK**—Semi-wooded CAMPGROUND with open & shaded sites. *From north city limits: Go .4 km/1/4 mi N on CR 21 (Sauble Falls Rd).*
◆◆◆◆FACILITIES: 725 sites, most common site width 40 feet, 715 full hookups, (15,30 & 50 amp receptacles), 10 no hookups, seasonal sites, 8 pull-thrus, a/c allowed, heater allowed, cable TV, tenting available, laundry, public phone, grocery store, RV supplies, LP gas refill by weight, ice, tables, patios, fire rings, wood, traffic control gate.

◆◆◆◆RECREATION: rec hall, rec room/area, coin games, swim pool (indoor) (heated), whirlpool, basketball hoop, playground, planned group activities, movies, recreation director, badminton, sports field, volleyball.

Open May 1 through Sep 15. Rate in 1995 $23-24 for 2 persons. Visa accepted. Member of OPCA. Phone: (519) 422-1161.
**SEE AD FRONT OF BOOK PAGE 140 AND AD THIS PAGE**

## SAULT STE. MARIE—D-4

***See listings at Goulais River & Thessalon***

SAULT STE. MARIE—Continued

**BELL'S POINT BEACH**—Scenic CAMPGROUND with shaded & open sites. *From jct Int. Bridge & Hwy 17B: Go 6.4 km/4 mi E on Hwy 178, then 4.8 km/3 mi E on Hwy 17.*
◆◆FACILITIES: 251 sites, most common site width 35 feet, 7 full hookups, 77 water & elec (15 & 30 amp receptacles), 167 no hookups, seasonal sites, 12 pull-thrus, a/c allowed, heater allowed, tenting available, group sites for tents/RVs, RV storage, sewage disposal, laundry, public phone, limited grocery store, RV supplies, ice, tables, fire rings, grills, wood, traffic control gate/guard.

◆◆◆RECREATION: river swimming, boating, canoeing, ramp, dock, 3 row/3 canoe/7 motor boat rentals, water skiing, river fishing, basketball hoop, playground, sports field, horseshoes, volleyball. Recreation open to the public.

Open all year. Facilities fully operational mid May through mid Oct. Rate in 1995 $12-18.50 per family. Reservations recommended Jul through Aug. Member of OPCA. Phone: (705) 759-1561.
**SEE AD TRAVEL SECTION PAGES 975, 976 AND 977**

**GLENVIEW VACATION HOMES & CAMPGROUND**—CAMPGROUND in wooded setting with modern cottages. *Located on Hwy 17, 9.6 km/6 mi N of International Bridge and city center.*
◆◆◆◆FACILITIES: 58 sites, most common site width 35 feet, 12 full hookups, 30 water & elec (15 & 30 amp receptacles), 16 no hookups, 21 pull-thrus, a/c allowed, heater allowed, tenting available, group sites for tents/RVs, cabins, sewage disposal, laundry, public phone, limited grocery store, ice, tables, fire rings, wood.

◆◆◆◆RECREATION: rec room/area, swim pool (heated), sauna, whirlpool, basketball hoop, 2 bike rentals, playground, horseshoes, hiking trails, volleyball, cross country skiing, snowmobile trails.

Open all year. Facilities fully operational mid May through Oct 1. Rate in 1995 $16-18 for 2 persons. Master Card/Visa accepted. Member of OPCA. Phone: (705) 759-3436.
**SEE AD TRAVEL SECTION PAGES 975, 976 AND 977**

KOA-Sault Ste. Marie—A wooded, grassy CAMPGROUND. *From jct Hwy 550, Hwy 7-B & Hwy 17: Go 4.8 km/3 mi N on Hwy 17, then .8 km/1/2 mi W on 5th Line Rd.* ◆◆◆◆FACILITIES: 150 sites, most common site width 35 feet, 19 full hookups, 79 water & elec (15,30 & 50 amp receptacles), 52 no hookups, 86 pull-thrus, tenting available, sewage disposal, laundry, public phone, limited grocery store, LP gas refill by weight/by meter, ice, tables, fire rings, grills, wood. ◆◆◆◆RECREATION: rec room/area, equipped pavilion, swim pool (heated), mini-golf ($), playground, planned group activities, horseshoes, hiking trails. Open May 1 through Oct 15. Rate in 1995 $19-24.75 for 2 persons. Phone: (705) 759-2344. KOA 10% value card discount.

**PINE CREST CAMPGROUND**—*From jct I-75 & Int Bridge: Go 1.6 km/1 mi E over Int Bridge, then 80 km/50 mi E on Hwy 17.*
**SEE PRIMARY LISTING AT THESSALON AND AD TRAVEL SECTION, MI PAGE 412**

**WAWA RV RESORT & CAMPGROUND KOA**—*From International Bridge: Go 227 km/142 mi W on Hwy 17.*
**SEE PRIMARY LISTING AT WAWA AND AD WAWA PAGE 1024**

**WOODY'S RESTAURANT**—*From jct Hwy 550, Hwy 17-B & Hwy 17: Go 10 km/6 1/2 mi N on Hwy 17.* New restaurant specializing in home-cooked meals for breakfast, lunch & dinner in conjunction with RV SPACES & tenting area. Open all year.
**SEE AD TRAVEL SECTION PAGES 975, 976 AND 977**

**WOODY'S RESTAURANT & TRAILER PARK**—RV SPACES behind a restaurant. *From jct Hwy 550, Hwy 17-B & Hwy 17: Go 10.4 km/6 1/2 mi N on Hwy 17.*
◆◆◆FACILITIES: 36 sites, most common site width 40 feet, 30 ft. max RV length, 6 full hookups, 18 water & elec (15 amp receptacles), 12 no hookups, 6 pull-thrus, tenting available, sewage disposal, limited grocery store, ice, tables, fire rings, wood.

RECREATION: hiking trails.

Open all year. Facilities fully operational mid May through Oct 1. Rate in 1995 $10.50-14.50 for 2 persons. Phone: (705) 777-2638.
**SEE AD TRAVEL SECTION PAGES 975, 976 AND 977**

## SCHREIBER—B-2

RAINBOW FALLS PROVINCIAL PARK—*From town: Go 12 3/4 km/8 mi W on Hwy 17.* FACILITIES: 97 sites, 28 elec, 69 no hookups, tenting available, handicap restroom facilities, sewage disposal, laundry, tables, wood. RECREATION: swimming, fishing, hiking trails. Open early Jun through mid Sep. Phone: (807) 824-2298.

SCHREIBER—Continued on next page

SCHREIBER—Continued

**Travel Rest Tent & Trailer Park**—CAMPGROUND near restaurants & stores. *At west end of town on Hwy 17.* ◆◆FACILITIES: 50 sites, most common site width 40 feet, 14 full hookups, 18 water & elec (15 amp receptacles), 18 no hookups, 18 pull-thrus, tenting available, limited grocery store, ice, tables, fire rings, wood. ◆RECREATION: swim pool (heated), horseshoes. Open mid May through mid Oct. Rate in 1995 $14-16 for 2 persons. Phone: (807) 824-2617.

## SEAFORTH—I-2

**FAMILY PARADISE CAMPGROUND**—Shaded or sunny sites on a lake. *From business center: Go 12 km/7 1/2 mi N on Main St (Huron CR 12), then 4.8 km/3 mi E on 12 & 13th Concession.*

WELCOME

◆◆◆◆FACILITIES: 175 sites, most common site width 40 feet, 130 full hookups, 28 water & elec, 12 elec (15 amp receptacles), 5 no hookups, seasonal sites, a/c allowed ($), heater allowed ($), tenting available, group sites for tents/RVs, RV storage, handicap restroom facilities, sewage disposal, laundry, public phone, grocery store, LP gas refill by weight, ice, tables, fire rings, wood, traffic control gate.

◆◆◆◆RECREATION: rec hall, rec room/area, pavilion, coin games, swim pool (heated), lake swimming, whirlpool, boating, no motors, canoeing, dock, 4 pedal boat rentals, pond fishing, basketball hoop, playground, 2 shuffleboard courts, planned group activities, movies, recreation director, sports field, horseshoes, volleyball. Recreation open to the public.

Open May 15 through Oct 15. Rate in 1995 $15.50-18.50 per family. Visa accepted. Member of OPCA. Phone: (519) 527-0629. FCRV 10% discount.

SEE AD TRAVEL SECTION PAGES 975, 976 AND 977

## SELKIRK—I-3

HALDIMAND AREA (Long Point Region Conservation Auth.)—*From town: Go 4 3/4 km/3 mi W on Regional Rd 3, then 4 3/4 km/3 mi S on Regional Rd 62, then W on Lakeshore Rd.* FACILITIES: 250 sites, 50 full hookups, 140 water & elec, 60 no hookups, tenting available, sewage disposal, laundry, tables, wood. RECREATION: rec hall, pavilion, lake swimming, boating, lake fishing, playground, shuffleboard court, hiking trails, volleyball. Recreation open to the public. Open Victoria Day through Oct 9. Phone: (519) 428-4623.

SELKIRK PROVINCIAL PARK—*From town: Go 3 1/4 km/2 mi W off Rainham Rd.* FACILITIES: 142 sites, 44 elec, 98 no hookups, tenting available, handicap restroom facilities, sewage disposal, tables, wood. RECREATION: swimming, boating, canoeing, fishing, playground, hiking trails. Open mid Jun through early Sep. Phone: (416) 776-2600.

## SHARBOT LAKE—G-5

SHARBOT LAKE PROVINCIAL PARK—*From jct Hwy 7 & Hwy 38: Go 4 3/4 km/3 mi W on Hwy 7.* FACILITIES: 195 sites, 20 ft. max RV length, 30 elec, 165 no hookups, tenting available, handicap restroom facilities, sewage disposal, laundry, tables, wood. RECREATION: swimming, boating, canoeing, ramp, lake fishing, playground, hiking trails. Open mid May through early Sep. Phone: (613) 335-2814.

## SHEGUIANDAH—F-1

**BATMAN'S COTTAGES, TENT & TRAILER PARK**—A bayside CAMPGROUND in a wooded area. *From south city limits: Go 3.2 km/2 mi S on Hwy 6.*

WELCOME

◆◆◆◆FACILITIES: 142 sites, most common site width 35 feet, 35 full hookups, 85 water & elec (15 amp receptacles), 22 no hookups, seasonal sites, tenting available, cabins, RV storage, sewage disposal, laundry, public phone, grocery store, RV supplies, marine gas, ice, tables, fire rings, grills, wood.

◆◆◆◆RECREATION: rec hall, coin games, lake swimming, boating, canoeing, ramp, dock, 2 row/2 canoe/5 motor boat rentals, water skiing, lake fishing, basketball hoop, playground, shuffleboard court,

SHEGUIANDAH—Continued
BATMAN'S COTTAGES, TENT & TRAILER PARK—Continued

planned group activities, badminton, sports field, horseshoes, hiking trails, volleyball. Recreation open to the public.

Open mid May through Sep 30. Rate in 1995 $17-20 per family. Master Card/Visa accepted. Phone: (705) 368-2180.

SEE AD THIS PAGE

**GREEN ACRES TENT & TRAILER PARK**—Campground on Sheguiandah Bay convenient to airport. *From jct Hwy 540 & Hwy 6: Go 10.4 km/6 1/2 mi S on Hwy 6.*

WELCOME

◆◆FACILITIES: 100 sites, most common site width 35 feet, 50 water & elec (15 amp receptacles), 50 no hookups, seasonal sites, 5 pull-thrus, tenting available, group sites for tents, RV storage, sewage disposal, laundry, public phone, grocery store, LP gas refill by weight/by meter, gasoline, ice, tables, fire rings, wood, traffic control gate.

◆◆◆RECREATION: rec room/area, lake swimming, boating, canoeing, ramp, dock, water skiing, lake fishing, horseshoes.

Open mid Apr through mid Oct. Rate in 1995 $13-16 per family. Reservations recommended during Jul. American Express/Master Card/Visa accepted. Phone: (705) 368-2428.

SEE AD TRAVEL SECTION PAGE 983

**Whitehaven Resort**—RV SPACES in a resort area. *From jct Hwy 540 & Hwy 6: Go 9.6 km/6 mi S on Hwy 6, then .4 km/1/4 mi E on Sheguiandah Bay Rd.* FACILITIES: 12 sites, most common site width 35 feet, 5 full hookups, 7 water & elec (15 amp receptacles), seasonal sites, tenting available, public phone, limited grocery store, ice, tables. RECREATION: lake swimming, boating, canoeing, ramp, dock, 2 canoe/2 pedal/20 motor boat rentals, lake fishing, horseshoes. Open May 1 through mid Oct. Rate in 1995 $12-15. Phone: (705) 368-2554.

## SHELBURNE—H-3

**Primrose Park**—Rolling, wooded CAMPGROUND with sunny & shaded sites. Many sites occupied by seasonal campers. *From east jct Hwy 89 & Hwy 10/24: Go .4 km/.25 mi S on Hwy 10/24.* ◆◆◆FACILITIES: 240 sites, most common site width 35 feet, 72 full hookups, 68 water & elec (15 amp receptacles), 100 no hookups, seasonal sites, 35 pull-thrus, tenting available, sewage disposal, laundry, public phone, grocery store, ice, tables, fire rings, wood. ◆◆◆RECREATION: rec room/area, swim pool (heated), playground, planned group activities (weekends only), badminton, sports field, horseshoes, volleyball. Recreation open to the public. Open May 15 through Oct 15. Rate in 1995 $16-22.50 per family. Phone: (519) 925-2848. FCRV 10% discount.

## SIMCOE—I-3

HAY CREEK AREA (Long Point Region Conservation Auth.)—*From town: Go 6 1/2 km/4 mi S on Hwy 24, then 1 1/2 km/1 mi E on Radical Rd.* FACILITIES: 43 sites, 43 no hookups, tenting available, tables, wood. RECREATION: pavilion, lake swimming, boating, no motors, fishing, playground, hiking trails. Recreation open to the public. Open Victoria Day through Labour Day. Phone: (519) 428-4623.

NORFOLK AREA (Long Point Region Conservation Auth.)—*From town: Go 8 km/5 mi S on Hwy 24, follow signs to Lakeshore Rd.* FACILITIES: 232 sites, 12 full hookups, 160 water & elec, 60 no hookups, tenting available, sewage disposal, limited grocery store, ice, tables, wood. RECREATION: pavilion, lake swimming, boating, fishing, playground, shuffleboard court, volleyball. Recreation open to the public. Open Victoria Day through Oct 9. Phone: (519) 428-4623.

TURKEY POINT PROVINCIAL PARK—*From town: Go 8 km/5 mi S on Hwy 24, then 6 1/2 km/4 mi SW on Hwy 24, then 3 1/4 km/2 mi SE on CR 10 (Turkey Point).* FACILITIES: 200 sites, 50 elec, 150 no hookups, tenting available, handicap restroom facilities, sewage disposal, laundry, tables, grills, wood. RECREATION: lake swimming, lake fishing, playground, hiking trails. Open early May through early Sep. Phone: (519) 426-3239.

## SIOUX LOOKOUT—D-2

**Abram Lake Tent and Trailer Park**—Lakeside CAMPGROUND. *From jct Hwy 664 & Hwy 72: Go 1.2 km/3/4 mi on Hwy 72, then E on Baver-Fenelon Rd.* ◆◆◆FACILITIES: 90 sites, most common site width 40 feet, 16 full hookups, 46 water & elec (15 & 30 amp receptacles), 28 no hookups, 36 pull-thrus, tenting available, laundry, public phone, limited grocery store, ice, tables, fire rings, grills, wood. ◆◆◆RECREATION: lake swimming, boating, canoeing, ramp, dock, 2 canoe/6 motor boat rentals, lake fishing. Open all year. Facilities fully operational May 15 through Oct 1. Rate in 1995 $14.50-18 for 2 persons. Phone: (807) 737-1247.

OJIBWAY PROVINCIAL PARK—*From town: Go 20 3/4 km/13 mi S on Hwy 72.* FACILITIES: 45 sites, 17 elec, 28 no hookups, tenting available, handicap restroom facilities, sewage disposal, tables, wood. RECREATION: swimming, boating, canoeing, ramp, fishing, playground, hiking trails. Open mid May through early Sep. Phone: (807) 737-2033.

## SIOUX NARROWS—D-1

**Laughing Water Trailer Park**—CAMPGROUND on Lake of The Woods. *From north city limits: Go 6.4 km/4 mi N on Hwy 71, then 1.6 km/1 mi W on Laughing Water Rd.* ◆◆FACILITIES: 25 sites, most common site width 20 feet, 30 ft. max RV length, 4 full hookups, 9 water & elec (15 amp receptacles), 12 no hookups, tenting available, public phone, limited grocery store, LP gas refill by weight, ice, tables, fire rings, wood. ◆◆◆RECREATION: lake swimming, boating, canoeing, ramp, dock, 15 row/1 pedal/15 motor boat rentals, lake fishing, playground, horseshoes, volleyball. Open May 15 through Sep 30. Rate in 1995 $13.50-19 for 4 persons. Phone: (807) 226-5462.

**PARADISE POINT RV PARK & MARINA**—Lakeside CAMPGROUND. *From south city limits: Go 1.6 km/1 mi S on Hwy 71, then 1.6 km/1 mi W on Fickas Rd.*

WELCOME

◆◆◆FACILITIES: 39 sites, most common site width 35 feet, 31 full hookups, (15,20 & 30 amp receptacles), 8 no hookups, seasonal sites, a/c allowed, tenting available, public phone, limited grocery store, gasoline, marine gas, ice, tables, fire rings, wood.

◆◆◆RECREATION: rec room/area, lake swimming, boating, canoeing, ramp, dock, 1 canoe/1 pedal/4 motor boat rentals, water skiing, lake fishing, playground, horseshoes.

PARADISE POINT RV PARK & MARINA—Continued on next page
SIOUX NARROWS—Continued on next page

SIOUX NARROWS—Continued
PARADISE POINT RV PARK & MARINA—Continued

Open May 1 through Sep 30. Rate in 1995 $16-18 for 2 persons. Visa accepted. Phone: (807) 226-5269.

**SEE AD PAGE 1017**

**PARADISE POINT RV PARK & MARINA**—*From south city limits: Go 1.6 km/1 mi S on Hwy 71, then 1.6 km/1 mi W on Fickas Rd.* Full service marina specializing in all repairs of Mercury outboard products. Open all year. Visa accepted. Phone: (807) 226-5269.

**SEE AD PAGE 1017**

**Tomahawk Trailer Park Resort**—A grassy, lakeside CAMPGROUND. *From south city limits: Go 1.6 km/1 mi S on Hwy 71, then .8 km/1/2 mi E on Tomahawk Rd.* ◆◆◆FACILITIES: 60 sites, most common site width 35 feet, 45 full hookups, 10 water & elec (15 & 30 amp receptacles), 5 no hookups, seasonal sites, 20 pull-thrus, tenting available, laundry, public phone, limited grocery store, ice, tables, fire rings, wood. ◆◆◆RECREATION: lake swimming, boating, canoeing, ramp, dock, 15 row/2 canoe/2 pedal/12 motor boat rentals, lake fishing, playground, horseshoes, hiking trails, volleyball. Open May 1 through Oct 1. Rate in 1995 $20-24 for 4 persons. Phone: (807) 226-5622.

## SMITHVILLE—I-3

**Meadow Brook Camping Park**—Level CAMPGROUND in countryside. *From center of town: Go 11.2 km/7 mi W on Hwy 20, then 1.6 km/1 mi S on S Grimsby Rd 18.* ◆◆FACILITIES: 100 sites, most common site width 35 feet, 80 full hookups, (15 amp receptacles), 20 no hookups, seasonal sites, 4 pull-thrus, tenting available, sewage disposal, public phone, ice, tables, fire rings, wood. ◆◆◆RECREATION: rec hall, swim pool, boating, canoeing, 1 pedal boat rentals, stream fishing, playground, planned group activities (weekends only), sports field, horseshoes. Open mid May through mid Oct. Rate in 1995 $18-22 per family. No refunds. Phone: (905) 643-2333.

## SOMBRA—I-1

CATHCART PARK (St. Clair Parkway Commission)—*From town: Go 3 1/4 km/2 mi N on CR 33 (St. Clair Pkwy).* FACILITIES: 66 sites, 66 water & elec, tenting available, sewage disposal, public phone, limited grocery store, ice, tables, fire rings, grills, wood. RECREATION: pavilion, river swimming, boating, ramp, dock, river fishing, playground. Open May 24 through Oct 15. Phone: (519) 892-3342.

LAMBTON-CUNDICK (St. Clair Parkway Commission)—*From town: Go 1 1/2 km/1 mi N on CR 33 (St. Clair Pkwy).* FACILITIES: 50 sites, 50 water & elec, tenting available, sewage disposal, public phone, ice, tables, fire rings, grills, wood. RECREATION: river swimming, boating, ramp, river fishing, playground, sports field. Open May 24 through Oct 15. Phone: (519) 892-3968.

## SOUTH BAYMOUTH—F-1

**SOUTH BAY RESORT**—Family CAMPGROUND on South Baymouth with open and wooded sites. *From ferry dock at South Baymouth & Hwy 6: Go .8 km/1/2 mi N on Hwy 6.*

◆◆◆FACILITIES: 77 sites, most common site width 35 feet, 60 water & elec (15 & 30 amp receptacles), 17 no hookups, seasonal sites, 5 pull-thrus, tenting available, cabins, sewage disposal, ice, tables, fire rings, grills, wood.

◆◆◆RECREATION: lake swimming, boating, canoeing, ramp, dock, 2 sail/5 canoe/5 pedal boat rentals, water skiing, lake fishing, playground, badminton, horseshoes.

Open mid May through mid Sep. Rate in 1995 $13.50-18 per family. Master Card accepted. Member of OPCA. Phone: (705) 859-3106.

**SEE AD TRAVEL SECTION PAGES 975, 976 AND 977**

## SOUTH RIVER—F-3

MIKISEW PROVINCIAL PARK—*From Hwy 11 in town: Go 16 km/10 mi W on Township Rd.* FACILITIES: 265 sites, 265 no hookups, 11 pull-thrus, tenting available, handicap restroom facilities, wood. RECREATION: lake swimming, boating, canoeing, ramp, lake fishing, playground, hiking trails. Open mid Jun through early Sep. Phone: (705) 386-7762.

## SPANISH—F-1

**Mitchells' Camp**—Level, grassy RV SPACES in conjunction with boat slips on the Spanish River. *From town: Go .8 km/1/2 mi S to Spanish River & follow signs.* FACILITIES: 15 sites, most common site width 35 feet, 15 water & elec (15 amp receptacles), seasonal sites, 2 pull-thrus, tenting available, sewage disposal, public phone, tables, grills. RECREATION: lake swimming, boating, canoeing, ramp, dock, 2 motor boat rentals, lake fishing, hiking trails. Open mid May through Aug 31. Rate in 1995 $12-13 per family. Phone: (705) 844-2202.

SPANISH—Continued

**VANCE'S COTTAGES-CAMPGROUND & MARINE**—RV SPACES on the Spanish River. *From town center: Go 152 m/500 feet S on Trunk Rd, then follow signs.*

FACILITIES: 16 sites, 16 full hookups, (15 & 30 amp receptacles), seasonal sites, 16 pull-thrus, a/c allowed, heater allowed, tenting available, cabins, laundry, public phone, gasoline, ice, tables, wood.

RECREATION: rec room/area, lake swimming, boating, canoeing, ramp, dock, 8 row/8 motor boat rentals, lake fishing, fishing guides, sports field, horseshoes.

Open mid May through mid Oct. Rate in 1995 $10-20 per family. Phone: (705) 844-2442.

**SEE AD TRAVEL SECTION PAGES 975, 976 AND 977**

**Waterfalls Park Lodge & Camping**—CAMPGROUND on a chain of clear water lakes. *From Spanish: Go 4.8 km/3 mi E on Hwy 17, then 4.8 km/3 mi N on Waterfalls Rd following signs.* ◆◆FACILITIES: 100 sites, most common site width 30 feet, 30 ft. max RV length, 24 full hookups, 36 water & elec (15 amp receptacles), 40 no hookups, seasonal sites, 7 pull-thrus, tenting available, sewage disposal, laundry, public phone, limited grocery store, ice, tables, fire rings, wood. ◆◆◆RECREATION: lake swimming, boating, canoeing, ramp, dock, 3 canoe/2 pedal/25 motor boat rentals, lake fishing, horseshoes, hiking trails, volleyball. Open mid May through mid Oct. Rate in 1995 $15-20 per family. Phone: (705) 844-2169.

## SPRAGGE—F-1

**KOA-North Channel Campground**—CAMPGROUND convenient to major highway. *From jct Hwy 108 & Hwy 17: Go 1.6 km/1 mi W on Hwy 17.* ◆◆◆FACILITIES: 143 sites, 9 full hookups, 94 water & elec (15 & 30 amp receptacles), 40 no hookups, seasonal sites, 55 pull-thrus, tenting available, sewage disposal, laundry, public phone, grocery store, LP gas refill by weight/by meter, ice, tables, fire rings, grills, wood. ◆◆◆RECREATION: rec hall, rec room/area, swim pool (heated), boating, canoeing, ramp, dock, river fishing, playground, horseshoes, volleyball. Open May 1 through Oct 15. Rate in 1995 $17-22 for 2 persons. Phone: (705) 849-2210. KOA 10% value card discount.

## SPRING BAY—F-1

**Fred's Camp**—RV SPACES in a summer resort on Kagawong Lake. *From jct CR 542 & Perivale Rd: Go 4.8 km/3 mi N on Perivale Rd.* FACILITIES: 12 sites, most common site width 35 feet, 8 water & elec (15 amp receptacles), 4 no hookups, tenting available, tables, fire rings. RECREATION: lake swimming, boating, dock, lake fishing, horseshoes. Open mid May through end of Nov. Facilities fully operational mid May through mid Oct. Rate in 1995 $18. Phone: (705) 377-4512.

**Mac's Camp**—CAMPGROUND near a lake. *From jct CR 542 & Perivale Rd: Go 8.8 km/5 1/2 mi N on Perivale Rd.* ◆◆◆FACILITIES: 15 sites, 30 ft. max RV length, 1 full hookups, 11 water & elec (15 & 30 amp receptacles), 3 no hookups, 12 pull-thrus, tenting available, sewage disposal, laundry, ice, tables, fire rings, wood. ◆◆◆RECREATION: lake swimming, boating, canoeing, 2 row/2 canoe/1 pedal/6 motor boat rentals, lake fishing, horseshoes, hiking trails, volleyball. Open Jun 1 through mid Oct. Rate in 1995 $18-20 per family. Phone: (705) 377-4537.

## STONECLIFFE—F-4

**Pine Valley Campground & Cottages**—Treed CAMPGROUND on a river. *From east village limits: Go .8 km/1/2 mi E on Hwy 17, then follow signs.* ◆◆◆FACILITIES: 20 sites, most common site width 35 feet, 12 full hookups, 8 water & elec (15 & 30 amp receptacles), seasonal sites, 12 pull-thrus, tenting available, handicap restroom facilities, sewage disposal, laundry, ice, tables, fire rings, wood. ◆◆◆RECREATION: rec room/area, river swimming, boating, canoeing, ramp, dock, 2 canoe/4 motor boat rentals, river fishing, horseshoes, volleyball. Open mid May through mid Oct. Rate in 1995 $18-20 per family. Phone: (613) 586-2621.

## STONEY CREEK—I-3

FIFTY POINT (Hamilton Reg. Conservation Auth.)—*From jct QEW & Hwy 56: Go 270 meters/300 yards N on N Service Rd, then 270 meters/300 yards W on Baseline Rd.* FACILITIES: 47 sites, 47 full hookups, (30 amp receptacles), 30 pull-thrus, tenting available, handicap restroom facilities, sewage disposal, laundry, public phone, ice, tables. RECREATION: pavilion, lake swimming, boating, canoeing, lake/pond fishing, playground, sports field, hiking trails, volleyball. Open Apr through Nov. Phone: (905) 643-2103.

## STOUFFVILLE—H-3

**CEDAR BEACH PARK**—CAMPGROUND at Musselman's Lake. *From jct Hwy 48 & York Rd 15: Go 2 km/1 1/4 mi E on York Rd 15 & follow signs.*

◆◆◆◆FACILITIES: 565 sites, most common site width 40 feet, 540 full hookups, 25 water & elec (15 & 30 amp receptacles), seasonal sites, 16 pull-thrus, a/c allowed ($), heater

STOUFFVILLE—Continued
CEDAR BEACH PARK—Continued

allowed, tenting available, RV storage, sewage disposal, public phone, grocery store, RV supplies, LP gas refill by weight, ice, tables, fire rings, wood, church services, traffic control gate.

◆◆◆◆◆RECREATION: rec hall, rec room/area, coin games, 3 swim pools (heated), wading pool, lake swimming, boating, no motors, canoeing, dock, 6 row/1 sail/9 canoe boat rentals, lake fishing, basketball hoop, playground, 4 shuffleboard courts, planned group activities, movies, 2 tennis courts, sports field, horseshoes, hiking trails, volleyball. Recreation open to the public.

Open Apr through Nov. Rate in 1995 $22-25 per family. Reservations recommended Jun 20 through Labor Day. Member of OPCA. Phone: (905) 642-1700.

**SEE AD TORONTO PAGE 1021**

## STRATFORD—I-2

**Stratford Fairgrounds and Trailer Park**—RV SPACES on Fairgrounds. *In town at 20 Glastonbury Drive (fairgrounds).* FACILITIES: 282 sites, 12 full hookups, 20 water & elec (15 & 30 amp receptacles), 250 no hookups, tenting available, public phone, tables. RECREATION: rec hall, planned group activities. Open mid May through mid Oct. Rate in 1995 $12-14. Phone: (519) 271-5832.

**STRATFORD TOURISM DEPARTMENT**—*From jct Hwy 8 & 21: Go 1 block S on Downie St, then 3/4 block W on Wellington.* This full service tourism department provides information on the famous Stratford Festival as well as tourist attractions, accommodations, etc. Open all year. Phone: (800) 561-SWAN.

**SEE AD FRONT OF BOOK PAGE 140 AND AD TRAVEL SECTION PAGE 978**

WILDWOOD CONSERVATION AREA (Upper Thames River Conservation Authority)—*From west city limits: Go 11 1/4 km/7 mi W on Hwy 7.* FACILITIES: 450 sites, 300 water & elec (15 & 30 amp receptacles), 150 no hookups, seasonal sites, handicap restroom facilities, sewage disposal, public phone, limited grocery store, ice, tables, fire rings, wood. RECREATION: rec room/area, pavilion, swim pool, lake swimming, boating, canoeing, ramp, dock, lake fishing, playground, planned group activities, recreation director, sports field, horseshoes, hiking trails. Open May through Oct 10. Day use only for winter sports Phone: (519) 284-2292.

**WILLOW LAKE PARK**—*From jct Hwy 19/7/8: Go 12 km/7 1/2 mi E on Hwy 7/8 (Shakespeare Rd), then 28.8 km/18 mi S on Hwy 59.*

**SEE PRIMARY LISTING AT WOODSTOCK AND AD WOODSTOCK PAGE 1026**

**WOODLAND LAKE CAMP & RV RESORT**—*From jct Hwy 19 & Hwy 8: Go 21 km/13 mi W on Hwy 8, then 8 km/5 mi N on Hwy 23, then 5 km/3 mi W on Logan Concession Rd 10/11 to park entrance.*

**SEE PRIMARY LISTING AT BORNHOLM AND AD TRAVEL SECTION PAGES 975, 976 AND 977**

## STRATHROY—I-2

**TROUT HAVEN PARK**—Quiet CAMPGROUND with shaded & open sites with trout fishing and fresh running streams. *From jct Hwy 402 (exit 65) & Hwy 81: Go 5.6 km/3 1/2 mi S on Hwy 81, then 1.2 km/3/4 mi W on Carroll St, then .4 km/1/4 mi N on Park St.*

◆◆◆FACILITIES: 70 sites, most common site width 35 feet, 60 full hookups, 10 water & elec (15 & 30 amp receptacles), seasonal sites, 3 pull-thrus, a/c allowed ($), heater not allowed, tenting available, RV rentals, RV storage, handicap restroom facilities, sewage disposal, laundry, public phone, ice, tables, fire rings, wood.

◆◆◆RECREATION: rec hall, swim pool, pond fishing ($), playground, 2 shuffleboard courts, planned group activities (weekends only), horseshoes.

Open Apr 15 through Oct 30. Rate in 1995 $14 per family. Member of OPCA. Phone: (519) 245-4070.

**SEE AD TRAVEL SECTION PAGES 975, 976 AND 977**

## STURGEON FALLS—F-3

**Big Oak Tent & Trailer Park & Cottages**—Secluded lakeside CAMPGROUND with open or shady sites. *From jct Hwy 17 & Nipissing St: Go 3.2 km/2 mi S on Nipissing St, then .8 km/1/2 mi W on CR.* ◆◆◆FACILITIES: 50 sites, most common site width 40 feet, 35 full hookups, 5 water & elec (15 amp receptacles), 10 no hookups, seasonal sites, 5 pull-thrus, tenting available, sewage disposal, laundry, public phone, limited grocery

BIG OAK TENT & TRAILER PARK & COTTAGES—Continued on next page
STURGEON FALLS—Continued on next page

STURGEON FALLS—Continued
BIG OAK TENT & TRAILER PARK & COTTAGES—Continued

store, ice, tables, fire rings, grills, wood. ◇◇RECREATION: rec hall, lake swimming, boating, canoeing, ramp, dock, 2 canoe/1 pedal/1 motor boat rentals, lake fishing, planned group activities, horseshoes, hiking trails. Open May 15 through Oct 15. Rate in 1995 $13.50-17 for 5 persons. Member of OPCA. Phone: (705) 753-0679.

**Cache Bay Tent & Trailer Park**—Grassy, open and shaded sites on Lake Nipissing. *From west city limits: Go 3.2 km/2 mi W on Hwy 17, then .4 km/1/4 mi S on Levac Rd, then 1.2 km/3/4 mi S on Cache St, then 100 yards W on Railway St, then follow signs.* ◇◇◇FACILITIES: 75 sites, most common site width 30 feet, 40 full hookups, 20 water & elec (15 & 30 amp receptacles), 15 no hookups, seasonal sites, 12 pull-thrus, tenting available, sewage disposal, ice, tables, fire rings, wood. ◇◇◇RECREATION: swim pool, boating, ramp, dock, lake fishing, playground, 2 tennis courts, sports field, horseshoes. Open mid May through mid Oct. Rate in 1995 $16 per family. Phone: (705) 753-2592.

**Dutrisac Cottages & Camping**—CAMPGROUND on Lake Nipissing. *From east town limits on Hwy 17: Go 2.8 km/1 3/4 mi S on Dutrisac Rd, then .8 km/1/2 mi W on gravel road.* ◇◇◇FACILITIES: 135 sites, most common site width 35 feet, 132 full hookups, 3 water & elec (15 & 50 amp receptacles), seasonal sites, 6 pull-thrus, tenting available, handicap restroom facilities, public phone, limited grocery store, ice, tables, fire rings, wood. ◇◇◇RECREATION: pavilion, lake swimming, boating, canoeing, ramp, dock, 43 motor boat rentals, lake fishing, playground, planned group activities (weekends only), horseshoes, hiking trails. Open May 1 through Oct 15. Rate in 1995 $10-16 per family. Phone: (705) 753-2419.

**GLENROCK COTTAGES & TRAILER PARK**—Shaded and grassy sites in a CAMPGROUND on Lake Nipissing. *From jct Hwy 17 & Nipissing St: Go 3.2 km/2 mi S on Nipissing, then 1.6 km/1 mi W on Marleau Rd, then .4 km/1/4 mi S on Des Erables Rd.*

◇◇◇FACILITIES: 88 sites, 56 full hookups, 16 water & elec (15 & 30 amp receptacles), 16 no hookups, seasonal sites, 18 pull-thrus, a/c allowed, heater allowed, tenting available, group sites for tents/RVs, RV storage, sewage disposal, laundry, public phone, grocery store, RV supplies, gasoline, marine gas, ice, tables, fire rings, wood.

◇◇◇RECREATION: rec room/area, coin games, lake swimming, boating, canoeing, ramp, dock, 2 pedal/8 motor boat rentals, water skiing, lake fishing, fishing guides, basketball hoop, playground, shuffleboard court, planned group activities (weekends only), badminton, sports field, horseshoes, volleyball.

Open May 1 through Oct 15. Rate in 1995 $17-20 per family. Master Card/Visa accepted. Member of OPCA. Phone: (705) 753-2150.

**SEE AD TRAVEL SECTION PAGE 981**

**Riverside Lodge**—*From jct Hwy 17 & Nippissing Rd: Go 4.8 km/3 mi S on Nippissing Rd, then 3.2 km/2 mi W on Quesnel Rd.* FACILITIES: 18 sites, most common site width 40 feet, 16 full hookups, 2 water & elec (15 & 30 amp receptacles), seasonal sites, tenting available, sewage disposal, public phone, limited grocery store, ice, tables, fire rings, wood. RECREATION: river swimming, boating, 1 canoe/10 motor boat rentals, lake/river fishing, horseshoes. Recreation open to the public. Open mid May through mid Oct. Rate in 1995 $10-18 per family. Phone: (705) 753-0509.

**Sunshine Motel Campground & RV Park**—RV SPACES behind a motel. *From west city limits: Go 1.6 km/1 mi W on Hwy 17.* FACILITIES: 40 sites, most common site width 25 feet, 15 full hookups, (15 amp receptacles), 25 no hookups, 15 pull-thrus, tenting available, laundry, public phone, ice. RECREATION: swim pool, horseshoes. Open all year. Facilities fully operational mid May through mid Oct. Rate in 1995 $16 per family. Phone: (705) 753-0560.

## SUDBURY—D-5

**CAROL CAMPSITE**—CAMPGROUND on Richard Lake. *From west jct Hwy 17 & Hwy 69S: Go 3.2 km/2 mi S on Hwy 69S.*

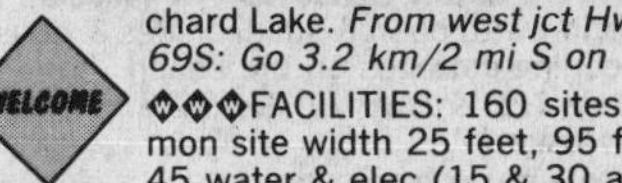

◇◇◇FACILITIES: 160 sites, most common site width 25 feet, 95 full hookups, 45 water & elec (15 & 30 amp receptacles), 20 no hookups, seasonal sites, 20 pull-thrus, a/c allowed, heater allowed, tenting available, group sites for tents/RVs, RV storage, handicap restroom facilities, sewage disposal, public phone, limited grocery store, RV supplies, LP gas refill by weight, ice, tables, fire rings, grills, wood.

◇◇◇RECREATION: rec hall, lake swimming, boating, canoeing, ramp, dock, 2 canoe/2 pedal/2 motor boat rentals, water skiing, lake fishing, basketball hoop, playground, planned group activities (weekends only), horseshoes, volleyball. Recreation open to the public.

Open May 15 through Oct 15. Rate in 1995 $16-17 for 4 persons. Master Card/Visa accepted. Member of OPCA. Phone: (705) 522-5570.

**SEE AD THIS PAGE**

**MINE MILLS CAMPGROUND**—Level sites on the banks of Richard Lake. *From west jct Hwy 17 & Hwy 69: Go 11 km/7 mi S on Hwy 69.*

◇◇FACILITIES: 150 sites, most common site width 40 feet, 150 water & elec (15 & 30 amp receptacles), seasonal sites, 150 pull-thrus, a/c allowed, heater allowed, tenting available, group sites for tents, sewage disposal, public phone, limited grocery store, ice, tables, fire rings, wood.

◇◇◇RECREATION: lake swimming, boating, canoeing, dock, water skiing, lake fishing, basketball hoop, planned group activities, sports field, horseshoes, volleyball. Recreation open to the public.

Open May 1 through Sep 30. Rate in 1995 $14-15 per family. Master Card accepted. Phone: (705) 522-5076.

**SEE AD THIS PAGE**

WINDY LAKE PROVINCIAL PARK—*From town: Go 43 1/4 km/27 mi N on Hwy 144, then 1 1/2 km/1 mi E on Hwy 544 (Levack).* FACILITIES: 85 sites, 56 elec, 29 no hookups, tenting available, handicap restroom facilities, sewage disposal, laundry, tables, wood. RECREATION: swimming, boating, canoeing, ramp, fishing, playground, hiking trails. Open mid May through early Sep. Phone: (705) 966-2315.

## SUNDERLAND—H-3

**TROUT WATER FAMILY CAMPING**—CAMPGROUND on the Beaver River. *From jct Hwy 12 & Hwy 7: Go 1.6 km/1 mi E on Hwy 7.*

◇◇◇FACILITIES: 144 sites, most common site width 50 feet, 81 full hookups, 22 water & elec (15 & 30 amp receptacles), 41 no hookups, seasonal sites, 6 pull-thrus, phone hookups, tenting available, group sites for tents/RVs, RV storage, sewage disposal, laundry, public phone, limited grocery store, LP gas refill by weight, ice, tables, patios, fire rings, wood, traffic control gate.

◇◇◇◇RECREATION: rec room/area, coin games, swim pool, wading pool, boating, no motors, canoeing, dock, 3 canoe/4 pedal boat rentals, river fishing, playground, planned group activities (weekends only), movies, badminton, sports field, horseshoes, hiking trails, volleyball.

Open May 5 through Oct 15. Rate in 1995 $16-21 per family. Visa accepted. Member of OPCA. Phone: (705) 357-1754.

**SEE AD THIS PAGE**

## SUNDRIDGE—F-3

**Lake Bernard Park**—Grassy, lakeside CAMPGROUND with open & shaded sites. *From south city limits: Go 8 km/5 mi S on Hwy 11, then 4.8 km/3 mi E on South Lake Bernard Rd.* ◇◇FACILITIES: 330 sites, most

SUNDRIDGE—Continued
LAKE BERNARD PARK—Continued

common site width 40 feet, 273 water & elec (15 & 30 amp receptacles), 57 no hookups, seasonal sites, 53 pull-thrus, tenting available, sewage disposal, laundry, public phone, grocery store, LP gas refill by weight, ice, tables, fire rings, wood. ◇◇◇RECREATION: rec hall, lake swimming, boating, canoeing, ramp, dock, 3 row/4 canoe/2 pedal/4 motor boat rentals, lake fishing, mini-golf ($), playground, shuffleboard court, planned group activities, badminton, sports field, horseshoes, hiking trails, volleyball. Recreation open to the public. Open May 1 through Oct 15. Rate in 1995 $14-18 per family. Member of NOTO; OPCA. Phone: (705) 384-5455.

## SUTTON—H-3

**ELM GROVE TRAILER PARK**—Open & shaded, level sites among mostly seasonal sites. *From jct of Woodbine Ave (Base Line): Go .4 km/1/4 mi W to Catering Rd, then 3.2 km/2 mi S.*

◇◇◇◇FACILITIES: 128 sites, 128 full hookups, (30 amp receptacles), seasonal sites, 5 pull-thrus, a/c allowed, heater allowed, phone hookups, tenting available, public phone, tables, fire rings, wood.

◇◇◇◇RECREATION: rec hall, pond swimming, boating, canoeing, river fishing, playground, planned group activities (weekends only), sports field, horseshoes, hiking trails, volleyball.

Open mid May through mid Oct. Rate in 1995 $18-20 per family. Member of OPCA. Phone: (905) 722-3693.

**SEE AD TRAVEL SECTION PAGES 975, 976 AND 977**

SIBBALD POINT PROVINCIAL PARK—*From town: Go 8 km/5 mi E on Hwy 48, then 3 1/4 km/2 mi N on CR 18.* FACILITIES: 636 sites, 117 elec, 519 no hookups, tenting available, handicap restroom facilities, sewage disposal, laundry, tables, wood. RECREATION: lake swimming, boating, canoeing, ramp, lake fishing, playground, hiking trails. Open mid May through early Oct. Phone: (905) 722-8061.

## SWASTIKA—C-6

CULVER PARK (City Park)—*In town on Hwy 66.* FACILITIES: 100 sites, 75 elec, 25 no hookups, seasonal sites, tenting available, handicap restroom facilities, sewage disposal, laundry, public phone, limited grocery store, ice, tables, fire rings, grills, wood. RECREATION: rec hall, lake swimming, boating, canoeing, ramp, dock, lake/stream fishing, playground, sports field, hiking trails. Recreation open to the public. Open Jun 15 through Sep 15. Phone: (705) 567-5215.

## SYDENHAM—H-5

**Glen-Lor**—Lakeside lodge & RV and tent CAMPGROUND occupied mostly by seasonals. *From Hwy 401 (exit 613) & CR 9: Go 16 km/10 mi N on CR 9 to end, then 3.2 km/2 mi E on CR 5. Follow signs.* ◇◇◇FACILITIES: 80 sites, most common site width 30 feet, 25 full hookups, 25 water & elec (15 & 30 amp receptacles), 30

GLEN-LOR—Continued on next page
SYDENHAM—Continued on next page

SYDENHAM—Continued
GLEN-LOR—Continued

no hookups, seasonal sites, tenting available, sewage disposal, laundry, public phone, grocery store, LP gas refill by weight, ice, tables, fire rings, wood. ◈◈◈RECREATION: rec room/area, lake swimming, boating, canoeing, ramp, dock, 5 canoe/2 pedal/14 motor boat rentals, lake fishing, playground, badminton, sports field, horseshoes, volleyball. Open early May through mid Oct. Rate in 1995 $16-21 per family. Phone: (613) 376-3020.

## TECUMSEH—J-1

✱ **LEISURE TRAILER SALES**—*From jct Hwy 2 & CR 19: Go 3.2 km/2 mi E on Hwy 2.* SALES: travel trailers, park models, 5th wheels, fold-down camping trailers. SERVICES: RV appliance mechanic, emergency road service business hours, RV towing, LP gas refill by weight/by meter, RV storage, sells parts/accessories, sells camping supplies, installs hitches. Open all year. Master Card/Visa accepted. Phone: (519) 727-3400.

**SEE AD WINDSOR PAGE 1025**

## TEMAGAMI—D-6

FINLAYSON POINT PROVINCIAL PARK—*From town: Go 1 1/2 km/1 mi S on Hwy 11, then 3/4 km/1/2 mi W on Finlayson.* FACILITIES: 113 sites, 14 elec, 99 no hookups, tenting available, handicap restroom facilities, sewage disposal, tables. RECREATION: lake swimming, boating, canoeing, ramp, dock, fishing, playground, hiking trails. Open mid May through early Sep. Phone: (705) 569-3205.

## THESSALON—D-4

**Brownlee Tent & Trailer Park**—Lakeside CAMPGROUND. *From jct Hwy 129 & Hwy 17: Go 9.6 km/6 mi E on Hwy 17, then 1.6 km/1 mi N on Brownlee Rd.* ◈◈FACILITIES: 85 sites, most common site width 30 feet, 25 full hookups, 40 water & elec (15 & 30 amp receptacles), 20 no hookups, seasonal sites, tenting available, sewage disposal, public phone, ice, tables, grills, wood. ◈◈◈RECREATION: lake swimming, boating, canoeing, ramp, dock, 10 row/2 canoe/2 pedal boat rentals, lake fishing, horseshoes, hiking trails. Open all year. Facilities fully operational Apr 1 through Nov 1. Rate in 1995 $11-12 per family. Phone: (705) 842-2118.



THESSALON—Continued

**PINE CREST CAMPGROUND**—A lakeside location with open & shaded sites & housekeeping cottages on the beach. *From jct Hwy 129 & Hwy 17: Go 3.2 km/2 mi W on Hwy 17.*

◈◈◈FACILITIES: 82 sites, most common site width 35 feet, 72 water & elec (15 & 30 amp receptacles), 10 no hookups, seasonal sites, 10 pull-thrus, a/c allowed ($), heater allowed ($), tenting available, group sites for tents, cabins, sewage disposal, laundry, public phone, limited grocery store, LP gas refill by weight/by meter, ice, tables, fire rings, wood.

◈◈◈RECREATION: lake swimming, boating, canoeing, 2 canoe/7 pedal/2 motor boat rentals, water skiing, lake fishing, basketball hoop, playground, sports field, horseshoes.

Open mid May through mid Oct. Rate in 1995 $11.40-13.88 per family. Reservations recommended during Jul. Master Card/Visa accepted. Phone: (705) 842-2635.

**SEE AD TRAVEL SECTION, MI PAGE 412**

THESSALON LAKESIDE PARK (City Park)—*In town on Stanley St.* FACILITIES: 80 sites, 16 full hookups, 40 water & elec (20 amp receptacles), 34 no hookups, seasonal sites, 25 pull-thrus, tenting available, sewage disposal, public phone, tables, fire rings, wood. RECREATION: lake swimming, boating, playground, sports field, hiking trails. Recreation open to the public. Open May 15 through Oct 15. Phone: (705) 842-2523.

## THORNBURY—H-2

**WILLIAM STEWART & DAUGHTERS FAMILY CAMPING**—CAMPGROUND with open & shaded, level sites. *From Thornbury: Go .8 km/1/2 mi E on Hwy 26, then .4 km/1/4 mi S on Grey Rd 2.*

◈◈◈FACILITIES: 146 sites, most common site width 35 feet, 37 full hookups, 39 water & elec (15 & 30 amp receptacles), 70 no hookups, seasonal sites, a/c allowed, heater not allowed, tenting available, group sites for tents/RVs, RV rentals, RV storage, sewage disposal, public phone, limited grocery store, RV supplies, LP gas refill by weight, ice, tables, fire rings, wood.

◈◈◈RECREATION: rec hall, coin games, swim pool (heated), river fishing, mini-golf ($), basketball hoop,



THORNBURY—Continued
WILLIAM STEWART & DAUGHTERS FAMILY CAMPING—Continued

planned group activities (weekends only), movies, horseshoes, volleyball.

Open all year. Facilities fully operational mid May through mid Oct. Rate in 1995 $18-20 per family. Reservations recommended Jul through Aug. Visa accepted. Member of OPCA. Phone: (519) 599-3800.

**SEE AD TRAVEL SECTION PAGES 975, 976 AND 977**

## THUNDER BAY—B-1

**CHIPPEWA PARK (City Park)**—*From jct Hwy 61 & Hwy 61B: Go 3.2 km/2 mi SE on Hwy 61B to City Rd, then follow signs.*

FACILITIES: 150 sites, 40 water & elec, 20 elec (15 amp receptacles), 90 no hookups, 40 pull-thrus, tenting available, sewage disposal, laundry, public phone, limited grocery store, ice, tables, fire rings, grills, wood.

RECREATION: rec hall, coin games, lake swimming, boating, dock, lake fishing, playground, sports field, horseshoes. Recreation open to the public.

Open May 16 through Labour Day. Master Card/Visa accepted. Phone: (807) 623-3912.

**SEE AD THIS PAGE**

**HAPPY LAND CAMPGROUND**—A level, semi-wooded CAMPGROUND with open or shaded sites. *From west city limits: Go 25.6 km/16 mi W on Hwy 17.*

◈◈◈FACILITIES: 100 sites, most common site width 35 feet, 26 full hookups, 26 elec (15,30 & 50 amp receptacles), 48 no hookups, seasonal sites, 85 pull-thrus, a/c allowed, heater allowed, tenting available, RV storage, sewage disposal, laundry, public phone, RV supplies, ice, tables, grills, wood.

◈◈◈RECREATION: rec room/area, coin games, swim pool (heated), playground, sports field, horseshoes, hiking trails.

Open Apr 15 through Oct 15. Rate in 1995 $15.50-20 for 2 persons. Master Card/Visa accepted. Member of OPCA. Phone: (807) 473-9003.

**SEE AD THIS PAGE**

⚑ **HAPPY LAND GIFT SHOP**—*From west city limits: Go 25.6 km/16 mi W on Hwy 17.* Specialty gift shop featuring beautiful amethyst specimans and jewelry, large selection of local crafts, moccasins, souvenir items, caps, T-shirts and sweatshirts. Open Apr 15 through Oct 15. Master Card/Visa accepted. Phone: (807) 473-9003.

**SEE AD THIS PAGE**

**KOA-Thunder Bay**—CAMPGROUND convenient to a major highway, with Kamper Kabins. *From jct Hwy 11-17 & Hwy 527: Go .4 km/1/4 mi S on Spruce River Rd.* ◈◈FACILITIES: 181 sites, most common site width 30 feet, 76 full hookups, 65 water & elec (15,30 & 50 amp receptacles), 40 no hookups, seasonal sites, 106

KOA-THUNDER BAY—Continued on next page
THUNDER BAY—Continued on next page

THUNDER BAY—Continued
KOA-THUNDER BAY—Continued

pull-thrus, tenting available, sewage disposal, laundry, public phone, limited grocery store, ice, tables, fire rings, wood. ◆◆RECREATION: rec room/area, pond fishing, playground, horseshoes, hiking trails. Open Apr 15 through Oct 15. Rate in 1995 $15-20 for 2 persons. Phone: (807) 683-6221. KOA 10% value card discount.

**LEN'S RV SALES**—*In town at 1189 Carrick St.* SALES: travel trailers, park models, truck campers, 5th wheels, motor homes, mini-motor homes, fold-down camping trailers. SERVICES: RV appliance mechanic full-time, RV storage, sells parts/accessories, installs hitches. Open all year. Master Card/Visa accepted. Phone: (807) 939-2585.
**SEE AD PAGE 1020**

MIDDLE FALLS PROVINCIAL PARK—*From town: Go 56 km/35 mi S on Hwy 61.* FACILITIES: 23 sites, 23 no hookups, tenting available, tables, wood. RECREATION: fishing. Open early Jun through early Sep. No showers. Phone: (807) 964-2097.

**ONTARIO GEM MINING COMPANY**—*From east city limits: Go 72 km/45 mi E on Hwy 17/11, then 3.2 km/2 mi S on Dorion Amethyst Mine Rd.* Open pit quarry extracting amethyst plus other minerals on site. Custom made jewelery and related gift shop. Open mid May through Oct 1. Master Card/Visa accepted. Phone: (807) 854-1041.
**SEE AD TRAVEL SECTION PAGE 983**

**TROWBRIDGE FALLS (City Park)**—*From jct Hwys 11 & 17 & Hodder Ave (Hwy 11B & 17B): Go 4 km/1/4 mi N on Copenhagen Rd.*
FACILITIES: 150 sites, 74 elec (15 amp receptacles), 76 no hookups, 20 pull-thrus, tenting available, sewage disposal, laundry, public phone, grocery store, ice, tables, fire rings, grills, wood.
RECREATION: river swimming, river fishing, playground, hiking trails.
Open May 16 through Labour Day. Phone: (807) 683-6661.
**SEE AD PAGE 1020**

## TILLSONBURG—I-2

**Red Oak Travel Park**—Shaded CAMPGROUND convenient to a major highway. *From jct Hwy 19 & Hwy 3: Go 13 km/8 mi W on Hwy 3.* ◆◆◆FACILITIES: 120 sites, most common site width 30 feet, 59 full hookups, 41 water & elec (15 & 30 amp receptacles), 20 no hookups, seasonal sites, 2 pull-thrus, tenting available, sewage disposal, laundry, limited grocery store, ice, tables, fire rings, wood. ◆◆◆◆RECREATION: rec hall, rec room/area, swim pool, mini-golf, playground, 2 shuffleboard courts, planned group activities (weekends only), horseshoes, volleyball. Recreation open to the public. Open May 2 through Oct 15. Rate in 1995 $18-22 per family. Member of OPCA. Phone: (519) 866-3504.

## TIMMINS—B-5

**Horseshoe Lake Park**—Open & shaded, level sites. *From jct Hwy 101 & Hwy 576: Go 3.2 km/2 mi W on Hwy 576, then .8 km/1/2 mi N on Horseshoe Lake Park Rd.* ◆◆FACILITIES: 90 sites, most common site width 30 feet, 50 water & elec, 40 elec (15 amp receptacles), seasonal sites, 15 pull-thrus, tenting available, sewage disposal, limited grocery store, ice, tables, fire rings, wood. ◆◆RECREATION: lake swimming, boating, electric motors only, canoeing, 2 pedal boat rentals, horseshoes, hiking trails. Open May 15 through Sep 15. Rate in 1995 $16 per family. Phone: (705) 268-2033.

**NIGHTHAWK RETREAT**—Semi-wooded CAMPGROUND overlooking the lake. *From jct Hwy 67 & Hwy 101: Go 4 km/2 1/2 mi W on Hwy 101, then 1.2 km/3/4 mi S on Nighthawk Retreat Rd.*
◆◆FACILITIES: 60 sites, most common site width 25 feet, 43 full hookups, (15 amp receptacles), 17 no hookups, seasonal sites, tenting available, group sites for tents, sewage disposal, laundry, limited grocery store, tables, fire rings, wood.
◆◆RECREATION: lake swimming, boating, canoeing, ramp, dock, 1 row/1 canoe boat rentals, lake fishing, hiking trails. Recreation open to the public.
Open all year. Facilities fully operational May 1 through Oct 15. Rate in 1995 $12 per family. Phone: (705) 363-2191.
**SEE AD TRAVEL SECTION PAGE 981**

## TIVERTON—H-2

**Pine Tree Tourist Park**—CAMPGROUND at west edge of town in a rural area. *From jct Hwy 21 & CR 15: Go .8 km/1/2 mi W on CR 15.* ◆◆◆FACILITIES: 75 sites, most common site width 30 feet, 50 full hookups, 15 elec (15 & 30 amp receptacles), 10 no hookups, seasonal sites, 1 pull-thrus, tenting available, sewage disposal, ice, tables, fire rings, wood. ◆◆◆RECREATION:

TIVERTON—Continued
PINE TREE TOURIST PARK—Continued

rec hall, planned group activities (weekends only), sports field, horseshoes, hiking trails. Open May 1 through Nov 1. Rate in 1995 $16 per family. Phone: (519) 368-7951.

## TOBERMORY—G-2

**Happy Hearts Tent & Trailer Park**—A semi-wooded CAMPGROUND. *From south city limits: Go 90 m/100 yards N on Hwy 6, then 1.2 km/3/4 mi W on Cape Hurd Rd.* ◆◆◆FACILITIES: 95 sites, most common site width 25 feet, 25 full hookups, (15 amp receptacles), 70 no hookups, seasonal sites, tenting available, sewage disposal, limited grocery store, ice, tables, fire rings, wood. ◆◆◆RECREATION: rec hall, rec room/area, swim pool, mini-golf ($), playground, horseshoes, volleyball. Open mid May through mid Oct. Rate in 1995 $16.25-18.25 per family. Phone: (519) 596-2455.

**LANDS END PARK**—Secluded, wooded CAMPGROUND in a natural setting. *From south city limits: Go 1.6 km/1 mi N on Hwy 6, then 2.4 km/1 1/2 mi W on Hay Bay Rd.*
◆◆◆◆FACILITIES: 100 sites, most common site width 30 feet, 50 water & elec (15 & 30 amp receptacles), 50 no hookups, seasonal sites, 15 pull-thrus, a/c allowed, heater allowed, tenting available, group sites for tents, cabins, RV storage, sewage disposal, public phone, limited grocery store, ice, tables, fire rings, grills, wood.
◆◆◆RECREATION: lake swimming, boating, canoeing, ramp, dock, 3 row/2 sail/5 canoe/2 pedal boat rentals, water skiing, lake fishing, playground, badminton, sports field, horseshoes, volleyball.
Open May 1 through mid Oct. Rate in 1995 $17-20 per family. Reservations recommended all season. Master Card/Visa accepted. Member of OPCA. Phone: (519) 596-2523.
**SEE AD TRAVEL SECTION PAGES 975, 976 AND 977**

**Tobermory Village Campground**—A CAMPGROUND with level sites. *On Hwy 6 (3.2 km/2 mi S of Ferry).* ◆◆◆FACILITIES: 154 sites, most common site width 40 feet, 34 full hookups, 40 water & elec (15 & 30 amp receptacles), 80 no hookups, seasonal sites, tenting available, sewage disposal, ice, tables, fire rings, wood. ◆◆RECREATION: pavilion, swim pool (heated), pond swimming, pond fishing, sports field, horseshoes, volleyball. Open May 1 through Oct 30. Rate in 1995 $14.50-18.50. Phone: (800) 459-5620.

## TORONTO—H-3

***See listings at Bolton, Bradford, Campbellville, Milton, Pickering, Stouffville, Sunderland, Thornhill & Waterdown***

### TORONTO AREA MAP

***Symbols on map indicate towns within a 64 km/40 mi radius of Toronto where campgrounds (diamonds), attractions (flags), & RV service centers & camping supply outlets (gears) are listed. Check listings for more information.***

**CAMPARK RESORTS**—*From jct Hwy 427 & Hwy QEW: Go 128 km/80 mi SW on QEW, then .4 km/1/4 mi W on Hwy 20 (Lundy's Lane).*
**SEE PRIMARY LISTING AT NIAGARA FALLS AND AD NIAGARA FALLS PAGE 1004**

TORONTO—Continued

**HEIDIS' CAMPGROUND & RV TRAILER SALES**—*From jct Hwy 401 & Hwy 400: Go 88 km/55 mi N on Hwy 400, then 14.4 km/9 mi N on Hwy 11, then .4 km/1/4 mi N on CR 11 (Hawkstone exit).*
**SEE PRIMARY LISTING AT BARRIE AND AD BARRIE PAGE 987**

INDIAN LINE CAMPGROUND (Metro Toronto & Region Cons. Auth.)—*From jct Hwy 401 (exit 348) & Hwy 427: Go 5 km/3 mi N on Hwy 427, then 1/2 km/3/10 mi W on Finch.* FACILITIES: 222 sites, most common site width 35 feet, 180 water & elec (15 & 30 amp receptacles), 42 no hookups, seasonal sites, 90 pull-thrus, tenting available, handicap restroom facilities, sewage disposal, laundry, public phone, ice, tables, fire rings, grills, wood. RECREATION: swim pool, pond fishing, playground, horseshoes, hiking trails. Recreation open to the public. Open May 5 through Oct 9. Phone: (905) 678-1233.

**KOA-BARRIE**—*From jct Hwy 401 & Hwy 400: Go 88 km/55 mi N on Hwy 400, then 14.4 km/9 mi N on Hwy 11, then 11.2 km/7 mi N on Hwy 93.*
**SEE PRIMARY LISTING AT BARRIE AND AD BARRIE PAGE 986**

**KOA-TORONTO WEST**—*From jct Hwy 401 (exit 312) & Guelph Line: Go 1.6 km/1 mi N on Guelph Line, then 1.6 km/1 mi W on 10th Side Rd, then 1.6 km/1 mi S on Second Line Rd.*
**SEE PRIMARY LISTING AT CAMPBELLVILLE AND AD NEXT PAGE**

TORONTO—Continued on next page

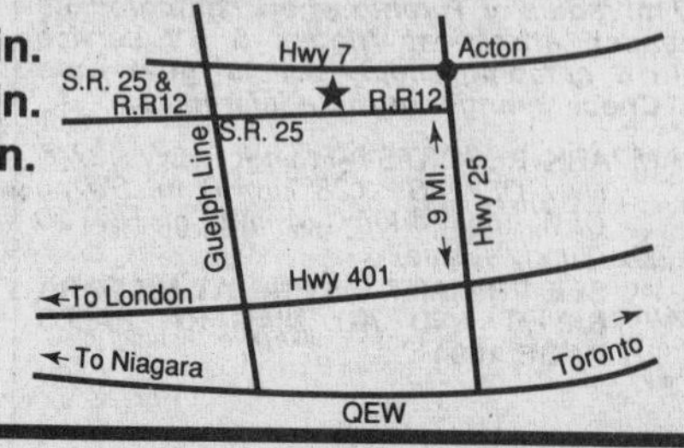


TORONTO—Continued

**LEISURE TIME PARK**—*From jct Hwy 401 & Hwy 400: Go 40 km/25 mi N on Hwy 400, then 16 km/10 mi W on Hwy 9.* WELCOME SEE PRIMARY LISTING AT BOLTON AND AD TRAVEL SECTION PAGES 975, 976 AND 977

**MILTON HEIGHTS CAMPGROUND**—*From jct Hwy 401 (exit 320) & Hwy 25 (Milton): Go 1.6 km/1 mi N on Hwy 25, then 2.4 km/1 1/2 mi W on Campbellville Rd, then 90 m/100 yards S on Townline Rd 22.* WELCOME
SEE PRIMARY LISTING AT MILTON AND AD THIS PAGE

**TORONTO NORTH CAMPGROUNDS & RV RESORT**—*From jct Hwy 401 & Hwy 400: Go 32 km/20 mi N on Hwy 400 to Hwy 88 (exit 64B), then 1000 feet W on Hwy 88.* WELCOME
SEE PRIMARY LISTING AT BRADFORD AND AD THIS PAGE

## TOTTENHAM—H-3

TOTTENHAM CONSERVATION AREA (Town of New Tecumseth)—*In town (New Tecumseth) on Mill St (Concession Rd 4).* FACILITIES: 87 sites, 37 water & elec (15 & 30 amp receptacles), 50 no hookups, seasonal sites, tenting available, handicap restroom facilities, tables, wood. RECREATION: equipped pavilion, pond swimming, canoeing, 3 canoe/3 pedal boat rentals, pond fishing, playground, horseshoes, hiking trails, volleyball. Open May 24 through Sep 1. Phone: (705) 435-6219.

## TRENTON—H-4

*See listings at Brighton, Carrying Place & Frankford*

## TWEED—H-5

**Fox's Lakeside Trailer Park**—Family CAMPGROUND on large shaded or sunny sites. *From jct Hwys 7 & 37: Go 8 km/5 mi S on Hwy 37 (in town), then 4.8 km/3 mi E on Sulphide Rd & follow signs.* ◇◇◇FACILITIES: 65 sites, most common site width 40 feet, 20 full hookups, 37 water & elec (15 & 30 amp receptacles), 8 no hookups, seasonal sites, 10 pull-thrus, tenting available, sewage disposal, public phone, limited grocery store, ice, tables, fire rings, wood. ◇◇◇RECREATION: lake swimming, boating, canoeing, dock, 1 canoe/2 motor boat rentals, lake fishing, playground, horseshoes, volleyball. Open mid May through mid Sep. Rate in 1995 $15 per family. Phone: (613) 478-3620.

**Swiss Pine Park**—Secluded CAMPGROUND with large grassy sites separated by trees. *From jct Hwy 37 & Hwy 7: Go 6.4 km/4 mi E on Hwy 7, then .4 km/1/4 mi N on Varty Rd.* ◇◇FACILITIES: 40 sites, most common site width 50 feet, 25 water & elec (15 & 30 amp receptacles), 15 no hookups, seasonal sites, tenting available, sewage disposal, laundry, ice, tables, fire rings, wood. ◇◇RECREATION: pavilion, river swimming, boating, no motors, canoeing, river fishing, sports field, horseshoes, volleyball. Recreation open to the public. Open mid May through mid Oct. Rate in 1995 $12-18 for 4 persons. Member of OPCA. Phone: (613) 478-6844. FCRV 10% discount.

## UPSALA—B-1

**Camp Saw Mill Bay**—CAMPGROUND with open sites on Northern Lake. *From town: Go 24 km/15 mi E on Hwy 17, then .8 km/1/2 mi S on Sawmill Bay Rd.* ◇◇◇FACILITIES: 57 sites, most common site width 30 feet, 35 full hookups, 12 water & elec (15 & 30 amp receptacles), 10 no hookups, seasonal sites, 4 pull-thrus, tenting available, sewage disposal, public phone, tables,

CAMP SAW MILL BAY—Continued on next page
UPSALA—Continued on next page

UPSALA—Continued
CAMP SAW MILL BAY—Continued

fire rings. ◆◆RECREATION: lake swimming, boating, ramp, dock, 2 motor boat rentals, lake fishing, horseshoes. Open May 15 through Oct 1. Rate in 1995 $20-22 per family. Phone: (807) 986-2327.

**Cushing Lake Resort**—Level sites on natural terrain near a lake. *From east town limits on Hwy 17: Go 6.4 km/4 mi E on Hwy 17, then 11.2 km/7 mi S on Lac Des Mille Lac Rd.* ◆◆FACILITIES: 30 sites, most common site width 25 feet, 30 water & elec (15 amp receptacles), seasonal sites, 2 pull-thrus, tenting available, non-flush toilets, sewage disposal, public phone, limited grocery store, ice, tables, fire rings, wood. ◆◆RECREATION: lake swimming, boating, canoeing, ramp, dock, 8 motor boat rentals, lake fishing. Open all year. Facilities fully operational mid May through mid Oct. No showers. Rate in 1995 $16 per family. Phone: (807) 986-2368.

INWOOD PARK (Upsala Regional Dev. Assn.)—*From east town limits: Go 2 1/2 km/1 1/2 mi E on Hwy 17.* FACILITIES: 86 sites, 86 no hookups, tenting available, non-flush/marine toilets, handicap restroom facilities, sewage disposal, tables, fire rings, wood. RECREATION: lake swimming, boating, no motors, canoeing, lake fishing, hiking trails. Open mid May through mid Oct. Phone: (807) 986-2425.

**OPEN BAY COTTAGES & CAMPGROUND**—Terraced campground with level, open & shaded sites beside a lake. *From east town limits on Hwy 17: Go 6.4 km/4 mi E on Hwy 17, then 16.8 km/10 1/2 mi S on Lac Des Mille Lac Rd.*

◆◆◆FACILITIES: 30 sites, 30 water & elec (15 amp receptacles), seasonal sites, tenting available, cabins, sewage disposal, laundry, public phone, grocery store, gasoline, marine gas, ice, tables, fire rings, grills, wood.

◆◆◆RECREATION: lake swimming, boating, canoeing, ramp, dock, 2 pedal/13 motor boat rentals, lake fishing.

Open mid May through end Sep. Rate in 1995 $14.50 for 2 persons. Phone: (807) 986-2356.

**SEE AD TRAVEL SECTION PAGES 975, 976 AND 977**

**Pine Point Resort**—A lakeside CAMPGROUND. *From east town limits: Go 6.4 km/4 mi E on Hwy 17, then 27.2 km/17 mi S on Lac Des Mille Lac Rd.* ◆◆◆FACILITIES: 80 sites, most common site width 35 feet, 23 full hookups, 44 water & elec, 3 elec (15 amp receptacles), 10 no hookups, seasonal sites, 26 pull-thrus, tenting available, sewage disposal, laundry, public phone, limited grocery store, ice, tables, fire rings, wood. ◆◆◆RECREATION: lake swimming, boating, canoeing, ramp, dock, 20 motor boat rentals, lake fishing, horseshoes, hiking trails. Recreation open to the public. Open all year. Facilities fully operational May 1 through Sep 30. Rate in 1995 $17.50-24.25 for 2 persons. Phone: (807) 986-1300.

**Savanne River Resort**—CAMPGROUND with open, level sites along the Savanne River. *From town: Go 19.3 km/12 mi E on Hwy 17.* ◆◆◆FACILITIES: 125 sites, most common site width 40 feet, 125 water & elec (15 & 30 amp receptacles), seasonal sites, 10 pull-thrus, tenting available, laundry, public phone, grocery store, ice, tables, fire rings, grills, wood. ◆◆◆RECREATION: rec room/area, river swimming, boating, canoeing, ramp, dock, 2 canoe/9 motor boat rentals, lake/river fishing, horseshoes. Open all year. Facilities fully operational May 1 through Oct 31. Rate in 1995 $14-18.50 per family. Phone: (800) 663-5852.

**Thousand Lakes Resort**—CAMPGROUND with gently rolling landscape on Lake Lac Des Mille Lac. *From east town limits on Hwy 17: Go 6.4 km/4 mi E on Hwy 17, then 11 km/7 mi S on Lac Des Mille Lac Rd.* ◆◆FACILITIES: 64 sites, most common site width 20 feet, 53 water & elec (15 amp receptacles), 11 no hookups, seasonal sites, 6 pull-thrus, tenting available, sewage disposal, public phone, limited grocery store, ice, tables, fire rings, wood. ◆◆◆RECREATION: lake swimming, boating, dock, 6 row/1 canoe/3 pedal/8 motor boat rentals, lake fishing, horseshoes. Open mid May through mid Oct. Rate in 1995 $14-19 for 2 persons. Phone: (807) 986-1600.

**Thunderbird Resort**—A semi-wooded, lakeside CAMPGROUND. *From east town limits on Hwy 17: Go 6.4 km/4 mi E on Hwy 17, then 11.2 km/7 mi S on Lac Des Mille Lac Rd.* ◆◆◆FACILITIES: 35 sites, most common site width 30 feet, 16 water & elec, 19 elec (15 & 30 amp receptacles), seasonal sites, tenting available, sewage disposal, public phone, limited grocery store, ice, tables, fire rings, wood. ◆◆RECREATION: lake swimming, boating, canoeing, ramp, dock, 1 canoe/1 pedal/38 motor boat rentals, lake fishing. Open May 15 through Oct 5. Rate in 1995 $18 for 2 persons. Phone: (807) 986-2332.

## UPTERGROVE—G-3

MCRAE POINT PROVINCIAL PARK—*From jct Hwy 12 & Muley Point Rd: Go 16 km/10 mi SE on Muley Point Rd.* FACILITIES: 202 sites, 125 elec (15 & 30 amp receptacles), 77 no hookups, 125 pull-thrus, tenting available, handicap restroom facilities, sewage disposal, tables, wood. RECREATION: lake swimming, boating, canoeing, ramp, lake fishing, hiking trails. Open mid May through mid Oct. Phone: (705) 325-7290.

## VERMILION BAY—D-1

**BLUE BIRD TRAILER & CAMPSITE**—CAMPGROUND at Eagle Lake. *From jct Hwy 105 & Hwy 17: Go 1.6 km/1 mi E on Hwy 17, then .4 km/1/4 mi S on Myers Rd.*

◆◆◆FACILITIES: 85 sites, most common site width 30 feet, 25 full hookups, 60 water & elec (15 & 30 amp receptacles), seasonal sites, 6 pull-thrus, a/c allowed ($), heater allowed ($), tenting available, group sites for tents, cabins, sewage disposal, laundry, public phone, gasoline, marine gas, ice, tables, fire rings, grills, wood.

◆◆◆RECREATION: lake swimming, boating, canoeing, ramp, dock, 1 canoe/2 pedal/9 motor boat rentals, water skiing, lake fishing, fishing guides, mini-golf ($), 5 bike rentals, horseshoes. Recreation open to the public.

Open May 15 through Sep 30. Rate in 1995 $19-20.56 per family. Master Card/Visa accepted. Phone: (807) 227-2042.

**SEE AD TRAVEL SECTION PAGES 975, 976 AND 977**

BLUE LAKE PROVINCIAL PARK—*From jct Hwy 17 & Hwy 647: Go 8 km/5 mi NW on Hwy 647.* FACILITIES: 188 sites, 75 elec (15 & 30 amp receptacles), 113 no hookups, 60 pull-thrus, tenting available, handicap restroom facilities, sewage disposal, tables, wood. RECREATION: lake swimming, boating, canoeing, ramp, lake fishing, playground, hiking trails. Open mid May through mid Sep. Phone: (807) 227-2601.

**Nixon Lake Resort**—Open & shaded sites on the banks of Nixon Lake. *From jct Hwy 105 & Hwy 17: Go 11.2 km/7 mi W on Hwy 17.* ◆◆FACILITIES: 16 sites, most common site width 25 feet, 28 ft. max RV length, 12 water & elec (15 amp receptacles), 4 no hookups, tenting available, public phone, tables, fire rings, wood. ◆◆RECREATION: lake swimming, boating, canoeing, ramp, 1 canoe/1 pedal boat rentals, lake fishing, horseshoes. Open mid May through mid Oct. Rate in 1995 $13-15 per family. Phone: (807) 227-2880.

**WOGENSTAHL'S CANADIAN RESORT & TRAILER PARK**—RV PARK with grassy sites on Cedar Lake. *From jct Hwy 17 & Hwy 105: Go 40.2 km/25 mi N on Hwy 105, then 1.6 km/1 mi E on Camp Robinson Rd.*

◆◆◆◆FACILITIES: 68 sites, most common site width 30 feet, 36 full hookups, (20 & 30 amp receptacles), 32 no hookups, seasonal sites, 33 pull-thrus, tenting available, cabins, sewage disposal, laundry, public phone, grocery store, RV supplies, gasoline, marine gas, ice, tables, fire rings, wood.

◆◆◆◆RECREATION: rec room/area, pavilion, lake swimming, boating, canoeing, ramp, dock, 4 canoe/33 motor boat rentals, water skiing, float trips, lake fishing, fishing guides, playground, planned group activities, badminton, horseshoes, hiking trails, volleyball. Recreation open to the public.

Open May 15 through Oct 15. Rate in 1995 $16.50-27 per family. Master Card/Visa accepted. Phone: (807) 529-6561.

**SEE AD FRONT OF BOOK PAGE 142 AND AD TRAVEL SECTION, CO PAGE 185 AND AD THIS PAGE**

## VERONA—H-5

**Desert Lake Family Resort**—Grassy, lakeside CAMPGROUND with open & Shaded sites. *From jct Hwy 401 (exit 611) & Hwy 38: Go 27.2 km/17 mi N on Hwy 38, then 9.6 km/6 mi E on Desert Lake Rd.* ◆◆◆FACILITIES: 150 sites, most common site width 35 feet, 125 water & elec (15 & 30 amp receptacles), 25 no hookups, seasonal sites, 30 pull-thrus, tenting available, handicap restroom facilities, sewage disposal, laundry, public phone, full service store, LP gas refill by weight, ice, tables, fire rings, wood. ◆◆◆RECREATION: equipped pavilion, lake swimming, boating, canoeing, ramp, dock, 4 canoe/4 pedal/8 motor boat rentals, lake fishing, mini-golf ($), playground, 2 shuffleboard courts, planned group activities, recreation director, badminton, sports field, horseshoes, hiking trails, volleyball. Open all year. Facilities fully operational Apr 15 through Oct 15. Rate in 1995 $18-21 for 2 persons. Member of OPCA. Phone: (613) 374-2196.

SECOND DEPOT LAKE (Napanee Reg. Conserv. Auth.)—*From town: Go 1 1/2 km/1 mi N on Hwy 38, then 4 3/4 km/3 mi W on Snider Rd, then 1 1/2 km/1 mi N on local road, then 1 1/2 km/1 mi W on local road.* FACILITIES: 60 sites, 60 no hookups, tenting available, handicap restroom facilities, sewage disposal, public phone, LP gas refill by meter, ice, tables, fire rings, grills, wood. RECREATION: pavilion, lake/river swimming, boating, canoeing, ramp, dock, 2 row/3 canoe/3 pedal boat rentals, lake/river fishing, playground, horseshoes, hiking trails. Recreation open to the public. Open May 20 through Sep 6. Phone: (613) 374-2945.

## VINELAND—I-3

**INDIAN LAKE CAMPGROUNDS**—Open & shaded sites in CAMPGROUND with a private lake. *From jct QEW (exit 57) & Regional Rd 24: Go 17.7 km/11 mi S on Regional Rd 24.*

◆◆◆FACILITIES: 163 sites, most common site width 30 feet, 25 full hookups, 120 water & elec (15 & 30 amp receptacles), 18 no hookups, seasonal sites, a/c allowed, heater not allowed, phone hookups, tenting available, group sites for tents/RVs, RV storage, sewage disposal, public phone, ice, tables, fire rings, wood, traffic control gate.

◆◆◆RECREATION: rec hall, coin games, swim pool, boating, canoeing, dock, 9 canoe boat rentals, playground, shuffleboard court, planned group activities (weekends only), badminton, horseshoes, hiking trails, volleyball.

Open May 1 through Oct 1. Rate in 1995 $22-24 per family. Phone: (905) 892-7982.

**SEE AD NIAGARA FALLS PAGE 1004**

## WARSAW—H-4

WARSAW CAVES (Otonabee Region Conservation Authority)—*From town: Go 4 km/2 1/2 mi N on CR 4.* FACILITIES: 65 sites, 65 no hookups, tenting available, non-flush toilets, public phone, tables, wood. RECREATION: river swimming, canoeing, 2 canoe boat rentals, river fishing, hiking trails. Open Jul 1 through Sep 4. No showers. Phone: (705) 652-3161.

## WASAGA BEACH—H-3

**Jell-E-Bean Campground**—Level CAMPGROUND with open & shaded areas. *Located on Hwy 26 at the W city limits.* ◆◆FACILITIES: 140 sites, most common site width 35 feet, 110 full hookups, 30 water & elec (15 & 30 amp receptacles), seasonal sites, tenting available, sewage disposal, public phone, limited grocery store, ice, tables, fire rings, grills, wood. ◆◆◆RECREATION: equipped pavilion, swim pool, playground, planned group activities (weekends only), badminton, horseshoes, volleyball. No pets. Open May 1 through early Oct. Rate in 1995 $26.17-28.04 per family. Member of OPCA. Phone: (705) 429-5418.

**KOA-Wasaga Beach**—Level, semi-wooded CAMPGROUND. *From east city limits: Go 6 km/3 3/4 mi E on Hwy 92.* ◆◆◆◆FACILITIES: 247 sites, most common site width 45 feet, 145 full hookups, 55 water & elec (15 amp receptacles), 47 no hookups, seasonal sites, 35 pull-thrus, tenting available, sewage disposal, laundry, public phone, grocery store, LP gas refill by weight, ice, tables, fire rings, wood. ◆◆◆◆RECREATION: rec room/area, equipped pavilion, swim pool (heated), mini-golf ($), playground, planned group activities, recreation director, badminton, sports field, horseshoes, volleyball. Open mid May through mid Oct. Rate in 1995 $24-27.50 per family. Member of OPCA. Phone: (800) KOA-5882. KOA 10% value card discount.

**Wasaga Campground Resort**—Modern campground with spacious shaded campsites. *In town at east*

WASAGA CAMPGROUND RESORT—Continued on next page
WASAGA BEACH—Continued on next page

WASAGA BEACH—Continued
WASAGA CAMPGROUND RESORT—Continued

*city limits on Hwy 92.* ◆◆◆FACILITIES: 340 sites, most common site width 50 feet, 250 full hookups, 45 water & elec (15 & 30 amp receptacles), 45 no hookups, seasonal sites, tenting available, handicap restroom facilities, sewage disposal, laundry, public phone, limited grocery store, LP gas refill by weight, ice, tables, fire rings, wood. ◆◆◆◆RECREATION: rec hall, swim pool (heated), boating, no motors, canoeing, pond fishing, playground, planned group activities, recreation director, 2 tennis courts, sports field, horseshoes, volleyball. Open May 1 through Oct 31. Rate in 1995 $20-24 for 2 persons. Member of OPCA. Phone: (705) 429-5267.

## WASHAGO—G-3

**BLACK RIVER WILDERNESS PARK**—A CAMPGROUND with shaded, riverside campsites. *From jct Hwy 11 & Hwy 169S: Go 8 km/5 mi S on Hwy 169S.*

◆◆◆FACILITIES: 91 sites, 28 full hookups, 12 water & elec (15 amp receptacles), 51 no hookups, seasonal sites, a/c allowed ($), heater allowed ($), tenting available, group sites for tents, sewage disposal, ice, tables, fire rings, wood.

◆◆RECREATION: swim pool, boating, canoeing, river fishing, playground, horseshoes, hiking trails.

Open mid May through mid Oct. Rate in 1995 $15-20 per family. Member of OPCA. Phone: (705) 689-1543.

**SEE AD TRAVEL SECTION PAGES 975, 976 AND 977**

## WATERDOWN—I-3

**OLYMPIA VILLAGE TRAILER PARK**—Quiet, grassy CAMPGROUND. *From jct Hwy 403 & Hwy 46: Go 3.2 km/2 mi N on Hwy 6, then 9.6 km/6 mi W on 4th Concession Rd.*

◆◆◆FACILITIES: 262 sites, most common site width 40 feet, 50 full hookups, 162 water & elec (15 & 30 amp receptacles), 50 no hookups, seasonal sites, 10 pull-thrus, tenting available, sewage disposal, laundry, public phone, limited grocery store, LP gas refill by weight, ice, tables, fire rings, wood, traffic control gate.

◆◆◆RECREATION: rec hall, equipped pavilion, coin games, swim pool, pond fishing, playground, planned group activities (weekends only), movies, sports field, horseshoes, volleyball.

Open May 1 through Oct 15. Rate in 1995 $15-22.50 per family. Visa accepted. Member of OPCA. Phone: (905) 627-1923.

**SEE AD TRAVEL SECTION PAGES 975, 976 AND 977**

## WATERLOO—I-2

**Green Acre Park**—A CAMPGROUND with grassy open and tree shaded sites. *From jct Hwy 401 & Hwy 8: Go 8 km/5 mi W on Hwy 8, then 10.4 km/6 1/2 mi N on Hwy 86, then 3.2 km/2 mi W on Northfield Dr, then .8 km/1/2 mi N on Westmound Rd, then 1.6 km/1 mi W on Conservation Dr, then 90 m/100 yards S on Beaver Creek Rd. (Follow signs)* ◆◆◆◆FACILITIES: 360 sites, 335 full hookups, 25 water & elec (15,30 & 50 amp receptacles), seasonal sites, 40 pull-thrus, tenting available, sewage disposal, laundry, public phone, limited grocery store, LP gas refill by weight/by meter, ice, tables, patios, fire rings, wood. ◆◆◆◆RECREATION: rec hall, rec room/area, pavilion, swim pool (heated), mini-golf ($), playground, 4 shuffleboard courts, planned group activities (weekends only), badminton, sports field, horseshoes, volleyball. Open all year. Facilities fully operational May 1 through Oct 31. Rate in 1995 $21.50-23 per family. Member of OPCA. Phone: (519) 885-1758. FCRV 10% discount.

## WAUBAUSHENE—G-3

**Mariner's Paradise**—Quiet CAMPGROUND located on Georgian Bay. *From jct Hwy 12, Hwy 400 & Hwy 69: Go .8 km/1/2 mi N on Hwy 69 (exit 59-Quarry Rd), then .4 km/1/4 mi S on E service road.* ◆◆FACILITIES: 87 sites, most common site width 40 feet, 12 full hookups, 50 water & elec (15 amp receptacles), 25 no hookups, seasonal sites, tenting available, sewage disposal, limited grocery store, ice, tables, fire rings, wood. ◆◆◆RECREATION: rec room/area, lake swimming, boating, canoeing, ramp, dock, lake fishing, sports field, horseshoes. Open mid May through mid Oct. Rate in 1995 $15-21 per family. Member of OPCA. Phone: (705) 538-2590.

## WAWA—C-3

AGAWA BAY CAMPGROUND (Lake Superior Provincial Park)—*From town: Go 88 km/55 mi S on Hwy 17.* FACILITIES: 164 sites, 164 no hookups, tenting available, handicap restroom facilities, sewage disposal, laundry, tables, wood. RECREATION: swimming, fishing, hiking trails. Open mid May through late Sep. Phone: (705) 856-2284.

CRESCENT LAKE CAMPGROUND (Lake Superior Provincial Park)—*From town: Go 96 km/60 mi S on Hwy 17.* FACILITIES: 25 sites, 25 no hookups, tenting available, non-flush toilets, sewage disposal, tables, wood. RECREATION: swimming, boating, no motors, canoeing, ramp, lake fishing, hiking trails. Open late Jun through early Sep. No showers. Phone: (705) 856-2284.

**Oski-Wawa Camp**—CAMPGROUND among evergreen trees. *From jct Hwy 101 & Hwy 17: Go 5.6 km/3 1/2 mi S on Hwy 17, then 9 m/100 yards W on Michipicoton Rd.* ◆◆FACILITIES: 80 sites, most common site width 50 feet, 5 full hookups, 35 water & elec (15 amp receptacles), 40 no hookups, 80 pull-thrus, tenting available, sewage disposal, ice, tables, fire rings, wood. ◆RECREATION: river swimming, boating, river fishing, hiking trails. Open mid May through mid Oct. Rate in 1995 $13-15 for 2 persons. Phone: (705) 856-2413.

RABBIT BLANKET LAKE CAMPGROUND (Lake Superior Provincial Park)—*From town: Go 30 1/2 km/19 mi S on Hwy 17.* FACILITIES: 60 sites, 60 no hookups, tenting available, handicap restroom facilities, tables, wood. RECREATION: swimming, boating, canoeing, lake fishing, hiking trails. Open early May through late Oct. Phone: (705) 856-2284.

**WAWA RV RESORT & CAMPGROUND KOA**—CAMPGROUND on the Magpie River. *From jct Hwy 101 & Hwy 17: Go 1.6 km/1 mi W on Hwy 17.*

◆◆◆◆FACILITIES: 98 sites, most common site width 35 feet, 19 full hookups, 48 water & elec (15 & 30 amp receptacles), 31 no hookups, 24 pull-thrus, a/c allowed, heater allowed, tenting available, group sites for tents/RVs, RV rentals, cabins, handicap restroom facilities, sewage disposal, laundry, public phone, grocery store, RV supplies, LP gas refill by weight, ice, tables, fire rings, wood.

◆◆◆RECREATION: rec room/area, pavilion, swim pool (heated), sauna, boating, canoeing, dock, 2 row/7 canoe boat rentals, river fishing, mini-golf ($), basketball hoop, playground, planned group activities, movies, hiking trails.

Open May 1 through mid Oct. Pool open Jun 15 through Sep 1. Rate in 1995 $18-23 for 2 persons. Master Card/Visa accepted. Member of OPCA. Phone: (705) 856-4368. KOA 10% value card discount.

**SEE AD THIS PAGE AND AD FRONT OF BOOK PAGES 68 AND 69**

## WEBBWOOD—F-2

CHUTES PROVINCIAL PARK—*From town: Go 16 km/10 mi W on Hwy 17, then 3 1/4 km/2 mi N on Hwy 553 (Massey).* FACILITIES: 134 sites, 56 elec, 78 no hookups, tenting available, handicap restroom facilities, sewage disposal, tables, wood. RECREATION: swimming, boating, canoeing, fishing, playground, hiking trails. Open mid May through late Sep. Phone: (705) 865-2021.

## WESTPORT—G-5

**CANOE LAKE TENT & TRAILER PARK**—Secluded, semi-wooded, lakeside family CAMPGROUND. *From jct Hwy 42/CR 10/CR 12: Go 5.6 km/3 1/2 mi W on CR 12, then 6.4 km/4 mi W on CR 8, then 1.6 km/1 mi S on Canoe Lake Rd.*

◆◆◆FACILITIES: 80 sites, most common site width 35 feet, 65 full hookups, (15 amp receptacles), 15 no hookups, seasonal sites, 4 pull-thrus, a/c not allowed, heater not allowed, phone hookups, tenting available, sewage disposal, ice, tables, fire rings, wood.

◆◆RECREATION: lake swimming, boating, canoeing, ramp, 7 row/1 canoe/7 motor boat rentals, water skiing, lake fishing, playground, hiking trails.

Open all year. Facilities fully operational May 15 through Oct 15. Reservation required during winter season. Rate in 1995 $13-16 per family. Phone: (613) 273-5232.

**SEE AD TRAVEL SECTION PAGES 975, 976 AND 977**

WESTPORT—Continued

**Sunnyside Campground**—Lakeside location on a Waterway system. *From east city limits: Go 3.2 km/2 mi E on Hwy 42, then 1.6 km/1 mi N on Golf Course Rd.* ◆◆◆FACILITIES: 180 sites, most common site width 40 feet, 180 water & elec (15 amp receptacles), seasonal sites, 20 pull-thrus, tenting available, sewage disposal, laundry, public phone, limited grocery store, ice, tables, fire rings, grills, wood. ◆◆◆RECREATION: lake swimming, boating, canoeing, ramp, dock, 8 row/5 canoe/4 motor boat rentals, lake fishing, playground, 2 shuffleboard courts, badminton, sports field, horseshoes, volleyball. Open May 15 through Oct 15. Rate in 1995 $18-21 per family. Member of OPCA. Phone: (613) 273-3124.

WESTPORT MUNICIPAL TRAILER PARK—*From town: Go 1 1/2 km/1 mi W on Mountain Rd.* FACILITIES: 60 sites, 20 full hookups, 20 water & elec (15 amp receptacles), 40 no hookups, seasonal sites, 31 pull-thrus, tenting available, sewage disposal, tables, fire rings, grills, wood. RECREATION: lake swimming, boating, canoeing, ramp, dock, lake fishing, hiking trails. Open May 15 through Sep 15. Phone: (613) 273-2191.

## WHEATLEY—J-1

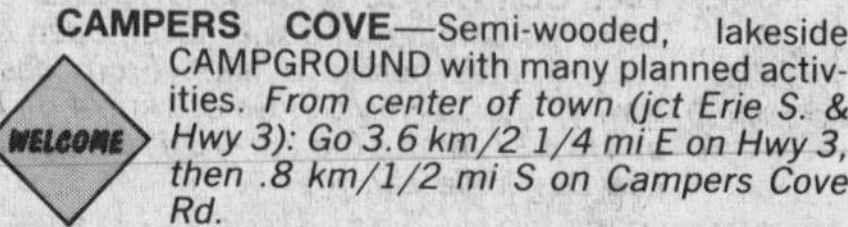

**CAMPERS COVE**—Semi-wooded, lakeside CAMPGROUND with many planned activities. *From center of town (jct Erie S. & Hwy 3): Go 3.6 km/2 1/4 mi E on Hwy 3, then .8 km/1/2 mi S on Campers Cove Rd.*

◆◆◆◆FACILITIES: 326 sites, most common site width 50 feet, 231 full hookups, 85 water & elec (15 & 30 amp receptacles), 10 no hookups, seasonal sites, 5 pull-thrus, a/c allowed ($), tenting available, group sites for tents/RVs, RV storage, sewage disposal, laundry, public phone, grocery store, RV supplies, LP gas refill by weight, ice, tables, fire rings, wood, church services, traffic control gate/guard.

◆◆◆◆◆RECREATION: rec room/area, equipped pavilion, coin games, lake swimming, boating, 2 canoe boat rentals, water skiing, lake fishing, basketball hoop, playground, 2 shuffleboard courts, planned group activities, movies, recreation director, badminton, sports field, horseshoes, hiking trails, volleyball.

Open mid May through Sep 30. Rate in 1995 $18-22 per family. Reservations recommended Jun through Aug. Master Card/Visa accepted. Member of OPCA. Phone: (800) 265-5833.

**SEE AD WINDSOR NEXT PAGE**

**Holiday Harbour Resort**—Open and shaded, level sites in a CAMPGROUND with half mile sandy beach on Lake Erie. *From jct Hwy 3 & Erie St: Go 5 blocks S on Erie St, then E on 2nd concessio then S on Pier Rd.* ◆◆FACILITIES: 57 sites, 8 full hookups, 49 water & elec (30 amp receptacles), seasonal sites, tenting available, sewage disposal, public phone, limited grocery store, ice, tables, fire rings, wood. ◆◆◆RECREATION: rec room/area, lake swimming, boating, lake fishing, playground, horseshoes, volleyball. Open mid May through mid Oct. Rate in 1995 $14-18 per family. Member of OPCA. Phone: (519) 825-7396.

**Lakeside Village Motel & Campground**—RV SPACES on the lake behind a motel. *From east city limits: Go 9.6 km/6 mi E on Hwy 3.* FACILITIES: 170 sites, 70 full hookups, 50 water & elec (15 & 30 amp receptacles), 50 no hookups, seasonal sites, tenting available, sewage disposal, laundry, public phone, limited grocery store, ice, tables, fire rings, wood. RECREATION: lake swimming, lake fishing. Open May through Oct. Rates available upon request. Phone: (519) 825-4307.

WHEATLEY PROVINCIAL PARK—*From town: Go 1 1/2 km/1 mi E on Hwy 3, then 3/4 km/1/2 mi S on Lake St.* FACILITIES: 210 sites, 52 elec, 158 no hookups, tenting available, handicap restroom facilities, sewage disposal, tables, wood. RECREATION: swimming, fishing, playground, hiking trails. Open mid May through early Oct. Phone: (519) 825-4659.

## WHITEFISH—F-2

FAIRBANK PROVINCIAL PARK—*From town: Go 4 3/4 km/3 mi W on Hwy 17, then 20 3/4 km/13 mi N on Hwy 658 (Worthington).* FACILITIES: 160 sites, 160 no hookups, tenting available, handicap restroom facilities, sewage disposal, laundry, tables, wood. RECREATION: swimming, boating, canoeing, ramp, fishing, playground, hiking trails. Open mid May through early Sep. Phone: (705) 866-0530.

**Holiday Beach Campground**—Camping sites on McCharles Lake. *From jct Hwy 17 & Regional Rd 55 (Old Hwy 17): Go 5.6 km/3 mi E on Regional Rd 55.* ◆◆FACILITIES: 130 sites, 90 water & elec (15 & 30 amp receptacles), 40 no hookups, seasonal sites, 40 pull-thrus, tenting available, sewage disposal, laundry, public phone, limited grocery store, ice, tables, fire rings, wood. ◆◆RECREATION: lake swimming, boating, canoeing, ramp, dock, 1 canoe/3 pedal/1 motor boat rentals, lake fishing, horseshoes, hiking trails. Recreation open to the public. Open mid May through mid Oct. Rate in 1995 $13-17 per family. Phone: (705) 866-0303.

## WHITE RIVER—B-3

OBATANGA PROVINCIAL PARK—*From town: Go 35 1/4 km/22 mi S on Hwy 17.* FACILITIES: 132 sites, 20 elec, 112 no hookups, tenting available, handicap restroom facilities, sewage disposal, laundry, tables, wood. RECREATION: swimming, boating, canoeing, ramp, fishing, playground, hiking trails. Open early Jun through early Sep. Phone: (807) 822-2592.

WHITE LAKE PROVINCIAL PARK—*From town: Go 36 3/4 km/23 mi N on Hwy 17.* FACILITIES: 187 sites, 24 elec, 163 no hookups, tenting available, handicap restroom facilities, sewage disposal, laundry, tables, wood. RECREATION: swimming, boating, canoeing, ramp, fishing, playground, hiking trails. Open mid May through late Sep. Phone: (807) 822-2447.

## WHITESTONE—F-3

**Lazy Acres Resort**—Open & wooded sites on Lake DeBois with excellent fishing at this CAMPGROUND on secluded natural terrain. *From west jct Hwy 124 & Hwy 520: Go 21 km/13 mi N on Hwy 520.* ◆◆FACILITIES: 152 sites, 35 ft. max RV length, 100 water & elec (15 amp receptacles), 52 no hookups, seasonal sites, 25 pull-thrus, tenting available, sewage disposal, laundry, public phone, ice, tables, fire rings, wood. ◆◆◆RECREATION: rec hall, lake swimming, boating, canoeing, ramp, dock, 3 row/3 canoe/3 motor boat rentals, lake fishing, mini-golf, sports field, horseshoes, hiking trails. Open May 1 through mid Oct. No showers. Rate in 1995 $14-16 per family. Phone: (705) 389-1466.

## WIARTON—G-2

BLUEWATER PARK (City Park)—*From jct Hwy 6 & William St: Go 1/2 km/1/4 mi E on William St.* FACILITIES: 63 sites, 33 ft. max RV length, 13 full hookups, 14 water & elec (15 amp receptacles), 36 no hookups, tenting available, sewage disposal, ice, tables, fire rings, wood. RECREATION: pavilion, swim pool (heated), lake swimming ($), boating, ramp, dock, lake fishing, playground, shuffleboard court, 4 tennis courts, sports field, horseshoes, hiking trails, volleyball. Recreation open to the public. Open May 15 through Oct 15. Phone: (519) 534-2592.

**CEDARHOLME CAMPGROUNDS**—CAMPGROUND on Hope Bay. *From north city limits: Go 1.6 km/1 mi N on Hwy 6, then 17.6 km/11 mi N on Bruce Rd 9, then .8 km/1/2 mi E on Hope Bay Rd.*

WELCOME

◆◆◆FACILITIES: 81 sites, most common site width 40 feet, 44 full hookups, 8 water & elec (15 & 30 amp receptacles), 29 no hookups, seasonal sites, a/c allowed, heater allowed, tenting available, RV storage, sewage disposal, laundry, public phone, grocery store, ice, tables, fire rings, grills, wood, traffic control gate.

◆◆RECREATION: lake swimming, boating, canoeing, ramp, dock, 1 canoe/1 pedal/3 motor boat rentals, water skiing, lake fishing, planned group activities (weekends only), horseshoes.

Open all year. Facilities fully operational May 1 through Oct 31. Rate in 1995 $15.42-19.63 per family. Visa accepted. Member of OPCA. Phone: (519) 534-1208.

SEE AD TRAVEL SECTION PAGE 983

**ROTH PARK**—Wooded CAMPGROUND at Berford Lake. *From north city limits: Go 1.6 km/1 mi N on Hwy 6, then .4 km/1/4 mi E on Bruce Rd 9, then 5.6 km/3 1/2 mi N on Berford Lake Rd.*

WELCOME

◆◆◆FACILITIES: 126 sites, most common site width 50 feet, 34 ft. max RV length, 115 water & elec (15 amp receptacles), 11 no hookups, seasonal sites, a/c allowed ($), heater allowed ($), tenting available, RV rentals, sewage disposal, laundry, public phone, limited grocery store, gasoline, marine gas, ice, tables, fire rings, wood.

◆◆◆RECREATION: rec hall, lake swimming, boating, canoeing, ramp, dock, 2 canoe/5 pedal/3 motor boat rentals, lake fishing, playground, planned group activities (weekends only), horseshoes.

Open May 1 through Sep 15. Rate in 1995 $13.50-17 per family. Reservations recommended all season. Member of OPCA. Phone: (519) 534-0145.

SEE AD TRAVEL SECTION PAGE 982



WIARTON—Continued

**Trillium Woods Camp**—Rustic, wooded sites in a CAMPGROUND on natural terrain. *From jct Hwy 6 & CR 21: Go 10.4 km/6 1/2 mi W on CR 21, then 1.2 km/3/4 mi N on paved road.* ◆◆◆FACILITIES: 112 sites, most common site width 40 feet, 104 water & elec (15 & 30 amp receptacles), 8 no hookups, seasonal sites, tenting available, sewage disposal, laundry, limited grocery store, ice, tables, fire rings, wood. ◆◆◆RECREATION: rec hall, lake swimming, boating, canoeing, dock, 1 row/3 canoe/1 pedal boat rentals, lake fishing, planned group activities (weekends only), badminton, sports field, horseshoes, hiking trails, volleyball. Open May 15 through Oct 15. Rate in 1995 $18 per family. Member of OPCA. Phone: (519) 534-2555.

## WILBERFORCE—G-4

**Moonlight Bay Tent & Trailer Park**—CAMPGROUND with spacious open or treed sites. *From west jct Hwy 121 & Hwy 648: Go 3.6 km/2 1/4 mi N on Hwy 648, then .4 km/1/4 mi E on Earles Rd.* ◆◆FACILITIES: 50 sites, most common site width 35 feet, 50 water & elec (15 amp receptacles), seasonal sites, tenting available, handicap restroom facilities, sewage disposal, laundry, ice, tables, fire rings, wood. ◆◆RECREATION: rec room/area, lake swimming, boating, canoeing, ramp, dock, 1 row/3 canoe boat rentals, lake fishing, badminton, sports field, horseshoes, hiking trails, volleyball. Recreation open to the public. Open May 15 through Oct 15. Rate in 1995 $16 per family. Phone: (705) 448-2525.

WILBERFORCE—Continued
MOONLIGHT BAY TENT & TRAILER PARK—Continued

## WINDSOR—J-1

***See listings at Amherstburg, Leamington, McGregor & Wheatley***

**KOA-Windsor/401**—Grassy, level CAMPGROUND near a major highway. *From jct Hwy 401 (exit 14) & Essex Rd 46: Go 3.2 km/2 mi E on Essex Rd 46, then 1.6 km/1 mi N on Conc. 9 (following signs).* ◆◆◆FACILITIES: 178 sites, most common site width 30 feet, 110 full hookups, 57 water & elec (15,30 & 50 amp receptacles), 11 no hookups, seasonal sites, 67 pull-thrus, tent-

KOA-WINDSOR/401—Continued on next page
WINDSOR—Continued on next page

WINDSOR—Continued
KOA-WINDSOR/401—Continued

ing available, handicap restroom facilities, sewage disposal, laundry, public phone, grocery store, LP gas refill by weight/by meter, ice, tables, fire rings, wood. ◆◆◆RECREATION: rec hall, rec room/area, equipped pavilion, swim pool, pond fishing, mini-golf ($), playground, planned group activities (weekends only), badminton, sports field, horseshoes, hiking trails, volleyball. Open Apr 1 through Nov 1. Rate in 1995 $23-29 per family. Member of OPCA. Phone: (519) 735-3660. KOA 10% value card discount.

## WOLFE ISLAND—H-5

**HI LO HICKORY FAMILY CAMPGROUND**—Riverside CAMPGROUND on Wolfe Island with grassy sites. *Take Kingston free ferry at Barrack St dock to Marysville Wolfe Island, then 11.2 km/7 mi E on Hwy 96, then 1.6 km/1 mi E on Hogan Rd.*

◆◆◆FACILITIES: 35 sites, most common site width 40 feet, 17 water & elec (15 & 30 amp receptacles), 18 no hookups, a/c allowed ($), heater allowed ($), tenting available, group sites for tents/RVs, RV storage, handicap restroom facilities, sewage disposal, ice, tables, fire rings, wood.

◆◆◆RECREATION: river swimming, boating, canoeing, ramp, dock, 2 row/1 motor boat rentals, water skiing, river fishing, horseshoes, volleyball.

Open mid May through mid Oct. Rate in 1995 $16-18 per family. Visa accepted. Member of OPCA. Phone: (613) 385-2430.

**SEE AD TRAVEL SECTION PAGES 975, 976 AND 977**

## WOODSTOCK—I-2

**HIDDEN VALLEY PARK** (SEASON LEASE ONLY)—Secluded, grassy, lakeside CAMPGROUND. *From jct Hwy 401 (exit 232-B) & Hwy 59: Go 14.8 km/9 1/4 mi N on Hwy 59.*

FACILITIES: 200 sites, most common site width 50 feet, 65 full hookups, 75 water & elec (15 amp receptacles), 60 no hookups, seasonal sites, a/c allowed ($), heater allowed ($), tenting available, group sites for tents/RVs, RV storage, sewage disposal, public phone, ice, tables, fire rings, wood, traffic control gate.

WOODSTOCK—Continued
HIDDEN VALLEY PARK—Continued

RECREATION: rec hall, pavilion, lake swimming, boating, canoeing, lake fishing, playground, sports field, horseshoes, volleyball. Recreation open to the public.

Open May 1 through mid Oct. Rate in 1995 $14-20 per family. Visa accepted. Member of OPCA. Phone: (519) 462-2596.

**SEE AD TRAVEL SECTION PAGES 975, 976 AND 977**

PITTOCK CONSERVATION AREA (Upper Thames River Conservation Authority)—*From jct Hwy 401 (exit 28) & Hwy 59: Go 4 3/4 km/3 mi N on Hwy 59.* FACILITIES: 238 sites, 144 water & elec (15 & 20 amp receptacles), 94 no hookups, seasonal sites, tenting available, sewage disposal, public phone, limited grocery store, ice, tables, wood. RECREATION: pavilion, swim pool (heated), lake swimming, boating, canoeing, ramp, dock, lake fishing, playground, planned group activities, recreation director, sports field, horseshoes, hiking trails. Open May through Oct 10. Phone: (519) 539-5088.

**WILLOW LAKE PARK**—Grassy CAMPGROUND with open & tree shaded sites. *From jct Hwy 401 (exit 230) & Sweaburg Rd: Go 3.2 km/2 mi N on Mill St, then 30 m/100 feet E on Hwy 2, then 3.2 km/2 mi N on Hwy 59.*

◆◆◆◆FACILITIES: 100 sites, most common site width 40 feet, 70 full hookups, 25 water & elec (15 & 30 amp receptacles), 5 no hookups, seasonal sites, 16 pull-thrus, a/c allowed ($), phone hookups, tenting available, RV rentals, cabins, RV storage, sewage disposal, laundry, public phone, limited grocery store, ice, tables, fire rings, wood, traffic control gate.

◆◆◆◆RECREATION: rec hall, rec room/area, coin games, swim pool (heated), whirlpool, basketball hoop, playground, shuffleboard court, planned group activities (weekends only), movies, badminton, sports field, horseshoes, volleyball.

Open May 1 through mid Oct. Rate in 1995 $18-21 for 4 persons. Reservations recommended during Jul. Master Card/Visa accepted. Member of OPCA. Phone: (519) 537-7301.

**SEE AD THIS PAGE**

## WYOMING—I-1

**COUNTRY VIEW RESORT-MOTEL & CAMPING** (NOT VISITED)—*From jct Hwy 21 & Hwy 7: Go 30 m/100 feet E on Hwy 7.*

FACILITIES: 36 sites, 28 full hookups, 8 water & elec (15 & 30 amp receptacles), tenting available, sewage disposal.

Open mid Apr through end Oct. Rate in 1995 $12-20 per family. Phone: (519) 845-3394.

**SEE AD TRAVEL SECTION PAGES 975, 976 AND 977**

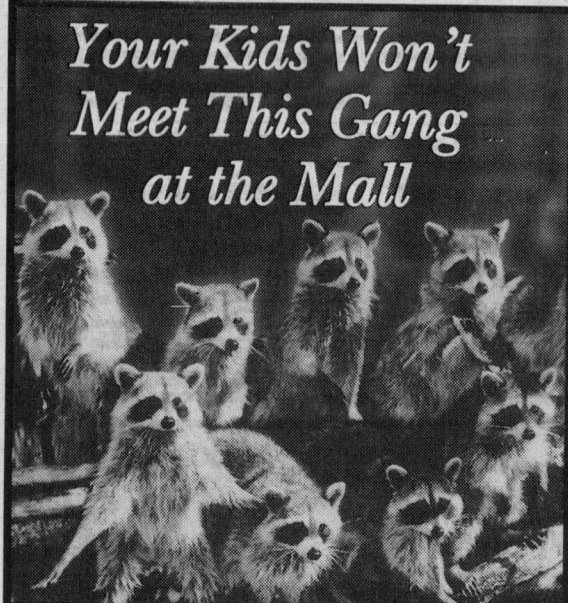

# WOODALL'S ALPHABETICAL QUICK REFERENCE

**For Your Convenience Facilities are Listed Alphabetically by Name within each State.**

**Types of Facilities Listed:**

**Bold Type – Campground, RV Park Advertisers/ ★ RV Service Centers/ ● Attractions**

**Special Services Indicated:**

**□ Cabin Rentals ® RV Rentals △ Tent Rentals**

## CONNECTICUT

Acorn Acres Campsites — ***NORWICH C-5***
American Legion State Forest (Austin F. — ***PLEASANT VALLEY A-3***
Black Rock State Park — ***THOMASTON B-2***
**★ ® Blonstein's Camping Center** — ***VERNON B-4***
® Branch Brook Campground — ***THOMASTON B-2***
® Brialee RV & Tent Park — ***ASHFORD A-5***
Burr Pond State Park - Taylor Brook Campground — ***TORRINGTON B-2***
Chamberlain Lake Campground — ***WOODSTOCK A-6***
**Charlie Brown Campground** — ***PHOENIXVILLE A-5***
**® □ Circle C Campground** — ***VOLUNTOWN C-6***
Del-Air Camp — ***TOLLAND A-5***
Devil's Hopyard State Park — ***EAST HADDAM C-4***
Gentiles Campground — ***PLYMOUTH B-3***
Hammonasset Beach State Park — ***MADISON D-4***
**Hemlock Hill Camp Resort** — ***LITCHFIELD B-2***
**★ ® Hemlock Hill RV Sales & Service** — ***LITCHFIELD B-2***
**★ ® Hemlock Hill RV Sales & Service** — ***NEW MILFORD C-2***
**® □ Hidden Acres Family Campground** — ***NORWICH C-5***
Hide-A-Way Cove — ***EAST KILLINGLY A-6***
Highland Campground — ***SCOTLAND B-5***
**® Highland Orchards Resort Park** — ***NORTH STONINGTON C-6***
**★ Highland Orchards Trailer Sales** — ***NORTH STONINGTON C-6***
Hopeville Pond State Park — ***JEWETT CITY B-6***
Housatonic Meadows State Park — ***CORNWALL BRIDGE B-2***
Kettletown State Park — ***SOUTHBURY C-2***
Lake Waramaug State Park — ***NEW PRESTON B-2***
Lake Williams Campground — ***LEBANON B-5***
**® □ Lone Oak Campsites** — ***CANAAN A-2***
Macedonia Brook State Park — ***KENT B-1***
Markam Meadows Campground — ***EAST HAMPTON C-4***
Mashamoquet Brook State Park — ***ABINGTON A-6***
**® Mineral Springs Family Campground** — ***STAFFORD SPRINGS A-5***
® Mohawk Campground — ***GOSHEN B-2***
® Moosemeadow Camping Resort — ***WEST WILLINGTON A-5***
Natures Campsites — ***VOLUNTOWN C-6***
Nelson's Family Campground — ***EAST HAMPTON C-4***
Nickerson Park — ***WILLIMANTIC B-5***
**□ Odetah Campground** — ***NORWICH C-5***
Pachaug State Forest — ***VOLUNTOWN C-6***
Peppertree Camping — ***PHOENIXVILLE A-5***
**Pleasant Acres Trailer Park** — ***NEW HAVEN D-3***
Rainbow Acres Family Campground — ***WILLINGTON A-5***
**★ ® Rent N' Roam RV Rentals** — ***HARTFORD B-4***
® △ □ River Bend Campground — ***ONECO B-6***
**® Riverdale Farm Campsites** — ***CLINTON D-4***
River Road Campground — ***CLINTON D-4***
Rocky Neck State Park — ***NIANTIC D-5***
Ross Hill Park — ***JEWETT CITY B-6***
**★ RV Parts & Electric** — ***WATERBURY C-3***
**® Salem Farms Campground** — ***SALEM C-5***
Salt Rock Family Campground — ***BALTIC B-5***
**® △ Seaport Campground** — ***MYSTIC D-6***
® □ Stateline Campresort — ***EAST KILLINGLY A-6***
Sterling Park Campground — ***STERLING B-6***
**® Strawberry Park Resort Campground** — ***PRESTON CITY C-6***
Sunrise Resort — ***MOODUS C-4***
® △ Treetops Campresort — ***KENT B-1***
® □ Valley in the Pines — ***GOSHEN B-2***
**® Waters Edge Campground** — ***LEBANON B-5***
West Thompson Lake (Corps of Eng. - West Thompson — ***THOMPSON A-6***
White Memorial Family Campground (White Foundation) — ***LITCHFIELD B-2***
**® White Pines Campsites** — ***WINSTED A-3***
Witch Meadow Lake Campground — ***SALEM C-5***
Wolf's Den Family Campground — ***EAST HADDAM C-4***
Ye Olde Countryside Campground — ***VOLUNTOWN C-6***

## MAINE

Abol Bridge Campground — ***MILLINOCKET C-3***
Acadia National Park (Blackwoods Campground) — ***BAR HARBOR E-4***
Acadia National Park (Seawall Campground) — ***SOUTHWEST HARBOR E-4***
**® □ Acres of Wildlife** — ***STEEP FALLS E-1***
**Aldus Shores Lakeside Camping** — ***SEARSMONT E-3***
® Allen Pond Campground — ***GREENE E-2***
Apache Campground — ***SANFORD F-1***
Apple Valley Campground — ***ACTON F-1***
**Arndt's Aroostook River Lodge & Campground** — ***PRESQUE ISLE B-4***
**Aroostook River Camping & Recreation** — ***CARIBOU A-4***
Aroostook State Park — ***PRESQUE ISLE B-4***
**® Augusta-West Lakeside Resort Kampground** — ***WINTHROP E-2***
Balsam Cove Campground — ***BUCKSPORT D-3***
□ Balsam Woods Campground — ***ABBOT D-3***
B & B Family Camping — ***SOUTH LEBANON F-1***
**® Barcadia Campground** — ***BAR HARBOR E-4***
**Bar Harbor Campground** — ***BAR HARBOR E-4***
**® Bass Harbor Campground** — ***BASS HARBOR E-4***
**® △ Bayley's Pine Point Resort** — ***SCARBOROUGH F-2***
**□ Bay of Naples Family Camping** — ***NAPLES E-1***
Bayview Campground — ***MILBRIDGE D-4***
**Beach Acres Campground** — ***WELLS F-1***
□ Bear Mountain Village Cabins & Campground — ***HARRISON E-1***
**Beaver Brook Camping Area** — ***NORTH MONMOUTH E-2***
**® Beaver Dam Campground** — ***BERWICK F-1***
® Big Skye Acres Campground — ***FREEPORT E-2***
□ Birch Point Lodge Campground & Cottage Resort — ***ISLAND FALLS B-4***
**Black Brook Cove Campground** — ***RANGELEY D-1***
Blackburn's Campground — ***WATERBORO CENTER F-1***
**Blueberry Pond Campground** — ***FREEPORT E-2***
Bradbury Mountain State Park — ***POWNAL E-2***
**★ Brake Service & Parts** — ***BANGOR D-3***
® Bunganut Lake Camping Area — ***ALFRED F-1***
**★ ® Call of the Wild** — ***OXFORD E-1***
Camden Hills State Park — ***CAMDEN E-3***
□ Camp Eaton — ***YORK HARBOR F-1***
Campers Cove Campground — ***BOOTHBAY E-2***
Camper's Paradise — ***PRESQUE ISLE B-4***

**MAINE — Continued**

Camp Seguin — ***GEORGETOWN E-2***
Canal Bridge Campground — ***FRYEBURG E-1***
Cape Neddick Oceanside Campground — ***CAPE NEDDICK F-1***
Cascadia Park — ***SACO F-2***
**□ Casey's Spencer Bay Camps** — ***GREENVILLE C-3***
Cathedral Pines (Stratton-Eustis Dev. Corp.) — ***STRATTON D-2***
**® Cedar Haven Campground** — ***FREEPORT E-2***
Chewonki Campgrounds — ***WISCASSET E-2***
**□ Christie's Campground & Cottages** — ***NEWPORT D-3***
Cobscook Bay State Park — ***DENNYSVILLE D-5***
® Colonial Mast — ***NAPLES E-1***
Cupsuptic Campground — ***RANGELEY D-1***
**★ Custom Land Yachts** — ***WINDHAM E-2***
**□ Deer Farm Camps & Campground** — ***KINGFIELD D-2***
**Desert Dunes of Maine** — ***FREEPORT E-2***
**• Desert of Maine** — ***FREEPORT E-2***
**Dixon's Campground** — ***OGUNQUIT F-1***
**★ Don's Campers** — ***BREWER D-3***
**★ Don's Trailer Sales** — ***SKOWHEGAN D-2***
Down East Family Camping — ***WISCASSET E-2***
**□ Duck Puddle Family Campground** — ***DAMARISCOTTA E-3***
Durham Leisure Center & Campground — ***FREEPORT E-2***
**★ East Coast RV Supply** — ***WELLS F-1***
**Family-N-Friends Campground** — ***SEBAGO LAKE E-1***
**The Flying Dutchman Campground** — ***BUCKSPORT D-3***
**Flying Point Campground** — ***FREEPORT E-2***
**® Four Seasons Camping Area** — ***NAPLES E-1***
Fran-Mort Campground — ***KENNEBUNK F-1***
□ Frost Pond Camps — ***MILLINOCKET C-3***
**★ △ Gagnon's Auto & RV Sales** — ***CARIBOU A-4***
**□ The Gatherings Family Campground,** — ***ELLSWORTH D-4***
**★ Good Times Unlimited** — ***FARMINGTON D-2***
**□ Gray Homestead Oceanfront Camping** — ***BOOTHBAY HARBOR E-2***
Great Pond Campground — ***BELGRADE E-2***
Greenland Cove Campground — ***DANFORTH C-4***
**® Greenlaw's RV & Tenting Park** — ***STONINGTON E-3***
Green Valley Campground — ***VASSALBORO E-2***
Greenwood Acres RV Park & Campground — ***BREWER D-3***
Gregoire's Campground — ***WELLS F-1***
**Hadley's Point Campground** — ***BAR HARBOR E-4***
□ Happy Horseshoe Campground — ***NORTH NEW PORTLAND D-2***
**Hebron Pines Campground** — ***HEBRON E-2***
Hermit Island — ***SMALL POINT E-2***
**Hid'n Pines** — ***OLD ORCHARD BEACH F-2***
**Hilltop Campground** — ***ROBBINSTON D-5***
Indian Pond Campground — ***THE FORKS C-2***
Jackman Landing Campground — ***JACKMAN C-2***
John's Trailer Park & Four Season Campground — ***JACKMAN C-2***
**® △ □ Katahdin Shadows Campground** — ***MEDWAY C-4***
**Keene's Lake Campground** — ***CALAIS D-5***
**Kennebunkport Camping** — ***KENNEBUNKPORT F-2***
**® Kezar Lake Camping Area** — ***LOVELL E-1***
**® □ Kings-Queens Court Vacation Resort** — ***EAST LEBANON F-1***
**★ Kinney RV's Sales & Service** — ***KENNEBUNK F-1***
**® Knowlton's Seashore Campground** — ***PERRY D-5***
**□ KOA-Augusta/Gardiner** — ***GARDINER E-2***
**△ □ KOA-Skowhegan-Canaan** — ***CANAAN D-3***
**® Kokatosi Campground** — ***RAYMOND E-2***
K's Family Circle Campground — ***NAPLES E-1***
**□ Lake Pemaquid Camping** — ***DAMARISCOTTA E-3***
Lake St. George State Park — ***LIBERTY E-3***
**® □ Lakeside Pines Campground** — ***BRIDGTON E-1***
Lamoine State Park — ***ELLSWORTH D-4***
**★ ® △ Lee's Family Trailer Sales & Service** — ***WINDHAM E-2***
**Libby's Oceanside Camp** — ***YORK HARBOR F-1***
Lily Bay State Park (Moosehead Lake) — ***GREENVILLE C-3***
Littlefield Beaches — ***LOCKE MILLS E-1***
**Little Ponderosa Campground** — ***BOOTHBAY E-2***
® △ □ Loon Echo Campground — ***JACKMAN C-2***
® □ Loon's Cry Campground — ***WARREN E-3***
Mainayr Campground — ***STEUBEN D-4***
Maine Roads Camping — ***NORRIDGEWOCK D-2***
△ □ Maine Wilderness Camps & Campground — ***SPRINGFIELD C-4***
Martin Stream Campsites — ***TURNER E-2***
Masthead Family Campground — ***BUCKSPORT D-3***
□ Matagamon Wilderness Campground — ***PATTEN B-4***
**★ McCluskey's Trailer Sales** — ***PRESQUE ISLE B-4***
**★ McKay's RV Center** — ***BREWER D-3***
**Meadowbrook Camping Area** — ***BATH E-2***
**□ Megunticook Campground By The Sea** — ***ROCKPORT E-3***
**□ Mic Mac Cove** — ***UNION E-3***
△ MILITARY PARK (Schoodic Point Rec. Area - — ***WINTER HARBOR E-4***
△ MILITARY PARK (Sprague Neck Campsites) — ***EAST MACHIAS D-5***
**The Moorings** — ***BELFAST E-3***
**Moosehead Family Campground** — ***GREENVILLE C-3***
**• Moosehead Marine Museum/Katahdin Cruises** — ***GREENVILLE C-3***
® Moose River Campground — ***JACKMAN C-2***
**★ Mountain Road RV** — ***SABATTUS E-2***
□ Mountain View Campground — ***DANFORTH C-4***
Mountainview Campground — ***SULLIVAN D-4***
Mount Blue State Park — ***WELD D-2***
Mousam River Campground — ***KENNEBUNK F-1***
Mt. Desert Campground — ***MT. DESERT E-4***
**Mt. Desert Narrows Camping Resort** — ***BAR HARBOR E-4***
**My Brothers Place** — ***HOULTON B-4***
**® □ Narrows Too Camping Resort** — ***BAR HARBOR E-4***
**® Neil E Michaud Campground** — ***PRESQUE ISLE B-4***
NE'RE Beach Family Campground — ***OLD ORCHARD BEACH F-2***
Nor'-40-Campsite — ***FARMINGTON D-2***
Northern Pride Lodge & Campground — ***KOKADJO C-3***
**Northport Travel Park** — ***BELFAST E-3***
□ Ocean Overlook Campground — ***WELLS F-1***
**□ Ocean View Cottages & Camping** — ***WELLS F-1***
® □ Ocean View Park Campground — ***POPHAM BEACH E-2***
**Ocean Wood Campground** — ***BIRCH HARBOR E-4***
□ Old Massachusetts Homestead — ***LINCOLNVILLE E-3***
**□ Old Mill Campground** — ***ROCKWOOD C-2***
Old Orchard Beach Camping — ***OLD ORCHARD BEACH F-2***
**□ Orr's Island Campground** — ***ORR'S ISLAND E-2***
□ Packard's Moorings Camping Area — ***SEBEC LAKE C-3***
**Palmyra Golf Course & RV Resort** — ***PALMYRA D-3***
**® □ Papoose Pond Resort** — ***NORTH WATERFORD E-1***

**MAINE — Continued**

Paradise Park Resort Campground — ***OLD ORCHARD BEACH F-2***
□ Patten Pond Camping Resort — ***ELLSWORTH D-4***
**Paul Bunyan Campground** — ***BANGOR D-3***
Peaks-Kenny State Park — ***DOVER-FOXCROFT D-3***
Pinederosa Camping Area — ***OGUNQUIT F-1***
□ Pine Grove Campground & Cottages — ***MEDWAY C-4***
△ □ Pine Ridge Campground & Cabins — ***LIBERTY E-3***
**® Pleasant Hill Campground** — ***BANGOR D-3***
Pleasant Point Campground — ***OAKLAND D-2***
Pleasant River Campground — ***BETHEL E-1***
**® Point Sebago** — ***CASCO E-1***
**Poland Spring Campground** — ***POLAND SPRING E-2***
**△ Powder Horn Camping** — ***OLD ORCHARD BEACH F-2***
Pray's Big Eddy Wilderness Campground — ***MILLINOCKET C-3***
® △ □ Quietside Campground — ***TREMONT E-4***
Rangeley State Park — ***RANGELEY D-1***
**® Range Pond Campground** — ***POLAND E-2***
Recompence Shore Campsites (University of Maine) — ***FREEPORT E-2***
**★ Rec Tech** — ***BREWER D-3***
**Red Barn Campground** — ***BREWER D-3***
® Riverbend Campground — ***LEEDS E-2***
River Run Canoe & Camping — ***BROWNFIELD E-1***
**Riverside Campground** — ***WELLS F-1***
Robert's Roost Campground — ***ROCKPORT E-3***
**Rol-lin Hills Campground** — ***LIVERMORE FALLS E-2***
**□ Saco/Portland South KOA** — ***SACO F-2***
**® Saltwater Farm Campground** — ***THOMASTON E-3***
□ Salty Acres Camp Grounds — ***KENNEBUNKPORT F-2***
Sandy Beach Campground — ***MADISON D-2***
Scott's Cove Camp Area — ***ALFRED F-1***
**Sea Breeze Campground & Motel** — ***WELLS F-1***
**Searsport Shores Camping Resort** — ***SEARSPORT E-3***
**® □ The Seaview** — ***EASTPORT D-5***
**Sea Vu Campground** — ***WELLS F-1***
**□ Sebago Lake Resort & Campground** — ***SEBAGO LAKE E-1***
Sebago Lake State Park — ***NAPLES E-1***
□ Seboomook Wilderness Campground — ***ROCKWOOD C-2***
® Sennebec Lake Campground — ***APPLETON E-3***
□ Shady Acres RV & Campground — ***CARMEL D-3***
**□ Shady Oaks Campground** — ***BUCKSPORT D-3***
Shamrock RV Park — ***BIDDEFORD F-1***
® Sherman Lake View Camping Area — ***NEWCASTLE E-3***
□ Sherwood Forest Campsite — ***NEW HARBOR E-3***
□ Shin Pond Village Camping — ***PATTEN B-4***
**Shore Hills Campground** — ***BOOTHBAY E-2***
Smitty's Campground — ***MADISON D-2***
® Smuggler's Den Campground — ***SOUTHWEST HARBOR E-4***
Somes Sound View Camp Ground — ***MT. DESERT E-4***
**South Arm Campground** — ***ANDOVER D-1***
South Bay Campground — ***LUBEC D-5***
**□ Spruce Lodge Tent/Trailer Park** — ***OLD ORCHARD BEACH F-2***
**® Spruce Valley Campground** — ***BAR HARBOR E-4***
**Stadig Campground** — ***WELLS F-1***
® Stetson Shores Campground — ***STETSON D-3***
**Stony Brook Recreation** — ***HANOVER D-1***
Sunkhaze Campground — ***JONESBORO D-5***
□ Sunset Point Campground — ***HARRINGTON D-4***
Sunset Point RV Trailer Park — ***LUBEC D-5***
® Sunshine Campground — ***DEER ISLE E-3***
**□ Tent Village Travel Trailer Park** — ***NEWPORT D-3***
**Timberland Acres RV Park** — ***ELLSWORTH D-4***
**Twin Brooks Camping Area** — ***GRAY E-2***
**□ Twin Pond Campground** — ***FARMINGTON D-2***
® □ Two Lakes Muskegon Camping Area — ***OXFORD E-1***
**Two Rivers Campground** — ***SKOWHEGAN D-2***
Vacationland Campsites — ***HARRISON E-1***
The Villa Vaughn — ***ORONO D-3***
**® Virginia Park** — ***OLD ORCHARD BEACH F-2***
Wagon Wheel Camping & Trailer Park — ***OLD ORCHARD BEACH F-2***
**Walnut Grove Campground** — ***ALFRED F-1***
**Wassamki Springs** — ***PORTLAND F-2***
**Wee Holme Campground** — ***BREWER D-3***
**Wells Beach Resort** — ***WELLS F-1***
Wheeler Stream Camping Area — ***BANGOR D-3***
Whispering Pines Campground — ***BUCKSPORT D-3***
White Birches Campground — ***SOUTHWEST HARBOR E-4***
**Wild Acres Tent & Trailer Park** — ***OLD ORCHARD BEACH F-2***
Wild Duck Camping Area — ***SCARBOROUGH F-2***
**® △ Woodland Acres Camp 'N Canoe** — ***BROWNFIELD E-1***
**• Woodland Acres Camp 'N Canoe** — ***BROWNFIELD E-1***
**Yogi Bear's Jellystone Park Camp-Resort** — ***WELLS F-1***
**Yonder Hill Family Campground** — ***SKOWHEGAN D-2***
York Beach Camper Park — ***YORK BEACH F-1***
York County Campsite Park — ***CORNISH E-1***
**Zen Farm RV Resort** — ***FRYEBURG E-1***

## MASSACHUSETTS

Airline Mobile Home Park — ***SOUTH DENNIS D-6***
**Applewood Campgrounds** — ***CHARLTON C-3***
**® □ Atlantic Oaks** — ***EASTHAM C-6***
**Bay View Campground** — ***BOURNE D-5***
**Berkshire Green Acres** — ***PLAINFIELD B-1***
**Black Bear Campgrounds** — ***SALISBURY A-5***
® □ Bonnie Brae Cabins & Campsites — ***PITTSFIELD B-1***
Boston Harbor Islands State Park — ***HINGHAM B-5***
**Bourne Scenic Park (Municipal Park)** — ***BOURNE D-5***
**★ Bradford RV Center** — ***BROCKTON C-5***
**★ Bradford RV Center** — ***RAYNHAM C-4***
**® Camper's Haven** — ***DENNISPORT D-6***
**• Camper Tours** — ***BOSTON B-5***
**Canoe River Campground** — ***MANSFIELD C-4***
**Cape Ann Camp Site** — ***GLOUCESTER B-5***
® Cape Cod Campresort — ***EAST FALMOUTH D-5***
**Circle CG Farm Adult RV Park** — ***BELLINGHAM C-4***
Clarksburg State Park — ***NORTH ADAMS A-1***
**Coastal Acres Camping Court** — ***PROVINCETOWN C-6***
**Country Aire Campground** — ***CHARLEMONT B-2***
**® Crystal Springs Campground** — ***BOLTON B-4***

## MASSACHUSETTS — Continued

D.A.R. State Forest — ***GOSHEN B-2***
★ **Diamond RV Centre** — ***HATFIELD B-2***
**Dunes' Edge Campground** — ***PROVINCETOWN C-6***
□ **Dunroamin' Trailer Park** — ***SANDWICH D-5***
Ellis Haven — ***PLYMOUTH C-5***
Erving State Forest — ***ERVING B-2***
Granville State Forest — ***GRANVILLE C-2***
□ **Grindell's Ocean View Park** — ***DENNISPORT D-6***
Harold Parker State Forest — ***ANDOVER A-4***
**Historic Valley Campground (Municipal Park)** — ***NORTH ADAMS A-1***
Horseneck Beach State Reservation — ***WESTPORT D-5***
**Horton's Camping Resort** — ***NORTH TRURO C-6***
★ **Hunter's RV Sales & Service** — ***HANSON C-5***
**Indianhead Resort** — ***PLYMOUTH C-5***
□ **Jellystone Park-Sturbridge** — ***STURBRIDGE C-3***
□ Jolly Whaler Trailer Park — ***BREWSTER D-6***
★ **Kent RV Service Center** — ***BUZZARDS BAY D-5***
**Knight & Look Campgrounds** — ***ROCHESTER D-5***
□ **KOA-Boston Hub** — ***WRENTHAM C-4***
□ **KOA-Minuteman** — ***LITTLETON B-4***
□ **KOA-Plymouth Kampground** — ***MIDDLEBORO C-5***
KOA-Sturbridge Webster Family Kampground — ***WEBSTER C-3***
Lake Dennison State Recreation Area — ***WINCHENDON A-3***
**Lakeside Resort** — ***BROOKFIELD C-3***
® □ Lamb City Campground — ***PHILLIPSTON B-3***
★ **Macdonald's RV Center** — ***PLAINVILLE C-4***
★ **Major's RV Service Center** — ***BOURNE D-5***
★ ® **Mann's Trailer Sales** — ***RUTLAND B-3***
Maple Park Family Camping — ***EAST WAREHAM D-5***
® □ **Martha's Vineyard Family** — ***MARTHA'S VINEYARD E-5***
Masasoit State Park — ***TAUNTON C-4***
□ Maurice's Campground — ***SOUTH WELLFLEET C-6***
★ ® **MCD RV Center** — ***HYANNIS D-6***
MILITARY PARK (Fourth Cliff Rec. Area-Hanscom AFB) — ***HUMAROCK C-5***
MILITARY PARK (Hanscom AFB FAMCAMP) — ***BEDFORD B-4***
□ Mohawk Trail State Forest — ***CHARLEMONT B-2***
Mt. Greylock State Reservation — ***NORTH ADAMS A-1***
Myles Standish State Forest — ***SOUTH CARVER C-5***
® **Normandy Farm Family Campground** — ***FOXBORO C-4***
★ **Normandy Farm RV Service** — ***FOXBORO C-4***
North of Highland Camping Area — ***NORTH TRURO C-6***
North Truro Camping Area — ***NORTH TRURO C-6***
**Norwell Campsites** — ***NORWELL C-5***
**Oak Haven Campground** — ***WALES C-3***
October Mountain State Forest — ***LEE B-1***
The Old Holbrook Place — ***WEST SUTTON C-3***
**The Old Saw Mill Campground** — ***WEST BROOKFIELD C-3***
Otter River State Forest — ***WINCHENDON A-3***
**Paine's Campground** — ***SOUTH WELLFLEET C-6***
**Partridge Hollow Camping Area** — ***MONSON C-2***
Pearl Hill State Park — ***WEST TOWNSEND A-3***
® △ □ **Peters Pond Park** — ***SANDWICH D-5***
® **Pine Acres Family Campground** — ***OAKHAM B-3***
**Pines Camping Area** — ***SALISBURY A-5***
® □ **Pinewood Lodge Campground** — ***PLYMOUTH C-5***
★ **Pinewood Lodge RV Service** — ***PLYMOUTH C-5***
Pittsfield State Forest — ***PITTSFIELD B-1***
• **Plymouth County Attractions** — ***PLYMOUTH C-5***
**Pout & Trout Campground** — ***NORTH RUTLAND B-3***
□ Prospect Lake Park — ***NORTH EGREMONT C-1***
Purple Meadow Campground — ***BERNARDSTON A-2***
® **Quinebaug Cove Campsite** — ***BRIMFIELD C-3***
★ ® **Rent 'N Roam RV Rentals** — ***SHREWSBURY B-3***
Roland C Nickerson State Park — ***BREWSTER D-6***
★ ® **Rousseau's RV Center** — ***LAKEVILLE C-5***
**Rusnik Campground** — ***SALISBURY A-5***
Salisbury Beach State Reservation — ***SALISBURY A-5***
Sandy Pond Campground — ***PLYMOUTH C-5***
□ Savoy State Forest — ***FLORIDA A-1***
Scusset Beach State Park — ***SAGAMORE D-5***
**Shady Acres Campground** — ***SOUTH CARVER C-5***
® □ **Shady Knoll Campground** — ***BREWSTER D-6***
® □ **Shady Pines Campground** — ***SAVOY B-1***
Shawme Crowell State Forest — ***SANDWICH D-5***
★ **Silver City Ford & RV Center** — ***RAYNHAM C-4***
□ **Sippewissett Cabins & Campground** — ***FALMOUTH D-5***
® Sodom Mountain Campground — ***SOUTHWICK C-2***
Southwick Acres — ***SOUTHWICK C-2***
**Springbrook Family Camping Area** — ***SHELBURNE FALLS B-2***
® **Summit Hill Campground** — ***WASHINGTON B-1***
**Sunsetview Farm Camping Area** — ***MONSON C-2***
Sutton Falls Camping Area — ***WEST SUTTON C-3***
**Sweetwater Forest** — ***BREWSTER D-6***
★ **Sweetwater Forest RV** — ***BREWSTER D-6***
Tolland State Forest — ***OTIS C-1***
Travelers Woods of New England — ***BERNARDSTON A-2***
**Village Green Family Campground** — ***BRIMFIELD C-3***
® △ **Wagon Wheel Camping Area** — ***WARWICK A-2***
® **Walker Island Family Camping** — ***CHESTER B-1***
Webb's Camping Area — ***MARTHA'S VINEYARD E-5***
Wells State Park — ***STURBRIDGE C-3***
Westport Camping Grounds — ***WESTPORT D-5***
★ **Westport RV** — ***SOUTH CARVER C-5***
**White Birch Campground** — ***SOUTH DEERFIELD B-2***
Willard Brook State Forest — ***WEST TOWNSEND A-3***
**Winding Brook Campground** — ***DOUGLAS C-3***
Windsor State Forest — ***WINDSOR B-1***
**Windy Acres Camping** — ***WESTHAMPTON B-2***
Winter Island Park (City Park) — ***SALEM B-5***
Wompatuck State Park — ***HINGHAM B-5***
**The Wood Lot Campground** — ***CHARLTON C-3***
**Wyman's Beach** — ***WESTFORD B-4***

# NEW HAMPSHIRE

Ames Brook Campground — ***ASHLAND D-3***
Ammonoosuc Campground — ***TWIN MOUNTAIN C-3***
□ **Angle Pond Grove** — ***SANDOWN F-4***
Apple Hill Campground — ***BETHLEHEM C-3***
**Arcadia Campground** — ***CENTER HARBOR D-3***
• **Attitash Alpine Slide & Aquaboggan** — ***BARTLETT C-4***
Autumn Hills Campground — ***WEARE E-3***
□ Ayer's Lake Farm Campground — ***BARRINGTON E-4***
□ Barrington Shores Campground — ***BARRINGTON E-4***
**The Beach Camping Area** — ***CONWAY D-4***
**Beachwood Shores Campground** — ***EAST WAKEFIELD D-4***
Bear Brook State Park — ***ALLENSTOWN E-4***
**Beaver Hollow Campground** — ***OSSIPEE D-4***
**Beaver Trails Campground** — ***LANCASTER B-3***
□ Beech Hill Campground — ***TWIN MOUNTAIN C-3***
® **Bethel Woods Campground** — ***HOLDERNESS D-3***
Blake's Brook Campground — ***EPSOM E-4***
® **Branch Brook Campground** — ***CAMPTON D-3***
Calef Lake Camping Area — ***AUBURN F-4***
• **Cannon Aerial Tramway/Franconia Notch State** — ***FRANCONIA C-3***
® □ **Chocorua Camping Village** — ***CHOCORUA D-4***
® **Circle 9 Ranch** — ***EPSOM E-4***
• **Clark's Trading Post** — ***NORTH WOODSTOCK C-3***
® **Clearwater Campground** — ***MEREDITH D-3***
**Cold Brook Campground** — ***WEBSTER E-3***
Cold Spring Camp — ***LINCOLN C-3***
Cold Springs Campground — ***WEARE E-3***
Coleman State Park — ***COLEBROOK B-3***
Connecticut Lakes State Forest (Deer Mountain — ***PITTSBURG A-3***
• **Conway Scenic Railroad** — ***NORTH CONWAY C-4***

## NEW HAMPSHIRE — Continued

△ Cove Camping Area on Conway Lake — ***CONWAY D-4***
Crawford Notch General Store & Campground — ***BARTLETT C-4***
Crawford Notch State Park (Dry River Campground) — ***BARTLETT C-4***
® **Crazy Horse Campground** — ***LITTLETON C-3***
® **Crescent Campsite** — ***CANAAN D-2***
Crown Point Campground — ***ROCHESTER E-4***
**The Crow's Nest Campground** — ***NEWPORT E-2***
Davidson's Countryside Campground — ***BRISTOL D-3***
Eastern Slope Camping Area — ***CONWAY D-4***
Ellacoya State Park — ***GILFORD D-4***
**Epsom Valley Campground** — ***EPSOM E-4***
**The Exeter Elms Family Campground** — ***EXETER F-4***
Ferndale Acres Campground — ***LEE E-4***
**Field and Stream Travel Trailer Park** — ***BROOKLINE F-3***
Field 'N Forest Recreation Area — ***HANCOCK F-2***
• **The Flume/Franconia Notch State Park** — ***FRANCONIA NOTCH C-3***
® The Foothills Campground — ***TAMWORTH D-4***
Forest Glen — ***LEE E-4***
**Forest Lake Campground** — ***WINCHESTER F-2***
Franconia Notch State Park (Echo Lake RV Park) — ***FRANCONIA C-3***
Franconia Notch State Park (Lafayette Campground) — ***FRANCONIA C-3***
Fransted Campground — ***FRANCONIA C-3***
**Friendly Beaver Campground** — ***NEW BOSTON F-3***
★ ® **Gary's Rte 4 RV's** — ***CONCORD E-3***
★ **Gilman's NH Coach & Camper** — ***PLYMOUTH D-3***
**Glen Ellis Family Campground** — ***GLEN C-4***
**Goose Hollow Campground** — ***CAMPTON D-3***
® **Great Bay Camping Village** — ***NEWFIELDS F-4***
Greenfield State Park — ***GREENFIELD F-3***
The Green Gate Camping Area — ***EXETER F-4***
**Green Meadow Camping Area** — ***GLEN C-4***
**Gunstock (Belknap County Park)** — ***GILFORD D-4***
Hack-Ma-Tack Family Campground — ***WEIRS BEACH D-3***
Hampton Beach State Park — ***HAMPTON BEACH F-5***
® □ **Harbor Hill Camping Area** — ***MEREDITH D-3***
• **Hart's Turkey Farm Restaurant** — ***MEREDITH D-3***
• **Heritage New Hampshire** — ***GLEN C-4***
**Hidden Valley RV & Golf Park** — ***DERRY F-4***
□ **Hillcrest Campground** — ***CONCORD E-3***
Hilltop Campground — ***SULLIVAN F-2***
® **Jacobs Brook Campground** — ***ORFORD D-2***
**Jefferson Campground** — ***JEFFERSON HIGHLANDS C-3***
★ **Jefferson Campground** — ***JEFFERSON HIGHLANDS C-3***
® Keyser Pond Campground — ***HENNIKER E-3***
□ **KOA-Broken Branch** — ***WOODSTOCK D-3***
□ KOA-Cherry Mountain — ***TWIN MOUNTAIN C-3***
□ KOA-Littleton/Lisbon — ***LITTLETON C-3***
Lake Francis State Park — ***PITTSBURG A-3***
® **Lake Ivanhoe Campground** — ***EAST WAKEFIELD D-4***
Lake Massasecum Campground — ***BRADFORD E-3***
Lamprey River Campground — ***LEE E-4***
The Lantern Campground — ***JEFFERSON C-3***
**Laurel Lake Campground** — ***FITZWILLIAM F-2***
Lazy River Camping Area — ***EPSOM E-4***
Living Water Campground — ***TWIN MOUNTAIN C-3***
**Long Island Bridge Campground** — ***CENTER HARBOR D-3***
• **Loon Mountain Park** — ***LINCOLN C-3***
• **Lost River** — ***NORTH WOODSTOCK C-3***
□ **Lost River Valley Campground** — ***NORTH WOODSTOCK C-3***
□ Maple Haven Camping, Cottages & Lodge — ***NORTH WOODSTOCK C-3***
**Mascoma Lake Camping Area** — ***LEBANON D-2***
® **Meredith Woods 4 Season Camping Area** — ***MEREDITH D-3***
**Mile Away Campground** — ***HENNIKER E-3***
Mink Brook Family Campground — ***LISBON C-3***
® **Mi-Te-Jo Campground** — ***MILTON E-4***
Mohawk Valley Camping Area — ***COLEBROOK B-3***
Mollidgewock State Park — ***ERROL B-4***
Monadnock State Park — ***JAFFREY F-2***
Moose Brook State Park — ***GORHAM C-4***
® **Moose Hillock Campground** — ***WARREN D-3***
□ **Mountain Lake Campground** — ***LANCASTER B-3***
• **Mount Washington Cruise** — ***WEIRS BEACH D-3***
• **Mt. Washington Auto Road** — ***GORHAM C-4***
• **Mt. Washington Cog Railway** — ***MOUNT WASHINGTON C-4***
• Museum of Family Camping — ***ALLENSTOWN E-4***
New Hampshire Seacoast Campground — ***SEABROOK F-5***
Northstar Campground — ***NEWPORT E-2***
**Old Stage Campground** — ***DOVER E-4***
Otter Lake Campground — ***NEW LONDON E-2***
**Oxbow Campground** — ***HILLSBORO E-3***
**The Pastures** — ***ORFORD D-2***
Paugus Bay Campground — ***WEIRS BEACH D-3***
Pawtuckaway State Park — ***RAYMOND F-4***
Pemi River Campground — ***THORNTON D-3***
Pillsbury State Park — ***WASHINGTON E-2***
® **Pine Acres Family Campground** — ***RAYMOND F-4***
Pine Grove Campground — ***FRANKLIN E-3***
**Pine Haven Campground** — ***WENTWORTH D-3***
**Pine Hollow Camping World** — ***WEIRS BEACH D-3***
**Pine-Knoll Campground & RV Resort** — ***CONWAY D-4***
• **Polar Caves Park** — ***PLYMOUTH D-3***
Provident Winnipesaukee Campground — ***CENTER HARBOR D-3***
Rand Pond Campground — ***GOSHEN E-2***
**Roger's Campground** — ***LANCASTER B-3***
**Saco River Camping Area** — ***NORTH CONWAY C-4***
• **Santa's Village** — ***JEFFERSON C-3***
**Scenic View Campground** — ***WARREN D-3***
® Scott's Big Rock Camping Area — ***NORTH STRATFORD B-3***
Seven Maples Camping Area — ***HANCOCK F-2***
Shel-Al Campground — ***HAMPTON F-5***
® **Shir-Roy Camping Area** — ***RICHMOND F-2***
® △ **Silver Lake Park Campground** — ***LACONIA E-3***
△ Silver Springs Campground — ***BARTLETT C-4***
• **Six Gun City** — ***JEFFERSON HIGHLANDS C-3***
Snowy Mountain Campground — ***BETHLEHEM C-3***
Squam Lakes Marina & Camp Resort — ***HOLDERNESS D-3***
**Storrs Pond Recreation Area** — ***HANOVER D-2***
• **Story Land** — ***GLEN C-4***
Surry Mountain Camping Area — ***KEENE F-2***
Swanzey Lake Camping Area — ***KEENE F-2***
® **Tamworth Camping Area** — ***TAMWORTH D-4***
□ Tarry-Ho Campground — ***TWIN MOUNTAIN C-3***
□ **Terrace Pines** — ***CENTER OSSIPEE D-4***
**Thousand Acres Family Campground** — ***FRANKLIN E-3***
**Tidewater Campground** — ***HAMPTON F-5***
**Timberland Camping Area** — ***GORHAM C-4***
® **Tuxbury Pond Camping Area** — ***SOUTH HAMPTON F-4***
□ Twin Mountain Motor Court & RV Park — ***TWIN MOUNTAIN C-3***
® **Twin Tamarack Family Camping and RV Resort** — ***MEREDITH D-3***
□ Umbagog Lake Campground — ***ERROL B-4***
® **Wakeda Campground** — ***HAMPTON FALLS F-5***
Waterest Campground — ***WOODSTOCK D-3***
Weirs Beach Tent and Trailer Park — ***WEIRS BEACH D-3***
**Westward Shores Camping Area** — ***WEST OSSIPEE D-4***
• **The Whale's Tale Water Park** — ***LINCOLN C-3***
® △ **White Birches Camping Park** — ***GORHAM C-4***
White Lake State Park — ***WEST OSSIPEE D-4***
• **White Mountain Attractions & Chamber** — ***NORTH WOODSTOCK C-3***
White Mountain National Forest (Big Rock Campground) — ***LINCOLN C-3***
White Mountain National Forest (Blackberry Crossing — ***CONWAY D-4***
White Mountain National Forest (Campton Campground) — ***CAMPTON D-3***
White Mountain National Forest (Covered Bridge — ***CONWAY D-4***
White Mountain National Forest (Dolly Copp Campground) — ***GORHAM C-4***
White Mountain National Forest (Hancock Campground) — ***LINCOLN C-3***
White Mountain National Forest (Jigger Johnson — ***BARTLETT C-4***
White Mountain National Forest (Passaconaway — ***CONWAY D-4***
White Mountain National Forest (Russell — ***NORTH WOODSTOCK C-3***
White Mountain National Forest (Sugarloaf I — ***TWIN MOUNTAIN C-3***

## NEW HAMPSHIRE — Continued

White Mountain National Forest (Sugarloaf II — ***TWIN MOUNTAIN C-3***
White Mountain National Forest (Waterville Campground) — ***CAMPTON D-3***
White Mountain National Forest (White Ledge — ***CONWAY D-4***
White Mountain National Forest (Wildwood — ***NORTH WOODSTOCK C-3***
Wildwood Campground — ***NEW BOSTON F-3***
**Wolfeboro Campground** — ***WOLFEBORO D-4***
**Woodmore Campground** — ***RINDGE F-2***
® □ **Yogi Bear's Jellystone Park Camp Resort** — ***ASHLAND D-3***

# NEW YORK

Ace of Diamonds — ***MIDDLEVILLE D-7***
Adirondack Camping Village — ***LAKE GEORGE D-9***
Adirondack Gateway Campground (Not Visited) — ***COLD BROOK D-7***
□ Allegany State Park (Quaker Area) — ***SALAMANCA F-2***
□ Allegany State Park (Red House Area) — ***SALAMANCA F-2***
® **Allen's Boat Livery Marina and** — ***SACKETS HARBOR C-6***
★ ® **All-Season RV Service Center** — ***BUFFALO E-2***
® **Alpine Lake Camping Resort** — ***CORINTH D-9***
★ **Alpin Haus** — ***AMSTERDAM E-9***
**Alps Family Campground** — ***AVERILL PARK E-10***
® American Family Campground — ***GODEFFROY B-1***
**Aqua Vista Valley Campground** — ***PETERSBURGH E-10***
**Arrowhead Camping Area** — ***DELEVAN E-2***
**Arrowhead Marina & RV Park** — ***SCHENECTADY E-9***
• **Ausable Chasm** — ***AUSABLE CHASM B-10***
® Ausable Pines Campground — ***PERU B-9***
Ausable Point Campground (Adirondack State Forest) — ***PERU B-9***
® **Ausable River Campsite** — ***KEESEVILLE B-10***
® □ **Babcock Hollow Campground** — ***BATH F-4***
® Baker's Acres — ***SARANAC B-9***
Battenkill Sports Quarters — ***CAMBRIDGE D-10***
Battle Row Campground (Nassau County Park) — ***OLD BETHPAGE C-3***
Bear Spring Mountain (Catskill State Forest) — ***WALTON F-7***
□ Bear's Sleepy Hollow RV Park — ***PULASKI D-6***
Beaverkill Campground (Catskills State Forest) — ***LIVINGSTON MANOR F-8***
Beaver Pond Campground (Harriman State Park) — ***STONY POINT B-2***
□ Belvedere Lake Campground — ***ROSEBOOM E-8***
□ **Black Bear Campground** — ***FLORIDA B-2***
® Blue Mountain Campground — ***SAUGERTIES F-9***
Blydenburgh Park (Suffolk County Park) — ***SMITHTOWN B-4***
Bowman Lake State Park — ***OXFORD F-7***
Breezy Point Campsite — ***WELLSVILLE F-3***
® **Brennan Beach RV Park** — ***PULASKI D-6***
Bristol Woodlands Campground — ***BRISTOL CENTER E-4***
**Broken Wheel Campground** — ***PETERSBURGH E-10***
® Brook-N-Wood Family Campground — ***ELIZAVILLE A-3***
Brown Tract Pond Campground (Adirondack — ***RAQUETTE LAKE C-8***
Buck Pond (Adirondack State Forest) — ***GABRIELS B-9***
® △ **Buckridge Nudist Park** — ***CANDOR F-6***
Buck's Woods Campsites — ***MORRISVILLE E-7***
Bulwagga Bay Campsite (City Park) — ***PORT HENRY C-10***
Burnham Point State Park — ***CAPE VINCENT C-6***
□ Buttermilk Falls State Park — ***ITHACA F-5***
**Camp at Ferenbaugh** — ***CORNING F-4***
**Camp Bell Campground** — ***CAMPBELL F-4***
**Camp Chautauqua Camping Resort** — ***CHAUTAUQUA F-1***
★ **Camp Chautauqua RV** — ***CHAUTAUQUA F-1***
★ **Campers Barn of Kingston** — ***KINGSTON F-9***
® Canaan Campground — ***HUBBARDSVILLE E-7***
□ **Canandaigua-Rochester KOA** — ***CANANDAIGUA E-4***
Caroga Lake Campground (Adirondack State — ***CAROGA LAKE D-8***
□ Catskill Mtn. Kampground — ***DOWNSVILLE F-7***
• **Cattaraugus-Allegany County Tourist Bureau** — ***SALAMANCA F-2***
□ Cayuga Lake State Park — ***SENECA FALLS E-5***
® Cedar Grove Campgrounds — ***CATSKILL F-9***
Cedar Point State Park — ***CLAYTON B-6***
Cedar Point (Suffolk County Park) — ***EAST HAMPTON B-5***
• **Central Leatherstocking Country, N.Y.** — ***HERKIMER E-7***
• **Chautauqua County Tourist Information Center** — ***MAYVILLE F-1***
• **Chautauqua County Visitors Bureau** — ***MAYVILLE F-1***
□ Chautauqua Heights Campground — ***DEWITTVILLE F-1***
**Cheerful Valley Campground** — ***PHELPS E-5***
□ Chenango Valley State Park — ***BINGHAMTON F-6***
® **Cherry Grove Campground** — ***WOLCOTT D-5***
® **Christy's Beaver Spring Lake Campsites** — ***DAVENPORT E-8***
□ Cinderella Campsite & Motel — ***NIAGARA FALLS D-2***
Clarence Fahnestock Memorial State Park — ***COLD SPRING B-2***
**Cliff & Ed's Trailer Park** — ***CUTCHOGUE B-5***
Coles Creek State Park — ***WADDINGTON A-7***
® **Conesus Lake Campground** — ***LAKEVILLE E-4***
Cool-Lea Camp — ***ODESSA F-5***
® □ **Cooperstown Beaver Valley Campground** — ***COOPERSTOWN E-8***
□ Cooperstown Ringwood Farms Campground — ***COOPERSTOWN E-8***
® **Cooperstown Shadow Brook Campground** — ***COOPERSTOWN E-8***
□ Copake Falls Area (Taconic State Park) — ***MILLERTON F-10***
**Country Hills Campground** — ***MARATHON F-6***
® **Country Roads Campsites** — ***GILBOA F-8***
® Covered Bridge Campsite — ***LIVINGSTON MANOR F-8***
Cranberry Lake Campground (Adirondack State — ***CRANBERRY LAKE B-8***
Creek Side Campsite — ***CANANDAIGUA E-4***
Crown Point Reservation Campground (Adirondack — ***CROWN POINT C-10***
• **Crystal Chandelier Restaurant** — ***HERKIMER E-7***
Crystal Grove Campsite — ***ST. JOHNSVILLE E-8***
® □ Crystal Lake Park — ***GARRATTSVILLE E-7***
Cumberland Bay State Park — ***PLATTSBURGH B-10***
Daggett Lake Campsites (Not Visited) — ***WARRENSBURG D-9***
® Darien Lake Camping Resort — ***DARIEN CENTER E-3***
Darien Lake State Park — ***DARIEN CENTER E-3***
★ **Dave Foster's RV Center** — ***WATERTOWN C-6***
□ **Deer River Campsite** — ***DUANE B-8***
® **Deer Run Campgrounds** — ***MECHANICVILLE E-9***
Delaware Valley Campsite — ***DOWNSVILLE F-7***
Delta Lake State Park — ***ROME D-7***
**Dingmans Family Campground** — ***NASSAU E-9***
★ **Doug Gordon RV Repairs** — ***CAMBRIDGE D-10***
Eagle Point Campground (Adirondack State Forest) — ***POTTERSVILLE C-9***
Earlton Hill Campsites/Ministries (Not Visited) — ***EARLTON F-9***
® **Eastern Long Island Kampground** — ***GREENPORT B-5***
Eighth Lake (Adirondack State Forest) — ***RAQUETTE LAKE C-8***
**Elmtree Campsites** — ***UTICA D-7***
Evangola State Park — ***ANGOLA E-2***
® **Evergreen Camping Resort** — ***LAKE GEORGE D-9***
□ Fair Haven Beach State Park — ***FAIR HAVEN D-5***
□ Fillmore Glen State Park — ***MORAVIA E-5***
® △ Fire Fox Resorts — ***GLEN AUBREY F-6***
Fire Island National Seashore (Watch Hill Campground) — ***PATCHOGUE C-4***
Fish Creek Ponds Campground (Adirondack State — ***TUPPER LAKE B-8***
Flint Creek Campgrounds — ***POTTER E-4***
★ **Foland Sales** — ***SYRACUSE D-6***
**Foland's Trailer Park** — ***SYRACUSE D-6***
□ Forest Haven Campground — ***KENNEDY F-2***
Forest Hill Lake Park — ***WINDSOR F-7***
Forked Lake Campground (Adirondack State Forest) — ***DEERLAND C-8***
Fort Ann Campground — ***FORT ANN D-10***
Four Mile Campsite (Fort Niagara State Park) — ***YOUNGSTOWN D-2***
**Four Winds Campground** — ***PORTAGEVILLE E-3***
**Frost Ridge Campground** — ***LEROY E-3***
• **Fulton County Tourism Office** — ***GLOVERSVILLE D-9***
® **Gardner Hill Campground** — ***LOWMAN F-5***
★ ® **Gary Johnston's RV Center** — ***PALMYRA D-4***
□ **Genesee Country Campground** — ***CALEDONIA E-3***
□ Gilbert Lake State Park — ***ONEONTA E-7***
Glimmerglass State Park — ***EAST SPRINGFIELD E-8***
Golden Beach (Adirondack State Forest) — ***RAQUETTE LAKE C-8***

## NEW YORK — Continued

Golden Hill State Park — BARKER D-2
Grass Point State Park — ALEXANDRIA BAY B-6
Green Acres by the Brook — HAGUE C-10
□ Green Lakes State Park — FAYETTEVILLE E-6
Hamlin Beach State Park — HAMLIN D-3
Hearthstone Point Campground (Adirondack State — LAKE GEORGE D-9
Heckscher State Park — EAST ISLIP C-4
• Herkimer Diamond Mine — HERKIMER E-7
★ ® Herman's Trailer Sales — WALTON F-7
® □ Hickory Hill Camping Resort — BATH F-4
□ Hickory Lake Campground — HOUGHTON F-3
Hidden Valley Camping Area — JAMESTOWN F-1
® Hide-A-Way Campsites — CENTRAL BRIDGE E-8
High Falls Park — CHATEAUGAY A-9
Higley Flow State Park — SOUTH COLTON B-8
△ Hill 'N Hollow Campsites — HAMMONDSPORT F-4
Hither Hills State Park — MONTAUK B-5
® □ Holiday Hill Campground — SPRINGWATER E-4
★ Holiday on Wheels — PATTERSON A-3
Holiday Travel Park — AUSABLE CHASM B-10
• Howe Caverns — HOWES CAVE E-8
Hunter Lake Campground — PARKSVILLE F-8
★ ® Hyde's RV and Boats — REXFORD E-9
Ideal Campground — POTTERSVILLE C-9
® □ Idlewood on the Lake — SODUS POINT D-5
Indian Island Park (Suffolk County Park) — RIVERHEAD B-4
△ □ Indian Ridge Campsites — CATSKILL F-9
® Interlake Farm Campground & Trailer Sales — RHINEBECK F-9
★ Interlake Trailer Sales — RHINEBECK F-9
Iroquois RV Park & Campground — PERU B-9
Jacques Cartier State Park — OGDENSBURG B-7
JJ's Pope Haven Campground — RANDOLPH F-2
Junction Campsite — SARANAC LAKE B-9
Kayuta Lake Campground — FORESTPORT D-7
Keewaydin State Park — ALEXANDRIA BAY B-6
Kelly's RV Park — WATERTOWN C-6
Kellystone Park Campsite — AFTON F-7
Kenneth L. Wilson Campground (Catskills State Forest) — PHOENICIA F-8
Keuka Lake State Park — KEUKA PARK E-4
Kittatinny Campgrounds — BARRYVILLE A-1
• Kittatinny Canoes — BARRYVILLE A-1
□ KOA-Ausable Chasm — AUSABLE CHASM B-10
□ KOA-Cooperstown — COOPERSTOWN E-8
□ KOA-Herkimer Diamond Campground — HERKIMER E-7
□ KOA-Lake George — LAKE LUZERNE D-9
□ KOA-Lake Placid-Whiteface Mountain — WILMINGTON B-9
□ KOA-Massena — MASSENA A-8
® □ KOA-Mexico — MEXICO D-6
® □ KOA-Natural Bridge/Watertown — NATURAL BRIDGE C-7
□ KOA-Newburgh/New Paltz — NEWBURGH A-2
□ KOA-Niagara Falls — NIAGARA FALLS D-2
□ KOA-Niagara Falls North — LEWISTON D-2
□ KOA-Old Forge — OLD FORGE C-7
□ KOA-Rome/Verona — VERONA D-7
□ KOA-Saugerties/Woodstock — SAUGERTIES F-9
□ KOA-Syracuse — BALDWINSVILLE D-6
® □ KOA-Thousand Islands — OGDENSBURG B-7
® □ KOA-Unadilla/I-88/Oneonta — UNADILLA F-7
□ KOA-Watkins Glen/Corning — WATKINS GLEN F-5
□ KOA-Westfield-Lake Erie — WESTFIELD F-1
□ Kring Point State Park — ALEXANDRIA BAY B-6
Lake Bluff Campground — LAKE BLUFF D-5
Lake Chalet Campground & Motel — BRIDGEWATER E-7
• Lake Champlain Ferries — ESSEX B-10
• Lake Champlain Ferries — PLATTSBURGH B-10
• Lake Champlain Ferries — PORT KENT B-10
Lake Durant (Adirondack State Forest) — BLUE MOUNTAIN LAKE C-8
Lake Eaton Campground (Adirondack State Forest) — LONG LAKE C-8
Lake Erie State Park — BROCTON F-1
® Lake George/Schroon Valley Resort — WARRENSBURG D-9
Lake George Battleground Campground — LAKE GEORGE D-9
® Lake George Campsite — LAKE GEORGE D-9
★ Lake George Campsite RV Sales — LAKE GEORGE D-9
® Lake George RV Park — LAKE GEORGE D-9
• Lake George Steamboat Company — LAKE GEORGE D-9
Lake Harris Campground (Adirondack State Forest) — LONG LAKE C-8
® Lake Lauderdale Campground — CAMBRIDGE D-10
Lakeside Beach State Park — ALBION D-3
□ Lakeside Campground — WINDSOR F-7
□ Lake Taghkanic State Park — HUDSON F-9
The Landing Campground — SYLVAN BEACH D-6
® Lazy "G" Campground — WOODRIDGE A-1
Lebanon Reservoir Campground — MORRISVILLE E-7
Ledgeview Village RV Park — LAKE GEORGE D-9
★ ® Leisure Trailer Sales — LAKEVILLE E-4
® □ LEI-TI Campground — BATAVIA E-3
★ Lei-Ti RV Sales & Service — BATAVIA E-3
□ Letchworth State Park — CASTILE E-3
Lewey Lake Public Campground (Adirondack State — INDIAN LAKE C-8
Limekiln Lake (Adirondack State Forest) — INLET C-8
Little Pond Campground (Catskill State Forest) — LIVINGSTON MANOR F-8
Little Sand Point (Adirondack State Forest) — LAKE PLEASANT D-8
Locust Park — CENTRAL BRIDGE E-8
Long Point State Park (Thousand Islands Region) — THREE MILE BAY C-6
Luzerne Public Campground (Adirondack State — LAKE LUZERNE D-9
Macomb Reservation State Park — SCHUYLER FALLS B-9
Magic Pines Family Campground — LEWIS B-9
★ Mantelli Trailer Sales — LOCKPORT D-2
Max V. Shaul State Park — MIDDLEBURGH E-8
McConchies Heritage Acres — GALWAY D-9
Meacham Lake Campground (Adirondack State Forest) — DUANE B-8
Meadowbrook Campground (Adirondack State — SARANAC LAKE B-9
® Meadow-Vale Campsites — COOPERSTOWN E-8
® Merry Knoll 1000 Islands Campground — CLAYTON B-6
△ MILITARY CAMPGROUND (Round Pond Recreation — NEWBURGH A-2
MILITARY PARK (Griffiss AFB FAMCAMP) — ROME D-7
□ Mills-Norrie State Park — POUGHKEEPSIE A-2
Moffitt Beach Campground (Adirondack State — LAKE PLEASANT D-8
® Mohawk Campground — CHERRY VALLEY E-8
Mohawk Camping on Lake George — LAKE GEORGE D-9
Mongaup Pond (Catskills State Forest) — LIVINGSTON MANOR F-8
Moreau Lake State Park — GLENS FALLS D-9
Mountaindale Park (City Park) — MOUNTAINDALE A-2
Mt. Kenyon Family Campground — LAKE LUZERNE D-9
• New York City Tours - KOA-Newburgh/New — NEWBURGH A-2
• New York City Tours-KOA Newburgh/New — NEW YORK CITY C-2
□ Niagara County Camping Resort — LOCKPORT D-2
Niagara Falls Campground & Motel — NIAGARA FALLS D-2
® □ Niagara Hartland Campgrounds — GASPORT D-2
Nickerson Park Campground — GILBOA F-8
Nick's Lake Campground (Adirondack State Forest) — OLD FORGE C-7
North/South Lake Campground (Catskills State — HAINES FALLS F-9
Northampton Beach Campground (Adirondack State — NORTHVILLE D-9
□ North Pole Campground — WILMINGTON B-9
★ Northway Travel Trailers — MALTA E-9
Oakland Valley Campground — CUDDEBACKVILLE A-1
□ Oak Orchard Marina & Campground — SENECA FALLS E-5
Oquaga Creek State Park — BAINBRIDGE F-7
• Oswego County Dept. of Promotion & Tourism — OSWEGO D-5
Ox-Bow Campsites — EAST BRANCH F-7
® □ Paradise Park Campground — WATKINS GLEN F-5
® □ Paradise Pines Camping Resort — NORTH HUDSON C-9
Paradox Lake Campground (Adirondack State — TICONDEROGA C-10
Pine Crest Camping — WINDSOR F-7
Pine Hollow Campground — PALENVILLE F-9
Pine Valley Campground — ENDICOTT F-6
Plaza Court Motel Campground — NIAGARA FALLS D-2
Point Comfort Campground (Adirondack State — LAKE PLEASANT D-8

## NEW YORK — Continued

Poke-O-Moonshine Campground (Adirondack State — KEESEVILLE B-10
□ Pop's Lake Campground — GALWAY D-9
★ Price Rite Trailer Sales — MONTGOMERY A-2
Putnam Pond Campsite (Adirondack State Forest) — TICONDEROGA C-10
Rainbow View Family Campground — LAKE GEORGE D-9
Red Barn Family Campground — HANKINS A-1
Rip Van Winkle Campground — SAUGERTIES F-9
Riverforest Park — WEEDSPORT E-5
® □ River Road Campground — CORINTH D-9
Riverside RV Camping — BAINBRIDGE F-7
□ Robert H Treman State Park — ITHACA F-5
Robert Moses State Park — MASSENA A-8
Rogers Rock Campground (Adirondack State — TICONDEROGA C-10
Rollins Pond Campground (Adirondack State Forest) — TUPPER LAKE B-8
□ Rosemond Campground & Motel — WOODRIDGE A-1
Royal Mountain Campsite — JOHNSTOWN E-8
□ Rudd Pond (Taconic State Park) — MILLERTON F-10
® Russell Brook Campsite — ROSCOE F-8
Sacandaga Campground (Adirondack State Forest) — NORTHVILLE D-9
Sampson State Park — KENDAIA E-5
® Scenic View Campground — BOLTON LANDING D-9
□ Schroon River Campsite — WARRENSBURG D-9
Schuyler Yacht Basin — SCHUYLERVILLE D-9
Sears Bellows (Suffolk County Park) — HAMPTON BAYS B-5
□ Selkirk Shores State Park — PULASKI D-6
Shangri-La Camping Sites — FRANKLINVILLE F-3
Sharp Bridge Campground (Adirondack State — SCHROON LAKE C-9
□ Singing Waters Campground — OLD FORGE C-7
Skybrook Campground — DANSVILLE E-4
Skyline Resort Campground — DARIEN CENTER E-3
★ Skyline RV Sales & Service — DARIEN CENTER E-3
® Skyway Camping Resort — ELLENVILLE A-2
★ Skyway RV Sales — ELLENVILLE A-2
Smith Point Park (Suffolk County Park) — SHIRLEY C-4
Southaven (Suffolk County Park) — BROOKHAVEN C-4
Southwick Beach State Park — WOODVILLE C-6
Southwoods RV Resort — BYRON D-3
® □ Spruce Row Campsite & RV Resort — ITHACA F-5
Stewart's Pond Campsite — HADLEY D-9
Stony Brook State Park — DANSVILLE E-4
□ Sugar Creek Glen Campground — DANSVILLE E-4
• Sullivan County-Office of Public Information — MONTICELLO A-1
Sunset Park — BALDWINSVILLE D-6
□ Ta-Ga-Soke Campgrounds — SYLVAN BEACH D-6
□ Taughannock Falls State Park — ITHACA F-5
Thompson's Lake State Park — ALTAMONT E-9
Timberline Lake Park — LEROY E-3
Trail's End Campsite (Not Visited) — HINCKLEY D-7
★ Triple-R Campground — FRANKLINVILLE F-3
□ Triple-R Campground — FRANKLINVILLE F-3
Tumble Hill Campground — COHOCTON E-4
• Turning Stone Casino — VERONA D-7
Upper Delaware Campgrounds — CALLICOON A-1
Verona Beach State Park — ONEIDA D-7
Vickio's Deerfield Park — WATKINS GLEN F-5
The Villages of Turning Stone RV Park — VERONA D-7
Wagon Wheel Campground — PRATTSBURGH E-4
□ Wakonda Family Campground — POTTERSVILLE C-9
★ Walton H Bull Recreation Barn — PLATTSBURGH B-10
• Warren County Department of Tourism — LAKE GEORGE D-9
® Warrensburg Travel Park — WARRENSBURG D-9
Watkins Glen State Park — WATKINS GLEN F-5
□ Welcome Traveler Trailer Court — WATERLOO E-5
□ Wellesley Island State Park — ALEXANDRIA BAY B-6
Wescott Beach State Park — SACKETS HARBOR C-6
® □ West Canada Creek Campsites — POLAND D-7
★ W.E.S. Trailer Sales — WADING RIVER B-4
Whetstone Gulf State Park — LOWVILLE C-7
Whip-O-Will Campsite — ACRA F-9
Whippoorwill Campground — LAKE GEORGE D-9
□ Whispering Pines Campground — LAKE PLACID B-9
White Birches Campsites — WINDHAM F-9
® Whiteface Terrace Campsite — WILMINGTON B-9
Wigwam Campground — EUCLID D-6
□ Wigwam Keuka Lake Campground — PENN YAN E-4
Wildwood State Park — WADING RIVER B-4
Wilmington Notch Campground (Adirondack State — WILMINGTON B-9
Winding Hills Park (Orange County Park) — MONTGOMERY A-2
® Woodland Hills Campground — AUSTERLITZ F-10
Woodland Valley Campground (Catskill State Forest) — PHOENICIA F-8
® Woods Road Campsites — CATSKILL F-9
® Woodstream Campsite — GAINESVILLE E-3
Yawger Brook Family Campsites — AUBURN E-5
□ Yogi Bear's Jellystone Park — PORT KENT B-10
★ Yogi Bear's Jellystone Park/Flatrock — MEXICO D-6
® △ □ Yogi Bear's Jellystone Park/Flatrock — MEXICO D-6
® □ Yogi Bear's Jellystone Park at Birchwood — ELLENVILLE A-2
□ Yogi Bear's Jellystone Park Camp Resort — NORTH JAVA E-3
® □ Yogi Bear's Jellystone Park Camp-Resort at — GARDINER A-2

# RHODE ISLAND

Arlington RV Supercenter — WARWICK C-4
★ ® Arlington RV Supercenter — WARWICK C-4
Bowdish Lake Camping Area — CHEPACHET A-2
Burlingame State Park — CHARLESTOWN E-2
Charlestown Breachway (State Camping Area) — CHARLESTOWN E-2
Echo Lake Campground — PASCOAG A-2
Fishermen's Memorial State Park — NARRAGANSETT D-3
Frontier Family Camper Park — ASHAWAY D-2
George Washington Management Area (State Park) — CHEPACHET A-2
Ginny-B Family Campground — FOSTER B-2
® □ Greenwood Hill Family Campground — HOPE VALLEY D-2
Hickory Ridge Campground — COVENTRY C-2
Holiday Acres Campground — GREENVILLE B-3
Long Cove Marina & Campsites — NARRAGANSETT D-3
Meadowlark — NEWPORT D-4
Melville Ponds Campground (City Park) — PORTSMOUTH C-4
Oak Embers Campground — EXETER C-3
Peeper Pond Campground — EXETER C-3
Wawaloam Campground — EXETER C-3
Whippoorwill Hill Family Campground — FOSTER B-2
® Whispering Pines — HOPE VALLEY D-2
Worden Pond Family Campground — WAKEFIELD D-3

# VERMONT

Alburg RV Resort & Trailer Sales — ALBURG A-1
Allis State Park — RANDOLPH C-3
® Apple Tree Bay Resort — SOUTH HERO B-1
Ascutney State Park — ASCUTNEY E-3
Bald Mountain Campground — TOWNSHEND F-3
Barrewood Campground — WESTFIELD A-3
Bomoseen State Park — BOMOSEEN D-2
Branbury State Park — SALISBURY C-2
Brighton State Park — ISLAND POND A-4
Burton Island State Park — ST. ALBANS BAY A-2
Button Bay State Park — VERGENNES C-1
Camperama Family Campground — TOWNSHEND F-3
Camping on The Battenkill — ARLINGTON E-2
□ Camp Skyland — SOUTH HERO B-1
□ Carry Bay Campground — NORTH HERO A-1

## VERMONT — Continued

® Caton Place Campground — CAVENDISH E-3
® Char-Bo Campground — DERBY CENTER A-4
Coolidge State Park — PLYMOUTH UNION D-2
Country Village Campground — BRANDON D-2
Crown Point Camping Area — PERKINSVILLE E-3
DAR State Park — ADDISON C-1
Dorset RV Park — DORSET E-2
★ Ehler's RV — ESSEX CENTER B-2
Elmore State Park — MORRISVILLE B-3
Emerald Lake State Park — NORTH DORSET E-2
Fort Dummer State Park — BRATTLEBORO F-3
Gifford Woods State Park — KILLINGTON D-2
Gold Brook Campground — STOWE B-3
Goose Point Campground — ALBURG A-1
□ Grand Isle State Park — GRAND ISLE A-1
Green Mountain National Forest (Hapgood Pond Campground) — PERU E-2
Green Valley Campground — MONTPELIER B-3
Greenwood Lodge and Campsites — BENNINGTON F-1
Groton Forest Road Campground — MARSHFIELD B-3
Half Moon Pond State Park — HUBBARDTON D-2
□ Harvey's Lake Cabins & Campground — WEST BARNET B-4
Hidden Acres RV Park & Campground — BRATTLEBORO F-3
® Homestead Campgrounds — GEORGIA CENTER A-2
® Horseshoe Acres — ANDOVER E-3
Howell's Camping Area — ARLINGTON E-2
Iroquois Land Family Camping — RUTLAND D-2
Jamaica State Park — JAMAICA E-2
Killington Campground at Alpenhof Lodge — KILLINGTON D-2
KOA-Brattleboro North — BRATTLEBORO F-3
® △ Lake Bomoseen Campground — BOMOSEEN D-2
□ Lake Carmi State Park — ENOSBURG FALLS A-2
® Lake Champagne Campground — RANDOLPH CENTER C-3
• Lake Champlain Ferries — BURLINGTON B-2
• Lake Champlain Ferries — CHARLOTTE B-1
• Lake Champlain Ferries — GRAND ISLE A-1
□ Lake Dunmore Kampersville — MIDDLEBURY C-2
Lake St. Catherine State Park — POULTNEY D-1
® Lakeview Camping Area — EDEN MILLS A-3
Lazy Lions Campground — BARRE C-3
® □ Limehurst Lake Campground — BARRE C-3
Little River State Park — WATERBURY B-2
® Lone Pine Campsites — COLCHESTER B-2
Maidstone State Park — BLOOMFIELD A-5
Malletts Bay Camp Ground — COLCHESTER B-2
Maple Grove Campground — FAIRFAX A-2
Maple Leaf Motel and Campground — WHITE RIVER JUNCTION D-3
Mobile Acres — RANDOLPH C-3
Molly Stark State Park — WILMINGTON F-2
Moose River Campground — ST. JOHNSBURY B-4
Mountain Trails — ROCHESTER C-2
□ Mountain View Campground and Cottages — MORRISVILLE B-3
New Discovery Campground (Groton State Forest) — GROTON C-4
North Hero State Park — NORTH HERO A-1
Old Lantern Campground — CHARLOTTE B-1
Onion River Camping Area — MARSHFIELD B-3
Otter Creek Campground — DANBY E-2
® Pine Hollow Camping — POWNAL F-1
Pine Valley RV Resort — QUECHEE D-3
Prouty Beach Campground (City Park) — NEWPORT A-4
Quechee Gorge State Park — QUECHEE D-3
Rest N' Nest — THETFORD D-3
Ricker Campground (Groton State Forest) — GROTON C-4
® Rivers Bend Campground — MIDDLEBURY C-2
Running Bear Camping Area — ASCUTNEY E-3
Shelburne Camping Area — SHELBURNE B-1
□ Silver Lake Family Campground — BARNARD D-3
Silver Lake State Park — BARNARD D-3
Smoke Rise Diner and Campground — BRANDON D-2
Smugglers Notch Campground (Mount Mansfield State — STOWE B-3
South Hill Riverside Campground — UNDERHILL B-2
Stillwater Campground (Groton State Forest) — GROTON C-4
Townshend State Forest — TOWNSHEND F-3
Tree Farm Campground — SPRINGFIELD E-3
★ ® Vermont Traveler — BRATTLEBORO F-3
White Caps Campground — WESTMORE A-4
White River Valley Camping — GAYSVILLE D-3
Wilgus State Park — ASCUTNEY E-3
® Will-O-Wood Campground — ORLEANS A-4
Winhall Brook Camping Area (Corps of — SOUTH LONDONDERRY E-2
Woodford State Park — BENNINGTON F-1

# ONTARIO

□ Abram Lake Tent and Trailer Park — SIOUX LOOKOUT D-2
Adolphustown Park — ADOLPHUSTOWN H-5
Agawa Bay Campground (Lake Superior Provincial Park) — WAWA C-3
Agimac's Lakeview Cabins & RV Park — IGNACE D-2
□ Ahmic Lake Resort — AHMIC HARBOUR F-3
Aintree Trailer Park — KINCARDINE H-2
Albion Hills Conservation Area (Metro Toronto & Region — BOLTON H-3
Algonquin Trails Resort — DWIGHT G-3
□ All Star Resort Tent & Trailer Park — MADAWASKA F-4
□ Almaguin Parklands Campground — KATRINE F-3
® Alpine RV Resort - Campsite — LINDSAY H-4
® Anchor Bay Camp — ENNISMORE H-4
Antler's Kingfisher Lodge — DEUX RIVIERES F-4
Arrowhead Provincial Park — HUNTSVILLE G-3
A.W. Campbell (St. Clair Region Conservation Auth.) — ALVINSTON I-1
Awenda Provincial Park — PENETANGUISHENE G-3
Backus Heritage Conservation Area (Long Point — PORT ROWAN J-2
Bailey's Bay Resort — PETERBOROUGH H-4
Bala Woodlands — BALA G-3
Balsam Lake Provincial Park — COBOCONK G-4
Bancroft Campground — BANCROFT G-4
Bancroft Tent & Trailer Camp — BANCROFT G-4
Bass Cove Park — ADOLPHUSTOWN H-5
Bass Lake Provincial Park — ORILLIA G-3
□ Batman's Cottages, Tent & Trailer Park — SHEGUIANDAH F-1
□ Bayfort Camp — MIDLAND G-3
□ Bayview Camp & Cottages — CALLANDER F-3
Beavermead (City Park) — PETERBOROUGH H-4
Bell's Point Beach — SAULT STE. MARIE D-4
□ Bensfort Bridge Resort — BAILIEBORO H-4
The Big Apple RV Park — COLBORNE H-4
□ Big Oak Tent & Trailer Park & Cottages — STURGEON FALLS F-3
Big Otter Marina & Campgrounds — PORT BURWELL J-2
® Bingemans Park — KITCHENER I-2
® Birch Bark Tent & Trailer Park — GRAND BEND I-2
Birch Cliff Lodge — BANCROFT G-4
Birchland Trailer Park — DRYDEN D-2
□ Birchwood Cottages Tent & Trailer Park — NIPISSING F-3
Birchwood Gift House and RV Park — NIPIGON B-2
® Bissell's Hideaway Resort — FONTHILL I-3
Black River Wilderness Park — WASHAGO G-3
□ Black Rock Resort — MANITOWANING F-2
Blueberry Hill Motel & Campground — GOULAIS RIVER D-4
□ Blue Bird Trailer & Campsite — VERMILION BAY D-1
® Blue Heron Trailer Park — DUNNVILLE I-3
Blue Lake Provincial Park — VERMILION BAY D-1
Bluewater Park (City Park) — WIARTON G-2
Bluewater Trailer Park (City Park) — KINCARDINE H-2
Blythwood Acres Trailer Park — COLBORNE H-4
□ Bob & Gale's Rainbow Camp & Trailer Park — PERRAULT FALLS D-2
Bon Echo Provincial Park — CLOYNE G-5
Bonnechere Provincial Park — ROUND LAKE CENTRE F-4

## ONTARIO — Continued

Bonnie Lake Camping — BRACEBRIDGE G-3
Booster Park (City Park) — MARMORA H-4
Bracebridge Camping & Trailer Park — BRACEBRIDGE G-3
Brandy's Hideaway Campground — GODERICH H-2
Brant Conservation Area (Grand River — BRANTFORD I-3
★ Brock RV Centre — PORT PERRY H-3
Brownlee Tent & Trailer Park — THESSALON D-4
Brucedale Conservation Area (Saugeen Valley — PORT ELGIN H-2
Bruce Mines Municipal Park — BRUCE MINES D-4
Busy Beaver Campground — HILTON BEACH D-4
Byng Island (Grand River Conservation Authority) — DUNNVILLE I-3
Cache Bay Tent & Trailer Park — STURGEON FALLS F-3
Caliper Lake Provincial Park — NESTOR FALLS E-1
Camel Chute Campground — GRIFFITH G-5
□ Camelot Tent & Trailer Park — MACKEY F-4
□ Campark Resorts — NIAGARA FALLS I-3
® □ Camp Barcovan — CARRYING PLACE H-4
□ Camp Bragmore — MANITOWANING F-2
Campers Cove — WHEATLEY J-1
Camp Hither Hills — OTTAWA G-6
□ Camp Saw Mill Bay — UPSALA B-1
Canisbay Lake Campground (Algonquin — ALGONQUIN PARK F-4
Canoe Lake Tent & Trailer Park — WESTPORT G-5
Carleton's Cove Tourist Trailer Park and Camping — BELLEVILLE H-5
Carol Campsite — SUDBURY D-5
• Carruther's Memorial Conservation Area — AVENING H-3
Carson's Camp — SAUBLE BEACH G-2
Castleton Hills Trailer Park — CASTLETON H-4
Cathcart Park (St. Clair Parkway Commission) — SOMBRA I-1
Cecile's Campsite — HEARST A-4
Cedar Beach Park — STOUFFVILLE H-3
Cedar Creek Campground — BRIGHTON H-4
Cedar Haven Tent & Trailer Park — COBDEN F-5
Cedarholme Campgrounds — WIARTON G-2
Cedar Valley Resort — ORONO H-4
Champlain Tent & Trailer Park — NORTH BAY F-3
Charleston Lake Provincial Park — LYNDHURST G-5
Chippawa Creek (Niagara Peninsula Conservation Auth.) — DUNNVILLE I-3
Chippewa Park (City Park) — THUNDER BAY B-1
Chutes Provincial Park — WEBBWOOD F-2
□ Clarke & Crombie Camps — NESTOR FALLS E-1
Claybanks Marina & Trailer Park — DRYDEN D-2
□ Cobblestone Lodge — IGNACE D-2
Cobden Municipal Park — COBDEN F-5
Cobourg East Campground — GRAFTON H-4
® Conestoga Family Campgrounds — ARTHUR H-2
Conestogo Lake (Grand River Conservation Authority) — ELMIRA I-2
Confederation Park (Hamilton Reg. Conservation Auth.) — HAMILTON I-3
□ Cookstown Toronto North KOA — COOKSTOWN H-3
Country View Resort-Motel & Camping — WYOMING I-1
Craigleith Provincial Park — COLLINGWOOD H-3
□ Crawford's Crow Lake Resort — NESTOR FALLS E-1
Crescent Lake Campground (Lake Superior Provincial Park) — WAWA C-3
Culver Park (City Park) — SWASTIKA C-6
Curry Hill Park — LANCASTER G-6
□ Cushing Lake Resort — UPSALA B-1
Darlington Provincial Park — OSHAWA H-4
Davy Lake Campground — IGNACE D-2
Deer Creek Area (Long Point Region Conservation Auth.) — LANGTON I-2
Delmar Campground — IRON BRIDGE F-1
□ Desert Lake Family Resort — VERONA H-5
Double "M" RV Park & Campground — LINDSAY H-4
□ Down Home Campgrounds — ECHO BAY D-4
Dreany Haven Campground — NORTH BAY F-3
Dressel's Jordon Valley Campground — ST. CATHARINES I-3
® Dressel's Still Acres — PORT COLBORNE I-3
Driftwood Provincial Park — DEEP RIVER F-4
Drury Park (Municipal Park) — COCHRANE B-5
® The Dunes Oakridge Park — GRAND BEND I-2
Durham Conservation Area (Saugeen Valley — DURHAM H-2
□ Dutrisac Cottages & Camping — STURGEON FALLS F-3
Duttona Trailer Park — DUTTON J-2
Dwyer Hill RV Resort — ASHTON G-5
Earl Rowe Provincial Park — ALLISTON H-3
• Edenvale Conservation Area — EDENVALE H-3
Edgewater Park — BLOOMFIELD H-5
Elm Grove Trailer Park — SUTTON H-3
Elora Gorge (Grand River Conservation Authority) — ELORA H-2
Emily Provincial Park — OMEMEE H-4
Esker Lakes Provincial Park — KIRKLAND LAKE C-6
Evergreen Park — ALFRED F-6
Fairbank Provincial Park — WHITEFISH F-2
Fairfield's Resort & Family Camping — CHERRY VALLEY H-5
△ Fairview Park Camping & Marina — NORTH BAY F-3
Falls Reserve (Maitland Valley Conservation Auth.) — GODERICH H-2
Family Paradise Campground — SEAFORTH I-2
Fanshawe Conservation Area (Upper Thames River — LONDON I-2
Ferris Provincial Park — CAMPBELLFORD H-4
□ Fiddlehead Resort — SAUBLE BEACH G-2
Fifty Point (Hamilton Reg. Conservation Auth.) — STONEY CREEK I-3
Finlayson Point Provincial Park — TEMAGAMI D-6
Fish Bay Yacht Club & Marina — NIPISSING F-3
The Fisheries Resort — FORT FRANCES E-1
Fisherman's Cove Tent & Trailer Park — KINCARDINE H-2
Fitzroy Provincial Park — ARNPRIOR F-5
• Fort Henry — KINGSTON H-5
Fox's Lakeside Trailer Park — TWEED H-5
Frankford Tourist Park (Village Park) — FRANKFORD H-4
Franklin Motel Tent & Trailer Park — NORTH BAY F-3
□ Fred's Camp — SPRING BAY F-1
Fushimi Lake Provincial Park — HEARST A-4
Galbraith Conservation Area (Maitland Valley — LISTOWEL H-2
□ Gawley's Parkview Camp — PERRAULT FALLS D-2
Georgian Bay Islands National Park (Cedar — HONEY HARBOUR G-3
□ Glen Allan Park — MARMORA H-4
□ Glencannon Resort — CLOYNE G-5
Glengarry Park (Parks of the St. Lawrence) — LANCASTER G-6
□ Glen-Lor — SYDENHAM H-5
Glenrock Cottages & Trailer Park — STURGEON FALLS F-3
□ Glenview Vacation Homes & — SAULT STE. MARIE D-4
Goff's Pakwash Camp — EAR FALLS C-2
□ Golden Beach Resort and Trailer Park — ROSENEATH H-4
□ Golden Hook Camp — RED LAKE C-1
□ Golden Lake Camp Ground & Marina — GOLDEN LAKE F-5
Graham Lake Campground — BROCKVILLE G-6
Grainger's Tent & Trailer Park — ARNPRIOR F-5
Grand Oaks Park — CAYUGA I-3
® Grand River RV Resort — DUNNVILLE I-3
Grangeways Trailer Park — SANDFORD H-3
® Green Acre Park — WATERLOO I-2
Green Acres Family Camp — KINCARDINE H-2
Green Acres Tent & Trailer Park — SHEGUIANDAH F-1
Greenpines Campground & RV Park — IGNACE D-2
Greenwater Provincial Park — COCHRANE B-5
® □ Grenville Park — PRESCOTT G-6
Grundy Lake Provincial Park — BRITT F-2
Guelph Lake (Grand River Conservation Authority) — GUELPH I-3
Guelph Township Recreational Park — GUELPH I-3
□ Gullwing Lake Tent & Trailer Park — BALA G-3
Haldimand Area (Long Point Region Conservation Auth.) — SELKIRK I-3
Halfway Lake Provincial Park — CARTIER D-5
Happy Green Acres Tent & Trailer Park — BROCKVILLE G-6
Happy Hearts Tent & Trailer Park — TOBERMORY G-2
® Happy Holiday Family Campground — FOREST I-1
Happy Land Campground — THUNDER BAY B-1
• Happy Land Gift Shop — THUNDER BAY B-1
Harrison Park (City Park) — OWEN SOUND G-2
Hay Creek Area (Long Point Region Conservation Auth.) — SIMCOE I-3

## ONTARIO — Continued

Heber Down Conservation Area (Central Lake Cons. Auth.) — OSHAWA H-4
Heidis' Campground — BARRIE H-3
★ Heidis' Campground & RV Trailer Sales — BARRIE H-3
Hidden Glen Trailer Park — PORT SEVERN G-3
Hidden Valley Park — WOODSTOCK I-2
Hideaway Trailer Park — BLOOMFIELD H-5
Highland Tent & Trailer Park — DUNNVILLE I-3
Hi Lo Hickory Family Campground — WOLFE ISLAND H-5
Holiday Beach Campground — WHITEFISH F-2
Holiday Beach Conservation Area (Essex Region — AMHERSTBURG J-1
Holiday Harbour Resort — WHEATLEY J-1
□ Holiday Haven Trailer Park & Resort — MANITOWANING F-2
Holiday Village Campground — FORT FRANCES E-1
The Homestead Trailer Park — BANCROFT G-4
Hope Mill (Otonabee Region Conservation Authority) — KEENE H-4
□ Horseshoe Lake Camp & Cottages — PARRY SOUND G-3
Horseshoe Lake Park — TIMMINS B-5
□ Huber's Lone Pine Lodge — DRYDEN D-2
• Huronia Historical Parks — MIDLAND G-3
Indian Lake Campgrounds — VINELAND I-3
Indian Line Campground (Metro Toronto & Region Cons. — TORONTO H-3
Inwood Park (Upsala Regional Dev. Assn.) — UPSALA B-1
Ipperwash Provincial Park — RAVENSWOOD I-1
Iroquois Municipal Park — IROQUOIS G-6
Island View Cottages & Campground — COE HILL G-4
Ivanhoe Lake Provincial Park — FOLEYET C-5
Ivy Lea Campsite (Parks of the St. Lawrence) — GANANOQUE H-5
Jay Lake Campground & RV Park — MINDEN G-4
Jell-E-Bean Campground — WASAGA BEACH H-3
® Jellystone Park — AMHERSTBURG J-1
Jolly Roger Campsite — BANCROFT G-4
Jubalee Beach Park — GRAFTON H-4
Kakabeka Falls Provincial Park — KAKABEKA FALLS B-1
Kap-Kig-Iwan Provincial Park — ENGLEHART C-6
Kearney Lake Campground (Algonquin — ALGONQUIN PARK F-4
® Kel-Mac Family Camping Resort — KEARNEY F-3
Kelso Beach (City Park) — OWEN SOUND G-2
Kenorus Quiet RV Resort — PORT ELGIN H-2
Kettle Lakes Provincial Park — IROQUOIS FALLS B-6
Killarney Provincial Park — KILLARNEY F-2
Killbear Provincial Park — BRITT F-2
King Waldorf's Tent & Trailer Park — NIAGARA FALLS I-3
Kittawa Camping — LIMOGES G-6
Knight's Beach — DUNNVILLE I-3
Knight's Hide-Away Park — NIAGARA FALLS I-3
□ KOA-Barrie — BARRIE H-3
KOA-Brighton/401 — BRIGHTON H-4
® □ KOA-Cardinal — CARDINAL G-6
□ KOA-Gravenhurst Muskoka — GRAVENHURST G-3
□ KOA-Heritage Place — KENORA D-1
□ KOA-Ivy Lea — GANANOQUE H-5
□ KOA-Kingston — KINGSTON H-5
□ KOA-London/401 — LONDON I-2
® □ KOA-Marmora — MARMORA H-4
□ KOA-Niagara Falls — NIAGARA FALLS I-3
□ KOA-North Channel Campground — SPRAGGE F-1
□ KOA-Owen Sound — OWEN SOUND G-2
□ KOA-Renfrew — RENFREW F-5
® □ KOA-Sault Ste. Marie — SAULT STE. MARIE D-4
□ KOA-Thousand Islands — MALLORYTOWN G-6
□ KOA-Thunder Bay — THUNDER BAY B-1
® □ KOA-Toronto West — CAMPBELLVILLE I-3
KOA-Wasaga Beach — WASAGA BEACH H-3
□ KOA-Windsor/401 — WINDSOR J-1
® Lafontaine Campground & RV Park — PENETANGUISHENE G-3
La Fortune (Town of Haldimand) — CALEDONIA I-3
□ Lagoon Tent & Trailer Park — HUNTSVILLE G-3
□ Lake Apsey Resort & Trailer Park — ESPANOLA F-2
® □ Lake Avenue Park — CHERRY VALLEY H-5
Lake Bernard Park — SUNDRIDGE F-3
Lake Dore Tent & Trailer Park — EGANVILLE F-5
Lakefield Park (City Park) — LAKEFIELD H-4
Lake Nipigon Provincial Park — BEARDMORE A-2
Lake of Two Rivers Campground (Algonquin — ALGONQUIN PARK F-4
Lake of the Woods Provincial Park — RAINY RIVER E-1
Lake Ontario Park (City Park) — KINGSTON H-5
Lake Saint Peter Provincial Park — LAKE ST. PETER G-4
Lakeside Summer Resort — ST. MARY'S I-2
Lakeside Village Motel & Campground — WHEATLEY J-1
Lambton-Cundick (St. Clair Parkway Commission) — SOMBRA I-1
Lancaster Park Outdoor Resort — LANCASTER G-6
The Landon Bay Centre — GANANOQUE H-5
□ Lands End Park — TOBERMORY G-2
Last Duel Park (City Park) — PERTH G-5
Laughing Water Trailer Park — SIOUX NARROWS D-1
Laurel Creek (Grand River Conservation Authority) — KITCHENER I-2
Lawson Park — FREELTON I-3
Layzee Acres RV Park — ORILLIA G-3
□ Lazy Acres Resort — WHITESTONE F-3
Lecuyer's Tru-Tail Lodge — NESTOR FALLS E-1
Leisure Bay Campground & Marina — BLIND RIVER F-1
® Leisure Lake Campground — LEAMINGTON J-1
★ ® Leisure Lake Trailer Sales — LEAMINGTON J-1
Leisure Time Park — BOLTON H-3
★ Leisure Trailer Sales — TECUMSEH J-1
★ Len's RV Sales — THUNDER BAY B-1
Lillie Kup Kamp — KATRINE F-3
Link's Camping Grounds — CALLANDER F-3
Lion's Head Beach Park — LION'S HEAD G-2
Little Austria Family Campground — BURFORD I-2
Little Lake Area (Long Point Conservation Region) — NORWICH I-2
Little Pine Lake Campground — NESTOR FALLS E-1
□ Log Cabin Point — CHERRY VALLEY H-5
Long Beach (Niagara Peninsula Conservation — PORT COLBORNE I-3
□ Longbow Lake Camp & Trailer Park — KENORA D-1
Long Point Provincial Park — PORT ROWAN J-2
□ Loon's Landing — FRENCH RIVER F-2
L'orignal Park (City Park) — L'ORIGNAL F-6
Lorne C. Henderson Area (St. Clair Region Conservation — PETROLIA I-1
□ Lower Beverley Lake Township Park — DELTA G-5
MacGregor Point Provincial Park — PORT ELGIN H-2
® MacKenzie's Trailer Park — PORT ALBERT H-2
MacLeod Provincial Park — GERALDTON A-2
□ Mac's Camp — SPRING BAY F-1
Mal's Camping — LANARK G-5
Mara Provincial Park — ATHERLEY G-3
• Marineland — NIAGARA FALLS I-3
Marine Park (St. Clair Parkway Commission) — MITCHELL BAY J-1
Mariner's Paradise — WAUBAUSHENE G-3
□ Marsh Bay Resort Tent & Trailer Park — COBALT C-6
Marten River Provincial Park — MARTEN RIVER D-6
□ Martins Camp — FRENCH RIVER F-2
Martin's Outlet Park — CHERRY VALLEY H-5
Marydale Estates — NEWTONVILLE H-4
McCreary's Beach Vacation Resort — PERTH G-5
McCullough's Landing — PERTH G-5
McGowan Lake Campground — MABERLY G-5
McLaren Campsite (Parks of the St. Lawrence) — INGLESIDE G-6
McRae Point Provincial Park — UPTERGROVE G-3
Meadow Brook Camping Park — SMITHVILLE I-3
Meaford Memorial Park (City Park) — MEAFORD G-2
Mew Lake Campground (Algonquin Provincial — ALGONQUIN PARK F-4
Middle Falls Provincial Park — THUNDER BAY B-1
Mikisew Provincial Park — SOUTH RIVER F-3
Mille Roches Campsite (Parks of the St. Lawrence) — INGLESIDE G-6
Milton Heights Campground — MILTON I-3
□ Mindemoya Court Cottages & Campground — MINDEMOYA F-1
Mine Mills Campground — SUDBURY D-5

## ONTARIO — Continued

□ Minnehaha Camp Resort — PORT LORING F-3
Missinaibi Lake Provincial Park — CHAPLEAU C-4
□ Missinaibi Outfitters — MATTICE A-4
Mississagi Provincial Park — ELLIOT LAKE F-1
□ Mitchells' Camp — SPANISH F-1
Moonlight Bay Tent & Trailer Park — WILBERFORCE G-4
Munro Tent & Trailer Park — POWASSAN F-3
Murphy's Point Provincial Park — PERTH G-5
Nagagamisis Provincial Park — HORNEPAYNE B-3
Narrows Lock Campground — CROSBY G-5
New Lowell (Nottawasaga Vly. Conservation — NEW LOWELL H-3
Neys Provincial Park — MARATHON B-3
Niagara Glen-View Tent & Trailer Park — NIAGARA FALLS I-3
• The Niagara Parks Commission — NIAGARA FALLS I-3
Nighthawk Retreat — TIMMINS B-5
Nixon Lake Resort — VERMILION BAY D-1
Norfolk Area (Long Point Region Conservation Auth.) — SIMCOE I-3
Nor-Halton Park — ACTON H-3
The Northwestern Tent & Trailer Park — DRYDEN D-2
• Nottawasaga Bluffs Conservation Area — CREEMORE H-3
• Nottawasaga Valley Conservation Authority — ANGUS H-3
Oastler Lake Provincial Park — PARRY SOUND G-3
Obatanga Provincial Park — WHITE RIVER B-3
Ojibwa Landing Park (City Park) — PENETANGUISHENE G-3
Ojibway Provincial Park — SIOUX LOOKOUT D-2
The Old Homestead Limited — BAYFIELD I-2
□ Old Mill Camp — KATRINE F-3
Olympia Village Trailer Park — WATERDOWN I-3
• Ontario Gem Mining Company — THUNDER BAY B-1
□ Open Bay Cottages & Campground — UPSALA B-1
Orchard Grove Tent & Trailer Park — NIAGARA FALLS I-3
O'Reilly Lake Family Campground — MOUNTAIN GROVE G-5
Oriole Park Resort — LONDON I-2
Oski-Wawa Camp — WAWA C-3
★ ® Ottawa Camping Trailers — OTTAWA G-6
Ottawa-Nepean Municipal Tent & Trailer Park — OTTAWA G-6
® Our Ponderosa Family Campground & Golf Resort — FOREST I-1
Pakwash Provincial Park — EAR FALLS C-2
Pancake Bay Provincial Park — BATCHAWANA BAY D-3
□ Panorama Camp — LAVIGNE F-3
Paradise Point RV Park & Marina — SIOUX NARROWS D-1
• Paradise Point RV Park & Marina — SIOUX NARROWS D-1
Parkhill Conservation Area (Ausable-Bayfield Conservation — PARKHILL I-2
® □ Parkview RV Resort & Cottage Rental — NESTOR FALLS E-1
□ Parry Sound-KOA Kampground — PARRY SOUND G-3
Paul's Creek Campsite — MCDONALD'S CORNERS G-5
□ Percy Boom Lodge — CAMPBELLFORD H-4
★ Peterborough RV Centre — PETERBOROUGH H-4
• Petun Conservation Area — COLLINGWOOD H-3
Pickerel Park — ADOLPHUSTOWN H-5
★ Pickering Motorhomes — PICKERING H-3
® □ Pike Lake Campground & Resort — MOUNT FOREST H-2
□ Pine Cliff Resort — COMBERMERE G-4
□ Pine Cone Park — ROUND LAKE CENTRE F-4
□ Pine Crest Campground — THESSALON D-4
□ Pinecrest Resort — GANANOQUE H-5
Pinehurst Lake (Grand River Conservation Authority) — PARIS I-2
□ Pine Point Resort — UPSALA B-1
□ Pine Ridge Park & Resort — PEMBROKE F-5
Pinery Provincial Park — GRAND BEND I-2
Pine Tree Tourist Park — TIVERTON H-2
Pine Valley Campground & Cottages — STONECLIFFE F-4
Pine Valley Park — CAMBRIDGE I-3
Pittock Conservation Area (Upper Thames River — WOODSTOCK I-2
Pleasant Beach Trailer Park — PORT COLBORNE I-3
□ Pleasure Park — BROCKVILLE G-6
Pog Lake Campground (Algonquin Provincial — ALGONQUIN PARK F-4
Point Farms Provincial Park — GODERICH H-2
Poplar Grove Tourist Camp — OTTAWA G-6
□ Poplar Point Resort — RED LAKE C-1
Port Burwell Provincial Park — PORT BURWELL J-2
Port Elgin Municipal Tourist Camp — PORT ELGIN H-2
Port Glasgow Tent & Trailer Park (Township Park) — RODNEY J-2
Presqu'ile Provincial Park — BRIGHTON H-4
Primrose Park — SHELBURNE H-3
Prospect Hill Camping Grounds — GRANTON I-2
® □ Providence Bay Tent & Trailer Park — PROVIDENCE BAY F-1
Quetico Provincial Park — ATIKOKAN E-2
® Quinte's Isle Campark — CHERRY VALLEY H-5
Rabbit Blanket Lake Campground (Lake Superior Provincial — WAWA C-3
Rainbow Falls Provincial Park — SCHREIBER B-2
Recreationland Tent & Trailer Park — CUMBERLAND F-6
□ Redden's Trailer Park — KENORA D-1
Red Oak Travel Park — TILLSONBURG I-2
□ Red Pine Lodge — FOLEYET C-5
□ Red Setter Resort — HAVELOCK H-4
Rene Brunelle Provincial Park — KAPUSKASING B-5
Restoule Provincial Park — RESTOULE F-3
★ Rick Trailer Sales — KINCARDINE H-2
Rideau Acres Campground — KINGSTON H-5
Rideau River Provincial Park — KEMPTVILLE G-6
□ Rip's Sleepy Hollow Resort — HALIBURTON G-4
Riverbend Park — PAKENHAM G-5
® Riverland Camp and Outfitters — MADAWASKA F-4
River Place Park — MOUNT FOREST H-2
Riverside/Cedar Campsite (Parks of the St. — MORRISBURG G-6
Riverside Campground — ESPANOLA F-2
□ Riverside Lodge — STURGEON FALLS F-3
Riverside Park (City Park) — PEMBROKE F-5
Riverside Park Motel & Campground — NIAGARA FALLS I-3
Riverwood Park — LINDSAY H-4
Rock Lake Campground (Algonquin Provincial — ALGONQUIN PARK F-4
Rock Point Provincial Park — DUNNVILLE I-3
Rockwood (Grand River Conservation Authority) — GUELPH I-3
Rolling Acres Farm Campground — ALLISTON H-3
□ Roll-in-G Campsite — PARRY SOUND G-3
Rondeau Provincial Park — MORPETH J-1
® □ Rondeau Shores Trailer Park — MORPETH J-1
® Roth Park — WIARTON G-2
□ Royal Windsor — ORIENT BAY A-2
Rushing River Provincial Park — KENORA D-1
Russ Haven Resort — BURK'S FALLS F-3
® Rus-Ton Village Family Campground — GRAND BEND I-2
★ RV World — ST. THOMAS I-2
Ryan's Campsite — DEEP RIVER F-4
• Ryan's Gifts — DEEP RIVER F-4
St. Lawrence Islands National Park (Mallorytown — MALLORYTOWN G-6
Saint Lawrence Park (City Park) — BROCKVILLE G-6
• St. Lawrence Parks Commission — MORRISBURG G-6
Salmon Point Campground — CHERRY VALLEY H-5
Samuel De Champlain Provincial Park — MATTAWA F-4
Sandbanks Provincial Park — BLOOMFIELD H-5
Sandbar Lake Provincial Park — IGNACE D-2
□ Sand Bay Camp — COMBERMERE G-4
Sand Hill Park — PORT BURWELL J-2
□ Sandhurst — KEARNEY F-3
Sandview Campground — BLOOMFIELD H-5
□ Sandy Beach Resort & Trailer Court — FENELON FALLS H-4
Sauble Beach Resort Camp — SAUBLE BEACH G-2
Sauble Falls Provincial Park — SAUBLE BEACH G-2
Saugeen Bluffs (Saugeen Valley Conservation Auth.) — PAISLEY H-2
® △ Saugeen Cedars Campground — HANOVER H-2
□ Saugeen Springs RV Park — HANOVER H-2
• Saugeen Valley Conservation Authority — HANOVER H-2
□ Savanne River Resort — UPSALA B-1
□ Schell's Camp and Park — FRENCH RIVER F-2
Scott's Tent & Trailer Park — NIAGARA FALLS I-3
Second Depot Lake (Napanee Reg. Conserv. Auth.) — VERONA H-5

## ONTARIO — Continued

Selkirk Provincial Park — ***SELKIRK I-3***
Serpent Mounds Provincial Park — ***KEENE H-4***
Shady Pines Campground — ***AILSA CRAIG I-2***
® **Shalamar Lake Niagara** — ***NIAGARA FALLS I-3***
**Shangri-La Park Campground** — ***ST. CATHARINES I-3***
Sharbot Lake Provincial Park — ***SHARBOT LAKE G-5***
**Shelter Valley Tent & Trailer Park** — ***GODERICH H-2***
® **Sherkston Shores** — ***PORT COLBORNE I-3***
Sherwood Park Campground — ***CLOYNE G-5***
The Shoals Provincial Park — ***CHAPLEAU C-4***
Sibbald Point Provincial Park — ***SUTTON H-3***
☐ Sid Turcotte Park — ***MATTAWA F-4***
Silent Lake Provincial Park — ***BANCROFT G-4***
Silver Lake Provincial Park — ***MABERLY G-5***
☐ Silversands Family Resort — ***KEARNEY F-3***
® Silver Sands Tent & Trailer Park — ***HUNTSVILLE G-3***
Six Mile Lake Provincial Park — ***PORT SEVERN G-3***
☐ **Sky-View Trailer Park** — ***LONGLAC A-3***
Sleeping Giant Provincial Park — ***PASS LAKE B-1***
**Smith's Camp** — ***MIDLAND G-3***
☐ Smugglers Cove Campground — ***MILFORD H-5***
Snowshoe Dam Tent & Trailer Park — ***RED LAKE C-1***
☐ South Bay on Gullrock — ***RED LAKE C-1***
☐ **South Bay Resort** — ***SOUTH BAYMOUTH F-1***
® South Lake Trailer Park — ***MINDEN G-4***
☐ **Spring Valley Park** — ***MOUNT FOREST H-2***
Springwater Conservation Area (Catfish Creek Conservation — ***AYLMER I-2***
• **Stillwater Gift Shop** — ***NIPIGON B-2***
**Stillwater Trailer Park** — ***NIPIGON B-2***
Stratford Fairgrounds and Trailer Park — ***STRATFORD I-2***
• **Stratford Tourism Department** — ***STRATFORD I-2***
Sturgeon Bay Provincial Park — ***BRITT F-2***
**Sturgeon Woods Trailer Park & Marina** — ***LEAMINGTON J-1***
• **Sturgeon Woods Trailer Park & Marina** — ***LEAMINGTON J-1***
® ☐ **Summer House Park** — ***MILLER LAKE G-2***
Sunnibank Park — ***DUNNVILLE I-3***
☐ **Sunny Acres** — ***FENELON FALLS H-4***
® ☐ Sunnyside Campground — ***WESTPORT G-5***
® ☐ **Sunrise Tourist Trailer Park** — ***BEWDLEY H-4***
Sunshine Motel Campground & RV Park — ***STURGEON FALLS F-3***

## ONTARIO — Continued

Swiss Pine Park — ***TWEED H-5***
Taylor's Cove — ***FORT FRANCES E-1***
**Tay River Tent & Trailer Camp** — ***PERTH G-5***
Tea Kettle Campground — ***NOVAR G-3***
Tea Lake Campground (Algonquin Provincial — ***ALGONQUIN PARK F-4***
1000 Islands Camping Resort — ***GANANOQUE H-5***
Terra Cotta Conservation Area (Credit Valley Cons. — ***BRAMPTON H-3***
☐ Terrawoods on Horseshoe Lake — ***PARRY SOUND G-3***
**Thames River Trailer Park** — ***LIGHTHOUSE COVE J-1***
Thessalon Lakeside Park (City Park) — ***THESSALON D-4***
☐ Thousand Lakes Resort — ***UPSALA B-1***
☐ Thunderbird Resort — ***UPSALA B-1***
Tidewater Provincial Park — ***MOOSONEE A-5***
• **Tiffin Centre for Conservation** — ***BARRIE H-3***
**Timberland Campground** — ***RENFREW F-5***
® ☐ Tobermory Village Campground — ***TOBERMORY G-2***
Tomahawk Trailer Park Resort — ***SIOUX NARROWS D-1***
**Toronto North Campground & RV Resort** — ***BRADFORD H-3***
Tottenham Conservation Area (Town of New — ***TOTTENHAM H-3***
Tramore's Covered Bridge Park — ***ROUND LAKE CENTRE F-4***
Travel Rest Tent & Trailer Park — ***SCHREIBER B-2***
Trillium Woods Camp — ***WIARTON G-2***
® **Trout Haven Park** — ***STRATHROY I-2***
**Trout Water Family Camping** — ***SUNDERLAND H-3***
**Trowbridge Falls (City Park)** — ***THUNDER BAY B-1***
Turkey Point Provincial Park — ***SIMCOE I-3***
Twilight Resort — ***MONTREAL RIVER HARBOUR D-3***
**Twin Towers Trailer Park** — ***DRYDEN D-2***
Two Bridges Motel & Campground — ***KAPUSKASING B-5***
Upper Canada Campground — ***MORRISBURG G-6***
• **Upper Canada Golf Course** — ***MORRISBURG G-6***
Upper Canada Migratory Bird Sanctuary Campsite (Parks — ***INGLESIDE G-6***
• **Upper Canada Village** — ***MORRISBURG G-6***
**Utopia (Nottawasaga Vly. Conservation Area)** — ***BARRIE H-3***
Valens (Hamilton Reg. Conservation Authority) — ***CAMBRIDGE I-3***
® **Valley View Campground** — ***GLENCOE I-2***
☐ **Vance's Cottages-Campground & Marine** — ***SPANISH F-1***
Victoria County Centennial Park — ***KIRKFIELD G-3***
**Viking Tent & Trailer Park** — ***IRON BRIDGE F-1***
Voyageur Provincial Park — ***CHUTE-A-BLONDEAU F-6***

## ONTARIO — Continued

Wakami Lake Provincial Park — ***CHAPLEAU C-4***
Warsaw Caves (Otonabee Region Conservation Authority) — ***WARSAW H-4***
Warwick Area (St. Clair Region Conservation Auth.) — ***SARNIA I-1***
Wasaga Campground Resort — ***WASAGA BEACH H-3***
☐ Waterfalls Park Lodge & Camping — ***SPANISH F-1***
☐ Waterways Campground — ***PORTLAND G-5***
Wawanosh Park (Maitland Valley Conservation Authority) — ***BLYTH H-2***
® ☐ **Wawa RV Resort & Campground KOA** — ***WAWA C-3***
® ☐ **Wellers Bay Campground** — ***CARRYING PLACE H-4***
☐ **West Lake Willows** — ***BLOOMFIELD H-5***
Westport Municipal Trailer Park — ***WESTPORT G-5***
Westview Trailer Park (City Park) — ***ELLIOT LAKE F-1***
Wheatley Provincial Park — ***WHEATLEY J-1***
Whispering Pines Family Camping — ***BRACEBRIDGE G-3***
Whispering Pines Recreational Park — ***HEPWORTH G-2***
☐ Whitehaven Resort — ***SHEGUIANDAH F-1***
White Lake Provincial Park — ***WHITE RIVER B-3***
☐ Whitewing Resort — ***EAR FALLS C-2***
☐ **Wild Goose Lake Trailer Park** — ***GERALDTON A-2***
**Wildwood Campground** — ***KEMPTVILLE G-6***
Wildwood Conservation Area (Upper Thames River — ***STRATFORD I-2***
Wildwood Golf & RV Resort — ***MCGREGOR J-1***
® **William Stewart & Daughters Family Camping** — ***THORNBURY H-2***
® ☐ **Willow Lake Park** — ***WOODSTOCK I-2***
Wilson's Tent & Trailer Camp — ***LYNDHURST G-5***
☐ Windmill Point Park — ***FORT ERIE I-3***
Windy Lake Provincial Park — ***SUDBURY D-5***
☐ **Wogenstahl's Canadian Resort & Trailer** — ***VERMILION BAY D-1***
® Woodcrest Resort Park — ***NORTHBROOK G-5***
Woodland Camp Site — ***ENNISMORE H-4***
**Woodland Lake Camp & RV Resort** — ***BORNHOLM I-2***
Woodland Park — ***ST. WILLIAMS J-2***
**Woodland Park** — ***SAUBLE BEACH G-2***
Woodland's Campsite (Parks of the St. Lawrence) — ***INGLESIDE G-6***
• **Woody's Restaurant** — ***SAULT STE. MARIE D-4***
**Woody's Restaurant & Trailer Park** — ***SAULT STE. MARIE D-4***
☐ **Yogi Bear's Jellystone Park Camp-Resort** — ***NIAGARA FALLS I-3***
**Yonder Hill Campground** — ***COBDEN F-5***

# 1996 READER COMMENT FORM

**Woodall Publications Corporation**
**13975 W. Polo Trail Dr., P.O. Box 5000, Lake Forest, IL 60045-5000**
**Attn: Directory Customer Relations**

**Woodall's invites you to share with us your comments on any campground *listed in this Directory.* Your comments will be acknowledged and forwarded to our representative for review at the time of inspection.**

*Please print clearly.*

Campground Name ______________________ Date You Camped Here ____________

Listing Town ______________________ State ____________

Your comments, please ______________________

______________________

______________________

______________________

______________________

______________________

Signed ______________________ Date ____________

Address ______________________

City ______________ State ____________ Zip ____________

Camping Unit: ❑ RV or ❑ Tent Years You've Camped ____________

**CD**

## INSPECTION REQUEST FOR RV PARK/CAMPGROUND NOT LISTED IN 1996 DIRECTORY

**Woodall Publications Corporation**
**13975 W. Polo Trail Dr., P.O. Box 5000, Lake Forest, IL 60045-5000**

*Please print clearly.*

Name of Campgound ______________________ Date Opened ____________

Mailing Address ______________________

Nearest Town ______________________

Driving Directions from this town (Be specfic regarding distance and highway numbers) ____________

______________________

Number of RV Spaces ______________ Number of Tent Spaces ____________

# Electric hookups __________ # Water hookups __________ # Sewer hookups __________

Season ______________________

Type of park ownership: Private ________ Federal ________ State ________ County or City ________

Other (please specify) ______________________

______________________

Former Campground Name if Changed ______________________

Signed ______________________ Title ____________

Address ______________________

Phone ______________________ Date ____________

**CD**

# WOODALL'S®

# 1996 GUIDE TO SEASONAL SITES IN RV PARKS/CAMPGROUNDS

## WHAT EXACTLY DO WE MEAN BY "SEASONAL CAMPING"?

Maybe you are a family from Florida who wants to spend the summer in the cool north woods of Minnesota, or in British Columbia or Ontario, Canada. Maybe your home base is New York, and you want to spend a warm and sunny winter in Arizona or Texas.

You might want to spend a few weeks in California, and you'd like to know which parks offer a weekly camping rate, and which of those parks are nearest to some great attractions to visit. You also may be interested in learning what RV dealerships are nearby, so you can have your rig serviced, or shop for a new one.

## WOODALL'S SEASONAL SITES GUIDE HELPS YOU MAKE YOUR PLANS!

If you'd like some great recommendations on where you can camp for a week, a month or an entire season, and which parks, RV dealerships and attractions cater to seasonal campers, then WOODALL'S 1996 GUIDE TO SEASONAL SITES IN RVPARKS/CAMPGROUNDS is for you! It has been specially designed for snowbirds, sunbirds and full-timers.

## WHAT WILL I FIND IN THIS GUIDE TO SEASONAL SITES?

Throughout these pages, we have provided detailed listings and display advertising from RV parks and campgrounds that invite you to come stay with them. To be included in this guide, each facility has purchased display advertising.

The ADVERTISEMENTS show you what is unique about each listed facility. They provide special seasonal rates, and tell you what attractions are nearby. They expand on the information in the listings. For example, the listing will tell you how many sites there are at an RV park. Their ad might say: Waterfront sites, or extra-wide pull-thrus. Additional information about hospital services, special entertainment programs, park trailer sales, distances to lakes and beaches is often provided, too.

The Listings tell you the "nuts and bolts" about the RV parks and campgrounds. They provide detailed driving directions, on-site facilities including numbers of sites, types of hookups, laundry facilities, and more. The reference line at the bottom of each listing tells you exactly where to find their ad.

## HOW IS THIS GUIDE ORGANIZED?

The listings and advertisements in this Guide are organized alphabetically, first by state in the United States, then by Canadian province. Within each state and province, the towns are listed in alphabetical order, and within each town, the facilities are also organized alphabetically.

## WHAT DO THE NUMBERS MEAN AT THE BOTTOM OF EACH PAGE?

Reader Service Numbers are assigned to each advertiser in the SEASONAL SITES GUIDE. Look at the bottom of each page for these numbers. Then, turn to the Reader Service Card following page 16. In the spaces provided on the card, write the numbers of the facilities you are interested in. Drop the postage-paid card in the mail. It's that easy! You'll receive brochures and other information ... sent directly to your home.

If you choose to inquire by phone, please let the RV Park/Campground know you found out about them by using WOODALL'S.

## WHAT THE LISTINGS TELL YOU

**FACILITIES:** All of the facilities listed are available on site.

**RECREATION:** All recreation listed is available right at the campground.

**YOGI BEAR'S JELLYSTONE NEW ORLEANS-HAMMOND**—CAMPGROUND with open & wooded spaces in rural area. *From jct I-55 & I-12: Go 10 mi E on I-12, then 3 mi N on Hwy 445.*

WELCOME

FACILITIES: 316 sites, most common site width 35 feet, 169 full hookups, 147 water & elec (20 & 30 amp receptacles), 60 pull-thrus, a/c allowed, heater allowed, group sites for tents/RVs, cabins, RV storage, handicap restroom facilities, sewage disposal, laundry, public phone, grocery store, RV supplies, LP gas refill by weight/by meter, ice, tables, patios, fire rings, grills, wood, church services, traffic control gate.

RECREATION: rec hall, rec room/area, pavilion, coin games, 3 swim pools, wading pool, whirlpool, boating, no motors, canoeing, dock, 28 canoe/12 pedal boat rentals, lake fishing, mini-golf ($), basketball hoop, playground, 2 shuffleboard courts, planned group activities, movies, recreation director, sports field, horseshoes, hiking trails, volleyball, local tours. Recreation open to the public.

Open all year. Facilities fully operational Mar 15 through Nov 30. No refunds. Member of ARVC; LCOA. Phone: (504) 542-1507.

SEE AD THIS PAGE

**DESCRIPTIVE PHRASE:** Intended to "paint a word picture" for you.

**DIRECTIONS:** Detailed, easy-to-read driving information.

**SPECIAL INFO:** This area includes such information as no pets, age restrictions, and operating season. If listing doesn't state "No Pets," pets are allowed.

**ADVERTISER CROSS-REFERENCE:** This line will refer you to the specific page for this listing's advertisement.

# FREE CAMPING INFORMATION

# Seasonal Guide

**SAVE HOURS OF RESEARCH!**

The campgrounds/RV parks, RV service centers and attractions listed below want your business! Here is a quick and easy way to receive **free information** about seasonal camping, fun things to do, and where to service your RV or buy a new one. Simply enter their **Reader Service Number** (listed below) on the **Reader Service Card,** which is located opposite page 16. Your request will be forwarded to the names you've indicated. Then, **you'll receive brochures and/or pricing information,** sent directly to your home. It's the no-hassle way to shop for the campground, attraction or RV dealership you are interested in!

| Enter Number | |
|---|---|
| | **ALABAMA** |
| 149 | Lake Eufaula Campground |
| | **ARIZONA** |
| 789 | Fiesta Grande, An RV Resort |
| 151 | Gringo Pass RV Park |
| 790 | Quail Run RV Park |
| 515 | Roger's RV Resort Golf & Country Club |
| 791 | Silveridge RV Resort |
| 793 | Venture In RV Resort |
| 792 | Villa Alameda RV Resort |
| | **ARKANSAS** |
| 321 | Riverside Mobile & RV Park |
| | **CALIFORNIA** |
| 718 | Big River RV Park |
| 196 | The California RV Resort |
| 803 | Campland on the Bay |
| 875 | Carbonero Creek Travel Trailer Village |
| 802 | Circle RV Ranch |
| 174 | Clio's River's Edge Trailer Resort |
| 804 | De Anza Harbor Resort |
| 700 | Desert Trails RV Park & Country Club |
| 810 | East Shore RV Park |
| 173 | Emerald Desert Country Club |
| 805 | Escondido RV Resort |
| 874 | Fairplex RV Park |
| 873 | Far Horizons 49er Trailer Village |
| 811 | Golden Village RV Resort |
| 435 | Mammoth Mountain RV Park |
| 871 | Mountain Valley RV Park |
| 150 | Mountain View RV Park |
| 870 | Newport Dunes Resort |
| 800 | Oak Creek RV Park |
| 806 | Palm Canyon Resort RV Park |
| 801 | Paradise by the Sea RV Park |
| 809 | Rancho Casa Blanca |
| 799 | Rancho Los Coches RV Park |
| 172 | Salton City Spa & RV Park |
| 807 | Santee Lakes Regional Park & Campground |
| 876 | Sun & Fun RV Park |
| 482 | Tahoe Valley Campground |
| 808 | 29 Palms RV Resort |
| 872 | Valencia Travel Village |
| 950 | Yosemite Pines RV Park |

| Enter Number | |
|---|---|
| | **COLORADO** |
| 880 | Alpen–Rose RV Park |
| 878 | Coachlight RV Park & Motel |
| 877 | Conejos River Campground |
| 879 | Diamond Campground & RV Park |
| 513 | Garden of the Gods Campground |
| 881 | Monarch Valley Ranch |
| 522 | Navajo Trail Campgorund |
| 521 | Riversedge RV Resort |
| 882 | Stagecoach Campground & Lodging |
| 883 | Ute Bluff Lodge RV Park |
| | **CONNECTICUT** |
| 884 | Strawberry Park Resort Campground |
| | **FLORIDA** |
| 849 | Bryn Mawr Ocean Resort |
| 890 | Camp Mack's River Resort |
| 169 | Central Park |
| 893 | Crystal Lake Village |
| 894 | Emerald Pointe RV Resort |
| 842 | Holiday Campground |
| 850 | KOA-Punta Gorda/Charlotte Harbor Kampground |
| 888 | Many Mansions RV Park |
| 891 | Meadowlark Campground |
| 168 | Naples RV Resort |
| 414 | Orange Harbor Mobile Home & RV Park |
| 851 | Panacea RV Park |
| 845 | Quail Roost RV Campground |
| 170 | Road Runner Travel Resort |
| 892 | Rock Creek Campgrounds |
| 846 | Sarasota Bay Travel Trailer Park |
| 283 | Southern Comfort RV Resort |
| 843 | Sumter Oaks RV Park |
| 719 | Tampa East Green Acres RV Travel Park |
| 887 | Travel Towne Travel Trailer Resort |
| 279 | Travel World |
| 171 | Upriver Campground |
| 847 | Village Park Luxury RV Park |
| 889 | Woodsmoke Camping Resort |
| 844 | Yogi Bear's Jellystone Park Camp-Resort |

| Enter Number | |
|---|---|
| | **GEORGIA** |
| 868 | Cherokee Campground |
| 167 | Deen's RV Park |
| 524 | Lake Nottely RV Park |
| 710 | Pine Mountain Campground |
| 866 | South Prong Creek Campground & RV Park |
| 867 | Sugar Mill Plantation RV Park |
| | **ILLINOIS** |
| 896 | Hide-A-Way Lakes |
| 895 | Mendota Hills Campground |
| 486 | Shady Lakes Campground |
| | **INDIANA** |
| 897 | Elkhart Campground |
| 899 | Hidden Paradise Campground |
| 451 | KOA-Brown County/Nashville |
| 203 | Last Resort Campground |
| 326 | Manapogo Park |
| 898 | Mini Mountain Campground |
| 478 | Mohawk Campground & RV Park |
| 466 | Yogi Bear's Jellystone Park Camp-Resort |
| | **KENTUCKY** |
| 434 | Lakewood Resort |
| | **LOUISIANA** |
| 886 | Great Discovery Campgrounds |
| 166 | KOA-Baton Rouge East |
| 165 | KOA-New Orleans/Hammond |
| 885 | KOA-Vinton/Lake Charles |
| 900 | Yogi Bear's Jellystone New Orleans-Hammond |
| | **MAINE** |
| 903 | Beach Acres Campground |
| 904 | Libby's Oceanside Camp |
| 902 | Orr's Island Campground |
| | **MARYLAND** |
| 145 | Eagles Nest Park |
| | **MASSACHUSETTS** |
| 329 | Pout & Trout Campground |
| 901 | Springbrook Family Camping Area |
| 194 | Sweetwater Forest RV |
| 199 | Windy Acres Camping |
| | **MICHIGAN** |
| 195 | Andry's Acres on the Lake |

Enter Number

448 Birchwood Resort & Campground
146 Camelot Campground
906 Cedarville RV Park Campground
711 Creek Valley Campground
907 Greenwood Acres Family Campground
905 Juniper Hills
462 Sandy Oak RV Park & RV Sales
908 Sharp Park
459 White River Campground

**MINNESOTA**

331 Pelican Hills Park

**MONTANA**

910 The Elkhorn Guest Ranch
909 Yellowstone's Edge RV Park

**NEVADA**

164 Holiday Travel Park

**NEW HAMPSHIRE**

428 Angle Pond Grove
520 Beachwood Shores Campground
914 Chocorua Camping Village
588 Crazy Horse Campground
485 Friendly Beaver Campground
115 Goose Hollow Campground
477 Mile Away Campground
320 Oxbow Campground
589 Terrace Pines
429 Woodmore Campground

**NEW JERSEY**

915 Brookville Campground
831 Cape Island Campground
916 Echo Farm Campground
185 Indian Branch Park
274 Ocean View Resorts Campground
447 Pleasant Acres Farm Campground
201 Pleasantville Campground

**NEW MEXICO**

917 Little Creek RV Park

**NEW YORK**

595 Allen's Boat Livery Marina and Campground
518 Brennan Beach RV Park
709 Deer Run Campgrounds
920 Delaware Valley Campsite

**NORTH CAROLINA**

437 Camp Hatteras
280 Rivercamp USA

**OKLAHOMA**

962 Holliday Outt Mobile Home & RV Park

**OREGON**

481 Driftwood Village RV Park
449 Sweet Home/Foster Lake KOA

**PENNSYLVANIA**

935 Family Affair Campgrounds
937 The Locust Campground
938 Mountain Springs Camping Resort
939 Pocono Vacation Park
936 Round Top Campground
934 Shady Acres Camp Grounds

Enter Number

**SOUTH DAKOTA**

325 Lake Park Campground

**TEXAS**

983 Alamo-KOA
156 Ancient Oaks Campground
163 Austin Capitol-KOA
162 Autumn Acres RV & Mobile Home Park
942 Bahia Vista Waterfront RV Park
985 Bayside RV Park
158 Breeze Lake Campground
441 Cowtown RV Park
699 Fun N Sun
154 Guadalupe River RV Resort
159 Honeydale Mobile Home & RV Park
984 Lakeview Mobile Home & Travel Trailer Park
155 McAllen Mobile Park
986 Meadowlark Park
941 Palmdale RV Resort
160 Paul's RV Park
284 Port Isabel Park Center
161 Twin Palms RV Park

**UTAH**

153 Camp VIP
152 The Canyons RV Resort
157 Harrisburg Lakeside RV Resort

**VERMONT**

945 Apple Tree Bay Resort
519 Lone Pine Campsites

**VIRGINIA**

202 Blue Ridge Campground
944 Gloucester Point Campground
277 Inlet View Waterfront Family Campground
943 Tom's Cove Camping
198 Yogi Bear's Jellystone Park Camp-Resort

**WASHINGTON**

946 Elma RV Park
591 Ferndale Campground & RV Park
463 Fidalgo Bay Resort
136 Ponderosa Hill RV Park–A Park Washington Facility

**WISCONSIN**

947 Wilderness Campground

**WYOMING**

254 Big Horn Mountains RV Resort
949 Fountain of Youth RV Park
948 Greenway Trailer Park

**NEW BRUNSWICK**

423 Camper's City

**NOVA SCOTIA**

919 E & F Webber Lakeside
286 Green Valley Campgrounds
918 Holiday Haven
430 Klahanie Trailer Sales

**ONTARIO**

921 Ahmic Lake Resort

Enter Number

328 Alpine RV Resort-Campsite
439 Bensfort Bridge Resort
927 Campark Resorts
930 Cedar Beach Park
285 Double M RV Park & Campground
282 Dressel's Still Acres
925 The Dunes Oakridge Park
924 Duttona Trailer Park
431 Elm Grove Trailer Park
281 Grand River RV Resort
923 The Homestead Trailer Park
275 Indian Lake Campgrounds
929 Kenorus Quiet RV Resort
932 KOA-Sherwood Forest
928 LaFontaine Campground & RV Park
926 Marydale Estates
922 Nottawasaga Valley Conservation Authority
931 Ol Jo Mobile Village RV Park & Campground
933 Osprey Point RV Resort
200 Riverside Park Motel & Campground
322 Willow Lake Park
327 Woodland Lake Camp & RV Resort

**PRINCE EDWARD ISLAND**

940 Marco Polo Land

**QUEBEC**

461 Camping "Domaine Du Repos"
480 Camping Jardin du Campeur
453 Camping Tropicana
433 Camping Wigwam
442 Domaine Du Lac Louise

**BAJA MEXICO**

912 Baja Seasons Resort
913 Estero Beach Resort
602 Juanito's Garden RV Park
911 Vagabundos Del Mar RV Park
601 Villas De Loreto Resort

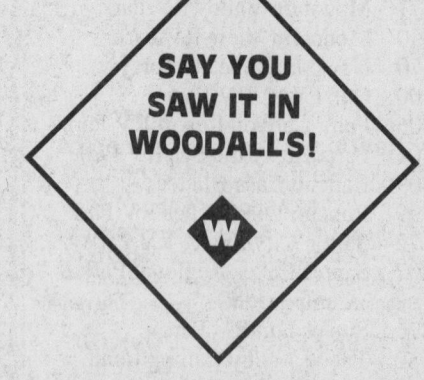

# SEASONAL SITE GUIDE

## ALABAMA

### EUFAULA

**LAKE EUFAULA CAMPGROUND**—A semi-wooded, lakeside CAMPGROUND with shaded sites. *From jct US 431 & US 82: Go 1/4 mi W on West Chewalla Creek Dr.*

WELCOME

FACILITIES: 100 sites, most common site width 20 feet, 88 full hookups, 12 water & elec (20 & 30 amp receptacles), 49 pull-thrus, a/c allowed, heater allowed ($), phone hookups, RV storage, sewage disposal, laundry, public phone, grocery store, RV supplies, ice, tables, wood.

RECREATION: rec room/area, pavilion, coin games, swim pool, boating, ramp, dock, lake fishing, fishing guides, playground.

Open all year. Phone: (334) 687-4425.

**SEE AD THIS PAGE**

## ARIZONA

### ARIZONA CITY

**QUAIL RUN RV PARK**—level, desert setting location. *From jct I-8 & I-10: Go 1 mi SE on I-10 (exit 200), then 3 1/2 mi S on Sunland Gin Rd, then 1/2 mi W on Santa Cruz.*

WELCOME

FACILITIES: 150 sites, accepts full hookup units only, 150 full hookups, (20,30 & 50 amp receptacles), a/c allowed, heater allowed, laundry, public phone, patios.

RECREATION: rec hall, rec room/area, swim pool (heated), 2 shuffleboard courts, planned group activities, recreation director, 2 tennis courts, horseshoes.

No tents/tent trailers. Age restrictions may apply. Open all year. Phone: (800) 466-6000.

**SEE AD CASA GRANDE THIS PAGE**

### CASA GRANDE

**FIESTA GRANDE AN RV RESORT**—A resort complex RV PARK in town. *From jct I-10 (exit 194) & Hwy 287: Go 1 8/10 mi W on Hwy 287 (Florence Blvd).*

WELCOME

FACILITIES: 581 sites, most common site width 36 feet, accepts full hookup units only, 581 full hookups, (30 & 50 amp receptacles),

CASA GRANDE, AZ—Continued
FIESTA GRANDE AN RV RESORT—Continued

30 pull-thrus, a/c allowed, heater allowed, phone hookups, handicap restroom facilities, laundry, public phone, patios, church services.

RECREATION: rec hall, rec room/area, swim pool (heated), whirlpool, 8 shuffleboard courts, planned group activities, movies, recreation director, horseshoes, local tours.

No tents/tent trailers. Age restrictions may apply. Open all year. Phone: (520) 836-7222.

**SEE AD THIS PAGE**

### LUKEVILLE

**GRINGO PASS RV PARK**—Shady, level sites at the US/Mexico border. *At Border: Go 150 feet N on Hwy 85.*

WELCOME

FACILITIES: 100 sites, most common site width 28 feet, 100 full hookups, (30 & 50 amp receptacles), 40 pull-thrus, a/c allowed, heater allowed, RV storage, sewage disposal, laundry, public phone, grocery store, RV supplies, LP gas refill by weight, ice, tables, patios, guard.

RECREATION: rec hall, rec room/area, pavilion, swim pool, whirlpool, basketball hoop, shuffleboard court, planned group activities, horseshoes.

Open all year. Facilities fully operational Apr through Oct. Swimming pool open Apr thru Oct. Phone: (602) 254-9284.

**SEE AD THIS PAGE**

► **GRINGO PASS TRAVELMALL**—*At border: Go 150 feet N on Hwy 85.* Groceries, Mexican vehicle insurance, motel, gasoline, LP gas, bar, duty free liquor, restaurant, laundry adjacent to RV park. Open all year. Phone: (602) 257-0887.

**SEE AD THIS PAGE**

**Three fires in a triangle signal distress.**

ARIZONA—Continued

### MESA

**SILVERIDGE RV RESORT**—A resort RV PARK with level, landscaped spaces. *From jct US 60 (Superstition Fwy, exit 189): Go 1/2 mi N on Sossaman Rd, then 1 mi E on Southern.*

WELCOME

FACILITIES: 687 sites, most common site width 36 feet, accepts full hookup units only, 687 full hookups, (30 & 50 amp receptacles), a/c allowed, heater allowed, cable TV, phone hookups, RV rentals, handicap restroom facilities, laundry, public phone, RV supplies, ice, patios, church services, traffic control gate/guard.

RECREATION: rec hall, rec room/area, swim pool (heated), whirlpool, driving range, putting green, 9 shuffleboard courts, planned group activities, movies, recreation director, 2 tennis courts, horseshoes, local tours.

No tents/tent trailers. Age restrictions may apply. Open all year. Facilities fully operational Oct through Apr. CPO. Member of ARVC; ATPA. Phone: (800) 354-0054.

**SEE AD THIS PAGE**

ARIZONA—Continued on next page

*Interstate 10, Exit 194, into Casa Grande*
*Then 1.8 miles West on the left.*
**Enjoy our relaxed 55+ Senior Resort**

- 18,000 + Sq. Ft. of Recreation Buildings
- Full Time Recreation Program w/Director
- LARGE 60' x 36' Lots
- Wood Dance Floor
- Large Pool and Spa
- City Fire Protection
- In Park Phone System

*Nearby*
Shopping Centers
2 Factory Outlet Malls
6 Golf Courses
Regional Medical Center

**1-520-426-7000 or 1-520-836-7222**
**1511 E. Florence Blvd., Casa Grande, AZ 85222**

SILVERIDGE
RV • RESORT

**8265 E. Southern Ave.**
**Mesa, AZ 85208**
**Mesa's Warmest RV Resort!**
**Exit 189 off 60 Freeway**

**Retiring? Check out our active "Retirement" lifestyle.**

**690 Spacious Lots**
**Free Cable T.V. / Phone Hookups**
**Recreation Complex / Sports**
**Heated Pool / Spa / Ex. Room**
**Special Lots available for year-round rentals**

**OFF-SEASON DISCOUNTS!**

**Call TOLL FREE**
**1-800-354-0054**

Lake Eufaula
West Chewalla Creek Dr.
82
Bridge
N
W E
S
431
See listing at Eufaula

**Lake Eufaula Campground**

- Pull thrus
- 100 Sites
- Full Hookups
- Tenting
- Rec Room
- Pavilion
- Pool
- Fishing

*Seasonal Rates*
*$225 Month*
*Includes*
*Elec./Water/Sewer*

**(334) 687-4425**

151 West Chewalla Creek Dr., Eufaula, AL 36027

**GRINGO PASS**
**RV PARK - LUKEVILLE**

**Gateway to Mexico - 65 Miles to Rocky Point**
**Mexican Auto/RV Insurance**
Base Camp for
ORGAN PIPE NAT'L MONUMENT
**GENERAL STORE - CAFE**
Laundromat - Gas - Propane
**(602) 254-9284 - RV Office**
**(602) 257-0887 - Insurance**
**P.O. Box 266**
**Lukeville, AZ 85341**

Only 10 Miles From Casa Grande

**"Enjoy Arizona in Arizona City"**

• Heated Swimming Pool • Tennis Courts
• Shuffleboard • 50 Amp Service • Cable TV
• Laundry • Nearby: Golf, Restaurants and Factory Outlet Shopping

**(520) 466-6000 or (800) 301-8114**
**RESERVATIONS ONLY**
**14010 South Amado Blvd., P.O. Box 1049,**
**Arizona City, AZ 85223**
See listing at Arizona City

### SHOW LOW

**VENTURE IN RV RESORT**—A resort RV PARK with open, level sites. Altitude 6300 ft. *From South jct US 60 & Hwy 260: Go 1 1/2 mi W on Hwy 260.*

WELCOME

FACILITIES: 399 sites, most common site width 33 feet, accepts full hookup units only, 399 full hookups, (30 & 50 amp receptacles), a/c allowed, heater allowed, cable TV, phone hookups, RV storage, handicap restroom facilities, laundry, public phone, patios.

RECREATION: rec hall, rec room/area, whirlpool, 4 shuffleboard courts, planned group activities, movies, recreation director, horseshoes, hiking trails.

No tents. Open early Apr through late Oct. Phone: (520) 537-4443.

**SEE AD THIS PAGE**

### YUMA

**ROGER'S RV RESORT GOLF & COUNTRY CLUB**—A resort RV PARK in a desert setting. *From jct I-8 (exit 12) & Fortuna Rd: Go 1 mi W on south frontage road.*

WELCOME

FACILITIES: 906 sites, most common site width 32 feet, accepts full hookup units



only, 906 full hookups, (20,30 & 50 amp receptacles), a/c allowed, heater allowed, cable TV, phone hookups, RV rentals, RV storage, handicap restroom facilities, sewage disposal, laundry, public phone, ice, patios, church services.

RECREATION: rec hall, rec room/area, swim pool (heated), whirlpool, golf ($), driving range ($), putting green, 8 shuffleboard courts, planned group activities, movies, recreation director, horseshoes, volleyball, local tours. Recreation open to the public.

No tents. Age restrictions may apply. Open all year. Phone: (520) 342-2992.

**SEE AD THIS PAGE**

**VILLA ALAMEDA RV RESORT**—An RV resort park in a former lemon grove with shaded, level sites. *From jct I-8 (exit 7) & Araby Rd: Go 1/2 mi S on Araby Rd, then 1 1/2 mi W on Hwy 80, then 1/2 mi S on Ave 5E.*

WELCOME

FACILITIES: 302 sites, most common site width 27 feet, accepts full hookup units only, 302 full hookups, (30 & 50 amp receptacles), a/c allowed,



cable TV, phone hookups, handicap restroom facilities, laundry, public phone, ice, patios, church services.

RECREATION: rec hall, rec room/area, swim pool (heated), whirlpool, putting green, 4 shuffleboard courts, planned group activities, movies, recreation director, horseshoes.

No tents. Age restrictions may apply. Open all year. Phone: (520) 344-8081.

**SEE AD THIS PAGE**

## ARKANSAS

### BULL SHOALS

**RIVERSIDE MOBILE & RV PARK**—Grassy, open and shaded RV AREA in a riverside mobile home park. *From SE end of Bull Shoals Dam: Go 1/10 mi SE on Hwy 178, then 1 mi W on asphalt road, then 1/2 mi S on CR 569 (River Rd).*

WELCOME

FACILITIES: 18 sites, 18 full hookups, (30 & 50 amp receptacles), 5 pull-thrus, a/c allowed, heater allowed ($), phone hookups, public phone, RV supplies, ice, tables, patios, grills.

RECREATION: pavilion, river fishing.

No tents. Open all year. Phone: (501) 431-8260.

**SEE AD THIS PAGE**

## CALIFORNIA

### ACTON

**THE CALIFORNIAN RV RESORT** (UNDER CONSTRUCTION)—*At intersection of Hwy 14 & Sierra Hwy (Soledad Canyon exit).*

WELCOME

**SEE AD LOS ANGELES PAGE 6**

### ANAHEIM—C-2

*See listing at Newport Beach*

CALIFORNIA—Continued on next page

CALIFORNIA—Continued

## BIG RIVER

**BIG RIVER RV PARK** (NOT VISITED)—*From jct Hwy 62 & Big River exit (Rio Mesa): Go 2 mi S on Rio Mesa, then 1 mi E on Capistrano, then 1/4 mi N on Marina.*

FACILITIES: 183 sites, 183 full hookups, (30 & 50 amp receptacles).

Open all year. Phone: (619) 665-9359.

**SEE AD THIS PAGE**

## BORREGO SPRINGS

**PALM CANYON RESORT RV PARK**—A formal RV PARK in the desert surrounded by mountains & vistas. *From center of town: Go 1 1/2 mi W on Palm Canyon Dr.*

FACILITIES: 138 sites, most common site width 20 feet, 138 full hookups, (30 amp receptacles), a/c allowed, heater allowed, cable TV, handicap restroom facilities, laundry, public phone, full service store, RV supplies, ice, tables, fire rings, grills, wood.

RECREATION: rec room/area, swim pool (heated), whirlpool, 4 tennis courts, horseshoes, hiking trails.

No tents. Open all year. Member of ARVC; CTPA. Phone: (619) 767-5341.

**SEE AD THIS PAGE**

## EL CAJON

**CIRCLE RV RANCH**—Formally developed, metro area RV PARK, close to interstate. *From jct I-8 & Greenfield Dr.: Go 1 block N on Greenfield Dr., then 1/4 mi E on Main St.*

FACILITIES: 179 sites, most common site width 20 feet, 179 full hookups, (30 & 50 amp receptacles), 5 pull-thrus, a/c allowed, heater allowed, cable TV, phone hookups, handicap restroom facilities, laundry, public phone, tables, patios.

RECREATION: rec hall, rec room/area, swim pool (heated), whirlpool, planned group activities, horseshoes.

No tents. Open all year. CPO. Member of ARVC; CTPA. Phone: (619) 440-0040.

**SEE AD SAN DIEGO PAGE 10**

EL CAJON, CA—Continued

**OAK CREEK RV PARK**—Paved, terraced sites with mountain & canyon views. *E'bound: From jct I-8 & Lake Jennings Park Rd exit: Continue 2 1/2 mi straight ahead on Olde Hwy 80. W'bound: From jct I-8 & Harbison Cyn/Dunbar Ln exit: Go 1 1/2 mi W on Olde Hwy 80.*

FACILITIES: 120 sites, most common site width 25 feet, accepts full hookup units only, 120 full hookups, (30 & 50 amp receptacles), a/c allowed, heater allowed, cable TV ($), phone hookups, group sites for RVs, handicap restroom facilities, laundry, public phone, ice, tables, patios.

RECREATION: rec hall, swim pool (heated), whirlpool, planned group activities, horseshoes.

No tents. Open all year. Member of ARVC; CTPA. Phone: (619) 390-7132.

**SEE AD SAN DIEGO PAGE 9**

**RANCHO LOS COCHES RV PARK**—Historic Spanish ranch and ancient Indian village site with level, gravel, landscaped sites. *From jct I-8 & Los Coches: Go 1/2 mi N on Los Coches, then 1/2 mi E on Business I-8.*

EL CAJON, CA—Continued

RANCHO LOS COCHES RV PARK—Continued

FACILITIES: 145 sites, most common site width 25 feet, 142 full hookups, 3 water & elec (20,30 & 50 amp receptacles), a/c allowed, heater allowed, cable TV, phone hookups, handicap restroom facilities, sewage disposal, laundry, public phone, RV supplies, tables, patios.

RECREATION: rec hall, equipped pavilion, swim pool (heated), whirlpool, horseshoes.

Open all year. CPO. Member of ARVC; CTPA. Phone: (619) 443-2025.

**SEE AD SAN DIEGO PAGE 9**

## EL CENTRO

**DESERT TRAILS RV PARK & COUNTRY CLUB**—Paved sites in a formal RV PARK surrounding a golf course, convenient to the Interstate. *From jct I-8 & 4th St: Go 1 block S on 4th St, then 700 feet E on Wake Ave.*

FACILITIES: 365 sites, most common site width 20 feet, 365 full hookups, (30 & 50 amp receptacles),

DESERT TRAILS RV PARK & COUNTRY CLUB—Continued on next page

EL CENTRO, CA—Continued on next page

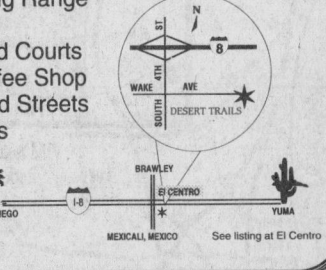

EL CENTRO, CA—Continued
DESERT TRAILS RV PARK & COUNTRY CLUB—Continued
71 pull-thrus, a/c allowed, heater allowed, cable TV, phone hookups, RV storage, handicap restroom facilities, laundry, public phone, tables, patios, church services.
RECREATION: rec hall, rec room/area, swim pool (heated), whirlpool, golf ($), driving range ($), putting green, 5 shuffleboard courts, planned group activities, recreation director, horseshoes, local tours. Recreation open to the public.
No tents. Open all year. Church services Jan through Mar only. Phone: (619) 352-7275.
SEE AD PAGE 3

CALIFORNIA—Continued

### ESCONDIDO

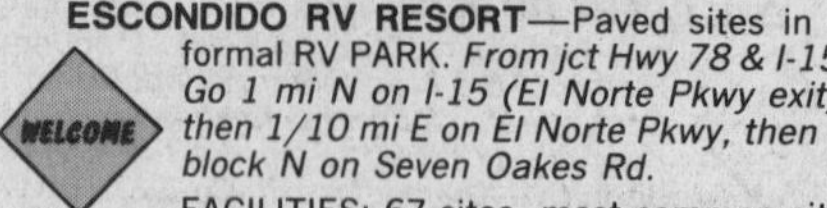

**ESCONDIDO RV RESORT**—Paved sites in a formal RV PARK. *From jct Hwy 78 & I-15: Go 1 mi N on I-15 (El Norte Pkwy exit), then 1/10 mi E on El Norte Pkwy, then 1 block N on Seven Oakes Rd.*
FACILITIES: 67 sites, most common site width 14 feet, 67 full hookups, (20,30 & 50 amp receptacles), a/c allowed, heater allowed, phone hookups, handicap restroom facilities, laundry, public phone, limited grocery store, RV supplies, LP gas refill by meter, ice, patios.
RECREATION: rec room/area, swim pool (heated), whirlpool.

ESCONDIDO, CA—Continued
ESCONDIDO RV RESORT—Continued
No tents. Open all year. Member of ARVC; CTPA. Phone: (619) 740-5000.
SEE AD THIS PAGE

### GRAEAGLE

**CLIO'S RIVERS EDGE TRAILER RESORT**—A riverside RV PARK in a mountainous region with pine shaded, level sites. Altitude 4300 ft. *From jct Hwy 70 & Hwy 89: Go 4 mi S on Hwy 89.*
FACILITIES: 222 sites, most common site width 32 feet, 222 full hookups, (30 amp receptacles), 25 pull-thrus, a/c allowed, heater not allowed, cable TV, group sites for RVs, laundry, public phone, patios, fire rings.
RECREATION: river fishing, badminton, horseshoes, volleyball.
No tents. Open Apr 15 through Oct 15. CPO. Phone: (916) 836-2375.
SEE AD THIS PAGE

### GROVELAND

**YOSEMITE PINES RV PARK**—Shaded, terraced RV PARK in the pines with level, gravel sites. Altitude 3000 ft. *From jct Hwy 108 & 120: Go 19 mi E on Hwy 120, then 1 mi E on Old Hwy 120.*
FACILITIES: 198 sites, most common site width 35 feet, 102 full hookups, 78 water & elec

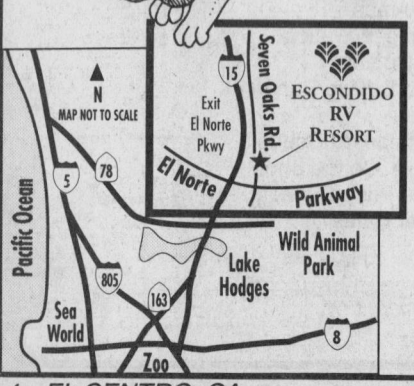

YOSEMITE PINES RV PARK—Continued on next page
GROVELAND, CA—Continued on next page

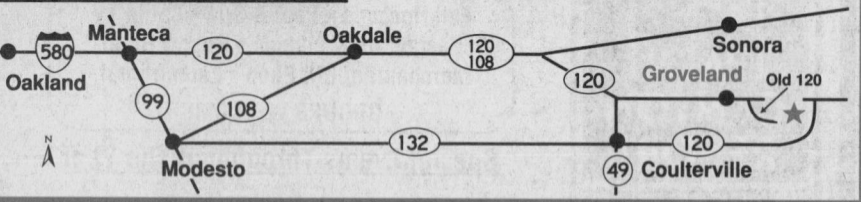

GROVELAND, CA—Continued
YOSEMITE PINES RV PARK—Continued

(20,30 & 50 amp receptacles), 18 no hookups, 60 pull-thrus, a/c allowed, heater allowed, cable TV ($), group sites for tents/RVs, RV storage, handicap restroom facilities, sewage disposal, laundry, public phone, grocery store, RV supplies, LP gas refill by meter, ice, tables, fire rings, grills, wood.

RECREATION: rec hall, swim pool (heated), basketball hoop, playground, planned group activities, horseshoes, volleyball.

Open all year. CPO. Phone: (209) 962-5042.

**SEE AD PAGE 4**

## HEMET

**GOLDEN VILLAGE RV RESORT**—Desert metro RV PARK with level open spaces. *From center of town (jct Hwy 74 & Hwy 79): Go 3 mi W on Hwy 74/Hwy 79.*

FACILITIES: 1041 sites, most common site width 35 feet, accepts full hookup units only, 1041 full hookups, (20 & 30 amp receptacles), 103 pull-thrus, a/c allowed, heater allowed, cable TV, phone hookups, handicap restroom facilities, laundry, public phone, ice, patios.

RECREATION: rec hall, rec room/area, 2 swim pools (heated), whirlpool, 8 shuffleboard courts, planned group activities, recreation director, badminton, horseshoes, volleyball, local tours.

No tents. Age restrictions may apply. Open all year. CPO. Member of ARVC; CTPA. Phone: (909) 925-2518.

**SEE AD THIS PAGE**

**MOUNTAIN VALLEY RV PARK**—RV PARK in metro area. *From center of town (jct Hwy 74 & Hwy 79): Go 1 3/4 mi W on Hwy 74/Hwy 79, then 1/8 mi S on Lyon.*

FACILITIES: 170 sites, most common site width 25 feet, 170 full hookups, (20,30 & 50 amp receptacles), a/c allowed, heater allowed, cable TV, phone hookups, handicap restroom facilities, laundry, public phone, ice, tables, patios, church services.

RECREATION: rec hall, equipped pavilion, swim pool (heated), whirlpool, 4 shuffleboard courts, planned group activities, movies, recreation director, horseshoes.

No tents. Open all year. Member of ARVC; CTPA. Phone: (909) 925-5812.

**SEE AD THIS PAGE**

## INDIO

**RANCHO CASA BLANCA**—A resort-oriented RV Park in a desert setting with a view of the mountains. *From I-10E (exit 111-86 Auto Center Dr): Go 1/2 mi N on Auto Center Dr, then 1 block E on Ave 44.*

FACILITIES: 200 sites, 200 full hookups, (30 & 50 amp receptacles), cable TV, phone hookups, handicap restroom facilities, laundry, public phone, ice, patios, traffic control gate/guard.

RECREATION: rec hall, rec room/area, 6 swim pools (heated), sauna, whirlpool, golf ($), putting green, shuffleboard court, planned group activities, movies, recreation director, 4 tennis courts, horseshoes.

No tents. Open all year. Minimum stay 2 nights. Minimum RV length 22 feet. Phone: (619) 347-1999.

**SEE AD PALM SPRINGS PAGE 7**

CALIFORNIA—Continued

## LOS ANGELES

*See listings at Acton, San Dimas & Valencia*

CALIFORNIA—Continued on next page

Stay With Woodall Advertised Campgrounds

**If you can't make a mistake, you can't make anything.**
***Marva Collins***

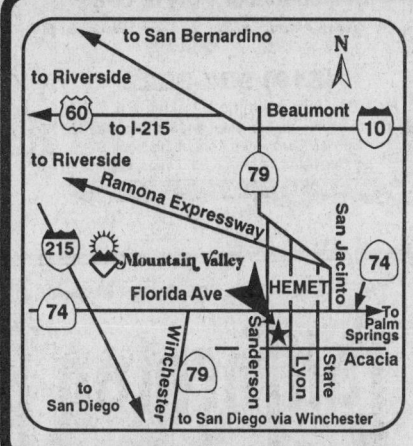

CALIFORNIA—Continued

## MAMMOTH LAKES

**MAMMOTH MOUNTAIN RV PARK**—Level sites among tall pines in the high Sierras. Altitude 7500 ft. *From jct US 395 & Hwy 203: Go 2 1/2 mi W on Hwy 203.*

WELCOME

FACILITIES: 164 sites, most common site width 20 feet, 20 full hookups, 132 water & elec (30 & 50 amp receptacles), 12 no hookups, a/c allowed, heater allowed, cable TV, group sites for tents, RV storage, handicap restroom facilities, sewage disposal, laundry, public phone, RV supplies, LP gas refill by meter, ice, tables, fire rings, grills.

RECREATION: rec hall, rec room/area, swim pool (indoor) (heated), whirlpool, 5 bike rentals, playground, hiking trails, cross country skiing, snowmobile trails.

Open all year. Water available on site Jun 1 through Oct 31. Member of ARVC;CTPA. Phone: (619) 934-3822.

SEE AD THIS PAGE

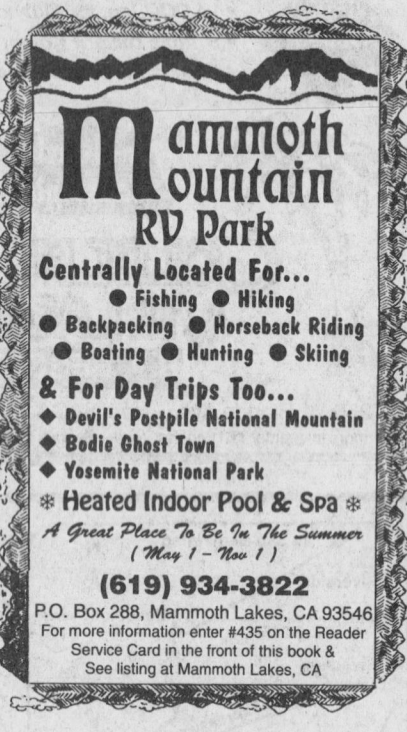

CALIFORNIA—Continued

## NEWPORT BEACH

**NEWPORT DUNES RESORT**—A scenic RV PARK on the bay with beach & active water sports. *From jct Hwy 55 & I-405: Go 1 3/4 mi SE on I-405, then 5 mi SW on Jamboree Rd, then 1 block W on Back Bay Dr. From jct Hwy 1 & Jamboree Rd: Go 1/4 mi NE on Jamboree Rd, then 1 block NW on Back Bay Dr.*

WELCOME

FACILITIES: 406 sites, most common site width 20 feet, 406 full hookups, (20,30 & 50 amp receptacles), a/c allowed, heater allowed, cable TV, RV storage, handicap restroom facilities, laundry, public phone, full service store, RV supplies, ice, tables, wood, traffic control gate/guard.

RECREATION: rec hall, rec room/area, pavilion, coin games, swim pool (heated), salt water swimming, whirlpool, boating, canoeing, ramp, dock, 5 sail/28 canoe/10 pedal/2 motor boat rentals, water skiing, salt water fishing, basketball hoop, 15 bike rentals, playground, planned group activities, movies, recreation director, horseshoes, hiking trails, volleyball. Recreation open to the public.

Open all year. Phone: (714) 729-3863.

SEE AD ANAHEIM PAGE 2

## OCEANSIDE

**PARADISE BY THE SEA RV PARK**—An RV PARK with paved parking and Ocean Beach access. *From jct I-5 & Hwy 78: Go 1/2 mi W on Vista Way, then 3/4 mi N on Hill St.*

WELCOME

FACILITIES: 102 sites, most common site width 25 feet, 102 full hookups, (20,30 & 50 amp receptacles), a/c allowed, heater allowed, cable TV, phone hookups, RV storage, sewage disposal,

PARADISE BY THE SEA RV PARK—Continued on next page
OCEANSIDE, CA—Continued on next page

OCEANSIDE, CA—Continued
PARADISE BY THE SEA RV PARK—Continued
laundry, public phone, limited grocery store, RV supplies, ice, tables, patios.

RECREATION: rec room/area, coin games, swim pool (heated), whirlpool.

No tents. Open all year. Member of ARVC;CTPA. Phone: (619) 439-1376.

**SEE AD PAGE 6**

## PALM DESERT

WELCOME

**EMERALD DESERT COUNTRY CLUB**—Formal RV PARK & golf course in a desert setting with mountain views. *From jct I-10 & Monterey Ave exit: Go 2 1/4 mi S on Monterey Ave, then 3 mi E on Frank Sinatra Dr.*

FACILITIES: 360 sites, most common site width 30 feet, accepts full hookup units only, 360 full hookups, (20,30 & 50 amp receptacles), a/c allowed, heater allowed, cable TV, phone hookups, cabins, RV storage, handicap restroom facilities, sewage disposal, laundry, public phone, limited grocery store, RV supplies, ice, patios, grills, traffic control gate.

RECREATION: rec hall, rec room/area, 2 swim pools (heated), whirlpool, golf ($), putting green, shuffleboard court, planned group activities, recreation director, 2 tennis courts, horseshoes, local tours.

No tents. Age restrictions may apply. Open all year. Planned group activities Nov through Mar. Member of ARVC; CTPA. Phone: (800) 426-4678.

**SEE AD PALM SPRINGS THIS PAGE**

## PALM SPRINGS

***See listings at Indio and Palm Desert***

## PLYMOUTH

WELCOME

**FAR HORIZONS 49ER TRAILER VILLAGE**—An RV PARK in rolling, historic area with formally developed, open sites. *From jct Hwy 16 & Hwy 49: Go 2 mi N on Hwy 49.*

FACILITIES: 329 sites, most common site width 33 feet, 329 full hookups, (20,30 & 50 amp receptacles), 16 pull-thrus, a/c allowed, heater allowed, cable TV, group sites for RVs, RV rentals, RV storage, sewage disposal, laundry, public phone, grocery store, RV supplies, LP gas refill by meter, ice, tables, patios.

RECREATION: rec hall, rec room/area, 2 swim pools (indoor) (heated), whirlpool, pond fishing, playground, 3 shuffleboard courts, planned group activities, movies, recreation director, badminton, horseshoes, volleyball, local tours.

No tents. Open all year. CPO. Member of ARVC; CTPA. Phone: (209) 245-6981.

**SEE AD THIS PAGE**

CALIFORNIA—Continued

## POMONA

WELCOME

**FAIRPLEX RV PARK**—Formal landscaped park on Los Angeles County Fairgrounds. *E'bound from jct Hwy 71 (Corona Expwy) & I-10: Go 2 1/2 mi NE on I-10, then 1 1/2 mi N on White Ave. W'bound from jct Hwy 83 & I-10: Go 5 1/2 mi W on I-10, then 1 block SW on Orange Grove Ave, then 1/2 mi NW on McKinley Ave, then 1 mi N on White Ave.*

◆◆◆◆ FACILITIES: 264 sites, most common site width 20 feet, 238 full hookups, 26 water & elec (30 & 50 amp receptacles), 177 pull-thrus, a/c allowed, heater allowed, phone hookups, group sites for RVs, handicap restroom facilities, sewage disposal, laundry, public phone, grocery store, RV supplies, ice, tables, guard.

◆◆RECREATION: rec room/area, swim pool (heated), whirlpool, movies, horseshoes.

No tents. Open all year. CPO. Member of ARVC; CTPA. Phone: (909) 593-8915.

**SEE AD NEXT PAGE**

CALIFORNIA—Continued on page 9

**Let our friendly, helpful guest service staff make your vacation convenient and enjoyable.**

# FAIRPLEX RV PARK

**2200 North White Avenue, Pomona, CA 91768**

**ADJACENT TO L.A. COUNTY FAIRGROUNDS & SHERATON SUITES FAIRPLEX HOTEL IN SUNNY CALIFORNIA**

## Facilities & Services

- Clubhouse
- Fully stocked market
- 24-hour roving security service
- Heated swimming pool & spa
- 24-hour laundry
- Hot showers
- Paved roads and parking
- Over 200 pull-thru or back-in sites
- Full hookups
- 50-30-20 amps
- Handicap parking
- Accommodates large RVs
- Grassy sites
- Large deck area
- Horseshoe pit
- Shuffleboard
- Pool tables & video games
- Video rentals
- 2 dump stations
- Weekly & monthly rates available

*We're easy to get to ... hard to leave.*

## Area Attractions

- Anaheim Stadium
- Disneyland
- Dodger Stadium
- Knotts Berry Farm
- Magic Mountain
- Winery Tours
- Art Galleries
- Movieland Wax Museum
- Raging Waters Theme Park
- Mountain Meadows Golf Course
- Satellite Wagering at Fairplex Park
- Universal City Studios
- Hot Air Balloon Flights
- Many Area Musuems
- Fishing, in area, Lakes & Streams
- Tennis courts & Bowling lanes Nearby
- Bike Trails
- Big Bear Lake & Lake Arrowhead
- Skiing & Snow Activities within 1 Hr Drive
- Warm, Sunny Beaches
- LA County Fair every Sept.

**09) 865-4318 • (909) 593-8915**

CALIFORNIA—Continued

## SALTON CITY

**SALTON CITY SPA & RV PARK**—A lakeview, desert RV AREA IN A MOBILE HOME PARK. *From jct Hwy 86 & South Marina Dr: Go 3 mi N & E on S Marina Dr, then 3/4 mi S on Sea View Dr.*

WELCOME

FACILITIES: 318 sites, 318 full hookups, (30 & 50 amp receptacles), 140 pull-thrus, a/c allowed, heater allowed, RV rentals, RV storage, handicap restroom facilities, laundry, public phone, ice, tables, patios, fire rings, grills.

RECREATION: rec hall, rec room/area, coin games, swim pool (heated), whirlpool, boating, salt water fishing, 75 bike rentals, 2 shuffleboard courts, planned group activities, tennis court, horseshoes, motorbike trails, volleyball.

Open all year. Phone: (619) 394-4333.

**SEE AD THIS PAGE**

## SAN DIEGO

**CAMPLAND ON THE BAY**—A scenic CAMPGROUND on the waterfront with prepared sites. *Southbound: From jct I-5 & Hwy 274 (Balboa-Garnet exit): Go 1/2 mi S on Mission Bay Dr. then 1 mi W on Grand Ave, then 1/4 mi S on Olney St.*

WELCOME

NEAR SAN DIEGO ATTRACTIONS

**Santee Lakes**

**Regional Park & Campground**

**Only 18 miles east of Downtown & close to beaches, mountains, deserts**

**NEW REC CENTER WITH KITCHEN**

**Over 190 Acres of Parkland**
- 152 Full Hookups
- Swimming • General Store
- Boating • Fishing

Daily - Weekly - Monthly Rates

**(619) 448-2482**

**TDD (619) 562-3477**

9040 Carlton Oaks Dr.
PO Box 719003 - Santee, CA 92072

For more information, enter #807 on the Reader Service Card in the front of this book and see listing at Santee

**Owned & Operated by**
**Padre Dam Municipal Water District**

SAN DIEGO, CA—Continued

CAMPLAND ON THE BAY—Continued

*Northbound: From jct I-5 & Garnet-Grand Ave: Go 1 mi W on Grand Ave, then 1/4 mi S on Olney St.*

FACILITIES: 702 sites, most common site width 20 feet, 528 full hookups, 40 water & elec (20 & 30 amp receptacles), 134 no hookups, 20 pull-thrus, a/c allowed, heater allowed, cable TV, phone hookups, group sites for tents/RVs, RV storage, sewage disposal, laundry, public phone, full service store, RV supplies, LP gas refill by meter, ice, tables, fire rings, grills, wood, church services, traffic control gate/guard.

RECREATION: rec hall, rec room/area, coin games, 2 swim pools (heated), salt water swimming, whirlpool, boating, canoeing, ramp, dock, 8 row/25 sail/8 canoe/16 pedal/1 motor boat rentals, water skiing, salt water fishing, 25 bike rentals, playground, planned group activities, movies, recreation director, sports field, horseshoes, volleyball, local tours. Recreation open to the public.

Open all year. Member of ARVC; CTPA. Phone: (800) 4-BAY-FUN.

**SEE ADS THIS PAGE**

SAN DIEGO, CA—Continued on next page

**Salton City**
**Spa & RV Park**

- Full Hook-ups
- Swimming Pool
- Large Clubhouse
- 20'x40' Heated Outdoor Spa
- Shaded Park
- Library
- Shuffleboard
- Sidewinder Golf Course
- Shower and Restroom Facilities
- Pool Room & Card Room
- Group Fire Ring
- Horseshoe Pit
- Brown Bag Bingo
- Weekly Dances

Boating
Water Skiing
Jet Skiing

**(619) 394-4333**
P.O. Box 5375
Salton City, CA 92274

See listing at Salton City

Good Sampark

**RESERVATIONS: (800) 365-1274**
**INFORMATION: (619) 390-7132**

**Close to metropolitan SAN DIEGO, we offer a quiet, country-like setting for resort-quality RV living.**

**See our ad at San Diego**

**For more information enter #800 on the reader service card in the front of the book**

**RANCHO LOS COCHES RV PARK**

Groups Welcome

***"Tucked away in an East San Diego County valley, nearly invisible from the road, is one of the neatest, most comfortable and most historic RV parks in Southern California."***

Walt Miller, RV Travel Writer
San Diego Tribune, April 1990

Good Sampark

**Pool • Spa • Clubhouse • Cable TV • Chapel**

**13468 Hwy 8 Business, Lakeside, CA 92040** (Olde Hwy 80)

**(619) 443-2025**

For more information enter #799 on the Reader Service Card

*Bievenidos! (Welcome)*

**In the quiet, laid back sector of San Diego... just 20 miles east, off I-8**

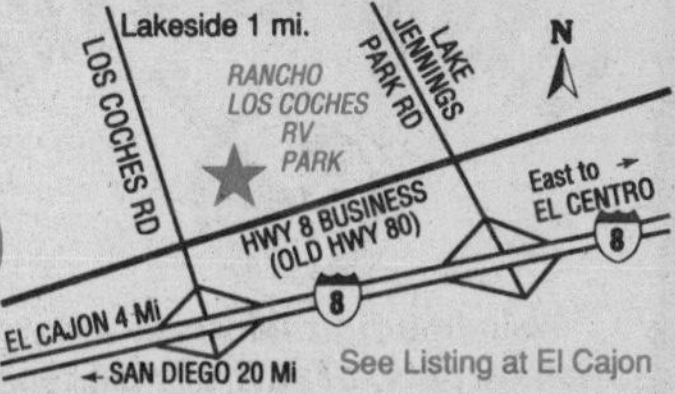


See Listing at El Cajon

*-- Before deciding, check the ratings --*

# FRIENDLY IS BACK!

BEACHFRONT Camping!
Recreational Activities!
Over 700 Sites!
Tents Welcome!
Boat & Bike Rentals!
Water Toy Rentals!

**Campland On the Bay**

2211 Pacific Beach Drive
San Diego, CA 92109

**1-800-4BAY FUN**
(1-800-422-9386)

**When in San Diego...**

**Every Site Comes with a Beach, a Bay and... A WHALE OF A GOOD TIME!**

**ASK ABOUT OUR SPECIAL SEA WORLD OFFER!**

**Campland On the Bay...**

The Family Wildlife!

Beach Front Camping
Recreational Activities
Boat & Bike Rentals
Water Toy Rentals
Boat Launch & Fishing

**1-800-4BAY FUN**

De Anza Bay Resort
SAN DIEGO ™

**De Anza Harbor Resort**

...Ahh, the Quiet Life!

Level Sites with Full Hook-ups
Relaxing Atmosphere
Golf Course Access
Horseshoe Pits

**1-800-942-PLAY**
(in California only)

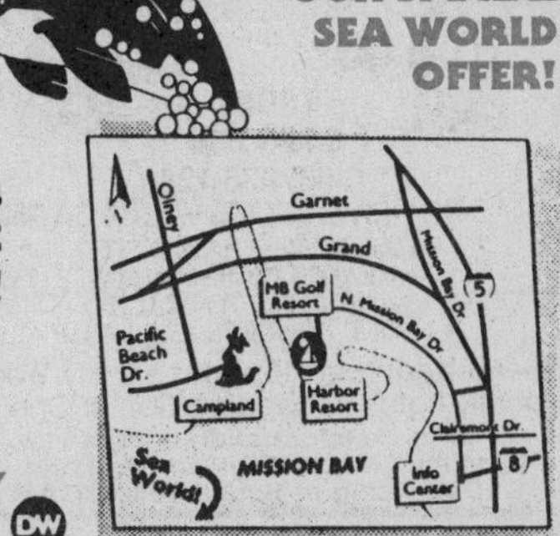

**DE ANZA HARBOR RESORT**—Waterfront scenic RV PARK with paved sites & sandy beach area. *From jct I-5 & Clairemont Dr: Go 1 block W on Clairemont Dr, then 1 mi N on N Mission Bay Dr, then 100 ft S on De Anza Dr.*

FACILITIES: 262 sites, most common site width 25 feet, 243 full hookups, (20 & 30 amp receptacles), 19 no hookups, a/c allowed, heater allowed, phone hookups, RV storage, handicap restroom facilities, sewage disposal, laundry, public phone, limited grocery store, LP gas refill by meter, ice, tables, grills, church services.

RECREATION: rec hall, salt water swimming, boating, ramp, salt water fishing, 20 bike rentals, playground, 2 shuffleboard courts, planned group activities, movies, recreation director, badminton, horseshoes, volleyball.

No tents. Open all year. Member of ARVC;CTPA. Phone: (619) 273-3211.

**SEE ADS PAGE 9**

## SAN DIMAS

**EAST SHORE RV PARK**—Scenic view; spacious, grassy sites with paved pads. *From jct I-210 & I-10: Go 1 1/2 mi E on I-10, then 1/2 mi NE on Fairplex Dr, then 3/4 mi NW on Via Verde (the Frank G Bonelli Regional County Park entrance road), then 1/2 mi NE on Camper View Rd (follow Bonelli Park signs).*







FACILITIES: 545 sites, 520 full hookups, (20,30 & 50 amp receptacles), 25 no hookups, 14 pull-thrus, a/c allowed, heater allowed, cable TV, phone hookups, group sites for tents/RVs, RV storage, handicap restroom facilities, sewage disposal, laundry, public phone, full service store, RV supplies, LP gas refill by meter, ice, tables, patios, fire rings, wood, guard.

RECREATION: rec hall, rec room/area, coin games, 2 swim pools, lake fishing, basketball hoop, playground, movies, horseshoes, hiking trails, volleyball.

Open all year. Member of ARVC; CTPA. Phone: (909) 599-8355.

**SEE AD LOS ANGELES PAGE 5**

## SANTA CRUZ

*See listing at Scotts Valley*

## SANTA PAULA

**MOUNTAIN VIEW RV PARK**—In town RV AREA in a mobile home park with paved sites in a rural citrus valley. *From jct US 101 & Hwy 126: Go 11 mi E on Hwy 126 (Peck Rd exit), then 1/4 mi N on Peck Rd, then 2 blocks E on Harvard Blvd.*

FACILITIES: 31 sites, most common site width 22 feet, accepts full hookup units only, 31 full hookups, (20 & 30 amp receptacles), 18 pull-thrus, a/c allowed, heater allowed, cable TV, public phone, patios.

RECREATION: whirlpool.

No tents. Open all year. Member of ARVC;CTPA. Phone: (805) 933-1942.

**SEE AD VENTURA NEXT PAGE**

## SANTEE

**SANTEE LAKES REGIONAL PARK & CAMPGROUND**—*From jct I-8 & Hwy 67: Go 2 mi N on Hwy 67 (Mission Gorge-Santee exit), then 50 feet W on Prospect, then 1/2 mi N on Magnolia, then 1 1/2 mi W on Mission Gorge, then 1/2 mi N on Carlton Hills Blvd, then 1/2 mi W on Carlton Oaks Dr.*

FACILITIES: 213 sites, 152 full hookups, (30 amp receptacles), 61 no hookups, 23 pull-thrus, a/c allowed, heater allowed, RV storage, handicap restroom facilities, sewage disposal, laundry, public phone, limited grocery store, RV supplies, LP gas refill by meter, ice, tables, patios, grills, traffic control gate/guard.

RECREATION: rec hall, swim pool, 10 row/8 canoe/25 pedal boat rentals, lake fishing ($), playground, horseshoes, volleyball. Recreation open to the public.

Open all year. Rental boats available weekends & holidays only. Pool closed in winter. No refunds. CPO. Member of ARVC; CTPA. Phone: (619) 448-2482.

**SEE AD SAN DIEGO PAGE 9**

**The California Condor can reach lengths of 55 inches.**



## SCOTTS VALLEY

**CARBONERO CREEK TRAVEL TRAILER PARK**—RV PARK convenient to a major highway with formal level sites. *From jct Hwy 1 & Hwy 17: Go 3 1/4 mi N on Hwy 17, then 3/4 mi W on Mt. Hermon Rd, then 3/4 mi N on Scotts Valley Dr to Disc Dr.*

FACILITIES: 114 sites, most common site width 22 feet, 104 full hookups, 10 water & elec (20 & 30 amp receptacles), 27 pull-thrus, a/c allowed, heater allowed, cable TV, phone hookups, laundry, public phone, LP gas refill by meter, ice, tables, patios.

RECREATION: rec room/area, swim pool (heated), whirlpool.

Open all year. Pool open Apr 1 to Dec 1. Member of ARVC: CTPA. Phone: (800) 546-1288.

**SEE AD SANTA CRUZ THIS PAGE**

## SOUTH LAKE TAHOE

**TAHOE VALLEY CAMPGROUND**—Level, shaded, natural sites in a pine wooded area near town. Altitude 6300 ft. *From north jct Hwy 89 & US 50: Go 1/4 mi SW on US 50.*

FACILITIES: 413 sites, most common site width 20 feet, 300 full hookups, 33 water & elec (15,20,30 & 50 amp receptacles), 80 no hookups, 40 pull-thrus, a/c allowed, heater allowed, cable TV ($), group sites for tents/RVs, RV storage, sewage disposal, laundry, public phone, full service store, RV supplies, LP gas refill by meter, ice, tables, grills, wood, guard.

RECREATION: rec hall, rec room/area, equipped pavilion, coin games, swim pool (heated), river swimming, river fishing, basketball hoop, playground, tennis court, badminton, horseshoes, hiking trails, volleyball, local tours.

Open Apr 15 through Oct 15. CPO. Member of ARVC;CTPA. Phone: (916) 541-2222.

**SEE AD THIS PAGE**

## TULARE

**SUN & FUN RV PARK**—Paved, landscaped sites in an RV PARK near a town & shopping. *From jct Hwy 137 & Hwy 99: Go 3 mi S on Hwy 99, then 1 block W on Ave 200.*

FACILITIES: 56 sites, most common site width 15 feet, 56 full hookups, (30 & 50 amp receptacles), a/c allowed, heater allowed, cable TV, phone hookups, handicap restroom facilities, sewage disposal, laundry, public phone, RV supplies, tables, patios, grills.

RECREATION: rec hall, swim pool, whirlpool, playground.

No tents. Open all year. Member of ARVC;CTPA. Phone: (209) 686-5779.

**SEE AD THIS PAGE**

## TWENTYNINE PALMS

**29 PALMS RV RESORT**—Formal RV PARK adjacent to golf course in a desert setting. *From the center of town at jct Adobe Rd & Hwy 62: Go 1 mi E on Hwy 62, then 2 mi N on Utah Trail Rd, then 1/2 mi W on Amboy Rd, then 1/2 block N on Desert Knoll Ave.*

FACILITIES: 197 sites, most common site width 25 feet, 197 full hookups, (30 & 50 amp receptacles), a/c allowed, heater allowed, phone hookups, RV storage, handicap restroom facilities, laundry, public phone, LP gas refill by meter, patios.

29 PALMS RV RESORT—Continued on next page
TWENTYNINE PALMS, CA—Continued on next page

**TWENTYNINE PALMS, CA—Continued**
**29 PALMS RV RESORT—Continued**

RECREATION: rec hall, rec room/area, swim pool (indoor) (heated), sauna, whirlpool, basketball hoop, 2 shuffleboard courts, planned group activities, tennis court, horseshoes.

Open all year. Member of ARVC; CTPA. Phone: (800) 874-4548.

**SEE AD THIS PAGE**

### VALENCIA

**VALENCIA TRAVEL VILLAGE**—Shaded, grassy sites in an active CAMPGROUND in the foothills. *From jct I-5 & Hwy 126: Go 1 1/2 mi W on Hwy 126.*

WELCOME

FACILITIES: 460 sites, 238 full hookups, 20 water & elec (20 & 30 amp receptacles), 202 no hookups, 150 pull-thrus, a/c allowed, heater allowed, cable TV, phone hookups, group sites for tents/RVs, RV storage, handicap restroom facilities, sewage disposal, laundry, public phone, full service store, RV supplies, LP gas refill by meter, ice, tables, patios, fire rings, grills, wood.

RECREATION: rec hall, rec room/area, coin games, 2 swim pools (heated), wading pool, whirlpool, basketball hoop, playground, 2 shuffleboard courts, planned group activities (weekends only), recreation director, tennis court, badminton, horseshoes, volleyball.

Open all year. CPO. Member of ARVC; CTPA. Phone: (805) 257-3333.

**SEE AD LOS ANGELES PAGE 6**

### VENTURA

***See listing at Santa Paula***

## COLORADO

### ALAMOSA

**NAVAJO TRAIL CAMPGROUND**—Open sites in an RV PARK convenient to a major highway. Altitude 7500 ft. *From jct US 285 & US 160: Go 1 1/2 mi W on US 285/US 160.*

WELCOME

FACILITIES: 46 sites, most common site width 18 feet, 46 full hookups, (20 & 30 amp receptacles), 20 pull-thrus, a/c allowed, heater allowed, phone hookups, handicap restroom facilities, laundry, public phone, limited grocery store, RV supplies, LP gas refill by weight/by meter, ice, tables, grills.

RECREATION: mini-golf ($), playground, horseshoes.

Open Apr 1 through Nov 1. Member of CACCL. Phone: (719) 589-9460.

**SEE AD THIS PAGE**

### ANTONITO

**CONEJOS RIVER CAMPGROUND**—CAMPGROUND with open & shaded sites in scenic setting near the foothills and overlooking the Conejos River. Altitude 8400 ft. *From jct US 285 & Hwy 17: Go 12 1/2 mi W on Hwy 17.*

WELCOME

FACILITIES: 58 sites, most common site width 25 feet, 30 full hookups, 28 water & elec (20,30 & 50 amp receptacles), 58 pull-thrus, a/c allowed ($), heater allowed ($), group sites for tents, cabins, RV storage, sewage disposal, laundry, limited grocery store, ice, tables, fire rings, grills, wood.

RECREATION: rec hall, rec room/area, coin games, swim pool (heated), whirlpool, mini-golf, basketball

**ANTONITO, CA—Continued**
**CONEJOS RIVER CAMPGROUND—Continued**

hoop, playground, badminton, sports field, horseshoes, hiking trails, volleyball.

Open May 15 through Nov 15. Member of CACCL. Phone: (719) 376-5943.

**SEE AD THIS PAGE**

### COLORADO SPRINGS

**GARDEN OF THE GODS CAMPGROUND**—Semi-wooded, family-oriented in metro area with planned activities. Altitude 6000 ft. *From jct I-25 (exit 141) & US 24: Go 2 1/2 mi W on US 24, then 1 block N on 31st St, then 6 blocks W on Colorado Ave to corner of Columbia & Colorado.*

FACILITIES: 300 sites, most common site width 16 feet, 200 full hookups, 50 water & elec (20,30 & 50 amp receptacles), 50 no hookups, a/c allowed, heater allowed, group sites for tents/RVs, cabins, handicap restroom facilities, sewage disposal, laundry, public phone, grocery store, RV supplies, LP gas refill by weight/by meter, ice, tables, patios, fire rings, grills, wood, guard.

GARDEN OF THE GODS CAMPGROUND—Continued on next page
**COLORADO SPRINGS, CO—Continued on next page**

**SAFETY TIP**
**Fires can create their own wind. Practice fire safety while camping. Before starting a fire, clean a 10-foot circle clear of forest debris.**

COLORADO SPRINGS, CO—Continued
GARDEN OF THE GODS CAMPGROUND—Continued

RECREATION: rec hall, rec room/area, pavilion, coin games, swim pool (heated), whirlpool, float trips, playground, planned group activities, horse riding trails, horse rental, local tours.

Open Apr 15 through Oct 15. Member of ARVC. Phone: (800) 248-9451.

SEE AD PAGE 11

## DURANGO

**ALPEN-ROSE RV PARK**—An RV PARK with level, grassy, shaded sites in a beautiful mountain setting. Altitude 6500 ft. *From West jct US 160/550: Go 6 1/2 mi N on US 550.*

FACILITIES: 110 sites, most common site width 28 feet, 100 full hookups, 10 water & elec (30 & 50 amp receptacles), 76 pull-thrus, a/c allowed, heater allowed, cable TV, group sites for tents/RVs, RV storage, handicap restroom facilities, sewage disposal, laundry, public phone, limited grocery store, RV supplies, ice, tables, grills.

RECREATION: rec hall, rec room/area, coin games, swim pool (heated), pond fishing ($), basketball hoop, playground, planned group activities, recreation director, badminton, sports field, horseshoes, volleyball, local tours.

Open Apr 15 through Oct 15. Member of CACCL. Phone: (970) 247-5540.

SEE AD THIS PAGE



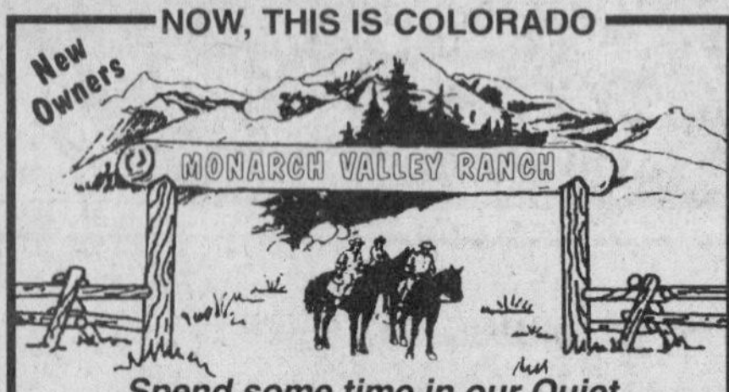

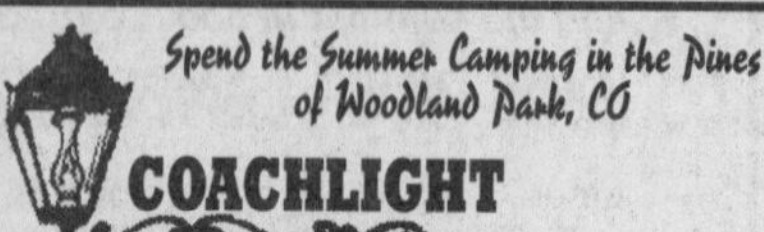




COLORADO—Continued

## GUNNISON

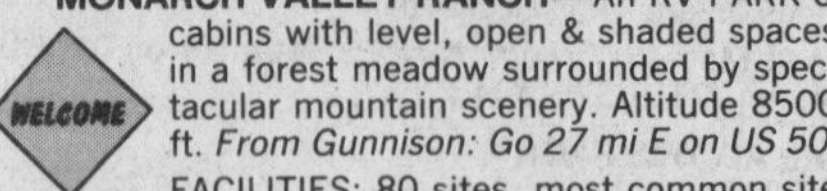

**MONARCH VALLEY RANCH**—An RV PARK & cabins with level, open & shaded spaces in a forest meadow surrounded by spectacular mountain scenery. Altitude 8500 ft. *From Gunnison: Go 27 mi E on US 50.*

FACILITIES: 80 sites, most common site width 40 feet, 65 full hookups, (20,30 & 50 amp receptacles), 15 no hookups, 65 pull-thrus, a/c allowed, heater allowed, group sites for tents/RVs, cabins, RV storage, sewage disposal, laundry, public phone, limited grocery store, RV supplies, LP gas refill by weight/by meter, ice, tables, grills.

RECREATION: rec room/area, coin games, lake swimming, whirlpool, lake/stream fishing, basketball hoop, playground, horse riding trails, horse rental, sports field, horseshoes, hiking trails, volleyball, cross country skiing, snowmobile trails. Recreation open to the public.

Open all year. Limited facilities in winter. Member of CACCL. Phone: (800) 869-9455.

SEE AD THIS PAGE

**MONARCH VALLEY STABLES**—*From Gunnison: Go 27 mi E on US 50.* Horseback riding featuring 1-hr through full day rental. Open May 1 through Nov 15. Master Card/Visa accepted. Phone: (800) 869-9455.

SEE AD THIS PAGE

**MONARCH VALLEY TROUT FISHING**—*From Gunnison: Go 27 mi E on US 50.* Trout fishing in a stocked lake or stream. Only state license required. Restaurant on site. Open May 1 through Nov 15. Master Card/Visa accepted. Phone: (800) 869-9455.

SEE AD THIS PAGE

## MEEKER

**STAGECOACH CAMPGROUND & LODGING**—Grassy, shaded sites in a CAMPGROUND on the White River. Altitude 6200 ft. *At jct Hwy 13 & Hwy 64.*

FACILITIES: 49 sites, most common site width 24 feet, 17 full hookups, 22 water & elec (20,30 & 50 amp receptacles), 10 no hookups, 20 pull-thrus, a/c allowed, heater allowed, phone hookups, group sites for tents/RVs, cabins, RV storage, sewage disposal, laundry, ice, tables, fire rings, wood.

RECREATION: river fishing, basketball hoop, horseshoes, volleyball.

Open all year. Facilities fully operational Apr 1 through Nov 30. Member of CACCL. Phone: (970) 878-4334.

SEE AD THIS PAGE

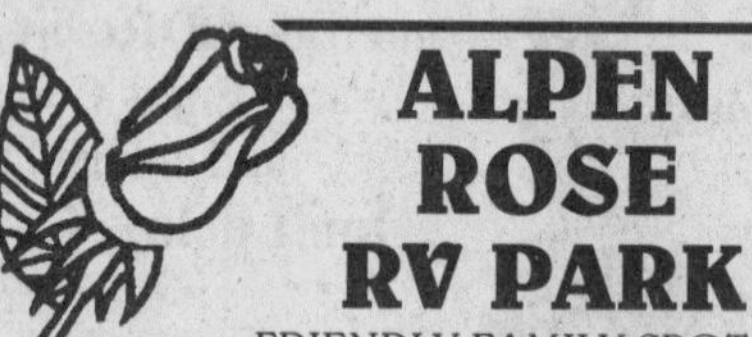





## SOUTH FORK

**RIVERSEDGE RV RESORT**—An RV PARK with pond sites or sites along the Rio Grande river. Altitude 8200 ft. *From jct Hwy 149 & US 160: Go 1 mi E on US 160.*

FACILITIES: 65 sites, most common site width 30 feet, 55 full hookups, 10 water & elec (20,30 & 50 amp receptacles), 7 pull-thrus, a/c allowed ($), heater allowed ($), group sites for tents, laundry, public phone, ice, tables, fire rings, wood.

RECREATION: rec hall, boating, 1 row/1 pedal boat rentals, river/pond fishing, fishing guides, planned group activities, recreation director, horseshoes, hiking trails.

Open all year. Phone: (719) 873-5993.

SEE AD THIS PAGE

**UTE BLUFF LODGE RV PARK**—Level RV SPACES beside a lodge. Altitude 8100 ft. *From jct Hwy 149 & US 160: Go 2 1/2 mi E on US 160.*

FACILITIES: 45 sites, most common site width 16 feet, 45 full hookups, (30 amp receptacles), 14 pull-thrus, a/c allowed, heater allowed ($), cable TV, phone hookups, cabins, sewage disposal, laundry, public phone, ice, tables, fire rings, grills.

RECREATION: rec room/area, whirlpool, basketball hoop, badminton, horseshoes, hiking trails, volleyball, snowmobile trails, local tours.

No tents. Open May 1 through Oct 1. Member of CACCL. Phone: (719) 873-5595.

SEE AD THIS PAGE

## WOODLAND PARK

**COACHLIGHT RV PARK & MOTEL**—Terraced, shaded sites in an RV PARK with moutainviews. Altitude 8400 ft. *From jct US 67 & US 24: Go 1 mi E on US 24.*

FACILITIES: 62 sites, most common site width 28 feet, 44 full hookups, (15,30 & 50 amp receptacles), 24 no hookups, a/c allowed, heater allowed ($), phone hookups, group sites for tents/RVs, RV rentals, sewage disposal, laundry, public phone, RV supplies, ice, tables, patios, fire rings, grills, wood.

RECREATION: horseshoes, hiking trails.

Open all year. Phone: (719) 687-8732.

SEE AD COLORADO SPRINGS THIS PAGE

**DIAMOND CAMPGROUND & RV PARK**—Wooded CAMPGROUND in moutainous area. Altitude 8500 ft. *From jct US 24 & Hwy 67: Go 3/4 mi N on Hwy 67.*

FACILITIES: 150 sites, most common site width 30 feet, 124 full hookups, 12 water & elec, 6 elec (20,30 & 50 amp receptacles), 8 no hookups, 30 pull-thrus, a/c allowed ($), heater allowed ($), group sites for RVs, RV rentals, sewage disposal, laundry, public phone, RV supplies, ice, tables, fire rings, grills, wood.

RECREATION: rec hall, playground, horseshoes, local tours.

Open May 10 through Oct 1. Member of CACCL. Phone: (719) 687-9684.

SEE AD COLORADO SPRINGS PAGE 11

# CONNECTICUT

## MYSTIC

*See listing at Preston City*

## PRESTON CITY

**STRAWBERRY PARK RESORT CAMPGROUND**—Level CAMPGROUND with shaded and open sites. *From jct Hwy 164 & Hwy 165: Go 1 mi E on Hwy 165, then 1/2 mi N on Pierce Rd.*

WELCOME

FACILITIES: 430 sites, most common site width 40 feet, 160 full hookups, 270 water & elec (20,30 & 50 amp receptacles), a/c allowed ($), heater allowed ($), cable TV, phone hookups, group sites for tents/RVs, RV rentals, RV storage, handicap restroom facilities, sewage disposal, laundry, public phone, full service store, RV supplies, LP gas refill by weight/by meter, ice, tables, fire rings, grills, wood, traffic control gate/guard.

RECREATION: rec hall, rec room/area, equipped pavilion, coin games, 3 swim pools, wading pool, sauna, whirlpool, basketball hoop, playground, 3 shuffleboard courts, planned group activities, movies, recreation director, horse riding trails, horse rental, badminton, sports field, horseshoes, hiking trails, volleyball, cross country skiing.

Open all year. Facilities fully operational Apr 1 through Oct 31. 3 day min. Holiday weekends. Weekend activities Labor Day thru Oct 31. No refunds. Member of ARVC; CCOA. Phone: (860) 886-1944.

**SEE AD MYSTIC THIS PAGE**

# FLORIDA

## BRADENTON

**SARASOTA BAY TRAVEL TRAILER PARK**—A grassy RV PARK with open, level sites with access to the Gulf. *From jct I-75 (exit 41) & Hwy 70: Go 12 mi W on Hwy 70/53rd Ave, then 3 mi W on Cortez Rd.*

WELCOME

FACILITIES: 240 sites, most common site width 25 feet, accepts full hookup units only, 240 full hookups, (20 & 30 amp receptacles), a/c allowed, heater not allowed, cable TV ($), phone hookups, RV rentals, sewage disposal, laundry, public phone, patios.

RECREATION: rec hall, rec room/area, boating, ramp, dock, salt water fishing, 4 shuffleboard courts, planned group activities, horseshoes.

No pets. No tents. Age restrictions may apply. Open all year. Planned activities winter only. Children welcome up to 2 weeks. Member of ARVC; FLARVC. Phone: (941) 794-1200.

**SEE AD THIS PAGE**

FLORIDA—Continued

## BUSHNELL

**SUMTER OAKS RV PARK**—RV PARK with shaded level sites. *From I-75 (exit 62) & Hwy 476B/673: Go 1 1/2 mi E on CR 673.*

WELCOME

FACILITIES: 124 sites, most common site width 35 feet, 124 full hookups, (20,30 & 50 amp receptacles), a/c allowed, heater allowed, phone hookups, handicap restroom facilities, laundry, public phone, grocery store, RV supplies, LP gas refill by weight/by meter, ice.

RECREATION: rec hall, rec room/area, swim pool (indoor) (heated), 2 shuffleboard courts, planned group activities, recreation director, horseshoes, volleyball.

Open all year. Planned activities winter only. Phone: (352) 793-1333.

**SEE AD THIS PAGE**

FLORIDA—Continued

## CLEARWATER

**TRAVEL TOWNE TRAVEL TRAILER RESORT**—RV PARK with grassy, semi-wooded sites. *From jct Hwy 60 & US 19: Go 5 mi N on US 19.*

WELCOME

FACILITIES: 360 sites, most common site width 25 feet, 360 full hookups, (20 & 30 amp receptacles), a/c allowed ($), heater not allowed, phone hookups, RV rentals, RV storage, sewage disposal, laundry, public phone, RV supplies, LP gas refill by weight/by meter, tables, patios, church services.

RECREATION: rec hall, swim pool (heated), playground, 10 shuffleboard courts, planned group activities, recreation director, horseshoes.

Open all year. Church & planned activities winter only. No refunds. Member of ARVC; FLARVC. Phone: (813) 784-2500.

**SEE AD THIS PAGE**

CLEARWATER, FL—Continued on next page

CLEARWATER, FL—Continued

**TRAVEL WORLD**—An RV PARK in town with open & grassy sites. *From jct I-275 & Hwy 688: Go 4 mi W on Hwy 688, then 1/2 mi S on S'bound frontage road (parallels US 19).*

FACILITIES: 340 sites, most common site width 28 feet, accepts full hookup units only, 340 full hookups, (20,30 & 50 amp receptacles), a/c allowed, heater allowed, phone hookups, laundry, public phone, LP gas refill by weight/by meter, ice, tables, patios.

RECREATION: rec hall, swim pool (heated), whirlpool, 12 shuffleboard courts, planned group activities, recreation director, horseshoes.

No tents. Age restrictions may apply. Open all year. No refunds. Phone: (813) 536-1765.

**SEE AD THIS PAGE**

## CRYSTAL RIVER

**QUAIL ROOST RV CAMPGROUND**—A CAMPGROUND with open sites. *From jct US 19 & Hwy 495 (N Citrus Ave): Go 7 1/2 mi NE on Hwy 495.*

FACILITIES: 40 sites, most common site width 30 feet, 40 full hookups, (30 amp receptacles), 27 pull-thrus, a/c allowed, heater allowed, phone hookups, RV storage, handicap restroom facilities, sewage disposal, laundry, public phone, tables.

RECREATION: rec room/area, equipped pavilion, planned group activities, horseshoes.

Open all year. Phone: (904) 563-0404.

**SEE AD THIS PAGE**

FLORIDA—Continued

## DADE CITY

**MANY MANSIONS RV PARK**—An RV PARK on rolling hills in a quiet, country location. *From jct US 301 & US 98: Go 3 mi SE on US 98 (Richland exit), then 1 mi S on Hwy 35A to Stewart Rd.*

FACILITIES: 233 sites, most common site width 20 feet, 233 full hookups, (20,30 & 50 amp receptacles), a/c allowed, heater allowed, phone hookups, RV rentals, RV storage, sewage disposal, laundry, public phone, LP gas refill by weight/by meter.

RECREATION: rec hall, 4 shuffleboard courts, planned group activities, horseshoes.

Age restrictions may apply. Open all year. Planned activities winter only. Children accepted for 2 weeks maximum stay. Phone: (800) 359-0135.

**SEE AD THIS PAGE**

## FORT MYERS

**ORANGE HARBOR MOBILE HOME & RV PARK**—RV AREA in a mobile home park. *From jct I-75 (exit 25) & Hwy 80E: Go 1/4 mi E on Hwy 80E.*

FACILITIES: 165 sites, accepts full hookup units only, 165 full hookups, (15 & 30 amp receptacles), a/c allowed, heater allowed, phone hookups, laundry, patios.

RECREATION: rec hall, rec room/area, swim pool (heated), boating, ramp, dock, salt water/river fishing, 9 shuffleboard courts, planned group activities, recreation director, local tours.

No pets. No tents. Age restrictions may apply. Open all year. Minimum 3 month stay. Phone: (941) 694-3707.

**SEE AD THIS PAGE**

FORT MYERS, FL—Continued

**UPRIVER CAMPGROUND**—An RV PARK with shady, grassy lots on the banks of Caloosahatchee River. *From jct I-75 (exit 26) & Hwy 78: Go 1 3/4 mi E on Hwy 78 (Bayshore Rd).*

FACILITIES: 296 sites, 296 full hookups, (20 & 30 amp receptacles), a/c allowed, heater allowed, cable TV, phone hookups, handicap restroom facilities, laundry, public phone, RV supplies, LP gas refill by weight/by meter, ice, tables, patios, church services.

RECREATION: rec hall, rec room/area, equipped pavilion, swim pool (heated), boating, ramp, dock, salt water/river fishing, golf, 6 shuffleboard courts, planned group activities, tennis court, horseshoes.

Age restrictions may apply Oct through Apr. Open all year. Group activities during winter season only. No refunds. Member of ARVC; FLARVC. Phone: (941) 543-3330.

**SEE AD THIS PAGE**

**WOODSMOKE CAMPING RESORT**—Quiet, secluded, wooded lakeside sites in an RV PARK. *From jct I-75 (exit 19) & Corkscrew Rd: Go 2 mi W on Corkscrew Rd, then 2 mi N on US 41.*

FACILITIES: 310 sites, most common site width 35 feet, 287 full hookups, 15 water & elec (20,30 & 50 amp receptacles), 8 no hookups, 15 pull-thrus, a/c allowed ($), heater not allowed, phone hookups, RV storage, handicap restroom facilities, sewage disposal, laundry, public phone, RV supplies, ice, tables, patios, church services.

RECREATION: rec hall, rec room/area, pavilion, coin games, swim pool (heated), whirlpool, boating, no motors, canoeing, 2 pedal boat rentals, lake fishing, playground, 5 shuffleboard courts, planned group activities, movies, recreation director, horseshoes, hiking trails, local tours.

WOODSMOKE CAMPING RESORT—Continued on next page
FORT MYERS, FL—Continued on next page

FORT MYERS, FL—Continued
WOODSMOKE CAMPING RESORT—Continued

Open all year. Planned group activities winter only. Member of ARVC; FLARVC. Phone: (941) 267-3456.

SEE AD THIS PAGE

## FORT PIERCE

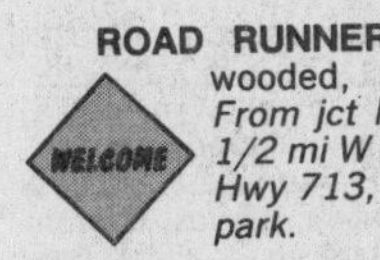


**ROAD RUNNER TRAVEL RESORT**—Semi-wooded, grassy, secluded RV PARK. *From jct I-95 (exit 66B) & Hwy 68: Go 1/2 mi W on Hwy 68, then 3 1/2 mi N on Hwy 713, then 1 1/4 mi E on CR 608 to park.*

FACILITIES: 450 sites, most common site width 20 feet, 450 full hookups, (20,30 & 50 amp receptacles), 25 pull-thrus, a/c allowed, heater allowed, phone hookups, RV rentals, RV storage, handicap restroom facilities, sewage disposal, laundry, public phone, full service store, RV supplies, LP gas refill by weight/by meter, ice, tables, patios, church services, traffic control gate.

RECREATION: rec hall, rec room/area, equipped pavilion, coin games, swim pool (heated), pond fishing, basketball hoop, 4 shuffleboard courts, planned group activities, recreation director, tennis court, badminton, horseshoes, volleyball, local tours.

Open all year. Member of ARVC; FLARVC. Phone: (800) 833-7108.

SEE AD THIS PAGE

## HAINES CITY

**CENTRAL PARK**—Open, rolling, grassy RV PARK. Most sites occupied by seasonal campers in winter. *From jct US 17 & 92 & US 27: Go 1/2 mi N on US 27, then 1/10 mi W on Commerce Ave.*

FACILITIES: 351 sites, most common site width 25 feet, 351 full hookups, (20 & 30 amp receptacles), 26 pull-thrus, a/c allowed ($), heater allowed ($), phone hookups, RV storage, sewage disposal, laundry, public phone, RV supplies, LP gas refill by weight, tables, patios, church services.

RECREATION: rec hall, swim pool (heated), pond fishing, 8 shuffleboard courts, planned group activities, movies, recreation director, horseshoes.

Open all year. Church services & most activities winter only. Phone: (941) 422-5322.

SEE AD THIS PAGE



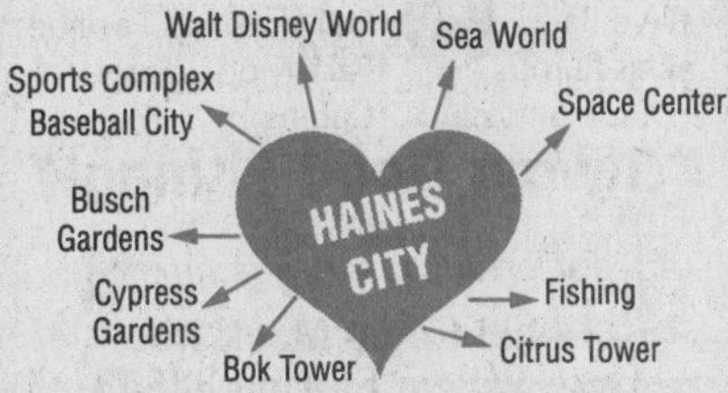




FLORIDA—Continued

**CENTRAL PARK II**—RV subdivision designed for park models. *From jct US 17 & 92 & US 27: Go 1/2 mi N on US 27, then 1 block W on Commerce Ave.*

FACILITIES: 129 sites, most common site width 35 feet, 129 full hookups, (30 & 50 amp receptacles), a/c allowed ($), heater allowed ($), phone hookups, laundry, public phone, LP gas refill by weight, tables.

RECREATION: rec hall, swim pool (heated), 4 shuffleboard courts, planned group activities, recreation director, horseshoes.

Age restrictions may apply. Open all year. Planned activities winter only. Phone: (941) 421-2622.

SEE AD THIS PAGE

## HOMESTEAD

**SOUTHERN COMFORT RV RESORT**—Grassy, semi-shaded CAMPGROUND convenient to a major highway. *From jct Hwy 27, US 1 & Southern Terminus of Florida Turnpike: Go 1 block E of US 1 on Palm Dr (344 St).*

FACILITIES: 356 sites, most common site width 26 feet, 350 full hookups, 6 water & elec (20,30 & 50 amp receptacles), 52 pull-thrus, a/c allowed, heater allowed, phone hookups, RV rentals, sewage disposal, laundry, public phone, limited grocery store, RV supplies, LP gas refill by weight/by meter, ice, tables, traffic control gate/guard.

HOMESTEAD, FL—Continued
SOUTHERN COMFORT RV RESORT—Continued

RECREATION: rec hall, equipped pavilion, swim pool (heated), 6 shuffleboard courts, planned group activities, movies, recreation director, horseshoes, local tours.

Open all year. No refunds. Member of ARVC; FLARVC. Phone: (305) 248-6909.

SEE AD THIS PAGE FLORIDA—Continued on next page

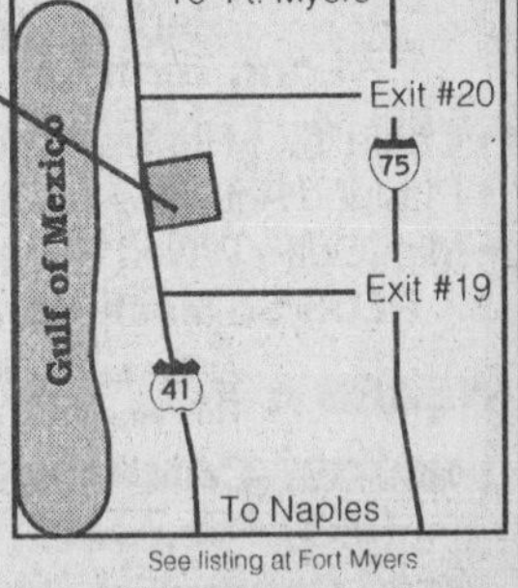

## LAKE BUENA VISTA

**YOGI BEAR'S JELLYSTONE PARK**—Lakeside, grassy CAMPGROUND. *From jct I-4 & US 192: Go 4 mi W on US 192.*

FACILITIES: 587 sites, most common site width 30 feet, 375 full hookups, 106 water & elec (20,30 & 50 amp receptacles), 106 no hookups, 150 pull-thrus, a/c allowed, heater allowed, phone hookups, group sites for tents, RV rentals, cabins, RV storage, handicap restroom facilities, sewage disposal, laundry, public phone, grocery store, RV supplies, LP gas refill by weight/by meter, ice, tables, church services.

RECREATION: rec hall, rec room/area, pavilion, coin games, swim pool (heated), wading pool, boating, ramp, dock, 3 row/4 canoe/12 pedal/motor boat

LAKE BUENA VISTA, FL—Continued
YOGI BEAR'S JELLYSTONE PARK—Continued

rentals, water skiing, lake fishing, mini-golf ($), basketball hoop, 50 bike rentals, playground, 4 shuffleboard courts, planned group activities, movies, recreation director, horseshoes, volleyball.

Open all year. Member of ARVC; FLARVC. Phone: (407) 239-4148.

**SEE AD ORLANDO NEXT PAGE**

## LAKE WALES

**CAMP MACK'S RIVER RESORT**—RV PARK next to a river. *From jct US 27 & Hwy 60: Go 9 mi E on Hwy 60, then 2 1/2 mi N on Boy Scout Rd, then 6 mi E on Camp Mack Rd.*

FACILITIES: 141 sites, most common site width 40 feet, 141 full hookups, (20,30 & 50 amp receptacles), 12 pull-thrus, a/c allowed, heater allowed, RV rentals, cabins, RV storage, public phone, limited grocery store, RV supplies, gasoline, marine gas, ice, tables.

RECREATION: lake/river fishing, fishing guides, driving range, planned group activities (weekends only), horseshoes.

Open all year. Phone: (941) 696-1108.

**SEE AD THIS PAGE**

## MOORE HAVEN

**MEADOWLARK CAMPGROUND** (NOT VISITED)—*From jct US 27 & Hwy 78: Go 8 mi W on Hwy 78, then S on CR 78A. Follow signs to park.*

FACILITIES: 155 sites, 155 full hookups.

Open all year. Phone: (941) 675-2243.

**SEE AD THIS PAGE**

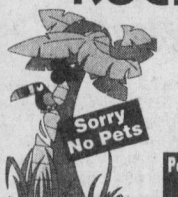



FLORIDA—Continued

## NAPLES

**NAPLES RV RESORT**—Level sites in an RV PARK resort adjacent to a major highway. *From jct I-75 (exit 15) & Hwy 951: Go 2/10 mi S on Hwy 951, then 1 mi E on Old Hwy 84 (Alligator Alley).*

FACILITIES: 314 sites, most common site width 33 feet, 314 full hookups, (30 & 50 amp receptacles), a/c allowed, heater not allowed, cable TV, phone hookups, sewage disposal, laundry, public phone, limited grocery store, RV supplies, LP gas refill by weight/by meter, ice, tables, patios, church services, traffic control gate/guard.

RECREATION: rec hall, swim pool (heated), whirlpool, mini-golf, basketball hoop, 6 shuffleboard courts, planned group activities, recreation director, badminton, horseshoes, volleyball.

No pets. No tents. Open all year. No refunds. Phone: (941) 455-7275.

**SEE AD THIS PAGE**

**ROCK CREEK CAMPGROUNDS**—AN RV PARK with level, grassy & semi-wooded spaces. *From jct US 41 & Hwy 84 (Davis Blvd): Go 1 1/2 mi NE on Hwy 84, then 1/2 mi N on Hwy 31 (Airport Rd).*

FACILITIES: 200 sites, most common site width 25 feet, 200 full hookups, (20,30 & 50 amp receptacles), 10 pull-thrus, a/c allowed, heater allowed, cable TV, phone hookups, RV storage, handicap restroom facilities, laundry, public phone, RV supplies, ice, tables, patios.

RECREATION: rec hall, rec room/area, pavilion, swim pool (heated), boating, canoeing, dock, salt water fishing, 2 shuffleboard courts, planned group activities, recreation director, horseshoes, local tours.

No pets. Age restrictions may apply. Open all year. Tents summer only. Children limited stay only. Group activities winter only. Member of ARVC; FLARVC. Phone: (941) 643-3100.

**SEE AD THIS PAGE**

## ORANGE CITY

**VILLAGE PARK LUXURY RV PARK**—Rolling terrain & wooded RV SPACES adjacent to 18 hole golf course. *From jct I-4 (exit 54): Go left at light.*

FACILITIES: 525 sites, most common site width 30 feet, accepts full hookup units only, 525 full hookups, (30 amp receptacles), a/c allowed, heater allowed, phone hookups, laundry, public phone, grocery store, RV supplies, LP gas refill by weight/by meter, ice.

RECREATION: rec hall, swim pool (heated), whirlpool, golf ($), mini-golf, 4 shuffleboard courts, planned group activities.

No tents. Open all year. Phone: (904) 775-2545.

**SEE AD THIS PAGE**

FLORIDA—Continued on next page

FLORIDA—Continued

## ORLANDO

**YOGI BEAR'S JELLYSTONE PARK**—Rustic, grassy, lakeside CAMPGROUND. *From jct Florida Tpk (exit 259) & I-4: Go 3 mi SW on I-4 (exit 29), then 1/10 mi W on Hwy 482, then 1 mi S on Turkey Lake Rd (north frontage road).*

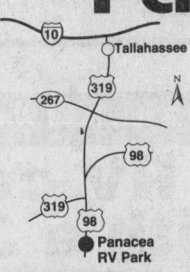

FACILITIES: 478 sites, most common site width 30 feet, 421 full hookups, 30 elec (20, 30 & 50 amp receptacles), 27 no hookups, 320 pull-thrus, a/c allowed, heater allowed, cable TV, phone hookups, group sites for tents/RVs, RV rentals, cabins, RV storage, handicap restroom facilities, sewage disposal, laundry, public phone, grocery store, RV supplies, LP gas refill by weight/by meter, ice, tables, patios.

RECREATION: rec hall, rec room/area, pavilion, coin games, swim pool (heated), wading pool, boating, ramp, dock, 2 row/8 canoe/5 pedal boat rentals, lake fishing, mini-golf ($), basketball hoop, 15 bike rentals, playground, 4 shuffleboard courts, planned group activities, movies, recreation director, horseshoes, volleyball.

Open all year. CPO. Member of ARVC; FLARVC. Phone: (407) 351-4394.

**SEE AD THIS PAGE**

## PANACEA

**PANACEA RV PARK**—CAMPGROUND with open & shaded sites. *From jct US 319 & US 98: Go 4 mi S on US 98.*

FACILITIES: 57 sites, most common site width 25 feet, 30 full hookups, 7 water & elec (30 & 50 amp receptacles), 20 no hookups, 5 pull-thrus, a/c allowed, heater allowed, phone hookups, group sites for tents, RV storage, handicap restroom facilities, sewage disposal, laundry, limited grocery store, RV supplies, LP gas refill by weight/by meter, ice, tables, fire rings.

RECREATION: rec hall, horseshoes.

Open all year. Phone: (904) 984-5883.

**SEE AD THIS PAGE**

## PUNTA GORDA

**KOA-PUNTA GORDA/CHARLOTTE HARBOR KAMPGROUND**—Campground with level sites surrounding lake. *From jct I-75 (exit 29) & US 17: Go 3/4 mi E on US 17, then right 1 mi on Golf Course Rd.*

FACILITIES: 131 sites, most common site width 28 feet, 125 full hookups, 6 elec (20,30 & 50 amp receptacles), 37 pull-thrus, a/c allowed, heater allowed, phone hookups, cabins, RV storage, handicap restroom facilities, laundry, public phone, grocery store, RV supplies, LP gas refill by weight/by meter, ice, tables, patios.

RECREATION: rec room/area, swim pool (heated), whirlpool, boating, electric motors only, 2 row/2 canoe/2 pedal boat rentals, lake fishing, playground, planned group activities, horseshoes, volleyball.

Open all year. Planned activities winter only. Member of ARVC; FLARVC. Phone: (800) KOA-4786.

**SEE AD THIS PAGE**

## ST. AUGUSTINE

**BRYN MAWR OCEAN RESORT**—CAMPGROUND with paved, landscaped spaces on the ocean beach. *From jct I-95 & Hwy 206: Go 7 mi E on Hwy 206, then 3 mi N on Hwy A1A.*

FACILITIES: 144 sites, most common site width 30 feet, accepts full hookup units only, 144 full hookups, (20 & 30 amp receptacles), 64 pull-thrus, a/c allowed, heater allowed, cable TV, phone hookups, group sites for RVs, RV rentals, RV storage, handicap restroom facilities, laundry, public phone, grocery store, RV supplies, LP gas refill by weight/by meter, ice, tables, patios, traffic control gate/guard.

RECREATION: rec hall, rec room/area, coin games, swim pool, salt water swimming, salt water fishing, basketball hoop, playground, 6 shuffleboard courts, planned group activities, movies, recreation director, 2 tennis courts, horseshoes, volleyball, local tours.

No tents. Open all year. CPO. Member of ARVC; FLARVC. Phone: (904) 471-3353.

**SEE AD THIS PAGE**

| FL | Highest Point is 345 ft. in Walton County | FL |
|---|---|---|

## ST. PETERSBURG

*See listing at Seminole*

## SEMINOLE

**HOLIDAY CAMPGROUND**—Semi-wooded grassy lots on the Bayou. *From jct I-275 (exit 15) & Hwy 694: Go 7 1/2 mi W on Hwy 694 (Gandy Blvd).*

WELCOME

FACILITIES: 723 sites, most common site width 25 feet, 580 full hookups, 113 water & elec (30 & 50 amp receptacles), 30 no hookups, a/c allowed, heater allowed, cable TV ($), phone hookups, group sites for RVs, RV storage, handicap restroom facilities, sewage disposal, laundry, public phone, limited grocery store, RV supplies, LP gas refill by weight/by meter, ice, tables, patios, church services, traffic control gate/guard.

RECREATION: rec hall, swim pool (heated), whirlpool, boating, ramp, dock, salt water fishing, basketball hoop, playground, 10 shuffleboard courts, planned group activities, recreation director, badminton, horseshoes, volleyball.

Open all year. Church & planned activities winter only. No refunds. Member of ARVC; FLARVC. Phone: (800) 354-7559.

**SEE AD ST. PETERSBURG THIS PAGE**

## TAMPA

**TAMPA EAST GREEN ACRES CAMPGROUND**—Quiet, level, grassy sites in suburban location. *From jct I-4 (exit 9) & McIntosh Rd: Go 1/4 mi S on McIntosh Rd, then 1/4 mi W on US 92.*

WELCOME

FACILITIES: 300 sites, most common site width 28 feet, 270 full hookups, 30 water & elec (20,30 & 50 amp receptacles), 50 pull-thrus, a/c allowed, phone hookups, group sites for tents/RVs, RV rentals, RV storage, sewage disposal, laundry, public phone, limited grocery store, RV supplies, LP gas refill by weight/by meter, ice, tables, patios, church services.

RECREATION: rec hall, rec room/area, swim pool (heated), pond fishing, playground, 8 shuffleboard courts, planned group activities, horseshoes, volleyball.

Open all year. Church winter only. CPO. Member of ARVC; FLARVC. Phone: (813) 659-0002.

**SEE AD THIS PAGE**

FL **State Flower: Orange Blossom** FL



**TAMPA EAST GREEN ACRES RV TRAVEL PARK**—RV PARK with level open and shaded sites. *From jct I-4 (exit 9) & McIntosh Rd: Go 1/10 mi S on McIntosh Rd.*

WELCOME

FACILITIES: 262 sites, most common site width 40 feet, 262 full hookups, (30 & 50 amp receptacles), 90 pull-thrus, a/c allowed, heater allowed, phone hookups, group sites for tents/RVs, RV storage, handicap restroom facilities, sewage disposal, laundry, public phone, limited grocery store, RV supplies, LP gas refill by weight/by meter, ice, tables, church services.

RECREATION: rec hall, swim pool (heated), pond fishing, basketball hoop, playground, 2 shuffleboard courts, planned group activities, horseshoes, volleyball.

Open all year. Church & planned activities winter only. CPO. Member of ARVC;FLARVC. Phone: (813) 659-0002.

**SEE AD THIS PAGE**

## WAUCHULA

**CRYSTAL LAKE VILLAGE** (NOT VISITED)—Semi-wooded RV PARK. *From jct Hwy 62 & US 17: Go 1/4 mi S on US 17.*

WELCOME

FACILITIES: 361 sites, 35 ft. max RV length, accepts full hookup units only, 361 full hookups, (30 & 50 amp receptacles), a/c allowed, heater allowed, phone hookups, RV storage, laundry, public phone, LP gas refill by weight, patios, church services.

RECREATION: rec hall, rec room/area, swim pool (heated), whirlpool, 6 shuffleboard courts, planned group activities, recreation director, horseshoes.

Open all year. Church & planned activities winter only. Phone: (941) 773-3582.

**SEE AD THIS PAGE**

FLORIDA—Continued on next page

FLORIDA—Continued

### ZEPHYRHILLS

**EMERALD POINTE RV RESORT** (UNDER CONSTRUCTION)—*From jct Hwy 54 & US 301: Go 7/10 mi S on US 301, then 4/10 mi E on Chancey Rd.*

WELCOME

Phone: (800) 315-1556.

**SEE AD THIS PAGE**

## GEORGIA

### BAXLEY

**DEEN'S RV PARK**—Large, shaded, level sites on a knoll overlooking the Altamaha River. For self-contained or full hookup units only. *From jct US 341 & US 1: Go 11 mi N on US 1, then 1 mi W on River Rd, then 1 mi N on Deen's Landing Rd.*

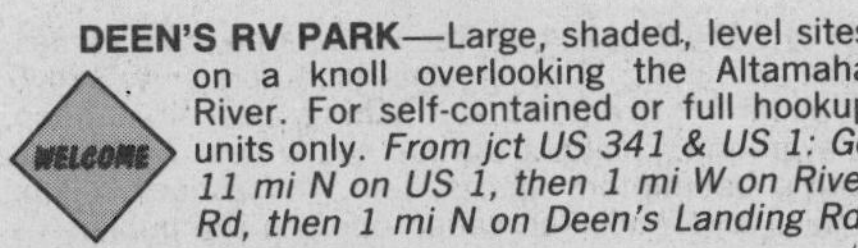

WELCOME

FACILITIES: 25 sites, most common site width 30 feet, accepts full hookup units only, 23 full hookups, 2 water & elec (15,20 & 30 amp receptacles), a/c allowed ($), heater allowed ($), phone hookups, tables.

RECREATION: boating, canoeing, ramp, water skiing, river fishing, playground, hiking trails.

No tents. Open all year. Phone: (912) 367-2949.

**SEE AD THIS PAGE**

### BLAIRSVILLE

**LAKE NOTTELY RV PARK**—Shaded, gravel, level sites on a wooded hillside overlooking a large lake. *From jct US 76/US 19/129: Go 2.2 mi W on US 76, then 1 1/10 mi N on Kiutuestia Creek Rd.*

WELCOME

FACILITIES: 75 sites, 75 full hookups, (20,30 & 50 amp receptacles), 3 pull-thrus, a/c allowed ($), heater allowed ($), phone hookups, group sites for RVs, laundry, tables.

RECREATION: equipped pavilion, lake swimming, boating, canoeing, ramp, dock, water skiing, lake fishing.

Age restrictions may apply. Open Apr 15 through Dec 15. Phone: (706) 745-4523.

**SEE AD THIS PAGE**

### HELEN

**CHEROKEE CAMPGROUND**—Level sites in a clearing in wooded hills. *From jct Hwy 75 & Chattahooche St in center of town (at Welcome Center): Go 1 mi W on Hwy 75, then 5 mi NE on HWy 356.*

WELCOME

FACILITIES: 58 sites, most common site width 35 feet, 47 full hookups, (20 & 30 amp receptacles), 11 no hookups, a/c allowed, heater allowed, phone hookups, group sites for tents/RVs, RV rentals, RV storage, handicap restroom facilities, laundry, public phone, ice, tables, fire rings, grills, wood.

RECREATION: pavilion, stream fishing, planned group activities (weekends only), horseshoes.

Open all year. Phone: (706) 878-CAMP.

**SEE AD THIS PAGE**

GEORGIA—Continued on next page

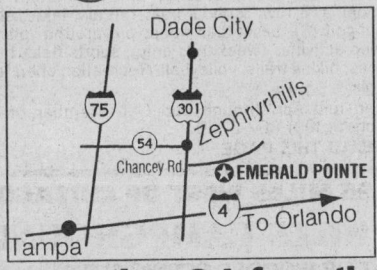

**Find a Campground Woodall's Does Not List? Tell Us About It!**

## PINE MOUNTAIN

**PINE MOUNTAIN CAMPGROUND**—Rolling, grassy CAMPGROUND with open & shaded sites. *From jct US 27 & Hwy 18: Go 1 mi N on US 27.*

FACILITIES: 158 sites, most common site width 30 feet, 41 full hookups, 117 water & elec (20,30 & 50 amp receptacles), 48 pull-thrus, a/c allowed ($), heater allowed, phone hookups, group sites for tents/RVs, RV storage, handicap restroom facilities, sewage disposal, laundry, public phone, limited grocery store, RV supplies, LP gas refill by weight/by meter, tables, fire rings, wood.

RECREATION: rec hall, pavilion, equipped pavilion, swim pool, whirlpool, pond fishing, basketball hoop, playground, badminton, sports field, horseshoes, volleyball.

Open all year. Member of ARVC. Phone: (706) 663-4329.

**SEE AD THIS PAGE**

## THOMASVILLE

**SUGAR MILL PLANTATION RV PARK**—CAMPGROUND with shaded, level sites in rural, wooded area. *From north jct US 84 & US 19: Go 7 mi N on US 19, then 500 feet W on McMillan Rd.*

FACILITIES: 43 sites, most common site width 35 feet, accepts full hookup units only, 43 full hookups, (20,30 & 50 amp receptacles), 22 pull-thrus, a/c allowed, heater allowed, phone hookups, group sites for RVs, cabins, RV storage, sewage dis-

posal, laundry, public phone, LP gas refill by weight/by meter, ice, tables, church services.

RECREATION: rec hall, boating, electric motors only, canoeing, 1 row boat rentals, pond fishing, basketball hoop, 2 shuffleboard courts, sports field, horseshoes, hiking trails.

No tents. Open all year. Phone: (912) 227-1451.

**SEE AD THIS PAGE**

## UNADILLA

**SOUTH PRONG CREEK CAMPGROUND & RV PARK**—Large, open and some shaded, grassy sites in a rural setting. *From jct I-75 (exit 40) & Hwy 230: Go 8 mi E on Hwy 230.*

FACILITIES: 100 sites, most common site width 25 feet, 2 full hookups, 65 water & elec (20 amp receptacles), 33 no hookups, a/c allowed ($), heater allowed ($), phone hookups, RV storage, handicap restroom facilities, sewage disposal, LP gas refill by weight/by meter, ice, tables, fire rings, grills, wood, church services.

RECREATION: rec room/area, pavilion, pond fishing, sports field, hiking trails.

Open all year. Phone: (800) BAR-BKUE.

**SEE AD THIS PAGE**

# ILLINOIS

## ALPHA

**SHADY LAKES CAMPGROUND**—A rural location with open & shaded sites. *From jct I-74 (exit 32) & Hwy 17: Go 2 mi W on Hwy 17, then 1/2 mi S on Hwy 150, then 4 mi W on Oxford Rd.*

FACILITIES: 290 sites, most common site width 30 feet, 250 full hookups, (20 & 30 amp receptacles), 40 no hookups, a/c allowed ($), heater allowed ($), group sites for tents/RVs, RV rentals, RV storage, sewage disposal, laundry, public phone, limited grocery store, RV supplies, LP gas refill by weight, ice, tables, wood.

RECREATION: rec hall, pavilion, coin games, swim pool, wading pool, boating, electric motors only, canoeing, 3 row/5 pedal boat rentals, lake fishing, mini-golf ($), basketball hoop, playground, planned group activities (weekends only), sports field, horseshoes, hiking trails, volleyball. Recreation open to the public.

Open mid Apr through mid Oct. Member of ICA. Phone: (309) 667-2709.

**SEE AD THIS PAGE**



## AMBOY

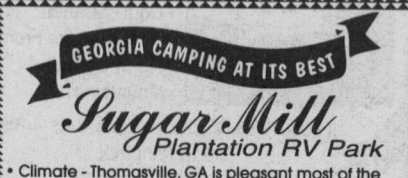

**MENDOTA HILLS CAMPGROUND**—Rolling grassy CAMPGROUND; some lakeside sites, some in the woods. *From jct US 30 & US 52: Go 6 1/2 mi S on US 52.*

FACILITIES: 250 sites, most common site width 28 feet, 100 full hookups, 100 water & elec (20 & 30 amp receptacles), 50 no hookups, 40 pull-thrus, a/c allowed ($), heater allowed ($), phone hookups, group sites for tents/RVs, RV rentals, RV storage, sewage disposal, laundry, public phone, limited grocery store, RV supplies, ice, tables, wood, church services.

RECREATION: rec hall, rec room/area, coin games, lake swimming, boating, electric motors only, 3 row/3 pedal boat rentals, lake fishing, basketball hoop, playground, planned group activities (weekends only), badminton, sports field, horseshoes, hiking trails, volleyball. Recreation open to the public.

Open all year. Facilities fully operational mid Apr through mid Oct. CPO. Member of ARVC; ICA. Phone: (815) 849-5930.

**SEE AD THIS PAGE**

## CHICAGO

*See listing at Yorkville*

## YORKVILLE

**HIDE-A-WAY LAKES**—A grassy CAMPGROUND with open or shaded sites beside a river. *From jct Hwy 34 & Hwy 47: Go 1 1/4 mi S on Hwy 47, then 2 mi E on Van Emmons St.*

FACILITIES: 1000 sites, most common site width 40 feet, 600 full hookups, 250 water & elec (20 & 30 amp receptacles), 150 no hookups, 80 pull-thrus, a/c allowed ($), heater allowed ($), group sites for tents/RVs, RV rentals, RV storage, sewage disposal, laundry, public phone, limited grocery store, RV supplies, LP gas refill by weight/by meter, ice, tables, fire rings, wood, church services.

RECREATION: rec hall, rec room/area, coin games, lake swimming, boating, 5 hp limit, canoeing, 6 canoe/4 pedal boat rentals, float trips, lake/river/pond fishing, basketball hoop, playground, planned group activities (weekends only), movies, badminton, sports field, horseshoes, hiking trails, volleyball, snowmobile trails.

Open all year. Facilities fully operational Mar 15 through Nov 15. Phone: (708) 553-6323.

**SEE AD CHICAGO THIS PAGE**

# INDIANA

## GREENFIELD

**MOHAWK CAMPGROUND & RV PARK**—Grassy, shaded sites in secluded rural area. *From jct I-70 & Hwy 9: Go 1/2 mi N on Hwy 9, then 1 1/4 mi W on CR 300 N, then 1 mi N on Fortville Rd, then 1/2 mi W on CR 375 N.*

FACILITIES: 129 sites, most common site width 30 feet, 13 full hookups, 66 water & elec (15,20 & 30 amp receptacles), 50 no hookups, 16 pull-thrus, a/c allowed ($), heater allowed ($), group sites for tents, RV rentals, RV storage, sewage disposal, laundry, public phone, tables, fire rings, wood.

RECREATION: swim pool, pond fishing, playground, badminton, sports field, horseshoes.

Open all year. Facilities fully operational Apr 1 through Oct 31. No refunds. Phone: (317) 326-3393.

**SEE AD INDIANAPOLIS THIS PAGE**

## HANNA

**LAST RESORT CAMPGROUND**—Open CAMPGROUND with grassy sites. *From jct US 30 & CR 1300 S: Go 1 mi N & W on CR 1300 S.*

FACILITIES: 91 sites, most common site width 35 feet, 47 full hookups, 38 water & elec (20 & 30 amp receptacles), 6 no hookups, 12 pull-thrus, a/c allowed ($), heater allowed ($), group sites for tents/RVs, sewage disposal, laundry, public phone, limited grocery store, RV supplies, LP gas refill by weight/by meter, ice, tables, fire rings, wood, church services.

RECREATION: rec room/area, coin games, swim pool (heated), boating, 1 row/2 pedal boat rentals, pond fishing, basketball hoop, 6 bike rentals, playground, planned group activities (weekends only), movies, badminton, sports field, horseshoes, volleyball. Recreation open to the public.

Age restrictions may apply. Open Apr 1 through Nov 1. Facilities fully operational Memorial Day through Labor Day. Phone: (219) 797-CAMP.

**SEE AD THIS PAGE**

## INDIANAPOLIS

***See listing at Greenfield***

## NASHVILLE

**KOA-BROWN COUNTY/NASHVILLE**—Hilltop CAMPGROUND with open or shaded sites. *From jct I-65 (Exit 68) & Hwy 46: Go 14 mi W on Hwy 46 (2 1/2 mi E of Nashville).*

FACILITIES: 143 sites, most common site width 35 feet, 73 full hookups, 70 water & elec (20 & 30 amp receptacles), 18 pull-thrus, a/c allowed ($), heater allowed ($), cable TV ($), group sites for tents/RVs, cabins, sewage disposal, laundry, public phone, grocery store, RV supplies, LP gas refill by weight/by meter, ice, tables, patios, fire rings, wood.

RECREATION: rec hall, rec room/area, pavilion, coin games, swim pool, basketball hoop, playground, planned group activities (weekends only), horseshoes, hiking trails.

Open Apr 1 through Nov 1. Member of ARVC. Phone: (812) 988-4475.

**SEE AD THIS PAGE**

## NEW CARLISLE

**MINI MOUNTAIN CAMPGROUND**—Open and shaded sites in a rolling, rural area. *From jct W Bypass US 31 & Hwy 2: Go 8 mi W on Hwy 2.*

FACILITIES: 184 sites, most common site width 28 feet, 115 full hookups, 49 water & elec (20 & 30 amp receptacles), 20 no hookups, 2 pull-thrus, a/c allowed ($), heater allowed ($), phone hookups, group sites for tents/RVs, RV rentals, sewage disposal, laundry, public phone, limited grocery store, RV supplies, LP gas refill by weight/by meter, ice, tables, patios, fire rings, wood.

RECREATION: rec room/area, coin games, swim pool (heated), pond fishing, mini-golf ($), basketball hoop, playground, planned group activities (weekends only), movies, badminton, sports field, horseshoes, hiking trails, volleyball. Recreation open to the public.

Open all year. Facilities fully operational Apr 1 through Nov 1. Member of ARVC; ICOA. Phone: (219) 654-3307.

**SEE AD SOUTH BEND NEXT PAGE**

## ORLAND

**MANAPOGO PARK**—Wooded, lakeside CAMPGROUND with grassy sites. *From jct Hwy 327 & Hwy 120: Go 3 1/4 mi E on Hwy 120, then 3/4 mi N on CR 650 W, then 1 mi E on CR 760 N.*

FACILITIES: 300 sites, most common site width 50 feet, 182 full hookups, 118 water & elec (20 & 30 amp receptacles), a/c allowed ($), heater allowed, group sites for tents/RVs, sewage disposal, laundry, public phone, grocery store, RV supplies, LP gas refill by weight, gasoline, ice, tables, fire rings, wood, church services, traffic control gate.

RECREATION: rec hall, rec room/area, coin games, lake swimming, boating, canoeing, ramp, dock, 4 row/2 canoe/1 pedal boat rentals, water skiing, lake fishing, basketball hoop, playground, 2 shuffleboard courts, planned group activities (weekends only), sports field, horseshoes, volleyball.

Open Apr 19 through Oct 13. Member of ARVC. Phone: (219) 833-3902.

**SEE AD THIS PAGE**

## PLYMOUTH

**YOGI BEAR'S JELLYSTONE PARK CAMP RESORT**—A CAMPGROUND in a semi-wooded area. Many additional sites are privately-owned. *From jct Hwy 17 & US 30: Go 4 mi W on US 30.*

FACILITIES: 160 sites, most common site width 40 feet, 160 full hookups, (20 & 30 amp receptacles), 2 pull-thrus, a/c allowed, heater allowed, group sites for tents, RV rentals, handicap restroom facilities, sewage disposal, laundry, public phone, grocery store, RV supplies, LP gas refill by weight/by meter, ice, tables, patios, fire rings, wood, church services, traffic control gate/guard.

RECREATION: rec hall, rec room/area, equipped pavilion, coin games, 2 swim pools, wading pool, lake swimming, whirlpool, dock, 4 pedal boat rentals, lake fishing, mini-golf ($), basketball hoop, playground, 2 shuffleboard courts, planned group activities, movies, recreation director, tennis court, badminton, sports field, horseshoes, volleyball. Recreation open to the public.

Open May 1 through Oct 1. Member of ARVC;IMHA. Phone: (219) 936-7851.

**SEE AD THIS PAGE**

INDIANA—Continued on next page

INDIANA—Continued

### ST. PAUL

**HIDDEN PARADISE CAMPGROUND**—Riverside, grassy, open & shaded sites. *From jct I-74 (Middletown-St Paul exit 123) & County Line Rd (800E): Go 2 mi S on County Line Rd, then 5 blocks SE on Jefferson St (cross river bridge).*

FACILITIES: 168 sites, most common site width 34 feet, 30 full hookups, 138 water & elec (20 & 30 amp receptacles), 53 pull-thrus, a/c allowed ($), heater allowed ($), phone hookups, group sites for tents/RVs, cabins, RV storage, sewage disposal, public phone, limited grocery store, RV supplies, LP gas refill by weight, ice, tables, fire rings, grills, wood, church services.

RECREATION: rec hall, rec room/area, equipped pavilion, coin games, river swimming, boating, canoeing, 3 canoe/6 pedal boat rentals, float trips, river fishing, basketball hoop, playground, planned group activities (weekends only), badminton, sports field, horseshoes, hiking trails, volleyball.

Open all year. Member of ARVC; IMHA. Phone: (317) 525-6582.

**SEE AD THIS PAGE**

INDIANA—Continued

### SOUTH BEND

*See listing at New Carlisle*

# KENTUCKY

### AURORA

**LAKEWOOD RESORT**—A wooded resort CAMPGROUND with open or shaded sites. Most sites occupied by seasonals. *From jct US 68 & Hwy 80: Go 2 3/4 mi NW on US 68, then follow signs 1/4 mi E.*

FACILITIES: 100 sites, most common site width 25 feet, 88 full hookups, 2 water & elec (15,20 & 30 amp receptacles), 10 no hookups, 10 pull-thrus, a/c allowed ($), heater allowed ($), cabins, sewage disposal, laundry, public phone, grocery store, RV supplies, ice, tables, patios, wood.

RECREATION: rec room/area, swim pool, boating, ramp, dock, 3 row/3 motor boat rentals, lake fishing, basketball hoop, playground, volleyball.

Open Mar 1 through Nov 1. Phone: (502) 354-9122.

**SEE AD THIS PAGE**

# LOUISIANA

### BATON ROUGE

**KOA-BATON ROUGE EAST**—A semi-wooded CAMPGROUND with concrete pads on sites. *From jct US 61 & I-12: Go 6 1/2 mi E on I-12 (exit 10), then 1/2 mi S on Hwy 3002, then 1/2 mi W on Hwy 1034.*

FACILITIES: 125 sites, most common site width 35 feet, 72 full hookups, 46 water & elec (20,30 & 50 amp receptacles), 7 no hookups, 59 pull-thrus, a/c allowed ($), heater allowed ($), cabins, handicap restroom facilities, sewage disposal, laundry, public phone, grocery store, RV supplies, LP gas refill by weight/by meter, ice, tables, patios, wood.

RECREATION: rec room/area, pavilion, coin games, swim pool, wading pool, whirlpool, basketball hoop, playground, horseshoes, local tours. Recreation open to the public.

Open all year. Pool open Apr 15 through Oct 1. Member of LCOA. Phone: (504) 664-7281.

**SEE AD THIS PAGE**

LOUISIANA—Continued

### HAMMOND

**KOA-NEW ORLEANS/HAMMOND**—An open, shaded, CAMPGROUND. Vehicles park on asphalt pads. *From jct I-12 & I-55: Go 1 mi S on I-55, then 1/2 mi N on US 51, then 3/4 mi W on asphalt road.*

FACILITIES: 59 sites, most common site width 20 feet, 44 full hookups, 15 water & elec (20,30 & 50 amp receptacles), 49 pull-thrus, a/c allowed ($), heater allowed ($), group sites for tents, cabins, RV storage, sewage disposal, laundry, public phone, grocery store, RV supplies, LP gas refill by weight/by meter, ice, tables, grills.

RECREATION: rec hall, coin games, swim pool, boating, electric motors only, 2 pedal boat rentals, lake fishing, basketball hoop, horseshoes, volleyball, local tours. Recreation open to the public.

Open all year. Pool open Apr 1-Sep 30. Member of LCOA. Phone: (504) 542-8094.

**SEE AD THIS PAGE**

**YOGI BEAR'S JELLYSTONE NEW ORLEANS-HAMMOND**—CAMPGROUND with open & wooded spaces in rural area. *From jct I-55 & I-12: Go 10 mi E on I-12, then 3 mi N on Hwy 445.*

FACILITIES: 316 sites, most common site width 35 feet, 169 full hookups, 147 water & elec (20 & 30 amp receptacles), 60 pull-thrus, a/c allowed, heater allowed, group sites for tents/RVs, cabins, RV storage, handicap restroom facilities, sewage disposal, laundry, public phone, grocery store, RV supplies, LP gas refill by weight/by meter, ice, tables, patios, fire rings, grills, wood, church services, traffic control gate.

RECREATION: rec hall, rec room/area, pavilion, coin games, 3 swim pools, wading pool, whirlpool, boating, no motors, canoeing, dock, 28 canoe/12 pedal boat rentals, lake fishing, mini-golf ($), basketball hoop, playground, 2 shuffleboard courts, planned group activities, movies, recreation director, sports field, horseshoes, hiking trails, volleyball, local tours. Recreation open to the public.

Open all year. Facilities fully operational Mar 15 through Nov 30. No refunds. Member of ARVC; LCOA. Phone: (504) 542-1507.

**SEE AD THIS PAGE**

LOUISIANA—Continued on next page



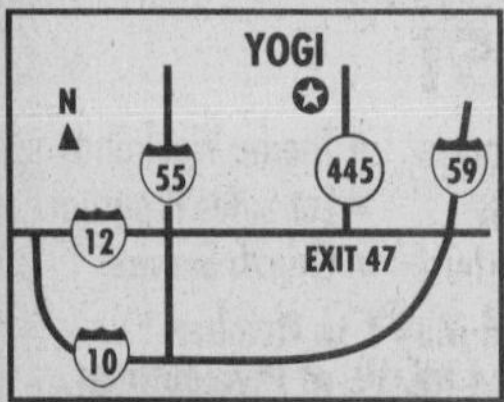

### KENTWOOD

**GREAT DISCOVERY CAMPGROUNDS**—Shaded and open grassy sites in a rural setting by a mobile home retirement village. *From jct I-55 (exit 61) & Hwy 38: Go 2 3/4 mi W on Hwy 38.*

FACILITIES: 48 sites, most common site width 40 feet, 16 full hookups, 32 water & elec (30 amp receptacles), 20 pull-thrus, a/c allowed, heater allowed, group sites for tents/RVs, cabins, handicap restroom facilities, sewage disposal, limited grocery store, RV supplies, tables, wood.

RECREATION: rec hall, pavilion, lake/pond fishing, badminton, sports field, horseshoes, hiking trails, volleyball.

Open all year. Member of LCOA. Phone: (504) 229-7194.

**SEE AD THIS PAGE**

### LAKE CHARLES

*See listing at Vinton*

### VINTON

**KOA-VINTON/LAKE CHARLES**—CAMPGROUND with open grassy sites. *From jct I-10 (exit 8 Vinton) & Hwy 108: Go 1/10 mi N on Hwy 108, then 1/10 mi W on Goodwin St.*

FACILITIES: 128 sites, most common site width 30 feet, 100 full hookups, 28 water & elec (20,30 & 50 amp receptacles), 67 pull-thrus, a/c allowed ($), heater allowed ($), group sites for RVs, cabins, handicap restroom facilities, sewage disposal, laundry, public phone, grocery store, RV supplies, LP gas refill by weight/by meter, ice, tables, grills.

RECREATION: rec hall, rec room/area, swim pool, mini-golf, basketball hoop, playground, shuffleboard court, horseshoes, volleyball, local tours.

Open all year. Member of ARVC; LCOA. Phone: (318) 589-2300.

**SEE AD LAKE CHARLES THIS PAGE**

## MAINE

### ORR'S ISLAND

**ORR'S ISLAND CAMPGROUND**—Island CAMPGROUND with shaded & open sites. *From jct US 1 & Hwy 24 (at Cook's Corner): Go 11 1/2 mi S on Hwy 24.*

FACILITIES: 70 sites, most common site width 24 feet, 35 full hookups, 18 water & elec (20 & 30 amp receptacles), 17 no hookups, 5 pull-thrus, a/c not allowed, heater not allowed, phone hookups, cabins, sewage disposal, laundry, public phone, ice, tables, fire rings, wood.





ORR'S ISLAND, ME—Continued
ORR'S ISLAND CAMPGROUND—Continued

RECREATION: salt water swimming, boating, 2 canoe boat rentals, salt water fishing, badminton, horseshoes, hiking trails, volleyball.

Open Memorial Day through mid Sep. Member of ARVC;MECOA. Phone: (207) 833-5595.

**SEE AD THIS PAGE**

### WELLS

**BEACH ACRES CAMPGROUND**—Level, open and wooded sites with some seasonal campers. *From jct I-95 (exit 2) & Hwy 109: Go 1 1/2 mi E on Hwy 109, then 2 mi S on US 1, then 1 block E on Eldridge Rd.*

FACILITIES: 400 sites, most common site width 40 feet, 320 full hookups, (20 & 30 amp receptacles), 80 no hookups, a/c allowed, phone hookups, RV storage, sewage disposal, laundry, public phone, limited grocery store, ice, tables, fire rings, traffic control gate/guard.

RECREATION: rec hall, swim pool, basketball hoop, playground, 2 shuffleboard courts, sports field, horseshoes.

No pets. Open Memorial Day through mid Sep. No refunds. Member of ARVC;MECOA. Phone: (207) 646-5612.

**SEE AD THIS PAGE**

### YORK HARBOR

**LIBBY'S OCEANSIDE CAMP**—An open, grassy, oceanside CAMPGROUND. *From I-95 ("The Yorks" exit): Go 1/4 mi S on US 1, then 3 mi NE on US 1A.*

FACILITIES: 95 sites, most common site width 18 feet, 88 full hookups, 7 water & elec (20 & 30 amp receptacles), a/c allowed ($), heater allowed ($), handicap restroom facilities, public phone, ice, tables.

RECREATION: rec room/area, salt water swimming, salt water fishing.

Open May 15 through Oct 15. CPO. Member of ARVC; MECOA. Phone: (207) 363-4171.

**SEE AD THIS PAGE**





# SEASONAL SITE GUIDE

## MARYLAND

### OCEAN CITY

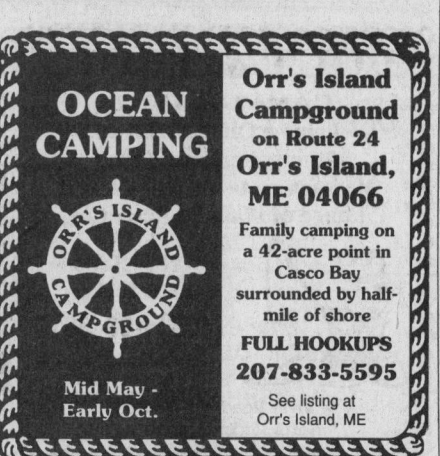

**EAGLE'S NEST PARK**—CAMPGROUND with shaded or covered patio sites. *From jct Hwy 528 & US 50: Go 1 mi W on US 50, then 1 mi S on Hwy 611, then 1 mi E on Eagle's Nest Rd.*

FACILITIES: 335 sites, most common site width 40 feet, 190 full hookups, 105 water & elec (20 & 30 amp receptacles), 40 no hookups, a/c allowed ($), cable TV, sewage disposal, laundry, public phone, grocery store, RV supplies, ice, tables, church services, traffic control gate.

RECREATION: rec hall, coin games, swim pool, salt water swimming, boating, ramp, 11 motor boat rentals, basketball hoop, planned group activities, horseshoes, volleyball.

Open all year. Phone: (410) 213-0097.

**SEE AD THIS PAGE**

# MASSACHUSETTS

## BREWSTER

**SWEETWATER FOREST**—Spacious, well separated, wooded sites in a family operated lakeside CAMPGROUND. *From jct US 6 (exit 10) & Hwy 124: Go 3 mi N on Hwy 124.*

FACILITIES: 300 sites, most common site width 30 feet, 64 full hookups, 171 water & elec (20 & 30 amp receptacles), 65 no hookups, cable TV, phone hookups, RV storage, handicap restroom facilities, sewage disposal, public phone, limited grocery store, RV supplies, LP gas refill by weight/by meter, ice, tables, traffic control gate.

RECREATION: rec hall, rec room/area, coin games, lake swimming, boating, 3 hp limit, canoeing, dock, 3 row/3 canoe boat rentals, lake fishing, basketball hoop, 10 bike rentals, playground, hiking trails, volleyball, cross country skiing.

Open all year. 3 day minimum reservation on holiday weekends. No refunds. Member of ARVC;MACO. Phone: (508) 896-3773.

**SEE AD CAPE COD THIS PAGE**

BREWSTER, MA—Continued

**SWEETWATER FOREST RV**—*From jct US 6 (exit 10) & Hwy 124: Go 3 mi N on Hwy 124.* SALES: park models. SERVICES: RV appliance mechanic full-time, LP gas refill by meter, sewage disposal, RV storage, sells parts/accessories, sells camping supplies, installs hitches. Open all year. Master Card/Visa accepted. Phone: (508) 896-3773.

**SEE AD CAPE COD THIS PAGE**

## CAPE COD

***See listing at Brewster***

## GREENFIELD

***See listing at Shelburne Falls***

## NORTH RUTLAND

**POUT & TROUT CAMPGROUND**—A rural setting with wooded or open grassy sites. Most sites occupied by seasonal campers. *From jct Hwy 56 & Hwy 68: Go 1/2 mi N on Hwy 68, then 3/4 mi NE on River Rd.*

FACILITIES: 156 sites, most common site width 35 feet, 70 full hookups, 76 water & elec (15,20 & 30 amp receptacles), 10 no hookups, a/c allowed ($), heater not allowed, phone hookups, group sites for tents/RVs, RV storage, sewage disposal, laundry, public phone, limited grocery store, LP gas refill by weight, ice, tables, fire rings, wood, traffic control gate.

RECREATION: rec hall, pavilion, coin games, swim pool, boating, no motors, canoeing, 3 row/2 pedal boat rentals, river/pond fishing, basketball hoop, playground, planned group activities, sports field, horseshoes.

Open mid Apr through Columbus Day. No refunds. Member of ARVC; MACO. Phone: (508) 886-6677.

**SEE AD THIS PAGE**

## SHELBURNE FALLS

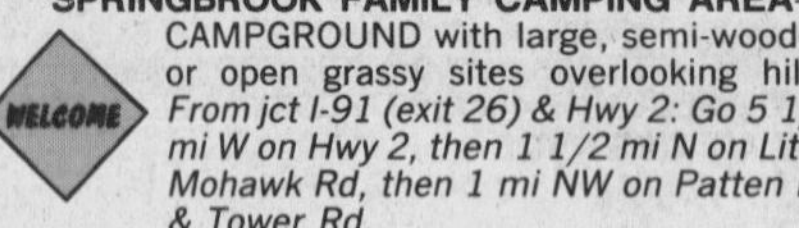

**SPRINGBROOK FAMILY CAMPING AREA**—CAMPGROUND with large, semi-wooded or open grassy sites overlooking hills. *From jct I-91 (exit 26) & Hwy 2: Go 5 1/2 mi W on Hwy 2, then 1 1/2 mi N on Little Mohawk Rd, then 1 mi NW on Patten Rd & Tower Rd.*

FACILITIES: 97 sites, most common site width 40 feet, 85 water & elec (15 & 20 amp receptacles), 12 no hookups, 10 pull-thrus, phone hookups, RV storage, sewage disposal, public phone, limited grocery store, RV supplies, LP gas refill by weight, ice, tables, fire rings, wood, traffic control gate.

SHELBURNE FALLS, MA—Continued
SPRINGBROOK FAMILY CAMPING AREA—Continued

RECREATION: rec room/area, coin games, swim pool, basketball hoop, playground, 2 shuffleboard courts, badminton, sports field, horseshoes, hiking trails, volleyball.

Open May 1 through Oct 15. Member of ARVC; MACO. Phone: (413) 625-6618.

**SEE AD GREENFIELD THIS PAGE**

## SPRINGFIELD

***See listing at Westhampton***

## WESTHAMPTON

**WINDY ACRES CAMPING**—Hillside CAMPGROUND in a rural area. *From jct Hwy 9 & Hwy 66: Go 9 mi W on Hwy 66, then 1 block N on South Rd.*

FACILITIES: 121 sites, most common site width 40 feet, 18 full hookups, 100 water & elec (15,20 & 30 amp receptacles), 3 no hookups, 4 pull-thrus, a/c allowed ($), heater not allowed, group sites for tents/RVs, RV storage, sewage disposal, laundry, public phone, limited grocery store, RV supplies, LP gas refill by weight/by meter, ice, tables, fire rings, traffic control gate.

RECREATION: rec room/area, equipped pavilion, coin games, pond swimming, playground, planned group activities (weekends only), badminton, sports field, horseshoes, volleyball.

Open May 1 through Oct 15. Member of ARVC; MACO. Phone: (413) 527-9862.

**SEE AD SPRINGFIELD THIS PAGE**

# MICHIGAN

## BATTLE CREEK

**CREEK VALLEY CAMPGROUND**—Mostly open, grassy RV SPACES in conjunction with a mobile home park. *From jct Hwy 89 & Hwy 37: Go 1 1/4 mi N on Hwy 37.*

FACILITIES: 22 sites, most common site width 25 feet, accepts full hookup units only, 22 full hookups, (30 amp receptacles), a/c allowed, heater allowed, cable TV ($), phone hookups, tables.

No tents. Open all year. Phone: (616) 964-9577.

**SEE AD THIS PAGE**

## BROOKLYN

**JUNIPER HILLS**—Wooded or grassy campsites in a rural area. *From jct Hwy 50 & US 12: Go 2 mi W on US 12.*

FACILITIES: 340 sites, most common site width 40 feet, 167 water & elec, 105 elec (20 & 30 amp receptacles), 68 no hookups, a/c allowed ($), heater allowed ($), group sites for tents/RVs, RV storage, sewage disposal, public phone, grocery store, ice, tables, wood.

RECREATION: rec hall, coin games, pond swimming, dock, pond fishing, basketball hoop, playground, planned group activities (weekends only), sports field, horseshoes, hiking trails, volleyball, snowmobile trails.

JUNIPER HILLS—Continued on next page
BROOKLYN, MI—Continued on next page

**BROOKLYN, MI—Continued**
JUNIPER HILLS—Continued

Open May 1 through Oct 30. Member of ARVC; MAPCO. Phone: (517) 592-6803.
**SEE AD THIS PAGE**

## CADILLAC

**BIRCHWOOD RESORT & CAMPGROUND**—An RV PARK with shady sites near large lake resort area with use of dock & lake facilities. *From South jct Hwy 55 & Hwy 115: Go 1 Block SE on Hwy 115.*

FACILITIES: 28 sites, 24 full hookups, 4 elec (20,30 & 50 amp receptacles), a/c allowed ($), heater not allowed, phone hookups, cabins, RV storage, public phone, ice, tables, patios, fire rings, wood, church services.

RECREATION: boating, dock, water skiing, lake fishing, basketball hoop, 5 bike rentals, playground, shuffleboard court, planned group activities (weekends only), movies, badminton, horseshoes, volleyball, cross country skiing, snowmobile trails. Recreation open to the public.

Open all year. Member of ARVC; MAPCO. Phone: (800) 299-9106.
**SEE AD THIS PAGE**

## CEDARVILLE

**CEDARVILLE RV PARK CAMPGROUND**—Level, open RV sites on Lake Huron. *From jct I-75 (exit 359) & Hwy 134: Go 17 mi E on Hwy 134 thru Cedarville, then 1 block S on Lake St.*

FACILITIES: 77 sites, most common site width 25 feet, 52 full hookups, 25 water & elec (20 & 30 amp receptacles), a/c allowed, heater allowed, phone hookups, RV storage, sewage disposal, laundry, public phone, tables, fire rings, wood.

RECREATION: rec hall, boating, ramp, dock, 3 row boat rentals, water skiing, lake fishing, planned group activities, recreation director.

Open May 1 through Oct 10. Member of ARVC; MAPCO. Phone: (906) 484-3351.
**SEE AD THIS PAGE**

## GRASS LAKE

**ANDRY'S ACRES ON THE LAKE**—CAMPGROUND with both level and hilly, shaded sites. *From jct I-94 (exit 150) & Mt Hope Rd: Go 4 mi N on Mt Hope Rd, then 1/4 mi W on entrance road.*

FACILITIES: 160 sites, most common site width 30 feet, 37 full hookups, 123 water & elec (20 & 30 amp receptacles), a/c allowed ($), heater not allowed, group sites for tents/RVs, sewage disposal, laundry, public phone, tables, fire rings, traffic control gate.

RECREATION: lake swimming, boating, canoeing, ramp, water skiing, lake fishing, playground, sports field.

Open May 1 through Oct 1. Phone: (517) 596-3117.
**SEE AD JACKSON THIS PAGE**

## HOUGHTON LAKE

✽ **SANDY OAK RV PARK & RV SALES**—*From jct US 27 & Hwy 55: Go 6 mi E on Hwy 55 (W Houghton Lake Dr), then 1 block S on Owens Rd.* SALES: park models. Open all year. Phone: (800) 323-0220.
**SEE AD THIS PAGE**

**SANDY OAK RV PARK & SALES**—Wooded CAMPGROUND with lots for sale or for rent. *From jct US 27 & Hwy 55: Go 6 mi E on Hwy 55 (W Houghton Lake Dr), then 1 block S on Owens Rd.*

FACILITIES: 258 sites, most common site width 40 feet, 258 full hookups, (30 amp receptacles), a/c allowed, heater allowed, cable TV, phone hookups, handicap restroom facilities, laundry, public phone, tables, fire rings, wood.



**HOUGHTON LAKE, MI—Continued**
SANDY OAK RV PARK & SALES—Continued

RECREATION: rec hall, swim pool (heated), whirlpool, pond fishing, playground, 2 shuffleboard courts, badminton, horseshoes, hiking trails, volleyball, cross country skiing, snowmobile trails.

No tents. Open all year. Phone: (800) 323-0220.
**SEE AD THIS PAGE**

## JACKSON

**GREENWOOD ACRES FAMILY CAMPGROUND**—CAMPGROUND with wide, grassy, level & open sites. *From I-94 (exit 147 Ann Arbor Rd): Go 7/10 mi W on Ann Arbor Rd, then 1 1/4 mi S on Portage Rd, then 1/2 mi E on Greenwood Rd, then N on Hilton to entrance.*

FACILITIES: 1160 sites, most common site width 50 feet, 580 full hookups, 580 water & elec (20 & 30 amp receptacles), a/c allowed ($), heater not allowed, group sites for RVs, sewage disposal, laundry, public phone, full service store, RV supplies, ice, tables, wood, church services, traffic control gate.

RECREATION: rec hall, pavilion, coin games, swim pool, lake swimming, boating, 5 hp limit, lake fishing, golf, mini-golf, driving range, basketball hoop, playground, planned group activities (weekends only), recreation director, 2 tennis courts, sports field, hiking trails, volleyball.

No tents. Open Easter through Halloween. Activities Memorial Day weekend thru Labor Day. CPO. Member of ARVC; MAPCO. Phone: (517) 522-8600.
**SEE AD THIS PAGE**

## JONES

**CAMELOT CAMPGROUND**—A CAMPGROUND with mostly open, hilly sites. *From jct Hwy 40 & Hwy 60: Go 2 1/2 mi W on Hwy 60.*

FACILITIES: 44 sites, most common site width 40 feet, 33 water & elec (20 & 30







**JONES, MI—Continued**
CAMELOT CAMPGROUND—Continued

amp receptacles), 11 no hookups, 1 pull-thrus, a/c allowed ($), heater allowed ($), group sites for tents, RV rentals, RV storage, handicap restroom facilities, sewage disposal, laundry, ice, tables, fire rings, wood.

RECREATION: rec hall, coin games, lake swimming, whirlpool, boating, canoeing, ramp, dock, 5 row boat rentals, lake fishing, badminton, horseshoes, volleyball.

Open Apr 1 through Oct 1. Phone: (616) 476-2473.
**SEE AD THIS PAGE**

MICHIGAN—Continued on next page

## MIDDLEVILLE

**SHARP PARK**—A shaded lakeside CAMPGROUND with many seasonal campers. *From center of town: Go 2 mi SE on Hwy 37, then 4 mi S on Yankee Springs Rd, then 1/2 mi W on Deep Lake Rd.*

FACILITIES: 114 sites, most common site width 30 feet, 83 full hookups, 20 elec (20 & 30 amp receptacles), 11 no hookups, a/c allowed, heater allowed, RV storage, sewage disposal, public phone, ice, tables, fire rings, traffic control gate.

RECREATION: pavilion, lake swimming, boating, canoeing, ramp, 9 row/2 canoe/3 pedal boat rentals, lake fishing, basketball hoop, playground, 2 shuffleboard courts, badminton, sports field, horseshoes, hiking trails, volleyball.

No pets. Open May 1 through Oct 15. Phone: (616) 795-3856.

**SEE AD THIS PAGE**

## MONTAGUE

**HAPPY MOHAWK CANOE LIVERY**—*From jct US 31 & Fruitvale Rd: Go 8 mi E on Fruitvale Rd (CR B-86).* Canoe, tube & raft rental and canoe livery on the White River in the Manistee National Forest. Open May 1 through Sep 30. Master Card/Visa accepted. Phone: (616) 894-4209.

**SEE AD THIS PAGE**

**WHITE RIVER CAMPGROUND**—A CAMPGROUND with shaded and open sites in the White River Recreation Area of the Manistee National Forest. *From jct US 31 & Fruitvale Rd: Go 5 mi E on CR B-86 (Fruitvale Rd).*

FACILITIES: 227 sites, most common site width 35 feet, 113 water & elec, 28 elec (20,30 & 50 amp receptacles), 86 no hookups, 15 pull-thrus, a/c allowed ($), heater allowed ($), group sites for tents/RVs, cabins, RV storage, sewage disposal, laundry, public phone, grocery store, RV supplies, LP gas refill by weight/by meter, ice, tables, fire rings, wood, church services.

RECREATION: rec hall, pavilion, coin games, swim pool (heated), canoeing, 200 canoe boat rentals, float trips, lake/river fishing, playground, planned group activities (weekends only), movies, horse riding trails, sports field, horseshoes, motorbike trails, hiking trails, volleyball, cross country skiing, snowmobile trails. Recreation open to the public.

Open all year. Facilities fully operational Memorial Day through Sep 30. Winter season by reservation only. CPO. Member of ARVC; MAPCO. Phone: (616) 894-4708.

**SEE AD THIS PAGE**

**About a pint or .47 litres of water is lost through the skin every day. If temperature rises or if exercising occurs, it is possible to sweat away 3 gallons of fluid in 24 hours.**

**SAY YOU SAW IT IN WOODALL'S!**

# MINNESOTA

## DETROIT LAKES

*See listing at Pelican Rapids*

## PELICAN RAPIDS

**PELICAN HILLS PARK**—A wooded CAMPGROUND with level sites. *S'bound from jct I-94 (exit 24) & Hwy 34A: Go 15 mi E on Hwy 34, then 2 1/2 mi N on CR 9. N'bound from jct I-94 (exit 50) & US 59: Go 17 mi N on US 59, then 6 1/2 mi N on CR 9, then 1 block E on Hwy 34, then 2 1/2 mi N on CR 9.*

FACILITIES: 57 sites, most common site width 30 feet, 17 full hookups, 12 water & elec, 10 elec (15,20 & 30 amp receptacles), 18 no hookups, 8 pull-thrus, a/c allowed, heater allowed, phone hookups, group sites for tents/RVs, cabins, RV storage, sewage disposal, public phone, grocery store, LP gas refill by weight, gasoline, ice, tables, fire rings, wood.

RECREATION: rec room/area, coin games, boating, canoeing, ramp, dock, water skiing, lake fishing, playground, sports field, horseshoes, hiking trails, volleyball.

Age restrictions may apply. Open May 1 through Sep 30. Member of MACO. Phone: (800) 430-2267.

**SEE AD DETROIT LAKES THIS PAGE**

# MONTANA

## CLINTON

**THE ELKHORN GUEST RANCH**—Wooded, riverside CAMPGROUND. *From jct I-90 (exit 126) and Rock Creek Rd: Go 3 1/2 mi S on Rock Creek Rd.*

FACILITIES: 120 sites, most common site width 30 feet, 55 full hookups, 30 water & elec (20 & 30 amp receptacles), 35 no hookups, 12 pull-thrus, a/c allowed, heater allowed, phone hookups, cabins, sewage disposal, laundry, public phone, limited grocery store, RV supplies, LP gas refill by weight/by meter, ice, tables, fire rings, wood.

RECREATION: swim pool (heated), river swimming, river fishing, fishing guides, playground, horse riding trails, horse rental, horseshoes, hiking trails, volleyball.

Open May 1 through Sep 30. Phone: (406) 825-3220.

**SEE AD MISSOULA THIS PAGE**

## LIVINGSTON

**YELLOWSTONE'S EDGE RV PARK**—Level sites next to a river with a scenic mountain view. Altitude 6000 ft. *From jct I-90 (exit 333) & US 89: Go 18 mi S on US 89.*

FACILITIES: 101 sites, most common site width 36 feet, 81 full hookups, (30 & 50 amp receptacles), 20 no hookups, 48 pull-thrus, a/c allowed, heater allowed, phone hookups, group sites for tents/RVs, handicap restroom facilities, sewage disposal, laundry, public phone, limited grocery store, RV supplies, LP gas refill by weight/by meter, ice, tables, fire rings, grills, wood.

RECREATION: rec room/area, coin games, boating, 9 hp limit, ramp, river fishing, sports field, horseshoes, volleyball.

Open May 1 through Nov 1. Phone: (406) 333-4036.

**SEE AD THIS PAGE**

## MISSOULA

*See listing at Clinton*

**A bear will usually dig his own den rather than inhabit an existing cave.**

*When I hear somebody sigh that "Life is hard," I am always tempted to ask, "Compared to what?"*

# NEVADA

## LAS VEGAS

**HOLIDAY TRAVEL PARK**—An RV PARK with level, hard surfaced back in & pull thru sites with a mountain view. *From jct US 93/95 Expressway & Boulder Hwy: Go 2 1/4 mi S on Boulder Hwy, then 1/4 mi NE on Nellis Blvd.*

FACILITIES: 402 sites, most common site width 30 feet, 402 full hookups, (30 & 50 amp receptacles), 120 pull-thrus, a/c allowed, heater allowed, phone hookups, laundry, public phone, ice, tables, grills, guard.

RECREATION: rec hall, rec room/area, swim pool (heated), sauna, whirlpool, shuffleboard court, horseshoes.

No pets. No tents. Age restrictions may apply. Open all year. CPO. Member of ARVC; CTPA. Phone: (702) 451-8005.

**SEE AD THIS PAGE**

# NEW HAMPSHIRE

## CAMPTON

**GOOSE HOLLOW CAMPGROUND**—Grassy and some shaded sites in a meadow surrounded by woods. *From jct I-93 (exit 28) & Hwy 49: Go 3 3/4 mi E on Hwy 49.*

FACILITIES: 165 sites, 48 full hookups, 17 water & elec (15,20 & 30 amp receptacles), 100 no hookups, group sites for tents/RVs, sewage disposal, public phone, ice, tables, fire rings.

RECREATION: rec hall, rec room/area, swim pool, river fishing, basketball hoop, horseshoes, volleyball.

Open all year. Phone: (800) 204-CAMP.

**SEE AD THIS PAGE**

NEW HAMPSHIRE—Continued

## CENTER OSSIPEE

**TERRACE PINES**—Level, wooded, prepared sites at a hilly CAMPGROUND on a lake. *From jct Hwy 16 & Center Ossipee Business District Rd: Go 500 feet W & 500 feet S, then 1/2 mi W on Main St to Center Ossipee Village, then 1 1/2 mi SW on Moultinville Rd, then 1 3/4 mi SW on Valley Rd, then 1/2 mi W on Bents Rd.*

FACILITIES: 183 sites, most common site width 45 feet, 29 ft. max RV length, 178 full hookups, 5 water & elec (20 & 30 amp receptacles), a/c allowed, heater allowed, phone hookups, cabins, sewage disposal, laundry, public phone, limited grocery store, LP gas refill by weight/by meter, ice, tables, fire rings, grills, wood, traffic control gate.

RECREATION: rec hall, rec room/area, coin games, lake swimming, boating, canoeing, ramp, dock, 2 row/4 canoe/1 pedal boat rentals, water skiing, lake fishing, basketball hoop, playground, badminton, horseshoes, hiking trails, volleyball.

Open May 15 through Columbus Day. Member of NE-HA-CA. Phone: (603) 539-6210.

**SEE AD THIS PAGE**

## CHOCORUA

**CHOCORUA CAMPING VILLAGE**—Lakeside CAMPGROUND on hilly terrain with shaded, prepared sites. *From jct Hwy 113 & Hwy 16: Go 3 mi S on Hwy 16.*

FACILITIES: 120 sites, most common site width 80 feet, 53 full hookups, 49 water & elec (15,20 & 30 amp receptacles), 18 no hookups, 8 pull-thrus, a/c allowed, heater allowed, phone hookups, group sites for tents, RV rentals, cabins, RV storage, handicap restroom facilities, sewage disposal, laundry, public phone, grocery store, RV supplies, LP gas refill by weight/by meter, ice, tables, fire rings, grills, wood, traffic control gate.

RECREATION: rec hall, rec room/area, coin games, lake swimming, boating, electric motors only, canoeing, dock, 2 row/2 canoe/1 pedal boat rentals, lake/river fishing, basketball hoop, playground, planned group activities, movies, recreation director, badminton, sports field, horseshoes, hiking trails, volleyball, cross country skiing, snowmobile trails.

Open all year. Member of NE-HA-CA. Phone: (603) 323-8536.

**SEE AD THIS PAGE**

NEW HAMPSHIRE—Continued

## EAST WAKEFIELD

**BEACHWOOD SHORES CAMPGROUND**—Large, sandy, shaded sites adjacent to a lake. *From jct Hwy 16 & Hwy 153N (Mountain Laurel Rd): Go 12 mi N on Hwy 153, then 2 mi W on Bonnymann Rd.*

FACILITIES: 87 sites, most common site width 40 feet, 87 full hookups, (20 & 30 amp receptacles), a/c allowed ($), heater not allowed, phone hookups, sewage disposal, laundry, public phone, limited grocery store, RV supplies, LP gas refill by weight, ice, tables, fire rings, grills, wood.

RECREATION: rec room/area, coin games, lake swimming, boating, canoeing, ramp, dock, 2 row/3 canoe boat rentals, water skiing, lake fishing, basketball hoop, planned group activities (weekends only), badminton, horseshoes, hiking trails, volleyball.

Open May 17 through Columbus Day. Member of ARVC; NE-HA-CA. Phone: (603) 539-4272.

**SEE AD THIS PAGE**

NEW HAMPSHIRE—Continued on next page

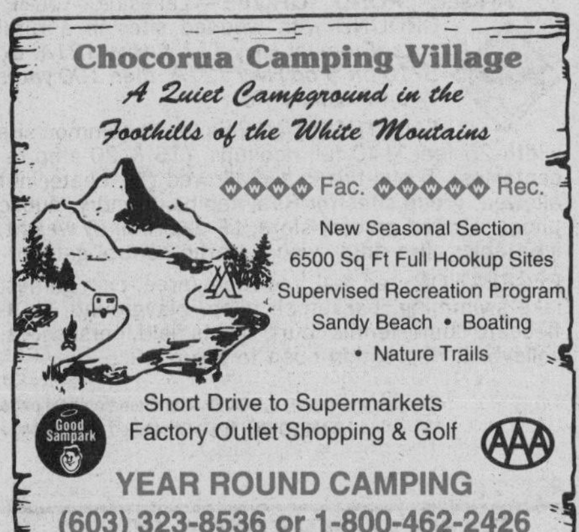

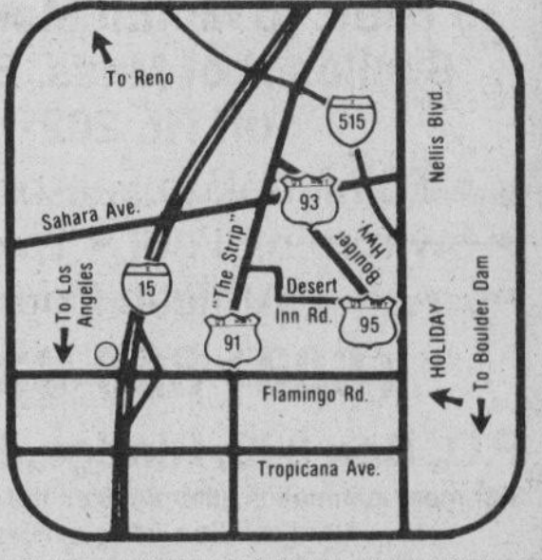

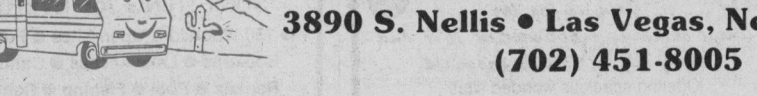

## HENNIKER

**MILE AWAY CAMPGROUND**—Rural, wooded CAMPGROUND. *From jct I-89 (exit 5) & Hwy 202: Go 5 mi W on Hwy 202, then 1 mi NE on Old West Hopkinton Rd.*

FACILITIES: 190 sites, most common site width 35 feet, 53 full hookups, 131 water & elec (20 & 30 amp receptacles), 6 no hookups, 2 pull-thrus, a/c allowed ($), heater allowed ($), phone hookups, group sites for tents/RVs, handicap restroom facilities, sewage disposal, laundry, public phone, limited grocery store, RV supplies, LP gas refill by weight/by meter, ice, tables, fire rings, wood.

RECREATION: rec hall, rec room/area, equipped pavilion, coin games, pond swimming, boating, 6 hp limit, canoeing, ramp, dock, 1 row/3 canoe/3 pedal boat rentals, pond fishing, mini-golf ($), basketball hoop, 2 shuffleboard courts, planned group activities





(weekends only), badminton, horseshoes, hiking trails, volleyball, cross country skiing, snowmobile trails.

Open all year. Facilities fully operational May 1 through Oct 31. Member of NE-HA-CA. Phone: (603) 428-7616.

**SEE AD THIS PAGE**

## HILLSBORO

**OXBOW CAMPGROUND**—Rolling terrain with level, wooded or open sites. *From jct US 202 & Hwy 149: Go 3/4 mi S on Hwy 149.*

FACILITIES: 74 sites, most common site width 35 feet, 60 full hookups, 5 elec (20 & 30 amp receptacles), 9 no hookups, 6 pull-thrus, a/c allowed ($), heater not allowed, cable TV ($), phone hookups, RV storage, laundry, public phone, ice, tables, fire rings, grills, wood.

RECREATION: rec hall, rec room/area, pavilion, pond swimming, basketball hoop, shuffleboard court, planned group activities (weekends only), badminton, sports field, horseshoes, hiking trails, volleyball.

Open May 15 through Oct 15. Member of NE-HA-CA. Phone: (603) 464-5952.

**SEE AD THIS PAGE**

## LITTLETON

**CRAZY HORSE CAMPGROUND**—CAMPGROUND with open & shaded sites in a rural setting. *From jct I-93 (exit 43) & Hwy 135: Go 100 yards E on Hwy 135, then 1 1/4 mi SW on Hwy 135/18, then 1 1/4 mi N on Hilltop Rd.*

FACILITIES: 150 sites, most common site width 24 feet, 17 full hookups, 83 water & elec (20,30 & 50 amp receptacles), 50 no hookups, 10 pull-thrus, a/c allowed, heater allowed, phone hookups, group sites for tents/RVs, RV rentals, RV storage, sewage disposal, laundry, limited grocery store, RV supplies, LP gas refill by weight/by meter, ice, tables, fire rings, grills, wood.

RECREATION: rec room/area, pavilion, coin games, swim pool, boating, canoeing, 6 canoe/1 pedal boat rentals, badminton, sports field, horseshoes, volleyball, cross country skiing, snowmobile trails.

Open all year. Member of NE-HA-CA. Phone: (800) 639-4107.

**SEE AD THIS PAGE**

## NEW BOSTON

**FRIENDLY BEAVER CAMPGROUND**—Wooded CAMPGROUND with some open grassy sites. *From jct Hwy 77 & Hwy 136 & Hwy 13 (Southwest corner): Go 2 mi W on Old Coach Rd.*

FACILITIES: 172 sites, most common site width 20 feet, 131 full hookups, 41 water & elec (15,20 & 30 amp receptacles), a/c allowed ($), heater not allowed, phone hookups, group sites for tents/RVs, RV storage, handicap restroom facilities, sewage disposal, laundry, public phone, limited grocery store, RV supplies, ice, tables, fire rings, wood.

RECREATION: rec hall, rec room/area, coin games, 3 swim pools (indoor) (heated), wading pool, whirlpool, basketball hoop, playground, planned group activities, recreation director, badminton, sports field, horseshoes, hiking trails, volleyball, snowmobile trails.

Open all year. Member of NE-HA-CA. Phone: (603) 487-5570.

**SEE AD THIS PAGE**

## RINDGE

**WOODMORE CAMPGROUND**—Shady, grassy, rural area near lakeside. *From west jct Hwy 119 & US 202: Go 1 mi N on US 202, then 1/4 mi E on Davis Crossing Rd, then 1/2 mi N on Woodbound Rd.*

FACILITIES: 130 sites, most common site width 50 feet, 90 full hookups, 20 water & elec (20 & 30 amp receptacles), 20 no hookups, 3 pull-thrus, a/c allowed ($), heater not allowed, group sites for tents/RVs, RV storage, sewage disposal, laundry, public phone, limited grocery store, RV supplies, LP gas refill by weight, ice, tables, fire rings, grills, wood, traffic control gate.

RECREATION: rec room/area, coin games, swim pool, boating, 35 hp limit, canoeing, 1 row/4 canoe/2 pedal boat rentals, water skiing, lake fishing, basketball hoop, playground, shuffleboard court, badminton, horseshoes, volleyball.

Open May 15 through Sep 20. Open weekends only Sep 20 to Columbus Day. Member of NE-HA-CA. Phone: (603) 899-3362.

**SEE AD THIS PAGE**

## SANDOWN

**ANGLE POND GROVE**—Lakeside CAMPGROUND with wooded sites in a rural area. *From jct Hwy 111 & Hwy 121A: Go 6/10 mi N on Hwy 121A, then 100 yards W on Pillsbury Rd.*

FACILITIES: 140 sites, most common site width 25 feet, 140 full hookups, (15 & 20 amp receptacles), 5 pull-thrus, a/c allowed ($), heater not allowed, group sites for RVs, cabins, laundry, public phone, limited grocery store, LP gas refill by weight, ice, tables, fire rings, wood, traffic control gate.

RECREATION: rec hall, rec room/area, coin games, lake swimming, basketball hoop, playground, shuffleboard court, tennis court, sports field, horseshoes, volleyball. Recreation open to the public.

ANGLE POND GROVE—Continued on next page
SANDOWN, NH—Continued on next page

WANT SOMETHING FREE?
TURN TO PAGE 16

SANDOWN, NH—Continued
ANGLE POND GROVE—Continued

No pets. No tents. Open May 15 through Oct 15. No refunds. Member of NE-HA-CA. Phone: (603) 887-4434.
**SEE AD THIS PAGE**

# NEW JERSEY

## ATLANTIC CITY

***See listing at Pleasantville***

## BARNEGAT

**BROOKVILLE CAMPGROUND**—Flat terrain with wooded sites in a rural setting. *E'bound: From jct Hwy 72 & CR 554: Go 1/4 mi E on CR 554, then 3/4 mi E on Brookville Rd, then 1/2 mi N on Jones Rd. S'bound: From Garden State Pkwy (exit 67): Go 4 mi W on CR 554, then 3/4 mi N on Brookville, then follow Girl Scout signs.*

FACILITIES: 100 sites, most common site width 35 feet, 72 full hookups, (20 & 30 amp receptacles), 28 no hookups, a/c allowed ($), heater allowed ($), phone hookups, RV rentals, RV storage, sewage disposal, public phone, ice, tables, wood.

RECREATION: rec hall, coin games, swim pool, lake fishing, basketball hoop, playground, badminton, horseshoes, volleyball.

Open May 1 through Oct 1. Member of ARVC;NJCOA. Phone: (609) 698-3134.
**SEE AD THIS PAGE**

## CAPE MAY

**CAPE ISLAND CAMPGROUND**—Sites well separated by high shrubbery. *From jct Hwy 109 & US 9: Go 1/2 mi N on US 9.*

FACILITIES: 455 sites, most common site width 35 feet, 310 full hookups, 127 water & elec (20 & 30 amp receptacles), 18 no hookups, 17 pull-thrus, a/c allowed, heater allowed, phone hookups, sewage disposal, laundry, public phone, grocery store, RV supplies, LP gas refill by weight, ice, tables, fire rings, wood, traffic control gate/guard.

**A fox can run as fast at 25 mph.**





CAPE MAY, NJ—Continued
CAPE ISLAND CAMPGROUND—Continued

RECREATION: rec hall, pavilion, coin games, 2 swim pools, wading pool, mini-golf ($), basketball hoop, playground, shuffleboard court, planned group activities, recreation director, 2 tennis courts, horseshoes, volleyball, local tours.

Open May 1 through Sep 30. 4 day min. stay with reservations in season. No refunds. Member of ARVC;NJCOA. Phone: (609) 884-5777.
**SEE AD THIS PAGE**

## HAMMONTON

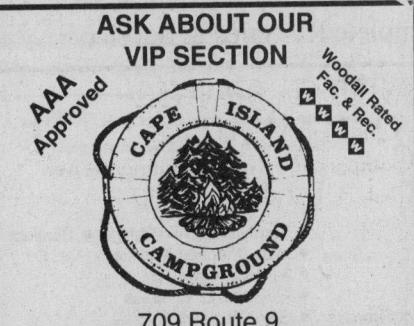

**INDIAN BRANCH PARK**—A Christian oriented, lakeside CAMPGROUND with wooded sites. *From jct Atlantic City Expressway & Hwy 54: Go 2 mi S on Hwy 54, then 3 1/2 mi E on US 322.*

FACILITIES: 214 sites, most common site width 40 feet, 134 full hookups, 80 water & elec (20 & 30 amp receptacles), a/c allowed ($), heater allowed, RV storage, sewage disposal, laundry, public phone, grocery store, RV supplies, LP gas refill by weight/by meter, ice, tables, fire rings, wood, church services, traffic control gate/guard.

RECREATION: rec hall, rec room/area, coin games, lake swimming, boating, electric motors only, canoeing, 12 canoe/3 pedal boat rentals, river fishing, basketball hoop, playground, 2 shuffleboard courts, planned group activities, recreation director, sports field, horseshoes, volleyball.

Open May 1 through Oct 1. 3 Day Min. Holiday Weekends Only by Reservation. Member of ARVC;NJCOA. Phone: (609) 561-4719.
**SEE AD THIS PAGE**

## OCEAN VIEW

**ECHO FARM CAMPGROUND**—Flat, sandy terrain with wooded sites. Most full hookup sites occupied by seasonals. *From jct Hwy 50 & US 9: Go 3/4 mi S on US 9.*

FACILITIES: 300 sites, most common site width 50 feet, 275 full hookups, 25 water & elec (20 & 30 amp receptacles), a/c allowed, cable TV, RV storage, sewage disposal, laundry, public phone, LP gas refill by weight, ice, tables, wood, traffic control gate.





OCEAN VIEW, NJ—Continued
ECHO FARM CAMPGROUND—Continued

RECREATION: rec hall, coin games, swim pool, wading pool, basketball hoop, playground, planned group activities (weekends only), horseshoes, volleyball.

Open Apr 15 through Oct 15. Minimum stay 1 week by reservations. Phone: (609) 624-3589.
**SEE AD NEXT PAGE**

**OCEAN VIEW RESORTS CAMPGROUND**—Destination resort with wooded sites on flat, sandy terrain and short drive to ocean. *S'bound: From jct Garden State Parkway (exit 17) & CR 625: Go 1/4 mi W on CR 625, then 1/4 mi N on US 9. N'bound: Use service area turnaround and follow S'bound directions.*

FACILITIES: 1175 sites, 1175 full hookups, (20,30 & 50 amp receptacles), 20 pull-thrus, a/c allowed ($), heater not allowed, cable TV ($), phone hookups, RV rentals, cabins, RV storage, laundry, public phone, grocery store, RV supplies, LP gas refill by weight/by meter, ice, tables, wood, guard.

OCEAN VIEW RESORTS CAMPGROUND—Continued on next page
OCEAN VIEW, NJ—Continued on next page

**Why is a drama teacher like Wells Fargo?**
***She's a stage coach.***

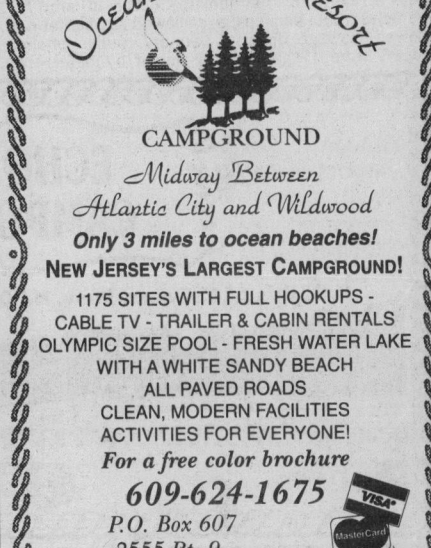

OCEAN VIEW, NJ—Continued
OCEAN VIEW RESORTS CAMPGROUND—Continued

RECREATION: rec hall, rec room/area, coin games, swim pool, lake swimming, boating, 6 pedal boat rentals, mini-golf ($), basketball hoop, playground, planned group activities, movies, recreation director, 2 tennis courts, badminton, sports field, volleyball, local tours.

Open Apr 15 through Oct 1. Weekends only Apr & May and after Labor Day. Member of ARVC;NJCOA. Phone: (609) 624-1675.

**SEE AD PAGE 29**

### PLEASANTVILLE

**PLEASANTVILLE CAMPGROUNDS**—CAMPGROUND with shaded & open sites. *From jct US 30 & US 9: Go 2 1/4 mi S on US 9.*

WELCOME

FACILITIES: 65 sites, most common site width 40 feet, 65 full hookups, (30 amp receptacles), 5 pull-thrus, a/c allowed, heater allowed, cable TV, sewage disposal, laundry, public phone, LP gas refill by weight/by meter, ice, tables.

Open Mar 1 through Nov 1. Phone: (609) 641-3176.

**SEE AD ATLANTIC CITY PAGE 29**

### SUSSEX

**PLEASANT ACRES FARM CAMPGROUND**—A rolling, scenic location with wooded and open sites. *From jct Hwy 284 & Hwy 23: Go 4 3/4 mi N on Hwy 23, then 1 mi E on Dewitt Rd.*

WELCOME

FACILITIES: 292 sites, most common site width 35 feet, 287 full hookups, (20 & 30 amp receptacles), 5 no hookups, a/c allowed ($), heater not allowed, sewage disposal, laundry, public phone, grocery store, LP gas refill by weight/by meter, ice,

SUSSEX, NJ—Continued
PLEASANT ACRES FARM CAMPGROUND—Continued

tables, wood, church services, traffic control gate.

RECREATION: rec hall, coin games, swim pool, wading pool, pond/stream fishing, mini-golf ($), basketball hoop, playground, planned group activities, recreation director, sports field, horseshoes, volleyball.

No tents. Open all year. 3 Day min. holiday weekends. Member of ARVC;NJCOA. Phone: (201) 875-4166.

**SEE AD THIS PAGE**

# NEW MEXICO

### RUIDOSO

**LITTLE CREEK RV PARK**—Level, gravel sites in a mountain setting. Altitude 7500 ft. *From jct US 70 & Hwy 48: Go 10 mi N on Hwy 48, then 2 mi E on Hwy 220.*

WELCOME

FACILITIES: 33 sites, most common site width 35 feet, accepts full hookup units only, 33 full hookups, (20 & 30 amp receptacles), a/c allowed, heater allowed ($), cable TV, phone hookups, group sites for RVs, public phone, RV supplies, ice, tables, patios, grills.

RECREATION: pavilion, swim pool (heated), whirlpool, horseshoes.

No tents. Open Apr 15 through Oct 31. Phone: (505) 336-4044.

**SEE AD THIS PAGE**

**Waxed paper is a good firestarter.**

# NEW YORK

### DOWNSVILLE

**DELAWARE VALLEY CAMPSITE**—Riverside CAMPGROUND with shaded sites. *From center of the village at jct Hwy 206 & Hwy 30: Go 3 3/4 mi S on Hwy 30.*

WELCOME

FACILITIES: 88 sites, most common site width 30 feet, 80 full hookups, (15 & 20 amp receptacles), 8 no hookups, 5 pull-thrus, a/c allowed, heater not allowed, phone hookups, RV storage, laundry, public phone, limited grocery store, ice, tables, fire rings, grills, wood.

RECREATION: river fishing, sports field, horseshoes, volleyball.

Open May 1 through Oct 15. Member of ARVC;CONY. Phone: (607) 363-2306.

**SEE AD THIS PAGE**

### MECHANICVILLE

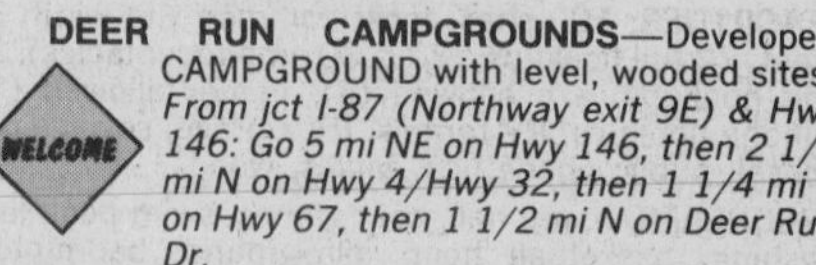

**DEER RUN CAMPGROUNDS**—Developed CAMPGROUND with level, wooded sites. *From jct I-87 (Northway exit 9E) & Hwy 146: Go 5 mi NE on Hwy 146, then 2 1/4 mi N on Hwy 4/Hwy 32, then 1 1/4 mi E on Hwy 67, then 1 1/2 mi N on Deer Run Dr.*

WELCOME

FACILITIES: 369 sites, most common site width 40 feet, 369 full hookups, (30 amp receptacles), 230 pull-thrus, a/c allowed ($), heater not allowed, RV rentals, RV storage, sewage disposal, laundry, public phone, limited grocery store, RV supplies, ice, tables, fire rings, wood.

RECREATION: rec hall, rec room/area, coin games, 3 swim pools (heated), wading pool, pond fishing, mini-golf ($), basketball hoop, playground, planned group activities, movies, recreation director, badminton, sports field, horseshoes, hiking trails, volleyball.

No tents. Open May 1 through Oct 15. Member of ARVC; CONY. Phone: (518) 664-2804.

**SEE AD SCHAGHTICOKE NEXT PAGE**

### PULASKI

**BRENNAN BEACH RV PARK**—CAMPGROUND on Lake Ontario with lakeside, wooded and open sites. *From jct Hwy 13 & Hwy 3: Go 1 mi N on Hwy 3, then follow signs 1/2 mi W on entry road.*

WELCOME

FACILITIES: 1400 sites, most common site width 40 feet, 1380 full hookups, 20 water & elec (20 & 30 amp receptacles), 150 pull-thrus, a/c allowed, heater allowed, phone hookups, RV rentals, handicap restroom facilities, sewage disposal, public phone, limited grocery store, RV supplies, LP gas refill by weight/by meter, ice, tables, patios, fire rings, wood, traffic control gate.

RECREATION: rec hall, rec room/area, coin games, 2 swim pools, wading pool, lake swimming, boating, canoeing, water skiing, lake/stream fishing, fishing

BRENNAN BEACH RV PARK—Continued on next page
PULASKI, NY—Continued on next page



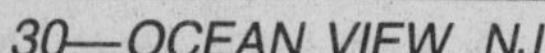

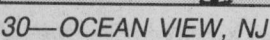

**PULASKI, NY—Continued**
**BRENNAN BEACH RV PARK—Continued**

guides, mini-golf ($), basketball hoop, playground, 4 shuffleboard courts, planned group activities, recreation director, 2 tennis courts, sports field, horseshoes, volleyball.

Open May 1 through Oct 15. Member of ARVC; CONY. Phone: (315) 298-2242.

**SEE AD PAGE 30**

### SACKETS HARBOR

**ALLEN'S BOAT LIVERY MARINA AND CAMPGROUND**—Sunny, grassy sites and wooded sites in a lakeside setting. *From jct I-81 (exit 45) & Hwy 3: Go 9 1/2 mi W on Hwy 3.*

WELCOME

FACILITIES: 215 sites, most common site width 30 feet, 155 full hookups, 35 water & elec (15,20 & 30 amp receptacles), 25 no hookups, a/c allowed ($), heater allowed ($), phone hookups, RV rentals, sewage disposal, public phone, grocery store, RV supplies, LP gas refill by weight/by meter, marine gas, ice, tables, fire rings, wood.

RECREATION: lake swimming, boating, canoeing, ramp, dock, 6 row/2 canoe/6 motor boat rentals, water skiing, lake/stream fishing, fishing guides, basketball hoop, playground, volleyball. Recreation open to the public.

Open May 1 through Oct 15. Phone: (315) 646-2486.

**SEE AD THIS PAGE**

### SCHAGHTICOKE

***See listing at Mechanicville***

# NORTH CAROLINA

### PINEY CREEK

**RIVERCAMP USA**—A riverside CAMPGROUND with open & shaded, grassy sites. *From jct US 221 & Hwy 113: Go 4 1/2 mi W on Hwy 113, then 1/2 mi W on South Fork Ch. Rd (CR 1316), then 2 mi W on Kings Creek Rd (CR 1308) to river (follow signs).*

WELCOME

FACILITIES: 74 sites, most common site width 35 feet, 24 full hookups, 50 water & elec (20 & 30 amp





**PINEY CREEK, NC—Continued**
**RIVERCAMP USA—Continued**

receptacles), a/c allowed ($), heater allowed ($), group sites for tents, RV rentals, cabins, sewage disposal, laundry, public phone, grocery store, RV supplies, ice, tables, fire rings, grills, wood.

RECREATION: pavilion, river swimming, boating, no motors, canoeing, 55 canoe boat rentals, float trips, river fishing, basketball hoop, 5 bike rentals, playground, horseshoes, hiking trails, volleyball. Recreation open to the public.

Open Apr 1 through Nov 1. Member of ARVC;NCCOA. Phone: (910) 359-2267.

**SEE AD THIS PAGE**

### RODANTHE

**CAMP HATTERAS**—Fifty-acre oceanfront & soundfront RV PARK & CAMPGROUND. *In town on Hwy 12.*

WELCOME

FACILITIES: 243 sites, most common site width 40 feet, 183 full hookups, 10 water & elec (30 & 50 amp receptacles), 50 no hookups, a/c allowed ($), heater allowed ($), cable TV ($), group sites for tents/RVs, RV storage, handicap restroom facilities, laundry, public phone, limited grocery store, RV supplies, ice, tables, patios, grills, church services, traffic control gate/guard.

RECREATION: rec hall, rec room/area, pavilion, coin games, 2 swim pools (indoor) (heated), wading pool, whirlpool, boating, canoeing, 4 sail/3 canoe/4 pedal boat rentals, salt water/pond fishing, mini-golf ($), basketball hoop, 6 bike rentals, playground, 4 shuffleboard courts, planned group activities, recreation director, tennis court, horseshoes, volleyball.

Open all year. Member of ARVC; NCCOA. Phone: (919) 987-2777.

**SEE AD THIS PAGE**





# OKLAHOMA

### OKLAHOMA CITY

**HOLLIDAY OUTT MOBILE HOME & RV PARK**—Large RV SPACES in a mobile home park. *From I-40 (exit 142): Go 1 mi N on Council Rd, then 1 mi W on 10th St, then 1/4 mi S on County Line Rd.*

WELCOME

FACILITIES: 50 sites, most common site width 30 feet, accepts full hookup units only, 50 full hookups, (30 & 50 amp receptacles), phone hookups.

No tents. Open all year. Phone: (405) 789-3423.

**SEE AD THIS PAGE**

***FASCINATING FACT***

**The Black-tailed Jack Rabbit will jump higher every 4th or 5th hop so it can get a better view of the surrounding area. They can jump as far as 20 feet.**

# SEASONAL SITE GUIDE

# OREGON

## BOARDMAN

**DRIFTWOOD VILLAGE RV PARK** (REBUILDING)—An RV PARK in a rural area. *From I-84 (exit 164) & Main St: Go 1 1/4 mi S on Main St, then 1 mi W on Kunze Rd, then 1/2 block N on Paul Smith Rd.*

FACILITIES: 62 sites, most common site width 25 feet, 42 full hookups, (20,30 & 50 amp receptacles), 20 no hookups, 42 pull-thrus, cable TV, phone hookups, handicap restroom facilities, sewage disposal, laundry, public phone, patios.

Open all year. Phone: (541) 481-2262.
**SEE AD THIS PAGE**

## CAVE JUNCTION

**OL JO MOBILE VILLAGE RV PARK & CAMPGROUND** (UNDER CONSTRUCTION)—Rural RV PARK in conjunction with mobile home park. *From US 199 & River St: Go 1/2 mi W on River St, then 1/4 mi N on Ollis Rd (follow signs).*

FACILITIES: 45 sites, most common site width 20 feet, 14 full hookups, 21 water & elec, 10 no hookups, 6 pull-thrus, cable TV, phone hookups, handicap restroom facilities, public phone, tables.

Open all year. Phone: (541) 592-2346.
**SEE AD THIS PAGE**









OREGON—Continued

## EUGENE

**KOA-SHERWOOD FOREST**—Semi-wooded CAMPGROUND with shaded sites. *From I-5 (Creswell exit 182): Go 1/2 block W on Oregon Ave.*

FACILITIES: 143 sites, most common site width 27 feet, 135 full hookups, (20 & 30 amp receptacles), 8 no hookups, 46 pull-thrus, a/c allowed ($), heater allowed ($), cable TV, phone hookups, cabins, sewage disposal, laundry, public phone, grocery store, RV supplies, ice, tables.

RECREATION: rec hall, rec room/area, coin games, swim pool (heated), whirlpool, mini-golf ($), basketball hoop, playground, horseshoes, volleyball.

Open all year. Pool open Jun 1-Sep 30. Phone: (541) 895-4110.
**SEE AD THIS PAGE**

## LAKESIDE

**OSPREY POINT RV RESORT**—An RV PARK on Ten Mile Lake. *From town center (N 8th St & N Lake Ave): Go 1/2 mi E on N Lake Ave, and follow signs.*

FACILITIES: 230 sites, 200 full hookups, (30 & 50 amp receptacles), 30 no hookups, 100 pull-thrus, RV rentals, handicap restroom facilities, sewage disposal, laundry, public phone, grocery store, tables.

RECREATION: rec hall, rec room/area, pavilion, lake swimming, boating, canoeing, ramp, dock, lake fishing, basketball hoop, 2 shuffleboard courts, sports field, hiking trails.

Open all year. Phone: (541) 759-2801.
**SEE AD REEDSPORT THIS PAGE**

## REEDSPORT

*See listing at Lakeside*

## SWEET HOME

**SWEET HOME/FOSTER LAKE KOA** (UNDER CONSTRUCTION)—Suburban CAMPGROUND overlooking a lake. *From east edge of town: Go 3 mi SE on Hwy 20 E.*

Phone: (541) 367-5629.
**SEE AD THIS PAGE**

# PENNSYLVANIA

## DOWNINGTOWN

**SHADY ACRES CAMP GROUNDS**—Streamside park with shaded sites. Sites available to seasonal campers only. *From jct Business US 30 & Hwy 282: Go 1 mi W on Hwy 282.*

FACILITIES: 50 sites, 50 full hookups, (30 amp receptacles), a/c allowed, heater allowed, cable TV, phone hookups, sewage disposal, laundry, public phone, tables, fire rings, traffic control gate.

RECREATION: pavilion, swim pool, wading pool, stream fishing, basketball hoop, playground, volleyball.

No tents. Open all year. Phone: (610) 269-1800.
**SEE AD THIS PAGE**

## ERIE

*See listing at North East*

## GETTYSBURG

**ROUND TOP CAMPGROUND**—Semi-wooded park with open and shaded sites near a major highway in a historic area. *From jct US 15 & Hwy 134: Go 1/8 mi N on Hwy 134, then 1/2 mi W on Knight Rd.*

FACILITIES: 260 sites, most common site

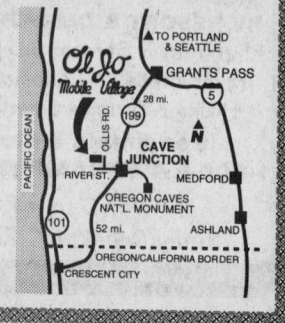


ROUND TOP CAMPGROUND—Continued on next page
GETTYSBURG, PA—Continued on next page

**GETTYSBURG, PA**—Continued
ROUND TOP CAMPGROUND—Continued

width 25 feet, 202 full hookups, 48 water & elec (20,30 & 50 amp receptacles), 10 no hookups, 8 pull-thrus, a/c allowed ($), heater allowed ($), RV storage, handicap restroom facilities, sewage disposal, laundry, public phone, full service store, RV supplies, LP gas refill by weight/by meter, ice, tables, fire rings, wood, church services.

RECREATION: rec hall, rec room/area, pavilion, coin games, swim pool, wading pool, mini-golf ($), basketball hoop, playground, 2 shuffleboard courts, planned group activities (weekends only), tennis court, badminton, sports field, horseshoes, volleyball, local tours.

Open all year. Phone: (800) 463-8321.

**SEE AD THIS PAGE**

### LEWISTOWN

**THE LOCUST CAMPGROUND**—Riverside CAMPGROUND with shaded sites. *From jct US 322 & US 22/522: Go 3 1/2 mi SW on US 22/522, then 1 mi S on Industrial Rd, then 1 mi SE on Locust Rd.*

WELCOME

FACILITIES: 260 sites, most common site width 25 feet, 134 full hookups, 66 water & elec (15,20 & 30 amp receptacles), 60 no hookups, a/c allowed ($), heater allowed ($), cable TV ($), RV storage, sewage disposal, laundry, public phone, ice, tables, fire rings, wood, church services, traffic control gate.

RECREATION: rec hall, rec room/area, coin games, boating, 7 hp limit, canoeing, dock, float trips, river fishing, basketball hoop, playground, planned group activities (weekends only), badminton, horseshoes, hiking trails, volleyball.

Open Apr 1 through Nov 1. Phone: (717) 248-3974.

**SEE AD THIS PAGE**

### NORTH EAST

**FAMILY AFFAIR CAMPGROUNDS**—Rolling grassy park with open and shaded sites. *From jct I-90 (exit 11) & Hwy 89: Go 3/4 mi S on Hwy 89, then 2 mi E on Cole Rd (gravel road), then 1 mi S on Hwy 426.*

WELCOME

FACILITIES: 250 sites, most common site width 21 feet, 200 water & elec (15,20 & 30 amp receptacles), 50 no hookups, 12 pull-thrus, a/c allowed ($), heater allowed ($), RV rentals, RV storage, sewage disposal, public phone, grocery store, LP gas refill by weight, ice, tables, fire rings, wood, church services.

RECREATION: rec hall, rec room/area, pavilion, coin games, 2 swim pools, boating, no motors, canoeing, 3 pedal boat rentals, lake fishing, mini-golf ($), basketball hoop, playground, planned group activities (weekends only), movies, sports field, motorbike trails, hiking trails, volleyball, snowmobile trails.

Open all year. Facilities fully operational Apr 1 through Nov 1. Member of ARVC; PCOA. Phone: (814) 725-8112.

**SEE AD ERIE PAGE 32**

### SHARTLESVILLE

**MOUNTAIN SPRINGS CAMPING RESORT**—Rolling CAMPGROUND with shaded & open sites. *From jct I-78/US 22 (exit 8) & Shartlesville Rd: Go 1 mi E on Mountain Rd.*

WELCOME

FACILITIES: 325 sites, most common site width 30 feet, 45 full hookups, 250 water & elec (20 amp receptacles), 30 no hookups, 18 pull-thrus, a/c allowed ($), heater not allowed, group sites for tents/RVs, cabins, sewage disposal, laundry, public phone, grocery store, RV supplies, LP gas refill by weight/by meter, ice, tables, fire rings, wood.

RECREATION: rec hall, rec room/area, pavilion, coin games, swim pool, wading pool, boating, no motors, canoeing, 2 canoe/4 pedal boat rentals, lake fishing, basketball hoop, playground, planned group activities (weekends only), movies, recreation director, badminton, sports field, horseshoes, hiking trails, volleyball.

Open Apr 1 through Nov 1. Member of ARVC; PCOA. Phone: (610) 488-6859.

**SEE AD THIS PAGE**

### STROUDSBURG

**POCONO VACATION PARK**—Rolling CAMPGROUND with grassy sites. Most sites occupied by seasonal campers. *From jct I-80 (exit 48) & Business US 209: Go 2 mi S on Business US 209, then 1/2 mi W on Shafer's School House Rd.*

WELCOME

FACILITIES: 225 sites, most common site width 23 feet, 175 full hookups, 40 water & elec (20 & 30 amp receptacles), 10 no hookups, 140 pull-thrus, a/c allowed, heater not allowed, cable TV, phone hookups, group sites for RVs, RV storage, sewage disposal, laundry, public phone, limited grocery store, LP gas refill by weight, ice, tables, fire rings, wood, church services.

RECREATION: rec hall, rec room/area, pavilion, coin games, swim pool, wading pool, basketball hoop, playground, planned group activities (weekends only), movies, tennis court, sports field, horseshoes, hiking trails, volleyball, snowmobile trails.

**STROUDSBURG, PA**—Continued
POCONO VACATION PARK—Continued

Open all year. Member of ARVC;PCOA. Phone: (717) 424-2587.

**SEE AD THIS PAGE**

## SOUTH DAKOTA

### RAPID CITY

**LAKE PARK CAMPGROUND**—Level, shaded sites by Canyon Lake. *From jct I-90 (exit 57) & US 16 W: Go 1 1/2 mi S on US 16 W, then 4 1/4 mi W on Hwy 44 (W on Omaha, S on Mt. View, W on Jackson Blvd), then 1,000 feet S on Chapel Lane (at Stavkirk sign).*

FACILITIES: 49 sites, most common site width 25 feet, 35 full hookups, 7 water & elec, 7 elec (20 & 30 amp receptacles), a/c allowed, heater allowed, phone hookups, group sites for tents/RVs, RV storage, sewage disposal, laundry, public phone, limited grocery store, RV supplies, ice, tables, church services.

RECREATION: rec room/area, coin games, swim pool (heated), boating, electric motors only, canoeing, 2 canoe boat rentals, lake/stream fishing, mini-golf ($), 8 bike rentals, playground, badminton, sports field, horseshoes, volleyball, cross country skiing, local tours.

Open all year. Phone: (800) 644-CAMP.

**SEE AD THIS PAGE**

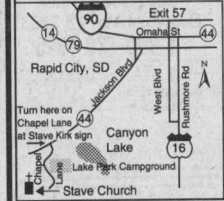

**The best way to keep camp pests, such as bears, away from your camp is to keep a clean campsite.**

**It's a good sign a storm is brewing if distant sounds are loud and hollow sounding.**

# TEXAS

## ALVIN

**MEADOWLARK PARK**—Shaded, grassy RV SPACES in a suburban mobile home park. *From jct Hwy 6 & Hwy 35: Go 1 1/10 mi S on Hwy 35, then 2 2/10 mi W on South St.*

FACILITIES: 21 sites, most common site width 30 feet, accepts full hookup units only, 21 full hookups, (30 & 50 amp receptacles), a/c allowed, heater allowed.

No tents. Open all year. Phone: (713) 331-5992.

**SEE AD THIS PAGE**

## AUSTIN

**AUSTIN CAPITOL-KOA**—Rolling, sunny & shaded sites in a CAMPGROUND along side of Interstate. *Northbound: Take exit 228 of I-35. Southbound: Take exit 226B of I-35, then follow signs to east side of frontage road.*

FACILITIES: 136 sites, 116 full hookups, 20 water & elec (20,30 & 50 amp receptacles), 56 pull-thrus, a/c allowed, heater allowed, cable TV ($), phone hookups, group sites for tents/RVs, cabins, handicap restroom facilities, sewage disposal, laundry, public phone, grocery store, RV supplies, LP gas refill by weight/by meter, gasoline, ice, tables, patios, grills.

RECREATION: rec hall, rec room/area, swim pool, basketball hoop, playground, planned group activities, recreation director, badminton, volleyball.

Open all year. Member of ARVC; TACO. Phone: (512) 444-6322.

**SEE AD THIS PAGE**

## BACLIFF

**BAYSIDE RV PARK**—Developed RV PARK with open sites on the bay. *From jct Hwy 146 & FM 646: Go 2 1/2 mi E on FM 646.*

FACILITIES: 87 sites, most common site width 25 feet, 87 full hookups, (30 & 50 amp receptacles), a/c allowed, heater allowed, phone hookups, handicap restroom facilities, laundry, public phone, full service store, RV supplies, LP gas refill by weight/by meter, ice, tables, patios, grills.

RECREATION: rec room/area, pavilion, equipped pavilion, coin games, salt water swimming, boating,

BACLIFF, TX—Continued
BAYSIDE RV PARK—Continued

ramp, dock, salt water fishing, planned group activities.

Open all year. Member of ARVC;TACO. Phone: (713) 339-2131.

**SEE AD HOUSTON NEXT PAGE**

## BROWNSVILLE

**AUTUMN ACRES RV & MOBILE HOME PARK**—Open, grassy sites in an RV AREA in a mobile home park oriented for retirees. *From jct US 83-77 & Boca Chica Blvd: Go 3 1/4 mi E on Boca Chica Blvd.*

FACILITIES: 126 sites, most common site width 30 feet, 126 full hookups, (30 & 50 amp receptacles), a/c allowed, heater allowed, phone hookups, laundry, public phone, patios.

RECREATION: rec hall, rec room/area, swim pool (heated), whirlpool, basketball hoop, 2 shuffleboard courts, planned group activities.

No tents. Age restrictions may apply. Open all year. Phone: (210) 546-4979.

**SEE AD THIS PAGE**

**BREEZE LAKE CAMPGROUND**—A quiet RV PARK with open & shaded lakeside sites. *From jct US 83-77 & FM 802: Go 5 1/2 mi E on FM 802, then 1/2 mi S on Vermillion.*

FACILITIES: 187 sites, most common site width 40 feet, 187 full hookups, (20 & 30 amp receptacles), 18 pull-thrus, a/c allowed ($), heater allowed ($), cable TV, phone hookups, laundry, public phone, limited grocery store, RV supplies, patios, traffic control gate.

RECREATION: rec hall, rec room/area, swim pool (heated), whirlpool, lake fishing, 2 shuffleboard courts, planned group activities, horseshoes, local tours.

Open all year. Member of ARVC; TACO. Phone: (210) 831-4427.

**SEE AD THIS PAGE**

**HONEYDALE MOBILE HOME & RV PARK**—Paved & grassy sites in a mobile home park. *From jct FM 802 & US 83/77: Go 2 mi S on US 83-77, then 1 3/4 mi W on Boca Chica, then 1/4 mi N on Honeydale Rd.*

FACILITIES: 185 sites, accepts full hookup units only, 185 full hookups, (20,30 & 50 amp receptacles), a/c allowed ($), heater allowed ($), RV storage, handicap restroom facilities, laundry, public phone, patios, traffic control gate.

RECREATION: rec hall, 3 shuffleboard courts, planned group activities, recreation director, horseshoes.

No pets. No tents. Age restrictions may apply. Open all year. Member of ARVC; TACO. Phone: (210) 542-9903.

**SEE AD THIS PAGE**

**PAUL'S RV PARK**—An RV PARK with shaded & open sites on the edge of town. *From jct US 83-77 & FM 802: Go 4 1/2 mi E on FM 802, then 1 1/2 mi S on Minnesota Ave (FM 313).*

FACILITIES: 135 sites, most common site width 30 feet, 135 full hookups, (20,30 & 50 amp receptacles), 17 pull-thrus, a/c allowed, heater allowed, cable TV, phone hookups, RV rentals, RV storage, laundry, public phone, limited grocery store, RV supplies, tables, patios, church services, guard.

RECREATION: rec hall, whirlpool, putting green, 3 shuffleboard courts, planned group activities, movies, recreation director, local tours.

PAUL'S RV PARK—Continued on next page
BROWNSVILLE, TX—Continued on next page

**BROWNSVILLE, TX**—Continued
PAUL'S RV PARK—Continued

Age restrictions may apply Nov 1 through Mar 1. Open all year. CPO. Member of ARVC;TACO. Phone: (210) 831-4852.
**SEE AD PAGE 34**

**RIO RV PARK**—RV park in conjunction with a mobile home park with open, grassy sites. *From jct US 83-77 & FM 802: Go 2 mi S on US 83-77, then 6 mi E on Boca Chica Blvd.*

WELCOME

FACILITIES: 112 sites, 112 full hookups, (20,30 & 50 amp receptacles), 18 pull-thrus, a/c allowed, heater allowed, cable TV, phone hookups, RV rentals, RV storage, laundry, public phone, limited grocery store, RV supplies, tables, patios, church services.

RECREATION: rec hall, swim pool (heated), whirlpool, 3 shuffleboard courts, planned group activities, movies, recreation director, horseshoes, local tours.

Open all year. CPO. Member of ARVC; TACO. Phone: (210) 831-4653.
**SEE AD PAGE 34**

## FORT WORTH

**COWTOWN RV PARK**—Paved, level RV sites convenient to interstate. *From jct Loop 820 W & I-20: Go 10 mi W on I-20 to exit 418 (Ranch House Rd), then 1 mi E on south access road.*

WELCOME

FACILITIES: 104 sites, most common site width 31 feet, 104 full hookups, (30 & 50 amp receptacles), 104 pull-thrus, a/c allowed, heater allowed, phone hookups, group sites for tents/RVs, RV storage, laundry, public phone, limited grocery store, RV supplies, LP gas refill by weight/by meter, ice, grills.

RECREATION: rec hall, rec room/area, equipped pavilion, swim pool, planned group activities, movies, recreation director, badminton, sports field, horseshoes, volleyball.

Open all year. Phone: (817) 441-7878.
**SEE AD THIS PAGE**

## HARLINGEN

***See listings at Rio Hondo and San Benito***

TEXAS—Continued

## HOUSTON

***See listing at Bacliff***

## KERRVILLE

**GUADALUPE RIVER RV RESORT**—Paved open & shaded sites in an RV PARK on the river. *From I-10 (exit 505): Go 2 1/2 mi S to Hwy 27, then 2 1/2 mi W on Hwy 27.*

WELCOME

FACILITIES: 120 sites, most common site width 35 feet, 120 full hookups, (30 & 50 amp receptacles), 66 pull-thrus, a/c allowed, heater allowed, cable TV ($), phone hookups, group sites for RVs, cabins, handicap restroom facilities, laundry, public phone, grocery store, RV supplies, LP gas refill by weight/by meter, ice, tables, patios, grills, wood.

RECREATION: rec hall, equipped pavilion, coin games, 3 swim pools (indoor) (heated), sauna, whirlpool, river fishing, putting green, playground, 2 shuffleboard courts, planned group activities, movies, recreation director, horseshoes, hiking trails, volleyball.

No tents/tent trailers. Open all year. Member of ARVC; TACO. Phone: (800) 582-1916.
**SEE AD THIS PAGE**

## LOS FRESNOS

**PALMDALE RV RESORT**—Level, grassy sites in a suburban RV PARK. *From jct FM 1847 & Hwy 100: Go 4 mi W on Hwy 100.*

WELCOME

FACILITIES: 200 sites, most common site width 40 feet, 200 full hookups, (30 & 50 amp receptacles), a/c allowed, heater allowed, phone hookups, group sites for RVs, handicap restroom facilities, laundry, public phone, RV supplies, ice.

PALMDALE RV RESORT—Continued on next page
LOS FRESNOS, TX—Continued on next page



A prairie chicken is a grouse.

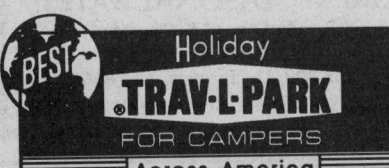

LOS FRESNOS, TX—Continued
PALMDALE RV RESORT—Continued

RECREATION: rec hall, rec room/area, swim pool (heated), whirlpool, 6 shuffleboard courts, planned group activities, recreation director, horseshoes, local tours.

No tents. Open all year. Phone: (210) 399-8694.
**SEE AD THIS PAGE**

## MC ALLEN

**MCALLEN MOBILE PARK**—An RV AREA in a mobile home park with grassy, shaded spaces in a rural setting. *From jct Hwy 336 & US 83: Go 3 1/2 mi E on US 83, then 1 3/4 mi N on US 281, then 1 3/4 mi W on Nolana Loop, then 1/2 mi N on McColl Rd.*

WELCOME

FACILITIES: 318 sites, most common site width 25 feet, 318 full hookups, (20 & 30 amp receptacles), 70 pull-thrus, a/c allowed, heater not allowed, phone hookups, RV storage, handicap restroom facilities, laundry, public phone, RV supplies, ice, patios, church services.

RECREATION: rec hall, rec room/area, swim pool (heated), whirlpool, 6 shuffleboard courts, planned group activities, recreation director, horseshoes, volleyball, local tours.

MC ALLEN, TX—Continued
MCALLEN MOBILE PARK—Continued

No pets. No tents. Open all year. Phone: (210) 682-3304.
**SEE AD THIS PAGE**

## PORT ISABEL

**PORT ISABEL PARK CENTER**—Waterfront RV PARK with large, sunny sites. *From jct Hwy 48 & Hwy 100: Go 3/4 mi E on Hwy 100, then 2 blocks S on Champion Ave.*

WELCOME

FACILITIES: 200 sites, most common site width 25 feet, 200 full hookups, (30 & 50 amp receptacles), a/c allowed, heater allowed, cable TV ($), phone hookups, group sites for tents/RVs, RV storage, laundry, public phone.

RECREATION: rec hall, boating, ramp, dock, salt water fishing, 4 shuffleboard courts, planned group activities, horseshoes.

Open all year. Member of ARVC; TACO. Phone: (210) 943-7340.
**SEE AD SOUTH PADRE ISLAND NEXT PAGE**

## RIO HONDO

**TWIN PALMS RV PARK**—Sunny sites with grass in a rural RV PARK. *From jct FM 345 & FM 106: Go 1/2 mi W on FM 106.*

WELCOME

FACILITIES: 81 sites, most common site width 20 feet, 81 full hookups, (30 & 50 amp receptacles), 79 pull-thrus, a/c allowed, heater allowed, phone hookups, laundry, public phone.

RECREATION: rec hall, rec room/area, whirlpool, 2 shuffleboard courts, planned group activities, recreation director, horseshoes, local tours.

Age restrictions may apply. Open all year. Tents accepted in summer only. Member of ARVC; TACO. Phone: (210) 748-2881.
**SEE AD HARLINGEN PAGE 35**

TEXAS—Continued

## ROCKPORT

**ANCIENT OAKS CAMPGROUND**—A grassy CAMPGROUND with live oak trees. *From jct FM 1069 & Hwy 35: Go 3/4 mi S on Hwy 35.*

WELCOME

FACILITIES: 99 sites, most common site width 25 feet, 79 full hookups, 20 water & elec (30 amp receptacles), 79 pull-thrus, a/c allowed, heater allowed, phone hookups, group sites for tents, RV storage, sewage disposal, laundry, public phone, limited grocery store, RV supplies, ice, tables.

RECREATION: rec hall, rec room/area, coin games, swim pool, basketball hoop, 2 shuffleboard courts, planned group activities, badminton, sports field, horseshoes, volleyball.

Open all year. Member of ARVC; TACO. Phone: (512) 729-5051.
**SEE AD THIS PAGE**

**BAHIA VISTA WATERFRONT RV PARK**—RV park with shaded sites on the Bay. *From FM 1069 & Hwy 35: Go 6 3/4 mi N on Hwy 35, then 1/2 mi W on FM 1781.*

WELCOME

FACILITIES: 57 sites, most common site width 30 feet, 57 full hookups, (20 & 30 amp receptacles), 21 pull-thrus, a/c allowed, heater allowed, phone hookups, laundry, public phone, tables.

RECREATION: rec hall, swim pool, salt water fishing, planned group activities, recreation director, horseshoes.

Open all year. Phone: (512) 729-1226.
**SEE AD THIS PAGE**

## SAN ANTONIO

**ALAMO-KOA**—A scenic riverside CAMPGROUND set among large trees. *From jct I-35 & Coliseum Rd: Go 1/2 mi S on Coliseum Rd, then 1 mi E on Gembler Rd. From I-10 & WW White Rd: Go 2 blocks N on WW White Rd, then 1 mi W on Gembler Rd.*

WELCOME

ALAMO-KOA—Continued on next page
SAN ANTONIO, TX—Continued on next page

ROCKPORT, TX

CAMPGROUND
Planned Activities & Fishing
Res: (800) 962-6134
Info: (512) 729-5051
1222 Bus. Hwy 35 S., Rockport, TX 78382
See listing at Rockport

In San Antonio It's
ALAMO KOA
"Deep in the Heart of Everything"
Over 30 Acres of Parkland with Shade Trees on the Salado River

• 20, 30 & 50 Amps • Phone Hookups • Laundries • 13 Public Phones • Scheduled Activities • Stocked Fishing Lake • Rec Room • Heated Pool • Spa • Free Nightly Movies • BBQ Wagon

**ON CITY BUS LINE TO** : Downtown, Alamo, Riverwalk & Missions

**CONVENIENT TO** : 18 Hole Golf Course, Convention Centers, Museums, Medical Centers, Restaurants, All City Services, Retama Park Race Track

***Discounts for Fiesta Texas & Sea World***

**Owned and Operated by the Rohde Family for 27 years**
***We Offer Personal Service and Attention***

**(210) 224-9296** **(800) 562-7783**
Reservation Line
**602 Gembler Rd., San Antonio, TX 78219**
For Free info, enter #983 on Reader Service Card
See listing at San Antonio, TX

McALLEN MOBILE PARK
Homey Atmoshpere, Friendly People
Over 300 RV Sites
Heated Pool/Spa
Large Lots with Trees
Rec Hall/Pool Room
Potlucks/Ice Cream Socials
No Pets
Shuffleboard
Planned Activities
Near Shopping,
Restaurants and
Medical Facilities
Family Owned & Operated
Member
Texas Recreational Vehicle Association
2061
281
McColl Rd
1/2 Mile
Nolana Loop
1-3/4 Mile
1-3/4 Mile
McAllen
BUS 83
83
Pharr
For Reservations Only: 1-800-847-6055
(210) 682-3304 • 4900 N. McColl Road, McAllen, TX 78504


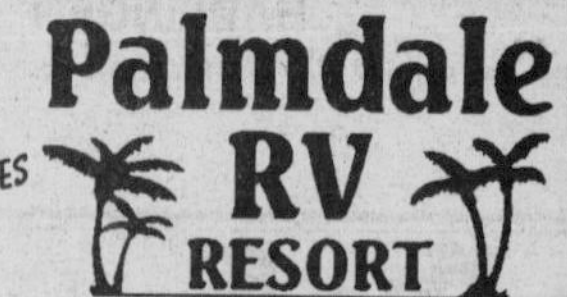

...WHERE THE "FUN" SHINES ON FOREVER & THE GOOD TIMES NEVER END!!


Palmdale RV RESORT

Quiet Country Living ❋ Minutes to Everything
Heated Pool & Spa ❋ Cable TV Available
6,000 Sq. Ft. Rec Center ❋ General Store/Gift Shop
Locked Postal Boxes ❋ Library/Card Room
Shuffleboard ❋ Pool Tables
Arts & Crafts ❋ Bingo
Line Dancing ❋ Exercise Groups
Special Events ❋ Dances ❋ Live Entertainment
Potlucks ❋ Saturday Breakfasts

***LOTS OF ACTIVITIES & LOADS OF FUN!***

HUGE 40' X 90' TEXAS-SIZE LOTS!


**Home of the Award-Winning "PALMDALE KITCHEN BAND"**
*In the Heart of the Rio Grande Valley*
*3 MI. EAST OF US 77-83 ON HIGHWAY 100*

**GREAT SEASONAL RATES!**
**Family Owned & Operated**
**PALMDALE RV RESORT**
**Box 308, Los Fresnos, TX 78566**
**(210) 399-8694 • Res: 1-800-456-7683**

**Bahia Vista Waterfront RV Park**
*Located on the Shores of Copano Bay*
• 300' Lighted Fishing Pier • Boat Tie Ups • Large Shaded Spaces • Full Hookups • • Pool • Clean, Hot Showers • Laundry • Recreation Hall • Hiking & Biking • Our nine acre park is nestled among thousands of ancient windswept Live Oak trees that provide shade and add rustic beauty to this peaceful bayside setting. Wildlife of all types abound in this area — a birders dream come true. Hike or bike the numerous trails and backroads along the bay. Spectacular sunrises & sunsets over beautiful Copano Bay are yours to behold from the bluffs.
***COME TO OUR PARK AND ENJOY REAL SOUTH TEXAS HOSPITALITY!***
5 mi N on Hwy 35, then W on FM 1781
**HCO 1, Box 239C, Rockport, TX 78382 • (512) 729-1226**

SAN ANTONIO, TX—Continued
ALAMO-KOA—Continued

FACILITIES: 350 sites, most common site width 25 feet, 220 full hookups, 130 water & elec (20,30 & 50 amp receptacles), 175 pull-thrus, a/c allowed ($), heater allowed ($), phone hookups, group sites for tents/RVs, cabins, sewage disposal, laundry, public phone, full service store, RV supplies, LP gas refill by weight/by meter, ice, tables, patios, fire rings, grills, wood, church services.

RECREATION: rec hall, coin games, swim pool (heated), whirlpool, lake/river fishing, basketball hoop, playground, planned group activities, movies, sports field, horseshoes, local tours.

Open all year. Member of ARVC; TACO. Phone: (210) 224-9296.

**SEE AD PAGE 36**

### SAN BENITO

**FUN N SUN**—RV PARK with open, grassy sites. *From jct US 83 & US 77: Go 3 mi S on US 83/77 to Helen Moore Road exit, then 1/2 mi S on West service road, then 1/2 mi W on FM 509.*

FACILITIES: 1402 sites, most common site width 35 feet, 1402 full hookups, (30 & 50 amp receptacles), 800 pull-thrus, a/c allowed, heater allowed, cable TV, phone hookups, group sites for RVs, handicap restroom facilities, laundry, public phone, LP gas refill by weight/by meter, ice, church services, traffic control gate/guard.

RECREATION: rec hall, rec room/area, swim pool (heated), whirlpool, driving range, putting green, 20 shuffleboard courts, planned group activities, movies, recreation director, 2 tennis courts, horseshoes, volleyball, local tours.

No tents. Age restrictions may apply. Open all year. Member of ARVC; TACO. Phone: (210) 399-5125.

**SEE AD HARLINGEN PAGE 35**

### SOUTH PADRE ISLAND

***See listing at Port Isabel***

### WESLACO

**LAKEVIEW MOBILE HOME & TRAVEL TRAILER PARK**—Shaded & open, grassy sites in an RV AREA IN A MOBILE HOME PARK surrounded by trees & birds. *From jct US 83 & FM 88: Go 2 mi E on US 83, then 2 1/2 mi S on FM 1015.*

FACILITIES: 164 sites, accepts full hookup units only, 164 full hookups, (30 amp receptacles), a/c allowed, heater allowed, phone hookups, RV storage, laundry, public phone, patios, church services.

RECREATION: rec hall, swim pool (heated), whirlpool, boating, ramp, dock, lake/pond fishing, 4 shuf-

WESLACO, TX—Continued
LAKEVIEW MOBILE HOME & TRAVEL TRAILER PARK—Continued

fleboard courts, planned group activities, horseshoes, hiking trails.

No tents. Age restrictions may apply. Open all year. Phone: (210) 565-5400.

**SEE AD THIS PAGE**

# UTAH

### HURRICANE

**THE CANYONS RV RESORT**—A CAMP RESORT with a mountain view offering luxury RV sites for sale. *From jct I-15 (exit 16) & Hwy 9: Go 6 1/2 mi E on Hwy 9.*

FACILITIES: 27 sites, most common site width 40 feet, 27 full hookups, (50 amp receptacles), a/c allowed ($), heater allowed ($), public phone, tables, patios.

RECREATION: rec room/area.

No tents/tent trailers. Open all year. Phone: (801) 635-0200.

**SEE AD ST. GEORGE THIS PAGE**

### ST. GEORGE

**HARRISBURG LAKESIDE RV RESORT**—A membership RV PARK with open & level sites with view of mountains. Currently accepting overnight guests. *From jct I-15 (exit 22) & Leeds: Go 2 mi S on east frontage road.*

FACILITIES: 138 sites, most common site width 20 feet, 138 full hookups, (20,30 & 50 amp receptacles), 75 pull-thrus, a/c allowed, heater allowed, cable TV, group sites for RVs, RV storage, handicap restroom facilities, sewage disposal, laundry, public phone, grocery store, RV supplies, gasoline, ice, tables.

RECREATION: rec room/area, swim pool (heated), whirlpool, playground, 2 shuffleboard courts, planned group activities, horseshoes, hiking trails.

No tents. Open all year. Member of ARVC. Phone: (801) 879-2212.

**SEE AD THIS PAGE**

UTAH—Continued

### SALT LAKE CITY

**CAMP VIP**—A CAMPGROUND in town with shade and a mountain view. Altitude 4250 ft. *From I-15 N' or S'bound or I-80 W'bound (exit 311 Airport-Reno): Go 1 1/2 mi W on I-80 (exit 118 Redwood Rd), then 1/4 mi N on Redwood Rd, then 1/4 mi E on N Temple. From I-80 E' bound (exit 115 N Temple): Stay on Temple and go 3 1/2 E on Temple.*

FACILITIES: 563 sites, most common site width 17 feet, 353 full hookups, 120 water & elec (20,30 & 50 amp receptacles), 90 no hookups, 259 pull-thrus, a/c allowed ($), heater allowed ($), phone hookups, group sites for tents/RVs, cabins, RV storage, handicap restroom facilities, sewage disposal, laundry, public phone, full service store, RV supplies, LP gas refill by meter, gasoline, ice, tables.

RECREATION: rec room/area, coin games, 2 swim pools (heated), wading pool, whirlpool, playground, horseshoes, local tours.

Open all year. Pool open Memorial Day through Labor Day. Member of ARVC; UCOA. Phone: (801) 328-0224.

**SEE AD THIS PAGE**

| UT | From the Indian meaning: "High in the Mountains" | UT |
|---|---|---|

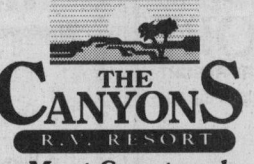

# VERMONT

## COLCHESTER

**LONE PINE CAMPSITES**—CAMPGROUND with paved roads & level, grassy sites. *N'bound from jct I-89 (exit 16) & US 2/7: Go 3 1/2 mi N on US 2/7, then 1 mi left on Bay Rd. S'bound from jct I-89 (exit 17) & US 2/7: Go 3 1/2 mi S on US 2/7, then 1 mi right on Bay Rd.*

FACILITIES: 260 sites, most common site width 30 feet, 165 full hookups, 95 water & elec (15 & 30 amp receptacles), a/c allowed ($), phone hookups, RV rentals, RV storage, handicap restroom facilities, sewage disposal, laundry, public phone, grocery store, RV supplies, LP gas refill by weight/by meter, ice, tables, fire rings, grills, wood.

RECREATION: rec room/area, equipped pavilion, coin games, 2 swim pools, mini-golf ($), basketball hoop, playground, shuffleboard court, planned group activities, 4 tennis courts, horseshoes, volleyball.

Open May 1 through Oct 15. 3 day minimum stay holiday weekends. No refunds. Member of VAPCOO. Phone: (802) 878-5447.

**SEE AD THIS PAGE**

***USE THE ALPHABETICAL QUICK REFERENCE INDEX AT THE END OF BOOK***





## SOUTH HERO

**APPLE TREE BAY RESORT**—Mostly open, rolling grassy terrain adjacent to lake and marina. *From I-89 (exit 17) & US 2: Go 6 mi NW on US 2.*

FACILITIES: 300 sites, most common site width 25 feet, 200 full hookups, 100 water & elec (30 amp receptacles), 20 pull-thrus, a/c allowed, phone hookups, group sites for tents/RVs, RV rentals, RV storage, sewage disposal, laundry, public phone, full service store, RV supplies, LP gas refill by weight/by meter, gasoline, marine gas, ice, tables, fire rings, grills, wood.

RECREATION: rec hall, rec room/area, coin games, swim pool (heated), lake swimming, boating, canoeing, ramp, dock, 3 row/4 sail/4 canoe/4 motor boat rentals, water skiing, lake/pond fishing, fishing guides, golf ($), basketball hoop, 4 bike rentals, playground, planned group activities, recreation director, badminton, horseshoes, volleyball. Recreation open to the public.

Open May 1 through Oct 25. Member of VAPCOO. Phone: (802) 372-5398.

**SEE AD THIS PAGE**

# VIRGINIA

## BURNT CHIMNEY

**BLUE RIDGE CAMPGROUND**—Lakeside, semi-wooded CAMPGROUND. *From jct Hwy 122 & CR 670: Go 8 1/2 mi SE on CR 670.*

FACILITIES: 102 sites, most common site width 25 feet, 76 full hookups, 26 water & elec (20 amp receptacles), a/c allowed ($), heater allowed ($), group sites for tents/RVs, sewage disposal, laundry, public phone, limited grocery store, RV supplies, LP gas refill by weight, ice, tables, grills, wood.

RECREATION: rec room/area, pavilion, coin games, lake swimming, boating, ramp, dock, lake fishing, playground, sports field, horseshoes, hiking trails, volleyball.

Open Apr 1 through Nov 1. Phone: (540) 721-3866.

**SEE AD THIS PAGE**

## CHINCOTEAGUE

**INLET VIEW WATERFRONT FAMILY CAMPGROUND**—Bayside CAMPGROUND with open & wooded sites. *From jct US 13 & Hwy 175: Go 11 mi E on Hwy 175, then 3 mi S on Main St.*

FACILITIES: 414 sites, most common site width 25 feet, 225 full hookups, 139 water & elec



(20 & 30 amp receptacles), 50 no hookups, a/c allowed ($), heater allowed ($), cable TV ($), phone hookups, group sites for tents/RVs, RV rentals, cabins, RV storage, sewage disposal, laundry, public phone, grocery store, RV supplies, LP gas refill by weight, ice, tables.

RECREATION: rec hall, coin games, boating, ramp, dock, salt water fishing, playground.

Open all year. Dec 1 - Mar 1 full hook-up units only. No refunds. Phone: (804) 336-5126.

**SEE AD THIS PAGE**

**TOM'S COVE CAMPING**—Waterfront CAMPGROUND with open & semi-wooded sites. *From jct US 13 & Hwy 175: Go 11 mi E on Hwy 175, then 1 1/4 mi S on Main St, then 1/2 mi E on Beebe Rd.*

FACILITIES: 888 sites, most common site width 35 feet, 633 full hookups, 200 water & elec (20 & 30 amp receptacles), 55 no hookups, 60 pull-thrus, a/c allowed ($), heater allowed ($), cable TV ($), group sites for tents/RVs, RV storage, handicap restroom facilities, sewage disposal, laundry, public phone, full service store, RV supplies, LP gas refill by weight/by meter, gasoline, ice, tables, wood, church services, guard.

RECREATION: rec hall, coin games, swim pool, salt water swimming, boating, ramp, dock, salt water fishing, 30 bike rentals, playground, sports field, horseshoes.

Open Mar 1 through Nov 30. Phone: (804) 336-6498.

**SEE AD THIS PAGE**

## GLOUCESTER POINT

**GLOUCESTER POINT CAMPGROUND**—Riverside with semi-wooded sites. *From jct Hwy 216 & US 17: Go 3 mi N on US 17, then 3 mi E on CR 636 (follow signs).*

FACILITIES: 230 sites, most common site width 30 feet, 165 full hookups, 65 water & elec (20 amp receptacles), a/c allowed ($), heater allowed ($), phone hookups, group sites for tents/RVs, RV rentals, sewage disposal, laundry, public phone, limited grocery store, RV supplies, LP gas refill by weight/by meter, ice, tables, fire rings, wood, church services.

RECREATION: rec room/area, pavilion, coin games, 2 swim pools, wading pool, boating, ramp, dock, salt water/pond fishing, basketball hoop, playground, planned group activities (weekends only), sports field, horseshoes, volleyball.

Open all year. Facilities fully operational Apr 1 through Nov 1. Phone: (804) 642-4316.

**SEE AD THIS PAGE**

# WASHINGTON

**FIDALGO BAY RESORT**—Level, grassy sites in a resort RV PARK on Fidalgo Bay. *From jct I-5 (exit 230) & Hwy 20: Go 12 mi W on Hwy 20, then 1 mi N on Fidalgo Bay Rd.*

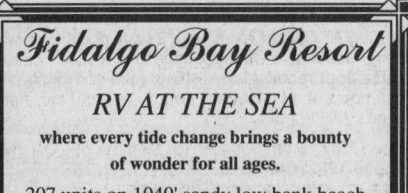

FACILITIES: 187 sites, most common site width 20 feet, 187 full hookups, (20,30 & 50 amp receptacles), 62 pull-thrus, a/c allowed, heater allowed, cable TV, group sites for RVs, handicap restroom facilities, laundry, public phone, limited grocery store, RV supplies.

RECREATION: rec hall, salt water swimming, boating, ramp, water skiing, salt water fishing, local tours.

No tents. Open all year. Member of ARVC; WARVC. Phone: (800) PARK-4-RV.

**SEE AD THIS PAGE**

## BELLINGHAM

**FERNDALE CAMPGROUND & RV PARK**—Family-oriented RV PARK with easy access to the interstate. *From I-5 (exit 263): Go 1 mi N on Portal Way.*

FACILITIES: 117 sites, most common site width 20 feet, 70 full hookups, 47 water & elec (20 & 30 amp receptacles), 111 pull-thrus, a/c allowed ($), heater allowed, cable TV ($), group sites for tents/RVs, RV storage, sewage disposal, laundry, public phone, grocery store, LP gas refill by meter, ice, tables, fire rings.

RECREATION: rec room/area, playground, badminton, sports field, horseshoes, volleyball.

Open all year. Phone: (360) 384-2622.

**SEE AD THIS PAGE**

## ELMA

**ELMA RV PARK**—Open, level, prepared sites in a rural RV PARK. *From jct US 8 & Hwy 12: Go 1/4 mi S on Hwy 12.*

FACILITIES: 87 sites, most common site width 25 feet, 40 full hookups, (30 & 50 amp receptacles), 47 no hookups, 102 pull-thrus, a/c allowed, heater allowed, cable TV, phone hookups, group sites for tents/RVs, RV storage, sewage disposal, laundry, public phone, LP gas refill by meter, tables.

RECREATION: badminton, horseshoes, volleyball.

Open all year. Member of ARVC; WARVC. Phone: (360) 482-4053.

**SEE AD THIS PAGE**

## SPOKANE

**PONDEROSA HILL RV PARK, A PARK WASHINGTON FACILITY**—Wooded RV PARK under towering pines with level, spacious sites. *From jct US 2/395 & I-90: Go 8 mi W on I-90 (exit 272), then cross overpass, then 1/8 mi E on Hallett Rd, then 7/8 mi NE on West Bow, turning back onto Hallett Rd, then 1/2 mi S on Mallon Rd.*

FACILITIES: 168 sites, most common site width 34 feet, 168 full hookups, (20,30 & 50 amp receptacles), 42 pull-thrus, a/c allowed, heater allowed, cable TV, phone hookups, group sites for RVs, laundry, public phone, LP gas refill by meter, ice, tables, traffic control gate.

SPOKANE, WA—Continued
PONDEROSA HILL RV PARK, A PARK WASHINGTON FACILITY—Continued

RECREATION: basketball hoop, playground, badminton, horseshoes, volleyball.

Open all year. Member of ARVC; WARVC. Phone: (509) 747-9415.

**SEE AD THIS PAGE**

# WISCONSIN

## MONTELLO

**WILDERNESS CAMPGROUND**—Shaded, grassy sites on the banks of 2 private lakes. *From jct Hwy 23 & Hwy 22 Southbound: Go 7 mi S on Hwy 22.*

FACILITIES: 300 sites, most common site width 45 feet, 70 full hookups, 190 water & elec (15,20 & 30 amp receptacles), 40 no hookups, 75 pull-thrus, a/c allowed ($), heater allowed ($), phone hookups, group sites for tents/RVs, RV storage, sewage disposal, laundry, public phone, grocery store, RV supplies, LP gas refill by weight/by meter, ice, tables, patios, fire rings, wood.

RECREATION: rec room/area, pavilion, coin games, lake swimming, boating, no motors, canoeing, ramp, 12 row/2 canoe/1 pedal boat rentals, lake fishing, mini-golf ($), basketball hoop, 12 bike rentals, playground, shuffleboard court, planned group activities (weekends only), movies, recreation director, badminton, sports field, horseshoes, hiking trails, volleyball.

Open Apr 23 through Oct 10. Member of ARVC; WACO. Phone: (608) 297-2002.

**SEE AD WISCONSIN DELLS THIS PAGE**



WISCONSIN—Continued

## WISCONSIN DELLS

*See listing at Montello*

**FASCINATING FACT**

***British sailors were ordered to sew short sleeves on their undershirts so that tender royal eyes wouldn't see the underside of life. Longshoremen unloading tea in the 17th century wore them and the "tea shirt" became "T-shirt."***

# WYOMING

## BUFFALO

**BIG HORN MTNS CAMPGROUND**—An RV PARK with open, grassy sites. Altitude 5000 ft. *From jct I-25 & US 16: Go 4 mi W on US 16.*

FACILITIES: 83 sites, most common site width 18 feet, 30 full hookups, 28 water & elec (20 & 30 amp receptacles), 25 no hookups, 22 pull-thrus, a/c allowed ($), heater allowed ($), group sites for tents/RVs, RV storage, sewage disposal, laundry, public phone, limited grocery store, RV supplies, ice, tables, grills, wood.

RECREATION: rec room/area, coin games, swim pool (heated), stream fishing, playground, sports field, horseshoes, hiking trails.

Open all year. Phone: (307) 684-2307.
**SEE AD THIS PAGE**

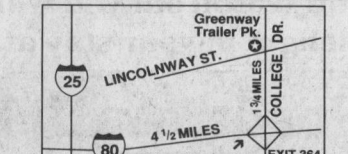





## CHEYENNE

**GREENWAY TRAILER PARK**—An open RV AREA in a mobile home park located in town. Altitude 6200 ft. *From jct I-25 & I-80: Go 4 1/2 mi E on I-80 (exit 364), then 1 3/4 mi N on College Dr.*

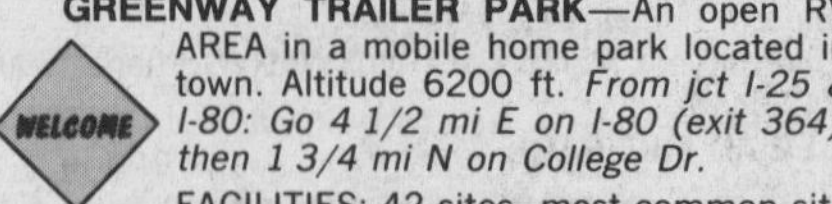

FACILITIES: 42 sites, most common site width 20 feet, 42 full hookups, (20,30 & 50 amp receptacles), 32 pull-thrus, a/c allowed, heater allowed, phone hookups, laundry, public phone, ice.

Open all year. Phone: (307) 634-6696.
**SEE AD THIS PAGE**

## THERMOPOLIS

**FOUNTAIN OF YOUTH RV PARK**—Shaded RV PARK with valley sites and a mineral pool. *From jct Hwy 120 & US 20: Go 2 mi N on US 20.*

FACILITIES: 62 sites, most common site width 18 feet, 35 ft. max RV length, 48





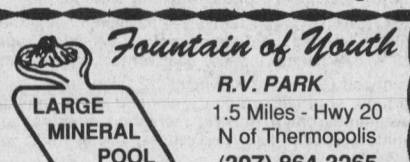

full hookups, 14 water & elec (20,30 & 50 amp receptacles), 62 pull-thrus, a/c allowed, heater allowed, phone hookups, RV storage, sewage disposal, laundry, public phone, RV supplies, LP gas refill by meter, ice, tables, patios, grills, guard.

RECREATION: swim pool (heated), boating, row boat rentals, river fishing, planned group activities, horseshoes, hiking trails, local tours.

Open Mar 1 through Nov 1. Member of WCA. Phone: (307) 864-3265.
**SEE AD THIS PAGE**



**SAFETY TIP**

**You can see frostbite (as a white spot on the skin) before you feel it. Your nose, ears and feet are the most vulnerable. Rub the skin next to the frostbitten area - not the frostbitten area itself.**

# CANADA

# NEW BRUNSWICK

## MONCTON

**CAMPER'S CITY**—A CAMPGROUND with open, grassy sites surrounded by woods near major highway. *From jct Hwy 126 & Hwy 2: Go 4.8 km/3 mi E on Hwy 2 (exit 492), then 1 block N on Mapleton Rd, then .4 km/1/4 mi E on Queens Way Dr.*

FACILITIES: 171 sites, 105 full hookups, 42 water & elec, 24 elec (15 amp receptacles), 42 pull-thrus, group sites for RVs, sewage disposal, laundry, public phone, limited grocery store, RV supplies, LP gas





refill by weight/by meter, gasoline, ice, tables, traffic control gate/guard.

RECREATION: rec hall, coin games, swim pool (heated), basketball hoop, playground, sports field, horseshoes, hiking trails, volleyball.

Open Jun 1 through Oct 15. Facilities fully operational Jun 1 through Sep 30. Phone: (506) 384-7867.
**SEE AD THIS PAGE**

# NOVA SCOTIA





## AYLESFORD

***See listing at Berwick***

## BERWICK

**KLAHANIE KAMPING**—CAMPGROUND with grassy sites, surrounded by pine & birch trees, in conjunction with an RV sales & service facility. *From jct Hwy 1 & Millville Rd: Go .8 km/1/2 mi S on Millville Rd.*

FACILITIES: 135 sites, most common site width 30 feet, 65 full hookups, 35 water & elec (15 amp receptacles), 35 no hookups, a/c allowed ($), heater allowed ($), cable TV ($), RV storage, sewage disposal, laundry, public phone, limited grocery store, RV supplies, LP gas refill by weight, ice, tables, fire rings, wood, traffic control gate.

RECREATION: rec room/area, 2 swim pools, lake swimming, boating, no motors, canoeing, 1 row/1 canoe/1 pedal boat rentals, lake fishing, mini-golf ($), basketball hoop, 2 shuffleboard courts, sports field, horseshoes, hiking trails.

Open May 15 through Oct 15. Member of COA of NS. Phone: (902) 847-9316.
**SEE AD AYLESFORD THIS PAGE**

**KLAHANIE TRAILER SALES**—*From jct Hwy 101 (exit 15 ) & Commercial St (Hwy 360): Go 1.6 km/1 mi S on Commercial St, then .4 km/1/4 mi E on Hwy 1.* SALES: travel trailers, 5th wheels, motor homes, mini-motor homes, fold down camping trailers. SERVICES: RV appliance mechanic full-time, emergency road service business hours, LP gas refill by weight, RV rentals, RV storage, sells parts/accessories, sells camping supplies, installs hitches. Open all year. Phone: (902) 538-7532.
**SEE AD AYLESFORD THIS PAGE**

NOVA SCOTIA—Continued on next page

NOVA SCOTIA—Continued

### KINGSTON

**HOLIDAY HAVEN**—CAMPGROUND with open grassy sites surrounded by trees. *E'bound from jct Hwy 101 (exit 17) & Marshall Rd: Go .8 km/1/2 mi N on Marshall Rd & follow signs. W'bound from Hwy 101 (exit 17): Go .8 km/1/2 mi N on Bishop Mountain Rd, then W on Pleasant St & follow signs for 2 km/1 1/4 mi.*

FACILITIES: 207 sites, most common site width 30 feet, 97 full hookups, 72 water & elec (15 amp receptacles), 38 no hookups, a/c allowed ($), heater allowed ($), group sites for RVs, cabins, sewage disposal, laundry, public phone, grocery store, RV supplies, ice, tables, fire rings, wood, traffic control gate.

RECREATION: rec hall, coin games, swim pool, wading pool, water slide, mini-golf ($), basketball hoop, playground, planned group activities, movies, recreation director, badminton, sports field, horseshoes, hiking trails, volleyball.

Open May 15 through Oct 15. Phone: (902) 765-2830.
**SEE AD THIS PAGE**

### LAKE CHARLOTTE

**E & F WEBBER LAKESIDE PARK**—Lakeside CAMPGROUND with wooded sites. *From Hwy 7: Go 4.8 km/3 mi N on Upper Lakeville Rd.*

FACILITIES: 66 sites, 48 full hookups, 4 water & elec (15 amp receptacles), 14 no hookups, 10 pull-thrus, tent rentals, laundry, public phone, limited grocery store, marine gas, ice, tables, fire rings, wood.

RECREATION: rec hall, lake swimming, boating, canoeing, ramp, dock, 1 row/2 canoe/2 pedal boat rentals, lake fishing, playground, sports field, horseshoes.

Open May 15 through Oct 15. Member of COA of NS. Phone: (902) 845-2340.
**SEE AD THIS PAGE**

### NINE MILE RIVER

**GREEN VALLEY CAMPGROUNDS**—Meadow CAMPGROUND on a river. Many sites occupied by seasonals. *From jct Hwy 14 & Renfrew Rd: Go 2.4 km/1 1/2 mi S on Renfrew Rd.*

FACILITIES: 220 sites, most common site width 30 feet, 56 full hookups, 120 water & elec (15 amp receptacles), 44 no hookups, a/c allowed, heater allowed, RV storage, sewage disposal, portable dump, laundry, public phone, limited grocery store, ice, tables, fire rings, wood, traffic control gate.

RECREATION: rec hall, rec room/area, coin games, swim pool, river swimming, canoeing, river fishing, basketball hoop, playground, planned group activites (weekends only), recreation director, sports field, horseshoes.

Open Victoria Day through Labour Day. Member of COA of NS. Phone: (902) 883-2617.
**SEE AD THIS PAGE**



## ONTARIO

### AHMIC HARBOUR

**AHMIC LAKE RESORT**—Secluded, lakeside CAMPGROUND. *From east jct Hwy 520 & Hwy 124: Go 6.5 km/4 mi W on Hwy 124.*

FACILITIES: 70 sites, most common site width 12 feet, 29 full hookups, 18 water & elec, 21 elec (15 & 30 amp receptacles), 2 no hookups, 4 pull-thrus, a/c not allowed, cabins, sewage disposal, laundry, public phone, limited grocery store, RV supplies, LP gas refill by weight, gasoline, marine gas, ice, tables, fire rings, wood.

RECREATION: lake swimming, boating, canoeing, ramp, dock, 2 row/12 canoe/1 pedal/8 motor boat rentals, water skiing, lake fishing, playground, planned group activities (weekends only), badminton, sports field, horseshoes, hiking trails, volleyball.

Open all year. Facilities fully operational May 15 through Oct 15. Member of OPCA. Phone: (705) 387-3853.
**SEE AD THIS PAGE**

### ANGUS

**NOTTAWASAGA VALLEY CONSERVATION AUTHORITY**—*From jct Hwy 400 & Hwy 90: Go 19 km/12 mi W on Hwy 90.* Administrator over 2 campgrounds and 9 day-use parks. Open all year. Phone: (705) 424-1479.
**SEE AD THIS PAGE**

### BAILIEBORO

**BENSFORT BRIDGE RESORT**—Rustic CAMPGROUND on the Otonabee River. *From jct Hwy 28 & CR 2: Go 6.4 km/4 mi E on CR 2, then 6.4 km/4 mi N to park.*

FACILITIES: 63 sites, most common site width 40 feet, 51 full hookups, 7 water & elec (30 amp receptacles), 5 no hookups, a/c allowed ($), heater allowed, phone hookups, cabins, sewage disposal, laundry, public phone, limited grocery store, marine gas, ice, tables, fire rings, wood, traffic control gate.

RECREATION: rec hall, lake swimming, boating, canoeing, ramp, dock, 2 row/2 canoe/5 motor boat rentals, water skiing, river fishing, planned group activities (weekends only), badminton, horseshoes, volleyball.

Open May 5 through Oct 15. Member of OPCA. Phone: (705) 939-6515.
**SEE AD PETERBOROUGH PAGE 44**

ONTARIO—Continued on next page



SAY YOU SAW IT IN WOODALL'S

**When baking at high altitudes, use more water, and lengthen the cooking time.**

ONTARIO—Continued

## BANCROFT

**THE HOMESTEAD TRAILER PARK**—Secluded lakeside CAMPGROUND with wooded & open sites. Most sites occupied by seasonal campers. *From south city limits: Go 29 km/18 mi S on Hwy 28, then 3.6 km/2 1/4 mi W on Dyno Rd, then 1.6 km/1 mi S on Road 10.*

FACILITIES: 150 sites, most common site width 40 feet, 150 full hookups, (15 & 30 amp receptacles), 2 pull-thrus, a/c allowed, heater allowed, cable TV, phone hookups, laundry, public phone, full service store, ice, tables, fire rings, wood.

RECREATION: rec hall, rec room/area, coin games, lake swimming, boating, canoeing, ramp, dock, 3 canoe/2 pedal/2 motor boat rentals, water skiing, lake fishing, basketball hoop, playground, planned group activities (weekends only), movies, badminton, sports field, horseshoes, volleyball.

Open May 1 through Oct 15. Member of OPCA. Phone: (613) 339-2500.

**SEE AD THIS PAGE**

## BARRIE

**UTOPIA (Nottawasaga Vly. Conservation Area)**—*From jct Hwy 400 & Hwy 90: Go 16 km/10 mi W on Hwy 90, then 4 km/2 1/2 mi S on Con Rd 6 of Essa Twp.*

FACILITIES: 80 sites, 10 full hookups, (30 amp receptacles), 70 no hookups, a/c allowed, heater allowed, RV storage, non-flush toilets, sewage disposal, tables, fire rings, grills, wood, guard.

RECREATION: equipped pavilion, lake swimming, boating, no motors, canoeing, pond fishing, sports field, horseshoes, hiking trails, cross country skiing. Recreation open to the public.

Open all year. Facilities fully operational May 1 through end Sep. No showers. Phone: (705) 424-6908.

**SEE AD ANGUS PAGE 41**



ONTARIO—Continued

## BORNHOLM

**WOODLAND LAKE CAMP & RV RESORT**—A CAMPGROUND with open and shaded sites overlooking a woodland lake. *From jct Hwy 8 & Hwy 23: Go 8 km/5 mi N on Hwy 23, then 4.8 km/3 mi W on Logan Concession Rd 10-11 to park.*

FACILITIES: 160 sites, most common site width 40 feet, 139 full hookups, 5 water & elec (15 & 30 amp receptacles), 16 no hookups, a/c allowed ($), heater allowed ($), laundry, public phone, limited grocery store, LP gas refill by weight, ice, tables, fire rings, wood, traffic control gate.

RECREATION: rec hall, rec room/area, lake swimming, boating, no motors, canoeing, 4 pedal boat rentals, lake fishing, basketball hoop, playground, planned group activities (weekends only), horse riding trails, sports field, horseshoes, hiking trails.

Open May 1 through mid Oct. Member of OPCA. Phone: (519) 347-2315.

**SEE AD THIS PAGE**

## DUNNVILLE

**GRAND RIVER RV RESORT**—Open & shaded sites in a CAMPGROUND on the Grand River. *From Hwy 3 in town center: Go .8 km/1/2 mi W on Hwy 3, then 9.6 km/6 mi S on Regional Rd 17.*

FACILITIES: 263 sites, 263 full hookups, (15 & 30 amp receptacles), 12 pull-thrus, a/c allowed ($), heater not allowed, phone hookups, RV rentals, handicap restroom facilities, portable dump, public phone, limited grocery store, RV supplies, LP gas refill by weight, gasoline, marine gas, ice, tables, fire rings, wood, traffic control gate.

RECREATION: rec room/area, coin games, swim pool, wading pool, boating, canoeing, ramp, dock, water skiing, river fishing, mini-golf, basketball hoop, playground, shuffleboard court, planned group activities, movies, sports field, horseshoes, volleyball, local tours.

No tents. Open May 1 through Oct 31. Phone: (905) 774-4257.

**SEE AD THIS PAGE**



ONTARIO—Continued

## DUTTON

**DUTTONA TRAILER PARK**—CAMPGROUND overlooking Lake Erie with shaded and open sites. *From Hwy 401 (exit 149): Go 4.8 km/3 mi S at exit 149, then 3.2 km/2 mi W on Hwy 3, then S on Coyne Rd.*

FACILITIES: 250 sites, most common site width 35 feet, 250 full hookups, (15 & 30 amp receptacles), 4 pull-thrus, RV storage, laundry, public phone, limited grocery store, RV supplies, LP gas refill by weight, ice, tables, patios, fire rings, wood, traffic control gate.

RECREATION: rec hall, rec room/area, coin games, swim pool, lake swimming, lake fishing, playground, 2 shuffleboard courts, planned group activities (weekends only), horseshoes, volleyball.

Open mid May through mid Oct. Phone: (519) 762-3643.

**SEE AD THIS PAGE**

## GRAND BEND

**THE DUNES OAKRIDGE PARK**—Open, shaded and level sites in a CAMPGROUND. Most sites occupied by seasonal campers. *From jct Hwy 81 & Hwy 21: Go 11 km/7 mi S on Hwy 21, then .4 km/1/4 mi W on Northville Crescent.*

FACILITIES: 208 sites, most common site width 40 feet, 119 full hookups, 9 water & elec (15 & 30 amp receptacles), 80 no hookups, a/c allowed, heater not allowed, phone hookups, group sites for tents, RV rentals, RV storage, sewage disposal, laundry, public phone, limited grocery store, RV supplies, LP gas refill by weight, ice, tables, fire rings, wood, traffic control gate.

RECREATION: rec hall, rec room/area, coin games, 2 swim pools, wading pool, basketball hoop, playground, planned group activities, movies, recreation director, horseshoes, hiking trails. Recreation open to the public.

Open all year. Facilities fully operational mid May through mid Oct. Member of OPCA. Phone: (519) 243-2500.

**SEE AD THIS PAGE**

## LINDSAY

**ALPINE RV RESORT - CAMPSITE**—Located on the Scugog River. Most sites occupied by seasonal campers. *From north jct Hwy 7 & Hwy 35: Go 4.8 km/3 mi N on Hwy 35, then 3.2 km/2 mi E on Kenrei Park Rd.*

FACILITIES: 122 sites, most common site width 50 feet, 102 full hookups, 20 water & elec (15 & 30 amp receptacles), 11 pull-thrus, a/c allowed, heater allowed ($), phone hookups, RV rentals, RV storage, handicap restroom facilities, sewage disposal, laundry, public phone, grocery store, ice, tables, fire rings, wood, traffic control gate.

RECREATION: rec hall, rec room/area, coin games, swim pool, boating, canoeing, ramp, dock, 2 canoe/1 pedal/3 motor boat rentals, water skiing, river fishing, basketball hoop, playground, planned group activities, movies, recreation director, badminton, sports field, horseshoes, volleyball.

Open May 12 through Oct 15. Member of OPCA. Phone: (705) 324-6447.

**SEE AD NEXT PAGE**

LINDSAY, ON—Continued on next page



**If you can't make a mistake, you can't make anything.** ***Marva Collins***

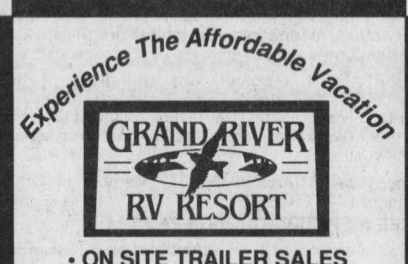

LINDSAY, ON—Continued

**DOUBLE "M" RV PARK & CAMPGROUND**—CAMPGROUND on the Scugog River. *From south jct Hwy 35 & Hwy 7: Go 1.2 km/3/4 mi W on Hwy 7, then .4 km/1/4 mi S on Victoria Rd 4.*

FACILITIES: 191 sites, most common site width 40 feet, 170 full hookups, 21 water & elec (15 & 30 amp receptacles), a/c allowed ($), heater not allowed, group sites for tents/RVs, RV storage, sewage disposal, laundry, public phone, limited grocery store, RV supplies, LP gas refill by weight, ice, tables, fire rings, wood, traffic control gate.

RECREATION: rec hall, rec room/area, coin games, river swimming, boating, canoeing, ramp, dock, river fishing, basketball hoop, playground, planned group activities (weekends only), movies, sports field, horseshoes, volleyball.

Open May 15 through mid Oct. Member of OPCA. Phone: (705) 324-9317.
**SEE AD THIS PAGE**

## NEW LOWELL

**NEW LOWELL (Nottawasaga Vly. Conservation Area)**—*From town center: Go 2 km/1.2 mi S on Mill St.*

FACILITIES: 98 sites, 49 water & elec (15 & 30 amp receptacles), 49 no hookups, group sites for tents/RVs, RV storage, handicap restroom facilities, sewage disposal, public phone, limited grocery store, ice, tables, fire rings, grills, wood, guard.

RECREATION: equipped pavilion, pond swimming, boating, no motors, canoeing, pond fishing, basketball hoop, playground, sports field, horseshoes, hiking trails, volleyball, cross country skiing, snowmobile trails. Recreation open to the public.

Open all year. Facilities full operational May 1 through end Sep. Phone: (705) 424-1479.
**SEE AD ANGUS PAGE 41**

## NEWTONVILLE

**MARYDALE ESTATES**—CAMPGROUND in a natural setting. *From jct Hwy 401 (exit 448) & Reg. Rd 18: Go .8 km/1/2 mi S to 1st Concession Rd, then follow signs 3.2 km/2 mi E .*

FACILITIES: 180 sites, most common site width 33 feet, 180 full hookups, (15 & 30 amp receptacles), a/c allowed, heater allowed, handicap restroom facilities, public phone, RV supplies, tables, fire rings, wood.

RECREATION: rec hall, swim pool, 2 shuffleboard courts, sports field, horseshoes, hiking trails, cross country skiing, snowmobile trails.

Open all year. Pool open May 15 thru Oct 15. Phone: (905) 786-2345.
**SEE AD THIS PAGE**

## NIAGARA FALLS

**CAMPARK RESORTS**—Quiet, level CAMPGROUND near tourist attractions. *From jct Queen Elizabeth Way & Hwy 420 (exit Lundy's Lane, Hwy 20): Go 2.4 km/1 1/2 mi W on Lundy's Lane.*

FACILITIES: 250 sites, most common site width 36 feet, 160 full hookups, 26 water & elec (15 & 30 amp receptacles), 64 no hookups, 7 pull-thrus, a/c allowed ($), heater allowed ($), phone hookups, group sites for tents/RVs, cabins, RV storage, sewage disposal, laundry, public phone, limited grocery store, RV supplies, ice, tables, fire rings, wood, traffic control gate.

RECREATION: rec hall, rec room/area, pavilion, coin games, swim pool (heated), basketball hoop, playground, planned group activities (weekends only), movies, recreation director, badminton, sports field, horseshoes, volleyball, local tours.

Open all year. Facilities fully operational May 1 through Oct 31. Member of OPCA. Phone: (905) 358-3873.
**SEE AD THIS PAGE**

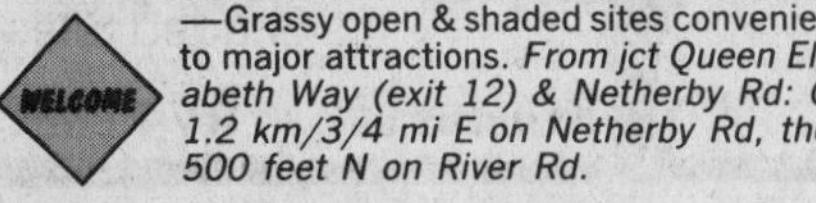

**RIVERSIDE PARK MOTEL & CAMPGROUND**—Grassy open & shaded sites convenient to major attractions. *From jct Queen Elizabeth Way (exit 12) & Netherby Rd: Go 1.2 km/3/4 mi E on Netherby Rd, then 500 feet N on River Rd.*

FACILITIES: 185 sites, most common site width 30

NIAGARA FALLS, ON—Continued
RIVERSIDE PARK MOTEL & CAMPGROUND—Continued

feet, 45 full hookups, 80 water & elec (15 & 30 amp receptacles), 60 no hookups, a/c allowed ($), heater not allowed, group sites for tents/RVs, RV storage, sewage disposal, laundry, public phone, limited grocery store, ice, tables, fire rings, wood.

RECREATION: rec room/area, coin games, swim pool, river swimming, boating, dock, river fishing, mini-golf ($), playground, sports field, horseshoes, hiking trails.

Open May 1 through Oct 15. Member of OPCA. Phone: (905) 382-2204.
**SEE AD THIS PAGE**

## PENETANGUISHENE

**LAFONTAINE CAMPGROUND & RV PARK**—Rustic CAMPGROUND in connection with winter skiing. *From jct Hwy 93 & CR 25: Go 6.4 km/4 mi W on CR 25, then 9.6 km/6 mi N on CR 6, then 1.6 km/1 mi E on CR 26.*

FACILITIES: 150 sites, most common site width 45 feet, 26 full hookups, 124 water & elec (15 & 30 amp

LAFONTAINE CAMPGROUND & RV PARK—Continued on next page
PENETANGUISHENE, ON—Continued on next page

PENETANGUISHENE, ON—Continued
LAFONTAINE CAMPGROUND & RV PARK—Continued

receptacles), a/c allowed, heater allowed, group sites for tents/RVs, RV rentals, sewage disposal, laundry, public phone, limited grocery store, ice, tables, fire rings, wood, guard.

RECREATION: rec hall, rec room/area, swim pool, sauna, whirlpool, basketball hoop, 20 bike rentals, playground, planned group activities (weekends only), movies, badminton, sports field, horseshoes, hiking trails, volleyball, cross country skiing. Recreation open to the public.

Open all year. Facilities fully operational May 1 through Oct 15. Member of OPCA. Phone: (705) 533-2961.

**SEE AD PAGE 43**

## PETERBOROUGH

***See listing at Bailieboro***

## PORT COLBORNE

**DRESSEL'S STILL ACRES** (REBUILDING)—CAMPGROUND with grassy, open and shaded sites. *From west town limits: Go 3.2 km/2 mi W on Hwy 3, then 1.6 km/1 mi S on Bessey Rd.*

WELCOME

FACILITIES: 91 sites, most common site width 30 feet, 81 water & elec (15 amp receptacles), 10 no hookups, 4 pull-thrus, a/c not allowed, heater not allowed, phone hookups, group sites for tents/

PORT COLBORNE, ON—Continued
DRESSEL'S STILL ACRES—Continued

RVs, RV rentals, RV storage, sewage disposal, ice, tables, fire rings, grills, wood.

RECREATION: rec hall, coin games, swim pool, lake swimming, basketball hoop, playground, planned group activities (weekends only), horseshoes, volleyball.

Open May 24 through Oct 31. Phone: (905) 834-0724.

**SEE AD THIS PAGE**

## PORT ELGIN

**KENORUS QUIET RV RESORT**—Grassy, shaded level CAMPGROUND convenient to a major highway. *From north city limits: Go 2.4 km/1 1/2 mi N on Hwy 21.*

WELCOME

FACILITIES: 247 sites, most common site width 30 feet, 241 full hookups, 6 water & elec (15 & 30 amp receptacles), 85 pull-thrus, a/c allowed ($), heater allowed ($), group sites for RVs, RV storage, handicap restroom facilities, sewage disposal, laundry, public phone, limited grocery store, RV supplies, LP gas refill by weight/by meter, ice, tables, patios, fire rings, wood, traffic control gate.

RECREATION: rec room/area, coin games, swim pool (heated), whirlpool, basketball hoop, playground, planned group activities (weekends only), sports field, horseshoes, volleyball.

Open May 1 through Oct 15. Member of OPCA. Phone: (519) 832-5183.

**SEE AD THIS PAGE**

## STOUFFVILLE

**CEDAR BEACH PARK**—CAMPGROUND at Musselman's Lake. *From jct Hwy 48 & York Rd 15: Go 2 km/1 1/4 mi E on York Rd 15 & follow signs.*

WELCOME

FACILITIES: 565 sites, most common site width 40 feet, 540 full hookups, 25 water & elec (15 & 30 amp receptacles), 16 pull-thrus, a/c allowed ($), heater allowed, RV storage, sewage disposal, public phone, grocery store, RV supplies, LP gas refill by weight, ice, tables, fire rings, wood, church services, traffic control gate.

RECREATION: rec hall, rec room/area, coin games, 3 swim pools (heated), wading pool, lake swimming, boating, no motors, canoeing, dock, 6 row/1 sail/9 canoe boat rentals, lake fishing, basketball hoop, playground, 4 shuffleboard courts, planned group

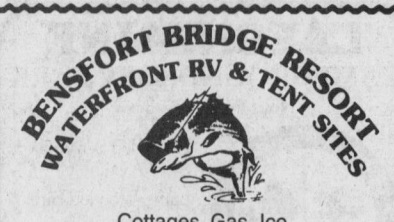

STOUFFVILLE, ON—Continued
CEDAR BEACH PARK—Continued

activities, movies, 2 tennis courts, sports field, horseshoes, hiking trails, volleyball. Recreation open to the public.

Open Apr through Nov. Member of OPCA. Phone: (905) 642-1700.

**SEE AD TORONTO THIS PAGE**

## SUTTON

**ELM GROVE TRAILER PARK**—Open & shaded, level sites among mostly seasonal sites. *From jct of Woodbine Ave (Base Line): Go .4 km/1/4 mi W to Catering Rd, then 3.2 km/2 mi S.*

WELCOME

FACILITIES: 128 sites, 128 full hookups, (30 amp receptacles), 5 pull-thrus, a/c allowed, heater allowed, phone hookups, public phone, tables, fire rings, wood.

RECREATION: rec hall, pond swimming, boating, canoeing, river fishing, playground, planned group activities (weekends only), sports field, horseshoes, hiking trails, volleyball.

Open mid May through mid Oct. Member of OPCA. Phone: (905) 722-3693.

**SEE AD THIS PAGE**

## TORONTO

***See listing at Stouffville***

## VINELAND

**INDIAN LAKE CAMPGROUNDS**—Open & shaded sites in CAMPGROUND with a private lake. *From jct QEW (exit 57) & Regional Rd 24: Go 17.7 km/11 mi S on Regional Rd 24.*

WELCOME

FACILITIES: 163 sites, most common site width 30 feet, 25 full hookups, 120 water & elec (15 & 30 amp receptacles), 18 no hookups, a/c allowed, heater not allowed, phone hookups, group sites for tents/RVs, RV storage, sewage disposal, public phone, ice, tables, fire rings, wood, traffic control gate.

RECREATION: rec hall, coin games, swim pool, boating, canoeing, dock, 9 canoe boat rentals, playground, shuffleboard court, planned group activities (weekends only), badminton, horseshoes, hiking trails, volleyball.

Open May 1 through Oct 1. Phone: (905) 892-7982.

**SEE AD NIAGARA FALLS PAGE 43**

## WOODSTOCK

**WILLOW LAKE PARK**—Grassy CAMPGROUND with open & tree shaded sites. *From jct Hwy 401 (exit 230) & Sweaburg Rd: Go 3.2 km/2 mi N on Mill St, then 30 m/100 feet E on Hwy 2, then 3.2 km/2 mi N on Hwy 59.*

WELCOME

FACILITIES: 100 sites, most common site width 40 feet, 70 full hookups, 25 water & elec (15 & 30 amp receptacles), 5 no hookups, 16 pull-thrus, a/c allowed ($), phone hookups, RV rentals, cabins, RV

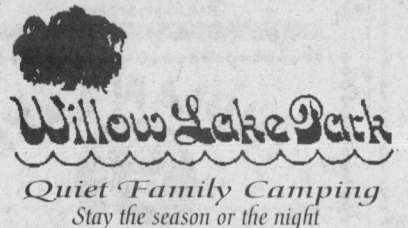

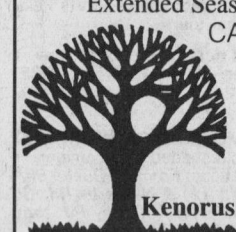

WILLOW LAKE PARK—Continued on next page
WOODSTOCK, ON—Continued on next page

**WOODSTOCK, ON—Continued**
**WILLOW LAKE PARK—Continued**

storage, sewage disposal, laundry, public phone, limited grocery store, ice, tables, fire rings, wood, traffic control gate.

RECREATION: rec hall, rec room/area, coin games, swim pool (heated), whirlpool, basketball hoop, playground, shuffleboard court, planned group activities (weekends only), movies, badminton, sports field, horseshoes, volleyball.

Open May 1 through mid Oct. Member of OPCA. Phone: (519) 537-7301.

**SEE AD PAGE 44**

# PRINCE EDWARD ISLAND

## CAVENDISH

**MARCO POLO LAND**—CAMPGROUND with open, grassy sites in a rural setting. *From jct Hwy 6 & Hwy 13: Go 1.6 km/1 mi S on Hwy 13.*

FACILITIES: 500 sites, most common site width 40 feet, 251 full hookups, 226 water & elec (15 & 30 amp receptacles), 23 no hookups, 41 pull-thrus, group sites for RVs, RV storage, sewage disposal, laundry, public phone, full service store, RV supplies, ice, tables, fire rings, wood, traffic control gate/guard.

RECREATION: rec hall, rec room/area, coin games, 2 swim pools (heated), mini-golf ($), basketball hoop, playground, planned group activities, movies, recreation director, 2 tennis courts, sports field, horseshoes, volleyball, local tours. Recreation open to the public.

Open May 30 through Sep 11. Facilities fully operational Jun 24 through Sep 4. Phone: (800) 665-2352.

**SEE AD THIS PAGE**

# QUEBEC

## DRUMMONDVILLE (ST-CHARLES)

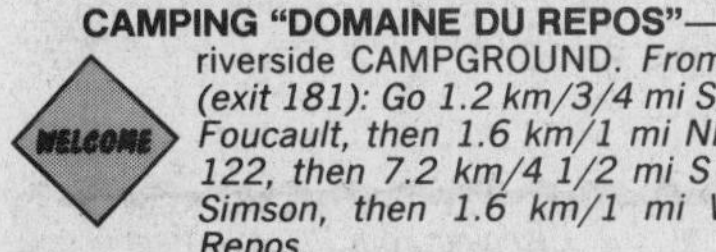

**CAMPING "DOMAINE DU REPOS"**—Wooded, riverside CAMPGROUND. *From Hwy 20 (exit 181): Go 1.2 km/3/4 mi SE on Boul Foucault, then 1.6 km/1 mi NE on Hwy 122, then 7.2 km/4 1/2 mi S on 3 Rg. Simson, then 1.6 km/1 mi W on Du Repos.*

FACILITIES: 83 sites, 80 full hookups, 3 water & elec (20 amp receptacles), group sites for tents/RVs, handicap restroom facilities, sewage disposal, laundry, public phone, full service store, ice, tables, fire rings, wood, church services, traffic control gate/guard.

RECREATION: rec hall, rec room/area, coin games, swim pool, boating, canoeing, ramp, dock, river fishing, basketball hoop, playground, badminton, horseshoes, hiking trails, volleyball.

Open all year. Facilities fully operational Apr 1 through Oct 30. Phone: (819) 478-1758.

**SEE AD THIS PAGE**

**QUEBEC—Continued**

## GRANBY

**CAMPING TROPICANA**—Semi-wooded CAMPGROUND. Most sites occupied by seasonal campers. *From jct Hwy 10 (exit 68) & Hwy 139: Go 8 km/5 mi N on Hwy 139, then 4.4 km/2 3/4 mi W on Hwy 112 (Principale St).*

FACILITIES: 880 sites, 805 full hookups, 75 water & elec (15 & 30 amp receptacles), 25 pull-thrus, a/c allowed, group sites for tents/RVs, RV rentals, sewage disposal, laundry, public phone, full service store, LP gas refill by weight, ice, tables, fire rings, wood, traffic control gate/guard.

RECREATION: rec hall, rec room/area, coin games, swim pool, lake swimming ($), water slide ($), 10 pedal boat rentals, mini-golf ($), basketball hoop, playground, planned group activities (weekends only), movies, recreation director, 3 tennis courts, sports field, horseshoes, volleyball. Recreation open to the public.

Open May 1 through Sep 15. Member of CQ. Phone: (514) 378-9410.

**SEE AD THIS PAGE**

## ST-LOUIS-DE-BLANDFORD

**DOMAINE DU LAC LOUISE**—Wooded CAMPGROUND. *From Hwy 20 (exit 235) & Hwy 263: Go 1.6 km/1 mi N on Hwy 263, then 1.2 km/3/4 mi E on dirt road (via Lemieux).*

FACILITIES: 210 sites, 150 full hookups, 60 water & elec (15 & 30 amp receptacles), 5 pull-thrus, group sites for tents/RVs, sewage disposal, laundry, public phone, limited grocery store, ice, tables, fire rings, wood, church services, guard.

RECREATION: rec hall, rec room/area, coin games, swim pool (heated), lake swimming, boating, 4 pedal boat rentals, basketball hoop, playground, planned group activities (weekends only), sports field, horseshoes, hiking trails, volleyball, cross country skiing. Recreation open to the public.

Open all year. Facilities fully operational May 1 through Nov 1. Member of CQ. Phone: (819) 364-7002.

**SEE AD THIS PAGE**

**QUEBEC—Continued**

## ST-VALLIER

**CAMPING JARDIN DU CAMPEUR**—A CAMPGROUND in a natural setting. *From Hwy 20E (exit 356): Go .4 km/1/4 mi E, then 2.8 km/1 3/4 mi S on Montee de la Station.*

FACILITIES: 149 sites, 40 ft. max RV length, 84 full hookups, 47 water & elec (15 & 30 amp receptacles), 18 no hookups, a/c allowed, heater allowed, group sites for tents/RVs, sewage disposal, laundry, public phone, limited grocery store, ice, tables, fire rings, wood, traffic control gate/guard.

RECREATION: rec room/area, pavilion, swim pool (heated), playground, 3 shuffleboard courts, planned group activities, sports field, horseshoes, volleyball. Recreation open to the public.

Open May 15 through Sep 30. Member of CQ. Phone: (418) 884-2270.

**SEE AD THIS PAGE**

## UPTON

**CAMPING WIGWAM**—Wooded CAMPGROUND on open terrain. *From Hwy 20 (exit 147): Go 10.4 km/6 1/2 mi SE on Hwy 116.*

FACILITIES: 250 sites, 250 full hookups, (15 & 30 amp receptacles), a/c allowed, heater not allowed, group sites for tents/RVs, RV rentals, laundry, public phone, grocery store, LP gas refill by weight, ice, tables, fire rings, wood, traffic control gate/guard.

RECREATION: rec room/area, coin games, swim pool, wading pool, boating, electric motors only, canoeing, ramp, dock, river fishing, mini-golf ($), playground, planned group activities (weekends only), badminton, sports field, horseshoes, volleyball. Recreation open to the public.

Open May 1 through Oct 31. Member of CQ. Phone: (514) 549-4513.

**SEE AD THIS PAGE**















**Tourist: "What beautiful scenery! Lived here all your life?"**
**Farmer: "Not yet."**

# MEXICO

## CABO SAN LUCAS

**VAGABUNDOS DEL MAR RV PARK**—Level, shaded, landscaped sites in an RV PARK. *From east edge of town: Go 3/4 mi E on Hwy 1.*

FACILITIES: 94 sites, most common site width 20 feet, 94 full hookups, (15 & 30 amp receptacles), 51 pull-thrus, a/c allowed, heater allowed, cable TV, laundry, public phone, ice, patios, guard.

RECREATION: swim pool (heated), salt water fishing, fishing guides, hiking trails, local tours.

Open all year. No refunds. Phone: 011-52-114-30290.

**SEE AD THIS PAGE**

## ENSENADA

**BAJA SEASONS RESORT**—Landscaped sites in an RV PARK and villas in a luxury resort on the beach overlooking the Pacific Ocean. *From south city limits of Rosarito Beach: Go 22 mi S on Hwy 1D to KM 72. Northbound from north city limits of Ensenada: Go 26 mi N on Hwy 1D to Los Alistos exit, then exit go under overpass & re-enter Hwy 1D heading S, then 4 mi S.*

FACILITIES: 134 sites, most common site width 25 feet, 134 full hookups, (30 amp receptacles), a/c allowed, heater allowed, cable TV, group sites for RVs, RV rentals, cabins, laundry, public phone, grocery store, RV supplies, ice, patios, grills, traffic control gate/guard.

RECREATION: rec room/area, swim pool, sauna, whirlpool, salt water fishing, mini-golf, putting green, playground, planned group activities, movies, 2 tennis courts, horse riding trails, horseshoes, volleyball, local tours.

No tents. Open all year. Phone: 800-754-4190.

**SEE AD THIS PAGE**

**ESTERO BEACH RESORT**—Oceanside RV PARK with wide, level landscaped sites. *From jct Hwy 1 & Estero Beach turnoff (Calle Jose Maria Morelos): Go 3/4 mi W, then 1/2 mi S.*

FACILITIES: 70 sites, most common site width 25 feet, 70 full hookups, (20 & 30 amp receptacles), a/c allowed, heater allowed, group sites for RVs, cabins, public phone, patios, traffic control gate/guard.

RECREATION: rec hall, rec room/area, coin games, salt water swimming, boating, canoeing, ramp, 2 row/4 canoe/4 pedal boat rentals, water skiing, salt water fishing, basketball hoop, 6 bike rentals, playground, 4 tennis courts, horse riding trails, horse rental, sports field, hiking trails, volleyball.

No tents. Open all year. Phone: 011-52-617-66230.

**SEE AD THIS PAGE**

**ESTERO EXHIBIT CENTER**—*From Hwy 1 & Estero Beach turnoff (Calle Jose Maria Morelos): Go 3/4 mi W, then 1/4 mi S to Estero Beach Resort.* A collection of Mexico's past treasures in a museum displaying the pre-Columbian splendor of Olmec, Aztec, Zapotec and Maya civilizations. Also, discover the treasure of Monte Alban, objects of the Mexican Colonial period, and fossils of Baja marine life. Open all year. Phone: 011-52-617-66230.

**SEE AD THIS PAGE**

## LORETO

**VILLAS DE LORETO RESORT**—Motel and RV PARK with open and shaded sites on the Sea of Cortez. *From jct Hwy 1 & Loreto turnoff: Go 1 1/2 mi E (to sign), then 3/4 mi S on partially paved road, then 1 block E to beach.*

FACILITIES: 36 sites, 18 full hookups, (15 & 30 amp receptacles), 18 no hookups, a/c allowed, heater allowed, cabins, sewage disposal, laundry, public phone.

RECREATION: swim pool, salt water swimming, boating, ramp, salt water fishing, 6 bike rentals, playground, horse rental, horseshoes, hiking trails, local tours.

Open all year. Phone: 011-52-113-50586.

**SEE AD THIS PAGE**

## LOS BARRILES

**JUANITO'S GARDEN RV PARK**—Modern RV park in landscaped park-like setting. *From jct Hwy 1 & Los Barriles turnoff: Go 1/2 mi W on paved road, then 1/4 mi N.*

FACILITIES: 30 sites, 30 full hookups, (15 amp receptacles), a/c allowed, heater allowed, cable TV, RV storage, laundry.

RECREATION: salt water swimming, salt water fishing, hiking trails.

No tents. Open all year. Phone: 011-52-114-10024.

**SEE AD THIS PAGE**











***A high density of desert light will cause you to have a decrease in night vision. You can help to reduce glare by using charcoal or soot to darken the skin around your eyes.***

# We Need Your Input!

**In order to continue to give you the most comprehensive Campground Directory possible we would like your input. Your experience will help us with future planning and improvements.**

**1. Are you a first-time user of *WOODALL'S*?**
❑ Yes ❑ No

**2. Which edition of this Directory did you take this survey from?**
❑ North American
❑ Eastern
❑ Western
❑ New York and New England
❑ Mid-Atlantic
❑ Great Lakes
❑ Great Plains and Mountain States
❑ Far West
❑ Frontier West
❑ The South
❑ Canada
❑ Guide to Seasonal Sites
❑ Discover
❑ Camping World President's Club

**3. If you have the North American edition, would you prefer that it be separated into 2 books (East and West) and then sold together as a package?**
❑ Yes ❑ No

**4. If you have the *Guide to Seasonal Sites,* where did you get it?**
❑ RV Show ❑ RV Dealer ❑ Direct from *WOODALL'S*

**5. If you have *Discover the Festival That Is North America,* where did you get it?**
❑ RV Show ❑ Premium with Subscription ❑ Direct from *WOODALL'S*

**6. When choosing a Campground/RV Park, rate the following in order of importance**

| | Very Important | Important | Somewhat Important | Not Important |
|---|---|---|---|---|
| Location | ❑ | ❑ | ❑ | ❑ |
| Facilities Rating | ❑ | ❑ | ❑ | ❑ |
| Types of Facilities | ❑ | ❑ | ❑ | ❑ |
| Type of Electric Hookups | ❑ | ❑ | ❑ | ❑ |
| Recreation Rating | ❑ | ❑ | ❑ | ❑ |
| Types of Recreation | ❑ | ❑ | ❑ | ❑ |
| Description of Park | ❑ | ❑ | ❑ | ❑ |
| Discounts Offered | ❑ | ❑ | ❑ | ❑ |
| Do They Advertise | ❑ | ❑ | ❑ | ❑ |
| Camping Fee | ❑ | ❑ | ❑ | ❑ |
| Nearby Facilities | ❑ | ❑ | ❑ | ❑ |
| Big Rig Accommodations | ❑ | ❑ | ❑ | ❑ |
| Other:____________ | ❑ | ❑ | ❑ | ❑ |

**7. Before reading this question, were you aware that there is a "How to Use this Directory" section on page I-XIII? (Does not apply to Guide to Seasonal Sites or Discover the Festival.)**
❑ Yes ❑ No

8. Is the "How to Use this Directory" section
❑ Very Important ❑ Somewhat Important ❑ Not Important

9. Before reading this question, were you aware that there is Guide to Seasonal Sites in the back of this Directory? (Does not apply to Discover the Festival or Guide to Seasonal Sites.)
❑ Yes ❑ No

10. Before reading this question, were you aware that there is an Alphabetical Listing Index in this Directory? (Does not apply to Discover the Festival or Guide to Seasonal Sites.)
❑ Yes ❑ No

11. How important to you are the following sections of this Directory?

| | Very Important | Important | Somewhat Important | Not Important |
|---|---|---|---|---|
| Magazine Article in Front of Book | ❑ | ❑ | ❑ | ❑ |
| State/Provincial Travel Sections | ❑ | ❑ | ❑ | ❑ |
| State/Provincial Maps | ❑ | ❑ | ❑ | ❑ |

12. Would the Campground/RV Park listings/ratings be more useful to you if they indicated a separate maintenance rating?
❑ Yes ❑ No

13. Do you use a Campground Directory other than *WOODALL'S?*
❑ Yes ❑ No
a. If yes, which one ______________________
b. What do you like best about this other Directory?
______________________

14. Would you utilize a trip routing service if provided by *WOODALL'S?*
❑ Yes ❑ No

15. Would you purchase information from *WOODALL'S* Campground Directory if it was available in a format for your computer?
a: ❑ Yes ❑ No
b: I would prefer
❑ Disk ❑ on-line service

16. If you could change or add to this Directory in 3 ways, what would they be?
1.______________________
2.______________________
3.______________________

17. Your Name: ______________________
Address: ______________________
______________________

Thank you so much for your time and your help!

**Please mail survey to:**

Deborah Spriggs
Woodall Publications Corp
13975 W. Polo Trail Dr., P.O. Box 5000
Lake Forest, IL 60045-5000